MANAGEMENT

TENTH CANADIAN EDITION

MANAGEMENT

STEPHEN P. ROBBINS
San Diego State University

MARY COULTER
Southwest Missouri State University

ED LEACH
Dalhousie University

MARY KILFOIL
Dalhousie University

PEARSON

Toronto

Vice-President, Editorial Director: Gary Bennett
Editor-in-Chief: Nicole Lukach
Acquisitions Editor: Nick Durie
Sponsoring Editor: Kathleen McGill
Marketing Manager: Cas Shields
Supervising Developmental Editor: Suzanne Schaan
Developmental Editor: Joanne Sutherland
Project Manager: Lesley Deugo
Production Editor: Tara Tovell
Copy Editor: Marcia Gallego
Proofreader: Patricia Jones
Compositor: Debbie Kumpf
Photo and Permissions Researcher: Amanda Campbell
Manufacturing Coordinator: Susan Johnson
Art Director: Julia Hall
Cover and Interior Designer: Anthony Leung
Cover Image: GettyImages

10 9 8 7 6 5 4 3 2 1 CKV

Library and Archives Canada Cataloguing in Publication
Management / Stephen P. Robbins ... [et al.]. — 10th Canadian ed.

Tenth Canadian ed. by: Stephen P. Robbins, Mary Coulter, Ed Leach, and Mary Kilfoil
Includes bibliographical references and index.
ISBN 978-0-13-211299-4
        1. Management—Textbooks. 2. Management—Canada—Textbooks.
I. Robbins, Stephen P., 1943-

HD31.M287 2011   658.4   C2011-901534-X

ISBN 978-0-13-211299-4

BRIEF CONTENTS

Preface   xiv
Acknowledgments   xxiii
About the Authors   xxiv

Part One   Defining the Manager's Terrain   1

CHAPTER 1: Introduction to Management and Organizations   2

    Supplement 1: History of Management Trends   28

CHAPTER 2: Organizational Culture and the Environment   38

CHAPTER 3: Managing in a Global Environment   69

CHAPTER 4: Managing Entrepreneurially   95

CHAPTER 5: Managing Responsibly and Ethically   119

Part Two   Planning   151

CHAPTER 6: Decision Making   152

CHAPTER 7: Foundations of Planning   184

CHAPTER 8: Strategic Management   207

CHAPTER 9: Planning Tools and Techniques   234

Part Three   Organizing   263

CHAPTER 10: Organizational Structure and Design   264

CHAPTER 11: Managers and Communication   289

CHAPTER 12: Managing Human Resources   321

CHAPTER 13: Managing Change and Innovation   353

Part Four   Leading   383

CHAPTER 14: Leadership   384

CHAPTER 15: Motivating Employees   416

CHAPTER 16: Managing Groups and Teams   447

Part Five   Controlling   475

CHAPTER 17: Foundations of Control   476

CHAPTER 18: Managing Operations   508

Video Case Incidents   533
Endnotes   543
Glossary/Subject Index   589
Name and Organization Index   607
List of Canadian Companies, by Province   615
List of International Companies, by Country   617
Photo Credits   620

CONTENTS

Preface   xiv
Acknowledgments   xxiii
About the Authors   xxiv

PART ONE
Defining the Manager's Terrain   1

CHAPTER 1
Introduction to Management and Organizations   2

Who Are Managers?   4
Types of Managers   4

What Is Management and What Do Managers Do?   5
Efficiency and Effectiveness   6
Management Functions   6
Management Roles   8

What Is an Organization?   10
The Size of Organizations   11
The Types of Organizations   12

What Challenges Do Managers Face?   12
Ethics and Social Responsibility   14
Workforce Diversity   14
Globalization   14
Managing in an E-business World   15
Customers   16

Why Build an Adaptable Organization?   17
Wicked Problems   17
Innovation   17
Knowledge Management and Learning Organizations   18

Why Study Management?   18
The Universality of Management   19
The Reality of Work   19
Self-Employment   20

Summary and Implications   20

MANAGEMENT @ WORK   22
Reading for Comprehension   22
Linking Concepts to Practice   22
Self-Assessment: How Motivated Am I to Manage?   22

Management for You Today   23
Working Together: Team-Based Exercise
A New Beginning   24
Ethics in Action   24
Case Application: Lipschultz Levin & Gray   24
Developing Your Diagnostic and Analytical Skills: Managing the Virus Hunters   25
Developing Your Interpersonal Skills: Mentoring   26

Supplement 1:
History of Management Trends   28

Historical Background of Management   29

Scientific Management   29
Important Contributions   29
How Do Today's Managers Use General Scientific Management?   31

General Administrative Theory   31
Important Contributions   31
How Do Today's Managers Use General Administrative Theory?   32

The Quantitative Approach   33
Important Contributions   33
How Do Today's Managers Use the Quantitative Approach?   33

Organizational Behaviour   33
Early Advocates   33
The Hawthorne Studies   34
How Do Today's Managers Use the Behavioural Approach?   35

The Systems Approach   35
The Systems Approach and Managers   35

The Contingency Approach   36
The Contingency Approach and Managers   36

Summarizing Management Theory   37

CHAPTER 2
Organizational Culture and the Organizational Environment   38

The Manager: Omnipotent or Symbolic?   39
The Omnipotent View   39
The Symbolic View   40
Reality Suggests a Synthesis   41

The Organization's Culture   41
What Is Organizational Culture?   42
Strong vs. Weak Cultures   43

Subcultures   44
The Source of Culture   44
How an Organization's Culture Continues   45
How Employees Learn Culture   46
How Culture Affects Managers   48

Current Organizational Culture Issues

Facing Managers   49
Creating an Ethical Culture   50
Creating an Innovative Culture   50
Creating a Customer-Responsive Culture   51
Creating a Culture That Supports Diversity   52

The Organizational Environment   53
Defining the External Environment   54
How the Organizational Environment Affects Managers   58

Summary and Implications   61

MANAGEMENT @ WORK   63
Reading for Comprehension   63
Linking Concepts to Practice   63
Self-Assessment: What's the Right Organizational Culture for Me?   63
Management for You Today   64
Working Together: Team-Based Exercise
Assessing the Organization's Environment   64
Ethics in Action   65
Case Application: Making You Say Wow   65
Developing Your Diagnostic and Analytical Skills: A Perfect Response to an Imperfect Storm   66
Developing Your Interpersonal Skills: Reading an Organization's Culture   67
Steps in Developing the Skill   67

CHAPTER 3
Managing in a Global Environment   69

What's Your Global Perspective?   71

Understanding the Global Environment   72
Regional Trading Alliances   73
BRICS   76
The World Trade Organization   76

Doing Business Globally   76
Different Types of International Organizations   77
How Organizations Go International   78

Managing in a Global Environment   80
The Legal–Political Environment   81
The Economic Environment   81
The Cultural Environment   82
The Pros and Cons of Globalization   85

Summary and Implications   87

MANAGEMENT @ WORK   89
Reading for Comprehension   89
Linking Concepts to Practice   89
Self-Assessment: Am I Well-Suited for a Career as a Global Manager?   89
Management for You Today   90
Working Together: Team-Based Exercise
Assessing People's Global Aptitudes   90
Ethics in Action   91
Case Application: National Basketball Association   91
Developing Your Diagnostic and Analytical Skills:
Yes Does Not Always Mean Yes, and No Does Not Always Mean No   92
Developing Your Interpersonal Skills: Becoming More Culturally Aware   93

CHAPTER 4
Managing Entrepreneurially   95

The Context of Entrepreneurship   96
What Is Entrepreneurship?   97
How Entrepreneurial Ventures Add Value to the Economy   97
The Nature of Opportunities and the Role of Entrepreneurial Managers   97
Why Is Entrepreneurship Important?   98
What Do Entrepreneurs Do?   98
Social Responsibility and Ethics Issues Facing Entrepreneurs   99

Start-Up and Planning Issues for an Entrepreneurial Venture   101
Identifying Environmental Opportunities and Competitive Advantage   101
Researching a Venture's Feasibility: Generating and Evaluating Ideas   103
Researching a Venture's Feasibility: Researching Competitors   104
Researching a Venture's Feasibility: Researching Financing   105
Planning a Venture: Developing a Business Plan   105

Issues in Organizing an Entrepreneurial Venture   106
Organizational Design and Structure   106
Human Resource Management   106
How to Stimulate and Make Changes   107
The Continuing Importance of Innovation   107

Issues in Leading an Entrepreneurial Venture   109
The Entrepreneur as Leader   109

Issues in Controlling an Entrepreneurial Venture   110
Managing Growth   111
Managing Downturns   111
Exiting the Venture   112

Summary and Implications   112

MANAGEMENT @ WORK   114
Reading for Comprehension   114
Linking Concepts to Practice   114
Self-Assessment: Am I Likely to Become and Entrepreneur?   114
Management for You Today   115
Working Together: Team-Based Exercise What Bugs You?   116
Ethics in Action   116
Case Application: Apple   116
Developing Your Diagnostic and Analytical Skills: Second Chance: The Business of Life   117
Developing Your Interpersonal Skills: Interviewing an Entrepreneur   117

CHAPTER 5
Managing Responsibly and Ethically   119

What Is Meant by Socially Responsible Management?   120
From Obligations to Responsiveness to Responsibility   121
The Evolution of Socially Responsible Management   124

Corporate Social Responsibility and Economic Performance   125

Sustainable Management Practices   126
Global Environmental Problems   127
How Organizations Manage Sustainably   127
Evaluating Sustainable Management   129

Values-Based Management   130
Purposes of Shared Values   131

Managerial Ethics   132
Four Views of Ethics   132
Factors That Affect Employee Ethics   133
Ethics in an International Context   137
Improving Ethical Behaviour   139

Summary and Implications   143

MANAGEMENT @ WORK   145
Reading for Comprehension   145
Linking Concepts to Practice   145
Self-Assessment: How Do My Ethics Rate?   145
Management for You Today   146
Working Together: Team-Based Exercise Assessing Ethical and Unethical Behaviour   147
Ethics in Action   147
Ethical Dilemma Exercise: Can an Environmental Organization Balance Its Values with Making Money?   147
Case Application: City of Ottawa   148
Developing Your Diagnostic and Analytical Skills: The Responsible Organization   149
Developing Your Interpersonal Skills: Building Trust   149

PART TWO
Planning   151

CHAPTER 6
Decision Making   152

The Decision-Making Process   153
Step 1: Identify a Problem   155
Step 2: Identify Decision Criteria   155
Step 3: Allocate Weights to Criteria   156
Step 4: Develop Alternatives   156
Step 5: Analyze Alternatives   156
Step 6: Select an Alternative   157
Step 7: Implement the Alternative   157
Step 8: Evaluate Decision Effectiveness   158

The Manager as Decision Maker   158
Making Decisions: Rationality   158
Making Decisions: Bounded Rationality   159
Making Decisions: The Role of Intuition   160

Types of Decisions and Decision-Making Conditions   161
Types of Decisions   161
Decision-Making Conditions   163

Decision-Making Styles   166
Group Decision Making   168
Individual and Group Decision Making: When Is One More Effective Than the Other?   169
Decision-Making Biases and Errors   169
Summing Up Managerial Decision Making   171

Effective Decision Making for Today's World   172

Summary and Implications   174

MANAGEMENT @ WORK   176
Reading for Comprehension   176
Reading for Comprehension   176
Linking Concepts to Practice   176
Self-Assessment: How Intuitive Am I?   176
Management for You Today   177
Working Together: Team-Based Exercise A Life or Death Situation   178
Ethics in Action   180
Case Application: C. F. Martin Guitar Company   180
Developing Your Diagnostic and Analytical Skills: Some Solutions Create More Problems   181
Developing Your Interpersonal Skills: Solving Problems Creatively   182
Managing Workforce Diversity: The Value of Diversity in Decision Making   183

CHAPTER 7
Foundations of Planning   184

What Is Planning?   183
Purposes of Planning   186
Planning and Performance   186

How Do Managers Plan?   187
Approaches to Establishing Goals   187
Developing Plans   193

Current Issues in Planning   197
Criticisms of Planning   197
Effective Planning in Dynamic Environments   197

Summary and Implications   200

MANAGEMENT @ WORK   201
Reading for Comprehension   201
Linking Concepts to Practice   201
Self-Assessment: What's My Attitude Toward Achievement?   201
Management for You Today   202
Working Together: Team-Based Exercise
Helping Design a Training Program   203
Ethics in Action   203
Case Application: Lend Lease Corporation   204
Developing Your Diagnostic and Analytical Skills: Ready or Not . . .   204
Developing Your Interpersonal Skills: Setting Goals   205

CHAPTER 8
Managing Strategically   207

The Importance of Strategic Management   208
What Is Strategic Management?   208
Why Is Strategic Management Important?   209

The Strategic Management Process   210
Step 1: Identify the Organization's Current Mission, Goals, and Strategies   211
Step 2: Conduct an Internal Analysis   211
Step 3: Conduct an External Analysis   212
Step 4: Formulate Strategies   213
Step 5: Implement Strategies   213
Step 6: Evaluate Results   214

Types of Organizational Strategies   214
Corporate Strategy   215
Business Strategy   219
Functional Strategy   224

Current Strategic Management Issues   224
Strategic Flexibility   225
New Directions in Organizational Strategies   225

Summary and Implications   228

MANAGEMENT @ WORK   229
Reading for Comprehension   229
Linking Concepts to Practice   229
Self-Assessment: How Well Do I Handle Ambiguity?   229
Management for You Today   230
Working Together: Team-Based Exercise
Identifying Organizational Strategies   231
Ethics in Action   231
Case Application: Haier Group   231
Developing Your Diagnostic and Analytical Skills: XXL No More!   232
Developing Your Interpersonal Skills: Scanning the Environment   233

CHAPTER 9
Planning Tools and Techniques   234

Techniques for Assessing the Environment   235
Environmental Scanning   235
Forecasting   238
Benchmarking   240

Techniques for Allocating Resources   241
Budgeting   242
Scheduling   244
Breakeven Analysis   248
Linear Programming   248

Contemporary Planning Techniques   251
Project Management   251
Scenario Planning   253

Summary and Implications   255

MANAGEMENT @ WORK   256
Reading for Comprehension   256
Linking Concepts to Practice   256
Self-Assessment: How Good Am I at Personal Planning?   256
Management for You Today   257
Working Together: Team-Based Exercise
Identifying Organizational Strategies   257
Ethics in Action   257
Case Application: Peerless Clothing   258
Developing Your Diagnostic and Analytical Skills: A New Pitch for an Old Classic   259
Developing Your Interpersonal Skills: Budgeting   260

PART THREE
Organizing 263

CHAPTER 10
Organizational Structure and Design 264

Defining Organizational Structure 265
  Work Specialization 266
  Departmentalization 266
  Chain of Command 268
  Span of Control 269
  Centralization and Decentralization 270
  Formalization 272

Organizational Design Decisions 273
  Mechanistic and Organic Organizations 273
  Contingency Factors 275

Common Organizational Designs 277
  Traditional Organizational Designs 277
  Contemporary Organizational Designs 278
  Today's Organizational Design Challenges 281
  A Final Thought 282

Summary and Implications 283

MANAGEMENT @ WORK 284
  Reading for Comprehension 284
  Linking Concepts to Practice 284
  Self-Assessment: What Type of Organizational Structure Do I Prefer? 284
  Management for You Today 285
  Working Together: Team-Based Exercise Delegating Effectively and Ineffectively 285
  Ethics in Action 286
  Case Application: Pfizer: A New Kind of Structure 286
  Developing Your Diagnostic and Analytical Skills: A Learning Organization at Svenska 287
  Developing Your Interpersonal Skills: Delegating 287

CHAPTER 11
Managers and Communication 289

Understanding Communication 290
  What Is Communication? 291
  Functions of Communication 292

Methods of Interpersonal Communication 292
  Channels for Interpersonal Communication Techniques 293

Effective Interpersonal Communication 294
  How Distortions Can Happen in Interpersonal Communication 296
  Barriers to Effective Interpersonal Communication 297
  Overcoming Barriers to Communication 300

Organizational Communication 302
  Formal vs. Informal Communication 302
  Direction of Communication Flow 302
  Organizational Communication Networks 303

Information Technology and Communication 305
  How Information Technology Affects Communication 306
  How Information Technology Affects Organizations 308
  Privacy Issues 308

Communications Issues in Today's Organizations 309
  Managing Communication in an Internet World 309
  Managing the Organization's Knowledge Resources 309
  The Role of Communication in Customer Service 310
  "Politically Correct" Communication 311

Summary and Implications 312

MANAGEMENT @ WORK 314
  Reading for Comprehension 314
  Linking Concepts to Practice 314
  Self-Assessment: What's My Face-to-Face Communication Style? 314
  Management for You Today 316
  Working Together: Team-Based Exercise Choosing the Right Communication Channel 317
  Ethics in Action 317
  Case Application: Voyant Technologies 318
  Developing Your Diagnostic and Analytical Skills: English-Only Rules 318
  Developing Your Interpersonal Skills: Active Listening 319

CHAPTER 12
Managing Human Resources 321

The Human Resource Management Process 321
  Why Human Resource Management Is Important 323
  Human Resources for Non–Human Resource Managers 323
  External Factors That Affect the HRM Process 324

Identifying and Selecting Competent Employees 327
  Human Resource Planning 327
  Recruitment and Decruitment 328
  Selection 330

Providing Employees with Needed Skills and Knowledge 334
  Employee Orientation 334
  Training 335

Retaining Competent and High Performance Employees 336

Employee Performance Management   337
What Happens When Performance Falls Short?   337
Compensation and Benefits   338
Career Development   339

Contemporary Issues in Managing Human
    Resources   340
Workforce Diversity   341
Managing Sexual Harassment   342
Managing Work–Life Balance   343
Helping Survivors Respond to Layoffs   345

Summary and Implications   345

MANAGEMENT @ WORK   347
Reading for Comprehension   347
Linking Concepts to Practice   347
Self-Assessment: How Good Am I at Giving Performance
    Feedback?   347
Management for You Today   348
Working Together: Team-Based Exercise
    Recruiting for Diversity   348
Ethics in Action   349
Case Application: Mitsubishi Motors North America   349
Developing Your Diagnostic and Analytical Skills:
    Busted   350
Developing Your Interpersonal Skills: Interviewing   351

CHAPTER 13
Managing Change and
Innovation   353

Forces for Change   354
External Forces   355
Internal Forces   356

Two Views of the Change Process   357
The Calm Waters Metaphor   357
The White-Water Rapids Metaphor   358
Putting the Two Views in Perspective   359

Managing Organizational Change   359
What Is Organizational Change?   360
Types of Change   360

Managing Resistance to Change   363
Why People Resist Change   363
Techniques for Reducing Resistance   364

Stimulating Innovation   365
Creativity vs. Innovation vs. Entrepreneurship   364
Stimulating and Nurturing Innovation   366

Current Issues in Managing Change   366
Changing Organizational Culture   366
Handling Employee Stress   371
Making Change Happen Successfully   373

Summary and Implications   375

MANAGEMENT @ WORK   377
Reading for Comprehension   377
Linking Concepts to Practice   377
Self-Assessment: How Well Do I Respond to Turbulent
    Change?   377
Management for You Today   379
Working Together: Team-Based Exercise
    Dealing with Stress   379
Ethics in Action   379
Case Application: Starwood Hotels: That Special Touch
    380
Developing Your Diagnostic and Analytical Skills: Changes
    in the Health Care Industry   380
Developing Your Interpersonal Skills: Managing Resistance
    to Change   381

PART FOUR
Leading   383

CHAPTER 14
Leadership   384

Who Are Leaders, and What Is Leadership?   385

Early Leadership Theories   386
Trait Theories   387
Behavioural Theories   388

Contingency Theories of Leadership   390
The Fiedler Model   391
Hersey and Blanchard's Situational Leadership®
    Theory   393
Path–Goal Theory   394

Contemporary Views of Leadership   396
Transformational vs. Transactional Leadership   397
Charismatic–Visionary Leadership   397
Team Leadership   399

Leadership Issues in the Twenty-First Century   400
Managing Power   401
Developing Trust   401
Providing Ethical Leadership   402
Empowering Employees   403
Leading Across Cultures   404
Understanding Gender Differences and Leadership   405
Becoming an Effective Leader   405

Summary and Implications   407

MANAGEMENT @ WORK   409
Reading for Comprehension   409
Linking Concepts to Practice   409
Self-Assessment: What's My Leadership Style?   409
Management for You Today   411

Working Together: Team-Based Exercise
Conveying Bad News   411
Ethics in Action   412
Case Application: Grafik Marketing Communications   412
Developing Your Diagnostic and Analytical Skills: Radical Leadership   413
Developing Your Interpersonal Skills: Acquiring Power   414

CHAPTER 15
Motivating Employees   416

What Is Motivation?   417

Early Theories of Motivation   418
Maslow's Hierarchy of Needs Theory   419
McGregor's Theory X and Theory Y   420
Herzberg's Motivation-Hygiene Theory   420
McClelland's Three-Needs Theory   422

Contemporary Theories of Motivation   422
Goal-Setting Theory   423
Reinforcement Theory   425
Job Design Theory   425
Equity Theory   428
Expectancy Theory   430
Integrating Contemporary Theories of Motivation   431

Current Issues in Motivation   433
Motivating a Diverse Workforce   433
Designing Effective Rewards Programs   436

From Theory to Practice: Suggestions for Motivating Employees   439

Summary and Implications   441

MANAGEMENT @ WORK   442
Reading for Comprehension   442
Linking Concepts to Practice   442
Self-Assessment: What Rewards Do I Value Most?   442
Management for You Today   443
Working Together: Team-Based Exercise
What Is Most Important to You in a Job?   443
Ethics in Action   444
Case Application: Best Buy   444
Developing Your Diagnostic and Analytical Skills: Google: Paradise Lost . . . or Gained?   445
Developing Your Interpersonal Skills: Designing Motivating Jobs   445

CHAPTER 16
Managing Groups and Teams   447

Groups and Group Development   449
What Is a Group?   449
Stages of Group Development   449

Work Group Performance and Satisfaction   451
External Conditions Imposed on the Group   452

Group Member Resources   452
Group Structure   452
Group Processes   456
Group Tasks   458

Turning Groups into Effective Teams   459
What Is a Work Team?   460
Types of Work Teams   460
Creating Effective Work Teams   461

Current Challenges in Managing Teams   463
Managing Global Teams   464
Understanding Social Networks   465

Summary and Implications   466

MANAGEMENT @ WORK   468
Reading for Comprehension   468
Linking Concepts to Practice   468
Self-Assessment: How Good Am I at Building and Leading a Team?   468
Management for You Today   469
Working Together: Team-Based Exercise
Puzzle Building   470
Ethics in Action   470
Case Application: Samsung Electronics   471
Developing Your Diagnostic and Analytical Skills: Team Ferrari   471
Developing Your Interpersonal Skills: Creating Effective Teams   472

PART FIVE
Controlling   475

CHAPTER 17
Foundations of Control   476

What Is Controlling, and Why Is It Important?   477
Performance Standards   478
Measures of Organizational Performance   478
Why Is Control Important?   479

The Control Process   480
Step 1: Measuring Performance   480
Step 2: Comparing Performance against Standard   481
Step 3: Taking Managerial Action   483
Summary of Managerial Decisions   484

Tools for Measuring Organizational Performance   485
Feedforward Control   485
Concurrent Control   486
Feedback Control   486

Methods of Control   487

Market Control   488
Bureaucratic Control   488
Clan Control   488

Financial and Information Controls   489
Traditional Financial Control Measures   490
Other Financial Control Measures   491
Information Controls   491

Current Issues in Control   493
Balanced Scorecard   494
Corporate Governance   495
Cross-Cultural Differences   496
Workplace Concerns   497
Customer Interactions   499

Summary and Implications   501

MANAGEMENT @ WORK   502
Reading for Comprehension   502
Linking Concepts to Practice   502
Self-Assessment: How Proactive Am I?   502
Management for You Today   503
Working Together: Team-Based Exercise
Controlling Cheating   503
Ethics in Action   504
Case Application: Baggage Blunders   504
Developing Your Diagnostic and Analytical Skills: A Control
Concern at BC Ferries   505
Developing Your Interpersonal Skills: Providing
Feedback   506

CHAPTER 18
Managing Operations   508

The Role of Operations Management   509
Services and Manufacturing   510
Managing Productivity   510
Strategic Role of Operations Management   511

What Is Value Chain Management, and Why Is It
Important?   512

What Is Value Chain Management?   513
Goal of Value Chain Management   514
Benefits of Value Chain Management   514

Managing Operations by Using Value Chain
Management   514
Requirements of Value Chain Management   515
Obstacles to Value Chain Management   518

Current Issues in Managing Operations   520
Technology's Role in Operations Management   520
Quality Initiatives   521
Quality Goals   523
Mass Customization   523

Summary and Implications   525

MANAGEMENT @ WORK   527
Reading for Comprehension   527
Linking Concepts to Practice   527
Self-Assessment: What Time of Day Am I Most
Productive?   527
Management for You Today   529
Working Together: Team-Based Exercise
Improving Personal Productivity   529
Ethics in Action   529
Case Application: Smooth Ride   530
Developing Your Diagnostic and Analytical Skills: Going
Postal   530
Developing Your Interpersonal Skills: Managing Operations
in an E-world Environment   531

Video Case Incidents   533
Endnotes   543
Glossary/Subject Index   589
Name and Organization Index   607
List of Canadian Companies by Province   615
List of International Companies by Country   617
Photo Credits   620

PREFACE

Welcome to the tenth Canadian edition of *Management*, by Stephen Robbins, Mary Coulter, Ed Leach, and Mary Kilfoil. This edition takes a fresh approach to management coverage through:

- relevant examples
- updated theory coverage
- a pedagogically sound design

What This Course Is About and Why It's Important

This course and this book are about management and managers. Managers are the one thing that all organizations—no matter the size, kind, or location—need. And there's no doubt that the world that managers face has changed, is changing, and will continue to change. The dynamic nature of today's organizations means both rewards and challenges for the individuals who will be managing those organizations. Management is a dynamic subject, and a textbook on it should reflect those changes to help prepare you to manage under the current conditions. Thus, we've written this tenth Canadian edition of *Management* to provide you with the best possible understanding of what it means to be a manager confronting change.

A New Approach for An Ever-Changing World

Today's students are deeply committed to making the world a better place and in this edition we have broadened the discussion of ethics and social responsibility to reflect this commitment. We have also moved beyond talking about managers being effective (doing the right thing) and being efficient (doing the right things well) to discuss the importance of being adaptable in our quickly-changing environment.

Some of the key changes we've made in our approach to this edition include:

- Increased emphasis on values-led management throughout the book
- Greater coverage of what it means to manage responsibly, with more examples of organizations that prioritize environmental and social responsibility, and a new section on the ISO 26000 standard on social responsibility
- Added discussion of adaptability—the need for managers to continuously scan for new opportunities and then act strategically to take advantage of them
- A new chapter on managing entrepreneurially, with a focus on why managers and organizations need to be flexible, nimble, and innovative

General Content and Approach

The underlying philosophy of our textbook is that "Management Is for Everyone." Students who are not managers, or do not envision themselves as managers, do not always understand why studying management is important or relevant. We use examples from a variety of settings and provide several different end-of-chapter applications, such as *Management for You Today*, to help you understand the relevance of studying management for your day-to-day life.

In this edition, we have continued to make enhancements that add to both learning and instruction:

- An emphasis on presenting a variety of managers, some in unusual (i.e., not large corporate) settings, and some with nontraditional decisions. Chapter openers present a range of real-life examples, from a pet food company facing challenges in a global economy to the CEO in charge of putting on the Olympics in Vancouver. It is hoped that these examples will highlight for students that management takes place in a variety of contexts.

- New profiles of Canadian organizations and managers who demonstrate a commitment to social responsibility and adaptability

- Up-to-date statistics wherever possible, and more discussion of the Canadian, rather than the U.S., scene

- Increased coverage of the impact of globalization, with more international examples provided

- Up-to-date theory and empirical findings in all chapters

- Greater emphasis on strategic management

- New and up-dated case materials and thought-provoking discussion questions

Chapter Pedagogical Features

We have continued to enhance the tenth Canadian edition through a rich variety of pedagogical features, including the following:

- Numbered learning outcomes at the opening of each chapter guide student learning. These are repeated in the margin at the start of each major chapter section to reinforce the learning outcome.

- A vignette opens each chapter and is threaded throughout the chapter to help students apply a story to the concepts they are learning.

- The vignette is followed by *Think About It* questions that give students a chance to put themselves into the shoes of managers in various situations.

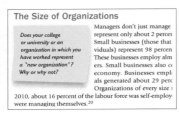

The Size of Organizations

Does your college
or university or an
organization in which you
have worked represent
a "new organization"?
Why or why not?

Managers don't just manage
represent only about 2 percer
Small businesses (those that
viduals) represent 98 percen
These businesses employ alm
ers. Small businesses also c
economy. Businesses empl
als generated about 29 perc
Organizations of every size r
2010, about 16 percent of the labour force was self-employ
were managing themselves.[20]

Q&A 8.3

PRISM 3.2

Diversity in Action 3.1

- Integrated questions (in the form of green notes) throughout the chapters help students relate management to their everyday lives.

- References in the margin to *Q&A, PRISM, and Diversity in Action* throughout the chapters enhance students' learning. These references refer students to the MyManagementLab website (www.pearsoned.ca/mymanagementlab), where students can complete exercises to better their understanding or learn more about a management concept or issue. For example, the *PRISM* (PRactical Interactive Skills Modules) feature consists of 12 interactive decision-tree–style skills exercises. The interactive decision-tree design of the management situations gives students the chance to try different management approaches and to learn why certain approaches are better than others.

- *Management Reflections* appear at appropriate places in chapters. These are longer examples designed to enhance student learning. While some of the *Reflections* are at a general managerial level, others focus on international issues, ethics, and innovation.

- *Tips for Managers* provides "take-aways" from each chapter—ideas that managers and would-be managers can start to put into action right now, based on what they have learned in the chapter.

- *Summary and Implications* are organized around the learning outcomes introduced at the beginning of each chapter.

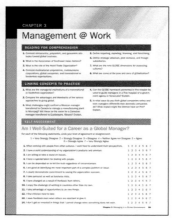

End-of-Chapter Applications

Taking the best of our end-of-chapter features from the ninth Canadian edition, we have maintained a rich section of applications, *Management @ Work*. This section provides students with a variety of opportunities to apply the material right now, even if they are not managers. It includes the following:

- *Reading for Comprehension.* Students can review their understanding of the chapter content.
- *Linking Concepts to Practice.* Students can see the application of theory to management situations.

- *Self-Assessment.* This feature includes one self-assessment exercise for the student to fill out, and refers students to the MyManagementLab website, where they can access additional interactive self-assessment exercises that will help them discover things about themselves, their attitudes, and their personal strengths and weaknesses. (For more details, see the Supplements section on pages xxi–xxii.)

- *Management for You Today.* Students can apply chapter material to their daily lives, helping them see that planning, leading, organizing, and controlling are useful in one's day-to-day life too. This feature is divided into two parts:

  - *Dilemma,* which presents an everyday scenario for students to resolve using management tools
  - *Becoming a Manager,* which provides suggestions for students on activities and actions they can do right now to help them in preparing to become a manager.

- *Working Together: Team-Based Exercise.* Students get a chance to work together in groups to solve a management challenge.

- New focus! *Ethics in Action.* This feature gives students an opportunity to consider ethical issues that relate to chapter material. This feature has been broadened to include a focus on values-led management and sustainability. It has two parts:

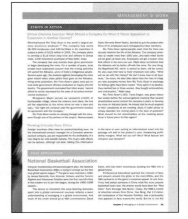

  - *Ethical Dilemma Exercise,* which focuses on ethical dilemmas that employees of organizations may face
  - *Thinking Critically About Ethics,* which encourages students to think critically about ethical issues they may encounter

- *Case Application.* This is a decision-focused case that asks students to determine what they would do if they were in the situation described.

- *Developing Your Diagnostic and Analytical Skills.* In this feature, students have the opportunity to apply chapter material to analyze a case. This feature effectively adds a second case to each chapter.

- *Developing Your Interpersonal Skills.* To reflect the importance being placed on skills, each chapter has this skills-based feature that encompasses the four management functions. The feature includes lessons about a particular skill, steps in developing the skill, a practice assignment to use the skill (often a mini-case), and a set of reinforcement assignments to further work on accomplishing the skill.

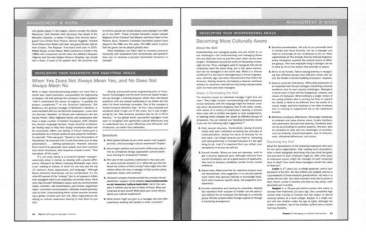

New to the Tenth Canadian Edition

In addition to the new pedagogical features highlighted above, we have introduced other new learning aids and made significant changes to content.

ScanLife™ Barcodes

ScanLife™ 2D Barcodes & Study on the Go: Featured at the beginning and end of each chapter, the ScanLife™ barcodes provide an unprecedented seamless integration between text and online content for students. The free, downloadable app (for instructions go to: http://web.scanlife.com/us_en/download-application) enables students to link to Pearson Canada's unique Study on the Go content directly from their smartphones, allowing them to study whenever and wherever they wish! Upon scanning, students can follow the online instructions to search the rich study assets, including glossary flashcards, audio summaries, and quizzes.

Video Cases

Ten video case incidents appear at the end of the book. A number of these come from the CBC television program *Venture*. The videos generally focus on several management issues within one of the book's five parts. Four new cases were carefully selected for this edition by David Delcorde of the University of Ottawa to provide instructors with audio-visual material to engage their students' attention. The videos are available in DVD format (978-0-13-270700-8).

Chapter-by-Chapter Highlights

Below, we highlight all the new material that has been added to each chapter.

Chapter 1: Introduction to Management and Organizations

- New! Introduction of adaptability as a core skill for successful organizations
- Broadened discussion of ethics to include social responsibility
- New! Discussion of innovation and creativity as contributors to building an adaptable organization

Chapter 2: Organizational Culture and the Organizational Environment

- New! Opening case on 3M as an example of how to build an innovative and adaptable culture
- New! Discussion of building a culture that supports diversity
- New! Discussion of springboard stories in sharing organizational culture and knowledge
- New! Expanded discussion of the impacts of an aging population in Canada and globally

Chapter 3: Managing in a Global Environment

- New! Section on the BRICS countries (Brazil, Russia, India and China, South Africa)

New! Chapter 4: Managing Entrepreneurially

- New! Discussion of entrepreneurship and why it's important
- New! Exploration of the nature of opportunity-seeking behaviour

- New! Examination of the importance of entrepreneurs' opportunity-seeking focus in enabling organizations to build cultures that are flexible, nimble, and innovative
- New! Examination of entrepreneurship from the perspective of the four managerial functions: planning, organizing, leading, and controlling
- New! Discussion of the continuing importance and forms of innovation
- New! *Developing Your Diagnostic and Analytical Skills:* "Second Chance: The Business of Life," which looks at the social return on Investment (SROI) of programs aimed at redirecting the entrepreneurial passions of youth in conflict with the law

Chapter 5: Managing Responsibly and Ethically

- Updated discussion of what it means to be a socially responsible manager
- New! Discussion of how managing responsibly contributes to organizational performance
- New! Examples of current sustainable management practices
- New! Discussion of the principles of values-based management
- New! An outline of current global ISO 14000 environmental standards for sustainability and the ISO 26000 standards for social responsibility released in November 2010.

Chapter 6: Decision Making

- New! Discussion of wicked problems as a context for unstructured problems
- New! *Management Reflection* on using IT to make better decisions

Chapter 7: Foundations of Planning

- New! Mention of SMART goals

Chapter 8: Managing Strategically

- Updated Indigo/Chapters opening case

Chapter 9: Planning Tools and Techniques

- Updated 2010 Olympic Games opening case
- Updated discussion of forecasting

Chapter 10: Organizational Structure and Design

- New! Updated discussion of project teams in creative organizations

Chapter 11: Managers and Communication

- New! Opening case on Lymbix: developing tone-checking software as vehicle for examining role of IT in communication
- New! Chapter restructured to focus on the role of managers in communication rather than the role of IT in communication
- Updated *Management Reflection* on the Yellow Pages
- Deepened discussion of active listening
- New! Discussion of privacy issues including PIPEDA (the Personal Information Protection and Electronic Documents Act)

Chapter 12: Managing Human Resources

- New! Number of learning outcomes reduced from nine to five and chapter reorganized around these learning outcomes
- New! Discussion of the impact of global aging on reducing the size of the workforce

Chapter 13: Managing Change and Innovation

- New! Chapter moved to Part Three: Organizing
- New! Discussion connected to material in Chapter 1 on building an adaptable organization and to Chapter 4: Managing Entrepreneurially

Chapter 14: Leadership

- Chapter streamlined and restructured to make it more digestable by students in terms of length and depth of coverage
- New! Showcases six Canadian leaders in different roles with a balance in gender rather than a single leader in a single context, including David Johnston as governor general, Phil Fontaine as chief of the Assembly of First Nations, Moya Greene as president of Canada Post, Annette Verschuren as president of Home Depot Canada, and David Cheesewright as president of Wal-Mart Canada

Chapter 15: Motivating Employees

- New! Discussion of McClelland's three needs theory
- New! Discussion of reinforcement theory

Chapter 16: Managing Groups and Teams

- Updated opening case on the Canadian men's Olympic hockey team
- Expanded discussion of effective group processes
- Expanded discussion on resolving conflict

Chapter 17: Foundations of Control

- New! Discussion of how controlling sometimes requires a change in direction to move beyond an existing plan, and can lead to increased opportunity recognition
- New! The competencies of a management accountant listed in three categories: accounting, management, and strategy

New! Chapter 18: Managing Operations

- New! Supplement on the subject converted to a full chapter, reinforcing managing operations as a core management skill
- Updated examples and increased emphasis on value chain management
- New! Opening case on Eldis Group and PartSelect: a pure e-commerce example to illustrate an application of value chain management
- New! Discussion of the use of analytics and "A" and "B" testing in managing operations
- New! Discussion of all three ISO quality standards: 9000 for operations, 14000 for sustainability, and the newly launched 26000 for social responsibility

Supplements

With this tenth edition of *Management*, we continue to offer MyManagementLab, which provides students with an assortment of tools to help enrich and expedite learning. MyManagementLab is an online study tool for students and an online homework and assessment tool for faculty. MyManagementLab lets students assess their understanding through auto-graded tests and assignments, develop a personalized study plan to address areas of weakness, and practise a variety of learning tools to master management principles. Some of these tools are described below:

- *Auto-Graded Tests and Assignments* MyManagementLab comes with two sample tests per chapter. These were prepared by Sandi Findlay, Mount Saint Vincent University. Students can work through these diagnostic tests to identify areas they have not fully understood. The sample tests generate a personalized study plan. Instructors can also assign these sample tests or create assignments, quizzes, or tests using a mix of publisher-supplied content and their own custom exercises.

- *Personalized Study Plan* In MyManagementLab, students are treated as individuals with specific learning needs. Students have limited study time, so it is important for them to be as effective as possible. A personalized study plan is generated from each student's results on sample tests and instructor assignments. Students can clearly see the topics they have mastered—and, more importantly, the concepts they need to work on.

- *eText* Students can study without leaving the online environment. They can access the eText online, including animated text figures. This interactive eText allows students to highlight sections, bookmark pages, or take notes electronically just as they might do with a traditional text. As an instructor, you can also add your own notes to the text that can be shared with your students.

- *Robbins OnLine Learning System (R.O.L.L.S.)* R.O.L.L.S. features the following tools:

  - *Robbins Self-Assessment Library*. The Self-Assessment Library helps students create a skills portfolio. It is an interactive library of 67 behavioural questionnaires that help students discover things about themselves, their attitudes, and their personal strengths and weaknesses. Learning more about themselves gives students interesting insights into how they might behave as a manager and motivates them to learn more about management theories and practices that can help them better understand what it takes to be a successful manager.

  - *Q&A*. The questions from each chapter that students ask most frequently are answered by the authors—in both written and audio format. It's like having an instructor standing over their shoulder at the times students need it the most.

  - *Diversity in Action*. These interactive exercises put students in the challenging role of a manager making decisions related to age, gender, or ethnic diversity.

  - *Passport: Managing in a Global Environment*. This multimedia module illustrates the globalization challenges that managers face. There are three to four global case scenarios that students can do at the end of each part. These cases span 13 different countries. Students will find a map and click a desired country to get information about that country (video and written information is provided). Using this information, students make decisions about the most appropriate ways to handle the managerial problems described in the case scenarios.

  - *Ethics*. In these interactive exercises, students are put in the role of a manager making decisions about current ethical issues.

  - *PRactical Interactive Skills Modules (PRISM)*. This module consists of 12 interactive decision-tree–style comprehensive exercises that provide students with an opportunity to try out different management skills and learn why certain approaches are better than others.

- *Glossary Flashcards* This study aid is useful for students' review of key concepts.

- *BizSkills Mini-Simulations* The BizSkills mini-simulations help students analyze and make decisions in common business situations; the simulations assess student choices and include reinforcement quizzes, outlines, and glossaries.
- *Careers in Management* These documents outline professional management associations in Canada and describe some key management positions and the skills students need to pursue specific careers.
- *Acadia/Pearson Business Insider Series Videos* The Acadia/Pearson video portal features interviews with more than 70 executives from a variety of companies. A list of the videos specifically correlated to the tenth Canadian edition of *Management* is available on MyManagementLab.
- *Management in the News* These mini cases were developed from current news articles and include questions for students to answer. These cases will be updated throughout the year.
- *Research Navigator* Research Navigator helps students quickly and efficiently make the most of their research time by providing four exclusive databases of reliable source content, including the EBSCO Academic Journal and Abstract Database, New York Times Search by Subject Archive, "Best of the Web" Link Library, and Financial Times Article Archive and Company Financials.

Additional Instructor Resources

For instructors, we have created an outstanding supplements package, all conveniently available online through MyManagementLab in the special instructor area, downloadable from our product catalogue at www.pearsoned.ca, or available on a single CD-ROM.

The Instructor's Resource CD-ROM (978-0-13-270698-8) contains the following:

- Instructor's Resource Manual (includes video teaching notes and detailed lecture outlines) prepared by Ed Leach and Mary Kilfoil, Dalhousie University
- PowerPoint Slides, prepared by Sandra Wellman, Seneca College
- Test Item File in Word, prepared by Ron Velin
- Video Guide, prepared by David Delcorde, University of Ottawa
- Image Library containing all exhibits in the text

MyTest

The new edition test bank comes with MyTest, a powerful assessment generation program that helps instructors easily create and print quizzes, tests, exams, as well as homework or practice handouts. Questions and tests can all be authored online, allowing instructors ultimate flexibility and the ability to efficiently manage assessments at any time, from anywhere. MyTest for *Management*, tenth Canadian edition, includes over 2500 questions in true/false, multiple-choice, and short-answer formats. These questions are also available in Microsoft Word format on the Instructor's Resource CD-ROM.

Video Cases

Video cases are available in DVD format (978-0-13-270700-8). These cases were prepared by David Delcorde, University of Ottawa. A complete video guide is available on the Instructor's Resource CD-ROM.

CourseSmart

CourseSmart goes beyond traditional expectations—providing instant, online access to the textbooks and course materials you need at a lower cost for students. And even as students save money, you can save time and hassle with a digital eTextbook that allows you to search for the most relevant content at the very moment you need it. Whether it's evaluating textbooks or creating lecture notes to help students with difficult concepts, CourseSmart can make life a little easier. See how when you visit www.coursesmart.com/instructors.

Technology Specialists

Pearson's Technology Specialists work with faculty and campus course designers to ensure that Pearson technology products, assessment tools, and online course materials are tailored to meet your specific needs. This highly qualified team is dedicated to helping schools take full advantage of a wide range of educational resources, by assisting in the integration of a variety of instructional materials and media formats. Your local Pearson Education sales representative can provide you with more details on this service program.

Acknowledgments

A number of people worked hard to give this tenth Canadian edition of *Management* a new look. The good humour, patience, and wisdom of our developmental editor, Joanne Sutherland, helped shape the final product and kept on us on track when we strayed. Thank you, Joanne!

We would like to thank Tara Tovell, the production editor for this project, who did an amazing job of making sure everything was in place and written clearly. Amanda Campbell was very helpful in doing the photo research, and made some incredible finds in the search for photos to highlight management concepts.

We enjoyed the opportunity to work with Marcia Gallego, the copy editor, and Patricia Jones, the proofreader on this project. Both were extremely diligent about checking for consistency throughout the text. Their keen eyes helped to make the pages as clean as they are. Together, they assisted us in understanding the value of virtual teams.

We received incredible support for this project from a variety of people at Pearson Education Canada. Karen Elliott and Nick Durie, acquisitions editors, stepped up and shared our vision for this edition. There are a number of other key contributors at Pearson who also played a major role in transforming the manuscript into the final product and delivering it into your hands. To all of them we extend our thanks. The Pearson sales team is an exceptional group, and we know they will do everything possible to make this book successful. We appreciate and value their support and interaction, particularly that of Kelly Brown, our local sales representative, who suggested we put in our proposal for this edition.

Finally, we want to acknowledge the many reviewers of this textbook for their detailed and helpful comments:

Jane Anderson, Lethbridge College

Sharon Archibald, Fleming College

Joanne Boothby, Grant MacEwan University

John Brownlee-Baker, Capilano University

Alok Dua, University of Manitoba

Denise Fortier, Bishop's University

Tim Hardie, Lakehead University

Sarah Holding, Vancouver Island University

Michelle Inness, University of Alberta

Robert MacDonald, Crandall University

Allan MacKenzie, Wilfrid Laurier University

Noufou Ouedraogo, Grant MacEwan University

Michael Pearl, Seneca College

Lisa Phillips, Douglas College

Kerry Rempel, Okanagan College

Kim Richter, Kwantlen Polytechnic University

Pat Sherlock, Nova Scotia Community College

Bryan Webber, Vancouver Island University

Claudia Zhang, Grant MacEwan University

We dedicate this book to our parents, Charles and Florence Leach and Gerald and Joan Kilfoil, who have taught us so much. In addition, we would like to thank our students, who have been the inspiration for this edition. Thank you all for keeping it so interesting!

Ed Leach and Mary Kilfoil
April 2011

ABOUT THE AUTHORS

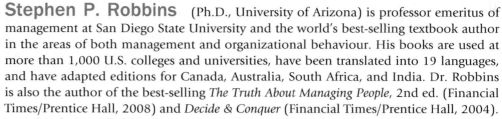

Stephen P. Robbins (Ph.D., University of Arizona) is professor emeritus of management at San Diego State University and the world's best-selling textbook author in the areas of both management and organizational behaviour. His books are used at more than 1,000 U.S. colleges and universities, have been translated into 19 languages, and have adapted editions for Canada, Australia, South Africa, and India. Dr. Robbins is also the author of the best-selling *The Truth About Managing People*, 2nd ed. (Financial Times/Prentice Hall, 2008) and *Decide & Conquer* (Financial Times/Prentice Hall, 2004).

In his "other life," Dr. Robbins actively participates in masters' track competitions. Since turning 50 in 1993, he's won 18 national championships, won 12 world titles, and set numerous U.S. and world age-group records at 60, 100, 200, and 400 metres. In 2005, Dr. Robbins was elected into the USA Masters' Track & Field Hall of Fame.

Mary Coulter received her Ph.D. in management from the University of Arkansas in Fayetteville. Before completing her graduate work, she held different jobs, including high school teacher, legal assistant, and government program planner. She has taught at Drury University, the University of Arkansas, Trinity University, and, since 1983, Missouri State University. Dr. Coulter's research interests have focused on competitive strategies for not-for-profit arts organizations and the use of new media in the educational process. Her research on these and other topics has appeared in such journals as *International Journal of Business Disciplines, Journal of Business Strategies, Journal of Business Research, Journal of Nonprofit and Public Sector Marketing,* and *Case Research Journal*. In addition to Management, Dr. Coulter has published other books with Prentice Hall, including *Strategic Management in Action*, now in its fourth edition, and *Entrepreneurship in Action*, which is in its second edition. When she's not busy teaching or writing, she enjoys puttering around in her flower gardens, trying new recipes, reading all different types of books, and enjoying many different activities with Ron, Sarah and James, and Katie and Matt.

Ed Leach received his Ph.D. in computing technology in education from Nova Southeastern University in Ft. Lauderdale and an MBA from the University of Western Ontario. Prior to completing his graduate work, Dr. Leach was an entrepreneur who also taught in the professional programs of the Society of Management Accountants and the Purchasing Management Association of Canada. His interest in working with entrepreneurs has continued since joining Dalhousie University, where Dr. Leach has mentored lead entrepreneurs during the start-up phase of their technology businesses, including two IPOs. Dr. Leach is an award-winning professor who developed the introductory management course at Dalhousie and has taught it since its inception in 1999. His research interests lie in the field of entrepreneurship and specifically the role of creativity in triggering innovation. Dr. Leach is the director of the Norman Newman Centre for Entrepreneurship, in the School of Business, Dalhousie University, and is a past president of the Canadian Council for Small Business and Entrepreneurship (CCSBE), 2006. When he is not busy teaching, he enjoys cooking and spending time with family, especially his and Mary's four grandchildren.

Mary Kilfoil received her Ph.D. from Dalhousie University and her master's degree from Carleton University, in economics. Dr. Kilfoil teaches the introductory management course in the Faculty of Management as well as courses in economics, program evaluation, and research methods at Dalhousie University. She has developed course curricula for the MBA Financial Services Program and the Executive Masters of Public Administration (MPA-M) Program offered to government employees across Canada. Dr. Kilfoil has more than 20 years' experience as a manager in the private sector and holds the position of senior economist and partner at Gardner Pinfold Consultants, one of Canada's leading firms specializing in economic analysis. She has extensive experience as a researcher, analyst, and report writer in the field of environmental and natural resource economics, economic impact analysis, and climate change policy, with some 75 major reports to her credit. She is also the co-director for the Dalhousie Shad Valley Program, a residential academic program for gifted youth. When she is not busy working, Mary enjoys spending time with family, gardening, outdoor recreational activities, and travelling.

PART ONE

DEFINING THE MANAGER'S TERRAIN

In PART ONE,
we look at the terrain in which managers operate and discuss the following topics:

Chapter 1	Introduction to Management and Organizations
Supplement 1	History of Management Trends
Chapter 2	Organizational Culture and the Organizational Environment
Chapter 3	Managing in a Global Environment
Chapter 4	Managing Entrepreneurially
Chapter 5	Managing Responsibly and Ethically

Welcome to the world of management! One thing is for certain: Organizations need managers. Good managers. No, not just good managers. They need *great* managers! They need people who can *set goals and plan* what needs to be done to achieve those goals. Organizations need people who can *organize and arrange* things so those goals can be met. They need people who can *lead and motivate* others in working toward those goals—who can pull up their sleeves and pitch in if needed. And they need people who can *evaluate* whether the goals were accomplished efficiently and effectively and who can change things when needed. Those people are managers. And great managers are essential for great organizations. We want to start you on your journey to being a *great* manager. What's it like to be a manager today?

Introduction to Management and Organizations

In this chapter, we'll introduce you to who managers are and what they do. One thing you'll discover is that the work managers do is vitally important to organizations. But you'll also see that being a manager—a good manager—isn't easy. The best companies and organizations are more flexible, more efficient, and more adaptable. After reading and studying this chapter, you will achieve the following learning outcomes.

Learning Outcomes

1 Understand what makes someone a manager.

2 Define management and describe what managers do.

3 Describe the characteristics of an organization.

4 Understand the challenges to managing.

5 Understand the importance of building an adaptable organization.

6 Explain the value of studying management.

▶ ▶ ▶ The celebration in 1984 of the 450th anniversary of explorer Jacques Cartier's arrival in Canada saw a small troupe of street performers put together a circus.[1] Who could have imagined at the time that this ragtag bunch of French-Canadian hippies would become the Cirque du Soleil ("circus of the sun") that we know today. Twenty-seven years later, Cirque du Soleil's big-budget, animal-free circuses are Canada's largest cultural export, pulling in an estimated $800 million a year in revenue. The dynamic between CEO Daniel Lamarre and company founder Guy Laliberté is an interesting one as the pragmatic (Lamarre) meets the creative (Laliberté). As Lamarre puts it, "I'm very lucky because we are so complementary. What Guy likes to do, I don't and what I like to do, he doesn't." Laliberté rather likes people with stratospheric ambitions. At a time when most businesses have reasonably modest expectations, Carmen Ruest, one of the original Cirque pioneers and now the company's director of creation, has been known to say, "The word *impossible* does not exist here."

Guy Laliberté created the ONE DROP Foundation in 2007 to fight global poverty by providing sustainable access to safe water. The ideals of the foundation reflect the values that have always been at the heart of Cirque du Soleil: the belief that life gives back what you have given and even the smallest gesture will make a difference. When Guy Laliberté became the first Canadian private space explorer, he dedicated his mission to raising awareness of water issues on Earth. As part of the first Poetic Social Mission in space, Laliberté hosted *Moving Stars and Earth for Water* from the International Space Station, a webcast concert featuring various artistic performances unfolding in 14 cities around the world.

Think About It

What kinds of skills do managers need? Put yourself in Guy Laliberté's shoes. What kinds of leadership skills would you need to manage 4000 employees in 40 countries? Is managing in a creative and artistic organization different from managing in any other organization? Do other organizations share Laliberté's belief that "life gives back what you have given"?

Guy Laliberté is a good example of what today's successful managers are like and the skills they must have to deal with the problems and challenges of managing in the twenty-first century. These managers may not be who or what you might expect. They range in age from under 18 to over 80. They run large corporations, as well as entrepreneurial start-ups. They are found in government departments, hospitals, small businesses, not-for-profit agencies, museums, schools, and even such nontraditional organizations as political campaigns and consumer cooperatives—in every country on the globe.

No matter where managers are found, the fact is that they have exciting and challenging jobs. Organizations need managers more than ever in these uncertain, complex, and chaotic times. *Managers do matter!* How do we know that managers matter to organizations? A Gallup Organization study based on interviews with 2 million employees at 700 companies found that the single most important variable in employee productivity and loyalty was not pay or benefits or workplace environment; it was the quality of the relationship between employees and their direct supervisors.[2] In addition, a KPMG/Ipsos Reid study of Canadian companies found that those that made the top 10 list for great human resource practices also scored high on financial performance and investment value. Six of the "Most Respected Corporations for Human Resources Management" placed in the top 10 on both financial measures, and nine scored in the top 10 of at least one of the financial measures.[3]

SCAN THIS

ScanLife™ Barcode: At the beginning and end of each chapter in the book, you will find a unique 2D barcode like the one above. Please go to http://web.scanlife.com/us_en/downloadapplication to see how you can download the ScanLife app to your smartphone for free. Once the app is installed, your phone will scan the code and link to a website containing Pearson Canada's Study on the Go content, including the popular study tools Glossary Flashcards, Audio Summaries, and Quizzes, which can be accessed anytime.

This textbook is about the important managerial work that Guy Laliberté, Daniel Lamarre, and the millions of other managers like them do. It recognizes the reality facing today's managers—new technologies and new ways of organizing work are altering old approaches. Today's successful managers must be able to blend tried-and-true management approaches with new ones. In this chapter, we introduce you to managers and management by looking at who managers are, what management is, what managers do, and what an organization is. We also consider the key challenges managers face today. Finally, we wrap up the chapter by discussing why it's important to study management.

Who Are Managers?

1. Understand what makes someone a manager.

MyManagementLab
Q&A 1.1

manager Someone who works with and through other people by coordinating their work activities in order to accomplish organizational goals.

It used to be fairly simple to define who managers were: They were the organizational members who told others what to do and how to do it. It was easy to differentiate *managers* from *nonmanagerial employees*. But it isn't quite so simple anymore. In many organizations, the changing nature of work has blurred the distinction between managers and nonmanagerial employees. Many nonmanagerial jobs now include managerial activities.[4] At General Cable Corporation's facility in Moose Jaw, Saskatchewan, for example, managerial responsibilities are shared by managers and team members. Most of the employees are cross-trained and multiskilled. Within a single shift, an employee may be a team leader, an equipment operator, a maintenance technician, a quality inspector, and an improvement planner.[5]

Today, how do we define who managers are? A **manager** is someone who works with and through other people by coordinating their work activities in order to accomplish organizational goals. A manager's job is not about *personal* achievement—it's about helping *others* do their work and achieve. That may mean coordinating the work of a departmental group, or it might mean supervising a single person. It could involve coordinating the work activities of a team composed of people from several different departments or even people outside the organization, such as temporary employees or employees who work for the organization's suppliers. Keep in mind, also, that managers may have other work duties not related to coordinating and integrating the work of others. For example, an insurance claims supervisor may also process claims in addition to coordinating the work activities of other claims clerks.

Types of Managers

first-line managers Managers at the lowest level of the organization who manage the work of nonmanagerial employees who are directly or indirectly involved with the production or creation of the organization's products.

middle managers Managers between the first-line level and the top level of the organization who manage the work of first-line managers.

top managers Managers at or near the top level of the organization who are responsible for making organization-wide decisions and establishing the plans and goals that affect the entire organization.

Is there some way to classify managers in organizations? In traditionally structured organizations (often pictured as being shaped like a pyramid where the number of employees is greater at the bottom than at the top), managers are often described as first-line, middle, or top (see Exhibit 1-1). Identifying exactly who the managers are in these organizations isn't difficult, although they may have a variety of titles. **First-line managers** are at the lowest level of management and manage the work of nonmanagerial employees who are directly or indirectly involved with the production or creation of the organization's products. They are often called *supervisors* but may also be called shift managers, district managers, department managers, office managers, or even foremen. **Middle managers** include all levels of management between the first-line level and the top level of the organization. These managers manage the work of first-line managers and may have titles such as regional manager, project leader, plant manager, or division manager. At or near the top of the organization are the **top managers**, who are responsible for making organization-wide decisions and establishing the plans and goals that affect the entire organization. These individuals typically have titles such as executive vice-president, president, managing director, chief operating officer, chief executive officer, or chair of the board. In the chapter-opening case, Guy Laliberté is the founder and driving creative force of Cirque du Soleil. He is involved in creating and implementing broad and comprehensive changes that affect the entire organization.

Not all organizations get work done using this traditional pyramidal form, however. Some organizations, for example, are more flexible and loosely structured with work being done by ever-changing teams of employees who move from one project to another as work

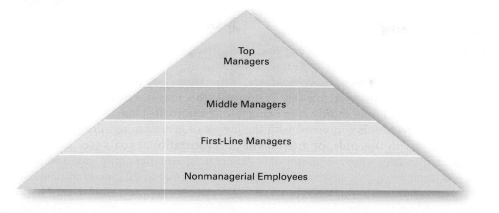

Exhibit 1-1

Managerial Levels

Top Managers

Middle Managers

First-Line Managers

Nonmanagerial Employees

demands arise. Although it's not as easy to tell who the managers are in these organizations, we do know that someone must fulfill that role—that is, there must be someone who works with and through other people by coordinating their work to accomplish organizational goals.

MyManagementLab
Q&A 1.2

What Is Management and What Do Managers Do?

▶ ▶ ▶ Managers plan, lead, organize, and control, and Daniel Lamarre, as chief executive officer of Cirque du Soleil, certainly carries out all these tasks. He has to coordinate the work activities of the entire company efficiently and effectively. But just as important to Lamarre is the creative side of Cirque—in fact, he sees his mission as finding work for artists. With operations in 40 countries, it might be tempting for Lamarre to try to arrive at consensus on issues, but at Cirque it is all about the power of the idea. Lamarre feels that the best ideas are lost if everyone has to compromise. So although it can be uncomfortable for some, debating ideas has become embedded in the company culture. "That is what we do," says Lamarre, "we are debating all of the time."[6]

2. Define management and describe what managers do.

Think About It

As a manager, Daniel Lamarre needs to plan, lead, organize, and control, and he needs to be efficient and effective. How might Lamarre balance the needs of efficiency and effectiveness with the creative and artistic mandate of his role as CEO of Cirque du Soleil? What skills are needed for him to plan, lead, organize, and control effectively? What challenges does he face performing these functions while running an international business?

Simply speaking, management is what managers do. But that simple statement does not tell us much, does it? A more thorough explanation is that **management** is coordinating work activities so that they are completed *efficiently* and *effectively* with and through other people. Management researchers have developed three specific categorization schemes to describe what managers do: functions, roles, and skills. In this section, we consider the challenges of balancing efficiency and effectiveness, and then examine the approaches that look at what managers do. In reviewing these categorizations, it might be helpful to understand that management is something that is a learned talent, rather than something that comes "naturally." Many people do not know how to be a manager when they first are appointed to that role.

management Coordinating work activities so that they are completed efficiently and effectively with and through other people.

Efficiency and Effectiveness

Efficiency refers to getting the most output from the least amount of inputs, or as management expert Peter Drucker explained, "doing things right."[7] Because managers deal with scarce inputs—including resources such as people, money, and equipment—they are concerned with the efficient use of those resources by getting things done at the least cost.

It's not enough just to be efficient, however. Management is also concerned with being effective, completing activities so that organizational goals are achieved. **Effectiveness** is often described as "doing the right things"—that is, those work activities that will help the organization reach its goals. For instance, hospitals may try to be efficient by reducing the number of days that patients stay in hospital. This may not be effective, however, if patients get sick at home shortly after being released from hospital.

Whereas efficiency is concerned with the means of getting things done, effectiveness is concerned with the ends, or attainment of organizational goals (see Exhibit 1-2). Management is concerned, then, not only with getting activities completed and meeting organizational goals (effectiveness) but also with doing so as efficiently as possible. In successful organizations, high efficiency and high effectiveness typically go hand in hand. Poor management is most often due to both inefficiency and ineffectiveness or to effectiveness achieved through inefficiency.

Management Functions

According to the functions approach, managers perform certain activities or duties as they efficiently and effectively coordinate the work of others. What are these activities or functions? In the early part of the twentieth century, a French industrialist named Henri Fayol first proposed that all managers perform five functions: planning, organizing, commanding, coordinating, and controlling.[8] Today, most management textbooks (including this one) are organized around the **management functions**: planning, organizing, leading, and controlling (see Exhibit 1-3). But you do not have to be a manager in order to have a need to plan, organize, lead, and control, so understanding these processes is important for everyone. Let's briefly define what each of these functions encompasses.

Planning

Think about a manager you have had. To what extent did he or she engage in planning, organizing, leading, and controlling?

If you have no particular destination in mind, then you can take any road. However, if you have someplace in particular you want to go, you have to plan the best way to get there. Because organizations exist to achieve some particular purpose, someone must clearly define that purpose and the means for its achievement. Managers performing the **planning** function define goals, establish an overall strategy for achieving those goals, and develop plans to integrate and

---

Exhibit 1-2

Efficiency and Effectiveness in Management

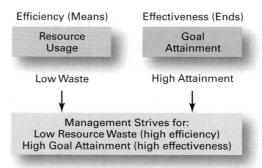

coordinate activities. This can be done by the CEO and senior management team for the overall organization. Middle-level managers often have a planning role within their units. First-line managers have a more limited role in the planning process, but may need to use planning to adequately schedule work and employees. Planning, by the way, is not just for managers. For instance, as a student, you need to plan for exams and your financial needs.

Organizing

Managers are also responsible for arranging work to accomplish the organization's goals. We call this function **organizing**. When managers organize, they determine what tasks are to be done, who is to do them, how the tasks are to be grouped, who reports to whom (that is, they define authority relationships), and where decisions are to be made. When you work in a student group, you engage in some of these same organizing activities—deciding on a division of labour, and what tasks will be carried out to get an assignment completed.

organizing A management function that involves determining what tasks are to be done, who is to do them, how the tasks are to be grouped, who reports to whom, and where decisions are to be made.

Leading

Every organization includes people, and a manager's job is to work with and through people to accomplish organizational goals. This is the **leading** function. When managers motivate subordinates, direct the work of individuals or teams, select the most effective communication channel, or resolve employee behaviour issues, they are leading. Knowing how to manage and lead effectively is an important, and sometimes difficult, skill as it requires the ability to successfully communicate. Leading is not just for managers, however. As a student, you might want to practise leadership skills when working in groups or club activities. You might also want to evaluate whether you need to improve your leadership skills in anticipation of the needs of future jobs.

leading A management function that involves motivating subordinates, directing the work of individuals or teams, selecting the most effective communication channels, and resolving employee behaviour issues.

Controlling

The final management function is **controlling**. After the goals are set (planning); the plans formulated (planning); the structural arrangements determined (organizing); and the people hired, trained, and motivated (leading), there has to be some evaluation of whether things are going as planned (controlling). To ensure that work is going as it should, managers must monitor and evaluate the performance of employees, technology, and systems. Actual performance must be compared with the previously set goals. If performance of individuals or units does not match the goals set, it's management's job to get performance back on track. This process of monitoring, comparing, and correcting is what we mean by the controlling function. Students, whether working in groups or alone, also face the responsibility of controlling; that is, they make sure the goals and actions are achieved and take corrective action when necessary.

controlling A management function that involves monitoring actual performance, comparing actual performance to a standard, and taking corrective action when necessary.

Just how well does the functions approach describe what managers do? Do managers always plan, organize, lead, and then control? In reality, what a manager does may not always happen in this logical and sequential order. But that does not negate the

---

Exhibit 1-3

Management Functions

Planning	Organizing	Leading	Controlling	
Defining goals, establishing strategy, and developing subplans to coordinate activities	Determining what needs to be done, how it will be done, and who is to do it	Directing and motivating all involved parties and resolving conflicts	Monitoring activities to ensure that they are accomplished as planned	*Lead to* Achieving the organization's stated purpose

importance of the basic functions that managers perform. Regardless of the order in which the functions are performed, the fact is that managers do plan, organize, lead, and control as they manage.

The continued popularity of the functions approach to describe what managers do is a tribute to its clarity and simplicity. But some have argued that this approach isn't appropriate or relevant.[9] So let's look at another perspective.

Management Roles

Henry Mintzberg, a prominent management researcher at McGill University in Montreal, studied actual managers at work. He says that what managers do can best be described by looking at the roles they play at work. His studies allowed him to conclude that managers perform 10 different but highly interrelated management roles.[10] The term **management roles** refers to specific categories of managerial behaviour. (Think of the different roles you play and the different behaviours you are expected to perform in these roles as a student, a sibling, an employee, a volunteer, and so forth.) As shown in Exhibit 1-4, Mintzberg's 10 management roles are grouped around interpersonal relationships, the transfer of information, and decision making.

The **interpersonal roles** involve working with people (subordinates and persons outside the organization) or performing duties that are ceremonial and symbolic in nature. The three interpersonal roles include being a figurehead, leader, and liaison. The **informational roles** involve receiving, collecting, and disseminating information. The three informational roles include monitor, disseminator, and spokesperson. Finally, the **decisional roles** involve making significant choices that affect the organization. The four decisional roles include entrepreneur, disturbance handler, resource allocator, and negotiator.

A number of follow-up studies have tested the validity of Mintzberg's role categories among different types of organizations and at different levels within given organizations.[11] The evidence generally supports the idea that managers—regardless of the type of organization or level in the organization—perform similar roles. However, the emphasis that managers give to the various roles seems to change with their organizational level.[12]

management roles Specific categories of managerial behaviour.

interpersonal roles Management roles that involve working with people or performing duties that are ceremonial and symbolic in nature.

informational roles Management roles that involve receiving, collecting, and disseminating information.

decisional roles Management roles that involve making significant choices that affect the organization.

Exhibit 1-4

Mintzberg's Management Roles

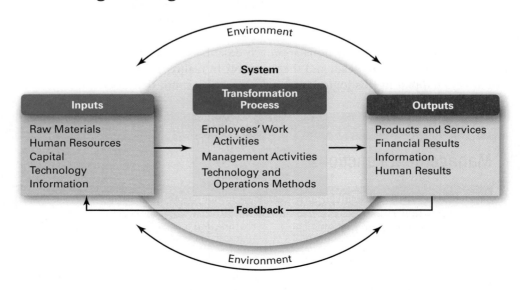

Source: H. Mintzberg, *The Nature of Managerial Work* (New York: Harper & Row, 1973), pp. 93–94. Copyright © 1973 by Henry Mintzberg. Reprinted by permission of Harper & Row, Publishers, Inc.

Specifically, the roles of disseminator, figurehead, negotiator, liaison, and spokesperson are more important at the higher levels of the organization, while the leader role (as Mintzberg defined it) is more important for lower-level managers than it is for either middle- or top-level managers.

Functions vs. Roles

So which approach to describing what managers do is better—functions or roles? Each has merit. However, the functions approach still represents the most useful way of conceptualizing the manager's job. "The classical functions provide clear and discrete methods of classifying the thousands of activities that managers carry out and the techniques they use in terms of the functions they perform for the achievement of goals."[13] Many of Mintzberg's roles align well with one or more of the functions. For instance, resource allocation is part of planning, as is the entrepreneurial role, and all three of the interpersonal roles are part of the leading function. Although most of the other roles fit into one or more of the four functions, not all of them do. The difference can be explained by the fact that all managers do some work that isn't purely managerial.[14]

Management Skills

Dell Inc. is one company that understands the importance of management skills.[15] It started an intensive five-day offsite skills-training program for first-line managers as a way to improve its operations. One of Dell's directors of learning and development thought this was the best way to develop "leaders who can build that strong relationship with their front-line employees." What did the supervisors learn from the skills training? Some things they mentioned were how to communicate more effectively and how to refrain from jumping to conclusions when discussing a problem with a worker.

Managers need certain skills to perform the duties and activities associated with being a manager. What types of skills does a manager need? Research by Robert L. Katz found that managers needed three essential skills: technical skills, human skills, and conceptual skills.[16]

Technical skills include knowledge of and expertise in a certain specialized field, such as engineering, computers, accounting, or manufacturing. These skills are more important at lower levels of management since these managers are dealing directly with employees doing the organization's work.

technical skills Knowledge of and expertise in a specialized field.

Human skills involve the ability to work well with other people, both individually and in a group. Because managers deal directly with people, this skill is crucial for managers at all levels! Managers with good human skills are able to get the best out of their people. They know how to communicate, motivate, lead, and inspire enthusiasm and trust. These skills are equally important at all levels of management. Management professor Jin Nam Choi, of McGill University, reports that research shows that 40 percent of managers either leave or stop performing within 18 months of starting at an organization "because they have failed to develop relationships with bosses, colleagues or subordinates."[17] Choi's comment underscores the importance of developing human skills.

human skills The ability to work well with other people, both individually and in a group.

Finally, **conceptual skills** involve the mental ability to analyze and generate ideas about abstract and complex situations. These skills help managers see the organization as a whole, understand the relationships among various subunits, and visualize how the organization fits into its broader environment. These skills are most important at the top management levels.

conceptual skills The mental ability to analyze and generate ideas about abstract and complex situations.

Exhibit 1-5 shows the relationship of the three skills to each level of management. Note that the three skills are important to more than one function. Additionally, in very flat organizations with little hierarchy, human, technical, and conceptual skills would be needed throughout the organization.

As you study the management functions in more depth, *Developing Your Diagnostic and Analytical Skills* and *Developing Your Interpersonal Skills*, found at the end of most chapters, will give you the opportunity to practise some of the key skills that are part of doing what a manager does. We feel that understanding and developing management skills is so important that we've included a skills feature in MyManagementLab. There, you'll find

Exhibit 1-5

Skills Needed at Different Management Levels

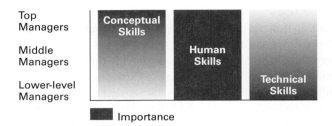

material on skill building as well as several interactive skills exercises. As you study the four management functions throughout the rest of the book, you'll be able to practise some key management skills. Although a simple skill-building exercise won't make you an instant expert, it can provide an introductory understanding of some of the skills you'll need to master in order to be an effective manager.

What Is an Organization?

3. Describe the characteristics of an organization.

organization A deliberate arrangement of people who act together to accomplish some specific purpose.

Managers work in organizations. But what is an organization? An **organization** is a deliberate arrangement of people who act together to accomplish some specific purpose. Your college or university is an organization; so are fraternities and sororities, government departments, churches, Amazon.ca, your neighbourhood video store, the United Way, the Toronto Raptors basketball team, your local co-op, and Canadian Tire. These are all organizations because they have three common characteristics, as shown in Exhibit 1-6:

1. *Distinct purpose.* This purpose is typically expressed in terms of a goal or a set of goals that the organization hopes to accomplish.

2. *Composed of people.* One person working alone is not an organization, and it takes people to perform the work that is necessary for the organization to achieve its goals.

3. *Deliberate structure.* Whether that structure is open and flexible or traditional and clearly defined, the structure defines members' work relationships.

Exhibit 1-6

Characteristics of Organizations

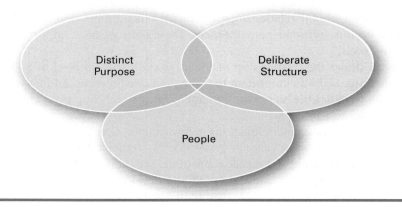

In summary, the term *organization* refers to an entity that has a distinct purpose, includes people or members, and has some type of deliberate structure.

Although these three characteristics are important to our definition of *what* an organization is, the concept of an organization is changing. It's no longer appropriate to assume that all organizations are going to be structured like Air Canada, Suncor Energy, or General Motors, with clearly identifiable divisions, departments, and work units. Just how is the concept of an organization changing? Exhibit 1-7 lists some differences between traditional organizations and new organizations. As these lists show, today's organizations are becoming more open, flexible, and responsive to changes.[18]

Why are organizations changing? Because the world around them has changed and continues to change. Societal, economic, political, global, and technological changes have created an environment in which successful organizations (those that consistently attain their goals) must embrace new ways of getting work done. As we stated earlier, even though the concept of organizations may be changing, managers and management continue to be important to organizations.

The Size of Organizations

Does your college or university or an organization in which you have worked represent a "new organization"? Why or why not?

Managers don't just manage in large organizations, which represent only about 2 percent of organizations in Canada. Small businesses (those that employ fewer than 100 individuals) represent 98 percent of all Canadian companies. These businesses employ almost half of all Canadian workers. Small businesses also contribute significantly to the economy. Businesses employing 50 or fewer individuals generated about 29 percent of total GDP in 2008.[19] Organizations of every size need managers. Moreover, in 2010, about 16 percent of the labour force was self-employed, meaning that these people were managing themselves.[20]

Managers are also not confined to manufacturing work, as only 12 percent of Canadians work in manufacturing organizations. Nineteen percent work in public sector jobs (those in the local, provincial, or federal government), while most Canadians (around 76 percent) work in the service sector of the economy.[21] The government is actually a large employer in Canada. For instance, Canada Post, a Crown corporation, is the fifth-largest employer in Canada, employing over 71 000, behind only Onex, Loblaw Companies, the Empire Company, the Royal Bank, and Magna International.[22]

Exhibit 1-7
The Changing Organization

Traditional Organization	New Organization
• Stable	• Dynamic
• Inflexible	• Flexible
• Job-focused	• Skills-focused
• Work is defined by job positions	• Work is defined in terms of tasks to be done
• Individual-oriented	• Team-oriented
• Permanent jobs	• Temporary jobs
• Command-oriented	• Involvement-oriented
• Managers always make decisions	• Employees participate in decision making
• Rule-oriented	• Customer-oriented
• Relatively homogeneous workforce	• Diverse workforce
• Workdays defined as 9 to 5	• Workdays have no time boundaries
• Hierarchical relationships	• Lateral and networked relationships
• Work at organizational facility during specific hours	• Work anywhere, anytime

The Types of Organizations

Managers work in a variety of situations, and thus the people to whom they are held accountable vary considerably. Large organizations in the **private sector** are often **publicly held**, which means that their shares are available on the stock exchange for public trading. Managers of these companies report to a board of directors that is responsible to shareholders (also known as stockholders). There are also numerous **privately held organizations** (whose shares are not available on the stock market), both large and small. Privately held organizations can be individually owned, family owned, or owned by some other group of individuals. A number of managers work in the **not-for-profit sector** (or nonprofit sector), where the emphasis is on providing charity or services rather than on making a profit. Examples of such organizations include the SPCA (Society for the Prevention of Cruelty to Animals), the Royal Ontario Museum, and Vancouver's Bard on the Beach Festival. Other organizational forms such as **NGOs** (nongovernmental organizations), partnerships, and cooperatives also require managers.

Many managers work in the **public sector** as **civil servants** for the provincial, federal, and local governments. The challenges of managing within government departments can be quite different from the challenges of managing in publicly held organizations. Critics argue that it is less demanding to work for governments because there are few measurable performance objectives, allowing employees to feel less accountable for their actions.

Some managers and employees work for **Crown corporations** such as Canada Post, the CBC, and the Business Development Bank of Canada. Crown corporations are structured like private sector corporations and have boards of directors, CEOs, and so on, but are owned by governments rather than shareholders. Employees in Crown corporations are not civil servants, and managers in Crown corporations are more independent than the senior bureaucrats who manage government departments.

Many of Canada's larger organizations are actually subsidiaries of American parent organizations (for example, Sears, Safeway, General Motors, and Ford Motor Company). These managers often report to American top managers and are not always free to set their own goals and targets. Conflicts can arise between how Canadian managers and the American managers to whom they report think things should be done.

What Challenges Do Managers Face?

▶ ▶ ▶ As CEO of Cirque du Soleil, Daniel Lamarre manages 4000 employees in 40 countries and also must manage his relationship with company founder Guy Laliberté, who is quite the character. "The reality is that Guy understands business and he understands that that is what he wants to do in life. . . . The first thing that you have to do when you work with someone like that, you have to like and love artists because Guy is an artist. If you are not able to work with an artist, you are in the wrong place."[23]

Think About It

Managing is far more complicated today than it ever was. Daniel Lamarre, like many managers, must deal with multicultural challenges, technological challenges, and the demand for more accountability from customers and clients. In the fall of 2008, Cirque and organizations around the world also had to deal with the global economic crisis. But unlike many other businesses, Cirque expected to maintain its profitability. How might managers in other organizations mimic the success of Cirque du Soleil in facing these challenges and create an adaptive organization that can react to the unexpected?

Managers have always had to deal with changes taking place inside and outside their organizations. In today's world, where managers everywhere are dealing with corporate ethics scandals, demands to be more socially responsible, challenges of managing a diverse workforce, and globalization, change is constant. We briefly describe these challenges below, and then throughout this textbook we discuss their impact on the way managers plan, organize, lead, and control.

---

private sector The part of the economy that is run by organizations which are free from direct government control; organizations in this sector operate to make a profit.

publicly held organization A company whose shares are available on the stock exchange for public trading.

privately held organization A company whose shares are not available on the stock exchange but are privately held.

not-for-profit sector The part of the economy that is run by organizations which operate for purposes other than making a profit (that is, providing charity or services).

NGO An organization that is independent from government control and whose primary focus is on humanitarian, development, and environmental sustainability activities.

public sector The part of the economy that is controlled by government.

civil servant A person who works in a local, provincial, or federal government department.

Crown corporation A commercial company owned by the government but independently managed.

4. Understand the challenges to managing.

Ethics and Social Responsibility

What do we mean by ethics? The term **ethics** refers to rules and principles that define right and wrong behaviour.[24] Unfortunately, the ethics of a situation are not always black and white. Consider the following: For some decisions, you can make choices exercising complete freedom of choice, with no regard to others. For other decisions, there is a set of laws that guides your behaviour. In between, there is a set of situations where you might want to consider the impact of your decision on others, even though there are no laws regarding your behaviour. This is the grey area of behaviour. Laws often develop because people did not act responsibly when they had a choice—for instance, not that long ago, drinking and driving did not have the penalties that it does now. Many people have talked about laws banning cellphones in various situations for much the same reason: Individuals do not think about the impact of their use on others.

ethics Rules and principles that define right and wrong behaviour.

The perception of what is an ethical decision can change with time. For example, in the nineteenth century, the Canadian federal government separated over 150 000 Aboriginal children from their families and communities to enrol them in residential schools. Two primary objectives of the residential school system were to remove children from the influence of their homes, families, traditions, and cultures, and to assimilate them into the dominant culture. These objectives were based on the assumption that Aboriginal cultures and spiritual beliefs were inferior. While the Canadian government undoubtedly felt it was doing what was right for Aboriginal children at the time, today, as Prime Minister Stephen Harper said in his formal speech of apology, "we recognize that this policy of assimilation was wrong, has caused great harm, and has no place in our country."[25]

What has happened to managerial ethics? This important aspect of managerial behaviour seems to have been forgotten or ignored when we see managers put their self-interest ahead of the interests of others who might be affected by their decisions. While most managers continue to behave in a highly ethical manner, recent widely publicized ethical abuses indicate a need to "upgrade" ethical standards. Efforts to improve the ethical behaviour of managers are being made at two levels. First, ethics education is being emphasized in university and college classrooms. Second, organizations themselves are taking a more active role in creating *and using* codes of ethics, providing ethics training programs, and hiring ethics officers. We want to prepare you to deal with the ethical dilemmas you are likely to face.

Beyond behaving ethically, today's managers are also challenged to be socially responsible when making decisions. In November 2010, the International Standards Organization

On June 11, 2008, Prime Minister Stephen Harper offered a public apology for the Canadian government's role in the administration of the residential school system. The purpose of the schools, which separated children from their families, was to forcibly assimilate First Nations children and has been described as "killing the Indian in the child." After their closing, the schools became notorious for allegations of physical, psychological, and sexual abuse and neglect.

social responsibility A business's intention, beyond its legal and economic obligations, to do the right things and act in ways that are good for society.

sustainable management The recognition by business of the close link between its decisions and activities and their impact on the natural environment.

(ISO) released its latest standard (ISO 26000), which "will help organizations for whom operating in a socially responsible manner is more than 'just a nice idea' to implement social responsibility in a pragmatic way that targets performance. It will be a powerful tool to help organizations move from good intentions about SR to good actions."[26] A *socially responsible* organization views things differently. It goes beyond what it's obligated to do or chooses to do because of some popular social need and does what it can to help improve society because it's the right thing to do. We define **social responsibility** as a business's efforts, beyond its legal and economic obligations, to do the right things and act in ways that are good for society.[27]

A key part of being socially responsible involves managing environmental resources in a responsible way. The recognition by business of the close link between its decisions and activities and their impact on the natural environment is referred to as **sustainable management**. Rachel Carson's *Silent Spring,* a book about the negative effects of pesticides on the environment that was published in 1962, is often cited as having launched the environmental movement. Until that time, few people (or organizations) paid attention to the environmental consequences of their decisions and actions.[28]

Business ethics, sustainability, and social responsibility are critical to all stakeholders and the performance of a company. We discuss ethics, social responsibility, and sustainable management extensively in Chapter 5. We have also included an *Ethical Dilemma Exercise* and a *Thinking Critically About Ethics* feature at the end of almost every chapter.

Workforce Diversity

workforce diversity The mix of people in organizations in terms of gender, race, ethnicity, disability, sexual orientation, and age, and demographic characteristics such as education and socio-economic status.

Another challenge facing managers is coordinating the work efforts of diverse organizational members in accomplishing organizational goals. Today's organizations are characterized by **workforce diversity**—the mix of people in organizations in terms of gender, race, ethnicity, disability, sexual orientation, and age, and demographic characteristics such as education and socio-economic status. Perhaps the most significant demographic force affecting workforce diversity during the next decade will be the aging of the population.[29]

Canada is a very diverse country, although this might not be apparent to everyone. Based on the 2006 census, on average, 19.8 percent of Canada's population is foreign-born.[30] This varies widely across the country, however. Ontario has the highest proportion of foreign-born individuals, 28.3 percent of its population. British Columbia is second, with 27.5 percent of its population being foreign-born. Toronto and Vancouver have much higher rates than their respective provinces. In these cities, foreign-born individuals make up about 45.7 and 39.6 percent of the population, respectively. By contrast, in Newfoundland and Labrador, only 1.7 percent of the population are foreign-born; in Nunavut, this figure is 1.5 percent; in Manitoba, it is 13.3 percent; and in Alberta, it is 16.2 percent. There are many more women and minorities—including people with disabilities and gays and lesbians—in the workforce than ever before, and most experts agree that diversity is steadily increasing.

The challenge for managers is to make their organizations more accommodating to diverse groups of people by addressing different lifestyles, family needs, and work styles. Smart managers recognize that diversity can be an asset because it brings a broad range of viewpoints and problem-solving skills to a company and also helps organizations better understand a diverse customer base.

Globalization

Management is no longer constrained by national borders and has to confront the challenges of operating in a global market.[31] Globalization has become such an important topic that we devote one chapter to it (Chapter 3) and integrate discussion of its impact on the various management functions throughout this textbook.

Canada has been slow historically to face the global challenge, although the relatively small size of many Canadian firms may be partly a factor in this.[32] The *Fortune* Global 500 ranks the largest global companies by revenue and in 2010 included only 11 Canadian firms, with Manulife being the top ranking at 208. The majority of the firms listed are American,

Textile workers in Italy are facing some of the challenges of globalization as inexpensive imports from Asia force the Italian clothing industry to cut jobs. But Italy's 120 000–member textile union, Filtea, is taking a controversial stand. The union leadership believes that the best way to protect Italian workers and their jobs is not to impose protective duties or quotas or to strike, but rather to press for better working conditions, tax breaks for corporate research, and ultimately better Italian products that will be more competitive through streamlined manufacturing processes.

but there are several entries from Britain, France, Germany, Japan, and China.[33] Managers who make no attempt to learn and adapt to changes in the global environment end up reacting rather than innovating; their organizations often become uncompetitive and fail.[34]

Managing in an E-business World

Can you imagine not using email? Do you expect advertisements to have web addresses included in their messages? Fifteen years ago email and web addresses were not the norm. Today's managers function in an e-business world. In fact, as a student, your learning may increasingly be taking place in an electronic environment. While critics have questioned the viability of Internet-based companies (dot-coms), especially after the high-tech collapse in 2000 and 2001, e-business is here for the long term. E-business offers many advantages to organizations—small or large, profit or not-for-profit, global or domestic—in all industries.[35]

E-business (electronic business) is a way of doing business that relies on electronic (Internet-based) linkages with employees, managers, customers, clients, suppliers, and partners to efficiently and effectively achieve goals. E-business includes **e-commerce (electronic commerce)**, which is essentially the sales and marketing component of e-business.[36] Firms such as Dell (computers), Indigo Books & Music, and Future Shop (electronics) are engaged in e-commerce, because they sell items over the Internet.

Not every organization is, or needs to be, a total e-business. Exhibit 1-8 illustrates three categories of e-business involvement.[37] The first category is an e-business *enhanced*

e-business (electronic business) A way of doing business that relies on electronic (Internet-based) linkages with employees, managers, customers, clients, suppliers, and partners to efficiently and effectively achieve goals.

e-commerce (electronic commerce) The sales and marketing component of e-business.

Exhibit 1-8

Categories of E-business Involvement

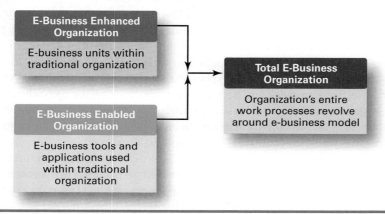

Amazon founder Jeff Bezos was a pioneer in the field of e-commerce when he founded the online bookseller. Today, Amazon has moved to a broader range of merchandise, including the Kindle, movies, electronics, computers, office equipment, clothing, shoes, and jewellery. Building on its expertise in e-commerce, the company now offers the Amazon Webstore, a "white label" website that allows companies to build an e-commerce business, combined with a fulfillment option that picks, packs, and ships their orders.

organization, a traditional organization that sets up e-business capabilities, usually e-commerce, while maintaining its traditional structure. Another category is an e-business *enabled* organization, which uses the Internet to perform its traditional business functions better, but not to sell anything. In other words, the Internet enables members of the organization to do their work more efficiently and effectively. Numerous organizations use electronic linkages to communicate with employees, customers, or suppliers, and to support them with information. The last category is a *total* e-business organization. Organizations such as Amazon.ca, Yahoo! Canada, Napster, and eBay are total e-business organizations; their whole existence revolves around the Internet.

Each of these different categories of e-business involvement presents unique management challenges, both in terms of managing employees and interacting with customers and clients. The high failure rate of the dot-coms underscores just how important good management is for e-business organizations.

Customers

Because of globalization and access to communications technology, especially the Internet, customers have access to more sources than ever before to find the supplies and services they want. Every organization needs customers. Without customers, most organizations would cease to exist. Yet focusing on customers has long been thought to be the responsibility of marketing types. "Let the marketers worry about customers" is how many managers have felt. We are discovering, however, that employee attitudes and behaviours play a big role in customer satisfaction. For instance, an analysis of a Qantas Airways passenger survey confirms this. Passengers were asked to rate their "essential needs" in air travel. Almost every factor listed by passengers was directly influenced by the actions of Qantas employees—from prompt baggage delivery, to courteous and efficient cabin crews, to assistance with connections, to quick and friendly check-ins.[38] Managers everywhere are beginning to understand that delivering consistent, high-quality service is essential for success and survival in today's competitive environment and that employees are an important part of that equation.[39] The implication is clear—managers must create a customer-responsive organization where employees are friendly and courteous, accessible, knowledgeable, prompt in responding to customer needs, and willing to do what is necessary to please customers.[40] We examine customer-service management and its importance to planning, organizing, leading, and controlling in several chapters.

Why Build an Adaptable Organization?

Earlier in the chapter, we distinguished between effectiveness and efficiency, but there is another point of view worthy of discussion. As early as 1972 it was suggested that the best companies in any field outshine their competitors in three areas: They are more flexible, more efficient, and more adaptable (see Exhibit 1-9).[41] Being flexible means reacting to events, while being adaptable means being proactive. An adaptable organization creates a set of skills, processes, and a culture that enable it to continuously look for new problems and offer solutions before the clients even realize they have a need.[42]

5. Understand the importance of building an adaptable organization.

Wicked Problems

The term **wicked problem** was first used in social planning in the 1960s to describe one that is impossible to solve because each attempt to create a solution changes the understanding of the problem.[43] Wicked problems are a continuing work in progress: They cannot be solved step by step because they are complex, and each possible solution may create a new problem. The world faces many wicked problems today, including climate change, poverty, pandemics such as AIDS, the fallout from the 2008 global financial crisis, terrorism, and environmental disasters like the 2010 massive oil spill in the Gulf of Mexico. All of these have an impact on how organizations do their business. A *Harvard Business Review* article suggests that many management strategy issues also are wicked problems as they have no easy solution.[44] How can these seemingly unsolvable problems be addressed, and what will be the impact on future management practice?

wicked problem A problem that is impossible to solve because each attempt to create a solution changes the understanding of the problem.

Innovation

> Now, economic progress depends more than ever on innovation. And the potential for technology innovation to improve lives has never been greater.[45]
>
> —*Bill Gates, co-founder of Microsoft*

When Apple came up with the Mac, IBM was spending at least 100 times more on R&D. According to Steve Jobs, co-founder of Apple, "It's not about money. It's about the people you have, how you're led, and how much you get it."[46]

In June 2010 the international Task Force on Business Schools and Innovation released its report, *Business Schools on an Innovation Mission.* The report suggested that innovation is about creating economic and social prosperity, and leadership and management are as

Exhibit 1-9

Characteristics of Effective Organizations

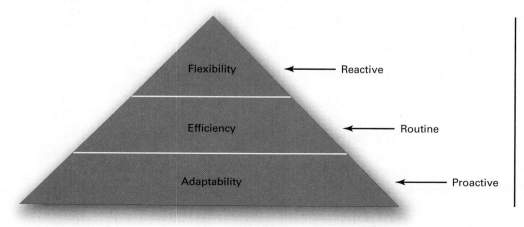

Flexibility ← Reactive

Efficiency ← Routine

Adaptability ← Proactive

Flexibility = Organizing to cope with the unexpected

Efficiency = Organizing for the expected

Adaptability = Organizing to anticipate new problems, trends, and opportunities

Source: Basadur Applied Creativity, Presentation March 18 and 19, 2010, Halifax, Nova Scotia.

essential to the process as science and technology. Innovation was seen as the bridge that connects business schools to a broader social purpose. The report observed that management innovation is "about the skills managers have in applying knowledge, judgment, and the ability to adapt and fashion new tools to solve problems."[47]

"Nothing is more risky than not innovating."[48] Innovation means doing things differently, exploring new territory, and taking risks. Innovation isn't just for high-tech and technologically advanced organizations. In today's world, organizational managers—at all levels and in all areas—need to encourage their employees to be on the lookout for new ideas and new approaches, not just in the products or services the organization provides, but in everything that is done. We examine the topic of building adaptable organizations and the role of innovation in accomplishing this objective in future chapters, where we discuss the core management competencies of planning, organizing, and leading.

Knowledge Management and Learning Organizations

Today's managers confront an environment in which change takes place at an unprecedented rate. As a result, many past management approaches and principles—created for a world that was more stable and predictable—no longer apply.

learning organization An organization that has developed the capacity to continuously learn, adapt, and change.

Organizations of the twenty-first century must be able to learn and respond quickly. They should be **learning organizations**—that is, ones that have developed the capacity to continuously learn, adapt, and change.[49] Such organizations need managers who can effectively challenge conventional wisdom, manage the organizations' knowledge bases, and make necessary changes. Exhibit 1-10 clarifies how a learning organization is different from a traditional organization.

knowledge management Cultivating a learning culture in which an organization's members systematically gather knowledge and share it with others in the organization to achieve better performance.

Part of a manager's responsibility is to understand the value of knowledge as an important resource, just like cash, raw materials, or office equipment. **Knowledge management** involves cultivating a learning culture in which an organization's members systematically gather knowledge and share it with others in the organization to achieve better performance.[50] For instance, accountants and consultants at Ernst & Young, a professional-services firm, document best practices they have developed, unusual problems they have dealt with, and other work information. This knowledge is then shared with all employees through computer-based applications and through COIN (community of interest) teams that meet regularly throughout the company.

Why Study Management?

6. Explain the value of studying management.

You may be wondering why you need to study management. If you are an accounting major, marketing major, or any major other than management, you may not understand

---

Exhibit 1-10

Learning Organization vs. Traditional Organization

	Traditional Organization	Learning Organization
Attitude toward change	If it's working, don't change it.	If you aren't changing, it won't be working for long.
Attitude toward new ideas	If it wasn't invented here, reject it.	If it was invented or reinvented here, reject it.
Who is responsible for innovation?	Traditional areas such as R&D	Everyone in organization
Main fear	Making mistakes	Not learning; not adapting
Competitive advantage	Products and service	Ability to learn; knowledge and expertise
Manager's job	Control others	Enable others

how studying management is going to help you in your career. We can explain the value of studying management by looking at the universality of management, the reality of work, and how management applies to anyone wanting to be self-employed.

MyManagementLab
Q&A 1.5

The Universality of Management

Just how universal is the need for management in organizations? We can say with absolute certainty that management is needed in all types and sizes of organizations, at all organizational levels, in all organizational work areas, and in all organizations, no matter what countries they are located in. This is known as the **universality of management** (see Exhibit 1-11). Managers in all these settings will plan, organize, lead, and control. However, this is not to say that management is done the same way in all settings. The differences in what a supervisor in a software applications testing facility at Microsoft does vs. what the CEO of Microsoft does are a matter of degree and emphasis, not of function. Because both are managers, both will plan, organize, lead, and control, but how they do so will differ.

universality of management
The reality that management is needed in all types and sizes of organizations, at all organizational levels, in all organizational work areas, and in organizations in all countries around the globe.

Since management is universally needed in all organizations, we have a vested interest in improving the way organizations are managed. Why? We interact with organizations every single day of our lives. Are you irritated when none of the salespeople in a department store seems interested in helping you? Do you get annoyed when you call your computer's technical help desk because your CD-ROM drive is no longer working, go through seven voice menus, and then get put on hold for 15 minutes? These are all examples of problems created by poor management. Organizations that are well managed—and we share many examples of these throughout the text—develop a loyal customer base, grow, and prosper. Those that are poorly managed find themselves with a declining customer base and reduced revenues. By studying management, you will be able to recognize poor management and work to get it corrected. In addition, you will be able to recognize good management and encourage it, whether it's in an organization with which you are simply interacting or whether it's in an organization in which you are employed.

The Reality of Work

Another reason for studying management is the reality that most of you, once you graduate and begin your career, will either manage or be managed. For those who plan on management careers, an understanding of the management process forms the foundation upon which to build your management skills. For those of you who don't see yourselves in management positions, you are still likely to have to work with managers. Also, assuming

Exhibit 1-11

Universal Need for Management

that you will have to work for a living and recognizing that you are very likely to work in an organization, you will probably have some managerial responsibilities even if you are not managers. Our experience tells us that you can gain a great deal of insight into the way your manager behaves and the internal workings of organizations by studying management. Our point is that you don't have to aspire to be a manager to gain something valuable from a course in management.

Self-Employment

You may decide that you want to run your own business rather than work for someone else. This will require that you manage yourself, and may involve managing other people as well. Thus, an understanding of management is equally important, whether you are a manager in someone else's business or running your own business.

SUMMARY AND IMPLICATIONS

1. Understand what makes someone a manager. Managers work with and through other people by coordinating employee work activities in order to accomplish organizational goals. The reality facing today's managers—new technologies and new ways of organizing work—are altering old approaches. Today's successful managers must be able to blend tried-and-true management approaches with new ones. Management is not about *personal* achievement—it's about helping *others* to achieve for the benefit of the organization as a whole.

▶ ▶ ▶ We saw that Guy Laliberté is both a visionary who guides the company and, together with Daniel Lamarre, a cheerleader who helps everyone in the organization do a better job.

2. Define management and describe what do managers do. Management is coordinating work activities so that they are done efficiently and effectively. *Efficiency* means "doing things right" and getting things done at the least cost. *Effectiveness* means "doing the right things" and refers to completing activities that will help achieve the organization's goals. To do their jobs, managers plan, organize, lead, and control. This means they set goals and plan how to achieve those goals; they figure out what tasks need to be done, and who should do them; they motivate individuals to achieve goals, and communicate effectively with others; and they put accountability measures into place to make sure that goals are achieved efficiently and effectively.

▶ ▶ ▶ In Daniel Lamarre's role as CEO of Cirque du Soleil, he manages the relationship with founder Guy Laliberté and, with managers in the rest of the organization, sets the goals for the overall organization.

3. Describe the characteristics of an organization. There is no single type of organization. Managers work in a variety of organizations, both large and small. They also work in a variety of industries, including manufacturing and the service sector. The organizations they work for can be publicly held (meaning shares are traded on the stock exchange and managers are responsible to shareholders), privately held (meaning shares of the company are not available to the public), public sector (where the government is the employer), or not-for-profit (where the emphasis is on providing charity or services rather than on making a profit).

▶ ▶ ▶ Cirque du Soleil is a privately held organization, and although 20 percent of the company is held by Dubai Ports, control rests with Guy Laliberté.

4. Understand the challenges to managing. Perhaps one of the greatest managerial challenges is the crisis in managing ethically, responsibly, and sustainably that is damaging confidence in today's organizations. Managers need to ensure that organizational members behave ethically. They also need to consider whether their own actions are socially responsible. Managers face the challenge of coordinating the work of a diverse workforce with differing needs. In addition, operating in today's global marketplace presents its own challenges and puts increasing pressure on managers. Customers and clients have access to more sources than ever before to meet their needs, particularly because of the growing number of e-businesses. Managers must be increasingly concerned with customer service and managing innovation to remain competitive. Finally, we live in a world of information overflow, and managers need to figure out how to manage all of that information and help their organizations become learning organizations. Even though all managers might not face all of these challenges, they should be aware of them, able to recognize them, and ready to handle them should they arise.

▶ ▶ ▶ With the establishment of the ONE DROP Foundation, Guy Laliberté, like many others, expanded his sense of responsibility beyond the company and its employees to the global community. The foundation works to fight poverty around the world by providing sustainable access to safe water.

5. Understand the importance of building an adaptable organization. The best companies in any field excel in three areas: They are more flexible, more efficient, and more adaptable than their competitors. Adaptable organizations create a set of skills, processes, and a culture that allows them to continuously look for new problems and offer solutions before the clients even realize they have a need. Organizations will continue to face wicked problems in the external environment and in strategy. Management innovation is "about the skills managers have in applying knowledge, judgment, and the ability to adapt and fashion new tools to solve problems" and has the potential to assist firms in managing responsibly and ethically.

▶ ▶ ▶ With operations in 40 countries, it would be tempting to try to arrive at consensus on issues, but at Cirque it is all about the power of the idea. "At Cirque, we say that it does not matter if it is your idea or my idea, at the end of the day the best idea has to prevail. In order to decide which one is the best idea, we have to debate. We have to agree that we disagree and then debate until we say, 'Okay, this is now what we think is the best idea.' That is a new culture that we like to impose on people because normally people are afraid to debate. So that is what we do, we are debating all of the time."

6. Explain the value of studying management. There are many reasons why students end up in management courses. Some of you are already managers, and are hoping to learn more about the subject. Some of you hope to be managers someday. And some of you might not have ever thought about being managers. Career aspirations are only one reason to study management, however. Any organization you encounter will have managers, and it is often useful to understand their responsibilities, challenges, and experience. Understanding management also helps us improve organizations.

CHAPTER 1

Management @ Work

READING FOR COMPREHENSION

1. How does a manager's job change with his or her level in the organization?

2. Why are efficiency, effectiveness, and adaptability important to management?

3. What are the four functions of management? Briefly describe each of them.

4. What are the three categories of management roles proposed by Mintzberg? Provide an example of each.

5. What are the three skills that affect managerial effectiveness?

6. What is an organization? Why are managers important to an organization's success?

7. Why is an understanding of management important even if you don't plan to be a manager?

8. How could an organization build an adaptive culture?

LINKING CONCEPTS TO PRACTICE

1. Is your instructor a manager? Discuss in terms of management functions, roles, and skills.

2. Is there one best "style" of management? Why or why not?

3. What characteristics of new organizations appeal to you? Why? Which do not? Why?

4. In today's economic environment, which is more important to organizations—efficiency, effectiveness, or adaptability? Explain your choice.

5. Can you think of situations where management does not matter to organizations? Explain.

6. How do societal trends (for example, social networking, or Baby Boomers reaching retirement age and leaving the workforce in unprecedented numbers) influence the practice of management? What are the implications for someone studying management?

SELF-ASSESSMENT

How Motivated Am I to Manage?

For each of the following statements, circle the level of agreement or disagreement that you personally feel:[51]

1 = Strongly Disagree 2 = Moderately Disagree 3 = Slightly Disagree 4 = Neither Agree nor Disagree 5 = Slightly Agree
6 = Moderately Agree 7 = Strongly Agree

1. I have a generally positive attitude toward those holding positions of authority over me.   1 2 3 4 5 6 7

2. I enjoy competition and striving to win for myself and my work group.   1 2 3 4 5 6 7

3. I like to tell others what to do and have no problem with imposing sanctions to enforce my directives.   1 2 3 4 5 6 7

4. I like being active, assertive, and protective of the members of my work group.   1 2 3 4 5 6 7

5. I enjoy the idea of standing out from the group, behaving in a unique manner, and being highly visible.   1 2 3 4 5 6 7

6. I am willing to perform routine, day-to-day administrative tasks and duties.   1 2 3 4 5 6 7

Scoring Key

Add up your responses to the six items.

Analysis and Interpretation

Not everyone is motivated to perform managerial functions. This instrument taps six components that have been found to be related to managerial success, especially in larger organizations. These are a favourable attitude toward authority; a desire to compete; a desire to exercise power; assertiveness; a desire for a distinctive position; and a willingness to engage in repetitive tasks.

Scores on this instrument will range from 6 to 56. Arbitrary cut-offs suggest that scores of 6 to 18 indicate low motivation to manage; 19 to 29 is moderate motivation; and 30 and above is high motivation.

What meaning can you draw from your score? It gives you an idea of how comfortable you would be doing managerial activities. Note, however, that this instrument emphasizes tasks associated with managing in larger and more bureaucratic organizations. A low or moderate score may indicate that you're more suited to managing in a small firm, in an organic organization, or in entrepreneurial situations.

More Self-Assessments   MyManagementLab

To learn more about your skills, abilities, and interests, go to the MyManagementLab website and take the following self-assessments:

- I.A.4.—How Well Do I Handle Ambiguity? (This exercise also appears in Chapter 8 on pages 229–230.)
- I.E.1.—What's My Emotional Intelligence Score?
- I.E.4.—Am I Likely to Become an Entrepreneur?
- III.C.1.—How Well Do I Respond to Turbulent Change? (This exercise also appears in Chapter 13 on pages 377–378.)

MANAGEMENT FOR YOU TODAY

Dilemma

Think about where you hope to be in your life five years from now (that is, your major goal). What is your competitive advantage for achieving your goal? What do you need to plan, organize, lead, and control to make sure that you reach your goal? Looking over Mintzberg's management roles (see Exhibit 1-4, on page 8), which roles seem comfortable for you? What areas need improvement?

Becoming a Manager

- Keep up with the current business news.
- Read books about good and bad examples of managing.
- Observe managers and how they handle people and situations.
- Talk to actual managers about their experiences—good and bad.

- In other classes you take, see what ideas and concepts potentially relate to being a good manager.
- Get experience in managing by taking on leadership roles in student organizations.
- Start thinking about whether or not you would enjoy being a manager.
- Stay informed about the current trends and issues facing managers.

WORKING TOGETHER: TEAM-BASED EXERCISE

A New Beginning

By this time in your life, all of you have had to work with individuals in managerial positions (or maybe you were the manager), either through work experiences or through other organizational experiences (social, hobby/interest, religious, and so forth). What do you think makes some managers better than others? Are there certain characteristics that distinguish good managers? Form groups of three or four individuals. Discuss your experiences with managers—good and bad. Draw up a list of the characteristics of those individuals you felt were good managers. For each characteristic, indicate which management function (planning, organizing, leading, and controlling) you think it falls under. Also identify which of Mintzberg's 10 roles the good managers seemed to fill. Were any of the roles missing from your list of characteristics? What explanation can you give for this? As a group, be prepared to explain the functions and roles that good managers are most likely to fill.

ETHICS IN ACTION

Ethical Dilemma Exercise: Are Canadian Executives Paid Too Much?

Are we paying executives too much? Is an average salary in 2008 of $7.35 million (down 29 percent from 2007 at $10.41 million) justifiable?[52] In any debate, there are two sides to the issue. One fact that supports paying this amount is that these executives have tremendous organizational responsibilities. They not only have to manage the organization in today's environment, but they also must keep it moving into the future. Their jobs are not 9-to-5 jobs, but rather 6 to 7 days a week, often 10 to 14 hours a day. If jobs are evaluated on the basis of skills, knowledge, abilities, and responsibilities, executives should be highly paid.[53] Furthermore, there is the issue of motivation and retention. If you want these individuals to succeed and stay with the company, you must provide a compensation package that motivates them to stay. Incentives based on various measures also provide the impetus for them to excel.

Most of the research done on executive salaries questions the linkage to performance. Even when profits are down, many executives are paid handsomely. In fact, Canadian corporate executives are some of the most highly paid people in the world (although American CEOs are paid more). Additionally, pay does not always seem directly related to performance.[54] If one takes into account company performance when evaluating a CEO's pay, Jeffrey Orr and Robert Gratton of Montreal-based Power Financial together were overpaid $66 888 000 in 2006; Ian Telfer and Robert McEwen of Vancouver-based Goldcorp together were overpaid $32 725 000; and David Stein of Markham, Ontario-based CoolBrands International was overpaid $8 072 000 for the same year.[55]

Do you believe that Canadian executives are overpaid? Explain your opinion.

Thinking Critically About Ethics

How far should a manager go to achieve efficiency or effectiveness? Suppose that you are the catering manager at a local country club and you are asked by the club manager to lie about information you have on your work group's efficiency. Suppose that by lying you will save ans employee's job. Is that okay? Is lying always wrong, or might it be acceptable under certain circumstances? What, if any, would those circumstances be? What about simply misrepresenting information that you have? Is that always wrong, or might it be acceptable under certain circumstances? When does "misrepresenting" become "lying"?

CASE APPLICATION

Lipschultz Levin & Gray

You might be surprised to find a passionate emphasis placed on people at an accounting firm.[56] Yet at Lipschultz Levin & Gray (**www.thethinkers.com**), self-described "head bean counter" Steven P. Siegel recognizes that his people make the organization. He describes his primary responsibility as ensuring that LLG's clients have the best professionals working for them. And the best way to do this, Siegel feels, is by developing the creativity, talent, and diversity of its staff so that new knowledge can be acquired and shared without getting hung up on formal organizational relationships or having employees shut away in corner offices.

Siegel's commitment to his people starts with the company's mission:

> LLG's goal is to be the pre-eminent provider of the highest quality accounting, tax and consulting services. We seek to accomplish this goal by leaving no stone unturned in exploring new and superior alternatives of supplying our services, and developing such methods on a global basis. Our environment promotes creativity, individual development, group interchange, diversity, good humour, family and community, all for the purpose of assisting in our clients' growth.

To further demonstrate that commitment, Siegel has implemented several significant changes at LLG. Because he is convinced that people do their best intellectual work in nontraditional settings, every telltale sign of what most people consider boring, dull accounting work has been eliminated. None of the firm's employees or partners has an office or desk to call his or her own. Instead, everyone is part of a nomadic arrangement where stuff (files, phones, laptops) is wheeled to a new spot every day. Everywhere you look in the company's office, you see versatility, comfort, and individuality. For instance, a miniature golf course is located in the middle of everything. The motivation behind this open office design is to create opportunities for professionals to gather—on purpose or by accident—without walls, cubicles, or offices to get in the way.

Visitors to LLG realize that the firm is different as soon as they walk in the door. A giant, wall-mounted abacus (remember the image of bean counters) decorates the interior. And visitors are greeted by a "Welcome Wall" with a big-screen television that flashes a continuous slide show of one-liners about business, life, and innovation. The setting may be fun and lighthearted, but the LLG team is seriously committed to serving its clients. So serious, in fact that they state:

> We have one goal. To "Delight" you. Good, even great, is not enough anymore. We will "Dazzle" you and we will guarantee it; We will deliver our service with integrity, honesty and openness in everything we do for you and with you; We will absolutely respect the confidentiality of our working relationship; We will return your phone calls, facsimiles and e-mails within 24 hours; We will always provide exceptional service, designed to help you add significant value to your business; We will meet the deadlines we set together with you; We will communicate with you frequently, building a win-win relationship with you; and You will always know in advance our fee arrangement for any service.

Yesterday, one of Siegel's new employees complained in an email to him that the work environment is too informal, and that employees need their own desks. This employee has done well in her first few months on the job. Siegel is meeting with her in an hour. What should he say to her?

DEVELOPING YOUR DIAGNOSTIC AND ANALYTICAL SKILLS

Managing the Virus Hunters

Imagine what life would be like if your product were never finished, if your work were never done, if your market shifted 30 times a day.[57] The computer-virus hunters at Symantec don't have to imagine. That is the reality of their daily work life. At the company's Response Lab in Santa Monica, California, described as the "dirtiest of all our networks at Symantec," software analysts collect viruses and other suspicious code and try to figure out how they work so security updates can be provided to the company's customers. By the door to the lab, there is even a hazardous materials box marked "Danger," where they put all the discs, tapes, and hard drives with the nasty viruses that need to be carefully and completely disposed of. Symantec's situation may seem unique, but the company, which makes content and network security software for both consumers and businesses, reflects the realities facing many organizations today: quickly shifting customer expectations and continuously emerging

global competitors that have drastically shortened product life cycles. Managing talented people in such an environment can be quite challenging as well.

Vincent Weafer, a native of Ireland, has been the leader of Symantec's virus-hunting team since 1999. Back then, he said, "There were less than two dozen people and . . . nothing really happened. We'd see maybe five new viruses a day and they would spread in a matter of months, not minutes." Now, Symantec's virus hunters around the world deal with some 20 000 virus samples each month, not all of which are unique, stand-alone viruses. The response-centre team is a diverse group whose members were not easy to find. Says Weafer, "It's not as if colleges are creating thousands of anti-malware or security experts every year that we can hire. If you find them in any part of the world, you just go after them." The response-centre team's makeup reflects that. For instance, one senior researcher is from Hungary;

another is from Iceland; and another works out of her home in Melbourne, Florida. But they all share something in common: They are all motivated by solving problems.

The launch of the Blaster.B worm in August 2003 changed the company's approach to dealing with viruses. The domino effect of Blaster.B and other viruses spawned by it meant the front-line software analysts were working around the clock for almost two weeks. The "employee burnout" potential made the company realize that its virus-hunting team would now have to be much deeper talent-wise. Now, the response centre's team numbers in the hundreds and managers can rotate people from the front lines, where they are responsible for responding to new security threats that crop up, into groups where they can help with new-product development. Others write internal research papers. Still others are assigned to develop new tools that will help their colleagues battle the next wave of threats. There is even an individual who tries to figure out what makes the virus writers tick—and the day never ends for these virus hunters. When Santa Monica's team finishes its day, colleagues in Tokyo take over. When the Japanese team finishes its day, it hands off to Dublin, who then hands back to Santa Monica for the new day. It's a frenetic, chaotic, challenging work environment that spans the entire globe. But Weafer says his goals are to "try to take the chaos out, to make the exciting boring," to have a predictable and well-defined process for dealing with the virus threats, and to spread work evenly to the company's facilities around the world. It's a managerial challenge that Weafer has embraced.

Questions

1. Keeping professionals excited about work that is routine and standardized *and* chaotic is a major challenge for Vincent Weafer. How could he use technical, human, and conceptual skills to maintain an environment that encourages innovation and professionalism among the virus hunters?

2. What management roles is Weafer playing as he (a) has weekly security briefing conference calls with co-workers around the globe, (b) assesses the feasibility of adding a new network security consulting service, and (c) keeps employees focused on the company's commitments to customers?

3. Go to Symantec's website (**www.symantec.com**) and look up information about the company. What can you tell about its emphasis on customer service and innovation? In what ways does the organization support its employees in servicing customers and in being innovative?

4. What could other managers learn from Vincent Weafer's and Symantec's approach?

DEVELOPING YOUR INTERPERSONAL SKILLS

Mentoring

About the Skill

A mentor is someone in the organization, usually older, more experienced, and in a higher-level position, who sponsors or supports another employee (a protégé) who is in a lower-level position in the organization. A mentor can teach, guide, and encourage. Some organizations have formal mentoring programs, but even if your organization does not, mentoring should be an important skill for you to develop.

Steps in Developing the Skill

You can be more effective at mentoring if you use the following six suggestions as you mentor another person:[58]

1. Communicate honestly and openly with your protégé. If your protégé is going to learn from you and benefit from your experience and knowledge, you are going to have to be open and honest as you talk about what you have done. Bring up the failures as well as the successes. Remember that mentoring is a learning process, and in order for learning to take place you are going to have to be open and honest in "telling it like it is."

2. Encourage honest and open communication from your protégé. You need to know as the mentor what your protégé hopes to gain from this relationship. You should encourage the protégé to ask for information and be specific about what he or she wants to gain.

3. Treat the relationship with the protégé as a learning opportunity. Don't pretend to have all the answers and all the knowledge, but do share what you have learned through your experiences. In your conversations and interactions with your protégé, you may be able to learn as much from that person as he or she does from you. So be open to listening to what your protégé is saying.

4. Take the time to get to know your protégé. As a mentor, you should be willing to take the time to get to know your protégé and his or her interests. If you are not willing to spend that extra time, you should probably not embark on a mentoring relationship.

5. Remind your protégé that there is no substitute for effective work performance. In any job, effective work performance is absolutely essential for success. It does not matter how much information you provide as a mentor if the protégé is not willing to strive for effective work performance.

6. **Know when it's time to let go.** Successful mentors know when it's time to let the protégé begin standing on his or her own. If the mentoring relationship has been effective, the protégé will be comfortable and confident in handling new and increasing work responsibilities. Just because the mentoring relationship is over does not mean that you never have contact with your protégé. It just means that the relationship becomes one of equals, not one of teacher and student.

Practising the Skill

Read the following scenario. Write some notes about how you would handle the situation described. Be sure to refer to the six suggestions for mentoring.

Scenario

Lora Slovinsky has worked for your department in a software design firm longer than any other of your employees. You value her skills and commitment, and you frequently ask for her judgment on difficult issues. Very often, her ideas have been better than yours and you have let her know through both praise and pay increases how much you appreciate her contributions. Recently, though, you have begun to question Lora's judgment. The fundamental problem is in the distinct difference in the ways you both approach your work. Your strengths lie in getting things done on time and under budget.

Although Lora is aware of these constraints, her creativity and perfectionism sometimes make her prolong projects, continually looking for the best approaches. On her most recent assignment, Lora seemed more intent than ever on doing things her way. Despite what you felt were clear guidelines, she was two weeks late in meeting an important customer deadline. While her product quality was high, as always, the software design was far more elaborate than what was needed at this stage of development. Looking over her work in your office, you feel more than a little frustrated and certain that you need to address matters with Lora. What will you say?

Reinforcing the Skill

The following activities will help you practise and reinforce the skills associated with mentoring:

1. If there are individuals on your campus who act as mentors (or advisers) to first-time students, make an appointment to talk to one of these mentors. They may be upper-division students, professors, or staff employees. Ask them about their roles as mentors and the skills they think it takes to be an effective mentor. How do the skills they mention relate to the behaviours described here?

2. Athletic coaches often act as mentors to their younger assistant coaches. Interview a coach about her or his role as a mentor. What types of things do coaches do to instruct, teach, advise, and encourage their assistant coaches? Could any of these activities be transferred to an organizational setting? Explain.

MyManagementLab

For more resources, please visit www.pearsoned.ca/mymanagementlab

SCAN THIS

History of Management Trends

Walk down almost any street in Vancouver, and you will spot a number of people carrying paper cups of coffee, picked up from one of the many local coffee shops found on many corners.[1] The per capita coffee consumption in Canada is high, an average of 402 cups of coffee per year, almost 25 percent more than Americans, and 161 percent more than Europeans. Vancouverites do their share to keep the numbers up.

Christine Corkan noticed the number of coffee drinkers and the coffee shops in Vancouver and realized that there were lots of places where one could not easily get a cup of coffee in the city. Trendy coffee shops tend not to be located next door to community parks, for instance, where people play soccer, baseball, and field hockey. From that observation, her business, Java Jazz Mobile Café, was born.

Java Jazz offers coffee, tea, and cold drinks, as well as baked goods, smoothies, and fresh fruit from the side of a cube van outfitted with a small kitchen run on a generator. Corkan aims to fill the niche where other concessions are not available, and can be hired for any private event in the area that wants to have coffee and beverages available on-site.

Corkan started developing her business with $35 000, almost all of it loaned to her by a friend at 5 percent interest. With the money, she had to purchase and furnish the van and buy beverages and serving cups.

In August, two months after starting the business, Corkan felt she was doing well. Her previous job was with Air Canada. "I made more in two days with Java Jazz than I make in a month at the airport," she said. "I have the first payment already saved for my loan and it's not due until November."

It is important for managers such as Corkan to understand how to run a business, a new experience for her, compared with working for Air Canada. Corkan would do well to learn more about different management theories, as they provide a framework for managing one's business, dealing with employees when she brings them on, and understanding the environment of the business. One of the keys to her success will be understanding as much as she can about how management works. Below, we review the history of management thought. As you read through it, you may want to identify some of the tips that would help you be a better manager.

Looking at management history can help us understand today's management theory and practice. It can help us see what did work and what did not. In this supplement, we introduce you to the origins of many contemporary management concepts and show how they have evolved to reflect the changing needs of organizations and society as a whole. Q&A S1.1

Historical Background of Management

Organized endeavours directed by people responsible for planning, organizing, leading, and controlling activities have existed for thousands of years. The Egyptian pyramids and the Great Wall of China, for instance, are tangible evidence that projects of tremendous scope, employing tens of thousands of people, were undertaken well before modern times. The pyramids are a particularly interesting example. The construction of a single pyramid occupied more than 100 000 workers for 20 years.[2] Who told each worker what to do? Who ensured that there would be enough stones at the site to keep workers busy? The answer to such questions is managers. Regardless of what managers were called at the time, someone had to plan what was to be done, organize people and materials to do it, lead and direct the workers, and impose some controls to ensure that everything was done as planned.

While organizations and managers have been around for thousands of years, two pre-twentieth-century events are particularly significant to the study of management.

First, in 1776, Adam Smith published *The Wealth of Nations*, in which he argued for the economic advantages that organizations and society would gain from the **division of labour**, the breakdown of

jobs into narrow and repetitive tasks. Using the pin industry as an example, Smith claimed that 10 individuals, each doing a specialized task, could together produce about 48 000 pins a day. However, if each person worked alone performing each task separately, it would be quite an accomplishment to produce even 10 pins a day! Smith concluded that division of labour increased productivity by increasing each person's skill and dexterity, by saving time lost in changing tasks, and by creating labour saving inventions and machinery. The continued popularity of job specialization—for example, specific tasks performed by members of a hospital surgery team, specific meal preparation tasks done by employees in restaurant kitchens, or specific positions played by players on a hockey team—is undoubtedly due to the economic advantages cited by Adam Smith.

The second important pre-twentieth-century influence on management is the **Industrial Revolution**. Starting in the eighteenth century in Great Britain, the revolution eventually crossed the Atlantic to North America. What the Industrial Revolution did was substitute machine power for human power. This made it more economical to manufacture goods in factories rather than at home. Managers were needed to forecast demand, ensure that enough material was on hand to make products, assign tasks to people, direct daily activities, and so forth. However, it was not until the early 1900s that the first major step was taken toward developing a formal theory to guide managers in running these large organizations.

In the next sections, we present the six major approaches to management: scientific management, general

administrative theory, quantitative, organizational behaviour, systems, and contingency (see Exhibit S1-1). Each of the six perspectives contributes to our overall understanding of management. However, each is also a limited view of a particular aspect of management. We begin our journey into management's past by looking at the first major theory of management—scientific management.

Scientific Management

If you had to pinpoint the year modern management theory was born, 1911 might be a logical choice. That was the year Frederick Winslow Taylor's *The Principles of Scientific Management* was published. Its contents were widely accepted by managers around the world. The book described the theory of **scientific management**: the use of scientific methods to define the "one best way" for a job to be done.

Important Contributions

Important contributions to scientific management theory were made by Frederick W. Taylor and Frank and Lillian Gilbreth. Let's look at what they did.

Frederick W. Taylor

Taylor did most of his work at the Midvale and Bethlehem Steel Companies in Pennsylvania. As a mechanical engineer with a Quaker and Puritan background, he was continually shocked at how employees performed. He observed that they used vastly different techniques to

division of labour The breakdown of jobs into narrow and repetitive tasks.

Industrial Revolution The substitution of machine power for human power, which led to mass production.

scientific management The use of the scientific method to determine the "one best way" for a job to be done.

SUPPLEMENT 1

Development of Major Management Theories

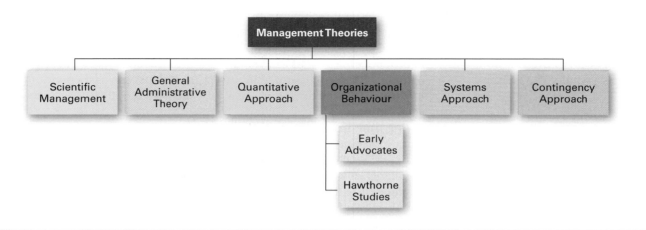

do the same job and were inclined to "take it easy" on the job. Taylor believed that employee output was only about one-third of what was possible. Virtually no work standards existed. Employees were placed in jobs with little or no concern for matching their abilities and aptitudes with the tasks they were required to do. Taylor set out to correct the situation by applying the scientific method to shop-floor jobs and spent more than two decades passionately pursuing the "one best way" for each job to be done.

Taylor's experiences at Midvale led him to define clear guidelines for improving production efficiency. He argued that four principles of management (see *Tips for Managers—Taylor's Four Principles of Management*) would result in prosperity for both employees and managers.[3] Through his studies of manual work using scientific principles, Taylor became known as the "father" of scientific management. His ideas spread in the United States, France, Germany, Russia, and Japan, and inspired others to study and develop methods of scientific management. His most prominent followers were Frank and Lillian Gilbreth. Q&A S1.2

Frank and Lillian Gilbreth

A construction contractor by trade, Frank Gilbreth gave up that career to study scientific management after hearing Taylor speak at a professional meeting. Frank and his wife, Lillian, a psychologist, studied work to eliminate wasteful hand and body motions. The Gilbreths also experimented with the design and use of the proper tools and equipment for optimizing work performance.[4]

Frank is probably best known for his experiments in bricklaying. By carefully analyzing the bricklayer's job, he reduced the number of motions in laying exterior brick from 18 to about 5, and on laying interior brick the motions were reduced from 18 to 2. Using Gilbreth's techniques, the bricklayer could be more productive and less fatigued at the end of the day.

The Gilbreths were among the first researchers to use motion pictures to study hand and body motions. They invented a device called a microchronometer, which recorded an employee's motions and the amount of time spent doing each motion. Wasted motions missed by the naked eye could be identified and eliminated. The Gilbreths also devised a classification scheme to label 17 basic hand motions (such as search, grasp,

TIPS FOR MANAGERS

Taylor's Four Principles of Management

- Develop a **science for each element of an individual's work**, which will replace the old rule-of-thumb method.

- **Scientifically select** and then train, teach, and develop employees.

- **Heartily cooperate with employees** so as to ensure that all work is done in accordance with the principles of the science that has been developed.

- **Divide work and responsibility almost equally** between management and employees. Management takes over all work for which it is better fitted than the employees.

hold), which they called **therbligs** ("Gilbreth" spelled backward with the *th* transposed). This scheme allowed the Gilbreths a more precise way of analyzing an employee's exact hand movements.

How Do Today's Managers Use Scientific Management?

The guidelines that Taylor and others devised for improving production efficiency are still used in organizations today.[5] When managers analyze the basic work tasks that must be performed, use time-and-motion study to eliminate wasted motions, hire the best qualified employees for a job, and design incentive systems based on output, they are using the principles of scientific management. But current management practice isn't restricted to scientific management. In fact, we can see ideas from the next major approach—general administrative theory—being used as well. Q&A S1.3

General Administrative Theory

Another group of writers looked at the subject of management but focused on the entire organization. These **general administrative theorists** developed more general theories of what managers do and what constitutes good management practice. Let's look at some important contributions that grew out of this perspective.

Important Contributions

The two most prominent theorists behind general administrative theory were Henri Fayol and Max Weber.

Henri Fayol

We mention Fayol in Chapter 1 because he described management

as a universal set of functions that included planning, organizing, commanding, coordinating, and controlling. Because his ideas were important, let's look more closely at what he had to say.[6]

Fayol wrote during the same time period as Taylor. While Taylor was concerned with first-line managers and the scientific method, Fayol's attention was directed at the activities of all managers. He wrote from personal experience because he was the managing director of a large French coal-mining firm.

Fayol described the practice of management as something distinct from accounting, finance, production, distribution, and other typical business functions. His belief that management was an activity common to all human endeavours in business, government, and even in the home led him to develop 14 **principles of management**—fundamental rules of management that could be taught in

therbligs A classification scheme for labelling 17 basic hand motions.

general administrative theorists Writers who developed general theories of what managers do and what constitutes good management practice.

principles of management Fundamental rules of management that could be taught in schools and applied in all organizational situations.

Exhibit S1-2

Weber's Ideal Bureaucracy

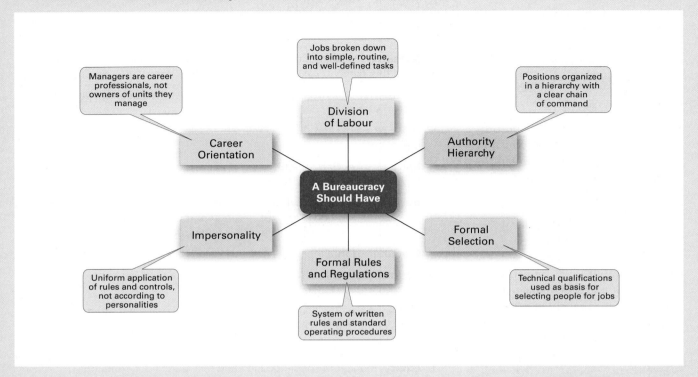

schools and applied in all organizational situations. These principles are shown in *Tips for Managers—Fayol's 14 Principles of Management*.

Managers today still employ many of Fayol's principles in building adaptable organizations where managers give ownership of the task to the individual, resulting in stronger motivation and commitment to the task. Managers like Guy Laliberté and Daniel Lamarre of Cirque du Soleil focus on building a strong team that supports the creative culture at the heart of Cirque du Soleil. Q&A S1.4

Max Weber

Weber (pronounced VAY-ber) was a German sociologist who studied organizational activity. Writing in the early 1900s, he developed a theory of authority structures and relations.[7] Weber described an ideal type of organization that he called a **bureaucracy**—a form of organization

characterized by division of labour, a clearly defined hierarchy, detailed rules and regulations, and impersonal relationships. Weber recognized that this "ideal bureaucracy" did not exist in reality. Instead, he intended it as a basis for theorizing about how work could be done in large groups. His theory became the model structural design for many of today's large organizations. The features of Weber's ideal bureaucratic structure are outlined in Exhibit S1-2.

Bureaucracy, as described by Weber, is a lot like scientific management in its ideology. Both emphasize rationality, predictability, impersonality, technical competence, and authoritarianism. Although Weber's writings were less operational than Taylor's, the fact that his "ideal type" still describes many contemporary

organizations attests to the importance of his work.

How Do Today's Managers Use General Administrative Theory?

Some of our current management ideas and practices can be directly traced to the contributions of the general administrative theorists. For instance, the functional view of the manager's job can be attributed to Fayol. In addition, his 14 principles serve as a frame of reference from which many current management concepts have evolved.

Weber's bureaucracy was an attempt to formulate an ideal prototype for organizations. Although many characteristics of Weber's bureaucracy

bureaucracy A form of organization characterized by division of labour, a clearly defined hierarchy, detailed rules and regulations, and impersonal relationships.

are still evident in large organizations, his model isn't as popular today as it was in the twentieth century. Many contemporary managers feel that bureaucracy's emphasis on strict division of labour, adherence to formal rules and regulations, and impersonal application of rules and controls takes away the individual employee's creativity and the organization's ability to respond quickly to an increasingly dynamic environment. However, even in highly flexible organizations of talented professionals—such as Calgary-based WestJet Airlines, Toronto-based ING Bank of Canada, or Ottawa-based Corel—some bureaucratic mechanisms are necessary to ensure that resources are used efficiently and effectively.

The Quantitative Approach

The **quantitative approach** involves the use of quantitative techniques to improve decision making. This approach also has been called *operations research* or *management science*.

Important Contributions

The quantitative approach evolved out of the development of mathematical and statistical solutions to military problems during World War II. After the war was over, many of the techniques that had been used to solve military problems were applied to businesses. One group of military officers, nicknamed the Whiz Kids, joined Ford Motor Company in the mid-1940s and immediately began using statistical methods and quantitative models to improve decision making. Two of these individuals whose names you might recognize are Robert McNamara (who went on to become president of Ford, US Secretary of Defense, and head of the World Bank and was recently featured in the documentary *The Fog of War*)

and Charles "Tex" Thornton (who founded Litton Industries).

What exactly does the quantitative approach do? It involves applications of statistics, optimization models, information models, and computer simulations to management activities. Linear programming, for instance, is a technique that managers use to improve resource allocation decisions. Work scheduling can be more efficient as a result of critical-path scheduling analysis. The economic order quantity model helps managers determine optimum inventory levels. Each of these is an example of quantitative techniques being applied to improve managerial decision making.

How Do Today's Managers Use the Quantitative Approach?

The quantitative approach contributes directly to management decision making in the areas of planning and control. For instance, when managers make budgeting, scheduling, quality control, and similar decisions, they typically rely on quantitative techniques. The availability of software programs has made the use of quantitative techniques somewhat less intimidating for managers, although they must still be able to interpret the results. We cover some of the more important quantitative techniques in Chapters 9 and 17.

The quantitative approach has not influenced management practice as much as the next approach we are going to discuss—organizational behaviour—for a number of reasons. These include the fact that many managers are unfamiliar with and intimidated by the quantitative tools, behavioural problems are more widespread and visible, and it is easier for most students and managers to relate to real, day-to-day people problems

than to the more abstract activity of constructing quantitative models.

Organizational Behaviour

As we know, managers get things done by working with people. This explains why some writers have chosen to look at management by focusing on the organization's human resources. The field of study concerned with the actions (behaviour) of people at work is called **organizational behaviour (OB)**. Much of what currently makes up the field of human resource management, as well as contemporary views on motivation, leadership, trust, teamwork, and conflict management, has come out of OB research.

Early Advocates

Although a number of people in the late 1800s and early 1900s recognized the importance of the human factor to an organization's success, four stand out as early advocates of the OB approach: Robert Owen, Hugo Münsterberg, Mary Parker Follett, and Chester Barnard. The contributions of these individuals were varied and distinct, yet they all believed that people were the most important asset of the organization and should be managed accordingly. Their approach was very different from the emphasis on bureaucracy and structured arrangements to improve workflow. In particular, their ideas provided the foundation for such management practices as employee selection procedures, employee motivation programs, employee work teams, and organization–environment management techniques. Exhibit S1-3 summarizes the most important ideas of the early advocates of OB.

quantitative approach The use of quantitative techniques to improve decision making.

organizational behaviour (OB) The field of study concerned with the actions (behaviour) of people at work.

SUPPLEMENT 1

Early Advocates of Organizational Behaviour (OB)

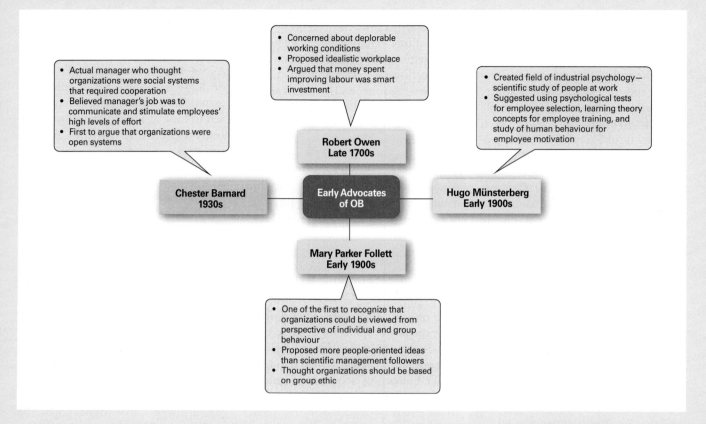

- Actual manager who thought organizations were social systems that required cooperation
- Believed manager's job was to communicate and stimulate employees' high levels of effort
- First to argue that organizations were open systems

- Concerned about deplorable working conditions
- Proposed idealistic workplace
- Argued that money spent improving labour was smart investment

- Created field of industrial psychology—scientific study of people at work
- Suggested using psychological tests for employee selection, learning theory concepts for employee training, and study of human behaviour for employee motivation

**Robert Owen
Late 1700s**

**Chester Barnard
1930s**

Early Advocates of OB

**Hugo Münsterberg
Early 1900s**

**Mary Parker Follett
Early 1900s**

- One of the first to recognize that organizations could be viewed from perspective of individual and group behaviour
- Proposed more people-oriented ideas than scientific management followers
- Thought organizations should be based on group ethic

The Hawthorne Studies

Without question, the most important contribution to the developing OB field came out of the **Hawthorne Studies**, a series of studies conducted at the Western Electric Company Works in Cicero, Illinois. These studies, which started in 1924, were initially designed by Western Electric industrial engineers as a scientific management experiment. They wanted to examine the effect of various illumination levels on employee productivity. As in any good scientific experiment, control and experimental groups were set up, with the experimental group being exposed to various lighting intensities and the control group working under a constant intensity. If you were the industrial engineers in charge of this experiment, what would you have

expected to happen? It's logical to think that individual output in the experimental group would be directly related to the intensity of the light. However, they found that as the level of light was increased in the experimental group, output for both groups increased. Then, much to the surprise of the engineers, as the light level was decreased in the experimental group, productivity continued to increase in both groups. In fact, a productivity decrease was observed in the experimental group *only* when the level of light was reduced to that of a moonlit night. What would explain these unexpected results? The engineers were not sure, but concluded that illumination intensity was not directly related to group productivity and that

something else must have contributed to the results. They were not able to pinpoint what that "something else" was, though.

In 1927, the Western Electric engineers asked Harvard professor Elton Mayo and his associates to join the study as consultants. Thus began a relationship that would last through 1932 and encompass numerous experiments in the redesign of jobs, changes in workday and workweek length, introduction of rest periods, and individual vs. group wage plans.[8] For example, one experiment was designed to evaluate the effect of a group piecework incentive pay system on group productivity. The results indicated that the incentive plan had less effect on an employee's output

Hawthorne Studies A series of studies during the 1920s and 1930s that provided new insights into individual and group behaviour.

than did group pressure, acceptance, and security. The researchers concluded that social norms, or group standards, were the key determinants of individual work behaviour.

Scholars generally agree that the Hawthorne Studies had a dramatic impact on management beliefs about the role of human behaviour in organizations. Mayo concluded that behaviour and attitudes are closely related, that group influences significantly affect individual behaviour, that group standards establish individual employee output, and that money is less a factor in determining output than are group standards, group attitudes, and security. These conclusions led to a new emphasis on the human behaviour factor in the management of organizations and the attainment of goals.

However, these conclusions were criticized. Critics attacked the research procedures, analyses of findings, and conclusions.[9] From a historical standpoint, it's of little importance whether the studies were academically sound or their conclusions justified. What *is* important is that they stimulated an interest in human behaviour in organizations. Q&A S1.5

How Do Today's Managers Use the Behavioural Approach?

The behavioural approach has largely shaped today's organizations. From the way managers design motivating jobs to the way they work with employee teams to the way they use open communication, we can see elements of the behavioural approach. Much of what the early OB advocates proposed and the conclusions from the Hawthorne Studies provided the foundation for our current theories of motivation, leadership, group behaviour and development, and numerous other behavioural topics that we address fully in later chapters.

The Systems Approach

During the 1960s, researchers began to analyze organizations from a systems perspective, a concept taken from the physical sciences. A **system** is a set of interrelated and interdependent parts arranged in a manner that produces a unified whole. The two basic types of systems are closed and open. **Closed systems** are not influenced by and do not interact with their environment. This is very much how Air Canada operated when it was a Crown corporation. Because it was in a regulated industry, it did not need to worry about competition. When the Canadian airline industry was deregulated, Air Canada was slow to adapt to the new competitive environment and went into bankruptcy protection in order to restructure its operations and attempt to become a more open system.[10]

Open systems dynamically interact with their environment. Today, when we describe organizations as systems, we mean open systems. Exhibit S1-4 shows a diagram of an organization from an open systems perspective. As you can see, an organization takes in inputs (resources) from the environment and transforms or processes these resources into outputs that are distributed into the environment. The organization is "open" to its environment and interacts with that environment.

The Systems Approach and Managers

How does the systems approach contribute to our understanding of management thinking? Systems researchers envisioned an organiza-

tion as being made up of "interdependent factors, including individuals, groups, attitudes, motives, formal structure, interactions, goals, status, and authority."[11] What this means is that managers coordinate the work activities of the various parts of the organization and ensure that all the interdependent parts of the organization are working together so that the organization's goals can be achieved. For example, the systems approach would recognize that, no matter how efficient the production department might be, if the marketing department does not anticipate changes in customer tastes and work with the product development department to create products customers want, the organization's overall performance will suffer. This approach is very different from the "silo" approach in some organizations, where each individual unit operates almost in isolation from other units.

In addition, the systems approach implies that decisions and actions taken in one organizational area will affect others and vice versa. For example, if the purchasing department does not acquire the right quantity and quality of inputs, the production department will not be able to do its job effectively.

Finally, the systems approach recognizes that organizations are not self-contained. They rely on their environments for essential inputs and as sources to absorb their outputs. No organization can survive for long if it ignores government regulations, supplier relations, or the varied external constituencies upon which it depends. (We cover these external forces in Chapter 2.)

How relevant is the systems approach to management? Quite relevant. Think, for example, of a

system A set of interrelated and interdependent parts arranged in a manner that produces a unified whole.

closed systems Systems that are not influenced by and do not interact with their environment.

open systems Systems that dynamically interact with their environment.

SUPPLEMENT 1

The Organization as an Open System

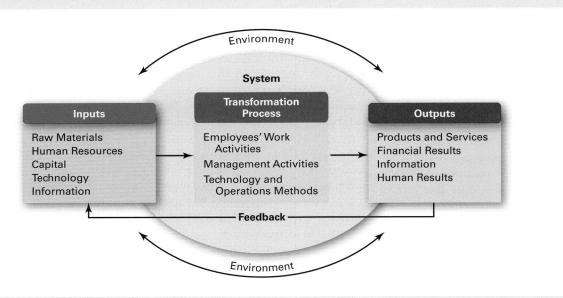

day-shift manager at a local Harvey's restaurant who every day must coordinate the work of employees filling customer orders at the front counter and the drive-through windows, direct the delivery and unloading of food supplies, and address any customer concerns that come up. This manager "manages" all parts of the "system" so that the restaurant meets its daily sales goals. **Q&A S1.6**

The Contingency Approach

Early management thinkers such as Taylor, Fayol, and Weber gave us principles of management that they generally assumed to be universally applicable. Later research found exceptions to many of their principles. For example, division of labour is valuable and widely used, but jobs can become *too* specialized. Bureaucracy is desirable in many situations, but in other cir-

cumstances, other structural designs are *more* effective. Management is not (and cannot be) based on simplistic principles to be applied in all situations. Different and changing situations require managers to use different approaches and techniques. The **contingency approach** (sometimes called the *situational approach*) says that organizations are different, face different situations (contingencies), and require different ways of managing.

The Contingency Approach and Managers

A contingency approach to management is intuitively logical because organizations and even units within the same organization are diverse—in size, goals, work, and the like. It would be surprising to find universally applicable management rules

that would work in *all* situations. But, of course, it's one thing to say that the method of managing "depends on the situation" and another to say what the situation is. Management researchers have been working to identify these "what" variables. Exhibit S1-5 describes four popular contingency variables. The list is by no means comprehensive—more than 100 different "what" variables have been identified—but it represents those most widely used and gives you an idea of what we mean by the term *contingency variable.* As you can see, the contingency variables can have a significant impact on managers. The primary value of the contingency approach is that it stresses there are no simplistic or universal rules for managers to follow. **Q&A S1.7**

contingency approach An approach that says that organizations are different, face different situations (contingencies), and require different ways of managing.

Popular Contingency Variables

Organization Size. As size increases, so do the problems of coordination. For instance, the type of organization structure appropriate for an organization of 50 000 employees is likely to be inefficient for an organization of 50 employees.

Routineness of Task Technology. To achieve its purpose, an organization uses technology. Routine technologies, such as assembly lines, require organizational structures, leadership styles, and control systems that differ from those required by customized or nonroutine technologies where individuals continually have to make decisions about how their jobs are to be done, such as in the emergency room of a hospital.

Environmental Uncertainty. The degree of uncertainty caused by environmental changes influences the management process. What works best in a stable and predictable environment may be totally inappropriate in a rapidly changing and unpredictable environment.

Individual Differences. Individuals differ in terms of their desire for growth, autonomy, tolerance of ambiguity, and expectations. These and other individual differences are particularly important when managers select motivation techniques, leadership styles, and job designs.

Summarizing Management Theory

It would not be unusual for you to read through this supplement on the history of management theory and wonder whether any of it is relevant to you. Theoretical perspectives and the research that is generated to help examine theories lead us to a more solid understanding of how managers should manage. The theories we present above appear in a historical sequence, but that does not mean that as a new theory was developed, the previous one became irrelevant. Instead, if you carefully consider the theories, you will note that they are somewhat self-contained, each addressing a separate aspect of the various considerations that managers face. Exhibit S1-6 highlights for you the different emphases of these theories, so that you can see how each contributes to a better understanding of management as a whole. Q&A S1.8

Emphases of Major Management Theories

Organizational Culture and the Organizational Environment

Are managers free to do whatever they want? In this chapter, we'll look at the factors that limit the discretion managers have in doing their jobs. These factors are both internal (the organization's culture) and external (the organizational environment). After reading and studying this chapter, you will achieve the following learning outcomes.

Learning Outcomes

1 Discuss the two differing views of how much control managers have.

2 Discuss the characteristics and importance of organizational culture.

3 Describe what kinds of cultures managers can create.

4 Describe the features of the specific and general organizational environments.

▶ ▶ ▶ Technical workers at 3M spend up to 15 percent of their time working on projects of their own choosing.[1] This is openly encouraged by 3M as long as the project has the potential to become an important breakthrough for the company. The "15 percent rule" has been a central part of 3M's overall culture of innovation since being introduced by company president William McKnight in 1948. The innovative culture is further encouraged by the "30 percent rule" that requires each division to produce 30 percent of its annual revenue from products that did not exist five years ago.

3M clearly prizes delegation and initiative, and has a strong tolerance for failure. Managers are directed to "hire the right people, and then get out of the way." The company culture emphasizes that a failure can turn into a success; there is no punishment for a product failing in the market. The human resources team also plays a pivotal role in reinforcing a stronger, customer-oriented culture through regular training programs that focus on the acronym

$E=MC^2$ (Engagement = More Customer Connect).

Implementation of these practices had built a company with over 76 000 employees and annual revenue of $23 billion, and has placed 3M at the forefront of innovative companies globally. After the bursting of the dot-com bubble in 2001, however, there was a shift in thinking at the company. James McNerney was hired from General Electric as president to deal with what

was felt to be too great a focus on innovation and creativity. He was asked to make the company more efficient using the Six Sigma discipline (a quality control philosophy) and to "whip the company into shape." McNerney left in 2005 to run Boeing, and the current CEO and president, George Buckley, was left with the task of rebuilding 3M's traditional innovative culture, which many felt had suffered as a result of the emphasis on process improvement.

Think About It

What would it be like to work at 3M? How would you feel about having 15 percent of your time to work on projects that meet your personal agenda? What kinds of resistance might James McNerney have encountered when he tried to establish a new culture of efficiency in the face of the established culture of innovation? What challenges might George Buckley have encountered when he became CEO in 2005? How does the 3M culture differ from the work cultures you have experienced?

SCAN THIS

The Manager: Omnipotent or Symbolic?

How much difference does a manager make in how an organization performs? The dominant view in management theory and society in general is that managers are directly responsible for an organization's success or failure. We will call this perspective the **omnipotent view of management**. In contrast, some observers have argued that much of an organization's success or failure is due to external forces outside managers' control. This perspective has been labelled the **symbolic view of management**. Let's look more closely at each of these perspectives so that we can try to clarify just how much credit or blame managers should receive for their organizations' performance.

The Omnipotent View

In Chapter 1 we discussed the importance of managers to organizations. This view reflects a dominant assumption in management theory: The quality of an organization's managers determines the quality of the organization itself. It's assumed that differences in an organization's effectiveness or efficiency are due to the decisions and actions of its managers.

1. Discuss the two differing views of how much control managers have.

omnipotent view of management The view that managers are directly responsible for an organization's success or failure.

symbolic view of management The view that managers have only a limited effect on substantive organizational outcomes because of the large number of factors outside their control.

Good managers anticipate change, exploit opportunities, correct poor performance, and lead their organizations toward their goals, which may be changed if necessary. When profits are up, managers take the credit and reward themselves with bonuses, stock options, and the like—even if they had little to do with the positive outcomes. When profits are down, top managers are often fired in the belief that "new blood" will bring improved results. The buck stops here! Following the oil spill in the Gulf of Mexico in April 2010, people were enraged when BP CEO Tony Hayward attended a weekend sailing event in which his yacht *Bob* was competing. The following Monday, Hayward was removed from direct responsibility for the cleanup. By early July 2010, there was speculation that the leadership at BP would be cleared out, including Hayward as well as Carl-Henric Svanberg, the Swedish chairman who in his apology to those affected by the spill referred to the "small people."[2]

MyManagementLab
Q&A 2.1

The view of managers as omnipotent is consistent with the stereotypical picture of the take-charge business executive who can overcome any obstacle in carrying out the organization's goals. This omnipotent view, of course, is not limited to business organizations. We can also use it to help explain the high turnover among college and professional sports coaches, who can be considered the "managers" of their teams. Coaches who lose more games than they win are seen as ineffective. They are fired and replaced by new coaches who, it is hoped, will correct the inadequate performance.

In the omnipotent view, when organizations perform poorly, someone has to be held accountable regardless of the reasons, and in our society, that "someone" is the manager. Of course, when things go well, we need someone to praise. So managers also get the credit—even if they had little to do with achieving positive outcomes.

The Symbolic View

When tunnelling for the Canada Line transit system started tearing up Vancouver's Cambie Street, a busy shopping area, customers stopped coming to the stores and restaurants. The street was noisy, there was no parking, and the area was a traffic nightmare. Facing a significant drop in customers, Christian Gaudreault, owner of Tomato Fresh Food Café, moved his restaurant elsewhere. Giriaj Gautam, who runs the Cambie General Store, found his sales down 25 percent and hoped he could hang on until construction finished up in the area, more than a year after it started. Was the declining revenue the result of decisions and actions by Gaudreault and Gautam, or was it the result of factors beyond their control? Similarly, when a massive power outage hit Ontario, mad cow disease struck

When both Home Hardware and Army and Navy closed their stores in downtown Regina, Blue Mantle, a thrift store in the same area, faced a loss of customer traffic and sales. As a result, Dave Barrett, the store's manager at the time, closed Blue Mantle soon after. He explained his decision: "When Home Hardware closed, and department store Army and Navy closed, that cut away a lot of our traffic to the store. We used to have lots of seniors that would swing over to our place." He also noted that the state of the economy was a factor in the store closing.[3] The Roman Catholic Archdiocese of Regina eventually re-opened Blue Mantle after receiving numerous requests from customers, and now runs the store with volunteers.

in Alberta, and the avian flu killed chickens in British Columbia, were these the result of managerial actions or circumstances outside managers' control? The symbolic view would suggest the latter.

The symbolic view says that a manager's ability to affect outcomes is influenced and constrained by external factors.[4] In this view, it's unreasonable to expect managers to significantly affect an organization's performance. Instead, an organization's results are influenced by factors managers do not control, such as the economy, customers, government policies, competitors' actions, industry conditions, control over proprietary technology, and decisions made by previous managers.

According to the symbolic view, managers merely symbolize control and influence.[5] How? They create meaning out of randomness, confusion, and ambiguity or try to innovate and adapt. Because managers have a limited effect on organizational outcomes, their actions involve developing plans, making decisions, and engaging in other managerial activities for the benefit of stockholders, customers, employees, and the public. However, the part that managers actually play in organizational success or failure is minimal.

Reality Suggests a Synthesis

In reality, managers are neither helpless nor all powerful. Internal and external constraints that restrict a manager's decision options exist within every organization. Internal constraints arise from the organization's culture, and external constraints come from the organization's environment.

MyManagementLab
Q&A 2.2

As Exhibit 2-1 shows, managers operate within the limits imposed by the organization's culture and environment. Yet, despite these constraints, managers are not powerless. They can still influence an organization's performance. In the remainder of this chapter, we discuss how an organization's culture and environment impose limits on managers. However, as we will see in other chapters, these constraints don't mean that a manager's hands are tied. As George Buckley of 3M recognized, managers can and do influence their culture and environment.

The Organization's Culture

▶ ▶ ▶ Every organization has a culture, a way that those in the organization interact with each other and with their clients or customers. When George Buckley was appointed president and CEO of 3M following the departure of James McNerney, he faced a crisis of confidence in what really mattered at 3M—either innovation or efficiency. McNerney had brought a passion for efficiency with him from GE, and the remnants of this new culture were still in place even as 3M declared a return to the focus on innovation. [6]

2. Discuss the characteristics and importance of organizational culture.

Think About It

What is organizational culture, and how does it affect both James McNerney's and George Buckley's ability to manage? Is the impact of culture different if the organization is a not-for-profit rather than a business organization?

Exhibit 2-1

Parameters of Managerial Discretion

| Organizational Environment | Managerial Discretion | Organizational Culture |

How does the culture of your college or university differ from that of your high school?

We know that every person has a unique personality—a set of relatively permanent and stable traits that influence the way we act and interact with others. When we describe someone as warm, open, relaxed, shy, or aggressive, we are describing personality traits. An organization, too, has a personality, which we call its *culture.*

What Is Organizational Culture?

Calgary-based EnCana was formed by a merger between Alberta Energy Company (AEC) and PanCanadian Energy Corporation.[7] It was not easy bringing the two companies together, as they were marked by two very different corporate cultures. PanCanadian was known as warm and fuzzy, with a risk-averse operating style. AEC was a much more aggressive company. "If you had to distill the two companies, PanCanadian managed for profitability while AEC managed for growth," says Brian Prokop, a research analyst with Calgary-based investment firm Peters & Co. Under the merger, EnCana retains AEC's culture of growth. Each EnCana employee must follow the written goals of a "principled meritocracy," which are spelled out in the company's corporate constitution. EnCana employees are not to become "egotistical or arrogant, cynical, unwilling to adapt or change or play internal politics or games but rather strive to be the best they can be." Thus, the organizational culture supports what EnCana and its CEO, Randall Eresman, are trying to achieve.

organizational culture A system of shared meaning and beliefs held by organizational members that determines, in large degree, how employees act.

What is **organizational culture**? It's a system of shared meaning and beliefs held by organizational members that determines, in large degree, how they act toward each other and outsiders. It represents a common perception held by an organization's members that influences how they behave. In every organization, there are values, symbols, rituals, myths, and practices that have evolved over time.[8] These shared values and experiences determine, in large degree, what employees perceive and how they respond to their world.[9] When faced with problems or issues, the organizational culture—the "way we do things around here"—influences what employees can do and how they conceptualize, define, analyze, and resolve issues. When considering different job offers, it makes sense to evaluate whether you can fit into the organization's culture.

MyManagementLab
Q&A 2.3, Q&A 2.4

Our definition of organizational culture implies three things:

- Culture is a *perception.* Individuals perceive the organizational culture on the basis of what they see, hear, or experience within the organization.

- Culture is *shared.* Even though individuals may have different backgrounds or work at different organizational levels, they tend to describe the organization's culture in similar terms.

- Culture is a *descriptive* term. It's concerned with how members perceive the organization, not with whether they like it. It describes rather than evaluates.

MyManagementLab
Q&A 2.5

Research suggests that seven dimensions capture the essence of an organization's culture.[10] These dimensions are described in Exhibit 2-2. Each dimension ranges from low (it's not very typical of the culture) to high (it's very typical of the culture). Appraising an organization on these seven dimensions gives a composite picture of the organization's culture. In many organizations, one of these cultural dimensions often is emphasized more than the others and essentially shapes the organization's personality and the way organizational members work. For instance, at Sony Corporation the focus is on product innovation. The company "lives and breathes" new-product development (outcome orientation), and employees' work decisions, behaviours, and actions support that goal. In contrast, WestJet Airlines has made its employees a central part of its culture (people orientation). Exhibit 2-3 describes how the dimensions can be combined to create significantly different organizations.

Exhibit 2-2

Dimensions of Organizational Culture

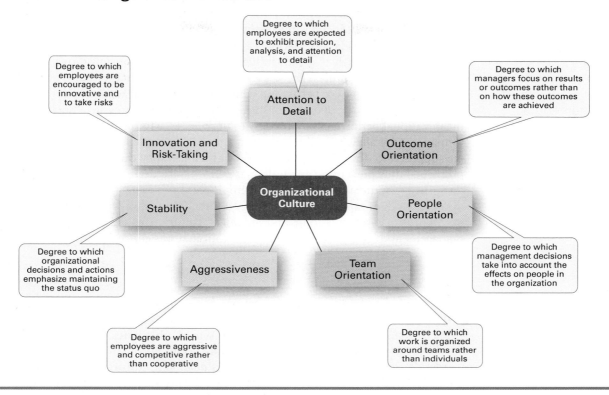

Exhibit 2-3

Contrasting Organizational Cultures

Organization A	Organization B
• Managers must fully document all decisions. • Creative decisions, change, and risks are not encouraged. • Extensive rules and regulations exist for all employees. • Productivity is valued over employee morale. • Employees are encouraged to stay within their own department. • Individual effort is encouraged.	• Management encourages and rewards risk-taking and change. • Employees are encouraged to "run with" ideas, and failures are treated as "learning experiences." • Employees have few rules and regulations to follow. • Productivity is balanced with treating its people right. • Team members are encouraged to interact with people at all levels and functions. • Many rewards are team-based.

Strong vs. Weak Cultures

Although all organizations have cultures, not all cultures have an equal impact on employees' behaviours and actions. **Strong cultures**—cultures in which the key values are deeply held and widely shared—have a greater influence on employees than do weak cultures. The more employees accept the organization's key values and the greater their commitment to those values, the stronger the culture is.

strong cultures Organizations in which the key values are deeply held and widely shared.

Whether an organization's culture is strong, weak, or somewhere in between depends on factors such as the size of the organization, how long it has been around, how much turnover there has been among employees, and the intensity with which the culture started.

At 3M, the 15 percent rule and the 30 percent rule make the cultural commitment to innovation crystal clear. Yet some organizations do not make clear what is important and what is not, and this lack of clarity is a characteristic of weak cultures. In such organizations, culture is unlikely to greatly influence managers. Most organizations, however, have moderate to strong cultures. There is relatively high agreement on what is important, what defines "good" employee behaviour, what it takes to get ahead, and so forth.

MyManagementLab
Q&A 2.6

An increasing body of evidence suggests that strong cultures are associated with high organizational performance.[11] It's easy to understand why a strong culture enhances performance. After all, when values are clear and widely accepted, employees know what they are supposed to do and what is expected of them, so they can act quickly to take care of problems, thus preventing any potential performance decline. The drawback is that the same strong culture also might prevent employees from trying new approaches, especially during periods of rapid change.[12] Strong cultures do not always yield *positive* results, however. Enron had a very strong, and unethical, culture. This enabled employees and top management to engage in unethical behaviour that was concealed from public scrutiny.

MyManagementLab
Q&A 2.7

Subcultures

Do the different instructors you have emphasize different things, such as innovative projects, a disciplined classroom, use of humour?

dominant culture A system of shared meanings that expresses the core values of a majority of the organization's members; it gives the organization its distinct personality.

subcultures Minicultures within an organization, typically defined by department designations and geographical separation.

Organizations do not necessarily have one uniform culture. In fact, most large organizations have a dominant culture and numerous sets of subcultures.[13]

When we talk about an organization's culture, we are referring to its *dominant* culture. A **dominant culture** expresses the core values that are shared by the majority of an organization's members. It's this macro view of culture that gives an organization its distinct personality.[14] **Subcultures** tend to develop in large organizations to reflect the common problems, situations, or experiences that members face. The existence of subcultures in an organization suggests that individual managers play a role in moulding a common culture in their own units. By conveying and then reinforcing core values, managers can influence the common culture of the employees in their unit.

core values The primary, or dominant, values that are accepted throughout the organization.

Subcultures are likely to be defined by department designations and geographical separation. An organization's marketing department, for example, can have a subculture that is uniquely shared by members of that department. It will include the **core values** of the dominant culture, plus additional values unique to members of the marketing department. Similarly, offices or units of the organization that are physically separated from the organization's main operations may take on a different personality. Again, the core values are essentially retained but modified to reflect the separated unit's distinct situation.

The Source of Culture

An organization's current customs, traditions, and general way of doing things are largely due to what it has done before and the degree of success it has had with those endeavours. The original source of an organization's culture usually reflects the vision or mission of the organization's founders. Their focus might be aggressiveness or it might be treating employees as family. The founders establish the early culture by projecting an image of what the organization should be. They are not constrained by previous customs or approaches. And the small size of most new organizations helps the founders instill their vision in all organizational members. Frank Stronach had a strong impact on the culture of the organization he founded, Magna International, as the following *Management Reflection* shows.

Magna Culture Creates Ownership

How much impact does a founder have on an organization's culture?
Frank Stronach, founder of Aurora, Ontario-based Magna International and currently chair of the board, still has a profound effect on Magna's culture, even though he is no longer CEO.[15] Magna's Corporate Constitution and the Employee's Charter provide the roadmap for the company's Fair Enterprise culture, first introduced by Stronach. Stronach believes that employees should show a "strong sense of ownership and entrepreneurial energy." To encourage a sense of ownership, 10 percent of pre-tax profits go toward profit-sharing programs for his employees. Managers' salaries are set "below industry standards" to encourage managers to earn more through profit-sharing bonuses. To further encourage managerial responsibility, Magna's managers are given considerable autonomy over buying, selling, and hiring. Stronach's policies of profit-sharing and empowerment have created a workforce that has made Magna one of the largest and most profitable companies in the country. ■

The impact of a founder on an organization's culture isn't unique to North America. At Hyundai Corporation, the giant Korean conglomerate, the culture reflects the fierce, competitive style of its founder, Chung Ju Yung. Other well-known contemporary examples of founders from Canada and other countries who have had an enormous impact on their organization's culture include Ted Rogers of Toronto-based Rogers Communications, Bill Gates of Microsoft, the late Anita Roddick of The Body Shop, and Richard Branson of the Virgin Group.

Though founders play an important role in establishing the culture of an organization, if an organization does not have a strong culture, any manager has some ability to create the culture he or she wants within the individual unit. By understanding how employees learn culture, which we discuss below, managers can shape the culture of their own units.

How an Organization's Culture Continues

Once a culture is in place, certain organizational practices help maintain it. For instance, during the employee selection process, managers typically judge job candidates not only on the requirements of the job but also on how well they might fit into the organization. At the same time, job candidates find out information about the organization and determine whether or not they are comfortable with what they see. (See *Developing Your Interpersonal Skills—Reading an Organization's Culture* at the end of the chapter.)

The actions of top executives also have a major impact on the organization's culture. Through what they say and how they behave, top-level managers establish norms that filter down through the organization. This can have a positive effect on employees' willingness to take risks or to provide exceptional customer service. At 3M George Buckley and other senior executives tolerate mistakes and enhance individual creativity by specifying goals while granting employees the right to pursue the goals they feel most committed to.[16] Managers' behaviour also can have the opposite effect if it is self-serving, as we saw in the subprime mortgage crisis of 2008.

Finally, an organization must help employees adapt to its culture through a process called **socialization**. Through the socialization process, new employees learn the organization's way of doing things. Socialization is more effective if companies hire individuals who fit into the culture. For instance, when potential job candidates look at the career section of Intuit Canada's website, they can determine whether or not they will fit into Intuit's culture.[17] The company informs job seekers that Intuit provides employees with "substantial work assignments." It also lets them know that it is looking for candidates who "are high performers, have the ability to work in teams and are willing and eager to learn and grow."

MyManagementLab
PRISM 3

socialization The process that adapts employees to the organization's culture.

At Stacy's Pita Chip Company, the environment is spotless but utilitarian, the equipment is used, and everything goes back into the business. Mark Andrus and Stacy Madison have bootstrapped their low-fat snack chip business to reach sales of over $1.3 million. The low-cost, hard-driving culture they have developed retains a sense of humour too, as is evident in the company's "dress code," shown here.

Socialization provides another benefit to organizations. It minimizes the possibility that new employees, who are unfamiliar with their new organization's culture, might disrupt the beliefs and customs that are in place.

Exhibit 2-4 summarizes how an organization's culture is established and maintained. The original culture is derived from the founders' philosophy. This, in turn, strongly influences the criteria used in hiring. The actions of the current top managers set the general expectations as to what is acceptable behaviour and what is not. Socialization processes, if successful, will match new employees' values to those of the organization during the selection process and provide support during that critical time when employees have joined the organization and are learning the ropes. (To determine what culture suits you, see *Self-Assessment—What's the Right Organizational Culture for Me?* at the end of the chapter.)

How Employees Learn Culture

Culture is transmitted to employees in a number of ways. The most significant are stories, rituals, material symbols, and language.

Stories

An organization's "stories" typically are related to significant people or events, such as the organization's founders, rule breaking, reactions to past mistakes, and so forth.[19] For instance, at 3M, the product innovation stories are legendary. There is the story about the 3M scientist who spilled chemicals on her tennis shoe and came up with Scotchgard. Then there is the story about Art Fry, a researcher who wanted a better way to mark the pages

Exhibit 2-4

How an Organization's Culture Is Established and Maintained

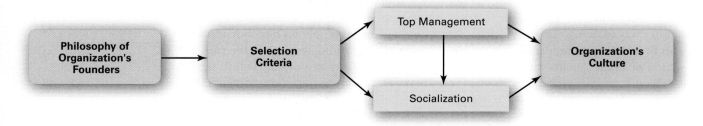

Taking its cue from the show *Survivor*, Osaka, Japan-based noodle maker Nissin Foods sent new managers on a wilderness survival trip recently. On a remote island, "managers had to dig toilets, make fire from dry leaves, catch fish and . . . make their own chopsticks out of bamboo." Company spokesman Masanaga Oguchi noted that the managers "would appreciate our product in a situation where they have to go through a lot of trouble just to make hot water." The socialization into management through the survival trip taught the new managers to work together as a team and introduced them to customers' needs.[18]

of his church hymnal and invented the Post-it Note. Such springboard stories "enable a leap in understanding by the audience so as to grasp how an organization or community or complex system may change."[20] These stories reflect what made 3M great and what it will take to continue that success.[21] An organization's stories help employees learn the culture by anchoring the present in the past, providing explanations and legitimacy for current practices, and showing what is important to the organization.[22]

Rituals

The annual employee golf tournament is an important ritual for Vancouver-based TrashBusters.com, an environmentally conscious company that removes people's clutter. Players have to find all their equipment from the garbage they have collected and are also expected to wear outrageous second-hand golf clothes. This ritual is in keeping with founder Mike McKee's philosophy of reducing environmental waste.

Corporate rituals are repetitive sequences of activities that express and reinforce the values of the organization, what goals are most important, and which people are important.[23] One of the best-known corporate rituals is Mary Kay Cosmetics' annual awards ceremony for its sales representatives.[24] Looking like a cross between a circus and a Miss America pageant, the ceremony takes place in a large auditorium, on a stage in front of a large, cheering audience, with all the participants dressed in glamorous evening clothes. Salespeople are rewarded for their success in achieving sales goals with a variety of flashy gifts including gold and diamond pins, furs, and pink Cadillacs. This "show" acts as a motivator by publicly acknowledging outstanding sales performance. In addition, the ritual aspect reinforces late founder Mary Kay's determination and optimism, which enabled her to overcome personal hardships, start her own company, and achieve material success. It conveys to salespeople that reaching their sales goals is important and that through hard work and encouragement they too can achieve success. With Mary Kay's passing in late 2001, the need to preserve her memory has become even stronger. Regional directors have been known to visit the Texas head office of the firm, where they can sit in her bathtub for good luck![25]

Material Symbols

When you walk into different businesses, do you get a "feel" for the place—formal, casual, fun, serious, and so forth? These feelings demonstrate the power of material symbols

One area where organizational culture influences employee behaviour is how employees dress for work. Look at what each of these four individuals is wearing. At what kinds of organizations do you think each of these styles is appropriate work wear? What do you think the cultures might be like at the organizations where each person works?

in creating an organization's personality. The layout of an organization's facilities, how employees dress, the types of automobiles provided to top executives, and the availability of corporate aircraft are examples of material symbols. Others include the size of offices, the elegance of furnishings, executive "perks" (extra "goodies" provided to managers such as health club memberships, use of company-owned resort facilities, and so forth), the existence of employee lounges or on-site dining facilities, and reserved parking spaces for certain employees. At Toronto-based Willow Manufacturing, everyone from the CEO down wears a uniform, to convey the message that everyone is a member of the team. Managers at Bolton, Ontario-based Husky Injection Molding Systems convey the sense of an egalitarian workplace by having employees and management share the parking lot, dining room, and even washrooms.

Material symbols convey to employees who is important, the degree of equality desired by top management, and the kinds of behaviour (for example, risk-taking, conservative, authoritarian, participative, individualistic) that are expected and appropriate.

Language

Many organizations and units within organizations use language as a way to identify members of a culture. By learning this language, members attest to their acceptance of the culture and their willingness to help preserve it. For instance, Microsoft employees have their own unique vocabulary: *work judo* (the art of deflecting a work assignment to someone else without making it appear that you are avoiding it); *eating your own dog food* (a strategy of using your own software programs or products in the early stages as a way of testing them even if the process is disagreeable); *flat food* (goodies from the vending machine that can be slipped under the door to a colleague who is working feverishly on deadline); *facemail* (actually talking to someone face-to-face, which is considered a technologically backward means of communicating); *death march* (the countdown to shipping a new product), and so on.[26]

Over time, organizations often develop unique terms to describe equipment, key personnel, suppliers, customers, processes, or products related to their business. New employees are frequently overwhelmed with acronyms and jargon that, after a short period of time, become a natural part of their language. Once learned, this language acts as a common denominator that unites members of a given culture.

How Culture Affects Managers

Because an organization's cultural norms define what its employees can and cannot do, they are particularly relevant to managers even though they are rarely explicitly stated or written down. It's unlikely that they will even be spoken. But they are there, and all managers quickly learn what to do and what not to do in their organization. For instance, you will not find the following values written down anywhere, but each comes from a real organization.

MyManagementLab
Q&A 2.8

- Look busy even if you are not.

- If you take risks and fail around here, you will pay dearly for it.

- Before you make a decision, run it by your manager so that he or she is never surprised.

- We make our product only as good as the competition forces us to.

- What made us successful in the past will make us successful in the future.

- If you want to get to the top here, you have to be a team player.

The link between values such as these and managerial behaviour is fairly straightforward. If an organization's culture supports the belief that profits can be increased by cost cutting and that the company's best interests are served by achieving slow but steady increases in quarterly earnings, managers are unlikely to pursue programs that are innovative, risky, long term, or expansionary. For organizations that value and encourage workforce diversity, the organizational culture, and thus managers' decisions and actions, will be supportive of diversity efforts. In an organization whose culture conveys a basic distrust of employees, managers are more likely to use an authoritarian leadership style than a democratic one. Why? The culture establishes for managers what is appropriate behaviour.

An organization's culture, especially a strong one, informs a manager's decision-making options in all four management functions. Exhibit 2-5 shows the major areas of a manager's job that are influenced by the culture in which he or she operates.

Current Organizational Culture Issues Facing Managers

Calgary-based WestJet Airlines is renowned for its attention to customers. Nike's innovations in running-shoe technology are legendary. Royal Bank (RBC Financial Group) consistently takes top honours for corporate responsibility and citizenship. How have these organizations achieved such reputations? Their organizational cultures have played a crucial role. Let's look at four current cultural issues managers should consider: creating an ethical culture, creating an innovative culture, creating a customer-responsive culture, and creating a culture that supports diversity.

3. Describe what kinds of cultures managers can create.

Exhibit 2-5

Managerial Decisions Affected by Organizational Culture

Planning
- The degree of risk that plans should contain
- Whether plans should be developed by individuals or teams
- The degree of environmental scanning in which management will engage

Leading
- The degree to which managers are concerned with increasing employee job satisfaction
- What leadership styles are appropriate
- Whether all disagreements—even constructive ones—should be eliminated

Organizing
- How much autonomy should be designed into employees' jobs
- Whether tasks should be done by individuals or in teams
- The degree to which department managers interact with each other

Controlling
- Whether to impose external controls or to allow employees to control their own actions
- What criteria should be emphasized in employee performance evaluations
- What repercussions will result from exceeding one's budget

Creating an Ethical Culture

The content and strength of an organization's culture influences its ethical climate and the ethical behaviour of its members.[27] A strong organizational culture will exert more influence on employees than a weak one. If the culture is strong and supports high ethical standards, it should have a very powerful and positive influence on employee behaviour. Likewise, a strong culture that encourages unethical behaviour will have a powerful influence on employees, as the following *Management Reflection* shows.

MANAGEMENT REFLECTION
► Focus on Ethics

Manager Rules with Iron Fist
Can a manager encourage individuals to act unethically?
At scandal-ridden WorldCom, Canadian-born CEO Bernie Ebbers ruled with an iron fist.[28] Hiding information from directors and auditors was an expected practice, with executives told to "follow orders." Employees were routinely criticized publicly if they did not follow orders. "Show those numbers to the [expletive deleted] auditors and I'll throw you out the [expletive deleted] window," a senior executive told an employee in an email. When company executives suggested that WorldCom needed a corporate code of conduct, Ebbers suggested that drafting one would be "a colossal waste of time." ■

TIPS FOR MANAGERS

Creating a More Ethical Culture

✎ Be a **visible role model.**

✎ Communicate **ethical expectations.**

✎ Provide **ethics training.**

✎ Visibly **reward ethical acts and punish unethical ones.**

✎ Provide **protective mechanisms** so employees can discuss ethical dilemmas and report unethical behaviour without fear.

An organizational culture most likely to shape high ethical standards is one that is high in risk tolerance, low to moderate in aggressiveness, and focused on means as well as outcomes. Managers in such a culture are supported for taking risks and innovating, are discouraged from engaging in uncontrolled competition, and will pay attention to *how* goals are achieved as well as to *what* goals are achieved.

What can managers do to create a more ethical culture? *Tips for Managers—Creating a More Ethical Culture* provides some suggestions.

Creating an Innovative Culture

You may not recognize IDEO's name, but you've probably used a number of its products. As a product design firm, it takes the ideas that corporations bring to it and turns them into reality. Some of its creations range from the first commercial mouse (for Apple Computer) to the first stand-up toothpaste tube (for Procter & Gamble) to the handheld personal organizer (for Palm). It's critical that IDEO's culture support creativity and innovation.[29] IDEO has won more *BusinessWeek*/DSA Industrial Design Excellence awards than any other firm. It also has been ranked by *BusinessWeek* in the top 25 most innovative companies and does consulting work for the other 24.[30] The company's emphasis is on simplicity, function, and meeting user needs. IDEO believes that the best ideas for creating or improving products or processes come from keen observation of how users work and play on a daily basis.[31]

Another innovative organization is Cirque du Soleil, the Montreal-based creator of circus theatre. Its managers state that the culture is based on involvement, communication, creativity, and diversity, which they see as keys to innovation.[32] Although these two companies are in industries where innovation is important (product design and entertainment), the fact is that any successful organization needs a culture that supports innovation. How important is culture to innovation? In a recent survey of senior executives, more than half said that the most important driver of innovation for companies was a supportive corporate culture.[33]

As we saw in Chapter 1, organizational culture is what makes Cirque du Soleil so special. Employees focus on solutions rather than blame. Consensus is not a virtue because CEO Daniel Lamarre feels that the best ideas get lost if everyone has to compromise. Lamarre encourages dissent, and tempers fly during discussions, but the results are the creative, dynamic shows that the Cirque produces.

What does an innovative culture look like? According to Swedish researcher Goran Ekvall, it is characterized by the following:

- *Challenge and involvement.* How much employees are involved in, motivated by, and committed to the long-term goals and success of the organization.

- *Freedom.* The degree to which employees can independently define their work, exercise discretion, and take initiative in their day-to-day activities.

- *Trust and openness.* The degree to which employees are supportive of and respectful to each other.

- *Idea time.* The amount of time individuals have to elaborate on new ideas before taking action.

- *Playfulness/humour.* How much spontaneity, fun, and ease there is in the workplace.

- *Conflict resolution.* The degree to which individuals make decisions and resolve issues based on the good of the organization vs. personal interest.

- *Debates.* How much employees are allowed to express their opinions and put forth their ideas for consideration and review.

- *Risk-taking.* How much managers tolerate uncertainty and ambiguity, and whether employees are rewarded for taking risks.[34]

Apple's risk-taking culture has helped it create such industry-changing innovations as the iPad and the iPhone. It also has made it number one on the World's 50 Most Innovative Companies list in 2007 and America's Most Admired Company in 2008. CEO Steve Jobs has been the catalyst behind his company's risk-taking culture.

Creating a Customer-Responsive Culture

Isadore Sharp, chair and CEO of Toronto-based Four Seasons Hotels and Resorts, believes keenly in customer service. Creating a customer-responsive culture starts with employee selection, where every candidate faces four or five interviews, to ensure they have the right attitude. As part of employee training, all new employees spend one night in the hotel as a guest to help them understand the perspective of the customer. Sharp notes that the hotel chain has "30 000 employees who are always thinking of new ways to make our guest experience more rewarding."[35]

TIPS FOR MANAGERS

Creating a More Customer-Responsive Culture

↗ Hire service-contact people with the **personality and attitudes consistent with customer service**—friendliness, enthusiasm, attentiveness, patience, concern about others, and listening skills.

↗ **Train customer-service people continually** by focusing on improving product knowledge, listening actively, showing patience, and displaying emotions.

↗ Socialize new service-contact people to the **organization's goals and values.**

↗ Design customer-service jobs so that **employees have as much control as necessary** to satisfy customers.

↗ Empower service-contact employees with the **discretion to make day-to-day decisions** on job-related activities.

↗ As the leader, **convey a customer-focused vision** and demonstrate through decisions and actions the commitment to customers.

Harrah's Entertainment, the Las Vegas–based national gaming company, is also devoted to customer service, and for good reason. Company research showed that customers who were satisfied with the service they received at a Harrah's casino increased their gaming expenditures by 10 percent, and those who were extremely satisfied increased their gaming expenditures by 24 percent. When customer service translates into these types of results, of course managers would want to create a customer-responsive culture![36]

But what does a customer-responsive culture look like? Research shows that six characteristics are routinely present in successful, service-oriented organizations:

- *Outgoing and friendly employees.* Successful service-oriented organizations hire employees who are outgoing and friendly.

- *Few rigid rules, procedures, and regulations.* Service employees need to have the freedom to meet changing customer service requirements.

- *Widespread use of empowerment.* Employees are empowered to decide what is necessary to please the customer.

- *Good listening skills.* Employees in customer-responsive cultures have the ability to listen to and understand messages sent by the customer.

- *Role clarity.* Service employees act as links between the organization and its customers, which can create considerable ambiguity and conflict. Successful customer-responsive cultures reduce employees' uncertainty about their roles and the best way to perform their jobs.

- *Employees attentive to customer needs.* They are willing to take the initiative, even when it's outside their normal job requirements, to satisfy a customer's needs.[37]

Based on these characteristics, what can managers do to make their cultures more customer-responsive? *Tips for Managers—Creating a More Customer-Responsive Culture* provides some suggestions.

In general, to create any type of culture (and to reinforce the culture), managers need to communicate the elements of the culture, model the appropriate behaviours, train employees to carry out the new actions, and reward desired behaviours, while creating negative incentives for straying from the desired behaviour.[38]

Creating a Culture That Supports Diversity

workforce diversity The mix of people in organizations in terms of gender, race, ethnicity, age, and other characteristics that reflect differences.

Today's organizations are characterized by **workforce diversity**, the mix of people in organizations in terms of gender, race, ethnicity, age, and other characteristics that reflect differences. Managers must look long and hard at their culture to see whether the shared meaning and beliefs that were appropriate for a more homogeneous workforce will accept and promote diverse views. Although organizations in the past may have supported diversity to meet federal hiring requirements, organizations today recognize that diversity-supportive cultures are good for business. Among other things, diversity contributes to more creative solutions and enhances employee morale. But how can such a culture be encouraged? The following *Management Reflection* discusses what managers can do.

MANAGEMENT REFLECTION

Creating an Inclusive Workplace Culture

How can managers create a culture that allows diversity to flourish?

Creating a workplace culture that supports and encourages the inclusion of diverse individuals and views is a major organizational effort.[39] There are two things managers can do. First, managers must show that they value diversity through their decisions and actions. As they plan, organize, lead, and control, they need to recognize and embrace diverse perspectives. For instance, at the Marriott Marquis Hotel in New York's Times Square, managers take required diversity-training classes, where they learn that the best way to cope with diversity-related conflict is by focusing on performance and not defining problems in terms of gender, culture, race, or disability. At Prudential, the annual planning process includes key diversity performance goals that are measured and tied to managers' compensation. The second thing managers can do is look for ways to reinforce employee behaviours that exemplify inclusiveness. Some suggestions include encouraging individuals to value and defend diverse views, creating traditions and ceremonies that celebrate diversity, rewarding "heroes" and "heroines" who accept and promote inclusiveness, and communicating formally and informally about employees who champion diversity issues. ∎

The Organizational Environment

▶ ▶ ▶ During the American stock market crash of 1929, the Dow Jones average fell by 54.7 percent.[40] Between October 11, 2007, and March 2, 2009, the market declined 50.2 percent! In the midst of the widespread market chaos during the recent market downturn, 3M reacted by aggressively managing costs and cash, as well as putting in place tighter operational discipline. In the fourth quarter of 2008, more than 2400 jobs were eliminated. Factory workers were temporarily laid off until production volumes returned to normal levels, pay raises were deferred in 2009, the policy of banking vacations was eliminated, and capital expenditures were cut back by 30 percent.[41]

4. Describe the features of the specific and general organizational environments.

Think About It

The financial collapse fuelled by the subprime mortgage crisis evolved quickly and soon became global. If you were a manager at 3M, could you have prepared for this eventuality?

In the supplement to Chapter 1, our discussion of an organization as an open system explained that an organization interacts with its environment as it takes in inputs and distributes outputs. Anyone who questions the impact of the external environment on managing should consider the following:

- A moratorium was placed on all offshore drilling in the Gulf of Mexico following the BP/Transocean Drilling oil spill in April 2010. Severe restrictions were placed on the Hebron well drilling off the coast of Newfoundland, and opposition mounted to allowing drilling on traditional fishing grounds such as George's Bank in offshore Nova Scotia.[42]

- During the Christmas rush of 2009, e-book sales surpassed traditional book sales for the first time at Amazon. On its busiest day of the season, December 14, Amazon processed 9.5 million items.[43]

As these two examples show, there are forces in the environment that play a major role in shaping managers' actions. In this section, we identify some of the critical environmental forces that affect managers and show how they impact managerial decision making.

Defining the External Environment

external environment Outside forces and institutions that potentially can affect the organization's performance.

The term **external environment** refers to forces and institutions outside the organization that potentially can affect the organization's performance. The external environment is made up of three components, as shown in Exhibit 2-6: the specific environment, the general environment, and the global environment. We discuss the first two types of external environment in this chapter. Today, globalization is one of the major factors affecting managers of both large and small organizations. We address the global environment in Chapter 3.

The Specific Environment

specific environment The part of the external environment that is directly relevant to the achievement of an organization's goals.

The **specific environment** includes those external forces that have a direct and immediate impact on managers' decisions and actions and are directly relevant to the achievement of the organization's goals. Each organization's specific environment is unique and changes with conditions. For instance, Timex and Rolex both make watches, but their specific environments differ because they operate in distinctly different market niches. What forces make up the specific environment? The main ones are customers, suppliers, competitors, and pressure groups.

Customers Organizations exist to meet the needs of customers. It's the customer or client who consumes or uses the organization's output. This is true even for government organizations and other not-for-profits.

Exhibit 2-6

The External Environment

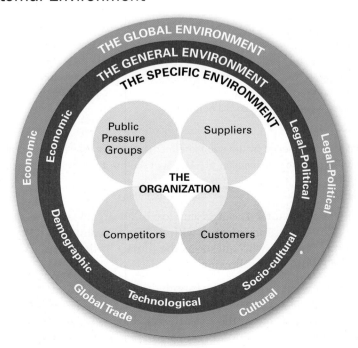

When the Internet search engine Google decided to accept heavy censorship of its Chinese site in compliance with Communist Party requirements, its founders said the widely criticized compromise was made to allow Internet access to a fifth of the world's population. Among those who disagreed with Google's compromise were these members of Students for a Free Tibet. In March of 2010 Google reconsidered its decision and withdrew its services from mainland China in protest of the self-censorship required as the price of doing business in China. [44]

Customers obviously represent potential uncertainty to an organization. Their tastes can change or they can become dissatisfied with the organization's products or service. Of course, some organizations face considerably more uncertainty as a result of their customers than do others. For example, what comes to mind when you think of Club Med? Club Med's image was traditionally one of carefree singles having fun in the sun at exotic locales. Club Med found, however, that as its target customers married and had children, these same individuals were looking for family-oriented vacation resorts where they could bring the kids. Although Club Med responded to the changing demands of its customers by offering different types of vacation experiences, including family-oriented ones, the company found it hard to change its image.

Suppliers When you think of an organization's suppliers, you typically think in terms of organizations that provide materials and equipment. For Canada's Wonderland, just outside of Toronto, that includes organizations that sell soft drinks, computers, food, flowers and other nursery stock, concrete, and paper products. But the term *suppliers* also includes providers of financial and labour inputs. Stockholders, banks, insurance companies, pension funds, and other similar organizations are needed to ensure a continuous supply of money. Labour unions, colleges and universities, occupational associations, trade schools, and local labour markets are sources of employees. When the sources of employees dry up, it can impact managers' decisions and actions. For example, a lack of qualified nurses, a serious problem plaguing the health care industry, is making it difficult for health care providers to meet demand and keep service levels high.

Competitors All organizations have one or more competitors. Even though it's a monopoly, Canada Post competes with FedEx, UPS, and other forms of communication such as the telephone, email, and fax. Nike competes with Reebok, Adidas, and Fila, among others. Coca-Cola competes with Pepsi and other soft drink companies. Not-for-profit organizations such as the Royal Ontario Museum and Girl Guides also compete for dollars, volunteers, and customers. One competitor that many managers ignore when launching new products or services is the status quo—customers tend to keep doing what they have always done unless there is a compelling reason to try something new. With this in mind, some would suggest that entering a new market with a new product is infinitely more risky than entering an established market where you find a compelling way to fulfill a need not now served by your competitors.

Public Pressure Groups Managers must recognize the special-interest groups that attempt to influence the actions of organizations. For instance, both Wal-Mart and Home Depot have had difficulty getting approval to build stores in Vancouver. Neighbourhood activists worry about traffic density brought about by big-box stores, and in the case of both

On May 31, 2010, Abitibi Bowater Inc.'s president, David Paterson, announced that the firm was poised to emerge from the bankruptcy filed in April 2010. The new firm will have a lower cost structure, less dependence on newsprint markets, and less debt. However, Abitibi Bowater is still greatly affected by the declining market for newsprint as consumers move from print-based media to the web, and it still must deal with a $1.3 billion pension deficit following the 2009 meltdown of equity markets.[46]

stores there is concern that local businesses will fail if the stores move in. Home Depot's director of real estate called Vancouver City Hall's review process "confusing and unfair" and "unlike anything in [his] experience."[45] Local hardware store owners and resident groups have lobbied against the store to city planners, hoping to keep big-box stores out of the Kitsilano neighbourhood.

As social and political attitudes change, so too does the power of public pressure groups. For example, through their persistent efforts, groups such as MADD (Mothers Against Drunk Driving) and SADD (Students Against Destructive Decisions) have managed to make changes in the alcoholic beverage and restaurant and bar industries, and raised public awareness about the problem of drunk drivers.

The General Environment

general environment Broad external conditions that may affect the organization.

The **general environment** includes the broad economic, legal–political, socio-cultural, demographic, and technological conditions that *may* affect the organization. Changes in any of these areas usually do not have as large an impact as changes in the specific environment do, but managers must consider them as they plan, organize, lead, and control.

Economic Conditions Interest rates, inflation, changes in disposable income, stock market fluctuations, and the stage of the general business cycle are some of the economic factors that can affect management practices in an organization. For example, many specialty retailers such as IKEA, Roots, Birks, and Williams-Sonoma are acutely aware of the impact consumer disposable income has on their sales. When consumers' incomes fall or when their confidence about job security declines, as happened following the subprime mortgage crisis in 2008, they will postpone purchasing anything that isn't a necessity. Even charitable organizations such as the United Way or the Heart and Stroke Foundation feel the impact of economic factors. During economic downturns, not only does the demand for their services increase, but also their contributions typically decrease.

Legal–Political Conditions Federal, provincial, and local governments influence what organizations can and cannot do. Some federal legislation has significant implications. For example, the Canadian Human Rights Act makes it illegal for any employer or provider of service that falls within federal jurisdiction to discriminate on the following grounds: race, national or ethnic origin, colour, religion, age, sex (including pregnancy and childbirth), marital status, family status, mental or physical disability (including previous or present drug or alcohol dependence), pardoned conviction, or sexual orientation. The act covers federal departments and agencies; Crown corporations; chartered banks; national airlines; interprovincial communications and telephone companies; interprovincial transportation companies; and other federally regulated industries, including certain mining operations.

Canada's Employment Equity Act of 1995 protects several categories of employees from employment barriers: Aboriginal peoples (whether First Nation, Inuit, or Métis); persons with disabilities; members of visible minorities (non-Caucasian in race or non-white in colour); and women. This legislation aims to ensure that members of these four groups are treated equitably. Employers covered by the Canadian Human Rights Act are also covered by the Employment Equity Act.

Many provinces have their own legislation, including employment equity acts, to cover employers in their provinces. Companies sometimes have difficulty complying with equity acts, as recent audits conducted by the Canadian Human Rights Commission show. In an audit of 180 companies, only Status of Women Canada; Elliot Lake, Ontario-based AJ Bus Lines; the National Parole Board; Canadian Transportation Agency; Les Méchins, Quebec-based Verreault Navigation; and Nortel Networks were compliant on their first try.[47]

The Competition Act of 1986 created the Bureau of Competition Policy (now called the Competition Bureau) to maintain and encourage competition in Canada. For example, if two major competing companies consider merging, they come under scrutiny from the bureau.

To protect farmers, the Canadian government has created marketing boards that regulate the pricing and production of such things as milk and eggs. Those who decide that they want to manufacture small amounts of cheese in Canada would have great difficulty doing so because the Canadian government does not open production quotas to new producers very often. Marketing boards restrict imports of some products, but the unintended result is that foreign governments oppose exports from Canada.

Organizations spend a great deal of time and money meeting government regulations, but the effects of these regulations go beyond time and money.[48] They also reduce managerial discretion by limiting the choices available to managers. In a 2004 COMPAS survey of business leaders, most respondents cited interprovincial trade barriers as a significant hurdle to doing business in this country, calling the barriers "bad economics."[49] An article published in May 2007 backed up the views of these Canadian business leaders, arguing that nearly half of the productivity advantage that the United States has over Canada could be accounted for by interprovincial trade barriers.[50]

Other aspects of the legal–political conditions are the political climate, the general stability of a country where an organization operates, and the attitudes that elected government officials hold toward business. This is discussed in more detail in Chapter 3.

Socio-cultural Conditions Vancouver-based A&W Food Services of Canada announced in January 2007 that it would become "the first national hamburger chain to provide customers across Canada with 'zero or significantly lower' trans fat in menu items." A&W marketing director Mike Atkinson explained the reason for the change: "Our customers wanted us to cut trans fats from our menu items so that's what we've done, without compromising taste and quality."[51] Burlington, Ontario-based Voortman Cookies was the first Canadian cookie maker to drop trans fats from its products. President and co-founder Harry Voortman said he dropped the trans fats after his daughter, Lynn, a naturopathic doctor, became concerned enough that she stopped eating her father's cookies altogether.[52] The *CBC Video Case Incident—The Fast-Food Industry and Trans Fats: Fad or Legitimate Concern for Society?* also explores the issue as it applies to managers in the food industry.

Why are A&W and Voortman changing their products? Because health officials and consumers are increasingly anxious about the link between TFAs (trans fatty acids) and heart disease.[53] Managers must adapt their practices to the changing expectations of the society in which they operate. As societal values, customs, and tastes change, managers also must change. For instance, as employees have begun seeking more balance in their lives, organizations have had to adjust by offering family leave policies, more flexible work hours, and on-site child care facilities. If an organization does business in other countries, managers need to be familiar with those countries' values and cultures, and manage in ways that recognize and embrace those specific socio-cultural aspects.

global aging The increase in the average age of the world's population.

Demographic Conditions Demographic conditions encompass trends in the physical characteristics of a population, such as gender, age, level of education, geographic location, income, and family composition. Changes in these characteristics will inform how managers plan, organize, lead, and control. In Canada, population researchers have labelled specific age cohorts. The average age of the world's population is increasing in a phenomenon known as **global aging.** Global aging is the result of both falling fertility rates (worldwide the fertility rate has fallen from 5.0 children per woman in the mid-1960s to 2.7 today) and rising longevity (the average life expectancy was 45 in 1945 and is 65 today). These trends are not the same across the globe. In the developed world, the fertility rate is 1.5 children per woman, or less than replacement, and in Japan and Italy life expectancy has approached 80 years. Fertility rates remain high in the less-developed world, but in emerging markets like China, fertility and longevity mirror the West.[54] While the developed world now accounts for 25 percent of the world's population, by the year 2030 it will account for less than 9 percent.

In Canada the proportion of the population older than 65 was 13.7 percent in the latest census[55] and is expected to increase to 26.5 percent by 2051.[56] This aging of the population will result in a labour shortage, and creative ways will need to be found to keep seniors working beyond the age of 65, along with pressure to increase immigration. Another effect will be a mounting fiscal burden, with fewer taxpayers to support each retired person (3.6 in Canada in 1995 and projected to be only 1.6 by 2050). We as a society and our politicians as our voice will be forced to make difficult choices to balance the needs of the aging population (for health care, in particular) and the needs of the general population (for education and social benefits such as welfare and employment insurance) with our capacity to pay for them. The aged will also face significant cultural challenges as they will have fewer children and grandchildren to care for them in family settings.[57]

Technological Conditions In terms of the general environment, the most rapid changes have occurred in technology. We live in a time of continuous technological change. For instance, the human genetic code has been cracked. It is predicted that by 2020, 3000 new pharmaceuticals will be brought to market based on the work of the human genome project, vs. the 500 that were introduced in 2000.[58] Information gadgets are getting smaller and more powerful. We have automated offices, electronic meetings, robotic manufacturing, lasers, integrated circuits, faster and more powerful microprocessors, synthetic fuels, and entirely new models of doing business in an electronic age. It is possible that nano sensors may someday be able to "smell" cancer, allowing physicians to employ a nano device rather than having to do a biopsy.[59] Companies that capitalize on technology, such as Research In Motion (RIM), eBay, and Google, prosper. In addition, many successful retailers such as Wal-Mart use sophisticated information systems to keep on top of current sales trends. Similarly, hospitals, universities, airports, police departments, and even military organizations that adapt to major technological advances have a competitive edge over those that do not. The whole area of technology is radically changing the fundamental ways that organizations are structured and the way that managers manage.

How the Organizational Environment Affects Managers

Knowing *what* the various components of the organizational environment are is important to managers. However, understanding *how* the organizational environment affects managers is equally important. The organizational environment affects managers through the degree of uncertainty that is present and through the various stakeholder relationships that exist between the organization and its external constituencies.

MyManagementLab
PRISM 4

environmental uncertainty The degree of change and the degree of complexity in an organization's environment.

Assessing Environmental Uncertainty

Not all environments are the same. They differ by what we call their degree of **environmental uncertainty**, which is the degree of change and the degree of complexity in an organization's environment (see Exhibit 2-7).

Exhibit 2-7

Environmental Uncertainty Matrix

Degree of Change		
	Stable	**Dynamic**
Simple	**Cell 1** Stable and predictable environment Few components in environment Components are somewhat similar and remain basically the same Minimal need for sophisticated knowledge of components	**Cell 2** Dynamic and unpredictable environment Few components in environment Components are somewhat similar but are in continual process of change Minimal need for sophisticated knowledge of components
Complex	**Cell 3** Stable and predictable environment Many components in environment Components are not similar to one another and remain basically the same High need for sophisticated knowledge of components	**Cell 4** Dynamic and unpredictable environment Many components in environment Components are not similar to one another and are in continual process of change High need for sophisticated knowledge of components

(Left axis label: **Degree of Complexity**)

The first of these dimensions is the degree of change. If the components in an organization's environment change frequently, we call it a *dynamic* environment. If change is minimal, we call it a *stable* one. A stable environment might be one in which there are no new competitors, few technological breakthroughs by current competitors, little activity by pressure groups to influence the organization, and so forth. For instance, Zippo Canada, best known for its Zippo lighters, faces a relatively stable environment. There are few competitors and there is little technological change. Probably the main environmental concern for the company is the declining trend in tobacco smokers, although the company's lighters have other uses and global markets remain attractive.

In contrast, the recorded music industry faces a dynamic (highly uncertain and unpredictable) environment. Digital formats and music-downloading sites have turned the industry upside down and brought uncertainty. If change is predictable, is that considered dynamic? No. Think of department stores that typically make one-quarter to one-third of their sales in December. The drop-off from December to January is significant. But because the change is predictable, we don't consider the environment to be dynamic. When we talk about degree of change, we mean change that is unpredictable. If change can be accurately anticipated, it's not an uncertainty that managers must confront.

The other dimension of uncertainty describes the degree of **environmental complexity**. The degree of complexity refers to the number of components in an organization's environment and the extent of the knowledge that the organization has about those components. For example, Hasbro, the second-largest toy manufacturer (behind Mattel), has simplified its environment by acquiring many of its competitors, such as Tiger Electronics, Wizards of the Coast, Kenner Toys, Parker Brothers, and Tonka Toys. The fewer competitors, customers, suppliers, government agencies, and so forth that an organization must deal with, the less complexity and therefore the less uncertainty there is in its environment.

Complexity is also measured in terms of the knowledge an organization needs to have about its environment. For instance, managers at the online brokerage E*TRADE must know a great deal about their Internet service provider's operations if they want to ensure that their website is available, reliable, and secure for their stock-trading customers. On the other hand, managers of grocery stores have a minimal need for sophisticated knowledge about their suppliers.

How does the concept of environmental uncertainty influence managers? Looking again at Exhibit 2-7, each of the four cells represents different combinations of the degree of complexity and the degree of change. Cell 1 (an environment that is stable and simple)

environmental complexity The number of components in an organization's environment and the extent of the organization's knowledge about those components.

represents the lowest level of environmental uncertainty. Cell 4 (an environment that is dynamic and complex) represents the highest. Not surprisingly, managers' influence on organizational outcomes is greatest in cell 1 and least in cell 4.

Because uncertainty is a threat to an organization's effectiveness, managers try to minimize it. Given a choice, managers would prefer to operate in environments such as those in cell 1. However, they rarely have full control over that choice. In addition, most industries today are facing more dynamic changes, making their environments more uncertain. The discipline of managing uncertainty is known as "risk management" and is deployed by managers in both for-profit and not-for-profit organizations.

Managing Stakeholder Relationships

Managers are also affected by the nature of the relationships they have with external stakeholders. The more obvious and secure these relationships become, the more influence managers will have over organizational outcomes.

Who are **stakeholders**? We define them as groups in the organization's external environment that are affected by and/or have an effect on the organization's decisions and actions. These groups have a stake in or are significantly influenced by what the organization does. In turn, these groups can influence the organization. For example, think of the groups that might be affected by the decisions and actions of Starbucks—coffee bean farmers, employees, specialty coffee competitors, local communities, and so forth. Some of these stakeholders also may impact decisions and actions of Starbucks' managers. The idea that organizations have stakeholders is now widely accepted by both management academics and practising managers.[60]

With what types of stakeholders might an organization have to deal? Exhibit 2-8 identifies some of the most common. Note that these stakeholders include internal and external groups. Why? Because both can affect what an organization does and how it operates. However, we are primarily interested in the external groups and their impact on managers' discretion in planning, organizing, leading, and controlling. This does not mean that the internal stakeholders are not important, but we explain these relationships, primarily with employees, throughout the rest of the book.

Why is stakeholder relationship management important? Why should managers even care about managing stakeholder relationships?[61] It can lead to improved predictability of environmental changes, more successful innovations, a greater degree of trust among

stakeholders Any constituencies in the organization's external environment that are affected by the organization's decisions and actions.

MyManagementLab
Q&A 2.9

Exhibit 2-8

Organizational Stakeholders

stakeholders, and greater organizational flexibility to reduce the impact of change. But does it affect organizational performance? The answer is yes! Management researchers who have looked at this issue are finding that managers of high-performing companies tend to consider the interests of all major stakeholder groups as they make decisions.[62]

Another reason given for managing external stakeholder relationships is that it's the "right" thing to do. What does this mean? It means that an organization depends on these external groups as sources of inputs (resources) and as outlets for outputs (goods and services), and managers should consider the interests of these external groups as they make decisions and take actions. We address this issue in more detail in Chapter 5 as we look at the concepts of managerial ethics and corporate social responsibility.

How can external stakeholder relationships be managed? There are four steps:

1. *Identify the organization's stakeholders.* Which of the various groups might be impacted by decisions that managers make and which groups might influence those decisions? Those groups that are likely to be influenced by and have influence on organizational decisions are the organization's stakeholders.

2. *Determine what particular interests or concerns the stakeholders might have.* These interests or concerns could be product quality, financial issues, safe working conditions, environmental protection, and so forth.

3. *Decide how critical each stakeholder is to the organization's decisions and actions.* Some stakeholders are more critical to the organization's decisions and actions than others. For instance, a critical stakeholder of the University of British Columbia would be the province's legislature since it controls how much budget money the university gets each year. On the other hand, the university's computer hardware and software suppliers are important but not critical.

4. *Determine how to manage the different stakeholder relationships.* This decision depends on how critical the stakeholder is to the organization and how uncertain the environment is.[63]

The more critical the stakeholder and the more uncertain the environment, the more managers need to rely on establishing explicit stakeholder partnerships rather than just acknowledging their existence.

SUMMARY AND IMPLICATIONS

1. Discuss the two differing views of how much control managers have. The omnipotent view of management suggests that managers are directly responsible for an organization's success or failure. While this is the dominant view of managers, there is another perspective. The symbolic view of management argues that much of an organization's success or failure is due to external forces outside managers' control. The reality is probably somewhere in between these two views, with managers often able to exert control, but also facing situations over which they have no control.

▶ ▶ ▶ At 3M, the 15 percent rule allows technical employees to work on projects they feel a personal commitment to (the omnipotent view). However, when markets collapsed in 2001 (after 9/11 and the dot-com bust) and again in late 2008 (as a result of the subprime mortgage crisis), the company found itself at the mercy of market forces beyond its managers' control (symbolic view).

2. Discuss the characteristics and importance of organizational culture. Culture influences how people within an organization act. A strong culture where everyone supports the goals of the organization makes it easier for managers to achieve goals. A weak culture, where people do not feel connected to the organization, can make things more difficult for managers. Managers can also influence culture, through how it is conveyed to employees, which employees are hired, and how rewards occur in organizations.

▶ ▶ ▶ The innovation culture at 3M was changed when James McNerney moved the cultural pendulum toward efficiency of operation and away from innovation. The pendulum swung back toward innovation with the appointment of George Buckley in 2005.

3. Describe what kinds of cultures managers can create. Managers can create a variety of cultures. In this chapter, we discussed ethical, innovative, customer-responsive, and diversity supportive cultures. By having a culture that is consistent with goals and values, managers can more easily encourage employees to achieve organizational goals.

▶ ▶ ▶ At 3M managers not only "talk the talk," they also "walk the talk" in their approach to collaboration and the incentives that support the stated cultural objectives.

4. Describe the features of the specific and general organizational environments. The organizational environment plays a major role in shaping managers' decisions and actions. Managers have to be responsive to customers and suppliers while being aware of competitors and public pressure groups. As well, economic, legal–political, socio-cultural, demographic, and technological conditions affect the issues managers face in doing their job.

▶ ▶ ▶ The 30 percent rule at 3M requiring that 30 percent of the current year's sales must come from products not in existence five years ago forces the company to proactively stay in touch with customers, competitors, and changes in the marketplace.

Management @ Work

READING FOR COMPREHENSION

1. Contrast the actions of managers according to the omnipotent and symbolic views.

2. What are the seven dimensions of organizational culture?

3. What is the impact of a strong culture on organizations and managers?

4. What is the source of an organization's culture? How does organizational culture continue?

5. How do employees learn an organization's culture?

6. What are the characteristics of an ethical culture, an innovative culture, an adaptable culture, a customer-responsive culture, and a diversity-supportive culture?

7. What forces influence the specific and the general organizational environments?

8. Discuss the two dimensions of organizational environmental uncertainty.

9. What are the four steps in managing external stakeholder relationships?

LINKING CONCEPTS TO PRACTICE

1. Classrooms have cultures. Describe your classroom culture using the seven dimensions of organizational culture. Does the culture constrain your instructor? How?

2. Refer to Exhibit 2-3 on page 43. How would a first-line manager's job differ in these two organizations? How about a top manager's job?

3. Can culture be a liability to an organization? Explain.

4. Why is it important for managers to understand the external forces that are acting on them and their organizations?

5. Describe an effective culture for (a) a relatively stable environment and (b) a dynamic environment. Justify your choices.

6. "Businesses are built on relationships." What do you think this statement means? What are the implications for managing the external organizational environment?

7. What would be the drawbacks in not managing stakeholder relationships?

SELF-ASSESSMENT

What's the Right Organizational Culture for Me?

For each of the following statements, circle the level of agreement or disagreement that you personally feel: [64]

1 = Strongly Agree 2 = Agree 3 = Uncertain 4 = Disagree 5 = Strongly Disagree

1. I like the thrill and excitement of taking risks.	1 2 3 4 5
2. I prefer managers who provide detailed and rational explanations for their decisions.	1 2 3 4 5
3. If a person's job performance is inadequate, it's irrelevant how much effort he or she made.	1 2 3 4 5
4. No person's needs should be compromised in order for a department to achieve its goals.	1 2 3 4 5
5. I like being part of a team and having my performance assessed in terms of my contribution to the team.	1 2 3 4 5
6. I like to work where there isn't a great deal of pressure and where people are essentially easygoing.	1 2 3 4 5
7. I like things to be stable and predictable.	1 2 3 4 5

Scoring Key

For items 1, 3, 4, 5, and 6, use marked scores. For items 2 and 7, reverse the score (that is, Strongly Agree = 5, Agree = 4, Uncertain = 3, Disagree = 2, Strongly Disagree = 1). Add up all the scores.

Analysis and Interpretation

Your total score will range from 7 to 35. Scores of 21 or lower indicate that you are more comfortable in a formal, mechanistic, rule-oriented, and structured culture. This is often associated with large corporations and government agencies. The lower your number, the stronger your preference for this type of culture. Scores above 22 indicate a preference for informal, humanistic, flexible, and innovative cultures, which are more likely to be found in high-tech companies, small businesses, research units, or advertising agencies. The higher your score above 22, the stronger your preference for these humanistic cultures.

Organizational cultures differ. So do individuals. The better you are able to match your personal preferences to an organization's culture, the more likely you are to find satisfaction in your work, the less likely you are to leave, and the greater the probability that you will receive positive performance evaluations.

More Self-Assessments MyManagementLab

To learn more about your skills, abilities, and interests, go to the MyManagementLab website and take the following self-assessment:

- III.B.3.—Am I Experiencing Work/Family Conflict?

MANAGEMENT FOR YOU TODAY

Dilemma

You are considering organizing an event to raise funds for a special cause (children living in poverty, breast cancer research, illiteracy, or another cause of your choice). Think about whom you might invite to this event (that is, your "customers"—those who will buy tickets to the event).

What type of event might appeal to them? What suppliers might you approach for help in organizing the event? What legal issues might you face in setting up this event? After considering all these specific environmental forces, describe the challenges you could face in holding this event.

Becoming a Manager

- When you read current business or general news stories, see if omnipotent or symbolic views of management are being described.

- Notice aspects of organizational culture as you interact with different organizations.

- Read books about different organizations and entrepreneurs to better understand how an organization's culture forms and how it's maintained.

- Start thinking about the type of organizational culture in which you are going to be most comfortable.

- If you belong to a student organization, evaluate its culture. What does the culture look like? How do new members learn the culture? How is the culture maintained?

- When you evaluate companies for class assignments (for this class and others you may be enrolled in), get in the habit of looking at the stakeholders that might be impacted by these companies' decisions and actions.

- Practise defining the general and specific environments of different organizations and notice how they are similar and different.

WORKING TOGETHER: TEAM-BASED EXERCISE

Assessing the Organization's Environment

All organizations are informed by the realities of their internal and external environments, yet the forces in their specific and general environments differ. Form a small group with three or four other class members and choose two

organizations in different industries. Describe the specific and general environmental forces that affect each organization. How are your descriptions different for the two organizations? How are they similar? Now, using the same two organizations, see if you can identify their important stakeholders. Also, indicate whether these stakeholders are critical for the organization and why they are or are not.

As a group, be prepared to share your information with the class and to explain your choices.

ETHICS IN ACTION

Ethical Dilemma Exercise: How Far Should a Company Go to Please Investors?

Managing relations with a variety of stakeholder groups is a challenge in any situation—but it's even more difficult when the culture tolerates or encourages ethically questionable behaviour.[65] This is what happened at Computer Associates, a provider of software solutions for business. When Computer Associates reported year after year of impressive sales growth, the stock price soared and investors cheered. During one quarter, however, the company failed to meet earnings expectations, and the stock price plummeted more than 40 percent in a single day as investors fled.

Because CEO Sanjay Kumar and a few top executives had wanted to please investors by keeping up the appearance of continued growth, they began booking software sales *before* the contracts were signed. They also told salespeople to change or remove dates on some contracts to clear the way for backdating those deals. Eventually the accounting irregularities made the press—touching off a lengthy investigation that eventually led to Kumar and four former executives pleading guilty to securities fraud.

Imagine this is your second day at work as a manager supervising a team of financial analysts in a major technology corporation. Your boss, the chief financial officer, calls you in and asks you to have your team find "creative" ways of improving sales figures. What should you do?

Thinking Critically About Ethics

Do you think it's possible for a manager with high ethical standards to live by the values in an organizational culture that tolerates, or even encourages, unethical practices? How could a manager deal with such situations?

CASE APPLICATION

Making You Say Wow

When you hear the name Ritz-Carlton Hotels, what words come to mind? Luxurious? Elegant? Formal, or maybe even stodgy? Way beyond my budget constraints? Three words that the company hopes comes to mind are *exemplary customer service*. Ritz-Carlton is committed to treating its guests like royalty. It has one of the most distinctive corporate cultures in the lodging industry, and employees are referred to as "our ladies and gentlemen." Its motto is printed on a card that employees carry with them: "We are Ladies and Gentlemen serving Ladies and Gentlemen." And these ladies and gentlemen of the Ritz have been trained in very precise standards and specifications for treating customers. These standards were established more than a century ago by founders Caesar Ritz and August Escoffier. Ritz employees are continually schooled in company lore and company values. Every day at 15-minute "line-up" sessions at each hotel property, managers reinforce company values and review service techniques. And these values are the basis for all employee training and rewards. Nothing is left to chance when it comes to providing exemplary customer service. Potential hires are tested both for cultural fit and for traits associated with an innate passion to serve. A company

executive says, "The smile has to come naturally." Although staff members are expected to be warm and caring, their behaviour toward guests had been extremely detailed and scripted. That's why a new customer service philosophy implemented in mid-2006 was such a radical departure from what the Ritz had been doing.

The company's new approach is almost the opposite from what the company had been doing: Don't tell employees how to make guests happy. Now they're expected to figure it out. Says Diana Oreck, vice-president, "We moved away from that heavily prescriptive, scripted approach and toward managing to outcomes." The outcome didn't change, though. The goal is still a happy guest who's wowed by the service received. However, under the new approach, staff member interactions with guests are more natural, relaxed, and authentic rather than sounding like they're recited lines from a manual.[66]

What is the culture like at Ritz-Carlton Hotels? Why do you think this type of culture might be important to a luxury hotel? What might be the drawbacks of such a culture? What challenges do you think the company faced in changing the culture? What is Ritz-Carlton doing to maintain this new culture? What kind of person do you think would be happiest and most successful in this culture? How do you think new employees "learn" the culture? What could other organizations learn from Ritz-Carlton about the importance of organizational culture?

DEVELOPING YOUR DIAGNOSTIC AND ANALYTICAL SKILLS

A Perfect Response to an Imperfect Storm

Twelve days.[67] That is how long it took for Mississippi Power to restore electric power to the heavily damaged areas of southern Mississippi after Hurricane Katrina slammed into the Mississippi Gulf Coast on August 29, 2005, with 233 kilometre-per-hour winds and pounding rain. That is remarkable, given the devastation that news photos and television newscasts so graphically displayed. It's something that even the federal and state governments could not accomplish. How bad was the damage company employees dealt with? One hundred percent of the company's customers were without power. Sixty-five percent of its transmission and distribution facilities were destroyed. And yet, this organization of 1250 employees did what it had to do, despite the horrible circumstances and despite the fact that more than half of its employees suffered substantial damage to their own homes. It speaks volumes about the cultural climate that the managers of Mississippi Power had created.

As a corporate subsidiary of utility holding company Southern Company, Mississippi Power provides electric services to more than 190 000 customers in the Magnolia State. When Hurricane Katrina turned toward Mississippi, managers at Mississippi Power swung into action with a swift and ambitious disaster plan. After Katrina's landfall, Mississippi Power's management team responded "with a style designed for speed and flexibility, for getting things done amid confusion and chaos." David Ratcliffe, senior executive of Southern Company, said, "I could not be prouder of our response." What factors led to the company's ability to respond as efficiently and effectively as it did?

One key element is the company's can-do organizational culture, which is evidenced by the important values inscribed on employees' identification tags: "Unquestionable Trust, Superior Performance, Total Commitment." Because the values were visible daily, employees knew their importance. They knew what was expected of them, in a disaster response or in just doing their everyday work. In addition, through employee training and managerial example, the organization had "steeped its culture" in Stephen Covey's book *The 7 Habits of Highly Effective People*. (The company's training building—the Covey Center—flooded during the storm.) These ingrained habits—be proactive; begin with the end in mind; put first things first; think win–win; seek first to understand, then to be understood; synergize; and sharpen the saw—also guided employee decisions and actions.

Another important element in the company's successful post-storm response was the clear lines of responsibility of the 20 "storm directors," who had clear responsibility and authority for whatever task they had been assigned. These directors had the power to do what needed to be done, backed by unquestionable trust from their bosses. Said one, "I don't have to ask permission."

Finally, the company's decentralized decision-making approach contributed to the way in which employees were able to accomplish what they did. The old approach of responding to a disaster with top-down decision making had been replaced by decision making being pushed further down to the electrical substation level, a distribution point that serves some 5000 people. Crews working to restore power reported to these substations and had a simple mission—get the power back on. "Even out-of-state line crews, hired on contract and working unsupervised, were empowered to engineer their own solutions." What the crews often did to "get the power back on" was quite innovative and entrepreneurial. For instance, one crew "stripped a generator off an ice machine to get a substation working." Mississippi Power's president, Anthony Topazi, said, "This structure made things happen faster than we expected. People were getting more done."

All in all, employees at Mississippi Power, working in difficult, treacherous, and often dangerous situations, did what they had to do. They got the job done. In recognition of the company's outstanding efforts to restore power in the wake of Hurricane Katrina, Mississippi Power was honoured with an "Emergency Response Award" by the Edison Electric Institute in January 2006. It's an award that all the company's employees can be proud of.

Questions

1. Using Exhibit 2-2 on page 43, describe the culture at Mississippi Power. Why do you think this type of culture might be important to an electric power company? On the other hand, what might be the drawbacks of such a culture?

2. Describe how you think new employees at Mississippi Power "learn" the company's culture.

3. What stakeholders might be important to Mississippi Power? What concerns might each of these stakeholders have? Would these stakeholders change if there was a disaster to which the company had to respond?

4. What could other organizations learn from Mississippi Power about the importance of organizational culture?

Reading an Organization's Culture

About the Skill

The ability to read an organization's culture can be a valuable skill. For instance, if you are looking for a job, you will want to choose an organization whose culture is compatible with your values and in which you will feel comfortable. If you can accurately assess a potential employer's culture before you make your job decision, you may be able to save yourself a lot of anxiety and reduce the likelihood of making a poor choice. Similarly, you will undoubtedly have business transactions with numerous organizations during your professional career, such as selling a product or service, negotiating a contract, arranging a joint work project, or merely seeking out who controls certain decisions in an organization. The ability to assess another organization's culture can be a definite plus in successfully performing those pursuits.

Steps in Developing the Skill

For the sake of simplicity, we are going to look at this skill from the perspective of a job applicant. We will assume that you are interviewing for a job, although this skill can be generalized to many situations. You can be more effective at reading an organization's culture if you use the following five suggestions:[68]

1. **Observe the physical surroundings.** Pay attention to signs, posters, pictures, photos, style of dress and length of hair, degree of openness between offices, and office furnishings and arrangements.

2. **Take note of those with whom you meet.** Did you meet the person who would be your immediate supervisor? Or did you meet with potential colleagues, managers from other departments, or senior executives? Based on what they revealed, to what degree do people interact with others who may not be in their particular work area or at their particular organizational level?

3. **Characterize the style of the people you meet.** Are they formal? Casual? Serious? Laid-back? Open? Not willing to provide information?

4. **Look at the organization's human resource manual.** Are formal rules and regulations printed there? If so, how detailed are these policies?

5. **Ask questions of the people with whom you meet.** The most valid and reliable information tends to come from asking the same questions of many people (to see how closely their responses align) and by talking with individuals whose jobs link them to the outside environment. Questions that will give you insights into organizational processes and practices might include: What is the background of the founders? What is the background of current senior managers? What are their functional specialties? Were they promoted from within or hired from outside? How does the organization integrate new employees? Is there a formal orientation program? Are there formal employee training programs? How does your manager define his or her job success? How would you define fairness in terms of reward allocations? Can you identify some people here who are on the "fast track"? What do you think has put them on the fast track? Can you identify someone in the organization who seems to be considered an oddball or deviant? How has the organization responded to this person? Can you describe a decision that someone made that was well received? Can you describe a decision that did not work out well? What were the consequences for the decision maker? Could you describe a crisis or critical event that has occurred recently in the organization? How did top management respond? What was learned from this experience?

Practising the Skill

Read the following scenario. Write some notes about how you would handle the situation described. Be sure to refer to the five suggestions for reading an organization's culture.

Scenario

You have spent the first three years after college graduation as a freelance graphic designer, and now you are looking at pursuing a job as an account executive at a graphic design firm. You feel that the scope of assignments and potential for technical training far exceed what you would be able to do on your own, and you are looking to expand your skills and meet a brand-new set of challenges. However, you want to make sure you "fit" into the organization where you are going to be spending more than eight hours every workday. What is the best way for you to find a place where you will be happy and where your style and personality will be appreciated?

Reinforcing the Skill

The following activities will help you practise and reinforce the skills associated with reading an organization's culture.

1. If you are taking more than one course, assess the culture of the various classes in which you are enrolled. How do the classroom cultures differ? Which culture(s) do you seem to prefer? Why?

2. Compare the atmosphere or feeling you get from various organizations. Because of the number and wide variety that you will find, it will probably be easiest for you to do this exercise using restaurants, retail stores, or banks. Based on the atmosphere that you observe, what type of organizational culture do you think these organizations might have? On what did you base your decision? Which type of culture do you prefer? Why? If you can, interview three employees at this organization for their descriptions of the organization's culture. Did their descriptions support your interpretation? Why or why not?

MyManagementLab

For more resources, please visit www.pearsoned.ca/mymanagementlab

SCAN THIS

Managing in a Global Environment

Every organization is affected in some way by the global environment. In this chapter, we'll look at what managers need to know about managing globally, including regional trading alliances, how organizations go international, and cross-cultural differences. After reading and studying this chapter, you will achieve the following learning outcomes.

Learning Outcomes

1 Compare and contrast the different views of global differences.

2 Describe the kinds of alliances that affect trade relations among countries in the world.

3 Describe how organizations do business globally.

4 Describe the challenges of doing business globally.

▶ ▶ ▶ Worry about pet food contamination swept across North America in February and March of 2007, upon news that at least 15 cats and 1 dog had died after eating possibly poisoned food.[1] There were also unconfirmed reports that hundreds of pets in Canada had suffered kidney failure. Though pet owners were reporting pet illnesses in February, the first recall of pet food did not occur until March 16, 2007, when Mississauga, Ontario-based Menu Foods asked retailers to remove 60 million packages of its wet pet foods off grocery and pet food store shelves. At the time, the company was not entirely sure why pets were getting sick, but something seemed to be wrong with its pet food.

For consumers, the pet food recall caused immediate confusion. There is no brand called "Menu Foods" on pet food shelves. Instead, 889 separate items under 100 different brand names had to be taken off grocery shelves. Menu Foods processes most of North America's most popular brands of wet pet food packaged in cans and foil pouches. It produces about 75 percent of private-label pet food brands in Canada (for companies such as Wal-Mart Canada, Sobeys, and Pet Valu) and between 40 and 50 percent of private-label pet food brands in the United States (for companies such as PetSmart, Safeway, and Wal-Mart).

At the time of the recall, Menu Foods was a virtually unknown company, particularly to consumers. Suddenly, this Canadian company had Americans worried about the wisdom of importing food from foreign sources, including Canada. Ironically, the contaminated ingredient in the recalled pet food came from an American company, Nevada-based ChemNutra, that had purchased the ingredient from a company in China.

On November 27, 2008, Canadian courts gave final approval to a $24 million (US) settlement to resolve more than 100 class action lawsuits against Menu Foods in the United States and Canada.

SCAN THIS

Think About It

Should large corporations have to report the source of all ingredients in the food products they manufacture? Put yourself in the shoes of Menu Foods' CEO. What responsibilities does an organization have when sourcing food ingredients globally?

The Menu Foods example illustrates that the global marketplace presents opportunities and challenges for managers. With the entire world as a market and national borders becoming increasingly irrelevant, the potential for organizations to grow expands dramatically. (To determine your fit for a position as an international manager, see *Self-Assessment—Am I Well-Suited for a Career as a Global Manager?* at the end of the chapter.)

However, as our opening dilemma also implies, even large, successful organizations with talented managers face challenges in managing in the global environment. Managers must deal with cultural, economic, and political differences. Meanwhile, new competitors can suddenly appear at any time from any place on the globe. Managers who don't closely monitor changes in their global environment or who don't take the specific characteristics of their location into consideration as they plan, organize, lead, and control are likely to find limited global success. In this chapter, we discuss the issues managers face in managing in a global environment.

MyManagementLab
Q&A 3.1

What's Your Global Perspective?

It's not unusual for Germans, Italians, or Indonesians to speak three or four languages. Japanese schoolchildren begin studying English in elementary school.[2] On the other hand, even though we are officially a bilingual country, many Canadians tend to think of English as the only international business language and don't see a need to study other languages.

1. Compare and contrast the different views of global differences.

How comfortable are you around people from different cultures?

Monolingualism is just one of the ways that people can be unfamiliar with the cultures of others. Successful global management requires enhanced sensitivity to differences in national customs and practices. Management practices that work in Vancouver might not be appropriate in Bangkok or Berlin. However, not everyone recognizes that others have different ways of living and working, particularly those who suffer from **parochialism**, which is viewing the world narrowly through one's own perspective.[3] Parochialism is a significant obstacle for managers working in a global business world. If managers fall into the trap of ignoring others' values and customs and rigidly applying an attitude of "ours is better than theirs" to foreign cultures, they will find it difficult to compete with other managers and organizations around the world that *are* seeking to understand foreign customs and market differences.

parochialism A narrow view of the world; an inability to recognize the differences of other people.

Individuals can take a variety of approaches in their attitudes toward other cultures.[4] Exhibit 3-1 summarizes the key points about three possible global attitudes. Let's look at each more closely.

MyManagementLab
Q&A 3.2

Exhibit 3-1

Key Information About Three Global Attitudes

Orientation	Ethnocentric Home Country	Polycentric Host Country	Geocentric World
Advantages	Simpler structure	Extensive knowledge of foreign market and workplace	Extensive understanding of global issues
	More tightly controlled	More support from host government	Balance between local and global objectives
		Committed local managers with high morale	Best people and work approaches used regardless of origin
Drawbacks	More ineffective management	Duplication of work	Difficult to achieve
	Inflexibility	Reduced efficiency	Managers must have both local and global knowledge
	Social and political backlash	Difficult to maintain global objectives because of intense focus on local traditions	

Reto Wittwer is the president and CEO of Kempinski Hotels. Born in Switzerland and educated in Catholic schools in France, he became a Buddhist when he fell in love with and married a Vietnamese woman after living in Asia for many years. Wittwer is a good example of a geocentric manager; in addition to German, French, Italian, and a Latin-based gypsy language called Rhaeto-Romanish, he speaks eight other languages.

ethnocentric attitude The belief that the best work approaches and practices are those of the home country.

polycentric attitude The view that the managers in the host country know the best work approaches and practices for running their businesses.

geocentric attitude A world-oriented view that focuses on using the best approaches and people from around the globe.

An **ethnocentric attitude** is the belief that the best work approaches and practices are those of the *home* country (the country in which the company's headquarters are located). Managers with an ethnocentric attitude believe that people in foreign countries do not have the skills, expertise, knowledge, or experience that people in the home country do. They would not trust foreign employees with key decisions or technology. While managers with a parochial outlook have a lack of knowledge about other cultures, managers who are ethnocentric believe that their home culture is better than any other.[5]

A **polycentric attitude** is the view that the managers in the *host* country (the foreign country in which the organization is doing business) know the best work approaches and practices for running their businesses. Managers with a polycentric attitude view every foreign operation as different and hard to understand. Thus, these managers are likely to leave their foreign facilities alone and let foreign employees figure out how best to do things.

The last type of global attitude that managers might have is a **geocentric attitude**, which is a *world-oriented* view that focuses on using the best approaches and people from around the globe. Managers with this type of attitude believe that it's important to have a global view both at the organization's headquarters in the home country *and* in the various foreign work facilities. For instance, the CEO of Home Décor (a disguised name), a fast-growing manufacturer of household accessories, is a Chinese immigrant who describes the company's strategy as "combining Chinese costs with Japanese quality, European design, and American marketing."[6] With a geocentric attitude, major issues and decisions are viewed globally by looking for the best approaches and people regardless of origin.

Later in this chapter and throughout the rest of the book, you will see how a geocentric attitude toward managing requires eliminating parochial attitudes and carefully developing an understanding of cultural differences between countries. It is important to realize that, while in some organizations all managers may express the same perspective toward the world (perhaps because the company has a strong culture), different views can also be held by individual managers; thus, the company does not necessarily present a unified front when dealing with people from another culture. However, the way that a company chooses to go global may indicate an overall perspective on the best way to do business in other countries.

Understanding the Global Environment

2. Describe the kinds of alliances that affect trade relations among countries in the world.

▶ ▶ ▶ After Menu Foods recalled its pet food, one legislator reminded Americans that it might not be safe to rely on foreign sources of food.[7] "We really don't know what else is out there and yet we've increased food imports and reduced inspections," said Bob Etheridge, a Democratic representative from North Carolina.

Some US legislators and farm groups called for fewer imports, a reconsideration of the free-trade agreement, fees from Canada and other countries so that the United States could conduct more inspections of food, and labels indicating country of origin on all food products. Should such legislation be passed, Menu Foods may find its dominant role in the pet food market shrinking.

The immediate impact of the pet food recall affected Menu Foods, but some were worried that the scandal would affect Canada's economy, which saw about $14 billion (US) in sales of food to the United States in 2006. "This is an ongoing issue that we have anxiety over," said David Emerson, the Canadian Minister of Trade at the time.

> **Think About It**
>
> Has the tainted pet food scandal affected the Canadian pet food industry's trade relations with the United States and Mexico?

As we discussed in Chapter 1, management is no longer constrained by national borders. Managers in all sizes and types of organizations are faced with the opportunities and challenges of managing in a global environment. For instance, managers at Menu Foods capitalized on the opportunity of the global environment by buying ingredients from companies around the world. This allowed them to make their company into a leading pet food manufacturer in North America. However, relying on ingredients that originated from China, which did not follow the same food product inspection standards as those in North American countries, has proven to be extremely costly to the company.

What is the global environment like? An important feature is global trade. Global trade is not new. Countries and organizations have been trading with each other for centuries. "Trade is central to human health, prosperity, and social welfare."[8] When trade is allowed to flow freely, countries benefit from economic growth and productivity gains because they specialize in producing the goods they are best at and importing goods that are more efficiently produced elsewhere. Global trade is being shaped by two forces: regional trading alliances and the agreements negotiated through the World Trade Organization.

Regional Trading Alliances

Just a few years ago, global competition was best described in terms of country against country—the United States vs. Japan, France vs. Germany, Mexico vs. Canada. Now, global competition has been reshaped by the creation of regional trading alliances, such as the European Union, the North American Free Trade Agreement, and the Association of Southeast Asian Nations.

The European Union

The signing of the Maastricht Treaty (named for the Dutch town where the treaty was signed) in February 1992 created the **European Union (EU)**, a unified economic and trade entity with 12 member countries—Belgium, Denmark, France, Greece, Ireland, Italy, Luxembourg, the Netherlands, Portugal, Spain, the United Kingdom, and Germany. By 2007, the EU comprised 27 countries. Four other countries (Croatia, Former Yugoslav Republic of Macedonia, Turkey, and Iceland) have submitted applications to join the EU.[9] The economic power represented by the EU is considerable. The original EU member countries cover a population base of 375 million people, and the current 27 member countries encompass a population of over 490 million.[10] (See Exhibit 3-2.)

Before the creation of the EU, each member country had border controls, taxes, and subsidies; nationalistic policies; and protected industries. Now, as a single market, the EU has no barriers to travel, employment, investment, and trade. The EU took an enormous step toward full unification in 1999 when 12 of its countries became part of the Economic and Monetary Union, the formal system responsible for the development of the **euro**, a single European currency. As of 2011, 17 EU countries had adopted the euro.[11] The primary reason these countries joined together was to assert their economic position against the strength of the United States and Japan. Working in separate countries with barriers

European Union (EU) A union of 27 European countries that forms an economic and political entity.

euro A single common European currency.

Exhibit 3-2

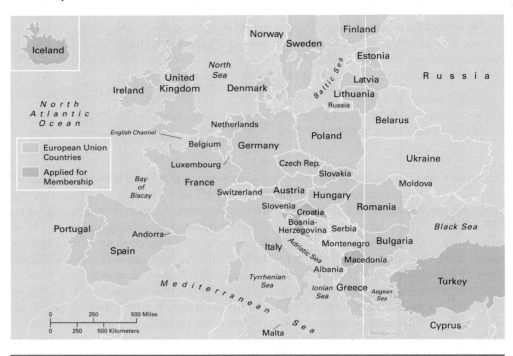

European Union Countries

against one another, European industries could not develop the efficiency of American and Japanese businesses.

On May 3, 2010, the **euro area** and the International Monetary Fund (IMF) agreed to a $146 billion bailout package for Greece in return for significant cuts in public spending. The immediate result was mass rioting in the streets of Athens.[12] When the bailout was announced, markets reacted to fears that the financial crisis would spread to countries like Portugal and Spain. On January 30, 2011, the Irish legislature passed a bill cutting $20.5 billion from its deficit spending over the next four years, marking an end to the economic boom dubbed the Celtic Tiger.[13] In spite of these challenges the EU has seen Unilever PLC of the United Kingdom emerge as a powerful force in consumer products, Daimler AG of Germany as a solid competitor in automobiles, and Nokia of Finland as a dominant player in cellphones.

North American Free Trade Agreement

When agreements in key issues covered by the **North American Free Trade Agreement (NAFTA)** were reached by the Canadian, US, and Mexican governments in August 1992, a vast economic bloc was created where barriers to free trade were reduced. Since NAFTA went into effect, Canada has become the United States' number one trading partner.[14] In 2009, Canadian exports to the United States were $271 billion, which accounted for almost 73 percent of our total exports.[15] Canada's exports to Mexico have quadrupled since the NAFTA agreement was signed, and its foreign investments in Mexico increased by a factor of five.[16] Westcoast Energy, Scotiabank, and BCE are just a few Canadian companies that have expanded their operations to Mexico. Many economists argue that reducing the barriers to trade (tariffs, import licensing requirements, customs user fees) has resulted in a strengthening of the economic power of all three countries. Free trade did not eliminate all trade problems between Canada and the United States, however, as shown by the softwood lumber dispute that ended in 2006.

Association of Southeast Asian Nations

The **Association of Southeast Asian Nations (ASEAN)** is a trading alliance of 10 Southeast Asian nations (see Exhibit 3-3). The ASEAN region has a population of about 590 million with a combined gross domestic product of $1499 billion (US).[17] This fast-growing region means ASEAN will be an increasingly important regional economic and political alliance whose impact eventually could rival that of both NAFTA and the EU.

Association of Southeast Asian Nations (ASEAN) A trading alliance of 10 Southeast Asian countries.

Other Trade Alliances

Other regions around the world continue to look at creating regional trading alliances. For instance, Latin American nations have moved to become part of free-trade blocs. Colombia, Mexico, and Venezuela led the way when all three signed an economic pact in 1994 eliminating import duties and tariffs (in 2006, Venezuela left the bloc and Panama asked to be included). Negotiators from 34 countries in the Caribbean region, South America, and Central America continue to work on a Free Trade Area of the Americas (FTAA) agreement, which was to have been operational no later than 2005.[18] However, at a November 2005 summit, the leaders of these 34 nations failed to reach any agreement, leaving the future of the FTAA up in the air.[19] The benefits to Canada of an FTAA are not clear. Most of these markets are quite small compared with Mexico and the United States. Already in existence is another free-trade bloc known as the Southern Cone Common Market, or Mercosur, which was formed in 1991 among Brazil, Argentina, Uruguay, and Paraguay. Ecuador and Peru are associate members, and Venezuela is in the process of gaining full membership.

The 53-nation African Union came into existence in July 2002.[20] Members of this alliance plan to create an economic development plan and work to achieve greater unity among Africa's nations. Like members of other trade alliances, these countries hope to gain economic, social, cultural, and trade benefits from their association.

Exhibit 3-3

ASEAN Members

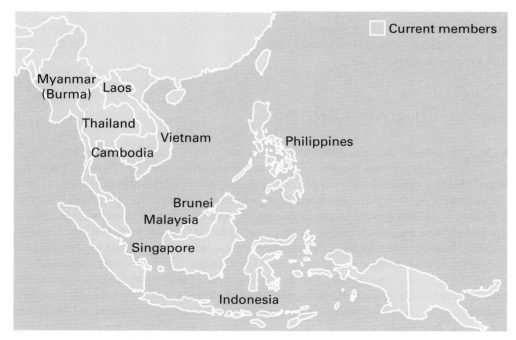

Source: Based on J. McClenahen and T. Clark, "ASEAN at Work," *IndustryWeek*, May 19, 1997, p. 42.

Also, the South Asian Association for Regional Cooperation (SAARC), composed of eight nations (India, Pakistan, Sri Lanka, Bangladesh, Bhutan, Nepal, Afghanistan, and the Maldives), started eliminating tariffs on January 1, 2006.[21] Its aim, like all the other regional trading alliances, is to allow for the free flow of goods and services.

BRICS

In 2001, global economist Jim O'Neill introduced the acronym BRIC when he argued that by 2050, Brazil, Russia, India, and China could be the world's dominant economies.[22] The acronym has since become a symbol of the shift in global economic power away from developed G7 nations toward countries with newly advanced economic development. Although no trade agreement yet exists among these countries, the BRIC group held its first summit in 2009 to discuss how they could work together to influence the global economy. South Africa became the fifth country to join in 2010, changing BRIC to **BRICS**, further demonstrating how quickly our global environment is changing.[23]

BRICS A grouping acronym that refers to the countries of Brazil, Russia, India, China, and South Africa, which are deemed to be at a similar stage of newly advanced economic development.

The World Trade Organization

Global growth and trade among nations does not just happen on its own. Systems and mechanisms are needed so that efficient and effective trading relationships can develop. Indeed, one of the realities of globalization is that countries are interdependent—that is, what happens in one can impact others, whether positively or negatively. For example, the severe Asian financial crisis in the late 1990s had the potential to totally disrupt economic growth around the globe and bring on a worldwide recession. But it did not. Why? Because there were mechanisms in place to prevent that from happening—mechanisms that encouraged global trade and averted the potential crisis. One of the most important of these mechanisms is the multilateral trading system called the **World Trade Organization (WTO)**.[24]

World Trade Organization (WTO) A global organization of 150 countries that deals with the rules of trade among nations.

The WTO was formed in 1995 and evolved from the General Agreement on Tariffs and Trade (GATT), an agreement in effect since the end of World War II. Today, the WTO is the only *global* organization dealing with the rules of trade among nations. Its membership consists of 153 member countries and 30 observer governments (which have a specific time frame within which they must apply to become members). At its core are the various trade agreements, negotiated and ratified by the vast majority of the world's trading nations. The goal of the WTO is to help businesses conduct trade between countries (importing and exporting) without undesired side effects. Although a number of vocal critics have staged visible protests and criticized the WTO, claiming that it destroys jobs and the natural environment, the WTO appears to play an important role in monitoring and promoting global trade.

Doing Business Globally

3. Describe how organizations do business globally.

▶ ▶ ▶ Menu Foods was founded in 1971 and bought its first US factory in New Jersey in 1977, hoping to use that factory to launch an expansion into the US market.[25] Today, the global company has three pet food processing plants, one in Streetsville, Ontario, and two in the United States (Emporia, Kansas, and Pennsauken, New Jersey). The company has processing plants in Canada and the United States so that it can process pet food products close to the areas it serves to reduce product costs, including freight costs. According to the company's website, "Menu's ability to serve [retailers] from three locations provides Menu with service and freight cost advantages compared to other single or two plant private-label competitors."

Menu Foods buys the ingredients for its pet food from a variety of companies, which in turn may buy ingredients for products from companies around the world. As the tainted pet food investigation found, an ingredient that originated from China was responsible for the deaths caused by Menu Foods' various pet foods. Because Menu Foods relies on suppliers for some of its ingredients, it may not always be aware of the original source of every ingredient it uses.

Think About It

How is Menu Foods structured to do business globally? Would it make sense for Menu Foods to form a strategic alliance or a joint venture, or to create a foreign subsidiary in countries that produce its ingredients? How might it choose partners to do so, if that strategy were chosen?

Organizations in different industries *and* from different countries are pursuing global opportunities. In this section, we look at different types of international organizations and how they do business in the global marketplace.

Different Types of International Organizations

Multinational Corporations

Organizations doing business globally are not anything new. DuPont started doing business in China in 1863. H.J. Heinz Company was manufacturing food products in the United Kingdom in 1905. Ford Motor Company set up its first overseas sales branch in France in 1908. By the 1920s, other companies, including Fiat, Unilever, and Royal Dutch Petroleum Company/Shell had gone international. But it was not until the mid-1960s that international companies became commonplace. Today, there are very few companies that do not have some type of international dealings. However, in spite of the fact that doing business internationally is so widespread, there is no one generally accepted approach to describing the different types of international companies—they are called different things by different authors. However, we are going to use the terms *multinational, multidomestic, global,* and *transnational* to describe the various types of international organizations.[26] A **multinational corporation (MNC)** is a broad term usually used to refer to any and all types of international companies that maintain operations in multiple countries.

> **multinational corporations (MNCs)** A broad term that refers to any and all types of international companies that maintain operations in multiple countries.

Multidomestic Corporations

A **multidomestic corporation** is an MNC that maintains significant operations in more than one country but decentralizes management to the local country. This type of organization does not attempt to manage foreign operations from its home country. Instead, local employees typically are hired to manage the business, and marketing strategies are tailored to that country's unique characteristics. This type of global organization reflects the polycentric attitude (see page 72). For example, Switzerland-based Nestlé can be described as a multidomestic corporation. With operations in almost every country on the globe, its managers match the company's products to its consumers. In parts of Europe, Nestlé sells products that are not available in North America or Latin America. Another example of a multidomestic corporation is Frito-Lay, a division of PepsiCo, which markets a Doritos chip in the British market that differs in both taste and texture from the Canadian and US versions. Many consumer companies manage their global businesses using this approach because they must adapt their products and services to meet the needs of the local markets.

> **multidomestic corporation** An international company that decentralizes management and other decisions to the local country.

Global Companies

A **global company** is an international company that centralizes its management and other decisions in the home country. These companies treat the world market as an integrated whole and focus on the need for global efficiency. Although these companies may have considerable global holdings, management decisions with company-wide implications are made from headquarters in the home country. This approach to globalization reflects the ethnocentric attitude (see page 72). Some examples of companies that can be considered global companies include Montreal-based transport manufacturer Bombardier, Montreal-based aluminum producer Rio Tinto Alcan, Tokyo-based consumer electronics firm Sony, Frankfurt-based Deutsche Bank AG, and New York City–based financial services provider Merrill Lynch.

> **global company** An international company that centralizes management and other decisions in the home country.

Transnational or Borderless Organizations

Many companies are going global by eliminating structural divisions that impose artificial geographical barriers. This type of global organization is called a **transnational**

> **transnational or borderless organization** A type of international company in which artificial geographical barriers are eliminated.

or borderless organization. The transnational or borderless organization approaches global business with a geocentric attitude. For example, IBM dropped its organizational structure based on country and reorganized into industry groups such as business solutions, software, IT services, and financing. Bristol-Myers Squibb changed its consumer business to become more aggressive in international sales and created a management position responsible for worldwide consumer medicines such as Bufferin and Excedrin. And Spain's Telefónica eliminated the geographic divisions between Madrid headquarters and its widespread phone companies. The company is organized, instead, along business lines such as Internet services, cellphones, and media operations. Borderless management is an attempt by organizations to increase efficiency and effectiveness in a competitive global marketplace.[27]

Born Globals

Our classification of different types of international organizations tends to describe large international businesses. However, there is an increasing number of businesses called **born globals** that choose to go global from inception.[28] These companies (also known as *international new ventures*, or *INVs*) commit resources (material, people, financing) upfront to doing business in more than one country and are likely to continue to play an increasingly important role in international business.

born global An international company that chooses to go global from inception.

How Organizations Go International

When organizations do go international, they often use different approaches depending on whether they are just starting or whether they have been doing business internationally for a while (see Exhibit 3-4). During the initial stages of going international, managers look at ways to get into a global market without having to invest a lot of capital. At this stage, companies may start with **global sourcing** (also called *global outsourcing*), which is purchasing materials or labour from around the world wherever it is cheapest. The goal: Take advantage of lower costs in order to be more competitive. For instance, in fall 2006, Montreal-based Bell Canada contracted with Sitel India and two other Indian companies to provide technical support and customer care to Canadian customers.[29] Although global sourcing is often the first step to going international, many organizations continue to use this approach even as they become more international because of the competitive advantages it offers. Beyond global sourcing, however, each successive stage of becoming more international requires more investment and thus entails more risk for the organization.

global sourcing Purchasing materials or labour from around the world wherever it is cheapest.

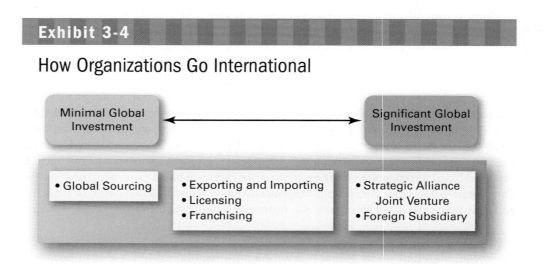

Exhibit 3-4

How Organizations Go International

Minimal Global Investment ⟷ Significant Global Investment

- Global Sourcing
- Exporting and Importing
- Licensing
- Franchising
- Strategic Alliance
- Joint Venture
- Foreign Subsidiary

Importing and Exporting

If a company wants to do business in other countries, what choices does it have?

An organization can go international by **exporting** its products to other countries—that is, by making products at home and selling them overseas. In addition, an organization can go international by **importing** products—that is, by selling products at home that are made abroad. Both exporting and importing are small steps toward being a global business and usually involve minimal investment and minimal risk. Many organizations start doing business globally this way. Many, especially small businesses, continue with exporting and importing as the way they do business globally. For instance, Haribhai's Spice Emporium, a small business in Durban, South Africa, exports spices and rice to customers all over Africa, Europe, and the United States. However, other organizations have built multimillion-dollar businesses by importing or exporting; that is what Montreal-based Mega Brands (formerly Mega Bloks) has done. Mega Brands is Canada's largest toy company, with sales in over 100 countries.[30] The company operates in 14 countries, with more than 1300 employees. Mega Brands is only one example of Canada's increasing reliance on export business. The value of merchandise exported from Canada totalled $369 billion in 2009, down from $490 billion in 2008.[31] Transportation equipment manufacturing, primary metal manufacturing, and paper manufacturing account for the largest volume of Canadian exports.

exporting An approach to going global that involves making products at home and selling them abroad.

importing An approach to going global that involves acquiring products made abroad and selling them at home.

Licensing and Franchising

Some managers use licensing or franchising in the early stages of doing business internationally. Licensing and franchising are similar in that they both involve one organization giving another the right to use its brand name, technology, or product specifications in return for a lump-sum payment or a fee usually based on sales. The only difference is that **licensing** is primarily used by manufacturing organizations that make or sell another company's products, and **franchising** is primarily used by service organizations that want to use another company's name and operating methods. For example, Russian consumers can enjoy McDonald's hamburgers because McDonald's Canada opened the first Russian franchise in Moscow. Franchises have also made it possible for Mexicans to dine on Richmond, BC-based Boston Pizza and Koreans to consume frozen yogourt from Markham, Ontario-based Coolbrands' Yogen Früz. Anheuser-Busch licenses the right to brew and market Budweiser beer to other brewers, such as Labatt in Canada, Modelo in Mexico, and Kirin in Japan. Licensing and franchising involve more investment and risk than exporting and importing because the company's brand is more at stake.

licensing An approach to going global in which a manufacturer gives another organization the right to use its brand name, technology, or product specifications.

franchising An approach to going global in which a service organization gives a person or group the right to sell a product, using specific business methods and practices that are standardized.

Strategic Alliances

Typically, once an organization has been doing business internationally for a while and has gained experience in international markets, managers may decide to make a more direct investment. One way they can do this is through **strategic alliances**, which are partnerships between a domestic and a foreign company in which both share resources and knowledge in developing new products or building production facilities. The partners also share the risks and rewards of this alliance. It is not always easy to find a partner, however. When Starbucks decided to open coffee shops in France, it was turned down by four major French food companies it approached as joint venture partners. Jean-Paul Brayer, former head of one of the food companies Starbucks approached, commented, "Their contract was way too expensive. It was a win–win situation—but only for Starbucks."[32] Starbucks ended up partnering with a Spanish firm, Grupo VIPS, and together they opened the first Parisian Starbucks in January 2004. By 2007, there were more than 50 Starbucks in Paris.[33]

A specific type of strategic alliance in which the partners agree to form a separate, independent organization for some business purpose is called a **joint venture**. For example, Hewlett-Packard has had numerous joint ventures with various suppliers around the globe to develop different components for its computer equipment, such as Tokyo-based Hitachi, which supplies hard drives for HP. These partnerships provide a faster and more inexpensive way for companies to compete globally than doing it on their own.

strategic alliances An approach to going global that involves a partnership between a domestic and a foreign company in which both share resources and knowledge in developing new products or building production facilities.

joint venture An approach to going global in which the partners agree to form a separate, independent organization for some business purpose; it is a type of strategic alliance.

Fast-food giant KFC, like many big franchise firms, is opening more new outlets overseas. Along the way, the company is making appropriate changes in its menu offerings, such as substituting juice and fruit for Coke and fries. This Shanghai promotion features new egg tarts.

Foreign Subsidiaries

foreign subsidiary An approach to going global that involves a direct investment in a foreign country by setting up a separate and independent production facility or office.

Managers can make a direct investment in a foreign country by setting up a **foreign subsidiary**, a separate and independent production facility or office. This subsidiary can be managed as a multidomestic corporation (foreign control), a global company (domestic control), or a transnational/borderless organization (global control). As you can probably guess, this arrangement involves the greatest commitment of resources and poses the greatest amount of risk. Many of the larger companies operating in Canada are actually subsidiaries of US corporations, including GM Canada, Procter & Gamble Canada, and McDonald's Canada. Canadian subsidiaries manage their operations and set their own targets and goals, but they also report to head office in the United States. Canada has been a good investment opportunity for American firms. The low Canadian dollar from the early 1990s until 2003 resulted in lower costs and higher productivity. However, the rise in the Canadian dollar may change the number of US companies doing business in Canada. Employers in Canada have long paid far less for health premiums for their employees than they would in the United States because of Canada's health care system. Prior to the collapse of the automobile industry in late 2008 and the subsequent bankruptcy of General Motors, the company agreed to a settlement with the United Auto Workers (UAW) in 2007 that brought into question whether Canada's health care advantage would continue. The American car manufacturer and the UAW agreed that the union would be responsible for paying its retired workers' health care costs going forward. This is expected to lower GM's labour and benefits costs to $55 an hour (from $75 an hour). This lower cost of benefits puts GM's costs close to Japan's $48-an-hour costs, and much lower than Canada's $70-an-hour costs for autoworkers.[34]

Managing in a Global Environment

4. Describe the challenges of doing business globally.

▶ ▶ ▶ Menu Foods was forced to remove 60 million packages of its wet pet foods off grocery and pet food store shelves in March 2007.[35] The pet food had been contaminated with melamine, a non-food product. Investigators found that the melamine had been mixed with wheat gluten (an ingredient in pet food) at XuZhou Anying factory in China. Employees apparently deliberately mixed the melamine into the wheat gluten because melamine mimics protein when mixed with gluten. The resulting product would then appear to have a higher nutrient value than it actually did.

China's animal feed producer had been supplementing the feed with melamine for a number of years. "Many companies buy melamine scrap to make animal feed, such as fish feed," says Ji Denghui, general manager of the Fujian Sanming Dinghui Chemical Company, which sells melamine. The additive is inexpensive, thus it reduces product costs. Ji also explains, "I don't know if there's a regulation on it. Probably not. No law or regulation says 'don't do it,' so everyone's doing it. The laws in China are like that, aren't they? If there's no accident, there won't be any regulation."

Think About It

How have the global legal–political and economic environments affected Menu Foods' ability to produce its pet food? What could Menu Foods do to protect itself from importing tainted ingredients from countries that have fewer regulations about food processing than Canada or the United States?

Assume for a moment that you are a manager going to work for a branch of a global organization in a foreign country. You know that your environment will differ from the one at home, but how? What should you be looking for?

As discussed in Chapter 2, managers must consider all areas of the general environment—the broad economic, legal–political, socio-cultural, demographic, and technological conditions—that may affect the organization. Any manager who finds himself or herself in a foreign country faces new challenges in the general environment that will impact their organizational decision making. In this section, we look at some of those challenges and offer guidelines for responding. Although our discussion is presented through the eyes of a Canadian manager, our analytical framework could be used by any manager who has to manage in a foreign environment, regardless of national origin.

MyManagementLab
Q&A 3.3

The Legal–Political Environment

Canadian managers are accustomed to stable legal and political systems. Changes are slow, and legal and political procedures are well established. The stability of laws governing the actions of individuals and institutions allows for accurate predictions. The same cannot be said for all countries. Managers in a global organization must stay informed of the specific laws in countries where they do business.

Also, some countries have a history of unstable governments. Managers of businesses in these countries face dramatically greater uncertainty as a result of political instability. For instance, political interference is a fact of life in some Asian countries. Many large businesses have postponed doing business in China because the government controls what organizations do and how they do it. As Chinese consumers gain more power, however, that attitude is likely to change.

The legal–political environment does not have to be unstable or revolutionary to be a concern to managers. Just the fact that a country's laws and political system differ from those of Canada is important. Managers must recognize these differences to understand the constraints under which they operate and the opportunities that exist.

The Economic Environment

The global manager must be aware of economic issues when doing business in other countries. First, it's important to have an understanding of the type of economic system under which the country operates. The two major types are a market economy and a command economy. A **market economy** is one in which resources are primarily owned and controlled by the private sector. A **command economy** is one in which all economic decisions are planned by a central government. In actuality, no economy is purely market or command. For instance, Canada and the United States are two countries at the market end of the spectrum, but their governments do have some control over economic activities. The economies of Vietnam and North Korea, however, would be more command-based. Then there is China, a country that is more command-based, but is moving to be more market-based. Why would managers need to know about a country's economic system? Because it has the potential to constrain decisions and actions. Other economic issues a manager might need to understand include currency exchange rates, inflation rates, and diverse tax policies.

market economy An economic system in which resources are primarily owned and controlled by the private sector.

command economy An economic system in which all economic decisions are planned by a central government.

The Cultural Environment

In what ways do you think culture affects doing business in other countries?

A large global oil company found that employee productivity in one of its Mexican plants was off 20 percent and sent a US manager to find out why. After talking to several employees, the manager discovered that the company used to have a monthly fiesta in the parking lot for all the employees and their families. Another US manager had cancelled the fiestas, saying they were a waste of time and money. The message employees were getting was that the company did not care about their families anymore. When the fiestas were reinstated, productivity and employee morale soared.

At Hewlett-Packard, a cross-global team of American and French engineers were assigned to work together on a software project. The American engineers sent long, detailed emails to their counterparts in France. The French engineers viewed the lengthy emails as patronizing and replied with quick, concise emails. This made the American engineers think that their French colleagues were hiding something from them. The situation spiralled out of control and negatively affected output until team members went through cultural training.[36]

national culture The values and attitudes shared by individuals from a specific country that shape their behaviour and beliefs about what is important.

Organizations have different cultures. Countries have cultures too. **National culture** is the values and attitudes shared by individuals from a specific country that shape their behaviour and beliefs about what is important.[37]

Which is more important to a manager—national culture or organizational culture? For example, is an IBM facility in Germany more likely to reflect German culture or IBM's corporate culture? Research indicates that national culture has a greater effect on employees than does their organization's culture.[38] German employees at an IBM facility in Munich will be influenced more by German culture than by IBM's culture. This means that as influential as organizational culture may be on managerial practice, national culture is even more influential.

MyManagementLab
Q&A 3.4

Legal, political, and economic differences among countries are fairly obvious. The Japanese manager who works in Canada or his or her Canadian counterpart in Japan can get information about a country's laws or tax policies without too much difficulty. Getting information about a country's cultural differences isn't quite that easy! The primary reason is that it's hard for natives to explain their country's unique cultural characteristics to someone else. For instance, if you are a Canadian raised in Canada, how would you characterize Canadian culture? In other words, what are Canadians like? When Wal-Mart moved to Japan, it had to rethink some of its approach to customer service, as the following *Management Reflection* shows.

National culture influences many aspects of competing abroad. India now has about 350 000 engineering graduates each year; the United States has 70 000. Organizations that need employees with engineering skills in order to be competitive are going to have to understand national cultures, such as that of India.

The Big Box Goes to Japan

What does Wal-Mart need to do to be successful in Japan? When Wal-Mart bought 38 percent of Seiyu, Japan's fourth-largest retailer, in 2003 to get a foothold in Japan, it tried to maintain the classic Wal-Mart culture, while attempting to meet the needs of Japanese customers.[39] Rather than loudly announcing its presence, Wal-Mart operated behind the Seiyu name. Employees at Seiyu had to adopt the Wal-Mart culture, however, starting the day much like their North American Wal-Mart counterparts, chanting "Give me an S" and eventually spelling out S-E-I-Y-U. The Japanese manager follows the chant by asking, "Who's number 1?" Employees respond with "Customers!" and punch their fists in the air.

The chant might have translated easily, but big-box stores in Japan are not an easy sell. Customers do not necessarily understand the concept of "everyday low prices." When Wal-Mart first came to town, Seiyu mailed circulars advertising low prices to local neighbourhoods, but Wal-Mart tried to stop the practice, as the company did not see the point of constantly advertising their everyday low prices. Unfortunately, Japanese customers are used to circulars announcing sales, and Seiyu had to continue the practice.

Wal-Mart faces several challenges in meeting customer needs in Japan. Homes are smaller, so bulk buying is less common, and many people rely on public transportation, making it difficult to bring big items home. Japanese customers demand high quality in clothing and have high standards for freshness in food. Richard Galanti, chief financial officer of Costco, which has also opened stores in Japan, notes that "the definition of fresh seafood in Japan is different than that in [North America]. Fresh means live in some cases."

By 2007, Wal-Mart had not successfully penetrated the Japanese market and had posted five years of losses. Wal-Mart then chose to grow their business in Japan through acquisitions. By 2010, Wal-Mart had purchased the 370-store Seiyu supermarket chain and was looking for additional acquisitions.[40] At Wal-Mart headquarters, executives remain hopeful that the company will fare better in Japan than it did in Germany and South Korea, two countries Wal-Mart exited in 2006 after it did not achieve expected sales. ■

Hofstede's Framework for Assessing Cultures

One of the most widely referenced approaches to helping managers better understand differences between national cultures was developed by Geert Hofstede. His research found that managers and employees vary on five dimensions of national culture, which are as follows:

- *Individualism vs. collectivism.* Individualism is the degree to which people in a country prefer to act as individuals rather than as members of groups. In an individualistic society, people are supposed to look after their own interests and those of their immediate family and do so because of the large amount of freedom that an individualistic society allows its citizens. The opposite is collectivism, which is characterized by a social framework in which people prefer to act as members of groups and expect others in groups of which they are a part (such as a family or an organization) to look after them and to protect them.

- *Power distance.* Hofstede used the term *power distance* as a measure of the extent to which a society accepts the fact that power in institutions and organizations is distributed unequally. A high power distance society accepts wide differences in power in organizations. Employees show a great deal of respect for those in authority. Titles, rank, and status carry a lot of weight. In contrast, a low power distance society plays down inequalities as much as possible. Superiors still have authority, but employees are not afraid of or in awe of the boss.

- *Uncertainty avoidance.* Uncertainty avoidance describes the degree to which people tolerate risk and prefer structured over unstructured situations. People in low uncertainty avoidance societies are relatively comfortable with risks. They are also relatively tolerant of behaviour and opinions that differ from their own because they don't feel threatened by them. On the other hand, people in a society that is high in uncertainty avoidance feel threatened by uncertainty and ambiguity and experience high levels of anxiety in such situations, which manifests itself in nervousness, high stress, and aggressiveness.

- *Achievement vs. nurturing.* The fourth cultural dimension, like individualism/collectivism, is a dichotomy. Achievement reflects the degree to which values such as assertiveness, the acquisition of money and material goods, and competition prevail. Nurturing is a national cultural attribute that emphasizes relationships and concern for others.[41]

- *Long-term and short-term orientation.* This cultural attribute looks at a country's orientation toward life and work. People in cultures with long-term orientation look to the future and value thrift and persistence. Also, in these cultures, leisure time is not so important, and it is believed that the most important events in life will occur in the future. A short-term orientation values the past and present and emphasizes respect for tradition and fulfilling social obligations. Leisure time is important, and it is believed that the most important events in life happen in the past and in the present.

Although we don't have the space to review Hofstede's entire results for all the countries he studied, we provide 12 examples of the first four variables in Exhibit 3-5. The long-term orientation variable isn't included in this table because scores for some of the countries were not reported. However, the top five countries with higher long-term orientation (LTO) scores are China, Hong Kong, Taiwan, Japan, and South Korea. Countries such as Sweden, Germany, Australia, United States, United Kingdom, and Canada had lower LTO scores, which reflect a more short-term orientation.[42] *Developing Your Interpersonal Skills—Becoming More Culturally Aware* on page 93 encourages you to think about how to become more comfortable when interacting with people from different cultures.

Exhibit 3-5

Examples of Hofstede's Cultural Dimensions

Country	Individualism/ Collectivism	Power Distance	Uncertainty Avoidance	Achievement/ Nurturing[a]
Australia	Individual	Small	Moderate	Strong
Canada	Individual	Moderate	Low	Moderate
England	Individual	Small	Moderate	Strong
France	Individual	Large	High	Weak
Greece	Collective	Large	High	Moderate
Italy	Individual	Moderate	High	Strong
Japan	Collective	Moderate	High	Strong
Mexico	Collective	Large	High	Strong
Singapore	Collective	Large	Low	Moderate
Sweden	Individual	Small	Low	Weak
United States	Individual	Small	Low	Strong
Venezuela	Collective	Large	High	Strong

[a]A weak achievement score is equivalent to high nurturing.

Source: Based on G. Hofstede, "Motivation, Leadership, and Organization: Do American Theories Apply Abroad?" *Organizational Dynamics,* Summer 1980, pp. 42–63.

The GLOBE Framework for Assessing Cultures

Although Hofstede's cultural dimensions have been the main framework for differentiating among national cultures, much of the data on which they are based are somewhat outdated. Since the time of Hofstede's original studies, there have been a number of changes in the global environment, suggesting the need for an updated assessment of cultural dimensions, which the GLOBE project provides.[43] The GLOBE (Global Leadership and Organizational Behavior Effectiveness) research program, which began in 1993, continues to investigate cross-cultural leadership behaviours. Using data from over 18 000 middle managers in 62 countries, the GLOBE research team identified nine dimensions on which national cultures differ:

- *Assertiveness.* The degree to which a society encourages people to be tough, confrontational, assertive, and competitive vs. modest and tender.

- *Future orientation.* The degree to which a society encourages and rewards future-oriented behaviours such as planning, investing in the future, and delaying gratification.

- *Gender differentiation.* The degree to which a society maximizes gender-role differences as measured by how much status and decision-making responsibilities women have.

- *Uncertainty avoidance.* The degree to which a society relies on social norms and procedures to alleviate the unpredictability of future events.

- *Power distance.* The degree to which members of a society expect power to be unequally shared.

- *In-group collectivism.* The degree to which members of a society take pride in membership in small groups, such as their family and circle of close friends, and the organizations in which they are employed, in contrast to focusing on societal institutions.

- *Performance orientation.* The degree to which a society encourages and rewards group members for performance improvement and excellence.

- *Humane orientation.* The degree to which a society encourages and rewards individuals for being fair, altruistic, generous, caring, and kind to others.

- *Individualism/collectivism.* The degree to which individuals are encouraged by societal institutions to be integrated into groups within organizations and society.

How do different countries rank on these nine dimensions? Exhibit 3-6 provides examples.

The Pros and Cons of Globalization

What is your attitude toward globalization? Is your attitude favourable or unfavourable?

Doing business globally today isn't easy! Advocates praise the economic and social benefits that come from globalization, yet that very globalization has created challenges and controversy because of the impact it can have on the world's poor (for instance, child labour has been used to produce North American goods). However, if one country's economy falters, it potentially could have a domino effect on other countries with which it does business.

Some have said that globalization is dead, including Canadian philosopher John Ralston Saul. However, Joel Bakan, a University of British Columbia law professor who wrote *The Corporation* and co-produced the documentary of the same name, claims, "It's overly optimistic to say globalization is dead."[44]

Although supporters of globalization praise it for its economic benefits, there are those who think that it is simply a euphemism for "Americanization"—that is, the way US cultural values and US business philosophy are said to be slowly taking over the world.[45]

Exhibit 3-6

GLOBE Rankings

Dimension	Low	Countries Rating Medium	High
Assertiveness	Sweden New Zealand Switzerland	Egypt Ireland Philippines	Spain United States Greece
Future orientation	Russia Argentina Poland	Slovenia Egypt Ireland	Denmark Canada Netherlands
Gender differentiation	Sweden Denmark Slovenia	Italy Brazil Argentina	South Korea Egypt Morocco
Uncertainty avoidance	Russia Hungary Bolivia	Israel United States Mexico	Austria Denmark Germany
Power distance	Denmark Netherlands South Africa	England France Brazil	Russia Spain Thailand
Individualism/collectivism (with the first column indicating the most collectivist and the last column indicating the most individualistic)	Denmark Singapore Japan	Hong Kong United States Egypt	Greece Hungary Germany
In-group collectivism	Denmark Sweden New Zealand	Japan Israel Qatar	Egypt China Morocco
Performance orientation	Russia Argentina Greece	Sweden Israel Spain	United States Taiwan New Zealand
Humane orientation	Germany Spain France	Hong Kong Sweden Taiwan	Indonesia Egypt Malaysia

Source: M. Javidan and R. J. House, "Cultural Acumen for the Global Manager: Lessons from Project GLOBE," *Organizational Dynamics*, Spring 2001, pp. 289–305. Copyright © 2001. Reprinted with permission from Elsevier.

Critics claim that this attitude of the "almighty American dollar wanting to spread the American way to every single country" has created many problems.[46] Exhibit 3-7 outlines the major pro- and anti-globalization arguments. Some of the dominant opponents of globalization include the International Institute for Sustainable Development; the International Forum on Globalization; Greenpeace; the Canadian-based Centre for Research on Globalization; and Canadian author, journalist, and activist Naomi Klein, who is well known for her book *No Logo: Taking Aim at the Brand Bullies*. Some of the main supporters of globalization include the London-based International Policy Network, the Washington-based Competitive Enterprise Institute, and the Cato Institute.

Because Canada is not seen as a country that wants to spread Canadian values and culture, Canadian managers may have some advantages over their American counterparts in doing business internationally. Managers will need to be aware of how their decisions and actions will be viewed, not only by those who may agree, but, more importantly, by

Exhibit 3-7

Woodward's Findings on Technology

Anti-Globalization Positions	**Pro-Globalization Positions**
• Globalization is a synonym for Western imperialism. • Trade liberalization may hinder economic development for poorer countries. • There are environmental, social, and economic costs to globalization. • Globalization erodes the power of local organizations and local decision-making methods. • Globalization can lead to the exploitation of workers' rights and human rights. • Globalization usually benefits wealthy countries at the expense of poor countries. • Lessening or removing trade regulations hurts the poor by pushing up the price of necessities, such as seeds for planting crops and medicine.	• Globalization promotes economic prosperity; it offers access to foreign capital, export markets, and advanced technology. • Globalization encourages the efficient use of natural resources and raises environmental awareness and, thus, helps protect the environment. • Globalization minimizes government intervention, which can hinder development, in business and in people's lives. • Globalization is a positive force that has encouraged the development of markets, which can bring about prosperity.

Source: Based on "Who Are the Players?" *Globalisation Guide*, http://www.globalisationguide.org/02.html (accessed July 6, 2007).

those who may disagree. They will need to adjust their leadership styles and management approaches to accommodate these diverse views. Yet, as always, they will need to do this while still being as efficient and effective as possible in reaching the organization's goals.

SUMMARY AND IMPLICATIONS

1. Compare and contrast the different views of global differences. We can view global differences from ethnocentric, polycentric, and geocentric perspectives. An ethnocentric attitude is the belief that the best work approaches and practices are those of the *home* country (the country in which the company's headquarters are located). The polycentric attitude is the view that the managers in the *host* country (the foreign country in which the organization is doing business) know the best work approaches and practices for running their businesses. The geocentric attitude, which is a *world-oriented* view, focuses on using the best approaches and people from around the globe.

▶ ▶ ▶ Menu Foods likely understood the best practices for doing business in Canada and the United States, but may not have taken enough precautions to understand that food regulations in China were almost nonexistent.

2. Describe the kinds of alliances that affect trade relations among countries in the world. Global trade is affected by two forces: regional trading alliances and the agreements negotiated through the World Trade Organization (WTO). Regional trading alliances include the European Union (EU), the North American Free Trade Agreement (NAFTA), the Association of Southeast Asian Nations (ASEAN), and others. These regional alliances specify how trade is conducted among countries. The goal of the WTO, which consists of 153 member countries and 30 observer governments, is to help businesses (importers and exporters) conduct their business through the various trade agreements, negotiated and ratified by the vast majority of the world's trading nations.

▶ ▶ ▶ Menu Foods used a variety of suppliers to get the ingredients to make its pet food, and some of these ingredients came from foreign countries with different quality standards. When things like this happen, there are often calls for more restrictive trade arrangements for countries with lower standards than North America.

3. Describe how organizations do business globally. Organizations can take on a variety of structures when they go global, including multinational corporations, multidomestic corporations, global companies, and transnational or borderless organizations. An organization can take lower-risk and lower-investment strategies for going global through importing or exporting, hiring foreign representation, or contracting with foreign manufacturers. It can also increase its presence in another country by joining with another business to form a strategic alliance or joint venture. Or it can set up a foreign subsidiary in order to have a full presence in the foreign country.

▶ ▶ ▶ Menu Foods is a global company that produces private-label and brand-name pet foods for retailers in Canada, the United States, and Mexico. Its headquarters are in Canada, and it has three manufacturing facilities in Canada and the United States. It processes pet food products close to the areas it serves to reduce product costs, including freight costs, so that it can remain competitive.

4. Describe the challenges of doing business globally. When managers do business in other countries, they will be affected by the global legal–political and economic environments of those countries. Differing laws and political systems can create constraints as well as opportunities for managers. The type of economic system in some countries can place restrictions on how foreign companies are able to conduct business. In addition, managers must be aware of the culture of the countries in which they do business to understand *how* business is done and what customers expect.

▶ ▶ ▶ Menu Foods learned the challenge of relying on pet food ingredients that originate from countries with different food safety standards and regulations. Though Menu Foods' ingredient supplier was American, that company was merely a distributor for Chinese-produced goods. As Menu Foods discovered, in a very unfortunate way, the wheat gluten its company had used in numerous brands was not produced according to the same food safety standards and regulations that exist in Canada and the United States.

Management @ Work

READING FOR COMPREHENSION

1. Contrast ethnocentric, polycentric, and geocentric attitudes toward global business.

2. What is the Association of Southeast Asian Nations?

3. What is the role of the World Trade Organization?

4. Contrast multinational corporations, multidomestic corporations, global companies, and transnational or borderless organizations.

5. Define importing, exporting, licensing, and franchising.

6. Define strategic alliances, joint ventures, and foreign subsidiaries.

7. What are the nine GLOBE dimensions for assessing cultures?

8. What are some of the pros and cons of globalization?

LINKING CONCEPTS TO PRACTICE

1. What are the managerial implications of a transnational or borderless organization?

2. Compare the advantages and drawbacks of the various approaches to going global.

3. What challenges might confront a Mexican manager transferred to Canada to manage a manufacturing plant in Winnipeg? Will these be the same for a Canadian manager transferred to Guadalajara, Mexico? Explain.

4. Can the GLOBE framework presented in this chapter be used to guide managers in a Thai hospital or a government agency in Venezuela? Explain.

5. In what ways do you think global companies select and train managers differently than domestic companies do? What impact might the Internet have on this? Explain.

SELF-ASSESSMENT

Am I Well-Suited for a Career as a Global Manager?

For each of the following statements, circle your level of agreement or disagreement:

1 = Very Strongly Disagree 2 = Strongly Disagree 3 = Disagree 4 = Neither Agree nor Disagree 5 = Agree
6 = Strongly Agree 7 = Very Strongly Agree

1. When working with people from other cultures, I work hard to understand their perspectives.	1 2 3 4 5 6 7
2. I have a solid understanding of my organization's products and services.	1 2 3 4 5 6 7
3. I am willing to take a stand on issues.	1 2 3 4 5 6 7
4. I have a special talent for dealing with people.	1 2 3 4 5 6 7
5. I can be depended on to tell the truth regardless of circumstances.	1 2 3 4 5 6 7
6. I am good at identifying the most important part of a complex problem or issue.	1 2 3 4 5 6 7
7. I clearly demonstrate commitment to seeing the organization succeed.	1 2 3 4 5 6 7
8. I take personal as well as business risks.	1 2 3 4 5 6 7
9. I have changed as a result of feedback from others.	1 2 3 4 5 6 7
10. I enjoy the challenge of working in countries other than my own.	1 2 3 4 5 6 7
11. I take advantage of opportunities to do new things.	1 2 3 4 5 6 7
12. I find criticism hard to take.	1 2 3 4 5 6 7
13. I seek feedback even when others are reluctant to give it.	1 2 3 4 5 6 7
14. I don't get so invested in things that I cannot change when something does not work.	1 2 3 4 5 6 7

Scoring Key

Reverse your scoring for item 12 (that is, 1 = 7, 2 = 6, 3 = 5, etc.), and then add up your total score. Your total score will range from 14 to 98. The higher your score, the greater your potential for success as an international manager.

Analysis and Interpretation

In today's global economy, being a manager often means being a global manager. But unfortunately, not all managers are able to transfer their skills smoothly from domestic environments to global ones. Your results here can help you assess whether your skills align with those needed to succeed as an international manager.

MANAGEMENT FOR YOU TODAY

Dilemma

You are part of a multicultural team of eight students, two from each of Canada, China, South Africa, and Germany. You are trying to put together a business plan for a small business that could be operated in your community. This is a course assignment, but winning proposals have the opportunity to be funded, up to $10 000. Your team is struggling to come up with a workable idea, and cannot even agree on a potential course of action to get the project completed. What might be some of the multicultural differences that could be getting in your way? What could you do to smooth over some of these differences? How might each student's global perspective be affecting team performance?

Becoming a Manager

- Learn as much as you can about other countries.
- Familiarize yourself with current global political, economic, and cultural issues.
- If given the opportunity, try to have your class projects or reports (in this class and other classes) cover global issues or global companies.
- Talk to instructors or students who may be from other countries and ask them what the business world is like in their countries.
- If you have the opportunity, travel to other countries.
- Go see a foreign film.

WORKING TOGETHER: TEAM-BASED EXERCISE

Assessing People's Global Aptitudes

Moving to a foreign country isn't easy, no matter how many times you have done it or how receptive you are to new experiences. Successful global organizations are able to identify the best candidates for global assignments, and one of the ways they do this is through individual assessments prior to assigning people to global facilities. Form groups of three to five individuals. Your newly formed team, the Global Assignment Task Force, has been given the responsibility for developing a global aptitude assessment form for Zara, the successful European clothing retailer.[48] The company is starting to become well known in North America, and Zara's managers have positioned the company for continued global success. That success is based on a simple principle—in fashion, nothing is as important as time to market.

Zara's store managers (more than 600 worldwide) offer suggestions every day on cuts, fabrics, and even new lines. After reviewing the ideas, a team at headquarters in A Coruña, Spain, decides what to make. Designers draw up the ideas and send them over the company's intranet to nearby factories. Within days, the cutting, dyeing, sewing, and assembling starts. In three weeks, the clothes will be in stores from Barcelona to Berlin to Bangkok. That is 12 times faster than its rivals. Zara has a twice-a-week delivery schedule that restocks old styles and brings in new designs. Rivals tend to get new designs once or twice a season.

Because Zara is expanding its global operations significantly, it wants to make sure that it's sending the best possible people to the various global locations. Your team's assignment is to come up with a rough draft of a form to assess people's global aptitudes. Think about the characteristics, skills, attitudes, and so on that you think a successful global employee would need. Your team's draft should be at least half a page but no longer than one page. Be prepared to present your ideas to your classmates and instructor.

ETHICS IN ACTION

Ethical Dilemma Exercise: What Should a Company Do When It Faces Opposition to Expansion in Another Country?

Montreal-based Rio Tinto Alcan is the world's largest primary aluminum producer.[49] The company has some 68 000 employees and 430 facilities in 61 countries; it posted a profit of $129 million in 2005. The company plans to develop a $1.8 billion strip mine and refinery in Orissa state, 1200 kilometres southeast of New Delhi, India.

The company has only recently been given permission to begin developing the mine. For a number of years, local people have expressed concern that the mining activities will uproot the Adivasis, some of India's indigenous people. Several years ago, the protests against developing the mine grew violent when state police fired guns at the Adivasis, killing three protesters. Rio Tinto Alcan's plans were put on hold while government officials conducted an inquiry into the deaths. The government concluded that tribal areas "cannot afford to remain backward for the sake of so-called environmental protection."

Bhagawan Majhi serves as sarpanch (chief) of Kucheipadar village, where the violence took place. He has led the opposition to the mines since he was a teen and says, "Our fight will continue until the government revokes its agreement with the company."

Rio Tinto Alcan insists on carrying through with the mine, even though one of its partners in the project, Norway-based

Hydro (formerly Norsk Hydro), decided to quit the project after three of its employees were kidnapped by tribal members.

Rio Tinto Alcan spokespeople claim that the mine can actually improve the life of the Adivasis. The company promises to create more than 1000 jobs, and each tribal family will be given at least one. Employees will get a health clinic that others in the area can use. Majhi does not believe that the Adivasis will be better off with the mine. For one thing, the Baphlimali Hill, which is sacred to them, will be ruined. He also says that land is more important than jobs. "What will we do with the money? We don't know how to do business," he notes. He also talks about how the lives of villagers who accepted money from Rio Tinto Alcan in exchange for drilling rights have been ruined: "They spent it on alcohol, they married two or three women, they bought wristwatches and motorcycles," Majhi says.

Rio Tinto Alcan's CEO, Travis Engen, was given notice two weeks before the annual general meeting that several shareholders would protest the company's plans to develop the mine on Adivasis lands. He knows that he must respond to their complaints at the meeting. Does it make sense to simply abandon the mining plans in the face of protests? What should he tell shareholders at the meeting about Alcan's future plans for the region?

Thinking Critically About Ethics

Foreign countries often have lax product-labelling laws. As the international product manager for a Canadian pharmaceutical company, you are responsible for the profitability of a new drug to be sold outside Canada. The drug's side effects can be serious, although not fatal. Adding this information

to the label or even putting an informational insert into the package will add to the product's cost, threatening profitability margins. What will you do? Why? What factors will influence your decision?

CASE APPLICATION

National Basketball Association

Using an exceptionally well-executed game plan, the National Basketball Association (NBA) is trying to emerge as the first truly global sports league.[50] The game was invented in 1891 by James Naismith, from Almonte, Ontario, and the Toronto Raptors and Vancouver Grizzlies were the first non-US cities in the modern era to join the league, during the 1995–1996 season.

The desire to transform the once-faltering domestic sport into a global commercial success reflects a keen understanding of managing in a global environment. And much of the credit should go to NBA commissioner David

Stern, who has been consciously building the NBA into a global brand.

Professional basketball sparked the interest of fans and players around the globe in the mid-1990s, and the NBA cashed in on the game's universal appeal. At one time, if you had asked someone in China what the most popular basketball team was, the answer would have been the "Red Oxen" from Chicago (the Bulls). Today, the NBA's centre of attention comes from China. Yao Ming, the 2.2-metre-tall centrepiece of the Houston Rockets, has a personality that appeals to fans around the world. But he is not the only global player in the league. Others include the Dallas Mavericks' Dirk Nowitzki from Germany; Pau Gasol of the Memphis Grizzlies, a native of Spain; San Antonio Spurs' guard Tony Parker from France; Denver Nuggets' forward Nenê Hilario from Brazil; and Utah Jazz guard Gordan Giricek from Croatia. The Raptors' first-round draft pick in 2004, Rafael Araujo, is from Brazil. What started as a trickle in the 1980s with occasional non-US stars like Hakeem Olajuwon (Nigeria) and the late Dražen Petrovic (Croatia), has turned into a flood. A total of 60 players from 28 countries and

territories outside the United States were playing in the NBA as of July 2007. These included Canadian players Jamaal Magloire of the Portland Trail Blazers and Steve Nash of the Phoenix Suns. Nineteen Canadian basketball players have played in the NBA over the years. The NBA wants to prove that the game can be played globally also.

What strategies can Stern take to increase consumer familiarity with basketball both domestically and globally? How can he develop a greater basketball presence in Canada?

DEVELOPING YOUR DIAGNOSTIC AND ANALYTICAL SKILLS

When Yes Does Not Always Mean Yes, and No Does Not Always Mean No

When a major chip-manufacturing project ran more than a month late, David Sommers, vice-president for engineering at Adaptec, felt that perhaps the company's Indian engineers "didn't understand the sense of urgency" in getting the project completed.[51] In the Scottish highlands, Bill Matthews, the general manager of McTavish's Kitchens, is quite satisfied with his non-Scottish employees—cooks who are German, Swedish, or Slovak and waitresses who are mostly Polish. Other highland hotels and restaurants also have a large number of Eastern European staff. Despite the obvious language barriers, these Scottish employers are finding ways to help their foreign employees adapt and be successful. When Lee Epting of Forum Nokia gave a presentation to a Finnish audience and asked for feedback, he was told, "That was good." Based on his interpretation of that phrase, he assumed that it must have been just an okay presentation . . . nothing spectacular. However, because Finns tend to be generally much quieter and more reserved than North Americans, that response actually meant, "That was great, off the scale."

It's not easy being a successful global manager, especially when it comes to dealing with cultural differences. Research by Wilson Learning Worldwide says there is an "iceberg of culture, of which we can only see the top 15 percent—food, appearance, and language." Although these elements themselves can be complicated, it's the other 85 percent of the "iceberg" that is not apparent initially that managers need to be especially concerned about. What does that include? Workplace issues such as communication styles, priorities, role expectations, work tempo, negotiation styles, nonverbal communication, attitudes toward planning, and so forth. Understanding these issues requires developing a global mindset and skill set. Many organizations are relying on cultural awareness training to help them do just that.

Having outsourced some engineering jobs to India, Axcelis Technologies had its North American–based employees go through a training program where they role-played scenarios with one person pretending to be Indian and the other his North American co-worker. One of the company's human resource directors said, "At first I was skeptical and wondered what I'd get out of the class, but it was enlightening for me. Not everyone operates like we do in North America." In our global world, successful managers must learn to recognize and appreciate cultural differences and to understand how to work effectively and efficiently with employees, no matter their nationality.

Questions

1. What global attitude do you think would most support, promote, and encourage cultural awareness? Explain.

2. Would legal–political and economic differences play a role as companies design appropriate cultural awareness training for employees? Explain.

3. Pick one of the countries mentioned in the case and do some cultural research on it. What did you find out about the culture of that country? How might this information affect the way a manager in that country plans, organizes, leads, and controls?

4. UK-based company Kwintessential has several cultural awareness "quizzes" on its website (**www.kwintessential. co.uk/resources/culture-tests.html**). Go to the company's website and try two or three of these. Were you surprised at your score? What does your score tell you about your cultural awareness?

5. What advice might you give to a manager who has little experience working with people in other countries?

DEVELOPING YOUR INTERPERSONAL SKILLS

Becoming More Culturally Aware

About the Skill

Understanding and managing people who are similar to us are challenges—but understanding and managing those who are *dissimilar from us and from each other* can be even tougher. Workplaces around the world are becoming increasingly diverse. Thus, managers need to recognize that not all employees want the same thing, act in the same manner, and can be managed in the same way. What is a diverse workforce? It's one that is heterogeneous in terms of gender, race, ethnicity, age, and other characteristics that reflect differences. Valuing diversity and helping a diverse workforce achieve its maximum potential are becoming indispensable skills for more and more managers.

Steps in Developing the Skill

The diversity issues an individual manager might face are many. They might include communicating with employees whose familiarity with the language might be limited; creating career development programs that fit the skills, needs, and values of a variety of employees; helping a diverse team cope with a conflict over goals or work assignments; or learning which rewards are valued by different groups of employees. You can improve your handling of diversity issues if you use the following eight suggestions:[52]

1. **Fully accept diversity.** Successfully valuing diversity starts with each individual accepting the principle of multiculturalism. Accept the value of diversity for its own sake—not simply because you have to. Accepting and valuing diversity is important because it's the right thing to do. And it's important that you reflect your acceptance in all you say and do.

2. **Recruit broadly.** When you have job openings, work to get a diverse applicant pool. Although referrals from current employees can be a good source of applicants, they tend to produce candidates similar to the current workforce.

3. **Select fairly.** Make sure that the selection process does not discriminate. One suggestion is to use job-specific tests rather than general aptitude or knowledge tests. Such tests measure specific skills, not subjective characteristics.

4. **Provide orientation and training for minorities.** Making the transition from outsider to insider can be particularly difficult for an employee who belongs to a minority group. Provide support either through a group or through a mentoring arrangement.

5. **Sensitize nonminorities.** Not only do you personally need to accept and value diversity, but as a manager you need to encourage all your employees to do so. Many organizations do this through diversity training programs, where employees examine the cultural norms of different groups. The most important thing a manager can do is show by his or her actions that diversity is valued.

6. **Strive to be flexible.** Part of valuing diversity is recognizing that different groups have different needs and values. Be flexible in accommodating employees' requests.

7. **Seek to motivate individually.** Motivating employees is an important skill for any manager; motivating a diverse workforce has its own special challenges. Managers must be more in tune with the background, cultures, and values of employees. What motivates a single mother of two young children who is working full time to support her family is likely to be different from the needs of a young, single, part-time employee or an older employee who is working to supplement his or her retirement income.

8. **Reinforce employee differences.** Encourage individuals to embrace and value diverse views. Create traditions and ceremonies that promote diversity. Celebrate diversity by accentuating its positive aspects. However, also be prepared to deal with the challenges of diversity, such as mistrust, miscommunication, lack of cohesiveness, attitudinal differences, and stress.

Practising the Skill

Read the descriptions of the following employees who work for the same organization. After reading each description, write a short paragraph describing what you think the goals and priorities of each employee might be. With what types of employee issues might the manager of each employee have to deal? How could these managers exhibit the value of diversity?

Lester is 57 years old, a college graduate, and a vice-president of the firm. His two children are married, and he is a grandparent of three beautiful grandchildren. He lives in a condo with his wife, who does volunteer work and is active in their church. Lester is healthy and likes to stay active, both physically and mentally.

Sanjyot is a 30-year-old clerical worker who came to Canada from Indonesia 10 years ago. She completed high school after moving to Canada and has begun to attend evening classes at a local college. Sanjyot is a single parent with two children under the age of eight. Although her health is excellent, one of her children suffers from a severe learning disability.

Yuri is a recent immigrant from one of the former Soviet republics. He is 42 years old, and his English communication skills are quite limited. He has an engineering degree from his country, but since he is not licensed to practise in Canada, he works as a parts clerk. He is unmarried and has no children but feels an obligation to his relatives back in his home country. He sends much of his paycheque to them.

Reinforcing the Skill

The following activities will help you practise and reinforce the skills associated with becoming more culturally aware:

1. Indicate which employees (age, gender, ethnicity, family status, and so forth) you think might be motivated by the following additional employee benefits: on-site daycare, fitness centre, tuition reimbursement, job sharing, English classes, having a mentor, being a mentor, performance bonus plan, more time off, flextime, enhanced retirement benefits, supervisory training, subsidized dependant care, discounts on company products, religious holidays, free candy and snacks in the employee break room, on-site physician, country club membership, and on-site dry cleaning services. Looking at your responses, what are the implications for a manager?

2. Ask friends from other cultures what kinds of biases they encounter in school or at work. Think about how you, as a manager, might deal with instances of these types of biases.

3. Come up with a list of suggestions that you personally can use to improve your sensitivity to diversity issues.

MyManagementLab

For more resources, please visit www.pearsoned.ca/mymanagementlab

SCAN THIS

Managing Entrepreneurially

In this chapter, we're going to look at the activities of entrepreneurs. We'll start by looking at how the opportunity focus of entrepreneurs enables organizations to build cultures that are flexible, nimble, and innovative. We will then examine entrepreneurship from the perspective of the four managerial functions: planning, organizing, leading, and controlling. After reading and studying this chapter, you will achieve the following learning outcomes.

Learning Outcomes

1. Describe entrepreneurship and why it's important.

2. Understand how to identify opportunities and build the business case for launching an entrepreneurial venture.

3. Understand the choices to be made in organizing an entrepreneurial venture.

4. Appreciate what is involved in leading an entrepreneurial venture.

5. Understand the unique challenges that need to be controlled if the entrepreneurial venture is to survive and prosper.

▶ ▶ ▶ At Research In Motion, it is claimed that "innovation knows no boundaries or borders."[1] RIM is the designer and manufacturer of the award-winning BlackBerry smartphone, used by millions of people around the world. RIM has also created applications to provide mobile access to email, applications, media, and the Internet through the BlackBerry.

The company was founded in 1984 in Waterloo, Ontario, by 23-year-old Michael Lazaridis and two friends, backed by funds from friends and family. Lazaridis had recently dropped out of the University of Waterloo, where he had been studying electrical engineering. The company's first contract came from General Motors. Moving from contract to contract, the company reached annual sales of $1 million and 12 employees by 1990. Contracts from Ericsson and GE Mobile followed. By 1992 Lazaridis realized that he was better at engineering than running the company, and he hired Jim Balsillie, a chartered accountant and Harvard graduate with an MBA, as co-

CEO. RIM's sales soared to $21 million by 1998, with profits of $400 000. In February 1999, the company launched the BlackBerry, marking the beginning of RIM's huge growth in the information and communication technologies market. In subsequent years the company has thrived under the combined leadership of Michael Lazaridis and Jim Balsillie and has become the world's biggest supplier of mobile devices.

SCAN THIS

Think About It

Why do you think Mike Lazaridis started his own business? Is it possible for an entrepreneur to be good at all the core skills needed for the business to succeed? What stresses might RIM's rapid growth have placed on the company? What role has innovation played in its success? What exit strategy would you suggest for the two CEOs?

The Context of Entrepreneurship

1. Describe entrepreneurship and why it's important.

It may seem odd that we have included a chapter on managing entrepreneurially in a section called *Defining the Manager's Terrain*. But, when you think about it, all organizations had a starting point, and if they were successful, they grew and had to go through the process of passing from the hands of the founders to the next generation of family or professional management. As we examine the natural cycle of organizational formation, we will learn some general lessons that can provide context for the discussion in later chapters on planning, organizing, leading, and controlling. In looking at the behaviour of entrepreneurs, we can build a stronger understanding of the role that managers play in building an innovative culture, such as the one at Cirque du Soleil (discussed in Chapter 1) and at 3M (discussed in Chapter 2). More importantly, the management lens of an entrepreneur, with its focus on opportunity, has a particularly valuable contribution to make to our understanding of what it takes to build an adaptive organization, as defined in Chapter 1.[2]

What Is Entrepreneurship?

Entrepreneurship is the process of starting new organizations, generally in response to opportunities. These new organizations may be for traditional for-profit purposes, but more and more often they are being started in response to needs within the community and are known as **social enterprises/ventures**. Entrepreneurs pursue opportunities by changing, revolutionizing, transforming, or introducing new products or services. For example, when RIM launched the BlackBerry smartphone, the world of communication changed forever, much to the chagrin of some family members, who took to referring to the addictive device as the "CrackBerry."

entrepreneurship The process of starting new organizations, generally in response to opportunities.

social enterprises/ventures Organizations that are started in response to needs within the community.

How Entrepreneurial Ventures Add Value to the Economy

There are two common and yet differing explanations of how entrepreneurs add value to an economy. One view, based on the work of Austrian economist Joseph Schumpeter, proposed that the entrepreneur creates an opportunity through innovation and then takes advantage of it. In the process of transformation that accompanies a radical innovation, the way things were done before is "destroyed." This process became known as **creative destruction**.[3] On the other hand, Israel Kirzner, another leading economist, suggested that entrepreneurs are able to perceive the opportunities for entrepreneurial profits by being sensitive to signals in the marketplace—they are **entrepreneurially alert.** The entrepreneur's role is to constantly look for imbalances in what people need and what is available (opportunities) and then take advantage of them.[4]

creative destruction The process of transformation that accompanies radical innovation, where the way things were done before is "destroyed."

entrepreneurially alert The ability to perceive opportunities for entrepreneurial profits by being sensitive to signals in the marketplace.

When Jim Balsillie and Mike Lazaridis introduced the BlackBerry, they created a disruptive technology that changed the rules of the game for everybody, under Schumpeter's theory. The person who buys goods from yard sales on the weekend and then posts them on eBay for sale at a higher price fits Kirzner's entrepreneurially alert model, which states that successful entrepreneurs have an uncanny ability to spot opportunities. Which of these two explanations is the best one? The answer is that they both explain how entrepreneurs create value.

The Nature of Opportunities and the Role of Entrepreneurial Managers

Because pursuing opportunity lies at the heart of our definition of entrepreneurship, it is important to better understand the nature of opportunity and strategies for identifying and commercializing it. How you best find an opportunity depends on the type of opportunity. Opportunities can be recognized, discovered, or enacted. A recognition strategy works best when both supply and demand are known. Using Kirzner's concept of entrepreneurial alertness, entrepreneurs *recognize* opportunities when they are alert to information in the environment. But if only supply or only demand is known, simply being alert will not help in finding opportunities. In this case, the entrepreneur relies on his or her experience and actively employs sophisticated search techniques to *discover* the opportunity. The assumption is that the opportunity exists—we just have to find it![5] An example is a mining company that employs geologists and seismic data to discover new deposits. The third type of opportunity occurs when neither supply nor demand is known and the entrepreneur creates something new, or *enacts* an opportunity. As the entrepreneur takes the idea to market, it may change as more information is gained. The entrepreneur begins to imagine (rather than recognize or actively search for) future opportunities. Why predict the future when you can create it![6]

Many people think that entrepreneurial ventures and small businesses are one and the same, but they're not. There are some key differences between the two. Entrepreneurs create **entrepreneurial ventures**—organizations that pursue opportunities, which are characterized by innovative practices, and have growth and profitability as their main goals. Entrepreneurs also pursue opportunities and create social ventures where the objective is to maximize social return on investment (SROI) rather than traditional return on investment (ROI). It should be noted that radical innovation of and by itself does not create the most value for an entrepreneur. Innovations in an existing marketplace well populated by competitors are often higher-value and lower-risk opportunities.

entrepreneurial ventures Organizations that are pursuing opportunities, are characterized by innovative practices, and have growth and financial viability as their main goals.

small business An organization that is independently owned, operated, and financed; has fewer than 100 employees; doesn't necessarily engage in any new or innovative practices; and has relatively little impact on its industry.

If you were starting a venture, would you look for gaps in the marketplace or would you improve on an existing idea?

On the other hand, a **small business** is a business that is independently owned, operated, and financed; has fewer than 100 employees; doesn't necessarily engage in any new or innovative practices; and has relatively little impact on its industry.[7] A small business isn't necessarily entrepreneurial just because it's small. The entrepreneurial business must be innovative and constantly seek out new opportunities. Even though entrepreneurial ventures may start small, they pursue growth. Some new small firms may grow, but many remain small businesses, by choice or by default.

Why Is Entrepreneurship Important?

Entrepreneurship and innovation are seen to be the cornerstones of a competitive national economy by governments. Because both are associated with "doing something new," in most countries entrepreneurship policies are closely tied to innovation policies. The entrepreneurial process introduces innovative products, processes, and organizational structures across an economy.[8] Its importance in Canada can be shown in three areas: innovation, number of new start-ups, and job creation.

Innovation

Innovation is a process of changing, experimenting, transforming, and revolutionizing, and it's a key aspect of entrepreneurial activity. The "creative destruction" process that characterizes innovation leads to technological changes and employment growth. Entrepreneurial firms act as "agents of change" by providing an essential source of new and unique ideas that may otherwise go untapped.[9] Statistics back this up. New small organizations generate 24 times more innovations per research and development dollar spent than do *Fortune* 500 organizations, and they account for more than 95 percent of new and "radical" product developments.[10] In the United States, small entrepreneurial firms produce 13 to 14 times more patents per employee than large patenting firms.[11]

Job Creation

Businesses with fewer than 50 employees represent 97.8 percent of the total business establishments in Canada. Forty-one percent of the Canadian workforce works in firms with fewer than 20 employees. In Canada, 2.7 million people, or 16 percent of the workforce, are self-employed.[12] Job creation is important to the overall long-term economic health of communities, regions, and nations. The latest figures show that small businesses accounted for most of the net new jobs.[13] Small organizations have been creating jobs at a fast pace, even as many of the world's largest and well-known global corporations have continued to downsize. These facts reflect the importance of entrepreneurial firms as job creators.

Global Entrepreneurship

What about entrepreneurial activity outside Canada and the United States? What kind of impact has it had? An annual assessment of global entrepreneurship called the Global Entrepreneurship Monitor (GEM) studies the impact of entrepreneurial activity on economic growth in various countries. The 2007 GEM report covered 42 countries that were divided into two clusters: high-income countries and middle- and low-income countries. Researchers found that in the high-income group, the highest levels of early-stage entrepreneurial activity were found in Iceland, Hong Kong, and the United States. In the middle- and low-income group, the highest levels of entrepreneurial activity were found in Thailand, Peru, and Colombia. The GEM report concluded that "the importance of entrepreneurship for economic development is widely acknowledged."[14]

What Do Entrepreneurs Do?

Describing what entrepreneurs do isn't an easy or simple task. No two entrepreneurs' work activities are exactly alike. In a general sense, entrepreneurs create something new, something different. They search for change, respond to it, and exploit it.[15]

Initially, an entrepreneur is engaged in assessing the potential for the entrepreneurial venture and then dealing with start-up issues. In exploring the entrepreneurial context, an entrepreneur gathers information, identifies potential opportunities, and pinpoints possible competitive advantage(s). Then, armed with that information, the entrepreneur researches the venture's feasibility—uncovering business ideas, looking at competitors, and exploring financing options.

After looking at the potential of a proposed venture and assessing the likelihood of pursuing it successfully, an entrepreneur proceeds to plan the venture. This includes such activities as developing a viable organizational mission, exploring organizational culture issues, and creating a well-thought-out business plan. When these planning issues have been resolved, the entrepreneur must look at organizing the venture, which involves choosing a legal form of business organization, addressing other legal issues such as patent or copyright searches, and coming up with an appropriate organizational design for structuring how work is going to be done.

Only after these start-up activities have been completed is the entrepreneur ready to actually launch the venture. This involves setting goals and strategies, as well as establishing the technology operations methods, marketing plans, information systems, financial accounting systems, and cash flow management systems.

When the entrepreneurial venture is up and running, the entrepreneur's attention switches to managing it. An important activity of managing the entrepreneurial venture is managing the various processes that are part of every business: making decisions, establishing action plans, analyzing external and internal environments, measuring and evaluating performance, and making needed changes. Also, the entrepreneur must perform activities associated with managing people, including selecting and hiring, appraising and training, motivating, managing conflict, delegating tasks, and being an effective leader. Finally, the entrepreneur must manage the venture's growth, including such activities as developing and designing growth strategies, dealing with crises, exploring various avenues for financing growth, placing a value on the venture, and perhaps even eventually exiting the venture.

Jeffrey Timmons, a professor at Babson College in Wellesley, Massachusetts, developed a model to explain the elements needed for entrepreneurial success (see Exhibit 4-1). The Timmons model of entrepreneurship considers opportunities, teams, and resources as the three critical factors available to an entrepreneur and holds that success depends on the ability of the entrepreneur to balance these critical factors.

Social Responsibility and Ethics Issues Facing Entrepreneurs

As they launch and manage their ventures, entrepreneurs are faced with the often-difficult issues of social responsibility and ethics. Just how important are these issues to entrepreneurs? The International Standards Organization has developed standards for sustainability and for social responsibility.[16] There are some entrepreneurs who take their social responsibilities seriously. For example, Jeff Skoll is a Canadian-born engineer who was the first employee and first president of eBay and owner of Participant Media, a producer of socially conscious movies such as *An Inconvenient Truth* and *Syriana*. Skoll donated over $1 billion of his eBay stock to found the Skoll Foundation in 1999. The foundation's mission is to drive large-scale change by investing in, connecting, and celebrating social entrepreneurs and other innovators dedicated to solving the world's most pressing problems. He defines social entrepreneurs as "society's change agents; creators of innovations that disrupt the status quo and transform our world for the better."[17]

Other entrepreneurs have pursued opportunities with products and services that protect the global environment. For example, Corporate Knights is an independent Canadian-based media company that works to prompt and reinforce sustainable development in Canada. Included in its "Cleantech 10" list are Westport Innovations of Vancouver, a leading developer of environmental technologies that enable vehicles to operate on

MyManagementLab
Q&A 4.1

Exhibit 4-1

The Timmons Model of the Entrepreneurial Process

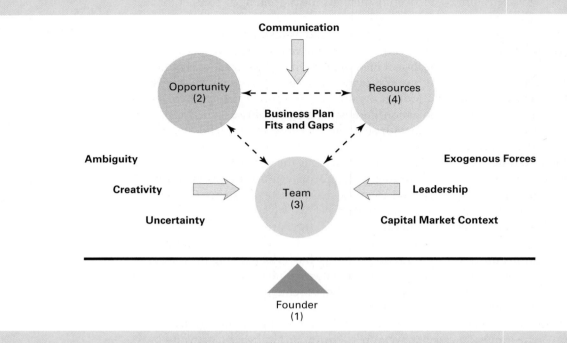

1. The Timmons Model bases itself on the founder (entrepreneur). Success of the venture depends on the ability of the founder to balance the critical factors of opportunity, team, and resources. The founder also has a commitment to sustainability for the environment, community, and society.

2. Unlike conventional entrepreneurship models that start with a business plan, the Timmons Model starts with a market opportunity and with the capacity of the founder to distinguish the difference between an idea and an opportunity.

3. Once the founder identifies an opportunity, he or she works to start a business by putting together the team. The founder's ability to build an effective team is a major factor in the success of the founder's vision in spite of the challenges to be faced.

4. The Timmons Model discounts the popular notion that extensive resources reduce the risk of starting a venture and encourages *bootstrapping* or starting with the bare minimal requirements as a way to attain competitive advantages. The founder works to "minimize and control" rather than "maximize and own."

Source: Based on the work of Jeffery Timmons in J. Timmons, S. Spinelli, and P. Ensign, *New Venture Creation*, 1st Canadian ed. (Toronto: McGraw-Hill Ryerson, 2009).

clean-burning alternative fuels, as well as Carmanah Technologies Corp. of Victoria, a solar LED lighting company.[18]

Ethical considerations also play a role in decisions and actions of entrepreneurs. Entrepreneurs need to be aware of the ethical consequences of what they do. The example they set—particularly for other employees—can be profoundly significant in influencing behaviour.

If ethics are important, how do entrepreneurs stack up? Unfortunately, not too well! In a survey of employees from different sizes of businesses who were asked whether they thought their organization was highly ethical, 20 percent of employees at companies with 99 or fewer employees disagreed.[19]

The Giving Pledge project, launched by Warren Buffett and Bill and Melinda Gates, invites the wealthiest individuals to give at least 50 percent of their money to charitable projects of their choosing. As part of his public pledge, Jeff Skoll stated, "The world is a vast and complicated place and it needs each of us doing all we can to ensure a brighter tomorrow for future generations. Conrad Hilton said it is the duty of successful people to give back to the society from which their success was derived. I feel privileged to have grown up in Canada and to now live in the US, two countries that value and reward education, hard work and good choices. I feel lucky to have been able to pursue my dreams and I hope that my contributions will in some small way lead to a sustainable world of peace and prosperity."

Start-Up and Planning Issues for an Entrepreneurial Venture

▶ ▶ ▶ Think back to 1984 when 23-year-old Michael Lazaridis and two friends launched RIM, primarily with money from friends and family. In the start-up stage, it is very common for the initial money to come from "friends, fools, and family."[20] As you read through this section, keep in mind the steps that Lazaridis went through as RIM procured its first contract with General Motors and grew into a million-dollar company, leading Lazaridis to hire Jim Balsillie in 1992 when he realized that he was better at engineering than running the business.

2. Understand how to identify opportunities and build the business case for launching an entrepreneurial venture.

Think About It

Why do you think Mike Lazaridis went to his friends and family for initial capital? Why wouldn't he just go the bank? As RIM grew, why would the company need to bring in leadership (Jim Balsillie) with a different skill set?

The first thing that entrepreneurs such as Michael Lazaridis must do is identify opportunities and possible competitive advantages. After they've done this, they're ready to start the venture by researching its feasibility and planning for its launch. In this section, we'll look at these start-up and planning issues.

Identifying Environmental Opportunities and Competitive Advantage

How important is the ability to identify environmental opportunities? Consider the fact that the life expectancy of Canadians is projected to grow from the 58 years in 1926 to 87.5 years in 2076. The combination of increased life expectancy and declining fertility rates makes it inevitable that the share of population 65 years and older will rise significantly in coming years. It is forecast that the ratio of prime-working-age Canadians (whose taxes will support health care and social benefits for those over 65) will fall from 5:1 in 2008 to 2:1 by 2070.[21] Sounds pretty ominous! Our definition of entrepreneurship focuses on opportunity, and in the midst of

TIPS FOR MANAGERS

Seven Questions to Ask When Identifying a New Opportunity (5Ws & 2Hs)

✔ **What** is your idea?

✔ **Who** will it matter to?

✔ **Why** will it matter to the people identified in the "Who"?

✔ **Where** will you do it?

✔ **When** will this happen?

✔ **How** will you pull off your "What"?

✔ **How much** will the people identified in the "Who" pay?

the looming crisis in health care there are significant opportunities in home care, health care delivery systems, and technology-enabled health care, particularly through electronic health records.[22]

MyManagementLab
Q&A 4.2

In 1994, when Jeff Bezos first saw that Internet usage was increasing by 2300 percent per month, he knew that something dramatic was happening. "I hadn't seen growth that fast outside of a Petri dish," he said. Bezos was determined to be a part of it. He quit his successful career as a stock market researcher and hedge fund manager on Wall Street and pursued his vision for online retailing, now Amazon.com.[23]

What would you have done had you seen that type of number somewhere? Ignored it? Written it off as a fluke? The skyrocketing Internet usage that Bezos observed and the recognition of the Baby Boomer demographic are prime examples of identifying environmental opportunities. In Chapter 8, which deals with strategy, we will point out that opportunities may arise from positive trends in external environmental factors. These trends provide unique and distinct possibilities for innovating and creating value. Entrepreneurs need to be able to pinpoint the pockets of opportunities that a changing context provides. After all, "organizations do not see opportunities, individuals do."[24] And they need to do so quickly, especially in dynamic environments, before those opportunities disappear or are exploited by others.[25] *Tips for Managers—Seven Questions to Ask When Identifying a New Opportunity* on page 101 provides some suggestions for considering opportunities.

The late Peter Drucker, a well-known management author, identified seven potential sources of opportunity that entrepreneurs might look for in the external context:[26]

Pam Cooley is president of CarShareHFX, Atlantic Canada's first multi-vehicle car-sharing service. Car sharing is a smart and practical alternative to car ownership. It provides the benefits of mobility with none of the hassles and commitments of owning a car, while reducing traffic congestion and emissions. Members access cars with an electronic key at any time via a state-of-the-art reservation system. CarShareHFX vehicles are located throughout downtown Halifax, typically no more than a 5- or 10-minute walk away.

1. *The unexpected*—When situations and events are unanticipated, opportunities can be found. An event may be an unexpected success (positive news) or an unexpected failure (bad news). Either way, there can be opportunities for entrepreneurs to pursue. For instance, the dramatic increase in greenhouse gases and the resulting emphasis on sustainable alternatives led Pam Cooley to found CarShareHFX so that clients could "have a smart and practical alternative to car ownership."[27]

2. *The incongruous*—When something is incongruous, there are inconsistencies and incompatibilities in the way it appears. Things "ought to be" a certain way but aren't. When conventional wisdom about the way things should be no longer holds true, for whatever reason, there are opportunities to capture. Entrepreneurs who are willing to "think outside the box"—that is, to think beyond the traditional and conventional approaches—may find pockets of potential profitability. Fred Smith, founder of FedEx, recognized in the early 1970s the inefficiencies in the delivery of packages and documents. His approach was: Why not? Who says that overnight delivery isn't possible? Smith's recognition of the incongruous led to the creation of FedEx, now a multibillion-dollar corporation.

3. *The process need*—What happens when technology doesn't immediately come up with the "big discovery" that's going to fundamentally change the very nature of some product or service? What happens is that there can be pockets of entrepreneurial opportunity in the various stages of the process as researchers and technicians continue to work for the monumental breakthrough. Because the full leap hasn't been possible, opportunities abound in the tiny steps. An example is the introduction of 3D television where, unlike digital television which required new hardware at both the home and the broadcast end, the technology is in the glasses used to view the program.

4. *Industry and market structures*—When changes in technology change the structure of an industry and market, existing firms can become obsolete if they're not attuned to the changes or are unwilling to change. Even changes in social values and consumer

tastes can shift the structures of industries and markets. The Internet arena provides several good examples of existing industries and markets being challenged by upstart entrepreneurial ventures. Pierre Omidyar and Jeff Skoll built eBay, which has prospered as an online go-between for buyers and sellers. As eBay's current CEO says, "The company's job is connecting people, not selling them things." And connect them, it does! The online auction firm has more than 90 million active registered users globally.[28]

5. *Demographics*—As we noted above in our discussion of identifying environmental opportunities, the characteristics of the world population are changing. There can be significant entrepreneurial opportunities in anticipating and meeting the changing needs of the population. For example, Thay Thida was one of three partners in Khmer Internet Development Services (KIDS) in Phnom Penh, Cambodia. She and her co-founders saw the opportunities in bringing Internet service to Cambodians and profited from their entrepreneurial venture.[29]

6. *Changes in perception*—Perception is one's view of reality. When changes in perception take place, the facts do not vary, but their meanings do. Changes in perception get at the heart of people's psychographic profiles—what they value, what they believe in, and what they care about. Changes in these attitudes and values create potential market opportunities for alert entrepreneurs. For example, think about your perception of healthy foods. As our perception of whether certain food groups are good for us has changed, there have been product and service opportunities for entrepreneurs to recognize and capture. John Mackey started Whole Foods Market in Austin, Texas, at the age of 25, as a place for customers to purchase food and other items free of pesticides, preservatives, sweeteners, and cruelty. Now, as the world's number one natural foods chain, Mackey's entrepreneurial venture consists of about 270 stores in the United States, Canada, and the United Kingdom.[30]

7. *New knowledge*—New knowledge is a significant source of entrepreneurial opportunity. Although not all knowledge-based innovations are significant, new knowledge ranks pretty high on the list of sources of entrepreneurial opportunity. It takes more than just having new knowledge, though. Entrepreneurs must be able to do something with that knowledge and need to protect important proprietary information from competitors. Tim Burke, founder of Halifax-based Tether, created an application that allowed cellphone users to connect their laptop or desktop to the Internet anywhere by accessing the data plan provided by their cellphone company.[31]

Being alert to entrepreneurial opportunities is only part of an entrepreneur's initial efforts. He or she must also understand competitive advantage. When an organization has a competitive advantage, it has something that other competitors don't, does something better than other organizations, or does something that others can't. Competitive advantage is a necessary ingredient for an entrepreneurial venture's long-term success and survival. Getting and keeping a competitive advantage is tough. However, it is something that entrepreneurs must consider as they begin researching a venture's feasibility.

Researching a Venture's Feasibility: Generating and Evaluating Ideas

It's important for entrepreneurs to research a venture's feasibility by generating and evaluating business ideas. Entrepreneurial ventures thrive on ideas. Generating ideas is an innovative, creative process. It's also one that takes time, not only in the beginning stages of the entrepreneurial venture but throughout the life of the business. Where do ideas come from?

Generating Ideas

Studies of entrepreneurs have shown that the sources of their ideas are unique and varied. One survey found that "working in the same industry" was the major source of ideas for an entrepreneurial venture (60 percent of respondents).[32] Other sources included personal interests or hobbies, familiar and unfamiliar products and services, and opportunities in external environmental sectors (technological, socio-cultural, demographics, economic, or legal–political).

What should entrepreneurs look for as they explore the sources of ideas? They should look for limitations of what is currently available, new and different approaches, advances and breakthroughs, unfilled niches, or trends and changes.

Evaluating Ideas

Evaluating entrepreneurial ideas involves personal and marketplace considerations. Each of these assessments will provide an entrepreneur with key information about the idea's potential. Exhibit 4-2 describes some questions that entrepreneurs might ask as they evaluate potential ideas.

A more structured evaluation approach that an entrepreneur might want to use is a **feasibility study**—an analysis of the various aspects of a proposed entrepreneurial venture, designed to determine its feasibility. Not only is a well-prepared feasibility study an effective evaluation tool to determine whether an entrepreneurial idea is a potentially successful one, but it can also serve as a basis for the all-important business plan.

A feasibility study should give descriptions of the most important elements of the entrepreneurial venture and the entrepreneur's analysis of the viability of these elements.

feasibility study An analysis of the various aspects of a proposed entrepreneurial venture that is designed to determine the feasibility of the venture.

Exhibit 4-2

Evaluating Potential Ideas

Personal Consideration:	Marketplace Consideration:
Do you have the capabilities to do what you've selected?	Have you educated yourself about financing issues?
Are you ready to be an entrepreneur?	Are you willing and prepared to do continual financial and other types of analyses?
Are you prepared emotionally to deal with the stresses and challenges of being an entrepreneur?	Who are the potential customers for your idea: who, where, how many?
Are you prepared to deal with rejection and failure?	What similar or unique product features does your proposed idea have compared to what's currently on the market?
Are you ready to work hard?	How and where will potential customers purchase your product?
Do you have a realistic picture of the venture's potential?	Have you considered pricing issues and whether the price you'll be able to charge will allow your venture to survive and prosper?
	Have you considered how you will need to promote and advertise your proposed entrepreneurial venture?

Researching a Venture's Feasibility: Researching Competitors

Part of researching a venture's feasibility is looking at the competitors. What would entrepreneurs like to know about their potential competitors? Exhibit 4-3 lists some possible questions to ask when evaluating potential competitors.

When an entrepreneur has information on competitors, he or she should assess how the proposed entrepreneurial venture is going to fit into its competitive arena. Will the entrepreneurial venture be able to compete successfully? In doing the analysis, remember that often the biggest competitors are the status quo (customers have no need to make a change) and substitutes (customers can use something else to satisfy their need). At the heart of every successful venture is the articulation of a compelling **value proposition**—an

value proposition An analysis of the benefits, costs, and value that an organization can deliver to customers and other groups within and outside of the organization.

Exhibit 4-3
Evaluating Potential Competitors

What types of products or services are competitors offering?

What are the major characteristics of these products or services?

What are the strengths and weaknesses of competitors' products?

How do competitors handle marketing, pricing, and distributing?

What do competitors attempt to do differently from other companies?

Do they appear to be successful at it? Why or why not?

What are they good at?

What competitive advantage(s) do they appear to have?

What are they not so good at?

What competitive disadvantage(s) do they appear to have?

How large and profitable are these competitors?

analysis of the benefits, costs, and value to the target customer and other groups within and outside of the organization.[33] This type of competitor analysis becomes an important part of the feasibility study and the business plan. If, after all this analysis, the situation looks promising, the final part of researching the venture's feasibility is to look at the various financing options. This isn't the final determination of how much funding the venture will need or where this funding will come from, but is simply the gathering of information about various financing alternatives.

Researching a Venture's Feasibility: Researching Financing

Getting financing isn't always easy. For instance, when William Carey first proposed building a liquor distributor business in Poland, more than 20 investment banking houses in New York passed on funding his idea. Carey recalls, "They didn't know Poland, and the business was small. We were ready to give up." Then, a New York investment banking boutique agreed to fund the venture. Today, Carey's company, CEDC (Central European Distribution), has more than 3000 employees and sales revenues of more than $1.1 billion (US).[34]

Planning a Venture: Developing a Business Plan

Planning is important to entrepreneurial ventures. Once a venture's feasibility has been thoroughly researched, the entrepreneur must look at planning the venture. The most important thing that an entrepreneur does in planning a venture is develop a **business plan**—a written document that summarizes a business opportunity and defines and articulates how the identified opportunity is to be seized and exploited.

For many would-be entrepreneurs, developing and writing a business plan seems like a daunting task. However, a good business plan is valuable. It pulls together all the elements of the entrepreneur's vision into a single coherent document. The business plan requires careful planning and creative thinking. If done well, it can be a convincing document that serves many functions. It serves as a blueprint and road map for operating the business. And the business plan is a "living" document that guides organizational decisions and actions throughout the life of the business, not just in the start-up stage.

business plan A written document that summarizes a business opportunity and defines and articulates how the identified opportunity is to be seized and exploited.

Issues in Organizing an Entrepreneurial Venture

3. Understand the choices to be made in organizing an entrepreneurial venture.

▶ ▶ ▶ Today Research In Motion is a $15 billion company with more than 14 000 employees. This success did not come all at once. The first milestone was when the first million-dollar sales year was recorded in 1990. A second milestone occurred in 1992, following the addition of Jim Balsillie, when sales grew to $21 million. A third milestone was reached with the launch of the BlackBerry in 1999.

Think About It

What organizational issues might Lazaridis and Balsillie have needed to address as they made the transition from start-up to small business, to mid-size business, to large business while experiencing rapid growth?

Once the start-up and planning issues for an entrepreneurial venture have been addressed, the entrepreneur is ready to begin organizing the entrepreneurial venture. There are four organizing issues an entrepreneur must address: organizational design and structure, human resource management, how to stimulate and make changes, and the continuing importance of innovation.

Organizational Design and Structure

The choice of an appropriate organizational structure is an important decision when organizing an entrepreneurial venture. At some point, successful entrepreneurs find that they can't do everything alone. More people are needed. The entrepreneur must then decide on the most appropriate structural arrangement for effectively and efficiently carrying out the organization's activities. Without some suitable type of organizational structure, the entrepreneurial venture may soon find itself in a chaotic situation.

In many small firms, the organizational structure tends to evolve with very little intentional and deliberate planning by the entrepreneur. For the most part, the structure may be very simple—one person does whatever is needed. As the entrepreneurial venture grows and the entrepreneur finds it increasingly difficult to go it alone, employees are brought on board to perform certain functions or duties that the entrepreneur can't handle. These individuals tend to perform those same functions as the company grows. As the entrepreneurial venture continues to grow, each of these functional areas may require managers and employees.

With the evolution to a more deliberate structure, an entrepreneur faces a whole new set of challenges. All of a sudden, he or she must share decision making and operating responsibilities. This is typically one of the most difficult things for an entrepreneur to do—let go and allow someone else to make decisions. *After all*, he or she reasons, *how can anyone know this business as well as I do?* Also, what might have been a fairly informal, loose, and flexible atmosphere that worked well when the organization was small may no longer be effective. But having a structured organization doesn't necessarily mean giving up flexibility, adaptability, and freedom. In fact, the structural design may be as fluid as the entrepreneur feels comfortable with and yet still have the rigidity it needs to operate efficiently.

Human Resource Management

As an entrepreneurial venture grows, additional employees will need to be hired to perform the increased workload. As employees are brought on board, an entrepreneur faces certain human resource management (HRM) issues. Two HRM issues of particular importance to entrepreneurs are employee recruitment and employee retention.

Employee Recruitment

Entrepreneurs, particularly, are looking for high-potential people who can perform multiple roles during various stages of venture growth. They look for individuals who buy into the venture's entrepreneurial culture—individuals who have a passion for the business.[35] They look for people who are exceptionally capable and self-motivated, flexible, and multi-skilled and who can help grow the entrepreneurial venture. Entrepreneurial managers are more concerned with matching characteristics of the person to the values and culture of the organization; that is, they focus on matching the person to the organization.[36]

Employee Retention

Getting competent and qualified people into a venture is just the first step in effectively managing the human resources. An entrepreneur wants to keep the people he or she has hired and trained. Many entrepreneurs understand the importance of having good people on board and keeping them. In the rough-and-tumble, intensely competitive world they operate in, entrepreneurs realize that the loss of talented employees can harm client services. To combat this, they often offer employees a wide array of desirable benefits, such as raises each year, profit sharing, trust funds for employees' children, paid sabbaticals, personal development funds, and so forth. This approach has the potential to keep employees loyal and productive.

MyManagementLab
PRISM 7

How to Stimulate and Make Changes

We know that entrepreneurs face dynamic change. Entrepreneurs need to be alert to problems and opportunities that may create the need for change. In fact, of the many hats an entrepreneur wears, that of change agent may be one of the most important.[37] If changes are needed in an entrepreneurial venture, often it is the entrepreneur who first recognizes the need for change and acts as the catalyst, coach, cheerleader, and chief change consultant. Even if a person is comfortable with taking risks—as entrepreneurs usually are—change can be difficult. That's why it's important for an entrepreneur to recognize the critical roles he or she plays in stimulating and implementing change.

Because organizational change of any type can be disruptive and scary, an entrepreneur must explain a change to employees and encourage change efforts by supporting employees, getting them excited about the change, building them up, and motivating them to put forth their best efforts. Finally, an entrepreneur may have to guide the actual change process as changes in strategy, technology, products, structure, or people are implemented. In this role, the entrepreneur answers questions, makes suggestions, gets needed resources, facilitates conflict, and does whatever else is necessary to get the change(s) implemented.

MyManagementLab
Q&A 4.3

The Continuing Importance of Innovation

In today's dynamically chaotic world of global competition, organizations must continually innovate new products and services if they want to compete successfully. Innovation is a key characteristic of entrepreneurial ventures and, in fact, is what makes an entrepreneurial venture "entrepreneurial." At Research In Motion, "innovation knows no boundaries or borders."[38] If you were a fly on the wall at RIM, you would likely see innovation taking place in several different forms:

MyManagementLab
Q&A 4.4

- **Curiosity-driven research**—Also referred to as basic research, this is research that is directed toward acquiring new knowledge rather than toward some more practical objective. The Perimeter Institute of Applied Physics was founded in 1999 based on a $100 million donation from Michael Lazaridis.[39] Researchers at this facility are dedicated to exploring the world around them without regard to solving problems that have commercial application. They are generating new knowledge in its purest form. Most curiosity-driven research occurs outside RIM at academic institutions or research institutes like the Perimeter Institute.

curiosity-driven research
Research directed toward acquiring new knowledge rather than toward some more practical objective (also referred to as basic research).

- **Applied research**—Applied research accesses, rather than generates, new knowledge and applies it to a practical or commercial purpose. At RIM it is common for

applied research Research that accesses, rather than generates, new knowledge and applies it to a practical or commercial purpose.

researchers to use some of the knowledge gained through curiosity-driven research and apply it to commercial problems.

● **Research and development (R&D)**—This includes investigative activities that an organization conducts to lead to discoveries that will help develop new products or procedures.[40] RIM invests in R&D in hopes of generating future profits. Some of the investment creates first-to-market competitive advantage through improving technology for the BlackBerry. These improvements are then protected by intellectual property rights. (As an illustration of the value of intellectual property, in 2006 RIM agreed to pay $612 million [US] to Chicago-based NTP to settle a patent infringement suit.) Another part of the R&D investment relates to improving internal manufacturing, marketing and support processes, and quality, as well as reducing costs.

Is there a systematic approach that an entrepreneurial venture can take to be more innovative? The following *Management Reflection—Finding Opportunity with Creativity* describes one approach.

MANAGEMENT REFLECTION
► Focus on Innovation

Finding Opportunity with Creativity

Can organizations use creativity to gain a competitive edge? Min Basadur is professor of innovation in the Michael G. DeGroote School of Business at McMaster University, in Hamilton, Ontario, and founder of Basadur Applied Creativity.[41] Basadur is recognized as a world leader in the field of applied creativity, with years of experience in building creative thinking, innovation, and problem-solving capabilities across organizations, including many *Fortune* 500 companies like PepsiCo, Procter & Gamble, and Pfizer.

Basadur's Simplex method combines three elements—process, skills, and profile—to find innovative solutions to fuzzy situations. The process includes eight steps, from formulating the problem through coming up with the solution, and finally implementing the solution. The three skills applied in each of the eight steps of the process ask participants to

● Use divergent thinking and brainstorming to come up with as many alternatives as possible.

● Defer judgment while brainstorming alternatives to allow the group to build on wild and crazy ideas, as well as the more practical ones.

● Use convergent and evaluative thinking to choose the alternative that fits best.

We all have a preferred way of solving problems, and Basadur uses the eight-step model to map out four problem-solving styles: generators, conceptualizers, optimizers, and implementers. Innovative organizations require a culture where all four approaches are represented on the problem-solving team. ■

Why are some companies able to consistently conceive of, create, and bring to market innovative and profitable new products and services while so many others struggle? It isn't the amount of money they spend on research and development. After all, the annual Global Innovation 1000 study, conducted by management consulting firm Booz & Company, has shown that there is no statistically significant relationship between financial performance and innovation spending—in terms of either total R&D dollars or R&D as a percentage of revenues.[42] As part of the research, a survey was conducted to explore the relationship between innovation capabilities, corporate strategy, and financial performance. More than 450 innovation leaders in over 400 companies and 10 industries were asked to name the three companies they considered to be the most innovative in the world. Apple captured 79 percent of the vote, followed by Google with 49 percent and 3M with 20 percent of the vote. Exhibit 4-4 provides the full list of the 10 most innovative firms.

Exhibit 4-4

Global Innovation 1000: The 10 Most Innovative Firms

		R&D Spending 2009		Sales 2009	Intensity (Spending as
		$US mil.	Rank	$US mil.	% of sales)
1	Apple	$1333	81	$42 905	3.1%
2	Google	$2843	44	$23 651	12.0%
3	3M	$1293	84	$23 123	5.6%
4	GE	$3300	35	$155 777	2.1%
5	Toyota	$7822	4	$204 363	3.8%
6	Microsoft	$9010	2	$58 437	15.4%
7	P&G	$2044	58	$79 029	2.6%
8	IBM	$5820	12	$95 759	6.1%
9	Samsung	$6002	10	$109 541	5.5%
10	Intel	$5653	13	$35 127	16.1%

What matters more than R&D is the particular combination of talent, knowledge, team structures, tools, and processes—the capabilities—that successful companies put together to enable innovation and create products and services they can successfully take to market. This means that companies must first choose the capabilities that matter most to their particular innovation strategy and then execute them well. Research conducted by Booz Allen Hamilton, a strategy and technology consulting firm based in the United States, suggests that companies often underperform at the commercialization stage. At this stage there are three customer- and market-oriented capabilities that matter most: gathering customer insights during the idea-generating stage, assessing market potential during the selection stage, and engaging with customers during the development stage.

Issues in Leading an Entrepreneurial Venture

As we noted at the beginning of the chapter, at RIM "innovation knows no boundaries or borders." Thus RIM invests in both applied research, often by putting resources toward R&D, and curiosity-driven research. The company also fosters a culture that supports innovation. Think back to the discussion of innovation in Chapter 1 where the report *Business Schools on an Innovation Mission* suggested that innovation is about creating economic and social prosperity, and leadership and management are as essential to the process as science and technology. Management innovation is "about the skills managers have in applying knowledge, judgment, and the ability to adapt and fashion new tools to solve problems."[43]

4. Appreciate what is involved in leading an entrepreneurial venture.

The Entrepreneur as Leader

Leading is an important function of entrepreneurs. As an entrepreneurial venture grows and people are brought on board, an entrepreneur takes on a new role—that of a leader. In this role, the entrepreneur has certain leadership responsibilities in leading the venture.

The 2010 movie *The Social Network* told the story of Mark Zuckerberg and the founding years of Facebook. As the company grew, enormous strains were put on personal relationships, the architecture needed to support the Facebook platform, and the financial and human resources of the company.

Today's successful entrepreneur must be like the leader of a jazz ensemble known for its improvisation, innovation, and creativity. Max DePree, former head of Herman Miller, Inc., a leading office furniture manufacturer known for its innovative leadership approaches, said it best in his book *Leadership Jazz*: "Jazz band leaders must choose the music, find the right musicians, and perform—in public. But the effect of the performance depends on so many things—the environment, the volunteers playing the band, the need for everybody to perform as individuals and as a group, the absolute dependence of the leader on the members of the band, the need for the followers to play well . . . The leader of the jazz band has the beautiful opportunity to draw the best out of the other musicians. We have much to learn from jazz band leaders, for jazz, like leadership, combines the unpredictability of the future with the gifts of individuals."[44]

The way an entrepreneur leads the venture should be much like the jazz band leader's job—drawing the best out of other individuals, even given the unpredictability of the situation. One way an entrepreneur does this is through the vision he or she creates for the organization. In fact, the driving force through the early stages of the entrepreneurial venture is often the visionary leadership of the entrepreneur. The entrepreneur's ability to articulate a coherent, inspiring, and attractive vision of the future is a key test of his or her leadership. But if an entrepreneur can do this, the results can be worthwhile. A study contrasting visionary and nonvisionary companies showed that visionary companies outperformed the nonvisionary ones 6 times over on standard financial criteria, and their stocks outperformed the general market 15 times over.[45]

MyManagementLab
Q&A 4.5

Issues in Controlling an Entrepreneurial Venture

5. Understand the unique challenges that need to be controlled if the entrepreneurial venture is to survive and prosper.

▶ ▶ ▶ "Speed Kills!" is a mantra often used to encourage safe driving habits. The same is often true for rapidly growing companies that are unable to manage the stresses and strains caused by growth, such as the need for cash injections, a growing workforce, and the need to figure out the logistics of invoicing customers and getting paid. Following the launch of the BlackBerry in 1999, RIM experienced massive growth, yet the company continues to thrive in the rapidly changing environment in which it operates.

Think About It

What challenges does a rapidly growing company face? How might the managers at RIM have dealt with these challenges?

Entrepreneurs must look at controlling the venture's operations in order to survive and prosper in both the short run and the long run. The unique control issues facing entrepreneurs include managing growth, managing downturns, and exiting the venture.

Managing Growth

Growth is a natural and desirable outcome for entrepreneurial ventures. Growth is what distinguishes an entrepreneurial venture. Entrepreneurial ventures pursue growth.[46] Growing slowly can be successful, but so can rapid growth. Growing successfully doesn't occur randomly or by luck. Successfully pursuing growth typically requires an entrepreneur to manage all the challenges associated with growing.

The best growth strategy is a well-planned one.[47] Ideally, the decision to grow doesn't come about spontaneously but instead is part of a venture's overall business goals and plan. Rapid growth without planning can be disastrous. Entrepreneurs need to address growth strategies as part of their business planning but shouldn't be overly rigid in that planning. The key challenges for an entrepreneur in organizing for growth include finding capital, finding people, and strengthening the organizational culture. Norbert Otto is the founder of Sport Otto, an online business based in Germany that has sold almost $2 million (US) worth of skates, skis, snowboards, and other sporting goods on eBay. As the company grows, Otto is finding that he has to be more organized.[48]

Having enough capital is a major challenge facing growing entrepreneurial ventures. The money issue never seems to go away, does it? Simply put, if you grow rapidly you will need to raise cash—rapid growth makes it almost impossible to fund the growth from annual profits. It takes capital to expand. The processes of finding capital to fund growth are much like those used for the initial financing of the venture. Hopefully, at this time the venture has a successful track record to back up the request. If it doesn't, it may be extremely difficult to acquire the necessary capital. That's why we said earlier that the best growth strategy is a planned one. As RIM grew at exponential rates, the company needed to arrange for ongoing rounds of financing and had to ensure that there was someone on board who knew this field intimately and could build a credible story for those providing the financing.

Another challenge that growing entrepreneurial ventures face is reinforcing already established organizational controls. Maintaining good financial records and financial controls over cash flow, inventory, customer data, sales orders, receivables, payables, and costs should be a priority of every entrepreneur—whether pursuing growth or not. However, it's particularly important to reinforce these controls when the entrepreneurial venture is expanding. It's all too easy to let things "get away" or to put them off when there's an unrelenting urgency to get things done. It's particularly important to have established procedures, protocols, and processes and to use them. Even though mistakes and inefficiencies can never be eliminated entirely, an entrepreneur should at least ensure that every effort is being made to achieve high levels of productivity and organizational effectiveness.

Managing Downturns

Although an entrepreneur hopes to never have to deal with organizational downturns, declines, or crises, there may come a time when he or she must do just that. After all, nobody likes to think about things going badly or taking a turn for the worse. But that's exactly what the entrepreneur should do—think about it *before* it happens by designing the control system to signal this to management early in the game.[49] It's important to have an up-to-date **contingency plan**, or **Plan B**, for dealing with a worst-case situation or crisis, just as you map exit routes from your home in case of a fire. An entrepreneur wants to be prepared before an emergency hits. This plan should focus on providing specific details for controlling the most fundamental and critical aspects of running the venture—cash flow, accounts receivable, costs, and debt. Beyond having a plan for controlling the venture's critical inflows and outflows, other actions would involve identifying specific strategies for cutting costs and restructuring the venture.

contingency plan A plan for dealing with a worst-case situation or crisis (often referred to as a Plan B).

Exiting the Venture

Exiting a venture is not something only entrepreneurs have to deal with. It is an issue that almost all organizations must face. When is the best time to plan your exit from the business? The answer may surprise you. The best time to plan an exit strategy is at the time you enter. Getting out of an entrepreneurial venture may seem to be a strange thing for entrepreneurs to do. However, there may come a point when the entrepreneur decides it's time to move on. That decision may be based on the fact that the entrepreneur hopes to capitalize financially on the investment in the venture—called **harvesting**—or on the fact that the entrepreneur is facing serious organizational performance problems and wants to get out, or even on the entrepreneur's desire to focus on other pursuits (personal or business). The issues involved with exiting the venture include choosing a proper business valuation method and knowing what's involved in the process of selling a business.

Setting a value on a business can be a little tricky. In many cases, the entrepreneur has sacrificed much for the business and sees it as his or her "baby." Calculating the value of the baby based on objective standards such as cash flow or some multiple of net profits can sometimes be a shock. That's why it's important for an entrepreneur who wishes to exit a venture to get a comprehensive business valuation prepared by professionals. Remember that if the value of the venture depends solely on the part the entrepreneur plays in the venture, it will have little value to prospective purchasers. A wise entrepreneur will build a venture whose value will persist after his or her departure.

Although the hardest part of preparing to exit a venture is valuing it, other factors should also be considered.[50] These include being prepared, deciding who will sell the business, considering the tax implications, screening potential buyers, and deciding whether to tell employees before or after the sale. The process of exiting an entrepreneurial venture should be approached as carefully as the process of launching it.

harvesting Exiting a venture when an entrepreneur hopes to capitalize financially on the investment in the venture.

SUMMARY AND IMPLICATIONS

1. Describe entrepreneurship and why it's important. Entrepreneurship is the process of starting new organizations, generally in response to opportunities. Entrepreneurs pursue opportunities by changing, revolutionizing, transforming, or introducing new products or services. Today, job growth and innovation are driven by entrepreneurial firms.

▶ ▶ ▶ Most of the innovation in society takes place in smaller firms like RIM, Microsoft, and Google, which were once tiny entrepreneurial start-ups. Innovation may lead to creative destruction, changing the way things were done before, as the BlackBerry technology has done. Other innovation builds on existing technology.

2. Understand how to identify opportunities and build the business case for launching an entrepreneurial venture. Once entrepreneurs have explored the entrepreneurial context and identified opportunities and possible competitive advantages, they must look at the issues involved in actually bringing an entrepreneurial venture to life. At the point of starting the venture, the entrepreneur needs to research the feasibility of the venture; develop a formal business plan; organize the financial, physical, and human resources; and then launch the venture.

▶ ▶ ▶ In 1984, 23-year-old Michael Lazaridis and two friends launched RIM with money that came primarily from friends and family. In the start-up stage, it is very common for the initial money to come from "friends, fools, and family."

3. Understand the choices to be made in organizing an entrepreneurial venture. Once the start-up and planning issues have been dealt with, the entrepreneur is ready to begin organizing the entrepreneurial venture. There are four organizing issues to be addressed: organizational design and structure, human resource management, how to stimulate and make changes, and the continuing importance of innovation.

▶▶▶ At Research In Motion, "innovation knows no boundaries or borders." This dedication to both applied and basic research helped propel RIM to the global stage. The choice to incorporate was a straightforward. After that it got complicated.

The company had to plan for a future that was largely unknown and in many ways unpredictable. The design and structure of the organization had to support its ability to be adaptable. At the same time, recruiting and retaining employees who would thrive in such an environment was core to RIM's success. It was vital to build a culture at RIM that embraced change and cherished innovation as a core organizational value.

4. Appreciate what is involved in leading an entrepreneurial venture. Leading is an important function of entrepreneurs. As an entrepreneurial venture grows and people are brought on board, an entrepreneur takes on a new role—that of a leader. No two entrepreneurs are the same, but they do share some common attributes, such as commitment and determination, strong leadership skills, an obsession with identifying opportunities, tolerance for risk and ambiguity, creativity, willingness to embrace building adaptable organizations, and finally a strong belief that what they do will make a difference (a strong internal locus of control). As the organization grows, it becomes impossible for the founder to be all things to all people and to be in all places at once. Empowering employees and developing effective work teams are effective ways of building management capacity in the entrepreneurial venture.

▶▶▶ As the firm grew, Research In Motion embraced the values of effective leadership. The founders made sure that they put an experienced board of advisers in place. They carefully chose the original venture capital investors to ensure that they brought more than money to the table. Finally, they articulated a shared vision for the organization.

5. Understand the unique challenges that need to be controlled if the entrepreneurial venture is to survive and prosper. Entrepreneurs must look at controlling the venture's operations in order to survive and prosper. Control issues that entrepreneurs face include managing growth, managing downturns, and exiting the venture.

▶▶▶ The BlackBerry was launched in 1999. By 2010, sales had grown to $15 billion and the company had 4000 employees. As they made the transition from start-up to small business, to mid-size business, to large business, Lazaridis and Balsillie had to manage aggressive growth and survive the collapse of the technology sector following 9/11, as well as the economic downturn in 2008. Despite these stressful times, Lazaridis and Balsillie were able to focus on their personal passion and create a legacy that will last beyond their lifetimes.

Management @ Work

READING FOR COMPREHENSION

1. What do you think would be the most difficult thing about being an entrepreneur? What do you think would be the most fun thing?

2. How does the concept of social entrepreneurship (see Chapter 5) relate to entrepreneurs and entrepreneurial ventures?

3. Would a good manager be a good entrepreneur? Discuss.

4. Why do you think many entrepreneurs find it difficult to step aside and let others manage their business?

5. Do you think a person can be taught to be an entrepreneur? Why or why not?

6. What do you think it means to be a successful entrepreneurial venture? How about a successful entrepreneur?

7. What is an entrepreneurial opportunity? How do entrepreneurs locate them?

8. What role does innovation play in the success of entrepreneurial ventures?

LINKING CONCEPTS TO PRACTICE

1. What is the difference between a small business and an entrepreneurial venture?

2. How do entrepreneurs add value to the economy?

3. Think about the entrepreneurs you have come in contact with. What makes them entrepreneurial?

4. What does an organizational culture that supports innovation look like?

5. How does the role of the entrepreneur change as the venture moves from start-up to operation, to growth, and finally to exit?

6. How does growth impact an entrepreneurial venture? Why do high-growth firms constantly require cash to support their growth?

7. Why do many entrepreneurs have problems creating an appropriate work–life balance?

SELF-ASSESSMENT

Am I Likely to Become an Entrepreneur?

For each of the following statements, circle the level of agreement or disagreement that you personally feel:

1 = Strongly Disagree 2 = Moderately Disagree 3 = Slightly Disagree 4 = Neither Agree nor Disagree 5 = Slightly Agree
6 = Moderately Agree 7 = Strongly Agree

1. I am constantly on the lookout for new ways to improve my life.	1 2 3 4 5 6 7
2. I feel driven to make a difference in my community and maybe the world.	1 2 3 4 5 6 7
3. I tend to let others take the initiative to start new projects.	1 2 3 4 5 6 7
4. Wherever I have been, I have been a powerful force for constructive change.	1 2 3 4 5 6 7
5. I enjoy facing and overcoming obstacles to my ideas.	1 2 3 4 5 6 7
6. Nothing is more exciting than seeing my ideas turn into reality.	1 2 3 4 5 6 7
7. If I see something I don't like, I fix it.	1 2 3 4 5 6 7
8. No matter what the odds, if I believe in something I will make it happen.	1 2 3 4 5 6 7
9. I love being a champion for my ideas, even against others' opposition.	1 2 3 4 5 6 7
10. I excel at identifying opportunities.	1 2 3 4 5 6 7

11. I am always looking for better ways to do things.   1 2 3 4 5 6 7

12. If I believe in an idea, no obstacle will prevent me from making it happen.   1 2 3 4 5 6 7

13. I love to challenge the status quo.   1 2 3 4 5 6 7

14. When I have a problem, I tackle it head on.   1 2 3 4 5 6 7

15. I am great at turning problems into opportunities.   1 2 3 4 5 6 7

16. I can spot a good opportunity long before others can.   1 2 3 4 5 6 7

17. If I see someone in trouble, I help out in any way I can.   1 2 3 4 5 6 7

Scoring Key

Reverse the score for item 3 (1 = 7, 2 = 6, 3 = 5, 4 = 4, 5 = 3, etc.). Add up all the scores.

Analysis and Interpretation

This scale assesses how proactive you are. It identifies the extent to which you will take action to influence your environment. Proactive personalities identify opportunities and act on them; they show initiative, take action, and persevere until they bring about the change. Research finds that a proactive personality is positively associated with entrepreneurial intentions.

The maximum score is 119 and the minimum score is 17. The higher your score, the stronger your proactive personality. For instance, scores above 85 indicate fairly high proactivity.

A number of factors have been found to be associated with becoming an entrepreneur. For instance, entrepreneurship tends to flourish in communities that encourage risk-taking and minimize the penalties attached to failures.

Having supportive parents is also a plus. Entrepreneurs typically have parents who encouraged them to achieve, to be independent, and to take responsibility for their actions. Entrepreneurs also tend to have parents who were self-employed or entrepreneurial themselves. But a high score on this questionnaire suggests a strong inclination toward becoming an entrepreneur.

More Self-Assessments MyManagementLab

To learn more about your skills, abilities, and interests, go to the MyManagementLab website and take the following self-assessments:

- I.A.5.—How Creative Am I?
- I.C.6.—How Confident Am I in My Abilities to Succeed?

MANAGEMENT FOR YOU TODAY

Dilemma

You have identified an entrepreneurial opportunity. What steps might you take to identify the benefits that will matter to the people you see as the primary users? What steps would you take to identify your competitors and their value proposition? How can you create a compelling value proposition that creates competitive advantage?

Becoming a Manager

- Identify an entrepreneur you admire and research his or her background.
- If you have a family member or family friend who is an entrepreneur, ask about his or her experiences.
- Visit a local support agency for small businesses outside of your educational institution. Ask about the services they provide to the entrepreneurial community and why those services are valued.
- If your college/university has an entrepreneurship or small business centre, go visit it.

- Identify seminars on small business and entrepreneurship available in your community and attend one.
- Invite an entrepreneur to lunch and use the opportunity to learn about his or her journey. In particular, explore how that person maintains a work–life balance.
- Take the time to think about what bugs you (what doesn't work as it is supposed to), and keep a journal for a week of everything you find. At the end of the week, pick one problem and come up with a solution that could lead to the creation of a venture.
- Imagine you are working for an entrepreneurial venture shortly after start-up. Describe what your typical day would be like.

What Bugs You?

Form groups of 3 or 4 individuals and think back over the events of the last 24 hours, including classes, commuting, social interactions, work, and family. Think about all of your interactions, including those with technology and appliances. For the next 5 minutes, list anything that did not work the way it was supposed to. Pick one of the problems your group has identified, and for the next 10 minutes, develop a solu-

tion that could result in a business opportunity. As a group, present your report to the class, identifying some of the problems from your original list, which problem you chose to develop a solution for, and why and how the solution you chose will add value for those affected by the problem (the value proposition).

Ethical Dilemma Exercise: Lifting the Corporate Veil

General Motors filed for bankruptcy on June 1, 2009, and announced that it would close 14 plants and 3 service centres. Following the announcement, General Motors was removed from the Dow Jones Industrial Average. In late 2008 and throughout 2009, Ontario—the industrial heartland of Canada—suffered more than the rest of the country. One of the fallouts from the collapse of industrial customers was

the bankruptcy of many small suppliers to the automotive industry. Imagine that you are the owner of a small incorporated business in rural Ontario and are forced to close your business and enter into bankruptcy. Because you are incorporated, you are not legally required to pay local suppliers, many of whom are your friends, neighbours, and extended family. What should you do?

Thinking Critically About Responsibility and Ethics

Is it possible run a social venture with the traditional bottom-line mindset? Are seeking to earn profits and the quest for efficiency compatible with doing the right thing?

Apple

Apple was named the top firm in the 2009 Global Innovation 1000 survey, beating Google, at second place, and 3M, at third, by a wide margin.[51] In the survey, Apple was held up as an example of the idea that innovation success is driven not by the amount of money spent, but rather by how and where it is spent. Apple is known for bringing innovative and stylish products to market.[52] Yet the company spends less than half the average percentage of sales on R&D as the rest of the computing and electronics industry, while earning a high return for shareholders. Winners in the innovation game are those who can innovate successfully without breaking the bank. At Apple, this was not always the case. In the 1990s, Apple invested precious human resources and billions of dollars in a succession of failed products, including the Newton PDA (personal digital assistant).[53] Following the return of Steve Jobs as CEO in 1997,[54] Apple has focused on the strengths that allow it to stand out from its competitors,

including a deep understanding of end-users, a high-touch consumer experience, intuitive user interfaces, sleek product design, and iconic branding.

The survey of the 2009 Global Innovation 1000 suggested that successful innovators follow one of three strategies. Need seekers build adaptable organizations that look for meaningful customer problems to solve and strive to be the first to market with those new offerings. Market readers invest in market intelligence on customers and competitors and focus on creating value through incremental change and by capitalizing on proven market trends. Technology drivers invest in R&D to develop leading-edge technology to solve customers' unstated needs. It is interesting to note that no one of these strategies was seen as better than the others.

In your opinion, which of these three innovation strategies is Apple using? As a manager at Apple, what would you need to do to keep the firm adaptable in the future?

Second Chance: The Business of Life

The Centre for Entrepreneurship Education and Development (CEED), through its Second Chance Program, gives youth who have been in conflict with the law the chance for a new start.[55] Many young people who break the law possess misdirected entrepreneurial characteristics. Second Chance provides participants between the ages of 15 and 30 with an opportunity to redirect their entrepreneurial energy and develop the life skills they need to become productive citizens—to manage the "business of life." Second Chance intends to break the cycle of criminal behaviour. One participant describes what that cycle is like:

> For most of my life, I've been involved in illegal activities and arrested at least once a month. I wound up on the streets at the early age of six, and had to learn how to fend for myself. Many of the skills I learned along the way kept me alive, but it was a one-sided life. I didn't trust anyone, care for anyone, or even love anyone, including myself. I was cursed to live a life of crime and emotional solitude.

Referrals for candidates for Second Chance are made by corrections officials, parole officers, and former participants. Perpetrators of violent crimes such as rape, murder, and assault with a deadly weapon are excluded. Applications always exceed the number of seats available. In 2009, 40 applications were made and 14 applicants were accepted. The recidivism rate (rate of reoffence) is around 5 percent for Second Chance graduates, compared to 60 percent for other offenders.

Social Return on Investment

It is becoming increasingly important to estimate the economic benefit of social programs such as Second Chance when attempting to secure public sector funding. The director of the Second Chance Program, Ed Matwawana, recently attended a conference where discussion focused on extending the measurement framework to include the social return on investment (SROI).

Ed Matwawana and CEED president and CEO Kathy Murphy make the business case for Second Chance by comparing the annual operating cost of the program ($300 000) with the annual cost of incarceration for a single inmate ($100 000), pointing out that the program breaks even when incarceration is reduced by three years.

Questions

Watch the Second Chance stories video at the Centre for Entrepreneurship and Education Development website (**www. ceed.ca**).

Think about how Ed Matwawana and Kathy Murphy can make the business case for funding based on earning a social return on investment for the participants and the community at large.

1. Is there a dollar value that you can assign to the reduction in community-based crime from the participants? What is the value for others in the community?

2. What other "social" values can you identify? How would you place a dollar value on them?

Interviewing an Entrepreneur

About the Skill

Many students are fearful that they are imposing upon the person they wish to interview. Experience shows otherwise. There is no greater compliment than to acknowledge others' wisdom and ask them to share it. Yes, some people will refuse the interview for a variety of reasons (they're too busy, there may be confidentiality issues, etc.), but you will find most very approachable.

Conducting interviews not only allows you to access the experience and knowledge of others but also helps you to build a network that will support your career. Before conducting your interview you need to set an objective and identify someone to interview; then conduct the interview and debrief it with your classmates.

Steps in Developing the Skill

Try to find a way to make both yourself and your interviewee comfortable. Be sure to explain who you are, why you are there, and what you expect. Tips include the following:

1. **Avoid closed-ended questions.** These are questions that allow a brief or simple yes or no response. Some examples are listed here:
   a. How old are you?
   b. How many children do you have?

c. Did your parents have a small business?

d. How many customers do you have?

e. Do you have any challenges in your business?

2. Use as many open-ended questions as possible. These kinds of responses will be rich in information. Some sample questions are listed here, and you are encouraged to develop your own.

a. Tell me about a time when . . .

b. You must have a lot of experience in . . . Which of those experiences had the most impact? Why?

c. I see from the pictures on your desk that you have several children. How have they affected the way you run the business?

d. You have stated that your parents also ran a business. How did this influence the way you run yours?

e. You seem to have a lot of customers. Which do you consider special? Why?

f. Of the challenges you face in your business, which are the most difficult? Why?

3. Try to use the laddering technique in your interview wherever possible. One response will allow you to drill deeper as answers are given to the original questions. The experience of most interviewers is that they have problems getting their subjects to stop talking, not the reverse.

The confidentiality of the interview must be respected. Do not share any of the matters discussed without the express permission of the interviewee. It is always a good idea to thank the interviewee and if appropriate send a summary of what you learned.

Practising the Skill

Find an entrepreneur you respect and ask that person to share his or her experiences with you. Many students interview their parents or other family members. Others interview small business advisers. It is important to conduct the interview face-to-face with your interviewee rather than by phone or email, as the face-to-face setting has a richness of communication that is absent in the other forms.

Reinforcing the Skill

After completing the interview, create a journal that details what you learned in the interview process and how you will be able to apply what you learned the next time you want to gather information from an expert. Remember to distinguish between the expected and the unexpected lessons learned. Many times the unexpected lessons are the most powerful.

- Identify the skills necessary to interview successfully.

- Reflect on the content of the interview to assimilate the knowledge gained. How does it apply or not apply to you?

- Identify what you expected to learn and identify any surprises/unexpected learning.

- Comment on the value of tacit (interviews) versus explicit (databases) techniques for gathering knowledge.

MyManagementLab _____

For more resources, please visit www.pearsoned.ca/mymanagementlab

SCAN THIS

Managing Responsibly and Ethically

How important is it for organizations and managers to be socially responsible and ethical? In this chapter, we'll look at what it means to be socially responsible and ethical and what role managers play in both. After reading and studying this chapter, you will achieve the following learning outcomes.

Learning Outcomes

1. Understand what it means to be a socially responsible manager.

2. Describe how managing responsibly contributes to organizational performance.

3. Identify sustainable management practices.

4. Understand the principles of values-based management.

5. Discuss current ethics issues.

▶ ▶ ▶ Since its founding in 1973 by Ray Anderson, Interface Inc., a manufacturer of carpet tiles, has grown into a billion-dollar business with 4000 employees.[1] In 1994, after reading Paul Hawken's *The Ecology of Commerce*, Anderson made a drastic change in course for his company. It became his mission to "turn the myth that you could do well in business or do good, but not both, on its head." Anderson believed that the classic "take, make waste" business model had to be replaced by one that respected the earth. Between 1996 and 1998, Interface reduced its greenhouse gas emissions by 71 percent while growing its sales by two-thirds and doubling its profits. Since 2003, Interface has manufactured 83 million yards of its carbon-neutral Cool Carpet—the company invests in renewable energy

and sequestration projects to offset the carbon footprint from manufacturing. Interface's dedication to sustainability has evolved into the company's Mission Zero commitment, a promise to eliminate any negative impact Interface has on the environment by 2020. Interface hopes its commitment will inspire other businesses to create their own Mission Zero journey to sustainability.

SCAN THIS

Think About It

What are the elements of corporate responsibility at Interface? What questions is Ray Anderson most often asked when he finishes his presentations—by shareholders, advocacy groups, and company employees? What balance between profitability and social responsibility might local Interface managers need to strike? In what ways might Interface's Mission Zero commitment create a competitive advantage?

Deciding how much social responsibility is enough—for instance, looking at when it's better to simply focus on profits—is just one example of the complicated types of ethical and social responsibility issues that managers may have to address as they plan, organize, lead, and control. As managers go about their business, social factors can and do influence their actions. In this chapter, we introduce you to the issues surrounding social responsibility and managerial ethics. Our discussion of these topics appears here in the textbook because both corporate social responsibility and ethics are responses to a changing environment and are influenced by organizational culture (Chapter 2); they have an influence on how we do business globally (Chapter 3); and they are important considerations when making decisions (Chapter 6).

What Is Meant by Socially Responsible Management?

1. Understand what it means to be a socially responsible manager.

By using digital technology and file-sharing websites, music and video users all over the world obtain and share many of their favourite recordings for free. Large global corporations lower their costs by outsourcing to countries where human rights are not a high priority and justify it by saying they're bringing in jobs and helping strengthen the local economies. Businesses facing a drastically changed industry environment offer employees early retirement and buyout packages. Are these companies being socially responsible? Managers regularly face decisions that have a dimension of social responsibility, such as those involving employee relations, philanthropy, pricing, resource conservation, product quality and safety, and doing business in countries that devalue human rights. What does it mean to be socially responsible?

MyManagementLab
Q&A 5.1

From Obligations to Responsiveness to Responsibility

The concept of *social responsibility* has been described in different ways. For instance, it has been called "profit making only," "going beyond profit making," "any discretionary corporate activity intended to further social welfare," and "improving social or environmental conditions."[2] We can understand it better if we first compare it to two similar concepts: social obligation and social responsiveness.[3]

The Classical View: Social Obligation

Social obligation is a firm's engaging in social actions because of its obligation to meet certain economic and legal responsibilities. The organization does what it's obligated to do and nothing more. This idea reflects the **classical view** of social responsibility, which says that management's only social responsibility is to maximize profits. The most outspoken advocate of this approach is economist and Nobel laureate Milton Friedman. He argued that managers' primary responsibility is to operate the business in the best interests of the stockholders, whose primary concerns are financial.[4] He also argued that when managers decide to spend the organization's resources for "social good," they add to the costs of doing business, which have to be passed on to consumers through higher prices or absorbed by stockholders through smaller dividends. You need to understand that Friedman doesn't say that organizations shouldn't be socially responsible. But his interpretation of social responsibility is to maximize profits for stockholders.

> *Would businesses be socially responsible if they weren't legally obligated to be so?"*

Joel Bakan, professor of law at the University of British Columbia, author of *The Corporation*, and co-director of the documentary of the same name, is more critical of organizations than Friedman. He finds that current laws support corporate behaviour that some might find troubling. Bakan suggests that today's corporations have many of the same characteristics as a psychopathic personality (for example, self-interested, lacking empathy, manipulative, and reckless in their disregard of others). Bakan notes that even though companies have a tendency to act psychopathically, this is not why they are fixated on profits. Rather, though they may have social responsibilities, the only *legal* responsibility corporations have is to maximize organizational profits for stockholders.[5] He suggests that more laws and more restraints need to be put in place if corporations are to behave more socially responsibly, as current laws direct corporations to be responsible to their shareholders, and make little mention of responsibility toward other stakeholders.

The Socio-economic View: Social Responsiveness and Social Responsibility

The other two concepts—social responsiveness and social responsibility—reflect the **socio-economic view**, which says that managers' social responsibilities go beyond making profits to include protecting and improving society's welfare. This view is based on the belief that corporations are *not* independent entities responsible only to stockholders. They also have a responsibility to the larger society that endorses their creation through various laws and regulations and supports them by purchasing their products and services. In addition, proponents of this view believe that business organizations are not just mere economic institutions. Society expects and even encourages businesses to become involved in social, environmental, political, and legal issues. For example, Avon Products was being socially responsible when it initiated its Breast Cancer Crusade to provide women with breast cancer education and early detection screening services, and which, after 14 years, has raised more than $450 million worldwide.[6]

Organizations around the world have embraced this view, as shown by a global survey of executives in which 84 percent said that companies must balance obligations to shareholders with obligations to the public good.[7] So how do the concepts of social responsiveness and social responsibility differ?

social obligation A firm's engaging in social actions because of its obligation to meet certain economic and legal responsibilities.

classical view The view that management's only social responsibility is to maximize profits.

MyManagementLab
Q&A 5.2

socio-economic view The view that management's social responsibility goes beyond making profits and includes protecting and improving society's welfare.

Social Responsiveness

social responsiveness A firm's engaging in social actions in response to some popular social need.

social need A need of a segment of society caused by factors such as physical and mental disabilities; language barriers; and cultural, social, or geographical isolation.

Social responsiveness means that a company engages in social actions in response to some popular **social need**. Managers in these companies are guided by social norms and values and make practical, market-oriented decisions about their actions.[8] For instance, managers at Toronto-based CIBC identified three themes—supporting youth, contributing to community development, and involving CIBC employees—to guide them in deciding which projects and organizations to support.[9] By making these choices, managers were "responding" to what they felt were important social needs; that is, things important to the community. Manulife Financial Canada strives to build stronger communities, promote health and wellness, enhance environmental sustainability, and harness the power of volunteering in the community. Manulife's corporate giving emphasizes giving back to the communities where it does business and encourages employees to do the same. Local managers choose the area of focus for philanthropy, identify partners, and determine how best to encourage employee involvement. By making these choices, managers respond to what they identify as important local needs.[10]

Many companies in Canada and around the world practise social responsiveness. For example, Mississauga, Ontario-based Purolator Courier developed its Tackle Hunger campaign because no major Canadian corporations were tackling this important issue. The program visits Canadian Football League (CFL) cities annually, and fans can have their picture taken with the Grey Cup if they bring a nonperishable food item or make a cash donation. In addition, Purolator donates the quarterback's weight in food to the local food bank whenever he gets sacked in a regular season game. Between 2003 and 2007, the program contributed almost 460 000 kilograms of food to food banks.[11]

Advocates believe that social responsiveness replaces philosophical talk with practical, market-oriented action. They see it as a more tangible and achievable goal than social responsibility.[12] Rather than assessing what is good for society in the long term and making moral judgments, managers in a socially responsive organization identify the prevailing social norms and then change their social involvement to respond to changing societal conditions. For instance, environmental stewardship seems to be an important social norm at present, and many companies are looking at ways to be environmentally responsible. Alcoa of Australia developed a novel way to recycle the used linings of aluminum smelting pots,[13] and Japanese auto parts manufacturer DENSO generates its own electricity and steam at many of its facilities. Other organizations are addressing other popular social issues. For instance, Indigo, Chapters, and Coles stores across Canada launched a fundraising drive in 2010 to rejuvenate the libraries at more than 132 public elementary schools from coast to coast through in-store activities.[14] These are examples of socially responsive actions for today.

Social Responsibility

social responsibility A business's intention, beyond its legal and economic obligations, to do the right things and act in ways that are good for society.

A *socially responsible* organization views things differently. It goes beyond what it's obligated to do or chooses to do because of some popular social need and does what it can to help improve society because it's the right thing to do. We define **social responsibility** as a business's efforts, beyond its legal and economic obligations, to do the right things and act in ways that are good for society.[15] Our definition assumes that a business obeys the law and cares for its stockholders, *and* it adds an ethical imperative to do those things that make society better and not to do those that make it worse, including environmental degradation. Note that this definition assumes that a firm has to differentiate between right and wrong. As Exhibit 5-1 shows, a socially responsible organization does what is right because it feels it has an ethical responsibility to do so. For example, the Royal Bank of Canada (RBC) has identified water stewardship as an environmental priority. Under the RBC Blue Water Project, the organization has committed $4.6 million to fresh water initiatives, announced significant grants to three universities for water research and programs, and pledged more than $21 million since 2007 to 223 organizations worldwide that are working to protect watersheds and provide access to clean drinking water.[16]

Social responsibility adds an ethical imperative to determine what is right or wrong and to engage in ethical business activities. A socially responsible organization does what is

Exhibit 5-1

Social Responsibility vs. Social Responsiveness

	Social Responsibility	Social Responsiveness
Major consideration	Ethical	Pragmatic
Focus	Ends	Means
Emphasis	Obligation	Responses
Decision framework	Long term	Medium and short term

Source: Adapted from S. L. Wartick and P. L. Cochran, "The Evolution of the Corporate Social Performance Model," *Academy of Management Review*, October 1985, p. 766.

right because it feels it has a responsibility to act that way. For example, Vancouver-based Mountain Equipment Co-op, which makes outdoor sports clothing and gear, has a green building policy. Its Ottawa and Winnipeg stores were the first and second Canadian retail buildings to comply with standards requiring a 50 percent reduction in energy consumption over regular buildings. CEO Peter Robinson says, "The bottom line is that sustainability is good business: for the ledger books and for the planet."[17] That's the attitude of a socially responsible manager and organization.

In 2010 Loblaw Companies, Canada's largest grocery chain operator, topped the *Corporate Knights* magazine ranking of corporate social responsibility in Canada.[18] As part of Ontario's Green Energy Act, Loblaws is installing solar panels in stores across the province, which will generate power for surrounding communities. Calgary-based Enbridge has pledged to plant a tree for every one it removes to build new facilities, conserve a hectare of natural land or wilderness for every hectare it impacts through construction, and generate a kilowatt of renewable power through its investments in renewable and alternative energy for every kilowatt its operations consume.[19] The Bank of Montreal launched its Clear Blue Skies Initiative in 2009 as a company-wide strategy of energy reduction and efficiency; waste management; and sustainable transport, materials, and procurement—all aimed at protecting and improving air quality.[20]

At Charlottetown, PEI-based APM Group, a construction and property development company, (from left) Terry Palmer, APM Group vice-president of finance; Tim Banks, president; Duane Lamont, vice-president of construction; and Pam Mullally, director of accounting, think about the bottom line when they review plans for new subdivisions APM might build. However, they also know that social responsibility is a guiding principle for the company. So they evaluate each project's impact on the environment, focus on design that promotes energy conservation, and strive to create a healthy economic community through the building plan.

Social Responsibility vs. Social Responsiveness

How should we view an organization's social actions? A Canadian business that meets federal pollution control standards or that doesn't discriminate against employees over age 40 in job promotion decisions is meeting its social obligation because laws mandate these actions. However, when it provides on-site child care facilities for employees; packages products using recycled paper; or announces that it will not purchase, process, or sell any tuna caught along with dolphins, it's being socially responsive. Why? Working parents and environmentalists have voiced these social concerns and demanded such actions.

For many businesses, their social actions are better viewed as being socially responsive than socially responsible (at least according to our definition). However, such actions are still good for society. For example, Wal-Mart Canada is a leader in the transition toward environmental sustainability in Canada's retail sector. Wal-Mart Canada's green plan includes a $25 million fund to support the restoration of community green space until 2015, hard targets for reductions in its carbon footprint and energy consumption, a commitment to being Canada's largest consumer of renewable energy, and a sustained program to offer environmentally efficient products and educate consumers about their benefits.[21]

Educational programs implemented by Brazilian cosmetics manufacturer Natura Cosmeticos SA in public primary schools in São Paulo to improve children's literacy and decision-making skills are also viewed as socially responsible.[22] Why? Through these programs, the company's managers are protecting and improving society's welfare. More and more organizations around the world are embracing the socio-economic view, as shown by a 2006 survey of more than 4200 managers in 116 countries in which respondents overwhelmingly agreed that the role of corporations in society goes far beyond just meeting stockholder obligations.[23] Some even try to measure their "Triple Bottom Line," which takes into account not only financial responsibilities, but social and environmental ones as well.[24]

The Evolution of Socially Responsible Management

Understanding the various socially responsible management strategies that exist today is easier if we think in terms of differing views on to whom organizations are responsible. Those supporting the socio-economic view would respond that managers should be responsible to any group affected by the organization's decisions and actions—that is, the stakeholders (such as employees and community members).[25] Classicists would say that shareholders, or owners, are the only legitimate concern. Exhibit 5-2 shows a four-stage model of the progression of an organization's social responsibility.[26]

At stage 1, managers are following the classical view of social responsibility and obey all laws and regulations while caring for stockholders' interests. At stage 2, managers expand their responsibilities to another important stakeholder group—employees. Because they want to attract, keep, and motivate good employees, stage 2 managers improve working conditions, expand employee rights, increase job security, and focus on human resource concerns.

Exhibit 5-2

To Whom Is Management Responsible?

At stage 3, managers expand their responsibilities to other stakeholders in the specific environment, primarily customers and suppliers. Socially responsible actions for these stakeholders might include fair prices, high-quality products and services, safe products, good supplier relations, and similar actions. Their philosophy is that they can meet their responsibilities to stakeholders only by meeting the needs of these other stakeholders.

> *Would you be willing to stop eating your favourite snack if you found out the company did not use environmentally friendly packaging for its products?*

Finally, at stage 4, which characterizes the highest socio-economic commitment, managers feel they have a responsibility to society as a whole. They view their business as a public entity and therefore feel that it's important to advance the public good. The acceptance of such responsibility means that managers actively promote social justice, preserve the environment, and support social and cultural activities. They do these things even if such actions may negatively affect profits.

MyManagementLab
Q&A 5.4

Corporate Social Responsibility and Economic Performance

▶ ▶ ▶ In his position as founder, CEO, and leader of the Interface journey toward sustainability, Ray Anderson says, "Our costs are down, our profits are up, and our products are the best they've ever been. It has rewarded us with more positive visibility and goodwill among our customers than the slickest, most expensive advertising or marketing campaign could possibly have generated. And a strong environmental ethic has no equal for attracting and motivating good people, galvanizing them around a shared higher purpose, and giving them a powerful reason to join and stay."[27]

Through its dedication to sustainability, Interface has created a working model that since 1996 has reduced greenhouse gas emissions by 71 percent and the wastewater stream by 72 percent, while growing sales by 60 percent and doubling earnings before interest and taxes.

2. Describe how managing responsibly contributes to organizational performance.

Think About It

Can a company be socially responsible and achieve good financial performance? Put yourself in Ray Anderson's shoes. What advantages does Interface gain through working toward its goal of a zero carbon footprint? Would you like to work for Interface? Why or why not? Is this a values-led organization? Why don't more businesses adopt the Interface model?

In this section, we look at the question: How do socially responsible activities affect a company's economic performance? Findings from a number of research studies can help us answer this question.[28]

The majority of studies show a positive relationship between social involvement and economic performance. However, we cannot generalize these findings because the studies haven't used standardized measures of social responsibility and economic performance.[29] Another concern in these studies has been causation: If a study showed that social involvement and economic performance were positively related, this didn't necessarily mean that social involvement *caused* higher economic performance. It could simply mean that high profits afforded companies the "luxury" of being socially involved.[30] Such methodological concerns can't be taken lightly. In fact, one study found that if the flawed empirical analyses in these studies were "corrected," social responsibility had a neutral impact on a company's financial performance.[31] Another found that participating in social issues not related to the organization's primary stakeholders was negatively associated with shareholder value.[32] However, a recent reanalysis of several studies concluded that managers can afford to be (and should be) socially responsible.[33]

social screening Applying social criteria (screens) to investment decisions.

Another way to view social involvement and economic performance is by looking at socially responsible investing (SRI) funds, which provide a way for individual investors to support socially responsible companies. Typically, these funds use some type of **social screening**; that is, they apply social and environmental criteria to investment decisions. For instance, SRI funds usually do not invest in companies that are involved in liquor, gambling, tobacco, nuclear power, weapons, price fixing, or fraud or in companies that have poor product safety, employee relations, or environmental track records. The SRI industry in Canada has grown significantly in the last few years, with new companies launching responsible investment funds and products.[34] (You can find a complete list of these funds, along with current performance statistics, at **www.socialinvestment.ca**.) The 2008 Canadian Socially Responsible Investment Review found that assets invested according to socially responsible guidelines increased from $503.61 billion in 2006 to $609.23 billion in 2008, a 21 percent increase over two years when markets generally experienced difficulty.[35]

We can also look at what consumers say about corporate social responsibility. A recent survey conducted by GlobeScan, which specializes in corporate issues, found that "83 percent of Canadians believe that corporations should go beyond their traditional economic role; 51 percent say they have punished a socially irresponsible company in the past year."[36] As for naming a socially responsible company, 43 percent of Canadians said they could not do so.

What conclusion can we draw from all of this? The most meaningful one is that there is little evidence to say that a company's social actions hurt its long-term economic performance. Given political and societal pressures on business to be socially involved, managers would be wise to take social goals into consideration as they plan, organize, lead, and control. Jason Mogus, president of Vancouver-based Communicopia, agrees: "The times that we are in right now are tough times for a lot of high-tech firms, and the ones that are thriving are the ones that really did build community connections and have strong customer and employee loyalty." Says Mogus, "If everyone's just there for the stock price and it goes underwater, then what you have is a staff of not very motivated workers."[37]

Sustainable Management Practices

3. Identify sustainable management practices.

▶ ▶ ▶ Interface sees itself as a restorative enterprise.[38] This includes a commitment to eliminate all forms of waste in every area of business, reduce greenhouse gases, and use renewable energy sources. Interface's goal is to ensure that by 2020, all fuels and electricity to operate manufacturing, sales, and office facilities will be from renewable sources, such as solar, wind, and geothermal energy. Products and processes have been redesigned to reduce and simplify the amount of resources used, so that material "waste" is remanufactured into the "nutrients" for the next cycle of production. In 2009, Interface diverted 25 million pounds of reclaimed carpet and postindustrial scrap from landfill.

At Interface, all nonrenewable energy is also considered waste. In three of its production facilities, the company generates green power on site, and it purchases additional requirements through green power. Interface started a company-wide waste reduction program called QUEST (Quality Utilizing Employee's Suggestions and Teamwork) and in the first three and a half years saved $67 million worldwide. Since 1999, the QUEST program has saved the company $433 million. Interface is also committed to creating a culture that uses sustainability principles to improve the lives and livelihoods of all its stakeholders—employees, partners, suppliers, customers, investors, and communities. This includes a commitment to transport people and products efficiently to eliminate waste and emissions.

Think About It

Why has Interface chosen to follow an approach to business that incorporates environmental sustainability? What benefits does managing sustainably provide to a company? What benefits does managing sustainably provide to society?

How might BP's 2010 oil leak in the Gulf of Mexico impact the public's commitment to sustainable management practices?

Rachel Carson's *Silent Spring,* a book about the negative effects of pesticides on the environment that was published in 1962, is often cited as having launched the environmental movement. Until that time, few people (and organizations) paid attention to the environmental consequences of their decisions and actions.[39] Although there were some groups concerned with conserving natural resources, about the only popular reference to saving the environment you would have seen was the ubiquitous printed request "Please Do Not Litter."

Since the publication of Carson's book, a number of highly publicized environmental disasters—mercury poisoning in Japan (from 1932 to 1968), the Three Mile Island (1979) and Chernobyl (1986) nuclear power plant accidents, the *Exxon Valdez* oil spill (1989), the BP oil spill (2010), and the Hungary toxic sludge disaster (2010)—have increased environmental awareness among individuals, groups, and organizations. Increasingly, managers began to confront questions about an organization's impact on the natural environment. The recognition by business of the close link between its decisions and activities and their impact on the natural environment is referred to as **sustainable management**. Let's look at some sustainability issues managers may have to address.

sustainable management The recognition by business of the close link between its decisions and activities and their impact on the natural environment.

Global Environmental Problems

Some of the more serious global environmental problems include global climate change, natural resource depletion, pollution (air, water, and soil), industrial accidents, and toxic wastes. How did these problems occur? Much of the blame can be placed on industrial activities in developed (economically wealthy) countries over the last half-century.[40] Various reports have shown that wealthy societies account for more than 75 percent of the world's energy and resource consumption and create most of the industrial, toxic, and consumer waste.[41] An equally unsettling picture is that as the world population continues to grow and as emerging countries become more market-oriented and well off, shortages in resources such as water and other global environmental problems can be expected to worsen.[42] But the good news is that things are changing. Increasingly, managers and organizations around the world have begun to consider the impact of their organizations on the natural environment and have embraced their responsibility to respect and protect the earth. For instance, IKEA encourages customers to use fewer bags and has cut the price of its large reusable totes from 99 cents to 59 cents. Tokyo-based Ricoh hires workers to sort through company trash to analyze what might be reused or recycled. And company employees have two cans—one for recycling and one for trash. If a recyclable item is found in a trash bin, it's placed back on the offender's desk for proper removal. These sustainable management practices, also known as green management practices, are increasingly being implemented by organizations.[43] What role *can* organizations play in addressing global environmental problems? In other words, how can they implement sustainable management practices?

How Organizations Manage Sustainably

Managers and organizations can do many things to protect and preserve the natural environment. Some do no more than what is required by law—that is, they fulfill their social obligation. However, others have made radical changes to make their products and production processes cleaner. For instance, Paris, France-based Total SA, one of the world's largest integrated oil companies, is cleaning up and greening up by implementing tough new rules on oil tanker safety and working with groups such as Global Witness and Greenpeace. UPS, the world's largest package delivery company, has taken numerous environmental actions, such as retrofitting its aircraft with advanced technology and fuel-efficient engines; developing a powerful computer network that efficiently dispatches its fleet of brown trucks; and using alternative fuel to run its trucks. There are many more examples of organizations committed to sustainable management. Although these examples are interesting, they don't tell us much about *how* organizations engage in sustainable management. One model of environmental responsibility uses the phrase *shades of green* to describe the different approaches that organizations take.[44] (See Exhibit 5-3.)

The first approach to sustainable management is the *legal* (or *light green*) *approach*—that is, simply doing what is required legally. Organizations that follow this approach exhibit little environmental sensitivity. They obey laws, rules, and regulations willingly and without legal challenge and may even try to use the law to their own advantage, but that is the extent of their implementation of sustainable management practices. For example, many durable product manufacturers have taken the legal approach and comply with the relevant environmental laws and regulations, but go no further. This approach is a good illustration of social obligation—these organizations simply follow the legal requirements to prevent pollution and protect the environment.

As an organization becomes more sensitive to environmental issues, it may adopt the *market approach*, where organizations respond to the environmental preferences of their customers. Whatever customers demand in terms of environmentally friendly products will be what the organization provides. For example, DuPont developed a new type of herbicide that helped farmers around the world reduce their annual use of chemicals by more than 20 million kilograms. By developing this product, the company was responding to the demands of its customers (farmers) who wanted to minimize the use of chemicals on their crops.

Organizations that follow the *stakeholder approach* work to meet the environmental demands of multiple stakeholders such as employees, suppliers, and the community. For instance, Hewlett-Packard has several corporate environmental programs in place for its supply chain (suppliers), product design and product recycling (customers and society), and work operations (employees and community). Both the market approach and the stakeholder approach are good illustrations of social responsiveness.

Finally, if an organization pursues an *activist* (also called a *dark green*) *approach to sustainable management*, it looks for ways to respect and preserve the earth and its natural resources. Organizations that follow the activist approach exhibit the highest degree of environmental sensitivity. For example, Ecover, a Belgian company that produces cleaning products from natural soaps and renewable raw materials, operates a near-zero-emissions factory. This ecological factory is an environmentally sound engineering marvel with a huge grass roof that keeps the factory cool in summer and warm in winter, and a water treatment system that runs on wind and solar energy. The company chose to build this type of facility because of its deep commitment to protecting and preserving the environment. The activist approach is an illustration of corporate social responsibility that goes beyond the usual definition of responsibility.

Exhibit 5-3

Approaches to Sustainable Management

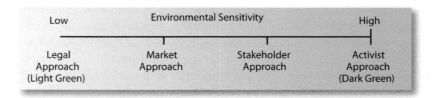

Source: Based on R. E. Freeman, J. Pierce, and R. Dodd, *Shades of Green: Business Ethics and the Environment* (New York: Oxford University Press, 1995).

Richard Kouwenhoven, manager of digital services of Burnaby, BC-based Hemlock Printers, founded by his father, has been one of the leaders in his generation's push to have the company, already known for its responsible management practices, become a leader in sustainable paper use.

Evaluating Sustainable Management

As organizations implement sustainable management practices, we find more and more of them issuing detailed reports on their environmental performance, many of them through the guidelines developed by the Global Reporting Initiative (GRI). Founded in 1997, the GRI is an independent entity that develops and disseminates globally applicable Sustainability Reporting Guidelines. Using G3 guidelines (reporting principles, reporting guidance, and standard disclosures), over 1000 organizations around the globe voluntarily report their efforts in promoting environmental sustainability. These reports, which can be found in the database on the GRI website, describe the numerous sustainable management practices these organizations are pursuing.

Another way that organizations can show their commitment to sustainable management practices is by adopting ISO standards. The nongovernmental ISO (International Organization for Standardization) is the world's largest developer of standards. Organizations that want to become ISO 14000 compliant must develop a total environmental management system for meeting environmental challenges. This means that the organization must minimize the effects of its activities on the environment and continually improve its environmental performance. The ISO 26000 social responsibility standards were released in November 2010. These standards provide guidance to business and public sector organizations on issues related to social responsibility. The ISO 26000 standards represent an international consensus on what social responsibility means and the issues that need to be addressed to implement it, based on broad stakeholder input, including developing countries, business, government, consumers, labour, and nongovernmental organizations.[45]

The final way to evaluate whether a company has incorporated sustainable management practices is by its inclusion in the list of the Global 100 Most Sustainable Corporations in the World, a project that was launched in 2005 as a collaboration between the Toronto-based media company Corporate Knights and the research firm Innovest Strategic Value Advisers. To be named to this list, a company must have displayed an ability to effectively manage environmental and social factors. The companies that comprise the Global 100 are announced each year at the renowned World Economic Forum in Davos, Switzerland. The Canadian companies on the 2010 list were Calgary-based Enbridge, TransCanada, Encana, Suncor Energy, and Nexen; Toronto-based Royal Bank of Canada, Toronto Dominion Bank, and Sun Life Financial; and Vancouver-based Telus.[46]

Values-Based Management

4. Understand the principles of values-based management.

▶ ▶ ▶ Interface practises values-based management. "Interface's values are our guiding principles."[47] As part of its values, the company is committed to sustainable management practices, with a zero carbon footprint as its goal. The company developed its model for sustainable business based on the "Seven Fronts of Mount Sustainability" and put in place a measurement framework, called Ecometrics, to monitor its progress and provide a framework that other organizations can use. Through its actions and deeds, Interface would like to not only demonstrate sustainable practices in all its dimensions—people, process, product, place, and profits—by 2020, but also become a "restorative" operation by returning more to the environment than it takes. As a first step, the organization strives to attain sustainability and a zero carbon footprint in its own business practices. To meet the higher goal of becoming a restorative business, it will work to help other organizations achieve sustainability. Interface believes that when stakeholders fully understand sustainability and the challenges that lie ahead, they will come together into a community of shared environmental and social goals.

Think About It

Do Interface's sustainable management practices create advantages for other companies? For society as a whole?

values-based management An approach to managing in which managers establish and uphold an organization's shared values.

Values-based management is an approach to managing in which managers establish and uphold an organization's shared values. An organization's values reflect what it stands for and what it believes in. As we discussed in Chapter 2, the shared organizational values form the organization's culture and serve many purposes.[48]

Vancouver-based Mountain Equipment Co-op (MEC) practises values-based management. MEC passionately pursues environmental preservation. Its strong environmental commitment influences employees' actions and decisions in areas such as product design, manufacturing, marketing, shipping, and store design. For instance, in designing its store in Montreal, the company favoured using recycled building materials.[49] Although contractors quoted cheaper prices for using new material, MEC held out, to be consistent with the company's values.

When Mountain Equipment Co-op opened its first Montreal store in 2003, the building was the first in Quebec to meet Natural Resource Canada's C-2000 standard. The store is much more energy efficient than conventional retail buildings. The building was made with reused building materials, and water for toilet flushing and landscape irrigation comes from roof water runoff. MEC has a high commitment to social and environmental responsibility, and its products come from factories that meet high labour, health, and safety standards.

Purposes of Shared Values

Exhibit 5-4 shows the four purposes of shared organizational values. One purpose is to guide managers' decisions and actions.[50] For instance, at Tom's of Maine, a manufacturer of all-natural personal care products, the corporate Statement of Beliefs guides managers as they plan, organize, lead, and control. One of the company's eight beliefs states, "We believe that different people bring different gifts and perspectives to the team and that a strong team is founded on a variety of gifts."[51] This statement expresses to managers the value of diversity—diversity of opinions, diversity of abilities—and serves as a guide for managing teams of people. Another belief states, "We believe in products that are safe, effective, and made of natural ingredients." Again, think how this statement might influence and guide company managers.

A second purpose of shared values is to shape employee behaviour by communicating what the organization expects of its members. Shared values also influence marketing efforts. Finally, shared values are a way to build team spirit in an organization.[52] When employees embrace the stated organizational values, they develop a deeper personal commitment to their work and feel obligated to take responsibility for their actions. Because the shared values influence the way work is done, employees become more enthusiastic about working together as a team to support the values they believe in. At companies such as Bolton, Ontario-based Husky Injection Molding, Vancouver-based Weyerhaeuser, Vancouver-based Vancity, Toronto-based Home Depot Canada, and numerous others, employees know what is expected of them on the job. The shared organizational values not only guide the way they work, but serve to unite them in a common quest. Just how do shared organizational values affect employee actions? They can promote employee loyalty in a hot job market, as the following *Management Reflection* shows.

MyManagementLab
Q&A 5.5

MANAGEMENT REFLECTION ► Focus on Ethics

Pacific Insight Electronics Values Its Employees

Can strong corporate values make a difference? With a strong economy and a shortage of workers throughout British Columbia, it's not easy for companies to attract or retain employees.[53] But Nelson, BC-based Pacific Insight Electronics (PI) has no trouble finding people who want to work for the company. PI finished at number 11 in *BCBusiness*'s Top 25 Best Companies to Work For in BC in 2006.

Employees praise the company for its strong corporate values related to "teamwork, respect, integrity, productivity and communication." The company is also praised for living by the Golden Rule: "Treat people how you want to be treated," says human resource manager Amanda Laurie.

Exhibit 5-4

Purposes of Shared Values

Employees receive birthdays off with pay, turkeys at Thanksgiving, and Christmas parties, which all help support the idea that they are treated well. The company also tries to provide flexibility for employees' personal needs by offering full- and part-time work. They also have a parent shift for those who need more options to manage their family lives. Even student schedules are considered. "We hire students for the summer, hire them back at Christmas . . . we work around their courses," says Laurie.

The company has a policy of promoting from within. Employees may start as production assistants, but they can advance to any number of other positions over time. "We have a lot of career paths," says Laurie.

Ultimately, PI's strong corporate values have contributed to the company's success. In 2006, the company doubled the previous year's earnings, achieving a record profit of $2.9 million. ■

Managerial Ethics

5. Discuss current ethics issues.

▶ ▶ ▶ Like many companies today, Interface has an ethics policy. The policy affirms the company's intention to act ethically in all its dealings. Employees and associates are expected to

- Engage in and promote honest and ethical conduct, including the ethical handling of actual or apparent conflicts of interest between personal and professional relationships

- Comply with applicable governmental laws, rules, and regulations

- Be committed to the full, fair, accurate, timely, and understandable disclosure in reports and documents that the Company files

- Promptly report any possible violation of this Code to the appropriate person or persons

Among the most common conflicts of interest at Interface are doing business with relatives, misuse of business time, competition with Interface, acceptance of gifts, illegal or improper payments, corporate opportunities, investment in other entities, and misuse of confidential information (insider trading).[54]

Think About It

Managers—at all levels, in all areas, and in all kinds of organizations—will face ethical issues and dilemmas. As managers plan, organize, lead, and control, they must consider ethical dimensions. How might an ethics policy provide guidance to employees, managers, leaders, and stakeholders?

ethics Rules and principles that define right and wrong behaviour.

What do we mean by ethics? As you may recall from Chapter 1, **ethics** refers to rules and principles that define right and wrong behaviour.[55] In this section, we examine the ethical dimensions of managerial decisions. Many decisions that managers make require them to consider who may be affected—in terms of the result as well as the process.[56] To better understand the complicated issues involved in managerial ethics, we look at four different views of ethics and the factors that influence a person's ethics, and offer some suggestions for what organizations can do to improve the ethical behaviour of employees.

MyManagementLab
Q&A 5.6

Four Views of Ethics

There are four views of ethics: the utilitarian view, the rights view, the theory of justice view, and the integrative social contracts theory.[57]

The Utilitarian View of Ethics

utilitarian view of ethics A view of ethics that says that ethical decisions are made solely on the basis of their outcomes or consequences.

The **utilitarian view of ethics** says that ethical decisions are made solely on the basis of their outcomes or consequences. Utilitarian theory uses a quantitative method for making ethical decisions by looking at how to provide the greatest good for the greatest number. Following the utilitarian view, a manager might conclude that laying off 20 percent of the workforce in her plant is justified because it will increase the plant's profitability, improve job security for the remaining 80 percent, and be in the best interest of stockholders. Utilitarianism encourages efficiency and productivity and is consistent with the goal of profit maximization. However, it can result in biased allocations of resources, especially when some of those affected by the decision lack representation or a voice in the decision. Utilitarianism can also result in the rights of some stakeholders being ignored.

The Rights View of Ethics

The **rights view of ethics** is concerned with respecting and protecting individual liberties and privileges such as the rights to privacy, freedom of conscience, free speech, life and safety, and due process. This would include, for example, protecting the free speech rights of employees who report legal violations by their employers. The positive side of the rights perspective is that it protects individuals' basic rights, but the drawback is that it can hinder productivity and efficiency by creating a work climate that is more concerned with protecting individuals' rights than with getting the job done. For instance, an individual's right to privacy might make it difficult to make special arrangements for employees who have an illness that prevents them from carrying out all their job responsibilities.

rights view of ethics A view of ethics that is concerned with respecting and protecting individual liberties and privileges.

The Theory of Justice View of Ethics

According to the **theory of justice view of ethics**, managers impose and enforce rules fairly and impartially and do so by following all legal rules and regulations. A manager following this view would decide to provide the same rate of pay to individuals who are similar in their levels of skills, performance, or responsibility and not base that decision on arbitrary differences such as gender, personality, race, or personal favourites. Using standards of justice also has pluses and minuses. It protects the interests of those stakeholders who may be underrepresented or lack power, but it can encourage a sense of entitlement that might make employees reduce risk-taking, innovation, and productivity.

theory of justice view of ethics A view of ethics in which managers impose and enforce rules fairly and impartially and do so by following all legal rules and regulations.

The Integrative Social Contracts Theory

The **integrative social contracts theory** proposes that ethical decisions be based on existing ethical norms in industries and communities in order to determine what constitutes right and wrong. This view of ethics is based on the integration of two "contracts": the general social contract that allows businesses to operate and defines the acceptable ground rules, and a more specific contract among members of a community that addresses acceptable ways of behaving. For instance, in deciding what wage to pay employees in a new factory in Ciudad Juarez, Mexico, Canadian managers following the integrative social contracts theory would base the decision on existing wage levels in the community, rather than paying what Canadians might consider a "fair wage" in that situation. Although this theory focuses on looking at existing practices, the problem is that some of these practices may be unethical.[58] Which approach to ethics do most businesspeople follow? Not surprisingly, most follow the utilitarian approach.[59] Why? It's consistent with such business goals as efficiency, productivity, and profits. However, that perspective needs to change because the world facing managers is changing. Trends toward individual rights, social justice, and community standards mean that managers need ethical standards based on nonutilitarian criteria. This is an obvious challenge for managers because making decisions on such criteria involves far more ambiguities than using utilitarian criteria such as efficiency and profits. The result, of course, is that managers increasingly find themselves struggling with the question of the right thing to do. The *CBC Video Case Incident—Stem Cell Research* on page 534 looks at some of the ethical questions surrounding stem cell research.

integrative social contracts theory A view of ethics that proposes that ethical decisions be based on existing ethical norms in industries and communities in order to determine what constitutes right and wrong.

Factors That Affect Employee Ethics

Whether a person acts ethically or unethically when faced with an ethical dilemma is the result of complex interactions between his or her stage of moral development and several moderating variables, including individual characteristics, the organization's structural design, organizational culture, and the intensity of the ethical issue (see Exhibit 5-5). People who lack a strong moral sense are much less likely to do the wrong things if they are constrained by rules, policies, job descriptions, or strong cultural norms that disapprove of such behaviours. Conversely, intensely moral individuals can be corrupted by an organizational structure and culture that permits or encourages unethical practices. Let's look more closely at the factors that influence whether individuals will behave ethically or unethically.

Stage of Moral Development

Research confirms the existence of three levels of moral development, each composed of two stages.[60] At each successive stage, an individual's moral judgment becomes less and less dependent on outside influences. The three levels and six stages are described in Exhibit 5-6.

Exhibit 5-5

Factors That Affect Ethical and Unethical Behaviour

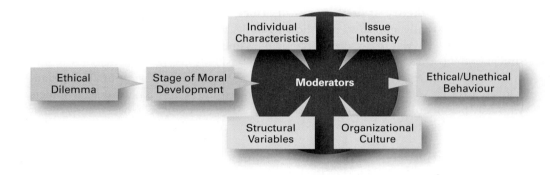

Exhibit 5-6

Stages of Moral Development

Level		Description of Stage
	Principled	6. Following self-chosen ethical principles even if they violate the law
		5. Valuing rights of others and upholding absolute values and rights regardless of the majority's opinion
	Conventional	4. Maintaining conventional order by fulfilling obligations to which you have agreed
		3. Living up to what is expected by people close to you
Preconventional		2. Following rules only when doing so is in your immediate interest
		1. Sticking to rules to avoid physical punishment

Source: Based on L. Kohlberg, "Moral Stages and Moralization: The Cognitive-Development Approach," in *Moral Development and Behavior: Theory, Research, and Social Issues*, ed. T. Lickona (New York: Holt, Rinehart & Winston, 1976), pp. 34–35.

The first level is labelled *preconventional.* At this level, a person's choice between right and wrong is based on the personal consequences involved, such as physical punishment, reward, or exchange of favours. Ethical reasoning at the *conventional* level indicates that moral values reside in maintaining expected standards and living up to the expectations of others. At the *principled* level, individuals make a clear effort to define ethical principles apart from the authority of the groups to which they belong or society in general.

We can draw some conclusions from research on the levels and stages of moral development.[61] First, people proceed through the six stages sequentially. They move up the moral ladder, stage by stage. Second, there is no guarantee of continued moral development. An individual's moral development can stop at any stage. Third, the majority of adults are at stage 4. They are limited to obeying the rules and will be inclined to behave ethically, although for different reasons. For instance, a manager at stage 3 is likely to make decisions that will receive peer approval; a manager at stage 4 will try to be a "good corporate citizen" by making decisions that respect the organization's rules and procedures; and a stage 5 manager is likely to challenge organizational practices that he or she believes to be wrong.

Individual Characteristics

Every person joining an organization has a relatively entrenched set of **values**. Our values—developed at a young age from parents, teachers, friends, and others—represent basic convictions about what is right and wrong. Thus, managers in the same organization often possess very different personal values.[62] Although *values* and *stage of moral development* may seem similar, they are not. Values are broad and cover a wide range of issues; the stage of moral development is a measure of independence from outside influences.

Two personality variables also have been found to influence an individual's actions according to his or her beliefs about what is right or wrong: ego strength and locus of control. **Ego strength** is a personality measure of the strength of a person's convictions. People who score high on ego strength are likely to resist impulses to act unethically and instead follow their convictions. That is, individuals high in ego strength are more likely to do what they think is right. We would expect employees with high ego strength to be more consistent in their moral judgments and actions than those with low ego strength.

Locus of control is a personality attribute that reflects the degree to which people believe they control their own fate. People with an *internal* locus of control believe that they control their own destinies; those with an *external* locus believe that what happens to them is due to luck or chance. How does this influence a person's decision to act ethically or unethically? Externals are less likely to take personal responsibility for the consequences of their behaviour and are more likely to rely on external forces to guide their actions. Internals, on the other hand, are more likely to take responsibility for consequences and rely on their own internal standards of right and wrong to guide their actions.[63] Also, employees with an internal locus of control are likely to be more consistent in their moral judgments and actions than those with an external locus of control.

Structural Variables

An organization's structural design influences whether employees behave ethically. Some structures provide strong guidance, whereas others create ambiguity and uncertainty. Structural designs that minimize ambiguity and uncertainty through formal rules and regulations and those that continuously remind employees of what is ethical are more likely to encourage ethical behaviour.

Other organizational mechanisms that influence ethics include performance appraisal systems and reward allocation procedures. Some organizational performance appraisal systems focus exclusively on outcomes, such as number of sales. Others evaluate means as well as ends, such as how customer-oriented employees are when customers speak with them. When employees are evaluated only on outcomes, they may be pressured to do "whatever is necessary" to look good on the outcome variables and not be concerned with how they got those results. Recent research suggests that "success may serve to excuse unethical behaviors."[64] Just think of the impact of this type of thinking. The danger is that,

values Basic convictions about what is right and wrong.

ego strength A personality measure of the strength of a person's convictions.

locus of control A personality attribute that reflects the degree to which people believe they control their own fate.

if managers take a more lenient view of unethical behaviours for successful employees, other employees will model their behaviour on what they see.

Closely associated with the performance appraisal system is the way rewards are allocated. The more that rewards or punishments depend on specific goal outcomes, the more pressure there is on employees to do whatever they must to reach those goals and perhaps compromise their ethical standards. Although these structural factors are important influences on employees, they are not the most important. What *is* the most important?

Research continues to show that the behaviour of managers is the single most important influence on an individual's decision to act ethically or unethically.[65] People look to see what those in authority are doing and use that as a benchmark for acceptable practices and expectations.

Organizational Culture

MyManagementLab
Q&A 5.7

The content and strength of an organization's culture also influence ethical behaviour.[66] An organizational culture most likely to encourage high ethical standards is one that is high in risk tolerance, control, and conflict tolerance. Employees in such a culture are encouraged to be aggressive and innovative, are aware that unethical practices will be discovered, and feel free to openly challenge expectations they consider to be unrealistic or personally undesirable.

As we discussed in Chapter 2, a strong culture will exert more influence on employees than a weak one. If the culture is strong and supports high ethical standards, it has a very powerful and positive influence on an employee's decision to act ethically or unethically. The Boeing Company, for example, has a strong culture that has long stressed ethical dealings with customers, employees, the community, and stockholders. To reinforce the importance of ethical behaviours, the company developed a series of serious and thought-provoking posters designed to get employees to recognize that their individual decisions and actions are important to the way the organization is viewed.

Issue Intensity

A student who would never consider breaking into an instructor's office to steal an accounting exam does not think twice about asking a friend who took the same course from the same instructor last semester what questions were on the exam. Similarly, a manager might think nothing about taking home a few office supplies yet be highly concerned about the possible embezzlement of company funds.

The Boeing Company's imaginative poster series reinforces the core values of integrity and ethical behaviour for its employees.

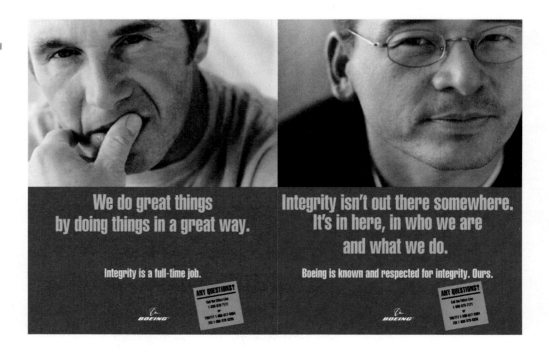

These examples illustrate the final factor that affects a manager's ethical behaviour: the intensity of the ethical issue itself.[67] As Exhibit 5-7 shows, six characteristics determine issue intensity: greatness of harm, consensus of wrong, probability of harm, immediacy of consequences, proximity to victim(s), and concentration of effect.[68] These six factors determine how important an ethical issue is to an individual. According to these guidelines, the larger the number of people harmed, the more agreement that the action is wrong, the greater the likelihood that the action will cause harm, the more immediately that the consequences of the action will be felt, the closer the person feels to the victim(s), and the more concentrated the effect of the action on the victim(s), the greater the issue intensity. When an ethical issue is important—that is, the more intense it is—the more we should expect employees to behave ethically.

Ethics in an International Context

Are ethical standards universal? Hardly! Social and cultural differences between countries are important factors that determine ethical and unethical behaviour. For example, the manager of a Mexican firm bribes several high-ranking government officials in Mexico City to secure a profitable government contract. Such a practice would be seen as unethical, if not illegal, in Canada, but is standard business practice in Mexico.

MyManagementLab
Q&A 5.8

Should Canadian companies operating in Saudi Arabia adhere to Canadian ethical standards, or should they follow local standards of acceptable behaviour? If Airbus (a European company) pays a "broker's fee" to a middleman to get a major contract with a Middle Eastern airline, should Montreal-based Bombardier be restricted from doing the same because such practices are considered improper in Canada?

In Canada and many other Western countries, engaging in bribery to conduct business in one's home country is considered unethical and often illegal. Bribing foreign public officials is widespread, however. The US government found bribery in more than 400 competitions for international contracts between 1994 and 2001.[69] Another study found that some Asian governments were far more tolerant of corruption than others. Singapore, Japan, and Hong Kong scored relatively low on corruption (0.83, 2.5, and 3.77 out of 10,

Exhibit 5-7

Determinants of Issue Intensity

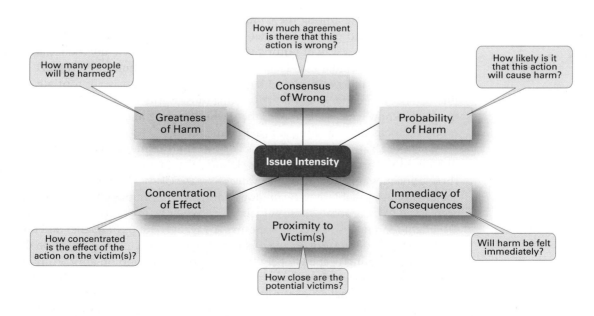

TIPS FOR MANAGERS

The Global Compact

Human Rights

Principle 1: Businesses should support and respect the protection of international human rights within their sphere of influence; and

Principle 2: make sure that they are not complicit in human rights abuses.

Labour Standards

Principle 3: Businesses should uphold the freedom of association and the effective recognition of the right to collective bargaining;

Principle 4: the elimination of all forms of forced and compulsory labour;

Principle 5: the effective abolition of child labour; and

Principle 6: the elimination of discrimination in respect of employment and occupation.

Environment

Principle 7: Businesses should support a precautionary approach to environmental challenges;

Principle 8: undertake initiatives to promote greater environmental responsibility; and

Principle 9: encourage the development and diffusion of environmentally friendly technologies.

Anti-Corruption

Principle 10: Businesses should work against corruption in all its forms, including extortion and bribery.

Source: United Nations Global Compact website, 2010 guidance documents on anti-corruption at http://www.unglobalcompact.org/Issues/transparency_anticorruption/Anti-Corruption_Guidance_Material.html (accessed November 11, 2010).

respectively), while Vietnam, Indonesia, India, the Philippines, and Thailand scored as the most corrupt of the 12 Asian countries surveyed.[70]

Canada has no national laws regarding codes of ethics, although a coalition of Canadian companies developed an international code of ethics in 1997.[71] The code is voluntary and deals with issues such as the environment, human rights, business conduct, treatment of employees, and health and safety standards. Supporters of the Canadian code include the Alliance of Manufacturers & Exporters Canada, the Conference Board of Canada, and the Canadian Council of Chief Executives (formerly the Business Council on National Issues). Montreal-based Rio Tinto Alcan, Calgary-based Komex International, Shell Canada, and Talisman Energy are among the companies that have signed the code. Former foreign affairs minister and current president of the University of Winnipeg Lloyd Axworthy viewed the code as a way of putting Canadian values into the international arena.[72] It's important for individual managers working in foreign cultures to recognize the various social, cultural, and political and legal influences on what is appropriate and acceptable behaviour.[73] And global organizations must clarify their ethical guidelines so that employees know what is expected of them while working in a foreign location, which adds another dimension to making ethical judgments.

The United Nations Global Compact documents outline principles for doing business globally in the areas of human rights, labour, the environment, and anti-corruption.[74] These principles are listed in *Tips for Managers—The Global Compact*, above. (The complete documents are available at **www.unglobalcompact.org/Issues**.) Global organizations have been asked to incorporate these guidelines into their business activities. The goal: a more sustainable and inclusive global economy. Today, over 3000 companies and international labour organizations from all regions of the world participate in the Global Compact. At the sixth meeting of the Global Compact Working Group on anticorruption, in June 2010, members reviewed progress made toward full embracement of the 10th principle. Organizations that make a commitment to the Global Compact and its 10 principles do so because they believe that the world business community plays a significant role in improving economic and social conditions.

Improving Ethical Behaviour

Managers can do a number of things if they are serious about reducing unethical behaviour in their organizations. They can seek to hire individuals with high ethical standards, establish codes of ethics and rules for decisions, lead by example, delineate job goals and undertake performance appraisals, provide ethics training, conduct independent social audits, and support individuals facing ethical dilemmas. Taken individually, these actions will probably not have much impact. But when all or most of them are implemented as part of a comprehensive ethics program, they have the potential to significantly improve an organization's ethical climate. The key term here, however, is *potential*. There are no guarantees that a well-designed ethics program will lead to the desired outcome. Sometimes corporate ethics programs can be little more than public relations gestures, having minimal influence on managers and employees. For instance, retailer Sears has a long history of encouraging ethical business practices and, in fact, has a corporate Office of Compliance and Ethics. However, the company's ethics programs did not stop managers from illegally trying to collect payments from bankrupt charge-account holders or from routinely deceiving automotive service centre customers in California into thinking they needed unnecessary repairs. (To help you think more about your own ethics, see *Self-Assessment—How Do My Ethics Rate?* at the end of the chapter.)

Employee Selection

Given that individuals are at different stages of moral development and possess different personal value systems and personalities, the selection process—interviews, tests, background checks, and so forth—could be used to eliminate ethically questionable applicants. The selection process should be viewed as an opportunity to learn about an individual's level of moral development, personal values, ego strength, and locus of control.[75] But it isn't easy! Even under the best circumstances, individuals with questionable standards of right and wrong will be hired. However, this should not be a problem if other ethics controls are in place.

Codes of Ethics and Rules for Decisions

Toronto-based Royal Bank of Canada has had a corporate code of conduct for more than 25 years. Christina Donely, the bank's senior adviser on employee relations and policy governance, says that the code "focuses on outlining behaviours that support honesty and integrity . . . and covers environmental [and] social issues."[76] However, that is not the way it is in all organizations. The Canadian Securities Administrators put into effect best corporate governance practices in March 2004 to crack down on business wrongdoing in publicly traded companies.[77] As well, the securities regulators of the 10 provinces and 3 territories have proposed that all public companies adopt written codes of ethics and conduct or explain why they do not have one.[78] But these proposals carry no enforcement requirements or mechanisms.

Ambiguity about what is and is not ethical can be a problem for employees. A **code of ethics**, a formal statement of an organization's primary values and the ethical rules it expects its employees to follow, is a popular choice for reducing that ambiguity. About 60 percent of Canada's 650 largest corporations have some sort of ethics code. Codes of ethics are also becoming more popular globally. A survey of business organizations in 22 countries found that 78 percent have formally stated ethics standards and codes of ethics.[79]

code of ethics A formal statement of an organization's primary values and the ethical rules it expects its employees to follow.

What should a code of ethics look like? It's been suggested that codes should be specific enough to show employees the spirit in which they are supposed to do things yet loose enough to allow for freedom of judgment.[80] A survey of companies' codes of ethics found their content tended to fall into three categories: (1) Be a dependable organizational citizen; (2) don't do anything unlawful or improper that will harm the organization; and (3) be good to customers.[81]

How well do codes of ethics work? In reality, they are not always effective in encouraging ethical behaviour in organizations. While no comparable Canadian data are available, a survey of employees in US businesses with ethics codes found that 75 percent of those surveyed had observed ethical or legal violations in the previous 12 months, including such things as deceptive sales practices, unsafe working conditions, sexual harassment, conflicts of interest, and environmental violations.[82] These findings suggest that companies with codes of ethics may not do enough monitoring. For instance, David Nitkin, president of Toronto-based EthicScan Canada, an ethics consultancy, notes that "only about 15% of [larger Canadian corporations with codes of ethics] have designated an ethics officer or ombudsman" or provide an ethics hotline and that less than 10 percent offer whistle-blower protection.[83] Whistle-blowing protection refers to provisions designed to encourage employees to report evidence essential for industry regulation and the prosecution of corporate wrongdoers by facilitating regulation and enforcement of laws. The 2009 UN Global Compact report *Reporting Guidance on the 10th Principle Against Corruption* provides businesses and organizations with a practical guideline for whistle-blowing effectively, as public reporting sends a strong signal to employees, investors, and consumers that a company is serious about ethical business practices.[84] Vancouver public employees were concerned enough about whistle-blower protection that it was one of the major stumbling blocks in reaching an agreement for a new collective agreement in summer 2007, leading to a 12-week strike.

Does this mean that codes of ethics should not be developed? No. But there are some suggestions managers can follow. First, an organization's code of ethics should be developed and then communicated clearly to employees. Second, all levels of management should continually affirm the importance of the code of ethics and the organization's commitment to it and consistently discipline those who break it. When managers consider the code of ethics important, regularly affirm its content, and publicly reprimand rule breakers, a code of ethics can supply a strong foundation for an effective corporate ethics program.[85] Finally, an organization's code of ethics might be designed around the 12 questions listed in Exhibit 5-8, which can be used to guide managers as they handle ethical dilemmas in decision making.[86]

Ethical Leadership

Doing business ethically requires a commitment from top managers. Why? Because it's the top managers who uphold the shared values and set the cultural tone. They are role models in terms of both words and actions, although what they *do* is far more important than what they *say*. If top managers, for example, take company resources for their personal use, inflate their expense accounts, or give favoured treatment to friends, they imply that such behaviour is acceptable for all employees. (To learn more about how trust works, see *Developing Your Interpersonal Skills—Building Trust* on pages 149–150.)

Top managers also set the cultural tone by their reward and punishment practices. The choices of who and what are rewarded with pay increases and promotions send a strong signal to employees. As we said earlier, when an employee is rewarded for achieving impressive results in an ethically questionable manner, it indicates to others that those ways are acceptable. When wrongdoing is uncovered, managers who want to emphasize their commitment to doing business ethically must punish the offender and publicize the fact by making the outcome visible to everyone in the organization. This practice sends a message that doing wrong has a price and it's not in employees' best interests to act unethically!

A 2002 ethics survey by KPMG found that 82 percent of Canadian organizations had initiatives that promoted ethical practices and about 56 percent had a senior manager responsible for handling ethical issues.[87]

Job Goals and Performance Appraisal

Employees in three Internal Revenue Service offices (the American equivalent of the Canada Revenue Agency) were found in the washrooms flushing tax returns and other related documents down the toilets. When questioned, they openly admitted doing it, but offered an interesting explanation for their behaviour. The employees' supervisors had been putting increasing pressure on them to complete more work in less time. If the piles

Exhibit 5-8

12 Questions Examining the Ethics of a Business Decision

1. Have you defined the problem accurately?

2. How would you define the problem if you stood on the other side of the fence?

3. How did this situation occur in the first place?

4. To whom and to what do you give your loyalty as a person and as a member of the corporation?

5. What is your intention in making this decision?

6. How does this intention compare with the probable results?

7. Whom could your decision or action injure?

8. Can you discuss the problem with the affected parties before you make the decision?

9. Are you confident that your position will be as valid over a long period of time as it seems now?

10. Could you disclose without qualm your decision or action to your boss, your chief executive officer, the board of directors, your family, society as a whole?

11. What is the symbolic potential of your action if understood? If misunderstood?

12. Under what conditions would you allow exceptions to your stand?

Source: Reprinted by permission of *Harvard Business Review.* An exhibit from "Ethics Without the Sermon" by L. L. Nash. November–December 1981, p. 81. Copyright © 1981 by the President and Fellows of Harvard College. All rights reserved.

of tax returns were not processed and moved off their desks more quickly, they were told, their performance reviews and salary raises would be adversely affected. Frustrated by few resources and an overworked computer system, the employees decided to "flush away" the paperwork on their desks. Although these employees knew what they did was wrong, it illustrates the impact of unrealistic goals and performance appraisals on behaviour.[88] Under the stress of unrealistic job goals, otherwise ethical employees may feel they have no choice but to do whatever is necessary to meet those goals.

Whether an individual achieves his or her job goals is usually a key issue in performance appraisal. Keep in mind, though, that if performance appraisals focus only on economic goals, ends will begin to justify means. If an organization wants its employees to uphold high ethical standards, the performance appraisal process should include this dimension. For example, a manager's annual review of employees might include a point-by-point evaluation of how their decisions measured up against the company's code of ethics, as well as how well job goals were met.

Ethical leadership starts with being a good role model. When Michael McCain, CEO of Maple Leaf Foods, learned of a listeriosis outbreak in one of the company's plants, he immediately took personal and organizational responsibility for the problem rather than trying to deflect the responsibility.

Ethics Training

More and more organizations are setting up seminars, workshops, and similar ethics training programs to encourage ethical behaviour. A 2002 ethics survey by KPMG found that 71 percent of Canadian corporations provided ethics training (up from 21 percent in 1997), although most provided fewer than eight hours per year.[89] But these training programs are not without controversy. The primary debate is whether you can actually teach ethics. Critics, for instance, stress that the effort is pointless because people establish their individual value systems when they are young. Proponents, however, note that several studies have found that values can be learned after early childhood. In addition, they cite evidence that shows that teaching ethical problem solving can make an actual difference in ethical behaviours;[90] that training has increased individuals' level of moral development;[91] and that, if it does nothing else, ethics training increases awareness of ethical issues in business.[92]

Ethics training sessions can provide a number of benefits.[93] They reinforce the organization's standards of conduct. They are a reminder that top managers want employees to consider ethical issues in making decisions. They clarify what practices are and are not acceptable. Finally, when employees discuss common concerns among themselves, they get reassurance that they are not alone in facing ethical dilemmas, which can strengthen their confidence when they have to take unpopular but ethically correct stances.

Independent Social Audits

An important element of deterring unethical behaviour is the fear of being caught. Independent social audits, which evaluate decisions and management practices in terms of the organization's code of ethics, increase the likelihood of detection. These social audits can be routine evaluations, performed on a regular basis just as financial audits are, or they can occur randomly with no prior announcement. An effective ethical program should probably have both. To maintain integrity, auditors should be responsible to the company's board of directors and present their findings directly to the board. This arrangement gives the auditors clout and lessens the opportunity for retaliation from those being audited.

Formal Protective Mechanisms

Our last recommendation is for organizations to provide formal mechanisms to protect employees who face ethical dilemmas so that they can do what is right without fear of reprimand. An organization might designate ethics counsellors. When employees face an

Chief Superintendent Fraser Macaulay was one of several RCMP officers who complained to Giuliano Zaccardelli, then RCMP commissioner, about how problems with the RCMP's pension and insurance plans were investigated. Consistent with the way many whistle-blowers are treated, Zaccardelli did not follow up with an investigation, and Macaulay was told that he "was on an island by [him]self."

ethics dilemma, they could go to these advisers for guidance. As a sounding board, the ethics counsellor would let employees openly state their ethics problem, the problem's cause, and their own options. After the options are clear, the adviser might take on the role of advocate who champions the ethically "right" alternatives. Other organizations have appointed ethics officers who design, direct, and modify the organization's ethics programs as needed.

It is important that managers assure employees who raise ethical concerns or issues to others inside or outside the organization that they will face no personal or career risks. These individuals, often called **whistle-blowers**, can be a key part of any company's ethics program because they are willing to step forward and expose unethical behaviour, no matter what the cost, professional or personal. Former prime minister Paul Martin tabled the Public Servants Disclosure Protection Act in March 2004 to protect those who expose government wrongdoings and financial mismanagement. Many critics complained that the act does not go far enough to protect whistle-blowers and hoped Parliament would have tabled a tougher bill.

whistle-blowers Individuals who raise ethical concerns or issues to others inside or outside the organization.

SUMMARY AND IMPLICATIONS

1. Understand what it means to be a socially responsible manager. We define corporate social responsibility as a business's obligation, beyond that required by law and economics, to pursue long-term goals that are good for society. Not everyone would agree that businesses have any responsibility to society. The classical view says that management's only responsibility is to maximize profits; stockholders, or owners, are the only legitimate concern. The socio-economic view says that management's responsibility goes beyond maximizing profits; any group affected by the organization's decisions and actions—that is, its stakeholders—are also its concern.

▶ ▶ ▶ Interface takes a socio-economic view toward corporate social responsibility. The company emphasizes being a good corporate citizen and helping to develop sustainable practices among its employees, suppliers, and competitors.

2. Describe how managing responsibly contributes to organizational performance. Some evidence suggests that socially responsible firms perform better, and they are certainly appreciated by many members of society. There is little evidence to say that a company's social actions hurt its long-term economic performance. Given political and societal pressures on business to be socially involved, managers would be wise to take social goals into consideration as they plan, organize, lead, and control.

▶ ▶ ▶ Interface has been able to be a successful company, even as it supports a socially responsible approach to doing business. "Our costs are down, our profits are up, and our products are the best they've ever been. It has rewarded us with more positive visibility and goodwill among our customers than the slickest, most expensive advertising or marketing campaign could possibly have generated. And a strong environmental ethic has no equal for attracting and motivating good people, galvanizing them around a shared higher purpose, and giving them a powerful reason to join and stay."[94]

3. Identify sustainable management practices. One model of environmental responsibility uses the phrase *shades of green* to describe the different approaches that organizations take to becoming environmentally responsible. Organizations that follow a *legal* (or *light green*) *approach* simply do what is required legally. Organizations that follow a *market approach* respond to the environmental preferences of their customers. Organizations that follow a *stakeholder approach* work to meet the environmental demands of multiple stakeholders such as employees, suppliers, and the community. Organizations that follow an *activist* (also called a *dark green*) *approach* look for ways to respect and preserve the earth and its natural resources.

▶ ▶ ▶ Interface's sustainable practices include a commitment to eliminate all forms of waste in every area of business, reduce and eliminate greenhouse gases, and operate facilities with renewable energy sources. Interface's goal is to ensure that by 2020, all fuels and electricity to operate manufacturing, sales, and office facilities will be from renewable sources. Products and processes have been redesigned to reduce and simplify the amount of resources used, so that material "waste" is remanufactured into new resources, providing technical "nutrients" for the next cycle of production.

4. Understand the principles of values-based management. An organization's values reflect what it stands for and what it believes in. Thus, an organization's values are reflected in the decisions and actions of employees. Shared values form an organization's culture and serve to (a) guide managers' decisions and actions, (b) shape employee behaviour, (c) influence marketing efforts, and (d) build team spirit.

▶ ▶ ▶ Interface not only talks the talk, it walks the walk. The corporate website provides a rich history of the journey up "Mount Sustainability" and shares the details of the journey with employees, stakeholders, suppliers, and competitors.[95]

5. Discuss current ethics issues. Ethics refers to rules and principles that define right and wrong behaviour. Ethical behaviour is encouraged (or discouraged) through organizational culture. A strong culture that supports ethical standards will have a powerful and positive influence on managers and employees. To improve ethical behaviour, managers can hire individuals with high ethical standards, design and implement a code of ethics, lead by example, delineate job goals and undertake performance appraisals, provide ethics training, perform independent social audits, and provide formal protective mechanisms for employees who face ethical dilemmas.

▶ ▶ ▶ Interface, like many companies, has an ethics policy to help guide the decisions and actions of its employees. In addition, Interface has made a commitment to support communities that are committed to the shared journey to sustainability.[96]

Management @ Work

READING FOR COMPREHENSION

1. Contrast the classical and socio-economic views of social responsibility.

2. Describe the evolution of responsible management.

3. Can being socially responsible help organizational performance?

4. What are some sustainable management practices that you have seen being implemented?

5. What is values-based management?

6. How do the four views of ethics differ?

7. What factors affect the ethical and unethical behaviour of employees?

8. How can managers encourage ethical behaviour in their organizations?

LINKING CONCEPTS TO PRACTICE

1. What does social responsibility mean to you personally? Do you think business organizations should be socially responsible? Explain.

2. Do you think values-based management is just a "do-gooder" ploy? Explain your answer.

3. Internet file-sharing programs are popular among college and university students. These programs work by allowing anyone to access any local network where desired files are located. These programs can severely limit the use of local networks by those working at colleges and universities if many students are exchanging music and video files at any given time. There is also

some question about whether sharing copyrighted files is legal. What ethical and social responsibilities does a college or university have in this situation? To whom does it have a responsibility? What guidelines might you suggest for campus decision makers?

4. What are some problems that could be associated with employee whistle-blowing for (a) the whistle-blower and (b) the organization?

5. Describe the characteristics and behaviours of someone you consider an ethical person. How could the types of decisions and actions this person engages in be encouraged in a workplace?

SELF-ASSESSMENT

How Do My Ethics Rate?

For each of the following statements, circle the level of agreement or disagreement that you personally feel:[97]

1 = Strongly Agree 2 = Agree 3 = Uncertain 4 = Disagree 5 = Strongly Disagree

1. The only moral of business is making money. 1 2 3 4 5

2. A person who is doing well in business does not have to worry about moral problems. 1 2 3 4 5

3. Act according to the law, and you cannot go wrong morally. 1 2 3 4 5

4. Ethics in business is basically an adjustment between expectations and the ways people behave. 1 2 3 4 5

5. Business decisions involve a realistic economic attitude and not a moral philosophy. 1 2 3 4 5

6. "Business ethics" is a concept for public relations only. 1 2 3 4 5

7. Competitiveness and profitability are important values. 1 2 3 4 5

8. Conditions of a free economy will best serve the needs of society. Limiting competition can only hurt society and actually violates basic natural laws. 1 2 3 4 5

9. As a consumer, when making an auto insurance claim, I try to get as much as possible regardless of the extent of the damage. 1 2 3 4 5

10. While shopping at the supermarket, it is appropriate to switch price tags on packages. 1 2 3 4 5

11. As an employee, I can take home office supplies; it doesn't hurt anyone. 1 2 3 4 5

12. I view sick days as vacation days that I deserve. 1 2 3 4 5

13. Employees' wages should be determined according to the laws of supply and demand. 1 2 3 4 5

14. The business world has its own rules. 1 2 3 4 5

15. A good businessperson is a successful businessperson. 1 2 3 4 5

Scoring Key

Compare your scores on each statement against the mean (average) scores of management students (N = 243).

Analysis and Interpretation

In comparing your scores to those of the average of a set of management students, determine whether you score higher or lower than the average student. What does this say about your ethics compared to others?

Statement	Management Students Mean	Statement	Management Students Mean
1	3.09	9	3.44
2	1.88	10	1.33
3	2.54	11	1.58
4	3.41	12	2.31
5	3.88	13	3.36
6	2.88	14	3.79
7	3.62	15	3.38
8	3.79		

More Self-Assessments MyManagementLab

To learn more about your skills, abilities, and interests, go to the MyManagementLab website and take the following self-assessments:

- #4—I.B.1.—What Do I Value?
- #4—I.C.3.—What Rewards Do I Value Most? (This exercise also appears in Chapter 15 on pages 442–443.)
- #4—III.B.1.—What's the Right Organizational Culture for Me? (This exercise also appears in Chapter 2 on pages 63–64.)
- #4—IV.E.4.—Am I an Ethical Leader?

MANAGEMENT FOR YOU TODAY

Dilemma

What things are you willing to do in order to be a more socially responsible citizen? Are there things that would be easy for you to give up in order to help promote the use of less energy and less packaging? Are there things that you would not give up, even though doing so might mean a more green environment for others?

Becoming a Manager

- Clarify your own personal views on how much social responsibility you think an organization should have.
- Research different companies' codes of ethics.
- Think about the organizational values that are important to you.

- When faced with an ethical dilemma, use the 12 questions in Exhibit 5-8 on page 141 to help you make a decision.
- Work through the *Ethics in Action* dilemmas found in each chapter in this textbook.

Assessing Ethical and Unethical Behaviour

You have obviously already faced many ethical dilemmas in your life—at school, in social settings, and even at work. Form groups of three to five individuals. Appoint a spokesperson to present your group's findings to the class. Each member of the group is to think of some unethical behaviours he or she has observed in organizations. The incidents could be something experienced as an employee, customer, or client, or an action observed informally.

Once everyone has identified some examples of ethically questionable behaviours, the group should identify three important criteria that could be used to determine whether a particular action is ethical. Think carefully about these criteria. They should differentiate between ethical and unethical behaviour. Write your choices down. Use these criteria to assess the examples of unethical behaviour described by group members.

When asked by your professor, the spokesperson should be ready to describe several of the incidents of unethical behaviour witnessed by group members, your criteria for differentiating between ethical and unethical behaviour, and how you used these criteria for assessing these incidents.

Ethical Dilemma Exercise: Can an Environmental Organization Balance Its Values with Making Money?

The Sierra Club lobbies for stricter antipollution regulations, pushes companies to use more eco-friendly products and techniques, and leads wilderness trips to promote appreciation for nature.[98] In short, the Sierra Club goes well beyond bare-minimum legal requirements by pursuing an activist approach to preserving the earth for future generations.

To raise money for its mission, the not-for-profit recently began licensing its name for a broad array of products, including jackets, coffee, and toys. The organization receives royalties of 5 percent to 20 percent of each product's retail price, and the manufacturers must include environmental advocacy information with every item. "We can raise money even as we promote environmentally conscious consumption," explained the executive director.

Imagine you are a manager reporting to Johanna O'Kelley, Sierra Club's director of licensing. O'Kelley wants to increase the number of environmentally friendly products on which the club's name appears. You get a bonus for each positive recommendation you make, based on the retail price of the product. A manufacturer has just proposed a Sierra Club bed cover containing organically grown cotton and coloured with vegetable dyes. However, the cover will have to contain some synthetic fibres to keep threads of the filler from working their way through the top. Bed covers sell for a lot more money than the coffee mugs you recently recommended for the club's logo. Should you recommend that the bed cover be licensed? Review Exhibit 5-7 on page 137 as you think about this dilemma.

Thinking Critically About Ethics

In an effort to be (or at least appear to be) socially responsible, many organizations donate money to philanthropic and charitable causes. In addition, many organizations ask their employees to make individual donations to these causes. Suppose you are the manager of a work team, and you know that several of your employees cannot afford to pledge money right now because of various personal and financial problems. You have also been told by your supervisor that the CEO has been known to check the list of individual contributors to see who is and is not "supporting these very important causes." What would you do? What ethical guidelines might you suggest for individual and organizational contributions to philanthropic and charitable causes?

City of Ottawa

Many Ottawa residents and some city councillors were up in arms after Richard Hewitt, deputy city manager of Public Works and Services, and some councillors and city employees were spotted at an Ottawa Senators game during the 2007 playoff season.[99] Hewitt and the others were seated in a corporate box owned by Waste Management of Canada.

Waste Management owns a dump at Carp Road and wants to either expand the dump or build a new incinerator there. Changes to the Carp Road site need city hall approval. However, the plans are opposed by nearby residents, the mayor, and the councillors who live in wards near the dump.

Hewitt's department is in charge of garbage collection and disposal. While ultimate approval for what happens at Carp Road will come from Ontario's Ministry of the Environment, Hewitt is supposed to represent the city's interests in the landfill expansion application process. Concerned citizens wondered whether Waste Management offered the tickets to get favourable treatment from the city.

The City of Ottawa has a code of employee ethics that states, "Employees shall neither offer nor accept any gifts, favours, hospitality or entertainment that could reasonably be construed as being given in anticipation of future, or recognition of past, 'special consideration' by the city."

Is accepting hockey playoff tickets a violation of this policy? Some citizens and councillors spoke out:

- "Sounds like a conflict of interest to me. It looks as if they're accepting a bribe. It doesn't look good," said Vivian Katz, a local citizen.

- "I think they should be able to take a break from their stressful jobs, I don't see a conflict of interest," said Steve Birk, a local citizen.

- "The city's code of conduct says staff aren't supposed to receive benefits from the people we do business with. It's clear, and I think accepting valuable, hard-to-get playoff tickets is a clear violation of the code," said Alex Cullen, a city councillor.

Hewitt defended his behaviour, however. "I feel I am in line with the city policy. I try to be cognizant of the policy on all occasions. There's a certain business element to these situations."

The city's ethics policy outlines possible exceptions to the general guidelines to not accept gifts: "Hospitality may be acceptable within strict limits as a part of some reciprocal business relationships or to develop a network which is of benefit to the city. An employee may pay for or accept customary business hospitality, such as meals." The policy cautions that entertainment activities must "clearly be seen as legitimately serving a definite business purpose," and be "appropriately related to the responsibilities of the individual."

Hewitt and the city staff who were at the game are governed by the city's ethics policy. Councillors, however, are not. There was widespread disagreement about whether councillors should be covered by the policy. Councillors Clive Doucet, Diane Holmes, and Rainer Bloess argued that the rules should apply to staff and councillors alike. "What's good for the goose is good for the gander," Bloess said.

Mayor Larry O'Brien suggested that elected officials needed more leeway, however. He feared that a strict policy might discourage corporations from sponsoring city events. He noted that earlier in the year he had been in a company's luxury box for a Senators game. Later in the year, he phoned that company, which then paid for the big-screen televisions that were installed in Sens Plaza outside city hall for the Stanley Cup playoff games. Citizens benefited by being able to watch the games in an enjoyable setting.

"Businesses do wonderful things for this community, and I think all councillors want to clarify the issues surrounding ethics," O'Brien said. "But we don't want to cut off our noses to spite our faces." Councillor Holmes disagrees. "Accepting things creates an obligation to return the favour. It's just human nature."

Are playoff tickets part of "the normal course of business"? Do such gifts influence a manager's decisions? Should elected officials be allowed to accept gifts of substantial value, and under what circumstances?

The Responsible Organization

Lynn Patterson is Director of Corporate Responsibility for the Royal Bank of Canada (RBC), a major Canadian corporation that has embraced "responsibility" as a core value within the framework of corporate citizenship. RBC has more than 15 million clients in 38 countries and employs over 70 000 people globally.[100]

RBC has a fundamental belief that corporate responsibility isn't only about how a company spends its money—it's also about how a company makes its money. According to the company's website, "Our goal is to be a responsible bank, acting with integrity every day and charting a stable course so that we are there for our clients, shareholders, employees and communities, today and tomorrow."

RBC's 2009 Corporate Responsibility Report and Public Accountability Statement identifies the four key elements of its corporate responsibility strategy: (1) generate a positive economic impact, (2) create a workplace of choice, (3) support community causes, and (4) promote environmental sustainability.

Lynn Patterson has a background in communications and is the public face for the bank's responsibility policy for consumers, investors, the press, and the public at large. In her presentations to shareholders and the public, Patterson points out that in 2000, RBC was the first Canadian bank to be named to the Dow Jones Sustainability Index. In 2003, RBC was the first Canadian bank to adopt the equator principles, which assess the social and environmental impacts of large-scale project finance deals, and in 2007, it was the only Canadian bank to be named one of the Global 100 Most Sustainable Corporations in the World.

Questions

1. Is RBC a responsible organization?

2. What is your best guess as to the initial reaction to this change in policy from clients, branch managers, the investment community, and activists?

3. Identify both the business case for acting responsibly and the ethical case for acting responsibly.

Building Trust

About the Skill

When individuals evaluate companies for their social responsibility policies, trust plays an important role in how the company is viewed. Trust is also important in the manager's relationships with his or her employees. Given the importance of trust, managers should actively seek to foster it within their work group.

Steps in Developing the Skill

You can be more effective at building trust among your employees if you use the following eight suggestions:[101]

1. **Practise openness.** Mistrust comes as much from what people don't know as from what they do. Being open with employees leads to trust. Keep people informed. Make clear the criteria you use in making decisions. Explain the rationale for your decisions. Be forthright and candid about problems. Fully disclose all relevant information.

2. **Be fair.** Before making decisions or taking actions, consider how others will perceive them in terms of objectivity and fairness. Give credit where credit is due. Be objective and impartial in performance appraisals. Pay attention to equity perceptions in distributing rewards.

3. **Speak your feelings.** Managers who convey only hard facts come across as cold, distant, and unfeeling. When you share your feelings, others will see that you are real and human. They will know you for who you are, and their respect for you is likely to increase.

4. **Tell the truth.** Being trustworthy means being credible. If honesty is critical to credibility, then you must be perceived as someone who tells the truth. Employees are more tolerant of hearing something "they don't want to hear" than of finding out that their manager lied to them.

5. **Be consistent.** People want predictability. Mistrust comes from not knowing what to expect. Take the time to think about your values and beliefs and let those values and beliefs consistently guide your decisions. When you know what is important to you, your actions will follow, and you will project a consistency that earns people's trust.

6. **Fulfill your promises.** Trust requires that people believe that you are dependable. You need to ensure that you keep your word. Promises made must be promises kept.

7. **Maintain confidences.** You trust those whom you believe to be discreet and those on whom you can rely. If people open up to you and make themselves vulnerable by telling you something in confidence, they need to feel assured you will not discuss it with others or betray that confidence. If people perceive you as someone who leaks personal confidences or someone who cannot be depended on, you have lost their trust.

8. **Demonstrate competence.** Develop the admiration and respect of others by demonstrating technical and professional ability. Pay particular attention to developing and displaying your communication, negotiation, and other interpersonal skills.

Practising the Skill

Read the following scenario. Write some notes about how you would handle the situation described. Bear in mind that the employees feel that they have been betrayed because the vacation that they had come to expect has been taken away from them. In determining what to do, be sure to refer to the eight suggestions for building trust.

Scenario

Donna Romines is the shipping department manager at Tastefully Tempting, a gourmet candy company based in New Brunswick. Orders for the company's candy come from around the world. Your six-member team processes these orders. Needless to say, the two months before Christmas are quite hectic. Everybody counts the days until December 24, when the phones finally stop ringing off the wall, at least for a few days.

When the company was first founded five years ago, after the holiday rush the owners would shut down Tastefully Tempting for two weeks after Christmas. However, as the business has grown and moved into Internet sales, that practice has become too costly. There is too much business to be able to afford that luxury. The rush for Valentine's Day starts as orders pour in the week after Christmas. Although the two-week post-holiday company-wide shutdown was phased out formally last year, some departments found it difficult to get employees to gear up once again after the Christmas break. The employees who came to work after Christmas accomplished little. This year, though, things have got to change. You know that the cultural "tradition" will not be easy to overcome, but your shipping team needs to be ready to tackle the orders that have piled up. How will you handle the situation?

Reinforcing the Skill

The following activities will help you practise and reinforce the skills associated with building trust:

1. Keep a one-week log describing ways that your daily decisions and actions encouraged people to trust you or to not trust you. What things did you do that led to trust? What things did you do that may have led to distrust? How could you have changed your behaviour so that the situations of distrust could have been situations of trust?

2. Review recent issues of a business periodical (for example, *BusinessWeek, Fortune, Forbes, Fast Company, IndustryWeek,* or the *Wall Street Journal*) for articles where trust (or lack of trust) may have played a role. Find two articles and describe the situation. Explain how the person(s) involved might have used skills in developing trust to handle the situation.

MyManagementLab

After you have completed the study of Part 1, do the following exercises at the MyManagementLab website (www.pearsoned.ca/mymanagementlab):

- You're the Manager: Putting Ethics into Action (Lindblad Expeditions)
- Passport, Scenario 1 (Paula Seeger, Java World), Scenario 2 (Charles Mathidi, QSI), and Scenario 3 (André Fasset, PhenomGaming)

VIDEO CASE INCIDENT

SCAN THIS

Please turn to the back of the book to see the Video Case Incidents available for Part 1.

PART TWO

PLANNING

**In PART TWO,
we look at the first management
function—planning—and discuss the
following topics:**

Chapter 6	Decision Making
Chapter 7	Foundations of Planning
Chapter 8	Managing Strategically
Chapter 9	Planning Tools and Techniques

Many have observed the importance of plans and planning, as demonstrated by the abundance of familiar quotes about it. From the noted Chinese philosopher Confucius, who said, "A man who does not plan long ahead will find trouble at his door," to the eighteenth-century British political writer who said, "I have never yet seen any plan which has not been mended by the observations of those who were much inferior in understanding to the person who took the lead in the business," we see how important planning is. *Great* managers need to learn how to plan and then do it. As novelist Richard Cushing said, "Always plan ahead. It wasn't raining when Noah built the ark." We can't resist one more quote about planning, this one from Benjamin Franklin: "By failing to prepare, you are preparing to fail."

Decision Making

Managers make decisions. And they want those decisions to be good decisions. In this chapter, we'll study the steps in the decision-making process. We'll also look at the various things that influence a manager as he or she makes decisions. After reading and studying this chapter, you will achieve the following learning outcomes.

Learning Outcomes

1 Describe the steps in the decision-making process.

2 Explain the different perspectives in management decision making.

3 Classify decisions and decision-making conditions.

4 Describe different decision-making styles and the impact of biases.

5 Identify effective decision-making techniques.

▶ ▶ ▶ Sandra Wilson, chair and CEO of Burnaby, BC-based Robeez Footwear, faced a very big decision in spring 2006.[1] At the time, Robeez was the leading worldwide manufacturer of soft-soled leather footwear for young children. Wilson wondered what the company should do next. Robeez was poised for growth, but needed outside capital in order to expand. Was it time to take on a new partner or sell the company? Would bringing in an outside investor take the company, which she considered her baby, out of her hands? Was there a company to which Wilson might sell Robeez that had the desire, drive, and expertise to achieve her vision for growth?

Wilson started her home-based business after she "stumbled across the idea to design baby shoes by watching [her] son and [her] friend's young children."

She received immediate encouragement from friends who saw her shoes. To test her idea in the marketplace, she made 20 pairs of shoes by hand, and took them to a retailer gift show. From that show she received orders from 15 retailers. This was enough to launch her business, Robeez Footwear, named for her young son, Robert.

Initially, Wilson handled all aspects of her business herself, from design to production to marketing and distribution. By 2006, however, 20 years after she had started the company, she employed 400 people and sold shoes in North America, Europe, and Australia. It was time for Wilson to decide the next steps for her business. "We experienced significant growth at Robeez, particularly over the last three or four years," said Wilson. "We have a real vision about where we want to take the Robeez brand

and we feel there is a lot of potential for growth with the brand."

Think About It

How do CEOs make important decisions? Put yourself in Sandra Wilson's shoes. What steps would you take to determine whether Robeez should take on a partner or be sold to another company? How could Wilson evaluate the effectiveness of the decision she is about to make? What decision criteria might she use?

SCAN THIS

Like managers everywhere, Sandra Wilson needs to make good decisions. Making good decisions is something that every manager strives to do, since the overall quality of managerial decisions has a major influence on organizational success or failure. In this chapter, we examine the concept of decision making and how managers make decisions.

The Decision-Making Process

It was the type of day that airline managers dread. A record-setting blizzard was moving up the East Coast, covering roads, railroads, and airport runways with as much as half a metre of snow. One of the major airlines that would have to deal with the storm, American Airlines, "has 85,000 employees who help make flights possible and four who cancel them." Danny Burgin, who works at the company's Fort Worth, Texas, control centre, is one of those four. But fortunately for Danny, snowstorms are fairly simple to deal with because they're usually "easier to predict and airline crews can work around them quickly with de-icers and snowploughs." But still, even this doesn't mean that the decisions he has to make are easy, especially when his decisions affect hundreds of flights and thousands of passengers.[2] Although most decisions managers make don't involve the weather, you can see that decisions play an important role in what an organization has to do or is able to do.

Managers at all levels and in all areas of organizations make **decisions**. That is, they make choices. For instance, top-level managers make decisions about their organization's goals, where to locate manufacturing facilities, or what new markets to move into. Middle- and lower-level managers make decisions about production schedules, product quality problems, pay raises, and employee discipline. Making decisions isn't something that just

1. Describe the steps in the decision-making process.

decision A choice from two or more alternatives.

managers do; all organizational members make decisions that affect their jobs and the organization they work for. But our focus is on how *managers* make decisions.

Although decision making is typically described as the act of choosing among alternatives, that view is simplistic. Why? Because decision making is a comprehensive process.[3] Even for something as straightforward as deciding where to go for lunch, you do more than just choose burgers or pizza. You may consider various restaurants, how you will get there, who might go with you. Granted, you may not spend a lot of time contemplating a lunch decision, but you still go through a process when making that decision. What *does* the decision-making process involve?

Exhibit 6-1 illustrates the **decision-making process**, a set of eight steps that begins with identifying a problem and decision criteria and allocating weights to those criteria; moves to developing, analyzing, and selecting an alternative that can resolve the problem; then moves to implementing the alternative; and concludes with evaluating the decision's effectiveness.

decision-making process A set of eight steps that includes identifying a problem, selecting an alternative, and evaluating the decision's effectiveness.

Exhibit 6-1

The Decision-Making Process

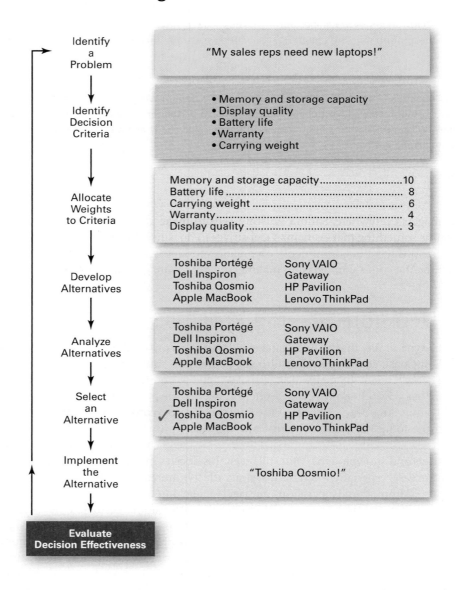

This process is as relevant to your personal decision about what movie to see on a Friday night as it is to a corporate action such as a decision to use technology in managing client relationships. Let's take a closer look at the process in order to understand what each step involves. We will use an example—a manager deciding which laptop computers are best to purchase—to illustrate.

Step 1: Identify a Problem

Do you follow these steps when making a decision?

The decision-making process begins with the existence of a **problem,** or, more specifically, a discrepancy between an existing and a desired state of affairs.[4] Take Amanda, a sales manager whose sales representatives need new laptops because their old ones are inadequate to do their jobs efficiently and effectively. For simplicity's sake, assume that Amanda has determined that it's not economical to simply add memory to the old laptops and that it's the organization's policy that managers purchase new computers rather than lease them. Now we have a problem. The sales reps' current laptops are not efficient or effective enough for sales reps to do their jobs properly. Amanda has a decision to make.

problem A discrepancy between an existing and a desired state of affairs.

How do managers identify problems? In the real world, most problems don't come with neon signs flashing "problem." When her reps started complaining about their computers, it was pretty clear to Amanda that something needed to be done, but few problems are that obvious. Managers also have to be cautious not to confuse problems with symptoms of a problem. Is a 5 percent drop in sales a problem? Or are declining sales merely a symptom of the real problem, such as poor-quality products, high prices, or bad advertising? Also, keep in mind that problem identification is subjective. What one manager considers a problem might not be considered a problem by another manager. In addition, a manager who resolves the wrong problem perfectly is likely to perform just as poorly as a manager who doesn't even recognize a problem and does nothing. As you can see, effectively identifying problems is important but not easy.[5]

Step 2: Identify Decision Criteria

Once a manager has identified a problem, the **decision criteria** important to resolving the problem must be identified. That is, managers must determine what is relevant in making a decision. Every decision maker has criteria, whether explicitly stated or not, that guide his or her decisions. These criteria are generally determined by one's objectives. In our laptop purchase example, Amanda has to assess what factors are relevant to her decision. These might include criteria such as price, convenience, multimedia capability, memory and storage capabilities, display quality, battery life, expansion capability, warranty, and carrying weight. After careful consideration, she decides that memory and storage capacity, display quality, battery life, warranty, and carrying weight are the relevant criteria in her decision.

decision criteria Criteria that define what is relevant in making a decision.

The choice of a new laptop relies on specific decision criteria like price, convenience, memory and storage capacity, display quality, battery life, warranty, and even carrying weight.

Step 3: Allocate Weights to Criteria

If the relevant criteria aren't equally important, the decision maker must weight the items in order to give them the correct priority in the decision. How? A simple way is to give the most important criterion a weight of 10 and then assign weights to the rest using that standard. Of course, you could use any number as the highest weight. The weighted criteria for our example are shown in Exhibit 6-2.

Step 4: Develop Alternatives

The fourth step requires the decision maker to list viable alternatives that could resolve the problem. No attempt is made to evaluate the alternatives, only to list them. Our sales manager, Amanda, identified eight laptops as possible choices (see Exhibit 6-3).

Step 5: Analyze Alternatives

Once the alternatives have been identified, a decision maker must critically analyze each one. How? By appraising it against the criteria established in steps 2 and 3. From this comparison, the strengths and weaknesses of each alternative become evident. Exhibit 6-3 shows the assessed values Amanda gave each of her eight alternatives after she had talked to some computer experts and read the latest information from computer magazines and from the web.

Keep in mind that the ratings given the eight laptop models listed in Exhibit 6-3 are based on the personal assessment made by Amanda. Some assessments can be done objectively. For instance, carrying weight is easy to determine by looking at descriptions online or in computer magazines. However, the assessment of display quality is more of a personal judgment. The point is that most decisions by managers involve judgments—

Exhibit 6-2

Criteria and Weights for Laptop Replacement Decision

Criterion	Weight
Memory and storage capacity	10
Battery life	8
Carrying weight	6
Warranty	4
Display quality	3

Exhibit 6-3

Assessed Values of Laptops Using Decision Criteria

	Memory and Storage Capacity	Battery Life	Carrying Weight	Warranty	Display Quality
Toshiba Portégé	10	3	10	8	5
Dell Inspiron	8	7	7	8	7
HP Pavilion	8	5	7	10	10
Apple MacBook	8	7	7	8	7
Sony VAIO	7	8	7	8	7
Gateway	8	3	6	10	8
Toshiba Qosmio	10	7	8	6	7
Lenovo ThinkPad	4	10	4	8	10

the criteria chosen in step 2, the weights given to the criteria in step 3, and the analysis of alternatives in step 5. This explains why two computer buyers with the same amount of money may look at two totally different sets of alternatives or even rate the same alternatives differently.

Exhibit 6-4 represents only an assessment of the eight alternatives against the decision criteria. It does not reflect the weighting done in step 3. If you multiply each alternative (Exhibit 6-3) by its weight (Exhibit 6-2), you get Exhibit 6-4. The sum of these scores represents an evaluation of each alternative against both the established criteria and weights. There are times when a decision maker might not have to do this step. If one choice had scored 10 on every criterion, you would not need to consider the weights. Similarly, if the weights were all equal, you could evaluate each alternative merely by summing up the appropriate lines in Exhibit 6-3. In this instance, for example, the score for the Toshiba Portégé would be 36 and the score for Gateway would be 35 (see Exhibit 6-4).

Step 6: Select an Alternative

> What does it mean if the "best" alternative does not feel right to you after going through the decision–making steps?

The sixth step in the decision-making process is choosing the best alternative or the one that generated the highest total in step 5. In our example (see Exhibit 6-4), Amanda would choose the Toshiba Qosmio because it scored highest (249 total).

That said, occasionally, when one gets to this step, the alternative that looks best according to the numbers may not feel like the best solution (for example, your intuition might suggest some other alternative). Often the reason is that the individual did not give the correct weight to one or more criteria (perhaps because one criterion was actually much more important than the individual realized initially, when assigning weights). Thus, if the individual finds that the "best alternative" does not seem like the right alternative, the decision maker needs to decide if a review of the criteria is necessary before implementing the alternative.

Step 7: Implement the Alternative

Step 7 is concerned with putting the decision into action. This involves conveying the decision to those affected by it and getting their commitment to it. Managers often fail to get buy-in from those around them before making a decision, even though successful implementation requires participation. One study found that managers used participation in only 20 percent of decisions, even though broad participation in decisions led to successful implementation 80 percent of the time. The same study found that managers most

Exhibit 6-4

Evaluation of Laptop Alternatives Against Weighted Criteria

	Memory and Storage Capacity	Battery Life	Carrying Weight	Warranty	Display Quality	Total
Toshiba Portégé	100	24	60	32	15	231
Dell Inspiron	80	56	42	32	21	231
HP Pavilion	80	40	42	40	30	232
Apple MacBook	80	56	42	32	21	231
Sony VAIO	70	64	42	32	21	229
Gateway	80	24	36	40	24	204
Toshiba Qosmio	100	56	48	24	21	249
Lenovo ThinkPad	40	80	24	32	30	206

MyManagementLab
Q&A 6.2

commonly tried to implement decisions through power or persuasion (used in 60 percent of decisions). These tactics were successful in only one of three decisions, however.[6] If the people who must carry out a decision participate in the process, they're more likely to enthusiastically support the outcome than if you just tell them what to do.

Step 8: Evaluate Decision Effectiveness

The last step in the decision-making process involves evaluating the outcome or result of the decision to see if the problem was resolved. If the evaluation showed that the problem still exists, then the manager needs to assess what went wrong. Was the problem incorrectly defined? Were errors made when evaluating alternatives? Was the right alternative selected but poorly implemented? The answers might lead you to redo an earlier step or might even require starting the whole process over.

MyManagementLab
Q&A 6.3

The Manager as Decision Maker

2. Explain the different perspectives in management decision making.

▶ ▶ ▶ Although Sandra Wilson had started Robeez as a home-based business and initially handled all aspects of her business, by 2006 the company employed 400 people and sold shoes in North America, Europe, and Australia.[7] Decision making had become dispersed across the organization and placed in the hands of managers.

Think About It

Although everyone in an organization makes decisions, decision making is particularly important to managers. As Exhibit 6-5 shows, it's part of all four managerial functions. In fact, that's why we say that decision making is the essence of management.[8] And that's why managers— when they plan, organize, lead, and control—are called *decision makers*. What management decisions are the managers at Robeez likely to be making in each of the four management areas in Exhibit 6-5?

The fact that almost everything a manager does involves making decisions doesn't mean that decisions are always time-consuming, complex, or evident to an outside observer. Most decision making is routine. Every day of the year, you make a decision about what to eat for dinner. It's no big deal. You've made the decision thousands of times before. It's a pretty simple decision and can usually be handled quickly. It's the type of decision you almost forget *is* a decision. And managers also make dozens of these routine decisions every day—for example, which employee will work what shift next week, what information should be included in a report, or how to resolve a customer's complaint. Keep in mind that even though a decision seems easy or has been faced by a manager a number of times before, it still is a decision. Let's look at three perspectives on how managers make decisions.

The decision-making process described in Exhibit 6-1 suggests that individuals make rational, carefully scripted decisions. But is this the best way to describe the decision-making situation and the person who makes the decisions? We look at those issues in this section. We start by looking at three perspectives on how decisions are made.

Making Decisions: Rationality

rational decision making Making decisions that are consistent and value-maximizing within specified constraints.

Our model of the decision-making process implies that individuals engage in **rational decision making**. By that we mean that people make consistent, value-maximizing choices within specified constraints.[9] What are the underlying assumptions of rationality, and how valid are those assumptions?

Assumptions of Rationality

A rational decision maker would be fully objective and logical. The problem faced would be clear and unambiguous, and the decision maker would have a clear and specific goal

Exhibit 6-5

Decisions in the Management Functions

Planning
- What are the organization's long-term objectives?
- What strategies will best achieve those objectives?
- What should the organization's short-term objectives be?
- How difficult should individual goals be?

Organizing
- How many employees should I have report directly to me?
- How much centralization should there be in the organization?
- How should jobs be designed?
- When should the organization implement a different structure?

Leading
- How do I handle employees who appear to be low in motivation?
- What is the most effective leadership style in a given situation?
- How will a specific change affect worker productivity?
- When is the right time to stimulate conflict?

Controlling
- What activities in the organization need to be controlled?
- How should those activities be controlled?
- When is a performance deviation significant?
- What type of management information system should the organization have?

Exhibit 6-6

Assumptions of Rationality

Lead to

- The problem is clear and unambiguous.
- A single, well-defined goal is to be achieved.
- All alternatives and consequences are known.
- Preferences are clear.
- Preferences are constant and stable.
- No time or cost constraints exist.
- Final choice will maximize payoff.

Rational Decision Making

and know all possible alternatives and consequences. Finally, making decisions rationally would consistently lead to selecting the alternative that maximizes the likelihood of achieving that goal. These assumptions apply to any decision—personal or managerial. However, for managerial decision making, we need to add one additional assumption: Decisions are made in the best interests of the organization. Most decisions that managers face in the real world don't meet the assumptions of rationality.[10] So how are most decisions in organizations usually made? The concept of bounded rationality can help answer that question.

Making Decisions: Bounded Rationality

Would you say you make decisions rationally or do you rely on gut instinct?

Most decisions that managers make don't fit the assumptions of perfect rationality (where all the steps above are followed, and all alternatives are known and fully understood). Instead, managers make those decisions under assumptions of **bounded rationality**. That is, they make decisions rationally, but are limited (bounded) by their ability to process information.[11] Because they cannot possibly analyze all

bounded rationality Limitations on a person's ability to interpret, process, and act on information.

satisfice To accept solutions that are "good enough."

MyManagementLab
Q&A 6.4

information on all alternatives, managers **satisfice** rather than maximize. Rather than carefully evaluate each alternative in great detail, managers settle on an alternative that is "good enough"—one that meets an acceptable level of performance. The first alternative that meets the "good enough" criterion ends the search.

Let's look at an example. Suppose that you are a finance major and upon graduation you want a job, preferably as a personal financial planner, with a minimum salary of $50 000 and within 100 kilometres of your hometown. You accept a job offer as a business credit analyst—not exactly a personal financial planner but still in the finance field—at a bank 50 kilometres from home at a starting salary of $55 000. A more comprehensive job search would have revealed a job in personal financial planning at a trust company only 25 kilometres from your hometown and starting at a salary of $57 000. Because the first job offer was satisfactory (or "good enough"), you behaved in a boundedly rational manner by accepting it, although according to the assumptions of perfect rationality, you did not maximize your decision by searching all possible alternatives and then choosing the best.

MyManagementLab
Q&A 6.5

Making Decisions: The Role of Intuition

Do you prefer to make decisions intuitively? Are these good decisions?

When managers at stapler maker Swingline saw the company's market share declining, they decided to use a logical scientific approach to help them address the issue. For three years, they exhaustively researched stapler users before deciding what new products to develop.

However, at newcomer Accentra, founder Todd Moses used a more intuitive decision approach to come up with his line of unique PaperPro staplers. His stapler sold 1 million units in 6 months in a market that sells only 25 million units in total annually—a pretty good result for a new product.[12]

Like Todd Moses, managers regularly use their intuition, which may actually help improve their decision making.[13] What is **intuitive decision making**? It's making decisions on the basis of experience, feelings, and accumulated judgment. Researchers studying managers' use of intuitive decision making identified five different aspects of intuition, which are described in Exhibit 6-7.[14]

Making a decision on intuition or "gut feeling" does not necessarily happen independently of rational analysis; rather, the two complement each other. A manager who has had experience with a particular, or even similar, type of problem or situation often can act quickly with what appears to be limited information. Such a manager does not rely on a systematic and thorough analysis of the problem or identification and evaluation of alternatives but instead uses his or her experience and judgment to make a decision.

intuitive decision making
Making decisions on the basis of experience, feelings, and accumulated judgment.

Intuition played a strong part in Barbara Choi's decision to locate her firm, a cosmetics and personal care products manufacturer, in Valley Springs Industrial Center in Los Angeles. In Chinese, the numbers of the building's address signify continued growth.

Exhibit 6-7

What Is Intuition?

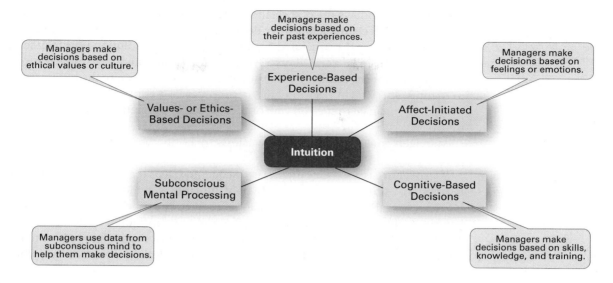

Source: Based on L. A. Burke and M. K. Miller, "Taking the Mystery Out of Intuitive Decision Making," *Academy of Management Executive*, October 1999, pp. 91–99.

How accurate is intuitive decision making? A recent study suggests that complex decisions may be better if made "in the absence of attentive deliberation."[15] (To discover your own intuitive abilities, see *Self-Assessment—How Intuitive Am I?* at the end of the chapter.)

MyManagementLab
Q&A 6.6

Types of Decisions and Decision-Making Conditions

▶ ▶ ▶ Managers at Robeez Footwear make decisions weekly about purchasing supplies and scheduling employee work shifts. It's something they have done numerous times. But there came a point when founder Sandra Wilson realized they faced a different kind of decision, one they had never encountered—they had maxed out their own capabilities and needed to find a way to move the company forward to the next level. This situation is not all that unusual.

3. Classify decisions and decision-making conditions.

Think About It

Managers in all kinds of organizations will face different types of problems and decisions as they do their jobs. Some problems are structured and recurring, while others are unstructured and nonrecurring. Can you think of some examples?

Types of Decisions

Structured Problems and Programmed Decisions

Some problems are straightforward. The goal of the decision maker is clear, the problem is familiar, and information about the problem is easily defined and complete. Examples of these types of problems could include what to do when a customer returns a purchase to a

structured problems Problems that are straightforward, familiar, and easily defined.

programmed decisions Repetitive decisions that can be handled by a routine approach.

procedure A series of interrelated sequential steps that a decision maker can use to respond to a structured problem.

rule An explicit statement that tells a decision maker what he or she can or cannot do.

policy A guideline for making a decision.

MyManagementLab
Q&A 6.7

unstructured problems Problems that are new or unusual and for which information is ambiguous or incomplete.

nonprogrammed decisions Decisions that are unique and nonrecurring and require custom-made solutions.

store, a supplier delivers an important product late, a news team wants to respond to a fast-breaking event, or a student wants to drop a class. Such situations are called **structured problems** because they are straightforward, familiar, and easily defined. When situations are structured, there is probably some standardized routine for handling problems that may arise. For example, when a restaurant server spills a drink on a customer's coat, the manager offers to have the coat cleaned at the restaurant's expense. This is what we call a **programmed decision**, a repetitive decision that can be handled by a routine approach. Why? Because once the structured problem is defined, the solution is usually self-evident or at least reduced to a few alternatives that are familiar and have proved successful in the past. The spilled drink on the customer's coat doesn't require the restaurant manager to identify and weight decision criteria or to develop a long list of possible solutions. Instead, the manager relies on one of three types of programmed decisions: procedure, rule, or policy.

Managers make programmed decisions by falling back on procedures, rules, and policies.

A **procedure** is a series of interrelated sequential steps that a decision maker can use to respond to a structured problem. The only difficulty is in identifying the problem. Once it's clear, so is the procedure. For instance, when bad weather grounds airplanes, airlines have procedures for helping customers who miss their flights. Customers may request being put up in hotels for the night. The customer service agent knows how to make this decision—follow the established airline procedure for dealing with customers when flights are grounded.

A **rule** is an explicit statement that tells a decision maker what he or she can or cannot do. Rules are frequently used because they are simple to follow and ensure consistency. For example, rules about lateness and absenteeism permit supervisors to make disciplinary decisions rapidly and fairly.

A **policy** is a guideline for making a decision. In contrast to a rule, a policy establishes general parameters for the decision maker rather than specifically stating what should or should not be done. Policies typically contain an ambiguous term that leaves interpretation up to the decision maker. "The customer always comes first and should always be *satisfied*" is an example of a policy statement. While ambiguity of policies is often intended to allow more flexibility in action, not all employees and customers are comfortable with flexibly determined policies.

Unstructured Problems and Nonprogrammed Decisions

Many organizational situations involve **unstructured problems**, which are problems that are new or unusual and for which information is ambiguous or incomplete. The toughest of these unstructured problems were introduced in Chapter 1 as wicked problems, which are characterized by the fact that the problem and the solution are interrelated, key stakeholders have wildly different perspectives and frames of reference, the constraints related to the problem and the resources needed to resolve it change over time, and the problem is never definitively solved—it is a continuing work in progress.

Nonprogrammed decisions are unique and nonrecurring and require custom-made solutions. For instance, if an office building were to be flooded because sprinklers went off accidentally, CEOs with businesses in the building would have to decide when and how to start operating again and what to do for employees whose offices were completely ruined. When a manager confronts an unstructured problem, there is no cut-and-dried solution. It requires a custom-made response through nonprogrammed decision making.

Few managerial decisions in the real world are either fully programmed or nonprogrammed. These are extremes, and most decisions fall somewhere in between. Few programmed decisions are designed to eliminate individual judgment completely. At the other extreme, even a unique situation requiring a nonprogrammed decision can be helped by programmed routines. It's best to think of decisions as *mainly* programmed or *mainly* nonprogrammed, rather than as completely one or the other.

The problems confronting managers usually become more unstructured as they move up the organizational hierarchy. Why? Because lower-level managers handle the routine

Many people believe that China will become the next big market for powerful brand-name products, and Zong Qinghou, founder of China's Wahaha beverage group, plans to be ready. But brand names are a new concept in Chinese markets, and Zong prefers his own first-hand information to market research. He will face many nonprogrammed decisions as he tries to make his brand a success at home and eventually abroad.

decisions themselves and let upper-level managers deal with the decisions they find unusual or difficult. Similarly, higher-level managers delegate routine decisions to their subordinates so that they can deal with more difficult issues.[16]

One of the more challenging tasks facing managers as they make decisions is analyzing decision alternatives (step 5 in the decision-making process). In the next section, we look at analyzing alternatives under different conditions.

MyManagementLab
Q&A 6.8

Decision-Making Conditions

When managers make decisions, they face three conditions: certainty, risk, and uncertainty. What are the characteristics of each?

Certainty

The ideal condition for making decisions is one of **certainty**, that is, a condition in which a decision maker can make accurate decisions because the outcome of every alternative is known. For example, when Saskatchewan's finance minister is deciding in which bank to deposit excess provincial funds, he knows the exact interest rate being offered by each bank and the amount that will be earned on the funds. He is certain about the outcomes of each alternative. As you might expect, most managerial decisions are not like this.

certainty A condition in which a decision maker can make accurate decisions because the outcome of every alternative is known.

Risk

How much risk and uncertainty affect your decisions?

A far more common condition is one of **risk**, a condition in which a decision maker is able to estimate the likelihood of certain outcomes. The ability to assign probabilities to outcomes may be the result of personal experiences or secondary information. With risk, managers have historical data that let them assign probabilities to different alternatives. Let's work through an example.

Suppose that you manage a ski resort in Whistler, BC. You are thinking about adding another lift to your current facility. Obviously, your decision will be influenced by the additional revenue that the new lift would generate, and additional revenue will depend on snowfall. The decision is made somewhat clearer because you have fairly reliable weather data from the past 10 years on snowfall levels in your area—three years of heavy snowfall, five years of normal snowfall, and two years of light snowfall. Can you use this information to help you make your decision about adding the new lift? If you have good information on the amount of revenues generated during each level of snow, the answer is yes.

risk A condition in which a decision maker is able to estimate the likelihood of certain outcomes.

Exhibit 6-8

Expected Value for Revenues from the Addition of One Ski Lift

Event	Expected Revenues	× Probability	= Expected Value of Each Alternative
Heavy snowfall	$850 000	0.3	$255 000
Normal snowfall	725 000	0.5	362 500
Light snowfall	350 000	0.2	70 000
			$687 500

You can calculate expected value—the expected return from each possible outcome—by multiplying expected revenues by snowfall probabilities. The result is the average revenue you can expect over time if the given probabilities hold. As Exhibit 6-8 shows, the expected revenue from adding a new ski lift is $687 500. Of course, whether that justifies a decision to build or not depends on the costs involved in generating that revenue. Making estimates of the probability of a set of outcomes is not a substitute for common sense. One of the contributing factors to the collapse of financial markets in the fall of 2008 was that "teams of math geniuses had used sophisticated algorithms to forecast default rates on sub-prime mortgages." The problem was that they looked at historical data that ignored the high-risk nature of the underlying financial instrument, and although the models predicted default rates of 10 to 12 percent, actual default rates were as high as 60 percent.[17]

Uncertainty

uncertainty A condition in which a decision maker is not certain about the outcomes and cannot even make reasonable probability estimates.

What happens if you have a decision where you are not certain about the outcomes and cannot even make reasonable probability estimates? We call such a condition **uncertainty**. Managers do face decision-making situations of uncertainty. Under these conditions, the choice of alternative is influenced by the limited amount of information available to the decision maker and by the psychological orientation of the decision maker. The optimistic manager will follow a *maximax* choice (maximizing the maximum possible payoff) in order to get the largest possible gain. The pessimist will follow a *maximin* choice (maximizing the minimum possible payoff) to make the best of a situation should the worst possible outcome occur. The manager who desires to minimize his maximum "regret" will opt for a *minimax* choice, to avoid having big regrets after decisions play out. Let's look at these different choice approaches using an example.

A marketing manager at Visa has determined four possible strategies (S_1, S_2, S_3, and S_4) for promoting the Visa card throughout western Canada. The marketing manager also knows that major competitor MasterCard has three competitive actions (CA_1, CA_2, CA_3) it's using to promote its card in the same region. For this example, we will assume that the Visa executive had no previous knowledge that would allow her to place probabilities on the success of any of the four strategies. She formulates the matrix shown in Exhibit 6-9 to show the various Visa strategies and the resulting profit to Visa depending on the competitive action used by MasterCard.

In this example, if our Visa manager is an optimist, she will choose S_4 because that could produce the largest possible gain: $28 million. Note that this choice maximizes the maximum possible gain (the *maximax* choice).

If our manager is a pessimist, she will assume that only the worst can occur. The worst outcome for each strategy is as follows: S_1 = $11 million; S_2 = $9 million; S_3 = $15 million; S_4 = $14 million. These are the most pessimistic outcomes from each strategy. Following the *maximin* choice, she would maximize the minimum payoff; in other words, she would select S_3 ($15 million is the largest of the minimum payoffs).

Exhibit 6-9

Payoff Matrix

(in millions of dollars)

Visa Marketing Strategy	MasterCard's Response		
	CA$_1$	CA$_2$	CA$_3$
S$_1$	13	14	11
S$_2$	9	15	18
S$_3$	24	21	15
S$_4$	18	14	28

In the third approach, managers recognize that once a decision is made, it will not necessarily result in the most profitable payoff. There may be a "regret" of profits given up—*regret* referring to the amount of money that could have been made had a different strategy been used. Managers calculate regret by subtracting all possible payoffs in each category from the maximum possible payoff for each given event, in this case for each competitive action. For our Visa manager, the highest payoff, given that MasterCard engages in CA$_1$, CA$_2$, or CA$_3$, is $24 million, $21 million, or $28 million, respectively (the highest number in each column). Subtracting the payoffs in Exhibit 6-9 from those figures produces the results shown in Exhibit 6-10.

The maximum regrets are S$_1$ = $17 million; S$_2$ = $15 million; S$_3$ = $13 million; and S$_4$ = $7 million. The *minimax* choice minimizes the maximum regret, so our Visa manager would choose S$_4$. By making this choice, she will never have a regret of giving up profits of more than $7 million. This result contrasts, for example, with a regret of $15 million had she chosen S$_2$ and MasterCard had taken CA$_1$.

Although managers will try to quantify a decision when possible by using payoff and regret matrices, uncertainty often forces them to rely more on intuition, creativity, hunches, and "gut feel." Anheuser-Busch uses Bud-Net and information technology (IT) to make better decisions, as the following *Management Reflection* shows.

(To learn more about creativity and decision making, see *Developing Your Interpersonal Skills—Solving Problems Creatively* at the end of the chapter.)

Regardless of the decision that needs to be made and the conditions that affect it, each manager has his or her own style of making decisions.

Exhibit 6-10

Regret Matrix

(in millions of dollars)

Visa Marketing Strategy	MasterCard's Response		
	CA$_1$	CA$_2$	CA$_3$
S$_1$	11	7	17
S$_2$	15	6	10
S$_3$	0	0	13
S$_4$	6	7	0

MANAGEMENT REFLECTION
► Focus on Innovation

Making Better Decisions with IT

BudNet is the "crown jewel of the King of Beers." What is it? It's Anheuser-Busch's (A-B's) powerful and sophisticated information system. Every night, data are collected from A-B distributors' computer servers. Each morning, managers can see what brands are selling in which packages, using which promotional materials and pricing discounts. According to "dozens of analysts, beer-industry veterans, and distributor executives . . . Anheuser has made a deadly accurate science out of finding out what beer lovers are buying, as well as when, where, and why." All this information allows A-B managers to continually adjust production and fine-tune marketing campaigns.

Most companies are "drowning in data" and don't know how to make sense out of it.[18] As this example shows, however, one of the primary uses for IT can be to help managers—and other employees—make better decisions by sorting through tons of data, looking for trends, patterns, and other insights. As we saw in our discussion of bounded rationality, a person's ability to process such a massive amount of information would be severely limited. So managers use IT to help make sense of all this information so they can make better decisions.

Another way that IT can help managers make better decisions is by using software tools that help them analyze data. Consultants estimate that some 75 percent of individual managers rely on personal productivity tools, such as spreadsheets, which can be used to gather and report information to help them make decisions in their own local area of responsibility. However, when you have each manager using his or her own data collection tools, there are no linkages or collaboration. Thus, on the organization-wide level, there's the more sophisticated **business performance management (BPM) software**, also sometimes called corporate performance management software, to help make decisions. BPM, which provides key performance indicators that help companies monitor efficiency of projects and employees, was initially believed to be the "silver bullet that had the potential to help corporate managers control their organization's performance in an increasingly volatile world." Although BPM software hasn't quite lived up to those lofty expectations, as it improves, it will increasingly be a tool managers use to help make better decisions. ■

business performance management (BPM) software
IT software that provides key performance indicators to help managers monitor efficiency of projects and employees. Also known as corporate performance management software.

Decision-Making Styles

4. Describe different decision-making styles and the impact of biases.

► ► ► As chair and CEO, Sandra Wilson needed to make a decision about the future of Robeez Footwear. "We recognized that if we wanted to execute the plans and achieve the vision for where we could take this company, we needed to look for . . . someone with the financial backing and expertise to help us continue to build Robeez," says Wilson.

Should Wilson seek a new partner for Robeez or sell the company? She weighed the pros and cons of each choice. For example, taking on a new partner would provide the company with the money to expand to more markets. The downside would be the possibility of losing control over the quality of the product. Selling Robeez to another company could provide Robeez with the resources and experience necessary to continue its momentum of growth. However, if Robeez were manufactured by another company, the corporate culture that underlies Robeez' success might change and negatively affect the brand.

Think About It

What biases might enter into Sandra Wilson's decision making, and how might she overcome these? How can Wilson improve her decision making, given that she is dealing with uncertainty and risk? How might escalation of commitment affect her decision?

Suppose that you were a new manager at Robeez Footwear. How would you make decisions? Decision-making styles differ along two dimensions.[19] The first dimension is an individual's *way of thinking*. Some of us are more rational and logical in the way we process information. A rational type processes information in order and makes sure that it's logical and consistent before making a decision. Others tend to be creative and intuitive. An intuitive type does not have to process information in a certain order and is comfortable looking at it as a whole.

The other dimension is an individual's *tolerance for ambiguity*. Some of us have a low tolerance for ambiguity. These types need consistency and order in the way they structure information so that ambiguity is minimized. On the other hand, some of us can tolerate high levels of ambiguity and are able to process many thoughts at the same time. (To assess your tolerance for ambiguity, see *Self-Assessment—How Well Do I Handle Ambiguity?* on pages 229–230, in Chapter 8.) When we diagram these two dimensions, four decision-making styles are evident: directive, analytic, conceptual, and behavioural (see Exhibit 6-11). Let's look more closely at each style.

Exhibit 6-11

Decision-Making Styles

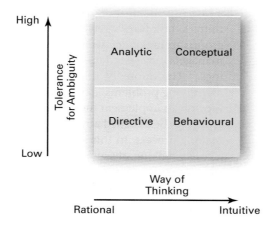

Source: S. P. Robbins and D. A. DeCenzo, *Supervision Today*, 2nd ed. (Upper Saddle River, NJ: Prentice Hall, 1998), p. 166.

- *Directive style.* Individuals with a **directive style** have a low tolerance for ambiguity and are rational in their way of thinking. They are efficient, logical, practical, and impersonal. Directive types make fast decisions and focus on the short run. Their efficiency and speed in making decisions often result in their making decisions with minimal information and assessing few alternatives.

- *Analytic style.* Individuals with an **analytic style** have much greater tolerance for ambiguity than do directive types. They want more information before making a decision and consider more alternatives than directive-style decision makers do. Analytic-style decision makers are characterized as careful decision makers with the ability to adapt to or cope with unique situations.

- *Conceptual style.* Individuals with a **conceptual style** tend to be very broad in their outlook and consider many alternatives. They are intuitive, focus on the long run, and are very good at finding creative solutions to problems. They are also adaptive and flexible.

directive style A decision-making style characterized by a low tolerance for ambiguity and a rational way of thinking.

analytic style A decision-making style characterized by a high tolerance for ambiguity and a rational way of thinking.

conceptual style A decision-making style characterized by a high tolerance for ambiguity and an intuitive way of thinking.

behavioural style A decision-making style characterized by a low tolerance for ambiguity and an intuitive way of thinking.

- *Behavioural style.* Individuals with a **behavioural style** have a low tolerance for ambiguity and an intuitive way of thinking. They are sociable, friendly, and supportive. They work well with others, are concerned about the achievements of those around them, and are receptive to suggestions from others. They often use meetings to communicate, although they try to avoid conflict. Acceptance by others is important to this decision-making style.

Although these four decision-making styles are distinct, most managers have characteristics of more than one style. It's probably more realistic to think of a manager's dominant style and his or her alternative styles. Although some managers will rely almost exclusively on their dominant style, others are more flexible and can shift their style depending on the situation.

MyManagementLab
Q&A 6.9, Q&A 6.10

Managers should also recognize that their employees may use different decision-making styles. Some employees may take their time, carefully weighing alternatives and considering riskier options (analytic style), while other employees may be more concerned about getting suggestions from others before making decisions (behavioural style). This does not make one approach better than the other. It just means that their decision-making styles are different. (See *Managing Workforce Diversity—The Value of Diversity in Decision Making* on page 183 for the issues associated with valuing diversity in decision making.)

Group Decision Making

> *Do you think individuals or groups make better decisions?*

Many organizational decisions are made by groups. It's a rare organization that does not at some time use committees, task forces, review panels, study teams, or similar groups to make decisions. In addition, studies show that managers may spend up to 30 hours a week in group meetings.[20] Undoubtedly, a large portion of that time is spent identifying problems, developing solutions, and determining how to implement the solutions. It's possible, in fact, for groups to be assigned any of the eight steps in the decision-making process. In this section, we look at the advantages and disadvantages of group decision making, discuss when groups would be preferred, and review some techniques for improving group decision making.

What advantages do group decisions have over individual decisions?

- *More complete information and knowledge.* A group brings a diversity of experience and perspectives to the decision process that an individual cannot.

- *More diverse alternative*s. Because groups have a greater amount and diversity of information, they can identify more diverse alternatives than an individual.

- *Increased acceptance of a solution.* Group members are reluctant to fight or undermine a decision they have helped develop.

- *Increased legitimacy.* Decisions made by groups may be perceived as more legitimate than decisions made unilaterally by one person.

If groups are so good at making decisions, how did the phrase "A camel is a horse put together by a committee" become so popular? The answer, of course, is that group decisions also have disadvantages:

- *Increased time to reach a solution.* Groups almost always take more time to reach a solution than it would take an individual.

- *Opportunity for minority domination.* The inequality of group members creates the opportunity for one or more members to dominate others. A dominant and vocal minority frequently can have an excessive influence on the final decision.

- *Ambiguous responsibility.* Group members share responsibility, but the responsibility of any single member is diluted.

- *Pressures to conform.* There can be pressures to conform in groups. This pressure undermines critical thinking in the group and eventually harms the quality of the final decision.[21]

Groupthink

Have you ever been in a situation in which several people were sitting around discussing a particular item and you had something to say that ran contrary to the consensus views of the group, but you remained silent? Were you surprised to learn later that others shared your views and also had remained silent? What you experienced is what Irving Janis termed **groupthink**.[22] This is a form of conformity in which group members withhold deviant, minority, or unpopular views in order to give the appearance of agreement. As a result, groupthink undermines critical thinking in the group and eventually harms the quality of the final decision.

Groupthink applies to a situation in which a group's ability to appraise alternatives objectively and arrive at a quality decision is jeopardized. Because of pressures for conformity, groups often deter individuals from critically appraising unusual, minority, or unpopular views. Consequently, an individual's mental efficiency, reality testing, and moral judgment deteriorate. How does groupthink occur? Groupthink manifests itself in a variety of ways.

Does groupthink really hinder decision making? Yes. Several research studies have found that groupthink symptoms were associated with poorer-quality decision outcomes, such as the *Challenger* space shuttle disaster.[23] But groupthink can be minimized if the group is cohesive, fosters open discussion, values diversity of opinion, and has an impartial leader who seeks input from all members.[24]

> **groupthink** The withholding by group members of different views in order to appear to be in agreement.

Individual and Group Decision Making: When Is One More Effective Than the Other?

Determining whether a group or an individual will be more effective in making a particular decision depends on the criteria you use to assess effectiveness.[25] The effectiveness of group decision making is also influenced by the size of the group. Although a larger group provides greater opportunity for diverse representation, it also requires more coordination and more time for members to contribute their ideas. So groups probably should not be too large. Evidence indicates, in fact, that groups of five, and to a lesser extent, seven, are the most effective.[26] Having an odd number in the group helps avoid decision deadlocks. Also, these groups are large enough for members to shift roles and withdraw from unfavourable positions but still small enough for quieter members to participate actively in discussions.

Decision-Making Biases and Errors

When managers make decisions, not only do they use their own particular style, but many use "rules of thumb," or **heuristics**, to simplify their decision making. Rules of thumb can be useful to decision makers because they help make sense of complex, uncertain, and ambiguous information.[27] Even though managers may use rules of thumb, that does not mean those rules are reliable. Why? Because they may lead to errors and biases in processing and evaluating information. Exhibit 6-12 identifies seven common decision-making biases and errors. Let's take a quick look at each.[28]

> **heuristics** Rules of thumb that managers use to simplify decision making.

- *Overconfidence bias.* Decision makers tend to think they know more than they do or hold unrealistically positive views of themselves and their performance. For instance, a sales manager brags that his presentation was so good that there is no doubt the sale will be his. Later he learns that he lost the sale because the client found him obnoxious.

Exhibit 6-12

Common Decision-Making Biases and Errors

- *Selective perception bias.* Decision makers selectively organize and interpret events based on their biased perceptions. This influences the information they pay attention to, the problems they identify, and the alternatives they develop. For instance, before Joanne meets with two job candidates, she learns that one went to her alma mater. She does not seriously consider the other job candidate because she believes that graduating from the same university as she did makes the candidate superior.

- *Confirmation bias.* Decision makers seek out information that reaffirms their past choices and discount information that contradicts past judgments. These people tend to accept at face value information that confirms their preconceived views and are critical and skeptical of information that challenges these views. For instance, Pierre continues to give business to the same supplier, even though the supplier has been late on several deliveries. Pierre thinks the supplier is a nice person, and the supplier keeps promising to deliver on time.

- *Sunk-costs error.* Decision makers forget that current choices cannot correct the past. They incorrectly fixate on past expenditures of time, money, or effort in assessing choices rather than on future consequences. For instance, Amita has spent thousands of dollars and several months introducing new procedures for handling customer complaints. Both customers and employees are complaining about the new procedures. Because of the investment in time and money she has already made, Amita does not want to consider the possibility that the procedures are needlessly complicated.

- *Escalation-of-commitment error.* Decisions can also be influenced by a phenomenon called **escalation of commitment**, which is an increased commitment to a previous decision despite evidence that it might have been wrong.[29] For example, studies of the events leading up to the space shuttle *Columbia* disaster in 2003 point to an escalation of commitment by decision makers to ignore the possible damage that foam striking the shuttle at takeoff might have had, even though the decision was questioned by certain individuals. Why would decision makers want to escalate commitment to a bad decision? Because they don't want to admit that their initial decision might have been flawed. Rather than search for new alternatives, they simply increase their commitment to the original solution.

escalation of commitment
An increased commitment to a previous decision despite evidence that it might have been wrong.

- *Self-serving bias.* Decision makers take credit for their successes and blame failure on outside factors. For instance, Jessie dismisses his team's efforts when he wins a contract, although he blames them for the small error that was in the final report.

- *Hindsight bias.* Decision makers falsely believe that they would have accurately predicted the outcome of an event once that outcome is actually known. For instance, after a client cancelled a contract that had been drawn up, Cindy tells her manager she knew ahead of time that was going to happen, even though she had had no such thoughts before the contract was cancelled. After the fact, some outcomes seem more obvious than they did beforehand.

How can managers avoid the negative effects of these decision-making errors and biases? The main thing is being aware of them and then trying not to exhibit them. Beyond that, managers also should pay attention to "how" they make decisions and try to identify the heuristics they typically use and critically evaluate how appropriate those are. Finally, managers might want to ask those around them to help identify weaknesses in their decision-making style and try to improve on them.

Summing Up Managerial Decision Making

How can we best sum up managerial decision making? Exhibit 6-13 provides an overview. Because it's in their best interests, managers *want* to make good decisions—that is, choose the "best" alternative, implement it, and determine whether or not it takes care of the problem—the reason a decision was needed in the first place. Their decision-making process is affected by four factors, including the decision-making approach being followed, the decision-making conditions, the type of problem being dealt with, and the decision maker's own style of decision making. In addition, certain decision-making errors and biases may impact the process. Each of these factors plays a role in determining how a manager makes a decision. So whether that decision involves addressing an employee's habitual tardiness, resolving a problem with product quality, or determining whether to enter a new market, remember that it has been shaped by a number of factors.

Exhibit 6-13

Overview of Managerial Decision Making

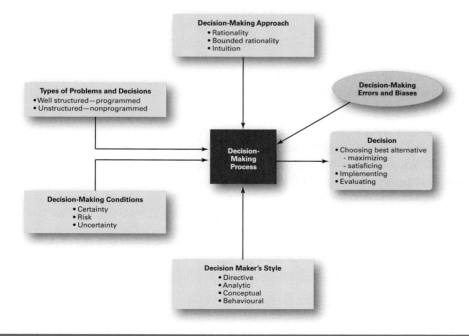

Effective Decision Making for Today's World

▶ ▶ ▶ On September 6, 2006, Sandra Wilson sold Robeez Footwear to Stride Rite, her largest client, for $30.5 million.[30] Wilson will stay on as a consultant to Stride Rite for the Robeez brand and help add children's accessories and clothing to the shoe line. As a consultant, she will be able to ensure that her vision for Robeez' design and brand continues.

The deal is also a coup for Stride Rite because it will help the company gain entry into the upscale department stores that carry Robeez. According to a financial analyst, "By having Robeez sold in stores like Saks and Bloomingdale's, that gives [Stride Rite] a better opportunity to also sell the Stride Rite product in those same retail channels."

Wilson found the decision to sell her company an emotional one. She signed the deal the same day her son Robert started high school. "I've had to say goodbye to two babies," she said. "This was probably the toughest decision I'm ever going to have to make, but I'm really looking forward to working with the Robeez team and Stride Rite in the next year."

Think About It

How can Sandra Wilson be sure she made the right decision?

Today's business world revolves around making decisions, often risky ones, usually with incomplete or inadequate information and under intense time pressure. In a recent survey of managers, 77 percent said that the number of decisions made during a typical workday had increased, and more than 43 percent said that the amount of time given to each decision had decreased.[31] Most managers are making one decision after another, and, as if that were not challenging enough, more is at stake than ever before. Bad decisions can cost millions. What do managers need to do to make effective decisions in today's fast-moving world? Here are a few guidelines:

- *Know when it's time to call it quits.* When it's evident that a decision is not working, don't be afraid to pull the plug. As we said earlier, many decision makers block or distort negative information because they don't want to believe that their decision was bad. They become so attached to the decision that they refuse to recognize when it's time to move on. In today's dynamic environment, this type of thinking simply will not work.

- *Practise the five whys.* When the environment is highly uncertain, one way to encourage good decision making is to get people to think more broadly and deeply about the issues. Because of the intense time pressure that managers face, it may be tempting to do just a superficial analysis. The "five whys" approach suggests that employees learn to ask "why" not just once, but five times.[32] Asking "why" this is happening usually results in a superficial explanation of the problem the first time; subsequent "whys" force decision makers to probe more deeply into the causes of the problem and possible solutions.

- *Use an effective decision-making process.* An effective decision-making process has these six characteristics: "(1) It focuses on what's important; (2) It's logical and consistent; (3) It acknowledges both subjective and objective thinking and blends analytical with intuitive thinking; (4) It requires only as much information and analysis as is necessary to resolve a particular dilemma; (5) It encourages and guides the gathering of relevant information and informed opinion; and (6) It's straightforward, reliable, easy to use, and flexible."[33]

The remaining suggestions for making decisions in today's world come from Karl Weick, an organizational psychologist who has made a career of studying organizations and how people work. This is similar to the discussion in Chapter 1 on the need to create organizations that are adaptive. He says that the best way for managers to respond to unpredictability and uncertainty is "by building an organization that expertly spots the unexpected when it crops up and then quickly adapts to the changed environment."[34] He calls these organizations *highly reliable organizations (HROs)* and says they share five habits:

- *They are not tricked by their success.* HROs are preoccupied with their failures. They are alert to the smallest deviations and react early and quickly to anything that does not fit with their expectations. Weick talks about navy aviators who describe "leemers—a gut feeling that something isn't right." Typically, these leemers turn out to be accurate. Something, in fact, is wrong. Organizations need to create climates where people feel safe trusting their leemers.

- *They defer to the experts on the front line.* Front-line employees—those who interact day in and day out with customers, products, suppliers, and so forth—have first-hand knowledge of what can and cannot be done, what will and will not work. Get their input. Let them make decisions.

- *They let unexpected circumstances provide the solution.* One of Weick's better-known works is his study of the Mann Gulch fire in Montana that killed 13 smoke jumpers in 1949. The event was a massive, tragic organizational failure. However, the reaction of the foreman illustrates how effective decision makers respond to unexpected circumstances. When the fire was nearly on top of his men, he invented the escape fire—a small fire that consumed all the brush around the team, leaving an area where the larger fire could not burn. His action was contrary to everything firefighters are taught (that is, you don't start fires—you extinguish them), but at the time it was the best decision.

- *They embrace complexity.* This characteristic is similar to the five whys we discussed earlier. Because business is complex, these organizations recognize that it "takes complexity to sense complexity." Rather than simplifying data, which we instinctively try to do when faced with complexity, these organizations aim for deeper understanding of the situation. They tap into their complexity to help them adapt more effectively.

- *They anticipate, but also anticipate their limits.* These organizations do try to anticipate as much as possible, but they recognize that they cannot anticipate everything. As Weick says, they don't "think, then act. They think by acting. By actually doing things, you'll find out what works and what doesn't."

Making decisions in today's fast-moving world is not easy. Successful managers have good decision-making skills to effectively and efficiently plan, organize, lead, and control.

MyManagementLab
PRISM 12

SUMMARY AND IMPLICATIONS

1. Describe the steps in the decision-making process. The steps include identifying a problem and the decision criteria; allocating weights to those criteria; developing, analyzing, and selecting an alternative that can resolve the problem; implementing the alternative; and evaluating the decision's effectiveness.

▶ ▶ ▶ Sandra Wilson, Robeez Footwear chair and CEO, identified that her company was poised for growth. She had to determine the relevant criteria and their weights to make a decision about whether or not to seek a new partner or sell the company. Which would be the best alternative?

2. Explain the different perspectives in management decision making. Decision making is particularly important to managers as it is part of all four managerial functions; decision making is the essence of management. The fact that almost everything a manager does involves making decisions doesn't mean that decisions are always time-consuming, complex, or evident to an outside observer. Most decision making is routine. Managers sometimes use intuition to enhance their decision-making process. Managers also need to decide whether they should make decisions themselves or encourage a team to help make the decision. Managers are affected by a variety of biases and errors: overconfidence bias, selective perception bias, confirmation bias, sunk-costs error, escalation-of-commitment error, self-serving bias, and hindsight bias.

▶ ▶ ▶ As Sandra's business grew, decisions were dispersed to managers in the field. While making decisions in each of the four areas of management (planning, organizing, leading, and controlling), they learned to employ the appropriate combination of decision-making perspectives—sometimes using intuition, sometimes rationality, and sometimes bounded rationality.

3. Classify decisions and decision-making conditions. Some problems are straightforward—these are known as structured problems. When situations are structured, there is often some standardized routine for handling problems that may arise, resulting in a programmed decision, a repetitive decision that can be handled by a routine approach. Many organizational situations involve unstructured problems, for which information is ambiguous or incomplete. The toughest of these unstructured problems are wicked problems, which are continuing works in progress.

▶ ▶ ▶ Managers at Robeez Footwear make decisions weekly about purchasing supplies and scheduling employee work shifts. It's something they have done numerous times and for which they used procedures and rules. But there came a point when founder Sandra Wilson realized they faced a different kind of decision, one they had never encountered—they had maxed out their own capabilities and needed to find a way to move the company forward to the next level. They were faced with a one-of-a-kind unstructured problem.

4. Describe different decision-making styles and the impact of biases. Decision-making styles differ along two dimensions. One is an individual's *way of thinking*—some of us are more rational and logical in the way we process information, while others tend to be creative and intuitive. The other dimension is an individual's *tolerance for ambiguity*—some managers need consistency and order, while others can tolerate high levels of ambiguity and are able to process many thoughts at the same time. When managers make decisions, they not only use their own particular style, but many use "rules of thumb," or heuristics, to simplify their decision making. In doing so, a variety of biases may once again lead to suboptimal choices.

▶ ▶ ▶ In making her choice of seeking a new partner, Sandra Wilson needed to be aware of the decision-making styles of the team advising her, as well as sensitive to the biases that could easily creep into the decision-making process.

5. Identify effective decision-making techniques. When making a decision, managers need to think broadly and deeply about issues and then know when it's time to call it quits. To be effective decision makers, they should focus on what is important; be logical and consistent; acknowledge both subjective and objective thinking; consider only as much information and analysis as is necessary; gather relevant information and informed opinion; and be flexible.

▶ ▶ ▶ Sandra Wilson was aware of a variety of positives and negatives in the decision to either bring in a new partner or sell Robeez. It was important for her to recognize that her preference for growth and the desire to see her creative vision for the brand continue might affect how she made her decision. Sandra Wilson decided that selling Robeez to Stride Rite was the right thing to do. There are advantages and disadvantages to most decisions, and it is important to weigh these thoroughly before reaching a conclusion.

Management @ Work

1. Why is decision making often described as the essence of a manager's job?

2. How is implementation important to the decision-making process?

3. What is a satisficing decision? How does it differ from a maximizing decision?

4. How do certainty, risk, and uncertainty affect decision making?

5. What is groupthink? How does it affect decision making?

6. Describe the decision-making biases and errors managers may exhibit.

7. How does escalation of commitment affect decision making? Why would managers make this type of error?

1. How might an organization's culture influence the way managers make decisions?

2. Would you call yourself a systematic or an intuitive thinker? What are the decision-making implications of these labels? What are the implications for choosing an employer?

3. All of us bring biases to the decisions we make. What would be the drawbacks of having biases? Could there be any advantages to having biases? Explain. What are the implications for decision making?

4. How can managers blend the guidelines for making effective decisions in today's world with the rationality and bounded rationality models of decision making, or can they? Explain.

5. Why do good managers sometimes make bad decisions? How can managers improve their decision-making skills?

How Intuitive Am I?

For each of the following questions, select the response that first appeals to you:[34]

1. When working on a project, I prefer to
  a. be told what the problem is, but be left free to decide how to solve it.
  b. get very clear instructions about how to go about solving the problem before I start.

2. When working on a project, I prefer to work with colleagues who are
  a. realistic.
  b. imaginative.

3. I most admire people who are
  a. creative.
  b. careful.

4. The friends I choose tend to be
  a. serious and hard-working.
  b. exciting and often emotional.

5. When I ask a colleague for advice on a problem I have, I
  a. seldom or never get upset if he/she questions my basic assumptions.
  b. often get upset if he/she questions my basic assumptions.

6. When I start my day, I
  a. seldom make or follow a specific plan.
  b. usually make a plan first to follow.

7. When working with numbers, I find that I
  a. seldom or never make factual errors.
  b. often make factual errors.

8. I find that I

a. seldom daydream during the day and really don't enjoy doing so when I do it.

b. frequently daydream during the day and enjoy doing so.

9. When working on a problem, I

a. prefer to follow the instructions or rules when they are given to me.

b. often enjoy circumventing the instructions or rules when they are given to me.

10. When I try to put something together, I prefer to have

a. step-by-step written instructions on how to assemble the item.

b. a picture of how the item is supposed to look once assembled.

11. I find that the person who irritates me the most is the one who appears to be

a. disorganized.

b. organized.

12. When an unexpected crisis comes up that I have to deal with, I

a. feel anxious about the situation.

b. feel excited by the challenge of the situation.

Scoring Key

For items 1, 3, 5, 6, and 11, score as follows: a = 1, b = 0
For items 2, 4, 7, 8, 9, 10, and 12, score as follows: a = 0, b = 1
Your total score will range between 0 and 12.

Analysis and Interpretation

Decision making isn't all systematic logic. Good decision makers also have developed, through experience, an intuitive ability that complements rational analysis. This ability is particularly valuable when decision makers face high levels of uncertainty, when facts are limited, when there is little previous precedent, when time is pressing, or when there are multiple plausible alternatives to choose among and there are good arguments for each.

If you have an intuitive score greater than 8, you prefer situations where there is a lack of structure and rules. You can handle uncertainty, spontaneity, and openness. Whether this ability is a plus in your job depends to a great extent on the culture of your organization. Where rationality is highly valued, reliance on intuition is likely to be seen as a negative quality. In open and creative-type cultures, intuitive ability is more likely to be valued.

More Self-Assessments MyManagementLab

To learn more about your skills, abilities, and interests, go to the MyManagementLab website and take the following self-assessments:

- I.A.4.—How Well Do I Handle Ambiguity? (This exercise also appears in Chapter 8 on pages 229–230.)
- I.D.1.—Am I a Procrastinator?
- III.C.1.—How Well Do I Respond to Turbulent Change? (This exercise also appears in Chapter 13 on pages 377–378.)
- IV.A.2.—Am I a Deliberate Decision Maker?

MANAGEMENT FOR YOU TODAY

Dilemma

Suppose your aunt said that she would help you open your own business. You are not sure whether you really want to run your own business, or work for a large consulting firm. However, you have always been interested in running a restaurant. How would you go about making a decision on what kind of restaurant you might open? How would you decide whether you should take your aunt up on her offer?

Becoming a Manager

- Pay close attention to decisions you make and how you make them.

- When you feel you have not made a good decision, assess how you could have made a better one. Which step of the decision-making process could you have improved?

- Work at developing good decision-making skills.

- Read books about decision making.

- Ask people you admire for advice on how they make good decisions.

WORKING TOGETHER: TEAM-BASED EXERCISE

A Life or Death Situation

The situation described in this problem is based on actual cases in which men and women lived or died depending upon the survival decision they made. Your "life" or "death" will depend on how well your group can share its present knowledge of a relatively unfamiliar problem, so that the group can make decisions that will lead to your survival.[36]

It is approximately 2:30 p.m. on October 5, and you have just crash-landed in a float plane on the east shore of Laura Lake in the subarctic region of the Northern Quebec–Newfoundland and Labrador border. The pilot was killed in the crash, but the rest of you are uninjured. Each of you is wet up to the waist and has perspired heavily. Shortly after the crash, the plane drifted into deep water and sank with the pilot's body pinned inside. The pilot was unable to contact anyone before the crash. However, ground sightings indicate that you are 48 kilometres south of your intended course and approximately 22 air miles east of Schefferville, your original destination and the nearest known habitation. Schefferville (pop. 240) is an iron ore–mining town approximately 300 air miles north of the St. Lawrence, 720 kilometres east of the James Bay/Hudson Bay area, 1290 kilometres south of the Arctic Circle, and 480 kilometres west of the Atlantic Coast. It is reachable only by air or rail, all roads ending a few kilometres from town. Your party was expected to return from northwestern Labrador to Schefferville no later than October 19 and filed a flight plan with Transport Canada via Schefferville radio to that effect.

The immediate area is covered with small evergreen trees (4 to 10 centimetres in diameter). Scattered in the area are a number of hills having rocky and barren tops. Tundra (treeless plains) makes up the valleys between the hills and consists only of small scrubs. Approximately 25 percent of the area in the region is covered by long, narrow lakes that run northwest to southeast. Innumerable streams and rivers flow into and connect the lakes. Temperatures during October vary between –4°C and 2°C, although it sometimes can go as high as 10°C and as low as –18°C. Heavy clouds cover the sky three-quarters of the time, with only one day in ten being fairly clear. Thirteen to eighteen centimetres of snow are on the ground. However, the actual depth varies enormously because the wind sweeps the exposed areas clear and builds drifts 0.9 to 1.5 metres deep in other areas. The wind speed averages 20 to 25 kilometres/hour and is mostly out of the west-northwest.

You are all dressed in insulated underwear, socks, heavy wool shirts, pants, knit gloves, sheepskin jackets, knitted wool toques, and heavy leather hunting boots. Collectively, your personal possessions include $150 in bills, 4 loonies, 4 quarters, 2 dimes, 1 nickel, and 3 pennies; 1 pocket knife (2 blades and an awl, which resembles an ice pick); 1 stub lead pencil; and an air map.

Before the plane drifted away and sank, you were able to salvage the 15 items listed on the attached chart. Your task is to rank these items according to their importance to your survival, from "1" for the most important up to "15" for the least important.

You may assume the following:

- The number of survivors is the same as the number on your team.

- You are the actual people in the situation.

- The team has agreed to stick together.

- All items are dry and in good condition.

Items	Step 1: Your ranking	Step 2: Team ranking	Step 3: Survival experts' ranking	Step 4: Difference between steps 1 and 3	Step 5: Difference between steps 2 and 3
A magnetic compass					
A 4-litre can of maple syrup					
A sleeping bag per person (arctic type; down-filled with liner)					
A bottle of water purification tablets					
A 6 m x 6 m piece of heavy-duty canvas					
13 wood matches in a metal screwtop, water-proof container					
75 m of 0.5-cm braided nylon rope, 20 kg test					
An operating 4-battery flashlight					
3 pairs of snowshoes					
A fifth of Bacardi rum (151 proof)					
Safety-razor shaving kit with mirror					
A wind-up alarm clock					
A hand axe					
1 aircraft inner tube for a 35-cm wheel (punctured)					
A book entitled *Northern Star Navigation*					
			Total	**Individual**	**Team**

ETHICS IN ACTION

Ethical Dilemma Exercise: Can Investment Advice Be "Perfectly Objective"?

Competitive problems are rarely well structured, as the managers at Greenfield Brokerage know.[37] Over the years, the firm has successfully competed with well-established rivals by making nonprogrammed decisions. For example, management decided to charge customers less for trading stocks, bonds, and mutual funds and to implement technology giving customers more trading choices. Because the competitive environment is constantly changing, Greenfield's advertising managers can never be certain about the outcome of decisions concerning how to promote the firm's competitive advantages.

Not long ago, some competing brokerage firms paid hefty fines to settle charges stemming from conflicts of interest involving their research and recommendations to customers. In the aftermath of these scandals, Greenfield's managers decided on an advertising campaign to stress that Greenfield does things differently. One tongue-in-cheek commercial took viewers behind the scenes at a fictitious competitor's office, where brokers chanted "Buy, buy, buy." A broker looked at a restaurant takeout menu as he told a customer on the phone, "I have your portfolio right here, and I think you should buy." Some networks rejected these aggressive commercials. The ads also raised questions about potential conflicts of interest created by Greenfield brokers steering business to in-house traders and mutual funds.

Imagine you are an advertising manager at Greenfield. Your advertising agency has suggested a newspaper ad in which a fictitious competing broker is quoted as saying, "My investment advice is perfectly objective, even though I work on commission." A Greenfield broker is then quoted as saying, "I don't work on commission like other brokers do, so my investment advice is perfectly objective." How certain are you that your advice is perfectly objective when Greenfield benefits from every client it gets? (Review Exhibits 6-12 on page 170 and 6-13 on page 171 as you think about this dilemma.)

Thinking Critically About Ethics

You are in charge of hiring a new employee to work in your area of responsibility, and one of your friends from college needs a job. You think he's minimally qualified for the position, and you feel that you could find a better-qualified and more experienced candidate if you kept looking. What will you do? What factors will influence your decision? What will you tell your friend?

CASE APPLICATION

C. F. Martin Guitar Company

The C. F. Martin Guitar Company (**www.mguitar.com**) has been producing acoustic instruments since 1833.[38] A Martin guitar is among the best that money can buy. Current CEO Christian Frederick Martin IV—better known as Chris—continues to be committed to the guitar maker's craft. During 2002, the company sold about 77 000 instruments and hit a record $77 million in revenue. Despite this success, Chris is facing some serious issues.

Martin Guitar is an interesting blend of old and new. Although the equipment and tools may have changed over the years, employees remain true to the principle of high standards of musical excellence. Building a guitar to meet these standards requires considerable attention and patience. In a 1904 catalogue, a family member explained, "How to build a guitar to give this tone is not a secret. It takes care and patience." Now, well over a century later, this statement is still an accurate reflection of the company's philosophy.

From the very beginning, quality has played an important role in everything that Martin Guitar does. Part of that quality approach includes a long-standing ecological policy. The company depends on natural wood products to make its guitars, but a lot of the wood supply is vanishing. Chris has long embraced the responsible use of traditional wood materials, going so far as to encourage suppliers to find alternative species. Based on thorough customer research, Martin Guitar introduced guitars that used structurally sound woods with natural cosmetic defects that were once considered unacceptable. In addition, Martin Guitar follows the directives of CITES, the Convention on International Trade in Endangered Species of Wild Fauna and Flora (**www.cites.org**), even though it has the potential to affect Martin Guitar's ability to produce the type of quality products it has in the past. This treaty barred the export of the much-desired Brazilian rosewood, which is considered endangered. A guitar built from the remaining supply of this popular wood has a hefty price tag—$39 999 and up. Similar prices may be in line for the leading alternative, Honduras mahogany. Chris says, "All of us who use wood for the tone [it makes] are scrambling. Options are limited."

Although the company is rooted in its past, Chris is wondering whether he should go in new directions. For instance, he could try selling guitars in the under-$800 segment, a segment that accounts for 65 percent of the acoustic guitar industry's sales. A less expensive guitar would not look,

smell, or feel like the company's pricier models. But Chris thinks that it would sound better than guitars in that price range made by other companies. Chris explains, "My fear is that if we don't look at alternatives, we'll be the company making guitars for doctors and lawyers. If Martin just worships its past without trying anything new, there won't be a Martin left to worship."

What should Chris do? Why?

DEVELOPING YOUR DIAGNOSTIC AND ANALYTICAL SKILLS

Some Solutions Create More Problems

With sentences handed down to executives involved in the Enron scandal, the conviction of Martha Stewart in March 2004 of lying to federal investigators during a stock-scandal investigation, and the conviction of Conrad Black for using millions of Hollinger International's profits between 1997 and 2004 for his own personal gain, being a CEO appears to be losing some of its lustre.[39] Why these individuals did what they did and why they made such decisions that proved to be so wrong is difficult to say. You just have to wonder what underlies the CEO decision-making process. Take the case of Robert Milton, CEO of Montreal-based Air Canada.

Air Canada has been struggling financially for a number of years. As the company went into bankruptcy in the early 2000s, Milton pleaded with the union leaders representing the company's 25 000 employees to consider accepting significant pay and benefits cuts. Milton built the case that this was a last resort and that without the employees' acceptance of the cuts, the company was doomed.

The company emerged from bankruptcy in late 2004, but employees have not seen pay raises in a while. Milton informed employees in spring 2006 that Air Canada would find it "hard" to increase wages in labour contract talks later in the year because other carriers have reduced pay. He added that expecting pay raises was not realistic, "given

that in most places around North America wages are going down very, very significantly."

Meanwhile, the company distributed $266 million to its shareholders, leading union members to conclude that the company was doing better than the CEO was acknowledging. That money, had it been distributed to employees, would have resulted in a $10 000 bonus for each one. Employees were furious, and demanded that Milton step down. However, Milton explained his logic for not giving that money to employees: "By providing a return of capital to our shareholders, the company is rewarding investors for their confidence while maintaining a firm foundation for future prosperity."

Questions

1. How do you think poor decision making contributed to the failures of Conrad Black and Robert Milton? Discuss.

2. How could the eight-step decision-making process have helped Milton make a better decision? Explain.

3. What role, if any, did escalation of commitment play in Milton's decision? Defend your opinion.

Solving Problems Creatively

About the Skill

Creativity is a frame of mind. You need to expand your mind's capabilities—that is, open up your mind to new ideas. Every individual has the ability to improve his or her creativity, but many people simply don't try to develop that ability. In a global business environment, where changes are fast and furious, organizations desperately need creative people. The uniqueness and variety of problems that managers face demand that they be able to solve problems creatively.

Steps in Developing the Skill

You can be more effective at solving problems creatively if you use the following 10 suggestions:[40]

1. **Think of yourself as creative.** Although this may be a simple suggestion, research shows that if you think you cannot be creative, you will not be. Believing in your ability to be creative is the first step in becoming more creative.

2. **Pay attention to your intuition.** Every individual has a subconscious mind that works well. Sometimes answers will come to you when you least expect them. Listen to that "inner voice." In fact, most creative people keep a notepad near their beds and write down ideas when the thoughts come to them. That way, they don't forget them.

3. **Move away from your comfort zone.** Every individual has a comfort zone in which certainty exists. But creativity and the known often do not mix. To be creative, you need to move away from the status quo and focus your mind on something new.

4. **Determine what you want to do.** This includes such things as taking time to understand a problem before beginning to try to resolve it, getting all the facts in mind, and trying to identify the most important facts.

5. **Look for ways to tackle the problem.** This can be accomplished by setting aside a block of time to focus on it; working out a plan for attacking it; establishing subgoals; imagining or actually using analogies wherever possible (for example, could you approach your problem like a fish out of water and look at what the fish does to cope? Or can you use the things you have to do to find your way when it's foggy to help you solve your problem?); using different problem-solving strategies such as verbal, visual, mathematical, theatrical (for example, you might draw a diagram of the decision or problem to help you visualize it better, or you might talk to yourself out loud about the problem, telling it as you

would tell a story to someone); trusting your intuition; and playing with possible ideas and approaches (for example, look at your problem from a different perspective or ask yourself what someone else, such as your grandmother, might do if faced with the same situation).

6. **Look for ways to do things better.** This may involve trying consciously to be original, not worrying about looking foolish, eliminating cultural taboos (like gender stereotypes) that might influence your possible solutions, keeping an open mind, being alert to odd or puzzling facts, thinking of unconventional ways to use objects and the environment (for instance, thinking about how you could use newspaper or magazine headlines to help you be a better problem solver), discarding usual or habitual ways of doing things, and striving for objectivity by being as critical of your own ideas as you would those of someone else.

7. **Find several right answers.** Being creative means continuing to look for other solutions even when you think you have solved the problem. A better, more creative solution just might be found.

8. **Believe in finding a workable solution.** Like believing in yourself, you also need to believe in your ideas. If you don't think you can find a solution, you probably won't.

9. **Brainstorm with others.** Creativity isn't an isolated activity. Bouncing ideas off others creates synergy.

10. **Turn creative ideas into action.** Coming up with creative ideas is only part of the process. Once the ideas are generated, they must be implemented. Keeping great ideas in your mind, or on papers that no one will read, does little to expand your creative abilities.

Practising the Skill

Read the following scenario. Write some notes about how you would handle the situation. Be sure to refer to the 10 suggestions for solving problems creatively.

Scenario

Every time the phone rings, your stomach clenches and your palms start to sweat. And it's no wonder! As sales manager for Brinkers, a machine tool parts manufacturer, you are besieged by calls from customers who are upset about late deliveries. Your manager, Carter Hererra, acts as both production manager and scheduler. Every time your sales representatives negotiate a sale, it's up to Carter to determine whether or not production can actually meet the delivery date the customer specifies. And Carter invariably says, "No problem." The good thing about this is that you make a lot of initial sales. The bad news is that production hardly ever meets the shipment dates that Carter authorizes. And he does not seem to be all that concerned about the aftermath of late deliveries. He says, "Our customers know they're getting outstanding quality at a great price. Just let them try to match that anywhere. It can't be done. So, even if they have to wait a couple of extra days or weeks, they're still getting the best deal they can." Somehow the customers don't see it that way, however. And they let you know about their unhappiness. Then it's up to you to try to soothe the relationship. You know this problem has to be taken care of, but what possible solutions are there? After all, how are you going to keep from making your manager or the customers angry?

Reinforcing the Skill

The following activities will help you practise and reinforce the skills associated with solving problems creatively:

1. Take out a couple of sheets of paper. How many words can you make using the letters in the word *brainstorm*? (There are at least 95.) If you run out of words before time is up, it's OK to quit early. But try to be as creative as you can.

2. List on a piece of paper some common terms that apply to both water and finance. How many were you able to come up with?

MANAGING WORKFORCE DIVERSITY

The Value of Diversity in Decision Making

Have you decided what your major is going to be? How did you decide? Do you feel your decision is a good one? Is there anything you could have done differently to make sure that your decision was the best one?[41]

Making good decisions is tough! Managers are continually making decisions—for instance, developing new products, establishing weekly or monthly goals, implementing advertising campaigns, reassigning employees to different work groups, resolving customers' complaints, or purchasing new laptops for sales representatives. One important suggestion for making better decisions is to tap into the diversity of the work group. Drawing upon the ideas of diverse employees can prove valuable to a manager's decision making. Why? Diverse employees can provide fresh perspectives on issues. They can offer differing interpretations on how a problem is defined and may be more open to trying new ways of doing things. Diverse employees usually are more creative in generating alternatives and more flexible in resolving issues. And getting input from diverse sources increases the likelihood of finding creative and unique solutions.

Even though diversity in decision making can be valuable, there are drawbacks. The lack of a common perspective usually means that more time is spent discussing the issues. Communication may be a problem, particularly if language barriers are present. In addition, seeking out diverse opinions can make the decision-making process more complex, confusing, and ambiguous. In addition, with multiple perspectives on the decision, it may be difficult to reach a single agreement or to agree on specific actions. Although these drawbacks are valid concerns, the value of diversity in decision making outweighs the potential disadvantages.

Now, about that decision on a major. Did you ask others for their opinions? Did you seek out advice from professors, family members, friends, or co-workers? Getting diverse perspectives on an important decision like this could help you make the best one! Managers also should consider the value to be gained from diversity in decision making.

MyManagementLab

For more resources, please visit www.pearsoned.ca/mymanagementlab

SCAN THIS

Foundations of Planning

In this chapter, we begin our study of the first of the management functions: planning. Planning is important because it establishes what an organization is doing. We'll look at how managers set goals, as well as how they establish plans. After reading and studying this chapter, you will achieve the following learning outcomes.

Learning Outcomes

1 Define the nature and purpose of planning.

2 Understand how managers set goals and develop plans.

3 Discuss contemporary issues in planning.

▶▶▶ Blue Man Group is one of the hottest performance groups today.[1] Its theatrical productions have run in New York, Boston, Chicago, and Las Vegas for years. Currently, the group has shows in Berlin, Oberhausen, Amsterdam, New York, Boston, Chicago, Las Vegas, and Orlando. It also opened a show in Toronto in 2005, which ran until 2007. Blue Man performances are a mix of mime, percussion music, and splashing paint.

The group was founded in 1988 by three guys who decided it was time to stage a funeral for the 1980s. They put on bald wigs, painted themselves blue, and carried a coffin filled with items representing the worst of the decade (such as yuppies and Rambo) into New York City's Central Park. MTV recorded the ceremony.

Encouraged by their friends, the trio (Chris Wink, Matt Goldman, and Phil Stanton) started giving small performances around the city. None of the three had formal training in music or acting. They really had not planned to become performers. Three years later, they had performed on national TV, spitting paint on *The Tonight Show* and *Live with Regis and Kathie Lee*. They also had an off-Broadway show called *Tubes*.

Wink, Goldman, and Stanton were also starting to burn out. They were working six days a week, had gone three years without a break, and performed 1200 consecutive shows. Once success started, the three just kept going, not giving thought to how to manage the show or their time. They did not have time to create new material, so they were just performing the same show over and over. They had a small crew who had "never worked in theater and [did not] have a clue, just like us," says Wink. They spent 90 minutes each night making themselves up before a performance. Then they were part of the cleanup crew. They were so tired that they did not have time for a personal life. How did they get into this situation? "We've never planned ahead," explained Wink.

Think About It

How much planning should organizations do? Put yourself in Blue Man Group's shoes. How can it make sure that the show goes on, should one of its members get injured?

Managers everywhere need to plan. In this chapter, we present the basics of planning: what it is, why managers plan, and how they plan. Then we conclude by looking at some contemporary issues in planning.

What Is Planning?

As we stated in Chapter 1, **planning** involves defining goals, establishing an overall strategy for achieving those goals, and developing a comprehensive set of plans to integrate and coordinate the work needed to achieve the goals. It's concerned both with ends (what's to be done) and means (how it's to be done). For instance, you and your classmates may want to organize a large graduation dinner dance. To do so, you would consider the goals, the strategy, and the plans and assign committees to get the work done.

Planning can be either formal or informal. In informal planning, nothing is written down, and there is little or no sharing of goals with others. Informal planning is general and lacks continuity. Although it's more common in smaller organizations, where the

1. Define the nature and purpose of planning.

planning A management function that involves defining goals, establishing a strategy for achieving those goals, and developing plans to integrate and coordinate activities.

MyManagementLab
Q&A 7.1

owner-manager has a vision of where he or she wants the business to go and how to get there, informal planning does exist in some large organizations as well. At the same time, some small businesses may have very sophisticated planning processes and formal plans. (To test your competence in planning, see *Self-Assessment—How Good Am I at Personal Planning?* on page 256, in Chapter 9.)

When we use the term *planning* in this book, we mean *formal* planning. In formal planning, specific goals covering a period of years are defined. These goals are written and shared with organization members. Then a specific action program for the achievement of these goals is developed; that is, managers clearly define the path they want to take to get the organization and the various work units from where they are to where the managers want them to be.

Setting goals, establishing strategies to achieve those goals, and developing a set of plans to integrate and coordinate activities seem pretty complicated. Given that fact, why should managers want to plan? Does planning impact performance? We address these issues in the following sections.

Purposes of Planning

Are you a planner or a doer? Do you prefer to make plans or just act?

We can identify at least four reasons for planning:

- *Planning provides direction to managers and nonmanagers alike.* When employees know where the organization or work unit is going and what they must contribute to reach goals, they can coordinate their activities, cooperate with each other, and do what it takes to accomplish those goals. Without planning, departments and individuals might work at cross purposes, preventing the organization from moving efficiently toward its goals.

- *Planning reduces uncertainty by forcing managers to look ahead, anticipate change, consider the impact of change, and develop appropriate responses.* Even though planning cannot eliminate change or uncertainty, managers plan in order to anticipate change and develop the most effective response to it.

- *Planning reduces overlapping and wasteful activities.* When work activities are coordinated around established plans, redundancy can be minimized. Furthermore, when means and ends are made clear through planning, inefficiencies become obvious and can be corrected or eliminated.

- *Planning establishes the goals or standards that are used in controlling.* If we are unsure of what we are trying to accomplish, how can we determine whether we have actually achieved it? In planning, we develop the goals and the plans. Then, through controlling, we compare actual performance against the goals, identify any significant deviations, and take any necessary corrective action. Without planning, there would be no way to control outcomes.

Ron Zambonini, former CEO of Ottawa-based Cognos (acquired by IBM in 2008), notes that planning went out of fashion during the dot-com years. He found that in both California and in Ottawa, entrepreneurs worked "90 hours a week, but the whole goal [was] not to build a business or a company. [All they really wanted was] someone to buy them out."[2] Unfortunately, many of those companies were not bought out, but folded. Planning might have helped them be more successful.

Planning and Performance

Is planning worthwhile? Do managers and organizations that plan outperform those that don't? Intuitively, you would expect the answer to be a resounding yes. While studies of performance in organizations that plan are generally positive, we cannot say that organizations that formally plan *always* outperform those that don't plan.

Victoria Hale founded the not-for-profit Institute for OneWorld Health with an informal plan. Inspired by a conversation with a cab driver about pharmaceutical science, Hale went back to an essay she had written years earlier about diseases that would benefit from drug development efforts. Using that as her preliminary business plan, she incorporated the institute the next day. The institute's goal is to persuade companies with important but not profitable drugs to donate those to the institute for tax and public relations benefits. The institute then uses grants and donations to distribute the drugs to needy patients around the world.

Are you skeptical of planning? Do you wonder whether planning really pays off?

Numerous studies have looked at the relationship between planning and performance.[3] We can draw the following four conclusions from these studies. First, generally speaking, formal planning is associated with higher profits, higher return on assets, and other positive financial results. Second, the quality of the planning process and the appropriate implementation of the plans probably contribute more to high performance than does the extent of planning. Third, in those studies in which formal planning did not lead to higher performance, the external environment often was the culprit. Government regulations, powerful labour unions, and other critical environmental forces constrain managers' options and reduce the impact of planning on an organization's performance. Fourth, the planning/performance relationship is influenced by the planning time frame. Organizations need at least four years of systematic formal planning before performance is affected.

MyManagementLab
Q&A 7.2

How Do Managers Plan?

▶ ▶ ▶ One evening, after three years of nonstop performing with Blue Man Group, Phil Stanton cut his hand with a router.[4] The group had never planned for what to do if one of them was injured. They had one understudy, one of the show's drummers, but only because their investors had insisted on it as a backup plan. While he had studied the show, he had never even rehearsed in it. When Stanton cut his hand, the drummer had to go onstage as a Blue Man. Because the group members wear bald wigs and paint themselves blue, no one in the audience knew that Stanton was missing. The show was a success even without him.

That success made the co-founders of Blue Man (Chris Wink, Matt Goldman, and Phil Stanton) realize that it would be quite easy to clone Blue Man, which would increase the number of shows they could do, and also give the co-founders time off. Finally, three years after they had started performing, they could think more about how to expand their show.

The group's next hurdle came when it opened a second venue, in Boston. The co-founders split their time between their New York venue and Boston, but it meant that they were less "hands on" at their shows. Quality started to slip. They finally realized they needed a specific plan to guide the 38 new performers they were bringing on board, so they locked themselves in an apartment and talked through their creative vision in great detail. The result? A

2. Understand how managers set goals and develop plans.

132-page operating manual that tells the story of the Blue Man show and allows the show to be reproduced by others. Ironically, by writing the plan, though it is a somewhat unorthodox one, the co-founders were able to express artistic ideals that had been understood among them but never stated before. Today, the former drummer who was their first understudy trains new Blue Man performers. Wink, Goldman, and Stanton make only occasional appearances onstage.

Think About It

How did planning make Blue Man Group performers more successful in their one existing show? How did planning allow the concept to be successfully replicated in other venues?

Planning is often called the primary management function because it establishes the basis for all the other functions that managers perform. Without planning, managers would not know what to organize, lead, or control. In fact, without plans, there would not be anything to organize, lead, or control! So how do managers plan?

Planning involves two important elements: goals and plans. **Goals** are desired outcomes for individuals, groups, or entire organizations.[5] Goals are objectives, and we use the two terms interchangeably. They provide the direction for all management decisions and form the criteria against which actual work accomplishments can be measured. That is why they are often called the foundation of planning. You have to know the desired target or outcome before you can establish plans for reaching it. **Plans** are documents that outline how goals are going to be met and that typically describe resource allocations, schedules, and other necessary actions to accomplish the goals. As managers plan, they are developing both goals and plans.

In the next section, we consider how to establish goals.

Approaches to Establishing Goals

Every organization has some purpose for being in business. This purpose is generally derived from an organization's mission statement, which answers the question: What is our reason for being in business? We describe mission statements more thoroughly in Chapter 8 when we discuss strategic management. For now, it is important to note that the organization's mission helps managers determine the organization's goals. Goals provide the direction for all management decisions and actions and form the criteria against which actual accomplishments are measured. Everything organizational members do should be oriented toward helping their work units and the organization achieve its goals. These goals can be established through a process of traditional goal setting or management by objectives.

Traditional Goal Setting

In **traditional goal setting**, goals are set at the top of the organization and then broken into subgoals for each organizational level. This traditional perspective works reasonably well when an organization is hierarchically structured. For example, the president of a manufacturing business tells the vice-president of production what he expects manufacturing costs to be for the coming year and tells the marketing vice-president what level he expects sales to reach for the year. These goals then are passed down to the next organizational level and written to reflect the work responsibilities of that level, passed down to the next level, and so forth. Then, at some later point, performance is evaluated to determine whether the assigned goals have been achieved. This traditional perspective assumes that top managers know what is best because they see the "big picture." Thus, the goals that are established and passed down to each succeeding level serve to direct and guide, and in some ways constrain, individual employees' work behaviours. Employees work to meet the goals that have been assigned in their areas of responsibility.

One of the problems with this traditional approach is that if top managers define the organization's goals in broad terms—achieving "sufficient" profits or increasing "market leadership"—these ambiguous goals have to be made more specific as they flow down

goals Desired outcomes for individuals, groups, or entire organizations.

plans Documents that outline how goals are going to be met and that describe resource allocations, schedules, and other necessary actions to accomplish the goals.

traditional goal setting An approach to setting goals in which goals are set at the top of the organization and then broken into subgoals for each organizational level.

Goals are the outcomes we desire. At the Bronx Zoo, where Patrick Thomas, curator of mammals, recently gazed into the eyes of Siberian tiger Taurus through a sheet of 2.5-centimetre-thick glass, "Our goal is to have animals engaged in normal behaviors." Thomas goes on to say of the new tiger habitat, "You want the exhibit to inspire visitors to care about saving tigers." The 1.2-hectare Tiger Mountain is particularly important: its 6 residents represent the mere 5000 tigers left in the wild.

through the organization. At each level, managers define the goals, applying their own interpretations and biases as they make them more specific. However, what often happens is that goals lose clarity and unity as they make their way down from the top of the organization to lower levels. Exhibit 7-1 illustrates what can happen in this situation.

When the hierarchy of organizational goals *is* clearly defined, however, it forms an integrated network of goals, or a **means–ends chain**. This means that higher-level goals (or ends) are linked to lower-level goals, which serve as the means for their accomplishment. In other words, the achievement of goals at lower levels becomes the means to reach the goals at the next level (ends), and the accomplishment of goals at that level becomes the means to achieve the goals at the next level (ends), and so forth and so on, up through the different levels of the organization. That is how the traditional goal-setting approach is supposed to work. For instance, if top management wants to increase sales by 10 percent for the year, the marketing and sales departments need to develop action plans that

means–ends chain An integrated network of goals in which the accomplishment of goals at one level serves as the means for achieving the goals, or ends, at the next level.

Exhibit 7-1

The Downside of Traditional Goal Setting

"We need to improve the company's performance."

"I want to see a significant improvement in this division's profits."

Top Management's Objective

Division Manager's Objective

"Increase profits regardless of the means."

Department Manager's Objective

"Don't worry about quality; just work fast."

Individual Employee's Objective

will yield these results. The manufacturing division needs to develop plans for how to produce more product. An individual salesperson may need to make more calls to new clients or convince current clients that they need more product. Thus, each of the lower levels (individual employee, sales, marketing, production) becomes means to achieving the corporate end of increasing sales.

Management by Objectives

management by objectives (MBO) An approach to setting goals in which specific performance goals are jointly determined by employees and their managers, progress toward accomplishing those goals is periodically reviewed, and rewards are allocated on the basis of this progress.

Instead of traditional goal setting, many organizations use **management by objectives (MBO)**, an approach in which specific performance goals are jointly determined by employees and their managers, progress toward accomplishing these goals is periodically reviewed, and rewards are allocated on the basis of this progress. Rather than using goals only as controls, MBO uses them to motivate employees as well. Employees will be more committed to goals that they help set.

Management by objectives consists of four elements: goal specificity, participative decision making, an explicit time period, and performance feedback.[6] Its appeal lies in its focus on the accomplishment of participatively set objectives as the reason for and motivation behind individuals' work efforts. Exhibit 7-2 lists the steps in a typical MBO program.

Do MBO programs work? Studies of actual MBO programs confirm that MBO increases employee performance and organizational productivity. A review of 70 programs, for example, found organizational productivity gains in 68 of them.[7] This same review also identified top management's commitment and involvement as important conditions for MBO to succeed.

One problem of MBO programs is that they may not be as effective in times of dynamic environmental change. An MBO program needs some stability for employees to work toward accomplishing the set goals. If new goals must be set every few weeks, there is no time for employees to work on accomplishing the goals and measuring that accomplishment. Another problem of MBO programs is that an employee's overemphasis on accomplishing his or her goals without regard to others in the work unit can be

Exhibit 7-2

Steps in a Typical MBO Program

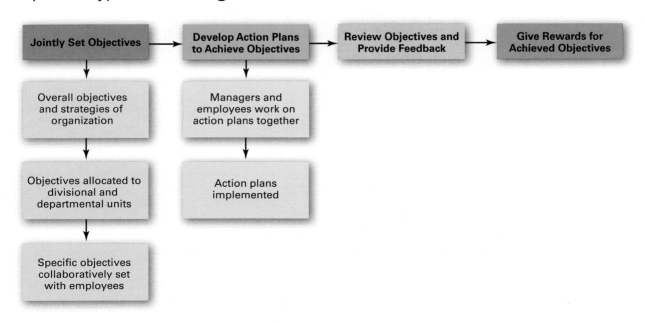

counterproductive. A manager must work closely with all members of the work unit to ensure that employees are not working at cross purposes. Finally, if MBO is viewed simply as an annual exercise in filling out paperwork, employees will not be motivated to accomplish the goals. (For a look at your response to achieving goals, see *Self-Assessment—What's My Attitude Toward Achievement?* on pages 201–202.)

MyManagementLab

Q&A 7.4

Characteristics of Well-Designed Goals

Goals are not all created equal! Some goals are better than others. How do you tell the difference? What makes a "well-designed" goal?[8] Exhibit 7-3 outlines the characteristics of well-designed goals.

A well-designed goal should be *written in terms of outcomes* rather than actions. The desired end result is the most important element of any goal and, therefore, the goal should be written to reflect this. Next, a goal should be *measurable and quantifiable*. It's much easier to determine if a goal has been met if it's measurable. For instance, suppose one of your goals is to "produce a high-quality product." What exactly do you mean by high quality? Because there are numerous ways to define quality, the goal should state specifically how you will measure whether or not the product is high quality. This means that even in areas where it may be difficult to quantify your intent, you should try to find some specific way or ways to measure whether that goal is accomplished. Why have the goal if you cannot measure whether it's been met?

Have you occasionally failed at your goals? How can you develop more achievable goals?

In addition to specifying a quantifiable measure of accomplishment, a well-designed goal should also be *clear as to a time frame*. Open-ended goals may seem preferable because of their flexibility. However, goals without a time frame make an organization less flexible because you are never sure when the goal has been met or when you should call it quits because the goal will never be met regardless of how long you work at it. A well-designed goal will specify a time frame for accomplishment. The mnemonic SMART is often used to describe well-designed goals that are specific, measurable, attainable, relevant, time-bound, and evaluated.[9]

A well-designed goal should also be *challenging but attainable*. Goals that are too easy to accomplish are not motivating, and neither are goals that are not attainable even with exceptional effort. A well-designed goal should also be *written down*. Although actually writing down goals may seem too time-consuming, the process of writing the goals forces people to think them through. In addition, the written goals become visible and tangible evidence of the importance of working toward something. Finally, a well-designed goal is *communicated to all organizational members* who need to know the goal. Why? Making people aware of goals ensures that they are all "on the same page" and working in ways to secure the accomplishment of the organization's goals. The following *Management Reflection* shows what can happen when an organization does not set goals for growth and must cope with booming sales.

Exhibit 7-3

Characteristics of Well-Designed Goals

- Written down
- Written in terms of outcomes rather than actions
- Measurable and quantifiable
- Clear time frame
- Challenging yet attainable
- Communicated to all necessary organizational members

Kicking Horse Coffee Learns the Benefits of Planning

Should a company plan for success? For Canada's top seller of organic coffee, Invermere, BC-based Kicking Horse Coffee, rapid growth and expansion meant that the company could not keep up with the soaring demand for its product.[10] As they started expanding into markets east of Manitoba, Kicking Horse founders Elana Rosenfeld (CEO) and Leo Johnson (president) did not really consider whether they had the capacity to meet an increase in demand. Rather, they focused on getting into new markets. Rosenfeld got a "wake-up call" about the need for planning. As a result, the founders developed detailed sales forecasts and considered capital needs. They also started to examine space, people, and equipment needs. The owners realized that they needed to be more disciplined about the opportunities they pursued, including deciding that they would not supply ground coffee to grocery stores.

The new strategic plan makes sure that demand for coffee can be met and that Kicking Horse can grow fast, while still keeping its promise to employees: "never any overtime." Rosenfeld explains why she has become so committed to planning: "Part of planning is articulating who you are and what you believe in so you can stay on the path." ■

Steps in Goal Setting

What steps should managers follow in setting goals? The goal-setting process consists of five steps.

mission The purpose of an organization.

1. *Review the organization's mission.* The **mission** is the purpose of an organization. The broad statement of what the organization's purpose is and what it hopes to accomplish provides an overall guide to what organizational members think is important. (We look more closely at organizational mission in Chapter 8.) It's important to review these statements before writing goals because the goals should reflect the intent of the company's mission.

Planning is definitely not just for managers. When families in the *Vancouver Sun*'s distribution area were asked to take the newspaper's "car-free challenge" for a month, they learned that planning became a much greater part of their lives. The three families pictured here took the challenge and found that figuring out how long a journey took and the best way to get there required being more aware of their schedules than when they could just grab their car keys and drive off.

2. *Evaluate available resources.* You don't want to set goals that are impossible to achieve given your available resources. Even though goals should be challenging, they should be realistic. After all, if the resources you have to work with will not allow you to achieve a goal no matter how hard you try or how much effort is exerted, that goal should not be set. That would be like the person with a $50 000 annual income and no other financial resources setting a goal of building an investment portfolio worth $1 million in three years. No matter how hard he or she works at it, it's not going to happen.

3. *Determine the goals individually or with input from others.* These goals reflect desired outcomes and should be consistent with the organization's mission and goals in other organizational areas. These goals should be measurable, specific, and include a time frame for accomplishment.

4. *Write down the goals and communicate them to all who need to know.* We have already explained the benefit of writing down and communicating goals.

5. *Review results and whether goals are being met.* If goals are not being met, make changes to the goals as needed, and in some cases make changes to the plan based on the new information at hand. For any plan to be effective, reviews need to be done, and this would be expected for any industry.

(For suggestions on setting work goals for employees, see *Developing Your Interpersonal Skills—Setting Goals* on pages 205–206.)

Developing Plans

Once goals have been established, written down, and communicated, a manager is ready to develop plans for pursuing the goals.

Types of Plans

The most popular ways to describe an organization's plans are by their breadth (strategic vs. operational), time frame (short term vs. long term), specificity (directional vs. specific), and frequency of use (single use vs. standing). These planning classifications are not independent. As Exhibit 7-4 illustrates, strategic plans are long term, directional, and single use. Operational plans are short term, specific, and standing. Let's describe each of these types of plans.

Strategic plans are plans that apply to the entire organization, establish the organization's overall goals, and seek to position the organization in terms of its environment. Plans that specify the details of how the overall goals are to be achieved are called **operational plans**. How do the two types of plans differ? Strategic plans tend to cover a longer time frame and a broader view of the organization. Strategic plans also include the formulation of goals, whereas operational plans define ways to achieve the goals. Also, operational plans tend to cover short time periods—monthly, weekly, and day to day.

The difference in years between short term and long term has shortened considerably. It used to be that long term meant anything over seven years. Try to imagine what you would like to be doing in seven years, and you can begin to appreciate how difficult it was for managers to establish plans that far in the future. As organizational environments have become more uncertain, the definition of *long term* has changed. We define **long-term plans** as those with a time frame beyond three years.[11] For instance, an organization may develop a five-year plan for increasing its sales in Asia. We define **short-term plans** as those with a time frame of one year or less. For instance, a company may decide that it will increase sales by 10 percent over the next year. The intermediate term is any time period in between. Although these time classifications are fairly common, an organization can designate any time frame it wants for planning purposes.

Intuitively, it would seem that specific plans would be preferable to directional, or loosely guided, plans. **Specific plans** are plans that are clearly defined and that leave no room for interpretation. They have clearly defined objectives. There is no ambiguity and

strategic plans Plans that apply to the entire organization, establish the organization's overall goals, and seek to position the organization in terms of its environment.

operational plans Plans that specify the details of how the overall goals are to be achieved.

long-term plans Plans with a time frame beyond three years.

short-term plans Plans with a time frame of one year or less.

specific plans Plans that are clearly defined and that leave no room for interpretation.

Exhibit 7-4

Types of Plans

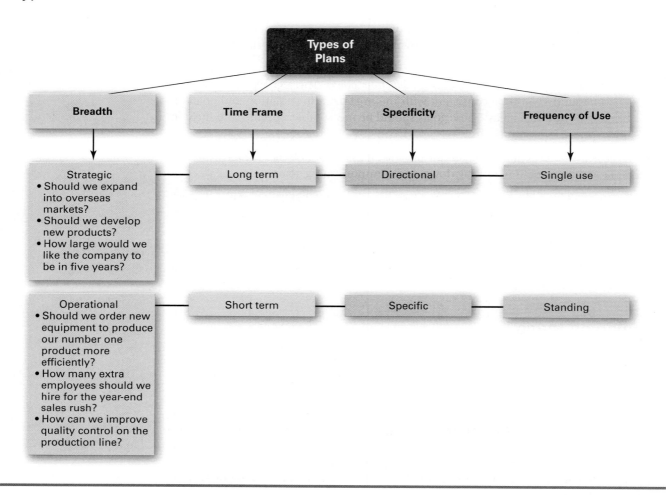

no problem with misunderstanding. For example, a manager who seeks to increase his or her unit's work output by 8 percent over a given 12-month period might establish specific procedures, budget allocations, and schedules of activities to reach that goal. The drawbacks of specific plans are that they require clarity and a sense of predictability that often do not exist. This clarity and predictability worked well for Blue Man Group, however, because they wanted to create a very uniform product.

When uncertainty is high and managers must be flexible in order to respond to unexpected changes, directional plans are preferable. **Directional plans** are flexible plans that set out general guidelines. They provide focus but don't lock managers into specific goals or courses of action. (Exhibit 7-5 illustrates how specific and directional plans differ, with the directional plan indicating only the intent to get from "A" to "B" and the specific plan identifying the exact route that one would take to go from "A" to "B.") Instead of detailing a specific plan to cut costs by 4 percent and increase revenues by 6 percent in the next six months, managers might formulate a directional plan for improving profits by 5 to 10 percent over the next six months. The flexibility inherent in directional plans must be weighed against the loss of clarity provided by specific plans.

Some plans that managers develop are ongoing, while others are used only once. A **single-use plan** is a one-time plan specifically designed to meet the needs of a unique situation. For instance, when Charles Schwab introduced its online discount stock-brokerage service, top-level executives used a single-use plan to guide the creation and

directional plans Plans that are flexible and that set out general guidelines.

single-use plan A one-time plan specifically designed to meet the needs of a unique situation.

Exhibit 7-5

Specific vs. Directional Plans

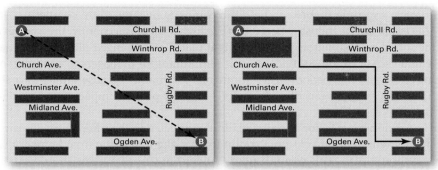

Directional Plan   **Specific Plan**

implementation of the new service. In contrast, **standing plans** are ongoing plans that provide guidance for activities performed repeatedly. Standing plans include policies, rules, and procedures, which we defined in Chapter 6. An example of a standing plan would be the discrimination and harassment policy developed by the University of Saskatchewan. It provides guidance to university administrators, faculty, and staff as they perform their job duties.

standing plans Ongoing plans that provide guidance for activities performed repeatedly.

MyManagementLab
Q&A 7.5

Contingency Factors in Planning

What kinds of plans are needed in a given situation? Will strategic or operational plans be needed? How about specific or directional plans? In some situations, long-term plans make sense; in others, they do not. What are these situations? The process of developing plans is influenced by three contingency factors: the level in the organization, the degree of environmental uncertainty, and the length of future commitments. It is also influenced by the planning approach followed.[12]

Exhibit 7-6 shows the relationship between a manager's level in the organization and the type of planning done. For the most part, operational planning dominates managers' planning efforts at lower levels. At upper organizational levels, planning becomes more strategy oriented.

Exhibit 7-6

Planning in the Hierarchy of Organizations

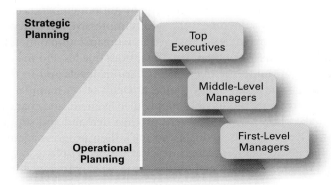

The second contingency factor that affects planning is environmental uncertainty. When environmental uncertainty is high, plans should be specific, but flexible. Managers must be prepared to amend plans as they are implemented. At times, managers may even have to abandon their plans.[13] For example, at Continental Airlines, former CEO Gordon M. Bethune and his management team established a specific goal of focusing on a key concern of customers—on-time flights—to help the company become more competitive in the highly uncertain airline industry. Because of the high level of uncertainty, the management team identified a "destination, but not a flight plan," and changed plans as necessary to achieve that goal of on-time service. Also, it's important for managers to continue formal planning efforts through periods of environmental uncertainty because studies have shown that it takes at least four years of such efforts before any positive impact on organizational performance is seen.[14]

The last contingency factor affecting planning is related to the time frame of plans. The more that current plans affect future commitments, the longer the time frame for which managers should plan. This **commitment concept** means that plans should extend far enough to meet those commitments made when the plans were developed. Planning for too long or too short a time period is inefficient and ineffective. To see how important the commitment concept is to planning, just look at the heated conversations that occurred throughout British Columbia's Lower Mainland when Vancouver was awarded the 2010 Olympic Winter Games. Planning for the event led to conflicts over public transportation. Some were fully committed to the construction of a rail-based rapid transit line (called the Canada Line), stating that the line would be needed when the Olympics came to town. Others raised concerns that the cost estimates for the line would prove to be too low and the public would be expected to pay for the additional costs. Many Lower Mainland residents thus worried that plans for the Canada Line had not adequately factored in all the costs and the promise to stay within budget would not be met.

commitment concept The idea that plans should extend far enough to meet those commitments made today.

Approaches to Planning

How an organization plans can best be understood by looking at *who* does the planning. In the traditional approach, planning is done entirely by top managers who are often assisted by a **formal planning department**, a group of planning specialists whose sole responsibility is to help write the various organizational plans. In this approach, plans developed by top managers flow down through other organizational levels, much like the traditional approach to goal setting. As they flow down through the organization, plans are tailored to the particular needs of each level. Although this approach helps make managerial planning thorough, systematic, and coordinated, all too often the focus is on developing "the plan," a thick binder (or binders) full of meaningless information that gets stuck away on a shelf and is never used by anyone for guiding or coordinating work efforts.

formal planning department A group of planning specialists whose sole responsibility is to help write the various organizational plans.

In a survey of managers about formal top-down organizational planning processes, over 75 percent said that their company's planning approach was unsatisfactory.[15] A common complaint was that "plans are documents that you prepare for the corporate planning staff and later forget." Although this traditional top-down approach to planning is still used by many organizations, it can be effective only if managers understand the importance of creating a workable, usable document that organization members actually draw on for direction and guidance, not a document that looks impressive but is never used.

Another approach to planning is to involve more organizational members in the process. In this approach, plans are not handed down from one level to the next, but instead are developed by organization members at the various levels and in the various work units to meet their specific needs. For instance, at Dell's server manufacturing facility in Austin, Texas, employees from production, supply management, and channel management meet weekly to make plans based on current product demand and supply. In addition, work teams set their own daily schedules and track their progress against those schedules. If a team falls behind, team members develop "recovery" plans to try to get back on schedule.[16] When organizational members are more actively involved in planning, they see that the plans are more than just something written down on paper. They can actually see that the plans are used in directing and coordinating work.

Current Issues in Planning

▶ ▶ ▶ When Blue Man Group started out, it was just three guys having fun, mocking the 1980s, and then working their ideas through mime and percussion.[17] They did not feel they had time to plan. Many people feel the same way. Recall, though, that the three co-founders (Chris Wink, Matt Goldman, and Phil Stanton) were able to do only as many shows as they could physically attend when they started out. By figuring out a way to clone themselves, they could do many more shows and have the opportunity to tour Canada and the United States, which they recently did in 2007. Touring has meant even more planning. The move to planning has certainly made the group successful: Blue Man Group Productions has about 450 employees, their productions attract 1 million people a year, and they bring in millions of dollars in revenues annually. Their first CD, *Audio,* was nominated for a Grammy in 1999, and one of their songs made the soundtrack for *Terminator 3: Rise of the Machines.*

However, Blue Man's time in Toronto was short-lived. The production closed only 18 months after it opened, although the group had planned to be there forever. The group's debut at Toronto's Panasonic Theatre got off to a rocky start. Four unions called on the public to boycott the production after Blue Man refused to negotiate a collective agreement with any of them and decided to use non-union performers instead. "We maybe made assumptions that were naive or, I hope not, arrogant," said Wink during a visit to Toronto. "But we assumed that things would be more like they were in the States."

Think About It

Blue Man Group clearly learned to develop plans in order to grow the company and create more opportunities. What could the group have done to better plan for their Toronto production? How did context contribute to the group's short run in Toronto?

3. Discuss contemporary issues in planning.

We conclude this chapter by addressing two contemporary issues in planning. Specifically, we look at criticisms of planning, and then at how managers can plan effectively in dynamic environments.

Criticisms of Planning

What if you really don't like to make plans?

Formalized organizational planning became popular in the 1960s and, for the most part, it is still popular today. It makes sense for an organization to establish some direction. But critics have challenged some of the basic assumptions underlying planning. What are the primary criticisms directed at formal planning?

- *Planning may create rigidity.*[18] Formal planning efforts can lock an organization into specific goals to be achieved within specific timetables. When these goals are set, the assumption may be that the environment will not change during the time period the goals cover. If that assumption is faulty, managers who follow a plan may face trouble. Rather than remaining flexible—and possibly throwing out the plan—managers who continue to do the things required to achieve the original goals may not be able to cope with the changed environment. Forcing a course of action when the environment is fluid can be a recipe for disaster.

- *Plans cannot be developed for a dynamic environment.*[19] Most organizations today face dynamic environments. If a basic assumption of making plans—that the environment will not change—is faulty, then how can you make plans at all? Today's business environment is often chaotic at best. By definition, that means random and unpredictable. Managing under those conditions requires flexibility, and that may mean not being tied to formal plans.

• *Formal plans cannot replace intuition and creativity.*[20] Successful organizations are typically the result of someone's innovative vision. But visions have a tendency to become formalized as they evolve. Formal planning efforts typically involve a thorough investigation of the organization's capabilities and opportunities and a mechanical analysis that reduces the vision to some type of programmed routine. That approach can spell disaster for an organization. Apple Inc. learned this the hard way. In the late 1970s and throughout the 1980s, Apple's success was attributed, in part, to the innovative and creative approaches of co-founder Steve Jobs. Eventually, Jobs was forced to leave, and with his departure came increased organizational formality, including detailed planning—the same things that Jobs despised so much because he felt that they hampered creativity. During the 1990s, the situation at Apple became so bad that Jobs was brought back as CEO to get Apple back on track. The company's renewed focus on innovation led to the debut of the iMac in 1998, the iPod in 2001, a radically new look for the iMac in 2002, an online music store in 2003, the iPhone in 2007, and the iPad in 2010.

• *Planning focuses managers' attention on today's competition, not on tomorrow's survival.*[21] Formal planning has a tendency to focus on how to capitalize on existing business opportunities within an industry. It often does not allow managers to consider creating or reinventing an industry. Consequently, formal plans may result in costly blunders and high catch-up costs when other competitors take the lead. On the other hand, companies such as Intel, General Electric, Nokia, and Sony have found success forging into uncharted waters, spawning new industries as they go.

MyManagementLab
Q&A 7.6

• *Formal planning reinforces success, which may lead to failure.*[22] It's hard to change or discard previously successful plans—to leave the comfort of what works for the anxiety of the unknown. Successful plans, however, may provide a false sense of security, generating more confidence in the formal plans than is warranted. Many managers will not face the unknown until they are forced to do so by environmental changes. By then, it may be too late!

• *Just planning is not enough.* It's not enough for managers just to plan. They have to start doing![23] When executives at the *Wall Street Journal* decided that they had to do something to respond to a prolonged slump in financial and technology advertising, they developed a plan for how best to accomplish that goal. Then they set about doing it. One of the first things they did was make some design changes by adding more colour to the paper's pages, redesigning the typeface, and making other format changes. Another thing they did to bring in more readers was launch a Saturday edition in September 2005. Next on the agenda: cutting down the size of the newspaper with the smaller format, starting in January 2007.[24] As this example shows, just planning to do something does not get it done. Planning to have enough money so you can retire at age 35 is not enough. You have to put that plan into motion and do it. Managers need to plan, but they also need to see that the plan is carried out.

How valid are these criticisms? Should managers forget about planning? No! Although the criticisms have merit when directed at rigid, inflexible planning, today's managers can be effective planners if they understand planning in dynamic, uncertain environments.

Effective Planning in Dynamic Environments

The external environment is continuously changing. For instance, Wi-Fi is revolutionizing all kinds of industries, from airlines to automobile manufacturing to consumer electronics. The power of the Internet also is being used by companies in new and unique ways, including product design and logistics. Consumers continue to increase the amounts they spend on eating out instead of cooking at home.

Terri Williamson put her background in chemistry and professional branding to good use when she decided to create a line of cosmetics under the brand name "Glow." She planned carefully, checking the Internet to be sure the product name was available, creating a distinctive look and feel for the packaging of her product line, hand-picking the Hollywood location of her store, and mixing and remixing essential oils and other ingredients in her home to come up with a distinctive sandalwood scent. Williamson's plans were coming to fruition in 2001 and 2002, with steadily rising sales among her celebrity clients, when everything changed. Jennifer Lopez unveiled her own new fragrance called "Glow by J.Lo," and Williamson's Glow Industries began a trademark infringement suit. The suit has since been settled out of court between the two parties.

How can managers effectively plan when the external environment is continually changing? We have already discussed uncertain environments as one of the main contingency factors that affect the types of plans managers develop. Because dynamic environments are more the norm than the exception for today's managers, let's revisit how to plan in an uncertain environment. (To determine your own reactions to continual change, see *Self-Assessment—How Well Do I Respond to Turbulent Change?* on pages 377–378, in Chapter 13.)

In an uncertain environment, managers need to develop plans that are specific, but flexible. Although this may seem contradictory, it's not. To be useful, plans need some specificity, but the plans should not be cast in stone. Managers must recognize that planning is an ongoing process; the plans serve as a road map, although the destination may be changing constantly due to dynamic market conditions. They should be willing to change directions if environmental conditions warrant. This flexibility is particularly important as plans are implemented. Managers must stay alert to environmental changes that could impact the effective implementation of plans and make changes as needed. Keep in mind, also, that it's important to continue formal planning efforts, even when the environment is highly uncertain, in order to see any effect on organizational performance. It's the persistence in planning efforts that contributes to significant performance improvement. Why? It seems that, as with most activities, managers "learn to plan" and the quality of their planning improves when they continue to do it.[25]

Finally, effective planning in dynamic environments means flattening the organizational hierarchy as the responsibility for establishing goals and developing plans is pushed to lower organizational levels, since there is little time for goals and plans to flow down from the top. Managers must train their employees in setting goals and establishing plans and then trust that they will do so. Doing so can lead to innovation, as the following *Management Reflection* shows.

MyManagementLab
Q&A 7.7

Employees Do Some of the Planning at Wipro

How do you move from an anonymous conglomerate to a global company? Just a short decade ago, Wipro in Bangalore, India, was "an anonymous conglomerate selling cooking oil and personal computers, mostly in India. Today, it is a US$2.3 billion-a-year global company, and most of its business comes from information-technology services."[26] Accenture, EDS, IBM, and the big US accounting firms know all too well the competitive threat Wipro represents. Not only are Wipro's employees low cost, but they are knowledgeable and skilled. They also play an important role in the company's planning. Since the information services industry is continually changing, employees are taught to analyze situations and to define the scale and scope of a client's problems in order to offer the best solutions. They are the ones on the front line with the clients, and it's their responsibility to establish what to do and how to do it. It's an approach that has positioned Wipro for success no matter how the industry changes. ■

SUMMARY AND IMPLICATIONS

1. Define the nature and purpose of planning. Planning is the process of defining specific goals that cover a period of years. These goals are written and shared with organizational members. Once the goals are agreed upon, specific action plans are created to achieve the goals. Planning's purpose is to provide direction, reduce uncertainty, reduce overlapping and wasteful activities, and establish the goals or standards used in controlling. Without planning, managers would not know what to organize, lead, or control.

▶ ▶ ▶ In Blue Man Group's case, lack of planning in the early years led to exhaustion and near burnout of its co-founders. The co-founders claimed they did not have time to plan.

2. Understand how managers set goals and develop plans. Planning involves two important elements: goals and plans. Goals are the desired outcomes for individuals, groups, or entire organizations. They provide the direction for all management decisions and form the criteria against which actual work accomplishments can be measured. Goals can be set at the top of the organization or through management by objectives (MBO), where employees and managers jointly develop goals. Once goals have been established, managers develop plans to achieve them, either on their own or with the help of employees. Plans outline how goals are going to be met. They typically describe resource allocations, schedules, and other necessary actions to accomplish the goals.

▶ ▶ ▶ Blue Man Group developed a very elaborate plan for their shows, enabling "clones" of the co-founders to deliver the same quality show wherever they performed.

3. Discuss contemporary issues in planning. Planning can lock people into a particular way of behaving, which might not be appropriate at a later point. Therefore, plans need to be somewhat flexible so that managers can respond to environmental changes. The more dynamic the environment, the more flexibility is needed.

▶ ▶ ▶ Blue Man Group acted as if its environment was not particularly dynamic. They assumed that they could recreate the same experience for showgoers with different performers, without thinking about the local environment. Thus, by writing clear plans for performers, they can produce a consistent show in any venue, but this may not be enough to guarantee that the show will go on.

Management @ Work

1. What are the benefits of planning?

2. Contrast formal with informal planning.

3. Compare an organization's mission with its goals.

4. Describe the differences between (a) strategic and operational plans, (b) short- and long-term plans, and (c) specific and directional plans.

5. Under what circumstances are short-term plans preferred? Under what circumstances are specific plans preferred?

6. How can managers plan effectively in dynamic environments?

LINKING CONCEPTS TO PRACTICE

1. If planning is so crucial, why do some managers choose not to do it? What would you advise these managers about planning?

2. Why would a manager use informal planning?

3. Explain how planning involves making decisions today that will have an impact later.

4. How might planning in a not-for-profit organization such as the Canadian Cancer Society differ from planning in a for-profit organization such as Molson?

5. What types of planning do you do in your personal life? Describe these plans in terms of being (a) strategic or operational, (b) short- or long-term, and (c) specific or directional.

6. "Organizations that fail to plan are planning to fail." Do you agree or disagree with this statement? Explain your position.

7. Will planning become more or less important to managers in the future? Why?

SELF-ASSESSMENT

What's My Attitude Toward Achievement?

For each of the following statements, circle the level of agreement or disagreement that you personally feel.[27] Try to minimize the use of answer #4.

1 = Disagree Very Much   2 = Disagree on the Whole   3 = Disagree a Little   4 = In Between or Don't Know
5 = Agree a Little   6 = Agree on the Whole   7 = Agree Very Much

1. People who are very successful deserve all the rewards they get for their achievements.	1 2 3 4 5 6 7
2. It's good to see very successful people fail occasionally.	1 2 3 4 5 6 7
3. Very successful people often get too big for their boots.	1 2 3 4 5 6 7
4. People who are very successful in what they do are usually friendly and helpful to others.	1 2 3 4 5 6 7
5. At school it's probably better for students to be near the middle of the class than the very top student.	1 2 3 4 5 6 7
6. People should not criticize or knock the very successful.	1 2 3 4 5 6 7
7. Very successful people who fall from the top usually deserve their fall from grace.	1 2 3 4 5 6 7
8. Those who are very successful ought to come down off their pedestals and be like other people.	1 2 3 4 5 6 7
9. The very successful person should receive public recognition for his/her accomplishments.	1 2 3 4 5 6 7
10. People who are very successful should be cut down to size.	1 2 3 4 5 6 7

11. One should always respect the person at the top.   1 2 3 4 5 6 7

12. One ought to be sympathetic to very successful people when they experience failure and fall from their very high positions.   1 2 3 4 5 6 7

13. Very successful people sometimes need to be brought down a peg or two, even if they have done nothing wrong.   1 2 3 4 5 6 7

14. Society needs a lot of very high achievers.   1 2 3 4 5 6 7

15. People who always do a lot better than others need to learn what it's like to fail.   1 2 3 4 5 6 7

16. People who are right at the top usually deserve their high position.   1 2 3 4 5 6 7

17. It's very important for society to support and encourage people who are very successful.   1 2 3 4 5 6 7

18. People who are very successful get too full of their own importance.   1 2 3 4 5 6 7

19. Very successful people usually succeed at the expense of other people.   1 2 3 4 5 6 7

20. Very successful people who are at the top of their fields are usually fun to be with.   1 2 3 4 5 6 7

Scoring Key

Add up your responses to items 2, 3, 5, 7, 8, 10, 13, 15, 18, and 19. Your score will range between 10 and 70. The higher your score here, the more you favour seeing very successful people fail.

Add up your responses to items 1, 4, 6, 9, 11, 12, 14, 16, 17, and 20. Your score will range between 10 and 70. The higher your score here, the more you favour rewarding very successful people.

Analysis and Interpretation

This instrument was developed to measure attitudes toward the success and achievement of others. Emphasis is on how you respond to the display of conspicuous success. It was developed in Australia, and although Australians value achievement, they are very ambivalent about its public expression. They tend to enjoy seeing the conspicuously successful fall from grace. In a sample of Australian adults, the average fall score was 38, and the average reward score was 45.

The results from this instrument can help you better understand why you react the way you do to others' success. It can also help you assess how important achievement is to your life goals.

More Self-Assessments MyManagementLab

To learn more about your skills, abilities, and interests, go to the MyManagementLab website and take the following self-assessments:

- I.E.2.—What Time of Day Am I Most Productive?
- I.E.3.—How Good Am I at Personal Planning? (This exercise also appears in Chapter 9 on page 256.)
- III.C.1.—How Well Do I Respond to Turbulent Change? (This exercise also appears in Chapter 13 on pages 377–378.)

MANAGEMENT FOR YOU TODAY

Dilemma

Think ahead to five years from now, to consider what it is that you might like to be doing with your life. Develop your own vision and mission statements. Establish a set of goals that will help you achieve your vision and mission.

Develop a five-year plan that maps out the steps you need to take in order to get to where you want to be with your life at that time.

Becoming a Manager

- Practise setting goals by doing so for various aspects of your personal life, such as academic studies, career preparation, family, and so forth.

- Be prepared to change your goals as circumstances change.

- For goals that you have set, write out plans for achieving those goals.

- Write a personal mission statement.

- If you are employed, talk to your manager(s) about the types of planning they do. Ask them for suggestions on how to be a better planner.

WORKING TOGETHER: TEAM-BASED EXERCISE

Helping Design a Training Program

People Power, a training company that markets its human resource programs to corporations around the globe, has had several requests to design a training program to teach employees how to use the Internet for researching information. This training program will then be marketed to potential corporate customers. Your team is spearheading this important project. There are three stages to the project: (1) researching corporate customer needs, (2) researching the Internet for specific information sources and techniques that could be used in the training module, and (3) designing and writing a specific training module. The first thing your team has to do is identify at least three goals for each stage. As you proceed with this task, you don't need to come up with specifics about "how" to proceed with these activities; just think about "what" you want to accomplish in each stage.

Form groups of three or four individuals. Complete your assigned work as described above. Be sure that your goals are well designed. Be prepared to share your team's goals with the rest of the class.

ETHICS IN ACTION

Ethical Dilemma Exercise: What Should Managers Do When Pressured to Deliver Results?

Some lower- and mid-level managers go to great lengths to achieve their goals rather than disrupt the means–ends chain that supports the accomplishment of higher-level goals.[28] But how far is too far? Coca-Cola has admitted that some personnel acted improperly when they took steps to manipulate the results of a product test at Burger King restaurants in Richmond, Virginia. If the test succeeded, the product—Frozen Coke—would have been introduced in more Burger King outlets. In turn, the prospect of higher sales was a milestone toward meeting Coca-Cola's overall revenue and profit goals.

Burger King executives and franchisees were not pleased when they found out about the manipulated test results. Coca-Cola's president sent a written apology to Burger King, noting: "These actions were wrong and inconsistent with the values of the Coca-Cola Company. Our relationships with Burger King and all our customers are of the utmost importance to us and should be firmly grounded in only the highest-integrity actions." Did Coca-Cola managers feel too much pressure to deliver results?

Imagine that you are a district manager with Coca-Cola and you are being promoted to a new position at the end of the month. Your area's sales are an important component of the corporation's provincial and national sales goals. However, this month's sales are running below the planned level. Should you ask area supermarkets to double their current monthly order and promise that any unsold Coca-Cola products can be returned during the following month?

Thinking Critically About Ethics

"I'm telling you. After my talk with my manager today about my work goals for the next quarter, I think our company's MBO program actually stands for 'manipulating by objectives,' not management by objectives," Carlos complained to his friend Sabrina. He went on, "She came in and outlined what she thought I should be working on, and then asked me what I thought of it. I guess that's her way of getting me to participate in the goal setting."

Is it unethical for a manager to enter a participative goal-setting session with a pre-established set of goals that he or she wants the employee to accept? Why or why not? Is it unethical for a manager to use his or her formal position to impose specific goals on an employee? Why or why not?

Lend Lease Corporation

"Every project we take on starts with a question: How can we do what's never been done before?"[29] That is the guiding philosophy of Australia's Lend Lease Corporation (**www.lendlease.com**). And it has done some pretty spectacular projects, including building the foundations for the Sydney Opera House, the Newington Olympic Village for the 2000 Summer Olympics, and soundstages for *The Matrix* and *Mission: Impossible 2.* But building is not the company's only business. It's also a market leader in terms of being a global, integrated real estate business with expertise in real estate investment, project management and construction, and property development. It currently manages more than $10 billion in global real estate assets.

Lend Lease is an Australian business success story and is seen as one of the most exciting companies to work for in Australia. In the mid-1990s, two Lend Lease executives—Chair Stuart Hornery and Director of Special Projects Malcolm Latham—stood at the edge of an abandoned limestone quarry about 32 kilometres outside London, surveying the barren landscape. Instead of seeing what most people would—an industrial wasteland—they envisioned a dramatic and unique civic space that would be a community gathering place in addition to a popular retail shopping centre. They made the decision to purchase the site from Blue Circle Industries, a British cement company that had been trying to develop it for more than eight years. Upon signing the deal, Lend Lease got a preapproved development plan that was in place for the site. However, company executives chose to abandon everything in this plan but the project's name: Bluewater.

Less than three weeks after that initial visit to the site, a team of Lend Lease employees, including Hornery, Latham, and six of the company's best retail, property, and project-management experts, met with Eric Kuhne, a well-respected US architect. The team's goal was to bring to life Hornery and Latham's vision for the Bluewater site. What they developed was an innovative, break-the-mould plan, simply titled The Bluewater Factors. The team's plan outlined a shopping complex featuring a glowing white roofscape; over 148 644 square metres of retail space; a 13 000-car parking garage; and more than 20 hectares of parks, 7 lakes, and more than 1 million trees and shrubs. The project's scale would be an enormous undertaking.

Put yourself in the position of Managing Director Greg Clarke during this planning stage. Clarke recognizes that effective managerial planning plays an important role in developing successful projects. He is considering using a project-control group (PCG) to help advise Hornery, Latham, and Kuhne on the project. Members of the PCG would not work on the project day-to-day, but would be accountable for it. Clarke has heard that PCGs can include as few as three or as many as fifteen members, who are chosen with consideration for the diverse mix of skills, intuition, and experiences they bring from both inside *and* outside the company. Members meet every six or seven weeks during a project's duration. Clarke thinks that having a PCG could be a good idea, but also worries that if the group becomes too seriously involved in giving advice and cannot reach agreement on what should be done, the company might have to pull the plug on Bluewater and move on.

Clarke is trying to decide whether to put together a PCG for this project and has come to you for advice. Would this level of planning help the project? What kind of team should he consider putting together for the PCG and why? What might be the downsides of using a PCG? (Note: Bluewater was completed in 1999.)

Ready or Not . . .

For once, governments and public health officials appear to be more prepared than businesses are.[30] They have spent billions preparing for a potential influenza pandemic by buying medicines, running disaster drills, and developing strategies for tighter border controls. On the other hand, a survey of global companies by London-based newsletter *Continuity Central* found that 72 percent had not even begun to get ready for a potential bird flu pandemic. Businesses in the United States seem to be particularly unprepared, compared with Canada. In a survey by Deloitte & Touche of 100 US executives, two-thirds said their companies had not yet prepared adequately for avian flu, and most had no one specifically in charge of such a plan. In Canada, perhaps because of the SARS (sudden acute respiratory syndrome) outbreak, more businesses have prepared plans to respond to a massive influenza pandemic, such as H1N1.

What the unprepared US businesses might not realize is how they potentially will be affected. For instance, how will they continue to do business if their workforce is ill or quarantined; if transportation, communication, utility services, or other necessary public infrastructure functions are not available or are available only in limited areas; or if financial services are curtailed? How will they earn revenues if the general public is sick or not able to venture out? It's a scenario with monumental implications for both the short term and the long term.

One company that has planned for a potential avian flu outbreak is Deutsche Bank. The steps it has taken include making sure employees in infected zones don't carry the disease to co-workers, moving others out of harm's way, communicating medical bulletins to far-flung offices, and preparing for the inevitable economic shocks as mass illness slows trade and undermines both public services and private commerce. Kenny Seow, Deutsche Bank's business continuity manager in Singapore, says, "The moment that there is human-to-human infection, we would execute a set of measures."

Businesses in Southeast Asia seem to be better prepared for a possible flu disaster. For one thing, many of these companies had to deal with the SARS outbreak in 2003—a situation that brought commerce in Hong Kong, Singapore, and Beijing to a near standstill. A survey of 80 corporate executives at a seminar held by the American Chamber of Commerce in Hong Kong found that nearly every company had someone in charge of avian flu policy and 60 percent had clearly stated plans that could be put in place immediately. One of the most prepared companies is global bank HSBC, which has made preparations for employees to work from home and is also preparing to divide work among multiple sites. Turner International Asia Pacific, a Time Warner unit in Hong Kong, is working on a mechanized cart that could automatically load tape after tape into a satellite transmission system so it could keep stations like Cartoon Network on the air—a boon if children were homebound for months. And even FedEx says that it has developed contingency plans down to every district or market in Asia Pacific.

What now? What about those businesses that have not begun to prepare for a possible outbreak? As the Deloitte report on avian flu concluded, "In a world where the global supply chain and real-time inventories determine almost everything we do, down to the food available for purchase in our grocery stores, the importance of advanced planning cannot be overstated."

Questions

1. What role do you think goals might play in a company's planning for any potential avian flu outbreak? List some goals that you think might be important.

2. What types of plans might companies need for this situation (for instance, short term, long term, or both)? Explain why you think these plans would be important.

3. How does this scenario reflect planning in a dynamic environment? What would managers need to do to make their planning effective in such an environment?

4. What could other businesses learn from Deutsche Bank's and HSBC's preparations?

5. Pick a company (any size, any kind, or any location) and describe how an influenza pandemic might affect it. Now, develop plans for this company to deal with such an outbreak.

DEVELOPING YOUR INTERPERSONAL SKILLS

Setting Goals

About the Skill

Employees should have a clear understanding of what they are attempting to accomplish. In addition, managers have the responsibility for seeing that this is done by helping employees set work goals. Setting goals is a skill every manager needs to develop.

Steps in Developing the Skill

You can be more effective at setting goals if you use the following eight suggestions:[31]

1. **Identify an employee's key job tasks.** Goal setting begins by defining what it is that you want your employees to accomplish. The best source for this information is each employee's job description.

2. **Establish specific and challenging goals for each key task.** Identify the level of performance expected of each employee. Specify the target toward which the employee is working.

3. **Specify the deadlines for each goal.** Putting deadlines on each goal reduces ambiguity. Deadlines, however, should not be set arbitrarily. Rather, they need to be realistic given the tasks to be completed.

4. **Allow the employee to actively participate.** When employees participate in goal setting, they are more likely to accept the goals. However, it must be sincere participation. That is, employees must perceive that you are truly seeking their input, not just going through the motions.

5. **Prioritize goals.** When you give someone more than one goal, it's important for you to rank the goals in order of importance. The purpose of prioritizing is to encourage the employee to take action and expend effort on each goal in proportion to its importance.

6. **Rate goals for difficulty and importance.** Goal setting should not encourage people to choose easy goals. Instead, goals should be rated for their difficulty and

importance. When goals are rated, individuals can be given credit for trying difficult goals, even if they don't fully achieve them.

7. **Build in feedback mechanisms to assess goal progress.** Feedback lets employees know whether their level of effort is sufficient to attain the goal. Feedback should be both self-generated and supervisor-generated. In either case, feedback should be frequent and regular.

8. **Link rewards to goal attainment.** It's natural for employees to ask, "What's in it for me?" Linking rewards to the achievement of goals will help answer that question.

Practising the Skill

Read the following scenario. Write some notes about how you would handle the situation described. Be sure to refer to the eight suggestions for setting goals.

Scenario

You worked your way through college while holding down a part-time job bagging groceries at the Food Town supermarket chain. You like working in the food industry, and when you graduated, you accepted a position with Food Town as a management trainee. Three years have passed and you have gained experience in the grocery store industry and in operating a large supermarket. About a year ago, you received a promotion to store manager at one of the chain's locations. One of the things you have liked about Food Town is that it gives store managers a great deal of autonomy in running their stores. The company provided very general guidelines to its managers. The concern was with the bottom line; for the most part, how you got there was up to you. Now that you are finally a store manager, you want to establish an MBO-type program in your store. You like the idea that everyone should have clear goals to work toward and then be evaluated against those goals.

Your store employs 90 people, although, except for the managers, most work only 20 to 30 hours per week. You have six people reporting to you: an assistant manager; a weekend manager; and grocery, produce, meat, and bakery managers. The only highly skilled jobs belong to the butchers, who have strict training and regulatory guidelines. Other, less-skilled jobs include cashier, shelf stocker, cleanup, and grocery bagger.

How would you go about setting goals in your new position? Include examples of goals for the jobs of butcher, cashier, and bakery manager.

Reinforcing the Skill

The following activities will help you practise and reinforce the skills associated with setting goals:

1. Where do you want to be in five years? Do you have specific five-year goals? Establish three goals you want to achieve in five years. Make sure these goals are specific, challenging, and measurable.

2. Set personal and academic goals you want to achieve by the end of this term. Prioritize and rate them for difficulty.

MyManagementLab

For more resources, please visit www.pearsoned.ca/mymanagementlab

SCAN THIS

Managing Strategically

In this chapter, we look at an important part of the planning that managers do: developing organizational strategies. Every organization has strategies for doing what it's in business to do, and managers must manage those strategies effectively. After reading and studying this chapter, you will achieve the following learning outcomes.

Learning Outcomes

1 Explain the role of strategic management.

2 Describe the role of managers in each strategic management step.

3 Describe organizational strategies.

4 Discuss current strategic management issues.

▶ ▶ ▶ Heather Reisman and husband Gerry Schwartz, owners of Toronto-based Indigo Books & Music, opened their first store in Burlington, Ontario, in September 1997.[1] By 2000, there were 14 locations across Canada. Indigo was the first book retailer in Canada to sell music and gifts and to include licensed cafés in its stores. The company faced stiff competition from Chapters, however, which was formed by the merger of SmithBooks and Coles in 1995. By 2000, Chapters was the top retail book brand in Canada, having achieved that rank from consumers for four consecutive years (from 1997 to 2000).

In November 2000, Reisman and Schwartz announced their bid to buy Chapters and, though a bitter battle ensued, the two companies merged in August 2001.

The merger was not a smooth one. Before the merger could be approved, the Competition Bureau imposed a number of conditions, including the sale or closing of 20 stores and a code of conduct for dealing with publishers. These rules affected the way Indigo/Chapters could do business until 2006.

Reisman has taken Canada's biggest book chain from a $48 million loss in 2002 to a $34.9 million profit in 2010, which represents an increase of 14 percent over 2009. With profit firmly part of her business plan, Reisman is now trying to determine a strategy that will lead to more growth.

SCAN THIS

Think About It

How does a bookselling company choose a strategy for growth in the digital age? Put yourself in Heather Reisman's shoes. What kinds of analyses can Reisman use to help her make good decisions that will lead to survival and growth?

The importance of having good strategies can be seen by the difficulties facing North American automotive manufacturers and traditional Canadian print media companies. By choosing effective strategies to attract customers, organizations can become prosperous and thrive. Improper strategies can lead to huge failures, however. This chapter examines various strategies that organizations can use to manage more effectively.

The Importance of Strategic Management

1. Explain the role of strategic management.

Effective managers around the world recognize the role that strategic management plays in their organizations' performance. For instance, using well-designed strategies, Swedish company Electrolux is the world's number one producer of household appliances and vacuum cleaners. It has "conquered" Europe and is looking to do the same in the US market. Hindustan Lever is India's largest consumer goods company and makes soaps, detergents, and food products. As a result of effective strategic management, it has achieved an average three-year total return to shareholders of 54 percent.[2] These companies illustrate the value of strategic management. In this section, we want to look at what strategic management is and why it's considered important to managers.

What Is Strategic Management?

Can the study of strategic management be used to plan a successful life for yourself?

To begin to understand the basics of strategy and strategic management, you need look no further than at what has happened in the discount retail industry. The industry's two largest competitors in Canada—Wal-Mart and Zellers—have battled for market dominance since Wal-Mart arrived in 1992. The two chains have some striking similarities: store atmosphere, markets served, and organizational purpose. Yet Wal-Mart's performance (financial and otherwise) has taken market share from Zellers every single year. Wal-Mart is the world's largest and most successful retailer, and Zellers is the second-largest discount retailer in Canada. Why the difference in performance? Organizations vary in how well they perform because of differences in their strategies and differences in competitive abilities.[3] Wal-Mart excels at strategic management, while Zellers struggles to find the right niche.

Strategic management is what managers do to develop the organization's strategies. What are an organization's **strategies**? They are the decisions and actions that determine the long-run performance of an organization. Strategies differ from plans, which we discussed in Chapter 7, in that strategies are the "big picture" decisions. Through strategic management, managers establish the game plan or road map—that is, the strategies—for how the organization will do whatever it's in business to do, how it will compete successfully, and how it will attract and satisfy its customers in order to achieve its goals.[4] It's an important task of managers and ultimately entails all the basic management functions—planning, organizing, leading, and controlling.

One term that is often used in conjunction with strategic management and strategies is **business model**, which is a strategic design for how a company intends to profit from its strategies, work processes, and work activities. A company's business model focuses on two things: (1) whether customers will value what the company is providing and (2) whether the company can make any money doing that.[5] For instance, Dell pioneered a new business model for selling computers to consumers directly on the Internet instead of through computer retailers, like all the other computer manufacturers. Did customers "value" that? Absolutely! Did Dell make money doing it that way? Absolutely! As managers think about strategies for their businesses, they need to give some thought to the economic viability of their business model.

Why Is Strategic Management Important?

In the summer of 2002, *American Idol*, a spin-off from a British television show, became one of the biggest shows in American television history. Seven seasons later, a large audience still tuned in, but in 2010 the audience ratings dropped for the first time in the show's history. With Simon Cowell no longer a judge, the show's creators had to work hard to come up with a strategy that would allow *Idol* to resume its place in the ratings charts.

Why is strategic management so important? One of the most significant reasons is that it can make a difference in how well an organization performs. The most fundamental questions about strategy address why firms succeed or fail, and why, when faced with the same environmental conditions, they have varying levels of performance. Studies of the factors that contribute to organizational performance have shown a positive relationship between strategic planning and performance.[6] In other words, it appears that organizations that use strategic management do have higher levels of performance. And that makes strategic management pretty important!

Another reason strategic management is important has to do with the fact that organizations of all types and sizes face continually changing situations. By following the steps in the strategic management process, managers examine relevant variables in deciding what to do and how to do it. When managers use the strategic management process, they can better cope with uncertain environments. (To understand your ability to deal with the ambiguity that managers often face, see *Self-Assessment—How Well Do I Handle Ambiguity?* on pages 229–230)

Finally, strategic management is important because it's involved in many of the decisions that managers make. Most of the significant current business events reported in the various business publications involve strategic management. For instance, Oakville, Ontario-based Tim Hortons introduced caramel-flavoured iced cappuccino, and Calgary-based WestJet Airlines hired bilingual flight attendants in anticipation of offering flights into Quebec City. Both of these events are examples of managers making strategic decisions.

How widespread is the use of strategic management? One survey of business owners found that 69 percent had strategic plans, and among those owners 89 percent responded that they found their plans effective.[7] They stated, for example, that strategic planning

strategic management What managers do to develop the organization's strategies.

strategies Plans for how an organization will do what it's in business to do, how it will compete successfully, and how it will attract and satisfy its customers in order to achieve its goals.

MyManagementLab
Q&A 8.1

business model A strategic design for how a company intends to profit from its strategies, work processes, and work activities.

gave them specific goals and provided their staff with a unified vision. Although a few management writers claim that strategic planning is "dead," most continue to emphasize its importance.[8]

Today, strategic management has moved beyond for-profit business organizations to include government agencies, hospitals, and other not-for-profit organizations. For instance, when Canada Post found itself in intense competitive battles with overnight package-delivery companies, courier services, and email, its CEO used strategic management to help pinpoint important issues and design appropriate strategic responses. Although strategic management in not-for-profits has not been as well researched as that in for-profit organizations, we know it's important for these organizations as well. The City of Vancouver, in collaboration with several other partners, has created a program to help not-for-profit organizations develop strategic plans, as the following *Management Reflection* shows.

MANAGEMENT REFLECTION

Helping Not-for-Profits Help Themselves

Can not-for-profit organizations benefit from strategic planning? Partners in Organizational Development (POD) believes so.[9] The organization provides grants to not-for-profit social services, arts, and environmental organizations in British Columbia to help them improve and change. Because not-for-profits may not have the internal resources needed to develop a strategic plan, funding is available that allows them to work with consultants to develop their plans.

The program was established in 1989 as a partnership of the Vancouver Foundation, United Way of the Lower Mainland, the Department of the Secretary of State, and the City of Vancouver. The program's aim is to help not-for-profit organizations adapt to an increasingly complex environment. Because of the "financial uncertainty, demographic shifts, heightened competition and growing service demands" that these groups face, strong management practices are essential, and the development of a strategic plan helps accomplish that. Not all of the funding goes to strategic planning initiatives, but the latest awards went to help a number of organizations create strategic plans, including the Kamloops Child Development Society, Nanaimo Community Gardens Society, Community Arts Council of Vancouver, Nanaimo Conservatory of Music, Chinook Institute for Community Stewardship, and Stanley Park Ecology Society. ■

The Strategic Management Process

2. Describe the role of managers in each strategic management step.

▶ ▶ ▶ As Heather Reisman considers the future of Indigo Books & Music, she recognizes that consumers have changed the way in which they get information and entertainment.[10] Book reading is down, as is television watching, while Internet use is up. Thus, Reisman has to respond to this new reality by figuring out ways to attract more consumers. Reisman started the equivalent of Facebook for book lovers and housed it on the Indigo website. As of November 2010, more than 250 000 customers had joined the online Indigo community. By creating a community of book lovers, she hopes to entice people to buy more books.

Think About It

What other strategies could Heather Reisman use to create more crossovers between books and the Internet? Would some strategies be more effective than others?

strategic management process A six-step process that encompasses strategic planning, implementation, and evaluation.

The **strategic management process**, as illustrated in Exhibit 8-1, is a six-step process that encompasses strategic planning, implementation, and evaluation. Although the first four steps describe the planning that must take place, implementation and evaluation are just as important! Even the best strategies can fail if management does not implement or evaluate them properly. Let's examine the six steps in detail.

Step 1: Identify the Organization's Current Mission, Goals, and Strategies

How would you develop a strategic plan for the next five or ten years of your life? What would be your mission, goals, and strategies?

Every organization needs a mission—a statement of the purpose of an organization. The mission answers the question, What is our reason for being in business? Defining the organization's mission forces managers to carefully identify the scope of its products or services. For example, Indigo Books & Music's mission statement is "to provide a service-driven, stress-free approach to satisfying the booklover."[11] The mission of WorkSafeBC (the Workers' Compensation Board of British Columbia) is to "promot[e] workplace health and safety for the workers and employers of [the] province."[12] The mission of eBay is "to build an online marketplace that enables practically anyone to trade practically anything almost anywhere in the world."[13] These statements provide clues to what these organizations see as their reason for being in business.

MyManagementLab
Q&A 8.2

It's also important for managers to identify goals and strategies consistent with the mission being pursued. As we explained in Chapter 7, goals are the foundation of planning. A company's goals provide the measurable performance targets that employees strive to reach. Knowing the company's current goals gives managers a basis for assessing whether those goals need to be changed. For the same reasons, it's important for managers to identify the organization's current strategies.

Step 2: Conduct an Internal Analysis

What are your strengths and weaknesses for developing a successful career?

The internal analysis provides important information about an organization's specific resources and capabilities. An organization's **resources** are its assets—financial, physical, human, intangible—that are used by the organization to develop, manufacture, and deliver products or services to its customers. Its **capabilities** are its skills and abilities in doing the work activities needed in its business. The major value-creating capabilities and skills of the organization are known as its **core competencies**.[14] Both resources and core competencies can determine the organization's competitive weapons. For instance, Fujio Cho, Toyota Motor Corporation's chair, called the company's Prius "a giant leap into the future," but the highly popular car is simply one more example of the company's resources and core competencies in product research and design,

resources An organization's assets—financial, physical, human, intangible—that are used to develop, manufacture, and deliver products or services to customers.

capabilities An organization's skills and abilities that enable it to do the work activities needed in its business.

core competencies An organization's major value-creating skills, capabilities, and resources that determine its competitive advantage.

MyManagementLab
Q&A 8.3

Exhibit 8-1

The Strategic Management Process

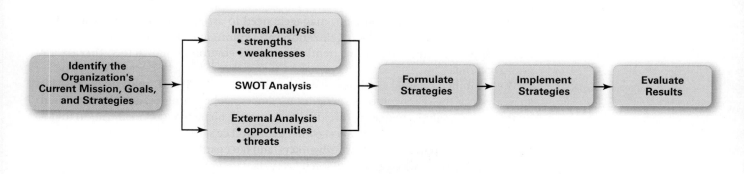

strengths Any activities the organization does well or any unique resources that it has.

weaknesses Activities the organization does not do well or resources it needs but does not possess.

MyManagementLab
Q&A 8.4

manufacturing, marketing, and managing its human resources. Experts who have studied the company point to its ability to nourish and preserve employee creativity and flexibility in a work environment that is fairly rigid and controlled.[15]

After doing the internal analysis, managers should be able to identify organizational strengths and weaknesses. Any activities the organization does well or any unique resources that it has are called **strengths**. **Weaknesses** are activities the organization does not do well or resources it needs but does not possess. This step forces managers to recognize that their organizations, no matter how large or successful, are constrained by the resources and capabilities they have.

Organizational culture, specifically, is one crucial part of the internal analysis that is often overlooked.[16] It's crucial because strong and weak cultures do have different effects on strategy, and the content of a culture has a major effect on strategies pursued. In a strong culture, almost all employees have a clear understanding of what the organization is about. This clarity makes it easy for managers to convey to new employees the organization's core competencies and strengths. The negative side of a strong culture, of course, is that it may be more difficult to change organizational strategies. Firms with "strategically appropriate cultures" outperformed corporations with less appropriate cultures.[17] What is a strategically appropriate culture? It's one that supports the firm's chosen strategy. For instance, Avis, the number two US car rental company, has for a number of years stood on top of its category in an annual survey of brand loyalty. By creating a culture where employees obsess over every step of the rental car experience, Avis has built an unmatched record for customer loyalty.[18]

Does the fact that Calgary-based WestJet Airlines made the list of Canada's 10 Most Admired Corporate Cultures for 2006 and again in 2008 mean anything? Does the fact that Coca-Cola has the world's most powerful global brand give it any edge? Studies of reputation and corporate performance show that it can have a positive impact.[19] As one researcher said, "A strong, well-managed reputation can and should be an asset for any organization."[20]

Step 3: Conduct an External Analysis

MyManagementLab
PRISM 3

What changes in the world are happening that might affect how your career may unfold over time? How might this affect your strategic plan?

MyManagementLab
Q&A 8.5

In Chapter 2, we described the external environment as informing a manager's actions. Analyzing that environment is a critical step in the strategy process. Managers in every organization need to do an external analysis. They need to know, for instance, what the competition is doing, what pending legislation might affect the organization, or what the labour supply is like in locations where it operates. In analyzing the external environment, managers should examine both the specific and general environments to see what trends and changes are occurring. At Indigo Books & Music, managers noted that individuals were reading fewer books and using the Internet more. This observation required Indigo to rethink how to encourage more people to rely on Indigo stores for gift items and connections with other book lovers. (To learn more about analyzing the environment, see *Developing Your Interpersonal Skills—Scanning the Environment* on page 233.)

After analyzing the environment, managers need to assess what they have learned in terms of opportunities that the organization can exploit, and threats that it must counteract. **Opportunities** are positive trends in external environmental factors; **threats** are negative trends.

opportunities Positive trends in external environmental factors.

threats Negative trends in external environmental factors.

SWOT analysis An analysis of the organization's strengths, weaknesses, opportunities, and threats.

The combined external and internal analyses are called the **SWOT analysis** because it's an analysis of the organization's *s*trengths, *w*eaknesses, *o*pportunities, and *t*hreats. Based on the SWOT analysis, managers can identify a strategic niche that the organization might exploit (see Exhibit 8-2). For instance, owner Leonard Lee started Ottawa-based Lee Valley Tools in 1982 to help individual woodworkers, and later gardeners, find just the right tools for their tasks. This niche strategy enabled Lee Valley to grow into one of North America's leading garden and woodworking catalogue companies for over 25 years.

Exhibit 8-2

Identifying the Organization's Opportunities

Organization's Resources/Capabilities

Organization's Opportunities

Opportunities in the Environment

SWOT analysis was very effective in keeping jobs at Procter & Gamble Canada's Brockville, Ontario, plant, as the following *Management Reflection* shows.

MANAGEMENT REFLECTION

Loss of Detergent Production Turns into Victory

How does a Canadian CEO convince his American bosses that there is advantage to staying in Canada? SWOT analysis saved the jobs of employees at Procter & Gamble Canada's Brockville, Ontario, plant.[21] Tim Penner, president of the Toronto-based company, knew that the parent company (based in Cincinnati, Ohio) planned to consolidate the production of laundry detergent in the United States, which would eliminate the jobs of the Brockville employees. Penner, in search of a new opportunity, suggested to head office that P&G move manufacture of fabric softener sheets and electrostatic cleaning sheets for the Swiffer sweeper to Brockville. Penner outlined the strengths of the Ontario plant, including a highly educated workforce known for its commitment and productivity. With Penner's strategic thinking, Brockville's loss of laundry detergent production turned into a victory for Canadian jobs. More recently, Penner convinced the US head office to allow the Brockville plant to produce Tide to Go. Penner says his job includes "aggressively selling Canada [to US head office] as a possible site for new products and reorganized operations." Penner's strategy has paid off. When he became president in 1999, P&G Canada was the seventh-largest revenue generator in the world for the US multinational. By 2007, Penner had taken the Canadian subsidiary to third place and increased annual sales from $1.5 billion to over $2.9 billion. ∎

Step 4: Formulate Strategies

Once the SWOT analysis is complete, managers need to develop and evaluate strategic alternatives and then select strategies that capitalize on the organization's strengths and exploit environmental opportunities, or that correct the organization's weaknesses and buffer it against threats. Strategies need to be established for the corporate, business, and functional levels of the organization, which we will describe shortly. This step is complete when managers have developed a set of strategies that gives the organization a relative competitive advantage over its rivals.

MyManagementLab
Q&A 8.6

Step 5: Implement Strategies

After strategies are formulated, they must be implemented. No matter how effectively an organization has planned its strategies, it cannot succeed if the strategies are not implemented properly.

MyManagementLab
Q&A 8.7

Exhibit 8-3

Ways to Implement Strategy

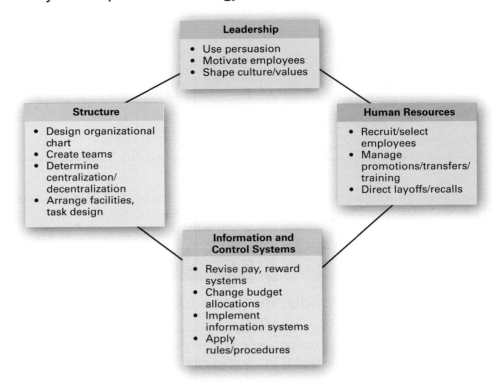

Leadership
- Use persuasion
- Motivate employees
- Shape culture/values

Structure
- Design organizational chart
- Create teams
- Determine centralization/ decentralization
- Arrange facilities, task design

Human Resources
- Recruit/select employees
- Manage promotions/transfers/ training
- Direct layoffs/recalls

Information and Control Systems
- Revise pay, reward systems
- Change budget allocations
- Implement information systems
- Apply rules/procedures

Source: Adapted from Jay R. Galbraith and Robert K. Kazanjian, *Strategy Implementation: Structure, Systems, and Process*, 2nd ed. (St. Paul, MN: West, 1986), p. 115.

Exhibit 8-3 indicates the different things organizations can do to implement a new strategy. The rest of the chapters in this book address a number of issues related to strategy implementation. For instance, in Chapter 10, we discuss the strategy–structure relationship. In Chapter 12, we show that if new strategies are to succeed, they often require hiring new people with different skills, transferring some current employees to new positions, or laying off some employees. Also, since more organizations are using teams, the ability to build and manage effective teams is an important part of implementing strategy (we cover teams in Chapter 16). Finally, top management leadership is a necessary ingredient in a successful strategy. So, too, is a motivated group of middle- and lower-level managers to carry out the organization's specific strategies. Chapters 14 and 15 discuss ways to improve leadership effectiveness and offer suggestions on motivating people.

Step 6: Evaluate Results

The final step in the strategic management process is evaluating results. How effective have the strategies been? What adjustments, if any, are necessary? We discuss this step in our coverage of the control process in Chapter 17.

MyManagementLab
Q&A 8.8

Types of Organizational Strategies

3. Describe organizational strategies.

▶ ▶ ▶ Indigo Books & Music first started to implement its expansion plans in 2001, by buying its major competitor, Chapters (and Chapters.ca).[22] This move gave Indigo a broader market base with a number of new stores, as well as the platform to launch a successful online business.

The plans Reisman contemplated in 2007 seek to further grow the company. Reisman planned to open at least 12 new stores by the end of 2008, with 6 of them in the large superstore format. She also hoped to expand some stores in Toronto and Montreal. To build stronger ties with consumers, she planned to create a social networking site for book lovers. She also planned to launch "Indigo TV," a channel that would broadcast author interviews and book-related programming throughout certain stores, and host an online photo album site where people can upload and display their pictures.

Think About It

Indigo Books & Music has chosen a growth strategy. What other ways might the company grow? What other strategies might you recommend to Heather Reisman?

There are three types of organizational strategy: corporate, business, and functional (see Exhibit 8-4). Managers at the top level of the organization typically are responsible for corporate strategies; for example, Heather Reisman plans Indigo Books & Music's growth strategy. Managers at the middle level typically are responsible for business strategies; for example, Indigo's executive vice-president, online, is responsible for the company's Internet business. Departmental managers typically are responsible for functional strategies; for example, Indigo's senior vice-president, human resource/organization development, is responsible for human resource policies, employee training, and staffing. Let's look at each level of organizational strategy.

Corporate Strategy

If you were to develop your own company, what business would it be in? Why?

Corporate strategy is a strategy that evaluates what businesses a company is in, should be in, or wants to be in, and what it wants to do with those businesses. It's based on the mission and goals of the organization and the roles that each business unit of the organization will play. Take PepsiCo, for instance. Its mission is to be a successful producer and marketer of beverage and packaged food products. At one time, PepsiCo had a restaurant division that included Taco Bell, Pizza Hut, and KFC and made a strategic decision to spin off that division as a separate and independent business entity, now known as YUM! Brands. What types of corporate strategies do organizations such as PepsiCo use?

corporate strategy An organizational strategy that evaluates what businesses a company is in, should be in, or wants to be in, and what it wants to do with those businesses.

In choosing what businesses to be in, senior management can choose among three main types of corporate strategies: growth, stability, and renewal. To illustrate, Wal-Mart, Ganong Bros., and General Motors are companies that seem to be going in different directions. Wal-Mart is rapidly expanding its operations and developing new business

Exhibit 8-4

Levels of Organizational Strategy

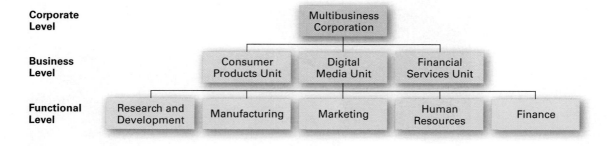

and retailing concepts. Managers at St. Stephen, New Brunswick-based Ganong Bros. ("Canada's Chocolate Family"), on the other hand, are content to maintain the status quo and focus on the candy industry. Meanwhile, sluggish sales and an uncertain outlook in the automobile industry have prompted GM to take drastic measures in dealing with its problems. Each of these organizations is using a different type of corporate strategy. Let's look closer at each type.

Growth

Wal-Mart, the world's largest retailer, continues to grow internationally and in the United States. With a **growth strategy**, an organization expands the number of markets served or products offered, either through its current business(es) or through new business(es). Because of its growth strategy, an organization may increase its revenues, number of employees, or market share. How can organizations grow? Through concentration, vertical integration, horizontal integration, or diversification.

growth strategy A corporate strategy that seeks to increase the organization's operations by expanding the number of products offered or markets served, either through its current business(es) or through new business(es).

Concentration Growth through *concentration* is achieved when an organization concentrates on its primary line of business and increases the number of products offered or markets served in this primary business. No other firms are acquired or merged with; instead, the company chooses to grow by increasing its own business operations. For instance, Oakville, Ontario-based Tim Hortons opens about 200 new stores a year, and is currently focusing most of its new openings on small-town western Canada, and Quebec. It had an aggressive expansion in the United States, where it had 288 stores in 2006 and 563 in 2008.[23]

Vertical Integration A company also might choose to grow by using vertical integration, either backward, forward, or both. In backward vertical integration, an organization becomes its own supplier so it can control its inputs. For instance, eBay owns an online payment business that helps it provide more secure transactions and control one of its most critical processes. In forward vertical integration, an organization becomes its own distributor and is able to control its outputs. For example, Apple has more than 80 retail stores to distribute its product.

Horizontal Integration In horizontal integration, a company grows by combining with other organizations in the same industry—that is, combining operations with competitors. Inbev of Belgium, which owns Labatt and Alexander Keith's, a Nova Scotia-based brewer, is the leading brewer in the world. Horizontal integration has been considered frequently in the Canadian banking industry in recent years as well.

Tim Hortons has signed a deal with Dubai-based Apparel Group to open up to 120 outlets in the Middle East, starting with five in 2011. The move is part of a wider plan to develop an international growth strategy. "Our top strategic priority is continuing to grow our Canadian and US businesses, which are the primary drivers of shareholder value," said Don Schroeder, the recently departed president and CEO of Tim Hortons.

Because combining with competitors might decrease the amount of competition in an industry, Competition Bureau Canada assesses the impact of proposed horizontal integration strategies and must approve such plans before they are allowed to go forward in this country. Other countries have similar bodies that protect fair competition. For instance, managers at Oracle Corporation had to get approval from the European Commission, the "watchdog" for the European Union, before it could acquire rival business-software maker PeopleSoft.

Diversification Finally, an organization can grow through *diversification*, either related or unrelated. In **related diversification** a company grows by merging with or acquiring firms in different, but related, industries. So, for instance, Toronto-based George Weston Foods is involved in the baking and dairy industries, while its ownership of Loblaw Companies provides for the distribution of Weston's food products. With **unrelated diversification**, a company combines with firms in different and unrelated industries. For instance, the Tata Group of India has businesses in chemicals, communications and IT (including the travel search engine Expedia), consumer products, energy, engineering, materials, and services. This is an odd mix, and in this case there's no strategic fit among the businesses.

Many companies use a combination of these approaches to grow. For instance, McDonald's has grown using the concentration strategy by opening more than 32 000 outlets in more than 100 countries, of which about 30 percent are company-owned. In addition, it's used horizontal integration by purchasing Boston Market, Chipotle Mexican Grill (which it spun off as a separate entity in 2006), and Donato's Pizza chains (which it sold in late 2003). It also has a minority stake in the UK-based sandwich shops Pret A Manger. McDonald's newest twist on its growth strategy is a move into the premium coffee market with its McCafé coffee shops.

> **related diversification** When a company grows by combining with firms in different, but related, industries.
>
> **unrelated diversification** When a company grows by combining with firms in different and unrelated industries.

Stability

A **stability strategy** is a corporate strategy characterized by an absence of significant change in what the organization is currently doing. Examples of this strategy include continuing to serve the same clients by offering the same product or service, maintaining market share, and sustaining the organization's business operations. The organization does not grow, but it does not fall behind, either.

Although it may seem strange that an organization might not want to grow, there are times when its resources, capabilities, and core competencies are stretched to their limits, and expanding operations further might jeopardize its future success. When might managers decide that the stability strategy is the most appropriate choice? One situation might be that the industry is in a period of rapid upheaval with external forces drastically changing and making the future uncertain. At times like these, managers might decide that the prudent course of action is to sit tight and wait to see what happens.

Owners and managers of small businesses, such as small neighbourhood grocers, often purposefully choose to follow a stability strategy. Why? They may feel that their business is successful enough just as it is, that it adequately meets their personal goals, and that they don't want the hassles of a growing business.

> **stability strategy** A corporate strategy characterized by an absence of significant change in what the organization is currently doing.

Renewal

The popular business periodicals frequently report stories of organizations that are not meeting their goals or whose performance is declining. When an organization is in trouble, something needs to be done. Managers need to develop strategies that address organizational weaknesses that are leading to performance declines. These strategies are called **renewal strategies**. There are two main types of renewal strategies, retrenchment and turnaround.

A **retrenchment strategy** reduces the company's activities or operations. Retrenchment strategies include cost reductions, layoffs, closing underperforming units, or closing entire product lines or services.[24] There is no shortage of companies that have pursued a retrenchment strategy. A partial list includes some big corporate names: Procter & Gamble, Sears Canada, Corel, and Nortel Networks. When an organization is facing minor performance

> **renewal strategy** A corporate strategy designed to address organizational weaknesses that are leading to performance declines.
>
> **retrenchment strategy** A short-run renewal strategy.

setbacks, a retrenchment strategy helps it stabilize operations, revitalize organizational resources and capabilities, and prepare to compete once again.

What happens if an organization's problems are more serious? What if the organization's profits are not just declining, but instead there are no profits, just losses? General Motors reported a net loss in 2005 of $3.4 billion.[25] Kodak had a $1.3 billion loss in 2005.[26] These types of situations call for a more drastic strategy. The **turnaround strategy** is a renewal strategy for times when the organization's performance problems are more critical.

For both renewal strategies, managers cut costs and restructure organizational operations. However, a turnaround strategy typically involves a more extensive use of these measures than does a retrenchment strategy.

Corporate Portfolio Analysis

When an organization's corporate strategy involves a number of businesses, managers can manage this collection, or portfolio, of businesses using a corporate portfolio matrix.[27] The first portfolio matrix—the **BCG matrix**—developed by the Boston Consulting Group, introduced the idea that an organization's businesses could be evaluated and plotted using a 2 × 2 matrix (see Exhibit 8-5) to identify which ones offered high potential and which were a drain on organizational resources.[28] The horizontal axis represents *market share*, which was evaluated as either low or high; and the vertical axis indicates anticipated *market growth*, which also was evaluated as either low or high. Based on its evaluation, businesses can be placed in one of four categories:

- *Cash cows* (low growth, high market share). Businesses in this category generate large amounts of cash, but their prospects for future growth are limited.

- *Stars* (high growth, high market share). These businesses are in a fast-growing market and hold a dominant share of that market. Their contribution to cash flow depends on their need for resources.

- *Question marks* (high growth, low market share). These businesses are in an attractive market, but hold a small share of that market. Therefore, they have the promise of performance, but need to be developed more for that to happen.

- *Dogs* (low growth, low market share). Businesses in this category do not produce, or consume, much cash. However, they hold no promise for improved performance.

Exhibit 8-5

The BCG Matrix and Strategic Implications

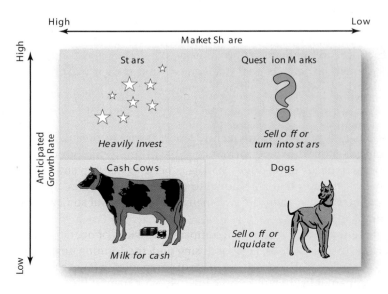

What are the strategic implications of the BCG matrix? Managers should "milk" cash cows for as much as they can, limit any new investment in them, and use the large amounts of cash generated to invest in stars and question marks with strong potential to improve market share. Heavy investment in stars will help take advantage of the market's growth and help maintain high market share. The stars, of course, will eventually develop into cash cows as their markets mature and sales growth slows. The hardest decision for managers is related to the question marks. After careful analysis, some will be sold off and others turned into stars. The dogs should be sold off or liquidated as they have low market share in markets with low growth potential.

A corporate portfolio matrix, such as the BCG matrix, can be a useful strategic management tool. It provides a framework for understanding diverse businesses and helps managers establish priorities for making resource allocation decisions.

Business Strategy

What might be the competitive advantage of a business you would like to create?

Now we move to the business level. A **business (or competitive) strategy** is a strategy focused on how an organization will compete in each of its businesses. For a small organization in only one line of business or the large organization that has not diversified into different products or markets, the competitive strategy simply describes how the company will compete in its primary or main market. For organizations in multiple businesses, however, each division will have its own competitive strategy that defines its competitive advantage, the products or services it will offer, the customers it wants to reach, and the like. For example, the French company LVMH Moët Hennessy-Louis Vuitton SA has different business-level strategies for its divisions, such as Donna Karan fashions, Louis Vuitton leather goods, Guerlain perfume, TAG Heuer watches, Dom Pérignon champagne, and other luxury products. Each division has developed its own unique approach for competing. When an organization is in several different businesses, these single businesses that are independent and formulate their own strategies are often called **strategic business units (SBUs)**.

business (or competitive) strategy An organizational strategy that focuses on how the organization will compete in each of its businesses.

strategic business units (SBUs) Single businesses of an organization in several different businesses that are independent and formulate their own strategies.

The Role of Competitive Advantage

Developing an effective business or competitive strategy requires an understanding of competitive advantage, a key concept in strategic management.[29] **Competitive advantage** is what sets an organization apart: that is, its distinct edge. That distinct edge comes from the organization's core competencies, which, as we know from earlier in this chapter, might be in the form of organizational capabilities—the organization does something that others cannot do or does it better than others can do it. WestJet Airlines has a competitive advantage because of its lower operating costs compared with rival Air Canada and its skills at giving passengers what they want—quick, convenient, and fun service. Those core competencies that lead to competitive advantage also can come from organizational assets or resources—the organization has something that its competitors do not have. For instance, Wal-Mart's state-of-the-art information system allows it to monitor and control inventories and supplier relations more efficiently than its competitors, which Wal-Mart has turned into a cost advantage. Harley-Davidson, Nike, and Coca-Cola all have well-known global trademarks that they use to get premium prices for their products.

competitive advantage What sets an organization apart: its distinct edge.

Quality as a Competitive Advantage

If implemented properly, quality can be a way for an organization to create a sustainable competitive advantage.[30] That is why many organizations apply quality management concepts to their operations in an attempt to set themselves apart from competitors.

To the degree that an organization can satisfy a customer's need for quality better than a competitor, it can attract and retain a loyal customer base. Moreover, constant improvement in the quality and reliability of an organization's products or services may result in a competitive advantage that cannot be taken away.[31]

Sustaining Competitive Advantage

Given the fact that every organization has resources and capabilities, what makes some organizations more successful than others? Why do some professional hockey teams consistently win championships or draw large crowds? Why do some organizations have consistent and continuous growth in revenues and profits? Why do some colleges, universities, or departments experience continually increasing enrolments? Why do some companies consistently appear at the top of lists ranking the "best," or the "most admired," or the "most profitable"? Although every organization has resources (assets) and capabilities (how work gets done) to do whatever it's in business to do, not every one is able to effectively exploit its resources and to develop the core competencies that can provide it with a competitive advantage. It's not enough for an organization simply to create a competitive advantage; it must be able to sustain it—that is, to keep its edge despite competitors' actions or evolutionary changes in the industry. But that is not easy to do. Market instabilities, new technology, and other types of significant but unpredictable changes can challenge managers' attempts at creating a long-term, sustainable competitive advantage. However, by using strategic management, managers can better position their organizations to get a sustainable competitive advantage.

Competitive Strategies

Many important ideas in strategic management have come from the work of Canadian Michael Porter.[32] Porter's major contribution has been to explain how managers can create and sustain a competitive advantage that will give a company above-average profitability. An important element in doing this is an industry analysis.

In any industry, five competitive forces dictate the rules of competition. Together, these five forces (see Exhibit 8-6) determine industry attractiveness and profitability. Managers assess an industry's attractiveness using these forces:

Exhibit 8-6

Forces in an Industry Analysis

Source: Based on M. E. Porter, *Competitive Strategy: Techniques for Analyzing Industries and Competitors* (New York: Free Press, 1980).

In trying to find a niche for his bread-making company, Dokse Perklin, founder of Mississauga, Ontario-based Le Bon Croissant, realized that he could do something that grocery stores and restaurants could not: ensure high-quality bakery products while controlling costs. "Hotels, grocery chains, restaurant chains [and] institutions just can't afford to bake on premises anymore," Perklin says. "They can't find the staff, they can't effectively control overheads, they can't ensure consistent quality." So Perklin filled that need and has created a bread-baking business that ships frozen unbaked and baked goods throughout Canada, the United States, the Caribbean, and Asia.

- *Threat of new entrants.* Factors such as economies of scale, brand loyalty, and capital requirements determine how easy or hard it is for new competitors to enter an industry.

- *Threat of substitutes.* Factors such as switching costs and buyer loyalty determine the degree to which customers are likely to buy a substitute product.

- *Bargaining power of buyers.* Factors such as number of customers in the market, customer information, and the availability of substitutes determine the amount of influence that buyers have in an industry.

- *Bargaining power of suppliers.* Factors such as the degree of supplier concentration and availability of substitute inputs determine the amount of power that suppliers have over firms in the industry.

- *Current rivalry.* Factors such as industry growth rate, increasing or falling demand, and product differences determine how intense the competitive rivalry will be among firms currently in the industry.

Once managers have assessed the five forces and determined what threats and opportunities exist, they are ready to select an appropriate competitive strategy. According to Porter, no firm can be successful by trying to be all things to all people. He proposes that managers select a strategy that will give the organization a competitive advantage, which he says arises out of either having lower costs than all other industry competitors or by being significantly different from competitors. On that basis, managers can choose one of three strategies: cost leadership, differentiation, or focus. Which one managers select depends on the organization's strengths and core competencies and its competitors' weaknesses.

Cost Leadership Strategy When an organization sets out to be the lowest-cost producer in its industry, it's following a **cost leadership strategy**. A low-cost leader aggressively searches out efficiencies in production, marketing, and other areas of operation. Overhead is kept to a minimum, and the firm does everything it can to cut costs. You will not find expensive art or interior décor at offices of low-cost leaders. For example, at Wal-Mart's headquarters in Bentonville, Arkansas, office furnishings are sparse and drab but functional.

Although low-cost leaders don't place a lot of emphasis on "frills," the product or service being sold must be perceived as comparable in quality to that offered by rivals or at least be acceptable to buyers. Examples of companies that have used the low-cost leader strategy include Wal-Mart, Hyundai, and WestJet Airlines.

cost leadership strategy A business strategy in which the organization sets out to be the lowest-cost producer in its industry.

Differentiation Strategy The company that seeks to offer unique products that are widely valued by customers is following a **differentiation strategy**. Sources of differentiation might be exceptionally high quality, extraordinary service, innovative design, technological capability, or an unusually positive brand image. The key to this competitive strategy is that whatever product or service attribute is chosen for differentiating must set the firm apart from its competitors and be significant enough to justify a price premium that exceeds the cost of differentiating. Vancouver-based Vancouver City Savings Credit Union differentiates itself from competitors through a focus on the community and the customer, as the following *Management Reflection* shows.

MANAGEMENT REFLECTION

Vancity Champions the Underdog

How does a small bank compete against the larger ones? Vancouver City Savings Credit Union (Vancity) does not hope to be like the country's Big Five banks.[33] It is much smaller, for one thing. Profit is not the bank's only goal, and only 20 percent of executive compensation is based on profit. Even so, the bank makes enough profit each year to return 30 percent of the profits to its members and the community. When Tamara Vrooman assumed the role of CEO in September 2007, she emphasized how Vancity is not simply about profit. "I am thrilled to be joining an organization that is well-known, successful, not afraid to take risks, and is thoughtful in terms of what it means to be a co-operative, a banker, an employer, and a member of the community."[34]

Vancity is sometimes mocked for its "left coast ways," but it is not afraid to be clear about its mission: The bank is committed to the community, social responsibility, and the environment. This is also what makes the bank unique. According to former CEO Dave Mowat: "Every day of our lives we're trading on our differentiation . . . We have to do it a little bit different, a little bit better to give value-added to draw people to our organization. There isn't an end point where we can win on scale." What the bank can win on is customer service, as Mowat explains, by providing "that extra bit of customization."

While Vancity has many wealthy clients, it likes to work with the less fortunate. It has set up a branch in Canada's poorest neighbourhood, East Vancouver, something other banks were reluctant to do. Mowat believes these clients can be just as trustworthy when you take the time to get to know them. Vancity is so dedicated to customer service that its customer satisfaction rating is at 85 percent, compared with 60 percent for the big banks. ∎

The Ortiz brothers, Nicolas, George, and Oliver, have earned almost $400 million in revenues in a country of only 3.5 million people by creating IKI, now the second-largest supermarket chain in Lithuania. IKI's 67 stores and 15 convenience outlets cater to the once-Communist country's long-unmet niche market for luxury goods like French cheese, North American personal-care products, free-range chickens, and gourmet mushrooms. The brothers recently opened IKI stores in Latvia and are planning to expand to Estonia.

Practically any successful consumer product or service can be identified as an example of the differentiation strategy: Calgary-based WestJet Airlines (customer service); Waterloo, Ontario-based Research In Motion, the maker of the BlackBerry (quality and innovative design); Vancouver-based Martha Sturdy (furniture design and brand image); and Ottawa-based Lee Valley Tools (product design).

Focus Strategy The first two of Porter's competitive strategies seek a competitive advantage in the broad marketplace. However, the **focus strategy** involves a cost advantage (cost focus) or a differentiation advantage (differentiation focus) in a narrow industry segment. That is, managers select a market segment in an industry and attempt to exploit it rather than serve the broad market. Segments can be based on product variety, type of end buyer, distribution channel, or geographical location of buyers. For example, at Compania Chilena de Fosforos SA, a large Chilean wood products manufacturer, Vice-Chair Gustavo Romero Zapata devised a focus strategy to sell chopsticks in Japan. Competitors, and even other company managers, thought he was crazy. However, by focusing on this segment, Romero's strategy managed to create more demand for his company's chopsticks than it had mature trees with which to make the products. Whether a focus strategy is feasible depends on the size of the segment and whether the organization can support the additional cost of focusing. Although research suggests that the focus strategy may be the most effective choice for small businesses because they typically do not have the economies of scale or internal resources to successfully pursue one of the other two strategies, there are large organizations that successfully use the focus strategy.[35] For example, Denmark's Bang & Olufsen, whose profit was over $56 million in 2005–2006, focuses on high-end audio equipment sales.[36] Whether a focus strategy is feasible depends on the size of the segment and whether the organization can make money serving that segment.

focus strategy A business strategy in which a company pursues a cost or differentiation advantage in a narrow industry segment.

Stuck in the Middle What happens if an organization is unable to develop a competitive advantage through either cost or differentiation? Porter uses the term **stuck in the middle** to describe those organizations that find it very difficult to achieve long-term success. Porter goes on to note that successful organizations frequently get into trouble by reaching

stuck in the middle A situation in which an organization is unable to develop a competitive advantage through cost or differentiation.

beyond their competitive advantage and ending up stuck in the middle. The Hudson's Bay Company department store in recent years seems to have had this strategy, avoiding the low-cost strategy of its sister store, Zellers, and avoiding the strategies of higher-end fashion boutiques such as Holt Renfrew.

However, research has shown that organizations *can* pursue a cost leadership and a differentiation strategy at the same time and achieve high performance.[37] But it's not easy to pull off! To do so successfully means an organization must be strongly committed to keeping costs low *and* establishing solid sources of differentiation. For example, companies such as Molson, Toyota, Intel, and Coca-Cola differentiate their products while at the same time maintaining low-cost operations.

Functional Strategy

functional strategy A strategy used by a functional department to support the business strategy of the organization.

Functional strategies are the strategies used by an organization's various functional departments to support the business strategy. Traditional functional departments include manufacturing, marketing, human resources, research and development, and finance.

Problems occur when employees and customers don't understand a company's strategy. For instance, Air Canada did not articulate a clear strategy in creating Tango and Zip to operate alongside the parent airline. By spring 2004, Tango had become a fare category rather than a brand, and it was announced that Zip would no longer operate as a separate carrier. By contrast, WestJet Airlines communicates a very clear strategy to its employees: enjoyable flights and an affordable experience for travellers. Employees are to ensure these while keeping costs down and improving turnaround time. Aware of the strategy, all WestJet employees know what is expected of them in a crisis, and all employees help in whatever ways are necessary to meet this strategy.

Current Strategic Management Issues

4. Discuss current strategic management issues.

▶ ▶ ▶ Indigo Books & Music is using its e-business to achieve growth.[38] While Amazon.ca has more visitors to its site, chapters.indigo.ca turns more of its visitors into buyers. By creating a social networking site, the company hopes consumers will share thoughts on their favourite books and, ultimately, encourage others to buy those books. While having a social networking site like Facebook would be a first for a book retailer, not everyone is sure this strategy will pay off. David Gray, president of Vancouver-based retail consultancy Sixth Line Solutions, notes that "everyone is rushing to do the next Facebook, and people only have so much time."

Think About It

Should Heather Reisman continue with her strategy of encouraging book lovers to interact more online? Or should she consider alternative ways of growing her business? How would a SWOT analysis help her arrive at a conclusion?

There is no better example of the strategic challenges faced by managers in today's dynamic environment than the recorded music industry. Global music sales tumbled 5 percent in 2006—the seventh drop in a row—and industry executives are braced for more declines.[39] However, digital sales were up 85 percent in the same year. As well, cell-phone ring-tone sales doubled from 2004 to 2005, but challenges still remain.[40] Rampant global piracy (according to the IFPI—an organization that represents the worldwide recording industry—one in three music discs sold worldwide is an illegal copy), economic uncertainty, and intense competition from other forms of entertainment have devastated the music industry. Its very nature continues to change, and managers are struggling to find strategies that will help their organizations succeed in such an environment.[41] But the music industry is not the only industry dealing with such enormous strategic challenges. Managers in all kinds of organizations face increasingly intense global competition and the increased demands of higher performance expectations by investors and customers.

How have managers responded to these new realities? In this section, we will look at some current issues in strategy, including the need for strategic flexibility, and how managers are designing strategies to emphasize e-business, customer service, and innovation.

Strategic Flexibility

Jürgen Schrempp, former CEO of DaimlerChrysler, stated, "My principle always was . . . move as fast as you can and [if] you indeed make mistakes, you have to correct them. It's much better to move fast, and make mistakes occasionally, than move too slowly."[42] You would not think that smart individuals who are paid lots of money to manage organizations would make mistakes when it comes to strategic decisions. But even when managers "manage strategically" by following the strategic management process, there is no guarantee that the chosen strategies will lead to positive outcomes. Reading any of the current business periodicals would certainly support this assertion. But the key for managers is responding quickly when it's obvious that the strategy is not working. In other words, they need **strategic flexibility**—the ability to recognize major external environmental changes, to quickly commit resources, and to recognize when a strategic decision is not working. Given the environment that managers face today—oftentimes, highly uncertain and changing—strategic flexibility seems absolutely necessary. What can managers do to enhance their ability to quickly shift strategies as needed? *Tips for Managers—Creating Strategic Flexibility* provides some suggestions.

strategic flexibility The ability to recognize major external environmental changes, to quickly commit resources, and to recognize when a strategic decision was a mistake.

New Directions in Organizational Strategies

What strategies are important for today's environment? We think there are three: e-business, customer service, and innovation.

E-business Strategies

As we discussed in Chapter 1, e-business techniques offer many advantages to organizations, whether simply through e-commerce (the sales and marketing component) or through being a total e-business.

There is no doubt that the Internet has changed and is changing the way organizations do business. Using the Internet, companies have, for instance, (1) created knowledge bases that employees can tap into anytime, anywhere; (2) turned customers into collaborative partners who help design, test, and launch new products; (3) become virtually paperless in specific tasks such as purchasing and filing expense reports; (4) managed logistics in real time; and (5) changed the nature of numerous work tasks throughout the organization.

Using e-business techniques, managers can formulate strategies that contribute to the development of a sustainable competitive advantage.[43] A cost leader can use e-business techniques to reduce costs in a variety of ways. It might use online bidding and order processing to eliminate the need for sales calls and to decrease salesforce expenses; it could use web-based inventory control systems that reduce storage costs; or it might use online testing and evaluation of job applicants. For example, General Electric applied e-business techniques as it initiated several Internet-based purchasing activities in order to reduce costs.

A differentiator needs to offer products or services that customers perceive and value as unique. How could e-business techniques contribute? The differentiator might use Internet-based knowledge systems to shorten customer response times; provide rapid online responses to service requests; or automate purchasing and payment systems so that customers have detailed status reports and purchasing histories. Dell is an excellent example of a company that has exploited the differentiation advantage made possible by e-business techniques.

TIPS FOR MANAGERS

Creating Strategic Flexibility

- Know what is happening with strategies currently being used by **monitoring and measuring results**.

- Encourage employees to **be open about disclosing and sharing negative information**.

- **Get new ideas and perspectives from outside** the organization.

- Have **multiple alternatives** when making strategic decisions.

- **Learn from mistakes**.

Source: Based on K. Shimizu and M. A. Hitt, "Strategic Flexibility: Organizational Preparedness to Reverse Ineffective Strategic Decisions," *Academy of Management Executive*, November 2004, pp. 44–59.

Finally, since the focuser targets a narrow market segment with customized products, it might provide chat rooms or discussion boards for customers to interact with others who have common interests; design niche websites that target specific groups with specific interests; or use websites to perform standardized office functions such as payroll or budgeting.

Research has shown that an important e-business strategy might be a clicks-and-bricks strategy. A clicks-and-bricks firm is one that uses both online (clicks) and traditional stand-alone locations (bricks).[44] A number of companies, such as Indigo Books & Music, London Drugs, and Canadian Tire, have stores as well as websites that allow consumers to shop online. Findings suggest that Canadians like to do their research on the web and then go to nearby stores to pick up items rather than have them shipped to their home. In 2009, Canadians spent $15.1 billion purchasing goods and services online, up from $12.8 billion in 2007 and $7.9 billion in 2005.[45] While online purchases by Canadians represent a small fraction of personal spending on goods and services, this area is growing. So stores' "clicks-and-bricks" strategy works . . . and works well!

Today's Internet-enriched environment provides managers with many opportunities to design strategies that can help their organizations achieve a sustainable competitive advantage. At their disposal are a variety of e-business tools and techniques. The key challenge for managers is to know which ones to use, where, and when. Well-chosen e-business strategies can help an organization succeed.

Customer Service Strategies

Companies that emphasize customer service need strategies that cultivate that atmosphere from top to bottom. What kinds of strategies does that take? It takes giving customers what they want, communicating effectively with them, and providing employees with customer service training. Let's look first at the strategy of giving customers what they want.

New Balance Athletic Shoe was the first of the athletic shoe manufacturers to give customers a truly unique product: shoes in varying widths. Previously, no other athletic shoe manufacturer had shoes for narrow or wide feet in almost any size.[46] It should come as no surprise that an important customer service strategy is giving customers what they want, a major aspect of an organization's overall marketing strategy.

Another important customer service strategy involves communication. Managers should know what is going on with customers. They need to find out what customers liked and did not like about their purchase encounter—from their interactions with employees to their experience with the actual product or service. But communication is not a one-way street. It's also important to let customers know what is going on with the organization that might affect future purchase decisions. Having an effective customer communication system is an important customer service strategy.

Finally, we have discussed previously the importance of an organization's culture in emphasizing customer service. And this requires that employees be trained to provide exceptional customer service. For example, Singapore Airlines is well known for its customer treatment. "On everything facing the customer, they do not scrimp," says an analyst based in Singapore.[47] Employees are expected to "get service right," leaving employees with no doubt about the expectations as far as how to treat customers. Singapore Airlines' service strategy is a good example of what managers must do if customer service is an important organizational goal and an important part of the company's culture.

Innovation Strategies

When Procter & Gamble purchased the Iams pet food business, it did what it always does—it used its renowned research division to look for ways to transfer technology from its other divisions to make new products.[48] One of the outcomes of this cross-divisional combination was a new tartar-fighting ingredient from toothpaste that is included in all of its dry adult pet foods.

As this example shows, innovation strategies are not necessarily focused on just the radical, breakthrough products. They can include the application of existing technology to new uses. Organizations of all kinds and sizes have successfully used both approaches. What types of innovation strategies do organizations need in today's environment? Those strategies should reflect their philosophy about innovation, which is shaped by two strategic decisions: innovation emphasis and innovation timing.

As discussed in Chapter 4, managers must first decide where the emphasis of their innovation effort will be. Is the organization's focus going to be basic scientific research, product development, or process improvement? Basic scientific research requires the heaviest commitment in terms of resources because it involves the nuts-and-bolts activities and work of scientific research. In numerous industries (for instance, genetics engineering, information technology, or pharmaceuticals), an organization's expertise in basic research is the key to a sustainable competitive advantage. However, not every organization requires this extensive commitment to scientific research to achieve high performance levels. Instead, many depend on product development strategies. Although this strategy also requires a significant resource investment, it's not in the areas associated with scientific research. Instead, the organization takes existing technology and improves on it or applies it in new ways, just as Procter & Gamble did when it applied tartar-fighting knowledge to pet food products. Both of these first two strategic approaches to innovation (basic scientific research and product development) can help an organization achieve high levels of differentiation, which is a significant source of competitive advantage.

Finally, the last strategic approach to innovation emphasis is a focus on process development. Using this strategy, an organization looks for ways to improve and enhance its work processes. The organization introduces new and improved ways for employees to do their work in all organizational areas. This innovation strategy can lead to an organization's lowering costs, which, as we know, can be a significant source of competitive advantage.

Once managers have determined the focus of their innovation efforts, they must decide on their innovation timing strategy. Some organizations want to be the first with innovations, whereas others are content to follow or mimic the innovations. An organization that is first to bring a product innovation to the market or to use a new process innovation is called a **first mover**. Being a first mover has certain strategic advantages and disadvantages, as shown in Exhibit 8-7. Some organizations pursue this route, hoping to develop a sustainable competitive advantage. Others have successfully developed a sustainable competitive advantage by being the followers in the industry. They let the first movers pioneer the innovations and then mimic their products or processes. Which approach managers choose depends on their organizations' innovation philosophies and specific resources and capabilities.

first mover An organization that is first to bring a product innovation to the market or to use a new process innovation.

Exhibit 8-7

First-Mover Advantages and Disadvantages

Advantages	Disadvantages
• Reputation for being innovative and industry leader	• Uncertainty over exact direction technology and market will go
• Cost and learning benefits	• Risk of competitors' imitating innovations
• Control over scarce resources and keeping competitors from having access to them	• Financial and strategic risks
• Opportunity to begin building customer relationships and customer loyalty	• High development costs

SUMMARY AND IMPLICATIONS

1. Explain the role of strategic management. Strategic management is that set of managerial decisions and actions that determines the long-run performance of an organization. It is an important task of managers and involves all the basic management functions—planning, organizing, leading, and controlling.

▶ ▶ ▶ Heather Reisman, CEO of Indigo Books & Music, announced a new growth strategy in June 2007 that recognizes the influence of the digital age on book sales. She hoped that the strategy she chose would pay off.

2. Describe the role of managers in each strategic management step. The strategic management process is a six-step process that encompasses planning, implementation, and evaluation. The first four steps involve planning: identifying the organization's current mission, goals, and strategies; analyzing the internal environment; analyzing the external environment; and formulating strategies. The fifth step is implementing the strategy, and the sixth step is evaluating the results of the strategy. Even the best strategies can fail if management does not implement or evaluate them properly.

▶ ▶ ▶ Indigo is currently building on its use of the Internet to help increase sales. The company will want to evaluate the success of its strategy over time and may want to reconsider it if online purchases do not increase significantly or fall.

3. Describe organizational strategies. There are three types of organizational strategy: corporate, business, and functional. They relate to the particular level of the organization that introduces the strategy. At the corporate level, organizations can engage in growth, stability, and renewal strategies. At the business level, strategies look at how an organization should compete in each of its businesses: through cost leadership, differentiation, or focus. At the functional level, strategies support the business strategy.

▶ ▶ ▶ Indigo is trying a differentiation strategy primarily by offering consumers a unique social-networking site for book lovers.

4. Discuss current strategic management issues. Managers face more uncertainty and risk and greater change in today's continually changing environment, making it necessary to scan the environment more frequently and adjust strategy accordingly. Important new strategies in today's environment are e-business, the need to be more customer focused, and an emphasis on the development of strategic innovation practices.

▶ ▶ ▶ Indigo's plan to place greater emphasis on online sales through its social networking site for book lovers focuses on all three new strategies mentioned. Changes in the environment can also lead to changes in an industry's regulations. In Indigo's case, its strategy is affected by government regulations that protect the Canadian book industry from foreign competition. If those regulations were revised to allow more foreign book retailers in Canada (Amazon.ca, a subsidiary of Amazon.com, was allowed to enter the Canadian market in 2002), Indigo may see more competition and might need to revise its strategy.

Management @ Work

READING FOR COMPREHENSION

1. Describe the six-step strategic management process.

2. What is a SWOT analysis?

3. Explain the three growth strategies.

4. Describe the role of competitive advantage in business strategies.

5. What are Porter's five competitive forces?

6. What are the three competitive strategies organizations can implement?

7. How can quality provide a competitive advantage? Give an example.

8. Describe the three new directions in organizational strategies.

LINKING CONCEPTS TO PRACTICE

1. Perform a SWOT analysis on a local business you think you know well. What, if any, competitive advantage does this organization have?

2. Should responsible management and ethical considerations be included in analyses of an organization's internal and external environments? Why or why not?

3. How might the process of strategy formulation, implementation, and evaluation differ for (a) large businesses, (b) small businesses, (c) not-for-profit organizations, and (d) global businesses?

4. How could the Internet be helpful to managers as they follow the steps in the strategic management process?

5. "The concept of competitive advantage is as important for not-for-profit organizations as it is for for-profit organizations." Do you agree or disagree with this statement? Explain your position, using examples to make your case.

6. Find examples of five different organizational mission statements. Using the mission statements, describe what types of corporate and business strategies each organization might use to fulfill that mission statement. Explain your rationale for choosing each strategy.

SELF-ASSESSMENT

How Well Do I Handle Ambiguity?

For each of the following statements, circle the level of agreement or disagreement that you personally feel:[49]

1 = Completely Disagree   4 = Neither Agree nor Disagree   7 = Completely Agree

1. An expert who does not come up with a definite answer probably does not know too much.	1 2 3 4 5 6 7
2. I would like to live in a foreign country for a while.	1 2 3 4 5 6 7
3. The sooner we all acquire similar values and ideals, the better.	1 2 3 4 5 6 7
4. A good teacher is one who makes you wonder about your way of looking at things.	1 2 3 4 5 6 7
5. I like parties where I know most of the people more than ones where all or most of the people are complete strangers.	1 2 3 4 5 6 7
6. Teachers or supervisors who hand out vague assignments give a chance for one to show initiative and originality.	1 2 3 4 5 6 7
7. A person who leads an even, regular life in which few surprises or unexpected happenings arise really has a lot to be grateful for.	1 2 3 4 5 6 7
8. Many of our most important decisions are based on insufficient information.	1 2 3 4 5 6 7

9. There is really no such thing as a problem that cannot be solved. 1 2 3 4 5 6 7

10. People who fit their lives to a schedule probably miss most of the joy of living. 1 2 3 4 5 6 7

11. A good job is one in which what is to be done and how it is to be done are always clear. 1 2 3 4 5 6 7

12. It is more fun to tackle a complicated problem than to solve a simple one. 1 2 3 4 5 6 7

13. In the long run, it is possible to get more done by tackling small, simple problems than large and complicated ones. 1 2 3 4 5 6 7

14. Often the most interesting and stimulating people are those who don't mind being different and original. 1 2 3 4 5 6 7

15. What we are used to is always preferable to what is unfamiliar. 1 2 3 4 5 6 7

16. People who insist upon a yes or no answer just don't know how complicated things really are. 1 2 3 4 5 6 7

Scoring Key

For odd-numbered questions, add the total points. For even-numbered questions, use reverse scoring (1 = 7, 2 = 6, 3 = 5, etc.) to determine your points. Your total score is the sum of the even- and odd-numbered questions.

Analysis and Interpretation

A completely tolerant person would score 15 and a completely intolerant person 105. Research shows that people typically score from 20 to 80, with a mean of 45.

In today's dynamic work environment, where changes occur at an ever-faster pace, the ability to tolerate ambiguity becomes a valuable asset. A high tolerance for ambiguity (scores lower than 40) makes you more likely to be able to function in a work world where there is less certainty about expectations, performance standards, and career progress. A low tolerance for ambiguity (scores higher than 60) makes you more likely to be comfortable in more stable, well-defined situations. People can work toward becoming more (or less) comfortable with ambiguity.

More Self-Assessments MyManagementLab

To learn more about your skills, abilities, and interests, go to the MyManagementLab website and take the following self-assessments:

- I.A.5.—How Creative Am I?
- III.C.1.—How Well Do I Respond to Turbulent Change? (This exercise also appears in Chapter 13 on pages 377–378.)

MANAGEMENT FOR YOU TODAY

Dilemma

In Chapter 7, you were asked to develop your personal vision and a mission statement. To supplement that exercise, develop a SWOT analysis for considering what you want to be doing in five years. What are your strengths and weaknesses? What are the opportunities and threats in carrying out this plan?

Becoming a Manager

- As you keep up with the current business news, pay attention to organizational strategies that managers are using. What types of strategies are the successful organizations using?

- Use SWOT analysis when you apply for jobs—after all, why would you want to work for some organization that has a lot of weaknesses or is facing significant threats?

- Talk to managers about strategy. Ask them how they know when it's time to try a different strategy.

Identifying Organizational Strategies

Examples of organizational strategies are found everywhere in business and general news periodicals. You should be able to recognize the different types of strategies from these news stories.

Form groups of three or four individuals. Using news stories in the business and popular press, find examples of five different organizational strategies. Determine whether the examples are corporate, business, or functional strategies, and explain why your group made that choice. Be prepared to share your examples with the class.

Ethical Dilemma Exercise: What Are the Real Costs of Selling Used Books?

What happens when a new entrant shakes up an entire industry and changes the competitive situation?[50] Consider the book retailing industry. In Japan, the Bookoff chain stirred up controversy by manoeuvring around the country's law forbidding discounts on new books. Instead, Bookoff buys used books from customers, cleans them up, and sells them for half the original price. Even as Bookoff has expanded to 700 stores, competitors are upset because they cannot legally cut their prices to compete. Moreover, the Japan Booksellers Federation complains that teenagers could be shoplifting books from other stores to sell to Bookoff.

In the United States, Amazon.com has used the Internet to successfully compete against long-established store chains such as Barnes & Noble. Amazon.com also allows dealers and individuals to sell used books alongside the new books posted on its online system.

Even though people buy and sell used books (and other items) through auctions on eBay—sales from which authors receive no royalties—Amazon.com is primarily a retailer competing with other retailers on and off the web. The practice of Amazon.com has drawn some protests. The Authors Guild in the United States wants its members to boycott Amazon.com because authors receive no royalties from sales of used books, only sales of new books.

Imagine that you are a manager for Indigo Books & Music with responsibility for expanding revenues by broadening the range of products offered in Indigo's stores. Although expanding further into the used book market might increase Indigo's sales, you are somewhat concerned about the impact this might have on author royalties. You are also worried that the Canadian Authors Association might decide to start a boycott if you sell significant numbers of used books. This could harm your in-store sales. What should you do? (Review Exhibit 8-6 on page 220 as you think about this challenge.)

Thinking Critically About Ethics

Many company websites have an "About Us" page that provides information about the company and its products or services—past, present, and often future. This information is available for anyone to read, even competitors. In an intensely competitive industry where it's difficult for a company to survive, much less be successful, would it be wrong for managers to include misleading, or even false information? Why or why not? Suppose that the industry was not intensely competitive. Would you feel different? Explain.

Haier Group

You may not be familiar with the Haier Group (sounds like "higher"), but if you have ever shopped for a refrigerator, microwave, wine cellar, or air conditioner at Wal-Mart, Sears, or Home Depot, you have undoubtedly seen, if not purchased, the company's products.[51] Haier's name surfaced in North American headlines in late 2005, when it made a bid to purchase domestic appliance maker Maytag, which operates in both Canada and the US. Haier exports its products to more than 100 countries and regions, and its revenue in 2005 was over $14 billion.

Haier Group is China's largest home-appliance maker, and CEO Zhang Ruimin has ambitious goals for his company.

Whereas the United States has General Electric, Germany has Mercedes-Benz, and Japan has Sony, China has yet to produce a comparable global competitor. Zhang is hoping to change that. Haier enjoys enviable prestige in China (a survey of "young, fashionable" Chinese ranked Haier as the country's third-most-popular brand behind Shanghai Volkswagen and Motorola, with Coca-Cola fourth), but Zhang is not satisfied. He wants to gain worldwide recognition, build the company into China's first truly global brand, and be listed on the *Fortune* Global 500. But accomplishing those goals may mean losing the "Chinese-ness." In an online survey conducted in 2005 by Interbrand, 79 percent of the respondents believed that a "made in China" label hurts Chinese brands, with the biggest challenge to Chinese companies being to change the impression of Chinese products as cheap, poor value, poor quality, and unreliable. Product recalls during 2007 have increased concern about products manufactured in China.

What can Zhang do to build his brand globally while addressing the concerns of those who worry about the quality and safety of Chinese products?

XXL No More!

For more than a decade, McDonald's was the leader in pioneering what it thought customers wanted—larger and larger portions.[52] Although its menu had remained relatively stable, McDonald's management was always looking for ways to improve sales and fend off strong competition from the likes of Wendy's and Burger King. It would also periodically add items to its menu to address small changes in people's fast-food desires, but these items often met with additional competition from other fast-food restaurants such as Taco Bell or even SUBWAY. The one thing that McDonald's did to boost sales and create a marketing coup was the addition of the Supersized Meal. Starting in the early 1990s, customers at McDonald's could add to their meal an extra-large soda and an extra-large order of french fries by simply saying, "Supersize it." Nearly 1 in 10 customers took advantage of the company's offer to "supersize" their meal for just 39 cents (US).

But since this expanded offering hit stores, McDonald's has come under fire. Public concern with the fattening of North America was often focused on McDonald's. The company's primary products were high in fat content, high in calories, and high in carbohydrates. Public pressure was mounting to the point that individuals sued McDonald's for causing their physical ailments brought about from obesity. Likened to the nicotine controversy surrounding cigarette smoking, lawyers were trying to make the connection that eating McDonald's food was addictive and a primary cause of obesity—especially among young people. Criticism reached its height early in 2004, when the effects of eating McDonald's food was the subject of an award-winning documentary. In it, producer Morgan Spurlock chronicled the 30-day effects of eating only McDonald's food for all of his meals. At the end of the month-long experiment, Spurlock spoke of his deteriorating health due solely to eating this fast food—and the 24 pounds he gained during this time frame.

Changes in public health consciousness and competitive pressures, along with this documentary film, led McDonald's to announce in March 2004 that it would eliminate all supersized offerings. McDonald's management claims that such action was warranted to simplify its menu offerings and to promote efficiency in the organization. Additionally, McDonald's has also begun altering its menu offerings. It now offers salads as an entrée meal, has reduced the fat content of its milk from 2 to 1 percent, and is attempting to promote itself as being more health conscious.

McDonald's action was largely driven by the reality that its sales had plummeted, as had its stock price. Competition from "health-friendly" alternatives was having a major effect on the company's revenues. McDonald's was losing market share and something had to be done. The company's announcement of the elimination of the supersized option and the addition of healthier substitutes is being viewed as a move that is entirely responsive to the changing market environment—something that executives at Burger King and Wendy's are watching very closely.

Questions

1. Explain how the environment affected McDonald's plans to discontinue offering supersized meals.

2. Describe how McDonald's can use the decision to stop selling supersized meals as a competitive advantage.

3. Would you classify this action by McDonald's as a growth strategy, a stability strategy, or a renewal strategy? Defend your choice.

4. Do you believe McDonald's was socially responsive in its actions to discontinue supersizing? Why or why not?

Scanning the Environment

About the Skill

Anticipating and interpreting changes that are taking place in the environment is an important skill that managers need. Information that comes from scanning the environment can be used in making decisions and taking actions. Managers at all levels of an organization need to know how to scan the environment for important information and trends.

Steps in Developing the Skill

You can be more effective at scanning the environment if you use the following five suggestions:[53]

1. **Decide which type of environmental information is important to your work.** Perhaps you need to know changes in customers' needs and desires, or perhaps you need to know what your competitors are doing. Once you know the type of information that you would like to have, you can look at the best ways to get that information.

2. **Regularly read and monitor pertinent information.** There is no scarcity of information to scan, but you need to read those information sources that are pertinent. How do you know information sources are pertinent? They are pertinent if they provide you with the information that you identified as important.

3. **Incorporate the information that you get from your environmental scanning into your decisions and actions.** Unless you use the information you are getting, you are wasting your time getting it. Also, the more that you find you are using information from your environmental scanning, the more likely it is that you will want to continue to invest time and other resources into gathering it. You will see that this information is important to your being able to manage effectively and efficiently.

4. **Regularly review your environmental scanning activities.** If you find that you are spending too much time getting nonuseful information, or if you are not using the pertinent information that you have gathered, you need to make some adjustments.

5. **Encourage your subordinates to be alert to information that is important.** Your employees can be your "eyes and ears" as well. Emphasize to them the importance of gathering and sharing information that may affect your work unit's performance.

Practising the Skill

Read the following scenario. Write some notes about how you would handle the situation described. Be sure to refer to the five suggestions for scanning the environment.

Scenario

You are the assistant to the president at your college or university. You have been asked to prepare a report outlining the external information that you think is important for her to monitor. Think of the types of information that the president would need in order to do an effective job of managing the college or university right now and over the next three years. Be as specific as you can in describing this information. Also, identify where this information could be found.

Reinforcing the Skill

The following activities will help you practise and reinforce the skills associated with scanning the environment:

1. Select an organization with which you are familiar either as an employee or perhaps as a frequent customer. Assume that you are the top manager in this organization. What types of information from environmental scanning do you think would be important to you? Where would you find this information? Now assume that you are a first-line manager in this organization. Would the types of information you would get from environmental scanning change? Explain.

2. Assume that you are a regional manager for a large bookstore chain. What types of environmental and competitive information are you able to identify using the Internet? For each source, what information did you find that might help you do your job better?

SCAN THIS

MyManagementLab

For more resources, please visit www.pearsoned.ca/mymanagementlab

Planning Tools and Techniques

In this chapter, we discuss some basic planning tools and techniques that managers in any business—large or small—can use. We begin by looking at some techniques for assessing the environment. Then we review techniques for allocating resources. Finally, we discuss some contemporary planning techniques, including project management and scenario planning. After reading and studying this chapter, you will achieve the following learning outcomes.

Learning Outcomes

1 Understand environmental scanning and how it is done.

2 Describe the tools managers can use to allocate resources effectively.

3 Appreciate how projects are managed.

▶▶▶ John Furlong (third from right in photo) had one of the most interesting and enviable jobs in the country—but also one of the most difficult and demanding.[1] He was the CEO of Vancouver 2010, the board of directors charged with getting everything ready for the 2010 Olympic Winter Games. The task was massive. He was appointed in early 2004, giving him six years to get everything ready for the 16-day event.

One of Furlong's early tasks was to put together his leadership team, shown here. The overall operating budget for the Olympics when Vancouver won the bid was about $1.5 billion. Projects included developing new transportation lines and building nearly $470 million worth of Olympic venues. Furlong hired staff, arranged for television rights, and mobilized thousands of volunteers. He could not miss his deadlines, as the dates of the games were already scheduled. And he was warned by the federal and provincial governments that he could not exceed budget.

The budget shortfalls from the 2004 Athens Summer Olympics gave Furlong reason to plan expenditures carefully. To the average Olympics visitor, the Athens games seemed well organized:

Everything happened on schedule, and there were no major problems. However, last-minute construction, trying to finish six stadiums on time, and security and terrorism-prevention costs resulted in "a bill that could have crippled the country's economy for a generation." The bill was more than twice the original amount budgeted for the games. Montreal served as another example for what happens when budgeting and planning is not kept under control. In

February 2006, Montreal announced that it had finally paid back its $2 billion debt for holding the 1976 Summer Olympic Games.

Being CEO of the Olympics is "an almost impossible job with a steep learning curve and little margin for error," said Furlong. Not one CEO had made it from start to finish in the past four Olympics, but Furlong proved to be the exception to the rule.

Think About It

With six years to plan, what did the CEO of the 2010 Olympics need to do to keep the project on task and on budget? Put yourself in John Furlong's shoes. What tools could he have used to keep the construction projects for the Olympic venues on track? How could he have made sure that everything was done on time? What planning tools might he have used to accomplish his goals?

SCAN THIS

Techniques for Assessing the Environment

In our description of the strategic management process in Chapter 8, we discussed the importance of assessing the organization's environment. In this section, we review three techniques to help managers do that: environmental scanning, forecasting, and benchmarking. There are a variety of software tools that can do the actual analysis of data, once collected. For instance, Ottawa-based Cognos (acquired by IBM in 2008), a world leader in business intelligence, has developed software that allows companies throughout the world to access their corporate data, analyze these data and prepare reports, plan budgets, and share information throughout the companies.

1. Understand environmental scanning and how it is done.

Environmental Scanning

How important is **environmental scanning**? While looking around on the company website of competitor Google, Bill Gates found a help-wanted page with descriptions of all the open jobs. What piqued his interest was that many of these posted jobs listed

environmental scanning The screening of large amounts of information to anticipate and interpret changes in the environment.

What kinds of information might you look for to learn about competition?

MyManagementLab
PRISM 3

qualifications that were identical to Microsoft's job requirements. He began to wonder why Google—a web search company—would be posting job openings for software engineers with backgrounds that "had nothing to do with web searches and everything to do with Microsoft's core business of operating-system design, compiler optimization, and distributed-systems architecture."[2] Gates emailed an urgent message to some of his top executives, saying that Microsoft had better be on its toes because it sure looked like Google was preparing to move into being more of a software company. (See *Developing Your Interpersonal Skills—Scanning the Environment* on page 233, in Chapter 8.)

Research has shown that companies with advanced environmental scanning systems have increased their profits and revenue growth.[3] Organizations that don't keep on top of environmental changes are likely to experience the opposite! For instance, Tupperware, the food-storage container company, enjoyed unprecedented success during the 1960s and 1970s, selling its products at home-hostessed parties where housewives played games, socialized, and saw product demonstrations. However, as North American society changed—more women working full time outside the home, an increasing divorce rate, and young adults waiting longer to marry—the popularity of Tupperware parties began to decline because no one had time to go to them. The company's North American market share fell from 60 percent to 40 percent while Rubbermaid, a competitor that marketed its plastic food-storage containers in retail outlets, increased its market share from 5 percent to 40 percent. By the early 1990s, most women had no desire to go to a Tupperware party, or knew how to find Tupperware products elsewhere. Yet Tupperware's president, obviously clueless about the changed environment, predicted that before the end of the decade, the party concept would be popular once again. In 2006, Tupperware was still struggling to find its niche.[4] This example shows how a once successful company can suffer by failing to recognize how the environment has changed.

Competitor Intelligence

competitor intelligence
Environmental scanning activity that seeks to identify who competitors are, what they are doing, and how their actions will affect the organization.

One of the fastest-growing areas of environmental scanning is **competitor intelligence**.[5] It's a process by which organizations gather information about their competitors and get answers to questions such as Who are they? What are they doing? and How will what they are doing affect us? Let's look at an example of how one organization used competitor intelligence in its planning.

On March 31, 2010, Marcel Lebrun, president of Radian6 of Fredericton, New Brunswick, announced the sale of his social-monitoring firm to Salesforce.com for $326 million. Radian6 tracks conversations on popular social media sites like Facebook, Twitter, LinkedIn, blogs, and online communities. Salesforce.com, a cloud computing company that provides software to manage customer relationships, believes that the purchase will allow customers to analyze the impact of their brand management efforts.

Dun & Bradstreet (D&B), a leading provider of business credit, marketing, and purchasing information, has an active business intelligence division. The division manager received a call from an assistant vice-president for sales in one of the company's geographic territories. This person had been on a sales call with a major customer and the customer happened to mention in passing that another company had visited and made a major presentation about its services. What was interesting was that, although D&B had plenty of competitors, this particular company wasn't one of them. The manager gathered together a team that sifted through dozens of sources (research services, Internet, personal contacts, and other external sources) and quickly became convinced that there was something to this—that this company was "aiming its guns right at us." Managers at D&B jumped into action to develop plans to counteract this competitive attack.[6]

Competitor intelligence experts suggest that 80 percent of what managers need to know about competitors can be found out from their own employees, suppliers, and customers.[7] Competitor intelligence does not have to involve spying. Customers, advertisements, promotional materials, marketing research, press releases, reports filed with government agencies, annual reports, want ads, newspaper reports, distributors, and industry studies are examples of readily accessible sources of information. Attending trade shows and debriefing the sales force can be other good sources of competitor information. Monitoring job ads by competitors gives some indication of the kinds of positions the competitor is trying to fill; the frequency of the ads may indicate that there is a lot of turnover, or that the company is expanding rapidly.[8] Many firms regularly buy competitors' products and have their own engineers study them (through a process called *reverse engineering*) to learn about new technical innovations. In addition, the Internet has opened up vast sources of competitor intelligence, as many corporate websites include new-product information and press releases. As Professor Marc-David Seidel of UBC's Sauder School of Business notes, "There are actually a lot of private firms that get hired to do this kind of work—the really dark stuff . . . These are ethical decisions. It's a fairly grey line."[9]

MyManagementLab

Q&A 9.1

The concerns about competitor intelligence pertain to the ways in which competitor information is gathered. For instance, at Procter & Gamble, executives hired competitive intelligence firms to spy on its competitors in the hair care business. At least one of these firms misrepresented themselves to competitor Unilever's employees, trespassed at Unilever's hair care headquarters in Chicago, and went through trash dumpsters to gain information. When P&G's CEO found out, he immediately fired the individuals responsible and apologized to Unilever.[10] Competitor intelligence becomes illegal corporate spying when it involves the theft of proprietary materials or trade secrets by any means. The difficult decisions about competitive intelligence arise because often there is a fine line between what is considered *legal and ethical* and what is considered *legal but unethical.* Although the top manager at one competitive intelligence firm contends that 99.9 percent of intelligence gathering is legal, there is no question that some people or companies will go to any lengths—many unethical—to get information about competitors.[11] Often participants will claim that what is legal or ethical is a grey area. For instance, when Air Canada accused WestJet Airlines of gathering information about its routes in an illegal manner, WestJet said that there was no indication the data were confidential, as the following *Management Reflection* shows.

MANAGEMENT REFLECTION
► Focus on Ethics

Air Canada Accuses WestJet Airlines of Espionage

Should managers access a competitor's website just because they can? When Jeffrey Lafond received a severance package from Air Canada in 2000, he was given a password for an Air Canada employee travel website that listed all of the company's flights and passenger loads.[12] The intended use for the password to the site was for Lafond to book two free flights of his choice every year through 2005.

Lafond subsequently became a financial analyst at WestJet Airlines. In March 2003, Mark Hill, WestJet co-founder and vice-president of strategic planning, saw Lafond accessing the Air Canada employee travel website. Intrigued, Hill asked for Lafond's password so that he could view the website himself.

Hill admits to spending about 90 minutes every night going into the website and counting Air Canada's load factors. He complained about this use of his time to Don Bell, WestJet's vice-president of customer service and another airline co-founder. As a result, Bell assigned Sven Hanson, a WestJet IT staff member, the task of developing a system to automatically download and analyze Air Canada's load factors. Air Canada claims that WestJet entered Air Canada's employee travel website 240 000 times between May 2003 and March 2004, using Lafond's password.

Lafond admits that he did ask WestJet to protect him financially, should Air Canada ever find out that he had given out his password. He was concerned: "I could have been liable for somebody else accessing the [Air Canada] database, I guess."

WestJet's lawyers rejected Air Canada's claims of corporate espionage. They said that while the website was password protected, "At all material times, there was nothing on the website stating it was confidential." They further argued that "Air Canada does not provide persons given access to the website any terms or conditions stating the information on the website is confidential or limiting the use of the information to a particular purpose."

In a countersuit, WestJet accused Air Canada of collecting garbage from Hill's house, in an effort to determine exactly how he was using Air Canada's data. Hill countersued Air Canada for trespassing. Neither airline denied the charges made against them, though both suggested that the harm to the other was minimal.

WestJet president and CEO Clive Beddoe apologized to shareholders in July 2004, and Hill resigned at the same time, stating that it was in his best interests and the best interests of the company. In May 2006, to put an end to the lawsuits, WestJet admitted that senior executives stole confidential information and apologized to Air Canada. It agreed to pay Air Canada $5.5 million for its legal fees and donate $10 million to children's charities in the name of both airlines. ■

Global Scanning

One type of environmental scanning that is particularly important is global scanning. Because world markets are complex and dynamic, managers have expanded the scope of their scanning efforts to gain vital information on global forces that might affect their organizations.[13] The value of global scanning to managers, of course, is largely dependent on the extent of the organization's global activities. For a company that has significant global interests, global scanning can be quite valuable. For instance, Mitsubishi has elaborate information networks and computerized systems to monitor global changes. This has led to the creation of one of the "most technologically advanced automotive-manufacturing facilities in the world."[14]

The sources that managers use for scanning the domestic environment are too limited for global scanning. Managers need to globalize their perspectives and information sources. For instance, they can subscribe to information-clipping services that review world newspapers and business periodicals and provide summaries of desired information. Also, there are numerous electronic services that provide topic searches and automatic updates in global areas of special interest to managers.

Forecasting

The second technique managers can use to assess the environment is forecasting. Forecasting is an important part of planning, and managers need forecasts that will allow them to predict future events effectively and in a timely manner. Environmental scanning establishes the basis for **forecasts**, which are predictions of outcomes. Virtually any component in the organization's environment can be forecasted. Let's look at how managers forecast and how effective forecasts are.

forecasts Predictions of outcomes.

MyManagementLab
Q&A 9.2

Forecasting Techniques

Forecasting techniques fall into two categories: quantitative and qualitative. **Quantitative forecasting** applies a set of mathematical rules to a series of past data to predict outcomes. These techniques are preferred when managers have sufficient hard data that can be used. **Qualitative forecasting**, in contrast, uses the judgment and opinions of knowledgeable individuals to predict outcomes. Qualitative techniques typically are used when precise data are limited or hard to obtain. Exhibit 9-1 describes some popular forecasting techniques.

Today, many organizations collaborate on forecasts by using Internet-based software known as CPFR®, which stands for collaborative planning, forecasting, and replenishment.[15] CPFR offers a standardized way for retailers and manufacturers to use the Internet to exchange data. Each organization relies on its own data about past sales trends, promotion plans, and other factors to calculate a demand forecast for a particular product. If their respective forecasts differ by a certain amount (say 10 percent), the retailer and manufacturer use the Internet to exchange more data and written comments until they arrive at a single and more accurate forecast. This collaborative forecasting helps both organizations do a better job of planning.

quantitative forecasting Forecasting that applies a set of mathematical rules to a series of past data to predict outcomes.

qualitative forecasting Forecasting that uses the judgment and opinions of knowledgeable individuals to predict outcomes.

Forecasting Effectiveness

The goal of forecasting is to provide managers with information that will facilitate decision making. On the one hand, it can be argued that despite forecasting's importance to planning, managers have had mixed success with it. In a survey of financial managers in

Exhibit 9-1

Forecasting Techniques

Technique	Description	Application
Quantitative		
Time series analysis	Fits a trend line to a mathematical equation and projects into the future by means of this equation	Predicting next quarter's sales on the basis of four years of previous sales data
Regression models	Predicts one variable on the basis of known or assumed other variables	Seeking factors that will predict a certain level of sales (for example, price, advertising expenditures)
Econometric models	Uses a set of regression equations to simulate segments of the economy	Predicting change in car sales as a result of changes in tax laws
Economic indicators	Uses one or more economic indicators to predict a future state of the economy	Using change in GNP to predict discretionary income
Substitution effect	Uses a mathematical formula to predict how, when, and under what circumstances a new product or technology will replace an existing one	Predicting the effect of HDTVs on the sale of traditional-style tube TVs
Qualitative		
Jury of opinion	Combines and averages the opinions of experts	Polling the company's human resource managers to predict next year's college and university recruitment needs
Sales force composition	Combines estimates from field sales personnel of customers' expected purchases	Predicting next year's sales of industrial lasers
Customer evaluation	Combines estimates from established customers' purchases	Surveying major car dealers by a car manufacturer to determine types and quantities of products desired

organizations in the United States, United Kingdom, France, and Germany, 84 percent of the respondents said their financial forecasts were inaccurate by 5 percent or more; 54 percent of the respondents reported inaccuracy of 10 percent or more.[16] On the other hand, the practice of forecasting requires managers to reflect on the factors that impact the decisions they make. It can be argued that the insights gained from the process of forecasting add as much value as the accuracy of the forecast.

MyManagementLab
Q&A 9.3

Forecasting techniques are most accurate when the environment is not rapidly changing. The more dynamic the environment, the more likely managers are to forecast ineffectively. Also, forecasting is relatively ineffective in predicting nonseasonal events such as recessions, unusual occurrences, discontinued operations, and the actions or reactions of competitors.

Although forecasting has a mixed record, there are ways to improve its effectiveness:[17]

- *Use simple forecasting methods.* They tend to do as well as, and often better than, complex methods that may mistakenly confuse random data for meaningful information. For instance, Brampton, Ontario-based Loblaw Companies did not need to use complex mathematical techniques to predict that Wal-Mart would be their next big competitor. Loblaw prepared for Wal-Mart's growing grocery inventory by increasing its proportion of nonfood items, and adding clothes, pharmaceuticals, and small appliances to a number of stores. Loblaw has also focused on customer convenience by forming "strategic alliances with coffee shops, fitness studios, photo marts, wine shops, dry cleaners and other companies to provide its customers with the convenience of one-stop-shopping in a Loblaws atmosphere."[18]

- *Look at involving more people in the process.* At *Fortune* 100 companies, it's not unusual to have 1000 to 5000 managers providing forecasting input. These businesses are finding that the more people are involved in the process, the more they can improve the reliability of the outcomes.[19]

- *Compare every forecast with "no change."* A no-change forecast is accurate approximately half the time.

- *Use rolling forecasts that look 12 to 18 months ahead, instead of using a single, static forecast.* These types of forecasts can help managers spot trends better and help their organizations be more adaptive in changing environments.[20]

- *Don't rely on a single forecasting method.* Make forecasts with several models and average them, especially when making long-range forecasts.

- *Don't assume that you can accurately identify turning points in a trend.* What is typically perceived as a significant turning point often turns out to be simply a random event.

- *Shorten the length of forecasts* to improve their accuracy because accuracy decreases as the period you are trying to predict increases.

Forecasting is a managerial skill and as such can be practised and improved. Forecasting software has made the task somewhat less mathematically challenging, although the "number crunching" is only a small part of the activity. Interpreting the forecast and incorporating that information into planning decisions is the challenge facing managers.

Benchmarking

benchmarking The search for the best practices among competitors or noncompetitors that lead to their superior performance.

Suppose that you are a talented pianist or gymnast. To make yourself better, you want to learn from the best, so you watch outstanding musicians or athletes for motions and techniques they use as they perform. That is what is involved in the final technique we are going to discuss for assessing the environment—**benchmarking**. This is the search for the best practices among competitors or noncompetitors that lead to their superior performance.[21] Does benchmarking work? Studies show that users have achieved 69 percent faster growth and 45 percent greater productivity.[22]

The basic idea behind benchmarking is that managers can improve performance by analyzing and then copying the methods of the leaders in various fields. Companies such as Sudbury, Ontario-based ABS Manufacturing and Distributing, a manufacturer of valves and gaskets for mining, and pulp and paper companies; Toronto-based Mr. Convenience, which leases furniture and appliances to Toronto consumers and businesses; and Mississauga, Ontario-based computer security firm BorderWare use benchmarking as a standard tool in their quest for performance improvement. Canadian business schools use benchmarking to set goals for where they want to rank. Rotman, Schulich, Ivey, and Sauder are just a few of the business schools that follow national and international rankings in their quest to be the "number one business school in Canada."

Some companies have chosen some pretty unusual benchmarking partners. Southwest Airlines, for example, studied Indy 500 pit crews, who can change a race-car tire in less than 15 seconds, to see how they could make gate turnarounds even faster. IBM studied Las Vegas casinos for ways to discourage employee theft. Even governments use benchmarking.

What does benchmarking involve? Exhibit 9-2 illustrates the four steps typically used in benchmarking.

Techniques for Allocating Resources

▶ ▶ ▶ As CEO of Vancouver 2010, John Furlong had to allocate a variety of resources properly.[23] Capital advances of $35 million went to the University of British Columbia for a curling centre and a hockey arena and to the City of Richmond for a speed skating oval. One athletes' village was built in the False Creek area of Vancouver and another was built in the Callahan Valley, near Whistler, along with a Nordic centre. At Whistler, construction included a centre for bobsled, skeleton, and luge. The convention centres in Vancouver and Whistler were expanded. There was a $600 million upgrade to the Sea-to-Sky Highway, the route to Whistler. The Canada Line (a rail-based rapid transit line) linking Vancouver International Airport to the downtown area was completed, causing frustration to shop owners along its path. These were just the major construction projects. Furlong also needed to hire hundreds of people, negotiate lucrative television deals, mobilize volunteers, and focus the world's attention on Vancouver and British Columbia for 16 days in February 2010. On June 29, 2007, exactly four years after Vancouver won the bid for the 2010 Winter Olympics, organizers were pleased with the planning to date. The budget was on track (with finances better than expected), and construction of many of the sporting venues was well ahead of schedule.

2. Describe the tools managers can use to allocate resources effectively.

Exhibit 9-2

Steps in Benchmarking

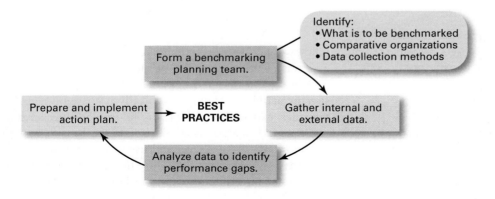

Source: Based on Y. K. Shetty, "Aiming High: Competitive Benchmarking for Superior Performance," *Long Range Planning*, February 1993, p. 42.

Furlong, and the Olympics themselves, had to avoid the scandals that often afflict Olympic games and their planning. He knew that he would face considerable political pressure from those who thought Olympic dollars would be better spent on improving the lives of Vancouver's homeless. How was Furlong able to get the job done on time and on budget?

Think About It

What tools did John Furlong use to keep this massive Olympic project on task and on budget? How did he make sure resources were allocated appropriately?

As we know from Chapter 7, once an organization's goals have been established, an important aspect of planning is determining how those goals are going to be accomplished. Before managers can organize and lead in order to implement the goals, they must have resources. How are these resources allocated effectively and efficiently so that organizational goals are met? That is what we want to look at in this section. Although managers can choose from a number of techniques for allocating resources (many of which are covered in courses on accounting, finance, human resources, and operations management), we discuss four techniques here: budgeting, scheduling, breakeven analysis, and linear programming. Exhibit 9-3 summarizes the differences among these techniques.

Exhibit 9-3

Techniques for Allocating Resources

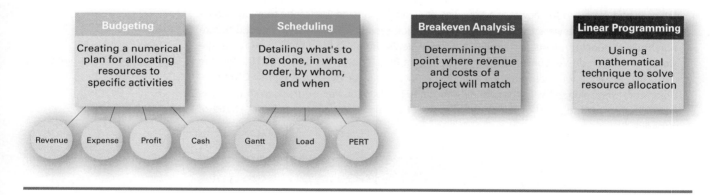

Budgeting

Have you ever made a budget? How difficult was it to create and follow it?

budget A numerical plan for allocating resources to specific activities.

Most of us have had some experience, as limited as it might be, with budgets. We probably learned at a very early age that unless we allocated our "revenues" carefully, our weekly allowance was spent on "expenses" before the week was half over.

A **budget** is a numerical plan for allocating resources to specific activities. Managers typically prepare budgets for revenues, expenses, and large capital expenditures such as equipment. It's not unusual, though, for budgets to be used for improving time, space, and use of material resources. These types of budgets substitute nondollar numbers for dollar amounts. For example, the costs of such items as person-hours, capacity use, or units of production can be budgeted for daily, weekly, or monthly activities. Exhibit 9-4 describes the different types of budgets that managers might use.

Why are budgets so popular? Probably because they are applicable to a wide variety of organizations and work activities within organizations. We live in a world in which

Exhibit 9-4

Types of Budgets

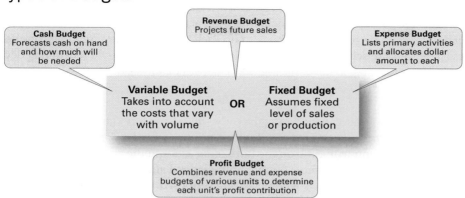

Revenue Budget
Projects future sales

Cash Budget
Forecasts cash on hand
and how much will
be needed

Expense Budget
Lists primary activities
and allocates dollar
amount to each

Variable Budget
Takes into account
the costs that vary
with volume

OR

Fixed Budget
Assumes fixed
level of sales
or production

Profit Budget
Combines revenue and expense
budgets of various units to determine
each unit's profit contribution

Source: Based on R. S. Russell and B. W. Taylor III, *Production and Operations Management* (Upper Saddle River, NJ: Prentice Hall, 1995), p. 287.

almost everything is expressed in monetary units. Dollars, pesos, euros, yen, and the like are used as a common measuring unit within a country. It seems only logical, then, that monetary budgets would be a useful tool for allocating resources and guiding work in such diverse departments as manufacturing and marketing research or at various levels in an organization. Budgets are one planning technique that most managers, regardless of organizational level, use. It's an important managerial activity because it forces financial discipline and structure throughout the organization.

Many managers don't like preparing budgets because they feel the process is time-consuming, inflexible, inefficient, and ineffective.[24] How can the budgeting process be improved? *Tips for Managers— Improving Budgeting* provides some suggestions. Organizations such as Texas Instruments, IKEA, Volvo, and Svenska Handelsbanken have incorporated several of these suggestions as they revamped their budgeting processes. (For an explanation of the mechanics of the budgeting process, see *Developing Your Interpersonal Skills—Budgeting* on pages 260–261.)

TIPS FOR MANAGERS

Improving Budgeting

- **Collaborate** and **communicate** with the stakeholders.
- **Be flexible** in setting targets.
- Understand that **goals should drive budgets**—budgets should not determine goals.
- **Coordinate budgeting** throughout the organization.
- **Use budgeting/planning software** when appropriate.
- Remember that **budgets are tools**.
- Remember that **profits result from smart management**, not because you budgeted for them.

Richard Hayne, founder and CEO of Urban Outfitters, sees his chain's budgeting process as "two sides of the brain working together." Budget controls at headquarters are tight, but the two brand presidents, who make quarterly plans determined by the budget and by fashion forecasts, have enough flexibility to change direction within a week based on what items are selling well. Despite daily monitoring, Urban Outfitters' individual merchandise buyers also have wide latitude; they can take markdowns when they need to instead of waiting for decisions from headquarters. "If you take the markdown when you need it," says the company's chief financial officer, "you have a better chance of selling it."

Scheduling

scheduling Detailing what activities have to be done, the order in which they are to be completed, who is to do each, and when they are to be completed.

Ann is a manager at a Roots store in Toronto. Every week, she determines employees' work hours and the store area where each employee will be working. If you observed any group of supervisors or department managers for a few days, you would see them doing much the same—allocating resources by detailing what activities have to be done, the order in which they are to be completed, who is to do each, and when they are to be completed. These managers are **scheduling**. In this section, we review some useful scheduling devices including Gantt charts, load charts, and PERT network analysis.

Gantt Charts

Gantt chart A scheduling chart developed by Henry Gantt that shows output, both planned and actual, over a period of time.

The **Gantt chart** was developed during the early 1900s by Henry Gantt, an associate of the scientific management expert Frederick Taylor. The idea behind a Gantt chart is simple. It's essentially a bar graph with time on the horizontal axis and the activities to be scheduled on the vertical axis. The bars show output, both planned and actual, over a period of time. The Gantt chart visually shows when tasks are supposed to be done and compares that with the actual progress on each. It's a simple but important device that lets managers detail easily what has yet to be done to complete a job or project and to assess whether an activity is ahead of, behind, or on schedule.

Exhibit 9-5 depicts a simplified Gantt chart for book production developed by a manager in a publishing company. Time is expressed in months across the top of the chart. The major work activities are listed down the left side. Planning involves deciding what activities need to be done to get the book finished, the order in which those activities need to be completed, and the time that should be allocated to each activity. Where a box sits within a time frame reflects its planned sequence. The shading represents actual progress. The chart also serves as a control tool because the manager can see deviations from the plan. In this example, both the design of the cover and the printing of first pages are running behind schedule. Cover design is about three weeks behind, and printing first pages is about two weeks behind schedule. Given this information, the manager might need to take some action to either make up for the two lost weeks or ensure that no further delays will occur. At this point, the manager can expect that the book will be published at least two weeks later than planned if no action is taken.

As John Furlong planned for the 2010 Olympics in Vancouver, he likely developed a similar chart that incorporated planning between 2005 and 2010. The chart would have indicated what needed to be done (goals), the actual progress (so he could keep track of whether projects such as building Olympic sites and housing were on schedule), and reporting dates for projects (so that those managing the projects kept him informed of progress and delays).

Exhibit 9-5

A Gantt Chart

Activity	Month
	1 2 3 4
Copy edit manuscript	
Design sample pages	
Draw artwork	
Print first pages	
Print final pages	
Design cover	

■ Actual progress
■ Goals

▲ Reporting Date

The trendy Zara clothing retailer continues to expand across Europe, the Americas, Asia, and Africa at a steady pace, its success relying heavily on its innovative product delivery schedule. New goods are shipped from the warehouse to Zara's more than 1000 stores every few days, instead of only once a season, as many competitors do. Maintaining the marketing advantage of this carefully managed schedule will be Zara's big challenge as it continues its global expansion.

Load Charts

A **load chart** is a modified Gantt chart. Instead of listing activities on the vertical axis, load charts list either entire departments or specific resources. This arrangement allows managers to plan and control capacity use. In other words, load charts schedule capacity by work areas.

For example, Exhibit 9-6 shows a load chart for six production editors at the same publishing company. Each editor supervises the production and design of several books. By reviewing a load chart, the executive editor, who supervises the six production editors, can see who is free to take on a new book. If everyone is fully scheduled, the executive editor might decide not to accept any new projects, to accept new projects and delay others, to have the editors work overtime, or to employ more production editors. In Exhibit 9-6, only Antonio and Maurice are completely scheduled for the next six months. The other editors have some unassigned time and might be able to accept new projects or be available to help other editors who get behind.

As John Furlong and his managers planned for the 2010 Olympics in Vancouver, they likely used load charts for the various groups working on Olympic projects. For instance, members of the organizing committee responsible for building Olympic housing in Vancouver and Whistler needed to coordinate with city governments of both locations and meet with architects, contractors, and building inspectors. To make sure that one person was not burdened with the responsibility of meeting with representatives of every area, a load chart could identify the committee members who would handle meetings, and then

load chart A modified Gantt chart that schedules capacity by entire departments or specific resources.

Exhibit 9-6

A Load Chart

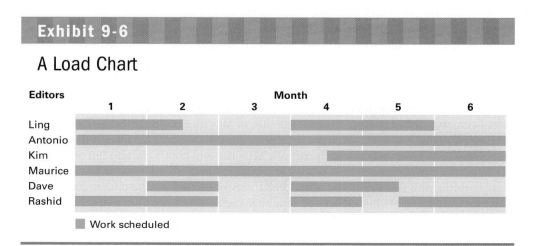

Work scheduled

people could be assigned accordingly. The load chart could also be used to ensure that someone was available for meetings and follow-up when particular decisions came due.

PERT Network Analysis

Gantt and load charts are useful as long as the activities being scheduled are few in number and independent of each other. But what if a manager had to plan a large project such as a departmental reorganization; the implementation of a cost-reduction program; the development of a new product that required coordinating inputs from marketing, manufacturing, and product design; or the Olympics? Such projects require coordinating hundreds and even thousands of activities, some of which must be done simultaneously and some of which cannot begin until preceding activities have been completed. If you are constructing a building, you obviously cannot start putting up the walls until the foundation is laid. How can managers schedule such a complex project? The Program Evaluation and Review Technique (PERT) is highly appropriate for such projects.

A **PERT network** is a flow chart diagram that depicts the sequence of activities needed to complete a project and the time or costs associated with each activity. With a PERT network, a manager must think through what has to be done, determine which events depend on one another, and identify potential trouble spots. PERT also makes it easy to compare the effects alternative actions might have on scheduling and costs. Thus, PERT allows managers to monitor a project's progress, identify possible bottlenecks, and shift resources as necessary to keep the project on schedule.

As John Furlong planned for the 2010 Olympics in Vancouver, he had many projects to coordinate, including building transportation lines, Olympic housing, and Olympic facilities. A PERT network helped him identify when projects needed to be completed and the goals that had to be met in order to make the completion date. For instance, the Canada Line, which links Vancouver International Airport to the downtown area, had to be completed about a year before the Olympics started in order to make sure that the system was working properly. Delays in approving the initial phase of the project in spring 2004 created worries that the project could not be completed in time. The original plan had assumed that approval would happen by March 2004, but approval came four months later, and only after two negative votes resulted in intense lobbying for the third round of voting to yield a positive outcome. The delays caused the provincial government to allocate more resources to the project in order to resolve the bottleneck created by concerns over whether the Canada Line planners had been realistic about their budget. Budget concerns continued to be an issue until completion of the line.

To understand how to construct a PERT network, you need to know four terms. **Events** are end points that represent the completion of major activities. **Activities** represent the time or resources needed to progress from one event to another. **Slack time** is the amount of time an individual activity can be delayed without delaying the whole project. The **critical path** is the longest or most time-consuming sequence of events and activities in a PERT network. Any delay in completing events on this path would delay completion of the entire project. In other words, activities on the critical path have zero slack time.

Developing a PERT network requires that a manager identify all key activities needed to complete a project, rank them in order of occurrence, and estimate each activity's completion time. Exhibit 9-7 explains the steps in this process.

Most PERT projects are complicated and include numerous activities. Such complicated computations can be done with specialized PERT software. However, let's work through a simple example. Assume that you are the superintendent at a construction company and have been assigned to oversee the construction of an office building. Because time really is money in your business, you must determine how long it will take to get the building completed. You have determined the specific activities and events. Exhibit 9-8 outlines the major events in the construction project and your estimate of the expected time to complete each. Exhibit 9-9 shows the actual PERT network based on the data in Exhibit 9-8. You have also calculated the length of time that each path of activities will take:

A-B-C-D-I-J-K (44 weeks)   →   A-B-C-E-G-H-J-K (47 weeks)

A-B-C-D-G-H-J-K (50 weeks)   →   A-B-C-F-G-H-J-K (47 weeks)

PERT network A flow chart diagram that depicts the sequence of activities needed to complete a project and the time or costs associated with each activity.

events End points that represent the completion of major activities in a PERT network.

activities The time or resources needed to progress from one event to another in a PERT network.

slack time The amount of time an individual activity can be delayed without delaying the whole project.

critical path The longest or most time-consuming sequence of events and activities in a PERT network.

Exhibit 9-7

Steps in Developing a PERT Network

1. *Identify every significant activity that must be achieved for a project to be completed.* The accomplishment of each activity results in a set of events or outcomes.

2. *Determine the order in which these events must be completed.*

3. *Diagram the flow of activities from start to finish, identifying each activity and its relationship to all other activities.* Use circles to indicate events and arrows to represent activities. This results in a flow chart diagram called a PERT network. (See Exhibit 9-9.)

4. *Compute a time estimate for completing each activity.* This is done with a weighted average that uses an *optimistic* time estimate (t_o) of how long the activity would take under ideal conditions, a *most likely* estimate (t_m) of the time the activity normally should take, and a *pessimistic* estimate (t_p) that represents the time that an activity should take under the worst possible conditions. The formula for calculating the expected time (t_e) is then

$$t_e = \frac{t_o + 4t_m + t_p}{6}$$

5. *Using the network diagram that contains time estimates for each activity, determine a schedule for the start and finish dates of each activity and for the entire project.* Any delays that occur along the critical path require the most attention because they can delay the whole project.

Exhibit 9-8

Outline of Major Events for Constructing an Office Building

Event	Description	Expected Time (in weeks)	Preceding Event
A	Approve design and get permits	10	None
B	Dig subterranean garage	6	A
C	Erect frame and siding	14	B
D	Construct floor	6	C
E	Install windows	3	C
F	Put on roof	3	C
G	Install internal wiring	5	D, E, F
H	Install elevator	5	G
I	Put in floor covering and panelling	4	D
J	Put in doors and interior decorative trim	3	I, H
K	Turn over to building management group	1	J

Exhibit 9-9

A PERT Network for Constructing an Office Building

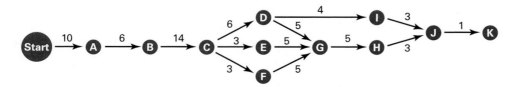

Your PERT network shows that if everything goes as planned, the total project completion time will be 50 weeks. This is calculated by tracing the project's critical path (the longest sequence of activities), A-B-C-D-G-H-J-K, and adding up the times. You know that any delay in completing the events on this path would delay the completion of the entire project. Taking six weeks instead of four to put in the floor covering and panelling (Event I) would have no effect on the final completion date. Why? Because that event is not on the critical path. However, taking seven weeks instead of six to dig the subterranean garage (Event B) would likely delay the total project. A manager who needed to get back on schedule or to cut the 50-week completion time would want to concentrate on those activities along the critical path that could be completed faster. How might the manager do this? He or she could look to see if any of the other activities *not* on the critical path had slack time in which resources could be transferred to activities that *were* on the critical path.

Breakeven Analysis

Managers at McCain Foods want to know how many units of its new Solo Gourmet pizzas must be sold in order to break even—that is, the point at which total revenue is just sufficient to cover total costs. **Breakeven analysis** is a widely used resource allocation technique to help managers determine breakeven point.[25]

breakeven analysis A technique for identifying the point at which total revenue is just sufficient to cover total costs.

Breakeven analysis is a simple calculation, yet it's valuable to managers because it points out the relationship between revenues, costs, and profits. To compute the breakeven point (BE), a manager needs to know the unit price of the product being sold (P), the variable cost per unit (VC), and total fixed costs (TFC). An organization breaks even when its total revenue is just enough to equal its total costs. But total cost has two parts: fixed and variable. *Fixed costs* are expenses that do not change regardless of volume. Examples include insurance premiums, rent, and property taxes. *Variable costs* change in proportion to output and include raw materials, labour costs, and energy costs.

Breakeven point can be computed graphically or by using the following formula:

$$BE = \frac{TFC}{P - VC}$$

This formula tells us that (1) total revenue will equal total cost when we sell enough units at a price that covers all variable unit costs and (2) the difference between price and variable costs, when multiplied by the number of units sold, equals the fixed costs. Let's work through an example.

Assume that Pierre's Photocopying Service charges $0.10 per photocopy. If fixed costs are $27 000 a year and variable costs are $0.04 per copy, Pierre can compute his breakeven point as follows: $27 000 ÷ ($0.10 − $0.04) = 450 000 copies, or when annual revenues are $45 000 (450 000 copies × $0.10). This same relationship is shown graphically in Exhibit 9-10.

As a planning tool, breakeven analysis could help Pierre set his sales goal. For example, he could determine his profit goal and then calculate what sales level is needed to reach that goal. Breakeven analysis could also tell Pierre how much volume has to increase to break even if he is currently operating at a loss or how much volume he can afford to lose and still break even.

Linear Programming

Kamie Bousman manages a manufacturing plant that produces two kinds of cinnamon-scented home fragrance products: wax candles and a wood-chip potpourri sold in bags. Business is good, and she can sell all of the products she can produce. This is her problem: Given that the bags of potpourri and the scented candles are manufactured in the same facility, how many of each product should she produce to maximize profits? Kamie can use **linear programming** to solve her resource allocation problem.

linear programming A mathematical technique that solves resource allocation problems.

Although linear programming can be used here, it cannot be applied to all resource allocation problems because it requires that there be limited resources, that the goal be

Exhibit 9-10

Breakeven Analysis

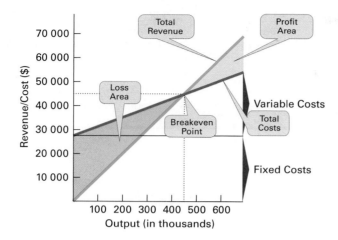

outcome optimization, that there be alternative ways of combining resources to produce a number of output mixes, and that there be a linear relationship between variables (a change in one variable must be accompanied by an exactly proportional change in the other).[26] For Kamie's business, that last condition would be met if it took exactly twice the amount of raw materials and hours of labour to produce two of a given home fragrance product as it took to produce one.

What kinds of problems can be solved with linear programming? Some applications include selecting transportation routes that minimize shipping costs, allocating a limited advertising budget among various product brands, making the optimal assignment of people among projects, and determining how much of each product to make with a limited number of resources. Let's return to Kamie's problem and see how linear programming could help her solve it. Fortunately, her problem is relatively simple, so we can solve it rather quickly. For complex linear programming problems, managers can use computer software programs designed specifically to help develop optimizing solutions.

First, we need to establish some facts about Kamie's business. She has computed the profit margins on her home fragrance products at $10 for a bag of potpourri and $18 for a scented candle. These numbers establish the basis for Kamie to be able to express her *objective function* as maximum profit = $10P + $18S, where P is the number of bags of potpourri produced and S is the number of scented candles produced. The objective function is simply a mathematical equation that can predict the outcome of all proposed alternatives. In addition, Kamie knows how much time each fragrance product must spend in production and the monthly production capacity (1200 hours in manufacturing and 900 hours in assembly) for manufacturing and assembly (see Exhibit 9-11). The production capacity numbers act as *constraints* on her overall capacity. Now Kamie can establish her constraint equations:

MyManagementLab

Q&A 9.5

$$2P + 4S \leq 1200$$
$$2P + 2S \leq 900$$

Of course, Kamie can also state that $P \geq 0$ and $S \geq 0$, because neither fragrance product can be produced in a volume less than zero.

Kamie has graphed her solution in Exhibit 9-12. The shaded area represents the options that don't exceed the capacity of either department. What does this mean? Well, let's look first at the manufacturing constraint line BE. We know that total manufacturing

Exhibit 9-11

Production Data for Cinnamon-Scented Products

| | Number of Hours Required (per unit) | | |
Department	Potpourri Bags	Scented Candles	Monthly Production Capacity (in hours)
Manufacturing	2	4	1200
Assembly	2	2	900
Profit per unit	$10	$18	

Exhibit 9-12

Graphical Solution to Linear Programming Problem

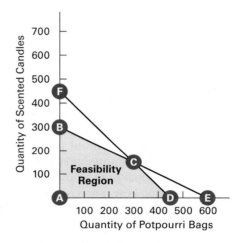

capacity is 1200 hours, so if Kamie decides to produce all potpourri bags, the maximum she can produce is 600 (1200 hours ÷ 2 hours required to produce a bag of potpourri). If she decides to produce all scented candles, the maximum she can produce is 300 (1200 hours ÷ 4 hours required to produce a scented candle). The other constraint Kamie faces is that of assembly, shown by line DF. If Kamie decides to produce all potpourri bags, the maximum she can assemble is 450 (900 hours' production capacity ÷ 2 hours required to assemble). Likewise, if Kamie decides to produce all scented candles, the maximum she can assemble is also 450 because the scented candles also take 2 hours to assemble. The constraints imposed by these capacity limits establish Kamie's *feasibility region.* Her optimal resource allocation will be defined at one of the corners within this feasibility region. Point C provides the maximum profits within the constraints stated. How do we know? At point A, profits would be 0 (no production of either potpourri bags or scented candles). At point B, profits would be $5400 (300 scented candles × $18 profit and 0 potpourri bags produced = $5400). At point D, profits would be $4500 (450 potpourri bags produced × $10 profit and 0 scented candles produced = $4500). At point C, however, profits would be $5700 (150 scented candles produced × $18 profit and 300 potpourri bags produced × $10 profit = $5700).

Contemporary Planning Techniques

▶ ▶ ▶ John Furlong was aware of the many projects he needed to complete before Vancouver could host the 2010 Olympics, but he could not possibly have known in advance all the possible distractions and problems that might crop up along the way.[27]

Furlong faced a few challenges. The residents of Vancouver were not unanimous in their support of the Olympics; some feared the possibility of soaring costs, and others felt that the money slotted for the Olympics would be better spent on assisting the homeless. The 20-member board of directors that Furlong oversaw represented seven different constituency groups: the Canadian Olympic Committee, federal and provincial governments, the City of Vancouver, the municipality of Whistler, the Canadian Paralympic Committee, and First Nations representatives. Furlong needed to ensure that these groups worked with each other in the best interests of the Olympics and set aside individual differences. He also had to meet the ongoing demand for information from the media and the public, who were following the Olympic preparations closely. In addition, a number of the shopkeepers whose stores had limited access because of the Canada Line construction lobbied the province to do something so that their businesses could survive road construction that kept customers away.

Furlong also had to plan for the unexpected. What if a project fell behind? What if the budget got out of hand because of rising construction costs? What if there was another terrorist attack in the United States in the year before the Olympics? What if a virus like SARS (sudden acute respiratory syndrome) arose in Vancouver as the Olympics began? What if city employees threatened to strike during the Olympics?

Think About It

What could John Furlong have done to improve his chances that the 2010 Olympics would run smoothly, without controversy and scandal? What tools should he have used to prepare for the unexpected?

Wi-Fi applications. Life-threatening epidemics. Dolby TrueHD audio. Deflation/inflation worries. Changing competition. Today's managers face the challenges of planning in an environment that is both dynamic and complex. Two planning techniques that are appropriate for this type of environment are project management and scenario planning. Both techniques emphasize *flexibility*, something that is important to make planning more effective and efficient in this type of organizational environment.

Project Management

You have a big project to complete. Can you list all the steps you need to take to complete it?

Different types of organizations, from manufacturers such as Bombardier and Boeing to software design firms such as Corel and Microsoft, take on projects. A **project** is a one-time-only set of activities that has a definite beginning and ending point in time.[28] Projects vary in size and scope—from Vancouver's plans for the Canada Line to go from the airport to downtown (which included a lengthy tunnel through the downtown area) to a sorority's holiday formal. **Project management** is the task of getting a project's activities done on time, within budget, and according to specifications.[29]

More and more organizations are using project management because the approach fits well with the need for flexibility and rapid response to perceived market opportunities. When organizations undertake projects that are unique, have specific deadlines, contain complex interrelated tasks requiring specialized skills, and are temporary in nature, they use project management methodology. These projects often do not fit into the standardized planning procedures that guide an organization's other routine work activities. Project management professionals are credentialed by the Project Management Institute (PMI)

3. Appreciate how projects are managed.

project A one-time-only set of activities that has a definite beginning and ending point in time.

project management The task of getting a project's activities done on time, within budget, and according to specifications.

MyManagementLab
Q&A 9.6

in specific areas such as project management, scheduling, and risk management.[30] What does the project management process involve?

The Project Management Process

In the typical project, work is done by a project team whose members are assigned from their respective work areas to the project and who report to a project manager. The project manager coordinates the project's activities with other departments. When the project team accomplishes its goals, it disbands and members move on to other projects or back to their permanent work areas.

The essential features of the project planning process are shown in Exhibit 9-13. The process begins by clearly defining the project's objectives. This step is necessary because the manager and the team members need to know what is expected. All activities in the project and the resources needed to do them must then be identified. What materials and labour are needed to complete the project? This step may be time-consuming and complex, particularly if the project is unique and there is no history or experience with similar projects. Once the activities and resources have been identified, the sequence of completion needs to be established. What activities must be completed before others can begin? Which can be done simultaneously? This step often uses flow chart diagrams such as a Gantt chart, a load chart, or a PERT network. Next, the project activities need to be scheduled. Time estimates for each activity are done, and these estimates are used to develop an overall project schedule and completion date. Then the project schedule is compared to the objectives, and any necessary adjustments are made. If the project completion time is too long, the manager might assign more resources to critical activities so they can be completed faster.

Today, the project management process can take place online, as a number of Internet-based project collaboration software packages are available. For instance, onProject provides web-based software that allows users to share and manage information associated with projects. Suppliers and customers can even be part of the process.[31]

The Role of the Project Manager

The temporary nature of projects makes managing them different from, say, overseeing a production line or preparing a weekly tally of costs on an ongoing basis. There is a specific job to be done. It has to be defined—in detail. And the project manager is responsible for how it's done. For instance, a variety of project managers were responsible for overseeing construction for the 2010 Olympics, some responsible for athletic venues, others responsible for road construction and housing. They were responsible for everything from developing plans to paying invoices.

Even with the availability of sophisticated computerized and online scheduling programs and other project management tools, the role of project manager remains difficult because he or she is managing people who typically are still linked to their permanent

MyManagementLab
Q&A 9.7

Exhibit 9-13

Project Planning Process

Source: Based on R. S. Russell and B. W. Taylor III, *Production and Operations Management* (Upper Saddle River, NJ: Prentice Hall, 1995), p. 287.

work areas. The only real influence project managers have is their communication skills and their powers of persuasion. To make matters worse, team members seldom work on just one project. They are usually assigned to two or three at any given time. So project managers end up competing with each other to focus an employee's attention on his or her particular project.

Scenario Planning

We already know how important it is that today's managers monitor and assess the external environment for trends and changes. As they assess the environment, issues and concerns that could affect their organization's current or planned operations are likely to be revealed. All of these will not be equally important, so it's usually necessary to focus on a limited set that are most important and to develop scenarios based on each.

A **scenario** is a consistent view of what the future is likely to be. Developing scenarios also can be described as *contingency planning;* that is, if this is what happens, then these are the actions we need to take. If, for instance, environmental scanning reveals increasing interest by the Alberta government in raising the provincial minimum wage, managers at SUBWAY could create multiple scenarios to assess the possible consequences of such an action. What would be the implications for its labour costs if the minimum wage was raised from its current $7.00 an hour to $7.25? How about $7.50 an hour? What effect would these changes have on the chain's bottom line? How might competitors respond? Different assumptions lead to different outcomes. The intent of scenario planning is not to try to predict the future but to reduce uncertainty by playing out potential situations under different specified conditions.[32] SUBWAY could, for example, develop a set of scenarios ranging from optimistic to pessimistic in terms of the minimum wage issue. It would then be prepared to implement new strategies to get and keep a competitive advantage. According to an expert in scenario planning, "Just the process of doing scenarios causes executives to rethink and clarify the essence of the business environment in ways they almost certainly have never done before."[33]

Although scenario planning is useful in anticipating events that *can be* anticipated, it's difficult to forecast random events—the major surprises that cannot be foreseen. The planning challenge comes from the totally random and unexpected events. For instance, the 9/11 terrorist attacks in New York, Washington, and Pennsylvania were random, unexpected, and a total shock to numerous organizations throughout the world. Scenario planning was of little use because no one could have envisioned this scenario. Similarly, the sudden spread of the SARS virus in Toronto caught everyone by surprise, and many businesses in Ontario learned the hard way about the importance of having contingency plans in place.[34] Over 75 percent of companies said that they did not have a contingency plan in place for public health crises.[35] When SARS hit Toronto, businesses were faced with employees ordered into quarantine. Some companies ordered employees to work from home; others required that key personnel remain on-site at all times, providing them with makeshift beds and other personal items. More companies have since thought about what to do if key employees are ordered to stay home from work, but can function. Toronto health officials also did not have a complete plan in place, but they had been working on a pandemic influenza plan for the city. Dr. Sheela Basrur, former chief medical officer of health for Ontario, noted how valuable it was to have a draft of the

scenario A consistent view of what the future is likely to be.

MyManagementLab
Q&A 9.8

The outbreak of SARS shows how unpredictable the environment can be for managers. Organizations had to develop contingency plans to ensure work could continue during a public health crisis.

plan available, and then test it with the SARS outbreak: "Although the official planning process had to take a backseat to the response to the actual outbreak, the outbreak has really well informed the plan, so it's now probably better than it ever would have been had we completed it and put it on a shelf before SARS hit."[36]

As difficult as it might be for managers to anticipate and deal with these random events, they're not totally vulnerable to the consequences. (See *Tips for Managers—Preparing for Unexpected Events.*) One suggestion that has been identified by risk experts as particularly important is to have an early warning system in place. (A similar idea is the tsunami warning systems in the Pacific and in Alaska, which alert officials to potentially dangerous tsunamis and give them time to take action.) Early warning indicators for organizations can give managers advance notice of potential problems and changes so managers can take action. Then, managers need to have appropriate responses (plans) in place if these unexpected events occur.

Planning tools and techniques can help managers prepare confidently for the future. However, managers should remember that all the tools we have described in this chapter are just that—tools. They will never replace a manager's skills and capabilities in using the information gained to develop effective and efficient plans.

SUMMARY AND IMPLICATIONS

1. Understand environmental scanning and how it is done. Environmental scanning screens large amounts of information to anticipate and interpret changes in the environment. One form of scanning is competitor intelligence, an activity that seeks to identify competitors, what they are doing, and how what they are doing will affect the organization. Forecasting and benchmarking are other ways of scanning the environment to provide information that facilitates decision making.

▶ ▶ ▶ As John Furlong prepared for the 2010 Olympic Winter Games, he developed benchmarks for the various projects that had to be completed before the games began, and he used forecasts to predict outcomes for his projects.

2. Describe the tools managers can use to allocate resources effectively. Managers can allocate resources more effectively through budgeting, scheduling, breakeven analysis, and linear programming.

▶ ▶ ▶ John Furlong had to use all of these techniques in order to keep the 2010 Olympics planning on track.

3. Appreciate how projects are managed. Project management is the task of completing a project's activities on time, within budget, and according to specifications. Managers and team members need to share information, which can be done through software or online through Internet-based collaboration. They also need to prepare for unexpected outcomes by using scenario planning.

▶ ▶ ▶ John Furlong had to be aware of the many factors that could change in the environment during the time leading up to the 2010 Olympics and develop alternative scenarios for problems that might arise and ways to respond to them.

Management @ Work

1. How can managers improve the effectiveness of forecasting?

2. What are the four steps in the benchmarking process?

3. Describe the different types of budgets.

4. Why is flexibility so important to today's planning techniques?

5. What are the steps in the project planning process?

6. Why has scenario planning become an important planning tool for managers?

1. Do intuition and creativity have any relevance in quantitative planning tools and techniques? Explain.

2. The *Globe and Mail*'s *Report on Business* and other business periodicals often carry reports of companies that have not met their sales or profit forecasts. What are some reasons a company might not meet its forecast? What suggestions could you make for improving the effectiveness of forecasting?

3. "It's a waste of time and other resources to develop a set of sophisticated scenarios for situations that may never occur." Do you agree or disagree? Explain your position.

4. In what ways is managing a project different from managing a department or other structured work area? In what ways are they the same?

5. "People can use statistics to prove whatever it is they want to prove." What do you think? What are the implications for managers and how they plan?

How Good Am I at Personal Planning?

For each of the following statements, circle your level of agreement or disagreement as it relates to your school and personal life:[37]

1 = Strongly Disagree   2 = Disagree   3 = Neither Agree nor Disagree   4 = Agree   5 = Strongly Agree

1. I am proactive rather than reactive.   1 2 3 4 5
2. I set aside enough time and resources to study and complete projects.   1 2 3 4 5
3. I am able to budget money to buy the things I really want without going broke. 1 2 3 4 5
4. I have thought through what I want to do in school.   1 2 3 4 5
5. I have a plan for completing my major.   1 2 3 4 5
6. My goals for the future are realistic.   1 2 3 4 5

Scoring Key

No overall scoring is necessary.

Analysis and Interpretation

A score of 5 on any item means that you are doing well in planning and goal setting in that area. The authors of this instrument suggest that any item you did not agree with (scores of 1 or 2) indicates you need to gain a better understanding of the importance of goal setting and what is involved in the process.

More Self-Assessments MyManagementLab

To learn more about your skills, abilities, and interests, go to the MyManagementLab website and take the following self-assessments:

- I.E.2.—What Time of Day Am I Most Productive?
- III.C.1.—How Well Do I Respond to Turbulent Change? (This exercise also appears in Chapter 13 on pages 377–378.)

MANAGEMENT FOR YOU TODAY

Dilemma

In Chapters 7 and 8, you were asked to develop your personal vision and mission statements, and to conduct a SWOT analysis to consider what you want to be doing in five years. What tools could you use to discover potential opportunities or threats that might occur during the next five years? How might you use forecasting techniques to evaluate whether your plan for five years from now makes sense? How could benchmarking help you improve the plan you have for your life?

Becoming a Manager

- Get into the habit of reading general news and business periodicals. Pay attention to events, trends, and changes that are written about.

- Practise competitor intelligence by visiting several different coffee shops in your neighbourhood and observing all the differences in service, product, and clientele across stores. Talk to employees about what they like about working for their employers.

- Take classes to learn about linear programming and forecasting techniques.

- Practise budgeting by applying it to your personal life.

- Try different scheduling tools when faced with class projects that need to be planned and managed.

WORKING TOGETHER: TEAM-BASED EXERCISE

Identifying Organizational Strategies

Benchmarking can be an important tool and source of information for managers. It also can be useful to students. Form groups of three or four individuals. In your small group, discuss study habits that each of you has found effective from your years of being in school. As a group, come up with a bulleted list of at least eight suggestions in the time period allotted by your instructor. When the instructor calls time, each group should combine with one other group and share your ideas, again in the time allotted by your instructor. In this larger group, be sure to ask questions about suggestions that each respective small group had. Each small group should make sure that it understands the suggestions of the other small group it's working with. When the instructor calls time, each small group will then present and explain the study habit suggestions of the other small group it was working with. After all groups have presented, the class will come up with what it feels are the "best" study habits of all the ideas presented.

ETHICS IN ACTION

Ethical Dilemma Exercise: What Factors Should Managers Consider When Making a Revenue Forecast?

Managers rely on forecasts for predicting many future events, especially when planning revenues and profits.[38] Forecasts are also important to financial analysts and investors assessing a company's investment potential and to bankers determining a company's ability to repay borrowed funds. For example, HealthSouth met many ambitious growth forecasts as it developed into a large chain of clinics and surgical centres across the United States with billions of dollars in annual revenues. Once its acquisitions slowed, however, HealthSouth had difficulty living up to lofty forecasts.

Then, according to a former chief financial officer, CEO Richard Scrushy pressured his managers: "If we weren't making the numbers, he'd say, 'Go figure it out.'" Even after repeatedly reassuring financial analysts that their estimates would be met, HealthSouth was forced to announce lower than expected results because of changes in government regulations. The stock price plummeted. Scrushy continued pushing his managers to find ways of avoiding disappointing results. During one high-level staff meeting, he reportedly told his executives, "I want each of the [divisional] presidents to email all of their people who miss their budget. I don't care whether it's by a dollar." Two weeks later, with government investigators gathering evidence of fraud, HealthSouth fired Scrushy. Ultimately, 11 former managers pleaded guilty to fraud charges, and Scrushy was named in a $1.4 billion fraud lawsuit.

Imagine you are the financial manager of a HealthSouth clinic preparing revenue forecasts for the coming quarter. Too high a number will set unrealistic expectations for senior managers, analysts, investors, and bankers to use in decision making; too low a number will make you and your facility look bad to upper management. What techniques should you consider in setting your revenue estimate? (Review Exhibit 9-1 on page 239 as you think about this ethical challenge.)

Thinking Critically About Ethics

Here are some techniques that have been suggested for gathering competitor information: (1) Get copies of lawsuits and civil suits that may have been filed against competitors. These court proceedings are public records and can expose surprising details. (2) Call the Better Business Bureau and ask if competitors have had complaints filed against them because of fraudulent product claims or questionable business practices. (3) Pretend to be a journalist and call competitors to ask questions. (4) Get copies of your competitors' in-house newsletters and read them. (5) Buy a single share of competitors' stock so you get the annual report and other information the company sends out. (6) Send someone from your organization to apply for a job at a competitor and have that person ask specific questions. (7) Dig through a competitor's trash.

Which, if any, of these are unethical? Defend your choices. What ethical guidelines would you suggest for competitor intelligence activities?

CASE APPLICATION

Peerless Clothing

At Montreal-based Peerless Clothing, chair and CEO Alvin Segal wonders about the future of manufacturing in Montreal.[39] The family-owned business is the largest domestic producer of fine tailored clothing in North America, manufacturing clothes under such labels as Calvin Klein, Ralph Lauren, and Izod, as well as private-label store brands. The garment industry has suffered setbacks in recent years, and while Peerless is known for the quality of its men's suits, continuing to manufacture suits in Montreal may not be the company's best strategy.

The company was founded in 1919 by Segal's late father, Moe. Segal started working in the family business in Montreal as a teenager in 1951. Although he started off on the factory floor, five years later he was the plant manager and then became president in 1970.

Segal took the opportunity to expand into the US market after the 1989 free-trade agreement, a decision that has paid off well. Eighty percent of the company's production is sold in the United States. With the rising strength of the Canadian dollar and much-lower-priced suits available from China, Segal and the others worry that they may not be able to compete effectively for much longer.

Corporate controller Tony Nardi thinks that if Peerless were a public company, responsible to outside shareholders, the company would be run quite a bit differently. It would also be a lot smaller, with less manufacturing done in Canada. "Dollar to dollar, it makes no sense to keep this factory open," he explains. "You make the same suit overseas and you make twice the amount of money."

Vice-chair Elliot Lifson believes that relying completely on overseas manufacturers to produce the company's suits could come with substantial risks. While production costs in China are lower, other problems arise when clothing is produced so far away. Because it takes longer for suits to be delivered, the company would need larger inventories, which in turn means building new and larger warehouses. A "Canadian operation can provide fast turnarounds for North American retailers," Lifson argues. In addition, the Montreal head office and the company's factory on Pie IX Boulevard represent knowledge and expertise that would be lost if the company downsized and outsourced the manufacturing of its suits.

In the past three years, Peerless has started outsourcing suits to overseas manufacturers, with about 65 percent of its product coming from Asia and being shipped directly to a warehouse in St. Albans, Vermont. This has turned out to be a successful strategy, and it is estimated that annual sales have grown about 20 percent in each of the past three years, to more than $500 million. However, while five years ago the Montreal factory used to produce 38 000 suits a week, production is down to about 23 000 suits a week because of increased production in Asia.

Remaining in Montreal is important to Segal, because his father started the business there and the company is well known for its corporate citizenship in the community. Peerless hires many new Canadians and Segal feels loyalty to his 1800 factory workers, who represent 60 cultural and linguistic groups. It is not uncommon for immigrants to "fly into Montreal one day, and show up at Peerless the next, often carrying a referral from a friend or family member who works there," Lifson reports. Twenty-two Peerless employees became Canadian citizens in the company's cafeteria in 2004.

Segal is known for innovation in the garment industry. He spent 15 years, starting in the late 1970s, buying about $1 million of computerized equipment that allowed assembly-line efficiencies for creating suits without the need of tailors. Instead, computer-assisted cutting, sewing, and gluing machines crank out high-quality suits at a lower cost. Segal was the first to bring this technology to North America, although it has been in use in Europe since after World War II. Segal, who thinks of himself as a manufacturing specialist, explains the benefit of the technology: "You produce a hand-tailored look without the hand tailoring." The focus on innovation meant that Segal was able to enter the US market quickly after the passage of the North American Free Trade Act and take a substantial share of the men's clothing market.

Now, however, he faces a new challenge. When Asian companies first started producing clothes for the North American market several years ago, production quality was low. Almost 90 percent of the clothing Peerless imported from Asia needed repairs before they could be shipped to customers. By 2007, however, only 10 percent of the clothing needed repairs.

Segal wonders how he can use planning tools and techniques to help him evaluate whether to keep his garment factory in Montreal operating, something he very much wants to do. He has come to you for advice.

DEVELOPING YOUR DIAGNOSTIC AND ANALYTICAL SKILLS

A New Pitch for an Old Classic

Andrew E. Friedman is a new breed of manager in America's favourite pastime—the classic game of baseball.[40] As the general manager of the Tampa Bay Rays (his formal title is executive vice-president of baseball operations), Friedman is responsible for overseeing and directing the team's overall baseball operations. And he is doing it his way—by relying on financial models and data mining to help improve the team's performance and valuation. For the 2006 season, *Sports Illustrated* ranked the team 24th overall out of the 30 MLB (Major League Baseball) teams. Its payroll of $35 million puts it at the bottom of the league in terms of players' salaries. However, Friedman uses his own numbers approach to assess the value of his team and to help it realize its maximum potential.

With a degree in management and finance from Tulane University in New Orleans, Friedman understands the language of business. He spent five years on Wall Street before joining the Rays organization as director of baseball development. Having played on Tulane's baseball team until an injury sidelined him, Friedman is no stranger to the game. However, in baseball, quantitative statistics-based methods of player talent assessment, team valuation, and contract negotiations are not the usual approach to doing business. That is why Friedman is not concerned about having the lowest payroll of any major league team; his assessment—based upon a valuation technique used on Wall Street—places the real value of the Rays' payroll at closer to $50 million.

Friedman also uses a quantitative approach to trading players. He says, "I am purely market driven. I love players I think that I can get for less than they are worth. It's positive arbitrage, the valuation asymmetry in the game." He and team owner Stuart Sternberg and team president Matt Silverman put their philosophy of quantitative, statistics-based talent assessment into action as they made their first big trade in 2006, "exchanging their all-star closer, Danys Báez, for two untested starting pitchers from the Los Angeles Dodgers, Edwin Jackson and Chuck Tiffany." The trio is betting that the two prospects will blossom into top-rated starting pitchers—"perhaps the most elusive and highly valued commodity in baseball today." Despite the emphasis on stats and quantitative analysis, the Rays management team understands that it "cannot be a substitute for old-fashioned scouting and talent assessment, an area it also wants to strengthen."

Although there may be a new pitch to an old classic, computers, BlackBerrys, and economic models cannot and will probably never provide all the answers. However, it is hoped that the tools and techniques can help the organization achieve, as its owner says, its maximum potential.

Questions

1. What other planning tools and techniques might be useful to Andrew Friedman as he oversees and directs the team's operations? Be specific.

2. In baseball, where the traditional approach to assessing player potential and performance has involved watching the individual play in different settings (scouting the player) and where most of the team management would not have a business background, how might you overcome the doubts of "traditionalists" about the benefits of using quantitative forecasting techniques?

3. What are some ways that Friedman might evaluate whether his quantitative forecasting techniques are working? Be specific.

Budgeting

About the Skill

Managers do not have unlimited resources to do their jobs. Most managers will have to deal with a budget, a numerical plan for allocating resources to specific activities. As planning tools, budgets indicate what activities are important and how many resources should be allocated to each activity. However, budgets are not used just in planning. They are also used in controlling. As control tools, budgets provide managers with quantitative standards against which to measure and compare resource consumption. By pointing out deviations between standard and actual consumption, managers can use the budget for control purposes.

Steps in Developing the Skill

You can develop your skills at budgeting if you use the following seven suggestions:[41]

1. **Determine which work activities are going to be pursued during the coming time period.** An organization's work activities are a result of the goals that have been established. Your control over which work activities your unit will be pursuing during a specific time period will depend on how much control you normally exercise over the work that must be done in order to meet those goals. In addition, the amount of control you have often depends on your managerial level in the organization.

2. **Decide which resources will be necessary to accomplish the desired work activities—that is, those that will ensure goals are met.** Although there are different types of budgets used for allocating resources, the most common ones involve monetary resources. However, you also may have to budget time, space, material resources, human resources, capacity utilization, or units of production.

3. **Gather cost information.** You will need accurate cost estimates of those resources you need. Old budgets may be of some help, but you will also want to talk with your manager, colleagues, and key employees, and use other contacts you have developed inside and outside your organization.

4. **Once you know which resources will be available to you, assign the resources as needed to accomplish the desired work activities.** In many organizations, managers are given a monthly, quarterly, or annual budget to work with. The budget will detail which resources are available during the time period. As the manager, you have to assign the resources in an efficient and effective manner to ensure that your unit goals are met.

5. **Review the budget periodically.** It's wise to do so. Don't wait until the end of the time period to monitor whether you are over or under budget.

6. **Take action if you find that you are not within your budget.** Remember that a budget also serves as a control tool. If resources are being consumed more quickly than budgeted, you may need to determine why and take corrective action.

7. **Use past experience as a guide when developing your budget for the next time period.** Although every budgeted time period will be different, it is possible to use past experience to pinpoint trends and potential problems. This knowledge can help you prepare for any circumstances that may arise.

Practising the Skill

Read the following scenario. Write some notes about how you would handle the situation described. Be sure to refer to the seven suggestions for budgeting.

Scenario

You have recently been appointed advertising manager for a new monthly health and lifestyle magazine, *Global Living for Life*, being developed by the magazine division of LifeTime Publications. You were previously an advertising manager on one of the company's established magazines. In this new position, you will report to the new magazine's publisher, Molly Tymon.

Estimates of first-year subscription sales for *Global Living for Life* are 125 000 copies. Newsstand sales should add another 5000 copies a month to that number, but your concern is with developing advertising revenue for the magazine.

You and Molly have set a goal of selling advertising space totalling $6 million during the magazine's first year. You think you can do this with a staff of 10 people. Because this is a completely new publication, there is no previous budget for your advertising group. You have been asked by Molly to submit a preliminary budget for your group.

Write up a report (no longer than two pages in length) that describes in detail how you would go about fulfilling this request by Molly. For example, where would you get budget categories? Whom would you contact? Present your best ideas for creating this budget for your department.

Reinforcing the Skill

The following activities will help you practise and reinforce the skills associated with budgeting:

1. Create a personal budget for the next month. Be sure to identify sources of income and planned expenditures. At the end of the month, answer the following questions:
   (a) Did your budget help you plan what you could and could not do this month?
   (b) Did unexpected situations arise that were not included in the budget? How did you handle those?
   (c) How is a personal budget similar to and different from a budget that a manager might be responsible for?

2. Interview three managers from different organizations. Ask them about their budgeting responsibilities and the "lessons" they have learned about budgeting.

MyManagementLab

After you have completed the study of Part 2, do the following exercises at the MyManagementLab website (www.pearsoned.ca/mymanagementlab):

- You're the Manager: Putting Ethics into Action (HealthSouth)
- Passport, Scenario 1 (Luke Castillo, Deere & Company), Scenario 2 (Yoko Sato, Toys "R" Us International), and Scenario 3 (Tomasso Perelli, Benito Sportswear)

VIDEO CASE INCIDENT

SCAN THIS

Please turn to the back of the book to see the Video Case Incidents available for Part 2.

PART THREE

ORGANIZING

In PART THREE,
we look at the management function of
organizing and discuss the following topics:

Chapter 10	Organizational Structure and Design
Chapter 11	Managers and Communication
Chapter 12	Managing Human Resources
Chapter 13	Managing Change and Innovation

Organizing is an important task of managers—one that's not always understood or appreciated. However, when the organization's goals and plans are in place, the organizing function sets in motion the process of seeing that those goals and plans are pursued. When managers organize, they're defining what work needs to get done and creating a structure that enables those work activities to be completed efficiently and effectively.

Organizational Structure and Design

Once managers are done planning, then what? This is when managers need to begin to "work the plan." And the first step in doing that involves designing an appropriate organizational structure. This chapter covers the decisions involved with designing that structure. After reading and studying this chapter, you will achieve the following learning outcomes.

Learning Outcomes

1 Define the major elements of organizational structure.

2 Describe the factors that affect organizational structure.

3 Compare and contrast traditional and contemporary organizational designs.

▶▶▶ Richard A. Peddie is the president and CEO of Maple Leaf Sports & Entertainment (MLSE), which owns the NHL's Toronto Maple Leafs, the NBA's Toronto Raptors, Major League Soccer's Toronto FC, the AHL's Toronto Marlies, Leafs TV, and Raptors NBA TV.[1] MLSE also owns the Air Canada Centre (where the Maple Leafs and Raptors play their home games). Peddie's job is complex—it includes responsibility for the business affairs of each team ("team operations, sales, marketing, finance, administration, event operations, broadcast, communications, and community development"). Peddie is also responsible for the operation of the Air Canada Centre, BMO Field, Ricoh Coliseum in Toronto, and General Motors Centre in Oshawa, Ontario.

To perform his job, Peddie needs a variety of people and departments to help him. One of his jobs, then, is to create an organizational structure for MLSE that supports the operations of the sports teams and the sports facilities. He has a great deal of flexibility in determining some parts of the structure, and less flexibility in determining others. For instance, the number of athletes that can fill positions on a hockey team is determined by the NHL. Through the draft and trades, Peddie and his managers have some ability to choose the particular players who fill these positions, however.

Peddie also oversees ticket sales for the four teams. In determining how to manage ticket sales, Peddie can consider whether there should be separate ticket sales departments for each team, whether marketing should be included with or separate from ticket sales, and whether ticket salespeople should be subdivided into specialties: corporate sales, season tickets, playoff tickets, etc.

(Note: At the time of writing, it had been announced that Peddie was to retire on December 31, 2011.)

Think About It

How do you run four sports teams and four sports facilities? Put yourself in Richard Peddie's shoes. He wants to continue to make Maple Leaf Sports & Entertainment successful. What can he do so that MLSE continues to adapt and change? What organizational structure can best ensure his goals?

SCAN THIS

Richard Peddie's desire to make Maple Leaf Sports & Entertainment successful illustrates how important it is for managers to design an organizational structure that helps accomplish organizational goals and objectives. In this chapter, we present information about designing appropriate organizational structures. We look at the various elements of organizational structure and the factors that influence their design. We also look at some traditional and contemporary organizational designs, as well as organizational design challenges that today's managers face.

MyManagementLab
Q&A 10.1

Defining Organizational Structure

No other topic in management has undergone as much change in the past few years as that of organizing and organizational structure. Traditional approaches to organizing work are being questioned and re-evaluated as managers search out structural designs that will best support and facilitate employees doing the organization's work—ones that can achieve efficiency but also have the flexibility that is necessary for success in today's dynamic environment. The challenge for managers is to design an organizational structure that allows employees to do their work effectively and efficiently (see Exhibit 10-1).

1. Define the major elements of organizational structure.

> ## Exhibit 10-1
> ## Purposes of Organizing
>
> - Divides work to be done into specific jobs and departments.
> - Assigns tasks and responsibilities associated with individual jobs.
> - Coordinates diverse organizational tasks.
> - Clusters jobs into units.
> - Establishes relationships among individuals, groups, and departments.
> - Establishes formal lines of authority.
> - Allocates and deploys organizational resources.

organizational structure How job tasks are formally divided, grouped, and coordinated within an organization.

organizational design The process of developing or changing an organization's structure.

work specialization The degree to which activities in an organization are subdivided into separate job tasks; also known as *division of labour*.

MyManagementLab
Q&A 10.2

Just what is **organizational structure**? It's the formal arrangement of jobs within an organization. When managers develop or change the structure, they are engaged in **organizational design**, a process that involves decisions about six key elements: work specialization, departmentalization, chain of command, span of control, centralization and decentralization, and formalization.[2]

Work Specialization

When you are working in a team on a course project, does it make sense to specialize tasks? What are the advantages and disadvantages?

Today we use the term **work specialization** to describe the degree to which activities in an organization are subdivided into separate job tasks. The essence of work specialization is that an entire job is not done by one individual but instead is broken down into steps, and each step is completed by a different person. Individual employees specialize in doing part of an activity rather than the entire activity.

During the first half of the twentieth century, managers viewed work specialization as an unending source of increased productivity. And for a time it was! Because it was not widely used, when work specialization *was* implemented, employee productivity rose. By the 1960s, however, it had become evident that a good thing could be carried too far. The point had been reached in some jobs where human diseconomies from work specialization—boredom, fatigue, stress, poor quality, increased absenteeism, and higher turnover—more than offset the economic advantages.

Today's View

Most managers today see work specialization as an important organizing mechanism but not as a source of ever-increasing productivity. They recognize the economies it provides in certain types of jobs, but they also recognize the problems it creates—including job dissatisfaction, poor mental health, and a low sense of accomplishment—when it's carried to extremes.[3] McDonald's uses high work specialization to efficiently make and sell its products, and most employees in health care organizations are specialized. However, other organizations, such as Bolton, Ontario-based Husky Injection Molding Systems and Ford Australia, have successfully increased job breadth and reduced work specialization. Still, specialization has its place in some organizations. No hockey team has anyone play both goalie and centre positions. Rather, players tend to specialize in their positions.

Departmentalization

Does your college or university have an office of student affairs? A financial aid or student housing department? Once job tasks have been divided up through work specialization, common job tasks have to be grouped back together so that they can be done in a coordinated way. The basis on which jobs are grouped together is called **departmentalization**. Every organization will have its own specific way of classifying and grouping work activities. Exhibit 10-2 shows the five common forms of departmentalization.

departmentalization The basis on which jobs are grouped together.

Exhibit 10-2

The Five Common Forms of Departmentalization

Functional Departmentalization

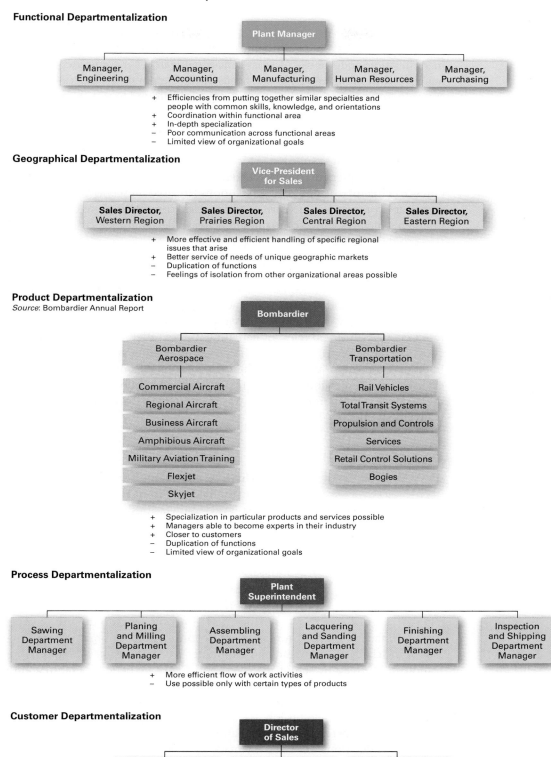

Plant Manager

Manager, Engineering | Manager, Accounting | Manager, Manufacturing | Manager, Human Resources | Manager, Purchasing

+ Efficiencies from putting together similar specialties and people with common skills, knowledge, and orientations
+ Coordination within functional area
+ In-depth specialization
− Poor communication across functional areas
− Limited view of organizational goals

Geographical Departmentalization

Vice-President for Sales

Sales Director, Western Region | Sales Director, Prairies Region | Sales Director, Central Region | Sales Director, Eastern Region

+ More effective and efficient handling of specific regional issues that arise
+ Better service of needs of unique geographic markets
− Duplication of functions
− Feelings of isolation from other organizational areas possible

Product Departmentalization

Source: Bombardier Annual Report

Bombardier

Bombardier Aerospace
- Commercial Aircraft
- Regional Aircraft
- Business Aircraft
- Amphibious Aircraft
- Military Aviation Training
- Flexjet
- Skyjet

Bombardier Transportation
- Rail Vehicles
- Total Transit Systems
- Propulsion and Controls
- Services
- Retail Control Solutions
- Bogies

+ Specialization in particular products and services possible
+ Managers able to become experts in their industry
+ Closer to customers
− Duplication of functions
− Limited view of organizational goals

Process Departmentalization

Plant Superintendent

Sawing Department Manager | Planing and Milling Department Manager | Assembling Department Manager | Lacquering and Sanding Department Manager | Finishing Department Manager | Inspection and Shipping Department Manager

+ More efficient flow of work activities
− Use possible only with certain types of products

Customer Departmentalization

Director of Sales

Manager, Retail Accounts | Manager, Wholesale Accounts | Manager, Government Accounts

+ Specialists able to meet customers' needs and problems
− Duplication of functions
− Limited view of organizational goals

Large organizations often combine forms of departmentalization. For example, a major Japanese electronics firm organizes each of its divisions along functional lines; its manufacturing units around processes; its sales units around seven geographic regions; and sales regions into four customer groupings.

Today's View

Two popular trends in departmentalization are the increasing use of customer departmentalization and the use of cross-functional teams. Customer departmentalization is being used to monitor customers' needs and to respond to changes in those needs. For example, Toronto-based Dell Canada is organized around four customer-oriented business units: home and home office; small business; medium and large business; and government, education, and health care. Burnaby, BC-based TELUS is structured around four customer-oriented business units: consumer solutions (focused on services to homes and individuals); business solutions (focused on services to small and medium-sized businesses and entrepreneurs); TELUS Québec (a TELUS company focused on services for the Quebec marketplace); and partner solutions (focused on services to wholesale customers, such as telecommunications carriers and wireless communications companies). Customer-oriented structures allow companies to better understand their customers and to respond faster to their needs.

cross-functional teams Work teams made up of individuals who are experts in various functional specialties together.

Managers use **cross-functional teams**—work teams made up of individuals who are experts in various functional specialties—to increase knowledge and understanding of some organizational tasks. For instance, Scarborough, Ontario-based Aviva Canada, a leading property and casualty insurance group, puts together catastrophe teams to more quickly help policyholders when a crisis occurs. The cross-functional teams, with trained representatives from all relevant departments, are called upon to provide services in the event of a crisis. During the BC wildfires of summer 2003, the catastrophe team worked on both local and corporate issues, including managing information technology, internal and external communication, tracking, resourcing, and vendors. This made it easier to meet the needs of policyholders as quickly as possible.[4] We discuss the use of cross-functional teams more fully in Chapter 16.

Chain of Command

chain of command The continuous line of authority that extends from the top of the organization to the lowest level and clarifies who reports to whom.

Have you ever worked in an organization where it was not clear what the chain of command was? What effect did this have on employees?

The **chain of command** is the continuous line of authority that extends from upper organizational levels to the lowest levels and clarifies who reports to whom. It helps employees answer questions such as, "Who do I go to if I have a problem?" or "To whom am I responsible?"

You cannot discuss the chain of command without discussing these other concepts: authority, responsibility, accountability, unity of command, and delegation. **Authority** refers to the rights inherent in a managerial position to tell people what to do and to expect them to do it.[5] To facilitate decision making and coordination, an organization's managers are part of the chain of command and are granted a certain degree of authority to meet their responsibilities. Some senior managers and CEOs are better at granting authority than others. For instance, when Richard Peddie hired Rob Babcock to be the general manager of the Raptors in 2004, some sportswriters raised concerns over whether Babcock would have enough autonomy to do his job. It was noted that Peddie "has a reputation for meddling with basketball operations."[6] When Babcock was fired in 2006, sportswriters observed that many of his decisions were actually made by senior management.[7]

authority The rights inherent in a managerial position to tell people what to do and to expect them to do it.

MyManagementLab
Q&A 10.3

responsibility The obligation or expectation to perform any assigned duties.

accountability The need to report and justify work to a manager's superiors.

As managers coordinate and integrate the work of employees, those employees assume an obligation to perform any assigned duties. This obligation or expectation to perform is known as **responsibility**. Responsibility brings with it **accountability**, which is the need to report and justify work to a manager's superiors. When John Muckler was dismissed as general manager of the Ottawa Senators in 2007, the team owner was signalling that he held Muckler accountable for failing to land top players who could have helped the team in their run at the Stanley Cup.[8]

The **unity of command** principle (one of Fayol's 14 principles of management discussed in the supplement *History of Management Trends*) helps preserve the concept of a continuous line of authority. It states that every employee should receive orders from only one superior. Without unity of command, conflicting demands and priorities from multiple managers can create problems.

Because managers have limited time and knowledge, they may choose to delegate some of their responsibilities to other employees. **Delegation** is the assignment of authority to another person to carry out specific duties, allowing the employee to make some of the decisions. Delegation is an important part of a manager's job, as it can ensure that the right people are part of the decision-making process. What can managers do to be better delegators? *Tips for Managers—Delegating Effectively* provides some suggestions.

unity of command The management principle that states every employee should receive orders from only one superior.

delegation The assignment of authority to another person to carry out specific duties, allowing the employee to make some of the decisions.

Today's View

Early management theorists (Fayol, Weber, Taylor, and others) were enamoured with the concepts of chain of command, authority, responsibility, and unity of command. However, times change, and so have the basic tenets of organizational design. Still, it's been hard for some organizations to give up the control that a formal chain of command represents.

In addition, concepts such as chain of command, authority, and so forth are considerably less relevant today because of things like information technology. In a matter of a few seconds, employees throughout the organization can access information that used to be available only to top managers. Also, with computers, employees communicate with anyone else anywhere in the organization without going through formal channels—that is, the chain of command. Moreover, as more organizations use self-managed and cross-functional teams and as new organizational designs with multiple bosses are implemented, these traditional concepts are less relevant.

TIPS FOR MANAGERS

Delegating Effectively

↗ Delegate **the whole task**.

↗ Select **the right person**.

↗ Ensure that **authority equals responsibility**.

↗ Give **thorough instructions**.

↗ Maintain **feedback**.

↗ **Evaluate** and **reward** performance.

Source: R. L. Daft, *Management*, 7th ed. (Mason, OH: Southwestern, 2005), p. 354.

Span of Control

How many employees can a manager efficiently and effectively manage? This question of **span of control** is important because, to a large degree, it determines the number of levels and managers an organization has. All things being equal, the wider or larger the span, the more efficient the organization. An example can show why.

Assume that we have two organizations, both of which have almost 4100 employees. As Exhibit 10-3 shows, if one organization has a uniform span of four and the other a span of eight, the wider span will have two fewer levels and approximately 800 fewer managers. If the average manager made $50 000 a year, the organization with the wider span would save $40 million a year in management salaries alone! Obviously, wider spans are more efficient in terms of cost. However, at some point, wider spans reduce effectiveness. When the span becomes too large, employee performance can suffer because managers may no longer have the time to provide the necessary leadership and support.

span of control The number of employees a manager can efficiently and effectively manage.

MyManagementLab
Q&A 10.4

Today's View

The contemporary view of span of control recognizes that many factors influence the appropriate number of employees that a manager can efficiently *and* effectively manage. These factors include the skills and abilities of the manager and the employees and characteristics of the work being done. For instance, the more training and experience employees have, the less direct supervision they need. Therefore, managers with well-trained and experienced employees can function quite well with a wider span. Other contingency variables that determine the appropriate span include similarity of employee tasks, the

Exhibit 10-3

Contrasting Spans of Control

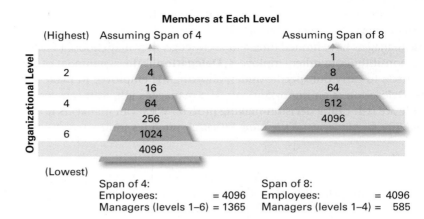

Members at Each Level

Span of 4:
Employees: = 4096
Managers (levels 1–6) = 1365

Span of 8:
Employees: = 4096
Managers (levels 1–4) =   585

complexity of those tasks, the physical proximity of subordinates, the degree to which standardized procedures are in place, the sophistication of the organization's information system, the strength of the organization's culture, and the preferred style of the manager.[9] Wider spans of control are also possible due to technology—it is easier for managers and their subordinates to communicate with each other, and there is often more information readily available to help employees perform their jobs.

The trend in recent years has been toward larger spans of control, which is consistent with managers' efforts to reduce costs, speed up decision making, increase flexibility, get closer to customers, and empower employees. However, to ensure that performance does not suffer because of these wider spans, organizations are investing heavily in employee training. Managers recognize that they can handle a wider span when employees know their jobs well or can turn to co-workers if they have questions.

Centralization and Decentralization

In some organizations, top managers make all the decisions and lower-level managers and employees simply carry out their orders. At the other extreme are organizations in which decision making is pushed down to the managers who are closest to the action. The former organizations are centralized, and the latter are decentralized.

Centralization describes the degree to which decision making is concentrated at a single point in the organization. If top managers make the organization's key decisions with little or no input from below, then the organization is centralized. We noted above that Richard Peddie tends to be closely involved in decisions regarding the Raptors. In contrast, the more that lower-level employees provide input or actually make decisions, the more **decentralization** there is. Keep in mind that the concept of centralization/ decentralization is relative, not absolute—that is, an organization is never completely centralized or decentralized. Few organizations could function effectively if all decisions were made by only a select group of top managers; nor could they function if all decisions were delegated to employees at the lowest levels. (To learn more about delegating, see *Developing Your Interpersonal Skills—Delegating* on pages 287–288.)

What determines whether an organization will move toward more centralization or decentralization? Exhibit 10-4 lists some of the factors that influence the amount of centralization or decentralization an organization uses.[10]

centralization The degree to which decision making is concentrated at a single point in the organization.

decentralization The degree to which lower-level employees provide input or actually make decisions.

MyManagementLab
PRISM 10

Many employees are asked to work in teams to get things done. These employees are a self-managed team. They make decisions about managing and scheduling production, and they monitor the quality of their output.

Exhibit 10-4

Factors That Influence the Amount of Centralization and Decentralization

More Centralization	More Decentralization
• Environment is stable.	• Environment is complex, uncertain.
• Lower-level managers are not as capable or experienced at making decisions as upper-level managers.	• Lower-level managers are capable and experienced at making decisions.
• Lower-level managers do not want to have a say in decisions.	• Lower-level managers want a voice in decisions.
• Decisions are significant.	• Decisions are relatively minor.
• Organization is facing a crisis or the risk of company failure.	• Corporate culture is open to allowing managers to have a say in what happens.
• Company is large.	• Company is geographically dispersed.
• Effective implementation of company strategies depends on managers' retaining say over what happens.	• Effective implementation of company strategies depends on managers' having involvement and flexibility to make decisions.

Today's View

As organizations become more flexible and responsive, there is a distinct trend toward decentralizing decision making. In large companies especially, lower-level managers are "closer to the action" and typically have more detailed knowledge about problems and how best to solve them than do top managers. For instance, the Bank of Montreal's approximately 1000 branches are organized into "communities"—a group of branches within a limited geographical area. Each community is led by a community area manager, who typically works within a 20-minute drive of the area's other branches. This area manager can respond faster and more intelligently to problems in his or her community than could some senior executive at the company's head office. As the company continues its southward expansion into the United States, it continues to use decentralization to successfully manage its various businesses.[11] The following *Management Reflection* considers the case of Cascades, a pulp and paper company, which illustrates a few of the reasons for having a decentralized structure.

MANAGEMENT REFLECTION

Brothers Decentralize to Increase Entrepreneurial Management

Does decentralization lead to better management? Kingsey Falls, Quebec-based Cascades, a leading manufacturer of packaging products and tissue paper, has more than 100 operating units located in Canada, the United States, and Europe.[12] Alain Lemaire is president and CEO, and his two brothers, Bernard and Laurent, are also senior executives in the business.

Cascades is composed of autonomous units: the Boxboard Group, the Containerboard Group–Norampac, the Specialty Products Group, and the Tissue Group. The companies produce coated boxboard and folding cartons, container-board packaging, specialty paper products, and tissues. Boralex, a company affiliated with Cascades, produces energy and is headed by Bernard Lemaire. The companies are treated as separate entities based on product and operate like a federation of small and medium-sized businesses. Each mill within a subsidiary operates as a separate business unit and is accountable for its own bottom line.

The company motivates its employees through profit sharing, although employees share only in the profits generated by their own mill. Because each mill is evaluated separately, managers have to be both more responsible and more accountable for their operations and encourage employees to take more ownership of their job performance. The Lemaires' emphasis on decentralized, entrepreneurial management has been copied by other Canadian forest products companies, such as Domtar. ■

---

employee empowerment Giving more authority to employees to make decisions.

Another term for increased decentralization is **employee empowerment**, which is giving more authority to employees to make decisions. We address empowerment more thoroughly in our discussion of leadership in Chapter 14.

Formalization

formalization The degree to which jobs within the organization are standardized and the extent to which employee behaviour is guided by rules and procedures.

Formalization refers to the degree to which jobs within the organization are standardized and the extent to which employee behaviour is guided by rules and procedures. If a job is highly formalized, then the person doing that job has little freedom to choose what is to be done, when it's to be done, and how he or she does it. Employees can be expected to handle the same input in exactly the same way, resulting in consistent and uniform output. In organizations with high formalization, there are explicit job descriptions, numerous organizational rules, and clearly defined procedures covering work processes. On the other hand, where formalization is low, job behaviours are relatively unstructured and employees have a great deal of freedom to choose how they do their work.

MyManagementLab
Q&A 10.5

The degree of formalization varies widely between organizations and even within organizations. For instance, at a newspaper, news reporters often have a great deal of discretion in their jobs. They may pick their news topics, find their own stories, research them the way they want, and write them up, usually within minimal guidelines. On the other hand, employees who lay out the newspaper pages don't have that type of freedom. They have constraints—both time and space—that standardize how they do their work.

Today's View

MyManagementLab
Q&A 10.6

Although some formalization is important and necessary for consistency and control, many of today's organizations seem to be less reliant on strict rules and standardization to guide and regulate employee behaviour. For instance, consider the following situation:

It is 2:37 p.m., and a customer at a branch of a large national drugstore chain is trying to drop off a roll of film for same-day developing. Store policy states that film must be dropped off by 2:00 p.m. for this service. The clerk knows that rules like this are supposed to be followed. At the same time, he wants to be accommodating to the customer, and he knows that the film could, in fact, be processed that day. He decides to accept the film and, in so doing, to violate the policy. He just hopes that his manager does not find out.[13]

Has this employee done something wrong? He did "break" the rule. But by breaking the rule, he actually brought in revenue and provided the customer good service: so good, in fact, that the customer may be satisfied enough to come back in the future.

Considering that there are numerous situations like these where rules may be too restrictive, many organizations have allowed employees some freedom to make those decisions that they feel are best under the circumstances. It does not mean that all organizational rules are thrown out the window, because there *will* be rules that are important for employees to follow—and these rules should be explained so employees understand why it's important to adhere to them. But for other rules, employees may be given some leeway in application.[14]

Organizational Design Decisions

Organizations don't have the same structures. A company with 30 employees is not going to look like one with 30 000 employees. But even organizations of comparable size don't necessarily have similar structures. What works for one organization may not work for another. How do managers decide what organizational design to use? That decision depends upon certain contingency factors. In this section, we look at two generic models of organizational design and then at the contingency factors that favour each.

2. Describe the factors that affect organizational structure.

Mechanistic and Organic Organizations

Exhibit 10-5 describes two organizational forms.[15] A **mechanistic organization** is a rigid and tightly controlled structure, much like McDonald's. It's characterized by high specialization, rigid departmentalization, a limited information network (mostly downward communication), narrow spans of control, little participation in decision making by lower-level employees, and high formalization.

mechanistic organization An organizational design that is rigid and tightly controlled.

Exhibit 10-5

Mechanistic vs. Organic Organization

Mechanistic	Organic
• High Specialization	• Cross-Functional Teams
• Rigid Departmentalization	• Cross-Hierarchical Teams
• Clear Chain of Command	• Free Flow of Information
• Narrow Spans of Control	• Wide Spans of Control
• Centralization	• Decentralization
• High Formalization	• Low Formalization

Mechanistic organizational structures tend to be efficiency machines and rely heavily on rules, regulations, standardized tasks, and similar controls. This organizational design tries to minimize the impact of differing personalities, judgments, and ambiguity because these human traits are seen as inefficient and inconsistent. Although there is no totally mechanistic organization, almost all large corporations and government agencies have some of these mechanistic characteristics.

organic organization An organizational design that is highly adaptive and flexible.

In direct contrast to the mechanistic form of organization is the **organic organization**, which is as highly adaptive and flexible a structure as the mechanistic organization is rigid and stable. This structure characterizes the Blue Water Café, a well-known Vancouver seafood restaurant. Rather than having standardized jobs and regulations, the organic organization is flexible, which allows it to change rapidly as needs require. Organic organizations have a division of labour, but the jobs people do are not standardized. Employees are highly trained and empowered to handle diverse job activities and problems, and these organizations frequently use cross-functional and cross-hierarchical teams. Employees in organic-type organizations require minimal formal rules and little direct supervision, instead relying on a free flow of information and wide span of control. Their high levels of skills and training and the support provided by other team members make formalization and tight managerial controls unnecessary.

Organizations can display a mix of mechanistic and organic features. Wikipedia, the online encyclopedia, is known for its creation and editing of entries by anyone who has Internet access. In this way, it displays a very organic structure. However, behind the scenes there is a more mechanistic structure, where individuals have some authority to monitor abuse and perform other functions to safeguard the credibility of entries and the website overall, as the following *Management Reflection* shows.

MANAGEMENT REFLECTION

Wikipedia's Structure Maintains Order in the Face of Anarchy

Why would a decentralized, free-wheeling website need an organizational structure? Even a seemingly democratic organization such as Wikipedia has an organizational structure.[16] The structure serves to help the online encyclopedia be as accurate as possible. At the bottom of that structure are the 4.6 million registered English-language users. These users are overseen by a group of about 1200 administrators, who have the power to "block other users from the site, either temporarily or permanently." One of their roles is to make sure that users are not vandalizing the site by adding incorrect information deliberately. To become an administrator, one must first be nominated, and then answer a series of five questions. Users then have seven days to register their approval or disapproval of the nominee. The administrators are overseen by a group called "bureaucrats." The bureaucrats can appoint administrators once they determine that users approve of a particular administrator nominee (this requires about a 70 percent approval rating by users). They can also change user names, and they make sure that bot policies (policies regarding automated or semi-automated processes that edit webpages) are followed. Above the bureaucrats are about 30 stewards, who are elected to this position. The stewards can provide (and take away) special access status to Wikipedia. Above the stewards is the seven-person Wikimedia Foundation board of trustees, who are "the ultimate corporate authority." At the top of the Wikipedia organizational chart is the "de facto leader," Jimmy Wales, one of the co-founders of Wikipedia. ■

When is a mechanistic structure preferable, and when is an organic one more appropriate? Let's look at the main contingency factors that influence the decision.

Contingency Factors

Top managers of most organizations typically put a great deal of thought into designing an appropriate structure. What that appropriate structure is depends on four contingency variables: the organization's strategy, size, technology, and degree of environmental uncertainty. It is important to remember that because these variables can change over the life cycle of the organization, managers should consider from time to time whether the current organizational structure is best suited for what the organization is facing.

MyManagementLab
Q&A 10.8

Strategy and Structure

An organization's structure should facilitate goal achievement. Because goals are an important part of the organization's strategies, it's only logical that strategy and structure are closely linked. Alfred Chandler initially researched this relationship.[17] He studied several large US companies and concluded that changes in corporate strategy led to changes in an organization's structure that support the strategy.

Research has shown that certain structural designs work best with different organizational strategies.[18] For instance, the flexibility and free-flowing information of the organic structure works well when an organization is pursuing meaningful and unique innovations. The mechanistic organization, with its efficiency, stability, and tight controls, works best for companies that want to tightly control costs.

Size and Structure

There is considerable evidence that an organization's size significantly affects its structure.[19] For instance, large organizations—those with 2000 or more employees—tend to have more specialization, departmentalization, centralization, and rules and regulations than do small organizations. However, the relationship is not linear. Rather, beyond a certain point, size becomes a less important influence on structure as an organization grows. Why? Essentially, once an organization has around 2000 employees, it's already fairly mechanistic. Adding 500 employees to an organization with 2000 employees will not have much of an impact. On the other hand, adding 500 employees to an organization that has only 300 members is likely to result in a shift toward a more mechanistic structure.

Technology and Structure

Every organization has at least one form of technology to convert its inputs into outputs. For instance, employees at FedEx Kinko's produce custom print jobs for individual customers. Employees at GM Canada's Oshawa, Ontario, plant build Chevrolet Impala, Chevrolet Monte Carlo, Buick Lacrosse/Allure, and Pontiac Grand Prix cars on a standardized assembly line. And employees at Bayer AG make aspirin and other pharmaceutical products using a continuous-flow production line. Each of these organizations uses a different type of technology.

MyManagementLab
Q&A 10.9

The initial interest in technology as a determinant of structure can be traced to the work of British scholar Joan Woodward.[20] She studied several small manufacturing firms in southern England to determine the extent to which structural design elements were related to organizational success. Woodward was unable to find any consistent pattern until she segmented the firms into three categories based on the size of their production runs. The three categories, representing three distinct technologies, have increasing levels of complexity and sophistication. The first category, **unit production**, describes the production of items in units or small batches. The second category, **mass production**, describes large-batch manufacturing. Finally, the third and most technically complex group, **process production**, describes the production of items in continuous processes. A summary of her findings is shown in Exhibit 10-6.

Since Woodward's initial work, numerous studies have been done on the technology–structure relationship. These studies generally demonstrate that organizations adapt their structures to their technology.[21] The processes or methods that transform an organization's inputs into outputs differ by their degree of routineness or standardization. In general, the more routine the technology, the more mechanistic the structure can be. Organizations

unit production The production of items in units or small batches.

mass production The production of items in large batches.

process production The production of items in continuous processes.

In his 2007 book *Wikinomics*, Don Tapscott suggested that more companies would follow the Procter & Gamble open innovation model and use mass collaboration and crowd sourcing to source more and more of their research and development externally.

A *BusinessWeek* and *New York Times* Business Bestseller

"An intriguing and important book that belongs on your shelf."
—*The Washington Post*

Facebook   Flickr

Wikipedia   Second Life

Linux   YouTube

InnoCentive   Human Genome Project

WIKINOMICS
How Mass Collaboration Changes Everything

WITH A NEW PREFACE

Don Tapscott
bestselling author of *The Digital Economy*
and Anthony D. Williams

with more nonroutine technology, such as custom furniture building or online education, are more likely to have organic structures because the product delivery cannot be standardized.[22]

Environmental Uncertainty and Structure

Some organizations face relatively stable and simple environments; others face dynamic and complex environments. Because uncertainty threatens an organization's effectiveness, managers will try to minimize it. One way to reduce environmental uncertainty is through adjustments in the organization's structure.[23] The greater the uncertainty, the more an organization needs the flexibility offered by an organic structure. On the other hand, in stable, simple environments, mechanistic structures tend to be most effective.

Today's View

The evidence on the environment–structure relationship helps explain why so many managers today are restructuring their organizations to be lean, fast, and flexible. Global competition, accelerated product innovation by competitors, and increased demands from customers for high quality and faster deliveries are examples of dynamic environmental forces. Mechanistic organizations are not equipped to respond to rapid environmental change and environmental uncertainty. As a result, we are seeing organizations designed to be more organic. However, a purely organic organization may not be ideal. One study found that organic structures may work more effectively if managers establish semistructures

---

Exhibit 10-6

Woodward's Findings on Technology, Structure, and Effectiveness

	Unit Production	Mass Production	Process Production
Structural Characteristics	• Low vertical differentiation	• Moderate vertical differentiation	• High vertical differentiation
	• Low horizontal differentiation	• High horizontal differentiation	• Low horizontal differentiation
	• Low formalization	• High formalization	• Low formalization
Most Effective Structure	• Organic	• Mechanistic	• Organic

Source: Based on J. Woodward, *Industrial Organization: Theory and Practice* (London: Oxford University Press, 1965).

that govern "the pace, timing, and rhythm of organizational activities and processes." Thus, introducing a bit of structure while keeping most of the flexibility of the organic structure may reduce operating costs.[24]

Common Organizational Designs

▶ ▶ ▶ Maple Leaf Sports & Entertainment (MLSE) is divided into four operating units: MLSE, Toronto Raptors, Toronto Maple Leafs (Toronto Marlies is an affiliate), and Toronto FC. Richard Peddie is the president and CEO of all four units.[25] The Raptors, the Maple Leafs, the Marlies, and Toronto FC each have their own general manager who manages the day-to-day operations of the team, develops recruiting plans, and oversees training. The general managers report to the CEO and have a number of managers who report to them. MLSE has a divisional structure, whereby its businesses operate separately, on a daily basis.

3. Compare and contrast traditional and contemporary organizational designs.

Think About It

Why do organizations vary in the types of structures they have? How do organizations choose their structures? Why does Maple Leaf Sports & Entertainment have the structure that it does?

What organizational designs do Ford Canada, Corel, McCain Foods, Procter & Gamble, and eBay have? In making organizational design decisions, managers can choose from traditional organizational designs and contemporary organizational designs.

Traditional Organizational Designs

In designing a structure to support the efficient and effective accomplishment of organizational goals, managers may choose to follow more traditional organizational designs. These designs—the simple structure, functional structure, and divisional structure—tend to be more mechanistic. Exhibit 10-7 summarizes the strengths and weaknesses of each of these designs.

Simple Structure

Most organizations start as entrepreneurial ventures with a simple structure consisting of owners and employees. A **simple structure** is an organizational structure with low departmentalization, wide spans of control, authority centralized in a single person, and little formalization.[26] This structure is most commonly used by small businesses in which the owner and manager are one and the same.

simple structure An organizational structure with low departmentalization, wide spans of control, authority centralized in a single person, and little formalization.

Exhibit 10-7

Strengths and Weaknesses of Common Traditional Organizational Designs

Structure	Strengths	Weaknesses
Simple Structure	Fast; flexible; inexpensive to maintain; clear accountability.	Not appropriate as organization grows; reliance on one person is risky.
Functional Structure	Cost-saving advantages from specialization (economies of scale, minimal duplication of people and equipment); employees are grouped with others who have similar tasks.	Pursuit of functional goals can cause managers to lose sight of what's best for overall organization; functional specialists become insulated and have little understanding of what other units are doing.
Divisional Structure	Focuses on results—division managers are responsible for what happens to their products and services.	Duplication of activities and resources increases costs and reduces efficiency.

As employees are added, however, most companies don't remain as simple structures. The structure tends to become more specialized and formalized. Rules and regulations are introduced, work becomes specialized, departments are created, levels of management are added, and the organization becomes increasingly bureaucratic. At this point, managers might choose a functional structure or a divisional structure.

Functional Structure

functional structure An organizational structure that groups similar or related occupational specialties together.

A **functional structure** is an organizational structure that groups similar or related occupational specialties together. It's the functional approach to departmentalization applied to the entire organization. For instance, Revlon is organized around the functions of operations, finance, human resources, and product research and development.

Divisional Structure

divisional structure An organizational structure that consists of separate business units or divisions.

The **divisional structure** is an organizational structure that consists of separate business units or divisions.[27] In this structure, each unit or division has relatively limited autonomy, with a division manager responsible for performance and with strategic and operational authority over his or her unit. In divisional structures, however, the parent corporation typically acts as an external overseer to coordinate and control the various divisions, and it often provides support services such as financial and legal. As we noted earlier, Maple Leaf Sports & Entertainment has four divisions, including Toronto's three major-league sports teams: the Raptors, the Maple Leafs, and Toronto FC.

Contemporary Organizational Designs

Managers in some contemporary organizations are finding that these traditional hierarchical designs often are not appropriate for the increasingly dynamic and complex environments they face. In response to marketplace demands for being lean, flexible, and innovative, managers are finding creative ways to structure and organize work and to make their organizations more responsive to the needs of customers, employees, and other organizational constituents.[28] Now, we want to introduce you to some of the newest concepts in organizational design. Exhibit 10-8 summarizes these contemporary organizational designs.

Exhibit 10-8

Contemporary Organizational Designs

Structure	Description	Advantages	Disadvantages
Team	A structure in which the entire organization is made up of work groups or teams.	Employees are more involved and empowered. Reduced barriers among functional areas.	No clear chain of command. Pressure on teams to perform.
Matrix– Project	Matrix is a structure that assigns specialists from different functional areas to work on projects but who return to their areas when the project is completed. Project is a structure in which employees continuously work on projects. As one project is completed, employees move on to the next project.	Fluid and flexible design that can respond to environmental changes. Faster decision making.	Complexity of assigning people to projects. Task and personality conflicts.
Boundaryless	A structure that is not defined by or limited to artificial horizontal, vertical, or external boundaries; includes *virtual* and *networked* types of organizations.	Highly flexible and responsive. Draws on talent wherever it's found.	Lack of control. Communication difficulties.

Team Structure

Larry Page and Sergey Brin, co-founders of Google, have created a corporate structure that "tackles most big projects in small, tightly focused teams."[29] In a **team structure**, the entire organization is made up of work groups or teams that perform the organization's work.[30] Needless to say, employee empowerment is crucial in a team structure because there is no line of managerial authority from top to bottom. Rather, employee teams are free to design work in the way they think is best. However, the teams are also held responsible for all work and performance results in their respective areas. Let's look at some other examples of organizations that are organized around teams.

In large organizations, the team structure complements what is typically a functional or divisional structure. This allows the organization to have the efficiency of a bureaucracy while providing the flexibility that teams provide. To improve productivity at the operating level, for instance, companies such as Toyota's CAPTIN plant (based in Delta, BC), Motorola, and Xerox extensively use self-managed teams. At Saturn and Hewlett-Packard, cross-functional teams are used to design new products or coordinate major projects.

team structure An organizational structure in which the entire organization is made up of work groups or teams.

MyManagementLab
Q&A 10.10

Matrix and Project Structures

Have you ever had to work for two managers at the same time? Was this a positive or negative experience?

In addition to the team structure, other popular contemporary designs are the matrix and project structures. In the **matrix structure**, specialists from different functional departments work on projects that are led by a project manager (see Exhibit 10-9). One unique aspect of this design is that it creates a *dual chain of command* in which employees have two managers—their functional area manager and their product or project manager—who share authority. The project manager has authority over the functional members who are part of his or her project team in areas related to the project's goals. However, any decisions about promotions, salary recommendations, and annual reviews typically remain the functional manager's responsibility. To work effectively, both managers have to communicate regularly, coordinate work demands on employees, and resolve conflicts together.

Many organizations are using a **project structure**, in which employees continuously work on projects. Unlike a matrix structure, a project structure has no formal departments where employees return at the completion of a project. Instead, employees take their specific skills, abilities, and experiences to other projects. Also, all work in project

matrix structure An organizational structure that assigns specialists from different functional departments to work on one or more projects.

MyManagementLab
Q&A 10.11

project structure An organizational structure in which employees continuously work on projects.

Exhibit 10-9

A Matrix Organization in an Aerospace Firm

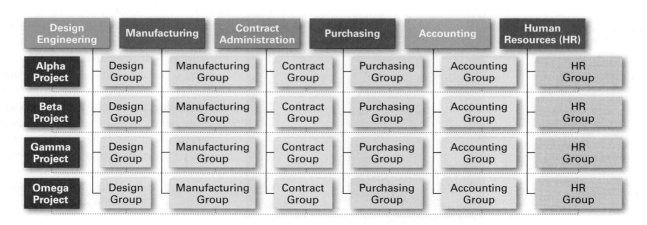

structures is performed by teams of employees. For instance, at design firm IDEO, project teams form, disband, and form again as the work requires. Employees "join" a project team because they bring needed skills and abilities to that project. Once a project is completed, however, they move on to the next one.[31]

Project structures tend to be fluid and flexible organizational designs. There is no departmentalization or rigid organizational hierarchy to slow down decision making or taking actions. In this type of structure, managers serve as facilitators, mentors, and coaches. They "serve" the project teams by eliminating or minimizing organizational obstacles and by ensuring that the teams have the resources they need to effectively and efficiently complete their work.

Boundaryless Organizations

Another contemporary organizational design is the **boundaryless organization**, which is an organization whose design is not defined by, or limited to, the horizontal, vertical, or external boundaries imposed by a predefined structure.[32] Former GE Chair Jack Welch coined the term because he wanted to eliminate vertical and horizontal boundaries within GE and break down external barriers between the company and its customers and suppliers. Although the idea of eliminating boundaries may seem odd, many of today's most successful organizations are finding that they can operate most effectively by remaining flexible and *un*structured—that the ideal structure for them is *not* having a rigid, bounded, and predefined structure.[33]

MyManagementLab
Q&A 10.12

What do we mean by *boundaries*? There are two types: (1) *internal*—the horizontal boundaries imposed by work specialization and departmentalization and the vertical ones that separate employees into organizational levels and hierarchies; and (2) *external*—the boundaries that separate the organization from its customers, suppliers, and other stakeholders. To minimize or eliminate these boundaries, managers might use virtual or network structural designs.

Virtual Organizations A **virtual organization** has elements of a traditional organization, but also relies on recent developments in information technology to get work done.[34] Thus, the organization could consist of a small core of full-time employees that temporarily hires outside specialists to work on opportunities that arise.[35] A virtual organization could also be formed of employees who work from their own home offices, connected by technology, but perhaps getting together face-to-face only rarely. An example of a virtual organization is Strawberry Frog, an international advertising agency based in Amsterdam. The small administrative staff accesses a network of about 50 people around the globe to complete advertising projects. By relying on this web of freelancers around the globe, the company enjoys a network of talent without all the unnecessary overhead and structural complexity.

The inspiration for virtual organizations comes from the film industry. If you look at the film industry, people are essentially "free agents" who move from project to project applying their skills—directing, talent search, costuming, makeup, set design—as needed.

Trend Micro, a maker of antivirus software, is a virtual organization with financial headquarters in Tokyo, product development people in Taiwan, and sales offices in Silicon Valley. Its computer-virus response centre is in Manila, and its smaller labs are scattered around the world from Munich to Tokyo. Says CEO Steve Chang, "With the Internet, viruses became global. To fight them, we had to become a global company." Trend Micro has responded to virus threats in as little as 30 minutes.

New Westminster, BC-based iGEN Knowledge Solutions uses its virtual form to bring technical solutions to its business clients. iGEN associates work from home offices, connected by wireless technologies, to solve client problems collaboratively. This structure allows faster idea implementation, product development, and service delivery. The company finds it easy to set up operations in different regions of the country without large overhead costs because of its virtual structure.

Network Organizations Another structural option for managers who want to minimize or eliminate organizational boundaries is the **network organization**, which is a small core organization that outsources major business functions.[36] This approach allows organizations to concentrate on what they do best and contract out other activities to companies that can do those activities best. Many large organizations use the network structure to outsource manufacturing. Companies like Cisco Systems, Nike, Ericsson, L.L. Bean, and Reebok have found that they can do hundreds of millions of dollars of business without owning manufacturing facilities. For instance, San Jose, California-based Cisco Systems is essentially a research and development company that uses outside suppliers and independent manufacturers to assemble the Internet routers its engineers design. Beaverton, Oregon-based Nike is essentially a product development and marketing company that contracts with outside organizations to manufacture its athletic footwear. And Stockholm, Sweden-based Ericsson contracts its manufacturing and even some of its research and development to more cost-effective contractors in New Delhi, Singapore, California, and other global locations.[37]

network organization A small core organization that outsources major business functions.

While many companies use outsourcing, not all are successful at it. Managers should be aware of some of the problems involved in outsourcing, such as the following:

- Choosing the wrong activities to outsource
- Choosing the wrong vendor
- Writing a poor contract
- Failing to consider personnel issues
- Losing control over the activity
- Ignoring the hidden costs
- Failing to develop an exit strategy (for either moving to another vendor, or deciding to bring the activity back in-house)

A review of 91 outsourcing activities found that the most likely reasons for an outsourcing venture to fail were writing a poor contract and losing control of the activity.[38]

Canadian managers say they are reluctant to outsource.[39] In a 2004 survey of 603 Canadian companies by Ipsos Reid, 60 percent were not eager to ship software development overseas. While a number of managers said they were concerned with controlling costs (36 percent), almost the same number said they preferred to keep jobs in Canada (32 percent), and one-third were also concerned about losing control of projects that went overseas.

Today's Organizational Design Challenges

As managers look for organizational designs that will best support and facilitate employees doing their work efficiently and effectively in today's dynamic environment, there are certain challenges with which they must contend. These include keeping employees connected, building a learning organization, and managing global structural issues.

Keeping Employees Connected

Many organizational design concepts were developed during the twentieth century, when work tasks were fairly predictable and constant, most jobs were full time and continued indefinitely, and work was done at an employer's place of business under a manager's supervision.[40] That is not what it's like in many organizations today, as you saw in our preceding discussion of virtual and network organizations. A major structural design challenge for managers is finding a way to keep widely dispersed and mobile employees connected to the organization. We cover information on motivating these employees in Chapter 13.

Building a Learning Organization

We first introduced the concept of a learning organization in Chapter 1 as we looked at some of the current issues facing managers. The concept of a learning organization does

MyManagementLab
Q&A 10.13

not involve a specific organizational design per se but instead describes an organizational mindset or philosophy that has design implications.

What is a learning organization? It's an organization that has developed the capacity to continuously learn, adapt, and change.[41] In a learning organization, employees continually acquire and share new knowledge and are willing to apply that knowledge in making decisions or performing their work. Some organizational theorists even go so far as to say that an organization's ability to do this—that is, to learn and to apply that learning—may be the only sustainable source of competitive advantage.[42] What structural aspects does a learning organization need?

MyManagementLab
Q&A 10.14

First, it's critical for members in a learning organization to share information and collaborate on work activities throughout the entire organization—across different functional specialties and even at different organizational levels. To do this requires minimal structural and physical barriers. In such a boundaryless environment, employees can work together and collaborate in doing the organization's work the best way they can and learn from each other. Finally, because of this need to collaborate, teams also tend to be an important feature of a learning organization's structural design. Employees work in teams that are empowered to make decisions about doing whatever work needs to be done or resolving issues. With empowered employees and teams, there is little need for "bosses" to direct and control. Instead, managers serve as facilitators, supporters, and advocates.

Managing Global Structural Issues

Are there global differences in organizational structures? Are Australian organizations structured like those in Canada? Are German organizations structured like those in France or Mexico? Given the global nature of today's business environment, this is an issue with which managers need to be familiar. Researchers have concluded that the structures and strategies of organizations worldwide are similar, "while the behavior within them is maintaining its cultural uniqueness."[43] What does this mean for designing effective and efficient structures? When designing or changing structure, managers may need to think about the cultural implications of certain design elements. For instance, one study showed that formalization—rules and bureaucratic mechanisms—may be more important in less economically developed countries, and less important in more economically developed countries, where employees may have higher levels of professional education and skills.[44] Other structural design elements may be affected by cultural differences as well.

A Final Thought

No matter what structural design managers choose for their organizations, the design should help employees do their work in the best—most efficient and effective—way they can. The structure should aid and facilitate organizational members as they carry out the organization's work. After all, the structure is simply a means to an end. (To understand your reaction to organizational structure, see *Self-Assessment—What Type of Organizational Structure Do I Prefer?* on pages 284–285.)

SUMMARY AND IMPLICATIONS

1. Define the major elements of organizational structure. Organizational structure is the formal arrangement of jobs within an organization. Organizational structures can vary due to six key elements: work specialization, departmentalization, chain of command, span of control, centralization and decentralization, and formalization. Decisions about these elements determine how work is organized; how many employees managers supervise; where in the organization decisions are made; and whether employees follow standardized operating procedures or have greater flexibility in how they do their work.

▶ ▶ ▶ For Maple Leafs Sports & Entertainment, it makes sense to separate the operation of the four sports teams because of the work specialization involved. For example, the general manager of the Raptors would not necessarily make good decisions about what Maple Leafs players should do to improve their game.

2. Describe the factors that affect organizational structure. There is no one best organizational structure. The appropriate structure depends upon the organization's strategy, its size, the technology it uses (unit production, mass production, or process production), and the degree of environmental uncertainty the organization faces.

▶ ▶ ▶ For Maple Leaf Sports & Entertainment, because hockey, basketball, and soccer are in different "industries" with different types of players, it makes sense to organize the teams by industry. Because sports teams are governed by formal rules, the teams have more of a mechanistic structure than an organic one. Each team has a similar organizational structure because size, technology, and environmental uncertainty would not differ in any meaningful way for the teams.

3. Compare and contrast traditional and contemporary organizational designs. The traditional structures of organizations are simple, functional, and divisional. Contemporary organizational designs include team structure, matrix and project structures, and boundaryless organizations.

▶ ▶ ▶ Maple Leaf Sports & Entertainment follows a traditional divisional structure for its sports teams. Other structures might be used to operate its sports facilities, such as a project structure or a boundaryless organization, because events and ticket sales can be managed in a variety of ways.

Management @ Work

READING FOR COMPREHENSION

1. Describe what is meant by the term *organizational design*.

2. In what ways can management departmentalize? When should one approach be considered over the others?

3. What is the difference between a mechanistic and an organic organization?

4. Why is the simple structure inadequate in large organizations?

5. Describe the characteristics of a boundaryless organization.

6. Describe the characteristics of a learning organization. What are its advantages?

LINKING CONCEPTS TO PRACTICE

1. Can an organization's structure be changed quickly? Why or why not?

2. Would you rather work in a mechanistic or an organic organization? Why?

3. What types of skills would a manager need to effectively work in a team structure? In a matrix and project structure? In a boundaryless organization?

4. "The boundaryless organization has the potential to create a major shift in the way we work." Do you agree or disagree with this statement? Explain.

5. With the availability of information technology that allows an organization's work to be done anywhere at any time, is organizing still an important managerial function? Why or why not?

SELF-ASSESSMENT

What Type of Organizational Structure Do I Prefer?

For each of the following statements, circle your level of agreement or disagreement:[45]

1 = Strongly Disagree   2 = Disagree Somewhat   3 = Undecided   4 = Agree Somewhat   5 = Strongly Agree

I prefer to work in an organization where:

1. Goals are defined by those at higher levels.   1 2 3 4 5
2. Clear job descriptions exist for every job.   1 2 3 4 5
3. Top management makes important decisions.   1 2 3 4 5
4. Promotions and pay increases are based as much on length of service as on level of performance.   1 2 3 4 5
5. Clear lines of authority and responsibility are established.   1 2 3 4 5
6. My career is pretty well planned out for me.   1 2 3 4 5
7. I have a great deal of job security.   1 2 3 4 5
8. I can specialize.   1 2 3 4 5
9. My boss is readily available.   1 2 3 4 5
10. Organization rules and regulations are clearly specified.   1 2 3 4 5
11. Information rigidly follows the chain of command.   1 2 3 4 5
12. There is a minimal number of new tasks for me to learn.   1 2 3 4 5
13. Work groups incur little turnover in members.   1 2 3 4 5
14. People accept authority of a leader's position.   1 2 3 4 5
15. I am part of a group whose training and skills are similar to mine.   1 2 3 4 5

Scoring Key

> Add up the numbers for each of your responses to get your total score.

Analysis and Interpretation

This instrument measures your preference for working in a mechanistic or organic organizational structure.

Scores above 60 suggest that you prefer a mechanistic structure. Scores below 45 indicate a preference for an organic structure. Scores between 45 and 60 suggest no clear preference.

Because the trend in recent years has been toward more organic structures, you are more likely to find a good organizational match if you score low on this instrument. However, there are few, if any, pure organic structures. Therefore, very low scores may also mean that you are likely to be frustrated by what you perceive as overly rigid structures of rules, regulations, and boss-centred leadership. In general, however, low scores indicate that you prefer small, innovative, flexible, team-oriented organizations. High scores indicate a preference for stable, rule-oriented, more bureaucratic organizations.

More Self-Assessments MyManagementLab

To learn more about your skills, abilities, and interests, go to the MyManagementLab website and take the following self-assessments:

- I.A.4.—How Well Do I Handle Ambiguity? (This exercise also appears in Chapter 8 on pages 229–230.)
- III.A.2.—How Willing Am I to Delegate?
- II.C.3.—How Good Am I at Playing Politics?
- IV.F.1.—Is My Workplace Political?

MANAGEMENT FOR YOU TODAY

Dilemma

Choose an organization for which you have worked. How did the structure of your job and the organization affect your job satisfaction? Did the tasks within your job make sense? In what ways could they be better organized? What structural changes would you make to this organization? Would you consider making this a taller or flatter organization? How would the changes you have proposed improve responsiveness to customers and your job satisfaction?

Becoming a Manager

- If you belong to a student organization or are employed, notice how various activities and events are organized through the use of work specialization, chain of command, authority, responsibility, and so forth.

- As you read current business periodicals, note what types of organizational structures businesses use and whether or not they are effective.

- Talk to managers about how they organize work and what they have found to be effective.

- Since delegating is part of decentralizing and is an important management skill, complete the *Developing Your Interpersonal Skills—Delegating* module on pages 287–288. Then practise delegating in various situations.

- Look for examples of organizational charts (a visual drawing of an organization's structure), and use them to try to determine what structural design the organization is using.

WORKING TOGETHER: TEAM-BASED EXERCISE

Delegating Effectively and Ineffectively

In relatively decentralized organizations, managers must delegate authority to another person to carry out specific duties. Read through *Developing Your Interpersonal Skills—Delegating* on pages 287–288. Form groups of three or four individuals. Your instructor will assign groups to either "effective delegating" or "ineffective delegating." Come up with a role-playing situation that illustrates what your group was assigned (effective or ineffective delegating), which you will present in class. Be prepared to explain how your situation was an example of effective or ineffective delegating.

ETHICS IN ACTION

Ethical Dilemma Exercise: Is "Just Following Orders" a Valid Defence?

Is a manager acting unethically by simply following orders within the chain of command?[46] One recent survey of human resource managers found that 52 percent of the respondents felt some pressure to bend ethical rules, often because of orders from above or to achieve ambitious goals. This might happen in any organization. At WorldCom, for example, Betty Vinson was a senior manager when she and others received orders, through the chain of command, to slash expenses through improper accounting. She argued against the move. Her manager said he had also objected and was told this was a one-time "fix" to make WorldCom's finances look better. Vinson reluctantly agreed, but she felt guilty and told her manager she wanted to resign. A senior executive persuaded her to stay, and she continued following orders to fudge the accounting.

Soon Vinson realized that the figures would need fudging for some time. After investigators started to probe WorldCom's finances, she and others cooperated with regulators and prosecutors. Ultimately, the company was forced into bankruptcy. Some managers were indicted; some (including Vinson) pleaded guilty to conspiracy and fraud.

Imagine that you are a salesperson at a major corporation. Your manager invites you to an expensive restaurant where she is entertaining several colleagues and their spouses. The manager orders you to put the meal on your expense account as a customer dinner. She says she will approve the expense so you are reimbursed, and higher-level managers will not know that managers and their spouses were in attendance. What would you do? (Review this chapter's *Chain of Command* section, on pages 268–269, as you consider your decision.)

Thinking Critically About Ethics

Changes in technology have cut the shelf life of most employees' skills. A factory or clerical worker used to be able to learn one job and be reasonably sure that the skills acquired to do that job would be enough for most of his or her work years. That is no longer the case. What ethical obligation do organizations have to assist employees whose skills have become obsolete? What about employees? Do they have an obligation to keep their skills from becoming obsolete? What ethical guidelines might you suggest for dealing with employee skill obsolescence?

CASE APPLICATION

Pfizer: A New Kind of Structure

Admit it. Sometimes the projects you're working on (school, work, or both) can get pretty monotonous. Wouldn't it be nice to have a magic button you could push to get someone else to do the detailed and time-consuming stuff for you? At Pfizer, such a button is a reality for a large number of employees.[47]

As a global pharmaceutical company, Pfizer is continually looking for ways to be more efficient and effective. The company's senior director of organizational effectiveness, Jordan Cohen, found that the "Harvard MBA staff we hired to develop strategies and innovate were instead Googling and making PowerPoints." Indeed, internal studies conducted to find out just how much time its valuable talent was spending on nonstrategic tasks was startling. The average Pfizer employee was spending 20 percent to 40 percent of his or her time on support work (creating documents, typing notes, doing research, manipulating data, scheduling meetings) and only 60 percent to 80 percent on knowledge work (strategy, innovation, networking, collaborating, critical thinking). And the problem wasn't just at lower levels. Even the highest-level employees were affected. That's when Cohen began looking for solutions. The solution he chose turned out to be the numerous knowledge-process outsourcing companies based in India.

Initial tests of outsourcing the support tasks didn't go well at all. However, Cohen continued to tweak the process until everything worked. Now Pfizer employees can click the OOF (Office of the Future) button in Microsoft Outlook, and they are connected to an outsourcing company where a single worker in India receives the request and assigns it to a team. The team leader calls the employee to clarify the request. The team leader then e-mails back a cost specification for the requested work. At this point, the Pfizer employee can say yes or no. Cohen says that the benefits of OOF are unexpected. Time spent on analysis of data has been cut—sometimes in half. The financial benefits are also impressive. And Pfizer employees love it. Cohen says, "It's kind of amazing. I wonder what they used to do."

Describe and evaluate what Pfizer is doing. What structural implications—good and bad—does this approach have? (Think in terms of the six organizational design elements.) Do you think this arrangement would work for other types of organizations? Why or why not? What role do you think organizational structure plays in an organization's efficiency and effectiveness?

DEVELOPING YOUR DIAGNOSTIC AND ANALYTICAL SKILLS

A Learning Organization at Svenska

Svenska Handelsbanken, Sweden's premier bank, is one of the largest banks in the Nordic region.[48] Pär Boman, Svenska's president and group chief executive, oversees a business that is organized around a decentralized structure. This structure has a network consisting of hundreds of branches in Sweden, Denmark, Finland, Norway, and Great Britain, as well as those located in 14 non-European countries such as China, Poland, and Russia. Boman believes that the bank's 30-plus years of developing its branch network have allowed it to consistently grow market share and achieve a return on equity that has been above the average of its competitors. Now these competitors are starting to copy Svenska's structure in an attempt to model the bank's success. But Boman believes the bank's competitive advantage is not simply from having more branches. Rather, he believes it comes from the degree of autonomy that branch managers have.

Svenska's branch managers can choose their customers and product offerings. They can also set staffing numbers and decide salary levels at their branch. All customers, private and corporate, no matter what their size, are the sole responsibility of the branch. That means, for example, that even a large global corporation such as Volvo is managed by a branch bank operation. Yet, to better facilitate customer service, each branch office can buy specialized services it may need in servicing such a large customer. Each branch manager is also responsible for branch performance, which is measured by a ratio of costs divided by revenues. At Svenska, this measure is used to benchmark every branch against each other. If a branch starts underperforming, the regional office will offer consultative services about what other branches are doing successfully. To stop predatory competition among its own branches, the company has set up strict geographical boundaries. Svenska's number of centralized staff is a relatively small percentage of what its competitors have, and guidelines from headquarters are few and seldom issued. The bank's flat management structure and emphasis on personal responsibility and consensus approach are well suited to the Swedish culture.

Boman wants to continue to build the learning organization the bank has started. He wants to improve its capacity to continuously learn, adapt, and change. That is an interesting goal for a 130-year-old bank that has proven to be successful in the industry.

Questions

1. What do you see as the advantages and disadvantages of Svenska Handelsbanken's structure?

2. Do you believe such a structure could work effectively in other cultures, such as that of the United States, in which there is less emphasis placed on consensus building?

3. What do you believe Pär Boman could do to enhance the learning organization concept at Svenska?

DEVELOPING YOUR INTERPERSONAL SKILLS

Delegating

About the Skill

Managers get things done through other people. Because there are limits to any manager's time and knowledge, effective managers need to understand how to delegate. *Delegation* is the assignment of authority to another person to carry out specific duties. It allows an employee to make some of the decisions. Delegation should not be confused with participation. In participative decision making, there is a sharing of authority. In delegation, employees make decisions on their own.

Steps in Developing the Skill

A number of actions differentiate the effective delegator from the ineffective delegator. You can be more effective at delegating if you use the following five suggestions:[49]

1. **Clarify the assignment.** Determine what is to be delegated and to whom. You need to identify the person who is most capable of doing the task, and then determine whether or not he or she has the time and motivation to do the task. If you have a willing and able employee, it's your responsibility to provide clear information on what is being delegated, the results you expect, and any time or performance expectations you may have. Unless there is an overriding need to adhere to specific methods, you should delegate only the results expected. Get agreement on what is to be done and the results expected, but let the employee decide the best way to complete the task.

2. **Specify the employee's range of discretion.** Every situation of delegation comes with constraints. Although

you are delegating to an employee the authority to perform some task or tasks, you are not delegating unlimited authority. You are delegating authority to act on certain issues within certain parameters. You need to specify what those parameters are so that employees know, without any doubt, the range of their discretion.

3. **Allow the employee to participate.** One of the best ways to decide how much authority will be necessary to accomplish a task is to allow the employee who will be held accountable for that task to participate in that decision. Be aware, however, that allowing employees to participate can present its own set of potential problems as a result of employees' self-interests and biases in evaluating their own abilities.

4. **Inform others that delegation has occurred.** Delegation should not take place behind the scenes. Not only do the manager and employee need to know specifically what has been delegated and how much authority has been given, but so does anyone else who is likely to be affected by the employee's decisions and actions. This includes people inside and outside the organization. Essentially, you need to communicate what has been delegated (the task and amount of authority) and to whom.

5. **Establish feedback channels.** To delegate without establishing feedback controls is to invite problems. The establishment of controls to monitor the employee's performance increases the likelihood that important problems will be identified and that the task will be completed on time and to the desired specifications. Ideally, these controls should be determined at the time of the initial assignment. Agree on a specific time for the completion of the task, and then set progress dates when the employee will report back on how well he or she is doing and any major problems that may have arisen. These controls can be supplemented with periodic checks to ensure that authority guidelines are not being abused, organizational policies are being followed, proper procedures are being met, and the like.

Practising the Skill

Read the following scenario. Write some notes about how you would handle the situation described. Be sure to refer to the five suggestions for delegating.

Scenario

Ricky Lee is the manager of the contracts group of a large regional office supply distributor. His manager, Anne Zumwalt, has asked him to prepare by the end of the month the department's new procedures manual, which will outline the steps followed in negotiating contracts with office products manufacturers who supply the organization's products. Because Ricky has another major project he is working on, he went to Anne and asked her if it would be possible to assign the rewriting of the procedures manual to Bill Harmon, one of his employees, who has worked in the contracts group for about three years. Anne said she had no problems with Ricky reassigning the project as long as Bill knew the parameters and the expectations for the completion of the project. Ricky is preparing for his meeting in the morning with Bill regarding this assignment. Prepare an outline of what Ricky should discuss with Bill to ensure the new procedures manual meets expectations.

Reinforcing the Skill

The following activities will help you practise and reinforce the skills associated with delegating:

1. Interview a manager regarding his or her delegation skills. What activities does he or she *not* delegate? Why?

2. Teach someone else how to delegate effectively. Be sure to identify to this person the behaviours needed to delegate effectively and explain why these behaviours are important.

MyManagementLab

For more resources, please visit www.pearsoned.ca/mymanagementlab

SCAN THIS

Managers and Communication

Without communication, nothing would ever get done in organizations. Managers are concerned with two types of communication: interpersonal and organizational. We look at both in this chapter and the role they play in a manager's ability to be efficient and effective. After reading and studying this chapter, you will achieve the following learning outcomes.

Learning Outcomes

1 Define the nature and function of communication.

2 Compare and contrast methods of interpersonal communication.

3 Identify barriers to effective interpersonal communication and how to overcome them.

4 Understand how communication flows in an organization.

5 Describe how technology affects managerial communication.

6 Discuss contemporary issues in communication.

▶ ▶ ▶ In July 2010, Lymbix released the beta version of ToneCheck, an add-in for Microsoft Outlook that identifies the emotional definition of words and phrases in order to help users improve the clarity of their communications.[1] It gauges words and phrases against eight levels of connotative feeling, allowing the user to make real-time corrections and adjust the overall tone of messages.

Matt Eldridge, president, and Josh Merchant, chief technology officer, are the co-founders of Moncton, New Brunswick–based Lymbix, whose mission is "to pioneer and become the world's leading provider of connotative solutions and be recognized as the thought-leader in enhanced awareness and control over text-based connotation." Eldridge found that emails meant to share genuine passions and energy sometimes were being taken as aggressive, and this was negatively affecting companies' sales.

By identifying emotionally charged phrases or sentences, Lymbix users can communicate more effectively—it's like running an emotional "spell check." One of the more interesting applications is in social media monitoring. Currently, companies use sentiment analysis and are limited to simplistic measures of

positive, negative, and neutral. The Lymbix connotative engine can actually determine the most intense emotions expressed in blogs, posts, email, and other social media. Companies get a deeper understanding of the market's perception of their product, brand, or organization, and can develop more targeted responses.[2]

In the summer of 2010, Microsoft announced that Lymbix had been invited to join BizSpark One, which seeks to

accelerate the growth of start-ups with high potential. In this unique, invite-only program, start-ups are paired with a dedicated relationship manager. This manager works with the start-up to promote visibility, expand its network of investors and mentors, expose it to business opportunities, and develop cutting-edge applications.[3]

SCAN THIS

Think About It

Have you sent email that was interpreted differently from how you intended? How common might this problem be in the commercial marketplace? Why would Microsoft invite Lymbix into the BizSpark One program? Is there a problem with how many of us use email as a communications tool? In what other forms of communication would an application like ToneCheck be useful?

Communication between managers and employees provides the information necessary to get work done effectively and efficiently in organizations. As such, there is no doubt that communication is fundamentally linked to managerial performance.[4] In this chapter, we present basic concepts in managerial communication. We describe the interpersonal communication process, channels for communicating, barriers to effective communication, and ways to overcome those barriers. We also look at organizational communication issues, including communication flow and communication networks. Finally, we discuss several contemporary communication issues facing managers.

Understanding Communication

1. Define the nature and function of communication.

If you have not studied communication before, you might think that it's a pretty normal process and that almost anyone can communicate effectively without much thought. So many things can go wrong with communication, though, that it's clear not everyone thinks about how to communicate effectively. For instance, unlike the character Bill Murray played in *Groundhog Day*, who kept waking up to start the same day over and over again, Neal L. Patterson, CEO of Cerner, a health care software development company based in Kansas City, probably wishes he *could* do over one particular day. Upset with the fact that employees did not seem to be putting in enough hours, he sent an angry and emotional email to about 400 company managers that said, in part:

> We are getting less than 40 hours of work from a large number of our K.C.-based EMPLOYEES. The parking lot is sparsely used at 8 a.m.; likewise at 5 p.m. As managers, you either do not know what your EMPLOYEES are doing, or you do not CARE. You have created expectations on the work effort which allowed this to happen inside Cerner, creating a very unhealthy environment. In either case, you have a problem and you will fix it or I will replace you . . . I will hold you accountable. You have allowed things to get to this state. You have two weeks. Tick, tock.[5]

Patterson had a message, and he wanted to get it out to his managers. Although the email was meant only for the company's managers, it was leaked and posted on a Yahoo! discussion site. The tone of the email surprised industry analysts, investors, and, of course, Cerner's managers and employees. The company's stock price dropped 22 percent over the next three days. Patterson apologized to his employees and acknowledged, "I lit a match and started a firestorm." This is a good example of why it's important for individuals to understand the impact of communication.

The importance of effective communication for managers cannot be overemphasized for one specific reason: Everything a manager does involves communicating. Not *some* things, but everything! A manager can't make a decision without information. That information has to be communicated. Once a decision is made, communication must again take place. Otherwise, no one would know that a decision was made. The best idea, the most creative suggestion, the best plan, or the most effective job redesign cannot take shape without communication. Managers need effective communication skills. We are not suggesting that good communication skills alone make a successful manager. We can say, however, that ineffective communication skills can lead to a continuous stream of problems for the manager.

What Is Communication?

Communication is the transfer and understanding of meaning. The first thing to note about this definition is the emphasis on the *transfer* of meaning. This means that if no information or ideas have been conveyed, communication has not taken place. The speaker who is not heard or the writer who is not read has not communicated.

More importantly, however, communication involves the *understanding* of meaning. For communication to be successful, the meaning must be conveyed and understood. A letter written in Portuguese addressed to a person who does not read Portuguese cannot be considered communication until it's translated into a language the person does read and understand. Perfect communication, if such a thing existed, would be the receiver's understanding of a transmitted thought or idea exactly as it was intended by the sender.

Another point to keep in mind is that *good* communication is often erroneously defined by the communicator as *agreement* with the message instead of clearly *understanding* the message.[6] If someone disagrees with us, many of us assume that the person just did not fully understand our position. In other words, many of us define good communication as having someone accept our views. But I can clearly understand what you mean and just *not agree* with what you say. In fact, many times, when a conflict has gone on for a long time, people will say it's because the parties are not communicating effectively. That assumption reflects the tendency to think that effective communication equals agreement.

The final point we want to make about communication is that it encompasses both **interpersonal communication**—communication between two or more people—and **organizational communication**—all the patterns, networks, and systems of communication within an organization. Both these types of communication are important to managers in organizations.

communication The transfer and understanding of meaning.

MyManagementLab
Q&A 11.1

interpersonal communication Communication between two or more people.

organizational communication All the patterns, networks, and systems of communication within an organization.

If you have ever had a bad haircut, you have probably never forgotten the experience. And you might never have returned to the stylist again. Dorys Belanger, owner of Montreal-based Au Premier Spa Urbain, says that a bad haircut should not be blamed on the stylist alone. Good communication is "50 percent up to the hairdresser, 50 percent up to the client," she says.

Functions of Communication

Why is communication important to managers and organizations? It serves four major functions: control, motivation, emotional expression, and information.[7]

Communication acts to *control* member behaviour in several ways. As we know from Chapter 10, organizations have authority hierarchies and formal guidelines that employees are required to follow. For instance, when employees are required to communicate any job-related grievance first to their immediate manager, or to follow their job description, or to comply with company policies, communication is being used to control. But informal communication also controls behaviour. When work groups tease or harass a member who is working too hard or producing too much (making the rest of the group look bad), they are informally controlling the member's behaviour.

Communication encourages *motivation* by clarifying to employees what is to be done, how well they are doing, and what can be done to improve performance if it's not up to par. As employees set specific goals, work toward those goals, and receive feedback on their progress, communication is required. Managers motivate more effectively if they show support for the employee by communicating constructive feedback, rather than mere criticism.

For many employees, their work group is a primary source of social interaction. The communication that takes place within the group is a fundamental mechanism by which members share frustrations and feelings of satisfaction. Communication, therefore, provides a release for *emotional expression* of feelings and for fulfillment of social needs.

Finally, individuals and groups need *information* to get things done in organizations. Communication provides that information.

No one of these four functions is more important than the others. For groups to work effectively, they need to maintain some form of control over members, motivate members to perform, provide a means for emotional expression, and make decisions. You can assume that almost every communication interaction that takes place in a group or organization is fulfilling one or more of these four functions.

Methods of Interpersonal Communication

2. Compare and contrast methods of interpersonal communication.

▶ ▶ ▶ Email is one form or channel of communicating at the interpersonal level. Matt Eldridge and Josh Merchant recognized a business opportunity in the unintended consequences that email communications can have, where the traditional solutions focused on the literal (denotative) meaning rather than the tone (connotative meaning). In this section, we will explore the channels that managers use to communicate with others.

Think About It

How might you unintentionally send the wrong message through your body language? Through your verbal intonation?

message A purpose to be conveyed.

encoding Converting a message into symbols.

channel The medium a message travels along.

Before communication can take place, a purpose, expressed as a **message** to be conveyed, must exist. It passes between a source (the sender) and a receiver. The message is converted to symbolic form (called **encoding**) and passed by way of some medium (**channel**) to the receiver, who retranslates the sender's message (called **decoding**). The result is the transfer of meaning from one person to another.[8]

Exhibit 11-1 illustrates the seven elements of the **interpersonal communication process**. In addition, the entire process is susceptible to **noise**—disturbances that interfere with the transmission, receipt, or feedback of a message. Typical examples of noise include illegible print, phone static, inattention by the receiver, and background sounds of machinery or co-workers. However, anything that interferes with understanding can be noise, and noise can create distortion at any point in the communication process.

Channels for Interpersonal Communication Techniques

Managers have a wide variety of communication channels from which to choose. These include face-to-face, telephone, group meetings, formal presentations, memos, postal (snail) mail, fax machines, employee publications, bulletin boards, social media, other company publications, audio files/DVD video, hotlines, email, computer conferences, voice mail, teleconferences, and videoconferences. It is interesting to note that small businesses/start-ups and not-for-profit organizations are using social media to reach a greater audience and to communicate with current and potential customers in ways that were not possible (affordable) previously. All of these communication channels include oral or written symbols, or both. How do you know which to use? Managers can use 12 questions to help them evaluate appropriate communication channels for different circumstances.[9]

1. *Feedback.* How quickly can the receiver respond to the message?
2. *Complexity capacity.* Can the method effectively process complex messages?
3. *Breadth potential.* How many different messages can be transmitted using this method?
4. *Confidentiality.* Can communicators be reasonably sure their messages are received only by those for whom they are intended?
5. *Encoding ease.* Can the sender easily and quickly use this channel?
6. *Decoding ease.* Can the receiver easily and quickly decode messages?
7. *Time–space constraint.* Do senders and receivers need to communicate at the same time and in the same space?
8. *Cost.* How much does it cost to use this method?
9. *Interpersonal warmth.* How well does this method convey interpersonal warmth?
10. *Formality.* Does this method have the needed amount of formality?
11. *Scanability.* Does this method allow the message to be easily browsed or scanned for relevant information?
12. *Time of consumption.* Does the sender or receiver exercise the most control over when the message is dealt with?

decoding A receiver's translation of a sender's message.

interpersonal communication process The seven elements involved in transferring meaning from one person to another.

noise Disturbances that interfere with the transmission, receipt, or feedback of a message.

MyManagementLab
Q&A 11.2

Exhibit 11-1

The Interpersonal Communication Process

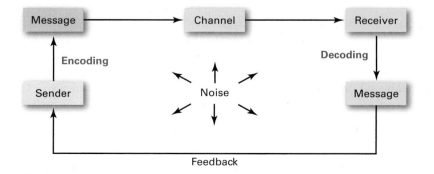

nonverbal communication
Communication transmitted
without words.

Exhibit 11-2 provides a comparison of the various communication methods on these 12 criteria. Which method a manager ultimately chooses should reflect the needs of the sender, the attributes of the message, the attributes of the channel, and the needs of the receiver. For instance, if you need to communicate to an employee the changes being made in her job, face-to-face communication would be a better choice than a memo since you want to be able to address immediately any questions and concerns that she might have. (To find out more about face-to-face communication, see *Self-Assessment—What's My Face-to-Face Communication Style?* on pages 314–315.)

We cannot leave the topic of interpersonal communication without looking at the role of **nonverbal communication**—that is, communication transmitted without words. Some of the most meaningful communications are neither spoken nor written. A loud siren or a red light at an intersection tells you something without words. When an instructor is teaching a class, she does not need words to tell her that her students are bored when their eyes are glazed over or they begin to read the school newspaper in the middle of class. Similarly, when students start putting their papers, notebooks, and books away, the message is clear: Class time is about over. The size of a person's office or the clothes he or she wears also convey messages to others. These are all forms of nonverbal communication. The best-known types of nonverbal communication are body language and verbal intonation.

Body language refers to gestures, facial expressions, and other body movements that convey meaning. A person frowning "says" something different from one who is smiling. Hand motions, facial expressions, and other gestures can communicate emotions or temperaments such as aggression, fear, shyness, arrogance, joy, and anger. Knowing the meaning behind someone's body movements and learning how to put forth your best body language can help you personally and professionally.[10] For instance, studies indicate that those who maintain eye contact while speaking are viewed with more credibility than those whose eye contact wanders. People who make eye contact are also deemed more competent than those who do not.

Be aware that what is communicated nonverbally may be quite different from what is communicated verbally. A manager may say it's a good time to discuss a raise, but then keep looking at the clock. This nonverbal signal may indicate that the manager has other things to do right now. Thus, actions can speak louder (and more accurately) than words.

A variety of popular books have been written to help one interpret body language. However, do use some care when interpreting their messages. For instance, while it is often thought that crossing one's arms in front of one's chest shows resistance to a message, it might also mean the person is feeling cold. Also remember that the meaning of body language can be different from one culture to another, as discussed in Chapter 3.

Verbal intonation (more appropriately called *paralinguistics*) refers to the emphasis someone gives to words or phrases that convey meaning. To illustrate how intonations can change the meaning of a message, consider the student who asks the instructor a question. The instructor replies, "What do you mean by that?" The student's reaction will vary, depending on the tone of the instructor's response. A soft, smooth vocal tone conveys interest and creates a different meaning from one that is abrasive and puts a strong emphasis on saying the last word. Most of us would view the first intonation as coming from someone sincerely interested in clarifying the student's concern, whereas the second suggests that the person is defensive or aggressive.

The fact that every oral communication also has a nonverbal message cannot be overemphasized. Why? Because the nonverbal component usually carries the greatest impact. "It's not *what* you said, but *how* you said it." People respond to *how* something is said, as well as *what* is said. Managers should remember this as they communicate.

body language Gestures, facial
expressions, and other body
movements that convey meaning.

verbal intonation An emphasis
given to words or phrases that
conveys meaning.

MyManagementLab
Q&A 11.3

Effective Interpersonal Communication

3. Identify barriers to effective
interpersonal communication
and how to overcome them.

▶ ▶ ▶ The first product released by Lymbix was TweetTone, a free application to filter the emotional noise on Twitter. "TweetTone tracks and analyzes the emotion behind the

Exhibit 11-2

Comparison of Communication Channels

Channel	Feedback Potential	Complexity Capacity	Breadth Potential	Confidentiality	Encoding Ease	Decoding Ease	Time–Space Constraint	Cost	Interpersonal Warmth	Formality	Scan-ability	Consumption Time
Face to face	1	1	1	1	1	1	1	2	1	4	4	S/R
Telephone	1	4	2	2	1	1	3	3	2	4	4	S/R
Group meetings	2	2	2	4	2	2	1	1	2	3	4	S/R
Formal presentations	4	2	2	4	3	2	1	1	3	3	5	Sender
Memos	4	4	2	3	4	3	5	3	5	2	1	Receiver
Postal mail	5	3	3	2	4	3	5	3	4	1	1	Receiver
Fax	3	4	2	4	3	3	5	3	3	3	1	Receiver
Publications	5	4	2	5	5	3	5	2	4	1	1	Receiver
Bulletin boards	4	5	1	5	3	2	2	4	5	3	1	Receiver
Audio files/ DVD videos	4	4	3	5	4	2	3	2	3	3	5	Receiver
Hotlines	2	5	2	2	3	1	4	2	3	3	4	Receiver
Email	3	4	1	2	3	2	4	2	4	3	4	Receiver
Computer conference	1	2	2	4	3	2	3	2	3	3	4	S/R
Voice mail	2	4	2	1	2	1	5	3	2	4	4	Receiver
Teleconference	2	3	2	5	2	2	2	2	3	3	5	S/R
Videoconference	3	3	2	4	2	2	2	1	2	3	5	S/R

Note: Ratings are on a 1–5 scale where 1 = high and 5 = low. Consumption time refers to who controls the reception of communication. S/R means the sender and receiver share control.

Source: P. G. Clampitt, *Communicating for Managerial Effectiveness* (Newbury Park, CA: Sage Publications, 1991), p. 136.

conversation on Twitter. We're different! Our connotative technology monitors the eight primary emotions—beyond positive, negative and neutral—so you can have a more precise understanding of exactly how people are feeling about your brand, campaign or your competition."[11] The authors entered the term "Dalhousie University," and in a sample of 100 tweets the dominant emotion was enjoyment/elation. Alternatively, in a sample of 100 tweets for "British Petroleum," the dominant emotion was fear/uneasiness at 42 percent and humiliation/shame at 23 percent.

Think About It

Tweets on Twitter must fit within the 140-character limit set by Twitter. Are you surprised that it is possible to measure the emotional tone of such a small communication? How can tools like TweetTone be used to measure the impact of communication strategy? What barriers to effective communication might distort your intended message?

How Distortions Can Happen in Interpersonal Communication

Distortions can happen with the sender, the message, the channel, the choice of channel, the receiver, or the feedback loop. Let's look at each.

Sender

A *sender* initiates a message by *encoding* a thought. Four conditions influence the effectiveness of that encoded message: the skills, attitudes, and knowledge of the sender, and the social–cultural system. How? We will use ourselves, as your textbook authors, as an example. If we don't have the required skills, our message won't reach you, the reader, in the form desired. Our success in communicating to you depends on our writing skills. In addition, any pre-existing ideas (attitudes) that we may have about numerous topics will affect how we communicate. For instance, our attitudes about managerial ethics or the importance of managers to organizations influence our writing. Next, the amount of knowledge we have about a subject affects the message(s) we are transferring. We cannot communicate what we don't know, and if our knowledge is too extensive, it's possible that our writing won't be understood by the readers. Finally, the socio-cultural system in which we live influences us as communication senders: Our beliefs and values (all part of culture) act to influence what and how we communicate.

Message

The *message* itself can distort the communication process, regardless of the kinds of supporting tools or technologies used to convey it. A message is the actual physical product encoded by the source. It can be a written document, a speech, or even the gestures and facial expressions we make. The message is affected by the symbols used to transfer meaning (words, pictures, numbers, etc.), the content of the message itself, and the decisions that the sender makes in selecting and arranging both the symbols and the content. Noise can distort the communication process in any of these areas.

Channel

Your instructor chooses to interact with all students via email rather than hold office hours. How effective do you think email is as the channel of communication in this context?

The *channel* chosen to communicate the message also has the potential to be affected by noise. Whether it's a face-to-face conversation, an email message, or a company-wide memorandum, distortions can and do occur. Managers need to recognize that certain channels are more appropriate for certain messages. (Think back to how Cerner's CEO, discussed earlier in this chapter, chose to communicate his frustration with his managers by email and whether that was an appropriate choice.) Obviously, if the office is on fire, a memo to convey the fact is inappropriate! And if something

Communication channels have multiplied with the spread of new technologies such as Wi-Fi, which provides wireless high-speed Internet access. Managers in some companies have saved time and money by switching to Wi-Fi for their internal communications. The devices mean that a manager can talk to customers, suppliers, or even his or her manager without having to hike across the aisles to the store's front-office telephone.

is important, such as an employee's performance appraisal, a manager might want to use multiple channels—perhaps an oral review followed by a written letter summarizing the points. This decreases the potential for distortion. In general, the type of channel chosen will affect the extent to which accurate emotional expression can be communicated. For instance, individuals often make stronger negative statements when using email than they would in holding a face-to-face conversation.[12] Additionally, individuals often give little thought to how their emails might be interpreted and assume that their intent will be readily apparent to the recipient, even though this is not always the case.[13]

Receiver

The *receiver* is the individual to whom the message is directed. Before the message can be received, however, the symbols in it must be translated into a form that the receiver can understand. This is the *decoding* of the message. Just as the sender was limited by his or her skills, attitudes, knowledge, and socio-cultural system, so is the receiver. And just as the sender must be skillful in writing or speaking, so the receiver must be skillful in reading or listening. A person's knowledge influences his or her ability to receive. Moreover, the receiver's attitudes and socio-cultural background can distort the message.

Feedback Loop

The final link in the communication process is a *feedback loop*. Feedback returns the message to the sender and provides a check on whether understanding has been achieved. Because feedback can be transmitted along the same types of channels as the original message, it faces the same potential for distortion. Many receivers forget that there is a responsibility involved in communication: to give feedback. For instance, if you sit in a boring lecture, but never discuss with the instructor ways that the delivery could be improved, you have not engaged in communication with your instructor.

When either the sender or the receiver fails to engage in the feedback process, the communication is effectively one-way communication. Two-way communication involves both talking and listening. Many managers communicate badly because they fail to use two-way communication.[14]

Barriers to Effective Interpersonal Communication

In addition to the general distortions identified in the communication process, managers face other barriers to effective communication.

Filtering

filtering The deliberate manipulation of information to make it appear more favourable to the receiver.

Filtering is the deliberate manipulation of information to make it appear more favourable to the receiver. For example, when a person tells his or her manager what the manager wants to hear, that individual is filtering information. Does this happen much in organizations? Yes, it does! As information is communicated up through organizational levels, it's condensed and synthesized by senders so those on top don't become overloaded with information. Those doing the condensing filter communications through their personal interests and their perceptions of what is important.

The extent of filtering tends to be a function of the number of vertical levels in the organization and the organizational culture. The more vertical levels there are in an organization, the more opportunities there are for filtering. As organizations become less dependent on strict hierarchical arrangements and instead use more collaborative, cooperative work arrangements, information filtering may become less of a problem. In addition, the ever-increasing use of email to communicate in organizations reduces filtering because communication is more direct as intermediaries are bypassed. Finally, the organizational culture encourages or discourages filtering by the type of behaviour it rewards. The more that organizational rewards emphasize style and appearance, the more managers will be motivated to filter communications in their favour.

MyManagementLab
Q&A 11.4

Emotions

How a receiver feels when a message is received influences how he or she interprets it. You will often interpret the same message differently, depending on whether you are happy or upset. Extreme emotions are most likely to hinder effective communication. In such instances, we often disregard our rational and objective thinking processes and substitute emotional judgments. It's best to avoid reacting to a message when you are upset because you are not likely to be thinking clearly.

Information Overload

information overload When the information we have to work with exceeds our processing capacity.

A marketing manager goes on a week-long sales trip to Spain and does not have access to his email. On his return, he is faced with 1000 messages. It's not possible to fully read and respond to each and every one of those messages without facing **information overload**—when the information we have to work with exceeds our processing capacity. Today's typical employee frequently complains of information overload. Email has added considerably to the number of hours worked per week, according to a recent study by Christina Cavanagh, professor of management communications at the University of Western Ontario's Richard Ivey School of Business.[15] Researchers calculate that 294 billion email messages circulate the globe each day. In 2001, that number was 5.1 billion email messages.[16] One researcher suggests that knowledge workers devote about 28 percent of their days to email.[17] The demands of keeping up with email, phone calls, faxes, meetings, and professional reading create an onslaught of data that is nearly impossible to process and assimilate. What happens when individuals have more information than they can sort and use? They tend to select out, ignore, pass over, or forget information. Or they may put off further processing until the overload situation is over. Regardless, the result is lost information and less effective communication.

MyManagementLab
Q&A 11.5

Selective Perception

MyManagementLab
Q&A 11.6

Individuals don't see reality; rather, they interpret what they see and call it "reality." These interpretations are based on an individual's needs, motivations, experience, background, and other personal characteristics. Individuals also project their interests and expectations when they are listening to others. For example, the employment interviewer who believes that young people spend too much time on leisure and social activities will have a hard time believing that young job applicants will work long hours.

Defensiveness

When people feel that they are being threatened, they tend to react in ways that reduce their ability to achieve mutual understanding. That is, they become defensive—engaging in behaviours such as verbally attacking others, making sarcastic remarks, being overly judgmental, and questioning others' motives.[18] When individuals interpret another's message as threatening, they often respond in ways that hinder effective communication.

Language

Words mean different things to different people. Age, education, and cultural background are three of the more obvious variables that influence the language a person uses and the definitions he or she gives to words. News anchor Peter Mansbridge and rap artist Nelly both speak English, but the language each uses is vastly different.

In an organization, employees typically come from diverse backgrounds and have different patterns of speech. Even employees who work for the same organization but in different departments often have different **jargon**—specialized terminology or technical language that members of a group use to communicate among themselves. Keep in mind that while we may speak the same language, our use of that language is far from uniform. Senders tend to assume that the words and phrases they use mean the same to the receiver as they do to them. This, of course, is incorrect and creates communication barriers. Knowing how each of us modifies the language would help minimize those barriers.

Montreal-based Yellow Pages learned that it could produce better printed telephone directories by studying how online users searched for things—demonstrating that customers and advertisers don't always use the same terms for the same categories, as the following *Management Reflection* shows.

Filtering, or shaping information to make it look good to the receiver, might not always be intentional. For John Seral, vice-president and chief information officer of GE Aviation and GE Energy, the problem was that "when the CEO asked how the quarter was looking, he got a different answer depending on whom he asked." Seral solved the problem by building a continuously updated database of the company's most important financial information that gives not just the CEO but also 300 company managers instant access to sales and operating figures on their PCs and BlackBerrys. Instead of dozens of analysts compiling the information, the new system requires only six.

jargon Specialized terminology or technical language that members of a group use to communicate among themselves.

MyManagementLab
Q&A 11.7

MANAGEMENT REFLECTION

Finding Sushi

Should we look under "sushi" or "restaurants—Japanese" in the phone book when we decide we want raw fish for dinner? Executives at Montreal-based Yellow Pages Group were in a quandary as to how to compete with Internet-based solutions for locating their current and prospective clients. The company has been in the phone book business for 100 years and, with the help of advertisers, has always determined the categories used by people searching the directory. The Internet has allowed Yellow Pages to better address user needs, however. "Now that we're seeing the trends through our online directories—the key words people use—it gives us a good idea of what they are looking for in the print book," says company spokeswoman Annie Marsolais.

In search engines like Google, products are found in one of two ways: organically or by paid advertising. For organic results, the behind-the-scenes search algorithm uses ranking criteria to display results. Firms that appear in the first three or four results will receive clicks, but after that the click rate drops dramatically. Firms wishing to improve their page ranking employ search engine optimization (SEO) techniques. Google's revenue model is based on selling advertising to those who want to have their results displayed at the top of the page or in the sidebar as paid advertising. It's not uncommon for advertisers to advertise on 10 000 or more search terms to ensure that their target customers can find them. The ranking of the paid ads that appear in response to any given search depends on who pays the most to Google for a particular search term.

Based on their research, Yellow Pages executives realized that in the short term they needed to revamp their current product, and in the longer term develop an online product. In looking at the current Yellow Pages directory they asked, "Should we look under "sushi" or "restaurants—Japanese" in the phone book when we decide we want raw fish for dinner? Paying attention to how people search for information online can give clearer insights into what organizations need to do to communicate more effectively.[19] ■

National Culture

In Chapter 3, we used the Hofstede and the GLOBE frameworks to examine cultural differences and learned that communication differences can also arise from the different languages that individuals use to communicate and the national culture they are part of. Interpersonal communication is not conducted the same way around the world. For example, let's compare countries that place a higher value on individualism (such as Canada) with countries where the emphasis is on collectivism (such as Japan).[20]

In Canada, communication patterns tend to be oriented to the individual and clearly spelled out. In collectivist countries, such as Japan, there is more interaction for its own sake. The Japanese manager, in contrast to the Canadian manager, engages in extensive verbal consultation with subordinates over an issue first and draws up a formal document later to outline the agreement that was made. The Japanese value decisions by consensus, and open communication is an inherent part of the work setting. Also, face-to-face communication is encouraged.

Cultural differences can affect the way a manager chooses to communicate. These differences undoubtedly can be a barrier to effective communication if not recognized and taken into consideration. Cultural differences also affect body language and such things as how closely people stand to each other. In China, for instance, it is not unusual to push in queues to get ahead, while in North America, there is an expectation that people will keep a greater distance between one another and stay in their position in a lineup.

Overcoming Barriers to Communication

On average, an individual must hear new information seven times before he or she truly understands.[21] This might explain why reading your textbook just once may not be enough. In light of this fact and the barriers to communication, what can we do to overcome these barriers? The following suggestions should help make your interpersonal communication more effective.

Use Feedback

Many communication problems can be directly attributed to misunderstanding and inaccuracies. These problems are less likely to occur if individuals use the feedback loop in the communication process, either verbally or nonverbally.

If a speaker asks a receiver, "Did you understand what I said?" the response represents feedback. Good feedback should include more than yes-and-no answers. The speaker can ask a set of questions about a message to determine whether or not the message was received and understood as intended. Better yet, the speaker can ask the receiver to restate the message in his or her own words. If the speaker hears what was intended, understanding and accuracy should improve. Feedback includes subtler methods than directly asking questions or having the receiver summarize the message. General comments can give the speaker a sense of the receiver's reaction to a message. (To learn more about giving feedback, see *Self-Assessment—How Good Am I at Giving Performance Feedback?* in Chapter 12).

Of course, feedback does not have to be conveyed in words. Actions *can* speak louder than words. A sales manager sends an email to his or her staff describing a new monthly sales report that all sales representatives will need to complete. If some of them don't turn in the new report, the sales manager has received feedback. This feedback suggests that the sales manager needs to clarify further the initial communication. Similarly, when you are talking to people, you watch their eyes and look for other nonverbal clues to tell whether they are getting your message or not.

Simplify Language

Because language can be a barrier, managers should choose words and structure their messages in ways that will make those messages clear and understandable to the receiver. Remember, effective communication is achieved when a message is both received and *understood.* Understanding is improved by simplifying the language used in relation to the audience intended. This means, for example, that a hospital administrator should always try to communicate in clear, easily understood terms. The language used in messages to the emergency room staff should be purposefully different from that used with office employees. Jargon can facilitate understanding when it's used within a group of those who know what it means, but it can cause many problems when used outside that group.

Listen Actively

Do you know the difference between hearing and listening? When someone talks, we hear. But too often we don't listen. Listening is an active search for meaning, whereas hearing is passive. In listening, two people are engaged in thinking: the sender *and* the receiver.

Many of us are poor listeners. Why? Because it's difficult, and it's usually more satisfying to be on the offensive. Listening, in fact, is often more tiring than talking. It demands intellectual effort. Unlike hearing, **active listening**, which is listening for full meaning without making premature judgments or interpretations, demands total concentration. The average person normally speaks at a rate of about 125 to 200 words per minute. However, the average listener can comprehend up to 400 words per minute.[22] The difference obviously leaves lots of idle time for the brain and opportunities for the mind to wander.

Active listening is enhanced by developing empathy with the sender—that is, by placing yourself in the sender's position. Because senders differ in attitudes, interests, needs, and expectations, empathy makes it easier to understand the actual content of a message. An empathetic listener reserves judgment on the message's content and carefully listens to what is being said. The goal is to improve your ability to receive the full meaning of a communication without having it distorted by premature judgments or interpretations. This involves accurately reflecting back what has been heard and asking "Do I have that right?" Once the answer is yes the next question needs to be "Is there more?" This loop continues until the sender indicates that the message has been accurately received and that all relevant issues have been covered. Other specific behaviours that active listeners demonstrate are listed in Exhibit 11-3. (To learn more about active listening, see *Developing Your Interpersonal Skills—Active Listening* on pages 319–320.)

active listening Listening for full meaning without making premature judgments or interpretations.

MyManagementLab
PRISM 11

Exhibit 11-3

Active Listening Behaviours

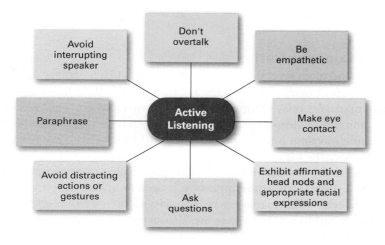

Source: Based on P. L. Hunsaker, *Training in Management Skills* (Upper Saddle River, NJ: Prentice Hall, 2001).

Constrain Emotions

It would be naive to assume that managers always communicate in a rational manner. We know that emotions can severely cloud and distort the transference of meaning. A manager who is emotionally upset over an issue is more likely to misconstrue incoming messages and fail to communicate clearly and accurately. What can the manager do? The simplest answer is to refrain from communicating until he or she has regained composure.

Watch Nonverbal Cues

If actions speak louder than words, then it's important to watch your actions to make sure they align with and reinforce the words that go along with them. The effective communicator watches his or her nonverbal cues to ensure that they convey the desired message.

Organizational Communication

4. Understand how communication flows in an organization.

An understanding of managerial communication is not possible without looking at the fundamentals of organizational communication. In this section, we look at several important aspects of organizational communication, including formal vs. informal communication, the direction of communication flow, and organizational communication networks.

Formal vs. Informal Communication

formal communication
Communication that follows the official chain of command or is part of the communication required to do one's job.

Communication within an organization is often described as formal or informal. **Formal communication** refers to communication that follows the official chain of command or is part of the communication required to do one's job. For example, when a manager asks an employee to complete a task, he or she is communicating formally. So is the employee who brings a problem to the attention of his or her manager. Any communication that takes place within prescribed organizational work arrangements would be classified as formal.

informal communication
Communication that is not defined by the organization's structural hierarchy.

Informal communication is communication that is not defined by the organization's structural hierarchy. When employees talk with each other in the lunch room, as they pass in hallways, or as they are working out at the company exercise facility, that is informal communication. Employees form friendships and communicate with each other. The informal communication system fulfills two purposes in organizations: (1) It permits employees to satisfy their need for social interaction, and (2) it can improve an organization's performance by creating alternative, and frequently faster and more efficient, channels of communication.

Direction of Communication Flow

Organizational communication can flow downward, upward, laterally, or diagonally. Let's look at each.

Downward Communication

Every morning, and often several times a day, managers at UPS package delivery facilities gather employees for mandatory meetings that last precisely three minutes. During those 180 seconds, managers relay company announcements and go over local information like traffic conditions or customer complaints. Then, each meeting ends with a safety tip. The three-minute meetings have proved so successful that many of the company's office employees are using the idea.[23]

downward communication
Communication that flows downward from managers to employees.

Any communication that flows downward from managers to employees is **downward communication**. Downward communication is used to inform, direct, coordinate, and evaluate employees. When managers assign goals to their employees, they are using downward communication. Managers are also using downward communication by providing employees with job descriptions, informing them of organizational policies and procedures, pointing out problems that need attention, or evaluating and giving feedback on their performance. Downward communication can take place through any of the communication methods we described earlier. Managers can improve the quality of the feedback they give to employees if they follow the advice given in *Tips for Managers— Suggestions for Giving Feedback.*

Upward Communication

Any communication that flows upward from employees to managers is **upward communication**. Managers rely on their employees for information. Reports are given to managers to inform them of progress toward goals and any current problems. Upward communication keeps managers aware of how employees feel about their jobs, their co-workers, and the organization in general. Managers also rely on upward communication for ideas on how things can be improved. Some examples include performance reports prepared by employees, suggestion boxes, employee attitude surveys, grievance procedures, manager–employee discussions, and informal group sessions in which employees have the opportunity to identify and discuss problems with their manager or even representatives of top management.

The extent of upward communication depends on the organizational culture. If managers have created a climate of trust and respect and use participative decision making or empowerment, there will be considerable upward communication as employees provide input to decisions. For instance, Ernst & Young encourages employees to evaluate the principals, partners, and directors on how well they create a positive work climate. A partner in the Montreal office was surprised to learn that people in her office found her a poor role model, and she took care to explain her actions more as a result.[24] In a highly structured and authoritarian environment, upward communication still takes place, but is limited in both style and content.

Lateral Communication

Communication that takes place among employees on the same organizational level is called **lateral communication**. In today's often chaotic and rapidly changing environment, horizontal (lateral) communication is frequently needed to save time and facilitate coordination. Cross-functional teams, for instance, rely heavily on this form of communication. However, it can create conflicts if employees don't keep their managers informed about decisions they have made or actions they have taken.

Diagonal Communication

Communication that cuts across both work areas *and* organizational levels is **diagonal communication**. When an analyst in the credit department communicates directly with a regional marketing manager—note the different department and different organizational level—about a customer problem, that is diagonal communication. In the interest of efficiency and speed, diagonal communication can be beneficial. Email facilitates diagonal communication. In many organizations, any employee can communicate by email with any other employee, regardless of organizational work area or level. However, just as with lateral communication, diagonal communication has the potential to create problems if employees don't keep their managers informed.

Organizational Communication Networks

The vertical and horizontal flows of organizational communication can be combined into a variety of patterns called **communication networks**. Exhibit 11-4 illustrates three common communication networks.

upward communication
Communication that flows upward from employees to managers.

TIPS FOR MANAGERS

Suggestions for Giving Feedback

Managers can use the following tips to give more effective feedback:

- "Relate feedback to existing **performance goals and clear expectations.**"

- "Give **specific feedback tied to observable behaviour or measurable results.**"

- "Channel feedback toward **key result areas.**"

- "Give feedback **as soon as possible.**"

- "Give positive **feedback for improvement, not just final results.**"

- "**Focus feedback on performance, not personalities.**"

- "Base feedback on **accurate and credible information.**"

Source: R. Kreitner and A. Kinicki, *Organizational Behavior,* 6th ed. (New York: McGraw-Hill/Irwin, 2004), p. 335. Reprinted by permission of McGraw-Hill Education.

---

lateral communication
Communication that takes place among employees on the same organizational level.

diagonal communication
Communication that cuts across both work areas and organizational levels.

communication networks The variety of patterns of vertical and horizontal flows of organizational communication.

Types of Communication Networks

In the *chain* network, communication flows according to the formal chain of command, both downward and upward. The *wheel* network represents communication flowing between a clearly identifiable and strong leader and others in a work group or team. The leader serves as the hub through whom all communication passes. Finally, in the *all-channel* network, communication flows freely among all members of a work team.

As a manager, which network should you use? The answer depends on your goal. Exhibit 11-4 also summarizes the effectiveness of the various networks according to four criteria: speed, accuracy, the probability that a leader will emerge, and the importance of member satisfaction. One observation is immediately apparent: No single network is best for all situations. If you are concerned with high member satisfaction, the all-channel network is best; if having a strong and identifiable leader is important, the wheel facilitates this; and if accuracy is most important, the chain and wheel networks work best.

Exhibit 11-4

Three Common Organizational Communication Networks and How They Rate on Effectiveness Criteria

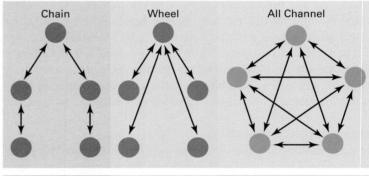

Criteria	Chain	Wheel	All Channel
Speed	Moderate	Fast	Fast
Accuracy	High	High	Moderate
Emergence of leader	Moderate	High	None
Member satisfaction	Moderate	Low	High

It looks like graffiti, but it's really informal communication at work. Dozens of whiteboards dot the hallways and common areas of Google's Mountain View head-quarters in California. Some of the boards are used by product teams swapping ideas, while the two largest are filled with cartoons and jokes. "It's collaborative art," says the company's director of communications and a frequent contributor. "When new hires see the boards, they get a quick, comprehensive snapshot of our personality."

The Grapevine We cannot leave our discussion of communication networks without discussing the **grapevine**—the informal organizational communication network. The grapevine is active in almost every organization. Is it an important source of information? You bet! One survey reported that 75 percent of employees hear about matters first through rumours on the grapevine.[25]

What are the implications for managers? Certainly, the grapevine is an important part of any group or organization communication network and well worth understanding.[26] It identifies for managers those bewildering issues that employees consider important and anxiety producing. It acts as both a filter and a feedback mechanism, picking up on the issues employees consider relevant. More importantly, from a managerial point of view, it *is* possible to analyze what is happening on the grapevine—what information is being passed, how information seems to flow along the grapevine, and what individuals seem to be key conduits of information on the grapevine. By being aware of the grapevine's flow and patterns, managers can stay on top of issues that concern employees, and, in turn, can use the grapevine to disseminate important information. Since the grapevine cannot be eliminated, managers should "manage" it as an important information network.

MyManagementLab
Q&A 11.8

Rumours that flow along the grapevine also can never be eliminated entirely. Managers can minimize the negative consequences of rumours by limiting their range and impact. How? By communicating openly, fully, and honestly with employees, particularly in situations where employees may not like proposed or actual managerial decisions or actions. Open and honest communication with employees can impact the organization in various ways. A study by Watson Wyatt Worldwide concluded that effective communication "connects employees to the business, reinforces the organization's vision, fosters process improvement, facilitates change, and drives business results by changing employee behavior." For those companies that communicated effectively, total returns to shareholders were 57 percent higher over a five-year period than for companies with less effective communication. And the study also showed that companies that were highly effective communicators were 20 percent more likely to report lower turnover rates.[27]

Information Technology and Communication

▶ ▶ ▶ Social networking websites such as Facebook and LinkedIn have become resources for employers seeking job candidates.[28] Companies large and small are using these resources to do research, form relationships, and fill positions. More than 350 companies broadcast their job listings to more than 10 million registered users of LinkedIn. A manager looking to fill a key position can use LinkedIn to view posted résumés, read an individual's postings, and even "check out a competitor's site for potential candidates."

5. Describe how technology affects managerial communication.

Brian Drum, president of executive search firm Drum Associates, uses social networking sites such as MySpace to see if there is any information about a job candidate's character that might suggest an inability to perform reliably. "Sometimes all we find is meaningless chitchat," says Drum, "but once in a while we'll turn up something useful, like an unflattering picture or a piece of information that really shows what the person is made of."

Some businesses are not just using social networking sites for recruiting, however. They have also added their own company profiles at such sites, where employees can interact with each other. They realize that a number of younger employees are using social networking sites, so they might as well encourage productive use of the medium.

Think About It

What are the benefits to employers of using a source like Facebook to screen job candidates? Should employers consider these postings just private musings and ignore them? Are there advantages to organizations in allowing employees to use social networking sites? If yes, do they outweigh the disadvantages?

Technology is changing the way we live and work. Take the following three examples: In a number of countries, employees, managers, housewives, and teens use wireless interactive web phones to send email, surf the web, swap photos, and play computer games. Service technicians at Ajax, Ontario-based Pitney Bowes Canada started using instant messaging rather than pagers, because "it's cheaper and it's two-way."[29] The company knows when messages are received. IBM's 320 000 employees regularly use instant messaging software for communicating and for workplace collaboration.[30]

The world of communication is not what it used to be. Managers are challenged to keep their organizations functioning smoothly while continually improving work operations *and* staying competitive even though both the organization and the environment are changing rapidly. Although changing technology has been a significant source of the environmental uncertainty facing organizations, these same technological advances have enabled managers to coordinate the work efforts of employees in ways that can lead to increased efficiency and effectiveness. Information technology now touches every aspect of almost every company's business. The implications for the ways individuals communicate are profound.

How Information Technology Affects Communication

Information technology has radically changed the way organizational members communicate. For example, it has

- significantly improved a manager's ability to monitor individual or team performance
- allowed employees to have more complete information to make faster decisions
- provided employees with more opportunities to collaborate and share information
- made it possible for employees to be fully accessible, any time, regardless of where they are

Information technology also creates opportunities for organizations. For instance, colleges and universities now have the capability of offering online courses and degrees. This could, over time, decrease the number of students taught in face-to-face contexts and increase the overall number of students because of the accessibility of online courses.

Three developments in information technology seem to be having the most significant impact on managerial communication today: email, instant messaging, and social networking websites.

Email

Have you ever emailed or instant-messaged someone who was just in the next office? Does the reliance on technology make it harder or easier to communicate with people?

Email is a quick and convenient way for organizational members to share information and communicate. Many people complain about email overload, however, and it is not always used effectively. A recent study found that opening nasty messages from your boss can harm your health over time.[31] While negative email messages from anyone had health consequences, those from superiors showed the most significant increase in a person's blood pressure.

Individuals should remember that email can be permanent, which means that a message sent in anger could come back to hurt the sender later on. Email is also not necessarily private communication, and organizations often take the position that they have the right to read your email.

To construct more effective emails, you might want to consider the following tips for writing and sending email offered by Professor Christina Cavanagh of the University of Western Ontario's Richard Ivey School of Business:[32]

- Don't send emails without a subject line.
- Be careful in your use of emoticons and acronyms for business communication.
- Write your message clearly and briefly.
- Copy emails to others only if they really need the information.
- Sleep on angry emails before sending to be sure you are sending the right message.

Instant Messaging

Instant messaging (IM) first became popular among teens and preteens who wanted to communicate online immediately with their friends. Now, it has moved to the workplace. According to the latest research, 11.4 billion IMs were sent worldwide each day in 2004, and this number was expected to increase to more than 45.8 billion by 2008.[33] However, there are a couple of drawbacks to IM. Unlike email, it requires users to be logged on to the organization's computer network in order to be able to communicate with one another. This leaves the network open to security breaches, and some organizations have limited which employees can use IM in the workplace as a result.

Social Networking Websites

Social networking websites such as Facebook, MySpace, and LinkedIn have drawn millions of subscribers who voluntarily post information about themselves that can be viewed by any other subscriber, unless the user deliberately sets privacy restrictions.

Employers and search firms are starting to check the postings of clients, and some even monitor employees to see if there is anything questionable in their character. Despite the public's concern that the government is not doing enough to protect individual privacy, many people feel free to post information (flattering and unflattering) about themselves online that is readily accessible to anyone.

Some employers post job offerings on sites such as Facebook; others post recruitment videos on sites such as YouTube. In a recent twist, some employers have done virtual interviews through Second Life, the online virtual community.[34] Job seekers create an "avatar," a computer-generated image that represents themselves, and then communicate with prospective employers through instant messaging. A recent virtual job fair on Second Life included employers Hewlett-Packard, Microsoft, Verizon, and Sodexho Alliance SA, a food and facilities-management services company.

Individuals who use websites such as Facebook may want to consider the lack of privacy such sites afford when it comes to employers and evaluations. Individuals may forget that once it's written on the web, it's difficult to erase. So while it might seem like a good idea to post photos of drunken partying, this might not leave a good impression on potential employers. As Deanna MacDougal, a partner at Toronto-based IQ Partners, notes, "If your potential employer Googles a name and sees your social life, that can be good but it can also hinder you. Even with password-protected sites, I think the youth need to be a little bit more careful." Geoff Bagg, president of Toronto-based The Bagg Group, adds, "I don't think you can segment your life and say, 'This is my private life and this is my work life.' They're all intertwined."[35]

Technology need not always reduce face-to-face communication. To make contact easier between employees, some companies are designing their offices with more common areas, which help bring employees together. At Skype Technologies SA's new office in Palo Alto, California (shown here), a pool table and foosball table sit next to nonfunctional phones on display as a joke in the employee recreation room. To make contact easier between employees at its call centre and in its information systems department, ASB, a New Zealand bank, adopted an open layout encompassing five areas on three different floors. There is a landscaped park area in the centre, a café, a minigolf green, a TV room, and a barbecue area. Since moving into the new design, bank managers have noted that the volume of interdepartmental emails has dropped, indicating that people are communicating in person more.

How Information Technology Affects Organizations

Employees—working in teams or as individuals—need information to make decisions and do their work. After describing the communications capabilities managers have at their disposal, it's clear that technology *can* significantly affect the way that organizational members communicate, share information, and do their work. The following *Management Reflection* explores how one Canadian firm reduced cost and improved service for customers using Voice over Internet Protocol (VoIP) technology.

MANAGEMENT REFLECTION
► Focus on Innovation

VoIP Improves Communication and Customer Service

Can saving money increase service? Johnson, a St. John's, Newfoundland and Labrador-based national insurance company founded in 1880, recently introduced the latest in long-distance telephone technology: Voice over Internet Protocol (VoIP).[36] The technology, purchased from Cisco Systems, treats long-distance calls as if they were local ones. With appropriate hardware, subscribers can use the same cable that connects their computer to the Internet to connect their telephone to make calls.

It is not just a cost-saving measure, though. C. C. Huang, Johnson's president and CEO, says, "We really believe in Voice over IP [Internet Protocol]. It's helping us provide better customer service, improve our productivity—and outperform the industry." The IP infrastructure allows voice, video, and data to be transferred on a single network.

When customers call in, the network can direct calls to staff members who have the appropriate skills and are available to handle the call. The network is also able to link a caller's phone number to his or her electronic file, making it immediately available to the employee handling the phone call. Employees are able to see their voice mail, email, and faxes on their telephone screens. Huang is enthusiastic about the system because, "We're actually spending less money—and doing more than we have before." ■

Communication and the exchange of information among organizational members are no longer constrained by geography or time. Collaborative work efforts among widely dispersed individuals and teams, information sharing, and the integration of decisions and work throughout an entire organization have the potential to increase organizational efficiency and effectiveness. While the economic benefits of information technology are obvious, managers must not forget to address the psychological drawbacks.[37] For instance, what is the psychological cost of an employee always being accessible? Will there be increased pressure for employees to "check in" even during their off hours? How important is it for employees to separate their work lives and their personal lives? While there are no easy answers to these questions, these are issues that managers will have to face.

Privacy Issues

The widespread use of voice mail and email at work has led to some ethical concerns as well. These forms of communication are not necessarily private, because employers have access to them. The federal Privacy Act (which protects the privacy of individuals and provides individuals with a right to access personal information about themselves) and the Access to Information Act (which allows individuals to access government information) apply to all federal government departments, most federal agencies, and some federal Crown corporations. However, many private sector employees are not covered by privacy legislation. Only Quebec's privacy act applies to the entire private sector. Managers need to clearly convey to employees the extent to which their communications will be monitored, and policies on such things as personal Internet and email use.

Managers need to ensure that their organizations conform to the Personal Information Protection and Electronic Documents Act (PIPEDA), which balances an individual's right to privacy with the need of organizations to collect, use, or disclose personal information for legitimate business purposes. Unlike the Privacy Act, PIPEDA applies to the Canadian private sector. Part one of the act outlines the ground rules for managing personal information, while parts two through five concern the use of electronic documents and signatures as legal alternatives to original documents and signatures.[38]

Communication Issues in Today's Organizations

Managing Communication in an Internet World

At eBay's headquarters, CEO Meg Whitman banned wireless devices such as BlackBerrys from Monday staff meetings. She said, "There was a little grumbling from the top execs who regularly attend the meetings. [However], personal interaction is much more important than instantly answering e-mails."[39]

6. Discuss contemporary issues in communication.

Managers are learning, the hard way sometimes, that all this new technology has created special communication challenges. The two main ones are (1) legal and security issues and (2) lack of personal interaction.

Chevron paid $2.2 million (US) to settle a sexual-harassment lawsuit stemming from inappropriate jokes being sent by employees over company email.[40] UK firm Norwich Union had to pay £450 000 in an out-of-court settlement after an employee sent an email stating that competitor Western Provident Association was in financial difficulties.[41]

Although email is a quick and easy way to communicate, managers need to be aware of potential legal problems from inappropriate email usage. Electronic information is potentially admissible in court. For instance, during the Enron trial, prosecutors entered into evidence emails and other documents they say showed that the defendants defrauded investors. Says one expert, "Today, e-mail and instant messaging are the electronic equivalent of DNA evidence."[42] But email's legal problems are not the only issue facing managers. Security concerns are another. Managers need to ensure that confidential information is kept confidential. Employee emails and blogs should not communicate—inadvertently or purposely—proprietary information. Corporate computer and email systems should be protected against hackers and spam. These are serious issues that managers and organizations must address if the benefits that communication technology offers are to be realized.

Another communication challenge posed by the Internet age we live and work in is the lack of personal interaction. Even when two people are communicating face-to-face, understanding is not always achieved. However, when communication takes place in a virtual environment, it can be *really* hard to achieve understanding and collaborate on getting work done. Some companies have gone so far as to ban email on certain days of the week. Others have simply encouraged employees to collaborate more in person. Yet, there are situations and times when personal interaction is not physically possible—for example, when your colleagues work across the continent or even across the globe. In those instances, real-time collaboration software (such as private workplace wikis, blogs, instant messengers, and other types of groupware) may be a better communication choice than sending an email and waiting for a response.[43]

Managing the Organization's Knowledge Resources

Kara Johnson is a materials expert at product design firm IDEO. To make finding the right materials easier, she built a master library of samples linked to a database that explains their properties and manufacturing processes.[44] What Johnson did was manage knowledge and make it easier for others at IDEO to "learn" and benefit from her knowledge. That is what today's managers need to do with the organization's knowledge resources—make it easy for employees to communicate and share their knowledge so they can learn from each other ways to do their jobs more effectively and efficiently. One way organizations can do this is to create online information databases that employees can access. This is one example of how managers can use communication tools to manage this valuable organizational resource called knowledge.

In addition to online information databases for sharing knowledge, some knowledge management experts suggest that organizations create **communities of practice**, which are "groups of people who share a concern, a set of problems, or a passion about a topic, and who deepen their knowledge and expertise in that area by interacting on an ongoing basis."[45] The keys to this concept are that the group must actually meet in some fashion on a regular basis and use its information exchanges to improve in some way. For example, repair technicians at Xerox tell "war stories" to communicate their experiences and to help others solve difficult problems with repairing machines.[46] This is not to say that communities of practice don't face challenges. They do. For instance, in large global organizations, keeping communities of practice going takes additional effort. To make these communities of practice work, it's important to maintain strong human interactions through communication. Interactive websites, email, and videoconferencing are essential communication tools. In addition, these groups face the same communication problems that individuals face—filtering, emotions, defensiveness, information overload, and so forth. However, groups can resolve these issues by focusing on the same suggestions we discussed earlier: using feedback, simplifying language, listening actively, constraining emotions, and watching nonverbal cues.

communities of practice Groups of people who share a concern, a set of problems, or a passion about a topic, and who deepen their knowledge and expertise in that area by interacting on an ongoing basis.

The Role of Communication in Customer Service

You have been a customer many times; in fact, you probably find yourself in a customer service encounter several times a day. So what does this have to do with communication? As it turns out, a lot! *What* communication takes place and *how* it takes place can have a significant impact on a customer's satisfaction with the service and the likelihood of being a repeat customer. Managers in service organizations need to make sure that employees who interact with customers are communicating appropriately and effectively with those customers. How? By first recognizing the three components in any service delivery process: the customer, the service organization, and the individual service provider.[47] Each plays a role in whether or not communication is working. Obviously, managers don't have a lot of control over what or how the customer communicates, but they can influence the other two.

An organization with a strong service culture already values taking care of customers— finding out what their needs are, meeting those needs, and following up to make sure that their needs were met satisfactorily. Each of these activities involves communication, whether face-to-face, by phone or email, or through other channels. In addition, communication is part of the specific customer service strategies the organization pursues. One strategy that many service organizations use is personalization. For instance, at Ritz-Carlton Hotels, customers are provided with more than a clean bed and room. Customers who have stayed at a location previously and indicated that certain items are important to them—such as extra pillows, hot chocolate, or a certain brand of shampoo—will find those items waiting in their room at arrival. The hotel's database allows service to be personalized to customers' expectations. In addition, all employees are asked to communicate information related to service provision. For instance, if a room attendant overhears guests talking about celebrating an anniversary, he or she is supposed to relay the information so something special can be done.[48] Communication plays an important role in the hotel's customer personalization strategy.

Communication also is important to the individual service provider or contact employee. The quality of the interpersonal interaction between the customer and that contact employee does influence customer satisfaction.[49] That is especially true when the service encounter is not up to expectations. People on the front line involved with those "critical service encounters" are often the first to hear about or notice service failures or breakdowns. They must decide *how* and *what* to communicate during these instances. Their ability to listen actively and communicate appropriately with the customer goes a long way in whether or not the situation is resolved to the customer's satisfaction or spirals out of control. Another important communication concern for the individual service provider is making sure that he or she has the information needed to deal with customers efficiently and effectively. If the service provider does not personally have the information, there should be some way to get the information easily and promptly.[50] Hudson's Bay Company uses online customer surveys to learn about customers' store experiences, as the following *Management Reflection* shows.

MANAGEMENT REFLECTION

Mystery Shoppers Dropped for Online Surveys

What is the best way to get feedback about customer service? Customers of The Bay, Zellers, and Home Outfitters can give feedback about their store experience by filling out an online survey at the Toronto-based Hudson's Bay Company's website.[51] Managers learned, for instance, that training was lacking in a specific department at a specific store after a customer described an experience where the clerk could not use the cash register properly or remove anti-theft tags from clothing.

The website for customer feedback is listed on sales receipts, encouraging customers who have had either negative or positive experiences to let the company know. Customers have submitted gripes about a number of issues at Hudson's Bay's stores, including "not enough sale items in stock . . . [and] no salesperson in sight when you really need one."

In the past, many retail outlets, including The Bay, have hired mystery shoppers to gather information about customer service. Companies are now questioning whether that is the best way to get adequate feedback, however. David Zinman, vice-president of corporate operations at Burnaby, BC-based Best Buy Canada, which owns Richmond, BC-based Future Shop, notes that "you get better-quality information from customers that are actually in there shopping and that aren't on your payroll."

The Texas-based Mystery Shopping Providers Association worries that stores are not getting the best feedback by relying on online surveys. Only about 10 percent of customers fill out the surveys, even though doing so can make them eligible to win 1 million HBC Rewards points. It is not obvious whether stores should continue to use online surveys or to use a mix of mystery shoppers and surveys. However, as we have suggested in this chapter, knowing how to communicate effectively also means knowing how to collect the best data for reliable feedback. ∎

Politically Correct Communication

Sears tells its employees to use phrases such as "person with a disability" instead of "disabled person" when writing or speaking about people with disabilities. It also suggests that when talking with a customer in a wheelchair for more than a few minutes, employees place themselves at the customer's eye level by sitting down to make a more comfortable atmosphere for everyone.[52] These suggestions, provided in an employee brochure that discusses assisting customers with disabilities, reflect the importance of politically correct communication. How you communicate with someone who is not like you, what terms you use in addressing a customer, or what words you use to describe a colleague who is wheelchair-bound can mean the difference between losing a client, an employee, a lawsuit, a harassment claim, or a job.[53]

Most of us are acutely aware of how our vocabulary has been modified to reflect political correctness. For instance, most of us refrain from using words like *handicapped, blind,* and *elderly,* and use instead terms like *physically challenged, visually impaired,* or *senior.* We must be sensitive to others' feelings. Certain words can and do stereotype, intimidate, and insult individuals. With an increasingly diverse workforce, we must be sensitive to how words might offend others. Although it's complicating our vocabulary and making it more difficult for people to communicate, it is something managers cannot ignore.

Words are the primary means by which people communicate. When we eliminate words from use because they are politically incorrect, we reduce our options for conveying messages in the clearest and most accurate form. For the most part, the larger the vocabulary used by a sender and a receiver, the greater the opportunity to accurately transmit messages. By removing certain words from our vocabulary, we make it harder to communicate accurately. When we further replace these words with new ones whose meanings are less well understood, we have reduced the likelihood that our messages will be received as we had intended them.

We must be sensitive to how our choice of words might offend or alienate others. But we need to acknowledge that politically correct language can restrict communication clarity. Nothing suggests that this increased communication ambiguity is likely to be reduced any time soon. This is just another communication challenge for managers.

SUMMARY AND IMPLICATIONS

1. Define the nature and function of communication. Communication serves four major functions: control, motivation, emotional expression, and information. In the control function, communication sets out the guidelines for behaviour. Communication motivates by clarifying to employees what is to be done, how well they are doing, and what can be done to improve performance if it's not up to par. Communication provides an opportunity to express feelings and also fulfills social needs. Finally, communication also provides the information to get things done in organizations.

▶ ▶ ▶ Lymbix has made a clear distinction between the denotative, or literal, meaning of a written communication and the connotative meaning, or tone, of a communication. For instance, "you are confused" and "you misunderstand" have the same literal meaning, yet the reader comes away with two different emotional responses. By running an emotional "spell check" to identify emotionally charged phrases or sentences, Lymbix users can communicate more effectively.

2. Compare and contrast methods of interpersonal communication. There are seven elements in the communication process. First there is a *sender* who has a message for a *receiver*. A *message* is a purpose to be conveyed. *Encoding* is converting a message into symbols. A *channel* is the medium a message travels along. *Decoding* is when the receiver retranslates a sender's message. Finally, there is *feedback*. Managers can evaluate the various communication methods according to their feedback, complexity capacity, breadth potential, confidentiality, encoding ease, decoding ease, time–space constraint, cost, interpersonal warmth, formality, scannability, and time of consumption. Communication methods include face-to-face communication, telephone communication, group meetings, formal presentations, memos, traditional mail, faxes, employee publications, bulletin boards, other company publications, audio- and videotapes, hotlines, email, computer conference, voice mail, teleconferences, and videoconferences.

▶ ▶ ▶ Lymbix focuses on analyzing digital communications but acknowledges that this is only one channel of communication. Managers need to take a holistic approach to managing which channels they use and when they use them.

3. Identify barriers to effective interpersonal communication and how to overcome them. When a message passes between a sender and a receiver, it needs to be converted into symbols (called *encoding*) and passed to the receiver by some channel. The receiver translates (*decodes*) the sender's message. At any point in this process, communication can become distorted through noise. A variety of other factors can also affect whether the message is interpreted correctly, including the degree of filtering, the sender's or receiver's emotional state, and whether too much information is being sent (information overload).

▶ ▶ ▶ The value of face-to-face communication is that one receives more information through body language. The rise of online communication, through such tools as email as well as social networking sites such as Facebook, means that communication is often more ambiguous. It also becomes harder to know whether too much information has been revealed because feedback mechanisms may not be as direct. TweetTone tracks and analyzes the emotion behind the conversation on Twitter. This is one tool organizations can use to measure the impact of their communication.

4. Understand how communication flows in an organization. Communication can be of the formal or informal variety. Formal communication follows the official chain of command or is part of the communication required to do one's job. Informal communication is not defined by the organization's structural hierarchy. Communication can flow downward, upward, laterally to those at the same organizational level, or diagonally, which means that the communication cuts across both work areas and organizational levels. Communication can also flow through networks and through the grapevine. The three types of communication networks are the chain, in which communication flows according to the formal chain of command; the wheel, in which communication flows between a clearly identifiable, strong leader and others in a work team; and the all-channel, in which communication flows freely among all members of a work team. Managers should manage the grapevine as an important information network. They can minimize the negative consequences of rumours by communicating with employees openly, fully, and honestly.

5. Describe how technology affects managerial communication. Information technology allows managers and employees more access to each other and to customers and clients. It provides more opportunities for monitoring, as well as a greater ability to share information. Information technology also increases flexibility and responsiveness. IT has an impact on organizations by affecting the way that organizational members communicate, share information, and do their work.

▶ ▶ ▶ Social networking websites such as Facebook and LinkedIn have become resources for employers seeking job candidates. Companies large and small are using these resources to do research, form relationships, and fill positions. A manager looking to fill a key position can use LinkedIn to view posted résumés, read an individual's postings, and even "check out a competitor's site for potential candidates."

6. Discuss contemporary issues in communication. The major issues covered in this chapter are managing in an Internet world, managing the organization's knowledge resources, communicating effectively and appropriately with customers, and understanding the importance of "politically correct" communication. Organizations today must figure out ways to help employees communicate with one another and share their knowledge to increase the effectiveness of the organization. Organizations have to consider the best ways to communicate with customers so that they can find out what their needs are, meet those needs, and follow up to make sure that their needs were met satisfactorily. Finally, dealing with the challenge of politically correct language means being sensitive to how words might offend others while realizing that sometimes clarity is lost.

Management @ Work

READING FOR COMPREHENSION

1. How is communication defined? What are the four functions of communication?

2. Identify four types of channels and when they might be best used. What steps can you take to make interpersonal communication more effective?

3. What can managers do to help them determine which communication channel to use in a given circumstance?

4. Describe the barriers to effective interpersonal communication. How can they be overcome?

5. How can the barriers to communication be overcome?

6. Which of the three common organizational networks listed in Exhibit 11-4 on page 304 would you feel most comfortable using? Why?

7. How has information technology enhanced a manager's communication effectiveness?

8. What are the two main challenges of communicating in the wired world?

LINKING CONCEPTS TO PRACTICE

1. Describe why effective communication is not synonymous with agreement between the communicating parties.

2. Which do you think is more important for a manager: speaking accurately or listening actively? Why?

3. "Ineffective communication is the fault of the sender." Do you agree or disagree with this statement? Explain your position.

4. How might a manager use the grapevine to his or her advantage? Support your response.

5. Is information technology helping managers to be more effective and efficient? Explain your position.

SELF-ASSESSMENT

What's My Face-to-Face Communication Style?

For each of the following statements, circle the level of agreement or disagreement that you personally feel:[54]

1 = Strongly Disagree   3 = Neither Agree nor Disagree   5 = Strongly Agree

1. I am comfortable with all varieties of people.		1 2 3 4 5
2. I laugh easily.		1 2 3 4 5
3. I readily express admiration for others.		1 2 3 4 5
4. What I say usually leaves an impression on people.		1 2 3 4 5
5. I leave people with an impression of me which they definitely tend to remember.		1 2 3 4 5
6. To be friendly, I habitually acknowledge verbally others' contributions.		1 2 3 4 5
7. I have some nervous mannerisms in my speech.		1 2 3 4 5
8. I am a very relaxed communicator.		1 2 3 4 5
9. When I disagree with somebody, I am very quick to challenge them.		1 2 3 4 5
10. I can always repeat back to a person exactly what was meant.		1 2 3 4 5

11. The sound of my voice is very easy to recognize. 1 2 3 4 5

12. I leave a definite impression on people. 1 2 3 4 5

13. The rhythm or flow of my speech is sometimes affected by nervousness. 1 2 3 4 5

14. Under pressure, I come across as a relaxed speaker. 1 2 3 4 5

15. My eyes reflect exactly what I am feeling when I communicate. 1 2 3 4 5

16. I dramatize a lot. 1 2 3 4 5

17. Usually, I deliberately react in such a way that people will know I am listening to them. 1 2 3 4 5

18. Usually, I do not tell people much about myself until I get to know them well. 1 2 3 4 5

19. Regularly, I tell jokes, anecdotes, and stories when I communicate. 1 2 3 4 5

20. I tend to constantly gesture when I communicate. 1 2 3 4 5

21. I am an extremely open communicator. 1 2 3 4 5

22. I am vocally a loud communicator. 1 2 3 4 5

23. In arguments, I insist upon very precise definitions. 1 2 3 4 5

24. In most social situations, I generally speak very frequently. 1 2 3 4 5

25. I like to be strictly accurate when I communicate. 1 2 3 4 5

26. Because I have a loud voice, I can easily break into a conversation. 1 2 3 4 5

27. Often, I physically and vocally act out when I want to communicate. 1 2 3 4 5

28. I have an assertive voice. 1 2 3 4 5

29. I readily reveal personal things about myself. 1 2 3 4 5

30. I am dominant in social situations. 1 2 3 4 5

31. I am very argumentative. 1 2 3 4 5

32. Once I get wound up in a heated discussion, I have a hard time stopping myself. 1 2 3 4 5

33. I am always an extremely friendly communicator. 1 2 3 4 5

34. I really like to listen very carefully to people. 1 2 3 4 5

35. Very often I insist that other people document or present some kind of proof for what they are arguing. 1 2 3 4 5

36. I try to take charge of things when I am with people. 1 2 3 4 5

37. It bothers me to drop an argument that is not resolved. 1 2 3 4 5

38. In most social situations I tend to come on strong. 1 2 3 4 5

39. I am very expressive nonverbally in social situations. 1 2 3 4 5

40. The way I say something usually leaves an impression on people. 1 2 3 4 5

41. Whenever I communicate, I tend to be very encouraging to people. 1 2 3 4 5

42. I actively use a lot of facial expressions when I communicate. 1 2 3 4 5

43. I very frequently verbally exaggerate to emphasize a point. 1 2 3 4 5

44. I am an extremely attentive communicator. 1 2 3 4 5

45. As a rule, I openly express my feelings and emotions. 1 2 3 4 5

Scoring Key

Step 1: Reverse the score on items 4, 17, and 26 (1 = 5, 2 = 4, 3 = 3, etc.).

Step 2: Add together the scores on the following items to get a final total for each dimension.

1. 5, 7, 9, 20, 44   = _____ (Dominant)
2. 22, 28, 30, 32, 39 = _____ (Dramatic)
3. 2, 10, 13, 37, 41 = _____ (Contentious)
4. 6, 21, 24, 34, 42 = _____ (Animated)
5. 11, 14, 18, 31, 40 = _____ (Impression leaving)
6. 4, 12, 16, 17, 36 = _____ (Relaxed)
7. 15, 23, 27, 29, 45 = _____ (Attentive)
8. 1, 25, 26, 33, 38 = _____ (Open)
9. 3, 8, 19, 35, 43   = _____ (Friendly)

Analysis and Interpretation

This scale measures the following dimensions of communication style:

Dominant—Tends to take charge of social interactions.

Dramatic—Manipulates and exaggerates stories and uses other stylistic devices to highlight content.

Contentious—Is argumentative.

Animated—Uses frequent and sustained eye contact, and many facial expressions, and gestures often.

Impression leaving—Is remembered because of the communicative stimuli that are projected.

Relaxed—Is relaxed and void of nervousness.

Attentive—Makes sure that the other person knows that he or she is being listened to.

Open—Is conversational, expansive, affable, convivial, gregarious, unreserved, somewhat frank, definitely extroverted, and obviously approachable.

Friendly—Ranges from being unhostile to showing deep intimacy.

For each dimension, your score will range from 5 to 25. The higher your score for any dimension, the more that dimension characterizes your communication style. When you review your results, consider to what degree your scores aid or hinder your communication effectiveness. High scores for being attentive and open would almost always be positive qualities. A high score for contentious, on the other hand, could be a negative in many situations.

More Self-Assessments   MyManagementLab

To learn more about your skills, abilities, and interests, go to the MyManagementLab website and take the following self-assessments:

- II.A.2.—How Good Are My Listening Skills?
- III.A.3.—How Good Am I at Giving Performance Feedback? (This exercise also appears in Chapter 12 on pages 347–348.)
- IV.E.3. —Am I a Gossip?

MANAGEMENT FOR YOU TODAY

Dilemma

Think of a person with whom you have had difficulty communicating. Using the barriers to effective interpersonal communication as a start, analyze what has gone wrong with the communication process with that person. What can be done to improve communication? To what extent did sender and receiver problems contribute to the communication breakdown? (Try taking the perspective of the receiver and then the sender.)

Becoming a Manager

- Practise being a good communicator—as a sender and a listener.
- When preparing to communicate, think about the most appropriate channel for your communication and why it may or may not be the most appropriate.
- Pay attention to your and others' nonverbal communication. Learn to notice the cues.
- Complete the Developing Your Interpersonal Skills—Active Listening module in this section.

WORKING TOGETHER: TEAM-BASED EXERCISE

Choosing the Right Communication Channel

Purpose

To reinforce the idea that some channels are more appropriate for certain communications than others.

Time Required

Approximately 20 minutes.

Procedure

Form groups of five or six individuals. Evaluate the most appropriate channel to use to deliver the following information to employees. Justify your choices.

1. The company has just been acquired by a large competitor, and 15 percent of the employees will be laid off within the next three months.

2. A customer has complained about an employee via email. You have investigated and found the complaint justified. How do you convey this to the employee?

3. The founder of the company, who is well liked, died of a heart attack last night.

4. Bonus decisions have been made. Not all individuals will receive a bonus.

5. An employee has gone above and beyond in meeting a customer's request. You want to acknowledge the employee's efforts.

ETHICS IN ACTION

Ethical Dilemma Exercise: Should CEOs Join the Blogger's World?

More and more organizational members are initiating messages through corporate blogs.[55] Officially known as *weblogs*, these are websites where an individual posts ideas, comments on contemporary issues, and offers other musings. Because anyone can visit the site and read the messages, companies have become concerned about messages that include sensitive data, criticize managers or competitors, use inflammatory language, or contain misrepresentations. Companies are also worried about the reaction of stakeholders who disagree with or are offended by blog postings. Corporate blogs are becoming so popular that companies such as Groove Networks have developed blog policies. In fact, CNN insisted that a reporter suspend a blog where he posted his conflicting thoughts about a career as a war correspondent, even though the reporter had a disclaimer saying the blog was "not affiliated with, endorsed by, or funded by CNN."

But what happens when a CEO sets up a blog? Jonathan Schwartz, CEO of Sun Microsystems, blogs about new technologies, management issues, and more (see **http://blogs. sun.com/jonathan**). Alan Meckler, the CEO of Jupitermedia,

started a blog as "a diary of the ups and downs of trying to do something monumental"—create a new industry-wide technology conference. This event put Jupitermedia squarely in competition with a well-established event known as Comdex. In early blog entries, Meckler talked bluntly about the competing conference's management. Based on legal advice (and negative feedback from a few conference exhibitors), he softened his tone in later entries. Although he still blogs, Meckler notes, "I'm not stirring the pot anymore, which isn't my nature." What is the most ethical way to deal with a corporate blog, especially one by a senior manager?

Imagine that you are Jupitermedia's public relations director. The CEO has just posted a blog message saying your conference was more financially successful than the competing conference. Because neither company releases profitability details, you know this statement cannot be verified. You don't want Jupitermedia to look bad; you also know that your CEO likes to express himself. What should you do about the CEO's blog? (Review Exhibit 11-1 on page 293 as you think about the ethical challenge posed by this blog communication.)

Thinking Critically About Ethics

According to a survey by Websense, 58 percent of employees spend time at non-work-related websites.[56] Another survey by salary.com and AOL found that personal Internet surfing was the top method of goofing off at work. Funny stories, jokes, and pictures make their way from one employee's email inbox to another's, to another's, and so forth. An elf bowling game sent by email was a favourite diversion during the holiday season. Although these may seem like fun and

harmless activities, it's estimated that such Internet distractions cost businesses over $54 billion annually. While there is a high dollar cost associated with using the Internet at work for other than business reasons, is there a psychological benefit to be gained by letting employees do something to relieve the stress of pressure-packed jobs? What are the ethical issues for both employees and organizations associated with widely available Internet access at work?

Voyant Technologies

Voyant Technologies makes teleconferencing technology that allows users to call various people at once and invite them to join a conference call.[57] A chance meeting in a headquarters hallway between company CEO Bill Ernstrom and his chief engineer led to the decision to have Voyant's engineers add streaming media to the company's flagship product. Four months and $200 000 later, Ernstrom wished he had never had that conversation, especially after a product manager who had learned of the project produced a marketing report that showed most customers had little interest in streaming anything. That incident underscored a communication challenge that had been ignored for too long: Top engineers were not listening to the product managers—and vice versa. According to Ernstrom, "We got a long way down the road,

built the code, got the engineers excited. Then we found out that we'd sell about 10 units."

The communication barriers experienced by Voyant are not all that unusual in high-tech organizations. The cultural and language gap between computer "geeks" and the more market/business-oriented colleagues happens time and time again. In these types of organizations, the early stages of a new project belong to the engineers. It's crucial to get the technology right, but what they produce is "often elegant technology that has no market, is too complicated, or doesn't match customers' expectations." Ernstrom's challenge is to get the two competing groups to collaborate. How might he do this?

English-Only Rules

Canada is a multicultural country.[58] "One in six Canadians in their 20s are immigrants, and one in five are the children of at least one immigrant parent." In 2006, 45.7 percent of Metropolitan Toronto's population, 39.6 percent of Vancouver's, and 30.7 percent of Montreal's were made up of immigrants.

The 2006 census found that 26 percent of Vancouver's population over age five spoke neither of the country's two official languages as their preferred language. The largest number of people who speak neither English or French as their preferred language speak Chinese (mainly Mandarin or Cantonese). The other dominant language in Vancouver is Punjabi, but many other languages are represented as well. Very few Vancouverites speak French, however (less than 8 percent).

Can an organization in BC require its employees to speak only English on the job? There are many sides to this issue. On the one hand, employers have identified the need to have a common language spoken in the workplace. Employers must be able to communicate effectively with all employees, especially when safety or productive efficiency matters are at stake. This, they claim, is a business necessity. Consequently, if it is a valid requirement of the job, the practice could be permitted. Furthermore, an employer's desire to have one language also stems from the fact that some employees may use bilingual capabilities to harass and insult other employees in a language they cannot understand. With today's increasing concern with protecting employees, especially women, from hostile environments, English-only rules serve as one means of reasonable care.

A counterpoint to this English-only rule firmly rests with the workforce diversity issue. Employees in today's organizations come from all nationalities and speak different languages. What about these individuals' desire to speak their language, to communicate effectively with their peers, and to maintain their cultural heritage? To them, English-only rules are discriminatory in terms of national origin in that they create an adverse impact for non-English-speaking individuals. Moreover, promoting languages of employees might be one way for organizations to avert marketing disasters. For example, marketing campaigns by Kentucky Fried Chicken and Coors have caused some embarrassment when these campaigns are translated literally in the global arena. Specifically, while Kentucky Fried Chicken's "Finger Licking Good" implies great-tasting fried chicken in North America, those same words in Chinese translate into "Eat Your Fingers Off." Likewise, Coors's marketing adage to "Turn It Loose," in Spanish means "Drink Coors and Get Diarrhea." Probably not the images the companies had in mind.

Questions

1. Should employers be permitted to require that only English be spoken in the workplace? Defend your position.

2. What suggestions for communication effectiveness, if any, would you give to organizations that market goods globally? Explain.

Active Listening

About the Skill

The ability to be an effective listener is often taken for granted. Hearing is often confused with listening, but hearing is merely recognizing sound vibrations. Listening is making sense of what we hear and requires paying attention, interpreting, and remembering. Effective listening is active rather than passive. Active listening is hard work and requires you to "get inside" the speaker's head in order to understand the communication from his or her point of view.

Steps in Developing the Skill

You can be more effective at active listening if you use the following eight suggestions:[59]

1. **Make eye contact.** Making eye contact with the speaker focuses your attention, reduces the likelihood that you will be distracted, and encourages the speaker.

2. **Exhibit affirmative nods and appropriate facial expressions.** The effective active listener shows interest in what is being said through nonverbal signals. Affirmative nods and appropriate facial expressions that signal interest in what is being said, when added to eye contact, convey to the speaker that you are really listening.

3. **Avoid distracting actions or gestures.** The other side of showing interest is avoiding actions that suggest your mind is elsewhere. When listening, don't look at your watch, shuffle papers, play with your pencil, or engage in similar distractions.

4. **Ask questions.** The serious active listener analyzes what he or she hears and asks questions. This behaviour provides clarification, ensures understanding, and assures the speaker you are really listening.

5. **Paraphrase.** Restate in your own words what the speaker has said. The effective active listener uses phrases such as "What I hear you saying is . . ." or "Do you mean . . .?" Paraphrasing is an excellent control device to check whether or not you are listening carefully and is also a control for accuracy of understanding.

6. **Avoid interrupting the speaker.** Let the speaker complete his or her thoughts before you try to respond. Don't try to second-guess where the speaker's thoughts are going. When the speaker is finished, you will know it.

7. **Don't overtalk.** Most of us would rather speak our own ideas than listen to what others say. While talking might be more fun and silence might be uncomfortable, you cannot talk and listen at the same time. The good active listener recognizes this fact and does not overtalk.

8. **Make smooth transitions between the roles of speaker and listener.** In most work situations, you are continually shifting back and forth between the roles of speaker and listener. The effective active listener makes transitions smoothly from speaker to listener and back to speaker.

Practising the Skill

Read the following scenario. Write some notes about how you would handle the situation described. Be sure to refer to the eight suggestions for active listening.

Scenario

Ben Lummis has always been one of the most reliable technicians at the car stereo shop you manage. Even on days when the frantic pace stressed most other employees, Ben was calm and finished his work efficiently and effectively. You don't know much about his personal life except that he likes to read books about model railroading during his lunch break and he has asked to listen to his favourite light jazz station on the shop radio for part of the day. Because his work has always been top-notch, you were happy to let him maintain his somewhat aloof attitude. But over the past month, you have wished you knew Ben better. He has been averaging about an absence a week, and he no longer spends his lunch break reading in the break room. When he returns from wherever it is he goes, he seems even more remote than when he left. You strongly suspect that something is wrong. Even his normally reliable work has changed. Several irate customers have returned with sound systems he installed improperly. At the time of these complaints, you reviewed each problem with him carefully, and each time he promised to be more careful. In addition, you checked the company's work absence records and found that Ben has enough time saved up to take seven more sick days this year. But things don't seem to be improving. Just this week, Ben took another suspicious sick day, and another angry customer has demanded that his improperly installed sound system be fixed. How would you discuss the matter with Ben?

Reinforcing the Skill

The following activities will help you practise and reinforce the skills associated with active listening:

1. In another lecture-format class, practise active listening for one session. Then ask yourself: Was this harder for me than a normal lecture? Did it affect my note taking? Did I ask more questions? Did it improve my understanding of the lecture's content?

2. For one week, practise active listening behaviours during phone conversations that you have with others. Keep a journal of whether listening actively was easy or difficult, what distractions there were, how you dealt with those distractions, and your assessment of whether or not active listening allowed you to get more out of the conversations.

MyManagementLab

For more resources, please visit www.pearsoned.ca/mymanagementlab

SCAN THIS

Managing Human Resources

Once an organization's structure is in place it's time to find the people to fill the jobs that have been created. That's where human resource management comes in. It's an important task that involves getting the right number of people in the right place at the right time. After reading and studying this chapter, you will achieve the following learning outcomes.

Learning Outcomes

1 Understand how managing human resources well contributes to the success of the organization.

2 Discuss the tasks associated with identifying and selecting competent employees.

3 Explain the different types of orientation and training.

4 Describe strategies for retaining competent, high-performing employees.

5 Discuss contemporary issues in managing human resources.

▶ ▶ ▶ Toronto-based Bank of Nova Scotia (also called Scotiabank), Canada's second-largest bank, provides retail, corporate, and investment banking services worldwide.[1]

Scotiabank has more than 1000 domestic branches and 1400 offices in 50 countries, mainly in the Caribbean and Central and South America. In fiscal year 2009, the bank had total assets of over $496 billion, making it the number two bank by market capitalization. Scotiabank has close to 68 000 employees, but President and CEO Rick Waugh worries that too many will be leaving within the next 5 to 10 years. He expects about half of the bank's senior management—vice-presidents and those at higher levels—will retire during that time.

Managing human resources so that an organization has the right people in place at the right time is often thought of as a key role of human resource managers. Waugh thinks that is not enough, however. "Responsibility for leadership development must begin at the very top. HR can and does play an important role facilitating the process,

but it must be owned and executed by current leaders," Waugh told attendees at a recent Conference Board of Canada's National Leadership Summit.

Waugh also wants to make sure that Scotiabank taps the full potential of its workforce. For instance, while women represent about 50 percent

of Scotiabank's management-level employees, they have much less representation at the executive level. Waugh will be working with senior managers to make sure that more qualified women get opportunities in senior management.

SCAN THIS

MyManagementLab
Q&A 12.1

Think About It

How do companies manage their human resources to achieve better performance? Put yourself in Rick Waugh's shoes. What policies and practices can he adopt to ensure that the bank has a high-quality workforce? What might he do to make sure that Scotiabank will have enough people to fill important roles as Baby Boomers retire?

The challenge facing Rick Waugh in making sure that Scotiabank recruits and retains high-quality employees reflects only a small aspect of the types of human resource management challenges facing today's managers. If an organization does not take its human resource management responsibilities seriously, work performance and goal accomplishment may suffer. The quality of an organization is, to a large degree, merely the sum of the quality of people it hires and keeps. Getting and keeping competent employees is critical to the success of every organization, whether the organization is just starting or has been in business for years. Therefore, part of every manager's job in the organizing function is human resource management.

The Human Resource Management Process

1. Understand how managing human resources well contributes to the success of the organization.

"Our people are our most important asset." Many organizations use this phrase, or something close to it, to acknowledge the important role that employees play in organizational success. These organizations also recognize that *all* managers must engage in some human resource management (HRM) activities—even in large ones that have a separate HRM department. These managers interview job candidates, orient new employees, and evaluate their employees' work performance.

Can HRM be an important strategic tool? *Can* it help establish an organization's sustainable competitive advantage? The answer to these questions seems to be yes. Various studies have concluded that an organization's human resources can be a significant source of competitive advantage.[2] And that is true for organizations around the world, not just Canadian firms. The Human Capital Index, a comprehensive global study of more than 2000 firms conducted by consulting firm Watson Wyatt Worldwide, concluded that people-oriented HR gives an organization an edge by creating superior shareholder value.[3]

Why Human Resource Management Is Important

Achieving competitive success through people requires a fundamental change in how managers think about their employees and how they view the work relationship. It involves working with and through people and seeing them as partners, not just as costs to be minimized or avoided. In addition to their potential importance as part of organizational strategy and their contribution to competitive advantage, an organization's HRM practices have been found to have a significant impact on organizational performance.[4] For instance, one study reported that significantly improving an organization's HRM practices could increase its market value by as much as 30 percent.[5] The term used to describe these practices that lead to such results is **high-performance work practices**. High-performance work practices lead to both high individual and high organizational performance. Exhibit 12-1 lists examples of high-performance work practices. The common thread in these practices is a commitment to improving the knowledge, skills, and abilities of an organization's employees; increasing their motivation; reducing loafing on the job; and enhancing the retention of quality employees while encouraging low performers to leave.

high-performance work practices Work practices that lead to both high individual and high organizational performance.

Human Resources for Non–human Resource Managers

Even if an organization doesn't use high-performance work practices, there are specific HRM activities that must be completed in order to ensure that the organization has qualified people to perform the work that needs to be done—activities that compose the **human resource management process**. Exhibit 12-2 shows the eight activities in this process. The first three activities ensure that competent employees are identified and selected, the next two involve providing employees with up-to-date knowledge and skills, and the final three ensure that the organization retains competent and high-performing employees. Before we discuss those specific activities, we need to look at external factors that affect the HRM process.

As a manager, it is important for you to be aware that federal and provincial legislation as well as company policies govern many aspects of the employment relationship. Because HR also involves appropriate ways for treating co-workers, even non-managers must be aware of basic HR principles and practices. You may also be interested in human resource issues as they help you understand and manage your own career.

human resource management process Activities necessary for staffing the organization and sustaining high employee performance.

MyManagementLab
Q&A 12.2

Exhibit 12-1

Examples of High-Performance Work Practices

- Self-managed teams
- Decentralized decision making
- Training programs to develop knowledge, skills, and abilities
- Flexible job assignments
- Open communication
- Performance-based compensation
- Staffing based on person–job and person–organization fit

Source: Based on W. R. Evans and W. D. Davis, "High-Performance Work Systems and Organizational Performance: The Mediating Role of Internal Social Structure," *Journal of Management*, October 2005, p. 760.

External Factors That Affect the HRM Process

The entire HRM process is influenced by the external environment. The factors that most directly influence it include employee labour unions, governmental laws and regulations, and demographic trends.

Labour Unions

MyManagementLab
Q&A 12.3

The Canada Labour Code covers employment by the federal government and Crown corporations and establishes the right of employees to join labour unions if they desire. The provinces and territories have similar legislation to cover workplaces within their areas. This legislation provides a general framework for fair negotiations between management and labour unions and also provides guidelines to make sure that labour disputes do not unduly inconvenience the public.

labour union An organization that represents employees and seeks to protect their interests through collective bargaining.

A **labour union** is an organization that represents employees and seeks to protect their interests through collective bargaining. Labour unions try to improve pay and benefits and working conditions for members. They also try to have greater control over the rules and procedures covering issues such as promotions, layoffs, transfers, and outsourcing.

In unionized organizations, many HRM decisions are regulated by the terms of collective agreements. These agreements usually define such things as recruitment sources; criteria for hiring, promotions, and layoffs; training eligibility; and disciplinary practices. About 31.4 percent of Canadian employees belong to labour unions, decreasing slightly from 33.7 percent in 1997. Slightly more women belong to unions. Older workers are also more likely to belong to unions: 38.2 percent of workers aged 55 to 64 are unionized, vs. 16.4 percent of workers aged 15 to 24.[6] By comparison, only about 12.5 percent of the workforce in the United States is unionized, although that percentage is higher in other countries. For instance, in Japan and Germany, respectively, 19.6 percent and 27 percent of the labour force belong to a union. In Mexico, 19 percent of employees belong to a union.[7] Individuals join a labour union for any number of reasons.[8] Wages, working conditions,

---

Exhibit 12-2

The Human Resource Management Process

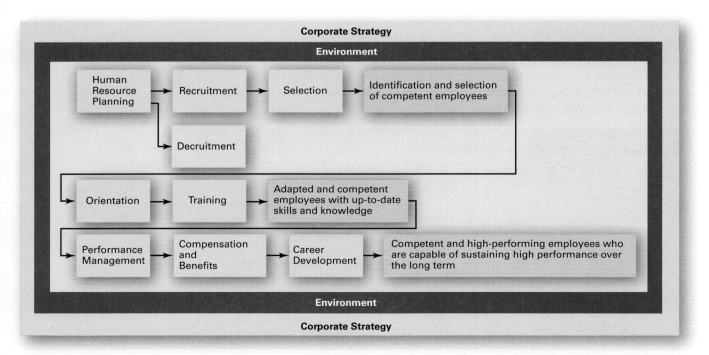

lack of respect by managers, unfair working hours, job security, and the desire for safer workplaces all contribute to unionization. For example, students working at Montreal's downtown Indigo Books, Music & Café were unhappy with their working conditions and voted to join the Confédération des syndicats nationaux in February 2003.[9]

Government Legislation

The federal government has greatly expanded its influence over HRM by enacting a number of laws and regulations, including the Canada Labour Code, employment standards legislation, the Charter of Rights and Freedoms, and the Canadian Human Rights Act. The provincial and territorial governments also have their own labour legislation that governs the workplace.

Legislation Affecting Workplace Conditions The Canada Labour Code covers employment by the federal government and Crown corporations and establishes the right of employees to join labour unions if they desire. Part II of this legislation outlines the health and safety obligations of federal employers to prevent accidents and injury to their employees.

Each province and territory has health and safety regulations that cover most non-federal workplaces in its region. This legislation is typically called the Occupational Health and Safety Act or something similar. The act generally does not cover work done in private homes or work done in farming operations (unless separate regulations have been added). There is separate legislation covering workplace hazards: the Workplace Hazardous Materials Information System (WHMIS). This is a comprehensive plan for providing information on the safe use of potentially hazardous materials in the workplace.

Employment standards legislation sets minimum employment standards in the private sector in Canada. It covers such things as the minimum age of employees, hours of work and overtime pay, minimum wages, equal pay, general holidays and annual vacations with pay, parental leave, and termination of employment.

The intent of the Canada Labour Code, Occupational Health and Safety Act, and employment standards legislation is to ensure that all employees have a safe work environment, that they are not asked to work too many hours, and that pay for jobs is not discriminatory.

Anti-Discrimination Legislation The Charter of Rights and Freedoms and the Canadian Human Rights Act require employers to ensure that equal employment opportunities exist for job applicants and current employees. (See Exhibit 12-3 for examples of prohibited grounds of discrimination in the provinces and territories.)

Trying to balance the "shoulds and should-nots" of these laws often falls within the realm of employment equity. The Employment Equity Act creates four "protected categories"—women, Aboriginal people, people with disabilities, and visible minorities. These groups must not be discriminated against by federally regulated employers and all employers who receive federal contracts worth more than $200 000.

Managers are not completely free to choose whom they hire, promote, or fire. Although these laws and regulations have significantly helped to reduce employment discrimination and unfair employment practices, they have, at the same time, reduced managers' discretion over human resource decisions. Because an increasing number of workplace lawsuits are targeting supervisors, as well as their organizations, managers need to be aware of what they can and cannot do by law.[10]

The Canadian Human Rights Act also covers discrimination in pay, under its pay equity guidelines. The act specifies that "it is a discriminatory practice for an employer to establish or maintain differences in wages between male and female employees employed in the same establishment who are performing work of equal value."[11] While it is not always easy to determine what "work of equal value" means, the Equal Wages Guidelines, 1986, helps employers sort this out.[12]

Demographic Trends

In 1971, only 8 percent of the Canadian population was 65 or older. In 2011, this is expected to increase to 14.4 percent and by 2051 to 26.5 percent (more than a quarter

MyManagementLab
Diversity in Action 1

MyManagementLab
Diversity in Action 3

MyManagementLab
Q&A 12.4

Exhibit 12-3

Prohibited Grounds of Discrimination in Employment*

Prohibited Grounds	FED	BC	ALTA	SASK	MAN	ONT	QUE	NB	PEI	NS	NFLD	NWT	YT
Race or colour	•	•	•	•	•	•	•	•	•	•	•	•	•
Religion	•	•	•	•	•	•	•	•	•	•	•	•	•
Age	•	(19–65)	(18+)	(18–64)	•	(18–65)	•	•	•	•	(19–65)	•	•
Sex (includes pregnancy or childbirth)	•	•	•	•	•[2]	•[2]	•	•	•	•	•	•	•
Marital status	•	•	•	•	•	•	•[3]	•	•	•	•	•	•
Physical/mental disability	•	•	•	•	•	•	•	•	•	•	•	•	•
Sexual orientation	•[4]	•	•	•	•	•	•	•	•	•	•	•	•
National or ethnic origin (includes linguistic background)	•	•		•[5]	•	•[6]	•[3]	•	•	•	•	•	•
Family status	•	•	•	•	•	•	•					•	•
Dependence on alcohol or drug	•	•[1]	•[1]	•[1]	•[1]	•[1]	•	•[1,7]	•[1]	•[7]			
Ancestry or place of origin		•	•	•	•	•	•	•	•[1]	•		•[5]	•
Political belief		•	•		•	•	•	•	•	•	•	•	•
Based on association				•	•	•	•		•	•		•	•
Pardoned conviction	•					•	•						
Record of criminal conviction		•					•						•
Source of income	•	•	•	•[8]	•	•			•	•	•	•	
Place of residence	•	•			•	•			•			•	
Assignment, attachment, or seizure of pay							•				•		
Social condition/origin							•				•		
Language	•					•	•						•

*Any limitation, exclusion, denial, or preference may be permitted if a bona fide occupational requirement can be demonstrated. Harassment on any of the prohibited grounds is considered a form of discrimination.

1 Complaints accepted based on policy.
2 In Manitoba, includes gender-determined characteristics; in Ontario, includes transgendered persons.
3 Quebec uses the term "civil status."
4 Pursuant to a 1992 Ontario Court of Appeal decision, the Canadian Human Rights Commission now accepts complaints on the grounds of sexual orientation.
5 Defined as nationality.
6 Ontario's code includes both "ethnicity" and "citizenship."
7 Previous dependence only.
8 Defined as "receipt of public assistance."

Source: Compiled from "Prohibited Grounds of Discrimination in Canada," *Canadian Human Rights Commission,* September 2006, http://www.chrc-ccdp.ca/publications/prohibitedgrounds-en.asp.

of the total population).[13] Faced with shortages of skilled workers and with much of the current knowledge base walking out the door, managers will need to find creative solutions to retaining employees and ensuring the transition of organizational knowledge to the next generation of employees. These and other demographic trends, such as a more educated workforce and more women working outside the home, are important because of the impact they're having on current and future HRM practices.

Identifying and Selecting Competent Employees

▶ ▶ ▶ As president and CEO of Scotiabank, Rick Waugh recognizes that providing good service means having good employees.[14] Scotiabank needs to recruit more employees to replace those who move into senior management positions in the next few years.

2. Discuss the tasks associated with identifying and selecting competent employees.

Think About It
How will changes in the age of the population affect how organizations hire people? How can Scotiabank and other organizations respond successfully? Canada is expected to experience a shortage of 1 million skilled workers by 2020, according to the Conference Board of Canada. Aware of these predictions, managers at many companies are developing plans to ensure that they will have enough qualified people to fulfill their human resource needs.

Every organization needs people to do whatever work is necessary for doing what the organization is in business to do. How do organizations get those people? And more importantly, what can they do to ensure that they get competent, talented people? This first phase of the HRM process involves three tasks: human resource planning, recruitment and decruitment, and selection.

Human Resource Planning

Human resource planning is the process by which managers ensure that they have the right number and kinds of people in the right places, and at the right times, who are capable of effectively and efficiently performing the tasks necessary to carry out the organization's strategy. Through planning, organizations can avoid sudden talent shortages and surpluses.[15] Human resource planning can be condensed into two steps: (1) assessing current human resources and (2) assessing future human resource needs and developing a program to meet those future needs.

Human resource planning works together with general management planning to make sure that the goals of the organization can be met. If management is planning an expansion, for instance, human resources needs to determine how to recruit more people. If management is planning downsizing, human resources determines how to lay off people in an efficient manner. If management is planning to introduce new technology, human resources should be examining the training needs required to make sure that the introduction of new technology will go smoothly. A human resource manager who thinks strategically will be sure that the skills and training of employees is consistent with where the organization is planning to go in the future.

human resource planning The process by which managers ensure that they have the right number and kinds of people in the right places, and at the right times, who are capable of effectively and efficiently performing assigned tasks.

Assessing Current Human Resources
Managers begin human resource planning by reviewing the organization's current human resource status, usually through a *human resource inventory*. This information is taken from forms filled out by employees, and includes things such as name, education, training, prior employment, languages spoken, special capabilities, and specialized skills. Many firms have introduced HR management information systems (HRMIS) to track employee information for policy and strategic needs. For instance, these systems can be used for salary and benefits administration. They can also be used to track absenteeism, turnover, and

health and safety data. More strategically, HRMIS can be used to keep track of employee skills and education and to match these to ongoing needs of the organization. The availability of sophisticated databases makes keeping and getting this information quite easy.

Another part of the assessment of current resources is the **job analysis**, which is an assessment that defines jobs and the behaviours necessary to perform them. For instance, what are the duties of a senior accountant who works for Suncor Energy? What knowledge, skills, and abilities are necessary to be able to adequately perform this job? How do these requirements compare with those for a junior accountant or for an accounting manager? Information for a job analysis can be gathered by directly observing or videotaping individuals on the job, interviewing employees individually or in a group, having employees complete a structured questionnaire, having job "experts" (usually managers) identify a job's specific characteristics, or having employees record their daily activities in a diary or notebook.

With information from the job analysis, managers develop or revise job descriptions and job specifications. A **job description** is a written statement of what a jobholder does, how it is done, and why it is done. It typically describes job content, environment, and conditions of employment. A **job specification** states the minimum qualifications that a person must possess to perform a given job successfully. It identifies the human traits, knowledge, skills, and attitudes needed to do the job effectively. The job description and the job specification are both important documents that aid managers in recruiting and selecting employees.

Meeting Future Human Resource Needs

Future human resource needs are determined by the organization's mission, goals, and strategies. Demand for employees is a result of demand for the organization's products or services. On the basis of its estimate of total revenue, managers can attempt to establish the number and mix of employees needed to reach that revenue. In some cases, however, that situation may be reversed. When particular skills are necessary but in short supply, the availability of appropriate human resources determines revenues.

After assessing both current capabilities and future needs, managers can estimate areas in which the organization will be understaffed or overstaffed. Then they're ready to proceed to the next step in the HRM process.

Recruitment and Decruitment

Once managers know their current human resource status and their future needs, they can begin to do something about any shortages or excesses. If one or more vacancies exist, they can use the information gathered through job analysis to guide them in **recruitment**—that is, the process of locating, identifying, and attracting capable applicants.[16] On the other hand, if human resource planning shows a surplus of employees, management may want to reduce the organization's workforce through **decruitment**.[17]

Recruitment

How would you go about recruiting team members to work on a course project?

Potential job candidates can be found through several sources, as Exhibit 12-4 shows.[18] Web-based recruiting, or e-recruiting, has become a popular choice for organizations and applicants. For instance, after the Vancouver Police Department examined the kinds of recruits that would be needed over the next several years, the department decided to launch a recruitment seminar inside Second Life, the online alternative universe. The police recruiters created their own avatars (Second Life personas) dressed "in a specially designed VPD uniform, badge, belt and radio." Inspector Kevin McQuiggen, head of the department's tech crimes division, explains why recruiting on Second Life makes sense: "If people are on Second Life, they're likely to be web-savvy, a quality the police department is looking for in new recruits." The department has seen an increasing number of Internet- and technology-related crimes in

job analysis An assessment that defines jobs and the behaviours necessary to perform them.

job description A written statement of what a jobholder does, how it is done, and why it is done.

job specification A statement of the minimum qualifications that a person must possess to perform a given job successfully.

recruitment The process of locating, identifying, and attracting capable applicants.

decruitment Techniques for reducing the organization's workforce.

Exhibit 12-4

Major Sources of Potential Job Candidates

Source	Advantages	Disadvantages
Internet	Reaches large numbers of people; can get immediate feedback	Generates many unqualified candidates
Employee Referrals	Knowledge about the organization provided by current employee; can generate strong candidates because a good referral reflects on the recommender	May not increase the diversity and mix of employees
Company Website	Wide distribution; can be targeted to specific groups	Generates many unqualified candidates
College/University Recruiting	Large centralized body of candidates	Limited to entry-level positions
Professional Recruiting Organizations	Good knowledge of industry challenges and requirements	Little commitment to specific organization

recent years, and hiring people who can help detect those crimes would be an advantage to the Vancouver police.[19]

Although e-recruiting has been gaining in popularity (Scotiabank, for instance, allows applicants to fill out an information form online and upload their résumé with the form), employers use other recruitment sources as well. Burnaby, BC-based Electronic Arts Canada, following the lead of some other Canadian companies, decided to recruit at universities in recent years to win "the best and the brightest" from computer science programs.[20] Pat York, director of human resources, is pleased with the results, as the interviews have led to hires more than a third of the time.

What recruiting sources have been found to produce superior candidates? The majority of studies have found that employee referrals generally produce the best candidates.[21] The explanation is intuitively logical. First, applicants referred by current employees are prescreened by these employees. Because the recommenders know both the job and the person being recommended, they tend to refer applicants who are well qualified. Also, because current employees often feel that their reputation is at stake with a referral, they tend to refer others only when they are reasonably confident that the referral will not make them look bad.

Decruitment

The other approach to controlling labour supply is through decruitment. Managers gain respect from their employees when termination is handled with transparency, timeliness, fairness, and respect for the individual being terminated. The decruitment options are shown in Exhibit 12-5. Obviously, people can be fired, but other choices may be more beneficial to the organization. Keep in mind that, regardless of the method used to reduce the number of employees in the organization, there is no easy way to do it, even though it may be absolutely necessary.

The Vancouver Police Department has started recruiting through an online presence on Second Life. They created special avatars (shown here) to interview prospective candidates.

Exhibit 12-5

Decruitment Options

Option	Description
Firing	Permanent involuntary termination
Layoffs	Temporary involuntary termination; may last only a few days or extend to years
Attrition	Not filling openings created by voluntary resignations or normal retirements
Transfers	Moving employees either laterally or downward; usually does not reduce costs but can reduce intraorganizational supply–demand imbalances
Reduced Workweeks	Having employees work fewer hours per week, share jobs, or perform their jobs on a part-time basis
Early Retirements	Providing incentives to older and more senior employees for retiring before their normal retirement dates
Job Sharing	Having employees share one full-time position

Selection

Once the recruiting effort has developed a pool of candidates, the next step in the HRM process is to determine who is best qualified for the job. This step is called the **selection process**, the process of screening job applicants to ensure that the most appropriate candidates are hired. Errors in hiring can have far-reaching implications. However, hiring the right people pays off.

What Is Selection?

Selection is an exercise in prediction. It seeks to predict which applicants will be successful if hired. Successful in this case means performing well on the criteria the organization uses to evaluate employees. In filling a sales position, for example, the selection process should be able to predict which applicants will generate a high volume of sales; for a position as a network administrator, it should predict which applicants will be able to effectively oversee and manage the organization's computer network.

Consider, for a moment, that any selection decision can result in four possible outcomes. As shown in Exhibit 12-6, two of these outcomes would be correct, and two would indicate errors.

Exhibit 12-6

Selection Decision Outcomes

		Selection Decision	
		Accept	**Reject**
Later Job Performance	**Successful**	Correct decision	Reject error
	Unsuccessful	Accept error	Correct decision

Karen Flavelle, president of Vancouver-based Purdy's Chocolates, agonizes over new hires because she really wants them to fit in with the company's culture. A search for a new personnel director took three years, until she could find someone who would support "the company's practice of rotating store clerks and plant workers into challenging projects to test their suitability for supervisory and management posts." Most managers at Purdy's are promoted from within.

A decision is correct when the applicant was predicted to be successful and proved to be successful on the job, or when the applicant was predicted to be unsuccessful and would be so if hired. In the first case, we have successfully accepted; in the second case, we have successfully rejected.

Problems arise when errors are made in rejecting candidates who would have performed successfully on the job (reject errors) or accepting those who ultimately perform poorly (accept errors). These problems can be significant. Given today's human resource laws and regulations, reject errors can cost more than the additional screening needed to find acceptable candidates. They can expose the organization to charges of discrimination, especially if applicants from protected groups are disproportionately rejected. The costs of accept errors include the cost of training the employee, the profits lost because of the employee's incompetence, the cost of severance, and the subsequent costs of further recruiting and screening. The major thrust of any selection activity should be to reduce the probability of making reject errors or accept errors while increasing the probability of making correct decisions. How do managers do this? By using selection procedures that are both valid and reliable.

Validity and Reliability

Any selection device that a manager uses should demonstrate **validity**, a proven relationship between the selection device and some relevant job criterion. For example, the law prohibits managers from using a test score as a selection device unless there is clear evidence that, once on the job, individuals with high scores on this test outperform individuals with low test scores. The burden is on managers to show that any selection device they use to differentiate between applicants is related to job performance.

In addition to being valid, a selection device must also demonstrate **reliability**, which indicates whether the device measures the same thing consistently. For example, if a test is reliable, any single individual's score should remain fairly consistent over time, assuming that the characteristics being measured are also stable. No selection device can be effective if it's low in reliability. Using such a device would be like weighing yourself every day on an erratic scale. If the scale is unreliable—randomly fluctuating, say four to seven kilos every time you step on it—the results will not mean much. To be effective predictors, selection devices must possess an acceptable level of consistency.

validity The proven relationship that exists between the selection device and some relevant job criterion.

reliability The ability of a selection device to measure the same thing consistently.

Types of Selection Devices

Managers can use a number of selection devices to reduce accept and reject errors. The best known include application forms, written tests, performance-simulation tests, interviews, background investigations, and, in some cases, physical examinations. Let's briefly review each of these devices. Exhibit 12-7 lists the strengths and weaknesses of each of these devices.[22]

What Works Best and When?

Many selection devices are of limited value to managers in making selection decisions. Exhibit 12-8 summarizes the validity of these devices for particular types of jobs. Managers should use those devices that effectively predict success for a given job.

In addition, managers who treat the recruiting and hiring of employees as if the applicants must be sold on the job and exposed only to an organization's positive characteristics are likely to have a workforce that is dissatisfied and prone to high turnover.[23]

One thing managers need to carefully watch is how they portray their organization and the work that an applicant will be doing. If they tell applicants only the good aspects, they're likely to have a workforce that's dissatisfied and prone to high turnover.[24] Negative

Exhibit 12-7

Selection Devices

Selection Device	Strengths	Weaknesses
Application Forms	Relevant biographical data and facts that can be verified have been shown to be valid performance measures for some jobs. When items on the form have been weighted to reflect job relatedness, this device has proved to be a valid predictor for diverse groups.	Usually only a couple of items on the form prove to be valid predictors of job performance, and then only for a specific job. Weighted-item applications are difficult and expensive to create and maintain.
Written Tests	Tests of intellectual ability, spatial and mechanical ability, perceptual accuracy, and motor ability are moderately valid predictors for many semi-skilled and unskilled lower-level jobs in manufacturing. Intelligence tests are reasonably good predictors for supervisory positions.	Intelligence and other tested characteristics can be somewhat removed from actual job performance, thus reducing their validity.
Performance-Simulation Tests	Tests are based on job analysis data and easily meet the requirement of job relatedness. Tests have proven to be valid predictors of job performance.	They are expensive to create and administer.
Interviews	Interviews must be structured and well organized to be effective predictors. Interviewers must use common questions to be effective predictors.	Interviewers must be aware of the legality of certain questions. Interviews are subject to potential biases, especially if they are not well structured and standardized.
Background Investigations	Verifications of background data are valuable sources of information.	Reference checks are essentially worthless as a selection tool.
Physical Examinations	Physical exams have some validity for jobs with certain physical requirements.	Managers must be sure that physical requirements are job related and do not discriminate.

TIPS FOR MANAGERS

Some Suggestions for Interviewing

↗ Structure a **fixed set of questions** for all applicants.

↗ Have **detailed information about the job** for which applicants are interviewing.

↗ **Minimize any prior knowledge** of applicants' backgrounds, experience, interests, test scores, or other characteristics.

↗ **Ask behavioural questions** that require applicants to give detailed accounts of actual job behaviours.

↗ Use a **standardized evaluation form**.

↗ **Take notes** during the interview.

↗ **Avoid short interviews** that encourage premature decision making.

Source: Based on D. A. DeCenzo and S. P. Robbins, *Human Resource Management*, 7th ed. (New York: Wiley, 2002), p. 200.

things can happen when the information an applicant receives is excessively inflated. First, mismatched applicants probably won't withdraw from the selection process. Second, inflated information builds unrealistic expectations, so new employees may quickly become dissatisfied and leave the organization. Third, new hires become disillusioned and less committed to the organization when they face the unexpected harsh realities of the job. In addition, these individuals may feel that they were misled during the hiring process and then become problem employees.

To increase employee job satisfaction and reduce turnover, managers should consider a **realistic job preview (RJP)**, which includes both positive and negative information about the job and the company. For instance, in addition to the positive comments typically expressed during an interview, the job applicant might be told that there are limited opportunities to talk to co-workers during work hours, that promotional advancement is unlikely, or that work hours are erratic and employees may have to work weekends. Research indicates that applicants who receive an RJP have more realistic expectations about the jobs they'll be performing and are better able to cope with the frustrating elements than are applicants who receive only inflated information.

realistic job preview (RJP) A preview of a job that includes both positive and negative information about the job and the company.

Exhibit 12-8

Quality of Selection Devices as Predictors

	Position			
Selection Device	**Senior Management**	**Middle and Lower Management**	**Complex Nonmanagerial**	**Routine Work**
Application Forms	2	2	2	2
Written Tests	1	1	2	3
Work Sampling	—	—	4	4
Assessment Centres	5	5	—	—
Interviews	4	3	2	2
Verification of Application Data	3	3	3	3
Reference Checks	1	1	1	1
Physical Exams	1	1	1	2

Note: Validity is measured on a scale from 5 (highest) to 1 (lowest). A dash means "not applicable."

Managers can make interviews more valid and reliable by following the approach presented in *Tips for Managers—Some Suggestions for Interviewing*. (See also *Developing Your Interpersonal Skills—Interviewing* on pages 351–352.)

Providing Employees with Needed Skills and Knowledge

3. Explain the different types of orientation and training.

▶ ▶ ▶ Thirty-year-old Roxann Linton is enthusiastic about her career at Scotiabank.[25] "Working with an international and diverse organization like Scotiabank, there are so many opportunities," says Linton. The young woman was chosen for Leading Edge, Scotiabank's fast-track leadership program. In the application process, she had to prepare a challenging business case analysis, go through psychometric testing, and be interviewed twice by a total of eight executives. The Leading Edge program prepares employees for senior management positions by rotating them through a series of assignments.

Linton worked for the bank for about five years in the bank's internal audit department in Kingston, Jamaica. She then transferred to Halifax and worked in commercial banking. During the first 15 months of the Leading Edge program, Linton managed more than 100 people in the electronic banking contact centre. Her next assignment was as director of special projects at Scotia Cassels Investment Counsel, part of the bank's wealth management division. She launched a new corporate bond fund during her first three months on that assignment. She will have one more 12- to 18-month assignment in another part of the bank, and then she can start applying for vice-president positions.

Think About It

What kinds of orientation and training methods do organizations use to help employees develop their skills and learn about their organization?

Organizations have to introduce new members to the work they will do and the organization. They do this through their orientation programs. As time goes by, employees may need to increase their skills. This is handled through training. We review the strategies that organizations use for orientation and training below.

Employee Orientation

Did you participate in some type of organized "introduction to campus life" when you started school? If so, you may have been told about your school's rules and regulations, the procedures for activities such as applying for financial aid, cashing a cheque, or registering for classes, and you were probably introduced to some of the campus administrators. A person starting a new job needs the same type of introduction to his or her job and the organization. This introduction is called **orientation**.

orientation Introduction of a new employee to his or her job and the organization.

There are two types of orientation. *Work unit orientation* familiarizes the employee with the goals of the work unit, clarifies how his or her job contributes to the unit's goals, and includes an introduction to his or her new co-workers. *Organization orientation* informs the new employee about the organization's objectives, history, philosophy, procedures, and rules. This should include relevant human resource policies and benefits such as work hours, pay procedures, overtime requirements, and fringe benefits. In addition, a tour of the organization's work facilities is often part of the organization orientation.

Managers have an obligation to make the integration of the new employee into the organization as smooth and as free of anxiety as possible. They need to openly discuss employee beliefs regarding mutual obligations of the organization and the employee.[26] It's in the best interests of the organization and the new employee to get the person up and running in the job as soon as possible. Successful orientation, whether formal or informal, results in an outsider–insider transition that makes the new member feel comfortable and fairly well adjusted, lowers the likelihood of poor work performance, and reduces the probability of a surprise resignation by the new employee only a week or two into the job.

Training

Employee training is an important HRM activity. As job demands change, employee skills have to be altered and updated. In 2006, US business firms budgeted over $55 billion on workforce formal training.[27] Canadian companies spend far less than American firms on training and development, about $852 per employee compared with $1273 by the Americans in 2006.[28] Managers, of course, are responsible for deciding what type of training employees need, when they need it, and what form that training should take.

MyManagementLab
Q&A 12.7

Types of Training

When organizations invest in employee training, what are they offering? Exhibit 12-9 describes the major types of training that organizations provide.[29] Some of the most popular types of training that organizations provide include sexual harassment, safety, management skills and development, and supervisory skills.[30] For many organizations, employee interpersonal skills training—communication, conflict resolution, team building, customer service, and so forth—is a high priority. For example, Shannon Washbrook, director of training and development for Vancouver-based Boston Pizza International, says, "Our people know the Boston Pizza concept; they have all the hard skills. It's the soft skills they lack." To address that, Washbrook launched Boston Pizza College, a training initiative that uses hands-on, scenario-based learning about many interpersonal skills topics.[31] SaskPower, like Scotiabank, uses training to develop leadership potential, as the following *Management Reflection* shows.

Toronto-based Labatt Breweries is putting its employees through beer school over the next few years. Beer "professors" at Labatt's beer school teach employees how to pour the perfect glass of beer and how to match food with certain beers.

MANAGEMENT REFLECTION

SaskPower Sends Its Leaders to Leadership School

Are leaders made or born? Managers at Regina-based SaskPower believe that leaders are developed, not born.[32] The company has developed a leadership program that is similar to a mini-MBA. It introduces participants to leadership skills and other areas of business. The company selects employees for the program based on leadership potential. Individuals can nominate themselves for the leadership-training program by persuading management with examples of why they would make great managers.

The program works better than the way managers were chosen previously at SaskPower. "It was unorganized, and the 'old boys' network' was still at work," said Bill Hyde, vice-president of human resources. The program also ensures that SaskPower continues to have a skilled workforce and trained managers for the future, when Baby Boomers start retiring in large numbers. ∎

Exhibit 12-9

Types of Training

Type	Includes
General	Communication skills, computer systems application and programming, customer service, executive development, management skills and development, personal growth, sales, supervisory skills, and technological skills and knowledge
Specific	Basic life/work skills, creativity, customer education, diversity/cultural awareness, remedial writing, managing change, leadership, product knowledge, public speaking/presentation skills, safety, ethics, sexual harassment, team building, wellness, and others

Source: Based on "2005 Industry Report—Types of Training," *Training*, December 2005, p. 22.

Training Methods

Is college or university training enough for the workplace, or do you need more?

Although employee training can be done in traditional ways, many organizations are increasingly relying on technology-based training methods because of their accessibility, cost, and ability to deliver information. Web-based or online training had been predicted just a few years ago to become the most popular method of training, but as Julie Kaufman, an industry analyst with Toronto-based IDC Canada, recently told attendees at a training and development conference, it simply has not lived up to expectations. Most organizations have not yet figured out how to make use of this type of training.[33] Exhibit 12-10 provides descriptions of the various traditional and technology-based training methods that managers might use. Of all these training methods, experts believe that organizations will increasingly rely on e-learning applications to deliver important information and to develop employees' skills.

Retaining Competent and High Performance Employees

4. Describe strategies for retaining competent, high-performing employees.

When an organization has invested significant money in recruiting, selecting, orienting, and training employees, it wants to keep those employees, especially the competent, high-performing ones! Two HRM activities that play a role in doing this are managing employee performance and developing an appropriate compensation and benefits program.

Exhibit 12-10
Employee Training Methods

Traditional Training Methods

- *On-the-job*—Employees learn how to do tasks simply by performing them, usually after an initial introduction to the task.

- *Job rotation*—Employees work at different jobs in a particular area, getting exposure to a variety of tasks.

- *Mentoring and coaching*—Employees work with an experienced worker who provides information, support, and encouragement; also called apprenticing in certain industries.

- *Experiential exercises*—Employees participate in role playing, simulations, or other face-to-face types of training.

- *Workbooks/manuals*—Employees refer to training workbooks and manuals for information.

- *Classroom lectures*—Employees attend lectures designed to convey specific information.

Technology-Based Training Methods

- *CD-ROM/DVD/videotapes/audiotapes*—Employees listen to or watch selected media that convey information or demonstrate certain techniques.

- *Videoconferencing/teleconferencing/satellite TV*—Employees listen or participate as information is conveyed or techniques demonstrated.

- *E-learning*—Internet-based learning where employees participate in multimedia simulations or other interactive modules.

Employee Performance Management

> *What techniques might you want to use if you had to evaluate the members of your student project group?*

Managers need to know whether their employees are performing their jobs efficiently and effectively or whether there is need for improvement. Employees are often compensated based on those evaluations. (For more on giving evaluations, see *Self-Assessment—How Good Am I at Giving Performance Feedback?* on pages 347–348)

Evaluating employee performance is part of a **performance management system**, which is a process of establishing performance standards and appraising employee performance in order to arrive at objective human resource decisions, as well as to provide documentation to support those decisions. Performance appraisal is a critical part of a performance management system. Some companies invest far more effort in it than others.

> **performance management system** A process of establishing performance standards and evaluating performance in order to arrive at objective human resource decisions, as well as to provide documentation to support those decisions.

Performance Appraisal Methods

More than 70 percent of managers admit that they have trouble giving a critical performance review to an underachieving employee.[34] Appraising someone's performance is never easy, especially with employees who aren't doing their jobs well, but managers can be better at it by using any of the seven different performance appraisal methods. A description of each of these methods, including advantages and disadvantages, is shown in Exhibit 12-11.

What Happens When Performance Falls Short?

So far, this discussion has focused on the performance management system. But what if an employee is not performing in a satisfactory manner? What can you do?

If, for some reason, an employee is not meeting his or her performance goals, a manager needs to find out why. If it is because the employee is mismatched for the job (a hiring error) or because he or she does not have adequate training, something relatively simple can be done: The manager can either reassign the individual to a job that better matches his or her skills or train the employee to do the job more effectively. If the problem is associated not with the employee's abilities but with his or her desire to do the job, it becomes a **discipline** problem. In that case, a manager can try **employee job counselling** and, if necessary, can take disciplinary action such as verbal and written warnings, suspensions, and even termination.

> **discipline** Actions taken by a manager to enforce an organization's standards and regulations.

> **employee job counselling** A process designed to help employees overcome performance-related problems.

Exhibit 12-11

Advantages and Disadvantages of Performance Appraisal Methods

Method	Advantage	Disadvantage
Written Essays	Simple to use	More a measure of evaluator's writing ability than of employee's actual performance
Critical Incidents	Rich examples; behaviourally based	Time-consuming; lack quantification
Graphic Rating Scales	Provide quantitative data; less time-consuming than others	Do not provide depth of job behaviour assessed
BARS	Focus on specific and measurable behaviours	Time-consuming; difficult to develop job behaviours
Multiperson Comparisons	Compare employees with one another	Unwieldy with large number of employees; legal concerns
MBO	Focuses on end goals; results oriented	Time-consuming
360-Degree Feedback	Thorough	Time-consuming

Compensation and Benefits

MyManagementLab
Q&A 12.8

How would you know whether your employer was paying you fairly?

Most of us expect to receive appropriate compensation from our employer. Developing an effective and appropriate compensation system is an important part of the HRM process.[35] Why? Because it helps attract and retain competent and talented individuals who help the organization accomplish its mission and goals. In addition, an organization's compensation system has been shown to have an impact on its strategic performance.[36]

Managers must develop a compensation system that reflects the changing nature of work and the workplace in order to keep people motivated. Organizational compensation can include many different types of rewards and benefits such as base wages and salaries, wage and salary add-ons, and incentive payments, as well as other benefits and services such as vacation time, extended health care, training allowances, and pensions. Benefits can often amount to one-third or more of an individual's base salary and should be viewed by the employee as part of the total compensation package.

How do managers determine who gets paid $9 an hour and who gets $350 000 a year? Several factors influence the differences in compensation and benefit packages for different employees. Exhibit 12-12 summarizes these factors, which are both job-based and business- or industry-based.

Many organizations use an alternative approach to determining compensation called **skill-based pay**. Under this type of pay system, an employee's job title does not define his or her pay category; skills do.[37] Research shows that this type of pay system seems to be more successful in manufacturing organizations than in service organizations and

skill-based pay A pay system that rewards employees for the job skills and competencies they can demonstrate.

Exhibit 12-12

Factors That Influence Compensation and Benefits

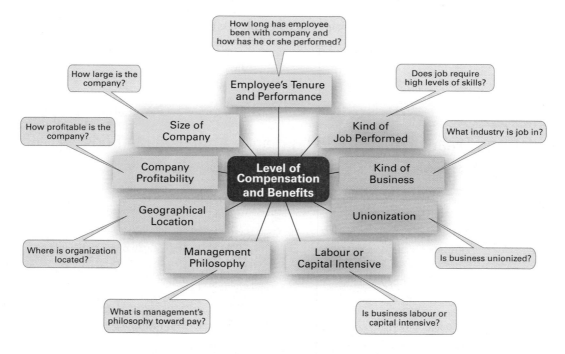

Sources: Based on R. I. Henderson, *Compensation Management*, 6th ed. (Upper Saddle River, NJ: Prentice Hall, 1994), pp. 3–24; and A. Murray, "Mom, Apple Pie, and Small Business," *Wall Street Journal*, August 15, 1994, p. A1.

organizations pursuing technical innovations.[38] Skill-based pay systems seem to mesh nicely with the changing nature of jobs and today's work environment. As one expert noted, "Slowly, but surely, we're becoming a skill-based society where your market value is tied to what you can do and what your skill set is. In this new world where skills and knowledge are what really count, it does not make sense to treat people as jobholders. It makes sense to treat them as people with specific skills and to pay them for these skills."[39] On the other hand, many organizations are using variable pay systems, in which an individual's compensation is contingent on performance—81 percent of Canadian and Taiwanese organizations use variable pay plans, and 78 percent of US organizations do.[40] In Chapter 13, we discuss how pay systems, such as pay-for-performance programs, can be used to motivate employees.

Although many factors influence the design of an organization's compensation system, flexibility is a key consideration. The traditional approach to paying people reflected a time of job stability when an employee's pay was largely determined by seniority and job level. Given the dynamic environments that many organizations face in which the skills that are absolutely critical to organizational success can change in a matter of months, the trend is to make pay systems more flexible and to reduce the number of pay levels. However, whatever approach managers take, they must establish a fair, equitable, and motivating compensation system that allows the organization to recruit and keep a productive workforce.

Career Development

For our purposes, we define a **career** as the sequence of positions held by a person during his or her lifetime.[41] Using this definition, it's apparent that we all have, or will have, a career. Moreover, the concept is as relevant to unskilled labourers as it is to software designers or physicians. But career development is not what it used to be![42]

career A sequence of positions held by a person during his or her lifetime.

The Way It Was

Career development programs were typically designed by organizations to help employees advance their work lives within a specific organization. The focus of such programs was to provide the information, assessment, and training needed to help employees realize their career goals. Career development was also a way for organizations to attract and retain highly talented people. Widespread organizational changes have led to uncertainty about the concept of a traditional organizational career. The individual—not the organization—is responsible for his or her own career! Both organizations and individuals are adjusting to the notion that organizational members have to look out for themselves and become more self-reliant.

Exhibit 12-13

What Do College and University Grads Want from Their Jobs?

Top Factors for Canadian Students	Top Factors for US Students	Top Factors for UK Students
• Opportunities for advancement in position	• Work–life balance	• International career opportunities
• Good people to work with	• Annual base salary	• Flexible working hours
• Good people to report to	• Job stability and security	• Variety of assignments
• Work–life balance	• Recognition for a job done well	• Paid overtime
• Initial salary	• Increasingly challenging tasks	
	• Rotational programs	

Sources: Based on E. Pooley, "Hire Education: How to Recruit Top University Graduates," *Canadian Business*, September 11–24, 2006; S. Shellenbarger, "Avoiding the Next Enron: Today's Crop of Soon-to-Be Grads Seeks Job Security," *Wall Street Journal*, February 16, 2006; "MBAs Eye Financial Services and Management Consulting," *HRMarketer.com*, June 7, 2005; and J. Boone, "Students Set Tighter Terms for Work," *FinancialTimes.com*, May 21, 2005.

TIPS FOR MANAGERS

Some Suggestions for a Successful Management Career

- Develop a **network**.
- Continue **upgrading** your skills.
- Consider **lateral career moves**.
- Stay **mobile**.
- Support your **boss**.
- Find a **mentor**.
- **Don't stay too long** in your first job.
- Stay **visible**.
- Gain control of **organizational resources**.
- Learn the **power structure**.
- Present **the right image**.
- Do **good work**.
- Select your **first job carefully**.

You and Your Career Today

The idea of increased personal responsibility for one's career has been described as a *boundaryless career* in which individuals rather than organizations define career progression, organizational loyalty, important skills, and marketplace value.[43] The challenge for individuals is that there are no norms and few rules to guide them in these new circumstances. Instead, individuals assume primary responsibility for career planning, career goal setting, and education and training.[44]

One of the first career decisions you have to make is a career choice. The optimum career choice is one that offers the best match between what you want out of life and your interests, abilities, and market opportunities. A good career match, then, is one in which you are able to develop a positive self-concept, to do work that you think is important, and to lead the kind of life you desire.[45] Exhibit 12-13 describes the factors Canadian, US, and UK college and university students are looking for in their jobs. As you look at these results, think about what is important to you.

Once you have identified a career choice, it's time to go to work! How do you survive and excel in your career? See *Tips for Managers—Some Suggestions for a Successful Management Career*.[46] By taking an active role in managing your career, your work life can be more exciting, enjoyable, and satisfying.

Contemporary Issues in Managing Human Resources

5. Discuss contemporary issues in managing human resources.

▶ ▶ ▶ Scotiabank prides itself on its work with the Aboriginal community.[47] The bank sponsors scholarships, events, and programs for community members, and also supports Aboriginal business initiatives.

The bank actively recruits from the Aboriginal community. Scotiabank's recruiting strategy is based "on the medicine wheel and the teachings of the medicine wheel, in terms of all the components [of the medicine wheel] need to exist in balance together," says Michele Baptiste, national manager of Aboriginal relations with Scotiabank. The bank has also approached the Aboriginal Human Resource Development Council of Canada to assist "in recruitment and retention of Aboriginal people across the country," according to Baptiste.

Think About It

How are companies managing diversity in their workplaces? To what extent are they addressing issues such as work–life balance? Should they be doing so?

Michele Baptiste, national manager of Aboriginal relations with Scotiabank, created the bank's Aboriginal employment strategy. It is based on the teachings of the medicine wheel (an example of which is shown here). The idea behind the medicine wheel is that the four major components of an individual (mental, spiritual, emotional, physical) have to be in balance. Baptiste emphasizes that Scotiabank takes a holistic approach to Aboriginal relations, bringing together employment, business, and community involvement.

We conclude this chapter by looking at some contemporary human resource issues facing today's managers: managing workforce diversity, dealing with sexual harassment, helping employees manage work–life balance, and managing downsizing.

Workforce Diversity

We have discussed the changing makeup of the workforce in several places throughout this textbook and provided insights in our *Managing Workforce Diversity* feature in several chapters. In this section, we consider how workforce diversity is directly affected by basic HRM activities, including recruitment, selection, and orientation and training.

Recruitment

To improve workforce diversity, managers need to widen their recruiting net. For example, the popular practice of relying on employee referrals as a source of job applicants tends to produce candidates who are similar to present employees. However, some organizations, such as Toronto-based Tele-Mobile (TELUS Mobility), have recruited and hired diverse individuals by relying on referrals from their current employees. But not every organization has the employee resources needed to achieve workforce diversity through employee referrals. Managers may have to look for job applicants in places where they might not have looked before. To increase diversity, managers from such companies as Calgary-based Suncor Energy; Saskatoon-based Cameco; and Toronto-based Scotiabank and TELUS Mobility are increasingly turning to nontraditional recruitment sources such as women's job networks, over-50 clubs, urban job banks, disabled people's training centres, ethnic newspapers, and gay rights organizations. This type of outreach should enable the organization to broaden its pool of diverse applicants. When IKEA went to Seville, Spain, it followed an alternative recruiting strategy, as the following *Management Reflection* shows.

MANAGEMENT REFLECTION
► Focus on International Issues

IKEA Taps into New Labour Force

Should you hire people with no previous experience? When Swedish-based IKEA opened up a store in Seville, its fifth location in Spain, the company decided to search for a different type of employee.[48] The company advertised for "single mothers, students, people with disabilities and long-term unemployed." They did not even require working experience. Andalusia, the region where the store was opening, has an 18.5 percent unemployment rate, and 30 000 applicants responded to IKEA's ads.

Employers in Spain had never recruited from these categories of workers before. IKEA's model for employment is unique: It targets people who really need jobs. The company provides training to its employees to help them overcome any initial hurdles from lack of experience. People with disabilities were hired for customer service, administration, and logistics. Juvencio Maeztu, the store manager, explained the store's hiring policy: "We were more interested in finding people with the right motivation than with the right college degrees."

IKEA's strategy of hiring the previously "unhirable" may well pay off in Spain. With the country's high unemployment rates and IKEA's plan to have 35 stores in Spain by 2015, those in Spain looking for jobs have renewed hope they will be able to find work. ■

Selection

Once a diverse set of applicants exists, efforts must be made to ensure that the selection process does not discriminate. Moreover, applicants need to be made comfortable with the organization's culture and be made aware of management's desire to accommodate their needs. For instance, at TD Canada Trust, managers are trained to respond positively to requests by employees who need a prayer room or whose religions require them to stop working by sundown.[49]

Orientation and Training

The outsider–insider transition is often more challenging for women and minorities than for white males. Many organizations provide special workshops to raise diversity awareness issues. For example, at a Kraft manufacturing facility, managers developed an ambitious diversity program that reflected the increased value the organization had placed on incorporating diverse perspectives. Among other things, they trained more than half of the plant's employees in diversity issues.[50]

Managing Sexual Harassment

Sexual harassment is a serious issue in both public and private sector organizations. A 2001 survey by York University found that 48 percent of working women in Canada reported they had experienced some form of "gender harassment" in the year before they were surveyed.[51] A 1996 RCMP survey found that 6 out of every 10 female Mounties said they had experienced sexual harassment.[52] In 2006, Nancy Sulz, who worked as an RCMP officer in British Columbia, was awarded $950 000 for her complaint against the detachment, which included claims of sexual harassment.[53] Barbara Orser, a research affiliate with the Conference Board of Canada, notes that "sexual harassment is more likely to occur in workplace environments that tolerate bullying, intimidation, yelling, innuendo and other forms of discourteous behaviour."[54] And sexual harassment is not a problem just in Canada. During 2005, more than 12 600 complaints were filed with the US Equal Employment Opportunity Commission (EEOC). Although most complaints are filed by women, the percentage of charges filed by males has risen every year but two since 1992.[55] Sexual harassment is a global issue: Charges have been filed against employers in such countries as Japan, Australia, the Netherlands, Belgium, New Zealand, Sweden, Ireland, and Mexico.[56]

Even though discussions of sexual harassment cases often focus on the large awards granted by a court, there are other concerns for employers. Sexual harassment creates an unpleasant work environment and undermines employees' ability to perform their jobs.

Sexual harassment is defined by the Supreme Court of Canada as unwelcome behaviour of a sexual nature in the workplace that negatively affects the work environment or leads to adverse job-related consequences for the employee.[57] Sexual harassment can occur between members of the opposite sex or of the same sex. Although such activity is generally covered under employment discrimination laws, in recent years this problem has gained more recognition. By most accounts, prior to the mid-1980s this problem was generally viewed as an isolated incident, with the individual at fault being solely responsible (if at all) for his or her actions.

Many problems associated with sexual harassment involve interpreting the Supreme Court's definition to determine exactly what constitutes illegal behaviour. For many organizations, conveying what an offensive or hostile environment looks like is not completely black and white. For instance, while it is relatively easy to focus on problems where an individual employee is harassed, this may not address more systemic problems in the workplace. Other employees can also be negatively affected when they witness offensive conduct.[58] Thus managers at all levels need to be attuned to what makes fellow employees uncomfortable—and if they don't know, they should ask.[59]

What can an organization do to protect itself against sexual harassment claims?[60] The courts want to know two things: Did the organization know about, or should it have known about, the alleged behaviour? and What did management do to stop it? With the number and dollar amounts of the awards against organizations increasing, there is a greater need for management to educate all employees on sexual harassment matters and have mechanisms available to monitor employees. Managers at all levels have a duty to create and maintain a harassment-free work environment. One final area of interest we want to discuss in terms of sexual harassment is workplace romances.

Workplace Romances

If you are employed, have you ever dated someone at work? If not, have you ever been attracted to someone in your workplace and thought about pursuing a relationship? Such

sexual harassment Any unwelcome behaviour of a sexual nature in the workplace that negatively affects the work environment or leads to adverse job-related consequences for the employee.

situations are more common than you might think—40 percent of employees surveyed by the *Wall Street Journal* said that they have had an office romance. And another survey found that 54 percent of single men and 40 percent of single women said they would be open to dating a co-worker.[61] The environment in today's organizations with mixed-gender work teams and working long hours is undoubtedly contributing to this situation. "People realize they're going to be at work such long hours, it's almost inevitable that this takes place," said one survey director. But a workplace romance is something that can potentially become a really big problem for organizations.[62] In addition to the potential conflicts and retaliation between co-workers who decide to stop dating or to end a romantic relationship, the more serious problems stem from the potential for sexual harassment accusations, especially when it's between supervisor and subordinate. The standard used by judicial courts has been that workplace sexual conduct is prohibited sexual harassment *if* it is unwelcome. If it's welcome, it still may be inappropriate, but usually is not unlawful. However, a recent ruling by the California Supreme Court concerning specifically a supervisor–subordinate relationship that got out of hand is worth noting. That ruling said the "completely consensual workplace romances can create a hostile work environment for others in the workplace."[63]

What should organizations do about workplace romances? The best bet is to have some type of policy regarding workplace dating among co-workers, particularly in terms of educating employees about the potential for sexual harassment. However, because possible liability is more serious when it comes to supervisor–subordinate relationships, organizations need to be more proactive in these situations in terms of discouraging such relationships and perhaps even requiring supervisors to report any such relationships to the HR department. At some point, the organization may even want to consider banning such relationships, although an outright ban may be difficult to put into practice.

Managing Work–Life Balance

> *What kinds of work–life balance issues are affecting your life right now?*

Professors Linda Duxbury of the Sprott School of Business at Carleton University and Chris Higgins of the University of Western Ontario are the leading Canadian researchers on the issue of work–life balance. Their research shows that employees are working long hours and are also increasingly being asked to work a number of unpaid hours a week.[64] This affects employees' abilities to manage their family lives.

What kinds of work–life balance issues can arise that might affect an employee's job performance? Here are some examples:

- Is it okay for someone to bring his baby to work because of an emergency crisis with normal child care arrangements?

- Is it okay to expect an employee to work 60 or more hours a week?

- Should an employee be given the day off to watch her child perform in a school event?

In the 1980s, organizations began to recognize that employees don't leave their families and personal lives behind when they walk into work. An organization hires a person who has a personal life outside the office, personal problems, and family commitments. Although managers cannot be sympathetic to every detail of an employee's family life, we *are* seeing organizations more attuned to the fact that employees have sick children, elderly parents who need special care, and other family issues that may require special arrangements. In response, most major organizations have taken actions to make their workplaces more family-friendly by offering **family-friendly benefits**, which include a wide range of work and family programs to help employees.[65] They have introduced programs such as on-site child care, summer day camps, flextime, job sharing, leaves for school functions, telecommuting, and part-time employment.

family-friendly benefits Benefits that accommodate employees' needs for work–life balance.

Does being rigid about not offering flextime harm employers? Surrey, BC, mom Sheila Whitehead thinks so. She quit her job as a marketing manager for a pharmaceuticals company when she could not get the flextime she needed to spend more time with her four-year-old daughter, Abigail, and her other two young children. She says that employers are "missing out on incredibly talented people who simply don't want the rigid nine-to-five hours." Whitehead created a website, **www.beyond9to5.com**, to help match employers with employees who want to have more flexible work hours.

Work–life conflicts are as relevant to male employees with children and women without children as they are for female employees with children. Heavy workloads and increased travel demands, for instance, are making it increasingly hard for many employees, male and female, to meet both work and personal responsibilities. A *Fortune* survey found that 84 percent of male executives surveyed said that "they'd like job options that let them realize their professional aspirations while having more time for things outside work." Also, 87 percent of these executives believed that any company that restructured top-level management jobs in ways that would both increase productivity and make more time available for life outside the office would have a competitive advantage in attracting talented employees.[66] Younger employees, particularly, put a higher priority on family and a lower priority on jobs, and are looking for organizations that give them more work flexibility.[67]

Today's progressive workplace is becoming more accommodating to the varied needs of a diverse workforce. It provides a wide range of scheduling options and benefits that allow employees more flexibility at work and allow employees to better balance or integrate their work and personal lives. Despite these organizational efforts, work–life programs have room for improvement. Workplace surveys still show high levels of employee stress stemming from work–life conflicts. And large groups of women and minority employees remain unemployed or underemployed because of family responsibilities and bias in the workplace.[68] So what can managers do?

Research on work–family life balance has provided some new insights. For instance, we are beginning to see evidence that there are positive outcomes when individuals are able to combine work and family roles.[69] As a participant in a recent study noted, "I think being a mother and having patience and watching someone else grow has made me a better manager. I am better able to be patient with other people and let them grow and develop in a way that is good for them."[70] In addition, individuals who have family-friendly workplace support appear to be more satisfied on the job.[71] This finding seems to strengthen the notion that organizations benefit by creating a workplace in which employee work–family life balance is possible. And the benefits show up in financial results as well. Research has shown a significant, positive relationship between work–family initiatives and an organization's stock price.[72]

However, managers need to understand that people do differ in their preferences for work–family life scheduling options and benefits.[73] Some people prefer organizational initiatives that better *segment* work from their personal lives. Others prefer programs that facilitate *integration*. For instance, flextime schedules segment because they allow employees to schedule work hours that are less likely to conflict with personal responsibilities. On the other hand, on-site child care integrates by blurring the boundaries between work and family responsibilities. People who prefer segmentation are more likely to be satisfied and committed to their jobs when offered options such as flextime, job sharing, and part-time hours. People who prefer integration are more likely to respond positively to options such as on-site child care, gym facilities, and company-sponsored family picnics.

Helping Survivors Respond to Layoffs

Downsizing is the planned elimination of jobs in an organization. When an organization has too many employees—which can happen when it needs to cut costs, is faced with declining market share, or has grown too aggressively—one option for shoring up profits is by eliminating some of those surplus employees through downsizing. Well-known companies such as Air Canada, Nortel, Shaw Communications, Domtar, BCE, and GM Canada and others have had to downsize in recent years.[74] How can managers best manage a downsized workplace? Expect disruptions in the workplace and in employees' personal lives. Stress, frustration, anxiety, and anger are typical reactions of both individuals being laid off and the job survivors. But are there things managers can do to lessen the pain? Yes.[75]

Open and honest communication is critical. Individuals who are being let go need to be informed as soon as possible. In providing assistance to employees being downsized, the law requires some form of severance pay in lieu of proper notice. Benefit extensions to help employees while they find new plans must also be covered for a specified period of time. Managers need to be sure they're following any laws that might affect the length of time pay and benefits must be offered and the types of pay and benefits that must be provided. In addition, many organizations provide job search assistance.

It may surprise you to learn that both victims and survivors experience feelings of frustration, anxiety, and loss.[76] But layoff victims get to start over with a clean slate and a clear conscience. Survivors don't. A new syndrome seems to be popping up in more and more organizations: **layoff-survivor sickness**, a set of attitudes, perceptions, and behaviours of employees who survive involuntary staff reductions.[77] Symptoms include job insecurity, perceptions of unfairness, guilt, depression, stress from increased workload, fear of change, loss of loyalty and commitment, reduced effort, and an unwillingness to do anything beyond the required minimum.

To address this survivor syndrome, managers may want to provide opportunities for employees to talk to counsellors about their guilt, anger, and anxiety.[78] Group discussions can also provide an opportunity for the survivors to vent their feelings. Some organizations have used downsizing as the spark to implement increased employee participation programs such as empowerment and self-managed work teams. In short, to keep morale and productivity high, every attempt should be made to ensure that those individuals who are still working in the organization know that they are needed and valuable.

downsizing The planned elimination of jobs in an organization.

layoff-survivor sickness A set of attitudes, perceptions, and behaviours of employees who remain after involuntary employee reductions; it includes insecurity, guilt, depression, stress, fear, loss of loyalty, and reduced effort.

SUMMARY AND IMPLICATIONS

1. Understand how managing human resources well contributes to the success of the organization. Studies show that an organization's human resources can be a significant competitive advantage. Often, employees are thought of as costs to be minimized or avoided. However, when employees are considered partners, they are more likely to be motivated, leading to greater organizational performance.

▶ ▶ ▶ Scotiabank is often rated as one of Canada's top employers and as a good place for women to work.

2. Discuss the tasks associated with identifying and selecting competent employees. Human resource managers do a human resource inventory to discover what skills and capabilities current employees have. They map that inventory against what might be needed in the future, based on the organization's mission, goals, and strategies. Organizations first need to assess their current and future needs for employees, to make sure they have enough of the right people to accomplish the organization's goals. When selecting new employees, organizations need to determine whether potential employees will be successful once they are on the job. To do this, managers use application forms, written tests, performance-simulation tests, interviews, background investigations, and, in some cases, physical examinations to screen employees. Managers need to make sure that they do not engage in discrimination in the hiring process.

▶ ▶ ▶ Because President and CEO Rick Waugh would like to see more women in senior management positions, Scotiabank needs to assess which of its female employees have the skills and leadership qualities to move into senior management. One way that Scotiabank identifies potential employees is through applications from its Careers webpage, which targets young graduates and encourages them to think about working for the bank.

3. Explain the different types of orientation and training. Organizations, particularly larger ones, have orientation programs for new employees. The orientation introduces the new employee to his or her job and to the organization. As job demands change, employees may need to have their skills updated through training programs. Companies use a variety of training methods, from on-the-job training to classroom work to technology-based training.

▶ ▶ ▶ Among other programs, Scotiabank has Leading Edge, the bank's fast-track leadership program.

4. Describe strategies for retaining competent, high-performing employees. Organizations develop compensation and benefit programs that will motivate employees to achieve high performance. Many organizations have implemented skill-based pay systems, which reward employees for the job skills and competencies they can demonstrate. A career is the sequence of positions held by a person during his or her lifetime. Career development programs used to be created by organizations to help employees advance within the organization. Today, employees are encouraged to create their own development programs, in addition to whatever their companies provide, because often employees work for multiple organizations during their careers. Thus, more responsibility rests on employees to manage their own careers.

5. Discuss contemporary issues in managing human resources. The major current issues in human resource management include managing workforce diversity, dealing with sexual harassment and workplace romances, helping employees manage work–life balance, and managing downsizing.

▶ ▶ ▶ Scotiabank prides itself on its work with the Aboriginal community, sponsoring scholarships, events, and programs for community members and also supporting Aboriginal business initiatives. The bank also permits flex hours, flex days, job sharing, and telecommuting so that employees can find the right "work life" to match their personal needs.

Management @ Work

READING FOR COMPREHENSION

1. Describe the environmental factors that most directly influence the human resource management process.

2. Contrast reject errors and accept errors. Which are more likely to open an employer to charges of discrimination? Why?

3. What is the relationship between job analysis, recruitment, and selection?

4. What are the major problems of the interview as a selection device?

5. What are the benefits and drawbacks of realistic job previews? (Consider this question from the perspective of both the organization and the employee.)

6. How are orientation and employee training alike? How are they different?

7. Describe three performance appraisal methods, as well as the advantages and disadvantages of each.

8. What is skill-based pay?

9. How do recruitment, selection, orientation, and training directly affect workforce diversity?

LINKING CONCEPTS TO PRACTICE

1. How does human resource management affect all managers?

2. Are there limits on how far a prospective employer should delve into an applicant's personal life by means of interviews or tests? Explain.

3. Should an employer have the right to choose employees without government interference in the hiring process? Explain your position.

4. Studies show that women's salaries still lag behind men's, and even with equal opportunity laws and regulations women are paid about 73 percent of what men are paid. How would you design a compensation system that would address this issue?

5. What drawbacks, if any, do you see in implementing flexible benefits? (Consider this question from the perspective of both the organization and the employee.)

6. What, in your view, constitutes sexual harassment? Describe how companies can minimize sexual harassment in the workplace.

SELF-ASSESSMENT

How Good Am I at Giving Performance Feedback?

For each of the following pairs, identify the statement that most closely matches what you normally do when you give feedback to someone else.[79]

1. a. Describe the behaviour. | **b.** Evaluate the behaviour.

2. a. Focus on the feelings that the behaviour evokes. | **b.** Tell the person what he or she should be doing differently.

3. a. Give specific instances of the behaviour. | **b.** Generalize.

4. a. Deal only with behaviour that the person can control. | **b.** Sometimes focus on something the person can do nothing about.

5. a. Tell the person as soon as possible after the behaviour. | **b.** Sometimes wait too long.

6. a. Focus on the effect the behaviour has on me. | **b.** Try to figure out why the individual did what he or she did.

7. a. Balance negative feedback with positive feedback. | **b.** Sometimes focus only on the negative.

8. a. Do some soul searching to make sure that the reason I am giving the feedback is to help the other person or to strengthen our relationship. | **b.** Sometimes give feedback to punish, win, or dominate the other person.

Scoring Key

Total the number of "a" responses, and then total the number of "b" responses, and then form an a/b ratio. For instance, if you have 6 "a" responses and 2 "b" responses, your a/b ratio would be 6/2.

Analysis and Interpretation

Along with listening skills, feedback skills compose the other primary component of effective communication. This instrument is designed to assess how good you are at providing feedback.

In this assessment instrument, the "a" responses are your self-perceived strengths and the "b" responses are your self-perceived weaknesses. By looking at the proportion of your "a" and "b" responses, you will be able to see how effective you feel you are when giving feedback and determine where your strengths and weaknesses lie.

More Self-Assessments MyManagementLab

To learn more about your skills, abilities, and interests, go to the MyManagementLab website and take the following self-assessments:

- I.B.3.—How Satisfied Am I with My Job?
- III.B.3.—Am I Experiencing Work–Family Conflict?
- IV.G.2.—How Much Do I Know About HRM?

MANAGEMENT FOR YOU TODAY

Dilemma

Your instructor has asked class members to form teams to work on a major class project. You have worked on teams before and have not always been pleased with the results. This time you are determined to have a good team experience. You have reason to believe that how people are recruited to and selected for teams might make a difference.

You also know that evaluating performance and giving feedback are important. You have heard that training can make a difference as well. With all of this in mind, write up a plan that indicates how you might recruit an excellent set of team members and make sure that they perform well throughout.

Becoming a Manager

- Using the Internet, research different companies that interest you and check out what they say about careers or their people.
- If you are working, note what types of human resource management activities your managers do. What do they do that seems to be effective? Ineffective? What can you learn from this?

- Do career research in your chosen career by finding out what it's going to take to be successful in that career.
- Complete this chapter's *Developing Your Interpersonal Skills—Interviewing* on pages 351–352 and *Developing Your Interpersonal Skills—Becoming More Culturally Aware* on pages 93–94, in Chapter 3.

WORKING TOGETHER: TEAM-BASED EXERCISE

Recruiting for Diversity

You work as director of human resources for a gift registry website based in Toronto. Your company currently has 30 employees, but due to the popularity of your site, the company is growing rapidly. To handle customer demand, at least 30 additional employees are going to be needed in the next three months. In filling those positions, the company's CEO is committed to increasing employee diversity because she feels that this will add unique perspectives on the types of gift services provided by the company. She has asked you to head up a team to propose some specific practices for recruiting diverse individuals.

Form teams of three or four individuals. Identify specific steps that your company can take to recruit diverse individuals. Be creative and be specific. Write down your proposed steps and be prepared to share your ideas with the class.

Ethical Dilemma Exercise: "But I Deserve an A!"

Everybody wants an A ranking; nobody wants a C ranking.[80] Yet the multiperson ranking system used by Goodyear Tire & Rubber Company forced managers to rank 10 percent of the workforce as A performers, 80 percent as B performers, and 10 percent as C performers. Those ranked as A performers were rewarded with promotions; those ranked as C performers were told they could be demoted or fired for a second C rating. Goodyear abandoned its 10-80-10 system just before some C employees who had been fired filed a lawsuit claiming age discrimination. "It is very unfair to start with the assumption that a certain percentage of your employees are unsatisfactory," said one of the plaintiffs. "It was very subjective and designed to weed out the older people."

Like Goodyear, a growing number of companies have followed the lead of General Electric in regularly ranking employees. Many companies give poor performers an opportunity to improve before taking action. However, critics say the ranking system forces managers to penalize employees on poorly performing teams. They also say the ranking system can lead to age, gender, or race discrimination. In response, companies are training managers to use more objective measures for appraisals, such as monitoring progress toward preset goals.

Imagine that you are a General Electric executive who must rank 20 percent of your subordinate managers as top performers, 70 percent as average, and 10 percent as needing improvement. Retaining incompetent or unmotivated managers is unfair to the rest of the staff and sends mixed signals. On the other hand, even if all your managers are competent, you must put 10 percent into the bottom category. Now it's appraisal time and you do not feel that any of your employees deserve to be in the bottom category. What should you do? (Review Exhibit 12-11 on page 337 as you consider this ethical challenge.)

Thinking Critically About Ethics

What you say online *can* come back to haunt you. Organizations are using Google, MySpace, and Facebook to check out applicants and current employees. In fact, some organizations see Google as a way to get "around discrimination laws, inasmuch as employers can find out all manner of information—some of it for a nominal fee—that is legally off-limits in interviews: your age, your marital status, fraternity pranks, stuff you wrote in college, political affiliations and so forth." And for those individuals who like to rant and rave about employers, there might be later consequences. That is why some individuals pull their Facebook profiles. What do you think of what these companies are doing? What positives and negatives are there to such behaviour? What are the ethical implications? What guidelines might you suggest for an organization's selection process?

Mitsubishi Motors North America

When Rich Gilligan took over as plant manager at Mitsubishi Motors North America's (MMNA) manufacturing facility in Normal, Illinois, in 1998, the plant had two notorious distinctions: It was one of the most automated yet least productive plants in the industry, and it was known as the place sued by the US government for the sexual harassment of its female employees.[81] That lawsuit was what most people knew about Mitsubishi Motors.

The high-profile case told the story of a dismal workplace: "sexual graffiti written on fenders about to pass female line employees; pornographic pictures taped on walls; male employees taunting women with wrenches and air compressors; women asked by male employees to bare their breasts; other women fondled; and women who complained of being fired or passed over for promotion." Almost from the beginning, the plant had a bad reputation regarding the employment of women. People in the local community looked with suspicion at plant employees. One of the shift managers said, "We had guys who had no bad marks asked to stop coaching girls' softball teams just because they worked at that plant." After numerous employee complaints, the Equal Employment Opportunity Commission (EEOC) entered the picture and filed suit on behalf of 500 female employees, charging the company with sexual harassment. The case dragged on for three years, further draining employee morale and damaging an already distant relationship between American employees and Japanese managers. That is the environment that Gilligan inherited.

Right before Gilligan was hired, MMNA settled the EEOC lawsuit for more than $44 million (US)—still the largest sexual harassment settlement in US history. The money was distributed to more than 400 women, many of whom still work at the plant. The EEOC settlement also dictated a makeover of the work environment.

Gilligan needs to change the culture of the plant, and improve productivity and quality. He knows that Mitsubishi's mission statement is "We are a spirited, diverse workforce. We are a culture that looks for, and rewards, hard work and dedication. We are winners." Although each member of the Mitsubishi Group is independent, they are supposed to share the guiding principles of the Sankoryo, first announced in the 1930s by founder Koyata Iwasaki and revised to reflect today's realities:

- *Shoki Hoko:* Strive to enrich society, both materially and spiritually, while contributing toward the preservation of the environment.
- *Shoji Komei:* Maintain principles of transparency and openness, conducting business with integrity and fairness.
- *Ritsugyo Boeki:* Expand business, based on an all-encompassing global perspective.

Conduct like this is not what was happening at MMNA as Gilligan took over. What could Gilligan do to improve the culture and increase productivity?

Busted

Like many other companies today, Scott's Miracle-Gro is facing the dilemma of persuading employees to take better care of themselves without diminishing employee morale or getting hit with employee lawsuits. It's on the leading edge of companies looking to monitor and change employee behaviour. But sometimes that edge can be razor sharp.[82]

Scott's Miracle-Gro's CEO, Jim Hagedorn, acknowledges that his company's wellness program is controversial. In 2000, he, like many other CEOs, watched as his company's health care costs skyrocketed. No help was in sight from either the US government or the health insurance industry, and the company's employees were, he said, "bingeing on health care." By February 2003, workers' health care insurance premiums had doubled, and employee morale had plummeted. Following his usual tell-it-like-it-is style, Hagedorn confronted the issue head-on with employees. He wanted them to know what they were up against: 20 percent of the company's net profits were going to health care. The company's health-risk assessment showed that half of the 6000 employees were overweight or morbidly obese and one-quarter of the employees smoked. After seeing a CNN program late one night in which a doctor was arguing that employers needed to get serious about employee obesity, smoking, and diabetes, Hagedorn knew what he had to do. Despite the late hour, he immediately called his HR chief and told her that he wanted to ban smoking and tackle obesity.

Getting that done wasn't so easy. The legal department worried that the plan might violate federal laws. Other advisers told Hagedorn not to do it or that he was moving too fast. But he wasn't easily dissuaded. He found a law firm that helped determine that in 21 states (including the company's home base in Ohio), it wasn't illegal to hire and fire people based on their smoking habits. Hagedorn also implemented a company-wide wellness program but realized that he needed a third party to run it so managers couldn't discriminate against employees based on their health.

Today, Scott's Miracle-Gro employees are encouraged to take exhaustive health-risk assessments. Those who don't pay $40 per month more in premiums. Each employee found to be at moderate to high risk is assigned to and works closely with a health coach. Those who don't comply pay an additional $67 per month on top of the $40. Many employees find the policy intrusive, but Hagedorn hasn't budged. He's adamant about bringing down health care costs and getting employees all the help they need to be healthy and lead healthier lives. One employee who was fired on his 30th birthday because he failed a drug test for nicotine use is suing the company. (The lawsuit is still proceeding through the court system.) However, another employee who was prodded by his health coach to see a doctor had his life saved when surgeons found a 95 percent blockage in his heart that would have killed him within five days without the stents that were inserted.

Discussion Questions

1. What do you think about Hagedorn's approach to controlling employee health care costs? Do you agree with it? Why or why not?

2. What benefits and drawbacks are there to this type of wellness program for (a) employees and (b) the company?

3. Research company wellness programs. What types of things are companies doing to encourage employee wellness? Are there any programs you found that you might recommend Hagedorn implement? Describe.

DEVELOPING YOUR INTERPERSONAL SKILLS

Interviewing

About the Skill

The interview is used almost universally as part of the employee selection process. Not many of us have ever gotten a job without having gone through one or more interviews. Interviews can be valid and reliable selection tools, but they need to be structured and well organized.

Steps in Developing the Skill

You can be an effective interviewer if you use the following seven suggestions for interviewing job candidates:[83]

1. **Review the job description and job specification.** Be sure that prior to the interview, you have reviewed pertinent information about the job. Why? Because this will provide you with valuable information on which to assess the job candidate. Furthermore, knowing the relevant job requirements will help eliminate interview bias.

2. **Prepare a structured set of questions you want to ask all job applicants.** By having a set of prepared questions, you ensure that you will get the information you want. Furthermore, by asking similar questions, you are able to better compare all candidates' answers against a common base.

3. **Before meeting a candidate, review his or her application form and résumé.** By doing this, you will be able to create a complete picture of the candidate in terms of what is represented on the résumé or application and what the job requires. You can also begin to identify areas to explore during the interview; that is, areas that are not clearly defined on the résumé or application but that are essential to the job can become a focal point in your discussion with the candidate.

4. **Open the interview by putting the applicant at ease and by providing a brief preview of the topics to be discussed.** Interviews are stressful for job candidates. Opening the discussion with small talk, such as the weather, can give the candidate time to adjust to the interview setting. By providing a preview of topics to come, you are giving the candidate an agenda. This helps the candidate begin framing what he or she will say in response to your questions.

5. **Ask your questions and listen carefully to the candidate's answers.** Select follow-up questions that flow naturally from the answers given. Focus on the candidate's responses as they relate to information

you need to ensure that the person meets your job requirements. If you are still uncertain, use a follow-up question to probe further for information.

6. **Close the interview by telling the applicant what is going to happen next.** Applicants are anxious about the status of your hiring decision. Be upfront with candidates regarding others who will be interviewed and the remaining steps in the hiring process. Let the person know your time frame for making a decision. In addition, tell the applicant how you will notify him or her about your decision.

7. **Write your evaluation of the applicant while the interview is still fresh in your mind.** Don't wait until the end of the day, after interviewing several people, to write your analysis of each person. Memory can (and often will) fail you! The sooner you write your impressions after an interview, the better chance you have of accurately noting what occurred in the interview and your perceptions of the candidate.

Practising the Skill

Read the following list and do the actions. Be sure to refer to the seven suggestions for conducting effective interviews.

1. Break into groups of three.

2. Take up to 10 minutes to compose five challenging job interview questions that you think should be relevant in the hiring of new graduates for a sales-management training program at Kraft Canada. Each hiree will spend 18 to 24 months as a sales representative calling on retail grocery and restaurant accounts. After this training period, successful performers can be expected to be promoted to the position of district sales supervisor.

3. Exchange your five questions with another group.

4. Each group should allocate one of the following roles to their three members: interviewer, applicant, and observer. The person playing the applicant should rough out a brief résumé of his or her background and experience and then give it to the interviewer.

5. Role play a job interview. The interviewer should include, but not be limited to, the five questions provided by the other group.

6. After the interview, the observer should evaluate the interviewer's behaviour in terms of the effective interview suggestions.

Reinforcing the Skill

The following activities will help you practise and reinforce the skills associated with interviewing:

1. On your campus, there is probably a job and career placement service provided for graduates. If possible, talk with two or three graduating students who have been interviewed by organizations through this campus service. Ask them to share what happened during their interviews. Then write a brief report describing what you found out and comparing the students' experiences with the suggestions for effective interviewing.

2. Interview a manager about the interview process he or she uses in hiring new employees. What types of information does the manager try to get during an interview? (Be sure that as you interview this manager, you are using the suggestions for good interviewing! Although you are not "hiring" this person, you are looking for information, which is exactly what managers are looking for during a job interview.)

MyManagementLab

For more resources, please visit www.pearsoned.ca/mymanagementlab

SCAN THIS

Managing Change and Innovation

Change is a constant for organizations and thus for managers. Because change can't be eliminated, managers must learn how to manage it successfully. Innovation is often closely tied to an organization's change efforts; thus, managers must know how to manage it as well. After reading and studying this chapter, you will achieve the following learning outcomes.

Learning Outcomes

1 Describe the forces that create the need for change.

2 Compare and contrast views of the change process.

3 Classify types of organizational change.

4 Explain how to manage resistance to change.

5 Describe techniques for stimulating innovation.

6 Discuss contemporary issues in managing change.

▶ ▶ ▶ By late 2006, Yahoo! was starting to lose its top position in providing web services to Internet users, facing stiff competition for visitors and advertisers from Google, Microsoft's MSN, America Online, and even MySpace.[1] Yahoo!'s shares were slumping, revenue growth was slowed, staff were leaving in alarming numbers, and a crucial project, code-name "Panama" (search marketing/campaign management software) was delayed. In 2005, Yahoo! and Google had the same market share, about 19 percent. A year later, Google's market share was about 25 percent of US online ad revenue, and Yahoo!'s had fallen to 18 percent.

In a memo that has been called "The Peanut Butter Manifesto," a Yahoo! senior vice-president, Brad Garlinghouse, expressed his concern to Yahoo!'s top executives that Yahoo! was losing ground. Garlinghouse argued that Yahoo! was spreading its resources too thin, "Thus we focus on nothing in particular." He recommended that the company undergo a deep reorganization, lay off 15 to 20 percent of the workforce, and make executives accountable for poor performance.

Industry analysts noted that Yahoo! lost its focus in 2005 and 2006, missing opportunities taken by YouTube,

Facebook, and MySpace. "Yahoo! had every single asset you would have needed to do those bigger, faster and sooner than anyone else," said Rob Norman, CEO of the WPP Group's GroupM Interaction unit, whose clients buy Yahoo! advertising.

About eight months after "The Peanut Butter Manifesto" was written, Yahoo! finally made a change industry analysts hoped would make the difference. On June 18, 2007, Terry Semel stepped down as Yahoo! CEO. In his place, the company appointed Jerry Yang, one of Yahoo!'s co-founders, as CEO and Susan Decker as president. High hopes were placed on the two to "cut through the bureaucracy and indecision" and lead Yahoo! back to the front of the pack. Six months later, Microsoft made an unsolicited bid to take over Yahoo! and in 2009 Jerry Yang was replaced as CEO by Carol Bartz.[2]

SCAN THIS

Think About It

Can large organizations be innovative at the same speed as smaller organizations? Put yourself in Jerry Yang's shoes. You are faced with major competition from several newer, smaller, and innovative organizations. Meanwhile, Yahoo! has grown so bureaucratic in recent years that it has stopped acting rapidly in the face of opportunities. How would you go about making Yahoo! respond more quickly?

Big companies and small businesses, universities and colleges, and governments at all levels are being forced to significantly change the way they do things. Although change has always been a part of the manager's job, it has become even more important in recent years. In this chapter, we describe why change is important and how managers can manage change. Since change is often closely tied to an organization's innovation efforts, we also discuss ways in which managers can stimulate innovation and increase their organization's adaptability. Then, we conclude by looking at some current issues in managing change.

Forces for Change

1. Describe the forces that create the need for change.

If it were not for change, the manager's job would be relatively easy. Planning would be simple because tomorrow would be no different from today. The issue of effective organizational design would also be solved because the environment would be free from uncertainty and there would be no need to adapt. Similarly, decision making would be dramatically streamlined because the outcome of each alternative could be predicted with almost certain accuracy. It would, indeed, simplify the manager's job if, for example, competitors did not introduce new products or services, if customers did not demand new and improved products, if government regulations were never modified, or if employees' needs never changed. But that is not the way it is. Change is an organizational reality[3] and managing change is an integral part of every manager's job. In Chapter 2, we pointed out the external and internal forces that constrain managers. These same forces also bring about the need for change. Let's briefly look at these forces.

External Forces

Are there external factors that might suggest to you that your college or university might think about doing things differently?

The external forces that create the need for change come from various sources. In recent years, the *marketplace* has affected firms such as Yahoo! as competition from Google, MySpace, and Ask Jeeves has intensified. These companies constantly adapt to changing consumer desires as they develop new search capabilities.

Government laws and regulations are a frequent impetus for change. For example, the Canadian Securities Administrators rules, which came into effect in March 2004, require Canadian companies to change the way they disclose financial information and to carry out corporate governance.

Technology also creates the need for change. For example, technological improvements in diagnostic equipment have created significant economies of scale for hospitals. Assembly-line technology in other industries is changing dramatically as organizations replace human labour with robots. In the greeting card industry, email and the Internet have changed the way people exchange greeting cards. Technological change from analog to digital recording has meant the shift from records to CDs, videotapes to DVDs, and film to digital cameras. In just 10 years, DVD players went from the test stage to virtually eliminating the videotape rental market. The companies that produced videotapes and the companies that rented them had to develop new strategies or go out of business.

The fluctuation in *labour markets* also forces managers to change. Organizations that need certain kinds of employees must change their human resource management activities to attract and retain skilled employees in the areas of greatest need. For instance, health care organizations facing severe nursing shortages have had to change the way they schedule work hours.

Profound changes taking place in the Chinese economy are creating labour shortages at hundreds of factories, as seen in the many public job postings at this location in Shenzhen, China. Managers around the world must expect that wages in China may go up as the middle class continues to grow, which will have an impact on the price of manufacturing goods. Some international companies are already considering moving to lower-wage countries such as Vietnam.

Economic changes, of course, affect almost all organizations. For instance, global recessionary pressures force organizations to become more cost efficient. But even in a strong economy, uncertainties about interest rates, federal budget deficits, and currency exchange rates create conditions that may force organizations to change.

Internal Forces

In addition to the external forces just described, internal forces also create the need for change. These internal forces tend to originate primarily from the internal operations of the organization or from the impact of external changes.

A redefinition or modification of an organization's *strategy* often introduces a host of changes. For instance, when Steve Bennett took over as CEO of Intuit (Quicken, QuickBooks, and QuickTax are its best-known products), the company was losing money. By orchestrating a series of well-planned and dramatic strategic changes, he turned Intuit into a profitable company with extremely committed employees, as the following *Management Reflection* shows.

MANAGEMENT REFLECTION
► Focus on Innovation

Steve Bennett Transforms Intuit

Can a company stay entrepreneurial and become more structured? When Steve Bennett was hired as Intuit's CEO in 2000, he had never worked for a high-tech firm.[4] He had spent his entire career with General Electric. Intuit's founder, Scott Cook, was looking for someone who could take Intuit to the next level. The company was struggling to break through the $1 billion (US) revenue wall, and Cook wanted the company to reach $10 billion (US) in revenue.

After he was hired, Bennett spent five weeks interviewing employees at many of Intuit's locations. He found a company still being run as haphazardly as a start-up venture. "The operation was a mess. It was losing money. Its technology was outdated. Execution was grindingly slow, and nothing was documented."[5] He discovered the organization had a democratic culture that nurtured employees to make sure they felt good. Managers chose whatever brand of PC they wanted to use, the employees were always holding meetings, and different units were responsible for the same product's development and sales support. Bennett felt the employees had to change how they viewed their work: "I wanted them to know that a company can be focused on high performance and still be a good place to work," he says.

Bennett introduced a number of changes, including putting business units in charge of development and customer service, introducing zero-based budgeting, and ordering the same computers for everyone to manage costs. He also flattened the organization, taking on 18 direct reports, rather than 8, so that he could drive change faster. "If you have that many direct reports, you don't have time to meddle in their business. My job is to conduct the orchestra, not to play all the instruments." He also introduced a new motto: "Mind your minutes." Employees were not to be involved in endless meetings, and they were to focus on the things that were really important. ■

In addition, an organization's *workforce* is rarely static. Its composition changes in terms of age, education, ethnic background, sex, and so forth. Take, for instance, an organization in which a large number of seasoned executives, because of financial reasons, decide to continue working instead of retiring. There might be a need to restructure jobs in order to retain and motivate younger managers. Also, the compensation and benefits system might need to be adapted to reflect the needs of this older workforce.

The introduction of new *equipment* represents another internal force for change. Employees may have their jobs redesigned, need to undergo training on how to operate the new equipment, or be required to establish new interaction patterns within their work group.

Finally, *employee attitudes* such as job dissatisfaction may lead to increased absenteeism, more voluntary resignations, and even labour strikes. Such events often lead to changes in management policies and practices.

Two Views of the Change Process

▶ ▶ ▶ For years, Yahoo!, which helped give birth to the commercial Internet in 1994, dominated the Internet services market.[6] Through 2004, things were going well for the company, but then it started to lose its competitive edge.

The company, well known for its banner and video ads, was targeted by both Google (who bought online ad firm DoubleClick) and Microsoft (who bought digital marketing firm aQuantive). Yahoo! tried to make a deal with Facebook but was not successful, while Google bought the leading video-sharing site, YouTube. Yahoo!'s response to competition has been comparatively slow, although it did buy 80 percent of advertising network RightMedia in April 2007.[7]

Because Yahoo! delayed its response to competition from Google, it faced a bigger challenge. In 2007, Google was worth $160 billion (US) on the stock market while Yahoo!'s shares were worth only $37 billion (US). Moreover, Yahoo! was facing a hostile takeover from Microsoft in early 2008 for $44.6 billion (US) that was subsequently rejected. In 2011, Yahoo had market value of $22.4 billion (US).[8]

Think About It

How does change happen in organizations? Is change a constant process, or can organizations take breaks from worrying about change, as Yahoo! seems to have done in the last few years?

2. Compare and contrast views of the change process.

We can use two very different metaphors to describe the change process.[9] One metaphor envisions the organization as a large ship crossing calm waters. The ship's captain and crew know exactly where they are going because they have made the trip many times before. Change comes in the form of an occasional storm, a brief distraction in an otherwise calm and predictable trip. In the other metaphor, the organization is seen as a small raft navigating a raging river with uninterrupted white-water rapids. Aboard the raft are half a dozen people who have never worked together before, who are totally unfamiliar with the river, who are unsure of their eventual destination, and who, as if things were not bad enough, are travelling at night. In the white-water rapids metaphor, change is an expected and natural state, and managing change is a continuous process. These two metaphors present very different approaches to understanding and responding to change. Let's take a closer look at each one.

The Calm Waters Metaphor

Up until the late 1980s, the calm waters metaphor pretty much described the situation that managers faced. It's best illustrated by Kurt Lewin's three-step description of the change process.[10] (See Exhibit 13-1.)

According to Lewin, successful change can be planned and requires *unfreezing* the status quo, *changing* to a new state, and *refreezing* to make the change permanent. The status quo can be considered an equilibrium state. To move from this equilibrium, unfreezing is necessary. Unfreezing can be thought of as preparing for the needed change. It can be achieved by increasing the *driving forces*, which are forces that drive change and direct behaviour away from the status quo; decreasing the *restraining forces*, which are forces that resist change and push behaviour toward the status quo; or combining the two approaches.

Once unfreezing is done, the change itself can be implemented. However, merely introducing change does not ensure that the change will take hold. The new situation needs to be *refrozen* so that it can be sustained over time. Unless this last step is taken, there is a strong chance that the change will be short-lived as employees revert back to the old equilibrium state—that is, the old ways of doing things. The objective of refreezing, then, is to stabilize the new situation by reinforcing the new behaviours.

Exhibit 13-1

The Change Process

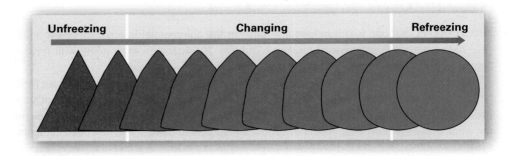

Note how Lewin's three-step process treats change simply as a break in the organization's equilibrium state. The status quo has been disturbed and change is necessary to establish a new equilibrium state. However, a calm waters environment is not what most managers face today.[11]

The White-Water Rapids Metaphor

The white-water rapids metaphor is consistent with our discussion of uncertain and dynamic environments in previous chapters. It's also consistent with a world that's increasingly dominated by information, ideas, and knowledge.[12] We can see how the metaphor applies to Yahoo!, which currently faces an uncertain and dynamic environment after dominating the Internet services industry for many years.

To get a feeling of what managing change might be like when you have to continuously manoeuvre in uninterrupted and uncertain rapids, consider attending a college or university that has the following rules: Courses vary in length. Unfortunately, when you sign up, you don't know how long a course will run. It might go for 2 weeks or 30 weeks. Furthermore, the instructor can end a course any time he or she wants, with no prior warning. If that is not bad enough, the length of the class changes each time it meets; sometimes the class lasts 20 minutes, other times it runs for 3 hours. And the time of the next class meeting is set by the instructor during this class. There is one more thing. All exams are unannounced, so you have to be ready for a test at any time. To succeed in this type of environment, you would have to be incredibly flexible and able to respond quickly to changing conditions. Students who are overly structured, "slow" to respond, or uncomfortable with change would not survive.

Growing numbers of managers are coming to accept that their job is much like what a student would face in such a college. The stability and predictability of the calm waters metaphor do not exist. Disruptions in the status quo are not occasional and temporary, and they are not followed by a return to calm waters. Many managers never get out of the rapids. They face constant change, bordering on chaos.

Is the white-water rapids metaphor an exaggeration? No! Although you would expect this type of chaotic and dynamic environment in high-tech industries, even organizations in non-high-tech industries are faced with constant change, as the following *Management Reflection* shows.

Navigating the Changing Waters at Electrolux

Is the white-water rapids metaphor an exaggeration? You might think that the home appliances industry wouldn't be all that difficult—after all, most households need the products, which are fairly uncomplicated—but that impression would be wrong. Electrolux's chief executive Hans Straberg has confronted several challenges.[13] First, there's the challenge of developing products that will appeal to a wide range of global customers. Then there's the challenge of less expensive alternatives flooding the market. In addition, Electrolux faces intense competition in the United States, where it gets 40 percent of its sales. Because approximately 80 percent of the workforce in Sweden belongs to a labour union, companies there face expectations in terms of how they treat their employees. However, Straberg recognized that his company was going to have to change if it was going to survive and prosper. One thing he did was shift production to lower-cost facilities in Asia and Eastern Europe. Then, to better grasp what today's consumers are thinking, the company held in-depth interviews with 160 000 customers from around the world. Using the information gained, a group of Electrolux employees gathered in Stockholm for a week-long brainstorming session to search for insights on what hot new products to pursue. Finally, to make the new product development process speedier, Straberg eliminated the structural divisions between departments. Designers, engineers, and marketers have to work together to come up with ideas. These changes were essential if Electrolux wanted to survive the white-water rapids environment in which it operates. ■

Putting the Two Views in Perspective

Does *every* manager face a world of constant and chaotic change? No, but the number who don't is dwindling. (See also *Self-Assessment—How Well Do I Respond to Turbulent Change?* on pages 377–378.) Managers in such businesses as telecommunications, computer software, and women's clothing have long confronted a world of white-water rapids. These managers used to envy their counterparts in industries such as banking, utilities, oil exploration, publishing, and air transportation, where the environment was historically more stable and predictable. However, those days of stability and predictability are long gone!

Today, any organization that treats change as the occasional disturbance in an otherwise calm and stable world runs a great risk. Too much is changing too fast for an organization or its managers to be complacent. It's no longer business as usual. And managers must be ready to efficiently and effectively manage the changes facing their organizations or their work areas. Nevertheless, managers have to be certain that change is the right thing to do at any given time. Companies need to carefully consider change strategies, as change can lead to failure. If change is the appropriate course of action, how should it be managed? That's what we'll discuss next.

MyManagementLab
Q&A 13.2

Managing Organizational Change

▶ ▶ ▶ With Jerry Yang back at the helm of Yahoo!, hopes were that he would be able to inspire the company's employees in a way that CEO Terry Semel did not seem able to do.[14] Many felt that Semel's background did not help him steer Yahoo! to a more visionary future. Semel was a Warner Bros. movie executive before joining Yahoo! in 2001. Yang was much quieter, but many of the successful Silicon Valley firms, such as Apple and Oracle, are run by their founders. "He's no Steve Jobs," says Ned May, an industry analyst. "But he's a founder. Putting a founder back in the reins will create excitement inside Yahoo!"

3. Classify types of organizational change.

Think About It
What advantages might come from bringing back a co-founder to help with the changes needed at Yahoo!?

What Is Organizational Change?

organizational change Any alteration of people, structure, or technology in an organization.

change agent Someone who acts as a catalyst and assumes the responsibility for managing the change process.

Most managers, at one point or another, will have to change some things in their workplace. We classify these changes as **organizational change**, which is any alteration of people, structure, or technology. Organizational changes often need someone to act as a catalyst and assume the responsibility for managing the change process—that is, a **change agent**. A change agent could be a manager within the organization or could be a non-manager—for example, a change specialist from the HR department or even an outside consultant. For major changes, an organization often hires outside consultants to provide advice and assistance. Because consultants are from the outside, they have an objective perspective that insiders may lack. But outside consultants have a limited understanding of the organization's history, culture, operating procedures, and people. They're also more likely than insiders to initiate drastic change because they don't have to live with the repercussions after the change is implemented. In contrast, internal managers may be more thoughtful but possibly overcautious because they must live with the consequences of their decisions.

Types of Change

What *can* a manager change? The manager's options fall into three categories: structure, technology, and people (see Exhibit 13-2).

Changing Structure

We discussed organizational structure issues in Chapter 10. Managers' organizing responsibilities include such activities as choosing the organization's formal design, allocating authority, and determining the degree of formalization. Once those structural decisions have been made, however, they are not final. Changing conditions or changing strategies bring about the need to make structural changes.

Exhibit 13-2

Three Categories of Change

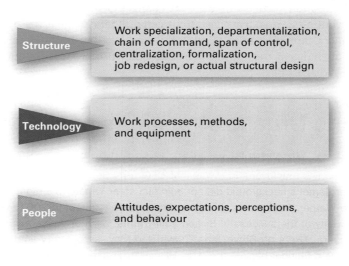

Structure → Work specialization, departmentalization, chain of command, span of control, centralization, formalization, job redesign, or actual structural design

Technology → Work processes, methods, and equipment

People → Attitudes, expectations, perceptions, and behaviour

What options does the manager have for changing structure? The manager has the same ones we introduced in our discussion of organizational structure and design. A few examples should make this clearer. Recall from Chapter 10 that an organization's structure is defined in terms of work specialization, departmentalization, chain of command, span of control, centralization and decentralization, and formalization. Managers can alter one or more of these *structural elements.* For instance, departmental responsibilities could be combined, organizational levels eliminated, or spans of control widened to make the organization flatter and less bureaucratic. Or more rules and procedures could be implemented to increase standardization. An increase in decentralization can be used to make decision making faster. Even downsizing involves changes in structure.

Another option would be to make major changes in the actual *structural design.* For instance, when Hewlett-Packard acquired Compaq, several structural changes were made as product divisions were dropped, merged, or expanded. Or structural design changes might include a shift from a functional to a product structure or the creation of a project structure design. Hamilton, Ontario-based Dofasco became a more profitable steel producer after revamping its traditional functional structure to a new design that arranges work around cross-functional teams. Some government agencies and private organizations are looking to new organizational ventures, forming public–private partnerships to deal with these changes, as the following *Management Reflection* shows.

MANAGEMENT REFLECTION
▶ Focus on Innovation

New Ways for Government to Get Jobs Done

Can public–private partnerships work? Federal and provincial governments are trying to come up with new ways to get much-needed projects completed.[15] Tony Fell, chair of Toronto-based RBC Capital Markets, notes that governments need help financing transportation, water, health care, and education systems, which are "deteriorating at an alarming rate." There is much talk about an innovative way of handling these projects: public–private partnerships (P3s), where the government and the private sector form companies to get things done. Unfortunately, to date most have not been successful. Almost four out of five P3s fail.

Whether they fail because the idea is unworkable, or whether they suffer from an inability of the public sector and the private sector to figure out appropriate ways to work together, is not entirely clear. Before leaving office, Gordon Campbell, premier of British Columbia, tried to find a successful model to make P3s work. Despite trying to get P3s started that would help with the "$2 billion in public capital projects built annually across the province," only one project has been signed. The private sector seems unwilling to take on risks that the government also does not want to assume.

One successful P3 is Toronto-based Teranet, formed in 1995 to create an electronic database of all the property title records in Ontario, so that lawyers could research and transfer titles in property deals from their office computers. The company has been profitable from the beginning. "The trouble was, if government tried it alone, it would probably take 30 to 40 years to get done and cost tens of millions of dollars," says Bonnie Foster, vice-president of corporate affairs and an original member of the Teranet management team.

The difficulties governments face in raising money for and managing large projects suggest that innovative ways to build public infrastructure still need to be found. Teranet may be one example of how to create joint ventures that work. ■

Changing Technology

Managers can also change the technology used to convert inputs into outputs. Most early studies in management—such as the work of Taylor and the Gilbreths described in the supplement to Chapter 1—dealt with efforts aimed at technological change. If you recall,

Computerization has been the engine for all kinds of changes in the business environment, including employee training. Cisco Systems' Internet Learning Solutions Group is charged with developing electronic training programs both for Cisco's own sales force and channel partners and for the company's hundreds of thousands of customers. The team, whose leaders are pictured here, has developed tools ranging from virtual classrooms to video server technology and content development templates. "We really believe that our e-learning programs are a more effective way to grow skills in high volume in a shorter time than in the past," says the group's director.

scientific management sought to implement changes that would increase production efficiency based on time-and-motion studies. Today, major technological changes usually involve the introduction of new equipment, tools, or methods; automation; or computerization.

Competitive factors or new innovations within an industry often require managers to introduce *new equipment, tools,* or *operating methods.* For example, coal mining companies in New South Wales, Australia, updated operational methods, installed more efficient coal-handling equipment, and made changes in work practices to be more productive. New innovations do not always inspire organizations to change, however. The Canadian Armed Forces has been criticized in recent years because it has not taken advantage of new technology to update its equipment.[16]

Automation is a technological change that uses machines for tasks previously done by people. It began in the Industrial Revolution and continues today as one of a manager's options for structural change. Automation has been introduced (and sometimes resisted) in organizations such as Canada Post, where automatic mail sorters are used, and in automobile assembly lines, where robots are programmed to do jobs that blue-collar workers used to perform.

Probably the most visible technological changes in recent years, though, have come through managers' efforts to expand *computerization.* Most organizations have sophisticated information systems. For instance, grocery stores and other retailers use scanners linked to computers that provide instant inventory information. Also, it's very uncommon for an office to not be computerized. At BP, employees had to learn how to deal with the personal visibility and accountability brought about by the implementation of an enterprise-wide information system. The integrative nature of this system meant that what any employee did on his or her computer automatically affected other computer systems on the internal network.[17] The Benetton Group uses computers to link its manufacturing plants outside Treviso, Italy, with the company's various sales outlets and a highly automated warehouse.[18]

Changing People

Changing people—that is, changing their attitudes, expectations, perceptions, and behaviours—is not easy. Yet, for over 30 years now, academic researchers and actual managers have been interested in finding ways for individuals and groups within organizations to work together more effectively. The term **organizational development (OD)**, though occasionally referring to all types of change, essentially focuses on techniques or programs to change people and the nature and quality of interpersonal work relationships.[19] The most popular OD techniques are described in Exhibit 13-3. The common thread in these techniques is that each seeks to bring about changes in the organization's people. For example, executives at Scotiabank, Canada's third-largest bank in terms of market capitalization, knew that the success of a new customer sales and service strategy depended on changing employee attitudes and behaviours. Managers used different OD techniques during the strategic change, including team building, survey feedback, and intergroup development. One indicator of how well these techniques worked in getting people to change was that every branch in Canada implemented the new strategy on or ahead of schedule.[20]

Global Organizational Development

Much of what we know about OD practices has come from North American research. However, managers need to recognize that although there may be some similarities in the

organizational development (OD) Techniques or programs to change people and the nature and quality of interpersonal work relationships.

Exhibit 13-3

Organizational Development Techniques

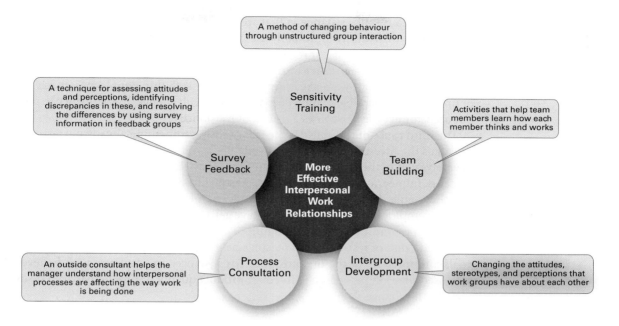

types of OD techniques used, some techniques that work for North American organizations may not be appropriate for organizations or organizational divisions based in other countries.[21] For instance, a study of OD interventions showed that "multirater (survey) feedback as practiced in the United States is not embraced in Taiwan" because the cultural value of "saving face is simply more powerful than the value of receiving feedback from subordinates."[22] What is the lesson for managers? Before using the same techniques to implement behavioural changes, especially across different countries, managers need to be sure that they have taken into account cultural characteristics and whether the techniques "make sense for the local culture."

Managing Resistance to Change

Change can be a threat to people in an organization. Organizations can build up inertia that motivates people to resist changing their status quo, even though change might be beneficial. Why do people resist change and what can be done to minimize their resistance?

4. Explain how to manage resistance to change.

Why People Resist Change

How would you feel if your company, two years after you started there, changed the software you used to enter your contact and sales information?

Resistance to change is well documented.[23] Why *do* people resist change? An individual is likely to resist change for the following reasons: uncertainty, habit, concern over personal loss, and the belief that the change is not in the organization's best interest.[24]

Change replaces the known with ambiguity and uncertainty. When you finish school, you will be leaving an environment where you know what is expected of you to join an organization where things are uncertain. Employees

MyManagementLab
Q&A 13.3

in organizations are faced with similar uncertainty. For example, when quality control methods based on sophisticated statistical models are introduced into manufacturing plants, many quality control inspectors have to learn the new methods. Some inspectors may fear that they will be unable to do so and may, therefore, develop a negative attitude toward the change or behave poorly if required to use the methods.

Another cause of resistance is that we do things out of habit. Every day, when you go to school or work, you probably go the same way. If you are like most people, you find a single route and use it regularly. As human beings, we are creatures of habit. Life is complex enough—we don't want to have to consider the full range of options for the hundreds of decisions we make every day. To cope with this complexity, we rely on habits or programmed responses. But when confronted with change, this tendency to respond in our accustomed ways becomes a source of resistance.

The third cause of resistance is the fear of losing something already possessed. Change threatens the investment you have already made in the status quo. The more that people have invested in the current system, the more they resist change. Why? They fear the loss of status, money, authority, friendships, personal convenience, or other economic benefits that they value. This helps explain why older employees tend to resist change more than younger employees. Older employees have generally invested more in the current system and thus have more to lose by changing.

A final cause of resistance is a person's belief that the change is incompatible with the goals and interests of the organization. For instance, an employee who believes that a proposed new job procedure will reduce product quality or productivity can be expected to resist the change.

Techniques for Reducing Resistance

When managers see resistance to change as dysfunctional, they can use a variety of actions to deal with it.[25] Exhibit 13-4 shows how to manage resistance at the unfreezing, changing, and refreezing stages. Actions include communicating the reasons for change, getting input

Exhibit 13-4

Helping Employees Accept Change

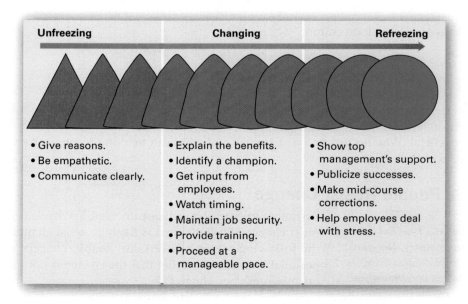

Source: J. Liebowitz and G. J. Iskat, "What to Do When Employees Resist Change," *Supervision* 57, no. 8 (August 1996), pp. 3–5. With permission.

from employees, choosing the timing of change carefully, and showing management support for the change process. Providing support to employees to deal with the stress of the change is also important. Depending on the type and source of the resistance, managers might choose to use any of these. In general, resistance is likely to be lower if managers involve people in the change, offer training where needed, and are open to revisions once the change has been implemented. (For more suggestions on reducing resistance, see *Developing Your Interpersonal Skills—Managing Resistance to Change* on pages 381–382.)

MyManagementLab
PRISM 5

Stimulating Innovation

5. Describe techniques for stimulating innovation.

▶ ▶ ▶ In order to improve its performance, Yahoo! must become more innovative.[26] The company was slow to catch on to the force that online social networking websites, such as Facebook, would become. Unlike Google, Yahoo! has been more interested in displaying content rather than creating content. Under the leadership of Terry Semel, the company became more product centred, turning out so many products that a senior vice-president commented that the company had spread itself too thin.

Yahoo! needs to develop a better technology platform that would integrate the company's entire network of products. It also needs to figure out what to do if MySpace surpasses Yahoo! in audience size (which seemed likely in 2007) and online social networking becomes more popular with advertisers.

Think About It

What can companies do to stimulate and nurture innovation?

"Winning in business today demands innovation."[27] Such is the stark reality facing today's managers. In the dynamic, chaotic world of global competition, organizations must create new products and services and adopt state-of-the-art technology if they are to compete successfully.[28]

MyManagementLab
Q&A 13.4

For instance, stores such as The Bay and Zellers have faced difficulty competing against Wal-Mart, because they have failed to either adapt or respond to retail industry practices. The Bay, for instance, has had difficulty identifying its target market and developing clothing lines appropriate to that market. A recent study of bankruptcies among Canadian wholesale and retail firms suggests that bankruptcies for older retailers may be the result of "Internet vendors and 'big-box' outlet stores . . . eroding the competitive position of established, traditional wholesale and retail businesses."[29] Meanwhile, fast-food restaurants like McDonald's and Krispy Kreme Doughnuts looked out of touch when the "low carb" fad swept the diet industry. How do companies keep up in a quickly changing environment?

When you think of successful innovators, you probably consider companies such as Sony, with its MiniDiscs, PlayStations, Cyber-Shot digital cameras, and OLED display TV. 3M continually introduces new types of Post-it Notes. Intel makes continual advances in chip designs. What is the secret to the success of these innovator champions? What, if anything, can other managers do to make their organizations more innovative? In the following pages, we will try to answer those questions as we discuss the factors behind innovation.

Creativity vs. Innovation vs. Entrepreneurship

Creativity refers to the ability to combine ideas in a unique way or to make unusual associations between ideas.[30] An organization that stimulates creativity develops unique ways to work or novel solutions to problems. But creativity by itself is not enough. Creative ideas need to be turned into useful products, services, or work methods; this process is defined as **innovation**. When innovations are turned into viable ventures, this is known as **entrepreneurship**. The innovative organization is characterized by its ability to channel creativity into useful outcomes. When managers talk about changing an organization to make it more creative, they usually mean they want to stimulate and nurture innovation.

creativity The ability to combine ideas in a unique way or to make unusual associations between ideas.

innovation The process of taking creative ideas and turning them into useful products, services, or work methods.

entrepreneurship The act of turning an innovation into a viable venture.

In Chapter 4, we pointed out that in today's dynamically chaotic world of global competition, organizations must continually innovate new products and services if they want to compete successfully. Innovation is a key characteristic of entrepreneurial ventures and, in fact, is what makes an entrepreneurial venture "entrepreneurial." In the same chapter, we pointed out that innovation can take place in three forms—curiosity-driven research, applied research, and research and development (R&D).

Sony, 3M, and Intel are aptly described as innovative because they take novel ideas and turn them into profitable products and work methods.

Stimulating and Nurturing Innovation

What has your employer done, if anything, to encourage innovation? Do you think more innovation could be encouraged?

MyManagementLab
Q&A 13.5

In Chapter 1, we discussed the value proposition for building adaptive organizations where successful organizations differentiate themselves from their competitors in three dimensions: They are more flexible, more efficient, and more adaptable. Flexibility is a reactive skill, while adaptability is proactive. Being adaptable requires an organization to create a set of skills, processes, and a culture that enables the organization to continuously look for new problems and offer solutions before the clients even realize they have a need.[31]

Using the systems approach we introduced in the supplement to Chapter 1, we can better understand how organizations become more innovative.[32] (See Exhibit 13-5.) We see from this model that getting the desired outputs (innovative products) involves both the inputs and the transformation of those inputs. Inputs include creative individuals and groups within the organization. But having creative individuals is not enough. It takes the right environment for the innovation process to take hold and prosper as the inputs are transformed. What does this "right" environment—that is, an environment that stimulates innovation—look like? We have identified three sets of variables that have been found to stimulate innovation: the organization's structure, culture, and human resource practices (see Exhibit 13-6).

Structural Variables

Research into the effect of structural variables on innovation shows five things.[33] First, organic structures positively influence innovation. Because this type of organization is low in formalization, centralization, and work specialization, organic structures facilitate the flexibility, adaptability, and cross-fertilization necessary in innovation. Second, the easy availability of plentiful resources provides a key building block for innovation. With an abundance of resources, managers can afford to purchase innovations, can afford the cost

Exhibit 13-5

Systems View of Innovation

Inputs	Transformation	Outputs
Creative individuals, groups, organizations	Creative environment, process, situation	Innovative product(s), work methods

Source: Adapted from R. W. Woodman, J. E. Sawyer, and R. W. Griffin, "Toward a Theory of Organizational Creativity," *Academy of Management Review*, April 1993, p. 309.

Exhibit 13-6

Innovation Variables

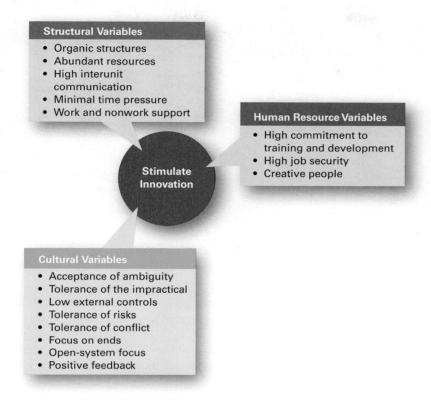

Structural Variables
- Organic structures
- Abundant resources
- High interunit communication
- Minimal time pressure
- Work and nonwork support

Human Resource Variables
- High commitment to training and development
- High job security
- Creative people

Stimulate Innovation

Cultural Variables
- Acceptance of ambiguity
- Tolerance of the impractical
- Low external controls
- Tolerance of risks
- Tolerance of conflict
- Focus on ends
- Open-system focus
- Positive feedback

of instituting innovations, and can absorb failures. Third, frequent interunit communication helps break down barriers to innovation.[34] Cross-functional teams, task forces, and other such organizational designs facilitate interaction across departmental lines and are widely used in innovative organizations. Fourth, innovative organizations try to minimize extreme time pressures on creative activities despite the demands of white-water-type environments. Although time pressures may spur people to work harder and may make them feel more creative, studies show that it actually causes them to be less creative.[35] Finally, studies show that when an organization's structure provides explicit support for creativity from work and nonwork sources, an employee's creative performance is enhanced. What kinds of support are beneficial? Things like encouragement, open communication, readiness to listen, and useful feedback.[36] Toronto-based Labatt Breweries, for instance, gathers employees from across the country to an annual "innovation summit" to allow them to present ideas.[37] At one summit, Don Perron, a power engineer from Labatt's Edmonton brewery, presented an idea to move pumps from the ceiling of the plant to the floor that was accepted. This impressed Perron, who said, "It gives you a sense of satisfaction." His co-workers have become enthusiastic about developing ideas as a result. "It has taken away some of the monotony [of production-line work]," Perron said. Labatt helps employees develop good ideas by investing time and money in the research and development of new ideas.

Cultural Variables

"Throw the bunny" is part of the lingo used by a project team at toy company Mattel. It refers to a juggling lesson in which team members try to learn to juggle two balls and a stuffed bunny. Most people easily learn to juggle two balls but cannot let go of that third

The toy industry is very competitive and picking the next great toy is not easy. Still, Toronto-based Spin Master is better than most at finding the most innovative new toys. Co-CEOs Anton Rabie and Ronnen Harary and executive vice-president Ben Varadi rely on intuition. They have also created a "culture of ideas" and pick everyone's brains for new ideas, "from inventors and licensing companies to distributors and retailers around the world." They give a prize to one employee each month for the best idea.

object. Creativity, like juggling, is learning to let go—that is, to "throw the bunny." For Mattel, having a culture in which people are encouraged to "throw the bunny" is important to its continued product innovations.[38]

Innovative organizations tend to have similar cultures.[39] They encourage experimentation, reward both successes and failures, and celebrate mistakes. An innovative culture is likely to have the following characteristics:

- *Acceptance of ambiguity.* Too much emphasis on objectivity and specificity constrains creativity. (To learn more about handling ambiguity, see *Self-Assessment—How Well Do I Handle Ambiguity?* on pages 229–230, in Chapter 8.)

- *Tolerance of the impractical.* Individuals who offer impractical, even foolish, answers to what-if questions are not stifled. What at first seems impractical might lead to innovative solutions.

- *Low external controls.* Rules, regulations, policies, and similar organizational controls are kept to a minimum.

- *Tolerance of risk.* Employees are encouraged to experiment without fear of consequences should they fail. Mistakes are treated as learning opportunities.

- *Tolerance of conflict.* Diversity of opinions is encouraged. Harmony and agreement between individuals or units are *not* assumed to be evidence of high performance.

- *Focus on ends.* Goals are made clear, and individuals are encouraged to consider alternative routes to meeting the goals. Focusing on ends suggests that there might be several right answers to any given problem.

- *Open-system focus.* Managers closely monitor the environment and respond to changes as they occur.

- *Positive feedback.* Managers provide positive feedback, encouragement, and support so employees feel that their creative ideas will receive attention.

Human Resource Variables

In this category, we find that innovative organizations actively promote the training and development of their members so their knowledge remains current; offer their employees high job security to reduce the fear of getting fired for making mistakes; and encourage individuals to become "champions" of change. **Idea champions** are individuals who actively and enthusiastically support new ideas, build support, overcome resistance, and ensure that innovations are implemented. Research finds that these idea champions have common personality characteristics: extremely high self-confidence, persistence, energy, and a tendency to take risks. Champions also display characteristics associated with dynamic leadership. They inspire and energize others with their vision of the potential of an innovation and through their strong personal conviction in their mission. They are also good at gaining the commitment of others to support their mission. In addition, champions have jobs that provide considerable decision-making discretion. This autonomy helps them introduce and implement innovations in organizations.[40] For instance, *Spirit* and *Opportunity*, the two golf-cart-sized exploration rovers that landed on Mars in 2004 to explore its surface, never would have been built had it not been for an idea champion by the name of Donna L. Shirley. As the head of Mars exploration in the 1990s at NASA's Jet Propulsion Laboratory in Pasadena, California, Shirley had been working since the early 1980s on the idea of putting roving vehicles on Mars. Despite ongoing funding and management support problems, she continued to champion the idea until it was approved in the early 1990s.[41]

idea champions Individuals who actively and enthusiastically support new ideas, build support, overcome resistance, and ensure that innovations are implemented.

Current Issues in Managing Change

▶ ▶ ▶ One of the most difficult challenges Yahoo! CEO Jerry Yang faced in moving the company forward was recapturing the organization's entrepreneurial culture, which it lost under Semel.[42] The culture had become bureaucratic, with lots of separate silos, when what was needed was a sleek, well-run organization. "Jerry won't be able to do much unless he can bring back that entrepreneurial spirit," notes Professor John Sullivan of San Francisco State University's business school.

6. Discuss contemporary issues in managing change.

Shortly after taking over the helm, Yang posted a description of his new job on Yahoo! His vision for the company moving forward included the following:

- A Yahoo! that executes with speed, clarity, and discipline.
- A Yahoo! that increases its focus on differentiating its products and investing in creativity and innovation.
- A Yahoo! that is better focused on what's important to its users, customers, and employees.

To accomplish his vision, Yang will need "to figure out how he wants the furniture broken," says Kevin Coyne, a strategy consultant and Harvard Business School lecturer.

Think About It

Is it possible to change a large organization's bureaucratic, slow-moving culture into an entrepreneurial, fast-paced culture?

Today's change issues—changing organizational culture, handling employee stress, and making change happen successfully—are critical concerns for managers. What can managers do to change an organization's culture when that culture no longer supports the organization's mission? What can managers do to handle the stress created by today's dynamic and uncertain environment? And how can managers successfully manage the challenges of introducing and implementing change? These are the topics we look at in this section.

Changing Organizational Culture

As we saw in Chapter 2, when W. James McNerney Jr. took over as CEO of 3M, he brought with him managerial approaches from his old employer, General Electric. He soon discovered that what was routine at GE was unheard of at 3M. For instance, he was the only one who showed up at meetings without a tie. His blunt, matter-of-fact, and probing style of asking questions caught many 3M managers off guard. McNerney soon realized that

MyManagementLab
Q&A 13.6

he would need to address the cultural issues before tackling any needed organizational changes.[43] The fact that an organization's culture is made up of relatively stable and permanent characteristics tends to make that culture very resistant to change.[44] A culture takes a long time to form, and once established it tends to become entrenched. Strong cultures are particularly resistant to change because employees have become so committed to them.

The explosion of the space shuttle *Columbia* in 2003 highlights how difficult changing an organization's culture can be. An investigation of the explosion found that the causes were remarkably similar to the reasons given for the *Challenger* disaster 20 years earlier.[45] Although foam striking the shuttle was the technical cause, NASA's organizational culture was the real problem. Joseph Grenny, a NASA engineer, noted that "the NASA culture does not accept being wrong." The culture does not accept that "there's no such thing as a stupid question." Instead, "the humiliation factor always runs high."[46] Consequently, people do not speak up. As this example shows, if, over time, a certain culture becomes inappropriate to an organization and a handicap to management, there might be little a manager can do to change it, especially in the short run. Even under favourable conditions, cultural changes have to be viewed in years, not weeks or even months.

Understanding the Situational Factors

What "favourable conditions" might facilitate cultural change? The evidence suggests that cultural change is most likely to take place when most or all of the following conditions exist:

- *A dramatic crisis occurs.* This can be the shock that weakens the status quo and makes people start thinking about the relevance of the current culture. Examples are a surprising financial setback, the loss of a major customer, or a dramatic technological innovation by a competitor.

- *Leadership changes hands.* New top leadership, who can provide an alternative set of key values, may be perceived as more capable of responding to the crisis than the old leaders were. Top leadership includes the organization's chief executive but might include all senior managers.

- *The organization is young and small.* The younger the organization, the less entrenched its culture. Similarly, it's easier for managers to communicate new values in a small organization than in a large one.

- *The culture is weak.* The more widely held the values and the higher the agreement among members on those values, the more difficult it will be to change. Conversely, weak cultures are more receptive to change than are strong ones.[47]

These situational factors help explain why a company such as Yahoo! faces challenges in reshaping its culture. For the most part, employees like the old ways of doing things and don't always see the company's problems as critical. This may also be why Yahoo! was slow to recognize the importance of Facebook and YouTube to the online scene.

How Can Cultural Change Be Accomplished?

Now we ask the question: If conditions are right, how do managers go about changing culture? The challenge is to unfreeze the current culture, implement the new "ways of doing things," and reinforce those new values. No single action is likely to have the impact necessary to change something that is so ingrained and highly valued. Thus, there needs to be a comprehensive and coordinated strategy for managing cultural change, as shown in *Tips for Managers—Strategies for Managing Cultural Change.*

TIPS FOR MANAGERS

Strategies for Managing Cultural Change

- Set the tone through management behaviour. Managers, particularly top management, need to be **positive role models.**

- Create **new stories, symbols, and rituals** to replace those currently in vogue.

- Select, promote, and support employees who **adopt the new values** that are sought.

- **Redesign socialization processes** to align with the new values.

- Change the reward system to **encourage acceptance** of a new set of values.

- Replace unwritten norms with **formal rules and regulations** that are tightly enforced.

- **Shake up current subcultures** through transfers, job rotation, and/or terminations.

- Work to get peer-group consensus through **employee participation** and creation of a climate with a high level of trust.

As you can see, these suggestions focus on specific actions that managers can take to change the ineffective culture. Following these suggestions, however, is no guarantee that a manager's change efforts will succeed. Organizational members don't quickly let go of values that they understand and that have worked well for them in the past. Managers must, therefore, be patient. Change, if it comes, will be slow. And managers must stay constantly alert to protect against any return to old, familiar practices and traditions.

Handling Employee Stress

As a student, you have probably experienced stress when finishing class assignments and projects, taking exams, or finding ways to pay rising tuition costs, which may mean juggling a job and school. Then, there is the stress associated with getting a decent job after graduation. Even after you have landed that job, your stress is not likely to stop. For many employees, organizational change creates stress. A dynamic and uncertain environment characterized by mergers, restructurings, forced retirements, and downsizing has created a large number of employees who are overworked and stressed out.[48] In fact, Ipsos Reid recently did a survey of 1500 Canadians with employer-sponsored health care plans. It found that 62 percent reported experiencing "a great deal of stress on the job." Workplace stress was bad enough to cause 34 percent of those surveyed to say that it had made them physically ill.[49] In this section, we review what stress is, what causes it, how to identify its symptoms, and what managers can do to reduce it.

What Is Stress?

Stress is the adverse reaction people have to excessive pressure placed on them from extraordinary demands, constraints, or opportunities.[50] Let's look more closely at what stress is.

Stress is not necessarily bad. Although it's often discussed in a negative context, stress does have a positive value, particularly when it offers a potential gain. Functional stress allows an athlete, stage performer, or employee to perform at his or her highest level in crucial situations.

However, stress is more often associated with fear of loss. When you take a test at school or have your annual performance review at work, you feel stress because you know that there can be either positive or negative outcomes. A good performance review may lead to a promotion, greater responsibilities, and a higher salary. But a poor review may keep you from getting the promotion. An extremely poor review might lead to your being fired.

Just because the conditions are right for stress to surface does not always mean it will. Stress is highest for individuals who are uncertain whether they will win or lose and lowest for individuals who think that winning or losing is a certainty. In addition, if winning or losing is unimportant, there is no stress. An employee who feels that keeping a job or earning a promotion is unimportant will experience no stress before a performance review.

MyManagementLab
Q&A 13.7

Causes of Stress

What are the things that cause you stress?

As shown in Exhibit 13-7, the causes of stress can be found in issues related to the organization or in personal factors that evolve out of the employee's private life. Clearly, change of any kind has the potential to cause stress. It can present opportunities, constraints, or demands. Moreover, changes are frequently created in a climate of uncertainty and around issues that are important to employees. It's not surprising, then, that change is a major stressor.

Symptoms of Stress

What signs indicate that an employee's stress level might be too high? Stress shows itself in a number of ways. For instance, an employee who is experiencing high stress may become depressed, accident prone, or argumentative; may have difficulty making routine decisions; may be easily distracted; and so on. As Exhibit 13-8 shows, stress symptoms can

Exhibit 13-7

Causes of Stress

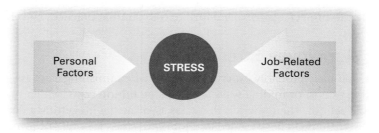

be grouped under three general categories: physical, psychological, and behavioural. Of these, the physical symptoms are least relevant to managers. Of greater importance are the psychological and behavioural symptoms, since these directly affect an employee's work.

In Japan, there is a stress phenomenon called *karoshi* (pronounced kah-roe-she), which is translated literally as "death from overwork." During the late 1980s, "several high-ranking Japanese executives still in their prime years suddenly died without any previous sign of illness."[51] As public concern increased, even the Japanese Ministry of Labour got involved, and it now publishes statistics on the number of *karoshi* deaths. As Japanese multinational companies expand operations to China, Korea, and Taiwan, it's feared that the *karoshi* culture may follow.

Reducing Stress

As we mentioned earlier, not all stress is dysfunctional. Since stress can never be totally eliminated from a person's life, either off the job or on, managers are concerned with reducing the stress that leads to dysfunctional work behaviour. How? Through controlling certain organizational factors to reduce organizational stress and, to a more limited extent, offering help for personal stress.

Exhibit 13-8

Symptoms of Stress

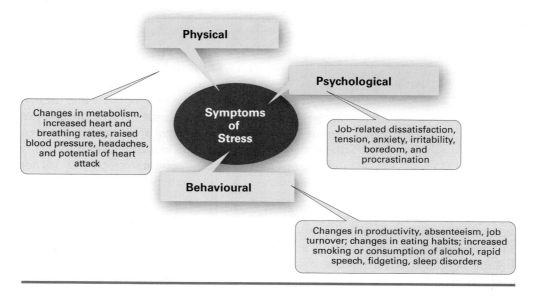

Things that managers can do in terms of organizational factors begin with employee selection. Managers need to make sure that an employee's abilities match the job requirements. When employees are in over their heads, their stress levels typically will be high. A realistic job preview during the selection process can minimize stress by reducing ambiguity about job expectations. Improved organizational communications will keep ambiguity-induced stress to a minimum. Similarly, a performance-planning program such as management by objectives will clarify job responsibilities, provide clear performance goals, and reduce ambiguity through feedback. Job redesign is also a way to reduce stress. If stress can be traced to boredom or to work overload, jobs should be redesigned to increase challenge or to reduce the workload. Redesigns that increase opportunities for employees to participate in decisions and to gain social support have also been found to reduce stress.[52]

Stress from an employee's personal life raises two problems. First, it's difficult for the manager to control directly. Second, there are ethical considerations. Specifically, does the manager have the right to intrude—even in the subtlest ways—in an employee's personal life? If a manager believes it's ethical and the employee is receptive, there are a few approaches the manager can consider. Employee *counselling* can provide stress relief. Employees often want to talk to someone about their problems, and the organization—through its managers, in-house human resource counsellors, or free or low-cost outside professional help—can meet that need. Companies such as BC Hydro and the University of British Columbia are just two of many organizations that provide extensive counselling services for their employees. A *time management program* can help employees whose personal lives suffer from a lack of planning that, in turn, creates stress sort out their priorities.[53] Still another approach is organizationally sponsored *wellness programs*. For example, Montreal-based Ericsson Canada, a telecommunications firm, insists that all employees take two weeks of holidays a year, in week-long increments. Peter Buddo, vice-president of human resources, explains his company's policy: "One day off a week is not going to do anyone any good." Hamilton, Ontario-based Dofasco's employees have access to three gyms, one at the plant, and the other two a 15-minute drive from the plant. There are 4000 visits a month to the three gyms combined. Montreal-based Hewlett-Packard Canada gives all its employees ergonomics training so that they will sit properly at their computer screens and avoid neck, shoulder, and arm injuries from keyboarding. The company also has four subsidized on-site fitness centres for staff in the Toronto area. Employees pay $20 a month for use of the centres at any time of the day, to take breaks and reduce stress.[54]

Making Change Happen Successfully

When changes are needed, who makes them happen? Who manages them? Although you may think that it's the responsibility of top managers, actually managers at *all* organizational levels are involved in the change process.

Even with the involvement of all levels of managers in change efforts, change processes don't always work the way they should. In fact, a global study of organizational change concludes that "hundreds of managers from scores of U.S. and European companies [are] satisfied with their operating prowess . . . [but] dissatisfied with their ability to implement change."[55] One of the reasons that change fails is that managers do not really know how to introduce change in organizations. Professor John Kotter of the Harvard Business School identifies a number of places where managers make mistakes when leading change. These are illustrated in Exhibit 13-9.

How can managers make change happen successfully? Managers can increase the likelihood of making change happen successfully in three ways. First, they should focus on making the organization ready for change. Exhibit 13-10 summarizes the characteristics of organizations that are ready for change.

Second, managers need to understand their own role in the process. They do this by creating a simple, compelling statement of the need for change; communicating constantly and honestly throughout the process; getting as much employee participation as possible; respecting employees' apprehension about the change but encouraging them to be flexible;

Exhibit 13-9

Mistakes Managers Make When Leading Change

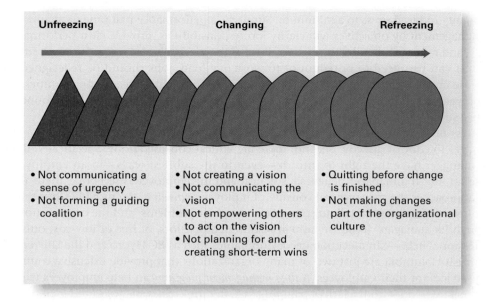

Unfreezing	Changing	Refreezing
• Not communicating a sense of urgency • Not forming a guiding coalition	• Not creating a vision • Not communicating the vision • Not empowering others to act on the vision • Not planning for and creating short-term wins	• Quitting before change is finished • Not making changes part of the organizational culture

Sources: J. P. Kotter, "Leading Change: Why Transformation Efforts Fail," *Harvard Business Review*, March–April 1995, pp. 56–67; and *Management*, First Canadian Edition by Williams/Kondra/Vibert. © 2004. Reprinted with permission of Nelson, a division of Thomson Learning: www.thomsonrights.com. FAX 800-730-2215.

Exhibit 13-10

Characteristics of Change-Capable Organizations

- *Link the present and the future.* Think of work as more than an extension of the past; think about future opportunities and issues and factor them into today's decisions.

- *Make learning a way of life.* Change-friendly organizations excel at knowledge sharing and management.

- *Actively support and encourage day-to-day improvements and changes.* Successful change can come from the small changes as well as the big ones.

- *Ensure diverse teams.* Diversity ensures that things won't be done the way they are always done.

- *Encourage mavericks.* Since their ideas and approaches are outside the mainstream, mavericks can help bring about radical change.

- *Shelter breakthroughs.* Change-friendly organizations have found ways to protect those breakthrough ideas.

- *Integrate technology.* Use technology to implement changes.

- *Build and deepen trust.* People are more likely to support changes when the organization's culture is trusting and managers have credibility and integrity.

Source: Based on P. A. McLagan, "The Change-Capable Organization," *Training & Development*, January 2003, pp. 50–58.

removing those who resist, but only after all possible attempts have been made to get their commitment to the change; aiming for short-term change successes, since large-scale change can be a long time coming; and setting a positive example.[56]

Third, managers need to encourage employees to be change agents—to look for those day-to-day improvements and changes that individuals and teams can make. For instance, a study of organizational change found that 77 percent of changes at the work-group level were reactions to a specific, current problem or to a suggestion from someone outside the work group; 68 percent of those changes occurred in the course of employees' day-to-day work.[57]

SUMMARY AND IMPLICATIONS

1. Describe the forces that create the need for change. Organizations are confronted with the need for change from both external and internal forces. Externally, the marketplace, government laws and regulations, technology, labour markets, and economic changes all put pressure on organizations to change. Internally, organizations may decide to change strategies. The introduction of new equipment can also lead to change. The workforce, both in terms of composition and attitudes, can also lead to demands for change.

▶ ▶ ▶ Yahoo! faces changes because it is a large organization experiencing challenges from ever-changing technology and fast-moving, smaller, and more aggressive organizations.

2. Compare and contrast views of the change process. Until the late 1980s, change was viewed as episodic, something that could be planned and managed readily. In between periods of change, organizations "stayed the course." In more recent years, environments have become more uncertain and dynamic, and this has led to more continuous demands for change.

▶ ▶ ▶ Yahoo! has had to respond to various changes in the online world (even as it introduced technological changes itself). To regain its leadership edge as the company moves forward, it has to be able to identify new opportunities on an ongoing basis and figure out a way to provide services that its competitors do not.

3. Classify types of organizational change. What *can* a manager change? The manager's options fall into three categories: structure, technology, and people (see Exhibit 13-2 on page 360). Changing *structure* includes any alteration in authority relations, coordination mechanisms, employee empowerment, job redesign, or similar structural variables. Changing *technology* encompasses modifications in the way work is performed or the methods and equipment that are used. Changing *people* refers to changes in employee attitudes, expectations, perceptions, and behaviour.

▶ ▶ ▶ Yahoo! replaced Terry Semel with Jerry Yang as CEO with the assumption that this change would put a founder back at the reins and inspire employees in a new way. At the same time, Yahoo! has had to create change within employees and its structure to take advantage of the new technologies that competitors are benefiting from.

4. Explain how to manage resistance to change. Managers can change an organization's structure, technology, and people. People tend to resist change, and there are a variety of reasons why they do so. The main reason is that change replaces the known with ambiguity and uncertainty. As well, people do not necessarily like their habits changed; they may fear losing something already possessed (such as status, money, or friendships); and they may believe that the change could actually reduce product quality or productivity.

▶ ▶ ▶ One of the challenges Yahoo! needs to manage is that employees have been used to working in separate silos, not always aware of the big picture of the organization. They may resist working "outside of the box" initially because they have been rewarded for working within subunits, rather than thinking of the overall strategic plan of the organization.

5. Describe techniques for stimulating innovation. Innovation is the process of taking creative ideas and turning them into useful products, services, or work methods. Organizations that have greater structural flexibility, encourage training and development of employees, and encourage risk-taking and new ideas are more likely to be innovative.

▶ ▶ ▶ At the outset, Yahoo! was a very innovative company, but in recent years its innovations have been more limited, which has allowed Google and Facebook to become serious competitors.

6. Discuss contemporary issues in managing change. One main consideration in managing change is determining how to introduce change in an existing organizational culture. An organization's culture can make it difficult to introduce change. Another major consideration is how to deal with employee stress while undergoing change.

▶ ▶ ▶ Yahoo!'s culture has been one of separate silos, and now it needs more teamwork from employees. This may create difficulties for CEO Jerry Yang, who has to figure out how to reward team activities rather than individual actions. However, because he was a co-founder of Yahoo!, he may be better suited to introducing such changes successfully than an outsider would be.

Management @ Work

READING FOR COMPREHENSION

1. Define *organizational change*.

2. What are the external and internal forces for change?

3. Why is handling change an integral part of every manager's job?

4. Describe Lewin's three-step change process. How is it different from the change process needed in the whitewater rapids metaphor of change?

5. Discuss what it takes to make change happen successfully.

6. Explain why people resist change and how resistance might be managed.

7. How do work overload, role conflict, and role ambiguity contribute to employee stress?

LINKING CONCEPTS TO PRACTICE

1. Can a nonmanagerial employee be a change agent? Explain your answer.

2. "Innovation requires allowing people to make mistakes. However, being wrong too many times can be fatal." Do you agree? Why or why not? What are the implications for nurturing innovation?

3. How are opportunities, constraints, and demands related to stress? (See the discussion in Chapter 4 on opportunity and innovation for background.) Give an example of each.

4. Planned change is often thought to be the best approach to take in organizations. Can unplanned change ever be effective? Explain.

5. Organizations typically have limits to how much change they can absorb. As a manager, what signs would you look for that might suggest that your organization has exceeded its capacity to change?

SELF-ASSESSMENT

How Well Do I Respond to Turbulent Change?

Listed below are a set of statements describing the characteristics of a managerial job. If your job had these features, how would you react to them?[58]

Use the following rating scale for your answers:

    1 = This feature would be very unpleasant for me.
    2 = This feature would be somewhat unpleasant for me.
    3 = I would have no reaction to this feature one way or another; or it would be about equally enjoyable and unpleasant.
    4 = This feature would be enjoyable and acceptable most of the time.
    5 = I would enjoy this feature very much; it's completely acceptable.

1. I regularly spend 30 to 40 percent of my time in meetings.   1 2 3 4 5

2. A year and a half ago, my job did not exist, and I have been essentially inventing it as I go along.   1 2 3 4 5

3. The responsibilities I either assume or am assigned consistently exceed the authority I have for discharging them.   1 2 3 4 5

4. I am a member of a team, and I have no more authority than anyone else on the team.   1 2 3 4 5

5. At any given moment in my job, I have on average about a dozen phone calls or emails to be returned.   1 2 3 4 5

6. My job performance is evaluated by not only my boss but also my peers and subordinates.   1 2 3 4 5

7. About three weeks a year of formal management training is needed in my job just to stay current.   1 2 3 4 5

8. My job consistently brings me into close working contact at a professional level with people of many races, ethnic groups, and nationalities, and of both sexes.   1 2 3 4 5

9. For many of my work colleagues, English is their second language.   1 2 3 4 5

10. My boss is from another country and has been in this country for only six months.   1 2 3 4 5

11. There is no objective way to measure my effectiveness.   1 2 3 4 5

12. I report to three different bosses for different aspects of my job, and each has an equal say in my performance appraisal.   1 2 3 4 5

13. On average, about a third of my time is spent dealing with unexpected emergencies that force all scheduled work to be postponed.   1 2 3 4 5

14. On average, I spend about a week every month out of town on business.   1 2 3 4 5

15. I frequently have to work until 8 p.m. to get my day's work completed.   1 2 3 4 5

16. When I have a meeting with the people who report to me, at least one or two will participate by phone or electronic conferencing.   1 2 3 4 5

17. The degree I earned in preparation for this type of work is now obsolete, and I probably should go back for another degree.   1 2 3 4 5

18. My job requires me to read 100 to 200 pages per week of technical materials.   1 2 3 4 5

19. My department is so interdependent with several other departments in the organization that all distinctions about which departments are responsible for which tasks are quite arbitrary.   1 2 3 4 5

20. I am unlikely to get a promotion any time in the near future.   1 2 3 4 5

21. There is no clear career path for me in this job and organization.   1 2 3 4 5

22. During the period of my employment here, either the entire organization or the division I worked in has been reorganized every year or so.   1 2 3 4 5

23. While I have many ideas about how to make things work better, I have no direct influence on either the business policies or the personnel policies that govern my division.   1 2 3 4 5

24. My organization is a defendant in an antitrust suit, and if the case comes to trial, I will probably have to testify about some decisions that were made a few years ago.   1 2 3 4 5

25. Sophisticated new technological equipment and software are continually being introduced into my division, necessitating constant learning on my part.   1 2 3 4 5

26. The computer I have in my office can be monitored by my bosses without my knowledge.   1 2 3 4 5

Scoring Key

To calculate your tolerance-of-change score, add up your responses to all 26 items.

Analysis and Interpretation

This instrument describes a number of characteristics of the changing workplace. The higher your score, the more comfortable you are with change.

The author of this instrument suggests an "average" score is around 78. If you scored over 100, you seem to be accepting the "new" workplace fairly well. If your score was below 70, you are likely to find the manager's job in the twenty-first century unpleasant, if not overwhelming.

More Self-Assessments MyManagementLab

To learn more about your skills, abilities, and interests, go to the MyManagementLab website and take the following self-assessments:

- I.A.4.—How Well Do I Handle Ambiguity? (This exercise also appears in Chapter 8 on pages 229–230.)
- I.A.5.—How Creative Am I?
- III.C.2.—How Stressful Is My Life?
- III.C.3.—Am I Burned Out?

MANAGEMENT FOR YOU TODAY

Dilemma

Think of something that you would like to change in your personal life. It could be your study habits, your fitness and nutrition, the way you interact with others, or anything else that is of interest to you. What values and assumptions have encouraged the behaviour that currently exists (that is, the one you want to change)?

What driving and restraining forces can you address in order to make the desired change?

Becoming a Manager

- Pay attention to how you handle change. Figure out why you resist certain changes and not others.

- Practise using different approaches to managing resistance to change at work or in your personal life.

- Read material that has been written about how to be a more creative person.

- Find ways to be innovative and creative as you complete class projects or work projects.

WORKING TOGETHER: TEAM-BASED EXERCISE

Dealing with Stress

Stress is something that all of us face, and college and university students particularly may have extremely stressful lives. How do you recognize when you are under a lot of stress? What do you do to deal with that stress?

Form teams of three or four individuals. Each person in the group should describe how he or she knows when he or she is under a lot of stress. What symptoms does each person show? Make a list of these symptoms and categorize them using Exhibit 13-8 on page 372. Then, each person should also describe things that he or she has found to be particularly effective in dealing with stress. Make a list of these stress-handling techniques. Out of that list, identify your top three stress reducers and be prepared to share these with the class.

ETHICS IN ACTION

Ethical Dilemma Exercise: How Can Managers Help Employees Embrace Responsible and Sustainable Management Practices?

What is the most ethical way to deal with change that will take away some employees' jobs or completely alter the work environment?[59] Andrew Souvaliotis is the chief impact officer and general manager of AIR MILES My Planet and leads AIR MILES for Social Change, a social venture within the AIR MILES Reward Program that aims to inspire greener, healthier, and more socially responsible lifestyle choices among Canadians. Souvaliotis was the founder of Green Rewards, the world's first environmental consumer loyalty program, which was ultimately acquired by LoyaltyOne in 2008. He has been trained by former US vice-president and Nobel laureate Al Gore to help raise public awareness of the impact of climate change and speaks frequently across Canada on the new green economy.[60]

AIR MILES introduced the My Planet program to inspire collectors to make more sutainable choices in grocery shopping, home energy, personal care products, and beauty products, and to reduce their use of chemicals. The program has added more than 100 new environmentally friendly rewards. At a keynote presentation at the Atlantic Eco Expo in Halifax, held in the fall of 2010, Souvaliotis traced his firm's journey in adopting sustainable practices, pointing out that with 9.5 million collectors and more than a hundred brand-name sponsors, AIR MILES and the collector community have the potential to make a difference for the planet.[61]

Imagine that you are the manager working for AIR MILES shortly after Souvaliotis has been tasked with the AIR MILES My Planet inititative. What would be your first reaction? How much stress might you experience as it becomes clear that you are expected to implement the program? What might be the best way to proceed to gain grassroots support for this strategic change within AIR MILES?

Thinking Critically About Ethics

Although numerous organizations provide stress-reduction programs, many employees choose not to participate. Why? Many employees are reluctant to ask for help, especially if a major source of that stress is job insecurity. After all, there is still a stigma associated with stress. Employees don't want to be perceived as unable to handle the demands of their jobs. Although they may need stress management now more than ever, few employees want to admit that they are stressed. What can be done about this paradox? Do organizations even have an ethical responsibility to help employees deal with stress?

Starwood Hotels: That Special Touch

Starwood is one of the world's largest hotel and leisure companies. Its well-known luxury and upscale brands include Four Points, Sheraton, Westin, St. Regis, and W Hotels. In an industry that's highly dependent on attracting and keeping customers, Starwood knows it has to be innovative. In 2006, the company's Westin chain spotted a market opportunity after a survey found that 34 percent of frequent travellers feel lonely away from home. The challenge was to be innovative in finding ways to exploit that opportunity. Again, showing its willingness to be different, the company took an unusual approach.

Instead of hiring the usual consultants, Starwood's management team turned to Six Sigma, a quality management process best known for increasing efficiency and reducing product defects. Many companies have had great success with Six Sigma, but it has often been described as a creativity killer. "Combining creativity and efficiency is a delicate managerial maneuver that few service companies can pull off." But that reputation didn't deter Starwood's managers. One thing they had in their favour was that the company already had a strong culture of creativity. In the 1990s, it designed its popular W Hotels as a blend of high fashion and high energy and captured a lot of attention and customers looking for a trendy experience.

Six Sigma at Starwood has helped increase financial performance by improving the quality of the guest experience. It provides the framework and tools needed to create a consistently superior guest experience at all properties while dramatically improving the bottom line.[62] Today, Starwood uses Six Sigma to dream up projects for its properties around the world. Since the program launched in 2001, 150 employees have been trained as "black belts" and 2700 as "green belts" in the art of Six Sigma. These employees are based mostly at the hotels, with the black belts overseeing the projects and the green belts taking care of the details. The Six Sigma specialists help hotel employees find ways to meet their goals. In fact, almost 100 percent of the creative ideas have come from in-house staff.

Starwood's innovation process starts with hotel teams who "pitch" the Six Sigma group on a new idea. A Six Sigma Council (composed of 13 people) evaluates the idea's merit, based on the goals and expected payoffs. If the council approves a project, the Six Sigma specialists are deployed to help the local hotel teams carry it out.[63]

Do you think Six Sigma's reputation as a "creativity killer" is justified? What does this say about what Starwood has accomplished with its Six Sigma program? What could other companies learn from Starwood's experience? How important do you think it is to have a culture of creativity? If a company doesn't have such a culture, what could managers do? What else might Starwood do to promote creativity and innovation? Do you think the hotel/resort industry environment is more calm waters or white-water rapids?

Changes in the Health Care Industry

When you think about the significant changes that have occurred in people's lives over the past five decades, clearly the advances in medical science would be at the top of such a list.[64] Diseases have been eradicated and medical procedures and devices have helped save thousands of lives. But don't be too quick to conclude that the health care industry is a model of innovation and efficiency.

Hospitals, in general, have one of the most archaic and costly operating systems of any group of large organizations. Nearly 95 percent of all hospitals currently use procedures and record-keeping systems that were implemented more than 50 years ago. It's the way it's always been done, and that is how most doctors and technicians prefer it. Individuals in this industry have been highly reluctant to accept and use new technologies.

Doctors and hospital administrators at Prairie General Hospital, however, refuse to be part of the "old guard." Consider the following that happened in the emergency room at Prairie General. A middle-aged patient was brought in by his wife to the emergency room. The patient, who was very overweight, was complaining of shortness of breath and dizziness. Although the patient claimed he was okay, his wife made him go to the hospital. Immediately, the staff at Prairie General went to work. While nurses hooked the patient up to heart-monitoring equipment and checked his vital signs, a resident wheeled over an emergency room cart, which contained a laptop computer. Logging in the patient's identification number, the ER doctor noticed that the patient had an EKG in the past year. Immediately reviewing the past EKG records and comparing it with current heart-monitoring results, the doctor determined the patient was in the midst of having a heart attack. Within 10 minutes of being seen, doctors had determined that the patient was suffering from a blocked artery. Clot-busting drugs were swiftly administered, and the patient was immediately taken to the cardiac lab, where an emergency angioplasty was performed to open up the clogged artery. Within a day, the patient was back on his feet and ready to go home. In most other hospitals, the patient may not have been so lucky!

Prairie General is unusual in the health care industry. This hospital is investing money in technology that enables it to provide better service at a lower cost. Through its system, called CareWeb, more than 1 million patient records are available. Within each of these records are all previous medical orders, such as lab test results and prescriptions, for each patient. When a patient comes to the hospital, that individual's health history is easily retrievable and can be used to assist in the current diagnosis.

What has been the effect of this technology change on Prairie General? The system is saving the hospital more than $1 million each year. It has reduced errors in patient care by more than 90 percent and reduced prescription errors and potential drug interactions by more than 50 percent. Patient charts are now available in moments rather than hours or days. And patients are now discharged more than 30 minutes faster than they had been before CareWeb was implemented.

Cost savings, time savings, increased patient care, and saved lives—all this makes you wonder why every hospital is not making such changes!

Questions

1. Describe the types of changes that have occurred at Prairie General in terms of structure, technology, and people. Cite examples.

2. Why do you believe there is resistance by the medical profession to systems such as CareWeb? Explain.

3. Assume you were going to make a presentation to a group of hospital staff (doctors and administrators) on why they should invest in technology such as CareWeb. How would you attempt to overcome their resistance to change and their attitude about continuing to do what they have always done? Discuss.

DEVELOPING YOUR INTERPERSONAL SKILLS

Managing Resistance to Change

About the Skill

Managers play an important role in organizational change— that is, they often serve as change agents. However, managers may find that change is resisted by employees. After all, change represents ambiguity and uncertainty, or it threatens the status quo. How can this resistance to change be effectively managed?

Steps in Developing the Skill

You can be more effective at managing resistance to change if you use the following three suggestions:[65]

1. **Assess the climate for change.** One major factor why some changes succeed and others fail is the readiness for change. Assessing the climate for change involves asking several questions. The more affirmative answers you get, the more likely it is that change efforts will succeed.

   - Is the sponsor of the change high enough in the hierarchy to have power to effectively deal with resistance?

   - Is senior management supportive of the change and committed to it?

   - Is there a strong sense of urgency from senior managers about the need for change, and is this feeling shared by others in the organization?

   - Do managers have a clear vision of how the future will look after the change?

   - Are there objective measures in place to evaluate the change effort, and have reward systems been explicitly designed to reinforce them?

   - Is the specific change effort consistent with other changes going on in the organization?

   - Are managers willing to sacrifice their personal self-interests for the good of the organization as a whole?

   - Do managers pride themselves on closely monitoring changes and actions by competitors?

   - Are managers and employees rewarded for taking risks, being innovative, and looking for new and better solutions?

   - Is the organizational structure flexible?

- Does communication flow both down and up in the organization?
- Has the organization successfully implemented changes in the recent past?
- Are employee satisfaction with and trust in management high?
- Is there a high degree of interaction and cooperation between organizational work units?
- Are decisions made quickly, and do decisions take into account a wide variety of suggestions?

2. **Choose an appropriate approach for managing the resistance to change.** There are five tactics that have been suggested for dealing with resistance to change. Each is designed to be appropriate for different conditions of resistance. They are *education and communication* (used when resistance comes from lack of information or inaccurate information); *participation* (used when resistance stems from people not having all the information they need or when they have the power to resist); *facilitation and support* (used when those with power will lose out in a change); *manipulation and cooptation* (used when any other tactic will not work or is too expensive); and *coercion* (used when speed is essential and change agents possess considerable power). Which one of these approaches will be most effective depends on the source of the resistance to the change.

3. **During the time the change is being implemented and after the change is completed, communicate with employees regarding what support you may be able to provide.** Your employees need to know that you are there to support them during change efforts. Be prepared to offer the assistance that may be necessary to help your employees enact the change.

Practising the Skill

Read the following scenario. Write some notes about how you would handle the situation described. Be sure to refer to the three suggestions for managing resistance to change.

Scenario

You are the nursing supervisor at a local hospital that employs both emergency room and floor nurses. Each of these teams of nurses tends to work almost exclusively with others doing the same job. In your professional reading, you have come across the concept of cross-training nursing teams and giving them more varied responsibilities, which in turn has been shown to improve patient care while lowering costs. You call the two team leaders, Sue and Scott, into your office to explain that you want the nursing teams to move to this approach. To your surprise, they are both opposed to the idea. Sue says she and the other emergency room nurses feel they are needed in the ER, where they fill the most vital role in the hospital. They work special hours when needed, do whatever tasks are required, and often work in difficult and stressful circumstances. They think the floor nurses have relatively easy jobs for the pay they receive. Scott, the leader of the floor nurse team, tells you that his group believes the ER nurses lack the special training and extra experience that the floor nurses bring to the hospital. The floor nurses claim they have the heaviest responsibilities and do the most exacting work. Because they have ongoing contact with patients and families, they believe they should not be called away from vital floor duties to help the ER nurses complete their tasks. What should you do about your idea to introduce more cross-training for the nursing teams?

Reinforcing the Skill

The following activities will help you practise and reinforce the skills associated with effectively managing resistance to change.

1. Think about changes (major and minor) that you have dealt with over the last year. Perhaps these changes involved other people and perhaps they were personal. Did you resist the change? Did others resist the change? How did you overcome your resistance or the resistance of others to the change?

2. Interview managers at three different organizations about changes they have implemented. What was their experience in implementing the change? How did they manage resistance to the change?

MyManagementLab

After you have completed the study of Part 3, do the following exercises at the MyManagementLab website (www.pearsoned.ca/mymanagementlab):

- *You're the Manager: Putting Ethics into Action* (Boston Scientific)
- Passport, Scenario 1 (Nelson Naidoo, Diamonds International), Scenario 2 (Kristen Mesicek, Global One Cellular), and Scenario 3 (Danny Lim, 88WebCom)

SCAN THIS

VIDEO CASE INCIDENT

CBC

Please turn to the back of the book to see the Video Case Incidents available for Part 3.

LEADING

After people are hired and brought into an organization, managers must oversee and coordinate their work so that organizational goals can be pursued and achieved. This is the leading function of management. Because this function involves an organization's people, it's an important one. However, precisely because it involves people, it can also be quite challenging. Managing people successfully involves understanding their attitudes, behaviours, personalities, motivation, and so forth. Understanding how people behave and why they do the things they do is downright difficult at times.

● **In PART FOUR,**
we look at the management function of
leading and discuss the following topics:

Chapter 14	Leadership
Chapter 15	Motivating Employees
Chapter 16	Managing Groups and Teams

Leadership

Leaders in organizations make things happen. But what makes leaders different from nonleaders? What's the most appropriate style of leadership? What can you do to be seen as a leader? Those are just a few of the questions we'll try to answer in this chapter. After reading and studying this chapter, you will achieve the following learning outcomes.

Learning Outcomes

1 Define leader and leadership.

2 Compare and contrast early theories of leadership.

3 Describe the three major contingency theories of leadership.

4 Describe modern views of leadership.

5 Discuss contemporary issues affecting leadership.

▶ ▶ ▶ Leadership is a multifaceted topic. As a result, the vignettes in this chapter will highlight five Canadian leaders identified as "master leaders" by Dr. Brad McRae, director of the Atlantic Leadership Institute.[1]

Dr. David Johnston was appointed Canada's governor general in July 2010 but served as the president of the University of Waterloo from 1999 through 2010. At the university, he was a forceful advocate for higher education, research, and innovation. He pointed out that three things distinguish the University of Waterloo from other universities: "We work very hard at innovation—we try constantly to reinvent ourselves. Secondly, we do a relatively small number of things exceedingly well—we have only six faculties, mathematics which is the largest in the world and engineering which is the largest in Canada. Thirdly, we believe deeply in the cooperative education model and employ it across our programs." A visionary at heart, Johnston has proposed the National Learning and Education Act as a national framework to ensure the well-being of the nation's talent. After all, he reasons, we have the Canada Health Act to protect and enhance the physical well-being of Canadians.

Universities are Canada's innovation engines. To reap the rewards of innovation, knowledge transfer, and the chance to shape and be shaped by the newest ideas in education, we must learn to build collaborative partnerships among the universities, the communities they serve, and local business partners. As Johnston puts it, "My definition of leadership is

recognizing your total dependence on the people around you."[2]

Think About It

What does it mean to be a leader for today's organizations? What kinds of challenges does someone like David Johnston face as a leader in the university environment where change is often glacially slow? What can such a person do to encourage other universities to emulate the Waterloo model?

SCAN THIS

Who Are Leaders, and What Is Leadership?

Let's begin by clarifying who leaders are and what leadership is. **Leaders** provide vision and strategy to the organization; managers implement that vision and strategy, coordinate and staff the organization, and handle the day-to-day problems that occur. **Leadership** is the process of influencing individuals or groups toward the achievement of goals.

Are all managers leaders? Because leading is one of the four management functions, ideally, all managers *should* be leaders; thus, we're going to study leaders and leadership from a managerial perspective.[3] However, even though we're looking at these from a managerial perspective, we're aware that groups often have informal leaders who emerge. Although these informal leaders may be able to influence others, they have not been the focus of most leadership research and are not the types of leaders we're studying in this chapter.

Leaders and leadership, like motivation, are organizational behaviour topics that have been researched a lot. Most of that research has been aimed at answering the question "What is an effective leader?" We'll begin our study of leadership by looking at some early leadership theories that attempted to answer that question.

1. Define leader and leadership.

leader A person who can influence others and provide vision and strategy to the organization.

leadership The process of influencing individuals or groups toward the achievement of goals.

Conservative MP Steven Fletcher is motivated to be a leader. A car accident left him quadriplegic when he was 23, and this inspired him to take charge of his life. He won his first political campaign, to be president of the University of Manitoba Students Union. He later became president of the Progressive Conservative Party of Manitoba. When he was elected MP, he defeated his riding's incumbent Liberal candidate. He says many of his constituents are not aware that he is quadriplegic until they meet him.

Early Leadership Theories

2. Compare and contrast early theories of leadership.

▶ ▶ ▶ Phil Fontaine is the former national chief of the Assembly of First Nations. The youngest son in an Ojibway family of 12 children, he served as chief of Sagkeeng First Nation at the tender age of 28 and set groundbreaking policies for his band. As national chief, Fontaine's crowning achievement was the negotiation of the $5.6 billion residential schools settlement, where he was known for opening lines of communication and building consensus to resolve complex and difficult issues. His focus for the future is the elimination of poverty; improvements in education, health care, and housing; and strengthening of cultural identity for First Nations people, the fastest-growing demographic segment in Canada.[4]

Think About It

In working toward a settlement for the residential schools abuses, Phil Fontaine had to work with an extraordinarily diverse group of stakeholders with competing agendas in the Assembly of First Nations and in the federal government. What traits would serve him well in this situation? What behaviours would serve him well in the negotiations?

People have been interested in leadership since they started coming together in groups to accomplish goals. However, it wasn't until the early part of the twentieth century that researchers actually began to study leadership. These early leadership theories focused on the *leader* (trait theories) and how the *leader interacted* with his or her group members (behavioural theories).

Trait Theories

Think about some of the managers you have encountered. How did their traits affect whether they were good or bad managers?

Even before the 2008 US presidential election, Barack Obama had captured the attention of political analysts and the public.[5] He had been compared to both Abraham Lincoln and Martin Luther King Jr. Many are saying that he has what it takes to be a leading political figure—characteristics such as self-awareness, clarity of speech, keen intellect, and an ability to relate to people. Is Obama a leader? The trait theories of leadership would answer this question by focusing on his traits.

MyManagementLab
Q&A 14.1

Leadership research in the 1920s and 1930s focused on isolating leader traits—that is, characteristics—that would differentiate leaders from nonleaders. Some of the traits studied included physical stature, appearance, social class, emotional stability, fluency of speech, and sociability. Despite the best efforts of researchers, it proved impossible to identify a set of traits that would *always* differentiate a leader (the person) from a nonleader. Maybe it was a bit optimistic to think that there could be consistent and unique traits that would apply universally to all effective leaders, no matter whether they were in charge of Toyota Motor Corporation, the Moscow Ballet, the country of France, a local collegiate chapter of Alpha Chi Omega, Ted's Malibu Surf Shop, or the University of Waterloo. However, later attempts to identify traits consistently associated with *leadership* (the process, not the person) were more successful. Seven traits associated with effective leadership include drive, the desire to lead, honesty and integrity, self-confidence, intelligence, job-relevant knowledge, and extroversion.[6] These traits are briefly described in Exhibit 14-1.

Researchers have begun organizing traits around the Big Five personality framework.[7] They have found that most of the dozens of traits that emerged in various leadership reviews fall under one of the Big Five personality traits (extroversion, agreeableness,

Exhibit 14-1

Seven Traits Associated with Leadership

1. **Drive.** Leaders exhibit a high effort level. They have a relatively high desire for achievement; they are ambitious; they have a lot of energy; they are tirelessly persistent in their activities; and they show initiative.

2. **Desire to lead.** Leaders have a strong desire to influence and lead others. They demonstrate the willingness to take responsibility.

3. **Honesty and integrity.** Leaders build trusting relationships between themselves and followers by being truthful or nondeceitful and by showing high consistency between word and deed.

4. **Self-confidence.** Followers look to leaders for an absence of self-doubt. Leaders, therefore, need to show self-confidence in order to convince followers of the rightness of their goals and decisions.

5. **Intelligence.** Leaders need to be intelligent enough to gather, synthesize, and interpret large amounts of information, and they need to be able to create visions, solve problems, and make correct decisions.

6. **Job-relevant knowledge.** Effective leaders have a high degree of knowledge about the company, industry, and technical matters. In-depth knowledge allows leaders to make well-informed decisions and to understand the implications of those decisions.

7. **Extroversion.** Leaders are energetic, lively people. They are sociable, assertive, and rarely silent or withdrawn.

Sources: S. A. Kirkpatrick and E. A. Locke, "Leadership: Do Traits Really Matter?" *Academy of Management Executive*, May 1991, pp. 48–60; and T. A. Judge, J. E. Bono, R. Ilies, and M. Werner, "Personality and Leadership: A Qualitative and Quantitative Review," *Journal of Applied Psychology*, August 2002, pp. 765–780.

conscientiousness, emotional stability, and openness to experience). This approach has resulted in consistent and strong support for traits as predictors of leadership.

Researchers eventually recognized that traits alone were not sufficient for identifying effective leaders because explanations based solely on traits ignored the interactions of leaders and their group members as well as situational factors. Possessing the appropriate traits only made it more likely that an individual would be an effective leader. Therefore, leadership research from the late 1940s to the mid-1960s concentrated on the preferred behavioural styles that leaders demonstrated. Researchers wondered whether there was something unique in what effective leaders *did*—in other words, in their *behaviour*.

Behavioural Theories

Rick Waugh, president and CEO of Scotiabank, has very little in common with his predecessors who led the bank before him. Both Cedric Ritchie, CEO in the 1970s and 1980s, and Peter Godsoe, who succeeded Ritchie, are described as "autocratic, undemocratic and one-man army" when others reflect on their leadership styles.[8] Waugh, who was appointed president and CEO in 2003, is seen as kinder and gentler. "He is always open to discussion," says Laurent Lemaire, executive vice-chairman of pulp-and-paper manufacturer Cascades and a member of Scotiabank's executive and risk committee and human resources committee. "He will listen to you bring ideas."[9] Scotiabank has been quite successful under different leaders, and moved from the number five to the number two bank in Canada under Godsoe. But this example shows that leaders can behave in very different ways, even when working for the same organization. What do we know about leader behaviour, and how can it help us in our understanding of what an effective leader is?

Researchers hoped that the behavioural theories approach would provide more definitive answers about the nature of leadership than did the trait theories. The four main leader behaviour studies are summarized in Exhibit 14-2.

Exhibit 14-2

Behavioural Theories of Leadership

	Behavioural Dimension	Conclusion
University of Iowa	*Democratic style:* involving subordinates, delegating authority, and encouraging participation *Autocratic style:* dictating work methods, centralizing decision making, and limiting participation *Laissez-faire style:* giving group freedom to make decisions and complete work	Democratic style of leadership was most effective, although later studies showed mixed results.
Ohio State	*Consideration:* being considerate of followers' ideas and feelings *Initiating structure:* structuring work and work relationships to meet job goals	High-high leader (high in consideration and high in initiating structure) achieved high subordinate performance and satisfaction, but not in all situations.
University of Michigan	*Employee oriented:* emphasizes interpersonal relationships and taking care of employees' needs *Production oriented:* emphasizes technical or task aspects of job	Employee-oriented leaders were associated with high group productivity and higher job satisfaction.
Managerial Grid	*Concern for people:* measures leader's concern for subordinates on a scale of 1 to 9 (low to high) *Concern for production:* measures leader's concern for getting job done on a scale of 1 to 9 (low to high)	Leaders performed best with a 9,9 style (high concern for production and high concern for people).

University of Iowa Studies

The University of Iowa studies explored three leadership styles to find which was the most effective.[10] The **autocratic** style described a leader who dictated work methods, made unilateral decisions, and limited employee participation. The **democratic** style described a leader who involved employees in decision making, delegated authority, and used feedback as an opportunity for coaching employees. Finally, the **laissez-faire** style described a leader who let the group make decisions and complete the work in whatever way it saw fit. The researchers' results seemed to indicate that the democratic style contributed to both good quantity and quality of work. Had the answer to the question of the most effective leadership style been found? Unfortunately, it wasn't that simple. Later studies of the autocratic and democratic styles showed mixed results. For instance, the democratic style sometimes produced higher performance levels than the autocratic style, but at other times, it didn't. However, more consistent results were found when a measure of employee satisfaction was used. Group members were more satisfied under a democratic leader than under an autocratic one.[11]

Now leaders had a dilemma! Should they focus on achieving higher performance or on achieving higher member satisfaction? This recognition of the dual nature of a leader's behaviour—that is, focus on the task and focus on the people—was also a key characteristic of the other behavioural studies.

The Ohio State Studies

The Ohio State studies identified two important dimensions of leader behaviour.[12] Beginning with a list of more than 1000 behavioural dimensions, the researchers eventually narrowed it down to just two that accounted for most of the leadership behaviour described by group members. The first dimension, called **initiating structure**, referred to the extent to which a leader defined his or her role and the roles of group members in attaining goals. It included behaviours that involved attempts to organize work, work relationships, and goals. The second dimension, called **consideration**, was defined as the extent to which a leader had work relationships characterized by mutual trust and respect for group members' ideas and feelings. A leader who was high in consideration helped group members with personal problems, was friendly and approachable, and treated all group members as equals. He or she showed concern for (was considerate of) his or her followers' comfort, well-being, status, and satisfaction. Research found that a leader who was high in both initiating structure and consideration (a **high-high leader**) sometimes achieved high group task performance and high group member satisfaction, but not always.

University of Michigan Studies

Leadership studies conducted at the University of Michigan at about the same time as those being done at Ohio State also hoped to identify behavioural characteristics of leaders that were related to performance effectiveness. The Michigan group also came up with two dimensions of leadership behaviour, which they labelled *employee oriented* and *production oriented*.[13] Leaders who were employee oriented were described as emphasizing interpersonal relationships. The production-oriented leaders, in contrast, tended to emphasize the task aspects of the job. Unlike the other studies, the Michigan studies concluded that leaders who were employee oriented were able to get high group productivity and high group member satisfaction.

The Managerial Grid

The behavioural dimensions from the early leadership studies provided the basis for the development of a two-dimensional grid for appraising leadership styles. This **managerial grid** used the behavioural dimensions "concern for people" and "concern for production" and evaluated a leader's use of these behaviours, ranking them on a scale from 1 (low) to 9 (high).[14] Although the grid (shown in Exhibit 14-3) had 81 potential categories into which a leader's behavioural style might fall, only 5 styles were named: impoverished management (1,1), task management (9,1), middle-of-the-road management (5,5), country

autocratic style A leadership style where the leader tends to centralize authority, dictate work methods, make unilateral decisions, and limit employee participation.

democratic style A leadership style where the leader tends to involve employees in decision making, delegate authority, encourage participation in deciding work methods and goals, and use feedback as an opportunity for coaching employees.

laissez-faire style A leadership style where the leader tends to give the group complete freedom to make decisions and complete the work in whatever way it sees fit.

MyManagementLab
Q&A 14.2

initiating structure The extent to which a leader defines his or her role and the roles of group members in attaining goals.

consideration The extent to which a leader has work relationships characterized by mutual trust and respect for group members' ideas and feelings.

high-high leader A leader high in both initiating structure and consideration behaviours.

managerial grid A two-dimensional grid of leadership behaviours—concern for people and concern for production—that results in five different leadership styles.

Exhibit 14-3

The Managerial Grid

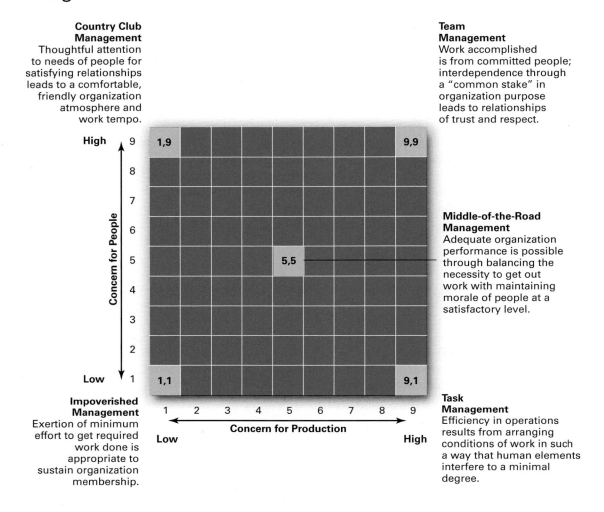

Country Club Management
Thoughtful attention to needs of people for satisfying relationships leads to a comfortable, friendly organization atmosphere and work tempo.

Team Management
Work accomplished is from committed people; interdependence through a "common stake" in organization purpose leads to relationships of trust and respect.

Middle-of-the-Road Management
Adequate organization performance is possible through balancing the necessity to get out work with maintaining morale of people at a satisfactory level.

Impoverished Management
Exertion of minimum effort to get required work done is appropriate to sustain organization membership.

Task Management
Efficiency in operations results from arranging conditions of work in such a way that human elements interfere to a minimal degree.

club management (1,9), and team management (9,9). Of these five styles, the researchers concluded that managers performed best when using a 9,9 style. Unfortunately, the grid offered no explanations about what made a manager an effective leader; it only provided a framework for conceptualizing leadership style. In fact, there's little substantive evidence to support the conclusion that a 9,9 style is most effective in all situations.[15]

Leadership researchers were discovering that predicting leadership success involved something more complex than isolating a few leader traits or preferable behaviours. They began looking at situational influences. Specifically, which leadership styles might be suitable in different situations, and what were these different situations?

Contingency Theories of Leadership

3. Describe the three major contingency theories of leadership.

▶ ▶ ▶ Moya Greene was appointed president of Canada Post on May 12, 2005, following a portfolio of difficult assignments—she was responsible for the privatization of CN Rail, helped deregulate the airline industry, and took a lead role in the overhaul of the unemployment insurance system. Because Greene did not come from a logistics or postal background, she had to learn the culture at Canada Post first-hand. Starting from the ground up, she worked at a variety of key tasks and gained a sense of how complex and difficult it is to move 40 million pieces of mail a day to 14 million mailboxes, and was quoted as saying, "Each of our executives has to do a specific number of front line operations quarterly."[16] After departing from Canada Post, Greene became CEO of the Royal Mail in the summer of 2010.

Think About It

How did Moya Greene's commitment to gaining front-line experience help her understand the context for decision making at Canada Post? How do different situations and contexts influence her leadership style?

Do you know what your leadership style is? What impact might that have on how you lead?

Contingency theories of leadership developed after it became clear that identifying traits or key behaviours was not enough to understand what made good leaders. Contingency researchers considered whether different situations required different styles of leadership. "The corporate world is filled with stories of leaders who failed to achieve greatness because they failed to understand the context they were working in."[17] Consider the fate of some of the Americans who have been recruited to run Canadian companies. Hudson's Bay Company hired Bill Fields and Zellers hired Millard Barron to replicate their US retail successes in Canada. Neither was able to do so. Successful Texas oilman J. P. Bryan was given two chances to restore profitability at Canadian companies—Gulf Canada Resources (now ConocoPhillips) and Canadian 88 Energy (now Pengrowth Energy Trust)—and failed in both attempts.[18] These examples suggest that one's leadership style may need to be adjusted for different companies and employees, and perhaps even for different countries.

In this section, we examine three contingency theories of leadership: the Fiedler contingency model, Hersey and Blanchard's Situational Leadership®/leader participation model, and path–goal theory. Each theory looks at defining leadership style and the situation, and attempts to answer *if–then* contingencies (that is, *if* this is the situation, *then* this is the best leadership style to use).

The Fiedler Model

The first comprehensive contingency model for leadership was developed by Fred Fiedler.[19] The **Fiedler contingency model** proposed that effective group performance depended on properly matching the leader's style and the amount of control and influence in the situation. The model was based on the premise that a certain leadership style would be most effective in different types of situations. The keys were to (1) define those leadership styles and the different types of situations and then (2) identify the appropriate combinations of style and situation.

Fiedler proposed that a key factor in leadership success was an individual's basic leadership style, either task oriented or relationship oriented. To measure a leader's style, Fiedler developed the **least-preferred co-worker (LPC) questionnaire**. This questionnaire contained 18 pairs of contrasting adjectives—for example, pleasant–unpleasant, cold–warm, boring–interesting, and friendly–unfriendly. Respondents were asked to think of all the co-workers they had ever had and to describe that one person they *least enjoyed* working with by rating him or her on a scale of 1 to 8 for each of the 18 sets of adjectives. (The 8 always described the positive adjective out of the pair, and the 1 always described the negative adjective out of the pair.)

If the leader described the least-preferred co-worker in relatively positive terms (in other words, a "high" LPC score—a score of 64 or above), then the respondent was primarily

Fiedler contingency model A leadership theory that proposed that effective group performance depended on the proper match between a leader's style and the degree to which the situation allowed the leader to control and influence.

least-preferred co-worker (LPC) questionnaire A questionnaire that measured whether a leader was task or relationship oriented.

interested in good personal relations with co-workers, and the style would be described as *relationship oriented*. In contrast, if the leader saw the least-preferred co-worker in relatively unfavourable terms (a low LPC score—a score of 57 or below), he or she was primarily interested in productivity and getting the job done; thus, the individual's style would be labelled *task oriented*. Fiedler acknowledged that a small number of people might fall in between these two extremes and not have a cut-and-dried leadership style. One other important point is that Fiedler assumed that a person's leadership style was fixed, regardless of the situation. In other words, if you were a relationship-oriented leader, you'd always be one, and if you were a task-oriented leader, you'd always be one.

After an individual's leadership style had been assessed through the LPC, it was time to evaluate the situation in order to be able to match the leader with the situation. Fiedler's research uncovered three contingency dimensions that defined the key situational factors in leader effectiveness:

leader–member relations One of Fiedler's situational contingencies that described the degree of confidence, trust, and respect employees had for their leader.

task structure One of Fiedler's situational contingencies that described the degree to which job assignments were formalized and structured.

position power One of Fiedler's situational contingencies that described the degree of influence a leader had over activities such as hiring, firing, discipline, promotions, and salary increases.

- **Leader–member relations**—The degree of confidence, trust, and respect employees had for their leader; rated as either good or poor.

- **Task structure**—The degree to which job assignments were formalized and structured; rated as either high or low.

- **Position power**—The degree of influence a leader had over activities such as hiring, firing, discipline, promotions, and salary increases; rated as either strong or weak.

Each leadership situation was evaluated in terms of these three contingency variables, which when combined produced eight possible situations that were either favourable or unfavourable for the leader. (See the bottom of Exhibit 14-4.) Situations I, II, and III were classified as highly favourable for the leader. Situations IV, V, and VI were moderately favourable for the leader. And situations VII and VIII were described as highly unfavourable for the leader.

Once Fiedler had described the leader variables and the situational variables, he had everything he needed to define the specific contingencies for leadership effectiveness.

Exhibit 14-4

The Fiedler Model

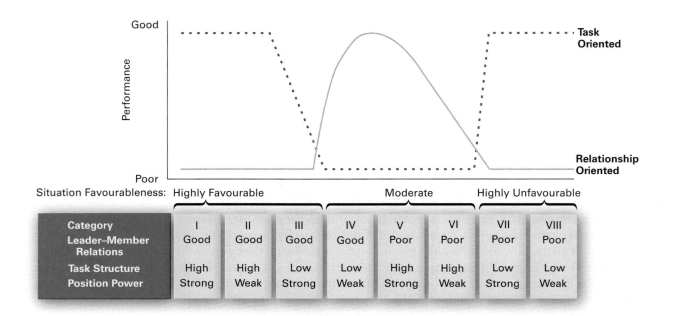

Category	I	II	III	IV	V	VI	VII	VIII
Leader–Member Relations	Good	Good	Good	Good	Poor	Poor	Poor	Poor
Task Structure	High	High	Low	Low	High	High	Low	Low
Position Power	Strong	Weak	Strong	Weak	Strong	Weak	Strong	Weak

To do so, he studied 1200 groups where he compared relationship-oriented versus task-oriented leadership styles in each of the eight situational categories. He concluded that task-oriented leaders performed better in very favourable situations and in very unfavourable situations. (See the top of Exhibit 14-4, where performance is shown on the vertical axis and situation favourableness is shown on the horizontal axis.) On the other hand, relationship-oriented leaders performed better in moderately favourable situations.

Because Fiedler treated an individual's leadership style as fixed, there were only two ways to improve leader effectiveness. First, you could bring in a new leader whose style better fit the situation. For instance, if the group situation was highly unfavourable but was led by a relationship-oriented leader, the group's performance could be improved by replacing that person with a task-oriented leader. The second alternative was to change the situation to fit the leader. This could be done by restructuring tasks; by increasing or decreasing the power that the leader had over factors such as salary increases, promotions, and disciplinary actions; or by improving the leader–member relations.

Research testing the overall validity of Fiedler's model has shown considerable evidence in support of the model.[20] However, his theory wasn't without criticisms. The major criticism is that it's probably unrealistic to assume that a person can't change his or her leadership style to fit the situation. Effective leaders can and do change their styles. Another is that the LPC wasn't very practical. Finally, the situation variables were difficult to assess.[21] Despite its shortcomings, the Fiedler model showed that effective leadership style needed to reflect situational factors.

MyManagementLab
Q&A 14.3

Hersey and Blanchard's Situational Leadership® Theory

Paul Hersey and Ken Blanchard developed a leadership theory that has gained a strong following among management development specialists.[22] This model, called **Situational Leadership® theory (SLT)**, is a contingency theory that focuses on followers' readiness. Before we proceed, there are two points we need to clarify: why a leadership theory focuses on the followers and what is meant by the term *readiness*.

The emphasis on the followers in leadership effectiveness reflects the reality that it *is* the followers who accept or reject the leader. Regardless of what the leader does, the group's effectiveness depends on the actions of the followers. This is an important dimension that most leadership theories have overlooked or underemphasized. **Readiness**, as defined by Hersey and Blanchard, refers to the extent to which people have the ability and willingness to accomplish a specific task.

SLT uses the same two leadership dimensions that Fiedler identified: task and relationship behaviours. However, Hersey and Blanchard go a step further by considering each as either high or low and then combining them into four specific leadership styles:

- *Telling* (high task–low relationship)—The leader defines roles and tells people what, how, when, and where to do various tasks.

- *Selling* (high task–high relationship)—The leader provides both directive and supportive behaviour.

- *Participating* (low task–high relationship)—The leader and followers share in decision making; the main role of the leader is facilitating and communicating.

- *Delegating* (low task–low relationship)—The leader provides little direction or support.

The final component in the SLT model is the four stages of follower readiness:

- *R1*—People are both *unable and unwilling* to take responsibility for doing something. Followers aren't competent or confident.

- *R2*—People are *unable but willing* to do the necessary job tasks. Followers are motivated but lack the appropriate skills.

- *R3*—People are *able but unwilling* to do what the leader wants. Followers are competent but don't want to do something.

- *R4*—People are both *able and willing* to do what is asked of them.

Situational leadership® theory (SLT) A leadership contingency theory that focuses on followers' readiness.

MyManagementLab
Q&A 14.4

readiness The extent to which people have the ability and willingness to accomplish a specific task.

Exhibit 14-5

Hersey and Blanchard's Situational Leadership®

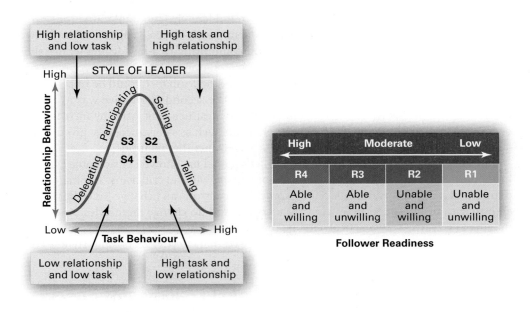

SLT essentially views the leader–follower relationship as like that of a parent and a child. Just as a parent needs to relinquish control when a child becomes more mature and responsible, so too should leaders. As followers reach higher levels of readiness, the leader responds not only by decreasing control over their activities but also by decreasing relationship behaviours. The SLT says if followers are at R1 (*unable and unwilling* to do a task), the leader needs to use the telling style and give clear and specific directions; if followers are at R2 (*unable and willing*), the leader needs to use the selling style and display high task orientation to compensate for the followers' lack of ability and high relationship orientation to get followers to "buy into" the leader's desires; if followers are at R3 (*able and unwilling*), the leader needs to use the participating style to gain their support; and if employees are at R4 (both *able and willing*), the leader doesn't need to do much and should use the delegating style.

SLT has intuitive appeal. It acknowledges the importance of followers and builds on the logic that leaders can compensate for ability and motivational limitations in their followers. However, research efforts to test and support the theory have generally been disappointing.[23] Possible explanations include internal inconsistencies in the model as well as problems with research methodology. Despite its appeal and wide popularity, we have to be cautious about any enthusiastic endorsement of SLT.

Path–Goal Theory

path–goal theory A leadership theory that says the leader's job is to assist followers in attaining their goals and to provide direction or support needed to ensure that their goals are compatible with those of the group or organization.

Currently, one of the most respected approaches to understanding leadership is **path–goal theory**, which states that the leader's job is to assist followers in attaining their goals and to provide direction or support needed to ensure that their goals are compatible with those of the group or organization. Developed by Robert House, path–goal theory takes key elements from the expectancy theory of motivation.[24] The term *path–goal* is derived from the belief that effective leaders clarify the path to help their followers get from where they are to the achievement of their work goals and make the journey along the path easier by reducing roadblocks and pitfalls.

House identified four leadership behaviours:

- *Directive leader*—The leader lets subordinates know what's expected of them, schedules work to be done, and gives specific guidance on how to accomplish tasks.

- *Supportive leader*—The leader shows concern for the needs of followers and is friendly.

- *Participative leader*—The leader consults with group members and uses their suggestions before making a decision.

- *Achievement-oriented leader*—The leader sets challenging goals and expects followers to perform at their highest level.

In contrast to Fiedler's view that a leader can't change his or her behaviour, House assumed that leaders are flexible and can display any or all of these leadership styles, depending on the situation.

As Exhibit 14-6 illustrates, path–goal theory proposes two situational or contingency variables that moderate the leadership behaviour–outcome relationship: those in the *environment* that are outside the control of the follower (factors including task structure, formal authority system, and the work group) and those that are part of the personal characteristics of the *follower* (including locus of control, experience, and perceived ability). Environmental factors determine the type of leader behaviour required if subordinate outcomes are to be maximized; personal characteristics of the follower determine how the environment and leader behaviour are interpreted. The theory proposes that a leader's behaviour won't be effective if it's redundant with what the environmental structure is providing or is incongruent with follower characteristics. For example, the following are some predictions from path–goal theory:

- Directive leadership leads to greater satisfaction when tasks are ambiguous or stressful than when they are highly structured and well laid out. The followers aren't sure what to do, so the leader needs to give them some direction.

MyManagementLab
PRISM 2

Exhibit 14-6

Path–Goal Model

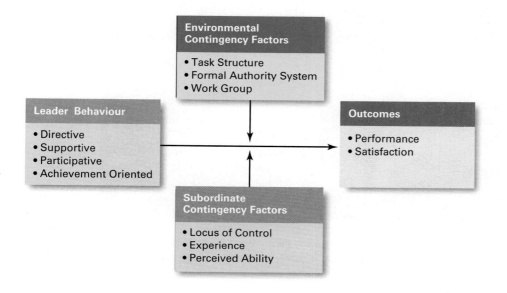

- Supportive leadership results in high employee performance and satisfaction when subordinates are performing structured tasks. In this situation, the leader only needs to support followers, not tell them what to do.

- Directive leadership is likely to be perceived as redundant among subordinates with high perceived ability or with considerable experience. These followers are quite capable, so they don't need a leader to tell them what to do.

- The clearer and more bureaucratic the formal authority relationships, the more leaders should exhibit supportive behaviour and de-emphasize directive behaviour. The organizational situation has provided the structure as far as what is expected of followers, so the leader's role is simply to support.

- Directive leadership will foster higher employee satisfaction when there is substantive conflict within a work group. In this situation, the followers need a leader who will take charge.

- Subordinates with an internal locus of control will be more satisfied with a participative style. Because these followers believe that they control what happens to them, they prefer to participate in decisions.

- Subordinates with an external locus of control will be more satisfied with a directive style. These followers believe that what happens to them is a result of the external environment, so they would prefer a leader who tells them what to do.

- Achievement-oriented leadership will increase subordinates' expectations that effort will lead to high performance when tasks are ambiguously structured. By setting challenging goals, followers know what the expectations are.

Research on the path–goal model is generally encouraging. Although not every study has found support for the model, the majority of the evidence supports the logic underlying the theory.[25] In summary, an employee's performance and satisfaction are likely to be positively influenced when a leader chooses a leadership style that compensates for shortcomings in either the employee or the work setting. However, if a leader spends time explaining tasks that are already clear or when an employee has the ability and experience to handle tasks without interference, the employee is likely to see such directive behaviour as redundant or even insulting.

MyManagementLab
Q&A 14.5

Contemporary Views of Leadership

4. Describe modern views of leadership.

▶ ▶ ▶ When David Cheesewright became president of Wal-Mart Canada, the organization was in the midst of implementing its sustainability strategy, under the banner of "the greener good." Lee Scott, president of Wal-Mart International, had set goals of zero waste to landfill (beginning with a 65 percent diversion rate by 2014), and a move to 100 percent renewable energy, with all Wal-Mart suppliers to be held to compliance standards supporting these initiatives. It was the company's intent to price products in a way that would reflect their true costs—including the environmental ones.[26]

Think About It

As president of Wal-Mart Canada, David Cheesewright is tasked with implementing a fundamental change in strategic direction. What tools might he use? What style of leadership would best support this transformation of the organizational culture? What types of resistance should he expect?

What are the latest views of leadership? There are three we want to look at: transformational vs. transactional leadership,[27] charismatic–visionary leadership, and team leadership.

Transformational vs. Transactional Leadership

Many early leadership theories viewed leaders as **transactional leaders**—that is, leaders who lead primarily by using social exchanges (or transactions). Transactional leaders guide or motivate followers to work toward established goals by exchanging rewards for their productivity.[28] But there's another type of leader—a **transformational leader**—who stimulates and inspires (transforms) followers to achieve extraordinary outcomes. Examples include Jim Goodnight of SAS Institute and Andrea Jung of Avon. They pay attention to the concerns and developmental needs of individual followers; they change followers' awareness of issues by helping those followers look at old problems in new ways; and they are able to excite, arouse, and inspire followers to exert extra effort to achieve group goals.

Transactional and transformational leadership shouldn't be viewed as opposing approaches to getting things done.[29] Transformational leadership develops from transactional leadership. Transformational leadership produces levels of employee effort and performance that go beyond what would occur with a transactional approach alone. Moreover, transformational leadership is more than charisma because a transformational leader attempts to instill in followers the ability to question not only established views but views held by the leader.[30] The four factors that characterize transformational leadership (the "four I's") are presented in *Tips for Managers—How to Be a Transformational Leader*. The evidence supporting the superiority of transformational leadership over transactional leadership is overwhelmingly impressive. For instance, studies that looked at managers in different settings, including the military and business, found that transformational leaders were evaluated as more effective, higher performers, more promotable than their transactional counterparts, and more interpersonally sensitive.[31] In addition, evidence indicates that transformational leadership is strongly correlated with lower turnover rates and higher levels of productivity, employee satisfaction, creativity, goal attainment, and follower well-being.[32]

transactional leaders Leaders who lead primarily by using social exchanges (or transactions).

transformational leaders Leaders who stimulate and inspire (transform) followers to achieve extraordinary outcomes.

TIPS FOR MANAGERS

How to be a Transformational Leader

- **Individualized consideration:** Pay attention to the needs of individual followers to help them reach their full potential.

- **Intellectual stimulation:** Provide "ways and reasons for followers to change the way they think about" things.

- **Inspirational motivation:** "Set an example of hard work, give 'pep' talks, [and] remain optimistic in times of crisis."

- **Idealized influence:** Show respect for others, building confidence and trust about the mission in followers.

Source: B. J. Avolio, D. A. Waldman, and F. J. Yammarino, "Leading in the 1990s: The Four I's of Transformational Leadership," *Journal of European Industrial Training* 15, no. 4 (1991), pp. 9–16.

Charismatic–Visionary Leadership

Have you ever encountered a charismatic leader? What was this person like?

Jeff Bezos, founder and CEO of Amazon.com, exudes energy, enthusiasm, and drive.[33] He's fun loving (his legendary laugh has been described as a flock of Canadian geese on nitrous oxide) but has pursued his vision for Amazon with serious intensity and has demonstrated an ability to inspire his employees through the ups and downs of a rapidly growing company. Bezos is what we call a **charismatic leader**—that is, an enthusiastic, self-confident leader whose personality and actions influence people to behave in certain ways.

charismatic leaders Enthusiastic, self-confident leaders whose personalities and actions influence people to behave in certain ways.

Characteristics of Charismatic Leaders

Several authors have attempted to identify personal characteristics of charismatic leaders.[34] The most comprehensive analysis identified five such characteristics: Charismatic leaders have a vision, ability to articulate that vision, willingness to take risks to achieve that vision, sensitivity to both environmental constraints and follower needs, and behaviours that are out of the ordinary.[35]

Effects of Charismatic Leadership

MyManagementLab
Q&A 14.6

An increasing body of evidence shows impressive correlations between charismatic leadership and high performance and satisfaction among followers.[36] Although one study found that charismatic CEOs had no impact on subsequent organizational performance, charisma is still believed to be a desirable leadership quality.[37]

Becoming Charismatic

If charisma is desirable, can people learn to be charismatic leaders? Or are charismatic leaders born with their qualities? Although a small number of experts still think that charisma can't be learned, most believe that individuals can be trained to exhibit charismatic behaviours.[38] For example, researchers have succeeded in teaching undergraduate students to "be" charismatic. How? The students have been taught to articulate a far-reaching goal, communicate high performance expectations, exhibit confidence in the ability of subordinates to meet those expectations, and empathize with the needs of their subordinates; they have learned to project a powerful, confident, and dynamic presence; and they have practised using a captivating and engaging tone of voice. The researchers have also trained student leaders to use charismatic nonverbal behaviours, including leaning toward the follower when communicating, maintaining direct eye contact, and having a relaxed posture and animated facial expressions. In groups with these "trained" charismatic leaders, members had higher task performance, higher task adjustment, and better adjustment to the leader and to the group than did group members who worked in groups led by noncharismatic leaders.

One last thing we should say about charismatic leadership is that it may not always be necessary to achieve high levels of employee performance. Charismatic leadership may be most appropriate when the follower's task has an ideological purpose or when the environment involves a high degree of stress and uncertainty.[39] This may explain why, when charismatic leaders surface, they're likely to crop up in politics, religion, or wartime, or when a business firm is starting up or facing a survival crisis. For example, Martin Luther King Jr. used his charisma to bring about social equality through nonviolent means, and Steve Jobs achieved unwavering loyalty and commitment from Apple's technical staff in the early 1980s by articulating a vision of personal computers that would dramatically change the way people lived.

Visionary Leadership

visionary leadership The ability to create and articulate a realistic, credible, and attractive vision of the future that improves on the present situation.

Although the term *vision* is often linked with charismatic leadership, **visionary leadership** is different because it's the ability to create and articulate a realistic, credible, and attractive vision of the future that improves on the present situation.[40] This vision, if properly selected and implemented, is so energizing that it "in effect jump-starts the future by calling forth the skills, talents, and resources to make it happen."[41]

An organization's vision should offer clear and compelling imagery that taps into people's emotions and inspires enthusiasm to pursue the organization's goals. It should be able to generate possibilities that are inspirational and unique and offer new ways of doing things that are clearly better for the organization and its members. Visions that are clearly articulated and have powerful imagery are easily grasped and accepted. For instance, Michael Dell of Dell Inc. created a vision of a business that sells and delivers customized PCs directly to customers in less than a week. The late Mary Kay Ash's vision of women as entrepreneurs selling products that improved their self-image gave impetus to her cosmetics company, Mary Kay Cosmetics.

Team Leadership

Because leadership is increasingly taking place within a team context and more organizations are using work teams, the role of the leader in guiding team members has become increasingly important. The role of a team leader *is* different from the traditional leadership role, as J. D. Bryant, a supervisor at the Texas Instruments Forest Lane plant in Dallas, discovered.[42] One day he was contentedly overseeing a staff of 15 circuit board assemblers. The next day he was told that the company was going to use employee teams, and he was to become a "facilitator." He said, "I'm supposed to teach the teams everything I know and then let them make their own decisions." Confused about his new role, he admitted, "There was no clear plan on what I was supposed to do." What *is* involved in being a team leader?

As chair and CEO of MTV Networks (MTV), Judy McGrath gets to rub shoulders with the likes of Jon Stewart, SpongeBob SquarePants, Bono, Michael Stipe, Mariah Carey, and John Legend. Today MTV is a $7 billion subsidiary of Viacom reaching more than 400 million households in nearly 170 countries. McGrath's challenge is keeping her employees focused on making sure MTV stays bold and experimental. Being a team leader calls on her "skillful management of talent and the chaos that comes with a creative enterprise." One of her most important leadership skills is her ability to listen to all the people in the organization, from interns to senior managers. Says one executive, "Judy's ability to concentrate on people is intense." (Note: McGrath left her position with MTV in 2011.)

MyManagementLab
Q&A 14.7

Many leaders are not equipped to handle the change to employee teams. As one consultant noted, "Even the most capable managers have trouble making the transition because all the command-and-control type things they were encouraged to do before are no longer appropriate. There's no reason to have any skill or sense of this."[43] This same consultant estimated that "probably 15 percent of managers are natural team leaders; another 15 percent could never lead a team because it runs counter to their personality—that is, they're unable to sublimate their dominating style for the good of the team. Then there's that huge group in the middle: Team leadership doesn't come naturally to them, but they can learn it."[44]

The challenge for many managers is learning how to become an effective team leader. They have to learn skills such as patiently sharing information, being able to trust others and give up authority, and understanding when to intervene. And effective team leaders have mastered the difficult balancing act of knowing when to leave their teams alone and when to get involved. New team leaders may try to retain too much control at a time when team members need more autonomy, or they may abandon their teams at times when the teams need support and help.[45]

One study looking at organizations that had reorganized themselves around employee teams found certain common responsibilities of all leaders. These included coaching, facilitating, handling disciplinary problems, reviewing team and individual performance, training, and communication.[46] However, a more meaningful way to describe the team leader's job is to focus on two priorities: (1) managing the team's external boundary and (2) facilitating the team process.[47] These priorities entail four specific leadership roles, as shown in Exhibit 14-7.

Exhibit 14-7

Team Leadership Roles

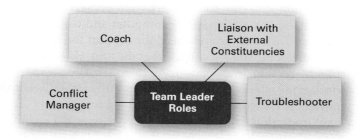

Leadership Issues in the Twenty-First Century

5. Discuss contemporary issues affecting leadership.

▶ ▶ ▶ In 2010, Annette Verschuren was inducted into Canada's Marketing Hall of Legends and the Nova Scotia Business Hall of Fame. Verschuren clearly demonstrated her superior leadership skills in her role as president of The Home Depot Canada. When she took on the role in March 2006, there were just 19 Home Depot stores in Canada, but by the time she stepped down in January 2011, that number had grown to 179! Verschuren also led the expansion of the company into China, acquiring a chain of 12 stores in December 2006.

Before working for The Home Depot, Verschuren's impressive titles included president and co-owner of Michael's of Canada (arts and crafts stores) and vice-president of corporate development at Imasco Ltd. (a holding company for Shoppers Drug Mart, Canada Trust, and Imperial Tobacco). In addition to her work in the private sector, Verschuren served as executive vice-president of Canada Development Investment Corporation, privatizing various Crown corporations.[48]

Think About It

How did Verschuren's prior experience in the private and public sectors prepare her as a leader to deal with managing power, developing trust, empowering employees, and leading across cultures at The Home Depot? How did her varied experience help her to understand gender differences and continuously improve the leadership skills of her and her team?

It's not easy being a chief information officer (CIO) today. This person, who is responsible for managing a company's information technology activities, faces a lot of external and internal pressures. Technology continues to change rapidly—almost daily, it sometimes seems. Business costs continue to rise. Rob Carter, CIO of FedEx, is on the hot seat facing such challenges.[49] He's responsible for all the computer and communication systems that provide around-the-clock and around-the-globe support for FedEx's products and services. If anything goes wrong, you know who takes the heat. However, Carter has been an effective leader in this seemingly chaotic environment.

For most leaders, leading effectively in today's environment is unlikely to involve the challenging circumstances Carter faces. However, twenty-first-century leaders do deal with some important leadership issues. In this section, we look at some of these issues: managing power, developing trust, empowering employees, leading across cultures, understanding gender differences in leadership, and becoming an effective leader.

Managing Power

Where do leaders get their power—that is, their capacity to influence work actions or decisions? Five sources of leader power have been identified: legitimate, coercive, reward, expert, and referent.[50]

Legitimate power and authority are the same. Legitimate power represents the power a leader has as a result of his or her position in the organization. Although people in positions of authority are also likely to have reward and coercive power, legitimate power is broader than the power to coerce and reward.

Coercive power is the power a leader has to punish or control. Followers react to this power out of fear of the negative results that might occur if they don't comply. Managers typically have some coercive power, such as being able to suspend or demote employees or to assign them work they find unpleasant or undesirable.

Reward power is the power to give positive rewards. These can be anything that a person values, such as money, favourable performance appraisals, promotions, interesting work assignments, friendly colleagues, and preferred work shifts or sales territories.

Expert power is power that's based on expertise, special skills, or knowledge. If an employee has skills, knowledge, or expertise that's critical to a work group, that person's expert power is enhanced.

Finally, **referent power** is the power that arises because of a person's desirable resources or personal traits. If I admire you and want to be associated with you, you can exercise power over me because I want to please you. Referent power develops out of admiration of another and a desire to be like that person.

Most effective leaders rely on several different forms of power to affect the behaviour and performance of their followers. For example, the commanding officer of one of Australia's state-of-the-art submarines, the HMAS *Sheean*, employs different types of power in managing his crew and equipment. He gives orders to the crew (legitimate), praises them (reward), and disciplines those who commit infractions (coercive). As an effective leader, he also strives to have expert power (based on his expertise and knowledge) and referent power (based on his being admired) to influence his crew.[51]

MyManagementLab
Q&A 14.8

legitimate power The power a leader has as a result of his or her position in an organization.

coercive power The power a leader has to punish or control.

reward power The power a leader has to give positive rewards.

expert power Power that's based on expertise, special skills, or knowledge.

referent power Power that arises because of a person's desirable resources or personal traits.

MyManagementLab
PRISM 5

MANAGEMENT REFLECTION
► Focus on Ethics

Is it always good to be friends? The definition of *friend* on social networking sites such as Facebook and MySpace is so broad that even strangers may tag you. But it doesn't feel weird because nothing really changes when a stranger does this. However, what if your boss, who isn't much older than you are, asks you to be a friend on these sites? What then? What are the implications if you refuse the offer? What are the implications if you accept? What ethical issues might arise because of this? What would you do? ■

Developing Trust

In today's uncertain environment, an important consideration for leaders is building trust and credibility—trust that can be extremely fragile. Before we can discuss ways leaders can build trust and credibility, we have to know what trust and credibility are and why they're so important.

The main component of credibility is honesty. Surveys show that honesty is consistently singled out as the number one characteristic of admired leaders. "Honesty is absolutely essential to leadership. If people are going to follow someone willingly, whether it be into battle or into the boardroom, they first want to assure themselves that the person is worthy of their trust."[52] In addition to being honest, credible leaders are competent and inspiring. They are personally able to effectively communicate their confidence and enthusiasm. Thus, followers judge a leader's **credibility** in terms of his or her honesty, competence, and ability to inspire.

credibility The degree to which followers perceive someone as honest, competent, and able to inspire.

Trust is closely entwined with the concept of credibility, and, in fact, the terms are often used interchangeably. **Trust** is defined as the belief in the integrity, character, and ability of a leader. Followers who trust a leader are willing to be vulnerable to the leader's actions because they are confident that their rights and interests will not be abused.[53] Research has identified five dimensions that make up the concept of trust:[54]

- *Integrity*—Honesty and truthfulness
- *Competence*—Technical and interpersonal knowledge and skills
- *Consistency*—Reliability, predictability, and good judgment in handling situations
- *Loyalty*—Willingness to protect a person, physically and emotionally
- *Openness*—Willingness to share ideas and information freely

Of these five dimensions, integrity seems to be the most critical when someone assesses another's trustworthiness.[55] Both integrity and competence came up in our earlier discussion of traits found to be consistently associated with leadership.

Workplace changes have reinforced why such leadership qualities are important. For instance, the trend toward empowerment (which we'll discuss shortly) and self-managed work teams has reduced many of the traditional control mechanisms used to monitor employees. If a work team is free to schedule its own work, evaluate its own performance, and even make its own hiring decisions, trust becomes critical. Employees have to trust managers to treat them fairly, and managers have to trust employees to conscientiously fulfill their responsibilities.

Also, leaders have to increasingly lead others who may not be in their immediate work group or even may be physically separated—members of cross-functional or virtual teams, individuals who work for suppliers or customers, and perhaps even people who represent other organizations through strategic alliances. These situations don't allow leaders the luxury of falling back on their formal positions for influence. Many of these relationships, in fact, are fluid and temporary. So the ability to quickly develop trust and sustain that trust is crucial to the success of the relationship.

Why is it important that followers trust their leaders? Research has shown that trust in leadership is significantly related to positive job outcomes, including job performance, organizational citizenship behaviour, job satisfaction, and organizational commitment.[56] Given the importance of trust to effective leadership, how can leaders build trust? *Tips for Managers—Suggestions for Building Trust* lists some ideas, which are explained in the skills module on developing trust found in MyManagementLab.[57]

Now, more than ever, managerial and leadership effectiveness depends on the ability to gain the trust of followers.[58] Downsizing, corporate financial misrepresentation, and the increased use of temporary employees have undermined employees' trust in their leaders and shaken the confidence of investors, suppliers, and customers. A survey found that only 39 percent of US employees and 51 percent of Canadian employees trusted their executive leaders.[59] Today's leaders are faced with the challenge of rebuilding and restoring trust with employees and with other important organizational stakeholders.

MyManagementLab
PRISM 4

TIPS FOR MANAGERS

Suggestions for Building Trust

- Practise **openness.**
- Be **fair.**
- Speak your **feelings.**
- Tell the **truth.**
- Show **consistency.**
- Fulfill your **promises.**
- Maintain **confidences.**
- Demonstrate **competence.**

Providing Ethical Leadership

The topic of leadership and ethics has received surprisingly little attention. Only recently have ethics and leadership researchers begun to consider the ethical implications in leadership.[60] Why now? One reason is a growing general interest in ethics throughout the field of management. Another, without a doubt, is the recent corporate financial scandals that have increased the public's and politicians' concerns about ethical standards.

Ethics is part of leadership in a number of ways. For instance, transformational leaders have been described as fostering moral virtue when they try to change the attitudes and behaviours of followers.[61] We can also see an ethical component to charisma. Unethical leaders may use their charisma to enhance their power over followers and use that power for self-serving purposes. On the other hand, ethical leaders may use their charisma in more socially constructive ways to serve others.[62] We also see a lack of ethics when leaders abuse their power and give themselves large salaries and bonuses while, at the same time, they seek to cut costs by laying off employees. And, of course, trust, which is important to ethical behaviour, explicitly deals with the leadership traits of honesty and integrity.

As we have seen recently, leadership is not values-free. Providing moral leadership involves addressing the *means* that a leader uses in trying to achieve goals, as well as the content of those goals. As a recent study concluded, ethical leadership is more than being ethical; it's reinforcing ethics through organizational mechanisms such as communication and the reward system.[63] Thus, before we judge any leader to be effective, we should consider both the moral content of his or her goals *and* the means used to achieve those goals. In Chapter 5, we examined ethical leadership, responsible leadership, values-led leadership, and leading with integrity. In Chapter 18, we will discuss the ISO standards 14001, which provide requirements for an environmental management system, and 26000, which provide guidance on social responsibility.

Empowering Employees

As we have described elsewhere in the text, managers are increasingly leading by empowering their employees. **Employee empowerment** involves giving more authority to employees to make decisions. Millions of individual employees and employee teams are making the key operating decisions that directly affect their work. They are developing budgets, scheduling workloads, controlling inventories, solving quality problems, and engaging in similar activities that until very recently were viewed exclusively as part of the manager's job.[64]

employee empowerment Giving more authority to employees to make decisions.

Why are more and more companies empowering employees? One reason is the need for quick decisions by those people who are most knowledgeable about the issues—often those at lower organizational levels. If organizations are to successfully compete in a dynamic global economy, they have to be able to make decisions and implement changes quickly. Another reason is the reality that organizational downsizing has left many managers with larger spans of control. In order to cope with the increased work demands, managers had to empower their people. Although empowerment is not appropriate for all circumstances, when employees have the knowledge, skills, and experience to do their jobs competently and when they seek autonomy and possess an internal locus of control, it can be beneficial. (To learn more about another way that managers cope with increased work demands, see *Developing Your Interpersonal Skills—Delegating* on pages 287–288, in Chapter 10.)

Empowerment should be used cautiously, however. Professor Jia Lin Xie of the University of Toronto's Rotman School of Management found that people who lack confidence can become ill from being put in charge of their own work. Xie and her colleagues found that "workers who had high levels of control at work, but lacked confidence in their abilities or blamed themselves for workplace problems, were more likely to have lower antibody levels and experienced more colds and flus."[65]

One of the difficulties with empowerment is that companies do not always introduce it properly. Professor Dan Ondrack of the University of Toronto's Rotman School of Management points out that for employees to be empowered, four conditions need to be met:[66]

- There must be a clear definition of the values and mission of the company.

- The company must help employees acquire the relevant skills.

- Employees need to be supported in their decision making and not criticized when they try to do something extraordinary.

- Employees need to be recognized for their efforts.

Paul Okalik (left) was the first sitting premier of Nunavut and was chosen to serve a second term. Okalik headed a nonpartisan government run by consensus, built from the principles of parliamentary democracy and Aboriginal values. Okalik's leadership skills include team building. He was the key negotiator in the settlement that led to the creation of Nunavut, and in his role as premier he balanced the needs of the Inuit and Qallunaaq (non-Inuit) residents in Nunavut.

Leading Across Cultures

One general conclusion that surfaces from leadership research is that effective leaders do not use a single style. They adjust their style to the situation. Although not mentioned explicitly, national culture is certainly an important situational variable in determining which leadership style will be most effective. What works in China isn't likely to be effective in France or Canada. For instance, one study of Asian leadership styles revealed that Asian managers preferred leaders who were competent decision makers, effective communicators, and supportive of employees.[67]

National culture affects leadership style because it influences how followers will respond. Leaders can't (and shouldn't) just choose their styles randomly. They're constrained by the cultural conditions their followers have come to expect. Exhibit 14-8 provides some findings from selected examples of cross-cultural leadership studies. Because most leadership theories were developed in the United States, they have an American bias. They emphasize follower responsibilities rather than rights; assume self-gratification rather than commitment to duty or altruistic motivation; assume centrality of work and democratic value orientation; and stress rationality rather than spirituality, religion, or superstition.[68] However, the GLOBE research program, first introduced in Chapter 3, is the most extensive and comprehensive cross-cultural study of leadership ever undertaken. The GLOBE study has found that there are some universal aspects to leadership. Specifically, a number of elements of transformational leadership appear to be associated with effective leadership, regardless of what country the leader is in.[69] These include vision, foresight, providing encouragement, trustworthiness, dynamism, positiveness, and proactiveness. The results led two members of the GLOBE team to conclude that "effective business leaders in any country are expected by their subordinates to provide a powerful and proactive vision to guide the company into the future, strong motivational skills to stimulate all employees to fulfill the vision, and excellent planning skills to assist in implementing the vision."[70] Some people suggest that the universal appeal of these transformational leader characteristics is due to the pressures toward common technologies and management practices, as a result of global competitiveness and multinational influences.

Exhibit 14-8

Selected Cross-Cultural Leadership Findings

- Korean leaders are expected to be paternalistic toward employees.
- Arab leaders who show kindness or generosity without being asked to do so are seen by other Arabs as weak.
- Japanese leaders are expected to be humble and speak frequently.
- Scandinavian and Dutch leaders who single out individuals with public praise are likely to embarrass, not energize, those individuals.
- Malaysian leaders are expected to show compassion while using more of an autocratic than a participative style.
- Effective German leaders are characterized by high performance orientation, low compassion, low self-protection, low team orientation, high autonomy, and high participation.

Sources: Based on J. C. Kennedy, "Leadership in Malaysia: Traditional Values, International Outlook," *Academy of Management Executive*, August 2002, pp. 15–17; F. C. Brodbeck, M. Frese, and M. Javidan, "Leadership Made in Germany: Low on Compassion, High on Performance," *Academy of Management Executive*, February 2002, pp. 16–29; M. F. Peterson and J. G. Hunt, "International Perspectives on International Leadership," *Leadership Quarterly*, Fall 1997, pp. 203–231; R. J. House and R. N. Aditya, "The Social Scientific Study of Leadership: Quo Vadis?" *Journal of Management* 23, no. 3 (1997), p. 463; and R. J. House, "Leadership in the Twenty-First Century," in *The Changing Nature of Work*, ed. A. Howard (San Francisco: Jossey-Bass, 1995), p. 442.

Understanding Gender Differences and Leadership

There was a time when the question "Do males and females lead differently?" could be seen as a purely academic issue—interesting, but not very relevant. That time has certainly passed! Many women now hold senior management positions, and many more around the world continue to join the management ranks despite the fact that women are still underrepresented in senior leadership roles. In a recent study of 600 companies in 20 countries, less than 5 percent had female chief executives.[71] Misconceptions about the relationship between leadership and gender can adversely affect hiring, performance evaluation, promotion, and other human resource decisions for both men and women. For instance, evidence indicates that a "good" manager is still perceived as predominantly masculine.[72]

A number of studies focusing on gender and leadership style have been conducted in recent years. Their general conclusion is that males and females use different styles. Specifically, women tend to adopt a more democratic or participative style. Women are more likely to encourage participation, share power and information, and attempt to enhance followers' self-worth. They lead through inclusion and rely on their charisma, expertise, contacts, and interpersonal skills to influence others. Women tend to use transformational leadership, motivating others by transforming their self-interest into organizational goals. Men are more likely to use a directive, command-and-control style. They rely on formal position authority for their influence. Men use transactional leadership, handing out rewards for good work and punishment for bad.[73]

There is an interesting qualifier to the findings just mentioned. The tendency for female leaders to be more democratic than males declines when women are in male-dominated jobs. Apparently, group norms and male stereotypes influence women, and in some situations, women tend to act more autocratically.[74]

Although it's interesting to see how male and female leadership styles differ, a more important question is whether they differ in effectiveness. Although some researchers have shown that males and females tend to be equally effective as leaders,[75] an increasing number of studies have shown that women executives, when rated by their peers, employees, and bosses, score higher than their male counterparts on a wide variety of measures.[76] (See Exhibit 14-9 for a summary.) Why? One possible explanation is that in today's organizations, flexibility, teamwork and partnering, trust, and information sharing are rapidly replacing rigid structures, competitive individualism, control, and secrecy. In these types of workplaces, effective managers must use more social and interpersonal behaviours. They listen, motivate, and provide support to their people. They inspire and influence rather than control. And women seem to do those things better than men.[77]

Although women seem to rate highly on the leadership skills needed to succeed in today's dynamic global environment, we don't want to fall into the same trap as the early leadership researchers who tried to find the "one best leadership style" for all situations. We know that there is no one *best* style for all situations. Instead, the most effective leadership style depends on the situation. So even if men and women differ in their leadership styles, we shouldn't assume that one is always preferable to the other.

Yale graduate Indra Nooyi, who played in an all-girl rock band while growing up in Chennai (India), is the savvy and irreverent chair and CEO of PepsiCo Inc. Drawn to PepsiCo as chief strategist almost 15 years ago by the chance to help turn around the company, she has helped the company double net profits to more than $5.6 billion (US) by focusing on better nutrition and by promoting workforce diversity. "Indra can drive as deep and hard as anyone I've ever met," says former CEO Roger Enrico, "but she can do it with a sense of heart and fun." Nooyi still sings in the office and has been known to go barefoot at work.

Becoming an Effective Leader

Organizations need effective leaders. Two issues pertinent to becoming an effective leader are leader training and recognizing that sometimes being an effective leader means *not* leading. Let's take a look at these issues.

Exhibit 14-9

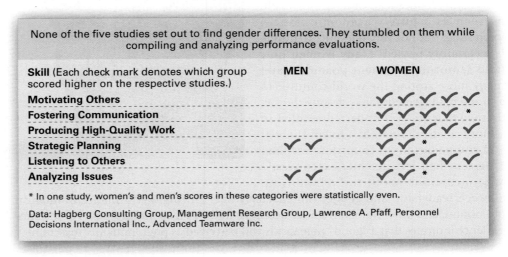

Where Female Managers Do Better: A Scorecard

None of the five studies set out to find gender differences. They stumbled on them while compiling and analyzing performance evaluations.		
Skill (Each check mark denotes which group scored higher on the respective studies.)	**MEN**	**WOMEN**
Motivating Others		✓ ✓ ✓ ✓ ✓
Fostering Communication		✓ ✓ ✓ ✓ *
Producing High-Quality Work		✓ ✓ ✓ ✓ ✓
Strategic Planning	✓ ✓	✓ ✓ *
Listening to Others		✓ ✓ ✓ ✓ ✓
Analyzing Issues	✓ ✓	✓ ✓ *

* In one study, women's and men's scores in these categories were statistically even.

Data: Hagberg Consulting Group, Management Research Group, Lawrence A. Pfaff, Personnel Decisions International Inc., Advanced Teamware Inc.

Source: R. Sharpe, "As Leaders, Women Rule," *BusinessWeek*, November 20, 2000, p. 75.

TIPS FOR MANAGERS

Getting Back to Basics

↗ Give people **a reason to come to work**.

↗ **Be loyal** to the organization's people.

↗ **Spend time with people** who do the real work of the organization—people down at the loading dock, or in the checkout line, or out on sales calls.

↗ **Be more open** and **more candid** about what business practices are acceptable and proper and how the unacceptable ones should be fixed.

Source: A. Webber, "Above-It-All CEOs Forget Workers," *USA Today*, November 11, 2002, p. 13A.

Leader Training

Organizations around the globe spend billions of dollars, yen, and euros on leadership training and development.[78] These efforts take many forms—from $50 000 leadership programs offered by universities such as Harvard to sailing experiences at the Outward Bound School. Although much of the money spent on leader training may provide doubtful benefits, our review suggests that there are some things managers can do to get the maximum effect from such training.[79]

First, let's recognize the obvious: Some people don't have what it takes to be a leader. Period. For instance, evidence indicates that leadership training is more likely to be successful with individuals who are high self-monitors than with low self-monitors. Such individuals have the flexibility to change their behaviour as different situations require. In addition, organizations may find that individuals with higher levels of a trait called *motivation to lead* are more receptive to leadership development opportunities.[80]

What kinds of things can individuals learn that might be related to being a more effective leader? It may be a bit optimistic to think that "vision-creation" can be taught, but implementation skills can be taught. People can be trained to develop "an understanding about content themes critical to effective visions."[81] We can also teach skills such as trust-building and mentoring. And leaders can be taught situational analysis skills. They can learn how to evaluate situations, how to modify situations to make them fit better with their style, and how to assess which leader behaviours might be most effective in given situations. *Tips for Managers—Getting Back to Basics* provides some suggestions for staying in touch with employees and being better leaders.

Substitutes for Leadership

Despite the belief that some leadership style will always be effective, regardless of the situation, leadership may not always be important! Research indicates that, in some situations, any behaviours a leader exhibits are irrelevant. In other words, certain individual, job, and organizational variables can act as "substitutes for leadership," negating the influence of the leader.[82]

For instance, follower characteristics such as experience, training, professional orientation, and need for independence can neutralize the effect of leadership. These characteristics can replace the employee's need for a leader's support or ability to create structure and reduce task ambiguity. Similarly, jobs that are inherently unambiguous and routine or that are intrinsically satisfying may place fewer demands on the leadership variable. Finally, such organizational characteristics as explicit formalized goals, rigid rules and procedures, and cohesive work groups can substitute for formal leadership.

SUMMARY AND IMPLICATIONS

1. Define leader and leadership. Leaders in organizations make things happen. But what makes leaders different from nonleaders? A leader is someone who can influence others and who has managerial authority. Leadership is a process of leading a group and influencing that group to achieve its goals.

▶ ▶ ▶ In his time as president of the University of Waterloo, David Johnston advanced his vision of universities as Canada's innovation engines. He employed his definition of leadership—recognizing your total dependence on the people around you—by building partnerships with the community and local business partners, most notably Research In Motion.

2. Compare and contrast early theories of leadership. Early attempts to define leadership traits were unsuccessful, although later attempts found seven traits associated with leadership. The University of Iowa studies explored three leadership styles. The only conclusion was that group members were more satisfied under a democratic leader than under an autocratic one. The Ohio State studies identified two dimensions of leader behaviour: initiating structure and consideration. A leader high in both those dimensions at times achieved high group task performance and high group member satisfaction, but not always. The University of Michigan studies looked at employee-oriented leaders and production-oriented leaders. They concluded that leaders who were employee oriented could get high group productivity and high group member satisfaction. The managerial grid looked at leaders' concern for production and concern for people and identified five leader styles. Although it suggested that a leader who was high in concern for production and high in concern for people was the best, there was no substantive evidence for that conclusion. The behavioural studies showed that a leader's behaviour has a dual nature: a focus on the task and a focus on the people.

▶ ▶ ▶ In reaching the residential schools settlement, Phil Fontaine needed to draw on the traits that first surfaced in his work as a band chief—his ability to open lines of communication and to build consensus.

3. Describe the three major contingency theories of leadership. Contingency theories acknowledge that different situations require different leadership styles. The theories suggest that leaders may need to adjust their style to the needs of different organizations and employees, and perhaps different countries.

▶ ▶ ▶ Because Moya Greene did not come from a logistics or postal background, she knew that she needed to learn Canada Post's culture first-hand. As her role at Canada Post evolved, she adjusted her style based on the context of the audience and the problem at hand.

4. Describe modern views of leadership. A transactional leader exchanges rewards for productivity, whereas a transformational leader stimulates and inspires followers to achieve goals. A charismatic leader is an enthusiastic and self-confident leader whose personality and actions influence people to behave in certain ways. People can learn to be charismatic. A visionary leader is able to create and articulate a realistic, credible, and attractive vision of the future. A team leader has two priorities: manage the team's external boundary and facilitate the team process. Four leader roles are involved: liaison with external constituencies, troubleshooter, conflict manager, and coach.

▶ ▶ ▶ David Cheesewright became president of Wal-Mart Canada as the company was implementing "the greener good" sustainability strategy. His role was to assist in transforming the organization into a truly sustainable one.

5. Discuss contemporary issues affecting leadership. The five sources of a leader's power are legitimate (authority or position), coercive (punish or control), reward (give positive rewards), expert (special expertise, skills, or knowledge), and referent (desirable resources or traits). Most effective leaders rely on several different sources of power—legitimate, coercive, reward, expert, and referent power—to affect the behaviour and performance of their followers. An important consideration for leaders today is building trust and credibility with employees. Trust in leadership has been found to have a significant effect on positive job outcomes, including job performance, organizational citizenship behaviour, job satisfaction, and organizational commitment.

▶ ▶ ▶ As Annette Verschuren performed her role in The Home Depot, she drew upon her prior experience to empower her performance and that of others in the organization. She was able to build trust with those she worked with and to adapt to the very different culture in the Asian operations.

Management @ Work

READING FOR COMPREHENSION

1. Discuss the strengths and weaknesses of trait theories of leadership.

2. What is the managerial grid? Contrast this approach to leadership with that developed by the Ohio State and University of Michigan studies.

3. How is a least-preferred co-worker (LPC) determined? What is the importance of one's LPC for the Fiedler contingency model for leadership?

4. What are the two contingency variables of the path–goal theory of leadership?

5. What similarities, if any, can you find among Fiedler's contingency model, Hersey and Blanchard's Situational Leadership®, and path–goal theory?

6. Describe the difference between a transactional leader and a transformational leader.

7. What sources of power are available to leaders? Which ones are most effective?

8. What are the five dimensions of trust?

LINKING CONCEPTS TO PRACTICE

1. What types of power are available to you? Which ones do you use most? Why?

2. Do you think that most managers in real life use a contingency approach to increase their leadership effectiveness? Discuss.

3. If you ask people why a given individual is a leader, they tend to describe the person in terms such as *competent, consistent*, *self-assured*, *inspiring a shared vision*, and *enthusiastic*. How do these descriptions fit with leadership concepts presented in the chapter?

4. What kinds of campus activities could a full-time student do that might lead to the perception that he or she is a charismatic leader? In pursuing those activities, what might the student do to enhance this perception of being charismatic?

5. Do you think trust evolves out of an individual's personal characteristics or out of specific situations? Explain.

SELF-ASSESSMENT

What's My Leadership Style?

The following items describe aspects of leadership behaviour.[83] Respond to each item according to the way you would be most likely to act if you were the leader of a work group. Use this scale for your responses:

A = Always   F = Frequently   O = Occasionally   S = Seldom   N = Never

1. I would most likely act as the spokesperson of the group. A F O S N

2. I would encourage overtime work. A F O S N

3. I would allow group members complete freedom in their work. A F O S N

4. I would encourage the use of uniform procedures. A F O S N

5. I would permit group members to use their own judgment in solving problems. A F O S N

6. I would stress being ahead of competing groups. A F O S N

7. I would speak as a representative of the group. A F O S N

8. I would needle group members for greater effort. A F O S N

9. I would try out my ideas in the group. A F O S N

10. I would let group members do their work the way they think best.   A   F   O   S   N

11. I would be working hard for a promotion.   A   F   O   S   N

12. I would be able to tolerate postponement and uncertainty.   A   F   O   S   N

13. I would speak for the group when visitors were present.   A   F   O   S   N

14. I would keep the work moving at a rapid pace.   A   F   O   S   N

15. I would turn group members loose on a job and let them go to it.   A   F   O   S   N

16. I would settle conflicts when they occur in the group.   A   F   O   S   N

17. I would get swamped by details.   A   F   O   S   N

18. I would represent the group at outside meetings.   A   F   O   S   N

19. I would be reluctant to allow group members any freedom of action.   A   F   O   S   N

20. I would decide what shall be done and how it shall be done.   A   F   O   S   N

21. I would push for increased production.   A   F   O   S   N

22. I would let some group members have authority that I should keep.   A   F   O   S   N

23. Things would usually turn out as I predicted.   A   F   O   S   N

24. I would allow the group a high degree of initiative.   A   F   O   S   N

25. I would assign group members to particular tasks.   A   F   O   S   N

26. I would be willing to make changes.   A   F   O   S   N

27. I would ask group members to work harder.   A   F   O   S   N

28. I would trust group members to exercise good judgment.   A   F   O   S   N

29. I would schedule the work to be done.   A   F   O   S   N

30. I would refuse to explain my actions.   A   F   O   S   N

31. I would persuade group members that my ideas are to their advantage.   A   F   O   S   N

32. I would permit the group to set its own pace.   A   F   O   S   N

33. I would urge the group to beat its previous record.   A   F   O   S   N

34. I would act without consulting the group.   A   F   O   S   N

35. I would ask that group members follow standard rules and regulations.   A   F   O   S   N

Scoring Key

1. Circle the numbers 8, 12, 17, 18, 19, 30, 34, and 35.

2. Write a 1 in front of the circled number if you responded Seldom or Never.

3. Also write a 1 in front of any remaining (uncircled) items if you responded Always or Frequently to these.

4. Circle the 1s that you have written in front of the following questions: 3, 5, 8, 10, 15, 18, 19, 22, 24, 26, 28, 30, 32, 34, and 35.

5. Count the circled 1s. This is your score for "Concern for People."

6. Count the uncircled 1s. This is your score for "Task."

Analysis and Interpretation

This leadership instrument taps the degree to which you are task or people oriented. Task orientation is concerned with getting the job done, whereas people orientation focuses on group interactions and the needs of individual members.

The cut-off scores separating high and low scores are approximately as follows. For task orientation, high is a score above 10; low is below 10. For people orientation, high is a score above 7; low is below 7.

The best leaders are ones who can balance their task/people orientation to various situations. A high score on both would indicate this balance. If you are too task oriented, you tend to be autocratic. You get the job done but at a high emotional cost. If you are too people oriented, your leadership style may be overly laissez-faire. People are likely to be happy in their work but sometimes at the expense of productivity.

Your score should also help you to put yourself in situations that increase your likelihood of success. For instance, evidence indicates that when employees are experienced and know their jobs well, they tend to perform best with a people-oriented leader. If you are people oriented, then this is a favourable situation for you. But if you are task oriented, you might want to pass on this situation.

More Self-Assessments MyManagementLab

To learn more about your skills, abilities, and interests, go to the MyManagementLab website and take the following self-assessments:

- II.B.2.—How Charismatic Am I?
- II.B.4.—Do Others See Me as Trustworthy?
- II.B.6.—How Good Am I at Building and Leading a Team? (This exercise also appears in Chapter 16 on pages 468–470.)
- IV.E.4.—Am I an Ethical Leader?
- IV.E.5.—What Is My LPC Score?

MANAGEMENT FOR YOU TODAY

Dilemma

Your school is developing a one-day orientation program for new students majoring in business. You have been asked to consider leading the group of students who will design and implement the orientation program. Develop a two- to three-page "handout" that shows whether the position is a natural fit for you. To do this (1) identify your strengths and weaknesses in the sources of power you can bring to the project; and (2) discuss whether you would be a transactional or transformational leader and why. Provide a strong concluding statement about whether or not you would be the best leader for this task.

Becoming a Manager

- As you interact with various organizations, note different leadership styles.
- Think of people you would consider effective leaders and try to determine why they are effective.
- If you have the opportunity, take leadership development courses.
- Practise building trust in relationships that you have with others.
- Read books on great leaders (not just business leaders) and on leadership development topics.

WORKING TOGETHER: TEAM-BASED EXERCISE

Conveying Bad News

You are the new manager of customer-service operations at Preferred Bank Card, a credit card issuer with offices throughout Ontario. Your predecessor, who was very popular with the customer-service representatives and who is still with the company, concealed from your team members how far behind they are on their goals this quarter. As a result, your team members are looking forward to a promised day off that they are not entitled to and will not be getting. It's your job to tell them the bad news. How will you do it?

Form groups of no more than four individuals. Discuss this situation and how you would handle it. Then create a role-playing situation that illustrates your group's proposed approach. Be ready to perform your role play in front of the class. Also, be prepared to provide the rest of the class with the specific steps that your group suggested be used in this situation.

Ethical Dilemma Exercise: Is "an Eye for an Eye" Fair Play?

What happens when a charismatic leader's relentless pursuit of a vision encourages extreme or even ethically questionable behaviour?[84] Consider the CEO of a company that hired an investigator to dive into other firms' dumpsters for information about their dealings with a major competitor. The same CEO's company has used precisely timed news releases as strategic weapons against particular rivals. And the same CEO's company once announced a hostile takeover bid for a direct competitor with the stated intention of not actively selling its products but acquiring its best customers and employees. This CEO, described by the *Wall Street Journal* as "a swashbuckling figure in Silicon Valley," is Larry Ellison of Oracle.

Ellison's charismatic leadership has built Oracle into a software powerhouse. Although it is locked in fierce competition with Microsoft and other giants, it does not ignore smaller rivals such as i2 Technologies. Oracle once issued a news release belittling i2's attempt at developing a certain type of software only minutes before i2's CEO was to meet with influential analysts. Such hardball tactics are hardly random or spontaneous. When Oracle pursued an unwelcome acquisition bid for rival PeopleSoft, the two CEOs traded barbed quotes for weeks as the companies battled in courtrooms and in the media. PeopleSoft's CEO, a former Oracle executive, described the situation as "enormously bad behaviour from a company that's had a history of it." Nevertheless, Oracle finally bought PeopleSoft in 2005.

Imagine that you are the CEO of i2 Technologies, which makes inventory and supply tracking systems that compete with Oracle's large-scale business software suites. In five minutes, you will be meeting with a roomful of financial analysts who make buy or sell recommendations to investors. Your goal is to showcase your company's accomplishments, outline your vision for its future, and encourage a positive recommendation so your stock price will go even higher. You just heard about Oracle's news release belittling your product in development—and you suspect the analysts also know about it. How will you handle the news release?

Thinking Critically About Ethics

Your boss is not satisfied with the way one of your colleagues is handling a project, and she reassigns the project to you. She tells you to work with this person to find out what he has done already and to discuss any other necessary information that he might have. She wants your project report by the end of the month. This person is pretty upset and angry over the reassignment and will not give you the information you need to even start, much less complete, the project. You will not be able to meet your deadline unless you get this information.

What type of power does your colleague appear to be using? What type of influence could you possibly use to gain his cooperation? What could you do to resolve this situation successfully, yet ethically?

Grafik Marketing Communications

When more seasoned employees take less experienced employees under their wings, we call this mentoring.[85] The wisdom and guidance of these seasoned individuals serve to assist less experienced employees in obtaining the necessary skills and socialization to succeed in the organization. It is also helpful in facilitating an individual's career progress. Technology, however, is starting to change some of this traditional mentoring process in terms of who does the mentoring. For Judy Kirpich, for example, technological advancements have resulted in significant increases in mentoring in her organization, Grafik Marketing Communications. However, the company's senior managers are the ones who need to be mentored. They do not have the technological savvy of the younger employees who have grown up on computers, resulting in what is called reverse mentoring.

Kirpich is considering introducing reverse mentoring, a practice started years ago at General Electric. Then-CEO Jack Welch recognized that his senior managers needed to become more proficient with using technology—especially the Internet. Accordingly, Welch had several hundred senior managers partner with younger employees in the organization. Not only were these managers able to learn about the Internet, but reverse mentoring also enhanced intergenerational understanding and gave senior decision makers a new perspective on younger consumer products and service needs. It also helped the organization in brainstorming for new and creative ideas.

Reverse mentoring, however, is not without drawbacks. For these younger employees to mentor properly, they must be trained. They must understand how to be patient with those individuals who may have a technology phobia. These reverse mentors need to recognize that their mentoring is limited to offering advice solely on relevant technology topics. They must also understand and acknowledge the need for confidentiality because many senior managers may be reluctant to have this mentoring relationship widely known. Reverse mentoring can also lead to the problem of subordinates forgetting that the leader is still in charge.

Furthermore, when reverse mentors exist, organizational members must be made aware that problems arising out of favouritism are a reality.

Kirpich wants to move reverse mentoring forward at Grafik Marketing Communications. However, she is aware of the many problems that could arise. What advice would you give her about successfully implementing reverse mentoring?

DEVELOPING YOUR DIAGNOSTIC AND ANALYTICAL SKILLS

Radical Leadership

Ricardo Semler, CEO of Semco Group of São Paulo, Brazil, is considered by many to be a radical. He has never been the type of leader that most people might expect to be in charge of a multimillion-dollar business.[86] Why? Semler breaks all the traditional "rules" of leading and managing. He is the ultimate hands-off leader who does not even have an office at the company's headquarters. As the "leading proponent and most tireless evangelist" of participative management, Semler says his philosophy is simple: Treat people like adults and they will respond like adults.

Underlying the participative management approach is the belief that "organizations thrive best by entrusting employees to apply their creativity and ingenuity in service of the whole enterprise, and to make important decisions close to the flow of work, conceivably including the selection and election of their bosses." And according to Semler, his approach works . . . and works well. But how does it work in reality?

At Semco, you will not find most of the trappings of organizations and management. There are no organization charts, no long-term plans, no corporate values statements, no dress codes, and no written rules or policy manuals. The company's 3000 employees decide their work hours and their pay levels. Subordinates decide who their bosses will be, and they also review their boss's performance. The employees also elect the corporate leadership and decide most of the company's new strategic initiatives. Each person has one vote—including Ricardo Semler.

At one of the company's plants outside São Paulo, there are no supervisors telling employees what to do. On any given day, an employee may decide to "run a grinder or drive a forklift, depending on what needs to be done." João Vendramin Neto, who is in charge of Semco's manufacturing,

says that "the workers know the organization's objectives and they use common sense to decide for themselves what they should do to hit those goals."

Why did Semler decide that his form of radical leadership was necessary, and does it work? Semler did not pursue such radical self-governance out of some altruistic ulterior motive. Instead, he felt it was the only way to build an organization that was flexible and resilient enough to flourish in chaotic and turbulent times. He maintains that this approach has enabled Semco to survive the roller-coaster nature of Brazilian politics and economy. Although the country's political leadership and economy have gone from one extreme to another and countless Brazilian banks and companies have failed, Semco has survived. And not just survived—prospered. Semler says, "If you look at Semco's numbers, we've grown 27.5 percent a year for 14 years." Semler attributes this fact to flexibility . . . of his company and, most importantly, of his employees.

Questions

1. Describe Ricardo Semler's leadership style. What do you think the advantages and drawbacks of his style might be?

2. What challenges might a radically "hands-off" leader face? How could those challenges be addressed?

3. How could future leaders be identified in this organization? Would leadership training be important to this organization? Discuss.

4. What could other businesses learn from Semler's approach to leadership?

Acquiring Power

About the Skill

The exercise of power is a natural process in any group or organization, and to perform their jobs effectively, managers need to know how to acquire and use power—the capacity of a leader to influence work actions or decisions. We discussed the concept of power earlier in the chapter and identified five different sources: legitimate, coercive, reward, expert, and referent power. Why is having power important? Because power makes you less dependent on others. When managers have power, they are not as dependent on others for critical resources. And if the resources managers control are important, scarce, and nonsubstitutable, their power will increase because others will be more dependent on them for those resources.

Steps in Developing the Skill

You can be more effective at acquiring power if you use the following eight suggestions:[87]

1. **Frame arguments in terms of organizational goals.** To be effective at acquiring power means camouflaging your self-interests. Discussions over who controls what resources should be framed in terms of the benefits that will accrue to the organization; do not point out how you personally will benefit.

2. **Develop the right image.** If you know your organization's culture, you already understand what the organization wants and values from its employees in terms of dress, associates to cultivate and those to avoid, whether to appear risk taking or risk aversive, the preferred leadership style, the importance placed on getting along well with others, and so forth. With this knowledge, you are equipped to project the appropriate image. Because the assessment of your performance is not always a fully objective process, you need to pay attention to style as well as substance.

3. **Gain control of organizational resources.** Controlling organizational resources that are scarce and important is a source of power. Knowledge and expertise are particularly effective resources to control. They make you more valuable to the organization and, therefore, more likely to have job security, chances for advancement, and a receptive audience for your ideas.

4. **Make yourself appear indispensable.** Because we are dealing with appearances rather than objective facts, you can enhance your power by appearing to be indispensable. You don't really have to be indispensable as long as key people in the organization believe that you are.

5. **Be visible.** If you have a job that brings your accomplishments to the attention of others, that is great. However, if you don't have such a job, you will want to find ways to let others in the organization know what you are doing by highlighting successes in routine reports, having satisfied customers relay their appreciation to senior executives, being seen at social functions, being active in your professional associations, and developing powerful allies who speak positively about your accomplishments. Of course, you will want to be on the lookout for those projects that will increase your visibility.

6. **Develop powerful allies.** To get power, it helps to have powerful people on your side. Cultivate contacts with potentially influential people above you, at your own level, and at lower organizational levels. These allies often can provide you with information that is otherwise not readily available. In addition, having allies can provide you with a coalition of support if and when you need it.

7. **Avoid "tainted" members.** In almost every organization, there are fringe members whose status is questionable. Their performance and/or loyalty may be suspect. Keep your distance from such individuals.

8. **Support your manager.** Your immediate future is in the hands of your current manager. Because he or she evaluates your performance, you will typically want to do whatever is necessary to have your manager on your side. You should make every effort to help your manager succeed, make her look good, support her if she is under siege, and spend the time to find out the criteria she will use to assess your effectiveness. Don't undermine your manager. And don't speak negatively of her to others.

Practising the Skill

Read the following scenario. Write some notes about how you would handle the situation described. Be sure to refer to the eight suggestions for acquiring power.

Scenario

You used to be the star marketing manager for Hilton Electronics. But for the past year, you have been outpaced again and again by Conor, a new manager in the design department, who has been accomplishing everything expected of her and more. Meanwhile, your best efforts to do your job well have been sabotaged and undercut by Leonila—your and Conor's manager. For example, before last year's international consumer electronics show, Leonila moved $30 000 from your budget to Conor's. Despite your best efforts, your marketing team could not complete all the marketing materials normally developed to showcase all of your organization's new products at this important industry show. Leonila has chipped away at your staff and budget ever since. Although you have been able to meet most of your goals with fewer staff and less budget, Leonila has continued to slice away resources of your group. Just last week, she eliminated two positions in your team of eight marketing specialists to make room for a new designer and some extra equipment for Conor. Leonila is clearly taking away your resources while giving Conor whatever she wants and more. You think it's time to do something, or soon you will not have any team or resources left. How should you approach the problem?

Reinforcing the Skill

The following activities will help you practise and reinforce the skills associated with acquiring power:

1. Keep a one-week journal of your behaviour describing incidents when you tried to influence others around you. Assess each incident by asking: Were you successful at these attempts to influence them? Why or why not? What could you have done differently?

2. Review recent issues of a business periodical (such as *BusinessWeek, Fortune, Forbes, Fast Company, IndustryWeek, Canadian Business, PROFIT,* or the *Wall Street Journal*). Look for articles on reorganizations, promotions, or departures from management positions. Find at least two articles where you believe power issues are involved. Relate the content of the articles to the concepts introduced in this *Developing Your Interpersonal Skills* feature.

MyManagementLab

For more resources, please visit www.pearsoned.ca/mymanagementlab

SCAN THIS

Motivating Employees

Motivating and rewarding employees is one of the most important and challenging activities that managers do. To get employees to put forth maximum work effort, managers need to know how and why they're motivated. After reading and studying this chapter, you will achieve the following learning outcomes.

Learning Outcomes

1 Define motivation.

2 Compare and contrast early theories of motivation.

3 Compare and contrast contemporary theories of motivation.

4 Discuss current issues in motivation.

5 Describe how managers can motivate employees.

▶ ▶ ▶ How do you motivate employees in an industry where absenteeism rates average 5 percent of all working hours, but can be as high as 10 percent in urban areas?[1] What do you do when the turnover rate of managers averages 20 percent, and the turnover rate of nonmanagerial employees averages 30 percent?

Sir Terry Leahy, CEO of UK-based Tesco, faces these problems daily. The company has over 4800 supermarkets, hypermarkets, and convenience stores in the United Kingdom, Ireland, Central Europe, and Asia. Once a discount supermarket, Tesco has built itself as a dressier, mid-market retailer while becoming the number one food retailer in the United Kingdom.

The company is trying to keep its Generation Y employees (Generation Y includes those born between 1979 and 1994) motivated, while also trying to accommodate the needs of other groups of employees, including ethnic minorities and mothers returning to the workplace. Not all of the jobs are interesting, and many can be quite repetitive.

Leahy believes in starting with the basics in dealing with employees. "We've built Tesco around sound values and principles," he says. Therefore, he makes sure that employees are treated with respect. But he is also concerned about performance: "If that's bad and there's no good reason, I get cross." (Note: Leahy retired from his position with Tesco in 2011.)

Think About It

What are the different motivation tools that managers use? Put yourself in Sir Terry Leahy's shoes. How should he motivate his managers so that he will have less turnover? What can he do to keep his shelf-stockers and cashiers motivated?

SCAN THIS

Motivating and rewarding employees is one of the most important and one of the most challenging activities that managers perform. Successful managers, like Sir Terry Leahy, understand that what motivates them personally may have little or no effect on others. Just because *you* are motivated by being part of a cohesive work team, don't assume everyone is. Or the fact that you are motivated by challenging work does not mean everyone is. Effective managers who want their employees to put forth maximum effort recognize that they need to know how and why employees are motivated and to tailor their motivational practices to satisfy the needs and wants of those employees.

In this chapter, we take a look at what motivation is, early motivation theories, and contemporary theories. Then, we discuss some current motivation issues and provide practical suggestions managers can use to motivate employees.

What Is Motivation?

All managers need to be able to motivate their employees, and that requires an understanding of what motivation is. Many people incorrectly view motivation as a personal trait—that is, a trait that some people have and others don't. Our knowledge of motivation tells us that we cannot label people that way. What we *do* know is that motivation is the result of the interaction between a person and a situation. Certainly, individuals differ in motivational drive, but, overall, motivation varies from situation to situation. For instance, your level of motivation probably differs among the various courses you take each term. As we analyze the concept of motivation, keep in mind that the level of motivation varies both between individuals and within individuals at different times.

Motivation refers to the process by which a person's efforts are energized, directed, and sustained toward attaining a goal.[2] This definition has three key elements: energy, direction, and persistence.[3] The *energy* element is a measure of intensity or drive. A motivated person puts forth effort and works hard. However, the quality of the effort must also be considered. High levels of effort don't necessarily lead to favourable job performance

1. Define motivation.

motivation The process by which a person's efforts are energized, directed, and sustained toward attaining a goal.

unless the effort is channelled in a *direction* that benefits the organization. Effort that's directed toward and consistent with organizational goals is the kind of effort we want from employees. Motivation also includes a *persistence* dimension. We want employees to persist in putting forth effort to achieve those goals. Finally, we will treat motivation as a *need-satisfying* process, as shown in Exhibit 15-1.

need An internal state that makes certain outcomes appear attractive.

A **need** is an internal state that makes certain outcomes appear attractive. An unsatisfied need creates tension, which an individual reduces by exerting effort. Because we are interested in work behaviour, this tension-reduction effort must be directed toward organizational goals. Therefore, inherent in our definition of motivation is the requirement that the individual's needs be compatible with the organization's goals. When the two don't match, individuals may exert high levels of effort that run counter to the interests of the organization. Incidentally, this is not all that unusual. Some employees regularly spend a lot of time talking with friends at work to satisfy their social need. There is a high level of effort, but little, if any, is being directed toward work.

What motivates you?

Finding ways to motivate employees to achieve high levels of performance is an important organizational problem, and managers keep looking for a solution. A Canadian Policy Research Network survey found that only 40 percent of Canadians are very satisfied with their jobs. By comparison, 47 percent of American workers are happy with their work, and 54 percent of Danish workers report high satisfaction.[4] In light of these results, it's no wonder that both academic researchers and practising managers want to understand and explain employee motivation.

Early Theories of Motivation

2. Compare and contrast early theories of motivation.

▶ ▶ ▶ Management at Tesco was interested in discovering what concerns their employees had and how these might be addressed.[5] They conducted research on their employees and found that many of their staff were single and worked mainly to have the money to travel overseas and participate in leisure activities. Their research also found that these employees "were unlikely to take much pride in their work, would lack commitment and would have little hesitation about going to work elsewhere if the pay were better."

Think About It

What kinds of needs do employees have? How can they be addressed?

Exhibit 15-1

The Motivation Process

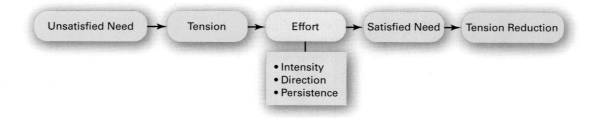

Unsatisfied Need → Tension → Effort → Satisfied Need → Tension Reduction

Effort:
• Intensity
• Direction
• Persistence

We begin by looking at four early motivation theories: *Maslow's hierarchy of needs theory, McGregor's Theory X and Theory Y, Herzberg's motivation-hygiene theory,* and *McClelland's three needs theory.* Although more valid explanations of motivation have been developed, these early theories are important because they represent the foundation from which contemporary motivation theories were developed and because many managers still use them.

Maslow's Hierarchy of Needs Theory

The best-known theory of motivation is probably Abraham Maslow's **hierarchy of needs theory**.[6] Maslow was a psychologist who proposed that within every person is a hierarchy of five needs:

1. **Physiological needs.** Food, drink, shelter, sexual satisfaction, and other physical requirements.

2. **Safety needs.** Security and protection from physical and emotional harm, as well as assurance that physical needs will continue to be met.

3. **Social needs.** Affection, belongingness, acceptance, and friendship.

4. **Esteem needs.** Internal esteem factors such as self-respect, autonomy, and achievement, and external esteem factors such as status, recognition, and attention.

5. **Self-actualization needs.** Growth, achieving one's potential, and self-fulfillment; the drive to become what one is capable of becoming.

Maslow argued that each level in the needs hierarchy must be substantially satisfied before the next is activated and that once a need is substantially satisfied, it no longer motivates behaviour. In other words, as each need is substantially satisfied, the next need becomes dominant. In terms of Exhibit 15-2, an individual moves up the needs hierarchy. From the standpoint of motivation, Maslow's theory proposed that, although no need is ever fully satisfied, a substantially satisfied need will no longer motivate an individual. Therefore, according to Maslow, if you want to motivate someone, you need to understand what level that person is on in the hierarchy and focus on satisfying needs at or above that level. Managers who accepted Maslow's hierarchy attempted to change their organizations and management practices so that employees' needs could be satisfied.

MyManagementLab
Q&A 15.1

hierarchy of needs theory Maslow's theory that there is a hierarchy of five human needs: physiological, safety, social, esteem, and self-actualization; as each need becomes satisfied, the next need becomes dominant.

physiological needs A person's need for food, drink, shelter, sexual satisfaction, and other physical requirements.

safety needs A person's need for security and protection from physical and emotional harm, as well as assurance that physical needs will continue to be met.

social needs A person's need for affection, belongingness, acceptance, and friendship.

esteem needs A person's need for internal esteem factors such as self-respect, autonomy, and achievement, and external esteem factors such as status, recognition, and attention.

self-actualization needs A person's need to grow and become what he or she is capable of becoming.

Exhibit 15-2

Maslow's Hierarchy of Needs

Maslow's needs theory received wide recognition during the 1960s and 1970s, especially among practising managers, probably because of its intuitive logic and ease of understanding. However, Maslow provided no empirical support for his theory, and several studies that sought to validate it could not.[7]

McGregor's Theory X and Theory Y

Do you need to be rewarded by others or are you a self-motivator?

Are individuals intrinsically or extrinsically motivated? Douglas McGregor tried to uncover the answer to this question through his discussion of Theory X and Theory Y.[8] **Extrinsic motivation** comes from outside the person and includes such things as pay, bonuses, and other tangible rewards. **Intrinsic motivation** reflects an individual's internal desire to do something, with motivation coming from interest, challenge, and personal satisfaction. Individuals show intrinsic motivation when they deeply care about their work, look for ways to improve the work, and are fulfilled by doing it well.[9]

McGregor's **Theory X** offers an essentially negative view of people. It assumes that employees have little ambition, dislike work, want to avoid responsibility, and need to be closely controlled to work effectively. It suggests that people are almost exclusively driven by extrinsic motivators. **Theory Y** offers a positive view. It assumes that employees can exercise self-direction, accept and actually seek out responsibility, and consider work a natural activity. It suggests that people are more intrinsically motivated. McGregor believed that Theory Y assumptions best captured the true nature of employees and should guide management practice.

What did McGregor's analysis imply about motivation? The answer is best expressed in the framework presented by Maslow. Theory X assumed that lower-order needs dominated individuals, and Theory Y assumed that higher-order needs dominated individuals. McGregor himself held to the belief that the assumptions of Theory Y were more valid than those of Theory X. Therefore, he proposed that participation in decision making, responsible and challenging jobs, and good group relations would maximize employee motivation.

Our knowledge of motivation tells us that neither theory alone fully accounts for employee behaviour. What we know is that motivation is the result of the interaction of the individual and the situation. Individuals differ in their basic motivational drive. As well, while you may find completing a homework assignment boring, you might enthusiastically plan a surprise party for a friend. These points underscore that the level of motivation varies both *between* individuals and *within* individuals at different times. They also suggest that managers should try to make sure that situations are motivating for employees.

Herzberg's Motivation-Hygiene Theory

Frederick Herzberg's **motivation-hygiene theory** proposes that intrinsic factors are related to job satisfaction and motivation, whereas extrinsic factors are associated with job dissatisfaction.[10] Findings from the survey work conducted by Herzberg are shown in Exhibit 15-3.

Herzberg concluded from his analysis that the replies people gave when they felt good about their jobs were significantly different from the replies they gave when they felt bad. Certain characteristics were consistently related to job satisfaction (factors on the left side of the exhibit), and others to job dissatisfaction (factors on the right side). Those factors associated with job satisfaction were intrinsic and included things such as achievement, recognition, and responsibility. When people felt good about their work, they tended to attribute these characteristics to themselves. On the other hand, when they were dissatisfied, they tended to cite extrinsic factors such as supervision, company policy, interpersonal relationships, and working conditions.

extrinsic motivation Motivation that comes from outside the person and includes such things as pay, bonuses, and other tangible rewards.

intrinsic motivation Motivation that comes from the person's internal desire to do something, due to such things as interest, challenge, and personal satisfaction.

Theory X The assumption that employees have little ambition, dislike work, want to avoid responsibility, and must be closely controlled to perform.

Theory Y The assumption that employees can exercise self-direction, accept and seek out responsibility, and consider work a natural activity.

MyManagementLab
Q&A 15.2

motivation-hygiene theory Herzberg's theory that intrinsic factors are related to job satisfaction and motivation, whereas extrinsic factors are related to job dissatisfaction.

Exhibit 15-3

Herzberg's Motivation-Hygiene Theory

Motivators	Hygiene Factors
• Achievement • Recognition • Work Itself • Responsibility • Advancement • Growth	• Supervision • Company Policy • Relationship with Supervisor • Working Conditions • Salary • Relationship with Peers • Personal Life • Relationship with Subordinates • Status • Security

Extremely Satisfied	Neutral	Extremely Dissatisfied

In addition, Herzberg believed that the data suggested that the opposite of satisfaction was not dissatisfaction, as traditionally had been believed. Removing dissatisfying characteristics from a job would not necessarily make that job more satisfying (or motivating). As shown in Exhibit 15-4, Herzberg proposed that his findings indicated the existence of a dual continuum: The opposite of "satisfaction" is "no satisfaction," and the opposite of "dissatisfaction" is "no dissatisfaction."

Therefore, managers who sought to eliminate factors that created job dissatisfaction could bring about workplace harmony but not necessarily motivation. The extrinsic factors that create job dissatisfaction were called **hygiene factors**. When these factors are adequate, people won't be dissatisfied, but they won't be satisfied (or motivated) either. To motivate people in their jobs, Herzberg suggested emphasizing **motivators**, the intrinsic factors such as achievement, recognition, and challenge that increase job satisfaction.

Herzberg's theory enjoyed wide popularity from the mid-1960s to the early 1980s, but criticisms arose concerning his procedures and methodology. Although today we say the theory was simplistic, it has had a strong influence on how we currently design jobs, as the following *Management Reflection* shows.

hygiene factors Factors that eliminate job dissatisfaction, but don't motivate.

motivators Factors that increase job satisfaction and motivation.

Exhibit 15-4

Contrasting Views of Satisfaction–Dissatisfaction

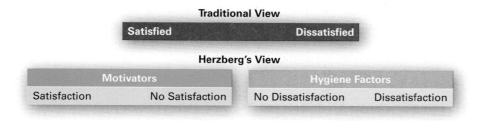

Machine Shop Cleans Up Its Act

Can the design of a machine shop affect employee morale? Langley, BC-based Pazmac Enterprises uses insights from Herzberg's theory to organize its workplace.[11] The employees at the machine shop enjoy perks often associated with employees in the high-tech industry. Owner Steve Scarlett provides opportunities for his employees to be involved in decision making. "I believe business needs to be planned diplomatically—we talk things out," says Scarlett. He ensures good relationships among employees, and he also shows concern about employees' hygiene needs, reflecting Herzberg. Usually machine shops are noisy and messy, the floors are covered with oil, and employees wear dirty overalls. Pazmac, however, is spotlessly clean. The lunch room is tastefully designed, and the men's washroom is plush, with potpourri bowls and paintings on the walls.

Scarlett believes that employees should be treated the way he himself would like to be treated, which explains why he provides an on-site swimming pool, personal trainers, weekly yoga classes, and professional counselling services for employees. Scarlett clearly considers both hygiene factors and motivator factors in dealing with his employees. His strategy has paid off. The company has had very little employee turnover in recent years, and a number of employees have worked there for more than 15 years. ■

McClelland's Three-Needs Theory

David McClelland and his associates proposed the **three-needs theory**, which says that three acquired (not innate) needs are major motivators in work.[12] These three needs are the **need for achievement (nAch)**, which is the drive to succeed and excel in relation to a set of standards; the **need for power (nPow)**, which is the need to make others behave in a way that they would not have behaved otherwise; and the **need for affiliation (nAff)**, which is the desire for friendly and close interpersonal relationships. Of these three needs, the need for achievement has been researched the most.

People with a high need for achievement strive for personal achievement rather than for the trappings and rewards of success. They have a desire to do something better or more efficiently than it's been done before.[13] They prefer jobs that offer personal responsibility for finding solutions to problems, in which they can receive rapid and unambiguous feedback on their performance in order to tell whether they're improving, and in which they can set moderately challenging goals. High achievers avoid what they perceive to be very easy or very difficult tasks. Also, a high need to achieve doesn't necessarily lead to being a good manager, especially in large organizations. That's because high achievers focus on their *own* accomplishments, while good managers emphasize helping *others* accomplish their goals.[14] McClelland showed that employees can be trained to stimulate their achievement need by being in situations where they have personal responsibility, feedback, and moderate risks.[15]

The other two needs in this theory haven't been researched as extensively as the need for achievement. However, we do know that the best managers tend to be high in the need for power and low in the need for affiliation.[16]

While needs theories give us some insights into motivating employees by stressing the importance of addressing individuals' needs, they don't provide a complete picture of motivation. For that we turn to some contemporary theories of motivation that explain the processes managers can use to motivate employees.

Contemporary Theories of Motivation

▶ ▶ ▶ One of the challenges of motivating employees is linking productivity to rewards. Compounding this challenge for Tesco is that some jobs are very boring.[17] Clare

---

three-needs theory McClelland's motivation theory, which says that three acquired (not innate) needs—achievement, power, and affiliation—are major motives in work.

need for achievement (nAch) The drive to succeed and excel in relation to a set of standards.

need for power (nPow) The need to make others behave in a way that they would not have behaved otherwise.

need for affiliation (nAff) The desire for friendly and close interpersonal relationships.

MyManagementLab
Q&A 15.3, Q&A 15.4

3. Compare and contrast contemporary theories of motivation.

Chapman, Tesco's director of human resources, says, "We're trying to take the routine out of the workplace, and build in more interest." The company eliminated the boring task of unloading soft drinks by ordering merchandising units that come fully stocked, ready to be wheeled into the store.

Tesco also encourages employees to buy shares of the company, so that staff can "share in the success they helped to create," says reward manager Helen O'Keefe. To help employees understand the potential benefits of shares, the annual benefit report includes share price graphs and a reward statement for staff. The benefit report helps employees see how the share price performs over the longer term and in comparison with the shares of other companies.

Sir Terry Leahy says he wants his employees to take four things from the job: "They find it interesting, they're treated with respect, they have the chance to get on, and they find their boss is helpful and not their biggest problem." All of these rewards make it easier for employees to perform well.

Think About It

How can you link productivity to rewards so that employees feel motivated? What other things can be done at Tesco to ensure that employees feel motivated?

The theories we look at in this section represent current explanations of employee motivation. Although these theories may not be as well known as those we just discussed, they are supported by research.[18] These contemporary motivation approaches are goal-setting theory, reinforcement theory, job design theory, equity theory, and expectancy theory.

Goal-Setting Theory

Before a big assignment or major class project presentation, has a teacher ever encouraged you to "just do your best"? What does that vague statement "do your best" mean? Would your performance on a class project have been higher had that teacher said you needed to score 93 percent to keep your A in the class? Research on goal-setting theory addresses these issues; the findings, as you'll see, are impressive in terms of the effect that goal specificity, challenge, and feedback have on performance.[19]

There is substantial research support for **goal-setting theory**, which says that specific goals increase performance and that difficult goals, when accepted, result in higher performance than do easy goals. What does goal-setting theory tell us?

First, working toward a goal is a major source of job motivation. Studies on goal setting have demonstrated that specific and challenging goals are superior motivating forces.[20] Such goals produce a higher output than does the generalized goal "do your best." The specificity of the goal itself acts as an internal stimulus. For instance, when a sales rep commits to making eight sales calls daily, this intention gives him a specific goal to try to attain.

It's not a contradiction that goal-setting theory says that motivation is maximized by *difficult* goals, whereas achievement motivation (from three-needs theory) is stimulated by *moderately challenging* goals.[21] First, goal-setting theory deals with people in general, while the conclusions on achievement motivation are based on people who have a high nAch. Given that no more than 10 to 20 percent of North Americans are high achievers (a proportion that's likely lower in underdeveloped countries), difficult goals are still recommended for the majority of employees. Second, the conclusions of goal-setting theory apply to those who accept and are committed to the goals. Difficult goals will lead to higher performance *only* if they are accepted.

Next, will employees try harder if they have the opportunity to participate in the setting of goals? Not always. In some cases, participatively set goals elicit superior performance; in other cases, individuals perform best when their managers assign goals. However, participation is probably preferable to assigning goals when employees might resist accepting difficult challenges.[22]

Finally, we know that people will do better if they get feedback on how well they're progressing toward their goals because feedback helps identify discrepancies between what

goal-setting theory The proposition that specific goals increase performance and that difficult goals, when accepted, result in higher performance than do easy goals.

MyManagementLab
Q&A 15.5

MyManagementLab
Q&A 15.6

Mark Cuban, who made a fortune selling his company Broadcast.com to Yahoo! and who owns the 2011 NBA champion Dallas Mavericks, appears to believe in the idea that people are motivated by having difficult goals. When all his ticket reps made their sales quotas, he rewarded them by saying, "Good. That's what you're supposed to do."

self-efficacy An individual's belief that he or she is capable of performing a task.

they have done and what they want to do. But all feedback isn't equally effective. Self-generated feedback—where an employee monitors his or her own progress—has been shown to be a more powerful motivator than feedback coming from someone else.[23] An example of this would be where an employee identifies the metrics they wish to measure and designs a customized report.

Three other contingencies besides feedback influence the goal–performance relationship: goal commitment, adequate self-efficacy, and national culture.

First, goal-setting theory assumes that an individual is committed to a goal. Commitment is most likely when goals are made public, when an individual has an internal locus of control, and when the goals are self-set rather than assigned.[24]

Next, **self-efficacy** refers to an individual's belief that he or she is capable of performing a task.[25] The higher your self-efficacy, the more confidence you have in your ability to succeed in a task. So, in difficult situations, we find that people with low self-efficacy are likely to reduce their effort or give up altogether, whereas those with high self-efficacy will try harder to master the challenge.[26] In addition, individuals with high self-efficacy seem to respond to negative feedback with increased effort and motivation, whereas those with low self-efficacy are likely to reduce their effort when given negative feedback.[27]

Finally, the value of goal-setting theory depends on the national culture. It's well adapted to North American countries because its main ideas align reasonably well with those cultures. It assumes that subordinates will be reasonably independent (not a high score on power distance), that people will seek challenging goals (low in uncertainty avoidance), and that performance is considered important by both managers and subordinates (high in assertiveness). Don't expect goal setting to lead to higher employee performance in countries where the cultural characteristics aren't like this.

Exhibit 15-5 summarizes the relationships among goals, motivation, and performance. Our overall conclusion is that the intention to work toward hard and specific goals is a powerful motivating force. Under the proper conditions, it can lead to higher performance. However, there is no evidence that such goals are associated with increased job satisfaction.[28]

Exhibit 15-5

Goal-Setting Theory

Reinforcement Theory

Reinforcement theory says that behaviour is a function of its consequences. Consequences that immediately follow a behaviour and increase the probability that the behaviour will be repeated are called **reinforcers**.

Reinforcement theory ignores factors such as goals, expectations, and needs. Instead, it focuses solely on what happens to a person when he or she does something. For instance, Wal-Mart improved its bonus program for hourly employees. Employees who provide outstanding customer service get a cash bonus. And all Wal-Mart hourly full- and part-time store employees are eligible for annual "My$hare" bonuses, which are allocated on store performance and distributed quarterly so that workers are rewarded more frequently.[29] The company's intent: Keep the workforce motivated.

According to B. F. Skinner, people will most likely engage in desired behaviours if they are rewarded for doing so. These rewards are most effective if they immediately follow a desired behaviour, and behaviour that isn't rewarded or that is punished is less likely to be repeated.[30]

Using reinforcement theory, managers can influence employees' behaviour by using positive reinforcers for actions that help the organization achieve its goals. Managers should ignore, not punish, undesirable behaviour. Although punishment eliminates undesired behaviour faster than nonreinforcement does, its effect is often temporary, and it may have unpleasant side effects, including dysfunctional behaviour such as workplace conflicts, absenteeism, and turnover. Although reinforcement is an important influence on work behaviour, it isn't the only explanation for differences in employee motivation.[31]

reinforcement theory The theory that behaviour is a function of its consequences.

reinforcers Consequences immediately following a behaviour that increase the probability that the behaviour will be repeated.

Job Design Theory

Have you ever had a job that was really motivating? What were its characteristics?

Because managers are primarily interested in how to motivate individuals on the job, we need to look at ways to design motivating jobs. If you look closely at what an organization is and how it works, you will find that it's composed of thousands of tasks. These tasks, in turn, are combined into jobs. We use the term **job design** to refer to the way tasks are combined to form complete jobs. The jobs that people perform in an organization should not evolve by chance. Managers should design jobs deliberately and thoughtfully to reflect the demands of the changing environ-

job design The way tasks are combined to form complete jobs.

MyManagementLab
Q&A 15.7

ment, the organization's technology, and its employees' skills, abilities, and preferences.[32] When jobs are designed with those things in mind, employees are motivated to work hard. What are some ways that managers can design motivating jobs?[33]

Job Enlargement

As we saw earlier, in Chapter 10, job design historically has concentrated on making jobs smaller and more specialized. Yet when jobs are narrow in focus and highly specialized, motivating employees is a real challenge. One of the earliest efforts at overcoming the drawbacks of job specialization involved the horizontal expansion of a job through increasing **job scope**—the number of different tasks required in a job and the frequency with which these tasks are repeated. For instance, a dental hygienist's job could be enlarged so that in addition to dental cleaning, he or she is pulling patients' files, re-filing them when finished, and cleaning and storing instruments. This type of job design option is called **job enlargement**.

Efforts at job enlargement that focused solely on increasing the number of tasks have had less than exciting results. As one employee who experienced such a job redesign said, "Before, I had one lousy job. Now, thanks to job enlargement, I have three lousy jobs!" However, one study that looked at how *knowledge* enlargement activities (expanding the scope of knowledge used in a job) affected employees found benefits such as more satisfaction, enhanced customer service, and fewer errors.[34] Even so, most job enlargement efforts provided few challenges and little meaning to employees' activities.

job scope The number of different tasks required in a job and the frequency with which these tasks are repeated.

job enlargement The horizontal expansion of a job through increasing job scope.

job enrichment The vertical expansion of a job by adding planning and evaluating responsibilities.

job depth The degree of control employees have over their work.

job characteristics model (JCM) A framework for analyzing jobs and designing motivating jobs that identifies five core job dimensions, their interrelationships, and their impact on employees.

skill variety The degree to which a job requires a variety of activities so that an employee can use a number of different skills and talents.

task identity The degree to which a job requires completion of a whole and identifiable piece of work.

task significance The degree to which a job affects the lives or work of other people.

autonomy The degree to which a job provides substantial freedom, independence, and discretion to the individual in scheduling work and determining the procedures to be used in carrying it out.

feedback The degree to which carrying out work activities required by a job results in the individual's obtaining direct and clear information about the effectiveness of his or her performance.

Job Enrichment

Another approach to designing motivating jobs is the vertical expansion of a job by adding planning and evaluating responsibilities—**job enrichment**. Job enrichment increases **job depth**, which is the degree of control employees have over their work. In other words, employees are empowered to assume some of the tasks typically done by their managers. Thus, the tasks in an enriched job should allow employees to do a complete activity with increased freedom, independence, and responsibility. These tasks should also provide feedback so that individuals can assess and correct their own performance. For instance, in an enriched job, our dental hygienist, in addition to dental cleaning, could schedule appointments (planning) and follow up with clients (evaluating). Although job enrichment can improve the quality of work, employee motivation, and satisfaction, the research evidence on the use of job enrichment programs has been inconclusive as to its usefulness.[35]

Job Characteristics Model

Even though many organizations have implemented job enlargement and job enrichment programs and experienced mixed results, neither of these job design approaches provided a conceptual framework for analyzing jobs or for guiding managers in designing motivating jobs. The **job characteristics model (JCM)** offers such a framework.[36] It identifies five core job dimensions, their interrelationships, and their impact on employee productivity, motivation, and satisfaction.

According to the JCM, any job can be described in terms of five core dimensions, defined as follows:

1. **Skill variety.** The degree to which a job requires a variety of activities so that an employee can use a number of different skills and talents.

2. **Task identity.** The degree to which a job requires completion of a whole and identifiable piece of work.

3. **Task significance.** The degree to which a job affects the lives or work of other people.

4. **Autonomy.** The degree to which a job provides substantial freedom, independence, and discretion to the individual in scheduling the work and determining the procedures to be used in carrying it out.

5. **Feedback.** The degree to which carrying out work activities required by a job results in the individual's obtaining direct and clear information about the effectiveness of his or her performance.

Exhibit 15-6 presents the JCM model. Notice how the first three dimensions—skill variety, task identity, and task significance—combine to create meaningful work. What we mean is that if these three characteristics exist in a job, we can predict that the person will view his or her job as important, valuable, and worthwhile. Notice, too, that jobs that possess autonomy give the job incumbent a feeling of personal responsibility for the results, and that if a job provides feedback, the employee will know how effectively he or she is performing.

From a motivational standpoint, the JCM suggests that internal rewards are obtained when an employee *learns* (knowledge of results through feedback) that he or she *personally* (experienced responsibility through autonomy of work) has performed well on a task that he or she *cares about* (experienced meaningfulness through skill variety, task identity, and/or task significance).[37] The more these three conditions characterize a job, the greater the

It is easy to identify the task that Manuela Frank and Erika Seres perform at Audi's headquarters in Ingolstadt, Germany. Their job is to ensure that new cars have no unappealing odours. "You can't smell more than six specimens at a time," says Seres (right), "because after that, you are not discerning. Like wine tasters, we have rules."

Exhibit 15-6

Job Characteristics Model

Source: J. R. Hackman and J. L. Suttle, eds., *Improving Life at Work* (Glenview, IL: Scott Foresman, 1977). With permission of the authors.

employee's motivation, performance, and satisfaction and the lower his or her absenteeism and likelihood of resigning. As the model shows, the links between the job dimensions and the outcomes are moderated by the strength of the individual's growth need (the person's desire for self-esteem and self-actualization). This means that individuals with a high growth need are more likely to experience the critical psychological states and respond positively when their jobs include the core dimensions than are individuals with a low growth need. This may explain the mixed results with job enrichment: Individuals with low growth needs don't tend to achieve high performance or satisfaction by having their jobs enriched. (For further insights into motivating employees, see *Developing Your Interpersonal Skills—Designing Motivating Jobs* on pages 445–446.)

The JCM provides specific guidance to managers for job redesign (see Exhibit 15-7).

MyManagementLab
PRISM 1

Exhibit 15-7

Guidelines for Job Redesign

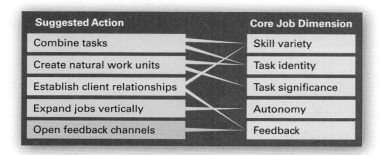

Source: J. R. Hackman and J. L. Suttle, eds., *Improving Life at Work* (Glenview, IL: Scott Foresman, 1977). With permission of the authors.

Equity Theory

Have you ever thought someone else's pay was unfair compared with yours?

After graduating from the University of New Brunswick, Mike Wilson worked in Northern Alberta as a civil engineer. He liked his job, but he became frustrated with his employer. "If you did a great job, you were treated just the same as if you did a poor job," he says.[38] Wilson decided to return home to work in the business his father had started in 1965—Dorchester, New Brunswick-based Atlantic Industries, which designs, fabricates, and builds corrugated steel structures. Wilson's hard work at Atlantic Industries has paid off: He received the 2005 Ernst & Young Entrepreneur of the Year Award for the Atlantic Region.

Wilson's decision to leave his job in Northern Alberta can be explained by equity theory. The term *equity* is related to the concept of fairness and equal treatment compared with others who behave in similar ways. There is considerable evidence that employees compare their job inputs and outcomes relative to others' and that inequities influence the degree of effort that employees exert.[39]

Equity theory, developed by J. Stacey Adams, proposes that employees perceive what they get from a job situation (outcomes) in relation to what they put into it (inputs) and then compare their inputs–outcomes ratio with the inputs–outcomes ratio of relevant others (see Exhibit 15-8). If an employee perceives her ratio to be equal to those of relevant others, a state of equity exists. In other words, she perceives that her situation is fair—that justice prevails. However, if the ratio is perceived as unequal, inequity exists and she views herself as under-rewarded or over-rewarded. Not all inequity (or equity) is real. It is important to underscore that it is the individual's *perception* that determines the equity of the situation.

What will employees do when they perceive an inequity? Equity theory proposes that employees might (1) distort either their own or others' inputs or outcomes, (2) behave in some way to induce others to change their inputs or outcomes, (3) behave in some way to change their own inputs or outcomes, (4) choose a different comparison person,

MyManagementLab
Q&A 15.8

equity theory The theory that an employee compares his or her job's inputs–outcomes ratio with that of relevant others and then responds to correct any inequity.

Exhibit 15-8

Equity Theory

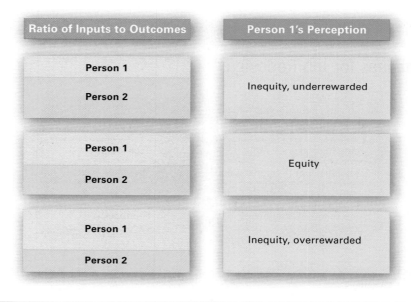

Ratio of Inputs to Outcomes	Person 1's Perception
Person 1 / Person 2	Inequity, underrewarded
Person 1 / Person 2	Equity
Person 1 / Person 2	Inequity, overrewarded

or (5) quit their jobs. These types of employee reactions have generally proved to be accurate.[40] A review of the research consistently confirms the equity thesis: Employee motivation is influenced significantly by relative rewards, as well as by absolute rewards. Whenever employees perceive inequity, they will act to correct the situation.[41] The result might be lower or higher productivity, improved or reduced quality of output, increased absenteeism, or voluntary resignation.

When Toronto city councillors faced inequity in their pay, they responded by voting themselves a raise, as the following *Management Reflection* shows.

MANAGEMENT REFLECTION
▶ Focus on Ethics

City Councillors End "Inequitable" Pay

What is fair pay for city councillors? Toronto city councillors voted themselves an 8.9 percent pay raise effective January 2007, shortly before it became obvious that extensive budget cuts were going to be needed to manage the city.[42] On a percentage basis, the pay raise seems high compared with what the average Ontarian received as a pay raise in 2006. Other government employees might have wondered if they should have raises as well.

But what should a municipal councillor be paid? In 2007, members of the Quebec National Assembly earned annual salaries of $82 073, heads of federal Crown corporations started at $109 000, Ontario premier Dalton McGuinty earned $198 620, and members of the BC legislature earned $98 000, plus expenses. With the raise, Toronto's councillors earn $95 000 a year. Despite working at different levels of government—federal, provincial, and local—all of these officials make complex decisions and need similar skills. Many of them could make more money working in the private sector.

When the Toronto councillors voted themselves a pay raise, they were not thinking about possible budget shortfalls. Instead, they were responding to the idea that they were underpaid compared with other government decision makers who performed duties similar to their own. As councillors for the largest city in the country, with the largest budget, they were advised by a consulting firm that they should rank in the "top 25 percent of salaries of councillors across the country." Their salary before the raise was one of the lowest in the country. ■

The **referent** against which individuals compare themselves is an important variable in equity theory.[43] Three referent categories have been defined: other, system, and self. The *other* category includes other individuals with similar jobs in the same organization but also includes friends, neighbours, or professional associates. On the basis of what they hear at work or read about in newspapers or trade journals, employees compare their pay with that of others. The *system* category includes organizational pay policies and procedures and the administration of the system. Whatever precedents have been established by the organization regarding pay allocation are major elements of this category. The *self* category refers to inputs–outcomes ratios that are unique to the individual. It reflects past personal experiences and contacts and is influenced by criteria such as past jobs or family commitments. The choice of a particular set of referents is related to the information available about the referents as well as to their perceived relevance. At Surrey, BC-based Back in Motion Rehab (named the #1 Best Workplace in Canada for 2007 by *Canadian Business*), management decided that the highest-paid director's base salary should be less than two times the salary of the average staff member.[44] Because this policy uses the average staff member's pay as a referent, it sends the message that the output of the average staff member is truly valued.

Historically, equity theory focused on **distributive justice**, which is the perceived fairness of the amount and allocation of rewards among individuals. Recent equity research has focused on looking at issues of **procedural justice**, which is the perceived fairness of the process used to determine the distribution of rewards. This research shows

referents Those things individuals compare themselves against in order to assess equity.

distributive justice Perceived fairness of the amount and allocation of rewards among individuals.

procedural justice Perceived fairness of the process used to determine the distribution of rewards.

that distributive justice has a greater influence on employee satisfaction than procedural justice, while procedural justice tends to affect an employee's organizational commitment, trust in his or her manager, and intention to quit.[45] What are the implications of these findings for managers? They should consider openly sharing information on how allocation decisions are made, follow consistent and unbiased procedures, and engage in similar practices to increase the perception of procedural justice. When managers increase the perception of procedural justice, employees are likely to view their managers and the organization as positive even if they are dissatisfied with pay, promotions, and other personal outcomes.

In conclusion, equity theory shows that, for most employees, motivation is influenced significantly by relative rewards, as well as by absolute rewards, but some key issues are still unclear.[46] For instance, how do employees define inputs and outcomes? How do they combine and weigh their inputs and outcomes to arrive at totals? When and how do the factors change over time? And how do people choose referents? Despite these problems, equity theory does have an impressive amount of research support and offers us some important insights into employee motivation. Managers need to pay attention to equity issues when making plans to motivate their employees.

Expectancy Theory

expectancy theory The theory that an individual tends to act in a certain way based on the expectation that the act will be followed by a given outcome and on the attractiveness of that outcome to the individual.

The most comprehensive and widely accepted explanation of employee motivation to date is Victor Vroom's **expectancy theory**.[47] Although the theory has its critics,[48] most research evidence supports it.[49]

Expectancy theory states that an individual tends to act in a certain way based on the expectation that the act will be followed by a given outcome and on the attractiveness of that outcome to the individual. It includes three variables or relationships (see Exhibit 15-9):

- *Expectancy, or effort–performance linkage.* The probability perceived by the individual that exerting a given amount of effort will lead to a certain level of performance.

- *Instrumentality, or performance–reward linkage.* The degree to which the individual believes that performing at a particular level is instrumental in attaining the desired outcome.

- *Valence, or attractiveness of reward.* The importance that the individual places on the potential outcome or reward that can be achieved on the job. Valence considers both the goals and needs of the individual. (See also *Self-Assessment—What Rewards Do I Value Most?* on pages 442–443.)

This explanation of motivation might sound complex, but it really is not. It can be summed up in these questions: How hard do I have to work to achieve a certain level of performance, and can I actually achieve that level? What reward will I get for working at

Exhibit 15-9

Simplified Expectancy Model

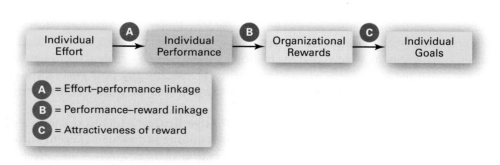

that level of performance? How attractive is the reward to me, and does it help me achieve my goals? Whether you are motivated to put forth effort (that is, to work) at any given time depends on your particular goals and your perception of whether a certain level of performance is necessary to attain those goals.

The key to expectancy theory is understanding an individual's goal and the link between effort and performance, between performance and rewards, and, finally, between rewards and individual goal satisfaction. Expectancy theory recognizes that there is no universal principle for explaining what motivates individuals and thus stresses that managers need to understand why employees view certain outcomes as attractive or unattractive. After all, we want to reward individuals with those things they value as positive. Also, expectancy theory emphasizes expected behaviours. Do employees know what is expected of them and how they will be evaluated? Finally, the theory is concerned with perceptions. Reality is irrelevant. An individual's own perceptions of performance, reward, and goal outcomes, not the outcomes themselves, will determine his or her motivation (level of effort). Exhibit 15-10 suggests how managers might increase employee motivation, using expectancy theory.

MyManagementLab
Q&A 15.9

Integrating Contemporary Theories of Motivation

We have presented three contemporary motivation theories. You might be tempted to view them independently, but doing so would be a mistake. Many of the ideas underlying the theories are complementary, and you will better understand how to motivate people if you see how the theories fit together.[50] Exhibit 15-11 presents a model that integrates much of what we know about motivation. Its basic foundation is the expectancy model. Let's work through the model, starting on the left.

The individual effort box has an arrow leading into it. This arrow flows from the individual's goals. Consistent with goal-setting theory, this goals–effort link is meant to illustrate that goals direct behaviour. Expectancy theory predicts that an employee will exert a high level of effort if he or she perceives that there is a strong relationship between effort and performance, performance and rewards, and rewards and satisfaction of personal goals. Each of these relationships is, in turn, influenced by certain factors. You can see from the model that the level of individual performance is determined not only by the level of individual effort but also by the individual's ability to perform and by whether the organization has a fair and objective performance evaluation system. The performance–reward relationship will be strong if the individual perceives that it is performance (rather than seniority, personal favourites, or some other criterion) that is rewarded. The final link in expectancy theory is the rewards–goals relationship. The traditional need theories come into play at this point. Motivation would be high to the degree that the rewards an individual received for his or her high performance satisfied the dominant needs consistent with his or her individual goals.

Exhibit 15-10

Steps to Increasing Motivation, Using Expectancy Theory

Improving Expectancy	Improving Instrumentality	Improving Valence
Improve the ability of the individual to perform.	**Increase the individual's belief that performance will lead to reward.**	**Make sure that the reward is meaningful to the individual.**
• Make sure employees have skills for the task. • Provide training. • Assign reasonable tasks and goals.	• Observe and recognize performance. • Deliver rewards as promised. • Indicate to employees how previous good performance led to greater rewards.	• Ask employees what rewards they value. • Give rewards that are valued.

Exhibit 15-11

Integrating Contemporary Theories of Motivation

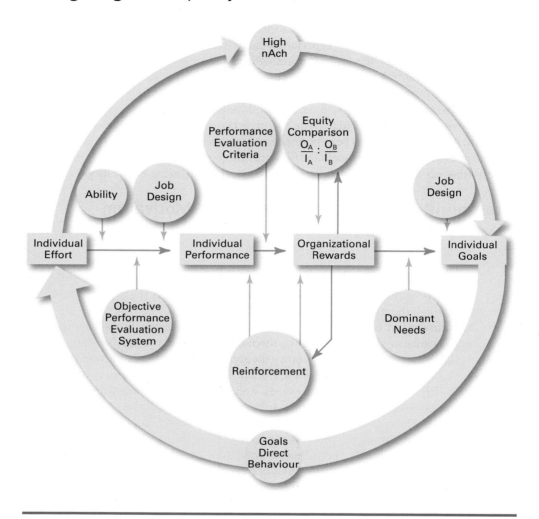

A closer look at the model also shows that it considers the achievement-need, reinforcement, equity, and JCM theories. The high achiever isn't motivated by the organization's assessment of his or her performance or organizational rewards; hence the jump from effort to individual goals for those with a high nAch. Remember that high achievers are internally driven as long as the jobs they're doing provide them with personal responsibility, feedback, and moderate risks. They're not concerned with the effort–performance, performance–reward, or rewards–goals linkages.

Reinforcement theory is seen in the model by recognizing that the organization's rewards reinforce the individual's performance. If managers have designed a reward system that is seen by employees as "paying off" for good performance, the rewards will reinforce and encourage continued good performance. Rewards also play a key part in equity theory. Individuals will compare the rewards (outcomes) they have received from the inputs or efforts they made with the inputs–outcomes ratio of relevant others. If inequities exist, the effort expended may be influenced.

Finally, the JCM is seen in this integrative model. Task characteristics (job design) influence job motivation at two places. First, jobs that are designed around the five job dimensions are likely to lead to higher actual job performance because the individual's motivation will be stimulated by the job itself—that is, these jobs will increase the linkage between effort and performance. Second, jobs that are designed around the five job dimensions increase an employee's control over key elements in his or her work. Therefore, jobs that offer autonomy, feedback, and similar task characteristics help to satisfy the individual goals of employees who desire greater control over their work.

Current Issues in Motivation

▶ ▶ ▶ One of the challenges managers at Tesco faced was how to motivate its many different employee groups: students, new graduates, mothers returning to the workplace, and ethnic minorities.[51] In a survey of its employees, the company found that older female employees wanted flexible hours and stimulating work, but they were not looking to be promoted. Young college graduates working in head office wanted a challenging, well-paid career and time to pursue personal interests and family life. Many employees noted they wanted managers who helped them.

Tesco has come up with a variety of practices to meet employee needs, including career breaks of up to eight months, discounts on family holidays, driving lessons, and magazine subscriptions. Tesco has a website that offers career and financial advice and discounts on meals, cinema tickets, and travel for its 16- to 24-year-old employees who are in school or have recently left school. The company created the "A-Level Options" program to give young people who did not want a post-secondary education the opportunity to be fast-tracked into management. Clare Chapman, Tesco's human resource director, says the company has not limited specific rewards for specific groups. "It's more a question of being mindful of the needs of all staff instead of catering for one or two types of attitude."

4. Discuss current issues in motivation.

Think About It

What factors need to be considered when motivating employees who have very different needs? Is there anything else Tesco can do to motivate young people?

So far, we have covered a lot of the theoretical bases of employee motivation. Understanding and predicting employee motivation continues to be one of the most popular areas in management research. However, even current studies of employee motivation are influenced by several significant workplace issues, such as motivating a diverse workforce and designing effective rewards programs. Let's take a closer look at each of these issues.

Motivating a Diverse Workforce

To maximize motivation among today's workforce, managers need to think in terms of *flexibility*. For instance, studies tell us that men place more importance on having autonomy in their jobs than do women. In contrast, the opportunity to learn, convenient and flexible work hours, and good interpersonal relations are more important to women.[52] Baby Boomers may need more flextime as they manage the needs of their children and their aging parents. Gen-Xers want employers to add to their experience so they develop portable skills. Meanwhile, Gen-Yers want more opportunities and the ability to work in teams.[53] Managers need to recognize that what motivates a single mother with two dependent children who is working full time to support her family may be very different from the needs of a single part-time employee or an older employee who is working only to supplement his or her retirement income. A diverse array of rewards is needed to motivate employees with such diverse needs.

Motivating Employees from Diverse Cultures

In today's global business environment, managers cannot automatically assume that motivational programs that work in one location are going to work in others. Most current motivation theories were developed in the United States by Americans about Americans.[54] Maybe the most blatant pro-American characteristic in these theories is the strong emphasis on individualism and quantity-of-life cultural characteristics. For instance,

434 **Part 4** Leading

It can be difficult or even misleading to apply Western theories of motivation to employees in other cultures. In Japan, for example, only a few thousand of all electronics workers are honoured with the title of "super technician," or *supaa ginosha*. These workers perform extraordinarily precise tasks, such as using a soldering iron to quickly and delicately repair tiny computer chips. In recognition of their expertise, these highly skilled workers receive certificates and pins, but seldom money. One of these super technicians, Rina Masuda (not shown here) of Sharp Corp., says, "The soldering I do by hand is far superior to anything that machines can do," her pride expressing the common view that recognition and honour are enough.

expectancy theory emphasizes goal accomplishment, as well as rational and individual thought. Let's look at several theories to see if there is any cross-cultural transferability.

Maslow's hierarchy of needs proposes that people start at the physiological level and then move progressively up the hierarchy in order. This hierarchy, if it has any application at all, aligns with American culture. In countries like Japan, Greece, and Mexico, where uncertainty-avoidance characteristics are strong (that is, individuals prefer structured situations), security needs would be on the top of the needs hierarchy. Countries that score high on quality-of-life characteristics (that is, individuals value relationships and are concerned with the welfare of others)—Denmark, Sweden, Norway, the Netherlands, and Finland—would have social needs on top.[55] We would predict, for instance, that group work will motivate employees more when a country's culture scores high on quality-of-life characteristics.

Equity theory has a relatively strong following in the United States. That is not surprising given that US-style reward systems are based on the assumption that employees are highly sensitive to equity in reward allocations. And in the United States, equity is meant to closely tie pay to performance. However, recent evidence suggests that even in collectivist cultures (where individuals expect that others will look after and protect them), especially in the former socialist countries of Central and Eastern Europe, employees expect rewards to reflect their individual needs, as well as their performance.[56] Moreover, consistent with a legacy of communism and centrally planned economies, employees exhibited a greater "entitlement" attitude—that is, they expected outcomes to be greater than their inputs.[57] These findings suggest that US-style pay practices may need modification, especially in Russia and former communist countries, in order to be perceived as fair by employees.

Despite these cross-cultural differences in motivation, don't assume there are no cross-cultural consistencies. For instance, the desire for interesting work seems important to almost all employees, regardless of their national culture. In a study of seven countries, employees in Belgium, Great Britain, Israel, and the United States ranked "interesting work" number one among 11 work goals. And this factor was ranked either second or third in Japan, the Netherlands, and Germany.[58] Similarly, in a study comparing job-preference outcomes among graduate students in the United States, Canada, Australia, and Singapore, growth, achievement, and responsibility were rated the top three and had identical rankings.[59] Both of these studies suggest some universality to the importance of intrinsic factors identified by Herzberg in his motivation-hygiene theory. Another recent study examining workplace motivation trends in Japan also seems to indicate that Herzberg's model is applicable to Japanese employees.[60]

Motivating Minimum-Wage Employees

MyManagementLab
Q&A 15.10

Suppose that in your first managerial position after graduating, you are responsible for managing a work group composed of minimum-wage employees. Offering more pay to these employees for high levels of performance is out of the question: Your company just cannot afford it.[61] In addition, these employees have limited education and skills. What are your motivational options at this point? One of the toughest motivational challenges facing many managers today is how to achieve high performance levels from minimum-wage employees.

One trap we often fall into is thinking that people are motivated only by money. Although money is important as a motivator, it's not the only reward that people seek and that managers can use. What are some other types of rewards? Many companies use employee recognition programs such as employee of the month, quarterly employee performance award ceremonies, or other celebrations of employee accomplishment. For instance, at many fast-food restaurants such as McDonald's and Wendy's, you will often see plaques hanging in prominent places that feature the "Crew Member of the Month."

These types of programs highlight employees whose performance has been of the type and level the organization wants to encourage. Many managers also recognize the power of praise, but you need to be sure that these "pats on the back" are sincere, unbiased (no favouritism), and done for the right reasons; otherwise, employees can interpret such actions as manipulative.

We know from the motivation theories presented earlier that rewards are only part of the motivation equation. We need to look at other elements, such as empowerment and career development assistance. We can look to job design and expectancy theories for these insights. In service industries such as travel and hospitality, retail sales, child care, and maintenance, where pay for front-line employees generally does not get much higher than the minimum-wage level, successful companies are empowering these front-line employees with more authority to address customers' problems. If we use the JCM to examine this change, we can see that this type of job redesign provides enhanced motivating potential because employees now experience increased skill variety, task identity, task significance, autonomy, and feedback. Also, employees facing this situation often want to better themselves professionally. They need guidance, assistance in self-assessment, and training. By providing these to minimum-wage employees, you are preparing them for the future—one that hopefully promises better pay. For many, this is a strong motivator![62]

At Vancouver-based Electronic Arts Canada, managers believe the company should pay attention to employee needs in order to motivate them. The cafeteria at Electronic Arts is well stocked with employee favourites, and employees can purchase takeout dinners at good prices for their families if they do not have time to cook dinner.

Motivating Professional and Technical Employees

Professionals are typically different from nonprofessionals.[63] They have a strong and long-term commitment to their field of expertise. Their loyalty is more often to their profession than to their employer. To keep current in their field, they need to regularly update their knowledge, and because of their commitment to their profession they rarely define their workweek as 8:00 a.m. to 5:00 p.m., five days a week.

What motivates professionals? Money and promotions typically are low on their priority list. Why? They tend to be well paid and enjoy what they do. In contrast, job challenge tends to be ranked high. They like to tackle problems and find solutions. Their chief reward in their job is the work itself. Professionals also value support. They want others to think that what they are working on is important.[64] That may be true for all employees, but professionals tend to be focused on their work as their central life interest, whereas nonprofessionals typically have other interests outside work that can compensate for needs not met on the job. The preceding points imply that managers should provide professional and technical employees with new assignments and challenging projects. Give them autonomy to follow their interests and allow them to structure their work in ways they find productive. Reward them with educational opportunities—training, workshops, conferences—that allow them to keep current in their field and to network with their peers. Also reward them with recognition.

Motivating Contingent Workers

As full-time jobs have been eliminated through downsizing and other organizational restructurings, the number of openings for part-time, contract, and other forms of temporary work have increased. Contingent workers don't have the security or stability that permanent employees have, and they don't identify with the organization or display the commitment that other employees do. Temporary employees also typically get little or no benefits such as health care or pensions.[65]

There is no simple solution for motivating contingent employees. For that small set of individuals who prefer the freedom of their temporary status—for instance, some students, working mothers, retirees—the lack of stability may not be an issue. In addition, temporariness might be preferred by highly compensated physicians, engineers, accountants, or financial planners who don't want the demands of a full-time job. But these are the exceptions. For the most part, temporary employees are not temporary by choice.

What will motivate involuntarily temporary employees? An obvious answer is the opportunity to become a permanent employee. In cases in which permanent employees are selected from a pool of temps, the temps will often work hard in hopes of becoming permanent. A less obvious answer is the opportunity for training. The ability of a temporary employee to find a new job is largely dependent on his or her skills. If the employee sees that the job he or she is doing can help develop marketable skills, then motivation is increased. From an equity standpoint, you should also consider the repercussions of mixing permanent and temporary workers when pay differentials are significant. When temps work alongside permanent employees who earn more and also get benefits for doing the same job, the performance of temps is likely to suffer. Separating such employees or perhaps minimizing interdependence between them might help managers decrease potential problems.[66]

Designing Effective Rewards Programs

Employee rewards programs play a powerful role in motivating for appropriate employee behaviour. In this section, we look at how managers can design effective rewards programs by using employee recognition programs and pay-for-performance programs. First, though, we should examine the issue of the extent to which money motivates.

The Role of Money

The most commonly used reward in organizations is money. As one author notes, "Money is probably the most emotionally meaningful object in contemporary life: only food and sex are its close competitors as common carriers of such strong and diverse feelings, significance, and strivings."[67]

Little research attention has been given to individual differences in people's feelings about money, although some studies indicate that money is not employees' top priority.[68] A survey of 2000 Canadians discovered that trustworthy senior management and a good balance between work and personal or family life mattered more than pay or benefits when it came to employee satisfaction.[69] In another survey that looked at Canadian attitudes about work, one respondent explained, "Of course money is important, but that's not what's going to make you jump out of bed in the morning." Another noted, "Everyone here would take more money and more time off—that's a given. But some of the things that really make the job a good or bad one are your relations with your boss."[70]

A number of studies suggest that an individual's attitude toward money is correlated with personality traits and demographic factors.[71] People who value money score higher on "attributes like sensation seeking, competitiveness, materialism, and control." People who desire money score higher on self-esteem, need for achievement, and Type A personality measures. Men seem to value money more than women. These studies suggest that individuals who value money will be more motivated by it than individuals who value other things.

What these findings suggest is that when organizations develop reward programs, they need to consider very carefully what individual employees value.

Employee Recognition Programs

employee recognition programs
Reward programs that provide managers with opportunities to give employees personal attention and express interest, approval, and appreciation for a job well done.

Employee recognition programs provide managers with opportunities to give employees personal attention and express interest, approval, and appreciation for a job well done.[72] These programs can take many forms. For instance, you can personally congratulate an employee in private for a good job. You can send a handwritten note or an email message acknowledging something positive that the employee has done. For employees with a strong need for social acceptance, you can publicly recognize accomplishments. To enhance group cohesiveness and motivation, you can celebrate team successes. For instance, you can throw a pizza party to celebrate a team's accomplishments.

A survey of Canadian firms by Hewitt Associates found that 35 percent of companies recognized individual or group achievements with cash or merchandise.[73] Do employees think employee recognition programs are important? You bet! One of the consistent themes that has emerged in the seven years that Hewitt Associates has studied the 50 Best Companies to Work for in Canada is the importance of recognition. A large number of the winning companies show appreciation for their employees frequently and visibly.[74] Most employee recognition programs are not financially based and hence impact motivation at little to no cost.

Pay-for-Performance Programs

What's in it for me? That is a question every person consciously or unconsciously asks before engaging in any form of behaviour. Our knowledge of motivation tells us that people act in order to satisfy some need. Before they do anything, therefore, they look for a payoff or reward. Although many different rewards may be offered by organizations, most of us are concerned with earning an amount of money that allows us to satisfy our needs and wants. In fact, a large body of research suggests that pay is far more motivational than some motivation theorists such as Maslow and Herzberg suggest.[75] Because pay is an important variable in motivation, we need to look at how we can use pay to motivate high levels of employee performance. This concern explains the logic behind pay-for-performance programs.

Pay-for-performance programs are variable compensation plans that pay employees on the basis of some performance measure.[76] Piece-rate pay plans, wage-incentive plans, profit-sharing plans, lump-sum bonuses, and stock option programs are examples. What differentiates these forms of pay from more traditional compensation plans is that instead of paying a person for time on the job, pay is adjusted to reflect some performance measure. These performance measures might include such things as individual productivity, team or work group productivity, departmental productivity, or the overall organization's profit performance.

Pay-for-performance is probably most compatible with expectancy theory. Specifically, individuals should perceive a strong relationship between their performance and the rewards they receive if motivation is to be maximized. If rewards are allocated only on nonperformance factors—such as seniority, job title, or across-the-board pay raises—then employees are likely to reduce their efforts.

Pay-for-performance programs are popular. The number of employees affected by variable pay plans has been rising in Canada. A 2007 survey of 314 firms by Hewitt Associates found that 80 percent of respondents have variable pay programs in place, compared with 43 percent in 1994.[77] Pay-for-performance programs are more common for non-unionized employees than unionized ones, although more than 30 percent of unionized companies had such plans in 2002.[78] Prem Benimadhu, an analyst with the Conference Board of Canada, notes, "Canadian unions have been very allergic to variable compensation."[79] In addition to wage uncertainty, employees may object to pay for performance if they feel that factors out of their control might affect the extent to which bonuses are possible.

In 2005, some 78 percent of large US companies had some form of variable pay plan.[80] About 22 percent of Japanese companies have company-wide pay-for-performance plans.[81] However, one Japanese company, Fujitsu, dropped its performance-based program after eight years because it proved to be "flawed and a poor fit with Japanese culture."[82] Management found that some employees set goals as low as possible for fear of falling short. Others set extremely short-term goals. As a result, Fujitsu executives felt that ambitious projects that could produce hit products were being avoided.

Do pay-for-performance programs work? The evidence is mixed, at best.[83] One recent study that followed the careers of 1000 top economists found that they put in more effort early in their careers, at a time when productivity-related incentives had a larger impact.[84] A recent study of Finnish white-collar employees found that higher levels of payment and more frequent payments positively affected productivity, while lower levels of payment did not improve productivity.[85] A Canadian study looked at both unionized and non-unionized workplaces and found that variable pay plans result in "increased productivity, a safer work environment, a better understanding of the business by employees, and little risk of employees losing base pay," according to Prem Benimadhu.[86] But there are studies that question the effectiveness of pay-for-performance approaches, suggesting they can lead to less group cohesiveness in the workplace.[87]

pay-for-performance programs
Variable compensation plans that pay employees on the basis of some performance measure.

MyManagementLab
Q&A 15.11, Q&A 15.12

If the organization uses work teams, managers should consider group-based performance incentives that will reinforce team effort and commitment. But whether these programs are individual based or team based, managers do need to ensure that they are specific about the relationship between an individual's pay and his or her expected level of appropriate performance. Employees must clearly understand exactly how performance—theirs and the organization's—translates into dollars on their paycheques.[88] Ottawa-based Lee Valley Tools uses quarterly newsletters to employees to let them know how much profit is forecast. This helps employees understand how hard work will pay off for them. Robin Lee, the company's president, says that "sharing information and profits promotes an atmosphere in which hard work, innovation and efficiency pay off for everybody."[89]

As mentioned earlier, organizations can use a variety of programs to reward employees for performance. The most common forms are profit-sharing and stock option programs.

Profit-Sharing Plans

profit-sharing plan An organization-wide plan in which the employer shares profits with employees based on a predetermined formula.

In a **profit-sharing plan**, the employer shares profits with employees based on a predetermined formula. Employees may receive direct cash bonuses or stock options. Though senior executives are most likely to be involved in profit-sharing plans, such plans can be applied to employees at any level.

Be aware that profit-sharing plans focus on past financial results. They don't necessarily focus employees on the future, because employees and managers look for ways to cut costs today, without considering future organizational needs.

Three Canadian studies by Professor Richard J. Long of the University of Saskatchewan's College of Commerce show that a profit-sharing plan is most effective in workplaces where there is more involvement by employees, more teamwork, and a managerial philosophy that encourages participation.[90]

Stock Option Programs

A 2006 study of the largest Canadian public companies by the Ontario Teachers' Pension Plan found little evidence that the amount paid to Canada's top executives was related to the performance of their companies.[91] Perceived abuses of executive compensation have led to the formation of organizations such as RiskMetrics Group (RMG) and the Canadian Coalition for Good Governance (CCGG), who act as advisers to large institutional investors who are feeling increased pressure to conduct thorough due diligence in voting their shares. Companies, in turn, are bringing practices into alignment with RMG's voting guidelines to ensure resolutions are successful.[92]

Executive bonus and stock option programs have come under fire because they seem to fly in the face of the belief that executive pay aligns with the organization's performance. What are stock option programs, and what are they designed to do?

stock options A financial incentive that gives employees the right to purchase shares of company stock, at some time in the future, at a set price.

employee stock ownership plan (ESOP) A company-established benefit plan in which employees acquire stock as part of their benefits.

Some companies try to encourage employees to adopt the perspective of top management by making them owners of their firms, either through stock options or employee stock ownership plans. **Stock options** are a financial incentive that gives employees the right to purchase shares of company stock, at some time in the future, at a set price. **Employee stock ownership plans (ESOPs)** are company-established benefit plans in which employees acquire stock as part of their benefits.

The original idea behind stock options was to turn employees into owners and give them strong motivation to work hard to make the company successful.[93] If the company was successful, the value of the stock went up, making the stock options valuable. In other words, there was a link between performance and reward. The popularity of stock options as a motivational and compensation tool skyrocketed during the dot-com boom in the late 1990s. Because many dot-coms could not afford to pay employees the going market-rate salaries, stock options were offered as performance incentives. However, the shakeout among dot-com stocks in 2000 and 2001 illustrated one of the inherent risks of offering stock options. As long as the market was rising, employees were willing to give up a large salary in exchange for stock options. However, when stock prices tanked, many individuals who joined and stayed with a dot-com for the opportunity to get rich through stock options found those stock options had become worthless. The declining stock market became a powerful demotivator.

Despite the risk of potential lost value and the widespread abuse of stock options, managers might want to consider them as part of their overall motivational program. An appropriately designed stock option program can be a powerful motivational tool for the entire workforce.[94] Exhibit 15-12 lists several recommendations for designing stock option programs.

From Theory to Practice: Suggestions for Motivating Employees

We have covered a lot of information about motivation. If you are a manager concerned with motivating your employees, what specific recommendations can you draw from the theories and issues presented in this chapter? Although there is no simple, all-encompassing set of guidelines, the following suggestions draw on what we know about motivating employees:

5. Describe how managers can motivate employees.

MyManagementLab
Q&A 15.13

- *Recognize individual differences.* Almost every contemporary motivation theory recognizes that employees are not identical.[95] They have different needs, attitudes, personalities, and other important individual variables. Managers may not be giving enough consideration to what employees really want in terms of pay and benefits from the workplace.

Exhibit 15-12

Recommendations for Designing Stock Option Programs

Design Question	Choices	Recommendations
Who receives them?	• Broad-based or restricted	• Match company growth prospects, management style, and organizational culture.
How many?	• Large or small percentage of employee income • Many or few options in previous grants	• Match company growth prospects. • Know that large previous grants may increase recipient risk aversion.
What terms?	• Vesting* • Maturity	• Should match business cycle. • Terms shorter than 10 years can create stronger pay-for-performance relationships.
How often?	• Fixed or variable schedule	• Predictable grants may reduce incentive alignment prospects. • Internal equity issues may result from schedules that result in a variety of exercise prices.
What price?	• Fair market value • Premium • Discounted • Indexed	• Employees must view stock option exercise prices as feasible and believe that chosen benchmarks are appropriate.
What ownership?	• Holding requirements after exercise • Ownership guidelines	• Requiring recipients to hold some of their shares after exercise encourages better incentive alignment. • Clear general ownership guidelines can also increase incentive alignment.

* Vesting refers to the time that must pass before a person can exercise the option.

Source: P. Brandes, R. Dharwadkar, and G. V. Lemesis, "Effective Employee Stock Option Design: Reconciling Stakeholder, Strategic, and Motivational Factors," *Academy of Management Executive,* February 2003, p. 84.

Andrew Robinson, who runs an information security company in Portland, Maine, has taken the idea of matching people to jobs a step further than most by matching future employees to potential jobs. Robinson runs a free after-school program to teach students like these about "ethical hacking," or the fine art of protecting computer systems by hacking them first. Of the 50 students in the program, Robinson says, "They have all the skills that they need to cause trouble, and some of them may have even started doing some of those things just for fun." His point to the students is, "Here's how you can do this legally, within a moral and ethical framework, and make a good amount of money doing it."

- *Match people to jobs.* There is a great deal of evidence showing the motivational benefits of carefully matching people to jobs. For example, high achievers should have jobs that allow them to participate in setting moderately challenging goals and that involve autonomy and feedback. Also, keep in mind that not everybody is motivated by jobs that are high in autonomy, variety, and responsibility.

- *Use goals.* The literature on goal-setting theory suggests that managers should ensure that employees have hard, specific goals and feedback on how well they're doing in achieving those goals. Should the goals be assigned by the manager or should employees participate in setting them? The answer depends on your perception of goal acceptance and the organization's culture. If you expect resistance to goals, participation should increase acceptance. If participation is inconsistent with the culture, use assigned goals.

- *Ensure that goals are perceived as attainable.* Regardless of whether goals are actually attainable, employees who see goals as unattainable will reduce their effort because they'll wonder why they should bother. Managers must be sure, therefore, that employees feel confident that increased efforts *can* lead to achieving performance goals.

- *Individualize rewards.* Because employees have different needs, what acts as a reinforcer for one may not for another. Managers should use their knowledge of employee differences to individualize the rewards they control, such as pay, promotions, recognition, desirable work assignments, autonomy, and participation.

- *Link rewards to performance.* Managers need to make rewards contingent on performance. Rewarding factors other than performance will reinforce only those other factors. Important rewards such as pay increases and promotions should be given for the attainment of specific goals. Managers should also look for ways to increase the visibility of rewards, making them potentially more motivating.

- *Check the system for equity.* Employees should perceive that rewards or outcomes are equal to the inputs. On a simple level, experience, ability, effort, and other obvious inputs should explain differences in pay, responsibility, and other obvious outcomes. And remember that one person's equity is another's inequity, so an ideal reward system should probably weigh inputs differently in arriving at the proper rewards for each job.

- *Show care and concern for employees.* Employees perform better for managers who care about them. Research done by Gallup with millions of employees and tens of thousands of managers consistently shows this simple truth: The best organizations create "caring" work environments.[96] When managers care about employees, performance results typically follow.

- *Use recognition.* Recognize the power of recognition. In a stagnant economy where cost cutting is widespread (as it was from 2001 to 2005), using recognition is a low-cost means to reward employees. And it's a reward that most employees consider valuable.

- *Don't ignore money.* It's easy to get so caught up in setting goals, creating interesting jobs, and providing opportunities for participation that you forget that money is a major reason why most people work. Some studies indicate that money is not the top priority of employees. Professor Graham Lowe at the University of Alberta and a colleague found that relationships in the workplace are more important than pay or benefits in determining job satisfaction.[97] Nevertheless, the allocation of performance-based wage increases, piecework bonuses, and other pay incentives is important in determining employee motivation. We are not saying that managers should focus solely on money as a motivational tool. Rather, we are simply stating the obvious—that is, if money is removed as an incentive, people are not going to show up for work. The same cannot be said for removing performance goals, enriched work, or participation.

SUMMARY AND IMPLICATIONS

1. Define motivation. Motivation refers to the process by which a person's efforts are energized, directed, and sustained toward attaining a goal, conditioned by the effort's ability to satisfy some individual need.

▶ ▶ ▶ At Tesco, one challenge was to motivate employees so that there would be less turnover.

2. Compare and contrast early theories of motivation. Four early motivation theories—Maslow's hierarchy of needs theory, McGregor's Theory X and Theory Y, Herzberg's two-factor theory, and McClelland's three needs theory—were discussed. Although more valid explanations of motivation have been developed, these early theories are important because they represent the foundation from which contemporary motivation theories were developed and because many practising managers still use them.

▶ ▶ ▶ Managers at Tesco discovered that different employee groups, such as students and mothers returning to the workplace, had different needs, and tried to address these needs to keep employees motivated.

3. Compare and contrast contemporary theories of motivation. It is possible to make jobs more motivating by designing them better. The job characteristics model proposes that employees will be more motivated if they have greater autonomy and feedback and the work is meaningful. Equity theory proposes that employees compare their rewards and their productivity with others, and then determine whether they have been treated fairly. Individuals who perceive that they are underrewarded will try to adjust their behaviour to correct this imbalance. Expectancy theory explores the link between people's belief in whether they can do the work assigned, their belief in whether they will get the rewards promised, and the extent to which the reward is something they value. Most research evidence supports expectancy theory. Goal-setting theory says that specific goals increase performance and that difficult goals, when accepted, result in higher performance than do easy goals. Reinforcement theory ignores factors such as goals, expectations, and needs. Instead, it focuses solely on what happens to a person when he or she does something.

▶ ▶ ▶ Tesco encourages employees to buy shares of the company, so that they can "share in the success they helped to create" and see the link between performance and reward.

4. Discuss current issues in motivation. Understanding and predicting employee motivation continues to be one of the most popular areas in management research. However, even current studies of employee motivation are influenced by several significant workplace issues—issues such as motivating a diverse workforce and designing effective rewards programs.

▶ ▶ ▶ One of Tesco's challenges was motivating employees who had somewhat repetitive jobs.

5. Describe how managers can motivate employees. Managers can motivate employees by recognizing individual differences, matching people to jobs, using goals, ensuring that goals are perceived as attainable, individualizing rewards, linking rewards to performance, checking the system for equity, using recognition, showing care and concern for their employees, and acknowledging that money is a major reason why most people work.

▶ ▶ ▶ Tesco has worked hard to recognize the different needs of students and mothers returning to the workplace. The company also uses recognition to motivate employees and reduce turnover.

Management @ Work

READING FOR COMPREHENSION

1. How do needs affect motivation?

2. Contrast lower-order and higher-order needs in Maslow's needs hierarchy.

3. Describe how Theory X and Theory Y managers approach motivation.

4. Define the five core dimensions of the job characteristics model.

5. What are some of the possible consequences of employees' perceiving an inequity between their inputs and outcomes and those of others?

6. What are some advantages of using pay-for-performance programs to motivate employee performance? Are there drawbacks? Explain.

7. What can an organization do to create a more motivating environment for employees?

LINKING CONCEPTS TO PRACTICE

1. Most of us have to work for a living, and a job is a central part of our lives. So why do managers have to worry so much about employee motivation issues?

2. Describe a task you have done recently for which you exerted a high level of effort. Explain your behaviour using the following motivation approaches: (1) the hierarchy of needs theory, (2) motivation-hygiene theory, (3) equity theory, and (4) expectancy theory.

3. If you had to develop an incentive system for a small company that makes tortillas, which elements from which motivation approaches or theories would you

use? Why? Would your choice be the same if it was a software design firm?

4. What motivation theories or approaches could be used to encourage and support workforce diversity efforts? Explain.

5. Many job design experts who have studied the changing nature of work say that people do their best work when they are motivated by a sense of purpose rather than by the pursuit of money. Do you agree? Explain your position.

SELF-ASSESSMENT

What Rewards Do I Value Most?

Below are 10 work-related rewards. For each, identify the number that best describes the value that a particular reward has for you personally. Use the following scale to express your feelings:[98]

1 = No Value at All 2 = Slight Value 3 = Moderate Value 4 = Great Value 5 = Extremely Great Value

1. Good pay 1 2 3 4 5

2. Prestigious title 1 2 3 4 5

3. Vacation time 1 2 3 4 5

4. Job security 1 2 3 4 5

5. Recognition 1 2 3 4 5

6. Interesting work 1 2 3 4 5

7. Pleasant conditions 1 2 3 4 5

9. Flexible schedule 1 2 3 4 5

10. Friendly co-workers 1 2 3 4 5

Scoring Key

To assess your responses, prioritize them into groups. Put all the rewards you gave a 5 together. Do the same for your other responses. The rewards you gave 5s or 4s are the ones that you most desire and which your employer should emphasize with you.

Analysis and Interpretation

What motivates you does not necessarily motivate me. So employers who want to maximize employee motivation should determine what rewards each employee individually values. This instrument can help you understand which work-related rewards have the greatest value to you.

Compare the rewards that your employer offers with your scores. The greater the disparity, the more you might want to consider looking for opportunities at another organization with a reward structure that better matches your preferences.

More Self-Assessments MyManagementLab

To learn more about your skills, abilities, and interests, go to the MyManagementLab website and take the following self-assessments:

- I.C.1.—What Motivates Me?
- I.C.4.—What's My View on the Nature of People?
- I.C.8.—What's My Job's Motivating Potential?

MANAGEMENT FOR YOU TODAY

Dilemma

You are in a team with six other management students, and you have a major case analysis due in four weeks. The case project will count for 25 percent of the course mark. You are the team's leader. Several team members are having difficulty getting motivated to get started on the project. Identify ways you could motivate your team members, using needs theories, expectancy theory, and equity theory. How will you motivate yourself?

Becoming a Manager

- Start paying attention to times when you are highly motivated and times when you are not as motivated. What accounts for the difference?
- When working on teams for class projects or on committees in student organizations, try different approaches to motivating others.
- If you are working, assess your job using the job characteristics model. How might you redesign your job to make it more motivating?

- As you visit various businesses, note what, if any, employee recognition programs these businesses use.
- Talk to practising managers about their approaches to employee motivation. What have they found works?

WORKING TOGETHER: TEAM-BASED EXERCISE

What Is Most Important to You in a Job?

List five criteria (for example: pay, recognition, challenging work, friendships, status, the opportunity to do new things, the opportunity to travel, and so forth) that would be most important to you in a job. Rank them by order of importance.

Break into small groups (three or four other class members) and compare your responses. What patterns, if any, did you find?

Ethical Dilemma Exercise: Are Some Employees More Deserving Than Others?

Employees who feel unfairly forced into accepting deep cuts in salary and benefits may not be the most motivated employees.[99] This is the situation facing many major North American airlines as they struggle for survival. To stay in business, management at Air Canada and other carriers have pressured unionized pilots, mechanics, and flight attendants for concessions on pay and work rules again and again.

Still, many North American airline employees were resentful that their compensation was unlikely to return to previous levels until the end of 2008—at the earliest. Air Canada employees were not even sure there would be an airline in 2008. Moreover, there was concern that cuts in management's compensation would not last as long as those for unionized employees. Many employees were bitter about what they saw as inequitable treatment. "We know we had to help the airline," says one flight attendant. "But we think they took more than they needed from us." This sense of inequity could dampen motivation and make a huge

difference in the way employees work together and the way they deal with customers.

Imagine that you were just promoted and now manage one of your airline's mechanical maintenance facilities at a regional airport. Your manager just told you that the airline has lost a large number of managers to jobs outside the industry. To stop defections and retain good managers, your company has decided to return managers to full pay and benefits within 12 months. However, employees must wait much longer. You sympathize with your employees' gripes about compensation cuts, and you know they have little hope of getting maintenance jobs at other airlines. Although you like your new job and would welcome full pay, you could easily move to another industry. What, if anything, would you do about the nonmanagerial employees who will continue working with the pay cuts? (Look back at this chapter's discussion of equity theory as you consider this ethical challenge.)

Thinking Critically About Ethics

You have been hired as a phone sales representative at G.A.P. Adventures in Toronto. In this job, you help customers who call in to book vacations by finding what works best for them and their needs. You check airline flights, times, and fares, and also help with rental car and hotel reservations.

Most car rental firms and hotels run contests for the sales representative who books the most cars or most hotel rooms. The contest winners receive very attractive rewards! For instance, if you book just 50 clients for one rental car company, your name is put in a draw for $1000. If you book 100 clients, the draw is for $2500. And if you book

200 clients, you receive an all-expenses-paid, one-week Caribbean vacation. So the incentives are attractive enough to encourage you to "steer" customers toward one of those companies even though it might not be the best or cheapest for them. Your manager does not discourage participation in these programs.

Do you see anything wrong with this situation? Explain. What ethical issues do you see for (a) the employee, (b) the organization, and (c) the customer? How could an organization design performance incentive programs that encourage high levels of performance without compromising ethics?

Best Buy

Customer-centricity.[100] That is the new strategic focus that Brad Anderson, CEO of Best Buy, is betting on to keep the company from becoming a retailing casualty like Woolworth or Kmart. What is customer-centricity? Simply, it's figuring out which customers are the most profitable and doing whatever it takes to please them so they want to come back often and spend money. As the biggest consumer electronics retailer in North America, Best Buy has a lot at stake. And its 100 000-plus employees will play a crucial role in this new approach, which shifts the focus from "pushing gadgets to catering to customers."

"At Best Buy, People Are the Engines That Drive Our Success." That is the upfront and central phrase on the company's web-based career centre. And to Best Buy, it's not an empty slogan. The company has tried to create an environment in which employees, wherever they are, have numerous opportunities to learn, work, play, and achieve. One way they do that is by providing facts and figures to employees on everything from new technology to industry changes to company actions. At store meetings or on the intranet, employees can get the information they need to do their jobs and do them well.

Like many other companies, Best Buy has "struggled to meet the demands of its business—how to do things better, faster, and cheaper than its competitors—with an increasingly stressed-out workforce." Its culture has always rewarded long hours and sacrifice. For instance, one manager used a plaque to recognize the employee "who turns on the lights in the morning and turns them off at night." However, that approach has been taking its toll on employees. Best Buy is having difficulty retaining its best and brightest managers and executives.

Anderson wants to know why the company does not have an "innovative incentive program to foster our innovative culture." He has come to you for advice. What is the best way for the company to get employees on board so that they will be more customer-centric in their approach?

DEVELOPING YOUR DIAGNOSTIC AND ANALYTICAL SKILLS

Google: Paradise Lost . . . or Gained?

A massage every other week, on-site laundry, swimming pool and spa, free delicious all-you-can-eat gourmet meals.[101] What more could an employee want? Sounds like an ideal job, doesn't it? However, at Google, many people are demonstrating by their decisions to leave the company that all those perks (and these are just a few) aren't enough to keep them there. As one analyst said, "Yes, Google's making gobs of money. Yes, it's full of smart people. Yes, it's a wonderful place to work. So why are so many people leaving?"

Google has been named the "best company to work for" by *Fortune* magazine for two years running, but make no mistake—Google's executives made the decision to offer all those fabulous perks for several reasons: to attract the best knowledge workers it can in an intensely competitive, cutthroat market; to help employees work long hours and not have to deal with time-consuming personal chores outside work; to show employees they are valued; and to have employees remain Googlers (the name used for employees) for many years. But a number of Googlers have jumped ship and given up these fantastic benefits to go out on their own.

For instance, Sean Knapp and two colleagues, brothers Bismarck and Belsasar Lepe, came up with an idea about how to handle web video. They left Google in April 2007, or as one person put it, "expelled themselves from paradise to start their own company." When the threesome left the company, Google wanted badly for them and their project to stay. Google offered them a "blank check." But they realized they would do all the hard work, and Google would own the product. So off they went, for the excitement of a start-up.

If this were an isolated occurrence, it would be easy to write off. But it's not. Other talented Google employees have done the same thing. In fact, so many of them have left that they've formed an informal alumni club of ex-Googlers turned entrepreneurs.

Questions

1. What's it like to work at Google? (Hint: Go to Google's website and click on About Google. Find the section Jobs at Google.) What's your assessment of the company's work environment?

2. Google is doing a lot for its employees, but obviously it's not done enough to retain several of its talented people. Using what you've learned from studying the various motivation theories, what does this situation tell you about employee motivation?

3. What do you think is Google's biggest challenge in keeping employees motivated?

4. If you were managing a team of Google employees, how would you keep them motivated?

DEVELOPING YOUR INTERPERSONAL SKILLS

Designing Motivating Jobs

About the Skill

As a manager, you may need to give input into the design or redesign of jobs at some point. How will you ensure that these jobs are motivating? What can you do regarding job design that will maximize your employees' motivation and performance? The job characteristics model, which defines five core job dimensions (skill variety, task identity, task significance, autonomy, and feedback) and their relationships to employee motivation, provides a basis for designing motivating jobs.

Steps in Developing the Skill

The following five suggestions, based on the job characteristics model, specify the types of changes in jobs you can make as a manager that are most likely to improve motivation in employees:[102]

1. **Combine tasks.** Put existing specialized and divided tasks back together to form a new, larger module of work. This step will increase skill variety and task identity.

2. **Create natural work units.** Design work tasks that form an identifiable and meaningful whole. This step will increase "ownership" of the work and will encourage employees to view their work as significant and important rather than as irrelevant and boring.

3. **Establish client relationships.** The client is the user of the product or service that is the basis for an employee's work. Whenever possible, establish direct relationships between employees and their clients. This step will increase skill variety, autonomy, and feedback for the employees.

4. **Expand jobs vertically.** Vertical expansion of a job means giving employees responsibilities and controls that were formerly the manager's. It partially closes the gap between the "doing" and "controlling" aspects of the job. This step will increase employee autonomy.

5. **Open feedback channels.** By increasing feedback, employees not only learn how well they are performing their jobs but also whether their performance is improving, deteriorating, or remaining at a constant level. Ideally, this feedback should be received directly as the employee does the job, rather than from his or her manager on an occasional basis.

Practising the Skill

Read the following scenario. Write some notes about how you would handle the situation described. Be sure to refer to the five suggestions for designing motivating jobs.

Scenario

You work for Sunrise Deliveries, a freight transportation company that makes local deliveries of products for your customers. In your position, you supervise Sunrise's six delivery drivers. Each morning, your drivers drive their preloaded trucks to their destinations and wait for the products to be unloaded. There is a high turnover rate in the job. In fact, most of your drivers don't stay longer than six months. Not only is this turnover getting expensive, but it's been hard to develop a quality customer-service program when you have constantly got new faces. You have also heard complaints from the drivers that "all they do is drive." What will you do to retain and motivate the delivery drivers?

Reinforcing the Skill

The following activities will help you practise and reinforce the skills associated with designing motivating jobs:

1. Think of the worst job you have ever had. Analyze the job according to the five dimensions identified in the job characteristics model. Redesign the job in order to make it more satisfying and motivating.

2. Interview two people in two different job positions on your campus. Ask them questions about their jobs, using the job characteristics model as a guide. Using the information provided, list recommendations for making the jobs more motivating.

MyManagementLab

For more resources, please visit www.pearsoned.ca/mymanagementlab

SCAN THIS

Managing Groups and Teams

Few trends have influenced how work gets done in organizations as much as the use of work teams. Organizations are increasingly structuring work around teams rather than individuals. Managers need to understand what influences team performance and satisfaction. After reading and studying this chapter, you will achieve the following learning outcomes.

Learning Outcomes

1 Define *group* and describe the stages of group development.

2 Describe the major components that influence group performance and satisfaction.

3 Define *team* and describe best practices for team performance.

4 Discuss contemporary issues in managing teams.

▶ ▶ ▶ Following the Canadian men's hockey team's disappointing result in Turin (their worst result in the Olympics since 1980), one reporter wrote, "How could an elite group of players who will be paid nearly $100 million in salaries, and that has scored 334 goals in NHL games already this season, look as dysfunctional as a bantam league team on its first road trip to Medicine Hat?"[1]

Planning for the 2010 Olympics, led by the executive team at Hockey Canada, began shortly after the Turin Olympics ended. In October 2008, 482 days before the start of the 2010 Olympics, Steve Yzerman, executive director of the Canadian men's Olympic hockey team, introduced his management team of Doug Armstrong, Ken Holland, and Kevin Lowe, with Wayne Gretzky as a special adviser. "We understand the gold medal is the expectation," Yzerman said, yet despite all the pressure, they would "try to remember this is just a game." Yzerman said the group was looking for players comfortable in all situations and in different positions. Offensive players had to also attend to defence and checking. The entire defence corps was expected to be capable of moving the puck and skating with it. As Yzerman

put it, "Stay-at-homes will stay at home. Literally."[2]

The coaching staff of Mike Babcock, head coach of the Detroit Red Wings, and associate coaches Lindy Ruff, Jacques Lemaire, and Ken Hitchcock was named in mid-June 2009. Two weeks later, the names of the 46 players invited to the summer tryout camp were announced. "We wanted to bring some different types of players, some guys that maybe aren't leading their teams in scoring, but are very good players in a different role," Yzerman said. "And in doing that, we had to remove a different type of player."[3]

Expectations ran high for the men's hockey team at the 2010 Vancouver Olympics. The Own the Podium program had predicted a record haul of medals, but in the early going, many doubted that this could be achieved, especially following the 5–3 loss to Team USA in the round robin tournament of men's hockey. All these doubts were erased, and on the final night of Olympic competition Sidney Crosby's winning goal in overtime put an exclamation point on the Canadians' success. In the end, Canada exceeded the ambitious goals set by Own the Podium.

SCAN THIS

Think About It

What is the best way to choose an effective team? Put yourself in Steve Yzerman's shoes. Are there other players he should have chosen instead? Could he have put together a better team? Why was Sidney Crosby not chosen for the 2006 team even though in his rookie year, at the age of 18, he amassed 102 points? Should younger and less experienced players have been recruited for the 2010 team with an eye on 2014? How might the pressure to win at home in Vancouver have influenced the selection of coaches and players?

You've probably had a lot of experience working in groups—on class project teams, maybe an athletic team, a fundraising committee, or even a sales team at work. Work teams are one of the realities—and challenges—of managing in today's dynamic global environment. Many organizations have made the move to restructure work around teams rather than individuals. Why? What do these teams look like? And, as with the challenge Steve Yzerman faced in preparing for the Vancouver 2010 Olympics, how can managers build effective teams? These are some of the questions we'll be answering in this chapter. Before we can understand teams, however, we first need to understand some basics about groups and group behaviour.

Groups and Group Development

Because most organizational work is done by individuals who are part of a work group, it's important for managers to understand group behaviour. Why? Because individuals act differently in groups than they do when they are alone. Therefore, if we want to understand organizational behaviour more fully, we need to study groups.

1. Define *group* and describe the stages of group development.

What Is a Group?

A **group** is defined as two or more interacting and interdependent individuals who come together to achieve specific goals. *Formal groups* are work groups defined by the organization's structure that have designated work assignments and specific tasks. In formal groups, appropriate behaviours are established by and directed toward organizational goals. Exhibit 16-1 provides some examples of different types of formal groups in today's organizations.

Informal groups are social groups. These groups occur naturally in the workplace in response to the need for social contact. For example, three employees from different departments who regularly eat lunch together are an informal group. Informal groups tend to form around friendships and common interests.

group Two or more interacting and interdependent individuals who come together to achieve particular goals.

Stages of Group Development

Have you ever noticed the stages a group goes through in learning how to work together?

Research has shown that groups develop through five stages.[4] As shown in Exhibit 16-2, these five stages are *forming, storming, norming, performing,* and *adjourning.* Understanding the progression of a group is useful for managers on many levels, one of them being the need to diagnose what actions must be taken in order to propel a group forward (e.g., if it is stuck in the forming phase, what needs to be done to take it into storming, etc.).

The **forming stage** has two phases. The first occurs as people join the group. In a formal group, people join because of some work assignment. After they've joined, the second phase begins: defining the group's purpose, structure, and leadership. This phase involves a great deal of uncertainty as members "test the waters" to determine what types of behaviour are acceptable. This stage is complete when members begin to think of themselves as part of a group.

forming stage The first stage of group development, in which people join the group and then define the group's purpose, structure, and leadership.

The **storming stage** is named because of the intragroup conflict that occurs over who will control the group and what the group needs to be doing. When this stage is complete, there is a relatively clear hierarchy of leadership and agreement on the group's direction.

storming stage The second stage of group development, which is characterized by intragroup conflict.

The **norming stage** is one in which close relationships develop and the group becomes cohesive. There's now a strong sense of group identity and camaraderie. This stage is complete when the group structure solidifies and the group has assimilated a common set of expectations (or norms) regarding member behaviour.

norming stage The third stage of group development, which is characterized by close relationships and cohesiveness.

Exhibit 16-1

Examples of Formal Groups

Command Groups: Groups that are determined by the organizational chart and composed of individuals who report directly to a given manager.

Task Groups: Groups composed of individuals brought together to complete a specific job task; their existence is often temporary because once the task is completed, the group disbands.

Cross-Functional Teams: Groups that bring together the knowledge and skills of individuals from various work areas, or groups whose members have been trained to do one another's jobs.

Self-Managed Teams: Groups that are essentially independent and, in addition to their own tasks, take on traditional managerial responsibilities such as hiring, planning and scheduling, and performance evaluations.

Exhibit 16-2

Stages of Group Development

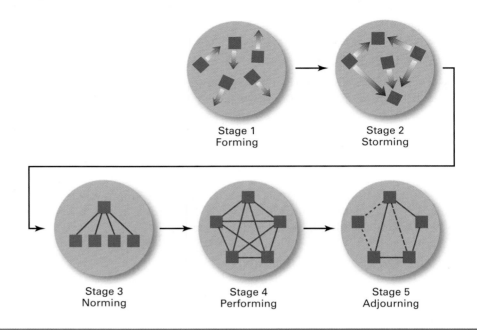

Stage 1
Forming

Stage 2
Storming

Stage 3
Norming

Stage 4
Performing

Stage 5
Adjourning

performing stage The fourth stage of group development, when the group is fully functional and works on the group task.

adjourning stage The final stage of group development for temporary groups, during which group members are concerned with wrapping up activities rather than task performance.

The fourth stage of group development is **performing**. The group structure is in place and accepted by group members. Their energies have moved from getting to know and understand each other to working on the group's task. This is the last stage of development for permanent work groups. However, for temporary groups—project teams, task forces, or similar groups that have a limited task to do—the final stage is **adjourning**. In this stage, the group prepares to disband. Attention is focused on wrapping up activities instead of task performance. Group members react in different ways. Some are upbeat, thrilled about the group's accomplishments. Others may be sad over the loss of camaraderie and friendships.

Many of you have probably experienced these stages as you've worked on a group project for a class. Group members are selected or assigned and then meet for the first time. There's a "feeling out" period to assess what the group is going to do and how it's going to be done. This is usually followed by a battle for control: Who's going to be in charge? When this issue is resolved and a "hierarchy" is agreed on, the group identifies specific work that needs to be done, who's going to do each part, and dates by which the assigned work needs to be completed. General expectations are established. These decisions form the foundation for what you hope will be a coordinated group effort culminating in a project that's been done well. When the project is complete and turned in, the group breaks up. Of course, some groups don't get much beyond the forming or storming stages. These groups may have serious interpersonal conflicts, turn in disappointing work, and get low grades.

Does a group become more effective as it progresses through the first four stages? Some researchers say yes, but it's not that simple.[5] That assumption may be generally true, but what makes a group effective is a complex issue. Under some conditions, high levels of conflict are conducive to high levels of group performance. There might be situations in which groups in the storming stage outperform those in the norming or performing stages. Also, groups don't always proceed sequentially from one stage to the next. Sometimes, groups are storming and performing at the same time. Groups even occasionally regress to previous stages. Therefore, it's not safe to assume that all groups precisely follow this

Senior vice-president Dadi Perlmutter leads a chip design group in Haifa, Israel, for the foremost semiconductor maker in the world, Intel. Perlmutter's group thrives on the kind of debate and confrontation typical of the storming stage of group development, but it achieves the kind of real-world results that usually characterize the performing stage. Recently, for instance, the group came up with a winning design for a processor chip for wireless computers that consumes half the power of other chips without sacrificing processing speed.

process or that performing is always the most preferable stage. It's better to think of this model as a general framework that underscores the fact that groups are dynamic entities and managers need to know the stage a group is in so they can understand the problems and issues that are most likely to surface.

Work Group Performance and Satisfaction

▶ ▶ ▶ After Canada scored in only one of its final 12 periods in Turin, defenceman Chris Pronger observed that playing six games in eight days did not leave a lot of time to practise and build a sense of team.[6] Mike Babcock, the coach for Team Canada 2010, reflected on how to build a team that would meet Steve Yzerman's objective of looking for players comfortable in all situations and in different positions. At the same time, Babcock had to balance this need with his personal style. Babcock's forceful personality was seen to be his greatest asset in an Olympic setting and was the opposite of Pat Quinn's style, who coached the 2006 Turin team.[7]

2. Describe the major components that influence group performance and satisfaction.

Think About It

How would group dynamics have changed as new groups of players from various NHL teams arrived for camp? What techniques could the coaching staff use to build the cohesiveness that Chris Pronger spoke of? How might Mike Babcock's different coaching style influence those players who had played for Pat Quinn?

Have you ever worked in a group that did not perform up to expectations? What are some of the reasons for this?

Many people consider them the most successful "group" of our times. Who? The Beatles. "The Beatles were great artists and entertainers, but in many respects they were four ordinary guys who, as a group, found a way to achieve extraordinary artistic and financial success and have a great time together while doing it. Every business team can learn from their story."[8]

Why *are* some groups more successful than others? Why do some groups achieve high levels of performance and high levels of member satisfaction and others do not? The answers are complex but include variables such as the abilities of the group's members, the size of the group, the level of conflict, and the internal pressures on members to conform to the group's norms. Exhibit 16-3 presents the major factors that determine group performance and satisfaction.[9] Let's look at each of them.

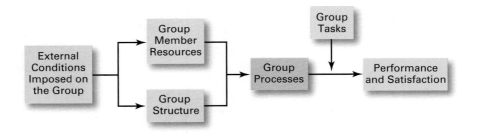

Exhibit 16-3

Group Performance Satisfaction Model

External Conditions Imposed on the Group

A work group is affected by the external conditions imposed on it. These include the organization's strategy, authority relationships, formal rules and regulations, the availability of resources, employee selection criteria, the performance management system and culture, and the general physical layout of the group's work space. For instance, some groups have modern, high-quality tools and equipment to do their jobs, while other groups don't. Or the organization might be pursuing a strategy of lowering costs or improving quality, which will affect what a group does and how it does it.

Group Member Resources

A group's performance potential depends to a large extent on the resources each individual brings to the group. These resources include knowledge, skills, abilities, and personality traits, and they determine what members can do and how effectively they will perform in a group. Interpersonal skills—especially conflict management and resolution, collaborative problem solving, and communication—consistently emerge as important for work groups to perform well.[10]

Personality traits also affect group performance because they strongly influence how an individual will interact with other group members. Research has shown that traits that are viewed as positive in our culture (such as sociability, self-reliance, and independence) tend to be positively related to group productivity and morale. In contrast, negative personality characteristics (such as authoritarianism, dominance, and unconventionality) tend to be negatively related to group productivity and morale.[11]

Group Structure

Work groups aren't unorganized crowds. They have an internal structure that shapes members' behaviour and influences group performance. The structure defines roles, norms, conformity, status systems, group size, group cohesiveness, and leadership. Let's look at the first six of these. Leadership was discussed in Chapter 14.

Roles

MyManagementLab
Q&A 16.1

We introduced the concept of roles in Chapter 1 when we discussed what managers do. (Remember Mintzberg's managerial roles.) Of course, managers aren't the only individuals in an organization who play various roles. The concept of roles applies to all employees and to their life outside an organization as well. (Think of the various roles you play: student, sibling, employee, spouse or significant other, etc.)

A **role** refers to behavioural patterns expected of someone occupying a given position in a social unit. In a group, individuals are expected to do certain things because of their position (role) in the group. These roles are generally oriented toward either getting work

role Behavioural patterns expected of someone occupying a given position in a social unit.

done or keeping group members happy.[12] Think about groups that you've been in and the roles that you played. Were you continually trying to keep the group focused on getting its work done? If so, you were in a task-accomplishment role. Or were you more concerned that group members had the opportunity to offer ideas and that they were satisfied with the experience? If so, you were performing a group member satisfaction role. Both roles are important to the group's ability to function effectively and efficiently.

A problem that arises is that individuals play multiple roles and adjust their roles to the group to which they belong at the time. Because of the different expectations of these roles, employees face *role conflicts*.

Norms

All groups have **norms**—standards or expectations that are accepted and shared by a group's members. Norms dictate things such as work output levels, absenteeism, promptness, and the amount of socializing on the job.

norms Standards or expectations that are accepted and shared by a group's members.

For example, norms dictate the "arrival ritual" among office assistants at Coleman Trust Inc., where the workday begins at 8 a.m. Most employees typically arrive a few minutes before and hang up their coats and put their purses and other personal items on their desk so everyone knows they're "at work." They then go to the break room to get coffee and chat. Anyone who violates this norm by starting work at 8 a.m. is pressured to behave in a way that conforms to the group's standard.

Although a group has its own unique set of norms, common organizational norms focus on effort and performance, dress, and loyalty. The most widespread norms are those related to work effort and performance. Work groups typically provide their members with explicit cues on how hard to work, level of output, when to look busy, when it's acceptable to goof off, and the like. These norms are very powerful influences on an individual employee's performance. They're so powerful that you can't predict someone's performance based solely on his or her ability and personal motivation. Dress norms frequently dictate what's acceptable to wear to work. If the norm is more formal dress, anyone who dresses casually may face subtle pressure to conform. Finally, loyalty norms will influence whether individuals work late, work on weekends, or move to locations they might not prefer to live.

MyManagementLab
Q&A 16.2, Q&A 16.3, Q&A 16.4

One negative thing about group norms is that being part of a group can increase an individual's antisocial actions. If the norms of the group include tolerating deviant behaviour, someone who normally wouldn't engage in such behaviour might be more likely to do so. For instance, one study found that those working in a group were more likely to lie, cheat, and steal than were individuals working alone.[13] Why? Because groups provide anonymity, thus giving individuals—who might otherwise be afraid of getting caught—a false sense of security.

MyManagementLab
Q&A 16.5

Conformity

Because individuals want to be accepted by groups to which they belong, they're susceptible to pressures to conform. Early experiments done by Solomon Asch demonstrated the impact that conformity has on an individual's judgment and attitudes.[14] In these experiments, groups of seven or eight people were asked to compare two cards held up by the experimenter. One card had three lines of different lengths, and the other had one line that was equal in length to one of the three lines on the other card (see Exhibit 16-4). Each group member was to announce aloud which of the three lines matched the single line. Asch wanted to see what would happen if members began to give incorrect answers. Would pressures to conform cause individuals to give wrong answers just to be consistent with the others? The experiment was "fixed" so that all but one of the members (the unsuspecting subject) was told ahead of time to start giving obviously incorrect answers after one or two rounds. Over many experiments and trials, the unsuspecting subject conformed over one-third of the time.

MyManagementLab
Q&A 16.6

Are these conclusions still valid? Research suggests that conformity levels have declined since Asch's studies. However, managers can't ignore conformity because it can still be a powerful force in groups.[15] Group members often want to be seen as one of the group

Exhibit 16-4

Examples of Asch's Cards

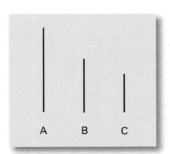

and avoid being visibly different. People tend to find it more pleasant to agree than to be disruptive, even if being disruptive may improve the group's effectiveness. So we conform. But conformity can go too far, especially when an individual's opinion differs significantly from that of others in the group. When this happens, the group often exerts intense pressure on the individual to align his or her opinion to conform to others' opinions, a phenomenon known as **groupthink**. Groupthink seems to occur when there is a clear group identity, members hold a positive group image that they want to protect, and the group perceives a collective threat to this positive image.[16]

groupthink A phenomenon in which a group exerts extensive pressure on an individual to align his or her opinion with others' opinions.

status A prestige grading, position, or rank within a group.

Status Systems

Status systems are an important factor in understanding groups. **Status** is a prestige grading, position, or rank within a group. As far back as researchers have been able to trace groups, they have found status hierarchies. Status can be a significant motivator with behavioural consequences, especially when individuals see a disparity between what they perceive their status to be and what others perceive it to be.

Status may be informally conferred by characteristics such as education, age, skill, or experience. Anything can have status value if others in the group evaluate it that way. Of course, just because status is informal doesn't mean that it's unimportant or that it's hard to determine who has it or who does not. Group members have no problem placing people into status categories and usually agree about who has high or low status.

Status is also formally conferred, and it's important for employees to believe that the organization's formal status system is congruent—that is, that there's consistency between the perceived ranking of an individual and the status symbols he or she receives from the organization. For instance, status incongruence would occur when a supervisor earns less than his or her subordinates, a desirable office is occupied by a person in a low-ranking position, or paid country club memberships are provided to division managers but not to vice-presidents. Employees expect the "things" an individual receives to be congruent with his or her status. When they're not, employees may question the authority of their managers and may not be motivated by job promotion opportunities.

Group Size

What's an appropriate size for a group? At Amazon.com, work teams have considerable autonomy to innovate and to investigate their ideas. And Jeff Bezos, founder and CEO, uses a "two-pizza" philosophy; that is, a team should be small enough that it can be fed with two pizzas. This "two-pizza" philosophy usually limits groups to five to seven people, depending, of course, on team member appetites.[17]

Group size affects performance and satisfaction, but the effect depends on what the group is supposed to accomplish.[18] Research indicates, for instance, that small groups are faster at completing tasks than are larger ones. However, for groups engaged in problem solving, large groups consistently get better results than smaller ones. What does this mean in terms of specific numbers? Large groups—those with a dozen or more members—are good for getting diverse input. Thus, if the goal of the group is to find facts, a larger group should be more effective. On the other hand, smaller groups—those with five to seven members—are better at doing something productive with those facts.

One important research finding related to group size concerns **social loafing**, which is the tendency for an individual to expend less effort when working collectively than when working individually.[19] Social loafing may occur because people believe that others in the group aren't doing their fair share. Thus, they reduce their work efforts in an attempt to make the workload fairer. Also, the relationship between an individual's input and the group's output is often unclear. Thus, individuals may become "free riders" and coast on the group's efforts because individuals believe that their contribution can't be measured.

social loafing The tendency for individuals to expend less effort when working collectively than when working individually.

The implications of social loafing are significant. When managers use groups, they must find a way to identify individual efforts. If they do not, group productivity and individual satisfaction may decline.[20]

Group Cohesiveness

MyManagementLab
Q&A 16.7

Cohesiveness is important because it has been found to be related to a group's productivity. Groups in which there's a lot of internal disagreement and lack of cooperation are less effective in completing their tasks than are groups in which members generally agree, cooperate, and like each other. Research in this area has focused on **group cohesiveness**, or the degree to which members are attracted to a group and share the group's goals.[21]

group cohesiveness The degree to which group members are attracted to one another and share the group's goals.

Research has generally shown that highly cohesive groups are more effective than less cohesive ones.[22] However, the relationship between cohesiveness and effectiveness is complex. A key moderating variable is the degree to which the group's attitude aligns with its goals or with the goals of the organization[23] (see Exhibit 16-5). The more cohesive the group, the more its members will follow its goals. If the goals are desirable (for instance, high output, quality work, cooperation with individuals outside the group), a cohesive group is more productive than a less cohesive group. But if cohesiveness is high and attitudes are unfavourable, productivity decreases. If cohesiveness is low but goals are supported, productivity increases, but not as much as when both cohesiveness and support are high. When cohesiveness is low and goals are not supported, there's no significant effect

Exhibit 16-5

Group Cohesiveness and Productivity

Alignment of Group and Organizational Goals	Cohesiveness: High	Cohesiveness: Low
High	Strong Increase in Productivity	Moderate Increase in Productivity
Low	Decrease in Productivity	No Significant Effect on Productivity

TIPS FOR MANAGERS

Increasing Group Cohesiveness

Increasing socio-emotional cohesiveness

✒ Keep the group relatively **small.**

✒ Strive for a **favourable public image** to increase the status and prestige of belonging.

✒ Encourage **interaction and cooperation.**

✒ Emphasize members' **common characteristics** and interests.

✒ **Point out environmental threats** (for example, competitors' achievements) to rally the group.

Increasing instrumental cohesiveness

✒ Regularly update and **clarify the group's goal(s).**

✒ Give every group member a **vital "piece of the action."**

✒ Channel each group member's special talents toward the **common goal(s).**

✒ **Recognize** and equitably reinforce **every member's contributions.**

✒ Frequently remind group members **they need each other** to get the job done.

Source: R. Kreitner and A. Kinicki, *Organizational Behaviour*, 6th ed. (New York: Irwin, 2004), p. 460. Reprinted by permission of McGraw-Hill Education.

on productivity. *Tips for Managers—Increasing Group Cohesiveness* indicates how to increase both socio-emotional and instrumental cohesiveness. Thinking back to the discussion of creativity and innovation in Chapter 4, it is interesting to note that in a study of 196 MBA students at McMaster University, in Hamilton, Ontario, nonhomogeneous groups came up with more creative solutions than did homogeneous groups. The nonhomogeneous groups also experienced higher levels of conflict.[24]

Group Processes

In addition to group member resources and structure, another factor that determines group performance and satisfaction concerns the processes that go on within a work group, such as communication, decision making, and conflict management. These processes are important to understanding work groups because they influence group performance and satisfaction positively or negatively. An example of a positive process factor is the synergy of four people on a marketing research team who are able to generate far more ideas as a group than the members could produce individually. However, the group may also have negative process factors, such as social loafing, high levels of conflict, or poor communication, that may hinder group effectiveness. We'll look at two important group processes: group decision making and conflict management.

Group Decision Making

It's a rare organization that doesn't use committees, task forces, review panels, study teams, or other similar groups to make decisions. Studies show that managers may spend up to 30 hours per week in group meetings.[25] Undoubtedly, a large portion of that time is spent formulating problems, developing solutions, and determining how to implement the solutions. It's possible, in fact, for groups to be assigned any of the eight steps in the decision-making process. (Refer to Chapter 6 to review these steps.)

What advantages do group decisions have over individual decisions? One is that groups generate more complete information and knowledge. They bring a diversity of experience and perspectives to the decision process that an individual cannot. In addition, groups generate more diverse alternatives because they have a greater amount and diversity of information. Next, groups increase acceptance of a solution. Group members are reluctant to fight or undermine a decision that they helped develop. Finally, groups increase legitimacy. Decisions made by groups may be perceived as more legitimate than decisions made by one person.

Group decisions also have disadvantages. One is that groups almost always take more time to reach a solution than would an individual. Another is that a dominant and vocal minority can heavily influence a group's final decision. In addition, groupthink can undermine critical thinking in a group and harm the quality of the final decision.[26] Finally, in a group, members share responsibility, but the responsibility of any single member is ambiguous.

Determining whether groups are effective at making decisions depends on the criteria used to assess effectiveness.[27] If accuracy, creativity, and degree of acceptance are important, then a group decision may work best. However, if speed and efficiency are important, then an individual decision may be the best. In addition, decision effectiveness is influenced by group size. Although a larger group provides more diverse representation, it also requires more coordination and time for members to contribute their ideas. Evidence indicates that groups of five, and to a lesser extent seven, are the most effective for making decisions.[28] Having an odd number in the group helps avoid decision deadlocks. Also, these groups are large enough for members to shift roles and withdraw from unfavourable positions but still small enough for quieter members to participate actively in discussions.

What techniques can managers use to help groups make more creative decisions? Exhibit 16-6 describes three possibilities.

Conflict Management

In addition to decision making, another important group process is how a group manages conflict. As a group performs its assigned tasks, disagreements inevitably arise. **Conflict** is *perceived* incompatible differences resulting in some form of interference or opposition. Whether the differences are real is irrelevant. If people in a group perceive that differences exist, then there is conflict.

Three different views have evolved regarding conflict.[29] The **traditional view of conflict** argues that conflict must be avoided—that it indicates a problem within the group. Another view, the **human relations view of conflict**, argues that conflict is a natural and inevitable outcome in any group and need not be negative, but has potential to be a positive force in contributing to a group's performance. The third and most recent view, the **interactionist view of conflict**, proposes that not only can conflict be a positive force in a group, but some conflict is *absolutely necessary* for a group to perform effectively.

The interactionist view doesn't suggest that all conflicts are good. Some conflicts—**functional conflicts**—are constructive and support the goals of the work group and improve its performance. Other conflicts—**dysfunctional conflicts**—are destructive and prevent a group from achieving its goals. Exhibit 16-7 illustrates the conflict challenges managers face.

When is conflict functional and when is it dysfunctional? Research indicates that it depends on the *type* of conflict.[30] **Task conflict** relates to the content and goals of the work. **Relationship conflict** focuses on interpersonal relationships. **Process conflict** refers to how the work gets done. Research has shown that *relationship* conflicts are almost always dysfunctional because the interpersonal hostilities increase personality clashes and decrease mutual understanding, and the tasks don't get done. On the other hand, low levels of process conflict and low to moderate levels of task conflict are functional. For *process* conflict to be productive, it must be minimal. Otherwise, intense arguments over who should do what may become dysfunctional because they can lead to uncertainty about task assignments, increase the time to complete tasks, and lead to members working at cross-purposes. However, a low to moderate level of *task* conflict consistently

conflict Perceived incompatible differences that result in interference or opposition.

traditional view of conflict The view that all conflict is bad and must be avoided.

human relations view of conflict The view that conflict is a natural and inevitable outcome in any group.

interactionist view of conflict The view that some conflict is necessary for a group to perform effectively.

MyManagementLab
Q&A 16.8

functional conflicts Conflicts that support a group's goals and improve its performance.

dysfunctional conflicts Conflicts that prevent a group from achieving its goals.

MyManagementLab
Q&A 16.9

task conflict Conflicts over content and goals of work.

relationship conflict Conflict based on interpersonal relationships.

process conflict Conflict over how work gets done.

Exhibit 16-6

Creative Group Decision Making

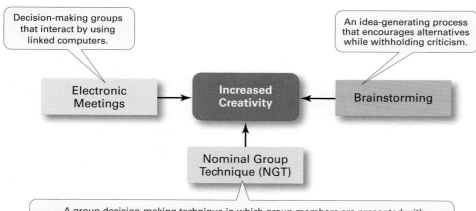

Decision-making groups that interact by using linked computers.

An idea-generating process that encourages alternatives while withholding criticism.

Electronic Meetings → Increased Creativity ← Brainstorming

↑ Nominal Group Technique (NGT)

A group decision-making technique in which group members are presented with a problem; each member independently writes down his or her ideas on the problem; and then each member presents one idea to the group until all ideas have been presented. No discussion takes place until all ideas have been presented.

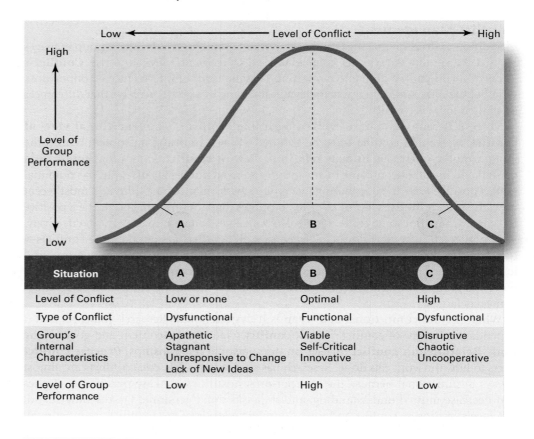

Exhibit 16-7

Conflict and Group Performance

Situation	A	B	C
Level of Conflict	Low or none	Optimal	High
Type of Conflict	Dysfunctional	Functional	Dysfunctional
Group's Internal Characteristics	Apathetic Stagnant Unresponsive to Change Lack of New Ideas	Viable Self-Critical Innovative	Disruptive Chaotic Uncooperative
Level of Group Performance	Low	High	Low

has a positive effect on group performance because it stimulates discussion of ideas that help groups be more innovative.[31] Because we don't yet have a sophisticated measuring instrument for assessing whether conflict levels are optimal, too high, or too low, a manager must try to judge that intelligently.

MyManagementLab
Q&A 16.10

When group conflict levels are too high, managers can select from five conflict management options: avoiding, accommodating, forcing, compromising, and collaborating.[32] (See Exhibit 16-8 for descriptions of these techniques.) Keep in mind that no one option is ideal for every situation. Which approach to use depends on the circumstances.

Group Tasks

At the QEII Health Sciences Centre in Halifax, Nova Scotia, daily reviews of each patient in each nursing unit are conducted in multidisciplinary rounds by teams of nurses, case managers, social workers, and an in-hospital doctor. These teams perform tasks such as prescribing drugs and recommending that patients be discharged. Employee teams at Lockheed Martin's Halifax facility custom build complex products such as ground-based radar systems using continuous quality improvement techniques. The three people in the Blue Man Group (see Chapter 7) perform their unique brand of performance art in multiple venues. Each of these groups has a different type of task to accomplish.

As the group performance/satisfaction model (see Exhibit 16-3 on page 452) shows, the impact that group processes have on group performance and member satisfaction is modified by the task the group is doing. More specifically, the *complexity* and *interdependence* of tasks influence a group's effectiveness.[33]

Exhibit 16-8

Conflict-Management Techniques

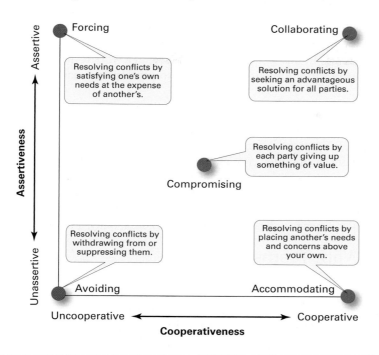

Tasks are either simple or complex. Simple tasks are routine and standardized. Complex tasks tend to be novel or nonroutine. It appears that the more complex the task, the more a group benefits from group discussion about alternative work methods. Group members don't need to discuss such alternatives for a simple task but can rely on standard operating procedures. Similarly, if there's a high degree of interdependence among the tasks that group members must perform, they'll need to interact more. Thus, effective communication and controlled conflict are most relevant to group performance when tasks are complex and interdependent.

Turning Groups into Effective Teams

▶ ▶ ▶ On November 4, 2009, exactly 100 days before the start of the Olympics, Steve Yzerman, along with Mike Babcock, convened a summit meeting in Detroit with his managerial team to review their scouting work a month into the new season. "At the August camp, the Olympics seemed so far away," he said. "Now, here we are, it's November, and it's time to really get at this. October just flew by. Here we are a dozen games into the season and I'm still thinking, 'Geez, I gotta get a better look at this guy or that guy' or see him in games against tougher competition."[34] In making their final selections, the group reflected on the objective of finding two-way players who would fit well with Coach Babcock's coaching philosophy and could come together quickly as a team.

3. Define *team* and describe best practices for team performance.

Think About It

How might Yzerman and his managerial team create a winning team with clear goals, relevant skills, and a level of mutual trust?

When companies such as W. L. Gore, Volvo, and Kraft Foods introduced teams into their production processes, they made news because no one else was doing it. Today, it's just the opposite—an organization that *doesn't* use teams would be newsworthy. It's estimated that some 80 percent of *Fortune* 500 companies have at least half of their employees on teams.[35] Teams are likely to continue to be popular. Why? Research suggests that teams typically outperform individuals when the tasks being done require multiple skills, judgment, and experience.[36] Organizations are using team-based structures because they've found that teams are more flexible and responsive to changing events than are traditional departments or other permanent work groups. Teams have the ability to quickly assemble, deploy, refocus, and disband. In this section, we'll discuss what a work team is, the different types of teams that organizations might use, and how to develop and manage work teams.

What Is a Work Team?

Most of you are probably familiar with teams, especially if you've watched or participated in organized sports. Work *teams* differ from work *groups* and have their own unique traits (see Exhibit 16-9). Work groups interact primarily to share information and to make decisions to help each member do his or her job more efficiently and effectively. There's no need or opportunity for work groups to engage in collective work that requires joint effort. On the other hand, **work teams** are groups whose members work intensely on a specific, common goal, using their positive synergy, individual and mutual accountability, and complementary skills.

Types of Work Teams

Teams can do a variety of things. They can design products, provide services, negotiate deals, coordinate projects, offer advice, and make decisions.[37] For instance, at Research In Motion (the maker of BlackBerrys), teams are used in new product development. At Ocean Nutrition (the world's leading producer of omega-3 fish oil) in Halifax, Nova Scotia, teams work on process optimization projects. And every summer weekend at any NASCAR race, you can see work teams in action during drivers' pit stops.[38] The four most common types of work teams are problem-solving teams, self-managed work teams, cross-functional teams, and virtual teams.

Problem-Solving Teams

When work teams first became popular, most were **problem-solving teams**, which are teams from the same department or functional area involved in efforts to improve work activities or to solve specific problems. Members share ideas or offer suggestions on how work processes and methods can be improved. However, these teams are rarely given the authority to implement any of their suggested actions.

work teams Groups whose members work intensely on a specific, common goal, using their positive synergy, individual and mutual accountability, and complementary skills.

problem-solving team A team from the same department or functional area that's involved in efforts to improve work activities or to solve specific problems.

Exhibit 16-9

Groups versus Teams

Work Teams	Work Groups
• Leadership role is shared	• One leader clearly in charge
• Accountable to self and team	• Accountable only to self
• Team creates specific purpose	• Purpose is same as broader organizational purpose
• Work is done collectively	• Work is done individually
• Meetings characterized by open-ended discussion and collaborative problem-solving	• Meetings characterized by efficiency; no collaboration or open-ended discussion
• Performance is measured directly by evaluating collective work output	• Performance is measured indirectly according to its influence on others
• Work is decided upon and done together	• Work is decided upon by group leader and delegated to individual group members

Source: J. R. Katzenbach and D. K. Smith, "The Wisdom of Teams," *Harvard Business Review*, July–August 2005, p. 161.

Self-Managed Work Teams

Although problem-solving teams were helpful, they didn't go far enough in getting employees involved in work-related decisions and processes. This led to another type of team, the **self-managed work team**, which is a formal group of employees who operate without a manager and are responsible for a complete work process or segment. A self-managed team is responsible for getting the work done *and* for managing itself. This usually includes planning and scheduling work, assigning tasks to members, collectively controlling the pace of work, making operating decisions, and taking action on problems. For instance, teams at Corning have no shift supervisors and work closely with other manufacturing divisions to solve production-line problems and coordinate deadlines and deliveries. The teams have the authority to make and implement decisions, finish projects, and address problems.[39] Other organizations, such as Xerox, Boeing, PepsiCo, and Hewlett-Packard, also use self-managed teams. It's estimated that about 30 percent of US employers now use this form of team; among large firms, the number is probably closer to 50 percent.[40] Most organizations that use self-managed teams find them to be effective.[41]

self-managed work team A type of work team that operates without a manager and is responsible for a complete work process or segment.

Cross-Functional Teams

The third type of team is the **cross-functional team**, which we introduced in Chapter 10 and defined as a work team composed of individuals from various specialties. Many organizations use cross-functional teams. For example, ArcelorMittal, the world's biggest steel company, uses cross-functional teams of scientists, plant managers, and salespeople to review and monitor product innovations.[42] The concept of cross-functional teams is even being applied in health care. For instance, at Suburban Hospital in Bethesda, Maryland, intensive care unit (ICU) teams composed of a doctor trained in intensive care medicine, a pharmacist, a social worker, a nutritionist, the chief ICU nurse, a respiratory therapist, and a chaplain meet daily with every patient's bedside nurse to discuss and debate the best course of treatment. The hospital credits this team care approach with reducing errors, shortening the amount of time patients spent in the ICU, and improving communication between families and the medical staff.[43]

cross-functional team A work team composed of individuals from various specialties.

MyManagementLab
Q&A 16.11

Virtual Teams

The final type of team is the **virtual team**, which is a team that uses technology to link physically dispersed members in order to achieve a common goal. For instance, a virtual team at Boeing-Rocketdyne played a pivotal role in developing a radically new product.[44] Another company, Decision Lens, uses a virtual team environment to generate and evaluate creative ideas.[45] In a virtual team, members collaborate online with tools such as wide-area networks, videoconferencing, fax, email, or websites where the team can hold online conferences.[46] Virtual teams can do all the things that other teams can do, including share information, make decisions, and complete tasks; however, they lack the normal give-and-take of face-to-face discussions. That's why virtual teams tend to be more task oriented, especially if the team members have never met in person.

virtual team A type of work team that uses technology to link physically dispersed members in order to achieve a common goal.

Creating Effective Work Teams

How do you build an effective team? Have you ever done so?

Teams are not always effective. They don't always achieve high levels of performance. However, research on teams provides insights into the characteristics typically associated with effective teams.[47] These characteristics are listed in Exhibit 16-10.

MyManagementLab
PRISM 9

Clear Goals

A high-performance team has a clear understanding of the goal to be achieved. Members are committed to the team's goals, know what they're expected to accomplish, and understand how they will work together to achieve these goals.

Exhibit 16-10

Characteristics of Effective Teams

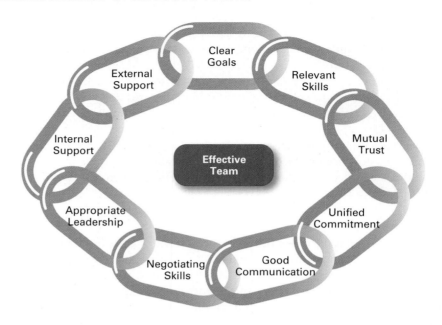

Relevant Skills

Effective teams are composed of competent individuals who have the necessary technical and interpersonal skills to achieve the desired goals while working well together. This last point is important because not everyone who is technically competent has the interpersonal skills to work well as a team member.

Mutual Trust

Effective teams are characterized by high mutual trust among members. That is, members believe in each other's ability, character, and integrity. But as you probably know from personal relationships, trust is fragile. Maintaining trust requires careful attention by managers.

Unified Commitment

Unified commitment is characterized by dedication to a team's goals and a willingness to expend extraordinary amounts of energy to achieve them. Members of an effective team exhibit intense loyalty and dedication to the team and are willing to do whatever it takes to help their team succeed.

Good Communication

Not surprisingly, effective teams are characterized by good communication. Members convey messages, verbally and nonverbally, between each other in ways that are readily and clearly understood. Also, feedback helps guide team members and correct misunderstandings. Like a couple who has been together for many years, members of high-performing teams are able to quickly and efficiently share ideas and feelings.

Negotiating Skills

Effective teams are continually making adjustments to who does what. This flexibility requires team members to possess negotiating skills. Because problems and relationships are regularly changing in teams, members need to be able to confront and reconcile differences.

All the work that employees do at Whole Foods Market is based around teamwork. Characteristics of effective teams, like job skills, commitment, trust, communication, and effective training and support, are important for making this kind of structure successful and contributing to the rapid growth of the organic-food retailer.

Appropriate Leadership

Effective leaders can motivate a team to follow them through the most difficult situations. How? By clarifying goals, demonstrating that change is possible by overcoming inertia, increasing the self-confidence of team members, and helping members to more fully realize their potential. Increasingly, effective team leaders are acting as coaches and facilitators. They help guide and support a team but don't control it.

Internal and External Support

The final condition necessary for an effective team is a supportive climate. Internally, the team should have a sound infrastructure, which means proper training, a clear and reasonable measurement system that team members can use to evaluate their overall performance, an incentive program that recognizes and rewards team activities, and a supportive human resource system. The right infrastructure should support members and reinforce behaviours that lead to high levels of performance. Externally, managers should provide the team with the resources needed to get the job done.

Current Challenges in Managing Teams

▶ ▶ ▶ As the Vancouver games unfolded, the early going was tough. "A shootout win over little Switzerland and that loss to the United States had fingers edging toward the panic button that screams for Royal Commissions and demands a complete ransacking and rebuilding of the entire hockey infrastructure—not to mention the firing of various coaches and the national stoning of whatever players happened to be on the ice or in the goal when the tide turned."[48] In the gold medal game, Canada won 3–2 on Sidney Crosby's goal in overtime.

4. Discuss contemporary issues in managing teams.

Think About It

As Hockey Canada prepares for the 2014 games, what impact might increasing numbers of international players have on the team dynamic? How will the team manager's role need to change? What role could social networks and social media play in building team success?

Few trends have influenced how work gets done in organizations as much as the use of work teams. The shift from working alone to working on teams requires employees to cooperate with others, share information, confront differences, and put aside personal interests for the greater good of the team. Managers can build effective teams by understanding what influences performance and satisfaction. However, managers also face some current challenges in managing teams, primarily those associated with managing global teams and with understanding organizational social networks.

Managing Global Teams

Two characteristics of today's organizations are obvious: They're global, and work is increasingly done by teams. This means that any manager is likely to have to manage a global team. What do we know about managing global teams? We know there are both drawbacks and benefits in using global teams (see Exhibit 16-11). Using our group model as a framework, we can see some of the issues associated with managing global teams.

Group Member Resources in Global Teams

In global organizations, understanding the relationship between group performance and group member resources is especially challenging because of the unique cultural characteristics represented by members of a global team. In addition to recognizing team members' knowledge, skills, abilities, and personality, managers need to be familiar with and clearly understand the cultural characteristics of the groups and the group members they manage.[49] For instance, is the global team from a culture in which uncertainty avoidance is high? If so, members will not be comfortable dealing with unpredictable and ambiguous tasks. Also, as managers work with global teams, they need to be aware of the potential for stereotyping, which can lead to problems.

Group Structure

Some of the structural areas where we see differences in managing global teams include conformity, status, social loafing, and cohesiveness.

Conformity. Are conformity findings generalizable across cultures? Research suggests that Asch's findings are culture bound.[50] For instance, as might be expected, conformity to social norms tends to be higher in collectivistic cultures than in individualistic cultures. Despite this, however, groupthink tends to be less of a problem in global teams because members are less likely to feel pressured to conform to the ideas, conclusions, and decisions of the group.[51]

Status. The importance of status also varies between cultures. The French, for example, are extremely status conscious. Furthermore, countries differ on the criteria that confer status. For instance, in Latin America and Asia, status tends to come from family position and formal roles held in organizations. In contrast, while status is important in countries such as the United States and Australia, it tends to be less "in your face." And it tends to be given based on accomplishments rather than on titles and family history. Managers must understand who and what holds status when interacting with people from a culture different from their own. A US manager who doesn't understand that office size isn't a measure of a Japanese executive's position or who fails to grasp the importance the British place on family genealogy and social class is likely to unintentionally offend others and reduce his or her interpersonal effectiveness.

Social Loafing. Social loafing has a Western bias. It's consistent with individualistic cultures, such as the United States and Canada, which are dominated by self-interest. It's not consistent with collectivistic societies, in which individuals are motivated by group goals. For instance, in studies comparing employees from the United States with employees from the People's Republic of China and Israel (both collectivistic societies), the Chinese and Israelis showed no propensity to engage in social loafing. In fact, they actually performed better in a group than when working alone.[52]

Cohesiveness. Cohesiveness is another group structural element with which managers may face special challenges. In a cohesive group, members are unified and "act as one." There's a great deal of camaraderie, and group identity is high. In global teams, however, cohesiveness is often more difficult to achieve because of higher levels of "mistrust, miscommunication, and stress."[53]

Exhibit 16-11

Drawbacks and Benefits of Global Teams

Drawbacks	Benefits
• Dislike team members	• Greater diversity of ideas
• Mistrust team members	• Limited groupthink
• Stereotyping	• Increased attention on understanding others' ideas, perspectives, etc.
• Communication problems	
• Stress and tension	

Source: Based on N. Adler, *International Dimensions in Organizational Behaviour*, 4th ed. (Cincinnati, OH: South-Western Publishing, 2002), pp. 141–147.

Group Processes

The processes that global teams use to do their work can be particularly challenging for managers. For one thing, communication issues often arise because not all team members may be fluent in the team's working language. This can lead to inaccuracies, misunderstandings, and inefficiencies.[54] However, research has also shown that a multicultural global team is better able to capitalize on the diversity of ideas represented if a wide range of information is used.[55]

Managing conflict in global teams isn't easy, especially when those teams are virtual teams. Conflict can interfere with how a team uses information. However, research has shown that in collectivistic cultures, a collaborative conflict management style can be most effective.[56]

The Manager's Role

Despite the challenges associated with managing global teams, there are things managers can do to provide a group with an environment in which efficiency and effectiveness are enhanced.[57] First, because communication skills are vital, managers should focus on developing those skills. Also, as mentioned earlier, managers must consider cultural differences when deciding what type of global team to use. For instance, evidence suggests that self-managed teams have not fared well in Mexico largely due to that culture's low tolerance of ambiguity and uncertainty and employees' strong respect for hierarchical authority.[58] Finally, it's vital that managers be sensitive to the unique differences of each member of a global team. But it's also important that team members be sensitive to each other.

Understanding Social Networks

We can't leave this chapter on managing teams without looking at the patterns of informal connections among individuals within groups—that is, at the **social network structure**.[59] What actually happens *within* groups? How *do* group members relate to each other, and how does work get done?

Managers need to understand the social networks and social relationships of work groups. Why? Because a group's informal social relationships can help or hinder its effectiveness. For instance, research on social networks has shown that when people need help getting a job done, they'll choose a friendly colleague over someone who may be more capable.[60] Another recent review of team studies showed that teams with high levels of interpersonal interconnectedness actually attained their goals better and were more committed to staying together.[61] Organizations are recognizing the practical benefits of knowing the social networks within teams. For instance, when Ken Loughridge, an IT manager with MWH Global, was transferred from Cheshire, England, to New Zealand, he had a "map" of the informal relationships and connections among company IT employees. This map had been created a few months earlier, using the results of a survey that asked

social network structure The patterns of informal connections among individuals within a group.

employees who they "consulted most frequently, who they turned to for expertise, and who either boosted or drained their energy levels." Not only did this map help him identify well-connected technical experts, it helped him minimize potential problems when a key manager in the Asia region left the company because Loughridge knew who this person's closest contacts were. Loughridge said, "It's as if you took the top off an ant hill and could see where there's a hive of activity. It really helped me understand who the players were."[62]

SUMMARY AND IMPLICATIONS

1. Define *group* and describe the stages of group development. A group is two or more interacting and interdependent individuals who come together to achieve specific goals. Formal groups are work groups that are defined by an organization's structure and have designated work assignments and specific tasks directed at accomplishing organizational goals. Informal groups are social groups.

The forming stage of group development consists of two phases: joining the group and defining the group's purpose, structure, and leadership. The storming stage involves intragroup conflict over who will control the group and what the group will be doing. In the norming stage, close relationships and cohesiveness develop as norms are determined. During the performing stage, group members begin to work on the group's task. At the adjourning stage, the group prepares to disband.

▶ ▶ ▶ When the Canadian men's hockey team started practising for the 2010 Winter Olympics, individual hockey players knew how to play the game and were used to playing for their own coaches and with their own teammates. The challenge for Team Canada was to meld these independent and autonomous groups into a team as quickly as possible.

2. Describe the major components that influence group performance and satisfaction. The major components that determine group performance and satisfaction are external conditions, group member resources, group structure, group processes, and group tasks. External conditions such as availability of resources and organizational goals affect work groups. Group member resources (knowledge, skills, abilities, and personality traits) can influence what members can do and how effectively they will perform in a group. Group roles generally involve getting group work done or keeping group members happy. Group norms are powerful influences on a person's performance and dictate factors such as work output levels, absenteeism, and promptness. Pressures to conform can heavily influence a person's judgment and attitudes. If carried to extremes, groupthink can be a problem. Status systems can be a significant motivator with individual behavioural consequences, especially if there's incongruence in status. What size group is most effective and efficient depends on the task the group is supposed to accomplish. Cohesiveness can affect a group's productivity positively or negatively. Group decision making and conflict management are important group processes that play a role in performance and satisfaction. If accuracy, creativity, and degree of acceptance are important, a group decision may work best. Relationship conflicts are almost always dysfunctional. Low levels of process conflict and low to moderate levels of task conflict are functional. Effective communication and controlled conflict are most relevant to group performance when tasks are complex and interdependent.

▶ ▶ ▶ After the 2006 Turin Olympic Games, Mike Babcock and Steve Yzerman built a team that met Yzerman's objective of looking for players who were comfortable in all game situations and in different positions, while fitting in with Babcock's philosophy of making sure that all the little things are done right. The players also had to be willing to accept Babcock's forceful personality. Babcock's coaching style was seen to be the opposite of Pat Quinn's, the coach of the 2006 Turin team.

3. Define *team* and describe best practices for team performance. Work groups have the following characteristics: a strong, clearly focused leader; individual accountability; a purpose that's the same as the broader organizational mission; an individual work product; efficient meetings; effectiveness measured by influence on others; and the ability to discuss, decide, and delegate together. Teams have the following characteristics: shared leadership roles; individual and mutual accountability; specific team purpose; collective work products; meetings with open-ended discussion and active problem solving; performance measured directly on collective work products; and the ability to discuss, decide, and do real work. A problem-solving team is a team that's focused on improving work activities or solving specific problems. A self-managed work team is responsible for a complete work process or segment and manages itself. A cross-functional team is composed of individuals from various specialties. A virtual team uses technology to link physically dispersed members in order to achieve a common goal. The characteristics of an effective team include clear goals, relevant skills, mutual trust, unified commitment, good communication, negotiating skills, appropriate leadership, and internal and external support.

▶ ▶ ▶ Many individuals resist being team players. To improve the odds that a team will function well, managers (like Steve Yzerman and coach Mike Babcock) can select the right people to be on a team, train individuals in how to work on teams, and make sure that rewards encourage individuals to be cooperative team players.

4. Discuss contemporary issues in managing teams. The challenges of managing global teams can be seen in the group member resources, especially the diverse cultural characteristics; group structure, especially conformity, status, social loafing, and cohesiveness; group processes, especially with communication and managing conflict; and the manager's role in making it all work. Managers need to understand the patterns of informal connections among individuals within groups because those informal social relationships can help or hinder the group's effectiveness.

Management @ Work

READING FOR COMPREHENSION

1. Think of a group to which you belong (or have belonged). Trace its development through the stages of group development shown in Exhibit 16-2 on page 450. How closely did its development parallel the group development model? How might the group development model be used to improve this group's effectiveness?

2. How do you explain the popularity of work teams in North America when the culture places such high value on individualism and individual effort?

3. A 20-year study done at Stanford University found that one quality fast-track executives had was the ability to function well as a member of a team. Do you think that everyone should be expected to be a team player, given the trends we're seeing in the use of teams? Discuss.

4. "To have a successful team, first find a great leader." What do you think of this statement? Do you agree? Why or why not?

5. Why do you believe mutual trust is important to developing high-performing work teams?

6. Why might a manager want to stimulate conflict in a group or team? How could conflict be stimulated?

LINKING CONCEPTS TO PRACTICE

1. In your experience, discuss the advantages and disadvantages of working in a team environment.

2. How do you think scientific management theorists would react to the increased reliance on teams in organizations? How would behavioural science theorists react?

3. "All work teams are work groups, but not all work groups are work teams." Do you agree or disagree with the statement? Discuss.

4. Would you prefer to work alone or as part of a team? Why? Support your response with data from your self-assessments.

5. Describe a situation in which individuals, acting independently, outperform teams in an organization.

SELF-ASSESSMENT

How Good Am I at Building and Leading a Team?

Use the following rating scale to respond to the 18 statements on building and leading an effective team:[63]

    1 = Strongly Disagree   2 = Disagree   3 = Slightly Disagree   4 = Slightly Agree   5 = Agree   6 = Strongly Agree

1. I am knowledgeable about the different stages of development that teams can go through in their life cycles.   1 2 3 4 5 6

2. When a team forms, I make certain that all team members are introduced to one another at the outset.   1 2 3 4 5 6

3. When the team first comes together, I provide directions, answer team members' questions, and clarify goals, expectations, and procedures.   1 2 3 4 5 6

4. I help team members establish a foundation of trust among one another and between themselves and me.   1 2 3 4 5 6

5. I ensure that standards of excellence, not mediocrity or mere acceptability, characterize the team's work.   1 2 3 4 5 6

6. I provide a great deal of feedback to team members regarding their performance. 1 2 3 4 5 6

7. I encourage team members to balance individual autonomy with interdependence among other team members. 1 2 3 4 5 6

8. I help team members become at least as committed to the success of the team as to their own personal success. 1 2 3 4 5 6

9. I help members learn to play roles that assist the team in accomplishing its tasks as well as building strong interpersonal relationships. 1 2 3 4 5 6

10. I articulate a clear, exciting, passionate vision of what the team can achieve. 1 2 3 4 5 6

11. I help team members become committed to the team vision. 1 2 3 4 5 6

12. I encourage a win-win philosophy in the team; that is, when one member wins, every member wins. 1 2 3 4 5 6

13. I help the team avoid groupthink or making the group's survival more important than accomplishing its goal. 1 2 3 4 5 6

14. I use formal process management procedures to help the group become faster, more efficient, and more productive, and to prevent errors. 1 2 3 4 5 6

15. I encourage team members to represent the team's vision, goals, and accomplishments to outsiders. 1 2 3 4 5 6

16. I diagnose and capitalize on the team's core competence. 1 2 3 4 5 6

17. I encourage the team to achieve dramatic breakthrough innovations, as well as small continuous improvements. 1 2 3 4 5 6

18. I help the team work toward preventing mistakes, not just correcting them after the fact. 1 2 3 4 5 6

Scoring Key

To calculate your total score, add up your scores on the 18 individual items.

Analysis and Interpretation

The authors of this instrument propose that it assesses team development behaviours in five areas: diagnosing team development (statements 1, 16); managing the forming stage (2–4); managing the norming stage (6–9, 13); managing the storming stage (10–12, 14, 15); and managing the performing stage (5, 17, 18). Your score will range between 18 and 108, with higher scores indicating greater ability at building and leading an effective team.

Based on a norm group of 500 business students, the following can help estimate where you are in relation to others.

Total score of 95 or more = You are in the top quartile
72–94 = You are in the second quartile
60–71 = You are in the third quartile
Less than 60 = You are in the bottom quartile

More Self-Assessments MyManagementLab

To learn more about your skills, abilities, and interests, go to the MyManagementLab website and take the following self-assessments:

- II.A.2.—How Good Are My Listening Skills?
- II.B.4.—Do Others See Me as Trustworthy?
- II.B.6.—How Good Am I at Building and Leading a Team?
- IV.E.1.—What's My Attitude Toward Working in Groups?

MANAGEMENT FOR YOU TODAY

Dilemma

One of your instructors has just informed your class that you will be working on a new major assignment worth 30 percent of your course mark. The assignment is to be done in teams of seven. Realistically, you will need to function as a virtual team, as it turns out that each of you has a different work and class schedule, so that there is almost no time when more than three people could meet face-to-face. As you know, virtual teams have benefits, but they can also have problems. How will you build group cohesiveness in this team? What norms might help the team function, and how should the norms be decided? What will you do to prevent social loafing?

Becoming a Manager

- Use any opportunities that come up to work in a group. Note things such as stages of team development, roles, norms, social loafing, and so forth.
- When confronted with conflicts, pay attention to how you manage or resolve them.
- In group projects, try different techniques for improving the group's creativity.
- When you see a successful team, try to assess what makes it successful.

WORKING TOGETHER: TEAM-BASED EXERCISE

Puzzle Building

What happens when a group is presented with a task that must be completed within a certain time frame? Does the group exhibit characteristics of the stages of team development? Your instructor will divide the class into groups and give you instructions about building a puzzle or watching others do so.

Note: Instructors can find the instructions for this exercise in the Instructor's Resource Manual.

ETHICS IN ACTION

Ethical Dilemma Exercise: Does Everyone Have to Be a Team Player?

You are a production manager at a Saturn plant. One of your newest employees in supply chain management is Barbara Petersen, who has a bachelor's degree in engineering and a master's degree in business.

You have recently been chosen to head up a cross-functional team to look at ways to reduce inventory costs. This team would essentially be a permanent task force. You have decided to have team members come from supplier relations, cost accounting, transportation, and production systems. You have also decided to include Barbara on the team. While she has been at Saturn only for four months, you have been impressed with her energy, smarts, and industriousness. You think this would be an excellent assignment for her to increase her visibility in the company and expand her understanding of the company's inventory system.

When you gave Barbara the good news, you were surprised by her response. "I'm not a team player. I didn't join clubs in high school. I was on the track team and I did well, but track is an individual sport. We were a team only in the sense that we rode together in the same bus to away meets. In university, I avoided the whole sorority thing. Some people may call me a loner. I don't think that's true. I can work well with others, but I hate meetings and committees. To me, they waste so much time. And when you work with a group, you've got all these different personalities that you have to adjust for. I'm an independent operator. Give me a job and I'll get it done. I work harder than anyone I know—and I give my employer 150 percent. But I don't want my performance to be dependent on the other people in my group. They may not work as hard as I will. Someone is sure to shirk some of their responsibilities. I just don't want to be a team player."

What do you do? Should you give Barbara the option of joining the inventory cost reduction team? Is it unethical for you to require someone like Barbara to do his or her job as part of a team?

Thinking Critically About Ethics

You have been hired as a summer intern in the events planning department of a public relations firm in Calgary. After working there about a month, you conclude that the attitude in the office is "anything goes." Employees know that supervisors will not discipline them for ignoring company rules. For example, employees have to turn in expense reports, but the process is a joke; nobody submits receipts to verify reimbursement, and nothing is ever said. In fact, when you tried to turn in your receipts with your expense report, you were told, "Nobody else turns in receipts and you don't really need to, either." You know that no expense cheque has ever been denied because of failure to turn in a receipt, even though the employee handbook says that receipts are required. Also, your co-workers use company phones for personal long-distance calls even though that is prohibited by the employee handbook. And one permanent employee told you to "help yourself" to any paper, pens, or pencils you might need here or at home. What are the norms of this group? Suppose that you were the supervisor in this area. How would you go about changing the norms?

Samsung Electronics

Samsung Electronics is now the world's largest and most profitable consumer electronics company.[64] In 2006, it ranked higher than Sony as the world's most valuable consumer electronics brand, according to the most recent valuable global brands survey done by the Interbrand Consulting Group. Its clever product designs have won over consumers and won numerous awards.

Samsung Group was founded as a trucking company in the 1930s, and in the 1960s became one of several *chaebol* (large conglomerates) "shaped by the Korean government and protected from foreign competition by import duties and other government-sponsored regulations." The electronics division, Samsung Electronics, is by far the largest and most global of the Samsung businesses.

At the company's design centre just a few blocks away from headquarters in Seoul, designers work in small teams with three to five members coming from various specialty areas and levels of seniority. Even though Korean culture has loosened up somewhat, respect for elders and a reluctance to speak out of turn are still the norm. But here at Samsung's design centre, there is no dress code and team members work as equals. Everyone—even the younger staffers, who often have their hair dyed green or pink—is encouraged to speak up and challenge their superiors.

Although Samsung Electronics is sitting on top now, Kim Byung Cheol, a senior executive, is worried about his company's future. Why? Because Samsung "still has not mastered one crucial factor: originality." Much of Samsung's success in electronics can be traced to its ability to mimic and enhance others' inventions, but it has never been the design innovator. Kim says, "We are at a pivotal moment for the company. If we don't become an innovator, we could end up like one of those Japanese companies, mired in difficulties." What can Kim and his managers do to encourage innovation and originality with the design centre teams?

Team Ferrari

Imagine working for an organization that employs more than 2000 individuals with each one having the identical focus.[65] Imagine, too, that company management in this organization wants you to work only so hard but still be the best at what you do. If you are employed by Ferrari, these elements are not hard to imagine.

Luca Cordero, president and managing director of Ferrari, believes that his employees truly make a difference in producing one of the world's greatest sports cars. Cordero recognizes that to be the best, he needs employees who understand how to work together and how to achieve common goals. That is because at Ferrari there are no assembly lines. Rather, teams of employees combine their efforts to produce an outstanding automobile noted for its quality in the automobile industry. You simply will not find traditional assembly lines in the Ferrari factory, nor will you find production quotas. Auto assembly time is not measured in seconds—rather, team tasks often last over 90 minutes for each portion of a car. Then the team proudly takes its finished work on to the next team so its work can begin.

Management of the company wants no more than 4000 Ferraris produced in each year, even though the company could sell considerably more.

Employees at Ferrari truly enjoy being part of a team. They cite the fact that working in a common direction is one of the most satisfying elements in their job. They also appreciate what management does for them. They are offered a state-of-the-art fitness centre, annual physicals at the company's on-site clinic, an employee cafeteria, and home-based training for employees to learn English. They feel as if Cordero and his team treat them as associates, not just as cogs in the Ferrari wheel. As one Ferrari employee stated, "For many of us, working for Ferrari is like working in the Vatican."

Is the team concept at Ferrari working? By all accounts it is. The company recently celebrated its first $1 billion year of sales, which resulted in over $60 million in profits. Profits over the past several years continue to rise, and more importantly for Ferrari's management, there is more than a two-year waiting list for most Ferrari models.

Questions

1. Why do you believe the team concept at Ferrari works so well? Cite specific examples to support your position.

2. Do you believe such a system could be replicated in other automotive manufacturers? If so, in what kind of organizations? If not, why not?

3. Using Exhibit 16-10 on page 462, describe each of the characteristics of effective teams as they relate to this case. Use examples when appropriate. If a characteristic was not specifically cited in the case, describe how it may have been part of this situation.

DEVELOPING YOUR INTERPERSONAL SKILLS

Creating Effective Teams

About the Skill

A team is different from a group because its members are committed to a common purpose, have a set of specific performance goals, and hold themselves mutually accountable for the team's results. Teams can produce outputs that are greater than the sum of the individual contributions of its members. The primary force that makes a work group an effective team—that is, a real high-performing team—is its emphasis on performance.

Steps in Developing the Skill

Managers and team leaders have a significant impact on a team's effectiveness. You can be more successful at creating an effective team if you use the following nine suggestions:[66]

1. **Establish a common purpose.** An effective team needs a common purpose to which all members aspire. This purpose is a vision. It's broader than any specific goals. This common purpose provides direction, momentum, and commitment for team members.

2. **Assess team strengths and weaknesses.** Team members will have different strengths and weaknesses. Knowing these strengths and weaknesses can help the team leader build upon the strengths and compensate for the weaknesses.

3. **Develop specific individual goals.** Specific individual goals help lead team members to achieve higher performance. In addition, specific goals facilitate clear communication and help maintain the focus on getting results.

4. **Get agreement on a common approach for achieving goals.** Goals are the ends a team strives to attain. Defining and agreeing upon a common approach ensures that the team is unified on the means for achieving those ends.

5. **Encourage acceptance of responsibility for both individual and team performance.** Successful teams make members individually and jointly accountable for the team's purpose, goals, and approach. Members understand what they are individually responsible for and what they are jointly responsible for.

6. **Build mutual trust among members.** When there is trust, team members believe in the integrity, character, and ability of each other. When trust is lacking, members are unable to depend on each other. Teams that lack trust tend to be short-lived.

7. **Maintain an appropriate mix of team member skills and personalities.** Team members come to the team with different skills and personalities. To perform effectively, teams need three types of skills. First, teams need people with technical expertise. Next, they need people with problem-solving and decision-making skills to identify problems, generate alternatives, evaluate those alternatives, and make competent choices. Finally, teams need people with good interpersonal skills.

8. **Provide needed training and resources.** Team leaders need to make sure that their teams have both the training and the resources to accomplish their goals.

9. **Create opportunities for small achievements.** Building an effective team takes time. Team members have to learn to think and work as a team. New teams cannot be expected to hit home runs every time they come to bat, especially at the beginning. Instead, team members should be encouraged to try for small achievements at the beginning.

Practising the Skill

Read the following scenario. Write some notes about how you would handle the situation described. Be sure to refer to the nine suggestions for creating effective teams.

Scenario

You are the leader of a five-member project team that has been assigned the task of moving your engineering firm into the new booming area of high-speed rail construction. You and your team have been researching the field, identifying business opportunities, negotiating alliances with equipment vendors, and evaluating high-speed rail experts and consultants from around the world. Throughout the process, Tonya, a highly qualified and respected engineer, has challenged everything you say during team meetings and in the workplace. For example, at a meeting two weeks ago, you presented the team with a list of 10 possible high-speed rail projects that had been identified by the team and started evaluating your organization's ability to compete for them. Tonya contradicted all your comments, questioned your statistics, and was pessimistic about the possibility of contracts. After this latest display of displeasure, two other group members, Liam and Ahmed, came to you and complained that Tonya's actions were damaging the team's effectiveness. You had put Tonya on the team for her unique expertise and insight. What should you say to Tonya, and how can you help get the team on the right track to reach its full potential?

Reinforcing the Skill

The following activities will help you practise and reinforce the skills associated with creating effective teams:

1. Interview three managers at different organizations. Ask them about their experiences in managing teams. What behaviours have they found successful in creating an effective team? What about those behaviours that have not been successful in creating an effective team?

2. After completing a team project for one of your classes, assess the team's effectiveness by answering the following questions: Did everyone on the team know exactly why the team did what it did? Did team members have a significant amount of input into or influence on decisions that affected them? Did team members have open, honest, timely, and two-way communications? Did everyone on the team know and understand the team's priorities? Did the team members work together to resolve destructive conflicts? Was everyone on the team working toward accomplishing the same thing? Did team members understand the team's unwritten rules of how to behave within the group?

MyManagementLab

After you have completed the study of Part 1, do the following exercises at the MyManagementLab website (www.pearsoned.ca/mymanagementlab):

- You're the Manager: Putting Ethics into Action (Avon Products)
- Passport, Scenario 1 (Robert Mathis, Daimler Chrysler), Scenario 2 (Mary Chang), and Scenario 3 (Jean Claude Moreau, Bon Appétit)

VIDEO CASE INCIDENT — CBC

Please turn to the back of the book to see the Video Case Incidents available for Part 4.

SCAN THIS

CONTROLLING

In **PART FIVE**, we look at the process of controlling and discuss the following topics:

| Chapter 17 | Foundations of Control |
| Chapter 18 | Managing Operations |

Managers must establish goals and plans, organize and structure work activities, and develop programs to motivate and lead people to put forth effort to accomplish those goals. Even when managers have finished these tasks, their job is not done. Quite the opposite! Managers must then monitor activities to make sure they're being done as planned and correct any significant deviations. This process is called *controlling*. It's the final link in the management process, and although controlling happens last in the process, that doesn't make it any less important than any of the other managerial functions.

Foundations of Control

Managers need to monitor the activities of the organization and determine whether they are accomplishing their planned goals. In evaluating outcomes, they are able to spot opportunities that sometimes require a change in direction. After reading and studying this chapter, you will achieve the following learning outcomes.

Learning Outcomes

1 Explain the nature and importance of control.

2 Describe the three steps in the control process.

3 Describe tools used to measure organizational performance.

4 Describe three methods of control.

5 Understand how financial and information controls help managers monitor performance.

6 Discuss contemporary issues in control.

▶ ▶ ▶ When Li Ka-shing first invested in Calgary-based Husky Oil (now Husky Energy) in 1986, buying 52 percent of its shares, the company had just posted its first year-end loss in the company's history.[1] The company had no cash on hand, shares had dropped to half of their 1981 value, and the company's debt was growing. Bob Blair, then the CEO at Husky, turned to Li. "We required a lot of capital, more than Husky could generate from its own cash flow," says Blair, in explaining why he approached his friend Li, a wealthy Hong Kong businessman, to invest in the company. In 1991, Li and his holding company bought 43 percent more of the company.

After the 1991 investment, Li immediately sent John Chin-Sung Lau (pictured) to Calgary to turn the company around. Li wanted to halt the company's large losses and "wild expansions" of Husky's previous management.

Appointed vice-president at the time, Lau had difficulty working with Husky president Art Price and found the culture at Husky to be a free-spending one.

Lau had a difficult task in front of him to make Husky profitable.

Think About It

What is organizational control? Put yourself in John Lau's shoes. How can he use control to make Husky successful? What did he need to do to turn Husky Energy into one of Canada's largest oil and gas enterprises?

SCAN THIS

In today's competitive global marketplace, managers want their organizations to achieve high levels of performance, and one way they can do that is by searching out the best practices successful organizations are using. By comparing themselves against the best, managers look for specific performance gaps and areas for improvement.

As we will see in this chapter, John Lau understands the importance of management strategy in making the right strategic choices. Lau also understands the role of management controls in supporting the choices made by Husky. No matter how thorough the planning, a decision still may be poorly implemented without a satisfactory control system in place. This chapter describes controls for monitoring and measuring performance. It also looks at how to create a well-designed organizational control system.

What Is Controlling, and Why Is It Important?

Imagine that a press operator at the Royal Canadian Mint in Ottawa noticed a flaw—an extra up leaf or an extra down leaf—on the new quarters being pressed at one of his five press machines. He stops the machine and leaves for a meal break. When he returns, he sees the machine running and assumes that someone has changed the die in the machine. However, after a routine inspection, the machine operator realizes that the die has not been changed. The faulty press has likely been running for over an hour, and thousands of the flawed coins are now co-mingled with unblemished quarters. As many as 50 000 of the faulty coins enter circulation, setting off a coin collector buying frenzy.[2] Can you see why ensuring that the process is under control (controlling) is such an important managerial function?

1. Explain the nature and importance of control.

Control is one of the four pillars of management (planning, leading, and organizing are the other three) and is a strategic activity that is infused across all activities within an organization. What is **controlling**? It's the process of monitoring activities to ensure that they are being accomplished as planned and correcting any significant deviations. All managers should be involved in the control function even if their units are performing as planned. Managers cannot really know whether their units are performing properly until they have evaluated what activities have been done and have compared the actual performance with the desired standard.[3] An effective control system ensures that activities are completed in ways that lead to the attainment of the organization's goals. The criterion that determines the effectiveness of a control system is how well it facilitates goal achievement. The more it helps managers achieve their organization's goals, the better the control system.[4]

Performance Standards

To achieve control, performance standards must exist. These standards are the specific goals created during the planning process. **Performance** is the end result of an activity. Whether that activity is hours of intense practice before a concert or race or whether it's carrying out job responsibilities as efficiently and effectively as possible, performance is what results from that activity. For example, the Society of Management Accountants of Canada requires three competencies of their members—accounting, management, and strategy. Within the accountability mandate, members are responsible for both performance (forward looking) and conformance (historic—assurance of compliance, performance, safeguarding of assets, and control of risk).[5]

Managers are concerned with **organizational performance**—the accumulated end results of all the organization's work activities. It's a complex but important concept. Managers need to understand the factors that contribute to high organizational performance. After all, they don't want (or intend) to manage their way to mediocre performance. They *want* their organizations, work units, or work groups to achieve high levels of performance, no matter what mission, strategies, or goals are being pursued.

Measures of Organizational Performance

All managers must know what organizational performance measures will give them the information they need. The most frequently used organizational performance measures include organizational productivity, organizational effectiveness, and industry and company rankings.

Organizational Productivity

Productivity is the overall output of goods or services produced divided by the inputs needed to generate that output. Organizations strive to be productive. They want the most goods and services produced using the least amount of inputs. Output is measured by the sales revenue an organization receives when those goods and services are sold (selling price × number sold). Input is measured by the costs of acquiring and transforming the organizational resources into the outputs.

Organizational Effectiveness

In Chapter 1, we defined managerial effectiveness as goal attainment. Can the same interpretation apply to organizational effectiveness? Yes, it can. **Organizational effectiveness** is a measure of how appropriate organizational goals are and how well an organization is achieving those goals. It's a common performance measure used by managers in designing strategies, work processes, and work activities, and in coordinating the work of employees.

Industry and Company Rankings

There is no shortage of different types of industry and company rankings. The rankings for each list are determined by specific performance measures. For instance, the companies listed in *Report on Business Magazine*'s Top 1000: Canada's Power Book are measured by assets. They are ranked according to after-tax profits in the most recent fiscal year,

controlling The process of monitoring activities to ensure that they are being accomplished as planned, and correcting any significant deviations.

MyManagementLab
Q&A 17.1, Q&A 17.2

performance The end result of an activity.

organizational performance The accumulated end results of all the organization's work activities.

MyManagementLab
Q&A 17.3

productivity The overall output of goods or services produced divided by the inputs needed to generate that output.

organizational effectiveness A measure of how appropriate organizational goals are and how well an organization is achieving those goals.

MyManagementLab
Q&A 17.4

excluding extraordinary gains or losses.[6] The companies listed in the 50 Best Employers in Canada are ranked based on answers given by managers to a leadership team survey, an employee opinion survey, and a human resource survey designed by Hewitt Associates, a compensation and benefits consultant.[7] The companies listed in the *PROFIT* 100: Canada's Fastest Growing Companies are ranked based on their percentage sales growth over the past five years. Private and publicly traded companies that are over 50 percent Canadian-owned and are headquartered in Canada nominate themselves, and then *PROFIT* editors collect further information about eligible companies.[8]

Why Is Control Important?

> *How can control help a team perform better on a course project?*

Planning can be done, an organizational structure can be created to efficiently facilitate the achievement of goals, and employees can be motivated through effective leadership. Still, there is no assurance that activities are going as planned and that the goals managers are seeking are, in fact, being attained. Control is important, therefore, because it's the final link in the four management functions. It's the only way managers know whether organizational goals are being met and, if not, the reasons why. The value of the control function lies in its relation to planning, empowering employees, and protecting the organization and workplace.

MyManagementLab
Q&A 17.5

In Chapter 7, we described goals as the foundation of planning. Goals give specific direction to managers. However, just stating goals or having employees accept your goals is no guarantee that the necessary actions to accomplish those goals have been taken. As the old saying goes, "The best-laid plans often go awry." The effective manager needs to follow up to ensure that what others are supposed to do is, in fact, being done and that their goals are in fact being achieved. In reality, managing is an ongoing process, and controlling activities provide the critical link back to planning (see Exhibit 17-1). If managers did not control, they would have no way of knowing whether their goals and plans were on target and what future actions to take.

Another reason control is important is employee empowerment. Many managers are reluctant to empower their employees because they fear employees will do something

Exhibit 17-1

The Planning–Controlling Link

wrong for which the manager will be held responsible. Thus, many managers are tempted to do things themselves and avoid empowering. This reluctance, however, can be reduced if managers develop an effective control system that provides information and feedback on employee performance.

The final reason that managers control is to protect the organization and the physical workplace.[9] Given today's environment, with heightened security alerts and surprise financial scandals, managers must have plans in place to protect the organization's employees, data, and infrastructure.

The Control Process

2. Describe the three steps in the control process.

control process A three-step process that includes measuring actual performance, comparing actual performance against a standard, and taking managerial action to correct deviations or inadequate standards.

The **control process** is a three-step process: measuring actual performance, comparing actual performance against a standard, and taking managerial action to correct deviations or inadequate standards (see Exhibit 17-2). The control process assumes that performance standards already exist, and they do. They're the specific goals created during the planning process. The control process for managers is similar to what you might do as a student at the beginning of the term: set goals for yourself for studying and marks, and then evaluate your performance after midterms, determining whether you have studied enough or need to study more in order to meet whatever goals you set for your marks. (To learn more about how proactive you are, see *Self-Assessment—How Proactive Am I?* on pages 502–503.)

Step 1: Measuring Performance

If you can't measure it, you can't manage it! To determine what actual performance is, a manager must acquire information about it. The first step in control, then, is measuring. Let's consider how we measure and what we measure.

How We Measure

Four sources of information frequently used by managers to measure actual performance are personal observations, statistical reports, oral reports, and written reports. Exhibit 17-3 summarizes the advantages and drawbacks of each approach. Most managers use a combination of these approaches.

Exhibit 17-2

The Control Process

Exhibit 17-3

Common Sources of Information for Measuring Performance

	Advantages	Drawbacks
Personal Observations (Management by Walking Around)	• Get first-hand knowledge • Information isn't filtered • Intensive coverage of work activities	• Subject to personal biases • Time-consuming • Can distract employees
Statistical Reports	• Easy to visualize • Effective for showing relationships	• Provide limited information • Ignore subjective factors
Oral Reports	• Fast way to get information • Allow for verbal and nonverbal feedback	• Information is filtered • Information cannot be documented
Written Reports	• Comprehensive • Formal • Easy to file and retrieve	• Take more time to prepare

What We Measure

What we measure is probably more critical to the control process than *how* we measure. Why? The selection of the wrong criteria can result in serious dysfunctional consequences. Besides, what we measure determines, to a great extent, what people in the organization will attempt to excel at.[10] For instance, if employees are evaluated by the number of big-ticket items they sell, they may not help customers who are looking for less expensive items.

Some control criteria can be used for any management situation. For instance, all managers deal with people, so criteria such as employee satisfaction or turnover and absenteeism rates can be measured. Keeping costs within budget is also a fairly common control measure. Other control criteria should recognize the different activities that managers supervise. For instance, a manager at a pizza delivery location might use measures such as number of pizzas delivered per day, average delivery time, or number of coupons redeemed. A manager in a governmental agency might use applications typed per day, client requests completed per hour, or average time to process paperwork.

Most work activities can be expressed in quantifiable terms, but when they can't, managers should use subjective measures. Although such measures may have limitations, having them is better than having no standards at all and doing no controlling.

Step 2: Comparing Performance against Standard

The comparing step determines the degree of variation between actual performance and the standard. Although some variation in performance can be expected in all activities, it's critical to determine the acceptable **range of variation** (see Exhibit 17-4). Deviations that exceed this range become significant and need the manager's attention. In the comparison stage, managers are particularly concerned with the size and direction of the variation. An example can help make this concept clearer.

range of variation The acceptable degree of variation between actual performance and the standard.

Chris Tanner is sales manager for Beer Unlimited, a distributor of specialty beers in the Prairies. Chris prepares a report during the first week of each month that describes sales for the previous month, classified by brand name. Exhibit 17-5 displays both the sales goal (standard) and the actual sales figures for the month of July.

Should Chris be concerned about July's sales performance? Sales were a bit higher than originally targeted, but does that mean there were no significant deviations? Even though overall performance was generally quite favourable, several brands might need to be examined more closely by Chris. However, the number of brands that deserve attention

Exhibit 17-4

Defining the Acceptable Range of Variation

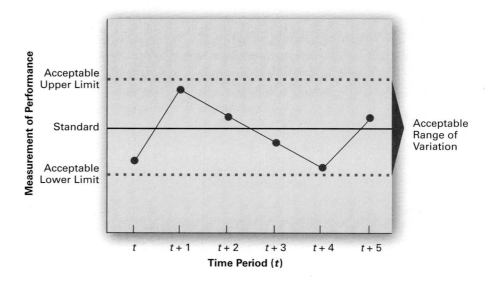

Exhibit 17-5

Sales Performance Figures for July, Beer Unlimited

Brand	Standard	(number of cases) Actual	Over (Under)
Premium Lager (Okanagan Spring, Vernon, BC)	1075	913	(162)
India Pale Ale (Alexander Keith's, Halifax)	800	912	112
Maple Brown Ale (Upper Canada Brewery, Guelph, ON)	620	622	2
Blanche de Chambly (Brasseries Unibroue, Quebec)	160	110	(50)
Full Moon (Alley Kat, Edmonton)	225	220	(5)
Black Cat Lager (Paddock Wood Brewing, Saskatoon, Saskatchewan)	80	65	(15)
Bison Blonde Lager (Agassiz, Winnipeg)	170	286	116
Total cases	**3130**	**3128**	**(2)**

depends on what Chris believes to be *significant.* How much variation should Chris allow before corrective action is taken?

The deviation on three brands (Maple Brown Ale, Full Moon, Black Cat Lager) is very small and does not need special attention. On the other hand, are the lower sales for Premium Lager and Blanche de Chambly brands significant? That is a judgment Chris must make. Premium Lager sales were 15 percent below Chris' goal. This deviation is significant and needs attention. Chris should look for a cause. In this instance, Chris attributes the decrease to aggressive advertising and promotion programs by the big domestic producers, Anheuser-Busch and Miller. Because Premium Lager is his company's number one selling microbeer, it's most vulnerable to the promotion clout of the big domestic producers. If the decline in sales of Premium Lager is more than a temporary slump (that is, if it happens again next month), then Chris will need to consider actions including cutting back on inventory in the short term and in the long term formulating strategies to combat his competitor's tactics.

Higher sales than anticipated can also be a problem. For instance, is the surprising popularity of Bison Blonde Lager (up 68 percent) a one-month anomaly, or is this brand becoming more popular with customers? If the brand is increasing in popularity, Chris will want to order more product to meet customer demand, so as not to run short and risk losing customers. Again, Chris will have to interpret the information and make a decision.

Benchmarking of Best Practices

We first introduced the concept of benchmarking in Chapter 9. In addition to comparing performance to internal goals, it is also worthwhile to compare performance to external exemplars. **Benchmarking** is the search for the best practices among competitors or non-competitors that lead to their superior performance. The **benchmark** is the standard of excellence against which to measure and compare.[11] At its most fundamental level, benchmarking means learning from others.[12] As a tool for monitoring and measuring organizational performance, benchmarking can be used to help identify specific performance gaps and potential areas of improvement.[13] To ensure the company is on track, Montreal-based BouClair, a home-decorating store, benchmarks everything against past performance and also against what other leading retailers are doing. "If a particular department or category is up 40% in sales over last year but we said we expected it to grow at 60%, then we are going to investigate and find out why," Gerry Goldberg, president and CEO, says.[14] "Then we look at our own same-store sales increases and compare them to the best companies out there. That's how we measure our efficiency and our productivity."

Managers should not look just at external organizations for best practices. It is also important for them to look inside their organization for best practices that can be shared. Research shows that best practices frequently already exist within an organization but usually go unidentified and unused.[15] In today's environment, organizations striving for high performance levels cannot afford to ignore such potentially valuable information. Some companies already have recognized the potential of internally benchmarking best practices as a tool for monitoring and measuring performance.

benchmarking The search for the best practices among competitors or noncompetitors that lead to their superior performance.

benchmark The standard of excellence against which to measure and compare.

Step 3: Taking Managerial Action

Managers can choose among three possible courses of action: they can do nothing; they can correct the actual performance; or they can revise the standard. Because "doing nothing" is fairly self-explanatory, let's look more closely at the other two options.

Correct Actual Performance

If the source of the performance variation is unsatisfactory work, the manager will want to take corrective action. Examples of such corrective action might include changing strategy, structure, compensation practices, or training programs; redesigning jobs; or firing employees. Toronto-based Celestica redesigned its manufacturing process to cut waste, as the following *Management Reflection* shows.

SYSCO is a food-services distribution firm, headquartered in Houston, Texas, that has more than 170 subsidiary companies. A recent innovation developed by its human resource department is the Innovation Key Metrics Benchmark System, which provides executives at all SYSCO's regional offices with scorecards showing how well their company has performed against others in the SYSCO family. A database of its business practices also lets SYSCO executives look up subsidiary companies of similar size and learn about what has made them strong in particular areas. Site visits to these benchmark firms are encouraged.

Celestica Works to Improve the Bottom Line

Can changing the manufacturing process reduce the bottom line? Toronto-based Celestica, an electronics manufacturer, has spent most of this decade introducing control mechanisms to improve the company's fortunes.[16] Between 2001 and 2005, the company cut 29 600 jobs and restructured its operations five times. The company saw its revenues decline significantly between 2001 and 2003 and finally started to see a profit at the end of 2006. The introduction of a number of controls is given credit for the turnaround.

One of the areas that Celestica worked on was improving manufacturing operations. It did so by watching how factory workers carried out their duties, and then designing more efficient processes. Workers at its Monterrey, Mexico, plant "reduced equipment setup time by 85 percent, shortened time between receiving an order and shipping it by 71 percent, reduced floor space used by 34 percent, reduced consumables by 25 percent, reduced scrap by 66 percent and reduced the investment in surface-mount technology (SMT) lines by 49 percent." ■

immediate corrective action Corrective action that corrects problems at once to get performance back on track.

basic corrective action Corrective action that looks at how and why performance deviated and then proceeds to correct the source of deviation.

MyManagementLab
Q&A 17.6

MyManagementLab
PRISM 8

A manager who decides to correct actual performance has to make another decision: Should immediate or basic corrective action be taken? **Immediate corrective action** corrects problems at once to get performance back on track. **Basic corrective action** looks at how and why performance has deviated and then proceeds to correct the source of deviation. It's not unusual for managers to rationalize that they don't have the time to take basic corrective action and therefore must be content to perpetually "put out fires" with immediate corrective action. Effective managers, however, analyze deviations and, when the benefits justify it, take the time to pinpoint and correct the causes of variance.

Revise the Standard

In some cases, variance may be a result of an unrealistic standard—a goal that's too low or too high. In this case, the standard—not the performance—needs corrective action.

If performance consistently exceeds the goal, then a manager should look at whether the goal is too easy and needs to be raised. On the other hand, managers must be cautious about revising a standard downward. It's natural to blame the goal when an employee or a team falls short. For instance, students who get a low score on a test often attack the grade cut-off standards as being too high; rather than accept the fact that their performance was inadequate, they will argue that the standards are unreasonable. Likewise, salespeople who don't meet their monthly quota often want to blame what they think is an unrealistic quota. The point is that when performance isn't up to par, you shouldn't immediately blame the goal or standard. If you believe the standard is realistic, fair, and achievable, tell employees that you expect future work to improve and then take the necessary corrective action to help make that happen.

Corrective action can take many forms. On the selling floor of Home Depot stores, where one contractor spent 20 minutes waiting for a Home Depot forklift operator to arrive so he could load some purchased drywall, the need to improve customer service led to changes in the composition of the workforce. Senior management realized that stores had hired too many part-time employees, whose commitment to the job and knowledge about the do-it-yourself business sometimes lagged behind those of full-timers. Home Depot scaled back from a 50-50 mix to a new balance of 40 percent part-time and 60 percent full-time employees, and customer service has since improved.

Summary of Managerial Decisions

Exhibit 17-6 summarizes the manager's decisions in the control process. Standards evolve out of goals that are developed during the planning process. These goals then provide the basis for the control process, which

Exhibit 17-6

Managerial Decisions in the Control Process

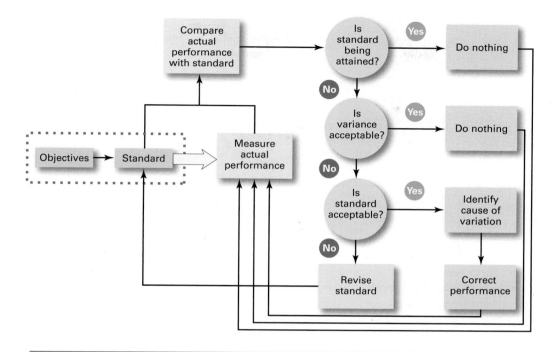

is essentially a continuous flow between measuring, comparing, and taking managerial action. Depending on the results of comparing, a manager's decision about what course of action to take might be to do nothing, revise the standard, or correct the performance.

Tools for Measuring Organizational Performance

Managers can implement controls *before* an activity begins, *during* the time the activity is going on, and *after* the activity has been completed. The first type is called *feedforward control*, the second is *concurrent control*, and the last is *feedback control* (see Exhibit 17-7).

3. Describe tools used to measure organizational performance.

Feedforward Control

When working on a project, do you anticipate problems ahead of time or wait until they occur?

The most desirable type of control—**feedforward control**—prevents anticipated problems since it takes place before the actual activity.[17] Let's look at some examples of feedforward control.

When McDonald's Canada opened its first restaurant in Moscow, it sent company quality control experts to help Russian farmers learn techniques for growing high-quality potatoes and bakers to learn processes for baking high-quality breads. Why? Because McDonald's strongly emphasizes product quality no matter what the geographical location. It wants a cheeseburger in Moscow to taste like one in Winnipeg. Still another example of feedforward control is the scheduled preventive maintenance programs on aircraft done by airlines. These are designed to detect and, it is hoped, to prevent structural damage that might lead to an accident.

feedforward control A type of control that focuses on preventing anticipated problems, since it takes place before the actual activity.

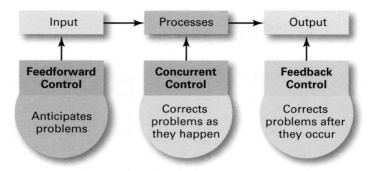

Exhibit 17-7

Types of Control

Input → Processes → Output

Feedforward Control — Anticipates problems

Concurrent Control — Corrects problems as they happen

Feedback Control — Corrects problems after they occur

The key to feedforward controls is taking managerial action *before* a problem occurs. Feedforward controls are desirable because they allow managers to prevent problems rather than having to correct them later after the damage (such as poor-quality products, lost customers, lost revenue, and so forth) has already been done. Unfortunately, these controls require timely and accurate information that often is difficult to get. As a result, managers frequently end up using the other two types of control.

Concurrent Control

Concurrent control, as its name implies, takes place while an activity is in progress. When control is enacted while the work is being performed, management can correct problems before they become too costly. Nicholas Fox is director of business product management at Google. He and his team keep a watchful eye on one of Google's most profitable businesses—online ads. They watch "the number of searches and clicks, the rate at which users click on ads, the revenue this generates—everything is tracked hour by hour, compared with the data from a week earlier and charted."[18] If they see something that's not working particularly well, they fine-tune it.

The best-known form of concurrent control is direct supervision. When managers use **management by walking around**, which is a term used to describe a manager being out in the work area, interacting directly with employees, they are using concurrent control. When a manager directly oversees the actions of employees, he or she can monitor their actions and correct problems as they occur. Although, obviously, there is some delay between the activity and the manager's corrective response, the delay is minimal. Problems usually can be addressed before much resource waste or damage has been done. Also, technical equipment (computers, computerized machine controls, and so forth) can be programmed for concurrent controls. For instance, you may have experienced concurrent control when using a computer program such as word-processing software that alerts you to misspelled words or incorrect grammatical usage. In addition, many organizational quality programs rely on concurrent controls to inform employees if their work output is of sufficient quality to meet standards.

MyManagementLab
Q&A 17.7

Feedback Control

The most popular type of control relies on feedback. In **feedback control**, the control takes place *after* the activity is done. For instance, when McDonald's executives learned that a suspected criminal ring had allegedly stolen millions of dollars in top prizes in their customer games, it was discovered through feedback control.[19] Even though the company took corrective action once it was discovered, the damage had already occurred.

Yun Jong-Yong, CEO of Samsung Electronics, describes how he practises an effective kind of concurrent control. "I spend much of my time visiting our domestic and overseas work sites to examine operations from the ground, receiving face-to-face reports and indicating areas for improvement. This gives me the opportunity to freely discuss matters with the person directly involved, from the top management to the junior staff of that work site . . . I still believe that no [technological] innovation can replace the valuable information that is gathered through direct discussions."

> *Have you used feedback with team members after completing a team project?*

As the McDonald's example shows, the major drawback of this type of control is that by the time the manager has the information, the problems have already occurred—leading to waste or damage. But for many activities, feedback is the only viable type of control available. For instance, financial statements are an example of feedback controls. If, for example, the income statement shows that sales revenues are declining, the decline has already occurred. So at this point, the manager's only option is to try to determine why sales have decreased and to correct the situation.

Feedback controls do have two advantages.[20] First, feedback provides managers with meaningful information on how effective their planning efforts were. Feedback that indicates little variance between standard and actual performance is evidence that the planning was generally on target. If the deviation is significant, a manager can use that information when formulating new plans to make them more effective. Second, feedback control can enhance employee motivation. People want information on how well they have performed, and feedback control provides that information. However, managers should be aware that recent research suggests that while individuals raise their goals when they receive positive feedback, they lower their goals when they receive negative feedback.[21] (To learn how to give feedback effectively, see *Developing Your Interpersonal Skills—Providing Feedback* on pages 506–507.)

Methods of Control

▶ ▶ ▶ Everyone seems to agree that John Lau, president and CEO of Husky Energy, is a difficult and demanding boss.[22] He represents the Li family's interests in the company, and the Li family "favours a top down, autocratic environment, crammed with checks and balances." As one former executive of the company noted, "If you want to learn manufacturing cost control, unit cost measurement, they are great at it." Lau, trained as an accountant, brought to Husky the financial models that Li uses with his own companies to control costs and improve performance. Husky gets top shareholder returns as a result, but the company is viewed as tough on its employees.

4. Describe three methods of control.

Think About It

What methods of control are available to managers? How do managers introduce controls? What impact might controls have on employees?

Ideally, every organization would like to efficiently and effectively reach its goals. Does this mean that the control systems organizations use are identical? In other words, would Matsushita, Husky Energy, and WestJet Airlines have the same types of control systems? Probably not. There are generally three approaches to designing control systems: market, bureaucratic, and clan controls.[23] (See Exhibit 17-8.)

Market Control

market control An approach to control that emphasizes the use of external market mechanisms, such as price competition and relative market share, to establish the standards used in the control system.

Market control is an approach to control that emphasizes the use of external market mechanisms, such as price competition and relative market share, to establish the standards used in the control system. Organizations that use the market control approach often have divisions that are set up as profit centres and evaluated by the percentage of total corporate profits contributed. For instance, at Japan's Matsushita, which supplies a wide range of products throughout the world, the various divisions (audiovisual and communication networks, components and devices, home appliances, and industrial equipment) are evaluated according to the profits each generates.

Bureaucratic Control

bureaucratic control An approach to control that emphasizes organizational authority and relies on administrative rules, regulations, procedures, and policies.

Another approach to control is **bureaucratic control**, which emphasizes organizational authority and relies on administrative rules, regulations, procedures, and policies. Husky Energy provides a good example of bureaucratic control. Although managers at Husky's various divisions are allowed some freedom to run their units as they see fit, they are expected to adhere closely to their budgets and stay within corporate guidelines.

Clan Control

clan control An approach to control in which employee behaviour is regulated by the shared values, norms, traditions, rituals, beliefs, and other aspects of the organization's culture.

Clan control is an approach to control in which employee behaviours are regulated by the shared values, norms, traditions, rituals, beliefs, and other aspects of the organization's culture. While market control relies on external standards and bureaucratic control is based on strict hierarchical mechanisms, clan control is dependent on the individuals and the groups in the organization (the clan) to identify appropriate and expected behaviours and performance measures. For instance, at Calgary-based WestJet Airlines, individuals are well aware of the expectations regarding appropriate work behaviour and performance standards, as the following *Management Reflection* shows.

Clan control requires careful selection and socialization of employees who will support the organization's culture.

Exhibit 17-8

Characteristics of Three Approaches to Designing Control Systems

Type of Control	Characteristics
Market	Uses external market mechanisms, such as price competition and relative market share, to establish standards used in system. Typically used by organizations whose products or services are clearly specified and distinct and that face considerable marketplace competition.
Bureaucratic	Emphasizes organizational authority. Relies on administrative and hierarchical mechanisms, such as rules, regulations, procedures, policies, standardization of activities, well-defined job descriptions, and budgets to ensure that employees exhibit appropriate behaviours and meet performance standards.
Clan	Regulates employee behaviour by the shared values, norms, traditions, rituals, beliefs, and other aspects of the organization's culture. Often used by organizations in which teams are common and technology is changing rapidly.

MANAGEMENT REFLECTION

WestJet Airlines' Employees Control Costs

Can employees be encouraged to think just like owners? WestJet Airlines' founder and former CEO, Clive Beddoe, encouraged his employees to keep costs low.[24] The airline has a much better profit margin than Air Canada and its other rivals. Beddoe introduced a generous profit-sharing plan to ensure that employees felt personally responsible for the profitability of the airline. The company's accountants insist that profit-sharing turns employees into "cost cops" looking for waste and savings. "We are one of the few companies that have to justify [to employees] its Christmas party every year," Derek Payne, vice-president of finance, boasts ruefully.

WestJet encourages teamwork and gives employees a lot of freedom to determine and carry out their day-to-day duties. There are no rigid job descriptions for positions, and employees are required to help with all tasks. Sometimes pilots are recruited to load baggage. When a plane reaches its destination, all employees onboard, even those not working the flight, are expected to prepare the plane for its next takeoff. The company saves $2.5 million annually in cleaning costs by having everyone work together. Planes get turned around much more quickly as well, usually within about a half-hour. When necessary, though, the employees have been able to do it in as little as six minutes. WestJet's profit-sharing program encourages employees to do their best because they see a clear link between their performance, the profits of the company, and their rewards. Not all companies that have profit-sharing programs provide employees with such clear links between behaviour and performance. ■

Financial and Information Controls

▶ ▶ ▶ For Husky Energy president and CEO John Lau, the bottom line is the measure of organizational performance.[25] When he started at Husky in 1991, it was not doing well financially. By 1993, it had a loss of $250 million on the books. In 2006, the company had $2.7 billion in net earnings, clearly an outstanding turnaround. Judith Romanchuk, an investment banker, notes that Lau has taken the company from "minor league player with a 'crumbling foundation' to a major producer" with holdings in both Canada and China.

Lau also measures performance by the number of barrels of oil equivalent (BOE) produced daily. When he started, Husky was producing 28 000 barrels daily. In 2006, the company produced 359 700 BOE daily. Lau has grown volume by 10 percent a year since 2004 and expected to reach 500 000 BOE daily by 2008. By 2020, he expects the company will extract half a million BOEs daily from the Alberta oil sands alone.

5. Understand how financial and information controls help managers monitor performance.

Think About It

How can managers use financial and information controls to make sure that their organizations are performing well?

One of the primary purposes of every business firm is to earn a profit. To achieve this goal, managers need financial controls and accurate information. Managers might, for instance, carefully analyze quarterly income statements for excessive expenses. They might also perform several financial ratio tests to ensure that sufficient cash is available to pay ongoing expenses, that debt levels have not risen too high, or that assets are being used productively. Or they might look at some newer financial control tools such as EVA (economic value added) to see if the company is creating economic value. Managers can control information and use it to control other organizational activities.

Traditional Financial Control Measures

Traditional financial control measures include ratio analysis and budget analysis. Exhibit 17-9 summarizes some of the most popular financial ratios used in organizations. Liquidity ratios measure an organization's ability to meet its current debt obligations. Leverage ratios examine the organization's use of debt to finance its assets and whether it's able to meet the interest payments on the debt. Activity ratios assess how efficiently the firm is using its assets. Finally, profitability ratios measure how efficiently and effectively the firm is using its assets to generate profits.

These ratios are calculated using information from the organization's two primary financial statements (the balance sheet and the income statement); they compare two figures and express them as a percentage or ratio. Because you have undoubtedly discussed these ratios in introductory accounting and finance courses, or you will in the near future, we are not going to elaborate on how they are calculated. Instead, we mention these ratios only briefly here to remind you that managers use such ratios as internal control devices for monitoring how efficiently and profitably the organization uses its assets, debt, inventories, and the like.

We discussed budgets as a planning tool in Chapter 9. When a budget is formulated, it's a planning tool because it gives direction to work activities. It indicates what activities are important and how much in resources should be allocated to each activity. But budgets are also used for controlling.

Budgets provide managers with quantitative standards against which to measure and compare resource consumption. By pointing out deviations between standard and actual

Exhibit 17-9

Popular Financial Ratios

Objective	Ratio	Calculation	Meaning
Liquidity	Current ratio	$\dfrac{\text{Current assets}}{\text{Current liabilities}}$	Tests the organization's ability to meet short-term obligations
	Acid test	$\dfrac{\text{Current assets less inventories}}{\text{Current liabilities}}$	Tests liquidity more accurately when inventories turn over slowly or are difficult to sell
Leverage	Debt to assets	$\dfrac{\text{Total debt}}{\text{Total assets}}$	The higher the ratio, the more leveraged the organization
	Times interest earned	$\dfrac{\text{Profits before interest and taxes}}{\text{Total interest charges}}$	Measures how far profits can decline before the organization is unable to meet its interest expenses
Activity	Inventory turnover	$\dfrac{\text{Sales}}{\text{Inventory}}$	The higher the ratio, the more efficiently inventory assets are being used
	Total asset turnover	$\dfrac{\text{Sales}}{\text{Total assets}}$	The fewer assets used to achieve a given level of sales, the more efficiently management is using the organization's total assets
Profitability	Profit margin on sales	$\dfrac{\text{Net profit after taxes}}{\text{Total sales}}$	Identifies the profits that various products are generating
	Return on investment	$\dfrac{\text{Net profit after taxes}}{\text{Total assets}}$	Measures the efficiency of assets to generate profits

consumption, they become control tools. If the deviations are judged to be significant enough to require action, the manager will want to examine what has happened and try to uncover the reasons behind the deviations. With this information, he or she can take whatever action is necessary. For example, if you use a personal budget for monitoring and controlling your monthly expenses, you might find one month that your miscellaneous expenses were higher than you had budgeted. At that point, you might cut back spending in another area or work extra hours to try to get more income.

Other Financial Control Measures

In addition to the traditional financial tools, managers are using measures such as EVA (economic value added) and MVA (market value added). The fundamental concept behind these financial tools is that companies are supposed to take in capital from investors and make it worth more. When managers do that, they have created wealth. When they take in capital and make it worth less, they have destroyed wealth.

Economic value added (EVA) is a tool that measures corporate and divisional performance. It's calculated by taking after-tax operating profit minus the total annual cost of capital.[26] EVA is a measure of how much economic value is being created by what a company does with its assets, less any capital investments the company has made in its assets. As a performance control tool, EVA focuses managers' attention on earning a rate of return over and above the cost of capital. About 30 percent of Canadian companies use EVA, including Montreal-based Rio Tinto Alcan; Montreal-based Domtar; Markham, Ontario-based Robin Hood Multifoods; and Montreal-based cable company Cogeco.[27] When EVA is used as a performance measure, employees soon learn that they can improve their organization's or business unit's EVA either by using less capital (that is, figuring out how to spend less) or by investing capital in high-return projects (that is, projects that will bring in more money, with fewer expenses). Former Molson CEO Daniel O'Neill was well rewarded for EVA improvement to the company in 2002. He "closed several breweries, laid off hundreds of staff and slashed overhead costs, using the savings to modernize remaining breweries," all of which sent Molson shares soaring. O'Neill received a $2.4 million bonus for his efforts.[28]

Market value added (MVA) adds a market dimension since it is a tool that measures the stock market's estimate of the value of a firm's past and expected capital investment projects. If the company's market value (value of all outstanding stock plus company's debt) is greater than all the capital invested in it (from shareholders, bondholders, and retained earnings), it has a positive MVA, indicating that managers have created wealth. If the company's market value is less than all the capital invested in it, the MVA will be negative, indicating that managers have destroyed wealth. Studies have shown that EVA is a predictor of MVA and that consecutive years of positive EVA generally lead to a high MVA.[29]

To understand that EVA and MVA measure different things, let's consider three companies that had the highest MVA in the United States in 2006 and the amount of wealth they created for their shareholders (in US dollars): General Electric ($281 billion), Exxon Mobil ($223 billion), and Microsoft ($221 billion). While these three companies had relatively similar MVA, they had very different real profits (measured by EVA). Exxon Mobil had the highest EVA ($28.9 billion), followed by Microsoft ($9.1 billion), and then GE ($8.2 billion). Microsoft, with a lower MVA than General Electric, delivered a higher EVA.[30]

Information Controls

Gordon Bobbitt found hundreds of phone records from Rogers littering the streets of Toronto in April 2007. These records contained contact information, financial details, and, in some cases, social insurance numbers. This case was just one instance of consumer records that were not handled properly. Earlier in 2007, CIBC and retailer TJX Companies (operator of Winners and Home Sense) had breaches of security with consumer data. In 2006, the RCMP processed about 7800 cases of identity theft, which represented $16.3 million in individual losses.[31]

economic value added (EVA)
A financial tool that measures corporate and divisional performance, calculated by taking after-tax operating profit minus the total annual cost of capital.

market value added (MVA) A financial tool that measures the stock market's estimate of the value of a firm's past and expected capital investment projects.

MyManagementLab
Q&A 17.8

There are two ways to view information controls: (1) as a tool to help managers control other organizational activities and (2) as an organizational area that managers need to control. Let's look first at information as a control tool.

How Is Information Used in Controlling?

Information is critical to monitoring and measuring an organization's activities and performance. Managers need the right information at the right time and in the right amount. Without information, they would find it difficult to measure, compare, and take action as part of the controlling process. Inaccurate, incomplete, excessive, or delayed information will seriously impede performance.

For instance, in measuring actual performance, managers need information about what is, in fact, happening within their area of responsibility and what the standards are in order to be able to compare actual performance with the standard and to help them determine acceptable ranges of variation within these comparisons. And they rely on information to help them develop appropriate courses of action if there are or are not significant deviations between actual and standard. Information can also be used to control costs, as the following *Management Reflection* shows.

MANAGEMENT REFLECTION

Air Canada Improves Maintenance Procedures

How can wireless technology make maintenance more efficient? Air Canada's former vice-president of IT and CIO, Alice Keung, found that maintenance costs at Air Canada were skyrocketing because line maintenance (unscheduled repairs to a plane's equipment, instruments, or body) was not handled very effectively.[32] In particular, pilots or mechanics would send a note to the Toronto maintenance facility by teletype or fax or put a note in the plane's log, noting a repair issue. Mechanics often would not get these notes, or the plane would arrive but the mechanic would not have the necessary parts to perform a quick maintenance procedure.

Keung realized that maintenance procedures could be significantly streamlined if mechanics had easy and immediate access to information about repairs that needed to be made, as well as maintenance manuals and diagrams. Mechanics were given tablet-sized display screens mounted on their trucks and connected to a wireless local area network. This made the information easily available, and the display was large enough to show maintenance diagrams when needed.

The technology significantly improved maintenance productivity. Mechanics spent less time travelling back and forth to the hangar to get additional parts, since they could determine what they needed more quickly. Mechanics could also make sure that parts were waiting when planes landed, so simple repairs could be performed without delaying flights. "That all has a bottom-line impact," Keung says. ■

As you can see, information is an important tool in monitoring and measuring organizational performance. Most of the information tools that managers use arise out of the organization's management information system.

Although there is no universally agreed-upon definition of a **management information system (MIS)**, we will define it as a system used to provide management with needed information on a regular basis. In theory, this system can be manual or computer-based, although all current discussions focus on computer-supported applications. The term *system* in MIS implies order, arrangement, and purpose. Further, an MIS focuses specifically on providing managers with *information,* not merely *data.* These two points are important and require elaboration. A **decision support system (DSS),** a subset of the management information system, is a computer-based information system that provides decision makers with information relevant to the decisions they are making.

management information system (MIS) A system used to provide management with needed information on a regular basis.

decision support system (DSS) A computer-based information system that provides decision makers with information relevant to the decisions they are making.

A library provides a good analogy. Although it can contain millions of volumes, a library does not do users much good if they cannot find what they want quickly. That is why librarians spend a great deal of time cataloguing a library's collections and ensuring that materials are returned to their proper locations. Organizations today are like well-stocked libraries. There is no lack of data. There is, however, an inability to process that data so that the right information is available to the right person when he or she needs it. Likewise, a library is almost useless if it has the book you need immediately, but either you cannot find it or the library takes a week to retrieve it from storage. An MIS, on the other hand, has organized data in some meaningful way and can access the information in a reasonable amount of time. **Data** are raw, unanalyzed facts, such as numbers, names, or quantities. Raw, unanalyzed facts are relatively useless to managers. When data are analyzed and processed, they become **information**. An MIS collects data and turns them into relevant information for managers to use.

data Raw, unanalyzed facts.

information Processed and analyzed data.

Controlling Information

As critically important as an organization's information is to everything it does, managers must have comprehensive and secure controls in place to protect that information. Such controls can range from data encryption to system firewalls to data backups and other techniques.[33] Problems can lurk in places that an organization might not even have considered, like search engines. Sensitive, defamatory, confidential, or embarrassing organizational information has found its way into search engine results. For instance, detailed monthly expenses and employee salaries on the National Speleological Society's website turned up in a Google search.[34] Laptop computers are also proving to be a weak link in an organization's data security. For instance, Boston-based mutual fund company Fidelity Investments disclosed that a stolen laptop had the personal information of almost 200 000 current and former Hewlett-Packard employees.[35] Even RFID (radio frequency identification) tags, now being used by more and more organizations to track and control products, may be vulnerable to computer viruses.[36] Needless to say, whatever information controls are used must be monitored regularly to ensure that all possible precautions are in place to protect the organization's important information.

Current Issues in Control

▶ ▶ ▶ Husky Energy, like all public organizations, has a board of directors that looks after the interests of shareholders.[37] In recent years, corporate governance has come under scrutiny because of corporate scandals. Many boards were not overseeing management as well as they might have.

Husky has strengthened its board policies in recent years. The primary duty of Husky's board is to "approve, monitor and provide guidance on the strategic planning process." While the president and CEO and senior management team create the strategic plan, the board has to review and approve it. The board's role also includes identifying the principal risks of Husky's business and managing and monitoring these risks, as well as approving Husky's strategic plans, annual budget, and financial plans.

6. Discuss contemporary issues in control.

Think About It

Why has corporate governance become so important in recent years? What are the advantages of having a strong corporate board? Would there be any disadvantages?

The employees of Tempe, Arizona-based Integrated Information Systems thought there was nothing wrong with exchanging copyrighted digital music over a dedicated office server they had set up. Like office betting on college basketball games, it was technically illegal but harmless, or so they thought. But after the company had to pay a $1.3 million (US) settlement to the Recording Industry Association of America, managers wished they had controlled the situation better.[38]

Control is an important managerial function. What types of control issues do today's managers face? We look at five: balanced scorecard, corporate governance, cross-cultural differences, workplace concerns, and customer interactions.

Balanced Scorecard

The balanced scorecard approach to performance measurement was introduced as a way to evaluate organizational performance from more than just the financial perspective.[39] The **balanced scorecard** is a performance measurement tool that examines four areas—financial, customer, internal business process, and learning/growth assets—that contribute to a company's performance. Exhibit 17-10 illustrates how the balanced scorecard is measured. The financial area looks at activities that improve the short- and long-term performance of the organization. The customer area looks at the customer's view of the organization, whether customers return, and whether they are satisfied. The internal business process looks at how production and operations, such as order fulfillment, are carried out. The learning and growth area looks at how well the company's employees are being managed for the company's future.

According to this approach, managers should develop goals in each of the four areas and then measure to determine if these goals are being met. For instance, a company might include cash flow, quarterly sales growth, and return on investment (ROI) as measures for success in the financial area. It might include percentage of sales coming from new products as a measure of customer goals. It might include dollars spent toward training or number of courses taken by employees as a measure of learning and growth. The intent of the balanced scorecard is to emphasize that all of these areas are important to an organization's success and that there should be a balance among them.

balanced scorecard A performance measurement tool that looks at four areas—financial, customer, internal business process, and learning and growth assets—that contribute to a company's performance.

MyManagementLab
Q&A 17.9

Exhibit 17-10

The Balanced Scorecard

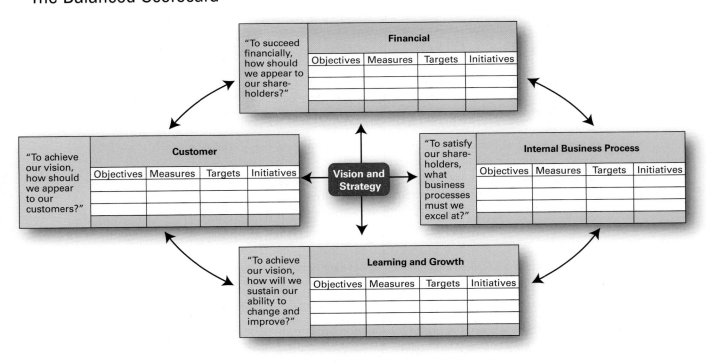

Source: R. S. Kaplan and D. P. Norton, "Using the Balanced Scorecard as a Strategic Management System," *Harvard Business Review* 74, no. 1 (January–February 1996), pp. 75–85.

Although a balanced scorecard makes sense, managers still tend to focus on areas that drive their organization's success.[40] Their scorecards reflect their strategies. If those strategies centre on the customer, for example, then the customer area is likely to get more attention than the other three areas. Yet you really cannot focus on measuring only one performance area because, ultimately, other performance areas will be affected.

Many companies are starting to use the balanced scorecard as a control mechanism, including Bell Canada, British Airways, and Hilton Hotels. In 2003, the Ontario Hospital Association developed a scorecard for 89 hospitals, designed to evaluate four main areas: clinical use and outcomes, financial performance and financial condition of the hospital, patient satisfaction, and how the hospital was investing for the future. The scorecard was purposefully designed to recognize the synergies among each of these measures. After hospitals were evaluated on the scorecard measures, the results of the scorecard evaluations were made available to patients, giving them an objective basis for choosing a hospital. The association provided the reports for every year up until 2007, except 2004, on its website.[41]

Corporate Governance

Although Andrew Fastow, Enron's former chief financial officer, had an engaging and persuasive personality, that still does not explain why Enron's board of directors failed to raise even minimal concerns about management's questionable accounting practices. The board even allowed Fastow to set up off-balance-sheet partnerships for his own profit at the expense of Enron's shareholders.

Corporate governance, the system used to govern a corporation so that the interests of corporate owners are protected, failed abysmally at Enron, as it did at many of the other companies caught in recent financial scandals. In the aftermath of these scandals, there have been increased calls for better corporate governance. Two areas in which corporate governance is being reformed are the role of boards of directors and financial reporting. The concern over corporate governance exists in Canada and globally.[42] For example, 75 percent of senior executives at US and Western European corporations expect their boards of directors to take a more active role in improving corporate governance.[43]

corporate governance The system used to govern a corporation so that the interests of corporate owners are protected.

The Role of Boards of Directors

The original purpose of a board of directors was to have a group, independent from management, looking out for the interests of shareholders who, because of the corporate structure, were not involved in the day-to-day management of the organization. However, it has not always worked that way in practice. Board members often enjoy a cozy relationship with managers in which board members "take care" of the CEO and the CEO "takes care" of the board members.

This quid pro quo arrangement is changing. In the United States, since the passage of the Sarbanes-Oxley Act in 2002, demands on board members of publicly traded companies have increased considerably.[44] The Canadian Securities Administrators rules, which came into effect in March 2004, strive to tighten board responsibility somewhat, though these rules are not as stringent as those developed in the United States. To help boards do their job better, researchers at the Corporate Governance Center at Kennesaw State University developed 10 governance principles for American public companies that have been endorsed by the Institute of Internal Auditors in the United States. These principles are equally relevant for Canadian public companies (see Exhibit 17-11 for a list of these principles).

Financial Reporting

In addition to expanding the role of boards of directors, the Canadian Securities Administrators rules require more financial disclosure by organizations but, unlike the Sarbanes-Oxley Act of the United States, do not require senior managers to provide a qualitative assessment of a company's internal compliance control. Still, these types of changes should lead to somewhat better information—that is, information that is more accurate and reflective of the firm's financial condition.

Exhibit 17-11

Twenty-First-Century Governance Principles for Public Companies

1. *Interaction:* Sound governance requires effective interaction among the board, management, the external auditor, and the internal auditor.

2. *Board purpose:* The board of directors should understand that its purpose is to protect the interests of the corporation's stockholders, while considering the interests of other stakeholders (for example, creditors and employees).

3. *Board responsibilities:* The board's major areas of responsibility should be monitoring the CEO, overseeing the corporation's strategy, and monitoring risks and the corporation's control system. Directors should employ healthy skepticism in meeting these responsibilities.

4. *Independence:* The major stock exchanges should define an "independent" director as one who has no professional or personal ties (either current or former) to the corporation or its management other than service as a director. The vast majority of the directors should be independent in both fact and appearance so as to promote arm's-length oversight.

5. *Expertise:* The directors should possess relevant industry, company, functional area, and governance expertise. The directors should reflect a mix of backgrounds and perspectives. All directors should receive detailed orientation and continuing education to assure they achieve and maintain the necessary level of expertise.

6. *Meetings and information:* The board should meet frequently for extended periods of time and should have access to the information and personnel it needs to perform its duties.

7. *Leadership:* The roles of board chair and CEO should be separate.

8. *Disclosure:* Proxy statements and other board communications should reflect board activities and transactions (e.g., insider trades) in a transparent and timely manner.

9. *Committees:* The nominating, compensation, and audit committees of the board should be composed only of independent directors.

10. *Internal audit:* All public companies should maintain an effective, full-time internal audit function that reports directly to the audit committee.

Source: P. D. Lapides, D. R. Hermanson, M. S. Beasley, J. V. Carcello, F. T. DeZoort, and T. L. Neal. Corporate Governance Center, Kennesaw State University, March 26, 2002.

Cross-Cultural Differences

The concepts of control that we have discussed so far are appropriate for an organization whose units are not geographically separated or culturally distinct. But what about global organizations? Will control systems be different, and what should managers know about adjusting controls for cross-cultural differences?

Methods of controlling people and work can be quite different in different countries. The differences we see in organizational control systems of global organizations are primarily in the measurement and corrective action steps of the control process. In a global corporation, managers of foreign operations tend to be less directly controlled by the home office, if for no other reason than that distance keeps managers from being able to observe work directly. Because distance creates a tendency to formalize controls, the home office of a global company often relies on extensive formal reports for control. The global company also may use the power of information technology to control work activities. For instance, the Japanese-based retailer Seven & i Holdings, which owns the 7-Eleven convenience store chain, uses automated cash registers not only to record sales and monitor inventory, but also to schedule tasks for store managers and to track managers' use of the built-in analytical graphs and forecasts. If managers don't use them enough, they are told to increase their activities.[45]

Technology's impact on control is most evident in comparisons of technologically advanced nations with those that are less technologically advanced. In countries such as Canada, the United States, Japan, Great Britain, Germany, and Australia, global managers use indirect control devices—especially computer-generated reports and analyses—in addition to standardized rules and direct supervision to ensure that work activities are going as planned. In less technologically advanced countries, managers tend to rely more on direct supervision and highly centralized decision making as means of control.

Also, constraints on what corrective actions managers can take may affect managers in foreign countries because laws in some countries do not allow managers the option of closing facilities, laying off employees, taking money out of the country, or bringing in a new management team from outside the country.

Finally, another challenge for global companies in collecting data for measurement and comparison is comparability. For instance, a company's manufacturing facility in Mexico might produce the same products as a facility in Scotland. However, the Mexican facility might be much more labour intensive than its Scottish counterpart (to take strategic advantage of lower labour costs in Mexico). If the top-level executives were to control costs by, for example, calculating labour costs per unit or output per employee, the figures would not be comparable. Global managers must address these types of control challenges.

Workplace Concerns

Today's workplace presents considerable control challenges for managers. From monitoring employees' computer use at work to protecting the workplace from disgruntled employees, managers must control the workplace to ensure that the organization's work can be carried out efficiently and effectively as planned. In this section, we look at two major workplace concerns: workplace privacy and employee theft.

Workplace Privacy

Do you think it is right for your employer to monitor your email and web surfing at work?

If you work, do you think you have a right to privacy at your workplace? What can your employer find out about you and your work? You might be surprised by the answers!

Employers can (and do), among other things, read your email (even those marked "personal" or "confidential"), tap your telephone, monitor your work by computer, store and review computer files, and monitor you in an employee washroom or dressing room. And these actions are not all that uncommon. Nearly 57 percent of Canadian companies have Internet-use policies restricting employees' personal use of the Internet.[46] Employees of the City of Vancouver are warned that their computer use is monitored, and a desktop agent icon of a spinning head reminds them that they are being watched. Exhibit 17-12 summarizes the percentage of employers engaging in different forms of workplace monitoring.

Why do managers feel they must monitor what employees are doing? A big reason is that employees are hired to work, not to surf the web checking stock prices, placing bets

Exhibit 17-12

Types of Workplace Monitoring by Employers

Internet use	54.7%
Telephone use	44.0%
Email messages	38.1%
Computer files	30.8%
Job performance using video cameras	14.6%
Phone conversations	11.5%
Voice mail messages	6.8%

Source: Based on S. McElvoy, "E-Mail and Internet Monitoring and the Workplace: Do Employees Have a Right to Privacy?" *Communications and the Law,* June 2002, p. 69.

at online casinos, or shopping for presents for family or friends. A 2003 Ipsos Reid poll found Canadians spend 1.6 billion hours a year online at work for personal reasons, an average of 4.5 hours a week per employee. The amount of personal time has doubled from 2000.[47] That is a significant cost to businesses.

Another reason that managers monitor employee email and computer use is that they don't want to risk being sued for creating a hostile workplace environment because of offensive messages or an inappropriate image displayed on a co-worker's computer screen. Concern about racial or sexual harassment is one of the reasons why companies might want to monitor or keep backup copies of all email. This electronic record can help establish what actually happened and can help managers react quickly.[48]

Finally, managers want to ensure that company secrets are not being leaked.[49] Although protecting intellectual property is important for all businesses, it's especially important in high-tech industries. Managers need to be certain that employees are not, even inadvertently, passing information on to others who could use that information to harm the company.

Even with the workplace monitoring that managers can do, Canadian employees do have some protection through the Criminal Code, which prohibits unauthorized interception of electronic communication. The Personal Information Protection and Electronic Documents Act, which went into effect in early 2004, gives employees some privacy protection, but it does not make workplace electronic monitoring illegal. Under existing laws, if an individual is aware of a corporate policy of surveillance and does not formally object, or remains at the job, the monitoring is acceptable.[50] Unionized employees may have a bit more privacy with respect to their computers. The Canada Labour Code requires employers operating under a collective agreement to disclose information about plans for technological change. This might provide unions with an opportunity to bargain over electronic surveillance.

Because of the potentially serious costs, and given the fact that many jobs now entail work that involves using a computer, many companies are developing and enforcing workplace monitoring policies. The responsibility for this falls on managers. It's important to develop some type of viable workplace monitoring policy. What can managers do to maintain control but do so in a way that is not demeaning to employees? They should develop a clear and unambiguous computer-use policy and make sure that every employee knows about it. For instance, managers should tell employees upfront that their computer use may be monitored at any time and provide clear and specific guidelines as to what constitutes acceptable use of company email systems and the web. The Bank of Montreal, for example, blocks access to "some of the dubious sites that are high risk," such as Playboy.com and other pornographic sites. The bank has developed policies about appropriate and inappropriate use of the Internet, which are emailed to all employees several times a year.[51]

Employee Theft

Would you be surprised to find out that up to 75 percent of Canadian organizations have reported experiencing employee theft and fraud?[52] It's a costly problem—Air Canada, which has run a campaign against employee theft, noted that the airline "is right in line with industry standards for employee theft, and that means as much as 9 per cent of stock such as office supplies and on-board products is taken each year."[53] Employee theft cost Canadian retail businesses more than $3 billion in 2008.[54]

employee theft Any unauthorized taking of company property by employees for their personal use.

Employee theft is defined as any unauthorized taking of company property by employees for their personal use.[55] It can range from embezzlement to fraudulent filing of expense reports to removing equipment, parts, software, and office supplies from company premises. While retail businesses have long faced serious potential losses from employee theft, loose financial controls at start-ups and small companies and the ready availability of information technology have made employee stealing an escalating problem in all kinds and sizes of organizations. It's a control issue that managers need to educate themselves about and that they must be prepared to deal with.[56]

Why do employees steal? The answer depends on whom you ask.[57] Experts in various fields—industrial security, criminology, clinical psychology—all have different perspectives. Industrial security people propose that people steal because the opportunity presents itself through lax controls and favourable circumstances. Criminologists say that it's because people have financial pressures (such as personal financial problems) or vice-based pressures (such as gambling debts). Clinical psychologists suggest that people steal because they can rationalize whatever they are doing as correct and appropriate behaviour ("everyone does it," "they had it coming," "this company makes enough money and they will never miss anything this small," "I deserve this for all that I put up with," and so forth).[58] Although each of these approaches provides compelling insights into employee theft and has been instrumental in program designs to deter it, unfortunately employees continue to steal.

What can managers do to deter or reduce employee theft or fraud? We can use the concepts of feedforward, concurrent, and feedback controls to identify actions managers can take.[59] Exhibit 17-13 summarizes several possible control measures.

Customer Interactions

Every month, every local branch of Enterprise Rent-a-Car conducts telephone surveys with customers.[60] Each branch earns a ranking based on the percentage of its customers who say they were "completely satisfied" with their last Enterprise experience—a level of satisfaction referred to as "top box." Top box performance is important to Enterprise because completely satisfied customers are far more likely to be repeat customers. And by using this service-quality index measure, employees' careers and financial aspirations are linked with the organizational goal of providing consistently superior service to each and every customer. Managers at Enterprise understand the connection between employees and customers and the importance of controlling these interactions.

There is probably no better area to see the link between planning and controlling than in customer service. If a company proclaims customer service as one of its goals, it quickly and clearly becomes apparent whether or not that goal is being achieved by seeing how satisfied customers are with their service. How can managers control the interactions between the goal and the outcome when it comes to customers? The concept of a service profit chain can help (see Exhibit 17-14).

Exhibit 17-13

Control Measures for Deterring or Reducing Employee Theft or Fraud

Feedforward	Concurrent	Feedback
Use careful prehiring screening.	Treat employees with respect and dignity.	Make sure employees know when theft or fraud has occurred—not naming names but letting people know this is not acceptable.
Establish specific policies defining theft and fraud and discipline procedures.	Openly communicate the costs of stealing.	
Involve employees in writing policies.	Let employees know on a regular basis about their successes in preventing theft and fraud.	Use the services of professional investigators.
Educate and train employees about the policies.	Use video surveillance equipment if conditions warrant.	Redesign control measures.
Have professionals review your internal security controls.	Install "lock-out" options on computers, telephones, and email.	Evaluate your organization's culture and the relationships of managers and employees.
	Use corporate hotlines for reporting incidents.	
	Set a good example.	

Sources: Based on A. H. Bell and D. M. Smith, "Protecting the Company Against Theft and Fraud," *Workforce Online*, December 3, 2000, www.workforce.com; J. D. Hansen, "To Catch a Thief," *Journal of Accountancy*, March 2000, pp. 43–46; and J. Greenberg, "The Cognitive Geometry of Employee Theft," in *Dysfunctional Behavior in Organizations: Nonviolent and Deviant Behavior*, eds. S. B. Bacharach, A. O'Leary-Kelly, J. M. Collins, and R. W. Griffin, pp. 147–193 (Stamford, CT: JAI Press, 1998).

Exhibit 17-14

The Service Profit Chain

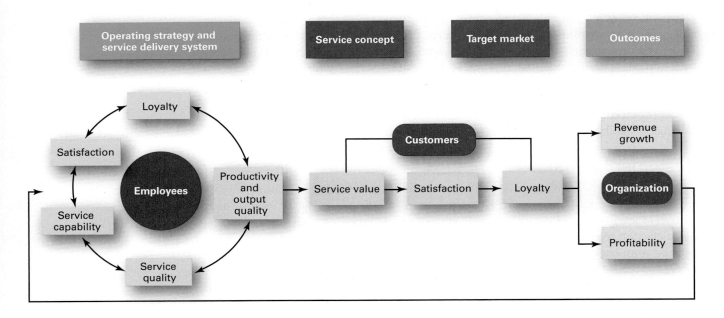

Sources: Adapted and reprinted by permission of *Harvard Business Review*. An exhibit from J. L. Heskett, T. O. Jones, G. W. Loveman, W. E. Sasser Jr., and L. A. Schlesinger, "Putting the Service Profit Chain to Work," *Harvard Business Review*, March–April 1994, p. 166. Copyright by the President and Fellows of Harvard College. All rights reserved. See also J. L. Heskett, W. E. Sasser, and L. A. Schlesinger, *The Service Profit Chain* (New York: Free Press, 1997).

---

service profit chain The service sequence from employees to customers to profit.

The **service profit chain** is the service sequence from employees to customers to profit.[61] According to this concept, the company's strategy and service delivery system influences how employees serve customers—their attitudes, behaviours, and service capability. Service capability, in turn, enhances how productive employees are in providing service and the quality of that service. The level of employee service productivity and service quality influences customer perceptions of service value. When service value is high, it has a positive impact on customer satisfaction, which leads to customer loyalty. And customer loyalty improves organizational revenue growth and profitability.

So what does the concept of a service profit chain mean for managers? Managers who want to control customer interactions should work to create long-term and mutually beneficial relationships among the company, employees, and customers. How? By creating a work environment that not only enables employees to deliver high levels of quality service, but makes them feel they are capable of delivering top-quality service. In such a service climate, employees are motivated to deliver superior service.

There is no better example of the service profit chain in action than WestJet Airlines. WestJet is the most consistently profitable Canadian airline, and its customers are fiercely loyal. This is because the company's operating strategy (hiring, training, rewards and recognition, teamwork, and so forth) is built around customer service. Employees consistently deliver outstanding service value to customers. And WestJet's customers reward the company by coming back. It's through efficiently and effectively controlling these customer interactions that companies like WestJet and Enterprise have succeeded.

SUMMARY AND IMPLICATIONS

1. Explain the nature and importance of control. Control is the process of monitoring activities to ensure that they are being accomplished as planned and correcting any significant deviations. Managers can measure a variety of performances, but the most frequently used ones are organizational productivity, organizational effectiveness, and industry rankings.

▶ ▶ ▶ When Li Ka-shing first bought Husky Energy, he immediately introduced financial controls to improve the company's bottom line. He also hired John Lau to stop the losses and halt the expansions that previous managers had introduced. These measures were put in place to make the company profitable.

2. Describe the three steps in the control process. The control process is a three-step process: measuring actual performance, comparing actual performance against a standard, and taking managerial action to correct deviations or inadequate standards.

3. Describe tools used to measure organizational performance. Managers can implement controls before an activity begins (feedforward control), during the time the activity is going on (concurrent control), and after the activity has been completed (feedback control).

4. Describe three methods of control. There are three different approaches to designing control systems: market, bureaucratic, and clan control. Market control emphasizes the use of external market mechanisms, such as price competition and relative market share, to establish the standards used in the control system. Bureaucratic control emphasizes organizational authority and relies on administrative rules, regulations, procedures, and policies. Under clan control, employee behaviours are regulated by the shared values, norms, traditions, rituals, beliefs, and other aspects of the organization's culture.

▶ ▶ ▶ Control is often needed to improve organizational performance, as John Lau found when he took over Husky Energy and had to halt the company's large losses and the "wild expansions" of the company's previous management.

5. Understand how financial and information controls help managers monitor performance. One of the primary purposes of every business firm is to earn a profit. To achieve this goal, managers need financial controls and accurate information. Managers can use financial and information controls to monitor performance. Traditional financial control measures include ratio analysis and budget analysis. There are two ways to view information controls: (1) as a tool to help managers control other organizational activities and (2) as an organizational area that managers need to control.

▶ ▶ ▶ At Husky Energy, John Lau uses traditional financial controls, as well as other measures, including the number of barrels of oil equivalent (BOE) produced by the company daily.

6. Discuss contemporary issues in control. Some important current issues in control include the balanced scorecard (looking at financial, customer, internal business process, and learning and growth assets), corporate governance, cross-cultural differences, workplace concerns, and customer interactions.

▶ ▶ ▶ Husky Energy has a board of directors that looks after the interests of shareholders. The primary duty of Husky's board is to "approve, monitor and provide guidance on the strategic planning process." The board also approves Husky's strategic plans, annual budget, and financial plans.

Management @ Work

READING FOR COMPREHENSION

1. What is the role of control in management?

2. Name four sources managers can use to acquire information about actual organizational performance.

3. What are three approaches to designing control systems?

4. Contrast immediate and basic corrective action.

5. What can management do to implement a benchmarking best-practices program?

6. What are the advantages and disadvantages of feedforward control?

7. Describe the financial control measures managers can use.

8. What challenges do managers of global organizations face with their control systems?

LINKING CONCEPTS TO PRACTICE

1. What would an organization have to do to change its dominant control approach from bureaucratic to clan? From clan to bureaucratic?

2. How could you use the concept of control in your own personal life? Be specific. (Think in terms of feedforward, concurrent, and feedback controls, as well as controls for the different areas of your life.)

3. When do electronic surveillance devices such as computers, video cameras, and telephone monitoring step over the line from "effective management controls" to "intrusions on employee rights"?

4. "Every individual employee in the organization plays a role in controlling work activities." Do you agree, or do you think control is something that only managers are responsible for? Explain.

5. Why do you think feedback control is the most popular type of control? Justify your response.

SELF-ASSESSMENT

How Proactive Am I?

For each of the following statements, circle the level of agreement or disagreement that you personally feel:[62]

1 = Strongly Disagree   4 = Neither Agree nor Disagree   7 = Strongly Agree

1. I am constantly on the lookout for new ways to improve my life.   1 2 3 4 5 6 7

2. I feel driven to make a difference in my community and maybe the world.   1 2 3 4 5 6 7

3. I tend to let others take the initiative to start new projects.   1 2 3 4 5 6 7

4. Wherever I have been, I have been a powerful force for constructive change.   1 2 3 4 5 6 7

5. I enjoy facing and overcoming obstacles to my ideas.   1 2 3 4 5 6 7

6. Nothing is more exciting than seeing my ideas turn into reality.   1 2 3 4 5 6 7

7. If I see something I don't like, I fix it.   1 2 3 4 5 6 7

8. No matter what the odds, if I believe in something I will make it happen.   1 2 3 4 5 6 7

9. I love being a champion for my ideas, even against others' opposition.   1 2 3 4 5 6 7

10. I excel at identifying opportunities.   1 2 3 4 5 6 7

11. I am always looking for better ways to do things.   1 2 3 4 5 6 7

12. If I believe in an idea, no obstacle will prevent me from making it happen.   1 2 3 4 5 6 7

13. I love to challenge the status quo.   1 2 3 4 5 6 7

14. When I have a problem, I tackle it head-on.   1 2 3 4 5 6 7

15. I am great at turning problems into opportunities.   1 2 3 4 5 6 7

16. I can spot a good opportunity long before others can.   1 2 3 4 5 6 7

17. If I see someone in trouble, I help out in any way I can.   1 2 3 4 5 6 7

Scoring Key

Add up the numbers for each of your responses to get your total score.

Analysis and Interpretation

This instrument assesses proactive personality. Research finds that the proactive personality is positively associated with entrepreneurial intentions.

Your proactive personality score will range between 17 and 149. The higher your score, the stronger your proactive personality. High scores on this questionnaire suggest you have strong inclinations toward becoming an entrepreneur.

More Self-Assessments MyManagementLab

To learn more about your skills, abilities, and interests, go to the MyManagementLab website and take the following self-assessments:

- I.E.2.—What Time of Day Am I Most Productive?
- II.B.5.—How Good Am I at Disciplining Others?
- III.A.2.—How Willing Am I to Delegate?
- III.A.3.—How Good Am I at Giving Performance Feedback? (This exercise also appears in Chapter 12 on pages 347–348.)

MANAGEMENT FOR YOU TODAY

Dilemma

Your parents have let you know that they are expecting a big party for their 25th wedding anniversary and that you are in charge of planning it. Develop a timeline for carrying out the project and then identify ways to monitor progress toward getting the party planned. How will you know that your plans have been successful? At what critical points do you need to examine your plans to make sure that everything is on track?

Becoming a Manager

- Identify the types of controls you use in your own personal life and whether they are feedforward, concurrent, or feedback controls.
- When preparing for major class projects, identify some performance measures that you can use to help you determine whether or not the project is going as planned.
- Try to come up with some ways to improve your personal efficiency and effectiveness.

WORKING TOGETHER: TEAM-BASED EXERCISE

Controlling Cheating

You are a professor in the School of Business at a local university. Several of your colleagues have expressed an interest in developing some specific controls to minimize opportunities for students to cheat on homework assignments and exams. You and some other faculty members have volunteered to write a report outlining some suggestions that might be used.

Form teams of three or four and discuss this topic. Write a bulleted list of your suggestions from the perspective of controlling possible cheating (1) before it happens, (2) while in-class exams or assignments are being completed, and (3) after it has happened. Please keep the report brief (no more than two pages). Be prepared to present your suggestions before the rest of the class.

Ethical Dilemma Exercise: Should Surfing Adult Websites on a Personal Laptop at Work Be Considered Private?

Pornography and offensive email are two major reasons why many companies establish strict policies and monitor their employees' use of the Internet.[63] Citing legal and ethical concerns, managers are determined to keep inappropriate images and messages out of the workplace. "As a company, if we don't make some effort to keep offensive material off our network, we could end up on the wrong end of a sexual harassment lawsuit or other legal action that could cost the company hundreds of thousands of dollars," says the technology manager at one small business. "To a company our size, that would be devastating." Another reason is cost. Unauthorized Internet activity not only wastes valuable work time but ties up network resources. Thus, many companies have installed electronic systems to screen email messages and monitor what employees do online. In some companies, one person is designated to review incoming emails and delete offensive messages.

Having a clear policy and a monitoring system are only first steps. Management must be sure that employees are aware of the rules—and understand that the company is serious about cleaning up any ethics violations. British Telecom (BT), for example, twice sent emails to remind all its employees that looking at online pornography was grounds for dismissal. Despite the warnings, management had to fire 200 employees in an 18-month period. Going further, the company told police about 10 employees' activities, and one has already been sentenced to prison. "We took this decision for the good of BT," explained a spokesperson, "and since we have taken this action, the problem has reduced dramatically."

Imagine that you are the administrative assistant for a high-ranking executive at BT. One afternoon you receive an urgent phone call for your manager. You knock on his office door but get no answer, so you open the door, thinking you will leave a note on his desk. Then you notice that your manager is absorbed in watching a very graphic adult website on his personal laptop. As you quietly back out of the office, you wonder how to handle this situation. Review the section *Workplace Privacy* on pages 497–498 as you consider this ethical challenge.

Thinking Critically About Ethics

Duplicating software for co-workers and friends is a widespread practice, but software in Canada is protected by copyright laws. Copying software is punishable by fines of up to $20 000. Businesses can be held accountable if their employees use unlicensed software on company computers.

Is reproducing copyrighted software ever an acceptable practice? Explain. Is it wrong for employees of a business to pirate software but permissible for struggling students who cannot afford to buy their own software? As a manager, what types of ethical guidelines could you establish for software use? What if you were a manager in another country where software piracy was an accepted practice?

Baggage Blunders

Terminal 5, built by British Airways for $8.6 billion (US), is Heathrow Airport's newest state-of-the-art facility. Made of glass, concrete, and steel, it's the largest freestanding building in the United Kingdom and has over 15 kilometres of belts for moving luggage. At the terminal's unveiling on March 15, 2008, Queen Elizabeth II called it a "twenty-first-century gateway to Britain." Alas . . . the accolades didn't last long! After two decades of planning and 100 million hours of labour, opening day didn't work out as planned.

Endless lines and severe baggage-handling delays led to numerous flight cancellations, stranding many irate passengers. Airport operators said the problems were triggered by glitches in the terminal's high-tech baggage-handling system.

With its massive automation features, Terminal 5 was planned to ease congestion at Heathrow and improve the flying experience for the 30 million passengers expected to pass through it annually. With 96 self-service check-in kiosks, more than 90 check-in fast bag drops, 54 standard check-in desks, and over 15 kilometres of suitcase-moving belts that were supposed to be able to process 12 000 bags per hour, the facility's design didn't seem to support those goals.

Within the first few hours of the terminal's operation, problems developed. Baggage workers, presumably under-staffed, were unable to clear incoming luggage fast enough. Many arriving passengers had to wait more than an hour to get their bags. There were problems for departing passengers, as well, as many tried in vain to check in for flights. Flights were allowed to leave with empty cargo holds. At one point that first day, the airline had no choice but to check in only those with no luggage. And it didn't help matters that the moving belt system jammed at one point. Lesser problems also became apparent: a few broken escalators, some hand dryers that didn't work, a gate that wouldn't function at the new Underground station, and inexperienced ticket sellers who didn't know the fares between Heathrow and various stations on the Piccadilly line. By the end of the first full day of operation, Britain's Department of Transportation released a statement calling for British Airways and the airport operator BAA to "work hard to resolve these issues and limit disruptions to passengers."

You might be tempted to think that all this could have been prevented if British Airways had only tested the system. But thorough runs of all systems "from toilets to check-in and seating" took place six months before opening, including four full-scale test runs using 16 000 volunteers.[64]

DEVELOPING YOUR DIAGNOSTIC AND ANALYTICAL SKILLS

A Control Concern at BC Ferries

Just after midnight on March 22, 2006, the *Queen of the North* ferry, part of the BC Ferries system, hit rocks off Gil Island, south of Prince Rupert.[65] It was immediately clear that the ferry was in trouble, and within 15 minutes, "all" the passengers and crew were off the ship and in the ferry's lifeboats. As local townspeople and the Coast Guard rescued the passengers from the lifeboats, the ferry sank, a little more than an hour after first striking the rocks. Initial media reports celebrated the fact that all 99 passengers and crew had managed to get off the ferry safely, and with no major injuries. The crew was widely praised for conducting an orderly evacuation, something employees practise and train for at regular intervals.

On day two, passengers were reported missing. How could the ferry crew not know that there had still been people onboard? While international regulations require that ferries record identifying information about all passengers (name, gender, and whether they are adults, children, or infants), Ottawa does not require BC's ferry fleet to meet international standards. Transport Canada guidelines also do not require the collection of passenger names. Ferry staff do not even take a head count after loading, so the number of passengers is only roughly determined by the number of tickets sold. Moreover, there is no system in place to count passengers as they move from the ship to lifeboats, should such a situation arise. Thus, the initial reports from BC Ferries that "all 99" passengers and crew survived were based on the simple belief that everyone had been evacuated.

In the days following the sinking, demands for explanations of what had gone wrong arose. Jackie Miller, president of the BC Ferry and Marine Workers Union, which represented the ferry employees, called for a public inquiry into safety issues of the entire ferry fleet, citing another ferry sinking and an engine room fire in recent years. "We have grave concerns," Miller said. "A lot of us have been continuously worried. BC Ferries has been incredibly lucky, thank God, that we haven't had a major loss of life as a result of the three major marine incidents."

However, Rod Nelson, regional director of communications for Transport Canada, reported that the *Queen of the North* passed an annual safety inspection less than three weeks earlier, including a lifeboat drill in March that required that passengers be evacuated in less than 30 minutes. "They did very well at it, and they obviously did very well when it happened for real," Nelson said.

The internal investigation BC Ferries conducted in the months after the sinking concluded that "human factors were the primary cause" of what happened. "The ship never altered course at all. It never changed its speed, it just ran ahead into Gil Island," BC Ferries' president, David Hahn, said. There were two people on the bridge that evening (from where the ship is navigated), the acting fourth officer and the quartermaster, who had not yet written her bridge watchman's exam. The report stated that the fourth officer "failed to make a necessary course alteration or verify such alteration was made in accordance with pre-established fleet routing directives and good seamanship."

During the investigation, crew members responsible for navigating the ship that night claimed that they were unfamiliar with newly installed steering equipment. In addition, they had turned off a monitor displaying their course, because they could not turn on the night settings. The bridge crew used the equipment "in a way different than as instructed," the report noted, although this was not cited as a cause of running aground. The report also concluded that the crew maintained a "casual watch-standing behaviour," had "lost situational awareness," and "failed to appreciate the vessel's impending peril." Transcripts of radio calls that evening noted that music was heard playing on the bridge.

Regarding the evacuation, though the crew was praised for acting quickly, several things made the evacuation more difficult than need be. There was no master key to the sleeping cabins; rather, multiple keys had to be tried. A chalk X is supposed to be drawn on searched cabin doors, but no one had chalk. As well, only 53 of the 55 cabins were confirmed to have been searched.

Questions

1. Describe the type(s) of control that could be used to improve the BC Ferries service to prevent an accident such as this occurring again. Give specific examples.

2. Assume that you are the president of BC Ferries. You have read the report of the investigation and noted some of the problems found. What would you do? Explain your reasoning.

3. Would some types of controls be more important than others in this situation?

Providing Feedback

About the Skill

Ask a manager how often he or she gives feedback to employees, and you are likely to get an answer followed by a qualifier! If the feedback is positive, it's likely to be given promptly and enthusiastically. However, negative feedback is often treated very differently and often avoided. Most of us don't enjoy receiving negative feedback, and managers don't particularly enjoy communicating bad news. They fear offending the other person or having to deal with the recipient's defensiveness. The result is that negative feedback is often avoided, delayed, or substantially distorted. However, it is important for managers to provide both positive and negative feedback. It is also important during formal reviews that managers bring up the good things employees have done over the evaluation period, even if they have already commented on them informally. Employees expect managers to remember these things and to be congratulated again.[66]

Steps in Developing the Skill

You can be more effective at providing feedback if you use the following six suggestions:[67]

1. **Focus on specific behaviours.** Feedback should be specific rather than general. Avoid such statements as, "You have a bad attitude" or "I'm really impressed with the good job you did." They are vague, and although they provide information, they don't tell the recipient enough to correct the "bad attitude" or on what basis you concluded that a "good job" had been done so the person knows what behaviours to repeat or to avoid.

2. **Keep feedback impersonal.** Feedback, particularly the negative kind, should be descriptive rather than judgmental or evaluative. No matter how upset you are, keep the feedback focused on job-related behaviours and never criticize someone personally because of an inappropriate action.

3. **Keep feedback goal oriented.** Feedback should not be given primarily to "unload" on another person. If you have to say something negative, make sure it's directed toward the recipient's goals. Ask yourself whom the feedback is supposed to help. If the answer is you, bite your tongue and hold the comment. Such feedback undermines your credibility and lessens the meaning and influence of future feedback.

4. **Time feedback well.** Feedback is most meaningful to a recipient when there is a very short interval between his or her behaviour and the receipt of feedback about that behaviour. Moreover, if you are particularly concerned with changing behaviour, delays in providing feedback on the undesirable actions lessen the likelihood that the feedback will be effective in bringing about the desired change. Of course, making feedback prompt merely for the sake of promptness can backfire if you have insufficient information, if you are angry, or if you are otherwise emotionally upset. In such instances, "well timed" could mean "somewhat delayed."

5. **Ensure understanding.** Make sure your feedback is concise and complete so that the recipient clearly and fully understands your communication. It may help to have the recipient rephrase the content of your feedback to find out whether or not it fully captured the meaning you intended.

6. **Direct negative feedback toward behaviour that the recipient can control.** There is little value in reminding a person of some shortcoming over which he or she has no control. Negative feedback should be directed at behaviour that the recipient can do something about. In addition, when negative feedback is given concerning something that the recipient can control, it might be a good idea to indicate specifically what can be done to improve the situation.

Practising the Skill

Read the following scenario. Write some notes about how you would handle the situation described. Be sure to refer to the six suggestions for providing feedback.

Scenario

Craig is an excellent employee whose expertise and productivity have always met or exceeded your expectations. But recently he has been making work difficult for other members of your advertising team. Like his co-workers, Craig researches and computes the costs of media coverage for your advertising agency's clients. The work requires laboriously leafing through several large reference books to find the correct base price and add-on charges for each radio or television station and time slot, calculating each actual cost, and compiling the results in a computerized spreadsheet. To make things more efficient and convenient, you have always allowed your team members to bring the reference books they are using to their desks while they are using them. Lately, however, Craig has been piling books around him for days and sometimes weeks at a time. The books interfere with the flow of traffic past his desk and other people have to go out of their way to retrieve the books from Craig's pile. It's time for you to have a talk with Craig. What will you say?

Reinforcing the Skill

The following activities will help you practise and reinforce the skills associated with providing feedback:

1. Think of three things that a friend or family member did well recently. Did you praise the person at the time? If not, why? The next time someone close to you does something well, give him or her positive feedback.

2. You have a good friend who has a mannerism (for instance, speech, body movement, style of dress, or whatever) that you think is inappropriate and detracts from the overall impression that he or she makes. Come up with a plan for talking with this person. What will you say? When will you talk with your friend? How will you handle his or her reaction?

MyManagementLab

For more resources, please visit www.pearsoned.ca/mymanagementlab

SCAN THIS

Managing Operations

Every organization "produces" something, whether it's a good or a service. This chapter focuses on how organizations do that through a process called *operations management*. We also look at the important role that managers play in managing those operations. After reading and studying this chapter, you will achieve the following learning outcomes.

Learning Outcomes

1 Explain the role of operations management.

2 Define the nature and purpose of value chain management.

3 Describe how value chain management is done.

4 Discuss contemporary issues in managing operations.

▶ ▶ ▶ David Ritacco is CEO of Truro, Nova Scotia–based Eldis Group, which serves the do-it-yourself (DIY) market for home appliance repair.[1] The company operates a family of DIY websites, including PartSelect. According to the company website, "We provide consumers with the parts and know-how to fix their major home appliances themselves, offering the internet's largest collection of step-by-step installation instructions and videos."

After completing a master's degree in computation at Oxford, Ritacco returned to the family business in Truro in 1999 and was assigned the task of dealing with a Y2K problem with the enterprise resource planning (ERP) software package. Ritacco later led the company's foray into the e-commerce market. Following a rocky start that targeted the repairman, the company switched from a business-to-business (B2B) model to a business-to-consumer (B2C) model, selling parts directly to consumers. Customers in Canada and the United States browse the websites to determine what part they need and

place their order online. The customer pays with a credit card, and a shipping ticket is printed automatically in one of the partner fulfillment centres, where the product is picked and shipped with an Eldis company logo and documentation. Eldis Group holds no inventory and relies on automation within its websites, allow-

ing the company to maintain a small staff. PartSelect, Eldis' flagship site, has more unique visitors monthly than Amazon.ca (405 992 versus 356 992).[2] A commitment to the principles of operations management has made Eldis a major player in its industry.

Think About It

What role is operations management playing at Eldis Group? How important might the role of operations management be in a manufacturing or service business? How might David Ritacco use operations management to achieve his objectives?

SCAN THIS

The Role of Operations Management

Inside Intel's factory in New Mexico, employee Trish Roughgarden is known as a "seed"—an unofficial title for technicians who transfer manufacturing know-how from one Intel facility to another.[3] Her job is to make sure that this factory works just like an identical one that opened earlier in Oregon. When another plant opened in Ireland, several hundred other seeds copied the same techniques. The company's facility in Arizona also benefited from "seeding." What the seeds do is part of a strategy known as "Copy Exactly," which Intel implemented after frustrating variations between factories hurt productivity and product quality. In the intensely competitive chip-making industry, Intel knows that how it manages operations will determine whether it succeeds.

What is **operations management**? The term refers to the design, operation, and control of the transformation process that converts resources into finished goods and services. Exhibit 18-1 portrays this process in a very simplified fashion. The system takes in inputs—people, technology, capital, equipment, materials, and information—and transforms them through various processes, procedures, work activities, and so forth into finished goods and services. Because every unit in an organization produces something, managers need to be familiar with operations management concepts in order to achieve goals efficiently and effectively.

1. Explain the role of operations management.

operations management The design, operation, and control of the transformation process that converts resources into goods and services.

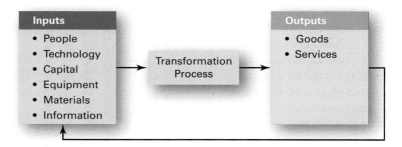

Exhibit 18-1

The Operations System

Operations management is important to organizations and managers for three reasons: It encompasses both services and manufacturing, it's important in effectively and efficiently managing productivity, and it plays a strategic role in an organization's competitive success. Let's look at each.

Services and Manufacturing

With a menu that offers over 200 items, The Cheesecake Factory restaurants rely on a finely tuned production system. One food-service consultant says, "They've evolved with this highly complex menu combined with a highly efficient kitchen."[4]

Every organization produces something. Unfortunately, this fact is often overlooked except in obvious cases, such as in the manufacturing of cars, cellphones, or lawnmowers. After all, **manufacturing organizations** produce physical goods. It's easy to see the operations management (transformation) process at work in these types of organizations because raw materials are turned into recognizable physical products. But that transformation process isn't as readily evident in **service organizations** because they produce nonphysical outputs in the form of services. For instance, hospitals provide medical and health care services that help people manage their personal health, airlines provide transportation services that move people from one location to another, cruise lines provides vacation and entertainment services, military forces provide defence capabilities, and the list goes on and on. Service organizations also transform inputs into outputs, although the transformation process isn't as easily recognizable as it is in manufacturing organizations. Take a university, for example. University administrators bring together inputs—professors, books, academic journals, technology materials, computers, classrooms, and similar resources—to transform "unenlightened" students into educated and skilled individuals who are capable of making contributions to society.

The reason we're making this point is that most of the world's developed countries are predominantly service economies. In Canada over 69 percent of all economic activity is in the services sector; in the United States, it's 78 percent.[5]

Managing Productivity

One jetliner has some 4 million parts. Efficiently assembling such a finely engineered product requires intense focus. Boeing and Airbus, the two major global manufacturers, have copied techniques from Toyota. However, not every technique can be copied because airlines demand more customization than do car buyers, and there are significantly more rigid safety regulations for jetliners than for cars.[6]

Although most organizations don't make products that have 4 million parts, improving productivity has become a major goal in virtually every organization. By **productivity**, we mean the overall output of goods or services produced divided by the inputs needed

manufacturing organizations Organizations that produce physical goods.

service organizations Organizations that produce nonphysical outputs in the form of services.

MyManagementLab
Q&A 18.1

productivity The overall output of goods or services produced divided by the inputs needed to generate that output.

to generate that output. For countries, high productivity can lead to economic growth and development. Employees can receive higher wages, and company profits can increase without causing inflation. For individual organizations, increased productivity provides a more competitive cost structure and the ability to offer more competitive prices.

MyManagementLab
Q&A 18.2

Organizations that hope to succeed globally are looking for ways to improve productivity. For example, McDonald's drastically reduced the amount of time it takes to cook its french fries—now only 65 seconds as compared with the 210 seconds it once took, saving time and other resources.[7] Toronto-based Canadian Imperial Bank of Commerce automated its purchasing function, saving several million dollars annually.[8] And [[Scaron]] koda, the Czech Republic car company owned by Germany's Volkswagen AG, improved its productivity through an intensive restructuring of its manufacturing process. The company recently produced its five-millionth car.[9]

Productivity is a composite of people and operations variables. To improve productivity, managers must focus on both. W. Edwards Deming, a management consultant and quality expert, believed that managers, not workers, were the primary source of increased productivity. He outlined 14 points for improving management's productivity (see Exhibit 18-2). A close look at these suggestions reveals Deming's understanding of the interplay between people and operations. High productivity cannot come solely from good "people management." The truly effective organization will maximize productivity by successfully integrating people into the overall operations system.

Strategic Role of Operations Management

The era of modern manufacturing originated over 100 years ago in North America, primarily in Detroit's automobile factories. The success that North American manufacturers

---

Exhibit 18-2

Deming's 14 Points for Improving Management's Productivity

1. Plan for the long-term future.

2. Never be complacent concerning the quality of your product.

3. Establish statistical control over your production processes and require your suppliers to do so as well.

4. Deal with the best and fewest number of suppliers.

5. Find out whether your problems are confined to particular parts of the production process or stem from the overall process itself.

6. Train workers for the job that you are asking them to perform.

7. Raise the quality of your line supervisors.

8. Drive out fear.

9. Encourage departments to work closely together rather than to concentrate on departmental or divisional distinctions.

10. Do not adopt strictly numerical goals.

11. Require your workers to do quality work.

12. Train your employees to understand statistical methods.

13. Train your employees in new skills as the need arises.

14. Make top managers responsible for implementing these principles.

Source: W. E. Deming, "Improvement of Quality and Productivity Through Action by Management," *National Productivity Review*, Winter 1981–1982, pp. 12–22. With permission. Copyright 1981 by Executive Enterprises, Inc., 22 West 21st St., New York, NY 10010-6904. All rights reserved.

A US citizen credited with improving production in the United States, W. Edwards Deming moved to Japan in 1950. There, he taught top management how to improve design and product quality; he is widely credited as being the force behind the innovative high-quality products that made Japan an industrial force in world markets.

experienced during World War II led manufacturing executives to believe that troublesome production problems had been conquered. These executives focused, instead, on improving other functional areas such as finance and marketing and gave manufacturing little attention.

However, as Canadian and US executives neglected production, managers in Japan, Germany, and other countries took the opportunity to develop modern, computer-based, and technologically advanced facilities that fully integrated manufacturing operations into strategic planning decisions. The competition's success realigned world manufacturing leadership. North American manufacturers soon discovered that foreign goods were being made not only less expensively but also with better quality. Finally, by the late 1970s, Canadian and American executives recognized that they were facing a true crisis, and they responded. They invested heavily in improving manufacturing technology, increased the corporate authority and visibility of manufacturing executives, and began incorporating existing and future production requirements into the organization's overall strategic plan. Today, successful organizations recognize the crucial role that operations management plays as part of the overall organizational strategy to establish and maintain global leadership.[10]

The strategic role that operations management plays in successful organizational performance can be seen clearly as more organizations move toward managing their operations from a value chain perspective, which we discuss next.

MyManagementLab
Q&A 18.3

What Is Value Chain Management, and Why Is It Important?

2. Define the nature and purpose of value chain management.

▶ ▶ ▶ Customers in Canada and the United States go to the PartSelect website, where they use the technology to determine what part they need and place their order online. The customer pays with a credit card, and a shipping ticket is printed automatically in one of the partner fulfillment centres, where the product is picked and shipped with the Eldis company logo and documentation. David Ritacco and his colleagues spend a significant amount of their time building and maintaining the relationships that support the many product lines they distribute.

Think About It

Why would a supplier want to do business with Eldis rather than sell the product themselves? Why would the customer choose Eldis rather than go directly to either the supplier or the manufacturer of the product? What are the benefits of value chain management to the supplier? To the customer? To Eldis?

It's 11 p.m., and you're reading a text message from your parents, saying they want to buy you a laptop for your birthday and that you should order it. You log on to Dell's website and configure your dream machine. You hit the order button, and within three or four days, your dream computer is delivered to your front door, built to your exact specifications, ready to set up and use immediately to write the management assignment that's due tomorrow. Or consider that Siemens AG's computed tomography manufacturing plant in Forcheim, Germany, has established partnerships with about 30 suppliers. These suppliers are partners in the truest sense as they share responsibility with the plant for overall process performance. This arrangement has allowed Siemens to eliminate all inventory warehousing and has reduced the number of times paper changes hands when parts are ordered from 18 to 1. At the Timken plant in Canton, Ohio, electronic purchase orders are sent across the street to an adjacent "Supplier City," where many of its key suppliers have set up shop. The process takes milliseconds and costs less than 50 cents per purchase order. And when Black & Decker extended its line of handheld tools to include a glue gun, it outsourced the entire design and production to the leading glue gun manufacturer. Why? Because the company understood that glue guns don't require motors, which was what Black & Decker did best.[11]

As these examples show, closely integrated work activities among many different players are possible. How? The answer lies in value chain management.

The concepts of value chain management have transformed operations management strategies and turned organizations around the world into finely tuned models of efficiency and effectiveness, strategically positioned to exploit competitive opportunities.

What Is Value Chain Management?

Every organization needs customers if it's going to survive and prosper. Even a not-for-profit organization must have "customers" who use its services or purchase its products. Customers want some type of value from the goods and services they purchase or use, and these customers decide what has value. Organizations must provide that value to attract and keep customers. **Value** is defined as the performance characteristics, features and attributes, and any other aspects of goods and services for which customers are willing to give up resources (usually money). For example, when you purchase Rihanna's new CD at Best Buy, a new pair of Australian sheepskin Ugg boots online at the company's website, a Wendy's bacon cheeseburger at the drive-through location near campus, or a haircut from your local hair salon, you're exchanging (giving up) money in return for the value you need or desire from these products—providing music during your evening study time, keeping your feet warm and fashionable during winter's cold weather, alleviating the lunchtime hunger pangs quickly since your next class starts in 15 minutes, or looking professionally groomed for the job interview you're going to next week.

How *is* value provided to customers? Through transforming raw materials and other resources into some product or service that end users need or desire when, where, and how they want it. However, that seemingly simple act of turning varied resources into something that customers value and are willing to pay for involves a vast array of interrelated work activities performed by different participants (suppliers, manufacturers, and even customers)—that is, it involves the value chain. The **value chain** is the entire series of organizational work activities that add value at each step, from raw materials to finished product. In its entirety, the value chain can encompass the supplier's suppliers to the customer's customers.[12]

Value chain management is the process of managing the sequence of activities and information along the entire value chain. In contrast to supply chain management, which

value The performance characteristics, features, and attributes, as well as any other aspects of goods and services for which customers are willing to give up resources.

MyManagementLab
Q&A 18.4

value chain The entire series of organizational work activities that add value at each step from raw materials to finished product.

value chain management The process of managing the sequence of activities and information along the entire value chain.

is *internally* oriented and focuses on efficient flow of incoming materials (resources) to the organization, value chain management is *externally* oriented and focuses on both incoming materials and outgoing products and services. Whereas supply chain management is efficiency oriented (its goal is to reduce costs and make the organization more productive), value chain management is effectiveness oriented and aims to create the highest value for customers.[13]

MyManagementLab
Q&A 18.5

Goal of Value Chain Management

Who has the power in the value chain? Is it the suppliers providing needed resources and materials? After all, they have the ability to dictate prices and quality. Is it the manufacturer who assembles those resources into a valuable product or service? Their contributions in creating a product or service are quite obvious. Is it the distributor that makes sure the product or service is available where and when the customer needs it? Actually, it's none of these! In value chain management, ultimately customers are the ones with power.[14] They're the ones who define what value is and how it's created and provided. Using value chain management, managers hope to find that unique combination where customers are offered solutions that truly meet their needs incredibly fast and at a price that competitors can't match.

The goal of value chain management is therefore to create a value chain strategy that meets and exceeds customers' needs and desires and allows for full and seamless integration among all members of the chain. A good value chain is one in which a sequence of participants work together as a team, each adding some component of value—such as faster assembly, more accurate information, better customer response and service, and so forth—to the overall process.[15] The better the collaboration among the various chain participants, the better the customer solutions. When value is created for customers and their needs and desires are satisfied, everyone along the chain benefits. For example, at Johnson Controls Inc., managing the value chain started first with improved relationships with internal suppliers and then expanded to external suppliers and customers. As the company's experience with value chain management improved, so did its connection with its customers, and this will ultimately pay off for all its value chain partners.[16]

Benefits of Value Chain Management

Collaborating with external and internal partners in creating and managing a successful value chain strategy requires significant investments in time, energy, and other resources, as well as a serious commitment by all chain partners. So why would managers ever choose to implement value chain management? A survey of manufacturers noted four primary benefits of value chain management: improved procurement, improved logistics, improved product development, and enhanced customer order management.[17]

MyManagementLab
Q&A 18.6

Managing Operations by Using Value Chain Management

3. Describe how value chain management is done.

▶ ▶ ▶ Ben Graham is the general manager at Eldis and works closely with David Ritacco to coordinate the building, maintenance, and management of the value chain. Both Graham and Ritacco are enthusiastic supporters of the value chain management approach and have embedded it in the organization's culture. At Eldis, enhancing the customer experience is emphasized to set the company apart from the competition. Thus, searches are based on what the customer knows—make, model, function, etc.—and are supported by an extensive library of images of parts and schematics by model. The website experience is further enhanced by customer feedback on installing the parts and user ratings. Eldis has made a large investment in software, hardware, and well-trained technical people to support its efforts. But, as noted above, making the change from a conventional supplier of parts to service people (B2B) to an online model (B2C) was not easy.

Think About It

What elements did David Ritacco and Ben Graham have to put in place to ensure the success of their value chain management approach? What obstacles might Eldis have had to overcome as it made the transition from conventional supplier to the sophisticated value chain management practices of today? Would the shift have been instantaneous or would it have been an evolution?

Managing an organization from a value chain perspective isn't easy. Approaches to giving customers what they want that may have worked in the past are likely no longer efficient or effective. Today's dynamic competitive environment demands new solutions from global organizations. Understanding how and why value is determined by the marketplace has led some organizations to experiment with a new business model, a concept we introduced in Chapter 8. For example, IKEA transformed itself from a small Swedish mail-order furniture operation into one of the world's largest furniture retailers by reinventing the value chain in that industry. The company offers customers well-designed products at substantially lower-than-typical prices in return for their willingness to take on certain key tasks traditionally done by manufacturers and retailers, such as getting furniture home and assembling it.[18] The company's creation of a new business model and its willingness to abandon old methods and processes has worked well.

Tips for Managers—Implementing Value Chain Management provides some suggestions for managers who are considering a value chain strategy.

Requirements of Value Chain Management

Exhibit 18-3 shows the six main requirements of a successful value chain strategy: coordination and collaboration, technology investment, organizational processes, leadership, employees, and organizational culture and attitudes.

Coordination and Collaboration

For the value chain to achieve its goal of meeting and exceeding customers' needs and desires, collaborative relationships must exist among all chain participants.[19] Each partner

TIPS FOR MANAGERS

Implementing Value Chain Management

⚡ **Identify successful examples** of value chain management within your industry.

⚡ **Arrange site visits** to those organizations who best match with what you plan to do.

⚡ **Identify the resources** you will need and place a dollar value on them.

⚡ **Build the business case** for implementing value chain management.

⚡ **Seek top management support** from your own organization and key suppliers.

⚡ **Allocate sufficient time and money** to sell the idea both internally and externally.

MyManagementLab
Q&A 18.7, Q&A 18.8

Exhibit 18-3

Value Chain Strategy Requirements

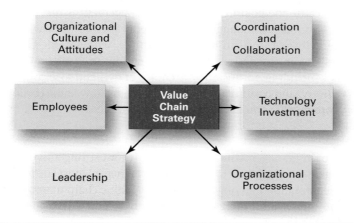

must identify things that they may not value but that customers do. And sharing information and being flexible in terms of who in the value chain does what are important steps in building coordination and collaboration. This sharing of information and analysis requires open communication among the various value chain partners. For example, Kraft Foods believes that better communication with customers and with suppliers has facilitated timely delivery of goods and services.[20]

Technology Investment

Successful value chain management isn't possible without a significant investment in information technology. The payoff from this investment, however, is that information technology can be used to restructure the value chain to better serve end users. For example, at American Standard's Trane facilities, a comprehensive IT strategy throughout its value chain, which extends globally, has helped it achieve significant work process improvements.[21]

Organizational Processes

organizational processes The ways that organizational work is done.

Value chain management radically changes **organizational processes**—that is, the ways that organizational work is done. When managers decide to manage operations using value chain management, old processes are no longer appropriate. All organizational processes must be critically evaluated, from beginning to end, to see where value is being added. Non-value-adding activities should be eliminated. Questions such as "Where can internal knowledge be leveraged to improve the flow of material and information?" "How can we better configure our product to satisfy both customers and suppliers?" "How can the flow of material and information be improved?" and "How can we improve customer service?" should be answered for each and every process. For example, when managers at Deere and Company implemented value chain management, a thorough process evaluation revealed that work activities needed to be better synchronized and interrelationships between multiple links in the value chain needed to be better managed. They changed numerous work processes division-wide in order to do this.[22] Three important conclusions can be made about organizational processes. First, better demand forecasting is necessary *and* possible because of closer ties with customers and suppliers. For example, in an effort to make sure that Listerine was on the store shelves when customers wanted it (known in the retail industry as *product replenishment rates*), Wal-Mart and Pfizer's Consumer Healthcare Group collaborated on improving product demand forecast information. Through their mutual efforts, the partners boosted Wal-Mart's sales of Listerine, an excellent outcome for both supplier and retailer. Customers also benefited because they were able to purchase the product when and where they wanted it.

Second, selected functions may need to be done collaboratively with other partners in the value chain. This collaboration may even extend to sharing employees. For instance, Saint-Gobain Performance Plastics places its own employees in customer sites and brings in employees of suppliers and customers to work on its premises.[23]

Finally, new measures are needed for evaluating performance of various activities along the value chain. Because the goal in value chain management is meeting and exceeding customers' needs and desires, managers need a better picture of how well this value is being created and delivered to customers. For example, when Nestlé USA implemented value chain management, it redesigned its metrics system to focus on one consistent set of measurements—including, for instance, accuracy of demand forecasts and production plans, on-time delivery, and customer service levels—that allowed the company to identify problem areas more quickly and take actions to resolve them.[24]

Leadership

Successful value chain management isn't possible without strong and committed leadership. From top organizational levels to lower levels, managers must support, facilitate, and promote the implementation and ongoing practice of value chain management. Managers must seriously commit to identifying what value is, how that value can best be provided, and how successful those efforts have been. A culture where all efforts are focused on delivering superb customer value isn't possible without serious commitment on the part of the organization's leaders.

Also, it's important that managers outline expectations for what's involved in the organization's pursuit of value chain management. Ideally, this starts with a vision or mission statement that expresses the organization's commitment to identifying, capturing, and providing the highest possible value to customers. For instance, when American Standard began using value chain management, the CEO held dozens of meetings across the United States to explain the new competitive environment and why the company needed to create better working relationships with its value chain partners in order to better serve the needs of its customers.[25]

Peter Tan was the marketing director of UPS's Beijing Olympics Project. Among his tasks was making sure the company got every package and piece of luggage to the right place on time . . . no mean feat when you consider that the Chinese government rebuilt much of the city just for the Olympics. Tan was prepared. "Our job was not simply moving things from point A to point B," he said. "We had to plot the entire city— every point, every hill, every traffic light—to determine route times. Everything had to be synchronized down to the second. That was our job." To help motivate his Chinese staff, Tan asked them to choose a team they wanted to sponsor; they chose the Chinese women's national volleyball team.

Then, managers should clarify expectations regarding each employee's role in the value chain. But clear expectations aren't important only for internal partners. Being clear about expectations also extends to external partners. For example, managers at American Standard identified clear requirements for suppliers and were prepared to drop any suppliers that couldn't meet the requirements, and they did so. The upside was that the suppliers that met the expectations benefited from more business, and American Standard had partners willing to work with them in delivering better value to customers.

MANAGEMENT REFLECTION
▶ Focus on Innovation

IT's Role in Managing the Value Chain

How can RFID technology assist partners in efficiently managing the value chain? Because value chain management requires such intensive collaboration among partners, getting and sharing information is critical.[26] One type of IT that many value chain partners are finding particularly relevant is RFID (radio-frequency identification). In fact, Wal-Mart has been phasing in an RFID program for its suppliers, who must comply by the company's deadlines.

What Is RFID? **RFID** is an automatic identification method in which information can be stored and remotely retrieved. It's similar to, but more sophisticated than, the old familiar bar code. Information is stored on and retrieved from RFID tags (sometimes called *chips*), which are like "little radio towers or transponders that send out information to a reader." An *active* RFID tag has a tiny battery in it that powers the internal circuits that store and send information at a pretty good distance. A *passive* tag has no internal power supply and must be "awakened" by a tag reader in order to send information. A complete RFID system usually requires tags, tag readers, computer servers, and software.

RFID An automatic identification method in which information can be stored and remotely retrieved.

What Are the Benefits of RFID? RFID technology has several benefits. First, it has the potential to streamline the supply chain, eliminate theft and waste, and solve logistics problems. Another benefit is that, unlike bar codes, RFID tags don't have to be in the line of sight in order to be read. (Think about a grocery store checkout, where the products have to be directly individually scanned by a laser.) RFID tags can be read at a distance, even through crates or other packing materials. In addition, RFID tags can be attached to each item in a shipment so that manufacturers, distributors, transportation companies, retailers, and marketers can track individual units across every step of the value chain.

What Are the Drawbacks of RFID? The main drawbacks of RFID technology are the cost of the chips, the lack of standardization of chips and the machines that read them, the challenge of analyzing the vast amounts of data that RFID produces, and the privacy concerns of customers.

How Are Organizations Using RFID? Many hospitals are experimenting with RFID in patient bracelets that hold medical information and in tracking doctors and nurses so they can be located quickly in an emergency. Law firms, libraries, and research centres are using RFID to track the movement of documents, files, and books. One of the most unusual applications is probably at the University of California, where RFID tags have been inserted into cadavers used for research to thwart the illegal selling of the corpses for profit. ■

Employees/Human Resources

We know from our discussions of management theories throughout this textbook that employees are the organization's most important resource. Without employees, there would be no products produced or services delivered—in fact, there would be no organized efforts in the pursuit of common goals. Not surprisingly, employees play an important role in value chain management. The three main human resource requirements for value chain management are flexible approaches to job design, effective hiring process, and ongoing training.

Flexibility is the key to job design in value chain management. Traditional functional job roles—such as marketing, sales, accounts payable, customer service, and so forth—don't work with value chain management. Instead, jobs must be designed around work processes that create and provide value to customers. It takes flexible jobs and flexible employees.

In a value chain organization, employees may be assigned to work teams that tackle particular processes and may be asked to do different things on different days, depending on need. In such an environment—where customer value is best delivered through collaborative relationships that may change as customer needs change and where there are no standardized processes or job descriptions—an employee's ability to be flexible is critical. Therefore, the organization's hiring process must be designed to identify employees who have the ability to learn and adapt.

Finally, the need for flexibility also requires that there be a significant investment in continual and ongoing employee training. Whether that training involves learning how to use information technology software, how to improve the flow of materials throughout the chain, how to identify activities that add value, how to make better decisions faster, or how to improve any number of other potential work activities, managers must see to it that employees have the knowledge and tools they need to do their jobs efficiently and effectively.

Organizational Culture and Attitudes

The last requirement for value chain management is having a supportive organizational culture and attitudes. From our extensive description of value chain management, you could probably guess the type of organizational culture that's going to support its successful implementation! Those cultural attitudes include sharing, collaboration, openness, flexibility, mutual respect, and trust. And these attitudes encompass not only the internal partners in the value chain but external partners as well.

Obstacles to Value Chain Management

As desirable as the benefits of value chain management may be, managers must tackle several obstacles in managing the value chain, including organizational barriers, cultural attitudes, required capabilities, and people (see Exhibit 18-4).

Exhibit 18-4

Obstacles to Value Chain Management

Organizational Barriers

Organizational barriers are among the most difficult obstacles to handle. These barriers include refusal or reluctance to share information, reluctance to shake up the status quo, and security issues. Without shared information, close coordination and collaboration is impossible. And the reluctance or refusal of employees to shake up the status quo can impede efforts toward value chain management and prevent its successful implementation. Finally, because value chain management relies heavily on a substantial information technology infrastructure, system security and Internet security breaches are issues that need to be addressed.

Cultural Attitudes

Unsupportive cultural attitudes—especially trust and control—can be obstacles to value chain management. The trust issue—both lack of trust and too much trust—is a critical one. To be effective, partners in a value chain must trust each other. There must be a mutual respect for, and honesty about, each partner's activities all along the chain. When that trust doesn't exist, the partners will be reluctant to share information, capabilities, and processes. But too much trust can also be a problem. Just about any organization is vulnerable to theft of **intellectual property**—that is, proprietary information that's critical to an organization's efficient and effective functioning and competitiveness. You need to be able to trust your value chain partners so your organization's valuable assets aren't compromised.[27] Another cultural attitude that can be an obstacle is the belief that when an organization collaborates with external and internal partners, it no longer controls its own destiny. However, this just isn't the case. Even with the intense collaboration that's important to value chain management, organizations still control critical decisions such as what customers value, how much value they desire, and what distribution channels are important.[28]

intellectual property Proprietary information that's critical to an organization's efficient and effective functioning and competitiveness.

Required Capabilities

We know from our earlier discussion of requirements for the successful implementation of value chain management that value chain partners need numerous capabilities. Several of these—coordination and collaboration, the ability to configure products to satisfy customers and suppliers, and the ability to educate internal and external partners—aren't easy. But they're essential to capturing and exploiting the value chain. Many of the companies we've described throughout this section endured critical, and oftentimes difficult, self-evaluations of their capabilities and processes in order to become more effective and efficient at managing their value chains.

People

The final obstacles to successful value chain management can be an organization's people. Without their unwavering commitment to do whatever it takes, value chain management won't be successful. If employees refuse to be flexible in their work—how and with whom they work—collaboration and cooperation throughout the value chain will be difficult to achieve.

In addition, value chain management takes an incredible amount of time and energy on the part of an organization's employees. Managers must motivate those high levels of effort from employees, which is not an easy thing to do.

Finally, a major human resource problem is a lack of experienced managers who can lead value chain management initiatives. Value chain management isn't very widespread, so there aren't a lot of managers who've done it successfully. However, this hasn't prevented progressive organizations from pursuing the benefits to be gained from value chain management.

Current Issues in Managing Operations

4. Discuss contemporary issues in managing operations.

▶ ▶ ▶ David Ritacco and Ben Graham use analytics to manage the day-to-day operations of their business and to manage the conversion rate of their customers (the percentage of visitors who proceed through the process to place an order). To do so, they use the visualization tool in Google Analytics (see *Developing Your Interpersonal Skills—Managing Operations in an E-world Environment* on pages 531–532). In addition to analytics, Ritacco and Graham use "A and B" testing to tweak performance of their site. For example, the company put an avatar on its website to speak with visitors (an actor from the United States who has played a minor role on the TV drama *Prison Break*). During the A and B test period, half the traffic to the website was directed to the conventional site, and half was driven to the site with the new avatar. Although Ritacco wasn't convinced that the avatar would work, Graham was in favour of it. At the end of the test period, they found a significant increase in conversion rate and order size on the website with the avatar. Based on these data, the avatar was incorporated into the customer experience.

Think About It

How might technology be used to increase productivity and support value chain management in a traditional manufacturer? A call centre? A not-for-profit organization?

Rowe Furniture has an audacious goal: Make a sofa in 10 days. It wants to "become as efficient at making furniture as Toyota is at making cars." Reaching that goal, however, requires revamping its operations management process to exploit technology *and* maintaining quality.[29] Rowe's actions illustrate three of today's most important operations management issues: technology, quality initiatives and goals, and mass customization.

Technology's Role in Operations Management

As we know from our previous discussion of value chain management, today's competitive marketplace has put tremendous pressure on organizations to deliver, in a timely manner, products and services that customers value. Smart companies are looking at ways to harness technology to improve operations management. Many fast-food companies are competing to see who can provide faster and better service to drive-through customers. With drive-through now representing a huge portion of sales, faster and better delivery can be a significant competitive edge. For instance, Wendy's has added awnings to some of its menu boards and replaced some of the text with pictures. Others use confirmation screens, a technology that helped McDonald's boost accuracy by more than 11 percent. And technology used by two national chains tells managers how much food they need to prepare by counting vehicles in the drive-through line and factoring in demand for current promotional and popular staple items.[30]

Although an organization's production activities are driven by the recognition that the customer is king, managers still need to be more responsive. For instance, operations managers need systems that can reveal available capacity, status of orders, and product quality while products are in the process of being manufactured, not just after the fact. To connect more closely with customers, production must be synchronized across the enterprise. To avoid bottlenecks and slowdowns, the production function must be a full partner in the entire business system.

Technology is making such extensive collaboration possible. Technology is also allowing organizations to control costs, particularly in the areas of predictive maintenance, remote diagnostics, and utility cost savings. For instance, new Internet-compatible equipment contains embedded web servers that can communicate proactively—for example, if a piece of equipment breaks or reaches certain preset parameters indicating that it's about to break, it asks for help. Technology can do more than sound an alarm or light up an indicator button. For instance, some devices have the ability to initiate email or signal a pager of a supplier, the maintenance department, or a contractor, describing the specific problem and requesting parts and service. How much is such e-enabled maintenance control worth? It can be worth quite a lot if it prevents equipment breakdowns and subsequent production downtime.

Managers who understand the power of technology to contribute to more effective and efficient performance know that managing operations is more than the traditional view of simply producing the product. Instead, the emphasis is on working together with all the organization's business functions to find solutions to customers' business problems.

Quality Initiatives

Quality problems are expensive. For example, even though Apple has had phenomenal success with its iPod, the batteries in the first three versions died after 4 hours instead of lasting up to 12 hours, as buyers expected. Apple's settlement with consumers cost close to $100 million (US). At Schering-Plough, problems with inhalers and other pharmaceuticals were traced to chronic quality control shortcomings, for which the company eventually paid a $500 million (US) fine. And in one recent year, the auto industry paid $14.5 billion (US) to cover the cost of warranty and repair work.[31]

Many experts believe that organizations unable to produce high-quality products won't be able to compete successfully in the global marketplace. What is quality? When you consider a product or service to have quality, what does that mean? Does it mean that the product doesn't break or quit working—that is, that it's reliable? Does it mean that the service is delivered in a way that you intended? Does it mean that the product does what it's supposed to do? Or does quality mean something else? Exhibit 18-5 provides a description of several quality dimensions. In this case, we define **quality** as the ability of a product or service to reliably do what it's supposed to do and to satisfy customer expectations.

How is quality achieved? That's an issue managers must address. A good way to look at quality initiatives is with the management functions—planning, organizing and leading, and controlling—that need to take place.

Planning for Quality

Managers must have quality improvement goals and strategies and plans to achieve those goals. Goals can help focus everyone's attention on some objective quality standard. For instance, Caterpillar has a goal of applying quality improvement techniques to help cut costs.[32] Although this goal is specific and challenging, managers and employees are partnering together to pursue well-designed strategies to achieve the goals, and they are confident they can do so.

Organizing and Leading for Quality

Because quality improvement initiatives are carried out by organizational employees, it's important for managers to look at how they can best organize and lead them. For instance, at the Moose Jaw, Saskatchewan, plant of General Cable Corporation, every

MyManagementLab
Q&A 18.9

quality The ability of a product or service to reliably do what it's supposed to do and to satisfy customer expectations.

Exhibit 18-5

Quality Dimensions of Goods and Services

Product Quality Dimensions

1. Performance—Operating characteristics
2. Features—Important special characteristics
3. Flexibility—Meeting operating specifications over some period of time
4. Durability—Amount of use before performance deteriorates
5. Conformance—Match with pre-established standards
6. Serviceability—Ease and speed of repair or normal service
7. Aesthetics—How a product looks and feels
8. Perceived quality—Subjective assessment of characteristics (product image)

Service Quality Dimensions

1. Timeliness—Performed in promised period of time
2. Courtesy—Performed cheerfully
3. Consistency—Giving all customers similar experiences each time
4. Convenience—Accessibility to customers
5. Completeness—Fully serviced, as required
6. Accuracy—Performed correctly each time

Sources: Adapted from J. W. Dean Jr. and J. R. Evans, *Total Quality: Management, Organization and Society* (St. Paul, MN: West Publishing, 1994); H. V. Roberts and B. F. Sergesketter, *Quality Is Personal* (New York: The Free Press, 1993); D. Garvin, *Managed Quality: The Strategic and Competitive Edge* (New York: The Free Press, 1988); and M. A. Hitt, R. D. Ireland, and R. E. Hoskisson, *Strategic Management*, 4th ed. (Cincinnati, OH: South-Western, 2001), p. 211.

employee participates in continual quality assurance training. In addition, the plant manager believes wholeheartedly in giving employees the information they need to do their jobs better. He says, "Giving people who are running the machines the information is just paramount. You can set up your cellular structure, you can cross-train your people, you can use lean tools, but if you don't give people information to drive improvement, there's no enthusiasm." As you might expect, this company shares production data and financial performance measures with all employees.[33]

Organizations with extensive and successful quality improvement programs tend to rely on two important people approaches: cross-functional work teams and self-directed, or empowered, work teams. Because all employees, from upper to lower levels, must participate in achieving product quality, it's not surprising that quality-driven organizations rely on well-trained, flexible, and empowered employees.

Controlling for Quality

Quality improvement initiatives aren't possible without a means of monitoring and evaluating their progress. Whether it involves standards for inventory control, defect rate, raw materials procurement, or other operations management areas, controlling for quality is important. For instance, at the Northrup Grumman Corporation plant in Rolling Meadows, Illinois, several quality controls have been implemented, such as automated testing and IT that integrates product design and manufacturing and tracks process quality improvements. Also, employees are empowered to make accept/reject decisions about products throughout the manufacturing process. The plant manager explains, "This approach helps build quality into the product rather than trying to inspect quality into the product." But one of the most important things the company does is "go to war" with its customers—soldiers preparing for war or in live-combat situations. Again, the plant manager says, "What discriminates us is that we believe if we can understand our customers' mission as well as they do, we can help them be more effective. We don't wait for our customer to ask us to do something. We find out what our customer is trying to do and then we develop solutions."[34]

These types of quality improvement success stories aren't limited to US operations. For example, at a Delphi assembly plant in Matamoros, Mexico, employees worked hard to improve quality and made significant strides. The customer reject rate on shipped products is now 10 ppm (parts per million), down from 3000 ppm—an improvement of almost 300 percent.[35] Quality initiatives at several Australian companies, including Alcoa of Australia, Wormald Security, and Carlton and United Breweries, have led to significant quality improvements.[36] And at Valeo Klimasystemme GmbH of Bad Rodach, Germany, assembly teams build different climate-control systems for high-end German cars, including Mercedes and BMW. Quality initiatives by Valeo's employee teams have led to significant improvements in various quality standards.[37]

Quality Goals

To publicly demonstrate their quality commitment, many organizations worldwide have pursued challenging quality goals, the two best known of which are ISO 9000 and Six Sigma. It is interesting to note that the ISO standards have been extended to include the issues discussed in Chapter 5—environmental performance and social responsibility.

MyManagementLab
Q&A 18.10

ISO 9000

ISO 9000 is a series of international quality management standards established by the International Organization for Standardization (**www.iso.org**), which sets uniform guidelines for processes to ensure that products conform to customer requirements. These standards cover everything from contract review to product design to product delivery. The ISO 9000 standards have become the internationally recognized standard for evaluating and comparing companies in the global marketplace. In fact, this type of certification can be a prerequisite for doing business globally. Achieving ISO 9000 certification provides proof that a quality operations system is in place.

A recent survey of ISO 9000 certificates—awarded in 170 countries—showed that the number of registered sites worldwide was almost 900 000, an increase of 16 percent over the previous year.[38]

ISO 9000, 14000, and 26000
A series of international quality management standards that set uniform guidelines for processes to ensure that products conform to customer requirements.

ISO 14000

ISO 14000 is a family of standards that address different aspects of environmental management, including environmental management systems (EMS) and encompassing both the requirements (ISO 14001:2004) and the guidelines (ISO 14004:2004). To be ISO 14001:2004 certified, an organization must commit to complying with applicable environmental legislation and regulations, as well as to continual improvement—for which the environmental management system provides the framework. The intent of ISO 14001:2004 "is to provide a framework for a holistic, strategic approach." The other standards in ISO 14000 address specific environmental aspects, including labelling, performance evaluation, life-cycle analysis communications, and auditing.[39]

ISO 26000

ISO 26000 (soon to be released) provides guidance on best practice in social responsibility (SR) worldwide for private and public sector organizations. ISO 26000 provides a guide to what SR means and what organizations can do to operate in a socially responsible way. It also refines best practices that already exist and makes the information available for the good of the international community.[40]

Six Sigma

Motorola popularized the use of stringent quality standards more than 30 years ago, through a trademarked quality improvement program called Six Sigma.[41] Very simply, **Six Sigma** is a quality standard that establishes a goal of no more than 3.4 defects per million units or procedures. What does the name mean? *Sigma* is the Greek letter that statisticians use to define a standard deviation from a bell curve. The higher the sigma, the fewer the deviations from the norm—that is, the fewer the defects. At One Sigma, two-thirds of whatever is being measured falls within the curve. Two Sigma covers about 95 percent. At Six Sigma, you're about as close to defect free as you can get.[42] It's an ambitious quality goal! Although Six Sigma is an extremely high standard to achieve, many quality-driven businesses are using it and benefiting from it. For instance, General Electric company executives estimate that the company has saved billions in costs since 1995.[43] Other well-known companies pursuing Six Sigma include ITT Industries, Dow Chemical, 3M Company, American Express, Sony Corporation, Nokia Corporation, and Johnson & Johnson. Although manufacturers seem to make up the bulk of Six Sigma users, service companies such as financial institutions, retailers, and health care organizations are beginning to apply it as well. What impact can Six Sigma have? Let's look at an example.

It used to take Wellmark Blue Cross & Blue Shield, a managed-care health care company, 65 days or more to add a new doctor to its medical plans. Thanks to Six Sigma, the company discovered that half the processes they were using were redundant. With those unnecessary steps gone, the job now gets done in 30 days or less, and with reduced staff. The company has also been able to reduce its administrative expenses by $3 million per year, an amount passed on to consumers through lower health insurance premiums.[44]

Quality Goals Summary

Although it's important for managers to recognize that many positive benefits come from obtaining ISO 9000, 14000, and 26000 certification or Six Sigma, the key benefit comes from the quality improvement journey itself. In other words, the goal of quality certification should be having work processes and an operations system in place that enable organizations to meet customers' needs and employees to perform their jobs in a consistently high-quality way.

Mass Customization

The term *mass customization* seems like an oxymoron. However, the design-to-order concept is becoming an important operations management issue for today's managers. **Mass customization** provides consumers with a product when, where, and how they want it.[45] Companies as diverse as BMW, Ford, Levi Strauss, Wells Fargo, Mattel, and Dell Computer are adopting mass customization to maintain or attain a competitive advantage. Mass customization requires flexible manufacturing techniques and continual customer dialogue.[46] Technology plays an important role in both.

With flexible manufacturing, companies have the ability to quickly readjust assembly lines to make products to order. Using technology such as computer-controlled factory equipment, intranets, industrial robots, bar-code scanners, digital printers, and logistics software, companies can manufacture, assemble, and ship customized products with customized packaging to customers in incredibly short time frames. Dell is a good example of a company that uses flexible manufacturing techniques and technology to custom-build computers to customers' specifications.

Technology is also important in the continual dialogue with customers. Using extensive databases, companies can keep track of customers' likes and dislikes. And the Internet has made it possible for companies to have ongoing dialogues with customers to learn about and respond to their exact preferences. For instance, on Amazon's website, customers are greeted by name and can get personalized recommendations of books and other products. The ability to customize products to a customer's desires and specifications starts an important relationship between the organization and the customer. If the customer likes

Six Sigma A quality standard that establishes a goal of no more than 3.4 defects per million units or procedures.

mass customization Providing customers with a product when, where, and how they want it.

The Ford Motor Company embraced Six Sigma as its primary method for managing quality. J. D. Power and Associates currently ranks five of Ford's vehicles in the top five in their category and fourteen of its vehicles in the top three in their category—evidence of the impact of Six Sigma and other quality initiatives at Ford.

the product and believes the customization provides value, he or she is more likely to be a repeat customer.

SUMMARY AND IMPLICATIONS

1. Explain the role of operations management. Operations management is the transformation process that converts resources into finished goods and services. Manufacturing organizations produce physical goods. Service organizations produce nonphysical outputs in the form of services. Productivity is a composite of people and operations variables. A manager should look for ways to successfully integrate people into the overall operations systems. Organizations must recognize the crucial role that operations management plays as part of their overall strategy in achieving successful performance.

▶ ▶ ▶ Eldis Group operates a family of DIY websites that "provide consumers with the parts and know-how to fix their major home appliances themselves, offering the internet's largest collection of step-by-step installation instructions and videos." Customers in Canada and the United States browse the websites to determine what parts they need and place their orders online.

2. Define the nature and purpose of value chain management. The value chain is the sequence of organizational work activities that add value at each step from raw materials to finished product. Value chain management is the process of managing the sequence of activities and information along the entire product chain. The goal of value chain management is to create a value chain strategy that meets or exceeds customers' needs and desires and that allows for full and seamless integration among all members of the chain. Value chain management has four benefits: improved procurement, improved logistics, improved product development, and enhanced customer order management.

▶ ▶ ▶ Customers in Canada and the United States go to the PartSelect website and place their online orders. The customer pays with a credit card, and a shipping ticket is printed automatically in one of the partner fulfillment centres, where the product is picked and shipped with the Eldis company logo and documentation.

3. Describe how value chain management is done. The six main requirements for successful value chain management are coordination and collaboration, investment in technology, organizational processes, leadership, employees or human resources, and organizational culture and attitudes. The obstacles to value chain management include organizational barriers (refusal to share information, reluctance to shake up the status quo, or security issues), unsupportive cultural attitudes, lack of required capabilities, and employee unwillingness or inability to do it.

▶ ▶ ▶ Ben Graham, general manager at Eldis, works closely with David Ritacco to coordinate the building, maintenance, and management of the value chain. Both are enthusiastic supporters of the value chain management approach and have embedded it in the organization's culture. The company emphasizes enhancing the customer experience to set it apart from competitors. Eldis has made a large investment in software, hardware, and well-trained technical people to support its efforts. The shift from a conventional supplier of parts to service people (B2B) to an online model (B2C) was not easy.

4. Discuss contemporary issues in managing operations. Companies are looking at ways to harness technology to improve their operations management through extensive collaboration and cost control. ISO 9000 is a series of international quality management standards that set uniform guidelines for processes to ensure that products conform to customer requirements. ISO 14001:2004 provides the general requirements for putting in place an environmental management system. ISO 26000 will provide guidance on best practice in social responsibility for all types of organizations. Six Sigma is a quality standard that establishes a goal of no more than 3.4 defects per million units or procedures. Mass customization provides customers with a product when, where, and how they want it. It requires flexible manufacturing techniques and continual customer dialogue.

▶ ▶ ▶ Ritacco and Graham use "A and B" testing to tweak performance of their site. For example, the company put an avatar on its website. During the A and B test period, half the traffic to the website was directed to the conventional site, and half was driven to the site with the new avatar. Although Ritacco wasn't convinced that the avatar would work, Graham was in favour. At the end of the test period, they found a significant increase in conversion rate and order size on the website with the avatar.

Management @ Work

READING FOR COMPREHENSION

1. Define operations management.

2. Discuss the strategic role of operations management and the manager in particular in improving productivity.

3. Define value chain and value chain management.

4. What are the benefits of value chain management?

5. Discuss the requirements for successful value chain management.

6. What obstacles do value chain management initiatives most often encounter?

7. Explain ISO standards (9000, 14000, and 26000) and Six Sigma.

8. Describe mass customization and the contribution made by operations management.

LINKING CONCEPTS TO PRACTICE

1. Contrast manufacturing and service organizations.

2. Describe the manager's role in improving productivity.

3. Select a company that you are familiar with and describe its value chain. Be as specific as possible in your description. Evaluate how it "uses" the value chain to create value.

4. Can you think of an example of how technology has enabled operations management practices?

5. Find three examples of mass customization products. Describe them, and then try describing what you think has to take place "behind the scenes" to create these products. Focus on the operations management aspects.

SELF-ASSESSMENT

What Time of Day Am I Most Productive?

1. Considering only your "feeling best rhythm," at what time would you get up if you were entirely free to plan your day?
   a. 5:00–6:30 a.m.
   b. 6:30–7:45 a.m.
   c. 7:45–9:45 a.m.
   d. 9:45–11:00 a.m.
   e. 11:00 a.m.–12:00 p.m.

2. Considering only your "feeling best rhythm," at what time would you go to bed if you were entirely free to plan your evening?
   a. 8:00–9:00 p.m.
   b. 9:00–10:15 p.m.
   c. 10:15 p.m.–12:30 a.m.
   d. 12:30–1:45 a.m.
   e. 1:45–3:00 a.m.

3. Assuming normal circumstances, how easy do you find it to get up in the morning?
   a. Not at all easy
   b. Slightly easy
   c. Fairly easy
   d. Very easy

4. How alert do you feel during the first half-hour after you wake up in the morning?
   a. Not at all alert
   b. Slightly alert
   c. Fairly alert
   d. Very alert

5. During the first half-hour after awakening in the morning, how tired do you feel?
   a. Very tired
   b. Fairly tired
   c. Fairly refreshed
   d. Very refreshed

6. You have decided to engage in some physical exercise. A friend suggests that you do this for one hour twice a week, and the best time for him is 7:00–8:00 a.m. Bearing in mind nothing else but your own "feeling best rhythm," how do you think you would perform?
   a. Would be in good form
   b. Would be in reasonable form
   c. Would find it difficult
   d. Would find it very difficult

7. At what time in the evening do you feel tired and, as a result, in need of sleep?
   a. 8:00–9:00 p.m.
   b. 9:00–10:15 p.m.
   c. 10:15 p.m.–12:30 a.m.
   d. 12:30–1:45 a.m.
   e. 1:45–3:00 a.m.

8. You wish to be at your peak performance for a test that you know is going to be mentally exhausting and will last for two hours. Considering only your own "feeling best rhythm," which one of the four testing times would you choose?
   a. 8:00–10:00 a.m.
   b. 11:00 a.m.–1:00 p.m.
   c. 1:00–3:00 p.m.
   d. 3:00–5:00 p.m.
   e. 7:00–9:00 p.m.

9. One hears about "morning" and "evening" types of people. Which one of these types do you consider yourself to be?
   a. Definitely a morning type
   b. More a morning than an evening type
   c. More an evening than a morning type
   d. Definitely an evening type

10. When would you prefer to rise if you were totally free to plan your time, knowing that you have a full day's work (8 hours) ahead?

   a. 5:00–6:30 a.m.
   b. 6:30–7:45 a.m.
   c. 7:45–9:45 a.m.
   d. 9:45–11:00 a.m.
   e. 11:00 a.m.–12:00 p.m.

11. If you always had to rise at 6:00 a.m., what do you think it would be like?
   a. Very difficult and unpleasant
   b. Rather difficult and unpleasant
   c. A little unpleasant but no great problem
   d. Easy and not unpleasant

12. How long does it usually take before you "recover" your senses in the morning after rising from a night's sleep?
   a. 0–10 minutes
   b. 11–20 minutes
   c. 21–40 minutes
   d. More than 40 minutes

13. Indicate the extent to which you are a morning or evening active individual.
   a. Very morning active (morning alert and evening tired)
   b. To some extent morning active
   c. To some extent evening active
   d. Very evening active (morning tired and evening alert)

Scoring Key

For items 1, 2, 7, 8, and 10, assign 5 points for a, 4 points for b, 3 points for c, 2 points for d, and 1 point for e.
For items 3, 4, 5, and 11, assign 1 point for a, 2 points for b, 3 points for c, and 4 points for d.
For items 6, 9, 12, and 13, assign 4 points for a, 3 points for b, 2 points for c, and 1 point for d.

Analysis and Interpretation

People differ in terms of when they are most alert and productive. This questionnaire taps your cycle to see whether you're more of a morning or an evening person. Score totals can range from 13 to 55. Scores of 22 and less indicate evening types; scores of 23 to 43 indicate intermediate types; and scores of 44 and above indicate morning types.

People have different cycles. Some of us do our best work early in the day, while others are most effective in the evening. You should know your personal cycle so you can organize your work accordingly. Don't fight your natural rhythms. If you don't already do this, you should adjust your activities so you undertake your most important and challenging activities when your cycle is high and do more mundane and routine activities when your cycle is low.

MANAGEMENT FOR YOU TODAY

Dilemma

Following the British Petroleum oil spill in the Gulf of Mexico in the summer of 2010, you have become more aware of the need for organizations to manage sustainably and responsibly. Two new ISO standards have been prepared. ISO 14001:2004 gives the general requirements for an environmental management system. It provides organizations with a common reference for communicating about environmental management issues with customers, regulators, the public, and other stakeholders. Organizations commit to compliance with environmental legislation and regulations, as well as to continual improvement—for

which the environmental management system provides the framework. ISO 26000 (guidance on social responsibility) will provide globally relevant guidance for private and public sector organizations and encourage the implementation of best practices in social responsibility worldwide.

What steps will you need to take to prepare yourself to work in organizations that adopt these principles? As you seek employment, how will you be able to differentiate organizations that simply "talk the talk" from those that actually "walk the walk"?

Becoming a Manager

- Go to the ISO site and review the standards on sustainability and social responsibility.

- Do some surfing to identify organizations that have embraced sustainability and social responsibility.

- Compare and contrast the sustainability pages for Wal-Mart and Interface Carpet.

- Identify a local organization that embraces either sustainable or socially responsible practices, or both. Visit the offices and talk with the staff.

- Explain your own opinion on these two issues and connect them your own values.

WORKING TOGETHER: TEAM-BASED EXERCISE

Improving Personal Productivity

Choose two tasks that you do every week, for example, shopping for groceries, hosting a poker game, cleaning your house/apartment, doing laundry. For each one, identify how you could:

a. Be more productive
b. Have higher-quality output from that task

ETHICS IN ACTION

Ethical Dilemma Exercise: Who Is Wearing the White Hat and Who Is Wearing the Black Hat?

Ben Graham, general manager of the Eldis Group, has often likened the current state of the Internet to the days of the "wild, wild west" where Google acts as the self-appointed town marshal or sheriff. Search engine optimization (SEO) techniques are employed by e-commerce businesses like Eldis to optimize the organic traffic—the traffic directed to the website by search engines like Google. The goal of optimizers is to have the company appear in the top three or four results on key search terms. In doing so, optimizers use "white hat" tactics that employ tried-and-tested methods, focus on long-term results, and comply with guidelines published by Google as well as with SEO practices recommended by experts. The problem is that the white hat approach is

slow, and there is no guarantee of a good ranking. "Black hat" tactics employ new and extreme (and sometimes unethical) methods to find loopholes in the search algorithms of the search engine providers.[47] There are three main techniques employed by black hat optimizers: cloaking, link farming, and keyword stuffing. In cloaking, content created specifically for search engine crawlers is hidden from normal view. Link farming is creating a network of interconnected pages with false content that is designed to look reputable. Keyword stuffing occurs when attackers exploit blogs and news sites that accept user input. Google is constantly looking for ways to identify and eliminate malware from its index through both manual and automated processes.[48]

Thinking Critically About Ethics

Both black hat and white hat search engine optimization techniques are present on the Internet. As the search engine of choice, Google is the primary gatekeeper. Should Google have the power to effectively close an Internet business down by excluding it from search results? How should ethical behaviour on the Internet be controlled? By industry associations? By Google? By legislation?

CASE APPLICATION

Smooth Ride

Big yellow school buses. They're a common sight at the beginning and end of the school day in many communities. One company that manufactures those school buses is Blue Bird North Georgia. School buses are a product in which quality is paramount. After all, that product is carrying precious cargo! However, achieving an organizational culture that's dedicated to quality and to efficient manufacturing isn't an easy thing to do.[49]

Blue Bird's plant in Lafayette, Georgia, started on its "lean" journey—that is, having a lean, efficient operation system—in 2003. The manager of engineering said, "Quality was at an all-time low. The plant was lacking in strategic systems and procedures to control quality, materials, production, finance, and human resources." In 2003, under new management, Blue Bird got serious about tackling its quality issues and implemented specific programs, including a material review board, a quality control lab equipped with a computerized maintenance management system, an employee suggestion system, weekly management roundtable meetings, and a safety incentive program. One key contributor to the company's success is measurement. Blue

Bird is determined to measure everything. The production manager said, "If you don't measure something, you don't know how well you're doing." Just how effective have these programs been?

The customer reject rate is now basically zero, with on-time delivery at 100 percent. The director of quality and risk management said, "Doing it right the first time takes a lot less time." Safety has also improved. The company's recordable injury rate was down 65 percent and time lost due to injuries was down 87 percent. After four years of hard work, the company achieved initial ISO 9001-2000 certification in March 2007. And it was named one of *Industry Week*'s best plants in 2007.

What has made Blue Bird's quality initiative successful? Discuss how you think each of the programs the company implemented contributed to what the company is today. How might value chain management concepts help Blue Bird become even more productive? What would the company have to do to benefit from managing its value chain? Research the concept of *lean manufacturing*. What does it mean? What benefits does "lean" offer?

DEVELOPING YOUR DIAGNOSTIC AND ANALYTICAL SKILLS

Going Postal

It's one of the oldest post offices in North America. Sepomex (Servicio Postal Mexicano), Mexico's state postal system, was established over four centuries ago in 1580. In August 1986, it became a semi-independent decentralized organization with the mandate to "serve as the public post office in Mexico." Carlos Rodarte is the head of regional operations for Sepomex, a job that entails many operational challenges.[50]

The Mexican postal system handles some 700 million letters a year, which may sound like a lot. But that number translates into just 7 pieces of mail per person. Compare that to Brazil, where the postal system handles 8 billion mailings a year, or 46 letters per person. It's clear that "Mexico's postal system is underused by a skeptical public." Data collected by a Mexican polling organization found that "a shocking 29 percent of Mexicans hadn't even heard of

Sepomex. Of those familiar with the mail service, 32 percent considered it to be slow and almost the same percentage preferred to use private messengers to hand-deliver documents, a common practice in Latin American cities."

Rodarte is trying to improve both the efficiency and the effectiveness of the country's postal system. He oversees Pantaco, the dispatch centre where most of the country's mail passes through at some point. He has made improvements there, including installing a new roof to make the building look more modern and investing in cutting-edge technology like security cameras, bar-code scanners, and machines that can read and sort 70 letters per minute. In addition, Mexico's Transport and Communications Ministry provided more funds to Sepomex, almost doubling capital outlays in 2005. These additional funds will go toward purchasing new vehicles, renovating dilapidated post offices, and making other infrastructure improvements. In addition, one of the things that Rodarte does to test his "own company's efficiency" is to send postcards to himself from almost every place he travels. However, there are still operational challenges to tackle, especially in the area of quality.

What is operations management? How might Carlos Rodarte use operations management to achieve his objectives?

Questions

1. Summarize the challenges that Rodarte faces in managing operations. Cite specific examples.

2. From the examples chosen above, develop metrics for measuring improvement—days to deliver a letter, processing time at the central postal station, etc.

3. What is the first problem you would attack? Why?

DEVELOPING YOUR INTERPERSONAL SKILLS

Managing Operations in an E-world Environment

About the Skill

If you can't measure it, you can't manage it! David Ritacco employs Google Analytics and other tools to manage the operations of PartSelect and the more than 400 000 unique monthly visits to the website. This is very different from the way companies have managed their relationships with customers in the past. What metrics might Ritacco look at to improve the operating results of the company?

Steps in Developing the Skill

Go to the Google Analytics home page (**www.google.com/ analytics**) and click on the Product tab and then Features. This page outlines the following enterprise-class features to practise "performance focused marketing":[51]

1. **Advertising ROI**
   a. Goals—Track sales and conversions and measure site engagement goals against self-defined threshold levels.
   b. Integrated AdWords and AdSense—View post-click data on keywords, search queries, etc., with AdWords, and use AdSense to see which site content generates the most revenue.
   c. Campaign-Tracking Capabilities—Track email campaigns, banner ads, offline ads, etc.

2. **Cross-Channel and Multimedia Marketing**
   a. Mobile Tracking—Track mobile websites, mobile apps, and web-enabled mobile devices.
   b. Internal Site Search—Find out what customers are really looking for and speed up time to conversion.
   c. Benchmarking—Compare key site usage metrics with those of your industry.
   d. Flash, Video, and Social Networking Tracking—Track usage by visitors to the website.

3. **Customized Reporting**
   a. Advanced Segmentation—Isolate and analyze subsets of your traffic and compare with current and historical data.
   b. Custom Reports—Create custom reports that are available for as long as you need them.
   c. Dashboards—Define a custom dashboard to manage the metrics you feel are most important.
   d. API and Developer Platform—Export data, create integration, and develop your own applications.
   e. Analytics Intelligence—Monitor client data and get automatic alerts of significant changes.

4. **Visualizing Data**
   a. Motion Charts—Choose appropriate metrics to expose data relationships that are difficult to see in traditional reports.
   b. Geo Reporting—Identify lucrative geographic markets.
   c. Funnels—Identify leaks by seeing which pages result in lost opportunities and where would-be customers go.
   d. Spark Lines—Create thumbnail-size graphics to save clicks and summarize data within a report.
   e. Score Cards—Provide summary metrics in the context of historical or site average data.

Practising and Reinforcing the Skill

The following activities will help you practise and reinforce the skills associated with managing operations in an e-world environment.

1. Make a list of the most popular websites that you visit. Pick the top 2 or 3 and go to the Compete website (**www.compete.com**). On the Compare Sites tab, compare the number of unique visitors to each site. Next, scroll down and look at the following metrics:
   a. How many unique visitors did each site have? Is this increasing or decreasing on an annual basis?
   b. How many search terms are in the top 10 search terms list for each of the sites? Click on top search terms and look at the other metrics columns available.

   c. Which of the sites you have chosen has a higher count in the following categories: referring sites, sites sending more traffic, sites sending less traffic, referring categories?

2. Based on your analysis above,
   a. Which site has the most traffic?
   b. What might account for this?
   c. What could each of the sites do to drive more traffic to their site?

3. Imagine that you built your own website. What metrics would you choose to measure? Why?

MyManagementLab

After you have completed the study of Part 5, do the following exercises at the MyManagementLab website (www.pearsoned.ca/mymanagementlab):

- You're the Manager: Putting Ethics into Action (Boston Scientific)
- Passport, Scenario 1 (Nelson Naidoo, Diamonds International), Scenario 2 (Kristen Mesicek, Global One Cellular), and Scenario 3 (Danny Lim, 88WebCom)

VIDEO CASE INCIDENT   CBC

SCAN THIS

Please turn to the back of the book to see the Video Case Incidents available for Part 5.

VIDEO CASE INCIDENTS

CBC ⟪⟫ CBC Video Case Incident

The Fast-Food Industry and Trans Fats: Fad or Legitimate Concern for Society?

Trans fats (such as partially hydrogenated oils) are fats that are artificially created through a chemical process that solidifies the oil and limits the body's ability to regulate cholesterol. These fats are considered to be the most harmful to one's health.

BanTransFats.com is an organization established to provoke a ban on the use of trans fats in food. The organization's 2003 lawsuit against Kraft resulted in the company's eliminating the use of trans fats in Oreo cookies and reducing or eliminating the use of trans fats in 650 other Kraft products. After the lawsuit, the US Food and Drug Administration (FDA) changed its labelling rule to include trans fats. This has had a significant effect on the elimination of trans fats in a range of fast foods in the United States and Canada.

On June 28, 2006, a task force formed by Health Canada recommended that total trans fats in vegetable oils and spreadable margarines be limited to 2 percent of total fat content. It also recommended that trans fats be limited to 5 percent of total fat content for all other foods. These recommendations have been publicly supported by the Canadian Restaurant and Foodservices Association (CRFA).

While banning trans fats is good for societal health, it is not as good for business; restaurants use trans fats because they are far cheaper than other fats. To preserve profits, restaurants may be forced to pass on the increased costs to consumers through higher prices. If regulations do not ultimately require a "ban" but only a "significant reduction," are fast-food companies moving toward eliminating trans fats due to a legitimate concern for society or to ensure that competitive ground is not lost? Are the increased costs to the food sector offset by health care savings? Given so much varying nutritional information and the realities of competition, how can the fast-food industry react to these changes, remain profitable, and be perceived as being socially responsible?

QUESTIONS

1. *For discussion:* How might the issue of trans fats be perceived by holders of the classical vs. the socio-economic views of corporate social responsibility?

2. *For debate:* "Since every person has the right to decide what to eat, ingesting trans fats seems to be more a matter of making informed decisions and, as such, the fast-food industry should not bear the entire responsibility for the illnesses that are believed to arise from eating its products." Do you agree or disagree with this statement?

3. *For analysis:* How does this case demonstrate the importance of stakeholder management?

4. *For application:* Pick a fast-food restaurant of your choice and, using the Internet and other sources, determine whether the elimination of trans fats from its products is mentioned in its corporate social responsibility activities. Based on your research, do you feel this company is eliminating trans fats out of genuine concern for society, for competitive advantage, to avoid or reduce government regulation, or some combination of these factors?

Sources: "Fast Food Fads," *CBC Venture*, January 30, 2005, 935, VA–2081 C; C. Ness, "Tiburon Lawyer Getting the Trans Fat Out," *San Francisco Chronicle*, February 4, 2007, http://sfgate.com/cgi-bin/article.cgi?f=/c/a/2007/02/04/LVGI5NRT291.DTL; www.bantransfats.com; "Diet Wars," *Frontline*, www.pbs.org/wgbh/pages/frontline/teach/diet/worksheet_pre2.html; and J. M. Hirsch, "Obesity Often Blamed on Food Companies," *CTV.ca*, March 20, 2006, www.ctv.ca/servlet/ArticleNews/story/CTVNews/20060320/food_obesity_ blame_060320?s_name=&no_ads=.

Stem Cell Research

Stem cells are undifferentiated cells that have the unique potential to produce any kind of cell in the body; they are "generic" cells with indefinite self-renewal capabilities. Stem cell research holds much promise in potentially curing diseases such as Alzheimer's and Parkinson's, diabetes, heart disease, arthritis, cancer, and spinal cord injuries.

In 2000, the federal government established the Canadian Institutes of Health Research (CIHR) as the premier funding agency for health research in Canada. To be eligible for funding, stem cells for research can be derived from only three major sources: very early embryos, fetal reproductive organs, and adult tissue. The conditions under which stem cell research would be eligible for CIHR funding include the use of pre-existing human embryonic stem cell lines; the use of surplus embryos originally created for reproductive purposes; when the persons for whom the embryos were created give free and informed consent for their use in research; and when there are no commercial transactions involved in embryo creation and use.

The ethical issues surrounding stem cell research are complex. As Peter Calamai states, "The ethical crux is usually framed as a dilemma: to potentially save the lives of people afflicted with degenerative diseases . . . through the use of embryonic stem cells, it appears necessary to sacrifice the potential life of an embryo."

Professor Ron Worton, a researcher in the genetics of human disease, noted that the embryos used would most likely die anyway since they are derived from "surplus" fertilized eggs remaining after treatment at fertility clinics. Professor Bernard Dickens, emeritus professor of health law and policy, noted that embryos have no legal rights in Canadian law; no one could be prosecuted for homicide for killing a fetus. Professor Abby Lipman, a professor of epidemiology, biostatistics, and occupational health, contended that the major threats to the health of Canadian women are from problems "much less exotic than the diseases being tackled by embryonic research," and the push by "vested interests" for such research means that poor women run the risk of being considered simply as producers of raw material for third parties.

In a *Science AAAS* article, Gretchen Vogel reports on the experience of the Bedford Stem Cell Research Foundation and its successful efforts to recruit donors of oocytes (eggs produced by the ovary before fertilization) for embryonic stem cell experiments. The group advertised in the *Boston Globe* in September 2000 and by word of mouth from 2003. By the end of 2005, 23 donors had yielded 274 oocytes at an average cost of $3673 per egg. Adding the costs of psychological and physical evaluations and medical expenses, the cost per woman of each completed donation cycle amounted to $27 200. The costs of obtaining materials for this research are obviously significant. Might ethical issues eventually emerge in biotechnology research in developing countries if poor women are transformed into producers of "raw materials" for third parties?

QUESTIONS

1. *For discussion:* Describe how each of the four perspectives of ethics applies to the ethics of stem cell research.

2. *For debate:* Do you feel that stem cell research is ethical? Would your position change if a loved one was afflicted by a disease that could potentially be cured through stem cell research?

3. *For analysis:* Professor Lipman contended that the major threats to the health of Canadian women are from poverty, abuse, and other woes, and that stem cell research means that poor women run the risk of being considered simply as producers of "raw material" for third parties. Do you agree or disagree with Professor Lipman?

4. *For application:* Using the Internet and other sources, define stem cell research. Given this definition, develop a "Code of Ethical Conduct" for a biotechnology lab engaged in stem cell research.

Sources: "Stem Cell," *CBC The National*, February 12, 2007; http://en.wikipedia.org/ wiki/Stem_cell_research; www.sciencecoalition.org; "Stem Cell Research and Ethics"; The Royal Society of Canada, www.rsc.ca/print.php?lang_id=1&page_id=195; "CIHR Releases Human Pluripotent Stem Cell Research Guidelines," Canadian Institutes of Health Research, March 4, 2002, www.cihr-irsc.gc.ca/ e/8000.html; www.repro-med.net/glossary.php; www.sciencemag.org/ cgi/content/full/313/5784/155b; and M. Bhardwaj and D. Macer, "Policy and Ethical Issues in Applying Biotechnology in Developing Countries," *Medical Science Monitor* 9, no. 2 (2003), www.MedSciMonit.com/pub/vol_9/no_2/3030.pdf.

Ben & Jerry's in Canada

In May 1978, Ben Cohen and Jerry Greenfield completed a $5 correspondence course on ice-cream making and started Ben & Jerry's in a converted abandoned gas station in Burlington, Vermont. They gambled their life savings of $8000 on a dream of making Vermont's best ice cream. By 1985, Ben & Jerry's had sales of more than $9 million, reaching almost $20 million the following year. Sales hit $237 million by the end of 1999, before the company was acquired by the Anglo-Dutch corporation Unilever in August 2000.

Ben & Jerry's operates on a corporate concept of *linked prosperity* anchored in three key parts to its mission statement. Its *product mission* calls for making, distributing, and selling "the finest quality all natural ice cream . . . with a continued commitment to incorporating wholesome, natural ingredients and promoting business practices that respect the earth . . . " Its *economic mission* is "to operate the company on a sustainable financial basis of profitable growth. " And its *social mission* is "to operate the company in a way that actively recognizes the central role that business plays in society by initiating innovative ways to improve the quality of life locally, nationally, and internationally."

Perhaps this is why Morrie Baker and his real estate partner were willing to risk over $1 million of their own money to develop Ben & Jerry's in Canada. But investors were worried that their $1 million could be eaten up very quickly. According to TheFranchiseMall.com, the total investment to open a single Ben & Jerry's franchise could run from $147 000 to $396 000. Planning and decision making are critical. Where should the franchises be set up? How much should be spent on a location? How much customer traffic is necessary to be profitable? Do the locations offer exclusivity, or would the location manager offer a site to competitors?

Morrie Baker now owns 20 Canadian shops and takes the view that success comes from execution and proper location choice. While Baker appears to be succeeding in Canada, it seems that elsewhere 10 percent of Ben & Jerry's shops close each year. Baker knows that a winning strategy requires the right decisions at the right times . . . within the confines of rationality!

QUESTIONS

1. *For discussion:* Which step of the decision-making process presents the greatest risk?

2. *For debate:* "Given the advances of information and communications technology, managerial decision making today is much easier since so much information is so quickly and easily available to aid in the decision-making process." Do you agree or disagree with this statement?

3. *For analysis:* In your view, which of the common decision-making biases and errors would most likely present the greatest risk to a manager deciding on a location for a Ben & Jerry's franchise?

4. *For application:* Using the Internet and other sources, identify some of the corporate social responsibility activities Ben & Jerry's has undertaken as a member of the Unilever company. What do you feel are the most important issues that affect the decision of the company to invest in these activities?

Sources: "Ben & Jerry's Ice Cream Moves into Canada," *CBC Venture*, January 30, 2005, 935, VA–2100 F; Ben & Jerry's website, www.benjerry.com/our_ company/our_history, www.benjerry.com/our_company/research_library/fin/ qtr/1999/Q4-99.html, www. benjerry.com/our_company/about_us/our_ history/timeline/index.cfm; "Unilever Acquisition of Ben & Jerry's," http://benjerry.custhelp.com/app/answers/detail/a_id/136/~/unilever-acquisition-of-ben-%26-jerry's; "Ben and Jerry's," Unilever, www.unileverusa.com/ourbrands/foods/benandjerrys.asp; "Ben and Jerry's Franchise," TheFranchiseMall.com, www. thefranchisemall.com/franchises/details/10816-0-Ben_and_Jerrys.htm; "Ben and Jerry's Franchise," FranchiseMarketplace.com, www.franchisemarket-place.com/franchisedetail.asp?aid=147&franchise=Ben_and_Jerry; and www.ethicalcorp.com/content.asp?ContentID=4538.

Joe Six-Pack and Four Canadian Entrepreneurs

Today, Canada's brewing industry comprises two dominant companies: Labatt Breweries of Canada, established in 1847, brewing 60 quality beers, employing 3200 Canadians, and operating six breweries from coast to coast; and Molson Breweries, Canada's oldest brewing company, established in 1786, employing 3000 employees across the country and operating six breweries. Molson Canada is now an integral part of the Molson Coors Brewing Company, which was formed by the 2005 merger of Molson and Coors.

In recent times, the Canadian market has seen the development of over 40 microbreweries and an endless influx of international beers. Risks for new market entrants are high. How could another start-up beer company and a micro-distillery promoting coolers ever hope to make it?

BLACK FLY BEVERAGE COMPANY

Black Fly Beverage Company is Ontario's first micro-distillery, founded by husband and wife team Rob Kelly and Cathy Siskind-Kelly in May 2005. Black Fly Coolers are made and bottled in London, Ontario. Setting up the enterprise required considerable funds, and major lenders were reluctant due to the very real risk of failure; most of the start-up funds were raised by the Kellys themselves. The production capacity of their 3300-square-foot "pilot" plant is limited to 2.5 million 400-millilitre bottles per year.

In January 2006, Black Fly's original cranberry–blueberry cooler was selling in 140 Liquor Control Board of Ontario (LCBO) outlets and bars in the London area. Today, the LCBO distributes the "all Canadian produced" cooler to 450 of its 600 stores. The Kellys are looking for a new plant with at least 10 times the capacity of the existing plant, and are considering expanding their market into all parts of Canada.

MOUNTAIN CREST BREWING COMPANY

Meet Manjit and Ravinder Minhas, petroleum-engineering graduates from the University of Calgary. The 20-something siblings started Calgary-based Mountain Crest Brewing Company in 2002. Their strategy is to underprice Molson and Labatt. To do so, they outsourced their brewing to Huber Brewing in Monroe, Wisconsin. Huber offered lower prices than any of the Canadian brewers they approached. In 2006, the siblings bought Huber Brewing to have long-term production stability, renaming it Minhas Craft Brewery in October 2007.

Mountain Crest beer is mainly sold in Alberta and other western provinces. In an effort to have a presence in eastern Canada, the Minhases incorporated Lakeshore Creek Brewing in Ontario in the summer of 2004, wanting to crack the large, highly competitive Ontario market with their Lakeshore Creek brand of premium but inexpensive beer.

Statistics Canada reports that Canadians bought around $7.9 billion worth of beer in 2003; it is estimated that 20 percent of that was spent on value beer. Ontario craft brewers such as Brick Brewery are posting record sales numbers. This is good news for the Minhases!

QUESTIONS

1. *For discussion:* Compare and contrast the Mountain Crest Brewing Company with the Black Fly Beverage Company using the strategic management process.

2. *For debate:* "The weakest part of the strategic management process undertaken by both the Mountain Crest Brewing Company and the Black Fly Beverage Company in their entry into the Ontario market was in their assessment of threats, or in the external analysis process." Do you agree or disagree with this statement?

3. *For analysis:* Which growth strategies would be best suited to each company in the long and short term?

4. *For application:* Using the Internet and other sources, identify two key competitors for both the Mountain Crest Brewing Company (in Ontario) and the Black Fly Beverage Company, and identify each company's sustainable competitive advantage over its key competitors.

Sources: "Joe Six Pack," *CBC Venture*, January 22, 2006, 6, NEP-14756; www.blackflycoolers.com; "Entrepreneur: Black Fly Beverage Co.," January 15, 2007, www.yoce.ca/entrepreneur_archives.php?sub=featureprofiles&issue=2&m=01&y=2007; www.macleans.ca/business/companies/article.jsp?content=200060529_127754_127754; T. Daykin, "Crafting Success," *Milwaukee Journal Sentinel*, October 29, 2007; H. Daniszewski, "Black Fly Grips Sales," *London Free Press*, January 18, 2006, www.lfpress.ca/cgi-bin/publish.cgi?p=120093&x=articles&s=shopping; M. Magnan, "Beer War," *Canadian Business*, July 2005, www.canadianbusiness.com/shared/print.jsp?content=20050718_69548_69548; "Siblings Brew Up Attack Plan on Big Beer," *Business Edge*, March 31, 2005, www.businessedge.ca/article.cfm/newsID/8963.cfm; and Mountain Crest Brewing Company website, www.damngoodbeer.ca/beer5.htm.

Information Technology: Massachusetts General Hospital

For over 50 years, Massachusetts General Hospital has been on the cutting edge of technology for the health industry. Located in Boston, it is the third-oldest hospital in the United States and boasts a state-of-the-art information system infrastructure that enables doctors and nurses to provide patients with the safest, most efficient health care available. Equipped with 16 000 personal computers, staff can locate one another, patients, and equipment in just seconds anywhere at any time. The emergency room can access patient histories and medical insurance records within seconds of a person's arrival. Updated lab results flash on a screen every 30 seconds, saving staff 20 to 30 minutes per patient. Doctors can even treat patients or manage hospital processes from home by entering a personal electronic signature when logging on to the hospital's intranet. While many institutions buy off-the-shelf software, Massachusetts General does its own innovative in-house development, bending the uses of new technologies to provide the best in health care to patients, families, and the community.

QUESTIONS

1. *For analysis:* How and why might "politically correct" communications be of particular interest to managers at Massachusetts General?

2. *For analysis:* As a hospital executive at Massachusetts General, how would you react to an Internet gripe site?

3. *For application:* What criteria would you use as an emergency room doctor to determine whether the information system was serving your needs and the needs of your staff and patients efficiently?

4. *For application:* Aside from the tracking system explained in the video, what other uses might there be for wireless capabilities at Massachusetts General?

5. *For debate:* Do you agree that Massachusetts General's innovative uses of technology for clinical processes create a safer environment for patients? Support your position.

Source: "Massachusetts General Hospital" (video), Pearson Prentice Hall Management Video Library.

Tamarack Lake Electric Boat Company

Montgomery Gisborne, a graduate of Ryerson Polytechnical University in Toronto, has a rich history in electric vehicles. Since 1994, Gisborne has served on the executive of the Electric Vehicle Society, Canada's largest electric vehicle organization. In 1997, an electric car he constructed placed tenth out of fifty entrants in the American Tour de Sol electric vehicle rally. In 2003, his car placed first.

In 2005, Gisborne formed the Tamarack Lake Electric Boat Company to bring electric boats to market. The Loon was a custom-designed, 20-foot pontoon-style prototype—a boat designed with 738 watts of solar panels overhead, serving as a source of solar energy and a roof. With a cruising speed of 5 knots, the 6-metre, eight-passenger Loon weighed in at 1000 kilograms, slightly heavier than a gas-powered version. Today, Tamarack Lake Electric Boat Company offers the commercial version of the Loon—22 feet, with a 1000-watt (peak) solar array and a top speed of 8 knots (9.5 mph)—and the Osprey—32 feet, with a 2000-watt (peak) solar array and the same top speed as the Loon.

Montgomery Gisborne has a lot of money riding on the successful commercialization of the electric boat—over a quarter of a million dollars. At $35 000 per Loon, almost twice the price of the gasoline engine–powered equivalent, the boat might be a tough sell, requiring a seasoned sales professional. The trouble is, Gisborne is the salesperson—and he's also the production engineer, the web page designer, and the advertising and promotions manager: a one-person show. So no small surprise that when he received his first order for 12 boats, his 18-hour days were not long enough!

Scrambling to buy enough materials to construct 12 Loons was a challenge. It was also a disappointment when his buyer was restricted to purchasing only five boats by his foreign government. Recognizing that he could no longer do it all himself, Gisborne hired some local talent to assist in production of the boats, as well as a part-time publicist to promote his creations. The publicity work has paid off, generating a significant order from Australia as well as deals from the Internet.

Now the question is, which organizational structure will best suit the Tamarack Lake Electric Boat Company?

QUESTIONS

1. *For debate:* Do you feel that a concerted effort to involve key stakeholders would offer the Tamarack Lake Electric Boat Company a sustainable competitive advantage?

2. *For analysis:* One possible organizational structure for the Tamarack Lake Electric Boat Company would be to hire a small number of full-time employees who "contract out" certain aspects of the work, such as hull fabrication, electronic components, boat interior components, advertising, accounting, and final assembly. Many aspects of running the company could be undertaken remotely. Would a network organization be an option for the Tamarack Lake Electric Boat Company?

3. *For application:* Using the Internet and other sources, research Montgomery Gisborne's competition and other successful small-volume, high-price manufacturers. How are his competitors and these other manufacturers organized? Does their approach to organizing give them any advantage over what you have recommended as an organizational structure for the Tamarack Lake Electric Boat Company?

Sources: "Solar Boat," *Venture's Dreamers and Schemers* (CBC), October 11, 2006; www.tamarackelectricboats.com/about_buffalo_solar_boats. html; and www.tamarackelectricboats.com/new_e_boats.html.

CBC **CBC Video Case Incident**

Millionaire on a Mission

Bill Young is a millionaire with a heart. After making millions leading high-growth entrepreneurial organizations, he decided to invest in helping others. He founded Toronto-based Social Capital Partners (SCP) in 2001. SCP provides support to businesses that hire people who often have difficulties finding employment: youths, single mothers, Aboriginal people, new immigrants, people with disabilities, and those with substance abuse issues.

SCP provides start-up capital to business ventures that it thinks will be able to grow and turn a profit within about three years. The business owners must commit to helping improve the lives of their employees by making them financially self-sufficient while providing training and other support as necessary.

The types of businesses supported by SCP are known as "social enterprises." They look like typical businesses, except most of their employees come from groups that rely heavily on government assistance to live and have found it nearly impossible to get full-time jobs for a variety of reasons. These businesses have a "double bottom line": "a financial bottom line like traditional businesses but also a social bottom line—getting people who have traditionally faced significant employment barriers back into the economic mainstream."

SCP funds a number of social enterprises, including Winnipeg-based Inner City Renovation (ICR). ICR, founded in August 2002, is a construction and renovation company that works mainly on not-for-profit housing projects. The company's work helps address the lack of affordable housing in Winnipeg and provides employment to Aboriginal people who live in the inner city. Employees often work on houses in their own neighbourhoods, which means that their work is also improving their local environment. ICR's employees earn a steady income and learn a skilled trade that they can use in the future. An Aboriginal social worker on staff helps employees address personal problems, including alcohol and chemical dependency.

By mid-2004, SCP and Winnipeg-based Community Ownership Solutions had invested $100 000 in ICR. The company generated almost $1 million in revenue after its first year, but also suffered a $350 000 loss. By the end of 2005, however, the company generated more than $1 million in revenue, with a loss of only $3000. Young acknowledges that ICR is a "wonderful learning experience. It's not like it's gone smoothly. It's such an exciting model, this notion of combining housing and employment. It's taking a radically different approach to structural social problems in a lot of urban areas. There are exciting implications, if we can make this work."

QUESTIONS

1. *For analysis:* What leadership style(s) might be effective when dealing with employees who have personal challenges, such as those who are employed by Inner City Renovation?

2. *For analysis:* From a leadership perspective, what are the advantages and disadvantages of leading a company identified as a social enterprise?

3. *For application:* Inner City Renovation would like to reduce the absenteeism and turnover rates of its employees. How should it go about doing this?

4. *For application:* What are some of the challenges that Bill Young faces in trying to identify social enterprises to invest in?

5. *For debate:* "Only money motivates employees. Inner City Renovation should pay its employees more in order to solve its turnover problems." Do you agree or disagree with this statement? Explain.

Sources: "Social Capitalist," *CBC Venture*, February 29, 2004, 916, VA–2050 D; www.socialcapitalpartners.ca/index.html (accessed January 23, 2005); M. Cook, "Chasing the Double Bottom Line: Series: The Charity Industry," *Ottawa Citizen*, March 1, 2004, p. D7; and www.socialcapitalpartners.ca/articles/.

Leading with Integrity: Quova's Marie Alexander

Founded in November 1999 by Rajat Bhargava, Derald Muniz, Dave Naffziger, Sumit Agarwal, Rahul Pathak, and Terry Duryea, Quova is headquartered in Mountain View, California. Quova's expertise lies in enabling online businesses to instantly identify where visitors to their website are geographically located. Online companies, including broadcasters, e-retailers, and banks, integrate Quova's geolocation data into their web applications to target advertising, detect fraud, and comply with local laws. Quova provides detailed demographic and other data with accuracy of 99.9 percent at the country level and up to 98.2 percent at the state level.

Quova was initially a privately held company with 70 employees. Since being acquired as a wholly owned subsidiary of Neustar in October 2010, Quova has worked with some impressive companies, such as BBC Worldwide and Continental Airlines. Such a fast-paced, leading-edge, and creative environment requires strong leadership.

Meet Marie Alexander, president and CEO of Quova. With a diverse educational background that includes a master of business information systems from Georgia State University and a bachelor of music therapy from Georgia College, and varied experience that includes managing an amusement park and working in mental institutions, Alexander might seem to be an unusual leader in such an environment. However, in her view this experience has informed her leadership style.

A recognized expert in Internet geolocation, Alexander believes that leadership is behavioural and practises what she refers to as "hands-under" leadership—a nurturing style that helps followers understand and reach their potential by "lifting and catching" them and emphasizing excellence with a heart. Alexander, who believes in leading with compassion, also has a comparably unsentimental view of conflict among subordinates. In her view, conflict is a good thing and demonstrates organizational growth. Without conflict, passive aggressiveness could prevail.

Alexander concedes that her nurturing approach is easier for a woman: Women are expected to portray a nurturing disposition, whereas men are not.

One of her greatest challenges is firing people, but she believes that as organizations change, changes in the workforce are often required. Knowing this, however, does not make firing someone and feeling responsible for the effect this will have on his or her life any easier.

QUESTIONS

1. *For debate:* "In today's highly competitive global environment, all effective managers at all organizational levels are good leaders; otherwise, the organizations they manage would not survive." Do you agree or disagree with this statement?

2. *For analysis:* Suppose that a major security leak in Quova's systems was discovered such that site visitors were being located and subsequently targeted by criminals. How might Marie Alexander publicly lead this company to preserve the support and confidence of investors, customers, and other key stakeholders?

3. *For application:* Using the Internet and other sources, select a CEO from two publicly traded, technology-related firms. Using their published bios and considering the nature of their companies, develop a possible leadership profile for each of these individuals. Compare and contrast these leadership profiles with the leadership style of Marie Alexander.

Sources: "Leading with Integrity" (video), Pearson Prentice Hall Management Video Library; www.linkedin.com/companies/quova; and www.quova.com/about-us/.

Eco-Preneurs: Easywash—the World's Most Eco-friendly Car Wash Company

The average Canadian washes his or her car three times per month, representing a car wash market in the order of $3.5 billion. That's a lot of money *and* a lot of water! Laura-Lee Normandeau and Geoff Baker's Vancouver, BC-based company Easywash would like a piece of that financial pie but in a way that is environmentally friendly and preserves a lot of that water. In a single year, the Easywash system would save 24 000 000 litres of clean drinking water now being used to wash cars, recycling nearly 85 percent of water used in the wash process from its own well.

This start-up company was formed with a view to franchise, the expectation being that each Easywash franchise would command a selling price of between $1 million and $2.5 million. The franchisee would benefit from assistance in setting up the car wash, a full training package on running the operation, marketing materials, and ongoing support. The challenge is that, while car washes are capital intensive by their nature, they are dominated by oil companies in Canada. Land costs are very high and there is a lack of financing opportunities. Undaunted, Normandeau and Baker have gambled everything—with $1.25 million from 60 shareholders and debt-servicing payments of $30 000 per month on $3.5 million. Construction costs on the initial site originally budgeted at $1.5 million have gone considerably over budget to around $2.3 million.

Like most environmentally friendly businesses and services, at Easywash going green is not cost free. Will customers be willing to pay a bit more for an environmentally friendly car wash? While the franchise will feature an express wash for $5 including taxes and will be the lowest-priced car wash in the marketplace, covering the operational costs and servicing the capital costs of the franchise would require an enormous number of car washes at $5. The full-service wash is significantly more expensive than its less green competitors'.

In the end, going bankrupt proved to be the only way to restart the company with a different debt/equity structure. The Easywash story suggests that a number of key controls are needed to ensure viability—both the controls and viability appear to have been in question.

QUESTIONS

1. For debate: "'Going green' is an admirable goal, but many customers are not willing to pay for it. Environmentally friendly, leading-edge companies such as Easywash represent considerably more risk than their less environmentally friendly competition, and this requires a much higher level of control." Do you agree with this statement?

2. *For analysis:* Traditional financial control measures include ratio analysis and budget analysis. Referring to the popular financial ratios presented in the text, which of those ratios, when calculated for Easywash, would be expected to reflect poor performance?

3. For application: Using the Internet and other sources, research Easywash's competition. Are there other eco-friendly car washes operating? Is their level of success superior to Easywash's? What is the nature of the control procedures put in place for these competitors? What can be learned from a review of competing car washes—eco-friendly or non-eco-friendly?

Sources: Fortune Hunters, Season One (CBC), January 12, 2008; http://corporate.easywash.com/; www.easywash.ca/section.asp?pageid=5716; *Octane*, January/February 2006, p. 62.

Who's Minding the Store?

Did you use your debit or credit card today? Do you feel secure knowing that technological advances have virtually assured privacy of your information? You may want to think again—welcome to the newest way of stealing credit card, debit card, and credit history information.

Thieves are breaking into stores, gas stations, and restaurants and stealing the hard drives attached to point-of-sale terminals used to swipe debit and credit cards. If not wiped clean every day, these hard drives are a repository of credit card numbers, debit card numbers, and encrypted pin numbers—everything needed to steal your credit and your money. Merchants are keeping it quiet and credit card companies will cover your losses, but your financial information and your identity are out there. For the thieves, this "open bank vault" is a windfall. The fraud statistics are staggering: In 2008, more than $400 million was lost in credit card fraud, almost half from counterfeit cards, and in 2009, $142.3 million was lost to debit card fraud.

Some major companies have been hit—Starbucks, Boston Pizza, Husky Oil, Red Robin, and many others who do not wish to be named. With 630 000 point-of-sale terminals in Canada, many open bank vaults are out there. In Abbotsford, British Columbia, 28 businesses were hit in 2010. One retail chain has been hit over 100 times. Stealing information from a hard drive is relatively easy, requiring only a card reader and a blank gift card. The gift card is loaded up and—presto! A new credit or debit card, with your account number, is available for use.

Merchants are expected to do everything possible to protect customers' information, including wiping clean the hard drives on their point-of-sale terminals every night. However, it appears that not all are doing this. Customers have every right to expect this practice, which would go a long way toward protecting credit and identity theft. Business practices have to change and better controls must be used. The question is, from a control point of view, what can be done to enhance the protection of customers' important information?

QUESTIONS

1. *For debate:* "One way of enhancing security would be to invest in advanced technology such as complicated data encryption that would serve as a control in protecting customers' information, even if the information is stolen. This additional expense would ultimately be borne by the customers and could result in price increases, but customers would be pleased to pay if they knew their personal information was secure. On the other hand, in the case of smaller companies with fewer resources, this increase in cost could force them out of business. The middle ground might be for each merchant to put in place controls to the level they can afford, taking into account the size and available resources of the organization." Do you agree with this statement?

2. *For analysis:* Suppose you operate a restaurant. How would you use bureaucratic control and clan control to enhance the security of your customers' financial information?

3. *For application:* Using the Internet and other sources, research the issue portrayed in this case. Discuss the controls that are being put in place to combat this type of fraud and to protect customers' personal information.

Source: "Who's Minding the Store?" *Marketplace* (CBC), March 29, 2010, www.cbc.ca/marketplace/2010/whos_minding_the_store/links. html.

ENDNOTES

Chapter 1

1. Based on "How Cirque du Soleil's Hippy Circus Took Over the World," *Guardian Unlimited*, September 4, 2009, www.guardian.co.uk/stage/2009/sep/04/cirque-du-soleil-circus; Cirque du Soleil home page, www.cirquedusoleil.com/CirqueDuSoleil/en/Pressroom/cirquedusoleil/biographies/Laliberté_guy.htm (accessed July 9, 2010); K. Moore, "Creativity No Laughing Matter at Cirque du Soleil," *Globe and Mail*, March 2, 2010, www.theglobeandmail.com; K. Moore, *"Daniel Lamarre: A CEO'sHigh-WireAct," Globe and Mail*, December 29, 2009.

2. K. A. Tucker and V. Allman, "Don't Be a Cat-and-Mouse Manager," *The Gallup Organization*, September 9, 2004, http://gmj.gallup.com.

3. "RBC Financial Group Again Selected by CEOs as Canada's Most Respected Corporation for 2003," *Canada NewsWire*, January 19, 2004.

4. D. J. Campbell, "The Proactive Employee: Managing Workplace Initiative," *Academy of Management Executive*, August 2000, pp. 52–66.

5. J. S. McClenahen, "Prairie Home Champion," *IndustryWeek*, October 2005, pp. 45–47.

6. K. Moore, *"Daniel Lamarre: A CEO'sHigh-WireAct," Globe and Mail*, December 29, 2009.

7. P. Drucker, *Management: Tasks, Responsibilities, Practices* (New York: Harper & Row, 1974).

8. H. Fayol, *Industrial and General Administration* (Paris: Dunod, 1916).

9. For a comprehensive review of this question, see C. P. Hales, "What Do Managers Do? A Critical Review of the Evidence," *Journal of Management*, January 1986, pp. 88–115.

10. H. Mintzberg, *The Nature of Managerial Work* (New York: Harper & Row, 1973); and J. T. Straub, "Put on Your Manager's Hat," *USA Today*, October 29, 2002, www.usatoday.com.

11. See, for example, L. D. Alexander, "The Effect Level in the Hierarchy and Functional Area Have on the Extent Mintzberg's Roles Are Required by Managerial Jobs," *Academy of Management Proceedings* (San Francisco, 1979), pp. 186–189; A. W. Lau and C. M. Pavett, "The Nature of Managerial Work: A Comparison of Public and Private Sector Managers," *Group and Organization Studies*, December 1980, pp. 453–466; M. W. McCall Jr. and C. A. Segrist, "In Pursuit of the Manager's Job: Building on Mintzberg," Technical Report No. 14 (Greensboro, NC: Center for Creative Leadership, 1980); C. M. Pavett and A. W. Lau, "Managerial Work: The Influence of Hierarchical Level and Functional Specialty," *Academy of Management Journal*, March 1983, pp. 170–177; C. P. Hales, "What Do Managers Do? A Critical Review of the Evidence," *Journal of Management*, January 1986, pp. 88–115; A. I. Kraut, P. R. Pedigo, D. D. McKenna, and M. D. Dunnette, "The Role of the Manager: What's Really Important in Different Management Jobs," *Academy of Management Executive*, November 1989, pp. 286–293; M. J. Martinko and W. L. Gardner, "Structured Observation of Managerial Work: A Replication and Synthesis," *Journal of Management Studies*, May 1990, pp. 330–357.

12. C. M. Pavett and A. W. Lau, "Managerial Work: The Influence of Hierarchical Level and Functional Specialty," *Academy of Management Journal*, March 1983, pp. 170–177.

13. S. J. Carroll and D. A. Gillen, "Are the Classical Management Functions Useful in Describing Managerial Work?" *Academy of Management Review*, January 1987, p. 48.

14. H. Koontz, "Commentary on the Management Theory Jungle—Nearly Two Decades Later," in *Management: A Book of Readings*, 6th ed. H. Koontz, C. O'Donnell, and H. Weihrich (New York: McGraw-Hill, 1984); S. J. Carroll and D. A. Gillen, "Are the Classical Management Functions Useful in Describing Managerial Work?" *Academy of Management Review*, January 1987, p. 48; and P. Allan, "Managers at Work: A Large-Scale Study of the Managerial Job in New York City Government," *Academy of Management Journal*, September 1981, pp. 613–619.

15. E. White, "Firms Step Up Training for Front-Line Managers," *Wall Street Journal*, August 27, 2007, p. B3.

16. R. L. Katz, "Skills of an Effective Administrator," *Harvard Business Review*, September–October 1974, pp. 90–102.

17. D. Nebenzahl, "People Skills Matter Most," *Gazette* (Montreal), September 20, 2004, p. B1.

18. H. G. Barkema, J. A. C. Baum, and E. A. Mannix, "Management Challenges in a New Time," *Academy of Management Journal*, October 2002, pp. 916–930; M. A. Hitt, "Transformation of Management for the New Millennium," *Organizational Dynamics*, Winter 2000, pp. 7–17; T. Aeppel, "Power Generation," *Wall Street Journal*, April 7, 2000, p. A11; "Rethinking Work," *Fast Company*, April 2000, p. 253; "Workplace Trends Shifting Over Time," *Springfield News Leader*, January 2, 2000, p. 7B1; "Expectations: The State of the New Economy," *Fast Company*, September 1999, pp. 251–264; T. J. Tetenbaum, "Shifting Paradigms: From Newton to Chaos," *Organizational Dynamics*, Spring 1998, pp. 21–33; T. A. Stewart, "Brain Power: Who Owns It . . . How They Profit from It," *Fortune*, March 17, 1997, pp. 105–110; G. P. Zachary, "The Right Mix," *Wall Street Journal*, March 13, 1997, p. A11; W. H. Miller, "Leadership at a Crossroads," *IndustryWeek*, August 19, 1996, pp. 42–56; M. Scott, "Interview with Dee Hock," *Business Ethics*, May–June 1996, pp. 37–41; and J. O. C. Hamilton, S. Baker, and B. Vlasic, "The New Workplace," *BusinessWeek*, April 29, 1996, pp. 106–117.

19. Industry Canada, "What Is the Contribution of Small Businesses to Canada's Gross Domestic Product?" *Small Business Research and Policy*, July 2010, www.ic.gc.ca/eic/site/sbrp-rppe.nsf/eng/rd02499.html (accessed November 11, 2010).

20. Statistics Canada, "Latest Release from the Labour Force Survey," *The Daily*, November 5, 2010, www.statcan.gc.ca/daily-quotidien/101105/dq101105a-eng.htm (accessed November 11, 2010).

21. Statistics Canada, "Latest Release from the Labour Force Survey," *The Daily*, November 5, 2010, www.statcan.gc.ca/daily-quotidien/101105/dq101105a-eng.htm (accessed November 11, 2010).

22. See "Highlights of the 2009 Annual Report," *Canada Post*, www.canadapost.ca/cpo/mc/aboutus/corporate/annualreport.jsf (accessed November 11, 2010); and "Top 1000 Publicly Traded Companies," *Report on Business*, http://v1.theglobeandmail.com/v5/content/tp1000-2009/index.php?sort=employee&order=DESC&industry=all&company=&x=11&y=7 (accessed November 11, 2010).

23. Karl Moore, *"Daniel Lamarre: A CEO'sHigh-WireAct," Globe and Mail*, December 29, 2009.

24. K. Davis and W. C. Frederick, *Business and Society: Management, Public Policy, Ethics*, 5th ed. (New York: McGraw-Hill, 1984), pp. 28–41, 76.

25. Indian and Northern Affairs Canada, "Prime Minister Harper Offers Full Apology on Behalf of Canadians for the Indian Residential

Schools System," June 11, 2008, www.ainc-inac.gc.ca/ai/rqpi/apo/index-eng.asp (accessed November 11, 2010).

26. International Organization for Standardization, "ISO's Social Responsibility Standard Approved for Publication," ISO News and Media, September 14, 2010, www.iso.org/iso/pressrelease.htm?refid=Ref1351 (accessed November 11, 2010).

27. S. L. Wartick and P. L. Cochran, "The Evolution of the Corporate Social Performance Model," *Academy of Management Review*, October 1985, p. 763.

28. R. Carson, *Silent Spring* (Boston: Houghton Mifflin, 1962); J. McCormack, *The Global Environmental Movement* (Chichester, UK: John Wiley, 1995).

29. R. W. Judy and C. D'Amico, *Workforce 2020* (Indianapolis: Hudson Institute, August 1999).

30. Information in this paragraph is based on http//www.statcan.ca/Daily/English/071204/d071204a.htm (accessed December 31, 2007); and http://www12.statcan.ca/english/census06/data/profiles/community/search/List/Page.cfm?Lang=E&GeoCode=48 (accessed December 31, 2007).

31. J. E. Garten, "Globalism without Tears," *Strategy+Business*, Fourth Quarter 2002, pp. 36–45; and L. L. Bierema, J. W. Bing, and T. J. Carter, "The Global Pendulum," *Training & Development*, May 2002, pp. 70–78; C. Taylor, "Whatever Happened to Globalization?" *Fast Company*, September 1999, pp. 228–236; and S. Zahra, "The Changing Rules of Global Competitiveness in the 21st Century," *Academy of Management Executive*, February 1999, pp. 36–42.

32. "Is Corporate Canada Being 'Hollowed Out'?" *CBCnews.ca*, May 27, 2007.

33. "Fortune Globe 500 2010," *Fortune*, http://money.cnn.com/magazines/fortune/fortune500/2010/index.html (accessed November 11, 2010).

34. A. Shama, "Management Under Fire: The Transformation of Management in the Soviet Union and Eastern Europe," *Academy of Management Executive* 7, no. 1 (1993), pp. 22–35.

35. T. J. Mullaney, H. Green, M. Arndt, R. D. Hof, and L. Himelstein, "The E-Biz Surprise," *BusinessWeek*, May 12, 2003, pp. 60–68; R. D. Hof and S. Hamm, "How E-Biz Rose, Fell, and Will Rise Anew," *BusinessWeek*, May 13, 2002, pp. 64–72; "Companies Leading Online," *IQ Magazine*, November–December 2001, pp. 54–63.

36. D. A. Menasce and V. A. F. Almeida, *Scaling for E-Business* (Upper Saddle River, NJ: Prentice Hall PTR, 2000).

37. D. A. Menasce and V. A. F. Almeida, *Scaling for E-Business* (Upper Saddle River, NJ: Prentice Hall PTR, 2000); M. Lewis, "Boom or Bust," *Business 2.0*, April 2000, pp. 192–205; J. Davis, "How It Works," *Business 2.0*, February 2000, pp. 112–115; and S. Alsop, "e or Be Eaten," *Fortune*, November 8, 1999, pp. 86–98.

38. Cited in E. Naumann and D. W. Jackson Jr., "One More Time: How Do You Satisfy Customers?" *Business Horizons*, May–June 1999, p. 73.

39. K. A. Eddleston, D. L. Kidder, and B. E. Litzky, "Who's the Boss? Contending with Competing Expectations from Customers and Management," *Academy of Management Executive*, November 2002, pp. 85–95.

40. See, for instance, M. D. Hartline and O. C. Ferrell, "The Management of Customer-Contact Service Employees: An Empirical Investigation," *Journal of Marketing*, October 1996, pp. 52–70; E. Naumann and D. W. Jackson Jr., "One More Time: How Do You Satisfy Customers?" *Business Horizons*, May–June 1999, p.

73; W. C. Tsai, "Determinants and Consequences of Employee Displayed Positive Emotions," *Journal of Management* 27, no. 4 (2001), pp. 497–512; S. D. Pugh, "Service with a Smile: Emotional Contagion in the Service Encounter," *Academy of Management Journal*, October 2001, pp. 1018–1027; S. D. Pugh, J. Dietz, J. W. Wiley, and S. M. Brooks, "Driving Service Effectiveness Through Employee-Customer Linkages," *Academy of Management Executive*, November 2002, pp. 73–84; K. A. Eddleston, D. L. Kidder, and B. E. Litzky, "Who's the Boss? Contending with Competing Expectations from Customers and Management," *Academy of Management Executive*, November 2002, pp. 85–95; and B. A. Gutek, M. Groth, and B. Cherry, "Achieving Service Success Through Relationships and Enhanced Encounters," *Academy of Management Executive*, November 2002, pp. 132–144.

41. P. E. Mott, *The Characteristics of Effective Organizations* (New York: HarperCollins, 1972).

42. M. Basadur, J. Conklin, and G. K. VanPatter, "Rethinking Wicked Problems Part 2: Unpacking Paradigms, Bridging Universes," *NextDJournal* 10, Conversation 10.3.

43. C. West Churchman introduced the concept of wicked problems in a guest editorial of *Management Science* 14, no. 4 (December 1967).

44. J. C. Camillus, "Strategy as a Wicked Problem," *Harvard Business Review* 86 (2008), pp. 98–101.

45. W. H. Gates, written testimony before US House of Representatives Committee on Science and Technology, March 2008.

46. D. Kirkpatrick, "The Second Coming of Apple," *Fortune*, November 9, 1998.

47. AACSB International, *Business Schools on an Innovation Mission: Report of the AACSB International Task Force on Business Schools and Innovation* (Tampa, FL: AACSB International, 2010).

48. R. A. Hattori and J. Wycoff, "Innovation DNA," *Training & Development*, January 2002, p. 24.

49. P. M. Senge, *The Fifth Discipline: The Art and Practice of Learning Organizations* (New York: Doubleday, 1990).

50. J. S. Brown and P. Duguid, "Balancing Act: How to Capture Knowledge without Killing It," *Harvard Business Review*, May–June 2000, pp. 73–80; J. Torsilieri and C. Lucier, "How to Change the World," *Strategy+Business*, Second Quarter, 2000, pp. 17–20; E. C. Wenger and W. M. Snyder, "Communities of Practice: The Organizational Frontier," *Harvard Business Review*, January–February 2000, pp. 139–145; S. R. Fisher and M. A. White, "Downsizing in a Learning Organization: Are There Hidden Costs?" *Academy of Management Review*, January 2000, pp. 244–251; R. Myers, "Who Knows?" *CFO*, December 1999, pp. 83–87; and M. T. Hansen, N. Nohria, and T. Tierney, "What's Your Strategy for Managing Knowledge?" *Harvard Business Review*, March–April 1999, pp. 106–116.

51. Based on J. B. Miner and N. R. Smith, "Decline and Stabilization of Managerial Motivation Over a 20-Year Period," *Journal of Applied Psychology*, June 1982, pp. 297–305; and J. B. Miner, B. Ebrahimi, and J. M. Wachtel, "How Deficiencies in Motivation to Manage Contribute to the United States' Competitiveness Problem (and What Can Be Done About It)," *Human Resource Management*, Fall 1995, pp. 363–386.

52. D. Flavelle, "Top Executives Still Raking It In," *Toronto Star*, January 5, 2010.

53. See, for example, "Executive Hires and Compensations: Performance Rules," *HRfocus*, July 2003, p. 1; and H. B. Herring, "At the Top, Pay and Performance Are Often Far Apart," *New York Times*, August 17, 2003, p. B9.

54. L. Lavelle, "CEO Pay: Nothing Succeeds Like Failure," *BusinessWeek*, September 11, 2000, p. 48.

55. D. Dias, "Bang for the Buck: CEO Scorecard" *National Post Business*, November 2006, pp. 23–28.

56. Information from Lipschultz Levin & Gray website, www. thethinkers.com (accessed March 15, 2003); and N. K. Austin, "Tear Down the Walls," *Inc.*, April 1999, pp. 66–76.

57. Information from Symantec website, www.symantec.com, December 14, 2005; N. Rothbaum, "The Virtual Battlefield," *Smart Money*, January 2006, pp. 76–80; S. H. Wildstrom, "Viruses Get Smarter—and Greedy," *BusinessWeek*, November 22, 2005, www.businessweek.com/technology/content/nov2005/tc20051122_735580.htm; and S. Kirsner, "Sweating in the Hot Zone," *Fast Company*, October 2005, pp. 60–65.

58. Based on H. Rothman, "The Boss as Mentor," *Nation's Business*, April 1993, pp. 66–67; J. B. Cunningham and T. Eberle, "Characteristics of the Mentoring Experience: A Qualitative Study," *Personnel Review*, June 1993, pp. 54–66; S. Crandell, "The Joys of Mentoring," *Executive Female*, March–April 1994, pp. 38–42; and W. Heery, "Corporate Mentoring Can Break the Glass Ceiling," *HRfocus*, May 1994, pp. 17–18.

Supplement 1

1. Based on "Coffee Crisis Prompts Action from Aid Groups," *CTV News*, September 19, 2002; www.java-jazz.ca/about_us.htm (accessed August 21, 2004); and G. Shaw, "No Turning Back Once the Money Rolls In: $30,000 Loan from a Friend Puts Jazzed-Up Coffee Van on the Road with Espresso Machine at the Ready," *Vancouver Sun*, August 21, 2004, p. J1.

2. C. S. George Jr., *The History of Management Thought*, 2nd ed. (Upper Saddle River, NJ: Prentice Hall, 1972), p. 4.

3. F. W. Taylor, *The Principles of Scientific Management* (New York: Harper, 1911), p. 44. For other information on F. W. Taylor, see M. Banta, *Taylored Lives: Narrative Productions in the Age of Taylor, Veblen, and Ford* (Chicago: University of Chicago Press, 1993); and R. Kanigel, *The One Best Way: Frederick Winslow Taylor and the Enigma of Efficiency* (New York: Viking, 1997).

4. See, for example, F. B. Gilbreth, *Motion Study* (New York: Van Nostrand, 1911); and F. B. Gilbreth and L. M. Gilbreth, *Fatigue Study* (New York: Sturgis and Walton, 1916).

5. G. Colvin, "Managing in the Info Era," *Fortune*, March 6, 2000, pp. F6–F9; and A. Harrington, "The Big Ideas," *Fortune*, November 22, 1999, pp. 152–153.

6. H. Fayol, *Industrial and General Administration* (Paris: Dunod, 1916).

7. M. Weber, *The Theory of Social and Economic Organizations*, ed. T. Parsons, trans. A. M. Henderson and T. Parsons (New York: Free Press, 1947).

8. E. Mayo, *The Human Problems of an Industrial Civilization* (New York: Macmillan, 1933); and F. J. Roethlisberger and W. J. Dickson, *Management and the Worker* (Cambridge, MA: Harvard University Press, 1939).

9. See, for example, A. Carey, "The Hawthorne Studies: A Radical Criticism," *American Sociological Review*, June 1967, pp. 403–416; R. H. Franke and J. Kaul, "The Hawthorne Experiments: First Statistical Interpretations," *American Sociological Review*, October 1978, pp. 623–643; B. Rice, "The Hawthorne Defect: Persistence of a Flawed Theory," *Psychology Today*, February 1982, pp. 70–74; J. A. Sonnenfeld, "Shedding Light on the Hawthorne Studies," *Journal of Occupational Behavior*, April 1985, pp. 111–130; S. R. G. Jones, "Worker Interdependence and Output: The Hawthorne Studies Reevaluated," *American Sociological Review*, April 1990, pp. 176–190; S. R. Jones, "Was There a Hawthorne Effect?" *American Sociological Review*, November 1992, pp. 451–468; and G. W. Yunker, "An Explanation of Positive and Negative Hawthorne Effects: Evidence from the Relay Assembly Test Room and Bank Wiring Observation Room Studies" (paper presented at Academy of Management annual meeting, Atlanta, Georgia, August 1993).

10. With thanks to a reviewer who provided this example.

11. K. B. DeGreene, *Sociotechnical Systems: Factors in Analysis, Design, and Management* (Englewood Cliffs, NJ: Prentice Hall, 1973), p. 13.

Chapter 2

1. Based on R. Chang, "At 3M Staff Get Time Off for Eureka Moments," *Straits Times*, Singapore, February 26, 2010; A. Nanavati, "Find a Middle Path," *Outlook Business India*, May 29, 2010; B. NNeji, "Improve Processes, Improve Innovation; Equally Critical: Process Improvement and Quality Must Work Together," *Advertising Age*, June 25, 2007.

2. "BP Braced for Shakeup at Top, "*Dow Jones International News*, July 3, 2010.

3. B. Cooper, "Blue Mantle Will Close on April 30: Other Closures Hurt Business," *Leader Post*, March 20, 2004, p. B2.

4. For insights into the symbolic view, see J. Pfeffer, "Management as Symbolic Action: The Creation and Maintenance of Organizational Paradigms," in *Research in Organizational Behavior*, vol. 3, ed. L. L. Cummings and B. M. Staw, pp. 1–52 (Greenwich, CT: JAI Press, 1981); D. C. Hambrick and S. Finkelstein, "Managerial Discretion: A Bridge between Polar Views of Organizational Outcomes," in *Research in Organizational Behavior*, vol. 9, ed. L. L. Cummings and B. M. Staw, pp. 369–406 (Greenwich, CT: JAI Press, 1987); J. A. Byrne, "The Limits of Power," *BusinessWeek*, October 23, 1987, pp. 33–35; J. R. Meindl and S. B. Ehrlich, "The Romance of Leadership and the Evaluation of Organizational Performance," *Academy of Management Journal*, March 1987, pp. 91–109; C. R. Schwenk, "Illusions of Management Control? Effects of Self-serving Attributions on Resource Commitments and Confidence in Management," *Human Relations*, April 1990, pp. 333–347; S. M. Puffer and J. B. Weintrop, "Corporate Performance and CEO Turnover: The Role of Performance Expectations," *Administrative Science Quarterly*, March 1991, pp. 1–19; and "Why CEO Churn Is Healthy," *BusinessWeek*, November 13, 2000, p. 230.

5. T. M. Hout, "Are Managers Obsolete?" *Harvard Business Review*, March–April 1999, pp. 161–168; and J. Pfeffer, "Management as Symbolic Action: The Creation and Maintenance of Organizational Paradigms," in *Research in Organizational Behavior*, vol. 3, ed. L. L. Cummings and B. M. Staw, pp. 1–52 (Greenwich, CT: JAI Press, 1981).

6. Based on R. Chang, "At 3M Staff Get Time Off for Eureka Moments," *Straits Times* (Singapore) February 26, 2010; A. Nanavati, "Find a Middle Path," *Outlook Business India*, May 29, 2010; B. NNeji, "Improve Processes, Improve Innovation; Equally Critical: Process Improvement and Quality Must Work Together," *Advertising Age*, June 25, 2007.

7. Example based on D. Yedlin, "Home Field Advantage," *Report on Business Magazine*, March 26, 2004, p. 51. See also EnCana's corporate constitution, www.encana.com/aboutus/constitution/ (accessed September 11, 2007).

8. L. Smircich, "Concepts of Culture and Organizational Analysis," *Administrative Science Quarterly*, September 1983, p. 339; D. R. Denison, "What Is the Difference between Organizational Culture and Organizational Climate? A Native's Point of View on a Decade of Paradigm Wars" (paper presented at Academy of Management Annual Meeting, Atlanta, Georgia, 1993); and M. J. Hatch, "The Dynamics of Organizational Culture," *Academy of Management Review*, October 1993, pp. 657–693.

9. K. Shadur and M. A. Kienzle, "The Relationship between Organizational Climate and Employee Perceptions of Involvement," *Group & Organization Management*, December 1999, pp. 479–503; and A. M. Sapienza, "Believing Is Seeing: How Culture Influences the Decisions Top Managers Make," in *Gaining Control of the Corporate Culture*, ed. R. H. Kilmann, M. J. Saxton, and R. Serpa (San Francisco: Jossey-Bass, 1985), p. 68.

10. C. A. O'Reilly III, J. Chatman, and D. F. Caldwell, "People and Organizational Culture: A Profile Comparison Approach to Assessing Person-Organization Fit," *Academy of Management Journal*, September 1991, pp. 487–516; and J. A. Chatman and K. A. Jehn, "Assessing the Relationship between Industry Characteristics and Organizational Culture: How Different Can You Be?" *Academy of Management Journal*, June 1994, pp. 522–553.

11. See, for example, D. R. Denison, *Corporate Culture and Organizational Effectiveness* (New York: Wiley, 1990); G. G. Gordon and N. DiTomaso, "Predicting Corporate Performance from Organizational Culture," *Journal of Management Studies*, November 1992, pp. 793–798; J. P. Kotter and J. L. Heskett, *Corporate Culture and Performance* (New York: Free Press, 1992), pp. 15–27; J. C. Collins and J. I. Porras, *Built to Last* (New York: HarperBusiness, 1994); J. C. Collins and J. I. Porras, "Building Your Company's Vision," *Harvard Business Review*, September–October 1996, pp. 65–77; R. Goffee and G. Jones, "What Holds the Modern Company Together?" *Harvard Business Review*, November–December 1996, pp. 133–148; and J. B. Sorensen, "The Strength of Corporate Culture and the Reliability of Firm Performance," *Administrative Science Quarterly* 47, no. 1 (2002), pp. 70–91.

12. J. B. Sorensen, "The Strength of Corporate Culture and the Reliability of Firm Performance," *Administrative Science Quarterly* 47, no. 1 (2002), pp. 70–91.

13. See J. M. Jermier, J. Slocum, L. Fry, and J. Gaines, "Organizational Subcultures in a Soft Bureaucracy: Resistance Behind the Myth and Facade of an Official Culture," *Organization Science*, May 1991, pp. 170–194; S. A. Sackmann, "Culture and Subcultures: An Analysis of Organizational Knowledge," *Administrative Science Quarterly*, March 1992, pp. 140–161; R. F. Zammuto, "Mapping Organizational Cultures and Subcultures: Looking Inside and Across Hospitals" (paper presented at the 1995 National Academy of Management Conference, Vancouver, BC, August 1995); and G. Hofstede, "Identifying Organizational Subcultures: An Empirical Approach," *Journal of Management Studies*, January 1998, pp. 1–12.

14. T. A. Timmerman, "Do Organizations Have Personalities?" (paper presented at the 1996 National Academy of Management Conference, Cincinnati, OH, August 1996).

15. See http://thecanadianencyclopedia.com/index.cfm?PgNm=TCE&Params=M1ARTM0011001; www.magna.com/magna/en/about/ (accessed September 11, 2007); and B. Simon, "Work Ethic and the Magna Carta," *Financial Post Daily*, March 20, 1997, p. 14.

16. J. Jamrong, M. Vickers, and D. Bear, "Building and Sustaining a Culture That Supports Innovation," *Human Resource Planning* 29, no. 3 (2006).

17. See www.intuit.ca/en/intuit/careers_college.jsp.

18. Caption based on information in H. Dolezalek, "Outwit, Outlast, Outlearn," *Training*, January 2004, p. 18.

19. J. Forman, "When Stories Create an Organization's Future," *Strategy+Business*, Second Quarter 1999, pp. 6–9; D. M. Boje, "The Storytelling Organization: A Study of Story Performance in an Office-Supply Firm," *Administrative Science Quarterly*, March 1991, pp. 106–126; C. H. Deutsch, "The Parables of Corporate Culture," *New York Times*, October 13, 1991, p. F25; and T. Terez, "The Business of Storytelling," *Workforce*, May 2002, pp. 22–24.

20. S. Denning, *The Springboard: How Storytelling Ignites Action in Knowledge Era Organizations* (Boston: Butterworth Heinemann, 2000).

21. J. Useem, "Jim McNerney Thinks He Can Turn 3M from a Good Company into a Great One—With a Little Help from His Former Employer, General Electric," *Fortune*, August 12, 2002, pp. 127–132.

22. A. M. Pettigrew, "On Studying Organizational Cultures," *Administrative Science Quarterly*, December 1979, p. 576.

23. A. M. Pettigrew, "On Studying Organizational Cultures," *Administrative Science Quarterly*, December 1979, p. 576.

24. Cited in J. M. Beyer and H. M. Trice, "How an Organization's Rites Reveal Its Culture," *Organizational Dynamics*, Spring 1987, p. 15; and "The 'Masculine' and 'Feminine' Sides of Leadership and Culture: Perception vs. Reality," *Knowledge@Wharton*, http://knowledge.wharton.upenn.edu/article.cfm?articleid=1287 (accessed July 3, 2007).

25. Thanks to one of my reviewers for reporting this story.

26. A. Bryant, "The New Power Breakfast," *Newsweek*, May 15, 2000, p. 52.

27. See B. Victor and J. B. Cullen, "The Organizational Bases of Ethical Work Climates," *Administrative Science Quarterly*, March 1988, pp. 101–125; L. K. Trevino, "A Cultural Perspective on Changing and Developing Organizational Ethics," in *Research in Organizational Change and Development*, vol. 4, ed. W. A. Pasmore and R. W. Woodman (Greenwich, CT: JAI Press, 1990); and M. W. Dickson, D. B. Smith, M. W. Grojean, and M. Ehrhart, "An Organizational Climate Regarding Ethics: The Outcome of Leader Values and the Practices That Reflect Them," *Leadership Quarterly*, Summer 2001, pp. 197–217.

28. P. P. Waldie and K. Howlett, "Reports Reveal Tight Grip of Ebbers on WorldCom," *Globe and Mail*, June 11, 2003, pp. B1, B7.

29. "The World's 50 Most Innovative Companies," *Fast Company*, March 2008, p. 93; T. Kelley and J. Littman, *The Ten Faces of Innovation: IDEO's Strategies for Defeating the Devil's Advocate and Driving Creativity Throughout Your Organization* (New York: Currency, 2005); C. Fredman, "The IDEO Difference," *Hemispheres*, August 2002, pp. 52–57; and T. Kelley and J. Littman, *The Art of Innovation* (New York: Currency, 2001).

30. B. Nussbaum, "IDEO Makes the Top 25 Global Innovators—Here's Why," *Businessweek*, April 17, 2006.

31. J. F. Suri, *Thoughtless Acts? Observations on Intuitive Design* (San Francisco: Chronicle Books, 2005).

32. "Cirque du Soleil: Creating a Culture of Extraordinary Creativity," InnovationNetwork, http://innovationnetwork.biz/inmembership/emergent-practices/cirque.html (accessed March 14, 2011).

33. J. Yang and R. W. Ahrens, "Culture Spurs Innovation," *USA Today*, February 25, 2008, p. 1B.

34. L. Simpson, "Fostering Creativity," *Training*, December 2001, p. 56.

35. K. Aaserud, C. Cornell, J. McElgunn, K. Shiffman, and R. Wright, "The Golden Rules of Growth: Isadore Sharp," *PROFIT*, May 2007, www.canadianbusiness.com/entrepreneur/managing/article.jsp?content=20070419_095326_4460.

36. L. Gary, "Simplify and Execute: Words to Live By in Times of Turbulence," *Harvard Management Update*, January 2003, p. 12.

37. Based on M. J. Bitner, B. H. Booms, and L. A. Mohr, "Critical Service Encounters: The Employee's Viewpoint," *Journal of Marketing*, October 1994, pp. 95–106; M. D. Hartline and O. C. Ferrell, "The Management of Customer-Contact Service Employees: An Empirical Investigation," *Journal of Marketing*, October 1996, pp. 52–70; M. L. Lengnick-Hall and C. A. Lengnick-Hall, "Expanding Customer Orientation in the HR Function," *Human Resource Management*, Fall 1999, pp. 201–214; B. Schneider, D. E. Bowen, M. G. Ehrhart, and K. M. Holcombe, "The Climate for Service: Evolution of a Construct," in *Handbook of Organizational Culture and Climate*, ed. N. M. Ashkanasy, C. P. M. Wilderom, and M. F. Peterson, pp. 21–36 (Thousand Oaks, CA: Sage, 2000); M. D. Hartline, J. G. Maxham III, and D. O. McKee, "Corridors of Influence in the Dissemination of Customer-Oriented Strategy to Customer Contact Service Employees," *Journal of Marketing*, April 2000, pp. 35–50; L. A. Bettencourt, K. P. Gwinner, and M. L. Mueter, "A Comparison of Attitude, Personality, and Knowledge Predictors of Service-Oriented Organizational Citizenship Behaviors," *Journal of Applied Psychology*, February 2001, pp. 29–41; R. C. Ford and C. P. Heaton, "Lessons from Hospitality That Can Serve Anyone," *Organizational Dynamics*, Summer 2001, pp. 30–47; S. D. Pugh, J. Dietz, J. W. Wiley, and S. M. Brooks, "Driving Service Effectiveness Through Employee-Customer Linkages," *Academy of Management Executive*, November 2002, pp. 73–84; K. A. Eddleston, D. L. Kidder, and B. E. Litzky, "Who's the Boss? Contending with Competing Expectations from Customers and Management," *Academy of Management Executive*, November 2002, pp. 85–95; and B. A. Gutek, M. Groth, and B. Cherry, "Achieving Service Success Through Relationships and Enhanced Encounters," *Academy of Management Executive*, November 2002, pp. 132–144.

38. Thanks to a reviewer, Dr. Michelle Inness, University of Alberta, for providing this insight.

39. This box is based on Y. Cole, "Holding Managers Accountable for Diversity Success," *DiversityInc.* Special Issue 2006, pp. 14–19; "Diversity Is Important to the Bottom Line," *HR Powerhouse*, www.hrpowerhouse.com, January 21, 2006; P. Rosinski, *Coaching Across Cultures: New Tools for Leveraging National, Corporate, and Professional Differences* (London: Nicholas Brealey, 2003); "Diversity at the Forefront," *BusinessWeek*, November 4, 2002, pp. 27–38; "Talking to Diversity Experts: Where Do We Go from Here?" *Fortune*, September 30, 2002, pp. 157–172; "Keeping Your Edge: Managing a Diverse Corporate Culture," *Fortune*, June 11, 2001, pp. S1–S18; "Diversity Today," *Fortune*, June 12, 2000, pp. S1–S24; O. C. Richard, "Racial Diversity, Business Strategy, and Firm Performance: A Resource-Based View," *Academy of Management Journal*, April 2000, pp. 164–177; A. Markels, "How One Hotel Manages Staff's Diversity," *Wall Street Journal*, November 20, 1996, pp. B1+; C. A. Deutsch, "Corporate Diversity in Practice," *New York Times*, November 20, 1996, pp. C1+; and D. A. Thomas and R. J. Ely,

"Making Differences Matter: A New Paradigm for Managing Diversity," *Harvard Business Review*, September–October 1996, pp. 79–90.

40. D. Kawamoto, "Dow Jones Decline Mimics Great Depression," *cnet News, Business Tech*, http://news.cnet.com/8301-1001_3-10185559-92.html (accessed July 3, 2010).

41. Information taken from the 2008 10-K annual report filed by 3M. *Bloomberg BusinessWeek* (accessed July 3, 2010).

42. C. Helman, "Chevron Drills First Deepwater Well Since BP Disaster," *Forbes.com*, October 2, 2010, www.ctv.ca/CTVNews/Canada/20101001/chevron-well-101002/ (accessed November 1, 2010).

43. M. Tabini, "Amazon: E-Book Sales Surpass Paper on Christmas Day," *Macworld*, December 28, 2009, www.macworld.com/article/145334/2009/12/amazon_ebooksales.html (accessed July 3, 2010).

44. C. MacLeod, "Chinese Divided Over Google Move," *Garnett News Service*, March 25, 2010.

45. J. Greenwood, "Home Depot Runs into Vancouver Red Tape," *Financial Post (National Post)*, May 10, 2004, pp. FP1, FP11.

46. B. Marotte, "Abitibi Bowater CEO Sees Slimmer, More Flexible Company," *Report on Business*, May 31, 2010.

47. D. Calleja, "Equity or Else," *Canadian Business*, March 19, 2001, p. 31.

48. T. S. Mescon and G. S. Vozikis, "Federal Regulation—What Are the Costs?" *Business*, January–March 1982, pp. 33–39.

49. J. Thorpe, "Inter-Provincial Trade Barriers Still a Concern for Executives 'Handicapping Country Economically,'" *Financial Post (National Post)*, September 13, 2004, p. FP2.

50. C. Sands, "Canada's Problem: Domestic Trade Barriers," *American*, May 22, 2007, www.american.com/archive/2007/may-0507/canada2019s-problem-domestic-trade-barriers.

51. B. Constantineau, "Trans Fats Come Off the Menu at A&W," *Vancouver Sun*, January 4, 2007, p. C1.

52. See www.ctv.ca/CTVNews/Health/20031125/voortmans_trans031125/.

53. G. Bonnell, "Food Industry Rushes to Drop Trans Fats," *Calgary Herald*, March 11, 2004, p. D1.

54. R. Jackson, N. Howe, and K. Nakashima, "Global Aging and the Future of Emerging Markets," Center for Strategic and International Studies, March 7, 2011, http://csis.org/publication/global-aging-and-future-emerging-markets (accessed March 13, 2011).

55. Statistics Canada, "Census Snapshot of Canada: Population (Age and Sex)," *Canadian Social Trends*, Cat. no. 11-008, www.statcan.gc.ca/pub/11-008-x/2007006/article/10379-eng.pdf (accessed July 5, 2010).

56. Human Resources and Skills Development Canada, "Canadians in Context—Aging Population," *Indicators of Well-Being in Canada*, www4.hrsdc.gc.ca/.3ndic.1t.4r@-eng.jsp?iid=33 (accessed July 5, 2010).

57. Center for Strategic and International Studies, *Global Aging Initiative*, http://csis.org/program/global-aging-initiative (accessed July 5, 2010).

58. D. Drell and A. Adamson, "Fast Forward to 2020: What to Expect in Molecular Medicine," Human Genome Project, 2003, www.ornl.

gov/sci/techresources/Human_Genome/medicine/tnty (accessed March 19, 2011).

59. "Application and Products: Putting Technology to Use," National Nanotechnology Initiative, www.nano.gov/html/facts/ nanoapplicationsandproducts.html (accessed March 19, 2011).

60. T. Donaldson and L. E. Preston, "The Stakeholder Theory of the Corporation: Concepts, Evidence, and Implications," *Academy of Management Review*, January 1995, pp. 65–91.

61. J. S. Harrison and C. H. St. John, "Managing and Partnering with External Stakeholders," *Academy of Management Executive*, May 1996, pp. 46–60.

62. A. J. Hillman and G. D. Keim, "Shareholder Value, Stakeholder Management, and Social Issues: What's the Bottom Line?" *Strategic Management Journal*, March 2001, pp. 125–139; and J. Kotter and J. Heskett, *Corporate Culture and Performance* (New York: Free Press, 1992).

63. J. S. Harrison and C. H. St. John, "Managing and Partnering with External Stakeholders," *Academy of Management Executive*, May 1996, pp. 46–60.

64. S. P. Robbins, *Organizational Behavior*, 8th ed. (Upper Saddle River, NJ: Prentice Hall, 1998), p. 617.

65. Situation adapted from information in "Two Admit to Securities Fraud," *Los Angeles Times*, April 25, 2006, p. C3; and "Software Chief Admits to Guilt in Fraud Case," *New York Times*, April 25, 2006, pp. A1+.

66. *The Ritz-Carlton*, March 10, 2008, http://corporate.ritzcarlton. com; R. Reppa and E. Hirsh, "The Luxury Touch," *Strategy+Business*, Spring 2007, pp. 32–37; and J. Gordon, "Redefining Elegance," *Training*, March 2007, pp. 14–20.

67. Based on www.southernco.com/mspower; Edison Electric Institute, "EEI Honors Mississippi Power with 'Emergency Response Award' for Hurricane Recovery Efforts," *PR Newswire*, January 11, 2006, www.prnewswire.com; S. Lewis, "Contractors to the Rescue," *Transmission & Distribution World*, December 1, 2005, http://tdworld.com/mag/power_contractors_rescue/index.html; D. Cauchon, "The Little Company That Could," *USA Today*, October 10, 2005, pp. 1B+; and S. Covey, *The 7 Habits of Highly Effective People* (New York: Free Press, 1989).

68. Based on N. Langton and S. P. Robbins, *Organizational Behavior*, 4th ed. (Toronto: Pearson Education Canada, 2007), p. 384.

Chapter 3

1. Based on D. Tetley, "Tension Rises as Recall List Grows," *Calgary Herald*, April 3, 2007, p. A3; and C. Gillis and A. Kingston, "The Great Pet Food Scandal," *Maclean's*, April 30, 2007, www.macleans.ca/business/companies/article. jsp?content=20070430_104326_104326 (accessed July 8, 2007); "Menu Foods Announces That Settlement Agreement in Pet Food Litigation Receives Final Approval by Canadian Courts," Menu Foods Income Fund, November 27, 2008, www.menufoods.com/Recall/; "Settlement Agreement in U.S. Pet Food Multidistrict Litigation Receives Final Approval," Menu Foods Income Fund, October 15, 2008, www.menufoods.com/Recall/.

2. M. Kato, "Elementary School English: Ready or Not —Teachers Fret Their Inadequate Skills, Others Dislike the Language," *Japan Times*, March 5, 2009, http://search.japantimes.co.jp/cgi-bin/ nn20090305f1.html (accessed February 3, 2011).

3. N. Adler, *International Dimensions of Organizational Behavior*, 3rd ed. (Cincinnati, OH: South-Western, 1996).

4. M. R. F. Kets De Vries and E. Florent-Treacy, "Global Leadership from A to Z: Creating High Commitment Organizations," *Organizational Dynamics*, Spring 2002, pp. 295–309; P. R. Harris and R. T. Moran, *Managing Cultural Differences*, 4th ed. (Houston, TX: Gulf Publishing, 1996); R. T. Moran, P. R. Harris, and W. G. Stripp, *Developing the Global Organization: Strategies for Human Resource Professionals* (Houston, TX: Gulf Publishing, 1993); Y. Wind, S. P. Douglas, and H. V. Perlmutter, "Guidelines for Developing International Marketing Strategies," *Journal of Marketing*, April 1973, pp. 14–23; and H. V. Perlmutter, "The Tortuous Evolution of the Multinational Corporation," *Columbia Journal of World Business*, January–February 1969, pp. 9–18.

5. M. Mendenhall, B. Punnett, and D. Ricks, *Global Management* (Cambridge, MA: Blackwell, 1995), p. 74.

6. A. K. Gupta and V. Govindarajan, "Cultivating a Global Mindset," *Academy of Management Executive*, February 2002, pp. 117–118.

7. "U.S. Legislators Could Side-Swipe Canada with Measures to Protect Food Supply," *Alaska Highway News*, May 11, 2007, p. C2; and R. Myers, "Food Fights: As Supply Chains Stretch to All Corners of the Globe, Producers Struggle to Guarantee Food Safety," *CFO Magazine*, June 1, 2007.

8. *World Trade Organization*, WTO Policy Issues for Parliamentarians, 2001, www.wto.org/english/res_e/booksp_e/parliamentarians_e.pdf (accessed September 3, 2004), p. 1.

9. B. Mitchener, "Ten New Members to Weigh in on Future of EU," *Wall Street Journal*, April 16, 2003, p. A16; C. Taylor, "Go East, Young Man," *Smart Money*, January 2003, p. 25; S. Miller and B. Grow, "A Bigger Europe? Not So Fast," *Wall Street Journal*, December 12, 2002, p. A15; and "Candidate Countries," Europa, http:// europa.eu/abc/european_countries/candidate_countries/index_en. htm (accessed July 5, 2007).

10. B. Mitchener, "A New EU, but No Operating Manual," *Wall Street Journal*, December 16, 2002, p. A10; and https://www.cia.gov/ library/publications/the-world-factbook/print/ee.html.

11. See "The Euro," European Central Bank, www.ecb.int/euro/ html/index.en.html (accessed March 10, 2011); H. Cooper, "The Euro: What You Need to Know," *Wall Street Journal*, January 4, 1999, p. A51.

12. Oxford Analytica, "Greece Bailout Reveals E.U. Problems," *Forbes.com*, May 4, 2010, www.forbes.com/2010/05/03/ eu-greece-bailout-business-oxford-analytica.html (accessed July 14, 2010).

13. "Irish Bailout Bill Passed," *The Statesman*, January 31, 2011, www.thestatesman.net/index.php?option=com_content&view=article &id=357363&catid=37 (accessed February 3, 2011).

14. U.S. Census Bureau, *Foreign Trade Statistics*, www.census.gov/ foreign-trade/statistics/highlights/index.html.

15. Statistics Canada, "Imports, Exports and Trade Balance of Goods on a Balance-of-Payments Basis, by Country or Country Grouping," *Summary Tables*, http://www40.statcan.gc.ca/l01/ cst01/gblec02a-eng.htm (accessed February 3, 2011).

16. "Goods Going South? Think Mexico," *Export Development Canada*, www.edc.ca/english/publications_9432.htm (accessed July 8, 2007).

17. "Selected Basic ASEAN Indicators," ASEAN website, www. aseansec.org/stat/Table1.pdf (accessed February 3, 2011).

18. "Ministerial Declaration," Free Trade Area of the Americas, January 23, 2006, www.ftaa-alca.org (accessed April 4, 2003);

and "NAFTA: Five-Year Anniversary," *Latin Trade*, January 1999, pp. 44–45.

19. "Ministerial Declaration," Free Trade Area of the Americas, January 23, 2006, www.ftaa-alca.org (accessed April 4, 2003); and M. Moffett and J. D. McKinnon, "Failed Summit Casts Shadow on Global Trade Talks," *Wall Street Journal*, November 7, 2005, pp. A1+.

20. D. Kraft, "Leaders Question, Praise African Union," *Springfield News-Leader*, July 10, 2002, p. 8A.

21. SAARC website, www.saarc-sec.org/ (accessed February 3, 2011).

22. B. Kowitt, "For Mr. BRIC, Nations Meeting a Milestone" *CNNMoney.com*, June 17, 2009, http://money.cnn.com/2009/06/17/news/economy/goldman_sachs_jim_oneill_interview.fortune/index.htm (accessed February 8, 2011).

23. "South Africa Invited to Join BRIC Group," *Reuters*, http://uk.reuters.com/article/2010/12/24/uk-bric-safrica-idUKTRE6BN1DX20101224 (accessed February 2, 2011).

24. This section is based on material from the World Trade Organization website, www.wto.org (accessed February 3, 2011).

25. C. Gillis and A. Kingston, "The Great Pet Food Scandal," *Maclean's*, April 30, 2007, www.macleans.ca/business/companies/article.jsp?content=20070430_104326_104326 (accessed July 8, 2007); see "Menu Foods Income Fund," *Bloomsberg Business Week*, 2011, http://investing.businessweek.com/research/stocks/snapshot/snapshot.asp?capId=3206215; D. George-Cosh, "Menu Foods Hammered as Customer Walks," *Globe and Mail*, June 13, 2007, p. B15; and "Facilities"and "Distribution Channels," Menu Foods Income Fund, www.menufoods.com/about_us/facilities.html (accessed February 3, 2011).

26. C. A. Barlett and S. Ghoshal, *Managing Across Borders: The Transnational Solution*, 2nd ed. (Boston: Harvard Business School Press, 2002); and N. J. Adler, *International Dimensions of Organizational Behavior*, 4th ed. (Cincinnati, OH: South-Western, 2002), pp. 9–11.

27. D. A. Aaker, *Developing Business Strategies*, 5th ed. (New York: John Wiley & Sons, 1998); and J. A. Byrne et al., "Borderless Management," *BusinessWeek*, May 23, 1994, pp. 24–26.

28. G. A. Knight and S. T. Cavusgil, "A Taxonomy of Born-Global Firms," *Management International Review* 45, no. 3 (2005), pp. 15–35; S. A. Zahra, "A Theory of International New Ventures: A Decade of Research," *Journal of International Business Studies*, January 2005, pp. 20–28; and B. M. Oviatt and P. P. McDougall, "Toward a Theory of International New Ventures," *Journal of International Business Studies*, January 2005, pp. 29–41.

29. See "Bell Canada Outsources Job to Sitel," *The Hindu Business Line*, October 16, 2006, www.blonnet.com/2006/10/17/stories/2006101701390400.htm.

30. Mega Brands, *Third Quarter Report, 2010*, www.megabrands.com/media/pdf/corpo/en/reports/2010_q3_en.pdf (accessed February 3, 2011).

31. Statistics Canada, "Imports, Exports and Trade Balance of Goods on a Balance-of-Payments Basis, by Country or Country Grouping," *Summary Tables*, http://www40.statcan.gc.ca/l01/cst01/gblec02a-eng.htm (accessed February 3, 2011).

32. L. Frost, "Starbucks Lures French Café Society," *Associated Press*, January 16, 2004.

33. E. Malkin, "Founder Sees Lots of Room for Lots More Starbucks, *New York Times*, September 22, 2007.

34. B. Brown, "UAW Deal Hurts Canada's Auto Towns," *Washington Times*, October 2, 2007.

35. Based on C. Gillis and A. Kingston, "The Great Pet Food Scandal," *Maclean's*, April 30, 2007, www.macleans.ca/business/companies/article.jsp?content=20070430_104326_104326 (accessed July 8, 2007); and D. Barboza and A. Barrionuevo, "Filler in Animal Feed Is Open Secret in China," *New York Times*, April 30, 2007.

36. Based on information from M. Javidan, P. W. Dorfman, M. S. deLuque, and R. J. House, "In the Eye of the Beholder: Cross-Cultural Lessons in Leadership from Project GLOBE," *Academy of Management Perspective*, February 2006, pp. 67–90; and M. Javidan, G. K. Stahl, F. Brodbeck, and C. P. M. Wilderon, "Cross-Border Transfer of Knowledge: Cultural Lessons from Project GLOBE," *Academy of Management Executive*, May 2005, pp. 59–76.

37. See G. Hofstede, *Culture's Consequences: International Differences in Work-Related Values*, 2nd ed. (Thousand Oaks, CA: Sage, 2001), pp. 9–15.

38. G. Hofstede, *Culture's Consequences: International Differences in Work-Related Values*, 2nd ed. (Thousand Oaks, CA: Sage, 2001), pp. 9–15; and G. Hofstede, "The Cultural Relativity of Organizational Practices and Theories," *Journal of International Business Studies*, Fall 1983, pp. 75–89.

39. Based on A. Daniels, "Wal-Mart Treading Softly in Japan: East Meets Western Retailer," *Arkansas Democrat-Gazette*, December 21, 2003, p. 67; K. Belson, "Wal-Mart Hopes It Won't Be Lost in Translation," *New York Times*, December 14, 2003, p. BU1; "Losses Increase at Wal-Mart Japan," *BBC News*, August 22, 2006, http://news.bbc.co.uk/2/hi/business/5273642.stm; and N. Maestri, "Wal-Mart Seeks Nimbler International Expansion," *Scotsman.com*, June 14, 2007, http://business.scotsman.com/latest.cfm?id=937142007.

40. "Wal-Mart Japan CEO: Will Actively Seek M&A," *Reuters*, February 23, 2010, www.reuters.com/article/2010/02/23/us-walmart-japan-idUSTRE61M1HC20100223 (accessed November 3, 2010).

41. Hofstede called this dimension *masculinity versus femininity*, but we have changed his terms because of their strong sexist connotation.

42. G. Hofstede, *Culture's Consequences: International Differences in Work-Related Values*, 2nd ed. (Thousand Oaks, CA: Sage, 2001), pp. 355–358.

43. R. J. House, P. J. Hanges, M. Javidan, P. W. Dorfman, and V. Gupta, *Culture Leadership, and Organizations: The GLOBE Study of 62 Societies* (Thousand Oaks, CA: Sage, 2004); M. Javidan, P. W. Dorfman, M. S. deLuque, and R. J. House, "In the Eye of the Beholder: Cross-Cultural Lessons in Leadership from Project GLOBE," *Academy of Management Perspective*, February 2006, pp. 67–90; and M. Javidan, G. K. Stahl, F. Brodbeck, and C. P. M. Wilderon, "Cross-Border Transfer of Knowledge: Cultural Lessons from Project GLOBE," *Academy of Management Executive*, May 2005, pp. 59–76.

44. O. Ward, "Pop Goes Globalization," *Toronto Star*, March 13, 2004, www.thestar.com (accessed March 21, 2004).

45. A. Kreamer, "America's Yang Has a Yen for Asia's Yin," *Fast Company*, July 2003, p. 58; D. Yergin, "Globalization Opens Door to New Dangers," *USA Today*, May 28, 2003, p. 11A; K. Lowrey Miller, "Is It Globaloney?" *Newsweek*, December 16, 2002, pp. E4–E8; L. Gomes, "Globalization Is Now a Two-Way Street—Good News for the

U.S.," *Wall Street Journal*, December 9, 2002, p. B1; J. Kurlantzick and J. T. Allen, "The Trouble with Globalism," *U.S. News & World Report*, February 11, 2002, pp. 38–41; and J. Guyon, "The American Way," *Fortune*, November 26, 2001, pp. 114–120.

46. J. Guyon, "The American Way," *Fortune*, November 26, 2001, pp. 114–120.

47. Adapted from G. M. Spreitzer, M. W. McCall Jr., and J. D. Mahoney, "Early Identification of International Executive Potential," *Journal of Applied Psychology*, February 1997, pp. 6–29.

48. Information from company website, www.inditex.com (accessed July 5, 2007); and M. Helft, "Fashion Fast-Forward," *Business 2.0*, May 2002, pp. 60–66.

49. Situation adapted from information in M. R. Cohn, "Indian Villagers Set to Battle Alcan," *Toronto Star*, July 3, 2004, pp. A1, A10–A12; A. Swift, "Alcan to Do Well in 2004, Says CEO," *Trail Times*, April 23, 2004, p. 14; L. Moore, "Alcan Sees Bright Year Ahead," *Gazette* (Montreal), April 23, 2004, p. B1; and www.alcan.com/web/publishing.nsf/Content/Alcan+Facts+2006 (accessed July 9, 2007).

50. See "Canadians in the NBA," NBA.com, June 30, 2004, www.nba.com/canada/Canadians_in_the_NBA-Canada_Generic_Article-18022.html (accessed September 15, 2007); D. Eisenberg, "The NBA's Global Game Plan," *Time*, March 17, 2003, pp. 59–63; J. Tyrangiel, "The Center of Attention," *Time*, February 10, 2003, pp. 56–60; "Spin Master Stern," *Latin Trade*, July 2000, p. 32; Information from NBA website, www.nba.com (accessed July 1, 2004); J. Tagliabue, "Hoop Dreams, Fiscal Realities," *New York Times*, March 4, 2000, p. B11; D. Roth, "The NBA's Next Shot," *Fortune*, February 21, 2000, pp. 207–216; A. Bianco, "Now It's NBA All-the-Time TV," *BusinessWeek*, November 15, 1999, pp. 241–242; and D. McGraw and M. Tharp, "Going Out on Top," *U.S. News & World Report*, January 25, 1999, p. 55.

51. M. A. Prospero, "Attitude Adjustment," *Fast Company*, December 2005, p. 107; D. Roberts and M. Arndt, "It's Getting Hotter in the East," *BusinessWeek*, August 22/29, 2005, pp. 78–81; M. Champion, "Scotland Looks East for Labor," *Wall Street Journal*, July 7, 2005, p. A11; L. Bower, "Cultural Awareness Aids Business Relations," *Springfield Business Journal*, April 4–10, 2005, p. 59; R. Rosmarin, "Mountain View Masala," *Business 2.0*, March 2005, pp. 54–56; and P.-W. Tam, "Culture Course," *Wall Street Journal*, May 25, 2004, pp. B1+.

52. C. Harvey and M. J. Allard, *Understanding and Managing Diversity: Readings, Cases, and Exercises*, 2nd ed. (Upper Saddle River, NJ: Prentice Hall, 2002); P. L. Hunsaker, *Training in Management Skills* (Upper Saddle River, NJ: Prentice Hall, 2001); and J. Greenberg, *Managing Behavior in Organizations: Science in Service to Practice*, 2nd ed. (Upper Saddle River, NJ: Prentice Hall, 1999).

Chapter 4

1. Based on Research In Motion home page, www.rim.com/company/ (accessed June 21, 2010).

2. P. E. Mott, *The Characteristics of Effective Organizations* (New York: HarperCollins, 1972).

3. J. A. Schumpeter, 1936), *The Theory of Economic Development*, 2nd ed. (Cambridge, MA: Harvard University Press, 1936).

4. I. M. Kirzner, *Competition and Entrepreneurship* (Chicago: University of Chicago Press, 1973).

5. J. O. Fiet, *The Systematic Search for Entrepreneurial Discoveries* (Westport, CT: Quorum Books, 2002); J. O. Fiet, V. G. H. Clouse,

and W. I. Norton, "Systematic Search by Repeat Entrepreneurs," in *Opportunity Identification and Entrepreneurial Behavior*, ed. E. B. John (Greenwich, CT: Information Age Publishing, 2004).

6. Y. Sarason, T. Dean, and J. F. Dillard, "Entrepreneurship as the Nexus of Individual and Opportunity: A Structuration View," *Journal of Business Venturing 21*, no. 3 (2006), pp. 286–305; S. D. Sarasvathy, "Causation and Effectuation: Toward a Theoretical Shift from Economic Inevitability to Entrepreneurial Contingency," *Academy of Management Review 26*, no. 2 (2001), pp. 243–263; S. D. Sarasvathy, N. Dew, R. Velamuri, and S. Venkataraman, "Three Views of Entrepreneurial Opportunity," *Handbook of Entrepreneurship Research 156* (2003), pp. 1–25.

7. J. W. Carland, F. Hoy, W. R. Boulton, and J. C. Carland, "Differentiating Entrepreneurs from Small Business Owners: A Conceptualization," *Academy of Management Review 9*, no. 2 (1984), pp. 354–359.

8. Organisation for Economic Co-operation and Development, "The Importance of Entrepreneurship," in *Measuring Entrepreneurship: A Digest of Indicators*, 2008, www.oecd.org/dataoecd/53/24/41664503.pdf (accessed November 18, 2010).

9. P. Almeida and B. Kogut, "The Exploration of Technological Diversity and Geographic Localization in Innovation: Start-up Firms in the Semiconductor Industry," *Small Business Economics*, 9, no. 1 (1997), pp. 21–31.

10. R. J. Arend, "Emergence of Entrepreneurs Following Exogenous Technological Change," *Strategic Management Journal 20*, no. 1 (1999), pp. 31–47.

11. U.S. Small Business Administration, Office of Advocacy, "Frequently Asked Questions," www.sba.gov, April 16, 2007.

12. Canadian Federation of Independent Business, "National Small Business Profile: Small Business Facts," www.cfib-fcei.ca/english/research/canada/33-small_business_facts/1148-small_business_facts.html (accessed November 18, 2010).

13. J. Timmons, S. Spinelli, and P. Ensign, *New Venture Creation: Entrepreneurship for the 21st Century*, 1st Canadian ed. (Toronto: McGraw Hill Ryerson, 2010).

14. N. Bosma, K. Jones, E. Autio, and J. Levie, *Global Entrepreneurship Monitor: 2007 Executive Report*, www.gemconsortium.org, p. 12.

15. P. F. Drucker, *Innovation and Entrepreneurship: Practice and Principles* (New York: Harper & Row, 1985).

16. International Organization for Standardization, "*ISO 14000 Essentials*," www.iso.org/iso/iso_catalogue/management_and_leadership_standards/environmental_management/iso_14000_essentials.htm (accessed October 7, 2010); International Organization for Standardization, "*ISO 26000: Social Responsibility*," www.iso.org/iso/iso_catalogue/management_and_leadership_standards/social_responsibility.htm (accessed October 7, 2010); International Organization for Standardization, "ISO's Social Responsibility Standard Approved for Publication," Ref: 1351, September 14, 2010, www.iso.org/iso/pressrelease.htm?refid=Ref1351 (accessed November 11, 2010).

17. Skoll Foundation, "About Us," www.skollfoundation.org/about/Ref1351 (accessed November 18, 2010).

18. Corporate Knights, "The 2010 Cleantech 10™," http://corporateknights.ca/report/cleantech-index-2010/2010-cleantech-10%E2%84%A2 (accessed November 18, 2010).

19. C. Sandlund, "Trust Is a Must," *Entrepreneur*, October 2002, pp. 70–75.

20. J. Timmons, S. Spinelli, and P. Ensign, *New Venture Creation: Entrepreneurship for the 21st Century*, 1st Canadian ed. (Toronto: McGraw Hill Ryerson, 2010).

21. Office of the Parliamentary Budget Officer, *Fiscal Sustainability Report*, February 18, 2010, http://www2.parl.gc.ca/Sites/PBO-DPB/documents/FSR_2010.pdf (accessed November 19, 2010).

22. Government of Canada, "Canada's Aging Population: Seizing the Opportunity," *Special Senate Committee Report on Aging: Final Report*, April 2009, www.parl.gc.ca/40/2/parlbus/commbus/senate/com-e/agei-e/rep-e/AgingFinalReport-e.pdf (accessed November 19, 2010).

23. G. B. Knight, "How Wall Street Whiz Found a Niche Selling Books on the Internet," *Wall Street Journal*, May 15, 1996, pp. A1+.

24. N. F. Krueger, Jr., "The Cognitive Infrastructure of Opportunity Emergence," *Entrepreneurship Theory and Practice*, Spring 2000, p. 6.

25. D. P. Forbes, "Managerial Determinants of Decision Speed in New Ventures," *Strategic Management Journal*, April 2005, pp. 355–366.

26. P. F. Drucker, *Innovation and Entrepreneurship: Practice and Principles* (New York: Harper & Row, 1985).

27. CarShare HFX home page, www.carsharehfx.ca/how.html (accessed November 19, 2010).

28. "Who We Are," eBay home page, www.ebayinc.com/who (accessed June 8, 2010).

29. S. McFarland, "Cambodia's Internet Service Is in Kids' Hands," *Wall Street Journal*, May 15, 2000, p. A9A.

30. "About Whole Foods Market," Whole Foods Market home page, www.wholefoodsmarket.com/company/ (accessed November 19, 2010).

31. Tether home page, http://tether.com/ (accessed November 19, 2010).

32. S. Greco, "The Start-up Years," *Inc. 500*, October 21, 1997, p. 57; R. P. Singh, G. E. Hills, and G. T. Lumpkin, "New Venture Ideas and Entrepreneurial Opportunities: Understanding the Process of Opportunity Recognition" (paper presented at the USASBE annual national conference: Sailing the Entrepreneurial Wave into the 21st Century, San Diego, CA, January 14–17, 1999); G. E. Hills, G. T. Lumpkin, and R. P. Singh, "Opportunity Recognition: Perceptions and Behaviors of Entrepreneurs," *Frontiers of Entrepreneurship Research* 17 (1997), 168–182.

33. C. Barnes, H. Blake, and D. Pinder, *Creating and Delivering Your Value Proposition: Managing Customer Experience for Profit* (London: Kogan Page, 2009).

34. A. Barrett, B. Turek, and C. Faivre d'Arcier, "Bottoms Up—and Profits, Too," *BusinessWeek*, September 12, 2005, pp. 80–82; and C. Hajim, "Growth in Surprising Places," *Fortune*, September 5, 2005, bonus section.

35. R. L. Heneman, J. W. Tansky, and S. M. Camp, "Human Resource Management Practices in Small and Medium-Sized Enterprises: Unanswered Questions and Future Research Perspectives," *Entrepreneurship Theory and Practice*, Fall 2000, pp. 11–26.

36. R. L. Heneman, J. W. Tansky, and S. M. Camp, "Human Resource Management Practices in Small and Medium-Sized Enterprises: Unanswered Questions and Future Research Perspectives," *Entrepreneurship Theory and Practice*, Fall 2000, pp. 11–26.

37. Based on G. Fuchsberg, "Small Firms Struggle With Latest Management Trends," *Wall Street Journal*, August 26, 1993, p. B2; M. Barrier, "Re-engineering Your Company," *Nation's Business*, February 1994, pp. 16–22; J. Weiss, "Re-engineering the Small Business," *Small Business Reports*, May 1994, pp. 37–43; and K. D. Godsey, "Back on Track," *Success*, May 1997, pp. 52–54.

38. RIM home page, www.rim.com/ (accessed June 3, 2010).

39. "History," Perimeter Institute for Theoretical Physics, www.perimeterinstitute.ca/About/History/History/(accessed June 3, 2010).

40. Definition from *Investopedia*, www.investopedia.com/terms/r/randd.asp (accessed June 10, 2010).

41. Based on Basadur Applied Creativity website, www.basadur.com/company/index.htm (accessed June 10, 2010).

42. B. Jaruzelski and K. Dehoff, "The Global Innovation 1000: How the Top Innovators Keep Winning," *strategy+business* 61 (November 3, 2010), www.strategy-business.com/article/10408?pg=0.

43. AACSB International, *Business Schools on an Innovation Mission: Report of the AACSB International Task Force on Business Schools and Innovation* (Tampa, FL: AACSB International, 2010).

44. M. DePree, *Leadership Jazz* (New York: Currency Doubleday, 1992), pp. 8–9.

45. J. C. Collins and J. I. Porras, *Built to Last: Successful Habits of Visionary Companies* (New York: Harper Business, 1994).

46. G. R. Merz, P. B. Weber, and V. B. Laetz, "Linking Small Business Management with Entrepreneurial Growth," *Journal of Small Business Management*, October 1994, pp. 48–60.

47. J. Bailey, "Growth Needs a Plan or Only Losses May Build," *Wall Street Journal*, October 29, 2002, p. B9; and L. Beresford, "Growing Up," *Entrepreneur*, July 1995, pp. 124–28.

48. R. D. Hof, "eBay's Rhine Gold," *BusinessWeek*, April 3, 2006, pp. 44–45.

49. C. Farrell, "How to Survive a Downturn," *BusinessWeek*, April 28, 1997, pp. ENT4-ENT6.

50. J. Bailey, "Selling the Firm and Letting Go of the Dream," *Wall Street Journal*, December 10, 2002, p. B6; P. Hernan, "Finding the Exit," *IndustryWeek*, July 17, 2000, pp. 55–61; D. Rodkin, "For Sale by Owner," *Entrepreneur*, January 1998, pp. 148–153; A. Livingston, "Avoiding Pitfalls When Selling a Business," *Nation's Business*, July 1998, pp. 25–26; and G. Gibbs Marullo, "Selling Your Business: A Preview of the Process," *Nation's Business*, August 1998, pp. 25–26.

51. B. Jaruzelski and K. Dehoff, "The Global Innovation 1000: How the Top Innovators Keep Winning," *Strategy+Business* 61, Winter 2010, www.strategy-business.com/article/10408?pg=0 (accessed April 5, 2011).

52. S. Thomke and B. Feinberg, "Design Thinking and Innovation at Apple," *Harvard Business Review*, January 9, 2009, http://hbr.org/product/design-thinking-and-innovation-at-apple/an/609066-PDF-ENG (accessed April 5, 2011).

53. "Apple/Newton Cancellation—2: No Layoffs Expected," Dow Jones Newswires, February 27, 1998.

54. C. Bayers, "Steve Jobs Comes Home to Apple," *Wired*, December 20, 1996, www.wired.com/techbiz/media/news/1996/12/1137 (accessed April 5, 2011).

55. Based on personal conversations and interviews with Kathy Murphy, CEO of CEED, and Ed Matwawana, director of the Second Chance Program; and Second Chance website, www.ceed.ca/default.asp?mn=1.247.241 (accessed November 19, 2010).

Chapter 5

1. Based on R. C. Anderson with R. White, *Confessions of a Radical Industrialist: Profits, People, Purpose—Doing Business by Respecting the Earth* (New York: St. Martin's Press, 2009); information retrieved from the Interface sustainability page on the Interface website, www.interfaceglobal.com/Sustainability.aspx (accessed November 13, 2010); interview with George Stroumboulopoulos, *The Hour*, CBC television, January 25, 2007; R. C. Anderson, presentation at the Power of Green Conference, Halifax, Nova Scotia, November 8, 2009.

2. M. L. Barnett, "Stakeholder Influence Capacity and the Variability of Financial Returns to Corporate Social Responsibility," *Academy of Management Review*, July 2007, pp. 794–816; A. Mackey, T. B. Mackey, and J. B. Barney, "Corporate Social Responsibility and Firm Performance: Investor Preferences and Corporate Strategies," *Academy of Management Review*, July 2007, pp. 817–835; and A. B. Carroll, "A Three-Dimensional Conceptual Model of Corporate Performance," *Academy of Management Review*, October 1979, p. 499.

3. See K. Basu and G. Palazzo, "Corporate Social Performance: A Process Model of Sensemaking," *Academy of Management Review*, January 2008, pp. 122–136; and S. P. Sethi, "A Conceptual Framework for Environmental Analysis of Social Issues and Evaluation of Business Response Patterns," *Academy of Management Review*, January 1979, pp. 68–74.

4. M. Friedman, *Capitalism and Freedom* (Chicago: University of Chicago Press, 1962); and M. Friedman, "The Social Responsibility of Business Is to Increase Profits," *New York Times Magazine*, September 13, 1970, p. 33.

5. J. Bakan, *The Corporation* (Toronto: Big Picture Media Corporation, 2003).

6. Information from Avon's website, www.avoncompany.com/women/avoncrusade/index.html (accessed July 10, 2007).

7. "The McKinsey Global Survey of Business Executives: Business and Society," *McKinsey Quarterly*, January 2006, www.mckinseyquarterly.com.

8. See, for example, D. J. Wood, "Corporate Social Performance Revisited," *Academy of Management Review*, October 1991, pp. 703–708.

9. Information from "How to Apply for Funding," CIBC website, www.cibc.com/ca/inside-cibc/cibc-your-community/how-to-apply-for-funding.html (accessed July 12, 2007).

10. "Building Our Communities Globally," Manulife Financial: Community Giving, www.manulife.com/public/about/index/0,,lang=en&navId=610014,00.html (accessed November 13, 2010).

11. Information from www.purolator.com/media/news/may_01_07.html; and http://cassies.ca/caselibrary/winners/2006pdfs/_559Purolator_Web_DR.pdf.

12. S. L. Wartick and P. L. Cochran, "The Evolution of the Corporate Social Performance Model," *Academy of Management Review*, October 1985, p. 763.

13. "Part of the Solution: One Man's Residue Is Another Man's Sand," *Alcoa Community E-news*, www.alcoa.com/australia/en/info_page/newsletter_200909_3.asp (accessed November 13, 2010).

14. Indigo Love of Reading Foundation website, http://adoptaschool.loveofreading.org/en_CA/home (accessed November 13, 2010).

15. See, for example, R. A. Buccholz, *Essentials of Public Policy for Management*, 2d ed. (Upper Saddle River, NJ: Prentice Hall, 1990).

16. RBC Blue Water Project website, http://bluewater.rbc.com/ (accessed November 13, 2010).

17. See www.mec.ca; and H. Hoag, "Blocks of Buildings of the Future," *Gazette* (Montreal), October 24, 2006, p. B3.

18. M. Straus, "Why Loblaws Takes Top Honours for Corporate Social Responsibility," *Globe and Mail*, June 20, 2010, www.theglobeandmail.com/report-on-business/managing/report-on-corporate-responsibil/why-loblaw-takes-top-honours-for-corporate-social-responsibility/article1605337/ (accessed November 13, 2010).

19. "Tree for a Tree," Enbridge website, www.enbridge.com/AboutEnbridge/CorporateSocialResponsibility/NeutralFootprint/TreeforaTree.aspx (accessed November 13, 2010).

20. "BMO Invests in Clear Blue Skies," *CNW*, November 23, 2009, www.newswire.ca/en/releases/archive/November2009/23/c3931.html (accessed November 13, 2010).

21. Based on D. Dias, "Giant Steps," *Financial Post Business*, July 7, 2008, www.financialpost.com/magazine/story.html?id=610758 (accessed November 13, 2010).

22. E. P. Lima, "Seeding a World of Transformation," *IndustryWeek*, September 6, 1999, pp. 30–31.

23. "The McKinsey Global Survey of Business Executives: Business and Society," *McKinsey Quarterly*, January 2006, www.mckinseyquarterly.com.

24. The Triple Bottom Line was first introduced in J. Elkington, *Cannibals with Forks: The Triple Bottom Line of 21st-Century Business* (Stony Creek, CT: New Society Publishers, 1998).

25. See, for example, A. B. Carroll, "The Pyramid of Corporate Social Responsibility: Toward the Moral Management of Organizational Stakeholders," *Business Horizons*, July–August 1991, pp. 39–48.

26. This section has been influenced by K. B. Boal and N. Peery, "The Cognitive Structure of Social Responsibility," *Journal of Management*, Fall–Winter 1985, pp. 71–82.

27. R. C. Anderson with R. White, *Confessions of a Radical Industrialist: Profits, People, Purpose—Doing Business by Respecting the Earth* (New York: St. Martin's Press, 2009), p. 76.

28. See, for instance, D. O. Neubaum and S. A. Zahra, "Institutional Ownership and Corporate Social Performance: The Moderating Effects of Investment Horizon, Activism, and Coordination," *Journal of Management*, February 2006, pp. 108–131; P. C. Godfrey, "The Relationship between Corporate Philanthropy and Shareholder Wealth: A Risk Management Perspective," *Academy of Management Review*, October 2005, pp. 777–798; D. K. Peterson, "The Relationship between Perceptions of Corporate Citizenship and Organizational Commitment," *Business & Society*, September 2004, pp. 296–319; B. Seifert, S. A. Morris, and B. R. Bartkus, "Having, Giving, and Getting: Slack Resources, Corporate Philanthropy, and Firm Financial Performance," *Business & Society*, June 2004, pp. 135–161; S. L. Berman, A. Wicks, S. Kotha, and T. Jones, "Does Stakeholder Orientation Matter? The Relationship between Stakeholder Management Models and Firm Financial Performance," *Academy of Management Journal*, October 1999, pp. 488–506; S. A. Waddock and S. B. Graves, "The Corporate Social Performance–Financial Performance Link," *Strategic Management Journal*, April 1997, pp. 303–319; D. B. Turban and D. W. Greening, "Corporate Social Performance and Organizational Attractiveness to Prospective Employees," *Academy of Management Journal*, June 1996, pp. 658–672; J. B. McGuire, A. Sundgren, and T. Schneeweis, "Corporate Social Responsibility and Firm Financial Performance," *Academy of Management Journal*, December 1988, pp. 854–872;

K. Aupperle, A. B. Carroll, and J. D. Hatfield, "An Empirical Examination of the Relationship between Corporate Social Responsibility and Profitability," *Academy of Management Journal*, June 1985, pp. 446–463; and P. Cochran and R. A. Wood, "Corporate Social Responsibility and Financial Performance," *Academy of Management Journal*, March 1984, pp. 42–56.

29. See J. Surroca and J. A. Tribo, "The Corporate Social and Financial Performance Relationship: What's the Ultimate Determinant?" *Academy of Management Proceedings* Best Conference Paper, 2005; D. J. Wood and R. E. Jones, "Stakeholder Mismatching: A Theoretical Problem in Empirical Research on Corporate Social Performance," *International Journal of Organizational Analysis*, July 1995, pp. 229–267; R. Wolfe and K. Aupperle, "Introduction to Corporate Social Performance: Methods for Evaluating an Elusive Construct," in J. E. Post (ed.), *Research in Corporate Social Performance and Policy* 12 (1991), pp. 265–268; and A. A. Ullmann, "Data in Search of a Theory: A Critical Examination of the Relationships among Social Performance, Social Disclosure, and Economic Performance of U.S. Firms," *Academy of Management Review*, July 1985, pp. 540–557.

30. B. Seifert, S. A. Morris, and B. R. Bartkus, "Having, Giving, and Getting: Slack Resources, Corporate Philanthropy, and Firm Financial Performance," *Business & Society*, June 2004, pp. 135–161; and J. B. McGuire, A. Sundgren, and T. Schneeweis, "Corporate Social Responsibility and Firm Financial Performance," *Academy of Management Journal*, December 1988, pp. 854–872.

31. A. McWilliams and D. Siegel, "Corporate Social Responsibility and Financial Performance: Correlation or Misspecification?" *Strategic Management Journal*, June 2000, pp. 603–609.

32. A. J. Hillman and G. D. Keim, "Shareholder Value, Stakeholder Management, and Social Issues: What's the Bottom Line?" *Strategic Management Journal* 22 (2001), pp. 125–139.

33. M. Orlitzky, F. L. Schmidt, and S. L. Rynes, "Corporate Social and Financial Performance," *Organization Studies* 24, no. 3 (2003), pp. 403–441.

34. "Socially Responsible Investing—Better Companies, Better Communities," *Green Money Journal*, Fall 2010, www.greenmoneyjournal.com/article.mpl?newsletterid=45&articleid=622 (accessed November 13, 2010).

35. Social Investment Organization, *Canadian Socially Responsible Investment Review 2008* (March 2009), www.socialinvestment.ca/documents/caReview2008.pdf (accessed November 11, 2010).

36. D. Macfarlane, "Why Now?" *Report on Business*, March 2004, pp. 45–46.

37. J. Jedras, "Social Workers," *Silicon Valley North*, July 30, 2001, p. 1.

38. Based on R. C. Anderson with R. White, *Confessions of a Radical Industrialist: Profits, People, Purpose—Doing Business by Respecting the Earth* (New York: St. Martin's Press, 2009); and information retrieved from the Interface sustainability page on the Interface website, www.interfaceglobal.com/Sustainability.aspx (accessed November 13, 2010).

39. This section is based on K. Buysse and A. Verbeke, "Proactive Environmental Strategies: A Stakeholder Management Perspective," *Strategic Management Journal*, May 2003, pp. 453–470; D. A. Rondinelli and T. London, "How Corporations and Environmental Groups Cooperate: Assessing Cross-Sector Alliances and Collaborations," *Academy of Management Executive*, February 2003, pp. 61–76; J. Alberto Aragon-Correa and S. Sharma, "A Contingent Resource-Based View of Proactive Corporate Environmental Strategy," *Academy of Management Review*, January 2003,

pp. 71–88; P. Christmann and G. Taylor, "Globalization and the Environment: Strategies for International Voluntary Environmental Initiatives," *Academy of Management Executive*, August 2002, pp. 121–135; P. Bansal, "The Corporate Challenges of Sustainable Development," *Academy of Management Executive*, May 2002, pp. 122–131; M. Stark and A. A. Marcus, "Introduction to the Special Research Forum on the Management of Organizations in the Natural Environment: A Field Emerging from Multiple Paths, with Many Challenges Ahead," *Academy of Management Journal*, August 2000, pp. 539–546; P. Bansal and K. Roth, "Why Companies Go Green: A Model of Ecological Responsiveness," *Academy of Management Journal*, August 2000, pp. 717–736; S. L. Hart, "Beyond Greening: Strategies for a Sustainable World," *Harvard Business Review*, January–February 1997, pp. 66–76; S. L. Hart, "A Natural-Resource-Based View of the Firm," *Academy of Management Review*, December 1995, pp. 986–1014; and P. Shrivastava, "Environmental Technologies and Competitive Advantage," *Strategic Management Journal*, Summer 1995, pp. 183–200.

40. J. L. Seglin, "It's Not That Easy Going Green," *Inc.*, May 1999, pp. 28–32; W. H. Miller, "What's Ahead in Environmental Policy?" *IW*, April 19, 1999, pp. 19–24; and P. Shrivastava, "Environmental Technologies and Competitive Advantage," *Strategic Management Journal*, Summer 1995, p. 183.

41. S. L. Hart, "Beyond Greening: Strategies for a Sustainable World," *Harvard Business Review*, January–February 1997, p. 68.

42. The Worldwatch Institute, *State of the World 2006: China and India Hold World in Balance*, www.worldwatch.org/node/3894 (accessed July 12, 2007); "Is There a Green Movement in the Air?" *Fortune*, December 12, 2005, pp. 69–78; A. Aston and B. Helm, "The Race Against Climate Change," *BusinessWeek*, December 12, 2005, pp. 58–66; J. Kluger and A. Dorfman, "The Challenges We Face," *Time*, August 26, 2002, pp. A6–A12; Worldwatch Institute, "Earth Day 2000: What Humanity Can Do Now to Turn the Tide," www.worldwatch.org/node/483 (accessed July 12, 2007); and L. Brown and Staff of the Worldwatch Institute, *State of the World* (New York: Norton, 1987–1996).

43. M. Conlin, "Sorry, I Composted Your Memorandum," *BusinessWeek*, February 18, 2008, p. 60; "Whole Foods Switching to Wind Power," *CBS News Online,* January 12, 2006, www.cbsnews.com; A. Aston and B. Helm, "Green Culture, Clean Strategies," *BusinessWeek*, December 12, 2005, p. 64; and J. Esty, "Never Say Never," *Fast Company*, July 2004, p. 34.

44. The concept of shades of green can be found in R. E. Freeman, J. Pierce, and R. Dodd, *Shades of Green: Business Ethics and the Environment* (New York: Oxford University Press, 1995).

45. International Organization for Standardization, "ISO's Social Responsibility Standard Approved for Publication," ISO News and Media, September 14, 2010, www.iso.org/iso/pressrelease.htm?refid=Ref1351 (accessed November 11, 2010).

46. Information from Global 100 website, www.global100.org (accessed November 13, 2010).

47. Based on R. C. Anderson with R. White, *Confessions of a Radical Industrialist: Profits, People, Purpose—Doing Business by Respecting the Earth* (New York: St. Martin's Press, 2009); and information retrieved from the Interface sustainability page on the Interface website, www.interfaceglobal.com/Sustainability.aspx (accessed November 13, 2010).

48. W. G. Bliss, "Why Is Corporate Culture Important?" *Workforce*, February 1999, pp. W8–W9; E. J. Giblin and L. E. Amuso, "Putting Meaning into Corporate Values," *Business Forum*, Winter 1997, pp. 14–18; R. Barrett, "Liberating the Corporate Soul," *HRfocus*, April 1997, pp. 15–16; K. Blanchard and M. O'Connor, *Managing by*

Values (San Francisco: Berrett-Koehler, 1997); and G. P. Alexander, "Establishing Shared Values Through Management Training Programs," *Training & Development*, February 1987, pp. 45–47.

49. Based on Mary Lamey, "A Monument to the Environment: Focus on Recycling: Mountain Equipment Is Building First 'Green' Retail Outlet in Quebec," *Gazette* (Montreal), November 22, 2002, www. Canada.com/montreal.

50. W. G. Bliss, "Why Is Corporate Culture Important?" *Workforce*, February 1999, pp. W8–W9; E. J. Giblin and L. E. Amuso, "Putting Meaning into Corporate Values," *Business Forum*, Winter 1997, pp. 14–18; R. Barrett, "Liberating the Corporate Soul," *HRfocus*, April 1997, pp. 15–16; K. Blanchard and M. O'Connor, *Managing by Values* (San Francisco: Berrett-Koehler, 1997); G. P. Alexander, "Establishing Shared Values Through Management Training Programs," *Training & Development*, February 1987, pp. 45–47; J. L. Badaracco Jr. and R. R. Ellsworth, *Leadership and the Quest for Integrity* (Boston: Harvard Business School Press, 1989); and T. Chappell, *Managing Upside Down: The Seven Intentions of Values-Centered Leadership* (New York: William Morrow, 1999).

51. Information from Tom's of Maine website, www.tomsofmaine. com/about/statement.asp (accessed July 11, 2007).

52. R. Kamen, "Values: For Show or for Real?" *Working Woman*, August 1993, p. 10.

53. D. West, "Number 11 with a Bullet: Pacific Insight Cruises Down the Road of Success Powered by Employees," *Nelson Daily News*, December 14, 2006, p. 1.

54. "Interface Code of Business Conduct and Ethics," Interface website, www.interfaceglobal.com/Investor-Relations/ Corporate-Governance.aspx (accessed July 15, 2010).

55. K. Davis and W. C. Frederick, *Business and Society: Management, Public Policy, Ethics*, 5th ed. (New York: McGraw-Hill, 1984), pp. 28–41, 76.

56. F. D. Sturdivant, *Business and Society: A Managerial Approach*, 3rd ed. (Homewood, IL: Richard D. Irwin, 1985), p. 128.

57. G. F. Cavanagh, D. J. Moberg, and M. Valasquez, "The Ethics of Organizational Politics," *Academy of Management Journal*, June 1981, pp. 363–374. See also F. N. Brady, "Rules for Making Exceptions to Rules," *Academy of Management Review*, July 1987, pp. 436–444, for an argument that the theory of justice is redundant with the prior two theories. See also T. Donaldson and T. W. Dunfee, "Toward a Unified Conception of Business Ethics: Integrative Social Contracts Theory," *Academy of Management Review*, April 1994, pp. 252–284; M. Douglas, "Integrative Social Contracts Theory: Hype Over Hypernorms," *Journal of Business Ethics*, July 2000, pp. 101–110; and E. Soule, "Managerial Moral Strategies—In Search of a Few Good Principles," *Academy of Management Review*, January 2002, pp. 114–124, for discussions of integrative social contracts theory.

58. E. Soule, "Managerial Moral Strategies—In Search of a Few Good Principles," *Academy of Management Review*, January 2002, p. 117.

59. D. J. Fritzsche and H. Becker, "Linking Management Behavior to Ethical Philosophy—An Empirical Investigation," *Academy of Management Journal*, March 1984, pp. 166–175.

60. L. Kohlberg, *Essays in Moral Development: The Philosophy of Moral Development*, vol. 1 (New York: Harper & Row, 1981); L. Kohlberg, *Essays in Moral Development: The Psychology of Moral Development*, vol. 2 (New York: Harper & Row, 1984); J. W. Graham, "Leadership, Moral Development, and Citizenship Behavior," *Business Ethics Quarterly*, January 1995, pp. 43–54; and T. Kelley,

"To Do Right or Just to Be Legal," *New York Times*, February 8, 1998, p. BU12.

61. See, for example, J. Weber, "Managers' Moral Reasoning: Assessing Their Responses to Three Moral Dilemmas," *Human Relations*, July 1990, pp. 687–702.

62. J. H. Barnett and M. J. Karson, "Personal Values and Business Decisions: An Exploratory Investigation," *Journal of Business Ethics*, July 1987, pp. 371–382; and W. C. Frederick and J. Weber, "The Value of Corporate Managers and Their Critics: An Empirical Description and Normative Implications," in *Business Ethics: Research Issues and Empirical Studies*, ed. W. C. Frederick and L. E. Preston, pp. 123–144 (Greenwich, CT: JAI Press, 1990).

63. L. K. Trevino and S. A. Youngblood, "Bad Apples in Bad Barrels: A Causal Analysis of Ethical Decision-Making Behavior," *Journal of Applied Psychology*, August 1990, pp. 378–385; and M. E. Baehr, J. W. Jones, and A. J. Nerad, "Psychological Correlates of Business Ethics Orientation in Executives," *Journal of Business and Psychology*, Spring 1993, pp. 291–308.

64. R. L. Cardy and T. T. Selvarajan, "Assessing Ethical Behavior Revisited: The Impact of Outcomes on Judgment Bias" (paper presented at the Annual Meeting of the Academy of Management, Toronto, Ontario, 2000).

65. B. Z. Posner and W. H. Schmidt, "Values and the American Manager: An Update," *California Management Review*, Spring 1984, pp. 202–216; R. B. Morgan, "Self- and Co-Worker Perceptions of Ethics and Their Relationships to Leadership and Salary," *Academy of Management Journal*, February 1993, pp. 200–214; G. R. Weaver, L. K. Trevino, and P. L. Cochran, "Corporate Ethics Programs as Control Systems: Influences of Executive Commitment and Environmental Factors," *Academy of Management Journal*, February 1999, pp. 41–57; and G. R. Weaver, L. K. Trevino, and P. L. Cochran, "Integrated and Decoupled Corporate Social Performance: Management Commitments, External Pressures, and Corporate Ethics Practices," *Academy of Management Journal*, October 1999, pp. 539–552.

66. B. Victor and J. B. Cullen, "The Organizational Bases of Ethical Work Climates," *Administrative Science Quarterly*, March 1988, pp. 101–125; J. B. Cullen, B. Victor, and C. Stephens, "An Ethical Weather Report: Assessing the Organization's Ethical Climate," *Organizational Dynamics*, Autumn 1989, pp. 50–62; B. Victor and J. B. Cullen, "A Theory and Measure of Ethical Climate in Organizations," in *BusinessEthics*, ed. W. Frederick and L. Preston, pp. 77–97 (Greenwich, CT: JAI Press, 1990); R. R. Sims, "The Challenge of Ethical Behavior in Organizations," *Journal of Business Ethics*, July 1992, pp. 505–513; and V. Arnold and J. C. Lampe, "Understanding the Factors Underlying Ethical Organizations: Enabling Continuous Ethical Improvement," *Journal of Applied Business Research*, Summer 1999, pp. 1–19.

67. T. M. Jones, "Ethical Decision Making by Individuals in Organizations: An Issue-Contingent Model," *Academy of Management Review*, April 1991, pp. 366–395; and T. Barnett, "Dimensions of Moral Intensity and Ethical Decision Making: An Empirical Study," *Journal of Applied Social Psychology*, May 2001, pp. 1038–1057.

68. T. M. Jones, "Ethical Decision Making by Individuals in Organizations: An Issue-Contingent Model," *Academy of Management Review*, April 1991, pp. 374–378.

69. M. McClearn, "African Adventure," *Canadian Business*, September 1, 2003.

70. "Corruption Still Tainting Asian Financial Picture, Study Says," *Vancouver Sun*, March 20, 2001, p. D18.

71. See www.transparency.ca/Readings/TI-C02.htm.

72. "Canadian Firms Ink New Ethics Code [for International Operations]," *Plant*, October 6, 1997, p. 4.

73. C. J. Robertson and W. F. Crittenden, "Mapping Moral Philosophies: Strategic Implications for Multinational Firms," *Strategic Management Journal*, April 2003, pp. 385–392.

74. Information from the Global Compact website, www.unglobalcompact.org (accessed July 11, 2007); J. Cohen, "Socially Responsible Business Goes Global," *In Business*, March–April 2000, p. 22; and C. M. Solomon, "Put Your Ethics to a Global Test," *Personnel Journal*, January 1996, pp. 66–74.

75. L. K. Trevino and S. A. Youngblood, "Bad Apples in Bad Barrels: A Causal Analysis of Ethical Decision-Making Behavior," *Journal of Applied Psychology*, August 1990, p. 384.

76. L. Bogomolny, "Good Housekeeping," *Canadian Business*, March 1, 2004, pp. 87–88.

77. See www.csa-acvm.ca/home.html.

78. W. Dabrowski, "Tighter Guidelines Issued on Disclosure: Canada's 'Sarbanes,'" *Financial Post (National Post)*, March 30, 2004, p. FP1.

79. "Global Ethics Codes Gain Importance as a Tool to Avoid Litigation and Fines," *Wall Street Journal*, August 19, 1999, p. A1; and J. Alexander, "On the Right Side," *World Business*, January–February 1997, pp. 38–41.

80. P. Richter, "Big Business Puts Ethics in Spotlight," *Los Angeles Times*, June 19, 1986, p. 29.

81. F. R. David, "An Empirical Study of Codes of Business Ethics: A Strategic Perspective" (paper presented at the 48th Annual Academy of Management Conference, Anaheim, California, August 1988).

82. "Ethics Programs Aren't Stemming Employee Misconduct," *Wall Street Journal*, May 11, 2000, p. A1.

83. L. Bogomolny, "Good Housekeeping," *Canadian Business*, March 1, 2004, pp. 87–88.

84. UN Global Compact, *Reporting Guidance on the 10th Principle Against Corruption* (New York: UN Global Compact Office, December 2009), www.unglobalcompact.org/Issues/transparency_anticorruption/Anti-Corruption_Guidance_Material.html.

85. A. K. Reichert and M. S. Webb, "Corporate Support for Ethical and Environmental Policies: A Financial Management Perspective," *Journal of Business Ethics*, May 2000; G. R. Weaver, L. K. Trevino, and P. L. Cochran, "Corporate Ethics Programs as Control Systems: Influences of Executive Commitment and Environmental Factors," *Academy of Management Journal*, February 1999, pp. 41–57; G. R. Weaver, L. K. Trevino, and P. L. Cochran, "Integrated and Decoupled Corporate Social Performance: Management Commitments, External Pressures, and Corporate Ethics Practices," *Academy of Management Journal*, October 1999, pp. 539–552; and B. Z. Posner and W. H. Schmidt, "Values and the American Manager: An Update," *California Management Review*, Spring 1984, pp. 202–216.

86. L. Nash, "Ethics Without the Sermon," *Harvard Business Review*, November–December 1981, p. 81.

87. J. B. Singh, "Ethics Programs in Canada's Largest Corporations," *Business and Society Review* 111, no. 2 (2006), pp. 119–136.

88. V. Wessler, "Integrity and Clogged Plumbing," *Straight to the Point*, newsletter of VisionPoint Corporation, Fall 2002, pp. 1–2.

89. J. B. Singh, "Ethics Programs in Canada's Largest Corporations," *Business and Society Review*111, no. 2 (2006), pp. 119–136; and K.

Doucet, "Canadian Organizations Not Meeting Ethics Expectations," *CMA Management* 74, no. 5 (2000), p. 10.

90. T. A. Gavin, "Ethics Education," *Internal Auditor*, April 1989, pp. 54–57.

91. L. Myyry and K. Helkama, "The Role of Value Priorities and Professional Ethics Training in Moral Sensitivity," *Journal of Moral Education* 31, no. 1 (2002), pp. 35–50; and W. Penn and B. D. Collier, "Current Research in Moral Development as a Decision Support System," *Journal of Business Ethics*, January 1985, pp. 131–136.

92. J. A. Byrne, "After Enron: The Ideal Corporation," *BusinessWeek*, August 19, 2002, pp. 68–71; D. Rice and C. Dreilinger, "Rights and Wrongs of Ethics Training," *Training & Development*, May 1990, pp. 103–109; and J. Weber, "Measuring the Impact of Teaching Ethics to Future Managers: A Review, Assessment, and Recommendations," *Journal of Business Ethics*, April 1990, pp. 182–190.

93. See, for instance, A. Wheat, "Keeping an Eye on Corporate America," *Fortune*, November 25, 2002, pp. 44–46; R. B. Schmitt, "Companies Add Ethics Training: Will It Work?" *Wall Street Journal*, November 4, 2002, p. B11; and P. F. Miller and W. T. Coady, "Teaching Work Ethics," *Education Digest*, February 1990, pp. 54–55.

94. R. C. Anderson with R. White, *Confessions of a Radical Industrialist: Profits, People, Purpose—Doing Business by Respecting the Earth* (New York: St. Martin's Press, 2009), p. 5.

95. "Our Progress,"Interface website, www.interfaceglobal.com/Sustainability/Progress-to-Zero.aspx (accessed July 15, 2010).

96. "Interface Support of Communities on the Shared Journey" Interface website, www.interfaceglobal.com/Sustainability/Social-Responsibility.aspx (accessed July 15, 2010).

97. Adapted from A. Reichel and Y. Neumann, *Journal of Instructional Psychology*, March 1988, pp. 25–53. With permission of the authors.

98. Situation adapted from information in C. H. Deutsch, "Green Marketing: Label with a Cause," *New York Times*, June 15, 2003, sec. 3, p. 6; and B. Lloy, "Sierra Club Hits the Apparel Trail," *Daily News Record*, February 17, 2003, p. 104.

99. Based on J. Rupert, "Ottawa Probes City Hall Gift Complaint," *Ottawa Citizen*, June 10, 2007, www.canada.com/ottawacitizen/news/story.html?id=a8964f19-b94e-49d0-bf3c-32d78424358a (accessed September 25, 2007); "City's Auditor Investigates After Firm Gives Staff Gifts," *CBCnews.ca*, June 11, 2007, www.cbc.ca/canada/ottawa/story/2007/06/11/ ticket-070611.html#skip300x250 (accessed September 25, 2007); and City of Ottawa, "The City's Employee Code of Conduct," March 2006, http://ottawa.ca/city_hall/policies/empl_codeconduct_ en.html#P217_23046 (accessed September 25, 2007).

100. Based on "Corporate Responsibility Isn't Only About How a Company Spends Its Money: It's About How a Company Makes Its Money," RBC Corporate Responsibility web page, www.rbc.com/responsibility/index.html (accessed November 13, 2010).

101. Based on F. Bartolome, "Nobody Trusts the Boss Completely—Now What?" *Harvard Business Review*, March–April 1989, pp. 135–142; and J. K. Butler Jr., "Toward Understanding and Measuring Conditions of Trust: Evolution of a Condition of Trust Inventory," *Journal of Management*, September 1991, pp. 643–663.

Chapter 6

1. Based on W. Stueck, "Builder of Toddler Shoe Empire Nudges Her Baby Out of the Nest," *Globe and Mail*, September 7, 2006, p. B1; D. Drew, "She Turned a Crisis into a Success," *Cowichan Valley Citizen*, November 29, 2006, p. 12; and G. Shaw, "Robeez Shoes Sold for $30.5 Million," *Vancouver Sun*, September 7, 2006, p. C1.

2. M. Trottman, "Choices in Stormy Weather," *Wall Street Journal*, February 14, 2006, p.B1+.

3. D. A. Garvin and M. A. Roberto, "What You Don't Know about Making Decisions," *Harvard Business Review*, September 2001, pp. 108–116.

4. W. Pounds, "The Process of Problem Finding," *Industrial Management Review*, Fall 1969, pp. 1–19.

5. R.J. Volkema, "Problem Formulation: Its Portrayal in the Texts," *Organizational Behavior Teaching Review* 11, no. 3 (1986–1987), pp. 113–126.

6. P. C. Nutt, *Why Decisions Fail: Avoiding the Blunders and Traps That Lead to Debacles* (San Francisco, CA: Berrett-Koehler, 2002).

7. W. Stueck, "Builder of Toddler Shoe Empire Nudges Her Baby Out of the Nest," *Globe and Mail*, September 7, 2006, p. B1; and Strategis, "Robeez Footwear, Better by Design," http://strategis.ic.gc.ca/epic/site/mfbs-gprea.nsf/en/lu00062e.html (accessed July 17, 2007).

8. T. A. Stewart, "Did You Ever Have to Make Up Your Mind?" *Harvard Business Review*, January 2006, p. 12; J. Pfeffer and R. I. Sutton, "Why Managing by Facts Works," *Strategy+Business*, Spring 2006, pp. 9–12; and E. Pooley, "Editor's Desk," *Fortune*, June 27, 2005, p. 16.

9. See H. A. Simon, "Rationality in Psychology and Economics," *Journal of Business*, October 1986, pp. 209–224; and A. Langley, "In Search of Rationality: The Purposes Behind the Use of Formal Analysis in Organizations," *Administrative Science Quarterly*, December 1989, pp. 598–631.

10. See, for example, J. G. March, *A Primer on Decision Making* (New York: Free Press, 1994), pp. 8–25; and A. Langley, H. Mintzberg, P. Pitcher, E. Posada, and J. Saint-Macary, "Opening Up Decision Making: The View from the Black Stool," *Organization Science*, May–June 1995, pp. 260–279.

11. See N. McK. Agnew and J. L. Brown, "Bounded Rationality: Fallible Decisions in Unbounded Decision Space," *Behavioral Science*, July 1986, pp. 148–161; B. E. Kaufman, "A New Theory of Satisficing," *Journal of Behavioral Economics*, Spring 1990, pp. 35–51; and D. R. A. Skidd, "Revisiting Bounded Rationality," *Journal of Management Inquiry*, December 1992, pp. 343–347.

12. W. Cole, "The Stapler Wars," *Time Inside Business*, April 2005, p. A5.

13. See K. R. Hammond, R. M. Hamm, J. Grassia, and T. Pearson, "Direct Comparison of the Efficacy of Intuitive and Analytical Cognition in Expert Judgment," in *IEEE Transactions on Systems, Man, and Cybernetics* SMC-17, no. 5 (1987), pp. 753–770; W. H. Agor, ed., *Intuition in Organizations* (Newbury Park, CA: Sage, 1989); O. Behling and N. L. Eckel, "Making Sense Out of Intuition," *The Executive*, February 1991, pp. 46–47; L. A. Burke and M. K. Miller, "Taking the Mystery Out of Intuitive Decision Making," *Academy of Management Executive*, October 1999, pp. 91–99; A. L. Tesolin, "How to Develop the Habit of Intuition," *Training & Development*, March 2000, p. 76; and T. A. Stewart, "How to Think with Your Gut," *Business 2.0*, November 2002, pp. 98–104.

14. See M. H. Bazerman and D. Chugh, "Decisions without Blinders," *Harvard Business Review*, January 2006, pp. 88–97; C. C. Miller and R. D. Ireland, "Intuition in Strategic Decision Making: Friend or Foe in the Fast-Paced 21st Century," *Academy of Management Executive*, February 2005, pp. 19–30; E. Sadler-Smith and E. Shefy, "The Intuitive Executive: Understanding and Applying 'Gut Feel' in Decision-Making," *Academy of Management Executive*, November 2004, pp. 76–91; T. A. Stewart, "How to Think with Your Gut," *Business 2.0*, November 2002, pp. 98–104; A. L. Tesolin, "How to Develop the Habit of Intuition," *Training & Development*, March 2000, p. 76; L. A. Burke and M. K. Miller, "Taking the Mystery Out of Intuitive Decision Making," *Academy of Management Executive*, October 1999, pp. 91–99; O. Behling and N. L. Eckel, "Making Sense Out of Intuition," *The Executive*, February 1991, pp. 46–47; W. H. Agor, ed., *Intuition in Organizations* (Newbury Park, CA: Sage, 1989); and K. R. Hammond, R. M. Hamm, J. Grassia, and T. Pearson, "Direct Comparison of the Efficacy of Intuitive and Analytical Cognition in Expert Judgment," *IEEE Transactions on Systems, Man, and Cybernetics* SMC-17, no. 5 (1987), pp. 753–770.

15. A. Dijksterhuis, M. W. Bos, L. F. Nordgren, R. B. van Baaren, "On Making the Right Choice: The Deliberation-without-Attention Effect," *Science* 311, no. 5763 (February 17, 2006), pp. 1005–1007.

16. K. R. Brousseau, M. J. Driver, G. Hourihan, and R. Larsson, "The Seasoned Executive's Decision-Making Style," *Harvard Business Review,* February 2006, pp. 111–121.

17. "Giant Pool of Money," *This American Life*, National Public Radio, September 5, 2008, www.thisamericanlife.org/radio-archives/episode/355/the-giant-pool-of-money (accessed July 20, 2010).

18. Information for this box from D. Jones and A. Shaw, "Slowing Momentum: Why BPM Isn't Keeping Pace with Its Potential," *BPM Magazine*, February 2006, pp. 4–12; B. Violino, "IT Directions," *CFO*, January 2006, pp. 68–72; D. Weinberger, "Sorting Data to Suit Yourself," *Harvard Business Review*, March 2005, pp. 16–18; and C. Winkler, "Getting a Grip on Performance," *CFO-IT*, Winter 2004, pp. 38–48.

19. A. J. Rowe and R. O. Mason, *Managing with Style* (San Francisco: Jossey-Bass, 1987); and A. J. Rowe, J. D. Boulgarides, and M. R. McGrath, *Managerial Decision Making, Modules in Management Series* (Chicago: SRA, 1984), pp. 18–22.

20. C. Shaffran, "Mind Your Meeting: How to Become the Catalyst for Culture Change," *Communication World*, February–March 2003, pp. 26–29.

21. I. L. Janis, *Victims of Groupthink* (Boston: Houghton Mifflin, 1972); R. J. Aldag and S. Riggs Fuller, "Beyond Fiasco: A Reappraisal of the Groupthink Phenomenon and a New Model of Group Decision Processes," *Psychological Bulletin,* May 1993, pp. 533–552; and T. Kameda and S. Sugimori, "Psychological Entrapment in Group Decision Making: An Assigned Decision Rule and a Groupthink Phenomenon," *Journal of Personality and Social Psychology*, August 1993, pp. 282–292.

22. I. L. Janis, *Victims of Groupthink* (Boston: Houghton Mifflin, 1972); R. J. Aldag and S. Riggs Fuller, "Beyond Fiasco: A Reappraisal of the Groupthink Phenomenon and a New Model of Group Decision Processes," *Psychological Bulletin,* May 1993, pp. 533–552; and T. Kameda and S. Sugimori, "Psychological Entrapment in Group Decision Making: An Assigned Decision Rule and a Groupthink Phenomenon," *Journal of Personality and Social Psychology*, August 1993, pp. 282–292.

23. D. D. Henningsen, M. L. M. Henningsen, J. Eden, and M. G. Cruz, "Examining the Symptoms of Groupthink and Retrospective Sensemaking," *Small Group Research* 37, no. 1 (2006), pp. 36–64; and R. S. Baron, "So Right It's Wrong: Groupthink and the

Ubiquitous Nature of Polarized Group Decision Making," *Advances in Experimental Social Psychology* 37 (2005), pp. 219–253.

24. Based on J. Brockner, *Self Esteem at Work* (Lexington, MA: Lexington Books, 1988), chapters 1–4.

25. See, for example, L. K. Michaelson, W. E. Watson, and R. H. Black, "A Realistic Test of Individual vs. Group Consensus Decision Making," *Journal of Applied Psychology* 74, no. 5 (1989), pp. 834–839; R. A. Henry, "Group Judgment Accuracy: Reliability and Validity of Postdiscussion Confidence Judgments," *Organizational Behavior and Human Decision Processes*, October 1993, pp. 11–27; P. W. Paese, M. Bieser, and M. E. Tubbs, "Framing Effects and Choice Shifts in Group Decision Making," *Organizational Behavior and Human Decision Processes*, October 1993, pp. 149–165; N. J. Castellan Jr., ed., *Individual and Group Decision Making* (Hillsdale, NJ: Lawrence Erlbaum Associates, 1993); and S. G. Straus and J. E. McGrath, "Does the Medium Matter? The Interaction of Task Type and Technology on Group Performance and Member Reactions," *Journal of Applied Psychology*, February 1994, pp. 87–97.

26. E. J. Thomas and C. F. Fink, "Effects of Group Size," *Psychological Bulletin*, July 1963, pp. 371–384; F. A. Shull, A. L. Delbecq, and L. L. Cummings, *Organizational Decision Making* (New York: McGraw-Hill, 1970), p. 151; A. P. Hare, *Handbook of Small Group Research* (New York: Free Press, 1976); M. E. Shaw, *Group Dynamics: The Psychology of Small Group Behavior*, 3rd ed. (New York: McGraw-Hill, 1981); and P. Yetton and P. Bottger, "The Relationships among Group Size, Member Ability, Social Decision Schemes, and Performance," *Organizational Behavior and Human Performance*, October 1983, pp. 145–159.

27. D. Kahneman and A. Tversky, "Judgment under Uncertainty: Heuristics and Biases," *Science* 185 (1974), pp. 1124–1131.

28. Information for this section is taken from S. P. Robbins, *Decide and Conquer* (Upper Saddle River, NJ: Financial Times/Prentice Hall, 2004).

29. See, for example, B. M. Staw, "The Escalation of Commitment to a Course of Action," *Academy of Management Review*, October 1981, pp. 577–587; D. R. Bobocel and J. P. Meyer, "Escalating Commitment to a Failing Course of Action: Separating the Roles of Choice and Justification," *Journal of Applied Psychology*, June 1994, pp. 360–363; C. F. Camerer and R. A. Weber, "The Econometrics and Behavioral Economics of Escalation of Commitment: A Re-examination of Staw's Theory," *Journal of Economic Behavior and Organization*, May 1999, pp. 59–82; V. S. Rao and A. Monk, "The Effects of Individual Differences and Anonymity on Commitment to Decisions," *Journal of Social Psychology*, August 1999, pp. 496–515; and G. McNamara, H. Moon, and P. Bromiley, "Banking on Commitment: Intended and Unintended Consequences of an Organization's Attempt to Attenuate Escalation of Commitment," *Academy of Management Journal*, April 2002, pp. 443–452.

30. Based on W. McLellan, "Soled! Born in a Basement, Robeez Matured into a Firm Worth $30.5M," *Province* (Vancouver), September 7, 2006, p. A29.

31. "Hurry Up and Decide!" *BusinessWeek*, May 14, 2001, p. 16.

32. J. Klayman, R. P. Larrick, and C. Heath, "Organizational Repairs," *Across the Board*, February 2000, pp. 26–31.

33. J. S. Hammond, R. L. Keeney, and H. Raiffa, *Smart Choices: A Practical Guide to Making Better Decisions* (Boston: Harvard Business School Press, 1999), p. 4.

34. This discussion is based on K. H. Hammonds, "5 Habits of Highly Reliable Organizations: An Interview with Karl Weick," *Fast Company*, May 2002, pp. 124–128.

35. Adapted from W. H. Agor, *AIM Survey* (El Paso, TX: ENP Enterprises, 1989), Part I. With permission.

36. Source unknown.

37. Situation adapted from information in N. Weinberg, "Holier Than Whom?" *Forbes*, June 23, 2003, p. 711; and E. Baum, "Schwab Campaign Bundles Controversy, Consistency," *Fund Marketing Alert*, March 10, 2003, p. 10.

38. Information from C. F. Martin's website, www.mguitar.com (accessed April 24, 2003, and July 18, 2007); D. Lieberman, "Guitar Sales Jam Despite Music Woes," *USA Today*, December 16, 2002, p. 2B; and S. Fitch, "Stringing Them Along," *Forbes*, July 26, 1999, pp. 90–91.

39. Based on A. Deslongchamps, "'Hard' to Raise Wages at Air Canada, ACE's Milton Warns," *National Post*, March 30, 2006, p. FP4; and "ACE Aviation to Pay Shareholders $266M in Aeroplan Units," *National Post*, February 17, 2006, p. FP6.

40. Based on J. Calano and J. Salzman, "Ten Ways to Fire Up Your Creativity," *Working Woman*, July 1989, p. 94; J. V. Anderson, "Mind Mapping: A Tool for Creative Thinking," *Business Horizons*, January–February 1993, pp. 42–46; M. Loeb, "Ten Commandments for Managing Creative People," *Fortune*, January 16, 1995, pp. 135–136; and M. Henricks, "Good Thinking," *Entrepreneur*, May 1996, pp. 70–73.

41. Information for this box comes from B. C. McDonald and D. Hutcheson, "Dealing with Diversity Is Key to Tapping Talent," *Atlanta Business Chronicle*, December 18, 1998, p. 45A1; P. M. Elsass and L. M. Graves, "Demographic Diversity in Decision-Making Groups: The Experience of Women and People of Color," *Academy of Management Review*, October 1997, pp. 946–973; and N. J. Adler, ed., *International Dimensions of Organizational Behavior*, 4th ed. (Cincinnati: South-Western College Publishing, 2001).

Chapter 7

1. Based on R. Ouzounian, "Down the Tube," *Toronto Star*, January 7, 2007, p. C6; S. Sperounes, "A Sensation Rises from Out of the Blue," *Edmonton Journal*, September 30, 2003, p. C1; "Masters of Splatter May Turn Your Mood Indigo," *People Weekly*, June 8, 1992, pp. 108–110; and Blue Man Group website, www.blueman.com (accessed July 20, 2007).

2. V. Pilieci, "The Lost Generation of Business Talent," *Vancouver Sun*, May 2, 2001, pp. D1, D9.

3. See, for example, D. K. Sinha, "The Contribution of Formal Planning to Decisions," *Strategic Management Journal*, October 1990, pp. 479–492; N. Capon, J. U. Farley, and J. M. Hulbert, "Strategic Planning and Financial Performance: More Evidence," *Journal of Management Studies*, January 1994, pp. 22–38; C. C. Miller and L. B. Cardinal, "Strategic Planning and Firm Performance: A Synthesis of More Than Two Decades of Research," *Academy of Management Journal*, March 1994, pp. 1649–1685; P. J. Brews and M. R. Hunt, "Learning to Plan and Planning to Learn: Resolving the Planning School/Learning School Debate," *Strategic Management Journal*, December 1999, pp. 889–913; and R. Wiltbank, N. Dew, S. Read, and S. D. Sarasvathy, "What to Do Next? The Case for Non-Predictive Strategy," *Strategic Management Journal* 27, no. 10 (October 2006), pp. 981–998.

4. S. Sperounes, "A Sensation Rises from Out of the Blue," *Edmonton Journal*, September 30, 2003, p. C1; K. Powers, "Blue Coup," *Forbes*, March 19, 2001, p. 136; and S. Hampson, "Blue Cogs in a Corporate Wheel," *Globe and Mail*, July 12, 2003, p. R3.

5. R. Molz, "How Leaders Use Goals," *Long Range Planning*, October 1987, p. 91.

6. P. N. Romani, "MBO by Any Other Name Is Still MBO," *Supervision*, December 1997, pp. 6–8; and A. W. Schrader and G. T. Seward, "MBO Makes Dollar Sense," *Personnel Journal*, July 1989, pp. 32–37.

7. P. N. Romani, "MBO by Any Other Name Is Still MBO," *Supervision*, December 1997, pp. 6–8; and R. Rodgers and J. E. Hunter, "Impact of Management by Objectives on Organizational Productivity," *Journal of Applied Psychology*, April 1991, pp. 322–336.

8. For additional information on goals, see, for instance, P. Drucker, *The Executive in Action* (New York: HarperCollins, 1996), pp. 207–214; and E. A. Locke and G. P. Latham, *A Theory of Goal Setting and Task Performance* (Upper Saddle River, NJ: Prentice Hall, 1990).

9. G. T. Doran, "There's a SMART Way to Write Management Goals and Objectives," *Management Review* 70, no. 11 (1981), pp. 35–36.

10. Based on J. McElgunn, "Staying on a Kicking Horse," *PROFIT*, November 2006, www.profitguide.com/article/3740—profit-w100-staying-on-a-kicking-horse.

11. J. D. Hunger and T. L. Wheelen, *Strategic Management and Business Policy*, 10th ed. (Upper Saddle River, NJ: Prentice Hall, 2006).

12. Several of these factors were suggested by J. S. Armstrong, "The Value of Formal Planning for Strategic Decisions: Review of Empirical Research," *Strategic Management Journal*, July–September 1982, pp. 197–211; and R. K. Bresser and R. C. Bishop, "Dysfunctional Effects of Formal Planning: Two Theoretical Explanations," *Academy of Management Review*, October 1983, pp. 588–599.

13. P. J. Brews and M. R. Hunt, "Learning to Plan and Planning to Learn: Resolving the Planning School/Learning School Debate," *Strategic Management Journal*, December 1999, pp. 889–913.

14. P. J. Brews and M. R. Hunt, "Learning to Plan and Planning to Learn: Resolving the Planning School/Learning School Debate," *Strategic Management Journal*, December 1999, pp. 889–913.

15. A. Campbell, "Tailored, Not Benchmarked: A Fresh Look at Corporate Planning," *Harvard Business Review*, March–April 1999, pp. 41–50.

16. J. H. Sheridan, "Focused on Flow," *IndustryWeek*, October 18, 1999, pp. 46–51.

17. J. K. Nestruck, "Blue Man Scoop: Founding Members Reveal How It All Began," *National Post*, June 8, 2005, p. AL1; S. Sperounes, "A Sensation Rises from Out of the Blue," *Edmonton Journal*, September 30, 2003, p. C1; K. Powers, "Blue Coup," *Forbes*, March 19, 2001, p. 136; and S. Hampson, "Blue Cogs in a Corporate Wheel," *Globe and Mail*, July 12, 2003, p. R3.

18. H. Mintzberg, *The Rise and Fall of Strategic Planning* (New York: Free Press, 1994).

19. H. Mintzberg, *The Rise and Fall of Strategic Planning* (New York: Free Press, 1994).

20. H. Mintzberg, *The Rise and Fall of Strategic Planning* (New York: Free Press, 1994).

21. G. Hamel and C. K. Prahalad, *Competing for the Future* (Boston: Harvard Business School Press, 1994).

22. D. Miller, "The Architecture of Simplicity," *Academy of Management Review*, January 1993, pp. 116–138.

23. M. C. Mankins and R. Steele, "Stop Making Plans—Start Making Decisions," *Harvard Business Review*, January 2006, pp. 76–84; L.

Bossidy and R. Charan, *Execution: The Discipline of Getting Things Done* (New York: Crown/Random House, 2002); and P. Roberts, "The Art of Getting Things Done," *Fast Company*, June 2000, p. 162.

24. Associated Press, "Dow Jones to Shrink 'Wall Street Journal,' Cut Some Data," *USA Today*, October 12, 2005, www.usatoday.com.

25. P. J. Brews and M. R. Hunt, "Learning to Plan and Planning to Learn: Resolving the Planning School/Learning School Debate," *Strategic Management Journal*, December 1999, pp. 889–913.

26. Information on Wipro Limited from Hoover's Online, www.hoovers.com (accessed March 21, 2006); R. J. Newman, "Coming and Going," *U.S. News & World Report*, January 23, 2006, pp. 50–52; T. Atlas, "Bangalore's Big Dreams," *U.S. News & World Report*, May 2, 2005, pp. 50–52; and K. H. Hammonds, "Smart, Determined, Ambitious, Cheap: The New Face of Global Competition," *Fast Company*, February 2003, pp. 90–97.

27. Adapted from N. T. Feather, "Attitudes toward the High Achiever: The Fall of the Tall Poppy," *Australian Journal of Psychology* 41 (1989), pp. 239–267.

28. Situation adapted from information in S. Leith, "Coke Faces Damage Control," *Atlanta Journal-Constitution*, June 19, 2003, p. C1; C. Terhume, "Coke Employees Acted Improperly in Marketing Test," *Wall Street Journal*, June 18, 2003, pp. A3, A6; and T. Howard, "Burger King, Coke May Face Off in Frozen Coke Suit," *USA Today*, June 6, 2003, www.usatoday.com/money/industries/food/_2003-06-04.bk_x.htm.

29. Based on information on Lend Lease from Hoover's Online, www.hoovers.com (accessed November 8, 2004); Lend Lease website, www.lendlease.com (accessed November 8, 2004 and July 20, 2007); P. LaBarre, "A Company without Limits," *Fast Company*, September 1999, pp. 160–186; "Lend Lease Building on Its Success," *Business Asia*, March 15, 1999, p. 11; and www.lendlease.com/llweb/bll/main.nsf/images/pdf_2005_annualreport.pdf/$file/pdf_2005_annualreport.pdf.

30. Based on "Corporate Canada Preparing for Influenza Pandemic," *Canadian Press*, January 22, 2006; M. Siegel, "Is Yesterday's Swine Flu Today's Bird Flu?" *USA Today*, March 22, 2006, p. 13A; M. Warner, "Preparing for the Avian Flu Threat in the U.S.," *New York Times*, March 21, 2006, www.nytimes.com; E. Rosenthal and K. Bradsher, "Is Business Ready for a Flu Pandemic?" *New York Times*, March 16, 2006, www.nytimes.com; Deloitte Center for Health Solutions, "Business Preparations for Pandemic Flu," Deloitte, December 2005, www.deloitte.com/dtt/cda/doc/content/PandemicFluSurvey%282%29.pdf (accessed July 20, 2007); and J. Carey, "Avian Flu: Business Thinks the Unthinkable," *BusinessWeek*, November 28, 2005, pp. 36–39.

31. Based on S. P. Robbins and D. A. DeCenzo, *Fundamentals of Management*, 4th ed. (Upper Saddle River, NJ: Prentice Hall, 2004), p. 85.

Chapter 8

1. Based on H. Shaw, "Indigo Pens Next Chapter," *Financial Post (National Post)*, June 22, 2007, www.canada.com/national post/financialpost/story.html?id=d1bc522d-712c-42f4-b2e4-fe71c0c5d0ba&k=68292 (accessed July 27, 2007); and Indigo Books & Music website, www.chapters.indigo.ca (accessed July 27, 2007).

2. See www.hll.com/mediacentre/annualreport2006.pdf.

3. J. W. Dean Jr. and M. P. Sharfman, "Does Decision Process Matter? A Study of Strategic Decision-Making Effectiveness," *Academy of Management Journal*, April 1996, pp. 368–396.

4. Based on A. A. Thompson Jr., A. J. Strickland III, and J. E. Gamble, *Crafting and Executing Strategy*, 14th ed. (New York: McGraw-Hill Irwin, 2005).

5. J. Magretta, "Why Business Models Matter," *Harvard Business Review*, May 2002, pp. 86–92.

6. E. H. Bowman and C. E. Helfat, "Does Corporate Strategy Matter?" *Strategic Management Journal* 22 (2001), pp. 1–23; P. J. Brews and M. R. Hunt, "Learning to Plan and Planning to Learn: Resolving the Planning School/Learning School Debate," *Strategic Management Journal*, December 1999, pp. 889–913; D. J. Ketchen Jr., J. B. Thomas, and R. R. McDaniel Jr., "Process, Content and Context; Synergistic Effects on Performance," *Journal of Management* 22, no. 2 (1996), pp. 231–257; C. C. Miller and L. B. Cardinal, "Strategic Planning and Firm Performance: A Synthesis of More Than Two Decades of Research," *Academy of Management Journal*, December 1994, pp. 1649–1665; and N. Capon, J. U. Farley, and J. M. Hulbert, "Strategic Planning and Financial Performance: More Evidence," *Journal of Management Studies*, January 1994, pp. 105–110.

7. "A Solid Strategy Helps Companies' Growth," *Nation's Business*, October 1990, p. 10.

8. See, for example, H. Mintzberg, *The Rise and Fall of Strategic Planning* (New York: Free Press, 1994); S. J. Wall and S. R. Wall, "The Evolution (Not the Death) of Strategy," *Organizational Dynamics*, Autumn 1995, pp. 7–19; J. A. Byrne, "Strategic Planning: It's Back!" *BusinessWeek*, August 26, 1996, pp. 46–52; and R. M. Grant, "Strategic Planning in a Turbulent Environment: Evidence from the Oil Majors," *Strategic Management Journal* 24, no. 6 (June 2003), pp. 491–517.

9. Based on information obtained from www.city.vancouver.bc.ca/commsvcs/socialplanning/_grants/PODGrants.htm; and www.centreforsustainability.ca/programs/ (accessed July 23, 2007).

10. Based on H. Shaw, "Indigo Pens Next Chapter," *Financial Post (National Post)*, June 22, 2007, www.canada.com/nationalpost/financialpost/story.html?id=d1bc522d-712c-42f4-b2e4-fe71c0c5d0ba&k=68292 (accessed July 27, 2007); and "Welcome to the Community: More than 250,000 members—Join the Conversation," chapters.indigo.ca, http://community.indigo.ca/find/community-groups/1.html (accessed November 9, 2010).

11. "About Our Company," Indigo Books & Music website, www.chapters.indigo.ca/About-Indigo-Books-Music-Inc/chaptersinc-art.html (accessed July 23, 2007).

12. "About Us," WorkSafeBC website, www.worksafebc.com/about_us/default.asp (accessed July 23, 2007).

13. "Company Overview," eBay, http://pages.ebay.ca/aboutebay/thecompany/companyoverview.html (accessed July 23, 2007).

14. C. K. Prahalad and G. Hamel, "The Core Competence of the Corporation," *Harvard Business Review*, May–June 1990, pp. 79–91.

15. A. Taylor, "How Toyota Does It," *Fortune*, March 6, 2006, pp. 107–124; C. Woodyard, "Slow and Steady Drives Toyota's Growth," *USA Today*, December 21, 2005, pp. 1B+; I. M. Kunii, C. Dawson, and C. Palmeri, "Toyota Is Way Ahead of the Hybrid Pack," *BusinessWeek*, May 5, 2003, p. 48; and S. Spear and H. K. Bowen, "Decoding the DNA of the Toyota Production System," *Harvard Business Review*, September–October 1999, pp. 96–106.

16. See, for example, H. J. Cho and V. Pucik, "Relationship between Innovativeness, Quality, Growth, Profitability, and Market Value," *Strategic Management Journal* 26, no. 6 (2005), pp. 555–575; W. F. Joyce, "Building the 4+2 Organization," *Organizational Dynamics*, May 2005, pp. 118–129; R. S. Kaplan and D. P. Norton, "Measuring the Strategic Readiness of Intangible Assets," *Harvard Business Review*, February 2004, pp. 52–63; C. M. Fiol, "Managing Culture as a Competitive Resource: An Identity-Based View of Sustainable Competitive Advantage," *Journal of Management*, March 1991, pp. 191–211; T. Kono, "Corporate Culture and Long-Range Planning," *Long Range Planning*, August 1990, pp. 9–19; S. Green, "Understanding Corporate Culture and Its Relation to Strategy," *International Studies of Management and Organization*, Summer 1988, pp. 6–28; C. Scholz, "Corporate Culture and Strategy—The Problem of Strategic Fit," *Long Range Planning*, August 1987, pp. 78–87; and J. B. Barney, "Organizational Culture: Can It Be a Source of Sustained Competitive Advantage?" *Academy of Management Review*, July 1986, pp. 656–665.

17. J. P. Kotter and J. L. Heskett, *Corporate Culture and Performance* (New York: Free Press, 1992).

18. K. E. Klein, "Slogans That Are the Real Thing," *BusinessWeek*, August 4, 2005, www.businessweek.com/smallbiz/content/aug2005/sb20050804_867552.htm (accessed July 27, 2007); and T. Mucha, "The Payoff for Trying Harder," *Business 2.0*, July 2002, pp. 84–85.

19. A. Carmeli and A. Tischler, "The Relationships between Intangible Organizational Elements and Organizational Performance," *Strategic Management Journal* 25 (2004), pp. 1257–1278; P. W. Roberts and G. R. Dowling, "Corporate Reputation and Sustained Financial Performance," *Strategic Management Journal*, December 2002, pp. 1077–1093; and C. J. Fombrun, "Corporate Reputations as Economic Assets," in *Handbook of Strategic Management*, ed. M. A. Hitt, R. E. Freeman, and J. S. Harrison, pp. 289–312 (Malden, MA: Blackwell, 2001).

20. Harris Interactive, "Johnson & Johnson Ranks No. 1 in National Corporate Reputation Survey for Seventh Consecutive Year," news release, December 7, 2005.

21. Based on G. Pitts, "Tide Turns for P&G Canada President," *Globe and Mail*, October 14, 2002, p. B3; S. Heinrich, "P&G Still the Best Step Up," *National Post*, April 14, 2003, p. FP4; and www.pg.com/en_CA/index.jhtml (accessed July 23, 2007).

22. Based on H. Shaw, "Indigo Pens Next Chapter," *Financial Post (National Post)*, June 22, 2007, www.canada.com/nationalpost/financialpost/story.html?id=d1bc522d-712c-42f4-b2e4-fe71c0c5d0ba&k=68292 (accessed July 27, 2007); and Indigo Books & Music website, www.chapters.indigo.ca.

23. See www.timhortons.com/ca/pdf/2010_Investor_Conference_FINAL.pdf (accessed October 30, 2010).

24. J. A. Pearce, II, "Retrenchment Remains the Foundation of Business Turnaround," *Strategic Management Journal* 15 (1994), pp. 407–417.

25. *GM 2006 Annual Report*, www.gm.com/company/investor_information/docs/fin_data/gm05ar/download/gm05ar.pdf (accessed July 25, 2007).

26. *Kodak 2005 Annual Report*, http://library.corporate-ir.net/library/11/115/115911/items/189563/annualReport05.pdf (accessed July 25, 2007).

27. H. Quarls, T. Pernsteiner, and K. Rangan, "Love Your Dogs," *Strategy+Business*, Spring 2006, pp. 58–65; and P. Haspeslagh, "Portfolio Planning: Uses and Limits," *Harvard Business Review*, January–February 1982, pp. 58–73.

28. Boston Consulting Group, *Perspective on Experience* (Boston: Boston Consulting Group, 1970).

29. R. Rumelt, "Towards a Strategic Theory of the Firm," in *Competitive Strategic Management*, ed. R. Lamb, pp. 556–570 (Upper Saddle River, NJ: Prentice Hall, 1984); M. E. Porter, *Competitive Advantage: Creating and Sustaining Superior Performance* (New York: Free Press, 1985); J. Barney, "Firm Resources and Sustained Competitive Advantage," *Journal of Management* 17, no. 1 (1991), pp. 99–120; M. A. Peteraf, "The Cornerstones of Competitive Advantage: A Resource-Based View," *Strategic Management Journal*, March 1993, pp. 179–191; and J. B. Barney, "Looking Inside for Competitive Advantage," *Academy of Management Executive*, November 1995, pp. 49–61.

30. T. C. Powell, "Total Quality Management as Competitive Advantage: A Review and Empirical Study," *Strategic Management Journal*, January 1995, pp. 15–37.

31. See R. J. Schonenberger, "Is Strategy Strategic? Impact of Total Quality Management on Strategy," *Academy of Management Executive*, August 1992, pp. 80–87; C. A. Barclay, "Quality Strategy and TQM Policies: Empirical Evidence," *Management International Review*, Special Issue (1993), pp. 87–98; T. E. Benson, "A Business Strategy Comes of Age," *IndustryWeek*, May 3, 1993, pp. 40–44; R. Jacob, "TQM: More Than a Dying Fad?" *Fortune*, October 18, 1993, pp. 66–72; R. Krishnan, A. B. Shani, R. M. Grant, and R. Baer, "In Search of Quality Improvement Problems of Design and Implementation," *Academy of Management Executive*, November 1993, pp. 7–20; B. Voss, "Quality's Second Coming," *Journal of Business Strategy*, March–April 1994, pp. 42–46; M. Barrier, "Raising TQM Consciousness," *Nation's Business*, April 1994, pp. 62–64; and special issue of *Academy of Management Review* devoted to TQM, July 1994, pp. 390–584.

32. See, for example, M. E. Porter, *Competitive Strategy: Techniques for Analyzing Industries and Competitors* (New York: Free Press, 1980); M. E. Porter, *Competitive Advantage: Creating and Sustaining Superior Performance* (New York: Free Press, 1985); G. G. Dess and P. S. Davis, "Porter's (1980) Generic Strategies as Determinants of Strategic Group Membership and Organizational Performance," *Academy of Management Journal*, September 1984, pp. 467–488; G. G. Dess and P. S. Davis, "Porter's (1980) Generic Strategies and Performance: An Empirical Examination with American Data—Part I: Testing Porter," *Organization Studies*, no. 1 (1986), pp. 37–55; G. G. Dess and P. S. Davis, "Porter's (1980) Generic Strategies and Performance: An Empirical Examination with American Data—Part II: Performance Implications," *Organization Studies*, no. 3 (1986), pp. 255–261; M. E. Porter, "From Competitive Advantage to Corporate Strategy," *Harvard Business Review*, May–June 1987, pp. 43–59; A. I. Murray, "A Contingency View of Porter's 'Generic Strategies,'" *Academy of Management Review*, July 1988, pp. 390–400; C. W. L. Hill, "Differentiation versus Low Cost or Differentiation and Low Cost: A Contingency Framework," *Academyof Management Review*, July 1988, pp. 401–412; I. Bamberger, "Developing Competitive Advantage in Small and Medium-Sized Firms," *Long Range Planning*, October 1989, pp. 80–88; D. F. Jennings and J. R. Lumpkin, "Insights between Environmental Scanning Activities and Porter's Generic Strategies: An Empirical Analysis," *Strategic Management Journal* 18, no. 4 (1992), pp. 791–803; N. Argyres and A. M. McGahan, "An Interview with Michael Porter," *Academy of Management Executive*, May 2002, pp. 43–52; and A. Brandenburger, "Porter's Added Value: High Indeed!" *Academy of Management Executive*, May 2002, pp. 58–60.

33. Based on W. Hanley, "Mowat's Lefty Ways Pay Big Dividends," *National Post*, February 28, 2004, p. IN01.

34. See www.peicreditunions.com/news/article.php?ID=594 (accessed September 26, 2007).

35. D. Miller and J. Toulouse, "Strategy, Structure, CEO Personality, and Performance in Small Firms," *American Journal of Small Business*, Winter 1986, pp. 47–62.

36. *Bang & Olufsen 2005–2006 Annual Report*, www.bang-olufsen.com/graphics/bogo/reports/annualreport_2005-06_uk.pdf (accessed July 25, 2007).

37. C. W. L. Hill, "Differentiation versus Low Cost or Differentiation and Low Cost: A Contingency Framework," *Academy of Management Review*, July 1988, pp. 401–412; R. E. White, "Organizing to Make Business Unit Strategies Work," in *Handbook of Business Strategy*, 2nd ed., ed. H. E. Glass, pp. 24.1–24.14 (Boston: Warren Gorham and Lamont, 1991); D. Miller, "The Generic Strategy Trap," *Journal of Business Strategy*, January–February 1991, pp. 37–41; S. Cappel, P. Wright, M. Kroll, and D. Wyld, "Competitive Strategies and Business Performance: An Empirical Study of Select Service Businesses," *International Journal of Management*, March 1992, pp. 1–11; and J. W. Bachmann, "Competitive Strategy: It's O.K. to Be Different," *Academy of Management Executive*, May 2002, pp. 61–65.

38. Based on H. Shaw, "Indigo Pens Next Chapter, *Financial Post (National Post)*, June 22, 2007, www.canada.com/nationalpost/financialpost/story.html?id=d1bc522d-712c-42f4-b2e4-fe71c0c5d0ba&k=68292 (accessed July 27, 2007).

39. See G. Masson, "Music Sales Continue to Fall," *Variety*, July 4, 2007, www.variety.com/article/VR1117968039.html?categoryid=19&cs=1 (accessed July 25, 2007).

40. E. Gunderson, "Ringtone Sales Ring Up Music Profits," *USA Today*, January 25, 2006, www.usatoday.com/life/music/news/2006-01-25-ringtones_x.htm (accessed July 25, 2007).

41. D. Leonard, "Songs in the Key of Steve," *Fortune*, May 12, 2003, pp. 52–62; L. Grossman, "It's All Free!" *Time*, May 5, 2003, pp. 60–67; and "Everybody Hurts: Music Sales Fall 7.2%," *USA Today*, April 9, 2003, p. 1B.

42. K. Shimizu and M. A. Hitt, "Strategic Flexibility: Organizational Preparedness to Reverse Ineffective Decisions," *Academy of Management Executive*, November 2004, p. 44.

43. G. T. Lumpkin, S. B. Droege, and G. G. Dess, "E-commerce Strategies: Achieving Sustainable Competitive Advantage and Avoiding Pitfalls," *Organizational Dynamics*, Spring 2002, pp. 325–340.

44. E. Kim, D. Nam, and J. L. Stimpert, "The Applicability of Porter's Generic Strategies in the Digital Age: Assumptions, Conjectures, and Suggestions," *Journal of Management* 30, no. 5 (2004), pp. 569–589.

45. "Online Retailers Don't Click with Canadian Shoppers, Study Finds," *CBCNews.ca*, December 22, 2006, www.cbc.ca/news/yourview/2006/12/online_retailers_dont_click_wi.html (accessed July 26, 2007); and R. Janelle, "More Canadians Shopping Online, but Spending Less: StatsCan," *Tech Vibes*, September 27, 2010, www.techvibes.com/blog/more-canadians-shopping-online-but-spending-less-statscan (accessed November 9, 2010).

46. J. Gaffney, "Shoe Fetish," *Business 2.0*, March 2002, pp. 98–99.

47. J. Doebele, "The Engineer," *Forbes*, January 9, 2006, pp. 122–124.

48. S. Ellison, "P&G to Unleash Dental Adult-Pet Food," *Wall Street Journal*, December 12, 2002, p. B4.

49. P. C. Nutt, "The Tolerance for Ambiguity and Decision Making," Working Paper Series, WP88-291, Ohio State University College of

Business, Columbus, Ohio; adapted from S. Budner, "Intolerance of Ambiguity as a Personality Variable," *Journal of Personality*, March 1962, pp. 29–50.

50. Situation adapted from information in J. Frederick, "War of Words," *Time International*, February 17, 2003, p. 33; and K. Regan, "Bugging Out Over Bezos' Bargain Book Bin," *E-commerce Times*, April 17, 2002, www.ecommercetimes.com.

51. Based on company information from Haier websites: www. haier.com, www.haieramerica.com, and www.haier.com.au (accessed March 30, 2006); S. Hamm and I. Rowley, "Speed Demons," *BusinessWeek*, March 27, 2006, pp. 68–76; E. Esfahani, "Thinking Locally, Succeeding Globally," *Business 2.0*, December 2005, pp. 96–98; Interbrand, "The Strategy for Chinese Brands," October 2005, www.brandchannel.com/images/papers/ 250_ChinaBrandStrategy.pdf (accessed July 27, 2007); Agence France-Presse, "Chinese Brands Coming to a Market Near You," *IndustryWeek*, April 14, 2005; and "Leadership in China: Haier's Zhang Ruimin," *Wharton Leadership Digest* 9, no. 6 (March 2005).

52. Based on B. Horovitz, "By Year's End, Regular Size Will Have to Do," *USA Today*, March 3, 2004, www.usatoday.com; and J. Woestendiek and A. Hirsch, "McDonald's to Trim Super Size," *Baltimore Sun*, March 4, 2004, www.baltimoresun.com.

53. Based on L. M. Fuld, *Monitoring the Competition* (New York: Wiley, 1988); E. H. Burack and N. J. Mathys, "Environmental Scanning Improves Strategic Planning," *Personnel Administrator*, 1989, pp. 82–87; and R. Subramanian, N. Fernandes, and E. Harper, "Environmental Scanning in U.S. Companies: Their Nature and Their Relationship to Performance," *Management International Review*, July 1993, pp. 271–286.

Chapter 9

1. Based on M. Hume, "On Time, On Budget: Games Cheaper Than Expected," *Globe and Mail*, May 8, 2007; D. Bramham, "Vancouver Games Hit First Hurdle," *Ottawa Citizen*, February 15, 2004, p. A12; D. Inwood, "Money Starts to Flow for Olympic Games," *Province* (Vancouver), February 18, 2004, p. A6; J. Lee, "John Furlong's Rockin' Life," *Vancouver Sun*, March 27, 2004, p. C1; J. Morris, "Long Road Ahead for 2010 Games," *Trail Times*, December 30, 2003, p. 4; "The Clock Is Ticking," *Maclean's*, July 14, 2003, p. 24; D. Saunders, "Olympics Put Greek Economy into a Tailspin," *Globe and Mail*, September 14, 2004, p. A1; and M. Bridge, "Athens Olympics May Have Been Best Ever," *Vancouver Sun*, October 15, 2004, p. B5.

2. F. Vogelstein, "Search and Destroy," *Fortune*, May 2, 2005, pp. 73–82.

3. S. C. Jain, "Environmental Scanning in U.S. Corporations," *Long Range Planning*, April 1984, pp. 117–128; see also L. M. Fuld, *Monitoring the Competition* (New York: John Wiley & Sons, 1988); E. H. Burack and N. J. Mathys, "Environmental Scanning Improves Strategic Planning," *Personnel Administrator*, April 1989, pp. 82–87; R. Subramanian, N. Fernandes, and E. Harper, "Environmental Scanning in U.S. Companies: Their Nature and Their Relationship to Performance," *Management International Review*, July 1993, pp. 271–286; B. K. Boyd and J. Fulk, "Executive Scanning and Perceived Uncertainty: A Multidimensional Model," *Journal of Management* 22, no. 1 (1996), pp. 1–21; D. S. Elkenov, "Strategic Uncertainty and Environmental Scanning: The Case for Institutional Influences on Scanning Behavior," *Strategic Management Journal* 18 (1997), pp. 287–302; K. Kumar, R. Subramanian, and K. Strandholm, "Competitive Strategy, Environmental Scanning and Performance: A Context Specific Analysis of Their Relationship," *International Journal of Commerce and Management*, Spring 2001,

pp. 1–18; and C. G. Wagner, "Top 10 Reasons to Watch Trends," *Futurist*, March–April 2002, pp. 68–69.

4. T. L. Wheelen and J. D. Hunger, *Strategic Management*, 8th ed. (Upper Saddle River, NJ: Prentice Hall, 2001), pp. 52–53; and J. Barrett, "Can a '50s Icon Do It Again?" *Newsweek*, March 20, 2006, p. E20.

5. B. Gilad, "The Role of Organized Competitive Intelligence in Corporate Strategy," *Columbia Journal of World Business*, Winter 1989, pp. 29–35; L. Fuld, "A Recipe for Business Intelligence," *Journal of Business Strategy*, January–February 1991, pp. 12–17; J. P. Herring, "The Role of Intelligence in Formulating Strategy," *Journal of Business Strategy*, September–October 1992, pp. 54–60; K. Western, "Ethical Spying," *Business Ethics*, September–October 1995, pp. 22–23; D. Kinard, "Raising Your Competitive IQ: The Payoff of Paying Attention to Potential Competitors," *Association Management*, February 2003, pp. 40–44; and K. Girard, "Snooping on a Shoestring," *Business 2.0*, May 2003, pp. 64–66.

6. C. Davis, "Get Smart," *Executive Edge*, October–November 1999, pp. 46–50.

7. B. Ettore, "Managing Competitive Intelligence," *Management Review*, October 1995, pp. 15–19.

8. S. Myburgh, "Competitive Intelligence: Bridging Organizational Boundaries," *Information Management Journal* 38, no. 2 (2004), pp. 46–53.

9. C. Sorensen, "Cloak & Dagger Inc.," *Financial Post (National Post)*, July 8, 2004, p. FP1.

10. A. Serwer, "P&G's Covert Operation," *Fortune*, September 17, 2001, pp. 42–44.

11. K. Western, "Ethical Spying," *Business Ethics*, September–October 1995, pp. 22–23.

12. P. Vieira, "The Airline, the Analyst and the Secret Password," *Financial Post*, June 30, 2004, p. FP1; C. Wong, "WestJet Disputes Air Canada Allegations of Corporate Espionage," *Canadian Press*, July 1, 2004; K. Macklem, "Spies in the Skies," *Maclean's*, September 20, 2004, pp. 20–23; and B. Jang and P. Waldie, "Late Nights, 'Hush-Hush' E-mails and 007 Project," *GlobeAdvisor*, October 3, 2006, www.globeadvisor.com/servlet/ArticleNews/story/gam/ 20061003/RWESTJETPROJECT03 (accessed July 27, 2007).

13. W. H. Davidson, "The Role of Global Scanning in Business Planning," *Organizational Dynamics*, Winter 1991, pp. 5–16.

14. T. L. Wheelen and J. D. Hunger, *Strategic Management*, 8th ed. (Upper Saddle River, NJ: Prentice Hall, 2001), p. 67; and www. mitsubishi-motors.ca/Company/WhoWeAre.aspx?lng=2 (accessed September 27, 2007).

15. "Is Supply Chain Collaboration Really Happening?" *ERI Journal*, January–February 2006, www.eri.com; L. Denend and H. Lee, "West Marine: Driving Growth through Shipshape Supply Chain Management, A Case Study," *Stanford Graduate School of Business*, April 7, 2005, www.vics.org; N. Nix, A. G. Zacharia, R. F. Lusch, W. R. Bridges, and A. Thomas, "Keys to Effective Supply Chain Collaboration: A Special Report from the Collaborative Practices Research Program," *Neeley School of Business, Texas Christian University*, November 15, 2004, www.vics.org; Collaborative, Planning, Forecasting, and Replenishment Committee website, www. cpfr.org (accessed May 20, 2003); and J. W. Verity, "Clearing the Cobwebs from the Stockroom," *BusinessWeek*, October 21, 1996, p. 140.

16. L. Brannen, "Upfront: Global Planning Perspectives," *Business Finance*, March 2006, pp. 12+.

17. P. N. Pant and W. H. Starbuck, "Innocents in the Forest: Forecasting and Research Methods," *Journal of Management*, June 1990, pp. 433–460; F. Elikai and W. Hall Jr., "Managing and Improving the Forecasting Process," *Journal of Business Forecasting Methods & Systems*, Spring 1999, pp. 15–19; M. A. Giullian, M. D. Odom, and M. W. Totaro, "Developing Essential Skills for Success in the Business World: A Look at Forecasting," *Journal of Applied Business Research*, Summer 2000, pp. 51–65; and T. Leahy, "Turning Managers into Forecasters," *Business Finance*, August 2002, pp. 37–40.

18. K. Moore and S. Caney, "A Real Food Fight," *National Post*, May 10, 2003, p. FP11.

19. T. Leahy, "Turning Managers into Forecasters," *Business Finance*, August 2002, pp. 37–40.

20. J. Hope, "Use a Rolling Forecast to Spot Trends," *Harvard Business School Working Knowledge*, March 13, 2006, http://hbswk.hbs.edu/archive/5250.html (accessed August 1, 2007).

21. This section is based on Y. K. Shetty, "Benchmarking for Superior Performance," *Long Range Planning* 26, no. 1 (1993), pp. 39–44; G. H. Watson, "How Process Benchmarking Supports Corporate Strategy," *Planning Review*, January–February 1993, pp. 12–15; S. Greengard, "Discover Best Practices," *Personnel Journal*, November 1995, pp. 62–73; J. Martin, "Are You as Good as You Think You Are?" *Fortune*, September 30, 1996, pp. 142–152; R. L. Ackoff, "The Trouble with Benchmarking," *Across the Board*, January 2000, p. 13; V. Prabhu, D. Yarrow, and G. Gordon-Hart, "Best Practice and Performance within Northeast Manufacturing," *Total Quality Management*, January 2000, pp. 113–121; "E-benchmarking: The Latest E-Trend," *CFO*, March 2000, p. 7; and E. Krell, "Now Read This," *Business Finance*, May 2000, pp. 97–103.

22. "Newswatch," *CFO*, July 2002, p. 26.

23. Based on J. Lee, "Finances Are in Great Shape, Vanoc Says," *Vancouver Sun*, June 29, 2007, p. B1; "Frequently Asked Questions," City of Vancouver website, www.city.vancouver.bc.ca/olympics/faq.htm (accessed June 28, 2007); D. Bramham, "Vancouver Games Hit First Hurdle," *Ottawa Citizen*, February 15, 2004, p. A12; D. Inwood, "Money Starts to Flow for Olympic Games," *Province*, February 18, 2004, p. A6; J. Lee, "John Furlong's Rockin' Life," *Vancouver Sun*, March 27, 2004, p. C1; J. Morris, "Long Road Ahead for 2010 Games," *Trail Times*, December 30, 2003, p. 4; and "The Clock Is Ticking," *Maclean's*, July 14, 2003, p. 24.

24. J. Hope and R. Fraser, "Who Needs Budgets?" *Harvard Business Review*, February 2003, pp. 108–115; T. Leahy, "The Top 10 Traps of Budgeting," *Business Finance*, November 2001, pp. 20–26; T. Leahy, "Necessary Evil," *Business Finance*, November 1999, pp. 41–45; J. Fanning, "Businesses Languishing in a Budget Comfort Zone?" *Management Accounting*, July–August 1999, p. 8; "Budgeting Processes: Inefficiency or Inadequate?" *Management Accounting*, February 1999, p. 5; A. Kennedy and D. Dugdale, "Getting the Most from Budgeting," *Management Accounting*, February 1999, pp. 22–24; G. J. Nolan, "The End of Traditional Budgeting," *Bank Accounting & Finance*, Summer 1998, pp. 29–36; and J. Mariotti, "Surviving the Dreaded Budget Process," *IndustryWeek*, August 17, 1998, p. 150.

25. See, for example, S. Stiansen, "Breaking Even," *Success*, November 1988, p. 16.

26. S. E. Barndt and D. W. Carvey, *Essentials of Operations Management* (Upper Saddle River, NJ: Prentice Hall, 1982), p. 134.

27. D. Bramham, "Vancouver Games Hit First Hurdle," *Ottawa Citizen*, February 15, 2004, p. A12; D. Inwood, "Money Starts to Flow for Olympic Games," *Province* (Vancouver), February 18,

2004, p. A6; J. Lee, "John Furlong's Rockin' Life," *Vancouver Sun*, March 27, 2004, p. C1; J. Morris, "Long Road Ahead for 2010 Games," *Trail Times*, December 30, 2003, p. 4; "The Clock Is Ticking," *Maclean's*, July 14, 2003, p. 24; and J. Lee, "Furlong Motivated by Olympic Challenge," *Vancouver Sun*, February 12, 2007, www.canada.com/vancouversun/features/2010/story.html?id=0b94e79e-433d-48ee-810b-0c5625684988 (accessed July 31, 2007).

28. E. E. Adam Jr. and R. J. Ebert, *Production and Operations Management*, 5th ed. (Upper Saddle River, NJ: Prentice Hall, 1992), p. 333.

29. See, for instance, C. Benko and F. W. McFarlan, *Connecting the Dots: Aligning Projects with Objectives in Unpredictable Times* (Boston: Harvard Business School Press, 2003); M. W. Lewis, M. A. Welsh, G. E. Dehler, and S. G. Green, "Product Development Tensions: Exploring Contrasting Styles of Project Management," *Academy of Management Journal*, June 2002, pp. 546–564; C. E. Gray and E. W. Larsen, *Project Management: The Managerial Process* (Columbus, OH: McGraw-Hill Higher Education, 2000); and J. Davidson Frame, *Project Management Competence: Building Key Skills for Individuals, Teams, and Organizations* (San Francisco: Jossey-Bass, 1999).

30. Project Management Institute website, www.pmi.org/Pages/default.aspx (accessed August 5, 2010).

31. For more information, see www.project-management-software.org; and P. Gordon, "Track Projects on the Web," *Information Week*, May 22, 2000, pp. 88–89.

32. L. Fahey, "Scenario Learning," *Management Review*, March 2000, pp. 29–34; S. Caudron, "Frontview Mirror," *Business Finance*, December 1999, pp. 24–30; and J. R. Garber, "What if . . . ?," *Forbes*, November 2, 1998, pp. 76–79.

33. S. Caudron, "Frontview Mirror," *Business Finance*, December 1999, p. 30.

34. L. Ramsay, "Lessons Learned from SARS Crisis," *Globe and Mail*, May 22, 2003, p. B16.

35. L. Ramsay, "Lessons Learned from SARS Crisis," *Globe and Mail*, May 22, 2003, p. B16.

36. T. Murray, "Independence Key for Ontario's New MOH," *Medical Post*, February 10, 2004, p. 47.

37. R. E. Quinn, S. R. Faerman, M. P. Thompson, and M. McGrath, *Becoming a Master Manager: A Competency Framework* (New York: Wiley, 1990), pp. 33–34.

38. Situation adapted from information in J. Helyar, "The Bizarre Reign of King Richard," *Fortune*, July 7, 2002, pp. 76–86; and R. Abelson, "Scrushy Chided Staff about Profits, Tape Reveals," *New York Times*, May 22, 2003, p. C1.

39. Based on G. Pitts, "Peerless Stays Nimble, But Montreal Pays the Cost," *Globe and Mail*, June 30, 2007, p. B5; www.peerless-clothing.com (accessed August 1, 2007); G. Pitts, "Peerless on a Mission: Stop China Now," *Globe and Mail*, January 14, 2005, p. B8; P. Donnelly, A. Kaptainis, and S. Dougherty, "Some Faces They Can't Miss: Montrealers Have Made a Big Splash in Everything From Food and Clothing to Theatre and Finance," *Gazette* (Montreal), October 29, 2000, p. A12; A. D. Gray, "Hitting the U.S. with Suits: Peerless Taps Giant Men's-Wear Market," *Gazette* (Montreal), November 12, 1990, p. TWIB3; and B. McKenna, "Canadian Suit Firm Threatens to Unravel NAFTA Talks," *Globe and Mail*, August 5, 1992, p. B1.

40. Based on information from team website, http://tampabay.devilrays.mlb.com/index.jsp?c_id=tb (accessed April 7, 2006); S. Kirchhoff, "Batter Up! Sports Economics Hits Field," *USA Today*, July 27, 2006, pp. 1B+; L. Thomas Jr., "Case Study: Fix a Baseball

Team," *New York Times*, April 2, 2006, www.nytimes.com; and A. Tillin, "Paul Podesta: The Stats Wonk Who Runs a Pro Sports Team," *Business 2.0*, November 2004, p. 103.

41. Based on R. N. Anthony, J. Dearden, and N. M. Bedford, *Management Control Systems*, 5th ed. (Homewood, IL: Irwin, 1984), Chapters 5–7.

Chapter 10

1. Based on "Corporate Info," Air Canada Centre websitse, www.theaircanadacentre.com/peddie.html (accessed August 1, 2007); "Richard Peddie, President and CEO, Maple Leaf Sports & Entertainment," Raptors website, www.nba.com/raptors/news/richardpeddie_bio.html (accessed August 2, 2007); "Ownership," MLSnet.com, http://toronto.fc.mlsnet.com/t280/about/ownership/ (accessed August 2, 2007); City of Toronto, "BMO Field Opens at Exhibition Place," news release, May 11, 2007, http://wx.toronto.ca/inter/it/newsrel.nsf/9da959222128b9e885256618006646d3/41b84cf6c5ef64fe852572db004bc010?OpenDocument (accessed August 2, 2007); "Maple Leaf Sports & Entertainment Unveils Toronto FC as 13th Major League Soccer Team," CanadaSoccer.com, May 11, 2006, www.canadasoccer.com/eng/media/viewArtical.asp?Press_ID=2445 (accessed August 2, 2007); and "Contact Us," Ricoh Coliseum website, www.ricohcoliseum.com/contact/ (accessed August 3, 2007).

2. See, for example, R. L. Daft, *Organization Theory and Design*, 6th ed. (St. Paul, MN: West Publishing, 1998).

3. S. Melamed, I. Ben-Avi, and M. S. Green, "Objective and Subjective Work Monotony: Effects on Job Satisfaction, Psychological Distress, and Absenteeism in Blue-Collar Workers," *Journal of Applied Psychology*, February 1995, pp. 29–42.

4. W. Hillier, "BC Forest Fires: A Time of Need," *Canadian Underwriter* 71, no. 1 (January 2004), pp. 22–23.

5. For a discussion of authority, see W. A. Kahn and K. E. Kram, "Authority at Work: Internal Models and Their Organizational Consequences," *Academy of Management Review*, January 1994, pp. 17–50.

6. B. Arthur, "Peddie Gives New GM 'Autonomy' for Change," *National Post*, June 8, 2004, p. S2.

7. See www.fan590.com/columnists/columnist1article.jsp?content=20060327_113940_4056 (accessed September 24, 2006).

8. "Senators Fire GM John Muckler: Report," *CBCnews.ca*, June 17, 2007, www.cbc.ca/sports/hockey/story/2007/06/17/senators-fire-muckler.html (accessed August 2, 2007); and C. Iorfida, "Less Is More for Muckler, Burke," *CBCnews.ca*, May 25, 2007, www.cbc.ca/sports/hockey/stanleycup2007/features/tradedeadline-fallout.html (accessed August 2, 2007).

9. D. Van Fleet, "Span of Management Research and Issues," *Academy of Management Journal*, September 1983, pp. 546–552.

10. See, for example, H. Mintzberg, *Power in and Around Organizations* (Upper Saddle River, NJ: Prentice Hall, 1983); and J. Child, *Organization: A Guide to Problems and Practices* (London: Kaiser & Row, 1984).

1. A. Ross, "BMO's Big Bang," *Canadian Business*, January 1994, pp. 58–63; and information on the company from Hoover's Online, www.hoovers.com (accessed May 25, 2003).

12. Based on L. Millan, "Who's Scoffing Now? The Lemaire Brothers Started Out Using Recycled Fibre in One Small Paper Mill in Rural Quebec," *Canadian Business*, March 27, 1998, pp. 74–77; "FAQ Corporate," Cascades, www.cascades.com/cas/en/0_0/0_2_1.jsp (accessed August 2, 2007); and *Cascades 2006 Annual Report*, www.cascades.com/document/en_129_2.pdf (accessed August 2, 2007).

13. E. W. Morrison, "Doing the Job Well: An Investigation of Pro-Social Rule Breaking," *Journal of Management*, February 2006, pp. 5–28.

14. E. W. Morrison, "Doing the Job Well: An Investigation of Pro-Social Rule Breaking," *Journal of Management*, February 2006, pp. 5–28.

15. T. Burns and G. M. Stalker, *The Management of Innovation* (London: Tavistock, 1961); and D. A. Morand, "The Role of Behavioral Formality and Informality in the Enactment of Bureaucratic versus Organic Organizations," *Academy of Management Review*, October 1995, pp. 831–872.

16. J. Dee, "All the News That's Fit to Print Out," *New York Times Magazine*, July 1, 2007, pp. 34–39; and wikipedia.com.

17. A. D. Chandler Jr., *Strategy and Structure: Chapters in the History of the Industrial Enterprise* (Cambridge, MA: MIT Press, 1962).

18. See, for instance, L. L. Bryan and C. I. Joyce, "Better Strategy Through Organizational Design," *The McKinsey Quarterly* no. 2 (2007), pp. 21–29; D. Jennings and S. Seaman, "High and Low Levels of Organizational Adaptation: An Empirical Analysis of Strategy, Structure, and Performance," *Strategic Management Journal*, July 1994, pp. 459–475; D. C. Galunic and K. M. Eisenhardt, "Renewing the Strategy–Structure–Performance Paradigm," in B. M. Staw and L. L. Cummings (eds.), *Research in Organizational Behavior*, vol. 16 (Greenwich, CT: JAI Press, 1994), pp. 215–255; R. Parthasarthy and S. P. Sethi, "Relating Strategy and Structure to Flexible Automation: A Test of Fit and Performance Implications," *Strategic Management Journal* 14, no. 6 (1993), pp. 529–549; H. A. Simon, "Strategy and Organizational Evolution," *Strategic Management Journal*, January 1993, pp. 131–142; H. L. Boschken, "Strategy and Structure: Re-conceiving the Relationship," *Journal of Management*, March 1990, pp. 135–150; D. Miller, "The Structural and Environmental Correlates of Business Strategy," *Strategic Management Journal*, January–February 1987, pp. 55–76; and R. E. Miles and C. C. Snow, *Organizational Strategy, Structure, and Process* (New York: McGraw-Hill, 1978).

19. See, for instance, P. M. Blau and R. A. Schoenherr, *The Structure of Organizations* (New York: Basic Books, 1971); D. S. Pugh, "The Aston Program of Research: Retrospect and Prospect," in *Perspectives on Organization Design and Behavior*, ed. A. H. Van de Ven and W. F. Joyce, pp. 135–166 (New York: John Wiley, 1981); and R. Z. Gooding and J. A. Wagner III, "A Meta-Analytic Review of the Relationship between Size and Performance: The Productivity and Efficiency of Organizations and Their Subunits," *Administrative Science Quarterly*, December 1985, pp. 462–481.

20. J. Woodward, *Industrial Organization: Theory and Practice* (London: Oxford University Press, 1965).

21. See, for instance, C. Perrow, "A Framework for the Comparative Analysis of Organizations," *American Sociological Review*, April 1967, pp. 194–208; J. D. Thompson, *Organizations in Action* (New York: McGraw-Hill, 1967); J. Hage and M. Aiken, "Routine Technology, Social Structure, and Organizational Goals," *Administrative Science Quarterly*, September 1969, pp. 366–377; and C. C. Miller, W. H. Glick, Y. D. Wang, and G. P. Huber, "Understanding Technology-Structure Relationships: Theory Development and Meta-Analytic Theory Testing," *Academy of Management Journal*, June 1991, pp. 370–399.

22. D. Gerwin, "Relationships between Structure and Technology," in *Handbook of Organizational Design*, vol. 2, ed. P. C. Nystrom and W. H. Starbuck, pp. 3–38 (New York: Oxford University Press, 1981); and D. M. Rousseau and R. A. Cooke, "Technology and Structure: The Concrete, Abstract, and Activity Systems of Organizations," *Journal of Management*, Fall–Winter 1984, pp. 345–361.

23. F. E. Emery and E. Trist, "The Causal Texture of Organizational Environments," *Human Relations*, February 1965, pp. 21–32; P. Lawrence and J. W. Lorsch, *Organization and Environment: Managing Differentiation and Integration* (Boston: Harvard Business School, Division of Research, 1967); and M. Yasai-Ardekani, "Structural Adaptations to Environments," *Academy of Management Review*, January 1986, pp. 9–21.

24. L. A. Perlow, G. A. Okhuysen, and N. P. Repenning, "The Speed Trap: Exploring the Relationship between Decision Making and Temporal Context," *Academy of Management Journal* 45 (2002), pp. 931–995.

25. Based on www.nba.com/raptors/news/mlsel_management. html; www.mapleleafs.com/team/Management.asp; http://mapleleafs. nhl.com/team/app/?service=page& page=NHLPage&id=12839; www.torontomarlies.com/news/News.asp?story_id=14; and www. torontomarlies.com/news/news.asp?story_id=433.

26. H. Mintzberg, *Structure in Fives: Designing Effective Organizations* (Upper Saddle River, NJ: Prentice Hall, 1983), p. 157.

27. R. J. Williams, J. J. Hoffman, and B. T. Lamont, "The Influence of Top Management Team Characteristics on M-Form Implementation Time," *Journal of Managerial Issues*, Winter 1995, pp. 466–480.

28. See, for example, R. E. Hoskisson, C. W. L. Hill, and H. Kim, "The Multidivisional Structure: Organizational Fossil or Source of Value?" *Journal of Management* 19, no. 2 (1993), pp. 269–298; I. I. Mitroff, R. O. Mason, and C. M. Pearson, "Radical Surgery: What Will Tomorrow's Organizations Look Like?" *Academy of Management Executive*, February 1994, pp. 11–21; T. Clancy, "Radical Surgery: A View from the Operating Theater," *Academy of Management Executive*, February 1994, pp. 73–78; M. Hammer, "Processed Change: Michael Hammer Sees Process as 'the Clark Kent of Business Ideas'—A Concept That Has the Power to Change a Company's Organizational Design," *Journal of Business Strategy*, November–December 2001, pp. 11–15; D. F. Twomey, "Leadership, Organizational Design, and Competitiveness for the 21st Century," *Global Competitiveness*, Annual 2002, pp. S31–S40; and G. J. Castrogiovanni, "Organization Task Environments: Have They Changed Fundamentally over Time?" *Journal of Management* 28, no. 2 (2002), pp. 129–150.

29. Q. Hardy, "Google Thinks Small," *Forbes*, November 14, 2005, pp. 198–202.

30. See, for example, H. Rothman, "The Power of Empowerment," *Nation's Business*, June 1993, pp. 49–52; B. Dumaine, "Payoff from the New Management," *Fortune*, December 13, 1993, pp. 103–110; J. A. Byrne, "The Horizontal Corporation," *BusinessWeek*, December 20, 1993, pp. 76–81; J. R. Katzenbach and D. K. Smith, *The Wisdom of Teams* (Boston: Harvard Business School Press, 1993); L. Grant, "New Jewel in the Crown," *U.S. News & World Report*, February 28, 1994, pp. 55–57; D. Ray and H. Bronstein, *Teaming Up: Making the Transition to a Self-Directed Team-Based Organization* (New York: McGraw Hill, 1995); and D. R. Denison, S. L. Hart, and J. A. Kahn, "From Chimneys to Cross-Functional Teams: Developing and Validating a Diagnostic Model," *Academy of Management Journal*, December 1996, pp. 1005–1023.

31. P. Kaihla, "Best-Kept Secrets of the World's Best Companies," *Business 2.0*, April 2006, p. 83; C. Taylor, "School of Bright Ideas,"

Time Inside Business, April 2005, pp. A8–A12; and B. Nussbaum, "The Power of Design," *BusinessWeek*, May 17, 2004, pp. 86–94.

32. See, for example, G. G. Dess, A. M. A. Rasheed, K. J. McLaughlin, and R. L. Priem, "The New Corporate Architecture," *Academy of Management Executive*, August 1995, pp. 7–20.

33. For additional readings on boundaryless organizations, see S. Rausch and J. Birkinshaw, "Organizational Ambidexterity: Antecedents, Outcomes, and Moderators," *Journal of Management*, June 2008, pp. 375–409; M. F. R. Kets de Vries, "Leadership Group Coaching in Action: The Zen of Creating High Performance Teams," *Academy of Management Executive*, February 2005, pp. 61–76; J. Child and R. G. McGrath, "Organizations Unfettered: Organizational Form in an Information-Intensive Economy," *Academy of Management Journal*, December 2001, pp. 1135–1148; M. Hammer and S. Stanton, "How Process Enterprises Really Work," *Harvard Business Review*, November–December 1999, pp. 108–118; T. Zenger and W. Hesterly, "The Disaggregation of Corporations: Selective Intervention, High-Powered Incentives, and Modular Units," *Organization Science* 8 (1997), pp. 209–222; R. Ashkenas, D. Ulrich, T. Jick, and S. Kerr, *The Boundaryless Organization: Breaking the Chains of Organizational Structure* (San Francisco: Jossey-Bass, 1997); R. M. Hodgetts, "A Conversation with Steve Kerr," *Organizational Dynamics*, Spring 1996, pp. 68–79; and J. Gebhardt, "The Boundaryless Organization," *Sloan Management Review*, Winter 1996, pp. 117–119. For another view of boundaryless organizations, see B. Victor, "The Dark Side of the New Organizational Forms: An Editorial Essay," *Organization Science*, November 1994, pp. 479–482.

34. S. C. Certo and S. T. Certo, *Modern Management*, 10th ed. (Upper Saddle River, NJ: Prentice Hall, 2006), p. 316; P. M. J. Christie and R. R. Levary, "Virtual Corporations: Recipe for Success," *Industrial Management*, July–August 1998, pp. 7–11; and C. C. Snow, R. E. Miles, and H. J. Coleman Jr., "Managing 21st Century Network Organizations," *Organizational Dynamics*, Winter 1992, pp. 5–20.

35. See, for instance, W. H. Davidow and M. S. Malone, *The Virtual Corporation* (New York: HarperCollins, 1992); H. Chesbrough and D. Teece, "When Is Virtual Virtuous? Organizing for Innovation," *Harvard Business Review*, January–February 1996, pp. 65–73; G. G. Dess, A. Rasheed, K. J. McLaughlin, and R. L. Priem, "The New Corporate Architecture," *Academy of Management Executive*, August 1995, pp. 7–20; M. Sawhney and D. Parikh, "Break Your Boundaries," *Business 2.0*, May 2000, pp. 198–207; D. Pescovitz, "The Company Where Everybody's a Temp," *New York Times Magazine*, June 11, 2000, pp. 94–96; W. F. Cascio, "Managing a Virtual Workplace," *Academy of Management Executive*, August 2000, pp. 81–90; D. Lyons, "Smart and Smarter," *Forbes*, March 18, 2002, pp. 40–41; and B. Hedberg, G. Dahlgren, J. Hansson, and N. Goran Olve, *Virtual Organizations and Beyond: Discovering Imaginary Systems* (New York: John Wiley, 2001).

36. R. E. Miles and C. C. Snow, "Causes of Failures in Network Organizations," *California Management Review* 34, no. 4 (1992), pp. 53–72; R. E. Miles and C. C. Snow, "The New Network Firm: A Spherical Structure Built on Human Investment Philosophy," *Organizational Dynamics*, Spring 1995, pp. 5–18; C. Jones, W. Hesterly, and S. Borgatti, "A General Theory of Network Governance: Exchange Conditions and Social Mechanisms," *Academy of Management Review*, October 1997, pp. 911–945; and R. E. Miles, C. C. Snow, J. A. Mathews, G. Miles, and H. J. Coleman, "Organizing in the Knowledge Age: Anticipating the Cellular Form," *Academy of Management Executive*, November 1997, pp. 7–24.

37. S. Reed, A. Reinhardt, and A. Sains, "Saving Ericsson," *BusinessWeek*, November 11, 2002, pp. 64–68.

38. J. Barthelemy and D. Adsit, "The Seven Deadly Sins of Outsourcing," *Academy of Management Executive* 17, no. 2 (2003), pp. 87–100.

39. K. Restivo, "Most Canadian Tech Firms Prefer Not to Outsource, Study Shows," *Financial Post (National Post)*, June 11, 2004, p. FP5.

40. C. E. Connelly and D. G. Gallagher, "Emerging Trends in Contingent Work Research," *Journal of Management*, November 2004, pp. 959–983.

41. P. M. Senge, *The Fifth Discipline: The Art and Practice of Learning Organizations* (New York: Doubleday, 1990).

42. A. N. K. Chen and T. M. Edgington, "Assessing Value in Organizational Knowledge Creation: Considerations for Knowledge Workers," *MIS Quarterly*, June 2005, pp. 279–309; K. G. Smith, C. J. Collins, and K. D. Clark, "Existing Knowledge, Knowledge Creation Capability, and the Rate of New Product Introduction in High-Technology Firms," *Academy of Management Journal*, April 2005, pp. 346–357; B. Marr, "How to Knowledge Management," *Financial Management*, February 2003, pp. 26–27; R. Cross, A. Parker, L. Prusak, and S. P. Borgati, "Supporting Knowledge Creation and Sharing in Social Networks," *Organizational Dynamics*, Fall 2001, pp. 100–120; M. Schulz, "The Uncertain Relevance of Newness: Organizational Learning and Knowledge Flows," *Academy of Management Journal*, August 2001, pp. 661–681; D. Zell, "Overcoming Barriers to Work Innovations: Lessons Learned at Hewlett-Packard," *Organizational Dynamics*, Summer 2001, pp. 77–86; G. Szulanski, "Exploring Internal Stickiness: Impediments to the Transfer of Best Practice within the Firm," *Strategic Management Journal*, Winter Special Issue, 1996, pp. 27–43; and J. M. Liedtka, "Collaborating Across Lines of Business for Competitive Advantage," *Academy of Management Executive*, April 1996, pp. 20–37.

43. N. M. Adler, *International Dimensions of Organizational Behavior*, 4th ed. (Cincinnati, OH: South-Western, 2002), p. 66.

44. P. B. Smith and M. F. Peterson, "Demographic Effects on the Use of Vertical Sources of Guidance by Managers in Widely Differing Cultural Contexts," *International Journal of Cross Cultural Management*, April 2005, pp. 5–26.

45. Based on J. F. Veiga and J. N. Yanouzas, *The Dynamics of Organization Theory: Gaining a Macro Perspective* (St. Paul, MN: West Publishing, 1979), pp. 158–160.

46. Situation adapted from information in "HR Pressured to Breach Ethics Policies, Says Survey," *HR Briefing*, June 1, 2003, p. 1; S. Pulliam, "A Staffer Ordered to Commit Fraud Balked, Then Caved," *Wall Street Journal*, June 23, 2003, pp. A1, A6; and J. Gilbert, "A Matter of Trust," *Sales & Marketing Management*, March 2003, pp. 30–31.

47. FAST COMPANY by A. Cohen. Copyright 2008 by Mansueto Ventures LLC. Reproduced with permission of Mansueto Ventures LLC in the format Textbook via Copyright Clearance Center.

48. Based on N. George, "The Virtues of Being Local," *Financial Times*, October 8, 2003, pp. 4–5; "Svenska Handelsbanken Branches Out in the UK," *European Banker*, November 2003, p. 6; Svenska's website, www.handelsbanken.se (accessed 2004); and N. George, "Counting on the Spirit of Independent Branches," *Financial Times*, November 5, 2001, p. 10.

49. Based on P. L. Hunsaker, *Training in Management Skills* (Upper Saddle River, NJ: Prentice Hall, 2001), pp. 135–136 and 430–432; R. T. Noel, "What You Say to Your Employees When You Delegate," *Supervisory Management*, December 1993, p. 13; and S. Caudron, "Delegate for Results," *IndustryWeek*, February 6, 1995, pp. 27–30.

Chapter 11

1. Based on Lymbix business plan, September 2010.

2. Lymbix products page, www.lymbix.com/products (accessed September 26, 2010).

3. Microsoft BizSpark One information page, www.bizspark.com/v2/ Programs/Pages/BizSpark.aspx (accessed September 26, 2010).

4. P. G. Clampitt, *Communicating for Managerial Effectiveness*, 3rd ed. (Thousand Oaks, CA: Sage, 2005); T. Dixon, *Communication, Organization, and Performance* (Norwood, NJ: Ablex, 1996), p. 281; P. G. Clampitt, *Communicating for Managerial Effectiveness* (Newbury Park, CA: Sage, 1991); and L. E. Penley, E. R. Alexander, I. E. Jernigan, and C. I. Henwood, "Communication Abilities of Managers: The Relationship to Performance," *Journal of Management*, March 1991, pp. 57–76.

5. "Electronic Invective Backfires," *Workforce*, June 2001, p. 20; and E. Wong, "A Stinging Office Memo Boomerangs," *New York Times*, April 5, 2001, p. C11.

6. C. O. Kursh, "The Benefits of Poor Communication," *Psychoanalytic Review*, Summer–Fall 1971, pp. 189–208.

7. W. G. Scott and T. R. Mitchell, *Organization Theory: A Structural and Behavioral Analysis* (Homewood, IL: Richard D. Irwin, 1976).

8. D. K. Berlo, *The Process of Communication* (New York: Holt, Rinehart & Winston, 1960), pp. 30–32.

9. P. G. Clampitt, *Communicating for Managerial Effectiveness* (Newbury Park, CA: Sage, 1991).

10. A. Warfield, "Do You Speak Body Language?" *Training & Development*, April 2001, pp. 60–61; D. Zielinski, "Body Language Myths," *Presentations*, April 2001, pp. 36–42; and "Visual Cues Speak Loudly in Workplace," *Springfield News-Leader*, January 21, 2001, p. 8B.

1. TweetTone Beta website, www.tweettone.com/ (accessed October 2, 2010).

12. T. R. Kurtzberg, C. E. Naquin, and L. Y. Belkin, "Electronic Performance Appraisals: The Effects of E-Mail Communication on Peer Ratings in Actual and Simulated Environments," *Organizational Behavior and Human Decision Processes* 98, no. 2 (2005), pp. 216–226.

13. J. Kruger, N. Epley, J. Parker, and Z.-W. Ng, "Egocentrism over E-Mail: Can We Communicate as Well as We Think?" *Journal of Personality and Social Psychology* 89, no. 6 (2005), pp. 925–936.

14. Thanks to an anonymous reviewer for providing this elaboration.

15. C. Cavanagh, *Managing Your E-Mail: Thinking Outside the Inbox* (Hoboken, NJ: John Wiley & Sons, 2003).

16. S. Radicati, ed. *Email Statistics Report 2010*, www. radicati.com/wp/wp-content/uploads/2010/04/ Email-Statistics-Report-2010-2014-Executive-Summary2.pdf (accessed January 22, 2011).

17. K. Macklem, "You've Got Too Much Mail," *Maclean's*, January 30, 2006, pp. 20–21.

18. D. K. Berlo, *The Process of Communication* (New York: Holt, Rinehart & Winston, 1960), p. 103.

19. Based on G. Robertson, "Goodbye, Buttonhole Makers. Hello, Tapas," May 22, 2007, *Globe and Mail*, p. B1.

20. A. Mehrabian, "Communication without Words," *Psychology Today*, September 1968, pp. 53–55.

21. L. Haggerman, "Strong, Efficient Leadership Minimizes Employee Problems," *Springfield Business Journal*, December 9–15, 2002, p. 23.

22. See, for instance, S. P. Robbins and P. L. Hunsaker, *Training in InterPersonal Skills*, 4th ed. (Upper Saddle River, NJ: Prentice Hall, 2006); M. Young and J. E. Post, "Managing to Communicate, Communicating to Manage: How Leading Companies Communicate with Employees," *Organizational Dynamics*, Summer 1993, pp. 31–43; J. A. DeVito, *The Interpersonal Communication Book*, 6th ed. (New York: HarperCollins, 1992); and A. G. Athos and J. J. Gabarro, *Interpersonal Behavior* (Upper Saddle River, NJ: Prentice Hall, 1978).

23. O. Thomas, "Best-Kept Secrets of the World's Best Companies: The Three Minute Huddle," *Business 2.0*, April 2006, p. 94.

24. V. Galt, "Top-Down Feedback," *Vancouver Sun*, February 15, 2003, pp. E1, E2.

25. Cited in "Heard It through the Grapevine," *Forbes*, February 10, 1997, p. 22.

26. See, for instance, A. Bruzzese, "What to Do about Toxic Gossip," *USA Today*, March 14, 2001, www.usatoday.com; N. B. Kurland and L. H. Pelled, "Passing the Word: Toward a Model of Gossip and Power in the Workplace," *Academy of Management Review*, April 2000, pp. 428–438; N. DiFonzo, P. Bordia, and R. L. Rosnow, "Reining in Rumors," *Organizational Dynamics*, Summer 1994, pp. 47–62; M. Noon and R. Delbridge, "News from Behind My Hand: Gossip in Organizations," *Organization Studies* 14, no. 1 (1993), pp. 23–26; and J. G. March and G. Sevon, "Gossip, Information and Decision Making," in *Decisions and Organizations*, ed. G. March, pp. 429–442 (Oxford: Blackwell, 1988).

27. "Effective Communication: A Leading Indicator of Financial Performance—2005/2006 Communication ROI Study," Watson Wyatt Worldwide, www.watsonwyatt.com.

28. B. McCrea, "A New Kind of Hookup," *Black Enterprise*, July 2007, p. 52; and M. Stopforth, "Why You Should Let Your Employees Use Facebook," *Moneyweb*, August 5, 1007, www.moneyweb.co.za/mw/view/mw/en/page71?oid=151800&sn=Detail&ccs_clear_ cache=1 (accessed October 9, 2007).

29. G. Buckler, "Instant Messaging Replacing Pagers in the Enterprise," *Computing Canada*, March 26, 2004, p. 18.

30. J. Rohwer, "Today, Tokyo: Tomorrow, the World," *Fortune*, September 18, 2000, pp. 140–152; J. McCullam and L. Torres, "Instant Enterprising," *Forbes*, September 11, 2000, p. 28; J. Guyon, "The World Is Your Office," *Fortune*, June 12, 2000, pp. 227–234; S. Baker, N. Gross, and I. M. Kunii, "The Wireless Internet," *BusinessWeek*, May 29, 2000, pp. 136–144; R. Lieber, "Information Is Everything . . . " *Fast Company*, November 1999, pp. 246–254; and "IM Is a Must in Lots of Offices," *MySA.com*, January 5, 2005, www.mysanantonio.com/business/stories/MYSA010205.1R.IM.55538bcc.html (accessed August 5, 2007).

31. M. Vallis, "Nasty E-mail from the Boss May Mean More Sick Days," *National Post*, January 9, 2004, pp. A1, A9. Study was done by George Fieldman, a psychologist at Buckinghamshire Chilterns University College, and presented at the 2004 Annual Occupational Psychology Conference of the British Psychological Society.

32. Derived from P. Kuitenbrouwer, "Office E-Mail Runs Amok," *Financial Post*, October 18, 2001, p. FP11.

33. F. Esker, "Employers Finding Business Applications for Instant Messaging" *New Orleans CityBusiness*, May 29, 2006, http://findarticles.com/p/articles/mi_qn4200/is_20060529/ai_n16432818 (accessed August 5, 2007).

34. Information on Second Life based on A. Athavaley, "A Job Interview You Don't Have to Show Up For," *Wall Street Journal*, June 20, 2007, p. D1.

35. "Be Careful about Your E-Trail," *Prince George Citizen*, June 22, 2007, p. 36.

36. M. Blanchard, "Johnson Inc. Relies on IP Telephony," *Globe and Mail*, May 13, 2004.

37. K. Hafner, "For the Well Connected, All the World's an Office," *New York Times*, March 30, 2000, p. D11.

38. "Personal Information Protection and the Electronic Documents Act (PIPEDA)—Part 1," Treasury Board of Canada Secretariat, www.tbs-sct.gc.ca/pgol-pged/piatp-pfefvp/course1/mod2/mod2-3-eng.asp (accessed September 30, 2010).

39. R. D. Hof, "Your Undivided Attention Please," *BusinessWeek*, January 19, 2004, p. 14.

40. C. Tice, "You've Got E-mail—and a Lawsuit on Your Hands," *Home Channel News*, October 26, 1998, http://findarticles.com/p/articles/mi_m0VCW/is_1998_Oct_26/ai_53425670 (accessed August 6, 2007).

41. R. Gaffney-Rhys, "Do You Need an Email Policy?" *I.T. Wales*, August 24, 2005, www.itwales.com/998242.htm (accessed August 6, 2007).

42. J. Eckberg, "E-Mail: Messages Are Evidence," *Cincinnati Enquirer*, July 27, 2004, www.enquirer.com.

43. M. Conlin, "E-Mail Is So Five Minutes Ago," *BusinessWeek*, November 28, 2005, pp. 111–112.

44. J. Scanlon, "Woman of Substance," *Wired*, July 2002, p. 27.

45. E. Wenger, R. McDermott, and W. Snyder, *Cultivating Communities of Practice: A Guide to Managing Knowledge* (Boston: Harvard Business School Press, 2002), p. 4.

46. E. Wenger, R. McDermott, and W. Snyder, *Cultivating Communities of Practice: A Guide to Managing Knowledge*(Boston: Harvard Business School Press, 2002), p. 39.

47. B. A. Gutek, M. Groth, and B. Cherry, "Achieving Service Success through Relationship and Enhanced Encounters," *Academy of Management Executive*, November 2002, pp. 132–144.

48. R. C. Ford and C. P. Heaton, "Lessons from Hospitality That Can Serve Anyone," *Organizational Dynamics*, Summer 2001, pp. 30–47.

49. M. J. Bitner, B. H. Booms, and L. A. Mohr, "Critical Service Encounters: The Employee's Viewpoint," *Journal of Marketing*, October 1994, pp. 95–106.

50. S. D. Pugh, J. Dietz, J. W. Wiley, and S. M. Brooks, "Driving Service Effectiveness through Employee-Customer Linkages," *Academy of Management Executive*, November 2002, pp. 73–84.

51. Based on M. Strauss, "Mining Customer Feedback, Firms Go Undercover and On-Line," *Globe and Mail*, May 13, 2004.

52. Sears, Roebuck and Company, *Assisting Customers with Disabilities: A Summary of Policies and Guidelines Regarding the Assistance of Customers with Disabilities for the Sears Family of Companies*, pamphlet obtained at Springfield, Missouri, Sears store, May 28, 2003.

53. M. L. LaGanga, "Are There Words That Neither Offend nor Bore?" *Los Angeles Times*, May 18, 1994, pp. 11–27; J. Leo, "Language in the Dumps," *U.S. News & World Report*, July 27, 1998, p. 16.

54. Reprinted from *Supervisory Management*, January 1989. American Management Association, New York. www.amanet.org. All rights reserved.

55. Situation adapted from information in T. Weidlich, "The Corporate Blog Is Catching On," *New York Times*, June 22, 2003, sec. 3, p. 12; and "CNN Shuts Down Correspondent's Blog," *EuropeMedia*, March 24, 2003, www.vandusseldorp.com.

56. Based on E. Frauenheim, "Stop Reading This Headline and Get Back to Work," *C/Net*, July 13, 2005, http://news.com.com/Stop+reading+this+headline+and+get+back+to+work/2100-1022_3-5783552.html (accessed August 7, 2007); and R. Breeden, "More Employees Are Using the Web at Work," *Wall Street Journal*, May 10, 2005, p. B4.

57. Information on Voyant Technologies from Hoover's Online, www.hoovers.com (accessed April 14, 2006); and S. Clifford, "How to Get the Geeks and the Suits to Play Nice," *Business 2.0*, May 2002, pp. 92–93.

58. Case based on D. D. Hatch, J. E. Hall, and M. T. Miklave, "New EEOC Guidance on National-Origin Discrimination," *Workforce*, April 2003, p. 76; A. Piech, "Going Global: Speaking in Tongues," *Inc.*, June 2003, p. 50; E. Anderssen and M. Valpy, "Face the Nation: Canada Remade," *Globe and Mail*, June 7, 2003, pp. A10–A11; and G. Schellenberg, *Immigrants in Canada's Census Metropolitan Areas*, Catalogue no. 89-613-MIE—No. 003 (Ottawa: Statistics Canada, August 2004).

59. Based on C. R. Rogers and R. E. Farson, *Active Listening* (Chicago: Industrial Relations Center of the University of Chicago, 1976); and P. L. Hunsaker, *Training in Management Skills* (Upper Saddle River, NJ: Prentice Hall, 2001), pp. 61–62.

Chapter 12

1. Based on Hoover's Online, www.hoovers.com (accessed December 5, 2010); R. Waugh, "Getting More Leaders Is Hard Enough, but the Job Skills Needed Are Changing, Too," *Canadian HR Reporter*, January 26, 2004, p. 18; J. Kirby, "In the Vault," *Canadian Business*, March 1–14, 2004, pp. 68–72; S. Greengard, "Brett Ellison," *IQ Magazine*, November–December 2002, p. 52; www.scotiabank.com/cda/content/0,1608,CID821_LIDen,00.html; http://cgi.scotiabank.com/annrep2006/en/pdf/ScotiaAR06_ConsolidatedFinancialStatements.pdf; and www.scotiabank.com/cda/content/0,1608,CID11095_LIDen,00.html.

2. P. M. Wright and G. C. McMahan, "Theoretical Perspectives for Strategic Human Resource Management," *Journal of Management* 18, no. 1 (1992), pp. 295–320; A. A. Lado and M. C. Wilson, "Human Resource Systems and Sustained Competitive Advantage," *Academy of Management Review*, October 1994, pp. 699–727; J. Pfeffer, *Competitive Advantage through People* (Boston: Harvard Business School Press, 1994); and J. Pfeffer, *The Human Equation* (Boston: Harvard Business School Press, 1998).

3. "Maximizing the Return on Your Human Capital Investment: The 2005 Watson Wyatt Human Capital Index® Report," "WorkAsia 2004/2005: A Study of Employee Attitudes in Asia," and "European Human Capital Index 2002," Watson Wyatt Worldwide, www.watsonwyatt.com.

4. See, for example, Y. Y. Kor and H. Leblebici, "How Do Interdependencies among Human-Capital Deployment, Development, and Diversification Strategies Affect Firms' Financial Performance?" *Strategic Management Journal*, October 2005, pp. 967–985; D. E. Bowen and C. Ostroff, "Understanding HRM—Firm Performance Linkages: The Role of the 'Strength' of the HRM System," *Academy of Management Review*, April 2004, pp. 203–221; R. Batt, "Managing Customer Services: Human Resource Practices, Quit Rates, and Sales Growth," *Academy of Management Journal*, June 2002, pp. 587–597; A. S. Tsui, J. L. Pearce, L. W. Porter, and A. M. Tripoli, "Alternative Approaches to the Employee–Organization Relationship: Does Investment in Employees Pay Off?" *Academy of Management Journal*, October 1997, pp. 1089–1121; M. A. Huselid, S. E. Jackson, and R. S. Schuler, "Technical and Strategic Human Resource Management Effectiveness as Determinants of Firm Performance," *Academy of Management Journal*, January 1997, pp. 171–188; J. T. Delaney and M. A. Huselid, "The Impact of Human Resource Management Practices on Perceptions of Organizational Performance," *Academy of Management Journal*, August 1996, pp. 949–969; B. Becker and B. Gerhart, "The Impact of Human Resource Management on Organizational Performance: Progress and Prospects," *Academy of Management Journal*, August 1996, pp. 779–801; M. J. Koch and R. G. McGrath, "Improving Labor Productivity: Human Resource Management Policies Do Matter," *Strategic Management Journal*, May 1996, pp. 335–354; and M. A. Huselid, "The Impact of Human Resource Management Practices on Turnover, Productivity, and Corporate Financial Performance," *Academy of Management Journal*, June 1995, pp. 635–672.

5. "Human Capital a Key to Higher Market Value," *Business Finance*, December 1999, p. 15.

6. "Indicators of Well-Being in Canada: Work—Unionization Rates," Human Resources and Skills Development Canada, www4.hrsdc.gc.ca/.3ndic.1t.4r@-eng.jsp?iid=17 (accessed December 5, 2010).

7. J. Visser, "Union Membership Statistics in 24 Countries," *Monthly Labor Review*, January 2006, pp. 38–49; and "Foreign Labor Trends—Mexico," US Department of Labor, 2002.

8. S. Premack and J. E. Hunter, "Individual Unionization Decisions," *Psychological Bulletin* 103, no. 2 (1988), pp. 223–234.

9. Based on M. King, "Union at Indigo," *Gazette* (Montreal), February 11, 2003, p. B3.

10. S. Armour, "Lawsuits Pin Target on Managers," *USA Today*, October 1, 2002, www.usatoday.com.

11. Canadian Human Rights Act, http://laws.justice.gc.ca/en/ShowFullDoc/cs/H-6///en.

12. See http://laws.justice.gc.ca/en/ShowDoc/cr/SOR-86-1082/bo-ga:s_1::bo-ga:s_2//en.

13. "Indicators of Well-Being in Canada: Canadians in Context—Aging Population," Human Resources and Skills Development Canada, www4.hrsdc.gc.ca/.3ndic.1t.4r@-eng.jsp?iid=33 (accessed December 5, 2010).

14. R. Waugh, "Getting More Leaders Is Hard Enough, But the Job Skills Needed Are Changing, Too," *Canadian HR Reporter*, January 26, 2004, p. 18.

15. J. Sullivan, "Workforce Planning: Why to Start Now," *Workforce*, September 2002, pp. 46–50.

16. T. J. Bergmann and M. S. Taylor, "College Recruitment: What Attracts Students to Organizations?" *Personnel*, May–June 1984, pp. 34–46; and A. S. Bargerstock and G. Swanson, "Four Ways to Build Cooperative Recruitment Alliances," *HR Magazine*, March 1991, p. 49.

17. J. R. Gordon, *Human Resource Management: A Practical Approach* (Boston: Allyn and Bacon, 1986), p. 170.

18. S. Burton and D. Warner, "The Future of Hiring—Top 5 Sources for Recruitment Today," *Workforce Vendor Directory*, 2002, p. 75.

19. C. Eustace, "VPD: Virtual Police Department," *Vancouver Sun*, May 29, 2007, pp. A1–A2.

20. G. Shaw, "An Offer That's Hard to Refuse," *Vancouver Sun*, November 12, 2003, p. D5.

21. See, for example, J. P. Kirnan, J. E. Farley, and K. F. Geisinger, "The Relationship between Recruiting Source, Applicant Quality, and Hire Performance: An Analysis by Sex, Ethnicity, and Age," *Personnel Psychology*, Summer 1989, pp. 293–308; and R. W. Griffeth, P. Hom, L. Fink, and D. Cohen, "Comparative Tests of Multivariate Models of Recruiting Sources Effects," *Journal of Management* 23, no. 1 (1997), pp. 19–36.

22. G. W. England, *Development and Use of Weighted Application Blanks*, rev. ed. (Minneapolis: Industrial Relations Center, University of Minnesota, 1971); J. J. Asher, "The Biographical Item: Can It Be Improved?" *Personnel Psychology*, Summer 1972, p. 266; G. Grimsley and H. F. Jarrett, "The Relation of Managerial Achievement to Test Measures Obtained in the Employment Situation: Methodology and Results," *Personnel Psychology*, Spring 1973, pp. 31–48; E. E. Ghiselli, "The Validity of Aptitude Tests in Personnel Selection," *Personnel Psychology*, Winter 1973, p. 475; I. T. Robertson and R. S. Kandola, "Work Sample Tests: Validity, Adverse Impact, and Applicant Reaction," *Journal of Occupational Psychology* 55, no. 3 (1982), pp. 171–183; A. K. Korman, "The Prediction of Managerial Performance: A Review," *Personnel Psychology*, Summer 1986, pp. 295–322; G. C. Thornton, *Assessment Centers in Human Resource Management* (Reading, MA: Addison-Wesley, 1992); C. Fernandez-Araoz, "Hiring without Firing," *Harvard Business Review*, July–August, 1999, pp. 108–120; and A. M. Ryan and R. E. Ployhart, "Applicants' Perceptions of Selection Procedures and Decisions: A Critical Review and Agenda for the Future," *Journal of Management* 26, no. 3 (2000), pp. 565–606.

23. See, for example, S. L. Premack and J. P. Wanous, "A Meta-Analysis of Realistic Job Preview Experiments," *Journal of Applied Psychology*, November 1985, pp. 706–720; J. A. Breaugh and M. Starke, "Research on Employee Recruitment: So Many Studies, So Many Remaining Questions," *Journal of Management* 26, no. 3 (2000), pp. 405–434; B. M. Meglino, E. C. Ravlin, and A. S. DeNisi, "A Meta-Analytic Examination of Realistic Job Preview Effectiveness: A Test of Three Counterintuitive Propositions," *Human Resource Management Review* 10, no. 4 (2000), pp. 407–434; and Y. Ganzach, A. Pazy, Y. Ohayun, and E. Brainin, "Social Exchange and Organizational Commitment: Decision-Making Training for Job Choice as an Alternative to the Realistic Job Preview," *Personnel Psychology*, Autumn 2002, pp. 613–637.

24. See, for example, Y. Ganzach, A. Pazy, Y. Ohayun, and E. Brainin, "Social Exchange and Organizational Commitment: Decision-Making Training for Job Choice as an Alternative to the Realistic Job Preview," *Personnel Psychology*, Autumn 2002, pp. 613–637; B. M. Meglino, E. C. Ravlin, and A. S. DeNisi, "A Meta-Analytic Examination of Realistic Job Preview Effectiveness: A Test of Three Counter Intuitive Propositions," *Human Resource Management Review* 10, no. 4 (2000), pp. 407–434; J. A. Breaugh and M. Starke, "Research on Employee Recruitment: So Many Studies, So Many Remaining Questions," *Journal of Management* 26, no. 3 (2000), pp. 405–434; and S. L. Premack and J. P. Wanous, "A Meta-Analysis of Realistic Job Preview Experiments," *Journal of Applied Psychology*, November 1985, pp. 706–720.

25. A. Wahl, "People Power," *Canadian Business*, March 29–April 11, 2004, p. 58.

26. D. G. Allen, "Do Organizational Socialization Tactics Influence Newcomer Embeddedness and Turnover?" *Journal of Management*, April 2006, pp. 237–256; C. L. Cooper, "The Changing Psychological Contract at Work: Revisiting the Job Demands–Control Model,"

Occupational and Environmental Medicine, June 2002, p. 355; D. M. Rousseau and S. A. Tijoriwala, "Assessing Psychological Contracts: Issues, Alternatives and Measures," *Journal of Organizational Behavior* 19 (1998), pp. 679–695; and S. L. Robinson, M. S. Kraatz, and D. M. Rousseau, "Changing Obligations and the Psychological Contract: A Longitudinal Study," *Academy of Management Journal*, February 1994, pp. 137–152.

27. "2006 Industry Report," *Training*, December 2006, www.trainingmag.com/managesmarter/images/pdfs/IndRep06.pdf (accessed September 6, 2007).

28. D. Sankey, "Canadian Companies Skimp on Training," Canada.com, June 27, 2007, www.canada.com/working/feeds/resources/atwork/story.html?id=30a5d031-8f8b-4f64-b607-2bcf11bead9d (accessed September 6, 2007); and "2006 Industry Report," *Training*, December 2006, www.trainingmag.com/managesmarter/images/pdfs/IndRep06.pdf (accessed September 6, 2007).

29. B. Hall, "The Top Training Priorities for 2003," *Training*, February 2003, p. 40; and T. Galvin, "2002 Industry Report," *Training*, October 2002, pp. 24–33.

30. H. Dolezalek, "2005 Industry Report," *Training*, December 2005, pp. 14–28.

31. B. Hall, "The Top Training Priorities for 2003," *Training*, February 2003, p. 40.

32. Based on K. Harding, "Once and Future Kings," *Globe and Mail*, April 9, 2003, pp. C1, C6.

33. L. Fowlie, "Online Training Takes the Slow Train: 'Next Big Thing' Fails to Live Up to Initial Hype," *Daily Townsman*, March 5, 2004, p. 11.

34. K. Sulkowicz, "Straight Talk at Review Time," *BusinessWeek*, September 10, 2007, p. 16.

35. This section is based on R. I. Henderson, *Compensation Management in a Knowledge-Based World*, 9th ed. (Upper Saddle River, NJ: Prentice Hall, 2003).

36. L. R. Gomez-Mejia, "Structure and Process of Diversification, Compensation Strategy, and Firm Performance," *Strategic Management Journal* 13 (1992), pp. 381–397; and E. Montemayor, "Congruence between Pay Policy and Competitive Strategy in High-Performing Firms," *Journal of Management* 22, no. 6 (1996), pp. 889–908.

37. J. D. Shaw, N. Gupta, A. Mitra, and G. E. Ledford Jr., "Success and Survival of Skill-Based Pay Plans," *Journal of Management*, February 2005, pp. 28–49; C. Lee, K. S. Law, and P. Bobko, "The Importance of Justice Perceptions on Pay Effectiveness: A Two-Year Study of a Skill-Based Pay Plan," *Journal of Management* 26, no. 6 (1999), pp. 851–873; G. E. Ledford, "Paying for the Skills, Knowledge and Competencies of Knowledge Workers," *Compensation and Benefits Review*, July–August 1995, pp. 55–62; and E. E. Lawler III, G. E. Ledford Jr., and L. Chang, "Who Uses Skill-Based Pay and Why," *Compensation and Benefits Review*, March–April 1993, p. 22.

38. J. D. Shaw, N. Gupta, A. Mitra, and G. E. Ledford Jr., "Success and Survival of Skill-Based Pay Plans," *Journal of Management*, February 2005, pp. 28–49.

39. M. Rowland, "It's What You Can Do That Counts," *New York Times*, June 6, 1993, p. F17.

40. Information from Hewitt Associates Studies, "Hewitt Study Shows Pay-for-Performance Plans Replacing Holiday Bonuses," December 6, 2005; "Salaries Continue to Rise in Asia Pacific," *Hewitt Annual Study Reports*, November 23, 2005; and "Hewitt Study Shows Base Pay Increases Flat for 2006 with Variable Pay Plans

Picking Up the Slack," *Hewitt Associates*, August 31, 2005, www.hewitt.com.

41. D. E. Super and D. T. Hall, "Career Development: Exploration and Planning," in *Annual Review of Psychology*, vol. 29, ed. M. R. Rosenzweig and L. W. Porter (Palo Alto, CA: Annual Reviews, 1978), p. 334.

42. A. K. Smith, "Charting Your Own Course," *U.S. News & World Report*, November 6, 2000, pp. 56–65; S. E. Sullivan, "The Changing Nature of Careers: A Review and Research Agenda," *Journal of Management* 25, no. 3 (1999), pp. 457–484; D. T. Hall, "Protean Careers of the 21st Century," *Academy of Management Executive*, November 1996, pp. 8–16; M. B. Arthur and D. M. Rousseau, "A Career Lexicon for the 21st Century," *Academy of Management Executive*, November 1996, pp. 28–39; N. Nicholson, "Career Systems in Crisis: Change and Opportunity in the Information Age," *Academy of Management Executive*, November 1996, pp. 40–51; and K. R. Brousseau, M. J. Driver, K. Eneroth, and R. Larsson, "Career Pandemonium: Realigning Organizations and Individuals," *Academy of Management Executive*, November 1996, pp. 52–66.

43. M. B. Arthur and D. M. Rousseau, *The Boundaryless Career: A New Employment Principle for a New Organizational Era* (New York: Oxford University Press, 1996).

44. M. Cianni and D. Wnuck, "Individual Growth and Team Enhancement: Moving toward a New Model of Career Development," *Academy of Management Executive*, February 1997, pp. 105–115.

45. L. K. Trevino, M. Brown, and L. P. Hartman, "A Qualitative Investigation of Perceived Executive Ethical Leadership: Perceptions from Inside and Outside the Executive Suite," *Human Relations*, January 2003, pp. 5–37.

46. R. Henkoff, "Winning the New Career Game," *Fortune*, July 12, 1993, pp. 46–49; "10 Tips for Managing Your Career," *Personnel*, October 1995, p. 106; A. Fisher, "Six Ways to Supercharge Your Career," *Fortune*, January 13, 1997, pp. 46–48; A. K. Smith, "Charting Your Own Course," *U.S. News & World Report*, November 6, 2000, pp. 56–65; and D. D. Dubois, "The 7 Stages of One's Career," *Training & Development*, December 2000, pp. 45–50.

47. Based on C. Petten, "Progressive Aboriginal Relations Important to Scotiabank," *Windspeaker*, March 2002, p. B7.

48. L. Crawford, "Motivation, Not a Degree Key at IKEA," *Financial Post (National Post)*, February 24, 2004, p. FP12; and interview with André de Wit, general manager of IKEA Ibérica, S.A., *Interes*, www.interes.org/icex/cda/controller/interes/0,5464,5322992_5325168_39745871_519802_0,00.html (accessed September 7, 2007).

49. A. Wahl, "Opening Doors," *Canadian Business*, March 29–April 11, 2004, p. 45.

50. R. Leger, "Linked by Differences," *Springfield (Missouri) News-Leader*, December 31, 1993, pp. B6+.

51. "Employers Underestimate Extent of Sexual Harassment, Report Says," *Vancouver Sun*, March 8, 2001, p. D6.

52. J. Monchuk, "Female Mounties Allege Sex Harassment Not Investigated to Protect RCMP," *Canadian Press Newswire*, September 26, 2003.

53. D. Spears, "Is a Well Drafted Harassment Policy Enough?" *Ottawa Business Journal*, February 20, 2006, www.ottawabusinessjournal.com/293617634517614.php (accessed October 14, 2007).

54. "Employers Underestimate Extent of Sexual Harassment, Report Says," *Vancouver Sun*, March 8, 2001, p. D6.

55. "Sexual Harassment Charges: FY 1992—FY 2005," U.S. Equal Employment Opportunity Commission, www.eeoc.gov.

56. "U.S. Leads Way in Sex Harassment Laws, Study Says," *Evening Sun*, November 30, 1992, p. A11; and W. Hardman and J. Heidelberg, "When Sexual Harassment Is a Foreign Affair," *Personnel*, April 1996, pp. 91–97.

57. *Janzen v. Platy Enterprises Ltd.* (1989), 10 C.H.R.R. D/6205 (S.C.C.).

58. "Facts About Sexual Harassment," U.S. Equal Employment Opportunity Commission, www.eeoc.gov (accessed June 1, 2003).

59. A. Fisher, "After All This Time, Why Don't People Know What Sexual Harassment Means?" *Fortune,* January 12, 1998, p. 68; and A. R. Karr, "Companies Crack Down on the Increasing Sexual Harassment by E-Mail," *Wall Street Journal*, September 21, 1999, p. A1.

60. See T. S. Bland and S. S. Stalcup, "Managing Harassment," *Human Resource Management*, Spring 2001, pp. 51–61; K. A. Hess and D. R. M. Ehrens, "Sexual Harassment—Affirmative Defense to Employer Liability," *Benefits Quarterly*, Second Quarter 1999, p. 57; J. A. Segal, "The Catch-22s of Remedying Sexual Harassment Complaints," *HR Magazine*, October 1997, pp. 111–117; S. C. Bahls and J. E. Bahls, "Hands-Off Policy," *Entrepreneur*, July 1997, pp. 74–76; J. A. Segal, "Where Are We Now?" *HR Magazine*, October 1996, pp. 69–73; B. McAfee and D. L. Deadrick, "Teach Employees to Just Say No," *HR Magazine*, February 1996, pp. 86–89; G. D. Block, "Avoiding Liability for Sexual Harassment," *HR Magazine*, April 1995, pp. 91–97; and J. A. Segal, "Stop Making Plaintiffs' Lawyers Rich," *HR Magazine*, April 1995, pp. 31–35.

61. S. Jayson, "Workplace Romance No Longer Gets the Kiss-Off," *USA Today*, February 9, 2006, p. 9D.

62. R. Mano and Y. Gabriel, "Workplace Romances in Cold and Hot Organizational Climates: The Experience of Israel and Taiwan," *Human Relations*, January 2006, pp. 7–35; J. A. Segal, "Dangerous Liaisons," *HR Magazine*, December 2005, pp. 104–108; "Workplace Romance Can Create Unforeseen Issues for Employers," *HR Focus*, October 2005, p. 2; C. A. Pierce and H. Aguinis, "Legal Standards, Ethical Standards, and Responses to Social-Sexual Conduct at Work," *Journal of Organizational Behavior*, September 2005, pp. 727–732; and C. A. Pierce, B. J. Broberg, J. R. McClure, and H. Aguinis, "Responding to Sexual Harassment Complaints: Effects of a Dissolved Workplace Romance on Decision-Making Standards," *Organizational Behavior and Human Decision Processes*, September 2004, pp. 66–82.

63. J. A. Segal, "Dangerous Liaisons," *HR Magazine*, December 2005, pp. 104–108.

64. I. Towers, L. Duxbury, C. Higgins, and J. Thomas, "Time Thieves and Space Invaders: Technology, Work and the Organization," *Journal of Organizational Change Management* 19, no. 5 (2006), pp. 593–618; and L. Duxbury and C. Higgins, "Work–Life Conflict in Canada in the New Millennium: A Status Report," *Australian Canadian Studies* 21, no. 2 (2003), pp. 41–72.

65. C. Oglesby, "More Options for Moms Seeking Work-Family Balance," *CNN.com*, May 10, 2001, www.cnn.com.

66. J. Miller and M. Miller, "Get A Life!" *Fortune,* November 28, 2005, pp. 108–124.

67. M. Elias, "The Family-First Generation," *USA Today*, December 13, 2004, p. 5D.

68. F. Hansen, "Truths and Myths about Work/Life Balance," *Workforce*, December 2002, pp. 34–39.

69. J. H. Greenhaus and G. N. Powell, "When Work and Family Are Allies: A Theory of Work–Family Enrichment," *Academy of Management Review*, January 2006, pp. 72–92; L. Duxbury, C. Higgins, and D. Coghill, "Voices of Canadians: Seeking Work–Life Balance," HRSDC, January 2003, www.hrsdc.gc.ca; and S. D. Friedman and J. H. Greenhaus, *Work and Family—Allies or Enemies?* (New York: Oxford University Press, 2000).

70. J. H. Greenhaus and G. N. Powell, "When Work and Family Are Allies: A Theory of Work–Family Enrichment," *Academy of Management Review*, January 2006, pp. 72–92.

71. L. B. Hammer, M. B. Neal, J. T. Newsom, K. J. Brockwood, and C. L. Colton, "A Longitudinal Study of the Effects of Dual-Earner Couples' Utilization of Family-Friendly Workplace Supports on Work and Family Outcomes," *Journal of Applied Psychology*, July 2005, pp. 799–810.

72. M. M. Arthur, "Share Price Reactions to Work–Family Initiatives: An Institutional Perspective," *Academy of Management Journal*, August 2003, pp. 497–505.

73. N. P. Rothbard, T. L. Dumas, and K. W. Phillips, "The Long Arm of the Organization: Work–Family Policies and Employee Preferences for Segmentation" (paper presented at the 61st Annual Academy of Management meeting, Washington, DC, August 2001).

74. L. T. Cullen, "Where Did Everyone Go?" *Time*, November 18, 2002, pp. 64–66.

75. S. Alleyne, "Stiff Upper Lips," *Black Enterprise*, April 2002, p. 59; C. Hymowitz, "Getting a Lean Staff to Do 'Ghost Work' of Departed Colleagues," *Wall Street Journal*, October 22, 2002, p. B1; and E. Krell, "Defusing Downsizing," *Business Finance*, December 2002, pp. 55–57.

76. P. P. Shah, "Network Destruction: The Structural Implications of Downsizing," *Academy of Management Journal*, February 2000, pp. 101–112.

77. See, for instance, K. A. Mollica and B. Gray, "When Layoff Survivors Become Layoff Victims: Propensity to Litigate," *Human Resource Planning*, January 2001, pp. 22–32.

78. S. Koudsi, "You're Stuck," *Fortune*, December 10, 2001, pp. 271–274.

79. L. A. Mainiero and C. L. Tromley, *Developing Managerial Skills in Organizational Behavior* (Upper Saddle River, NJ: Prentice Hall, 1994). Adapted by permission of Prentice Hall, Inc.

80. Situation adapted from information in J. Russell, "Older Goodyear Workers Who Say Age Played into Evaluations Get Day in Court," *Akron Beacon Journal*, July 3, 2003, www.ohio.com/bj; and K. Clark, "Judgment Day," *U.S. News & World Report*, January 13, 2003, pp. 31–32.

81. Information on company from Mitsubishi Motors North America website, www.mitsubishicars.com (accessed June 1, 2004); "Mitsubishi Plans Big Boost to U.S. Production," *IndustryWeek*, March 18, 2003, www.industryweek.com; D. Kiley, "Workplace Woes Almost Eclipse Mitsubishi Plant," *USA Today*, October 21, 2002, p. B11; "EEOC Responds to Final Report of Mitsubishi Consent Decree Monitors," Equal Employment Opportunity Commission, www.eeoc.gov (accessed May 23, 2001); and S. Greengard, "Zero Tolerance: Making It Work," *Workforce*, May 1999, pp. 28–34.

82. M. Freudenheim, "Seeking Savings, Employers Help Smokers Quit," *New York Times* online, www.nytimes.com, October 26, 2007; and M. Conlin, "Get Healthy or Else," *BusinessWeek*, February 26, 2007, pp. 58–69.

83. Based on S. P. Robbins and D. A. DeCenzo, Fundamentals of Management, 4th ed. (Upper Saddle River, NJ: Prentice Hall, 2004), p. 194.

Chapter 13

1. Based on K. J. Delaney, "Spreading Change: As Yahoo! Falters, Executive's Memo Calls for Overhaul," *Wall Street Journal*, November 18, 2006, p. A1; and R. D. Hof, "Back to the Future at Yahoo!" *BusinessWeek*, July 2, 2007, p. 34.

2. "Job Cuts Help Yahoo Profits Surge," *BBC News Online*, http://news.bbc.co.uk/2/hi/business/8317476.stm (accessed February 14, 2011).

3. C. R. Leana and B. Barry, "Stability and Change as Simultaneous Experiences in Organizational Life," *Academy of Management Review*, October 2000, pp. 753–759.

4. Based on L. Tischler, "Sudden Impact," *Fast Company*, September 2002, pp. 106–113.

5. E. Nee, "The Hottest CEO in Tech," *Business 2.0*, June 2003, p. 86.

6. Based on R. D. Hof, "Back to the Future at Yahoo!" *BusinessWeek*, July 2, 2007, p. 34.

7. See www.techcrunch.com/2007/04/29/panama-not-enough-to-battle-google-yahoo-acquires-rightmedia (accessed October 14, 2007).

8. "Yahoo Rejects Microsoft Approach," *BBC News Online*, http://news.bbc.co.uk/2/hi/business/7239220.stm (accessed February 14, 2011).

9. The idea for these metaphors came from J. E. Dutton, S. Ashford, K. O'Neill, and K. Lawrence, "Moves That Matter: Issue Selling and Organizational Change," *Academy of Management Journal*, August 2001, pp. 716–736; B. H. Kemelgor, S. D. Johnson, and S. Srinivasan, "Forces Driving Organizational Change: A Business School Perspective," *Journal of Education for Business*, January–February 2000, pp. 133–137; G. Colvin, "When It Comes to Turbulence, CEOs Could Learn a Lot from Sailors," *Fortune*, March 29, 1999, pp. 194–196; and P. B. Vaill, *Managing as a Performing Art: New Ideas for a World of Chaotic Change* (San Francisco: Jossey-Bass, 1989).

10. K. Lewin, *Field Theory in Social Science* (New York: Harper & Row, 1951).

11. For contrasting views on episodic and continuous change, see K. E. Weick and R. E. Quinn, "Organizational Change and Development," in *Annual Review of Psychology*, vol. 50, ed. J. T. Spence, J. M. Darley, and D. J. Foss, pp. 361–386 (Palo Alto, CA: Annual Reviews, 1999).

12. G. Hamel, "Take It Higher," *Fortune*, February 5, 2001, pp. 169–170.

13. A. Sains and S. Reed, "Electrolux Cleans Up," *BusinessWeek*, February 27, 2006, pp. 42–43.

14. Based on R. D. Hof, "Back to the Future at Yahoo!" *BusinessWeek*, July 2, 2007, p. 34; and J. Thaw and A. Levy, "Yahoo! CEO Digs in for Slugfest with Google," *The Vancouver Sun*, June 20, 2007, p. D3.

15. Based on T. Belford, "Half Public, Half Private, It Beats Odds," *Financial Post (National Post)*, June 9, 2003, p. BE4; S. Tafler, "BC + X = P3: BC Struggles with the Partnering Numbers," *Summit: Canada's Magazine for Public Sector Purchasing*, September 2002, pp. 16–18; and P. Vieira, "RBC Pushes Public-Private Partnerships," *Financial Post (National Post)*, November 26, 2002, p. FP10.

16. S. Crock and J. Carey, "Storming the Streets of Baghdad," *BusinessWeek*, October 21, 2002, pp. 46–47.

17. J. Jesitus, "Change Management: Energy to the People," *IndustryWeek*, September 1, 1997, pp. 37, 40.

18. D. Lavin, "European Business Rushes to Automate," *Wall Street Journal*, July 23, 1997, p. A14.

19. See, for example, T. C. Head and P. F. Sorensen, "Cultural Values and Organizational Development: A Seven-Country Study," *Leadership & Organization Development Journal*, March 1993, pp. 3–7; A. H. Church, W. W. Burke, and D. F. Van Eynde, "Values, Motives, and Interventions of Organization Development Practitioners," *Group & Organization Management*, March 1994, pp. 5–50; W. L. French and C. H. Bell Jr., *Organization Development: Behavioral Science Interventions for Organization Improvement*, 6th ed. (Upper Saddle River, NJ: Prentice Hall, 1998); N. A. Worren, K. Ruddle, and K. Moore, "From Organizational Development to Change Management," *Journal of Applied Behavioral Science*, September 1999, pp. 273–286; G. Farias, "Organizational Development and Change Management," *Journal of Applied Behavioral Science*, September 2000, pp. 376–379; W. Nicolay, "Response to Farias and Johnson's Commentary," *Journal of Applied Behavioral Science*, September 2000, pp. 380–381; and S. Hicks, "What Is Organization Development?" *Training & Development*, August 2000, p. 65.

20. T. White, "Supporting Change: How Communicators at Scotiabank Turned Ideas into Action," *Communication World*, April 2002, pp. 22–24.

21. M. Javidan, P. W. Dorfman, M. S. deLuque, and R. J. House, "In the Eye of the Beholder: Cross-Cultural Lessons in Leadership from Project GLOBE," *Academy of Management Perspective*, February 2006, pp. 67–90; and E. Fagenson-Eland, E. A. Ensher, and W. W. Burke, "Organization Development and Change Interventions: A Seven-Nation Comparison," *Journal of Applied Behavioral Science*, December 2004, pp. 432–464.

22. E. Fagenson-Eland, E. A. Ensher, and W. W. Burke, "Organization Development and Change Interventions: A Seven-Nation Comparison," *Journal of Applied Behavioral Science*, December 2004, p. 461.

23. See, for example, A. Deutschman, "Making Change: Why Is It So Hard to Change Our Ways?" *Fast Company*, May 2005, pp. 52–62; S. B. Silverman, C. E. Pogson, and A. B. Cober, "When Employees at Work Don't Get It: A Model for Enhancing Individual Employee Change in Response to Performance Feedback," *Academy of Management Executive*, May 2005, pp. 135–147; C. E. Cunningham, C. A. Woodward, H. S. Shannon, J. MacIntosh, B. Lendrum, D. Rosenbloom, and J. Brown, "Readiness for Organizational Change: A Longitudinal Study of Workplace, Psychological and Behavioral Correlates," *Journal of Occupational and Organizational Psychology*, December 2002, pp. 377–392; M. A. Korsgaard, H. J. Sapienza, and D. M. Schweiger, "Beaten Before Begun: The Role of Procedural Justice in Planning Change," *Journal of Management* 28, no. 4 (2002), pp. 497–516; R. Kegan and L. L. Lahey, "The Real Reason People Won't Change," *Harvard Business Review*, November 2001, pp. 85–92; S. K. Piderit, "Rethinking Resistance and Recognizing Ambivalence: A Multidimensional View of Attitudes toward an Organizational Change," *Academy of Management Review*, October 2000, pp. 783–794; C. R. Wanberg and J. T. Banas, "Predictors and Outcomes of Openness to Changes in a Reorganizing Workplace," *Journal of Applied Psychology*, February 2000, pp. 132–142; A. A. Armenakis and A. G. Bedeian, "Organizational Change: A Review of Theory and Research in the 1990s," *Journal of Management* 25, no. 3 (1999), pp. 293–315; and B. M. Staw, "Counterforces to Change,"
in *Change in Organizations*, ed. P. S. Goodman and Associates, pp. 87–121 (San Francisco: Jossey-Bass, 1982).

24. J. P. Kotter and L. A. Schlesinger, "Choosing Strategies for Change," *Harvard Business Review*, March–April 1979, pp. 107–109; P. Strebel, "Why Do Employees Resist Change?" *Harvard Business Review*, May–June 1996, pp. 86–92; J. Mariotti, "Troubled by Resistance to Change," *IndustryWeek*, October 7, 1996, p. 30; and A. Reichers, J. P. Wanous, and J. T. Austin, "Understanding and Managing Cynicism About Organizational Change," *Academy of Management Executive*, February 1997, pp. 48–57.

25. J. P. Kotter and L. A. Schlesinger, "Choosing Strategies for Change," *Harvard Business Review*, March–April 1979, pp. 106–111; K. Matejka and R. Julian, "Resistance to Change Is Natural," *Supervisory Management*, October 1993, p. 10; C. O'Connor, "Resistance: The Repercussions of Change," *Leadership & Organization Development Journal*, October 1993, pp. 30–36; J. Landau, "Organizational Change and Barriers to Innovation: A Case Study in the Italian Public Sector," *Human Relations*, December 1993, pp. 1411–1429; A. Sagie and M. Koslowsky, "Organizational Attitudes and Behaviors as a Function of Participation in Strategic and Tactical Change Decisions: An Application of Path-Goal Theory," *Journal of Organizational Behavior*, January 1994, pp. 37–47; V. D. Miller, J. R. Johnson, and J. Grau, "Antecedents to Willingness to Participate in a Planned Organizational Change," *Journal of Applied Communication Research*, February 1994, pp. 59–80; P. Pritchett and R. Pound, *The Employee Handbook for Organizational Change* (Dallas, TX: Pritchett, 1994); R. Maurer, *Beyond the Wall of Resistance: Unconventional Strategies That Build Support for Change* (Austin, TX: Bard Books, 1996); D. Harrison, "Assess and Remove Barriers to Change," *HRfocus*, July 1999, pp. 9–10; L. K. Lewis, "Disseminating Information and Soliciting Input during Planned Organizational Change," *Management Communication Quarterly*, August 1999, pp. 43–75; J. P. Wanous, A. E. Reichers, and J. T. Austin, "Cynicism About Organizational Change," *Group & Organization Management*, June 2000, pp. 132–153; K. W. Mossholder, R. P. Settoon, A. A. Armenakis, and S. G. Harris, "Emotion during Organizational Transformations," *Group & Organization Management*, September 2000, pp. 220–243; and S. K. Piderit, "Rethinking Resistance and Recognizing Ambivalence: A Multidimensional View of Attitudes toward an Organizational Change," *Academy of Management Review*, October 2000, pp. 783–794.

26. M. Helft, "Yahoo!, Aiming for Agility, Shuffles Executives," *Business Day*, December 6, 2006.

27. R. M. Kanter, "From Spare Change to Real Change: The Social Sector as Beta Site for Business Innovation," *Harvard Business Review*, May–June 1999, pp. 122–132.

28. J. E. Perry-Smith and C. E. Shalley, "The Social Side of Creativity: A Static and Dynamic Social Network Perspective," *Academy of Management Review*, January 2003, pp. 89–106; and P. K. Jagersma, "Innovate or Die: It's Not Easy, but It Is Possible to Enhance Your Organization's Ability to Innovate," *Journal of Business Strategy*, January–February 2003, pp. 25–28.

29. Statistics Canada, "Corporate Failures, 1996," *The Daily*, August 8, 2003.

30. These definitions are based on T. M. Amabile, *Creativity in Context* (Boulder, CO: Westview Press, 1996).

31. M. Basadur, J. Conklin, and G. K. VanPatter, "Rethinking Wicked Problems Part (2): Unpacking Paradigms, Bridging Universes," *NextD Journal* 10 (2007), Conversation 10.3.

32. R. W. Woodman, J. E. Sawyer, and R. W. Griffin, "Toward a Theory of Organizational Creativity," *Academy of Management Review*, April 1993, pp. 293–321.

33. T. M. Egan, "Factors Influencing Individual Creativity in the Workplace: An Examination of Quantitative Empirical Research," *Advances in Developing Human Resources*, May 2005, pp. 160–181; F. Damanpour, "Organizational Innovation: A Meta-Analysis of Effects of Determinants and Moderators," *Academy of Management Journal*, September 1991, pp. 555–590; S. D. Saleh and C. K. Wang, "The Management of Innovation: Strategy, Structure, and Organizational Climate," *IEEE Transactions on Engineering Management*, February 1993, pp. 14–22; G. R. Oldham and A. Cummings, "Employee Creativity: Personal and Contextual Factors at Work," *Academy of Management Journal*, June 1996, pp. 607–634; J. B. Sorensen and T. E. Stuart, "Aging, Obsolescence, and Organizational Innovation," *Administrative Science Quarterly*, March 2000, pp. 81–112; T. M. Amabile, C. N. Hadley, and S. J. Kramer, "Creativity Under the Gun," *Harvard Business Review*, August 2002, pp. 52–61; and N. Madjar, G. R. Oldham, and M. G. Pratt, "There's No Place Like Home? The Contributions of Work and Nonwork Creativity Support to Employees' Creative Performance," *Academy of Management Journal*, August 2002, pp. 757–767.

34. P. R. Monge, M. D. Cozzens, and N. S. Contractor, "Communication and Motivational Predictors of the Dynamics of Organizational Innovations," *Organization Science*, May 1992, pp. 250–274.

35. T. M. Amabile, C. N. Hadley, and S. J. Kramer, "Creativity Under the Gun," *Harvard Business Review*, August 2002, pp. 52–61.

36. N. Madjar, G. R. Oldham, and M. G. Pratt, "There's No Place Like Home? The Contributions of Work and Nonwork Creativity Support to Employees' Creative Performance," *Academy of Management Journal*, August 2002, pp. 757–767.

37. V. Galt, "Training on Tap," *Globe and Mail*, November 20, 2002, pp. C1, C8.

38. C. Salter, "Mattel Learns to 'Throw the Bunny,'" *Fast Company*, November 2002, p. 22.

39. See, for instance, J. E. Perry-Smith, "Social Yet Creative: The Role of Social Relationships in Facilitating Individual Creativity," *Academy of Management Journal*, February 2006, pp. 85–101; C. E. Shalley, J. Zhou, and G. R. Oldham, "The Effects of Personal and Contextual Characteristics on Creativity: Where Should We Go from Here?" *Journal of Management* 30, no. 6 (2004), pp. 933–958; M. Amabile, *Creativity in Context* (Boulder, CO: Westview Press, 1996); M. Tushman and D. Nadler, "Organizing for Innovation," *California Management Review*, Spring 1986, pp. 74–92; R. Moss Kanter, "When a Thousand Flowers Bloom: Structural, Collective, and Social Conditions for Innovation in Organization," in *Research in Organizational Behavior*, vol. 10, ed. B. M. Staw and L. L. Cummings, pp. 169–211 (Greenwich, CT: JAI Press, 1988); G. Morgan, "Endangered Species: New Ideas," *Business Month*, April 1989, pp. 75–77; S. G. Scott and R. A. Bruce, "Determinants of Innovative People: A Path Model of Individual Innovation in the Workplace," *Academy of Management Journal*, June 1994, pp. 580–607; T. M. Amabile, R. Conti, H. Coon, J. Lazenby, and M. Herron, "Assessing the Work Environment for Creativity," *Academy of Management Journal*, October 1996, pp. 1154–1184; A. deGues, "The Living Company," *Harvard Business Review*, March–April 1997, pp. 51–59; J. Zhou, "Feedback Valence, Feedback Style, Task Autonomy, and Achievement Orientation: Interactive Effects on Creative Behavior," *Journal of Applied Psychology* 83, no. 2 (1998), pp. 261–276; G. Hamel, "Reinvent Your Company," *Fortune*, June 12, 2000, pp. 98–118; J. M. George and J. Zhou, "When Openness to Experience and Conscientiousness Are Related to Creative Behavior:

An Interactional Approach," *Journal of Applied Psychology*, June 2001, pp. 513–524; and Perry-Smith and C. E. Shalley, "The Social Side of Creativity: A Static and Dynamic Social Network Perspective," *Academy of Management Review*, January 2003, pp. 89–106.

40. J. M. Howell and C. A. Higgins, "Champions of Change," *Business Quarterly*, Spring 1990, pp. 31–32; P. A. Carrow-Moffett, "Change Agent Skills: Creating Leadership for School Renewal," *NASSP Bulletin*, April 1993, pp. 57–62; T. Stjernberg and A. Philips, "Organizational Innovations in a Long-Term Perspective: Legitimacy and Souls-of-Fire as Critical Factors of Change and Viability," *Human Relations*, October 1993, pp. 1193–2023; and J. Ramos, "Producing Change That Lasts," *Across the Board*, March 1994, pp. 29–33.

41. Associated Press, "Mars Rover Is Launched on Voyage to Look for Water," *USA Today*, June 11, 2003, www.usatoday.com; NASA's website, www.nasa.gov (accessed June 11, 2003); and W. J. Broad, "A Tiny Rover, Built on the Cheap, Is Ready to Explore Distant Mars," *New York Times*, July 5, 1997, p. 9.

42. Based on K. J. Delaney and J. S. Lublin, "Can 'Chief Yahoo' Rise to Challenges as Yahoo Chief?" *Wall Street Journal*, June 20, 2007, p. B1; and http://yodel.yahoo.com/2007/06/18/my-new-job.

43. C. Hymowitz, "How Leader at 3M Got His Employees to Back Big Changes," *Wall Street Journal*, April 23, 2002, p. B1; and J. Useem, "Jim McNerney Thinks He Can Turn 3M from a Good Company into a Great One—With a Little Help from His Former Employer: General Electric," *Fortune*, August 12, 2002, pp. 127–132.

44. See T. H. Fitzgerald, "Can Change in Organizational Culture Really Be Managed?" *Organizational Dynamics*, Autumn 1988, pp. 5–15; B. Dumaine, "Creating a New Company Culture," *Fortune*, January 15, 1990, pp. 127–131; P. F. Drucker, "Don't Change Corporate Culture—Use It!" *Wall Street Journal*, March 28, 1991, p. A14; J. Martin, *Cultures in Organizations: Three Perspectives* (New York: Oxford University Press, 1992); D. C. Pheysey, *Organizational Cultures: Types and Transformations* (London: Routledge, 1993); C. G. Smith and R. P. Vecchio, "Organizational Culture and Strategic Management: Issues in the Strategic Management of Change," *Journal of Managerial Issues*, Spring 1993, pp. 53–70; P. Bate, *Strategies for Cultural Change* (Boston: Butterworth-Heinemann, 1994); and P. Anthony, *Managing Culture* (Philadelphia: Open University Press, 1994).

45. M. L. Wald and J. Schwartz, "Shuttle Inquiry Uncovers Flaws in Communication," *New York Times*, August 4, 2003, http://nytimes.com.

46. M. L. Wald and J. Schwartz, "Shuttle Inquiry Uncovers Flaws in Communication," *New York Times*, August 4, 2003, http://nytimes.com.

47. See, for example, R. H. Kilmann, M. J. Saxton, and R. Serpa, eds., *Gaining Control of the Corporate Culture* (San Francisco: Jossey-Bass, 1985); and D. C. Hambrick and S. Finkelstein, "Managerial Discretion: A Bridge between Polar Views of Organizational Outcomes," in *Research in Organizational Behavior*, vol. 9, ed. B. M. Staw and L. L. Cummings (Greenwich, CT: JAI Press, 1987), p. 384.

48. M. A. Cavanaugh, W. Boswell, M. Roehling, and J. Boudreau, "An Empirical Examination of Self-Reported Work Stress among U.S. Managers," *Journal of Applied Psychology*, February 2000, pp. 65–74; M. A. Verespej, "Stressed Out," *IndustryWeek*, February 21, 2000, pp. 30–34; J. Laabs, "Time-Starved Workers Rebel," *Workforce*, October 2000, pp. 26–28; and C. Daniels, "The Last Taboo," *Fortune*, October 28, 2002, pp. 137–144.

49. I. Phaneuf, "Drug Company Study Finds Rise in Work-Related Stress," *Vancouver Sun*, May 5, 2001, p. D15.

50. Adapted from R. S. Schuler, "Definition and Conceptualization of Stress in Organizations," *Organizational Behavior and Human Performance*, April 1980, p. 189. For an updated review of definitions, see R. L. Kahn and P. Byosiere, "Stress in Organizations," in *Handbook of Industrial and Organizational Psychology*, vol. 3, 2nd ed., ed. M. D. Dunnette and L. J. Hough, pp. 573–580 (Palo Alto, CA: Consulting Psychologists Press, 1992).

51. B. L. de Mente, "Karoshi: Death from Overwork," Asia Pacific Management Forum, May 2002, www.apmforum.com.

52. H. Benson, "Are You Working Too Hard?" *Harvard Business Review*, November 2005, pp. 53–58; B. Cryer, R. McCraty, and D. Childre, "Pull the Plug on Stress," *Harvard Business Review*, July 2003, pp. 102–107; C. Daniels, "The Last Taboo," *Fortune*, October 28, 2002, pp. 137–144; S. E. Jackson, "Participation in Decision Making as a Strategy for Reducing Job-Related Strain," *Journal of Applied Psychology*, February 1983, pp. 3–19; C. D. Fisher, "Boredom at Work: A Neglected Concept," *Human Relations*, March 1993, pp. 395–417; C. A. Heaney, B. A. Israel, S. J. Schurman, E. A. Baker, J. S. House, and M. Hugentobler, "Industrial Relations, Worksite Stress Reduction and Employee Well-Being: A Participatory Action Research Investigation," *Journal of Organizational Behavior*, September 1993, pp. 495–510; P. Froiland, "What Cures Job Stress?" *Training*, December 1993, pp. 32–36; C. L. Cooper and S. Cartwright, "Healthy Mind, Healthy Organization—A Proactive Approach to Occupational Stress," *Human Relations*, April 1994, pp. 455–471; and A. A. Brott, "New Approaches to Job Stress," *Nation's Business*, May 1994, pp. 81–82.

53. See R. S. Schuler, "Time Management: A Stress Management Technique," *Personnel Journal*, December 1979, pp. 851–855; and M. E. Haynes, *Practical Time Management: How to Make the Most of Your Most Perishable Resource* (Tulsa, OK: Penn Well Books, 1985).

54. "Employee Wellness," *Canadian HR Reporter*, February 23, 2004, pp. 9–12.

55. P. A. McLagan, "Change Leadership Today," *Training & Development*, November 2002, p. 29.

56. W. Pietersen, "The Mark Twain Dilemma: The Theory and Practice for Change Leadership," *Journal of Business Strategy*, September–October 2002, pp. 32–37; C. Hymowitz, "To Maintain Success, Managers Must Learn How to Direct Change," *Wall Street Journal*, August 13, 2002, p. B1; and J. E. Dutton, S. Ashford, K. O'Neill, and K. Lawrence, "Moves That Matter: Issue Selling and Organizational Change," *Academy of Management Journal*, August 2001, pp. 716–736.

57. P. A. McLagan, "The Change-Capable Organization," *Training & Development*, January 2003, pp. 50–58.

58. Adapted from P. B. Vaill, *Managing as a Performing Art: New Ideas for a World of Chaotic Change* (San Francisco: Jossey-Bass, 1989), pp. 8, 9.

59. Situation adapted from information in "HR Director Backs Team to Stay Focused During Boots Upheaval," *Personnel Today*, March 21, 2006, p. 2; "Boots' Revamp as Group to Shut 17 Depots," *Europe Intelligence Wire*, March 15, 2006.

60. "Speaker Profiles Atlantic Eco Expo," Atlantic Eco Expo website, www.atlanticecoexpo.com/greengala.html (accessed September 23, 2010).

61. "What Is AIR MILES My Planet?" AIR MILES website, https://www.airmiles.ca/arrow/MyPlanet?splashId=3800148 (accessed September 23, 2010).

62. "Career Paths—Six Sigma," Westin Hotels and Resorts website, www.starwoodhotels.com/westin/careers/paths/description.html?category=20000030 (accessed January 27, 2011).

63. S. A. Ante, "Rubbing Customers the Right Way," *Business Week*, October 8, 2007, pp. 88–89; and S. A. Ante, "Six Sigma Kick-Starts Starwood," *Business Week*, www.businessweek.com/ (accessed January 27, 2011).

64. Based on M. Warner, "Under the Knife," *Business 2.0*, February 2004, www.business20.com.

65. Based on J. P. Kotter and L. A. Schlesinger, "Choosing Strategies for Change," *Harvard Business Review*, March–April 1979, pp. 106–114; and T. A. Stewart, "Rate Your Readiness to Change," *Fortune*, February 7, 1994, pp. 106–110.

Chapter 14

1. Based on B. McRae, *The Seven Strategies of Master Leaders* (Toronto: Northbridge, 2009).

2. B. McRae, *The Seven Strategies of Master Leaders* (Toronto: Northbridge, 2009).

3. Most leadership research has focused on the actions and responsibilities of managers and extrapolated the results to leaders and leadership in general.

4. "B. McRae, *The Seven Strategies of Master Leaders* (Toronto: Northbridge, 2009).

5. P. Bacon Jr. and M. Calabresi, "The Up-and-Comers," *Time Canada*, April 24, 2006, p. 28; P. Bacon Jr., "The Exquisite Dilemma of Being Obama," *Time*, February 20, 2006, pp. 24–28; A. Stephen, "10 People Who Will Change the World," *New Statesman*, October 17, 2005, pp. 18–20; "Ten to Watch," *Fortune*, September 9, 2005, p. 282; P. Bacon Jr., "Barack Obama," *Time*, April 18, 2005, pp. 60–61; and A. Ripley, D. E. Thigpen, and J. McCabe, "Obama's Ascent," *Time*, November 11, 2004, pp. 74–78.

6. See S. A. Kirkpatrick and E. A. Locke, "Leadership: Do Traits Matter?" *Academy of Management Executive*, May 1991, pp. 48–60; and T. A. Judge, J. E. Bono, R. Ilies, and M. W. Gerhardt, "Personality and Leadership: A Qualitative and Quantitative Review," *Journal of Applied Psychology*, August 2002, pp. 765–780.

7. R. M. Stogdill and A. E. Coons, eds., *Leader Behavior: Its Description and Measurement*, Research Monograph No. 88 (Columbus: Ohio State University, Bureau of Business Research, 1951). For an updated literature review of Ohio State research, see S. Kerr, C. A. Schriesheim, C. J. Murphy, and R. M. Stogdill, "Toward a Contingency Theory of Leadership Based upon the Consideration and Initiating Structure Literature," *Organizational Behavior and Human Performance*, August 1974, pp. 62–82; and B. M. Fisher, "Consideration and Initiating Structure and Their Relationships with Leader Effectiveness: A Meta-Analysis," in *Proceedings of the 48th Annual Academy of Management Conference*, ed. F. Hoy, pp. 201–205 (Anaheim, CA, 1988).

8. J. Kirby, "In the Vault," *Canadian Business*, March 1–March 14, 2004, pp. 68–72.

9. J. Kirby, "In the Vault," *Canadian Business*, March 1–March 14, 2004, pp. 68–72.

10. K. Lewin and R. Lippitt, "An Experimental Approach to the Study of Autocracy and Democracy: A Preliminary Note," *Sociometry* 1 (1938), pp. 292–300; K. Lewin, "Field Theory and Experiment in Social Psychology: Concepts and Methods," *American Journal of Sociology* 44 (1939), pp. 868–896; K. Lewin, R. Lippitt, and R. K. White, "Patterns of Aggressive Behavior in Experimentally

Created Social Climates," *Journal of Social Psychology* 10 (1939), pp. 271–301; and R. Lippitt, "An Experimental Study of the Effect of Democratic and Authoritarian Group Atmospheres," *University of Iowa Studies in Child Welfare* 16 (1940), pp. 43–95.

11. B. M. Bass, *Stogdill's Handbook of Leadership* (New York: The Free Press, 1981), pp. 289–299.

12. R. M. Stogdill and A. E. Coons, eds., *Leader Behavior: Its Description and Measurement*, Research Monograph No. 88 (Columbus: Ohio State University, Bureau of Business Research, 1951). For an updated literature review of Ohio State research, see S. Kerr, C. A. Schriesheim, C. J. Murphy, and R. M. Stogdill, "Toward a Contingency Theory of Leadership Based upon the Consideration and Initiating Structure Literature," *Organizational Behavior and Human Performance*, August 1974, pp. 62–82; and B. M. Fisher, "Consideration and Initiating Structure and Their Relationships with Leader Effectiveness: A Meta-Analysis," in *Proceedings of the 48th Annual Academy of Management Conference*, ed. F. Hoy, pp. 201–205 (Anaheim, CA, 1988).

13. R. Kahn and D. Katz, "Leadership Practices in Relation to Productivity and Morale," in *Group Dynamics: Research and Theory*, 2nd ed., D. Cartwright and A. Zander (Elmsford, NY: Row, Paterson, 1960).

14. R. R. Blake and J. S. Mouton, *The Managerial Grid III* (Houston: Gulf Publishing, 1984).

15. L. L. Larson, J. G. Hunt, and R. N. Osborn, "The Great Hi-Hi Leader Behavior Myth: A Lesson from Occam's Razor," *Academy of Management Journal*, December 1976, pp. 628–641; and P. C. Nystrom, "Managers and the Hi-Hi Leader Myth," *Academy of Management Journal*, June 1978, pp. 325–331.

16. B. McRae, *The Seven Strategies of Master Leaders* (Toronto: Northbridge, 2009).

17. W. G. Bennis, "The Seven Ages of the Leader," *Harvard Business Review*, January 2004, p. 52.

18. R. McQueen, "The Long Shadow of Tom Stephens: He Branded MacBlo's Crew as Losers, Then Made Them into Winners," *Financial Post (National Post)*, June 22, 1999, pp. C1, C5.

19. E. Fiedler, *A Theory of Leadership Effectiveness* (New York: McGraw-Hill, 1967).

20. R. Ayman, M. M. Chemers, and F. Fiedler, "The Contingency Model of Leadership Effectiveness: Its Levels of Analysis," *Leadership Quarterly*, Summer 1995, pp. 147–167; C. A. Schriesheim, B. J. Tepper, and L. A. Tetrault, "Least Preferred Co-worker Score, Situational Control, and Leadership Effectiveness: A Meta-Analysis of Contingency Model Performance Predictions," *Journal of Applied Psychology*, August 1994, pp. 561–573; and L. H. Peters, D. D. Hartke, and J. T. Pholmann, "Fiedler's Contingency Theory of Leadership: An Application of the Meta-Analysis Procedures of Schmidt and Hunter," *Psychological Bulletin*, March 1985, pp. 274–285.

21. See E. H. Schein, *Organizational Psychology*, 3rd ed. (Upper Saddle River, NJ: Prentice Hall, 1980), pp. 116–117; and B. Kabanoff, "A Critique of Leader Match and Its Implications for Leadership Research," *Personnel Psychology*, Winter 1981, pp. 749–764.

22. P. Hersey and K. Blanchard, "So You Want to Know Your Leadership Style?" *Training and Development Journal*, February 1974, pp. 1–15; and P. Hersey and K. H. Blanchard, *Management of Organizational Behavior: Leading Human Resources*, 8th ed. (Upper Saddle River, NJ: Prentice Hall, 2001).

23. See, for instance, E. G. Ralph, "Developing Managers' Effectiveness: A Model with Potential," *Journal of Management Inquiry*, June 2004, pp. 152–163; C. L. Graeff, "Evolution of Situational Leadership Theory: A Critical Review," *Leadership Quarterly* 8, no. 2 (1997), pp. 153–170; and C. F. Fernandez and R. P. Vecchio, "Situational Leadership Theory Revisited: A Test of an Across-Jobs Perspective," *Leadership Quarterly* 8, no. 1 (1997), pp. 67–84.

24. R. J. House, "A Path–Goal Theory of Leader Effectiveness," *Administrative Science Quarterly*, September 1971, pp. 321–338; R. J. House and T. R. Mitchell, "Path–Goal Theory of Leadership," *Journal of Contemporary Business*, Autumn 1974, p. 86; and R. J. House, "Path–Goal Theory of Leadership: Lessons, Legacy, and a Reformulated Theory," *Leadership Quarterly*, Fall 1996, pp. 323–352.

25. J. C. Wofford and L. Z. Liska, "Path–Goal Theories of Leadership: A Meta-Analysis," *Journal of Management*, Winter 1993, pp. 857–876; and A. Sagie and M. Koslowsky, "Organizational Attitudes and Behaviors as a Function of Participation in Strategic and Tactical Change Decisions: An Application of Path–Goal Theory," *Journal of Organizational Behavior*, January 1994, pp. 37–47.

26. B. McRae, *The Seven Strategies of Master Leaders* (Toronto: Northbridge, 2009).

27. B. M. Bass and R. E. Riggio, *Transformational Leadership*, 2nd ed. (Mahwah, NJ: Lawrence Erlbaum Associates, 2006), p. 3.

28. B. M. Bass and R. E. Riggio, *Transformational Leadership*, 2nd ed. (Mahwah, NJ: Lawrence Erlbaum Associates, 2006), p. 3.

29. B. M. Bass, "Leadership: Good, Better, Best," *Organizational Dynamics*, Winter 1985, pp. 26–40; and J. Seltzer and B. M. Bass, "Transformational Leadership: Beyond Initiation and Consideration," *Journal of Management*, December 1990, pp. 693–703.

30. B. J. Avolio and B. M. Bass, "Transformational Leadership, Charisma, and Beyond." Working paper, School of Management, State University of New York, Binghamton, 1985, p. 14.

31. R. S. Rubin, D. C. Munz, and W. H. Bommer, "Leading from Within: The Effects of Emotion Recognition and Personality on Transformational Leadership Behavior," *Academy of Management Journal*, October 2005, pp. 845–858; T. A. Judge and J. E. Bono, "Five-Factor Model of Personality and Transformational Leadership," *Journal of Applied Psychology*, October 2000, pp. 751–765; B. M. Bass and B. J. Avolio, "Developing Transformational Leadership: 1992 and Beyond," *Journal of European Industrial Training*, January 1990, p. 23; and J. J. Hater and B. M. Bass, "Supervisors' Evaluation and Subordinates' Perceptions of Transformational and Transactional Leadership," *Journal of Applied Psychology*, November 1988, pp. 695–702.

32. A. E. Colbert, A. L. Kristof-Brown, B. H. Bradley, and M. R. Barrick, "CEO Transformational Leadership: The Role of Goal Importance Congruence in Top Management Teams," *Academy of Management Journal*, February 2008, pp. 81–96; R. F. Piccolo and J. A. Colquitt, "Transformational Leadership and Job Behaviors: The Mediating Role of Core Job Characteristics," *Academy of Management Journal*, April 2006, pp. 327–340; O. Epitropaki and R. Martin, "From Ideal to Real: A Longitudinal Study of the Role of Implicit Leadership Theories on Leader-Member Exchanges and Employee Outcomes," *Journal of Applied Psychology*, July 2005, pp. 659–676; J. E. Bono and T. A. Judge, "Self-Concordance at Work: Toward Understanding the Motivational Effects of Transformational Leaders," *Academy of Management Journal*, October 2003, pp. 554–571; T. Dvir, D. Eden, B. J. Avolio, and B. Shamir, "Impact of Transformational Leadership on Follower Development and Performance: A Field Experiment," *Academy of Management Journal*,

August 2002, pp. 735–744; N. Sivasubramaniam, W. D. Murry, B. J. Avolio, and D. I. Jung, "A Longitudinal Model of the Effects of Team Leadership and Group Potency on Group Performance," *Group and Organization Management*, March 2002, pp. 66–96; J. M. Howell and B. J. Avolio, "Transformational Leadership, Transactional Leadership, Locus of Control, and Support for Innovation: Key Predictors of Consolidated-Business-Unit Performance," *Journal of Applied Psychology*, December 1993, pp. 891–911; R. T. Keller, "Transformational Leadership and the Performance of Research and Development Project Groups," *Journal of Management*, September 1992, pp. 489–501; and B. M. Bass and B. J. Avolio, "Developing Transformational Leadership: 1992 and Beyond," *Journal of European Industrial Training*, January 1990, p. 23.

33. F. Vogelstein, "Mighty Amazon," *Fortune*, May 26, 2003, pp. 60–74.

34. J. M. Crant and T. S. Bateman, "Charismatic Leadership Viewed from Above: The Impact of Proactive Personality," *Journal of Organizational Behavior*, February 2000, pp. 63–75; G. Yukl and J. M. Howell, "Organizational and Contextual Influences on the Emergence and Effectiveness of Charismatic Leadership," *Leadership Quarterly*, Summer 1999, pp. 257–283; and J. A. Conger and R. N. Kanungo, "Behavioral Dimensions of Charismatic Leadership," in *Charismatic Leadership*, J. A. Conger, et al., pp. 78–97 (San Francisco: Jossey-Bass, 1988).

35. J. A. Conger and R. N. Kanungo, *Charismatic Leadership in Organizations* (Thousand Oaks, CA: Sage, 1998).

36. K. S. Groves, "Linking Leader Skills, Follower Attitudes, and Contextual Variables via an Integrated Model of Charismatic Leadership," *Journal of Management*, April 2005, pp. 255–277; J. J. Sosik, "The Role of Personal Values in the Charismatic Leadership of Corporate Managers: A Model and Preliminary Field Study," *Leadership Quarterly*, April 2005, pp. 221–244; A. H. B. deHoogh, et al., "Leader Motives, Charismatic Leadership, and Subordinates' Work Attitudes in the Profit and Voluntary Sector," *Leadership Quarterly*, February 2005, pp. 17–38; J. M. Howell and B. Shamir, "The Role of Followers in the Charismatic Leadership Process: Relationships and Their Consequences," *Academy of Management Review*, January 2005, pp. 96–112; J. Paul, et al., "The Effects of Charismatic Leadership on Followers' Self-Concept Accessibility," *Journal of Applied Social Psychology*, September 2001, pp. 1821–1844; J. A. Conger, R. N. Kanungo, and S. T. Menon, "Charismatic Leadership and Follower Effects," *Journal of Organizational Behavior* 21 (2000), pp. 747–767; R. W. Rowden, "The Relationship Between Charismatic Leadership Behaviors and Organizational Commitment," *Leadership & Organization Development Journal*, January 2000, pp. 30–35; G. P. Shea and C. M. Howell, "Charismatic Leadership and Task Feedback: A Laboratory Study of Their Effects on Self-Efficacy," *Leadership Quarterly*, Fall 1999, pp. 375–396; S. A. Kirkpatrick and E. A. Locke, "Direct and Indirect Effects of Three Core Charismatic Leadership Components on Performance and Attitudes," *Journal of Applied Psychology*, February 1996, pp. 36–51; D. A. Waldman, B. M. Bass, and F. J. Yammarino, "Adding to Contingent-Reward Behavior: The Augmenting Effect of Charismatic Leadership," *Group & Organization Studies*, December 1990, pp. 381–394; and R. J. House, J. Woycke, and E. M. Fodor, "Charismatic and Noncharismatic Leaders: Differences in Behavior and Effectiveness," in *Charismatic Leadership*, J. A. Conger, et al., pp. 103–104 (San Francisco: Jossey-Bass, 1988).

37. B. R. Agle, N. J. Nagarajan, J. A. Sonnenfeld, and D. Srinivasan, "Does CEO Charisma Matter? An Empirical Analysis of the Relationships Among Organizational Performance, Environmental Uncertainty, and Top Management Team Perceptions of CEO Charisma," *Academy of Management Journal*, February 2006, pp. 161–174.

38. R. Birchfield, "Creating Charismatic Leaders," *Management*, June 2000, pp. 30–31; S. Caudron, "Growing Charisma," *IndustryWeek*, May 4, 1998, pp. 54–55; and J. A. Conger and R. N. Kanungo, "Training Charismatic Leadership: A Risky and Critical Task," in *Charismatic Leadership*, J. A. Conger, et al., pp. 309–323 (San Francisco: Jossey-Bass, 1988).

39. J. G. Hunt, K. B. Boal, and G. E. Dodge, "The Effects of Visionary and Crisis-Responsive Charisma on Followers: An Experimental Examination," *Leadership Quarterly*, Fall 1999, pp. 423–448; R. J. House and R. N. Aditya, "The Social Scientific Study of Leadership: Quo Vadis?" *Journal of Management* 23, no. 3 (1997), pp. 316–323; and R. J. House, "A 1976 Theory of Charismatic Leadership," in *Leadership: The Cutting Edge,* ed. J. G. Hunt and L. Larson, pp. 189–207 (Carbondale, Illinois: Southern Illinois University Press), 1977.

40. This definition is based on M. Sashkin, "The Visionary Leader," in *Charismatic Leadership,* J. A. Conger, et al., pp. 124–125 (San Francisco: Jossey-Bass, 1988); B. Nanus, *Visionary Leadership* (New York: The Free Press, 1992), p. 8; N. H. Snyder and M. Graves, "Leadership and Vision," *Business Horizons*, January–February 1994, p. 1; and J. R. Lucas, "Anatomy of a Vision Statement," *Management Review*, February 1998, pp. 22–26.

41. B. Nanus, *Visionary Leadership* (New York: The Free Press, 1992), p. 8.

42. S. Caminiti, "What Team Leaders Need to Know," *Fortune*, February 20, 1995, pp. 93–100.

43. S. Caminiti, "What Team Leaders Need to Know," *Fortune*, February 20, 1995, p. 93.

44. S. Caminiti, "What Team Leaders Need to Know," *Fortune*, February 20, 1995, p. 100.

45. N. Steckler and N. Fondas, "Building Team Leader Effectiveness: A Diagnostic Tool," *Organizational Dynamics*, Winter 1995, p. 20.

46. R. S. Wellins, W. C. Byham, and G. R. Dixon, *Inside Teams* (San Francisco: Jossey-Bass, 1994), p. 318.

47. N. Steckler and N. Fondas, "Building Team Leader Effectiveness: A Diagnostic Tool," *Organizational Dynamics*, Winter 1995, p. 21.

48. B. McRae, *The Seven Strategies of Master Leaders* (Toronto: Northbridge, 2009).

49. G. Colvin, "The FedEx Edge," *Fortune*, April 3, 2006, pp. 77–84.

50. See J. R. P. French Jr. and B. Raven, "The Bases of Social Power," in *Group Dynamics: Research and Theory*, ed. D. Cartwright and A. F. Zander, pp. 607–623 (New York: Harper & Row, 1960); P. M. Podsakoff and C. A. Schriesheim, "Field Studies of French and Raven's Bases of Power: Critique, Reanalysis, and Suggestions for Future Research," *Psychological Bulletin*, May 1985, pp. 387–411; R. K. Shukla, "Influence of Power Bases in Organizational Decision Making: A Contingency Model," *Decision Sciences*, July 1982, pp. 450–470; D. E. Frost and A. J. Stahelski, "The Systematic Measurement of French and Raven's Bases of Social Power in Workgroups," *Journal of Applied Social Psychology*, April 1988, pp. 375–389; and T. R. Hinkin and C. A. Schriesheim, "Development and Application of New Scales to Measure the French and Raven (1959) Bases of Social Power," *Journal of Applied Psychology*, August 1989, pp. 561–567.

51. See the Royal Australian Navy website, www.navy.gov.au.

52. J. M. Kouzes and B. Z. Posner, *Credibility: How Leaders Gain and Lose It, and Why People Demand It* (San Francisco: Jossey-Bass, 1993), p. 14.

53. Based on F. D. Schoorman, R. C. Mayer, and J. H. Davis, "An Integrative Model of Organizational Trust: Past, Present, and Future," *Academy of Management Review*, April 2007, pp. 344–354; G. M. Spreitzer and A. K. Mishra, "Giving Up Control Without Losing Control," *Group & Organization Management*, June 1999, pp. 155–187; R. C. Mayer, J. H. Davis, and F. D. Schoorman, "An Integrative Model of Organizational Trust," *Academy of Management Review*, July 1995, p. 712; and L. T. Hosmer, "Trust: The Connecting Link between Organizational Theory and Philosophical Ethics," *Academy of Management Review*, April 1995, p. 393.

54. P. L. Schindler and C. C. Thomas, "The Structure of Interpersonal Trust in the Workplace," *Psychological Reports*, October 1993, pp. 563–573.

55. H. H. Tan and C. S. F. Tan, "Toward the Differentiation of Trust in Supervisor and Trust in Organization," *Genetic, Social, and General Psychology Monographs*, May 2000, pp. 241–260.

56. R. C. Mayer and M. B. Gavin, "Trust in Management and Performance: Who Minds the Shop While the Employees Watch the Boss?" *Academy of Management Journal*, October 2005, pp. 874–888; and K. T. Dirks and D. L. Ferrin, "Trust in Leadership: Meta-Analytic Findings and Implications for Research and Practice," *Journal of Applied Psychology*, August 2002, pp. 611–628.

57. See for example, K. T. Dirks and D. L. Ferrin, "Trust in Leadership: Meta-Analytic Findings and Implications for Research and Practice," *Journal of Applied Psychology*, August 2002, pp. 611–628; J. K. Butler Jr., "Toward Understanding and Measuring Conditions of Trust: Evolution of a Conditions of Trust Inventory," *Journal of Management*, September 1991, pp. 643–663; and F. Bartolome, "Nobody Trusts the Boss Completely—Now What?" *Harvard Business Review*, March–April 1989, pp. 135–142.

58. R. Zemke, "The Confidence Crisis," *Training*, June 2004, pp. 22–30; J. A. Byrne, "Restoring Trust in Corporate America," *BusinessWeek*, June 24, 2002, pp. 30–35; S. Armour, "Employees' New Motto: Trust No One," *USA Today*, February 5, 2002, p. 1B; J. Scott, "Once Bitten, Twice Shy: A World of Eroding Trust," *New York Times*, April 21, 2002, p. WK5; J. Brockner, et al., "When Trust Matters: The Moderating Effect of Outcome Favorability," *Administrative Science Quarterly*, September 1997, p. 558; and J. Brockner, et al., "When Trust Matters: The Moderating Effect of Outcome Favorability," *Administrative Science Quarterly*, September 1997, p. 558.

59. Watson Wyatt, "Weathering the Storm: A Study of Employee Attitudes and Opinions," *WorkUSA 2002 Study*, www.watsonwyatt. com.

60. This section is based on R. B. Morgan, "Self- and Co-Worker Perceptions of Ethics and Their Relationships to Leadership and Salary," *Academy of Management Journal*, February 1993, pp. 200–214; E. P. Hollander, "Ethical Challenges in the Leader–Follower Relationship," *Business Ethics Quarterly*, January 1995, pp. 55–65; J. C. Rost, "Leadership: A Discussion about Ethics," *Business Ethics Quarterly*, January 1995, pp. 129–142; R. N. Kanungo and M. Mendonca, *Ethical Dimensions of Leadership* (Thousand Oaks, CA: Sage, 1996); J. B. Ciulla, ed., *Ethics: The Heart of Leadership* (New York: Praeger, 1998); J. D. Costa, *The Ethical Imperative: Why Moral Leadership Is Good Business* (Cambridge, MA: Perseus Press, 1999); and N. M. Tichy and A. McGill, eds., *The Ethical Challenge: How to Build Honest Business Leaders* (New York: John Wiley & Sons, 2003).

61. J. M. Burns, *Leadership* (New York: Harper & Row, 1978).

62. J. M. Avolio, S. Kahai, and G. E. Dodge, "The Ethics of Charismatic Leadership: Submission or Liberation?" *Academy of Management Executive*, May 1992, pp. 43–55.

63. L. K. Trevino, M. Brown, and L. P. Hartman, "A Qualitative Investigation of Perceived Executive Ethical Leadership: Perceptions from Inside and Outside the Executive Suite," *Human Relations*, January 2003, pp. 5–37.

64. W. A. Randolph, "Navigating the Journey to Empowerment," *Organizational Dynamics*, Spring 1995, pp. 19–32; R. C. Ford and M. D. Fottler, "Empowerment: A Matter of Degree," *Academy of Management Executive*, August 1995, pp. 21–31; R. C. Herrenkohl, G. T. Judson, and J. A. Heffner, "Defining and Measuring Employee Empowerment," *Journal of Applied Behavioral Science*, September 1999, p. 373; C. Robert and T. M. Probst, "Empowerment and Continuous Improvement in the United States, Mexico, Poland, and India," *Journal of Applied Psychology*, October 2000, pp. 643–658; C. Gomez and B. Rosen, "The Leader-Member Link between Managerial Trust and Employee Empowerment," *Group & Organization Management*, March 2001, pp. 53–69; W. Alan Rudolph and M. Sashkin, "Can Organizational Empowerment Work in Multinational Settings?" *Academy of Management Executive*, February 2002, pp. 102–115; and P. K. Mills and G. R. Ungson, "Reassessing the Limits of Structural Empowerment: Organizational Constitution and Trust as Controls," *Academy of Management Review*, January 2003, pp. 143–153.

65. J. Schaubroeck, J. R. Jones, and J. L. Xie, "Individual Differences in Utilizing Control to Cope with Job Demands: Effects on Susceptibility to Infectious Disease," *Journal of Applied Psychology* 86, no. 2 (2001), pp. 265–278; and A. M. Owens, "Empowerment Can Make You Ill, Study Says," *National Post*, April 30, 2001, pp. A1, A8.

66. "Delta Promotes Empowerment," *Globe and Mail*, May 31, 1999, Advertising Supplement, p. C5.

67. F. W. Swierczek, "Leadership and Culture: Comparing Asian Managers," *Leadership & Organization Development Journal*, December 1991, pp. 3–10.

68. R. J. House, "Leadership in the Twenty-First Century," in *Culture and Leadership Across the World*, ed. J. S. Chhokar, F. C. Brodbeck, and R. J. House (Mahwah, NJ: Lawrence Erlbaum Associates, 2007); M. F. Peterson and J. G. Hunt, "International Perspectives on International Leadership," *Leadership Quarterly*, Fall 1997, pp. 203–231; and J. R. Schermerhorn and M. H. Bond, "Cross-Cultural Leadership in Collectivism and High Power Distance Settings," *Leadership & Organization Development Journal* 18, no. 4/5 (1997), pp. 187–193.

69. R. J. House, et al., "Culture Specific and Cross-Culturally Generalizable Implicit Leadership Theories: Are the Attributes of Charismatic/Transformational Leadership Universally Endorsed?" *Leadership Quarterly*, Summer 1999, pp. 219–256; and D. E. Carl and M. Javidan, "Universality of Charismatic Leadership: A Multi-Nation Study" (paper presented at the National Academy of Management Conference, Washington, DC, August 2001).

70. D. E. Carl and M. Javidan, "Universality of Charismatic Leadership: A Multi-Nation Study" (paper presented at the National Academy of Management Conference, Washington, DC, August 2001), p. 29.

71. N. Clark, "Women Still Missing Out on Top Jobs at World's Largest Companies," *The Independent*, March 9, 2010, www. independent.co.uk/news/business/news/ women-still-missing-out-on-top-jobs-at-worlds-largest-companies-1918433.html (accessed February 3, 2011).

72. G. N. Powell, D. A. Butterfield, and J. D. Parent, "Gender and Managerial Stereotypes: Have the Times Changed?" *Journal of Management* 28, no. 2 (2002), pp. 177–193.

73. See K. M. Bartol, D. C. Martin, and J. A. Kromkowski, "Leadership and the Glass Ceiling: Gender and Ethnic Influences on Leader Behaviors at Middle and Executive Managerial Levels," *Journal of Leadership & Organizational Studies*, Winter 2003, pp. 8–19; A. H. Eagly and S. J. Karau, "Role Congruity Theory of Prejudice Toward Female Leaders," *Psychological Review*, July 2002, pp. 573–598; J. Becker, R. A. Ayman, and K. Korabik, "Discrepancies in Self/Subordinates' Perceptions of Leadership Behavior: Leader's Gender, Organizational Context, and Leader's Self-Monitoring," *Group & Organization Management*, June 2002, pp. 226–244; N. Z. Selter, "Gender Differences in Leadership: Current Social Issues and Future Organizational Implications," *Journal of Leadership Studies*, Spring 2002, pp. 88–99; J. M. Norvilitis and H. M. Reid, "Evidence for an Association Between Gender-Role Identity and a Measure of Executive Function," *Psychological Reports*, February 2002, pp. 35–45; W. H. Decker and D. M. Rotondo, "Relationships Among Gender, Type of Humor, and Perceived Leader Effectiveness," *Journal of Managerial Issues*, Winter 2001, pp. 450–465; C. L. Ridgeway, "Gender, Status, and Leadership," *Journal of Social Issues*, Winter 2001, pp. 637–655; M. Gardiner and M. Tiggemann, "Gender Differences in Leadership Style, Job Stress and Mental Health in Male- and Female-Dominated Industries," *Journal of Occupational and Organizational Psychology*, September 1999, pp. 301–315; and F. J. Yammarino, A. J. Dubinsky, L. B. Comer, and M. A. Jolson, "Women and Transformational and Contingent Reward Leadership: A Multiple Levels-of-Analysis Perspective," *Academy of Management Journal*, February 1997, pp. 205–222.

74. M. Gardiner and M. Tiggemann, "Gender Differences in Leadership Style, Job Stress and Mental Health in Male- and Female-Dominated Industries," *Journal of Occupational and Organizational Psychology*, September 1999, pp. 301–315.

75. J. M. Norvilitis and H. M. Reid, "Evidence for an Association Between Gender-Role Identity and a Measure of Executive Function," *Psychological Reports*, February 2002, pp. 35–45; W. H. Decker and D. M. Rotondo, "Relationships Among Gender, Type of Humor, and Perceived Leader Effectiveness," *Journal of Managerial Issues*, Winter 2001, pp. 450–465; H. Aguinis and S. K. R. Adams, "Social-Role versus Structural Models of Gender and Influence Use in Organizations: A Strong Inference Approach," *Group & Organization Management*, December 1998, pp. 414–446; and A. H. Eagly, S. J. Karau, and M. G. Makhijani, "Gender and the Effectiveness of Leaders: A Meta-Analysis," *Psychological Bulletin* 117 (1995), pp. 125–145.

76. K. M. Bartol, D. C. Martin, and J. A. Kromkowski, "Leadership and the Glass Ceiling: Gender and Ethnic Influences on Leader Behaviors at Middle and Executive Managerial Levels," *Journal of Leadership & Organizational Studies*, Winter 2003, pp. 8–19; and R. Sharpe, "As Leaders, Women Rule," *BusinessWeek*, November 20, 2000, pp. 74–84.

77. K. M. Bartol, D. C. Martin, and J. A. Kromkowski, "Leadership and the Glass Ceiling: Gender and Ethnic Influences on Leader Behaviors at Middle and Executive Managerial Levels," *Journal of Leadership & Organizational Studies*, Winter 2003, pp. 8–19.

78. See, for instance, R. Lofthouse, "Herding the Cats," *EuroBusiness*, February 2001, pp. 64–65; and M. Delahoussaye, "Leadership in the 21st Century," *Training*, September 2001, pp. 60–72.

79. See, for instance, A. A. Vicere, "Executive Education: The Leading Edge," *Organizational Dynamics*, Autumn 1996, pp. 67–81; J. Barling, T. Weber, and E. K. Kelloway, "Effects of Transformational Leadership Training on Attitudinal and Financial Outcomes: A Field Experiment," *Journal of Applied Psychology*, December 1996, pp. 827–832; and D. V. Day, "Leadership Development: A Review in Context," *Leadership Quarterly*, Winter 2000, pp. 581–613.

80. K. Y. Chan and F. Drasgow, "Toward a Theory of Individual Differences and Leadership: Understanding the Motivation to Lead," *Journal of Applied Psychology*, June 2001, pp. 481–498.

81. M. Sashkin, "The Visionary Leader," in *Charismatic Leadership,* J. A. Congeret al., p. 150 (San Francisco: Jossey-Bass, 1988).

82. S. Kerr and J. M. Jermier, "Substitutes for Leadership: Their Meaning and Measurement," *Organizational Behavior and Human Performance*, December 1978, pp. 375–403; J. P. Howell, P. W. Dorfman, and S. Kerr, "Leadership and Substitutes for Leadership," *Journal of Applied Behavioral Science* 22, no. 1 (1986), pp. 29–46; J. P. Howell, et al., "Substitutes for Leadership: Effective Alternatives to Ineffective Leadership," *Organizational Dynamics*, Summer 1990, pp. 21–38; and P. M. Podsakoff, B. P. Niehoff, S. B. MacKenzie, and M. L. Williams, "Do Substitutes for Leadership Really Substitute for Leadership? An Empirical Examination of Kerr and Jermier's Situational Leadership Model," *Organizational Behavior and Human Decision Processes*, February 1993, pp. 1–44.

83. Adapted with permission from T. Sergiovanni, R. Metzcus, and L. Burden, "Toward a Particularistic Approach to Leadership Style: Some Findings," *American Educational Research Journal* 6, no. 1 (January 1969), American Educational Research Association, Washington, DC.

84. Situation adapted from information in J. Menn, "Ellison Talks Tough on Bid for PeopleSoft," *Los Angeles Times*, July 10, 2003, p. C11; M. Mangalindan, D. Clark, and R. Sidel, "Hostile Move Augurs High-Tech Consolidation," *Wall Street Journal*, June 9, 2003, p. A11; A. Pham, "Oracle's Merger Hurdles Get Higher," *Los Angeles Times*, June 30, 2003, p. C11; S. Pannill, "Smashmouth PR Meets High Tech," *Forbes*, May 28, 2001, p. 9; and F. Vogelstein, "Oracle's Ellison Turns Hostile," *Fortune*, June 23, 2003, p. 28.

85. Based on M. Henricks, "Kids These Days," *Entrepreneur*, May 2002, pp. 71–72.

86. L. M. Fisher, "Ricardo Semler Won't Take Control," *Strategy+Business*, Winter 2005, pp. 78–88; R. Semler, *The Seven-Day Weekend: Changing the Way Work Works* (New York: Penguin Group, 2004); A. J. Vogl, "The Anti-CEO," *Across the Board*, May–June 2004, pp. 30–36; G. Colvin, "The Anti-Control Freak," *Fortune*, November 26, 2001, p. 22; and R. Semler, "Managing without Managers," *Harvard Business Review*, September–October 1989, pp. 76–84.

87. Based on H. Mintzberg, *Power In and Around Organizations* (Upper Saddle River, NJ: Prentice Hall, 1983), p. 24; and P. L. Hunsaker, *Training in Management Skills* (Upper Saddle River, NJ: Prentice Hall, 2001), pp. 339–364.

Chapter 15

1. Based on Hoover's Online, www.hoover.com; S. Butcher, "Relentless Rise in Pleasure Seekers," *Financial Times*, July 6, 2003, http://news.ft.com (accessed July 7, 2003); C. Blackhurst, "The Chris Blackhurst Interview: Sir Terry Leahy," *Management Today*, February 2004, pp. 32–34; "Tesco at a Glance," and Tesco, www.tescocorporate.com/page.aspx?pointerid=A8E0E60508F94A8DBA909E2ABB5F2CC7 (accessed September 20, 2007); and *Tesco: Preliminary Results 2009/10,* www.tescoplc.com/plc/ir/pres_results/analyst_packs/ap2010/prelim10/prelim10.pdf (accessed February 14, 2011).

2. R. M. Steers, R. T. Mowday, and D. L. Shapiro, "The Future of Work Motivation Theory," *Academy of Management Review*, July 2004, pp. 379–387.

3. N. Ellemers, D. De Gilder, and S. A. Haslam, "Motivating Individuals and Groups at Work: A Social Identity Perspective on

Leadership and Group Performance," *Academy of Management Review*, July 2004, pp. 459–478.

4. G. Shaw, "Canada Lags World on Job Quality," *Vancouver Sun*, September 18, 2004, p. F5.

5. Based on S. Butcher, "Relentless Rise in Pleasure Seekers," *Financial Times*, July 6, 2003, http://news.ft.com (accessed July 7, 2003).

6. A. Maslow, *Motivation and Personality* (New York: McGraw-Hill, 1954); A. Maslow, D. C. Stephens, and G. Heil, *Maslow on Management* (New York: John Wiley & Sons, 1998); M. L. Ambrose and C. T. Kulik, "Old Friends, New Faces: Motivation Research in the 1990s," *Journal of Management* 25, no. 3 (1999), pp. 231–292; and "Dialogue," *Academy of Management Review*, October 2000, pp. 696–701.

7. See, for example, D. T. Hall and K. E. Nongaim, "An Examination of Maslow's Need Hierarchy in an Organizational Setting," *Organizational Behavior and Human Performance*, February 1968, pp. 12–35; E. E. Lawler III and J. L. Suttle, "A Causal Correlational Test of the Need Hierarchy Concept," *Organizational Behavior and Human Performance*, April 1972, pp. 265–287; R. M. Creech, "Employee Motivation," *ManagementQuarterly*, Summer 1995, pp. 33–39; J. Rowan, "Maslow Amended," *Journal of Humanistic Psychology*, Winter 1998, pp. 81–92; J. Rowan, "Ascent and Descent in Maslow's Theory," *Journal of Humanistic Psychology*, Summer 1999, pp. 125–133; and M. L. Ambrose and C. T. Kulik, "Old Friends, New Faces: Motivation Research in the 1990s," *Journal of Management* 25, no. 3 (1999), pp. 231–292.

8. D. McGregor, *The Human Side of Enterprise* (New York: McGraw-Hill, 1960). For an updated analysis of Theories X and Y, see R. J. Summers and S. F. Conshaw, "A Study of McGregor's Theory X, Theory Y and the Influence of Theory X, Theory Y Assumptions on Causal Attributions for Instances of Worker Poor Performance," in *Organizational Behavior*, ASAC 1988 Conference Proceedings, vol. 9, Part 5, ed. S. L. McShaneed (Halifax, NS: ASAC, 1988), pp. 115–123.

9. K. W. Thomas, *Intrinsic Motivation at Work* (San Francisco: Berrett-Koehler, 2000); and K. W. Thomas, "Intrinsic Motivation and How It Works," *Training*, October 2000, pp. 130–135.

10. F. Herzberg, B. Mausner, and B. Snyderman, *The Motivation to Work* (New York: John Wiley, 1959); F. Herzberg, *The Managerial Choice: To Be Effective or to Be Human*, rev. ed. (Salt Lake City: Olympus, 1982); R. M. Creech, "Employee Motivation," *Management Quarterly*, Summer 1995, pp. 33–39; and M. L. Ambrose and C. T. Kulik, "Old Friends, New Faces: Motivation Research in the 1990s," *Journal of Management* 25, no. 3 (1999), pp. 231–292.

11. Based on G. Bellett, "Firm's Secret to Success Lies in Treating Workers Right," *Vancouver Sun*, March 21, 2001, pp. D7, D11; V. Galt, "Getting Fit on the Job," *Globe and Mail*, November 6, 2002, p. C1; and C. Lochhead, "Healthy Workplace Programs at Pazmac Enterprises Ltd.," Canadian Labour and Business Centre, March 2002, www.clbc.ca/files/CaseStudies/pazmac.pdf (accessed September 20, 2007).

12. D. C. McClelland, *The Achieving Society* (New York: Van Nostrand Reinhold, 1961); J. W. Atkinson and J. O. Raynor, *Motivation and Achievement* (Washington, DC: Winston, 1974); D. C. McClelland, *Power: The Inner Experience* (New York: Irvington, 1975); and M. J. Stahl, *Managerial and Technical Motivation: Assessing Needs for Achievement, Power, and Affiliation* (New York: Praeger, 1986).

13. D. C. McClelland, *The Achieving Society* (New York: Van Nostrand Reinhold, 1961).

14. D. C. McClelland, *Power: The Inner Experience* (New York: Irvington, 1975); and D. C. McClelland and D. H. Burnham, "Power Is the Great Motivator," *Harvard Business Review*, March–April 1976, pp. 100–110.

15. D. Miron and D. C. McClelland, "The Impact of Achievement Motivation Training on Small Businesses," *California Management Review*, Summer 1979, pp. 13–28.

16. "McClelland: An Advocate of Power," *International Management*, July 1975, pp. 27–29.

17. Based on S. Butcher, "Relentless Rise in Pleasure Seekers," *Financial Times*, July 6, 2003, http://news.ft.com (accessed July 7, 2003); A. Nottage, "Tesco," *Human Resources*, May 2003, p. 10; and C. Blackhurst, "The Chris Blackhurst Interview: Sir Terry Leahy," *Management Today*, February 2004, pp. 32–34.

18. R. M. Steers, R. T. Mowday, and D. L. Shapiro, "The Future of Work Motivation Theory," *Academy of Management Review*, July 2004, pp. 379–387; E. A. Locke and G. P. Latham, "What Should We Do About Motivation Theory? Six Recommendations for the Twenty-First Century," *Academy of Management Review*, July 2004, pp. 388–403; and M. L. Ambrose and C. T. Kulik, "Old Friends, New Faces: Motivation Research in the 1990s," *Journal of Management* 25, no. 3 (1999), pp. 231–292.

19. M. L. Ambrose and C. T. Kulik, "Old Friends, New Faces: Motivation Research in the 1990s," *Journal of Management* 25, no. 3 (1999), pp. 231–292.

20. J. C. Naylor and D. R. Ilgen, "Goal Setting: A Theoretical Analysis of a Motivational Technique," in *Research in Organizational Behavior*, vol. 6, ed. B. M. Staw and L. L. Cummings, pp. 95–140 (Greenwich, CT: JAI Press, 1984); A. R. Pell, "Energize Your People," *Managers Magazine*, December 1992, pp. 28–29; E. A. Locke, "Facts and Fallacies About Goal Theory: Reply to Deci," *Psychological Science*, January 1993, pp. 63–64; M. E. Tubbs, "Commitment as a Moderator of the Goal–Performance Relation: A Case for Clearer Construct Definition," *Journal of Applied Psychology*, February 1993, pp. 86–97; M. P. Collingwood, "Why Don't You Use the Research?" *Management Decision*, May 1993, pp. 48–54; M. E. Tubbs, D. M. Boehne, and J. S. Dahl, "Expectancy, Valence, and Motivational Force Functions in Goal-Setting Research: An Empirical Test," *Journal of Applied Psychology*, June 1993, pp. 361–373; E. A. Locke, "Motivation Through Conscious Goal Setting," *Applied and Preventive Psychology* 5 (1996), pp. 117–124; M. L. Ambrose and C. T. Kulik, "Old Friends, New Faces: Motivation Research in the 1990s," *Journal of Management* 25, no. 3 (1999), pp. 231–292; E. A. Locke and G. P. Latham, "Building a Practically Useful Theory of Goal Setting and Task Motivation: A 35-Year Odyssey," *American Psychologist*, September 2002, pp. 705–717; Y. Fried and L. H. Slowik, "Enriching Goal-Setting Theory with Time: An Integrated Approach," *Academy of Management Review*, July 2004, pp. 404–422; and G. P. Latham, "The Motivational Benefits of Goal-Setting," *Academy of Management Executive*, November 2004, pp. 126–129.

21. J. B. Miner, *Theories of Organizational Behavior* (Hinsdale, IL: Dryden Press, 1980), p. 65.

22. J. A. Wagner III, "Participation's Effects on Performance and Satisfaction: A Reconsideration of Research and Evidence," *Academy of Management Review*, April 1994, pp. 312–330; J. George-Falvey, "Effects of Task Complexity and Learning Stage on the Relationship between Participation in Goal Setting and Task Performance," *Academy of Management Proceedings*, on disk, 1996; T. D. Ludwig and E. S. Geller, "Assigned Versus Participative Goal Setting and Response Generalization: Managing Injury Control among Professional Pizza Deliverers," *Journal of Applied Psychology*, April 1997, pp. 253–261; and S. G. Harkins and M. D. Lowe, "The Effects

of Self-Set Goals on Task Performance," *Journal of Applied Social Psychology*, January 2000, pp. 1–40.

23. J. M. Ivancevich and J. T. McMahon, "The Effects of Goal Setting, External Feedback, and Self-Generated Feedback on Outcome Variables: A Field Experiment," *Academy of Management Journal*, June 1982, pp. 359–372; and E. A. Locke, "Motivation Through Conscious Goal Setting," *Applied and Preventive Psychology* 5 (1996), pp. 117–124.

24. J. R. Hollenbeck, C. R. Williams, and H. J. Klein, "An Empirical Examination of the Antecedents of Commitment to Difficult Goals," *Journal of Applied Psychology*, February 1989, pp. 18–23; see also J. C. Wofford, V. L. Goodwin, and S. Premack, "Meta-Analysis of the Antecedents of Personal Goal Level and of the Antecedents and Consequences of Goal Commitment," *Journal of Management*, September 1992, pp. 595–615; M. E. Tubbs, "Commitment as a Moderator of the Goal–Performance Relation": A Case for Clearer Construct Definition," *Journal of Applied Psychology*, February 1993, pp. 86–97; J. W. Smither, M. London, and R. R. Reilly, "Does Performance Improve Following Multisource Feedback? A Theoretical Model, Meta-Analysis, and Review of Empirical Findings," *Personnel Psychology*, Spring 2005, pp. 171–203.

25. M. E. Gist, "Self-Efficacy: Implications for Organizational Behavior and Human Resource Management," *Academy of Management Review*, July 1987, pp. 472–485; and A. Bandura, *Self-Efficacy: The Exercise of Control* (New York: Freeman, 1997).

26. E. A. Locke, E. Frederick, C. Lee, and P. Bobko, "Effect of Self-Efficacy, Goals, and Task Strategies on Task Performance," *Journal of Applied Psychology*, May 1984, pp. 241–251; M. E. Gist and T. R. Mitchell, "Self-Efficacy: A Theoretical Analysis of Its Determinants and Malleability," *Academy of Management Review*, April 1992, pp. 183–211; A. D. Stajkovic and F. Luthans, "Self-Efficacy and Work-Related Performance: A Meta-Analysis," *Psychological Bulletin*, September 1998, pp. 240–261; and A. Bandura, "Cultivate Self-Efficacy for Personal and Organizational Effectiveness," in E. Locke (ed.), *Handbook of Principles of Organizational Behavior* (Malden, MA: Blackwell, 2004), pp. 120–136.

27. A. Bandura and D. Cervone, "Differential Engagement in Self-Reactive Influences in Cognitively-Based Motivation," *Organizational Behavior and Human Decision Processes*, August 1986, pp. 92–113; and R. Ilies and T. A. Judge, "Goal Regulation Across Time: The Effects of Feedback and Affect," *Journal of Applied Psychology*, May 2005, pp. 453–467.

28. See J. C. Anderson and C. A. O'Reilly, "Effects of an Organizational Control System on Managerial Satisfaction and Performance," *Human Relations*, June 1981, pp. 491–501; and J. P. Meyer, B. Schacht-Cole, and I. R. Gellatly, "An Examination of the Cognitive Mechanisms by Which Assigned Goals Affect Task Performance and Reactions to Performance," *Journal of Applied Social Psychology* 18, no. 5 (1988), pp. 390–408.

29. K. Maher and K. Hudson, "Wal-Mart to Sweeten Bonus Plans for Staff," *Wall Street Journal*, March 22, 2007, p. A11; and Reuters, "Wal-Mart Workers to Get New Bonus Plan," *CNNMoney.com*, March 22, 2007.

30. B. F. Skinner, *Science and Human Behavior* (New York: The Free Press, 1953); and B. F. Skinner, *Beyond Freedom and Dignity* (New York: Knopf, 1972).

31. The same data, for instance, can be interpreted in either goal-setting or reinforcement terms, as shown in E. A. Locke, "Latham vs. Komaki: A Tale of Two Paradigms," *Journal of Applied Psychology*, February 1980, pp. 16–23. Also see M. L. Ambrose and C. T. Kulik, "Old Friends, New Faces: Motivation Research in the 1990s," *Journal of Management* 25, no. 3 (1999), pp. 231–292.

32. See, for example, R. W. Griffin, "Toward an Integrated Theory of Task Design," in *Research in Organizational Behavior*, vol. 9, ed. B. Staw and L. L. Cummings, pp. 79–120 (Greenwich, CT: JAI Press, 1987); and M. Campion, "Interdisciplinary Approaches to Job Design: A Constructive Replication with Extensions," *Journal of Applied Psychology*, August 1988, pp. 467–481.

33. S. Caudron, "The De-Jobbing of America," *IndustryWeek*, September 5, 1994, pp. 31–36; W. Bridges, "The End of the Job," *Fortune*, September 19, 1994, pp. 62–74; and K. H. Hammonds, K. Kelly, and K. Thurston, "Rethinking Work," *BusinessWeek*, October 12, 1994, pp. 75–87.

34. M. A. Campion and C. L. McClelland, "Follow-Up and Extension of the Interdisciplinary Costs and Benefits of Enlarged Jobs," *Journal of Applied Psychology*, June 1993, pp. 339–351; M. L. Ambrose and C. T. Kulik, "Old Friends, New Faces: Motivation Research in the 1990s," *Journal of Management* 25, no. 3 (1999), pp. 231–292.

35. See, for example, J. R. Hackman and G. R. Oldham, *Work Redesign* (Reading, MA: Addison-Wesley, 1980); J. B. Miner, *Theories of Organizational Behavior* (Hinsdale, IL: Dryden Press, 1980), pp. 231–266; R. W. Griffin, "Effects of Work Redesign on Employee Perceptions, Attitudes, and Behaviors: A Long-Term Investigation," *Academy of Management Journal*, June 1991, pp. 425–435; J. L. Cotton, *Employee Involvement* (Newbury Park, CA: Sage, 1993), pp. 141–172; and M. L. Ambrose and C. T. Kulik, "Old Friends, New Faces: Motivation Research in the 1990s," *Journal of Management* 25, no. 3 (1999), pp. 231–292.

36. J. R. Hackman and G. R. Oldham, "Development of the Job Diagnostic Survey," *Journal of Applied Psychology*, April 1975, pp. 159–170; and J. R. Hackman and G. R. Oldham, "Motivation through the Design of Work: Test of a Theory," *Organizational Behavior and Human Performance*, August 1976, pp. 250–279.

37. J. R. Hackman, "Work Design," in *Improving Life at Work*, ed. J. R. Hackman and J. L. Suttle (Glenview, IL: Scott, Foresman, 1977), p. 129; M. L. Ambrose and C. T. Kulik, "Old Friends, New Faces: Motivation Research in the 1990s," *Journal of Management* 25, no. 3 (1999), pp. 231–292.

38. "Entrepreneur Profile," *National Post*, www.canada.com/nationalpost/entrepreneur/ail.html (accessed September 20, 2007).

39. J. S. Adams, "Inequity in Social Exchanges," in *Advances in Experimental Social Psychology*, vol. 2, ed. L. Berkowitz, pp. 267–300 (New York: Academic Press, 1965); and M. L. Ambrose and C. T. Kulik, "Old Friends, New Faces: Motivation Research in the 1990s," *Journal of Management* 25, no. 3 (1999), pp. 231–292.

40. See, for example, P. S. Goodman and A. Friedman, "An Examination of Adams' Theory of Inequity," *Administrative Science Quarterly*, September 1971, pp. 271–288; E. Walster, G. W. Walster, and W. G. Scott, *Equity: Theory and Research* (Boston: Allyn & Bacon, 1978); and J. Greenberg, "Cognitive Reevaluation of Outcomes in Response to Underpayment Inequity," *Academy of Management Journal*, March 1989, pp. 174–184.

41. See, for example, M. R. Carrell, "A Longitudinal Field Assessment of Employee Perceptions of Equitable Treatment," *Organizational Behavior and Human Performance*, February 1978, pp. 108–118; R. G. Lord and J. A. Hohenfeld, "Longitudinal Field Assessment of Equity Effects on the Performance of Major League Baseball Players," *Journal of Applied Psychology*, February 1979, pp. 19–26; and J. E. Dittrich and M. R. Carrell, "Organizational Equity Perceptions, Employee Job Satisfaction, and Departmental Absence and Turnover Rates," *Organizational Behavior and Human Performance*, August 1979, pp. 29–40.

42. Based on "Councillors Approve Own Pay Hike," *cbc.ca,* July 28, 2006; and Z. Ruryk, "Most T.O. Residents Against Council Raise," *TorontoSun.com*, September 9, 2007.

43. P. S. Goodman, "An Examination of Referents Used in the Evaluation of Pay," *Organizational Behavior and Human Performance*, October 1974, pp. 170–195; S. Ronen, "Equity Perception in Multiple Comparisons: A Field Study," *Human Relations*, April 1986, pp. 333–346; R. W. Scholl, E. A. Cooper, and J. F. McKenna, "Referent Selection in Determining Equity Perception: Differential Effects on Behavioral and Attitudinal Outcomes," *Personnel Psychology*, Spring 1987, pp. 113–127; and C. T. Kulik and M. L. Ambrose, "Personal and Situational Determinants of Referent Choice," *Academy of Management Review*, April 1992, pp. 212–237.

44. A. Wahl, "Canada's Best Workplaces: Overview," *Canadian Business*, April 26, 2007, www.canadianbusiness.com/managing/career/article.jsp?content=20070425_85420_85420 (accessed September 20, 2007).

45. See, for example, J. Brockner, "Why It's So Hard to Be Fair," *Harvard Business Review*, March 2006, pp. 122–129; J. A. Colquitt, "Does the Justice of One Interact with the Justice of Many? Reactions to Procedural Justice in Teams," *Journal of Applied Psychology*, August 2004, pp. 633–646; M. A. Konovsky, "Understanding Procedural Justice and Its Impact on Business Organizations," *Journal of Management* 26, no. 3 (2000), pp. 489–511; R. C. Dailey and D. J. Kirk, "Distributive and Procedural Justice as Antecedents of Job Dissatisfaction and Intent to Turnover," *Human Relations*, March 1992, pp. 305–316; and D. B. McFarlin and P. D. Sweeney, "Distributive and Procedural Justice as Predictors of Satisfaction with Personal and Organizational Outcomes," *Academy of Management Journal*, August 1992, pp. 626–637.

46. G. P. Latham and C. C. Pinder, "Work Motivation Theory and Research at the Dawn of the Twenty-First Century," *Annual Review of Psychology* 56, 2005, pp. 485–516; P. S. Goodman, "Social Comparison Process in Organizations," in *New Directions in Organizational Behavior*, ed. B. M. Staw and G. R. Salancik, pp. 97–132 (Chicago: St. Clair, 1977); and J. Greenberg, "A Taxonomy of Organizational Justice Theories," *Academy of Management Review*, January 1987, pp. 9–22.

47. V. H. Vroom, *Work and Motivation* (New York: John Wiley, 1964).

48. See, for example, H. G. Heneman III and D. P. Schwab, "Evaluation of Research on Expectancy Theory Prediction of Employee Performance," *Psychological Bulletin*, July 1972, pp. 1–9; and L. Reinharth and M. Wahba, "Expectancy Theory as a Predictor of Work Motivation, Effort Expenditure, and Job Performance," *Academy of Management Journal*, September 1975, pp. 502–537.

49. See, for example, V. H. Vroom, "Organizational Choice: A Study of Pre- and Postdecision Processes," *Organizational Behavior and Human Performance*, April 1966, pp. 212–225; L. W. Porter and E. E. Lawler III, *Managerial Attitudes and Performance* (Homewood, IL: Richard D. Irwin, 1968); W. Van Eerde and H. Thierry, "Vroom's Expectancy Models and Work-Related Criteria: A Meta-Analysis," *Journal of Applied Psychology*, October 1996, pp. 575–586; and M. L. Ambrose and C. T. Kulik, "Old Friends, New Faces: Motivation Research in the 1990s," *Journal of Management* 25, no. 3 (1999), pp. 231–292.

50. See, for instance, M. Siegall, "The Simplistic Five: An Integrative Framework for Teaching Motivation," *Organizational Behavior Teaching Review* 12, no. 4 (1987–1988), pp. 141–143.

51. S. Butcher, "Relentless Rise in Pleasure Seekers," *Financial Times*, July 6, 2003, http://news.ft.com (accessed July 7, 2003); "Tesco Pilots Student Benefits," *Employee Benefits*, November 7,

2003, p. P12; and www.tescocorporate.com/annualreview07/01_tescostory/tescostory3.html (accessed October 14, 2007).

52. J. R. Billings and D. L. Sharpe, "Factors Influencing Flextime Usage among Employed Married Women," *Consumer Interests Annual*, vol. 45 (Ames, IA: American Council on Consumer Interests, 1999), pp. 89–94; and I. Harpaz, "The Importance of Work Goals: An International Perspective," *Journal of International Business Studies*, First Quarter 1990, pp. 75–93.

53. N. Ramachandran, "New Paths at Work," *U.S. News & World Report*, March 20, 2006, p. 47; S. Armour, "Generation Y: They've Arrived at Work with a New Attitude," *USA Today*, November 6, 2005, pp. B1+; R. Kanfer and P. L. Ackerman, "Aging, Adult Development, and Work Motivation," *Academy of Management Review*, July 2004, pp. 440–458; and R. Bernard, D. Cosgrave, and J. Welsh, *Chips and Pop: Decoding the Nexus Generation* (Toronto: Malcolm Lester Books, 1998).

54. N. J. Adler, *International Dimensions of Organizational Behavior*, 4th ed. (Cincinnati, OH: South-Western, 2002), p. 174.

55. G. Hofstede, "Motivation, Leadership and Organization: Do American Theories Apply Abroad?" *Organizational Dynamics*, Summer 1980, p. 55.

56. J. K. Giacobbe-Miller, D. J. Miller, and V. I. Victorov, "A Comparison of Russian and U.S. Pay Allocation Decisions, Distributive Justice Judgments and Productivity Under Different Payment Conditions," *Personnel Psychology*, Spring 1998, pp. 137–163.

57. S. L. Mueller and L. D. Clarke, "Political-Economic Context and Sensitivity to Equity: Differences between the United States and the Transition Economies of Central and Eastern Europe," *Academy of Management Journal*, June 1998, pp. 319–329.

58. I. Harpaz, "The Importance of Work Goals: An International Perspective," *Journal of International Business Studies*, First Quarter 1990, pp. 75–93.

59. G. E. Popp, H. J. Davis, and T. T. Herbert, "An International Study of Intrinsic Motivation Composition," *Management International Review*, January 1986, pp. 28–35.

60. R. W. Brislin, B. MacNab, R. Worthley, F. Kabigting Jr., and B. Zukis, "Evolving Perceptions of Japanese Workplace Motivation: An Employee-Manager Comparison," *International Journal of Cross-Cultural Management*, April 2005, pp. 87–104.

61. P. Falcone, "Motivating Staff without Money," *HR Magazine*, August 2002, pp. 105–108.

62. P. Falcone, "Motivating Staff without Money," *HR Magazine*, August 2002, pp. 105–108.

63. See, for instance, S. R. Barley and G. Kunda, "Contracting: A New Form of Professional Practice," *Academy of Management Perspectives*, February 2006, pp. 45–66; T. J. Allen and R. Katz, "Managing Technical Professionals and Organizations: Improving and Sustaining the Performance of Organizations, Project Teams, and Individual Contributors," *Sloan Management Review*, Summer 2002, pp. S4–S5; G. Poole, "How to Manage Your Nerds," *Forbes ASAP*, December 1994, pp. 132–136; and M. Alpert, "The Care and Feeding of Engineers," *Fortune*, September 21, 1992, pp. 86–95.

64. "One CEO's Perspective on the Power of Recognition," *Workforce Management*, March 2, 2004, www.workforce.com; and R. Fournier, "Teamwork Is the Key to Remote Development—Inspiring Trust and Maintaining Motivation Are Critical for a Distributive Development Team," *InfoWorld*, March 5, 2001, p. 48.

65. R. J. Bohner Jr. and E. R. Salasko, "Beware the Legal Risks of Hiring Temps," *Workforce,* October 2002, pp. 50–57.

66. J. P. Broschak and A. Davis-Blake, "Mixing Standard Work and Nonstandard Deals: The Consequences of Heterogeneity in Employment Arrangements," *Academy of Management Journal,* April 2006, pp. 371–393; M. L. Kraimer, S. J. Wayne, R. C. Liden, and R. T. Sparrowe, "The Role of Job Security in Understanding the Relationship between Employees' Perceptions of Temporary Workers and Employees' Performance," *Journal of Applied Psychology,* March 2005, pp. 389–398; and C. E. Connelly and D. G. Gallagher, "Emerging Trends in Contingent Work Research," *Journal of Management,* November 2004, pp. 959–983.

67. D. W. Krueger, "Money, Success, and Success Phobia," in *The Last Taboo: Money as a Symbol and Reality in Psychotherapy and Psychoanalysis,* ed. D. W. Krueger, pp. 3–16 (New York: Brunner/Mazel, 1986).

68. T. R. Mitchell and A. E. Mickel, "The Meaning of Money: An Individual-Difference Perspective," *Academy of Management Review,* July 1999, pp. 568–578.

69. This paragraph is based on Graham Lowe, "21st Century Job Quality: Achieving What Canadians Want," *Canadian Policy Research Networks,* Research Report W|37, September 2007.

70. D. Grigg and J. Newman, "Labour Researchers Define Job Satisfaction," *Vancouver Sun,* February 16, 2002, p. E2.

71. This paragraph is based on T. R. Mitchell and A. E. Mickel, "The Meaning of Money: An Individual-Difference Perspective," *Academy of Management Review,* July 1999, pp. 568–578. The reader may want to refer to the myriad references cited in the article.

72. F. Luthans and A. D. Stajkovic, "Provide Recognition for Performance Improvement," in *Principles of Organizational Behavior,* ed. E. A. Locke, pp. 166–180 (Oxford, UK: Blackwell, 2000).

73. CNW Group, "Calgary Salary Increases Outpace Rest of Canada, According to Hewitt," news release, September 5, 2006, www.newswire.ca/en/releases/archive/September2006/05/c2519.html (accessed September 20, 2007).

74. "Secrets of Their Success (and Failure)," *Report on Business,* January 2006, pp. 54–55.

75. S. L. Rynes, B. Gerhart, and L. Parks, "Personnel Psychology: Performance Evaluation and Pay for Performance," *Annual Review of Psychology* 56, no. 1 (2005), p. 572; and A. M. Dickinson, "Are We Motivated by Money? Some Results from the Laboratory," *Performance Improvement* 44, no. 3 (March 2005), pp. 18–24.

76. R. K. Abbott, "Performance-Based Flex: A Tool for Managing Total Compensation Costs," *Compensation and Benefits Review,* March–April 1993, pp. 18–21; J. R. Schuster and P. K. Zingheim, "The New Variable Pay: Key Design Issues," *Compensation and Benefits Review,* March–April 1993, pp. 27–34; C. R. Williams and L. P. Livingstone, "Another Look at the Relationship between Performance and Voluntary Turnover," *Academy of Management Journal,* April 1994, pp. 269–298; and A. M. Dickinson and K. L. Gillette, "A Comparison of the Effects of Two Individual Monetary Incentive Systems on Productivity: Piece Rate Pay versus Base Pay Plus Incentives," *Journal of Organizational Behavior Management,* Spring 1994, pp. 3–82.

77. CNW Group, "Calgary Salary Increases Reach New Heights, According to Hewitt," news release, www.newswire.ca/en/releases/archive/September2007/06/c5734.html (accessed September 17, 2007); G. Teel, "City Leads Nation in Salary Increases," *Calgary Herald,* September 7, 2007, www.canada.com/calgaryherald/news/calgarybusiness/story.

html?id=ba2ca066-5d60-4a67-b24b-969c32bcedfa&p=1 (accessed September 17, 2007); Hewitt Associates, "Hewitt Study Shows Pay-for-Performance Plans Replacing Holiday Bonuses," news release, December 6, 2005, http://was4.hewitt.com/hewitt/resource/newsroom/pressrel/2005/12-06-05eng.pdf (accessed April 29, 2006); and P. Brieger, "Variable Pay Packages Gain Favour: Signing Bonuses, Profit Sharing Taking Place of Salary Hikes," *Financial Post (National Post),* September 13, 2002, p. FP5.

78. E. Beauchesne, "Pay Bonuses Improve Productivity, Study Shows," *Vancouver Sun,* September 13, 2002, p. D5; and the Conference Board of Canada, "Variable Pay Offers a Bonus for Unionized Workplaces," news release, September 12, 2002, www.conferenceboard.ca/press/2002/variable_pay.asp (accessed April 29, 2006).

79. "Hope for Higher Pay: The Squeeze on Incomes Is Gradually Easing Up," *Maclean's,* November 25, 1996, pp. 100–101.

80. Hewitt Associates, "Hewitt Study Shows Base Pay Increases Flat for 2006 with Variable Pay Plans Picking Up the Slack," August 31, 2005.

81. E. Beauchesne, "Pay Bonuses Improve Productivity, Study Shows," *Vancouver Sun,* September 13, 2002, p. D5; and "More Than 20 Percent of Japanese Firms Use Pay Systems Based on Performance," *Manpower Argus,* May 1998, p. 7.

82. M. Tanikawa, "Fujitsu Decides to Backtrack on Performance-Based Pay," *New York Times,* March 22, 2001, p. W1.

83. G. D. Jenkins Jr., N. Gupta, A. Mitra, and J. D. Shaw, "Are Financial Incentives Related to Performance? A Meta-Analytic Review of Empirical Research," *Journal of Applied Psychology,* October 1998, pp. 777–787.

84. T. Coupé, V. Smeets, and F. Warzynski, "Incentives, Sorting and Productivity Along the Career: Evidence from a Sample of Top Economists," *Journal of Law Economics & Organization* 22, no. 1 (April 2006), pp. 137–167.

85. A. Kauhanen and H. Piekkola, "What Makes Performance-Related Pay Schemes Work? Finnish Evidence," *Journal of Management and Governance* 10, no. 2 (2006), pp. 149–177.

86. E. Beauchesne, "Pay Bonuses Improve Productivity, Study Shows," *Vancouver Sun,* September 13, 2002, p. D5.

87. P. A. Siegel and D. C. Hambrick, "Pay Disparities within Top Management Groups: Evidence of Harmful Effects on Performance of High-Technology Firms," *Organization Science* 16, no. 3 (May–June 2005), pp. 259–276; S. Kerr, "Practical, Cost-Neutral Alternatives That You May Know, But Don't Practice," *Organizational Dynamics* 28, no. 1 (1999), pp. 61–70; E. E. Lawler, *Strategic Pay* (San Francisco: Jossey Bass, 1990); and J. Pfeffer, *The Human Equation: Building Profits by Putting People First* (Boston: Harvard Business School Press, 1998).

88. T. Reason, "Why Bonus Plans Fail," *CFO,* January 2003, p. 53; and "Has Pay for Performance Had Its Day?" *McKinsey Quarterly,* no. 4, 2002, via *Forbes* website, www.forbes.com/smallbusiness/2002/10/22/1022mckinsey.html (accessed September 20, 2007).

89. V. Sanderson, "Sweetening Their Slice: More Hardware and Lumberyard Dealers Are Investing in Profit-Sharing Programs as a Way to Promote Employee Loyalty," *Hardware Merchandising,* May–June 2003, p. 66.

90. R. J. Long, "Patterns of Workplace Innovations in Canada," *Relations Industrielles* 44, no. 4 (1989), pp. 805–826; R. J. Long, "Motives for Profit Sharing: A Study of Canadian Chief Executive Officers," *Relations Industrielles* 52, no. 4 (1997), pp. 712–723; and T. H. Wagar and R. J. Long, "Profit Sharing in Canada: Incidences and

Predictors," *Proceedings of the Administrative Sciences Association of Canada (Human Resources Division)*, 1995, pp. 97–105.

91. J. McFarland, "Missing Link: CEO Pay and Results," *Globe and Mail*, June 1, 2006, p. B1.

92. C. Howe, "Compensation Committees Face Increasing Challenges, Demands," *Canadian HR Reporter*, May 3, 2010.

93. W. J. Duncan, "Stock Ownership and Work Motivation," *Organizational Dynamics*, Summer 2001, pp. 1–11.

94. P. Brandes, R. Dharwadkar, and G. V. Lemesis, "Effective Employee Stock Option Design: Reconciling Stakeholder, Strategic, and Motivational Factors," *Academy of Management Executive*, February 2003, pp. 77–95; and J. Blasi, D. Kruse, and A. Bernstein, *In the Company of Owners: The Truth About Stock Options* (New York: Basic Books, 2003).

95. This paragraph is based on "Paying Workers Well Is Not Enough, Surveys Finds," *Financial Post (National Post)*, May 16, 2001, p. C10.

96. K. A. Tucker and V. Allman, "Don't Be a Cat-and-Mouse Manager," *Gallup Brain*, brain.gallup.com, September 9, 2004.

97. This paragraph is based on D. Grigg and J. Newman, "Labour Researchers Define Job Satisfaction," *Vancouver Sun*, February 16, 2002, p. E2.

98. J. Greenberg and R. Baron, *Behavior in Organizations*, 6th ed. (Upper Saddle River, NJ: Prentice Hall, 1995). Reprinted by permission of Prentice Hall, Inc., Upper Saddle River, NJ.

99. Situation adapted from information in W. Zellner, "They Took More Than They Needed from Us," *BusinessWeek*, June 2, 2003, p. 58; "Coffee, Tea, or Bile?" *BusinessWeek*, June 2, 2003, p. 56; "US Airways Pilots' Stand on Management," *New York Times*, May 24, 2003, p. C2; and "US Airways Flight Attendants Delay Concession Talks," *New York Times*, December 4, 2002, p. C4.

100. Based on J. Marquez, "Best Buy Offers Choice in Its Long-term Incentive Program to Keep the Best and Brightest," *Workforce Management*, April 24, 2006, pp. 42–43; M. Boyle, "Best Buy's Giant Gamble," *Fortune*, April 3, 2006, pp. 68–75; J. S. Lublin, "A Few Share the Wealth," *Wall Street Journal*, December 12, 2005, pp. B1+; J. Thotta, "Reworking Work," *Time*, July 25, 2005, pp. 50–55; and M. V. Copeland, "Best Buy's Selling Machine," *Business 2.0*, July 2004, pp. 92–102.

101. A. Lashinsky, "Where Does Google Go Next?" *CNNMoney.com*, May 12, 2008; K. Hafner, "Google Options Make Masseuse a Multimillionaire," *New York Times* online, www.nytimes.com, November 12, 2007; Q. Hardy, "Close to the Vest," *Forbes*, July 2, 2007, pp. 40–42; K. J. Delaney, "Start-ups Make Inroads with Google's Work Force," *Wall Street Journal* online, www.wsj.com, June 28, 2007; and "Perk Place: The Benefits Offered by Google and Others May Be Grand, but They're All Business," *Knowledge@Wharton*, http://knowledge.wharton.upenn.edu, March 21, 2007.

102. Based on J. R. Hackman, "Work Design," in *Improving Life at Work*, ed. J. R. Hackman and J. L. Suttle, pp. 132–133 (Santa Monica, CA: Goodyear, 1977)

Chapter 16

1. Based on D. Cox, "Team Canada Has It All: Depth, Experience and, Oh Yes, Talent," *Toronto Star*, December 22, 2005, p. A1; M. MacDonald, "Teamwork Key to Gold—On and Off the Ice," *Nanaimo Daily News*, January 27, 2003, p. A9; S. Burnside and B. Beacon, "Lafleur Says Team Canada Well Chosen, Even if There's No Canadiens," *Canadian Press*, May 18, 2004; and "Primeau Looks Like Conn Man," *Star Phoenix*, May 17, 2004, p. C2.

2. W. Scanlan, "All Eyes Will Be on Stevie 'Y's' Guys: Hockey Canada's Job of Mining Gold at the 2010 Olympics Began Yesterday," *Ottawa Citizen*, October 19, 2008.

3. "Yzerman Gets Ready for Any Type of Game," *National Post*, July 3, 2009.

4. B. W. Tuckman and M. C. Jensen, "Stages of Small-Group Development Revisited," *Group and Organizational Studies*, December 1977, pp. 419–427; and M. F. Maples, "Group Development: Extending Tuckman's Theory," *Journal for Specialists in Group Work*, Fall 1988, pp. 17–23.

5. L. N. Jewell and H. J. Reitz, *Group Effectiveness in Organizations* (Glenview, IL: Scott Foresman, 1981); and M. Kaeter, "Repotting Mature Work Teams," *Training*, April 1994, pp. 54–56.

6. A. Robinson, "Canada Left to Lick Its Wounds," *Pittsburgh Post Gazette,* February, 26, 2006.

7. C. Cole, "Babcock Has All the Right Stuff: Team Canada Head Coach's Forceful Personality Perfect for Star-Laden Roster," *Vancouver Sun,* August 27, 2009.

8. A. Sobel, "The Beatles Principles," *Strategy+Business*, Spring 2006, p. 42.

9. This model is based on the work of P. S. Goodman, E. Ravlin, and M. Schminke, "Understanding Groups in Organizations," in *Research in Organizational Behavior*, vol. 9, ed. L. L. Cummings and B. M. Staw, pp. 124–128 (Greenwich, CT: JAI Press, 1987); J. R. Hackman, "The Design of Work Teams," in *Handbook of Organizational Behavior*, ed. J. W. Lorsch, pp. 315–342 (Upper Saddle River, NJ: Prentice Hall, 1987); G. R. Bushe and A. L. Johnson, "Contextual and Internal Variables Affecting Task Group Outcomes in Organizations," *Group and Organization Studies*, December 1989, pp. 462–482; M. A. Campion, C. J. Medsker, and A. C. Higgs, "Relations Between Work Group Characteristics and Effectiveness: Implications for Designing Effective Work Groups," *Personnel Psychology*, Winter 1993, pp. 823–850; D. E. Hyatt and T. M. Ruddy, "An Examination of the Relationship Between Work Group Characteristics, and Performance: Once More into the Breach," *Personnel Psychology*, Autumn 1997, pp. 553–585; and P. E. Tesluk and J. E. Mathieu, "Overcoming Roadblocks to Effectiveness: Incorporating Management of Performance Barriers into Models of Work Group Effectiveness," *Journal of Applied Psychology*, April 1999, pp. 200–217.

10. G. L. Stewart, "A Meta-Analytic Review of Relationships Between Team Design Features and Team Performance," *Journal of Management*, February 2006, pp. 29–54; T. Butler and J. Waldroop, "Understanding 'People' People," *Harvard Business Review*, June 2004, pp. 78–86; J. S. Bunderson, "Team Member Functional Background and Involvement in Management Teams: Direct Effects and the Moderating Role of Power Centralization," *Academy of Management Journal*, August 2003, pp. 458–474; and M. J. Stevens and M. A. Campion, "The Knowledge, Skill, and Ability Requirements for Teamwork: Implications for Human Resource Management," *Journal of Management*, Summer 1994, pp. 503–530.

11. V. U. Druskat and S. B. Wolff, "The Link Between Emotions and Team Effectiveness: How Teams Engage Members and Build Effective Task Processes," *Academy of Management Proceedings*, on CD-ROM, 1999; D. C. Kinlaw, *Developing Superior Work Teams: Building Quality and the Competitive Edge* (San Diego: Lexington, 1991); and M. E. Shaw, *Contemporary Topics in Social Psychology* (Morristown, NJ: General Learning Press, 1976), pp. 350–351.

12. McMurry, Inc., "The Roles Your People Play," *Managing People at Work*, October 2005, p. 4; G. Prince, "Recognizing Genuine Teamwork," *Supervisory Management*, April 1989, pp. 25–36;

R. F. Bales, *SYMLOG Case Study Kit* (New York: The Free Press, 1980); and K. D. Benne and P. Sheats, "Functional Roles of Group Members," *Journal of Social Issues* 4 (1948), pp. 41–49.

13. A. Erez, H. Elms, and E. Fong, "Lying, Cheating, Stealing: Groups and the Ring of Gyges" (paper presented at the Academy of Management Annual meeting, Honolulu, HI, August 8, 2005).

14. S. E. Asch, "Effects of Group Pressure upon the Modification and Distortion of Judgments," in *Groups, Leadership and Men*, ed. H. Guetzkow, pp. 177–190 (Pittsburgh: Carnegie Press, 1951); and S. E. Asch, "Studies of Independence and Conformity: A Minority of One Against a Unanimous Majority," *Psychological Monographs: General and Applied* 70, no. 9 (1956), pp. 1–70.

15. R. Bond and P. B. Smith, "Culture and Conformity: A Meta-Analysis of Studies Using Asch's [1952, 1956] Line Judgment Task," *Psychological Bulletin*, January 1996, pp. 111–137.

16. M. E. Turner and A. R. Pratkanis, "Mitigating Groupthink by Stimulating Constructive Conflict," in *Using Conflict in Organizations*, ed. C. DeDreu and E. Van deVliert, pp. 53–71 (London: Sage, 1997).

17. A. Deutschman, "Inside the Mind of Jeff Bezos," *Fast Company*, August 2004, pp. 50–58.

18. See, for instance, E. J. Thomas and C. F. Fink, "Effects of Group Size," *Psychological Bulletin*, July 1963, pp. 371–384; and M. E. Shaw, *Group Dynamics: The Psychology of Small Group Behavior*, 3rd ed. (New York: McGraw-Hill, 1981).

19. R. C. Liden, S. J. Wayne, R. A. Jaworski, and N. Bennett, "Social Loafing: A Field Investigation," *Journal of Management*, April 2004, pp. 285–304; and D. R. Comer, "A Model of Social Loafing in Real Work Groups," *Human Relations*, June 1995, pp. 647–667.

20. S. G. Harkins and K. Szymanski, "Social Loafing and Group Evaluation," *Journal of Personality and Social Psychology*, December 1989, pp. 934–941.

21. C. R. Evans and K. L. Dion, "Group Cohesion and Performance: A Meta-Analysis," *Small Group Research*, May 1991, pp. 175–186; B. Mullen and C. Copper, "The Relation Between Group Cohesiveness and Performance: An Integration," *Psychological Bulletin*, March 1994, pp. 210–227; and P. M. Podsakoff, S. B. MacKenzie, and M. Ahearne, "Moderating Effects of Goal Acceptance on the Relationship Between Group Cohesiveness and Productivity," *Journal of Applied Psychology*, December 1997, pp. 974–983.

22. See, for example, L. Berkowitz, "Group Standards, Cohesiveness, and Productivity," *Human Relations*, November 1954, pp. 509–519; and B. Mullen and C. Copper, "The Relation Between Group Cohesiveness and Performance: An Integration," *Psychological Bulletin*, March 1994, pp. 210–227.

23. S. E. Seashore, *Group Cohesiveness in the Industrial Work Group* (Ann Arbor: University of Michigan, Survey Research Center, 1954).

24. M. Basadur and M. Head, "Team Performance and Satisfaction: A Link to Cognitive Style within a Process Framework," *Journal of Creative Behaviour* 35, no. 4 (2001), pp. 227–248.

25. C. Shaffran, "Mind Your Meeting: How to Become the Catalyst for Culture Change," *Communication World*, February–March 2003, pp. 26–29.

26. I. L. Janis, *Victims of Groupthink* (Boston: Houghton Mifflin, 1972); R. J. Aldag and S. Riggs Fuller, "Beyond Fiasco: A Reappraisal of the Groupthink Phenomenon and a New Model of Group Decision Processes," *Psychological Bulletin*, May 1993, pp. 533–552; and T. Kameda and S. Sugimori, "Psychological Entrapment in Group Decision Making: An Assigned Decision Rule and a Groupthink

Phenomenon," *Journal of Personality and Social Psychology*, August 1993, pp. 282–292.

27. See, for example, L. K. Michaelson, W. E. Watson, and R. H. Black, "A Realistic Test of Individual vs. Group Consensus Decision Making," *Journal of Applied Psychology* 74, no. 5 (1989), pp. 834–839; R. A. Henry, "Group Judgment Accuracy: Reliability and Validity of Postdiscussion Confidence Judgments," *Organizational Behavior and Human Decision Processes*, October 1993, pp. 11–27; P. W. Paese, M. Bieser, and M. E. Tubbs, "Framing Effects and Choice Shifts in Group Decision Making," *Organizational Behavior and Human Decision Processes*, October 1993, pp. 149–165; N. J. Castellan Jr., ed., *Individual and Group Decision Making* (Hillsdale, NJ: Lawrence Erlbaum Associates, 1993); and S. G. Straus and J. E. McGrath, "Does the Medium Matter? The Interaction of Task Type and Technology on Group Performance and Member Reactions," *Journal of Applied Psychology*, February 1994, pp. 87–97.

28. E. J. Thomas and C. F. Fink, "Effects of Group Size," *Psychological Bulletin*, July 1963, pp. 371–384; F. A. Shull, A. L. Delbecq, and L. L. Cummings, *Organizational Decision Making* (New York: McGraw-Hill, 1970), p. 151; A. P. Hare, *Handbook of Small Group Research* (New York: The Free Press, 1976); M. E. Shaw, *Group Dynamics: The Psychology of Small Group Behavior*, 3rd ed. (New York: McGraw-Hill, 1981); and P. Yetton and P. Bottger, "The Relationships Among Group Size, Member Ability, Social Decision Schemes, and Performance," *Organizational Behavior and Human Performance*, October 1983, pp. 145–159.

29. This section is adapted from S. P. Robbins, *Managing Organizational Conflict: A Nontraditional Approach* (Upper Saddle River, NJ: Prentice Hall, 1974), pp. 11–14. Also see D. Wagner-Johnson, "Managing Work Team Conflict: Assessment and Preventative Strategies," Center for the Study of Work Teams, University of North Texas, November 3, 2000, www.workteams.unt.edu/reports; and M. Kennedy, "Managing Conflict in Work Teams," Center for the Study of Work Teams, University of North Texas, November 3, 2000, www.workteams.unt.edu/reports.

30. See K. A. Jehn, "A Multimethod Examination of the Benefits and Detriments of Intragroup Conflict," *Administrative Science Quarterly*, June 1995, pp. 256–282; K. A. Jehn, "A Qualitative Analysis of Conflict Type and Dimensions in Organizational Groups," *Administrative Science Quarterly*, September 1997, pp. 530–557; K. A. Jehn, "Affective and Cognitive Conflict in Work Groups: Increasing Performance Through Value-Based Intragroup Conflict," in *Using Conflict in Organizations*, ed. C. DeDreu and E. Van deVliert, pp. 87–100 (London: Sage, 1997); K. A. Jehn and E. A. Mannix, "The Dynamic Nature of Conflict: A Longitudinal Study of Intragroup Conflict and Group Performance," *Academy of Management Journal*, April 2001, pp. 238–251; C. K. W. DeDreu and A. E. M. Van Vianen, "Managing Relationship Conflict and the Effectiveness of Organizational Teams," *Journal of Organizational Behavior*, May 2001, pp. 309–328; and J. Weiss and J. Hughes, "Want Collaboration? Accept—And Actively Manage—Conflict," *Harvard Business Review*, March 2005, pp. 92–101.

31. C. K. W. DeDreu, "When Too Little or Too Much Hurts: Evidence for a Curvilinear Relationship Between Task Conflict and Innovation in Teams," *Journal of Management*, February 2006, pp. 83–107.

32. K. W. Thomas, "Conflict and Negotiation Processes in Organizations," in *Handbook of Industrial and Organizational Psychology*, 2nd ed., vol. 3, ed. M. D. Dunnette and L. M. Hough, pp. 651–717 (Palo Alto, CA: Consulting Psychologists Press, 1992).

33. See, for example, J. R. Hackman and C. G. Morris, "Group Tasks, Group Interaction Process, and Group Performance Effectiveness: A Review and Proposed Integration," in *Advances in Experimental Social Psychology*, ed. L. Berkowitz, pp. 45–99 (New York: Academic

Press, 1975); R. Saavedra, P. C. Earley, and L. Van Dyne, "Complex Interdependence in Task-Performing Groups," *Journal of Applied Psychology*, February 1993, pp. 61–72; M. J. Waller, "Multiple-Task Performance in Groups," *Academy of Management Proceedings,* on disk, 1996; and K. A. Jehn, G. B. Northcraft, and M. A. Neale, "Why Differences Make a Difference: A Field Study of Diversity, Conflict, and Performance in Workgroups," *Administrative Science Quarterly*, December 1999, pp. 741–763.

34. E. Duhatschek, "Yzerman Making His List—and Checking It Twice," *Globe and Mail*, November 3, 2009.

35. Cited in T. Purdum, "Teaming, Take 2," *Industry-Week*, May 2005, p. 43; and C. Joinson, "Teams at Work," *HRMagazine*, May 1999, p. 30.

36. See, for example, S. A. Mohrman, S. G. Cohen, and A. M. Mohrman Jr., *Designing Team-Based Organizations* (San Francisco: Jossey-Bass, 1995); P. MacMillan, *The Performance Factor: Unlocking the Secrets of Teamwork* (Nashville, TN: Broadman & Holman, 2001); and E. Salas, C. A. Bowers, and E. Eden, eds., *Improving Teamwork in Organizations: Applications of Resource Management Training* (Mahwah, NJ: Lawrence Erlbaum, 2002).

37. See, for instance, E. Sunstrom, DeMeuse, and D. Futrell, "Work Teams: Applications and Effectiveness," *American Psychologist*, February 1990, pp. 120–133.

38. J. S. McClenahen, "Bearing Necessities," *IndustryWeek*, October 2004, pp. 63–65; P. J. Kiger, "Acxiom Rebuilds from Scratch," *Workforce*, December 2002, pp. 52–55; and T. Boles, "Viewpoint—Leadership Lessons from NASCAR," *IndustryWeek* online, May 21, 2002, www.industryweek.com.

39. M. Cianni and D. Wanuck, "Individual Growth and Team Enhancement: Moving Toward a New Model of Career Development," *Academy of Management Executive*, February 1997, pp. 105–115.

40. "Teams," *Training*, October 1996, p. 69; and C. Joinson "Teams at Work," *HRMagazine*, May 1999, p. 30.

41. G. M. Spreitzer, S. G. Cohen, and G. E. Ledford Jr., "Developing Effective Self-Managing Work Teams in Service Organizations," *Group & Organization Management*, September 1999, pp. 340–366.

42. "Meet the New Steel," *Fortune*, October 1, 2007, pp. 68–71.

43. J. Appleby and R. Davis, "Teamwork Used to Save Money; Now It Saves Lives," *USA Today* online, March 1, 2001, www.usatoday.com.

44. A. Malhotra, A. Majchrzak, R. Carman, and V. Lott, "Radical Innovation without Collocation: A Case Study at Boeing-Rocketdyne," *MIS Quarterly*, June 2001, pp. 229–249.

45. A. Stuart, "Virtual Agreement," *CFO*, November 2007, p. 24.

46. A. Malhotra, A. Majchrzak, and B. Rosen, "Leading Virtual Teams," *Academy of Management Perspectives*, February 2007, pp. 60–70; B. L. Kirkman and J. E. Mathieu, "The Dimensions and Antecedents of Team Virtuality," *Journal of Management*, October 2005, pp. 700–718; J. Gordon, "Do Your Virtual Teams Deliver Only Virtual Performance?" *Training*, June 2005, pp. 20–25; L. L. Martins, L. L. Gilson, and M. T. Maynard, "Virtual Teams: What Do We Know and Where Do We Go from Here?" *Journal of Management*, December 2004, pp. 805–835; S. A. Furst, M. Reeves, B. Rosen, and R. S. Blackburn, "Managing the Life Cycle of Virtual Teams," *Academy of Management Executive*, May 2004, pp. 6–20; B. L. Kirkman, B. Rosen, P. E. Tesluk, and C. B. Gibson, "The Impact of Team Empowerment on Virtual Team Performance: The Moderating Role of Face-to-Face Interaction," *Academy of Management Journal*, April 2004, pp. 175–192; F. Keenan and S. E. Ante, "The New Teamwork," *BusinessWeek e.biz*, February 18, 2002, pp. EB12–

EB16; and G. Imperato, "Real Tools for Virtual Teams," *Fast Company*, July 2000, pp. 378–387.

47. J. Mathieu, M. T. Maynard, T. Rapp, and L. Gilson, "Team Effectiveness 1997–2007: A Review of Recent Advancements and a Glimpse into the Future," *Journal of Management*, June 2008, pp. 410–476; S. W. Lester, B. W. Meglino, and M. A. Korsgaard, "The Antecedents and Consequences of Group Potency: A Longitudinal Investigation of Newly Formed Work Groups," *Academy of Management Journal*, April 2002, pp. 352–368; M. A. Marks, M. J. Sabella, C. S. Burke, and S. J. Zaccaro, "The Impact of Cross-Training on Team Effectiveness," *Journal of Applied Psychology*, February 2002, pp. 3–13; J. A. Colquitt, R. A. Noe, and C. L. Jackson, "Justice in Teams: Antecedents and Consequences of Procedural Justice Climate," *Personnel Psychology* 55 (2002), pp. 83–100; J. M. Phillips and E. A. Douthitt, "The Role of Justice in Team Member Satisfaction with the Leader and Attachment to the Team," *Journal of Applied Psychology*, April 2001, pp. 316–325; J. E. Mathieu, et al., "The Influence of Shared Mental Models on Team Process and Performance," *Journal of Applied Psychology*, April 2000, pp. 273–283; G. L. Stewart and M. R. Barrick, "Team Structure and Performance: Assessing the Mediating Role of Intrateam Process and the Moderating Role of Task Type," *Academy of Management Journal*, April 2000, pp. 135–148; J. D. Shaw, M. K. Duffy, and E. M. Stark, "Interdependence and Preference for Group Work: Main and Congruence Effects on the Satisfaction and Performance of Group Members," *Journal of Management* 26, no. 2 (2000), pp. 259–279; V. U. Druskat and S. B. Wolff, "The Link Between Emotions and Team Effectiveness: How Teams Engage Members and Build Effective Task Processes," *Academy of Management Proceedings*, on CD-ROM, 1999; R. Forrester and A. B. Drexler, "A Model for Team-Based Organization Performance," *Academy of Management Executive*, August 1999, pp. 36–49; A. R. Jassawalla and H. C. Sashittal, "Building Collaborative Cross-Functional New Product Teams," *Academy of Management Executive*, August 1999, pp. 50–63; and G. R. Jones and G. M. George, "The Experience and Evolution of Trust: Implications for Cooperation and Teamwork," *Academy of Management Review*, July 1998, pp. 531–546.

48. R. MacGregor, "Grezky and Yzerman Ranted, but Yzerman Remains Calm," *Globe and Mail*, February 23, 2010.

49. B. L. Kirkman, C. B. Gibson, and D. L. Shapiro, "Exporting Teams: Enhancing the Implementation and Effectiveness of Work Teams in Global Affiliates," *Organizational Dynamics*, Summer 2001, pp. 12–29; J. W. Bing and C. M. Bing, "Helping Global Teams Compete," *Training & Development*, March 2001, pp. 70–71; C. G. Andrews, "Factors That Impact Multi-Cultural Team Performance," Center for the Study of Work Teams, University of North Texas, November 3, 2000, www.workteams.unt.edu/reports/; P. Christopher Earley and E. Mosakowski, "Creating Hybrid Team Cultures: An Empirical Test of Transnational Team Functioning," *Academy of Management Journal*, February 2000, pp. 26–49; J. Tata, "The Cultural Context of Teams: An Integrative Model of National Culture, Work Team Characteristics, and Team Effectiveness," *Academy of Management Proceedings*, on CD-ROM, 1999; D. I. Jung, K. B. Baik, and J. J. Sosik, "A Longitudinal Investigation of Group Characteristics and Work Group Performance: A Cross-Cultural Comparison," *Academy of Management Proceedings*, on CD-ROM, 1999; and C. B. Gibson, "They Do What They Believe They Can? Group-Efficacy Beliefs and Group Performance Across Tasks and Cultures," *Academy of Management Proceedings*, on CD-ROM, 1996.

50. R. Bond and P. B. Smith, "Culture and Conformity: A Meta-Analysis of Studies Using Asch's [1952, 1956] Line Judgment Task," *Psychological Bulletin*, January 1996, pp. 111–137.

51. I. L. Janis, *Groupthink*, 2nd ed. (New York: Houghton Mifflin, 1982), p. 175.

52. See P. C. Earley, "Social Loafing and Collectivism: A Comparison of the United States and the People's Republic of China," *Administrative Science Quarterly*, December 1989, pp. 565–581; and P. C. Earley, "East Meets West Meets Mideast: Further Explorations of Collectivistic and Individualistic Work Groups," *Academy of Management Journal*, April 1993, pp. 319–348.

53. N. J. Adler, *International Dimensions of Organizational Behavior*, 4th ed. (Cincinnati, OH: South-Western, 2002), p. 142.

54. K. B. Dahlin, L. R. Weingart, and P. J. Hinds, "Team Diversity and Information Use," *Academy of Management Journal*, December 2005, pp. 1107–1123.

55. N. J. Adler, *International Dimensions of Organizational Behavior*, 4th ed. (Cincinnati, OH: South-Western, 2002), p. 142.

56. S. Paul, I. M. Samarah, P. Seetharaman, and P. P. Mykytyn, "An Empirical Investigation of Collaborative Conflict Management Style in Group Support System-Based Global Virtual Teams," *Journal of Management Information Systems*, Winter 2005, pp. 185–222.

57. S. Chang and P. Tharenou, "Competencies Needed for Managing a Multicultural Workgroup," *Asia Pacific Journal of Human Resources* 42, no. 1 (2004), pp. 57–74; and N. J. Adler, *International Dimensions of Organizational Behavior*, 4th ed. (Cincinnati, OH: South-Western, 2002), p. 142.

58. C. E. Nicholls, H. W. Lane, and M. Brehm Brechu, "Taking Self-Managed Teams to Mexico," *Academy of Management Executive*, August 1999, pp. 15–27.

59. J. Reingold and J. L. Yang, "The Hidden Workplace: What's Your OQ?" *Fortune*, July 23, 2007, pp. 98–106; and P. Balkundi and D. A. Harrison, "Ties, Leaders, and Time in Teams: Strong Inference About Network Structures' Effects on Team Viability and Performance," *Academy of Management Journal*, February 2006, pp. 49–68.

60. T. Casciaro and M. S. Lobo, "Competent Jerks, Lovable Fools, and the Formation of Social Networks," *Harvard Business Review*, June 2005, pp. 92–99.

61. P. Balkundi and D. A. Harrison, "Ties, Leaders, and Time in Teams: Strong Inference About Network Structures' Effects on Team Viability and Performance," *Academy of Management Journal*, February 2006, pp. 49–68.

62. J. McGregor, "The Office Chart That Really Counts," *BusinessWeek*, February 27, 2006, pp. 48–49.

63. Adapted from D. A. Whetten and K. S. Cameron, *Developing Management Skills*, 3rd ed. (New York: HarperCollins, 1995), pp. 534–535.

64. M. Fackler, "Raising the Bar at Samsung," *New York Times*, April 25, 2006, www.nytimes.com/2006/04/25/technology/25samsung.html (accessed September 21, 2007); B. Breen, "The Seoul of Design," *Fast Company*, December 2005, pp. 90–97; E. Ramstad, "Standing Firm," *Wall Street Journal*, March 16, 2005, pp. A1+; D. Rocks and M. Ihlwan, "Samsung Design," *BusinessWeek*, December 6, 2004, pp. 88–96; and Interbrand Consulting Group, "Best Global Brands 2006," www.ourfishbowl.com/images/surveys/BGB06Report_072706.pdf (accessed September 20, 2007).

65. Based on M. Moskowitz and R. Levering, "100 Best Companies to Work For: 10 Great Companies to Work for in Europe: Ferrari Good Food, Good People, Lots of Fun—Sounds Like a European Holiday? No, It's a Great Job," *Fortune*, January 7, 2003, www.fortune.com; and www.ferrari.com (accessed 2004).

66. Based on P. L. Hunsaker, *Training in Management Skills* (Upper Saddle River, NJ: Prentice Hall, 2001), chapter 12.

Chapter 17

1. Based on "Energy Roughneck," *Canadian Business*, August 1996, pp. 20+; Hoover's Online, www.hoovers.com; and C. Cattaneo, "Husky CEO Lau Reveals Intention to Retire," *National Post (Financial Post)*, April 23, 2004, p. FP4.

2. Based on B. Hagenbauh, "State Quarter's Extra Leaf Grew Out of Lunch Break," *USA Today*, January 20, 2006, p. 1B.

3. K. A. Merchant, "The Control Function of Management," *Sloan Management Review*, Summer 1982, pp. 43–55.

4. E. Flamholtz, "Organizational Control Systems as a Managerial Tool," *California Management Review*, Winter 1979, p. 55.

5. "The CMA Competency Map," *Certified Management Consultants*, www.cma-Canada.org/index.cfm/ci_id/2544/la_id/1.htm (accessed August 22, 2010).

6. "The Top 1000: Canada's Power Book," *Globe and Mail*, www.globeinvestor.com/series/top1000.

7. S. Brearton and J. Daly, "50 Best Employers in Canada," *Globe and Mail*, December 29, 2003, p. 33; and "Study Guidelines," *Best Employers in Canada*, http://was7.hewitt.com/bestemployers/canada/study_guidelines.htm (accessed September 21, 2007).

8. See http://list.canadianbusiness.com/rankings/profit100/2008/intro/Default.aspx?sp2=1&d1=d&sc1=9 (accessed March 27, 2011).

9. P. Magnusson, "Your Jitters Are Their Lifeblood," *BusinessWeek*, April 14, 2003, p. 41; S. Williams, "Company Crisis: CEO Under Fire," *Hispanic Business*, March 2003, pp. 54–56; T. Purdum, "Preparing for the Worst," *IndustryWeek*, January 2003, pp. 53–55; and S. Leibs, "Lesson from 9/11: It's Not About Data," *CFO*, September 2002, pp. 31–32.

10. S. Kerr, "On the Folly of Rewarding A, While Hoping for B," *Academy of Management Journal*, December 1975, pp. 769–783.

11. Y. F. Jarrar and M. Zairi, "Future Trends in Benchmarking for Competitive Advantage: A Global Survey," *Total Quality Management*, December 2001, pp. 906–912.

12. M. Simpson and D. Kondouli, "A Practical Approach to Benchmarking in Three Service Industries," *Total Quality Management*, July 2000, pp. S623–S630.

13. K. N. Dervitsiotis, "Benchmarking and Paradigm Shifts," *Total Quality Management*, July 2000, pp. S641–S646.

14. See www.canada.com/nationalpost/entrepreneur/bouclair.html.

15. T. Leahy, "Extracting Diamonds in the Rough," *Business Finance*, August 2000, pp. 33–37.

16. Based on R. Luciw, "Firm's Application of New Management Practices Draws Praise from Analyst," *Globe and Mail*, March 2, 2005, p. B16, and T. Harbert, "Lean, Mean Six Sigma Machines," *Design News*, December 11, 2006.

17. H. Koontz and R. W. Bradspies, "Managing through Feedforward Control," *Business Horizons*, June 1972, pp. 25–36.

18. M. Helft, "The Human Hands Behind the Google Money Machine," *New York Times* online, June 2, 2008, www.nytimes.com.

19. "An Open Letter to McDonald's Customers," *Wall Street Journal*, August 22, 2001, p. A5.

20. W. H. Newman, *Constructive Control: Design and Use of Control Systems* (Upper Saddle River, NJ: Prentice Hall, 1975), p. 33.

21. R. Ilies and T. A. Judge, "Goal Regulation across Time: The Effects of Feedback and Affect," *Journal of Applied Psychology* 90, no. 3 (May 2005), pp. 453–467.

22. Based on C. Cattaneo, "Li May Usher in Sea Change at Air Canada," *National Post (Financial Post)*, November 24, 2003, p. FP03.

23. W. G. Ouchi, "A Conceptual Framework for the Design of Organizational Control Mechanisms," *Management Science*, August 1979, pp. 833–838; and W. G. Ouchi, "Markets, Bureaucracies, and Clans," *Administrative Science Quarterly*, March 1980, pp. 129–141.

24. Based on P. Fitzpatrick, "Wacky WestJet's Winning Ways: Passengers Respond to Stunts That Include Races to Determine Who Leaves the Airplane First," *National Post*, October 16, 2000, p. C1.

25. C. Cattaneo, "Li May Usher in Sea Change at Air Canada," *National Post (Financial Post)*, November 24, 2003, p. FP03; C. Cattaneo, "Stranger in a Strange Land," *National Post (Financial Post)*, December 13, 2003, p. FP1F; Husky Energy, *Annual Report 2006*, p. 6, www.huskyenergy.ca/downloads/InvestorRelations/2006/HSE_Annual2006.pdf (accessed September 22, 2007); and "Husky Energy [The Investor 500]," *Canadian Business*, www.canadianbusiness.com/rankings/investor500/index.jsp?pageID=profile&profile=16&year=2007&type=profile (accessed September 22, 2007).

26. F. Hansen, "The Value-Based Management Commitment," *Business Finance*, September 2001, pp. 2–5.

27. M. Acharya and T. Yew, "A New Kind of Top 10," *Toronto Star*, June 30, 2002, p. C01.

28. M. Acharya and T. Yew, "A New Kind of Top 10," *Toronto Star*, June 30, 2002, p. C01.

29. K. Lehn and A. K. Makhija, "EVA and MVA as Performance Measures and Signals for Strategic Change," *Strategy & Leadership*, May–June 1996, pp. 34–38.

30. S. Taub, "MVPs of MVA: Which Companies Created the Most Wealth for Shareholders Last Year? *CFO*, July 1, 2003, www.cfo.com (accessed June 22, 2004); and "America's Best Wealth Creators—2007 edition," *EVA Dimensions*, www.evadimensions.com/2007top20RankingSummary.pdf (accessed September 22, 2007).

31. Debra Black, "Rogers Data on Clients Found in Lot," *Toronto Star*, April 8, 2007, www.thestar.com/News/article/200727 (accessed May 20, 2007).

32. "When Wireless Works," *CIO*, February 12, 2002, www.cio.de (accessed July 2, 2004).

33. J. McPartlin, "Hackers Find Backers," *CFO*, January 2006, pp. 75–77; J. Swartz, "Data Losses Push Businesses to Encrypt Backup Tapes," *USA Today*, June 13, 2005, p. 1B; J. Goff, "New Holes for Hackers," *CFO*, May 2005, pp. 64–73; B. Grow, "Hacker Hunters," *BusinessWeek*, May 30, 2005, pp. 74–82; J. Swartz, "Crooks Slither into Net's Shady Nooks and Crannies," *USA Today*, October 21, 2004, pp. 1B+; J. Swartz, "Spam Can Hurt in More Ways Than One," *USA Today*, July 7, 2004, p. 3B; and T. Reason, "Stopping the Flow," *CFO*, September 2003, pp. 97–99.

34. D. Whelan, "Google Me Not," *Forbes*, August 16, 2004, pp. 102–104.

35. J. Levitz and J. Hechinger, "Laptops Prove Weakest Link in Data Security," *Wall Street Journal*, March 24, 2006, pp. B1+.

36. J. Markoff, "Study Says Chips in ID Tags Are Vulnerable to Viruses," *New York Times*, March 15, 2006, www.nytimes.com/2006/03/15/technology/15tag.html (accessed September 25, 2007).

37. Based on "Corporate Governance," Husky Energy, www.huskyenergy.ca/abouthusky/corporategovernance/ (accessed September 22, 2007).

38. J. Yaukey and C. L. Romero, "Arizona Firm Pays Big for Workers' Digital Downloads," *Springfield News-Leader*, May 6, 2002, p. 6B.

39. R. S. Kaplan and D. P. Norton, "How to Implement a New Strategy without Disrupting Your Organization," *Harvard Business Review*, March 2006, pp. 100–109; L. Bassi and D. McMurrer, "Developing Measurement Systems for Managing in the Knowledge Era," *Organizational Dynamics*, May 2005, pp. 185–196; G. M. J. de Koning, "Making the Balanced Scorecard Work (Part 2), *Gallup Brain*, August 12, 2004, http://brain.gallup.com; G. M. J. de Koning, "Making the Balanced Scorecard Work (Part 1), *GallupBrain*, July 8, 2004, http://brain.gallup.com; *Balanced Scorecard Collaborative*, June 29, 2003, www.bscol.com; K. Graham, "Balanced Scorecard," *New Zealand Management*, March 2003, pp. 32–34; K. Ellis, "A Ticket to Ride: Balanced Scorecard," *Training*, April 2001, p. 50; T. Leahy, "Tailoring the Balanced Scorecard," *Business Finance*, August 2000, pp. 53–56; and R. S. Kaplan and D. P. Norton, "Using the Balanced Scorecard as a Strategic Management System," *Harvard Business Review*, 74, no. 1 (January–February 1996), pp. 75–85.

40. T. Leahy, "Tailoring the Balanced Scorecard," *Business Finance*, August 2000, pp. 53–56.

41. See www.oha.com/KnowledgeCentre/Library/HospitalReports/Pages/HospitalReports.aspx (accessed October 14, 2007); and T. Leahy, "Tailoring the Balanced Scorecard," *Business Finance*, August 2000, pp. 53–56.

42. "A Revolution Where Everyone Wins: Worldwide Movement to Improve Corporate-Governance Standards," *BusinessWeek*, May 19, 2003, p. 72.

43. J. S. McClenahen, "Executives Expect More Board Input," *IndustryWeek*, October 2002, p. 12.

44. D. Salierno, "Boards Face Increased Responsibility," *Internal Auditor*, June 2003, pp. 14–15.

45. N. Shirouzu and J. Bigness, "7-Eleven Operators Resist System to Monitor Managers," *Wall Street Journal*, June 16, 1997, p. B1.

46. E. O'Connor, "Pulling the Plug on Cyberslackers," *StarPhoenix*, May 24, 2003, p. F22.

47. E. O'Connor, "Pulling the Plug on Cyberslackers," *StarPhoenix*, May 24, 2003, p. F22.

48. D. Hawkins, "Lawsuits Spur Rise in Employee Monitoring," *U.S. News & World Report*, August 13, 2001, p. 53; L. Guernsey, "You've Got Inappropriate Mail," *New York Times*, April 5, 2000, p. C11; and R. Karaim, "Setting E-Privacy Rules," *Cnnfn Online*, December 15, 1999, www.cnnfn.com.

49. E. Bott, "Are You Safe? Privacy Special Report," *PC Computing*, March 2000, pp. 87–88.

50. E. O'Connor, "Pulling the Plug on Cyberslackers," *StarPhoenix*, May 24, 2003, p. F22.

51. A. Tomlinson, "Heavy-Handed Net Policies Push Privacy Boundaries," *Canadian HR Reporter*, December 2, 2002, pp. 1–2.

52. C. Sorensen, "Canada Ranks High in Employee Theft: Global Survey Findings," *National Post*, May 28, 2004, p. FP9.

53. A. Perry, "Back-to-School Brings Pilfering: Some Employees Raid Office for Kids," *Toronto Star*, August 30, 2003, p. B01.

54. See PricewaterhouseCoopers Canada, "Canadian Retailers Lose Over $3 Billion Annually to Crime: Retail Council of Canada, PricewaterhouseCoopers Survey," September 16, 2009, www.pwc.com/ca/en/media/release/2009-09-16-canadian-retailers-crime.jhtml (accessed March 30, 2011).

55. J. Greenberg, "The STEAL Motive: Managing the Social Determinants of Employee Theft," in *Antisocial Behavior in Organizations*, ed. R. Giacalone and J. Greenberg), pp. 85–108 (Newbury Park, CA: Sage, 1997.

56. "Crime Spree," *BusinessWeek*, September 9, 2002, p. 8; B. P. Niehoff and R. J. Paul, "Causes of Employee Theft and Strategies That HR Managers Can Use for Prevention," *Human Resource Management*, Spring 2000, pp. 51–64; and G. Winter, "Taking at the Office Reaches New Heights: Employee Larceny Is Bigger and Bolder," *New York Times*, July 12, 2000, p. C11.

57. This section is based on J. Greenberg, *Behavior in Organizations: Understanding and Managing the Human Side of Work*, 8th ed. (Upper Saddle River, NJ: Prentice Hall, 2003), pp. 329–330.

58. A. H. Bell and D. M. Smith, "Why Some Employees Bite the Hand That Feeds Them," *Workforce*, May 16, 2000, www.workforce.com (accessed December 3, 2000).

59. A. H. Bell and D. M. Smith, "Protecting the Company against Theft and Fraud," *Workforce*, May 18, 2000, www.workforce.com (accessed December 3, 2000); J. D. Hansen, "To Catch a Thief," *Journal of Accountancy*, March 2000, pp. 43–46; and J. Greenberg, "The Cognitive Geometry of Employee Theft," in *Dysfunctional Behavior in Organizations: Nonviolent and Deviant Behavior*, ed. S. B. Bacharach, A. O'Leary-Kelly, J. M. Collins, and R. W. Griffin, pp. 147–193 (Stamford, CT: JAI Press, 1998).

60. Information from company website, www.enterprise.com (accessed June 29, 2003); A. Taylor, "Driving Customer Satisfaction," *Harvard Business Review*, July 2002, pp. 24–25.

61. S. D. Pugh, J. Dietz, J. W. Wiley, and S. M. Brooks, "Driving Service Effectiveness through Employee-Customer Linkages," *Academy of Management Executive*, November 2002, pp. 73–84.

62. T. S. Bateman and J. M. Crant, "The Proactive Component of Organizational Behavior: A Measure and Correlates," *Journal of Organizational Behavior*, March 1993, p. 112; and J. M. Crant, "Proactive Behavior in Organizations," *Journal of Management* 26, no. 3 (2000), pp. 435–462.

63. Situation adapted from information in K. Cushing, "E-Mail Policy," *Computer Weekly*, June 24, 2003, p. 8; and "Spam Leads to Lawsuit Fears, Lost Time," *InternetWeek*, June 23, 2003, www.internetweek.com.

64. K. Capell, "British Airways Hit by Heathrow Fiasco," *BusinessWeek*, April 3, 2008, p. 6; The Associated Press, "Problems Continue at Heathrow's Terminal 5," *International Herald Tribune* online, www.iht.com, March 31, 2008; M. Scott, "New Heathrow Hub: Slick, but No Savior," *BusinessWeek*, March 28, 2008, p. 11; and G. Katz, "Flights Are Canceled, Baggage Stranded, as London's New Heathrow Terminal Opens," *The Seattle Times* online, seattletimes.nwsource.com, March 27, 2008.

65. Based on E. Baron and E. O'Connor, "Why So Far Off Course?" *Province*(Vancouver), March 23, 2006, p. A3; W. Boei, M. Bridge, and L. Pynn, "99 Escape after Ship Runs Aground, Slides into Depths," *Vancouver Sun*, March 23, 2006, p. A1; C. E. Harnett, "Ferry Brass," *Times Colonist*(Victoria), June 6, 2006, p. A3; C. E. Harnett, "Human Error Sank B.C. Ferry," *Calgary Herald*, March 27, 2007, p. A5; D. Meissner, "New Details in Queen of North Report," *Daily News*, March 27, 2007, p. 1; C. Montgomery, "Loose Manifest Rules Led to Miscount," *Province*(Vancouver), March 28, 2006, p. A4; C.

Montgomery and I. Austin, "Human Error Is Faulted for Ship Sinking," *Province*(Vancouver), March 27, 2007, p. A6; and "Union Will Defend Fired Ferry Workers," *Kamloops Daily News*, May 7, 2007, p. A5.

66. With thanks to Denise Fortier, Bishop's University, who provided this insight.

67. Based on P. L. Hunsaker, *Training in Management Skills* (Upper Saddle River, NJ: Prentice Hall, 2001), pp. 60–61.

Chapter 18

1. Based onEldis Group home page, http://eldisgroup.com (accessed October 8, 2010).

2. Data from the Compete website, www.compete.com/ (accessed October 5, 2010).

3. D. Clark, "Inside Intel, It's All Copying," Wall Street Journal, October 28, 2002, pp. B1+.

4. D. McGinn, "Faster Food," *Newsweek*, April 19, 2004, pp. E20–E22.

5. D. McGinn, "Faster Food," *Newsweek*, April 19, 2004, pp. E20–E22; and *World Fact Book 2006*, www.odci.gov/cia/publications.

6. D. Michaels and J. L. Lunsford, "Streamlined Plane Making," *Wall Street Journal*, April 1, 2005, pp. B1+.

7. J. Ordonez, "McDonald's to Cut the Cooking Time of Its French Fries," *Wall Street Journal*, May 19, 2000, p. B2.

8. C. Fredman, "The Devil in the Details," Executive Edge, April–May 1999, pp. 36–39.

9. Information from [[Scaron]]koda website, www.skoda-auto.com (accessed May 30, 2006); and T. Mudd, "The Last Laugh," IndustryWeek, September 18, 2000, pp. 38–44.

10. S. Levy, "The Connected Company," Newsweek, April 28, 2003, pp. 40–48; and J. Teresko, "Plant Floor Strategy," IndustryWeek, July 2002, pp. 26–32.

11. T. Laseter, K. Ramdas, and D. Swerdlow, "The Supply Side of Design and Development," *Strategy+Business*, Summer 2003, p. 23; J. Jusko, "Not All Dollars and Cents," *IndustryWeek*, April 2002, p. 58; and D. Drickhamer, "Medical Marvel," *IndustryWeek*, March 2002, pp. 47–49.

12. J. H. Sheridan, "Managing the Value Chain," IndustryWeek, September 6, 1999, pp. 1–4.

13. J. H. Sheridan, "Managing the Value Chain," IndustryWeek, September 6, 1999, p. 3.

14. . Teresko, "Forward, March!" *IndustryWeek*, July 2004, pp. 43–48; D. Sharma, C. Lucier, and R. Molloy, "From Solutions to Symbiosis: Blending with Your Customers," *Strategy+Business*, Second Quarter 2002, pp. 38–48; and S. Leibs, "Getting Ready: Your Suppliers," *IndustryWeek*, September 6, 1999.

15. D. Bartholomew, "The Infrastructure," IndustryWeek, September 6, 1999, p. 1.

16. T. Stevens, "Integrated Product Development," IndustryWeek, June 2002, pp. 21–28.

17. T. Vinas, "A Map of the World: IW Value-Chain Survey," IndustryWeek, September 2005, pp. 27–34.

18. R. Normann and R. Ramirez, "From Value Chain to Value Constellation," *Harvard Business Review on Managing the Value Chain* (Boston: Harvard Business School Press, 2000), pp. 185–219.

19. J. Teresko, "The Tough Get Going," *IndustryWeek*, March 2005, pp. 25–32; D. M. Lambert and A. M. Knemeyer, "We're in This Together," *Harvard Business Review*, December 2004, pp. 114–122; and V. G. Narayanan and A. Raman, "Aligning Incentives in Supply Chains," *Harvard Business Review*, November 2004, pp. 94–102.

20. D. Drickhamer, "Looking for Value," IndustryWeek, December 2002, pp. 41–43.

21. J. Teresko, "Tying IT Assets to Process Success," *IndustryWeek*, September 2005, p. 21.

22. J. H. Sheridan, "Managing the Value Chain," *IndustryWeek*, September 6, 1999, p. 3.

23. S. Leibs, "Getting Ready: Your Customers," IndustryWeek, September 6, 1999, p. 1.

24. G. Taninecz, "Forging the Chain," *IndustryWeek*, May 15, 2000, pp. 40–46.

25. S. Leibs, "Getting Ready: Your Customers," *IndustryWeek*, September 6, 1999, p. 1.

26. Information in this box from J. McPartlin, "Making Waves," CFO-IT, Spring 2005, pp. 32–37.

27. ASIS International and Pinkerton, *Top Security Threats and Management Issues Facing Corporate America: 2003 Survey of Fortune 1000 Companies*, www.asisonline.org/newsroom/surveys/pinkerton.pdf.

28. J. H. Sheridan, "Managing the Value Chain," *IndustryWeek*, September 6, 1999, p. 4.

29. R. Russell and B. W. Taylor, *Operations Management*, 5th ed. (New York: Wiley, 2005); C. Liu-Lien Tan, "U.S. Response: Speedier Delivery," *Wall Street Journal*, November 18, 2004, pp. D1+; and C. Salter, "When Couches Fly," *Fast Company*, July 2004, pp. 80–81.

30. S. Anderson, "Restaurants Gear Up for Window Wars," *Springfield (Missouri) News-Leader*, January 27, 2006, p. 5B.

31. D. Bartholomew, "Quality Takes a Beating," *IndustryWeek*, March 2006, pp. 46–54; J. Carey and M. Arndt, "Making Pills the Smart Way," *BusinessWeek*, May 3, 2004, pp. 102–103; and A. Barrett, "Schering's Dr. Feelbetter?" *BusinessWeek*, June 23, 2003, pp. 55–56.

32. T. Vinas, "Six Sigma Rescue," *IndustryWeek*, March 2004, p. 12.

33. J. S. McClenahen, "Prairie Home Companion," *IndustryWeek*, October 2005, pp. 45–46.

34. T. Vinas, "Zeroing In on the Customer," *IndustryWeek*, October 2004, pp. 61–62.

35. W. Royal, "Spotlight Shines on Maquiladora," *IndustryWeek*, October 16, 2000, pp. 91–92.

36. See B. Whitford and R. Andrew, eds., The Pursuit of Quality (Perth, UK: Beaumont, 1994).

37. D. Drickhamer, "Road to Excellence," IndustryWeek, October 16, 2000, pp. 117–118.

38. Information from International Organization for Standardization, The ISO Survey—*2006*, www.iso.org/iso/survey2006.pdf.

39. "ISO 14000 Essentials," www.iso.org/iso/iso_catalogue/management_and_leadership_standards/environmental_management/iso_14000_essentials.htm (accessed October 7, 2010).

40. "ISO 26000—Social Responsibility," www.iso.org/iso/iso_catalogue/management_and_leadership_standards/social_responsibility.htm (accessed October 7, 2010).

41. G. Hasek, "Merger Marries Quality Efforts," *IndustryWeek*, August 21, 2000, pp. 89–92.

42. M. Arndt, "Quality Isn't Just for Widgets," *BusinessWeek*, July 22, 2002, pp. 72–73.

43. E. White, "Rethinking the Quality Improvement Program," Wall Street Journal, September 19, 2005, p. B3.

44. M. Arndt, "Quality Isn't Just for Widgets," *BusinessWeek*, July 22, 2002, pp. 72–73.

45. S. McMurray, "Ford's F-150: Have It Your Way," Business 2.0, March 2004, pp. 53–55; "Made-to-Fit Clothes Are on the Way," USA Today, July 2002, pp. 8–9; and L. Elliott, "Mass Customization Comes a Step Closer," Design News, February 18, 2002, p. 21.

46. E. Schonfeld, "The Customized, Digitized, Have-It-Your-Way Economy," *Fortune*, October 28, 1998, pp. 114–120.

47. G. Krishnan, "White Hat, Black Hat," *New Straits Times* (Malaysia), August 2, 2010, p. 24.

48. B. Prince, "How Black Hat SEO Abuses Search Engines," eWeek.com, August 16, 2010, www.eweek.com/c/a/Security/How-Black-Hat-SEO-Abuses-Search-Engines-607182/.

49. Based on D. Blanchard, "Lean In for a Smooth Ride," IndustryWeek, January 2008, p. 38; and D. Blanchard, "Blue Bird North Georgia: IW Best Plants Profile 2007," January 1, 2008, www.industryweek.com.

50. Information from Sepomex website, www.sepomex.gob.mx (accessed February 24, 2006); and A. Guthrie, "Going Postal," *Latin Trade*, July 2005, pp. 84–85.

51. "Enterprise-Class Features Delivered on Google's World-Class Platform," Google Analytics, www.google.com/analytics/features.html (accessed October 10, 2010).

GLOSSARY/SUBJECT INDEX

Note: Page references in bold refer to pages on which key terms have been defined.

A

Access to Information Act, 308

Accountability. The need to report and justify work to a manager's superiors. **268**

Achievement, 84, 201–202, 422

Achievement-oriented leader, 395, 396

Acid test ratio, 490f

Active listening. Listening for full meaning without making premature judgments or interpretations. **301**, 301f, 319–320

Activist (dark green) approach, 128

Activities. The time or resources needed to progress from one event to another in a PERT network. **246**

Activity ratios, 490f

Adaptable organization, 17–18

Adjourning stage. The final stage of group development for temporary groups, during which group members are concerned with wrapping up activities rather than task performance. **450**

African Union, 75

Aging population, 58

Ambiguity, 229–230

"Americanization," 85–86

Analytic style. A decision-making style characterized by a high tolerance for ambiguity and a rational way of thinking. **167**

Anti-discrimination legislation, 325

Application forms, 332f, 333f

Applied research. Research that accesses, rather than generates, new knowledge and applies it to a practical or commercial purpose. **107**–108

Asian financial crisis, 76

Assertiveness, 85, 86f

Assessment centres, 333f

Association of Southeast Asian Nations (ASEAN). A trading alliance of 10 Southeast Asian countries. **75**, 75f

Attractiveness of reward, 430

Audiotape training, 336f

Australia, 342, 434

Authority. The rights inherent in a managerial position to tell people what to do and to expect them to do it. **268**

Autocratic style. A leadership style where the leader tends to centralize authority, dictate work methods, make unilateral decisions, and limit employee participation. **389**

Automation, 362

Autonomy. The degree to which a job provides substantial freedom, independence, and discretion to the individual in scheduling work and determining the procedures to be used in carrying it out. **426**

B

Background investigations, 332f

Balanced scorecard. A performance measurement tool that looks at four areas—financial, customer, internal business process, and learning and growth assets—that contribute to a company's performance. **494**–495, 494f

Bargaining power of buyers, 221

BARS, 337f

Basic corrective action. Corrective action that looks at how and why performance deviated and then proceeds to correct the source of deviation. **484**

Basic research, 107

BCG matrix. A strategy tool that guides resource allocation decisions on the basis of market share and growth rate of businesses. **218**–219, 218f

Behavioural style. A decision making style characterized by a low tolerance for ambiguity and an intuitive way of thinking. **168**

Behavioural theories, 388–390, 388f

Belgium, 342, 434

Benchmark. The standard of excellence against which to measure and compare. **483**

Benchmarking. The search for the best practices among competitors or noncompetitors that lead to their superior performance. 240–241, 241f, **483**

Benefits, 338–339, 338f, 343

Biases, in decision making, 169–171, 170f

Big Five personality framework, 387–388

Bilingualism, 71

Black hat tactics, 529

Blogs, 317

Boards of directors, 495

Body language. Gestures, facial expressions, and other body movements that convey meaning. **294**

Borderless organization. A type of international company in which artificial geographical barriers are eliminated. **77**–78

Born global. An international company that chooses to go global from inception. **78**

Boundaries, 280

Boundaryless career, 340

Boundaryless organization. An organization that is not defined by a chain of command, places no limits on spans of control, and replaces departments with empowered teams. **280**

Bounded rationality. Limitations on a person's ability to interpret, process, and act on information. **159**–160

Brazil, 76

Breadth potential, 293

Breakeven analysis. A technique for identifying the point at which total revenue is just sufficient to cover total costs. **248**, 249f

Breakeven point (BE), 248

BRICS. A grouping acronym that refers to the countries of Brazil, Russia, India, China, and South Africa that are deemed to be at a similar stage of newly advanced economic development. **76**

Budget. A numerical plan for allocating resources to specific activities. **242**

Budgeting, 242, 243f, 260–261

Bureaucracy. A form of organization characterized by division of labour, a clearly defined hierarchy, detailed rules and regulations, and impersonal relationships. **32**, 32f

Bureaucratic control. An approach to control that emphasizes organizational authority and relies on administrative rules, regulations, procedures, and policies. **488**, 488f

Business (competitive) strategy. An organizational strategy that focuses on how the organization will compete in each of its businesses. **219**–224

    competitive advantage, 219–220

    cost leadership strategy, 221

    differentiation strategy, 222–223

    focus strategy, 222–223

    stuck in the middle, 223–224

Business model. A strategic design for how a company intends to profit from its strategies, work processes, and work activities. **209**

Business performance management (BPM) software. IT Software that provides key performance indicators to help managers monitor efficiency of projects and employees. Also known as corporate performance management software. **166**

Business plan. A written document that summarizes a business opportunity and defines and articulates how the identified opportunity is to be seized and exploited. **105**

Business Schools on an Innovation Mission, 17

Buyers, bargaining power of, 221

C

Calm waters metaphor, 357–358

Canada

    age cohorts, 58

    aging population, 58

    bilingualism, 71

    demographic trends, 325–327

    diversity, 14

    health care system, and subsidiaries, 80

    manufacturing technology, 512

    motivation, 434

    small business in, 98

    unionized workers, 324

Canada Labour Code, 325

Canadian Human Rights Act, 56–57, 325

Capabilities. An organization's skills and abilities that enable it to do the work activities needed in its business. **211**

Career. A sequence of positions held by a person during his or her lifetime. **339**

Career development, 339–340, 339f

Cases

    Apple, 116

    baggage-handling system, 504–505

    Best Buy, 444–445

    Blue Bird, 530

    C.F. Martin Guitar Company, 180–181

City of Ottawa, 148

Grafik Marketing Communications, 412–413

Haier Group, 231–232

Lend Lease Corporation, 204

Lipschultz Levin & Gray, 24–25

Mitsubishi Motors North America, 349–350

National Basketball Association (NBA), 91–92

Peerless Clothing, 258–259

Pfizer, 286

Ritz-Carlton, 65–66

Samsung Electronics, 471

Starwood Hotels, 380

Voyant Technologies, 318

Cash cows, 218

CD-ROM training, 336f

Celtic Tiger, 74

Centralization. The degree to which decision making is concentrated at a single point in the organization. **270**–272, 271f

Certainty. A condition in which a decision maker can make accurate decisions because the outcome of every alternative is known. **163**

Chain of command. The continuous line of authority that extends from the top of the organization to the lowest level and clarifies who reports to whom. **268**–269

Challenge, 51

Challenges of management, 12–16

Change
calm waters metaphor, 357–358
change agent, 360
change-capable organizations, 374f
change management, 359–363, 369–375
change process, 357–359, 358f
employee stress, 371–373, 372f
external forces, 355–356
forces for change, 354–357
internal forces, 356–357
issues in change management, 369–375
mistakes when leading change, 374f
organizational change, 107, 360
organizational culture, changing, 369–371
people, 362
reducing resistance, 364–365, 364f
resistance to change, 363–365, 381–382
responding to turbulent change, 377–378
situational factors, 370
stimulating innovation, 365–369
structure, 360–361
successful change, 373–375
technology, 361–362
types of change, 360–363, 360f
views of the change process, 357–359
white-water rapids metaphor, 358, 359

Change agent. Someone who acts as a catalyst and assumes the responsibility for managing the change process. **360**

Change-capable organizations, 374f

Change management, 359–363, 369–375

Channel. The medium a message travels along. **292**, 293–294, 295f, 296–297

Charismatic leaders. Enthusiastic, self-confident leaders whose personalities and actions influence people to behave in certain ways. **397**–398, 412

Charter of Rights and Freedoms, 325

Chief information officer (CIO), 400

China, 76, 404

Civil servant. A person who works in a local, provincial, or federal government department. **12**

Clan control. An approach to control in which employee behaviour is regulated by the shared values, norms, traditions, rituals, beliefs, and other aspects of the organization's culture. **488,** 488f

Classical view. The view that management's only social responsibility is to maximize profits. **121**

Classroom lectures, 336f

Clicks-and-bricks strategy, 226

Closed systems. Systems that are not influenced by and do not interact with their environment. **35**

Coaching, 336f

Code of ethics. A formal statement of an organization's primary values and the ethical rules it expects its employees to follow. 13, 138, **139**–140

Coercive power. The power a leader has to punish or control. **401**

COIN (community of interest), 18

Collaboration, 515–516

Collectivism, 83, 85, 86f

Command economy. An economic system in which all economic decisions are planned by a central government. **81**

Command groups, 449f

Commitment concept. The idea that plans should extend far enough to meet those commitments made today. **196**

Communication. The transfer and understanding of meaning. **291**
active listening, 301, 301f
barriers, 297–300
body language, 294
channel, 292, 293–294, 295f, 296–297
and customer service, 227, 310–311
decoding, 293
defensiveness, 298–299
diagonal communication, 303
direction of communication flow, 302–303
distortions, 296–297
downward communication, 302–303
effective communication, 294–302
and effective teams, 462
emotions, 298, 302
encoding, 292
face-to-face communication style, 314–316
feedback, 300
feedback loop, 297
filtering, 298
formal communication, 302
functions of, 292

grapevine, 305

informal communication, 302

information overload, 298

and information technology, 305–309

and the Internet, 309

interpersonal communication, 291

interpersonal communication process, 293, 293f

issues, 309–312

knowledge resources, management of, 309–310

language, 299, 301

lateral communication, 303

message, 292, 296

methods of interpersonal communication, 292–294

national culture, 300

noise, 293

nonverbal communication, 294

nonverbal cues, 302

organizational communication, 291, 302–305

overcoming barriers to communication, 300–302

"politically correct" communication, 311–312

receiver, 297

selective perception, 298

sender, 296

understanding, 290–292

upward communication, 303

verbal intonation, 294

Communication networks. The variety of patterns of vertical and horizontal flows of organizational communication. **303**–305, 304f

Communities of practice. Groups of people who share a concern, a set of problems, or a passion about a topic, and who deepen their knowledge and expertise in that area by interacting on an ongoing basis. **310**

Company rankings, 478–479

Compensation, 338–339, 338f

Competence, 402

Competition Act, 57

Competitive advantage. What sets an organization apart: its distinct edge. 101–103, **219**–220

Competitive forces, 220–221, 220f

Competitive strategy. See business (competitive) strategy

Competitor intelligence. Environmental scanning activity that seeks to identify who competitors are, what they are doing, and how their actions will affect the organization. **236**–237

Competitors
competitive forces, 220–221, 220f
described, 55
researching, 104–105

Complexity capacity, 293

Complexity (environmental), 59

Computer-virus hunters, 25–26

Computerization, 362

Concentration, 216

Conceptual skills. The mental ability to analyze and generate ideas about abstract and complex situations. **9**

Conceptual style. A decision making style characterized by a high tolerance for ambiguity and an intuitive way of thinking. **167**

Concurrent control. A type of control that takes place while an activity is in progress. **486**, 499*f*

Confidentiality, 293

Confirmation bias, 170

Conflict. Perceived incompatible differences that result in interference or opposition. **457**

Conflict management, 457–458, 459*f*

Conflict resolution, 51

Conformity, 453–454, 464

Consideration. The extent to which a leader has work relationships characterized by mutual trust and respect for group members' ideas and feelings. **389**

Consistency, 402

Contemporary organizational designs, 278–281, 278*f*

Contemporary planning techniques, 251–254

    project management, 251–253

    scenario planning, 253–254

Contemporary theories of motivation, 422–433, 432*f*

Contemporary views of leadership, 396–399

Contingency approach. An approach that says that organizations are different, face different situations (contingencies), and require different ways of managing. **36**

Contingency factors, 195–196, 275–277

Contingency plan. A plan for dealing with a worst-case situation or crisis (often referred to as a Plan B). **111**

Contingency planning, 253

Contingency theories of leadership, 390–396

Contingency variable, 36, 37*f*

Contingent workers, 435–436

Control process. A three-step process that includes measuring actual performance, comparing actual performance against a standard, and taking managerial action to correct deviations or inadequate standards. **480**–485, 480*f*

    comparison of performance against standard, 481–483

    managerial action, 483–484

    measurement of performance, 480–481, 481*f*

    summary of managerial decisions, 484–485

Controlling. A management function that involves monitoring actual performance, comparing actual performance to a standard, and taking correct action when necessary; the process of monitoring activities to ensure that they are being accomplished as planned, and correcting any significant deviations. **7**–8, **478**

    balanced scorecard, 494–495, 494*f*

    and communication, 292

control process, 480–485

controls. *See* controls

corporate governance, 495, 496*f*

cross-cultural differences, 496–497

customer interactions, 499–500

employee theft, 498–499, 499*f*

entrepreneurial venture, 110–112

importance of, 479–480

information, use of, 492–493

issues in control, 493–500

and organizational culture, 49*f*

organizational performance, 478–479

performance standards, 478

planning-controlling link, 479*f*

for quality, 522–523

tools for measuring organizational performance, 485–487

workplace concerns, 497–499, 497*f*

workplace privacy, 497–498, 497*f*

Controls

    see also controlling

    approaches to design of control systems, 488, 488*f*

    bureaucratic control, 488, 488*f*

    clan control, 488, 488*f*

    concurrent control, 486, 499*f*

    feedback control, 486–487, 499*f*

    feedforward control, 485–486, 499*f*

    financial controls, 489–491

    information controls, 491–493

    market control, 488, 488*f*

    methods of control, 487–488

    types of, 486*f*

Conventional level, 135

Coordination, 515–516

Core competencies. An organization's major value-creating skills, capabilities, and resources that determine its competitive advantage. **211**–212

Core values. The primary, or dominant, values that are accepted throughout the organization. **44**

Corporate governance. The system used to govern a corporation so that the interests of corporate owners are protected. **495**, 496*f*

Corporate portfolio analysis, 218–219

Corporate rituals, 47

Corporate social responsibility. *See* social responsibility

Corporate strategy. An organizational strategy that evaluates what businesses a company is in, should be in, or wants to be in, and what it wants to do with those businesses. **215**–219

    BCG matrix, 218–219, 218*f*

    corporate portfolio analysis, 218–219

    growth strategy, 216–217

    renewal strategies, 217–218

    retrenchment strategy, 217–218

    stability strategy, 217

    turnaround strategy, 218

Corporate veil, 116

The Corporation (Bakan), 85, 121

Corrective action, 483–484

Corruption, 140

Cost leadership strategy. A business strategy in which the organization sets out to be the lowest-cost producer in its industry. 221, **221**

Costs, 293

Counselling, 373

Country club management, 389–390, 390*f*

Creative destruction. The process of transformation that accompanies radical innovation, where the way things were done before is "destroyed." **97**

Creative problem solving, 182–183

Creativity. The ability to combine ideas in a unique way or to make unusual associations between ideas. **365**–366

Credibility. The degree to which followers perceive someone as honest, competent, and able to inspire. **401**

Crises, 111

Critical incidents, 337*f*

Critical path. The longest or most time-consuming sequence of events and activities in a PERT network. **246**, 248

Cross-cultural differences, 496–497

Cross-cultural leadership, 404, 404*f*

Cross-functional teams. Work teams made up of individuals who are experts in various functional specialties together; a work team composed of individuals from various specialties. **268**, 449*f*, **461**

Crown corporations. A commercial company owned by the government but independently managed. **12**

Cultural attitudes. *See* organizational culture

Cultural awareness, 93

Cultural change, 369–371

Cultural environment, 82–85

Cultural variables, 367–368

Culture

    cultural environment, 82–85

    national culture, 82–85, 300, 404, 424

    organizational. *See* organizational culture

Curiosity-driven research. Research directed toward acquiring new knowledge rather than toward some more practical objective (also referred to as basic research). **107**

Current ratio, 490*f*

Customer departmentalization, 267*f*

Customer evaluation, 239*f*

Customer-responsive culture, 51–52

Customer-responsive organization, 16

Customer service

    and communication, 227, 310–311

    strategies, 226

Customers

    attentiveness to needs of, 52

    challenges of, 16

    interactions with, 499–500

    needs of, 16

    as specific environment, 54–55

Customs, 44

D

Dark green approach, 128

Data. Raw, unanalyzed facts. **493**

Debates, 51

Debt to assets ratio, 490f

Decentralization. The degree to which lower-level employees provide input or actually make decisions. 270–272, 271f

Decision. A choice from two or more alternatives. **153**

see also decision making

nonprogrammed decisions, 162–163

organizational design decisions, 273–277

programmed decision, 161–162

structured problems, 161–162

types of decisions, 161–163

unstructured problems, 162–163

Decision criteria. Criteria that define what is relevant in making a decision. **155**

Decision making

see also decisions

biases, 169–171, 170f

bounded rationality, 159–160

calling it quits, 172

certainty, 163

conditions, 163–166

decision-making process, 153–158, 172

effective decision making, 172–173

errors, 169–171, 170f

five whys, 172

group decision making, 168–169, 456–457, 457f

heuristics, 169–171

highly reliable organizations (HROs), 173

intuitive decision making, 160–161, 176–177

manager as decision maker, 158–161, 159f

overview, 171, 171f

rational decision making, 158–159, 159f

risk, 163–164

styles, 166–168

uncertainty, 164–166

and workforce diversity, 183

Decision-making process. A set of eight steps that includes identifying a problem, selecting an alternative, and evaluating the decision's effectiveness. 153–158, **154**, 154f, 172

Decision-making rules, 139–140

Decision-making styles, 166–168, 167f

analytic style, 167

behavioural style, 168

conceptual style, 167

directive style, 167

Decision support system (DSS). A computer-based information system that provides decision makers with information relevant to the decisions they are making. **492**

Decisional roles. Management roles that involve making significant choices that affect the organization. **8**

Decoding. A receiver's translation of a sender's message. **293**

Decoding ease, 293

Recruitment. Techniques for reducing the organization's workforce. **328,** 329, 330f

Defensiveness, 298–299

Delegation. The assignment of authority to another person to carry out specific duties, allowing the employee to make some of the decisions. **269,** 287–288

Democratic style. A leadership style where the leader tends to involve employees in decision making, delegate authority, encourage participation in deciding work methods and goals, and use feedback as an opportunity for coaching employees. **389**

Demographic conditions, 58

Demographic trends, 325–327

Demographics, 103

Denmark, 434

Departmentalization. The basis on which jobs are grouped together. **266**–268, 267f

Design. See organizational design

Desire to lead, 387f

Diagnostic and analytical skills

baseball, and management, 259

BC Ferries, 505

changes in health care industry, 380–381

corporate responsibility, 149

cultural differences, 92

decision-making, and problems, 181

English-only rules, 318

Ferrari, 471–472

Google, 445

McDonald's, and Supersized Meals, 232

Mexico's state postal system, 530–531

Mississippi Power, 66

pandemic protection, 204–205

radical leadership, 413

Second Chance Program, 117

Svenska, 287

virus hunters, 25–26

wellness program, 350

Diagonal communication. Communication that cuts across both work areas and organizational levels. **303**

Differentiation strategy. A business strategy in which a company seeks to offer unique products that are widely valued by customers. **222**

Directional plans. Plans that are flexible and that set out general guidelines. **194,** 195f

Directive leader, 395, 396

Directive style. A decision-making style characterized by a low tolerance for ambiguity and a rational way of thinking. **167**

Discipline. Actions taken by a manager to enforce an organization's standards and regulations. **337**

Discrimination, 325

Dissatisfaction, 421, 421f

Distortions in communication, 296–297

Distributive justice. Perceived fairness of the amount and allocation of rewards among individuals. **429**–430

Diversification, 217

Diversity. See workforce diversity

Division of labour. The breakdown of jobs into narrow and repetitive tasks. **29**

Divisional structure. An organizational structure that consists of separate business units or divisions. **278**

Dogs, 218

Dominant culture. A system of shared meanings that expresses the core values of a majority of the organization's members; it gives the organization its distinct personality. **44**

Downsizing. The planned elimination of jobs in an organization. **345**

Downturns, 111

Downward communication. Communication that flows downward from managers to employees. **302**–303

Drive, 387f

Driving forces, 357

DVD training, 336f

Dynamic environment, 59, 197, 198–199

Dysfunctional conflicts. Conflicts that prevent a group from achieving its goals. **457**

E

E-business (electronic business). A way of doing business that relies on electronic (Internet based) linkages with employees, managers, customers, clients, suppliers, and partners to efficiently and effectively achieve goals. **15**

see also Internet

categories of e-business involvement, 15f

clicks-and-bricks strategy, 226

enabled organization, 16

enhanced organization, 15–16

strategies, 225–226

total e-business organization, 16

E-commerce (electronic commerce). The sales and marketing component of e-business. **15**

E-learning, 336f

Econometric models, 239f

Economic changes, 355

Economic environment, 56, 81

Economic indicators, 239f

Economic performance, and social responsibility, 125–126

Economic value added (EVA). A financial tool that measures corporate and divisional performance, calculated by taking after-tax operating profit minus the total annual cost of capital. **491**

Effective organizations, 17f

Effectiveness. Completing activities so that organizational goals are achieved; referred to as "doing the right things." **6,** 6f

Efficiency. Getting the most output from the least amount of inputs; referred to as "doing things right." **6,** 6*f*

Efficient organizations, 17

Effort-performance linkage, 430

Ego strength. A personality measure of the strength of a person's convictions. **135**

Electronic business. *See* e-business (electronic business)

Electronic commerce. *See* e-commerce (electronic commerce)

Email, 306, 309

Emotions, 298, 302

Employee benefits, 338–339, 338*f*, 343

Employee compensation, 338–339, 338*f*

Employee empowerment. Giving more authority to employees to make decisions. 52, **272, 403**

Employee job counselling. A process designed to help employees overcome performance related problems. **337**

Employee-oriented leaders, 389

Employee recognition programs. Reward programs that provide managers with opportunities to give employees personal attention and express interest, approval, and appreciation for a job well done. **436**–437

Employee recruitment. *See* recruitment

Employee retention, 107, 336–340

Employee rewards programs, 436–439

Employee stock ownership plan (ESOP). A company-established benefit plan in which employees acquire stock as part of their benefits. **438**

Employee theft. Any unauthorized taking of company property by employees for their personal use. **498**–499, 499*f*

Employees

    attitudes, 357

    contingent workers, 435–436

    counselling, 373

    customer needs, attentiveness to, 52

    employee ethics, factors affecting, 133–137, 134*f*

    front-line employees, 173

    keeping employees connected, 281

    minimum-wage employees, 434–435

    monitoring, 497–498, 497*f*

    motivation. *See* motivation

    new employees, integration of, 334

    organizational culture, learning about, 46–48

    orientation, 334, 342

    professional employees, 435

    recruitment of, 107

    reducing resistance, 364–365, 364*f*

    retention of, 107

    selection, and ethics, 139

    in service-oriented organizations, 52

    and shared organizational values, 131–132

    stress, 371–373, 372*f*

    technical employees, 435

    temporary employees, 435–436

training, 335–336, 335*f*, 336*f*, 342

and value chain management, 518, 520

whistle-blowers, 140, 142

Employment Equity Act, 325

Employment standards legislation, 325

Empowerment. *See* employee empowerment

Encoding. Converting a message into symbols. **292**

Encoding ease, 293

Entrepreneurial ventures. Organizations that are pursuing opportunities, are characterized by innovative practices, and have growth and financial viability as their main goals. **97**–98

    see also entrepreneurship

    adding value to economy, 97

    business plan, 105

    competitive advantage, 101–103

    competitors, researching, 104–105, 105*f*

    control issues, 110–112

    downturns, management of, 111

    environmental opportunities, 101–103

    exiting a venture, 112

    financing, researching, 105

    growth management, 111

    harvesting, 112

    human resource management, 106–107

    idea evaluation, 104, 104*f*

    idea generation, 103–104

    innovation, 107–109

    leadership issues, 109–110

    organizational change, 107

    organizational design and structure, 106

    planning issues, 101–105

    start-up issues, 101–105

Entrepreneurially alert. The ability to perceive opportunities for entrepreneurial profits by being sensitive to signals in the marketplace. **97**

Entrepreneurship. The process of starting new organizations, generally in response to opportunities; the act of turning an innovation into a viable venture. **97, 365**

    see also entrepreneurial venture

    context of, 96–100

    creative destruction, 97

    entrepreneurial managers, role of, 97–98

    ethics, 99–100

    importance of, 98

    vs. innovation, 365–366

    opportunities, nature of, 97–98

    organizational issues, 106–109

    self-assessment, 114–115

    small business, 98

    social enterprises/ventures, 97

    social responsibility, 99–100

    Timmons Model of entrepreneurial process, 100*f*

    what entrepreneurs do, 98–100

Environment. *See* global environment; organizational environment

Environmental assessment, 235–241

benchmarking, 240–241, 241*f*

competitor intelligence, 236–237

environmental scanning, 235–236

forecasting, 238–240

global scanning, 238

Environmental complexity. The number of components in an organization's environment and the extent of the organization's knowledge about those components. **59**

Environmental issues. *See* sustainable management

Environmental opportunities, 101–103

Environmental scanning. The screening of large amounts of information to anticipate and interpret changes in the environment. **235**–236

Environmental uncertainty. The degree of change and the degree of complexity in an organization's environment. 37*f*, **58**–60, 59*f*, 276

Equal Wages Guidelines, 325

Equipment, changes in, 356, 362

Equity, 428, 440

Equity theory. The theory that an employee compares his or her job's inputs–outcomes ratio with that of relevant others and then responds to correct any inequity. **428**–430, 428*f*, 434

Errors, in decision making, 169–171, 170*f*

Escalation of commitment. An increased commitment to a previous decision despite evidence that it might have been wrong. **170**

Esteem needs. A person's need for internal esteem factors such as self-respect, autonomy, and achievement, and external esteem factors such as status, recognition, and attention. **419**

Ethics. Rules and principles that define right and wrong behaviour. **132**

    CEOs, and corporate blogs, 317

    charismatic leadership, 412

    code of ethics, 13, 138, 139–140

    decision-making rules, 139–140, 141*f*

    described, 13–14

    employee compensation, 444

    employee ethics, factors affecting, 133–137, 134*f*

    and employee selection, 139

    and entrepreneurs, 99–100

    environmental organizations, 147

    executive compensation, 24

    formal protective mechanisms, 142

    four views of ethics, 132–133

    Global Compact, 138

    global context, 137–138

    global expansion, 91

    improving ethical behaviour, 139–142

    independent social audits, 142

    and individual characteristics, 135

    integrative social contracts theory, 133

    issue intensity, 136–137, 137*f*

    job goals, 140–141

    "just following orders," 286

and leadership, 140, 402–403

lifting the corporate veil, 116

moral development, 134–135, 134*f*

multiperson comparisons, 349

objectivity of investment advice, 180

and organizational culture, 50, 136

performance appraisal, 140–141

pleasing investors, 65

pressure to deliver results, 203

revenue forecast, 257–258

rights view of ethics, 133

self-assessment, 145–146

SEO tactics, 529

and social responsibility, 122–123

socially responsible management practices, 379

structural variables, 135–136

surfing adult websites at work, 504

sustainable management practices, 379

team players, 470–471

theory of justice view of ethics, 133

training, 142

used books, sale of, 231

utilitarian view of ethics, 132–133

whistle-blowing protection, 140

Ethnocentric attitude. The belief that the best work approaches and practices are those of the home country. 71*f*, **72**

Euro. A single common European currency. **73**

Euro area. A group of 17 member states of the European Union that use the euro as their currency. **74**

European Union (EU). A union of 27 European countries that forms an economic and political entity. **73**–74, 74*f*, 434

Events. End points that represent the completion of major activities in a PERT network. **246**, 247*f*

Executive compensation, 24

Exiting a venture, 112

Expectancy, 430

Expectancy theory. The theory that an individual tends to act in a certain way based on the expectation that the act will be followed by a given outcome and on the attractiveness of that outcome to the individual. **430**–431, 430*f*, 431*f*, 437

Experiential exercises, 336*f*

Expert power. Power that's based on expertise, special skills, or knowledge. **401**

Exporting. An approach to going global that involves making products at home and selling them abroad. **79**

External analysis, 212–213

External boundaries, 280

External constraints, 41

External environment. Outside forces and institutions that potentially can affect the organization's performance. **54**–58, 54*f*

general environment, 56–58

specific environment, 54–56

External forces for change, 355–356

External locus of control, 135

Extrinsic motivation. Motivation that comes from outside the person and includes such things as pay, bonuses, and other tangible rewards. **420**

Extroversion, 387*f*

F

Facial expressions, 294

Family-friendly benefits. Benefits that accommodate employees' needs for work–life balance. **343**

Fayol, Henri, 31–32

Fayol's 14 principles of management, 31

Feasibility of venture

competitors, researching, 104–105, 105*f*

financing, researching, 105

idea evaluation, 104, 104*f*

idea generation, 103–104

Feasibility study. An analysis of the various aspects of a proposed entrepreneurial venture that is designed to determine the feasibility of the venture. **104**

Feedback. The degree to which carrying out work activities required by a job results in the individual's obtaining direct and clear information about the effectiveness of his or her performance. 293, 300, 303, 347–348, 423–424, **426**, 506–507

Feedback control. A type of control that takes place after a work activity is done. **486**–487, 499*f*

Feedback loop, 297

Feedforward control. A type of control that focuses on preventing anticipated problems, since it takes place before the actual activity. **485**–486, 499*f*

Female leadership styles, 405, 406*f*

Fiedler contingency model. A leadership theory that proposed that effective group performance depended on the proper match between a leader's style and the degree to which the situation allowed the leader to control and influence. **391**–393, 392*f*

Filtering. The deliberate manipulation of information to make it appear more favourable to the receiver. **298**

Financial controls, 489–491

Financial ratios, 490, 490*f*

Financial reporting, 495

Financing, 105

Finland, 434

First-line managers. Managers at the lowest level of the organization who manage the work of nonmanagerial employees who are directly or indirectly involved with the production or creation of the organization's products. **4**

First mover. An organization that is first to bring a product innovation to the market or to use a new process innovation. **227**, 227*f*

Fixed costs, 248

Flexibility, 17

Flexible manufacturing, 524

Focus strategy. A business strategy in which a company pursues a cost or differentiation advantage in a narrow industry segment. **223**

Forces for change, 354–357

Forecasting, 238–240, 239*f*

Forecasts. Predictions of outcomes. **238**

Foreign subsidiary. An approach to going global that involves a direct investment in a foreign country by setting up a separate and independent production facility or office. 12, **80**

Formal communication. Communication that follows the official chain of command or is part of the communication required to do one's job. **302**

Formal planning, 186

see also planning

Formal planning department. A group of planning specialists whose sole responsibility is to help write the various organizational plans. **196**

Formality, 293

Formalization. The degree to which jobs within the organization are standardized and the extent to which employee behaviour is guided by rules and procedures. **272**–273

Forming stage. The first stage of group development, in which people join the group and then define the group's purpose, structure, and leadership. **449**

Franchising. An approach to going global in which a service organization gives a person or group the right to sell a product, using specific business methods and practices that are standardized. **79**

Free Trade Area of the Americas (FTAA), 75

Freedom, 51

Front-line employees, 173

Functional conflicts. Conflicts that support a group's goals and improve its performance. **457**

Functional departmentalization, 267*f*

Functional strategy. A strategy used by a functional department to support the business strategy of the organization. **224**

Functional structure. An organizational structure that groups similar or related occupational specialties together. **278**

Functions of management. *See* management functions

Future orientation, 85, 86*f*

G

G3 guidelines, 129

Gantt chart. A scheduling chart developed by Henry Gantt that shows output, both planned and actual, over a period of time. **244**, 244*f*

Gender differences, and leadership, 405, 406*f*

Gender differentiation, 85, 86*f*

General administrative theorists. Writers who developed general theories of what managers do and what constitutes good management practice. **31**–33

General Agreement on Tariffs and Trade (GATT), 76

General environment. Broad external conditions that may affect the organization. **56**–58

General training, 335f

Geocentric attitude. A world oriented view that focuses on using the best approaches and people from around the globe. 71f, **72**

Geographical departmentalization, 267f

Germany, 324, 434, 512

Gestures, 294

Gilbreth, Frank, 30–31

Gilbreth, Lillian, 30–31

Giving Pledge project, 101f

Global 100 Most Sustainable Corporations, 129

Global aging. The increase in the average age of the world's population. **58**

Global attitudes, 71f

Global Compact, 138

Global company. An international company that centralizes management and other decisions in the home country. **77**

Global Entrepreneurship Monitor (GEM), 98

Global environment

    borderless organization, 77–78

    born globals, 78

    cross-cultural leadership, 404, 404f

    cultural environment, 82–85

    doing business globally, 76–80

    economic environment, 81

    entrepreneurship, 98

    environmental problems, 127

    ethics, 137–138

    exporting, 79

    foreign subsidiary, 80

    franchising, 79

    global company, 77

    global sourcing, 78

    global trade, 73

    going international, 78–80, 78f

    importing, 79

    joint venture, 79

    legal-political environment, 81

    licensing, 79

    management in, 80–87

    multidomestic corporation, 77

    multinational corporation (MNC), 77

    organizational development, 362–363

    pros and cons of globalization, 85–87, 87f

    regional trading alliances, 73–76

    self-assessment, 89–90

    strategic alliances, 79

    teams, management of, 464–465

    transnational organization, 77–78

    types of international organizations, 77–78

    understanding, 72–76

Global environmental problems, 127

Global Innovation 1000, 108

Global outsourcing, 78

Global perspective, 71–72

Global scanning, 238

Global sourcing. Purchasing materials or labour from around the world wherever it is cheapest. **78**

Global structural issues, 282

Global teams, 464–465

Global trade, 73

Globalization, 14–15, 85–87, 87f

    see also global environment

GLOBE cultural assessment framework, 85, 86f, 404

Goal-setting theory. The proposition that specific goals increase performance and that difficult goals, when accepted, result in higher performance than do easy goals. **423**–424, 424f, 440

Goals. Desired outcomes for individuals, groups, or entire organizations. **188**

    approaches to establishing goals, 188–193

    commitment, 424

    and effective teams, 461

    goal-setting, 192–193, 205–206

    goal-setting theory, 423–424, 424f, 440

    job goals, and ethics, 140–141

    management by objectives (MBO), 190–191, 190f

    organizational goals, 6

    and planning, 479

    quality goals, 523–524

    and strategic management process, 211

    traditional goal setting, 188–190, 189f

    well-designed goals, characteristics of, 191, 191f

Government

    as employer, 11

    legislation, 56–57, 325, 355, 495

    public sector, 12

    regulations, 57, 355

Grapevine. The informal organizational communication network. **305**

Graphic rating scales, 337f

Great Britain, 434

Greece, 434

Group. Two or more interacting and interdependent individuals who come together to achieve particular goals. **449**

    adjourning stage, 450

    conflict management, 457–458, 459f

    effective teams, turning into, 459–463

    external conditions, 452

    formal groups, 449, 449f

    forming stage, 449

    group-based performance incentives, 438

    group decision making, 168–169, 456–457, 457f

    group development, stages of, 449–451, 450f

    group performance satisfaction model, 452f

    group processes, 456–458, 465

    group structure, 452–456, 464–465

    group tasks, 458–459

    informal groups, 449

    member resources, 452, 464

    norming stage, 449

    performance and satisfaction, 451–459

    performing stage, 450

    personality traits, 452

    size, 454–455

    social loafing, 455, 464

    storming stage, 449

    vs. teams, 460f

Group cohesiveness. The degree to which group members are attracted to one another and share the group's goals. **455**–456, 455f, 464

Group decision making, 168–169, 456–457, 457f

Group processes, 456–458, 465

Group structure, 452–456

    conformity, 453–454, 464

    global teams, 464

    group cohesiveness, 455–456, 455f, 464

    group size, 454–455

    norms, 453

    roles, 452–453

    status systems, 454, 464

Group tasks, 458–459

Groupthink. The withholding by group members of different views in order to appear to be in agreement; a phenomenon in which a group exerts extensive pressure on an individual to align his or her opinion with others' opinions. **169, 454**

Growth management, 111

Growth strategy. A corporate strategy that seeks to increase the organization's operations by expanding the number of products offered or markets served, either through its current business(es) or through new business(es). **216**–217

Gut feeling, 160

H

Hand motions, 294

Harvesting. Exiting a venture when an entrepreneur hopes to capitalize financially on the investment in the venture. **112**

Hawthorne Studies. A series of studies during the 1920s and 1930s that provided new insights into individual and group behaviour. **34**–35

Health care industry, 380–381

Hersey and Blanchard's situational leadership theory (SLT), 393–394, 394f

Herzberg's motivation-hygiene theory, 420–421, 421f

Heuristics. Rules of thumb that managers use to simplify decision making. **169**

Hierarchy of needs theory. Maslow's theory that there is a hierarchy of five human needs: physiological, safety, social, esteem, and self-actualization; as each need becomes satisfied, the next need becomes dominant. **419**–420, 419f, 434

High-high leader. A leader high in both initiating structure and consideration behaviours. **389**

High-performance work practices. Work practices that lead to both high individual and high organizational performance. **323**, 323f

Highly reliable organizations (HROs), 173

Hindsight bias, 171

Hofstede's cultural assessment framework, 83–84, 84

Home country, 72

Honesty, 387f

Horizontal integration, 216–217

Host country, 72

HR management information systems (HRMIS), 327

Human relations view of conflict. The view that conflict is a natural and inevitable outcome in any group. **457**

Human resource management
  assessment of current human resources, 327–328
  benefits, 338–339, 338f, 343
  career development, 339–340, 339f
  compensation, 338–339, 338f
  decruitment, 328, 329, 330f
  demographic trends, 325–327
  employee orientation, 334, 342
  employee recruitment, 107
  employee retention, 107, 336–340
  employee training, 335–336, 335f, 336f, 342
  entrepreneurial ventures, 106–107
  external factors, 324–327
  high-performance work practices, 323, 323f
  HR management information systems (HRMIS), 327
  human resource inventory, 327
  human resource planning, 327–328
  identification and selection of competent employees, 327–334
  importance of, 323
  innovation, and human resource variables, 366–368
  issues in, 340–345
  labour unions, 324–325
  layoffs, 345
  managers and, 322
  meeting future human resource needs, 328
  for non-human resource managers, 323
  performance appraisal methods, 337, 337f
  performance management system, 337
  process, 322–327, 324f
  realistic job preview (RJP), 333
  recruitment, 107, 328–329, 341
  selection devices, 332–333, 332f, 333f
  selection process, 139, 330–334, 341
  sexual harassment, management of, 342–343
  sources of potential candidates, 329f
  unsatisfactory performance, 337
  value chain management, 518, 520
  work-life balance, 343–345
  workforce diversity, 341–342

Human resource management process. Activities necessary for staffing the organization and sustaining high employee performance. 322–327, **323**, 324f

Human resource planning. The process by which managers ensure that they have the right number and kinds of people in the right places, and at the right times, who are capable of effectively and efficiently performing assigned tasks. **327**–328

Human skills. The ability to work well with other people, both individually and in a group. **9**

Humane orientation, 85, 86f

Humour, 51

Hygiene factors. Factors that eliminate job dissatisfaction, but don't motivate. **421**

I

Idea champions. Individuals who actively and enthusiastically support new ideas, build support, overcome resistance, and ensure that innovations are implemented. **369**

Idea evaluation, 104, 104f

Idea generation, 103–104

Idea time, 51

Ideal bureaucracy, 32, 32f

Immediate corrective action. Corrective action that corrects problems at once to get performance back on track. **484**

Importing. An approach to going global that involves acquiring products made abroad and selling them at home. **79**

Impoverished management, 389, 390f

In-group collectivism, 85, 86f

Inclusive workplace culture, 53

Incongruous situations and events, 102

Independent social audits, 142

India, 76

Individual differences, 37f, 439

Individualism, 83, 85, 86f

Industrial Revolution. The substitution of machine power for human power, which led to mass production. **29**

Industry analysis, 220f

Industry rankings, 478–479

Industry structures, 102–103

Informal communication. Communication that is not defined by the organization's structural hierarchy. **302**

Informal groups, 449

Informal planning, 185–186

Information. Processed and analyzed data. **493**

Information controls, 491–493

Information overload. When the information we have to work with exceeds our processing capacity. **298**

Information technology
  and communication, 305–309
  email, 306, 309
  instant messaging (IM), 307

and organizations, 308
  privacy issues, 308–309
  social networking websites, 307

Informational roles. Management roles that involve receiving, collecting, and disseminating information. **8**

Initiating structure. The extent to which a leader defines his or her role and the roles of group members in attaining goals. **389**

Innovation. The process of taking creative ideas and turning them into useful products, services, or work methods. **365**
  vs. creativity, 365–366
  cultural variables, 367–368
  entrepreneurial ventures, 107–109
  and entrepreneurship, 97, 98
  vs. entrepreneurship, 365–366
  human resource variables, 366–368
  importance of, 17–18
  nurturing innovation, 366–369
  stimulating innovation, 365–369
  strategies, 226–227
  structural variables, 366–367
  systems view of, 366f
  variables, 366–369, 367f

Innovative culture, 50–51

Instant messaging (IM), 307

Instrumentality, 430

Integrative social contracts theory. A view of ethics that proposes that ethical decisions be based on existing ethical norms in industries and communities in order to determine what constitutes right and wrong. **133**

Integrity, 387f, 402

Intellectual property. Proprietary information that's critical to an organization's efficient and effective functioning and competitiveness. **519**

Intelligence, 387f

Interactionist view of conflict. The view that some conflict is necessary for a group to perform effectively. **457**

Internal analysis, 211–212

Internal boundaries, 280

Internal constraints, 41

Internal forces for change, 356–357

Internal locus of control, 135

International context. See global environment

International new ventures (INVs), 78

International organizations, 77–78
  see also global environment

Internet
  see also e-business (electronic business)
  changes resulting from, 225
  communication, management of, 309
  e-business enabled organization, 16
  SEO tactics, 529
  surfing adult websites at work, 504

Interpersonal communication. Communication between two or more people. **291**
  active listening, 301, 301f

barriers, 297–300

channel, 293–294, 295f, 296–297

defensiveness, 298–299

distortions, 296–297

effective interpersonal communication, 294–302

emotions, 298, 302

feedback, 300

feedback loop, 297

filtering, 298

information overload, 298

language, 299, 301

message, 296

methods, 292–294

national culture, 300

nonverbal cues, 302

overcoming barriers to communication, 300–302

receiver, 297

selective perception, 298

sender, 296

Interpersonal communication process. The seven elements involved in transferring meaning from one person to another. **293,** 293f

Interpersonal roles. Management roles that involve working with people or performing duties that are ceremonial and symbolic in nature. **8**

Interpersonal skills

active listening, 319–320

budgeting, 260–261

creative problem solving, 182–183

delegation, 287–288

effective teams, 472–473

feedback, 506–507

goal-setting, 205–206

interviewing an entrepreneur, 117–118

interviews, 351–352

mentoring, 26–27

motivating jobs, designing, 445–446

operations management in e-world environment, 531–532

power, acquisition of, 414–415

reading an organization's culture, 67–68

resistance to change, management of, 381–382

scanning the environment, 233

trust-building, 149–150

Interpersonal warmth, 293

Interviews, 332f, 333, 333f, 351–352

Intrinsic motivation. Motivation that comes from the person's internal desire to do something, due to such things as interest, challenge, and personal satisfaction. **420**

Intuitive decision making. Making decisions on the basis of experience, feelings, and accumulated judgment. **160**–161, 176–177

Inventory turnover ratio, 490f

Involvement, 51

Ireland, 342

ISO 9000, 14000, and 26000. A series of international quality management standards that set uniform guidelines for processes to ensure that products conform to customer requirements. **523**

ISO standards, 14, 129, 523

Israel, 434

Issue intensity, 136–137, 137f

J

Japan, 83, 324, 342, 434, 512

Jargon. Specialized terminology or technical language that members of a group use to communicate among themselves. **299**

Job analysis. An assessment that defines jobs and the behaviours necessary to perform them. **328**

Job characteristics model (JCM). A framework for analyzing jobs and designing motivating jobs that identifies five core job dimensions, their interrelationships, and their impact on employees. **426**–427, 427f, 432

Job creation, 98

Job depth. The degree of control employees have over their work. **426**

Job description. A written statement of what a jobholder does, how it is done, and why it is done. **328**

Job design. The way tasks are combined to form complete jobs. **425**

Job design theory, 425–427, 427f

Job enlargement. The horizontal expansion of a job through increasing job scope. **425**

Job enrichment. The vertical expansion of a job by adding planning and evaluating responsibilities. **426**

Job goals, and ethics, 140–141

Job-relevant knowledge, 387f

Job rotation, 336f

Job scope. The number of different tasks required in a job and the frequency with which these tasks are repeated. **425**

Job specification. A statement of the minimum qualifications that a person must possess to perform a given job successfully. **328**

Joint venture. An approach to going global in which the partners agree to form a separate, independent organization for some business purpose; it is a type of strategic alliance. **79**

Jury of opinion, 239f

K

Knowledge management. Cultivating a learning culture in which an organization's members systematically gather knowledge and share it with others in the organization to achieve better performance. **18**

Knowledge resources, 309–310

L

Labour markets, 355

Labour union. An organization that represents employees and seeks to protect their interests through collective bargaining. **324**–325

Laissez-faire style. A leadership style where the leader tends to give the group complete freedom to make decisions and complete the work in whatever way it sees fit. **389**

Language, 299, 301

Language, and organizational culture, 48

Lateral communication. Communication that takes place among employees on the same organizational level. **303**

Latin American nations, 75

Layoff-survivor sickness. A set of attitudes, perceptions, and behaviours of employees who remain after involuntary employee reductions; it includes insecurity, guilt, depression, stress, fear, loss of loyalty, and reduced effort. **345**

Layoffs, 345

Leader. A person who can influence others and provide vision and strategy to the organization. **385**

see also leadership; leading

achievement-oriented leader, 395, 396

charismatic leader, 397–398, 412

credibility, 401

directive leader, 395, 396

employee-oriented leaders, 389

high-high leader, 389

participative leader, 395, 396

production-oriented leaders, 389

supportive leader, 395, 396

training, 406

transactional leaders, 397

transformational leaders, 397

Leader–member relations. One of Fiedler's situational contingencies that described the degree of confidence, trust, and respect employees had for their leader. **392**

Leadership. The process of influencing individuals or groups toward the achievement of goals. **385**

see also leaders; leading

behavioural dimensions, 389

behavioural theories, 388–390, 388f

charismatic-visionary leadership, 397–398

contemporary views of leadership, 396–399

contingency theories of leadership, 390–396

cross-cultural leadership, 404, 404f

early leadership theories, 386–390

effective leadership, 405–407

employee empowerment, 403

ethical leadership, 140, 402–403

Fiedler contingency model, 391–393, 392f

gender differences, 405, 406f

issues, 400–407

leadership school, 335

leadership styles, 389, 393, 409–411

managerial grid, 388f, 389–390, 390f

Ohio State studies, 388f, 389

path-goal theory, 394–396, 395*f*

power, management of, 401

radical leadership, 413

situational leadership theory (SLT), 393–394, 394*f*

substitutes for, 406–407

team leadership, 399, 399*f*, 463

trait theories, 387–388, 387*f*

transformational *vs.* transactional leadership, 397

trust, development of, 401–402

University of Iowa studies, 388*f*, 389

University of Michigan studies, 388*f*, 389

and value chain management, 516–517

Leading. A management function that involves motivating subordinates, directing the work of individuals or teams, selecting the most effective communication channels, and resolving employee behaviour issues. **7**

see also leaders; leadership

entrepreneurial venture, 109–110

and organizational culture, 49*f*

for quality, 521–522

Learning organization. An organization that has developed the capacity to continuously learn, adapt, and change. **18,** 18*f*, 281–282

Least-preferred co-worker (LPC) questionnaire. A questionnaire that measured whether a leader was task or relationship oriented. **391**

Legal (light green) approach, 128

Legal-political environment, 56–57, 81

Legislation, 56–57, 325, 355, 495

Legitimate power. The power a leader has as a result of his or her position in an organization. **401**

Leverage ratios, 490*f*

Licensing. An approach to going global in which a manufacturer gives another organization the right to use its brand name, technology, or product specifications. **79**

Light green approach, 128

Linear programming. A mathematical technique that solves resource allocation problems. **248**–250, 250*f*

Liquidity ratios, 490*f*

Listening skills, 52

Load chart. A modified Gantt chart that schedules capacity by entire departments or specific resources. **245**–246, 245*f*

Locus of control. A personality attribute that reflects the degree to which people believe they control their own fate. **135**

Long-term orientation, 84

Long-term plans. Plans with a time frame beyond three years. **193**

Low-cost leaders, 221

Loyalty, 402

M

Maintenance procedures, 492

Male leadership styles, 405

Management. Coordinating work activities so that they are completed efficiently and effectively with and through other people. **5**

see also manager

challenges of, 12–16

described, 5–10

diagnostic and analytical skills. *See* diagnostic and analytical skills

effectiveness, 6, 6*f*

efficiency, 6, 6*f*

functions, 6–8

in global environment, 80–87

historical background, 29

interpersonal skills. *See* interpersonal skills

managerial discretion, parameters of, 41*f*

motivation to manage, 22–23

omnipotent view of management, 39–40

roles, 8–9

and self-employment, 20

skills, 9–10

and social responsibility, 120–125

of stakeholder relationships, 60–61

strategic management. *See* strategic management

study of management, 18–20

sustainable management. *See* sustainable management

symbolic view of management, 39, 40–41

theories. *See* management theories

trends, history of, 28–37

universality of management, 19, 19*f*

values-based management, 130–132

Management by objectives (MBO). An approach to setting goals in which specific performance goals are jointly determined by employees and their managers, progress toward accomplishing those goals is periodically reviewed, and rewards are allocated on the basis of this progress. **190**–191, 190*f*

Management by walking around. A term used to describe a manager being out in the work area, interacting directly with employees. 481*f*, **486**

Management challenges, 12–16

Management functions. Planning, organizing, leading, and controlling. **6,** 7*f*

controlling, 7–8

leading, 7

vs. management roles, 9

organizing, 7

planning, 6–7

Management information system (MIS). A system used to provide management with needed information on a regular basis. **492**

Management roles. Specific categories of managerial behaviour. **8**

decisional roles, 8

informational roles, 8

interpersonal roles, 8

vs. management functions, 9

Mintzberg's management roles, 8, 8*f*

Management skills, 10*f*

conceptual skills, 9

human skills, 9

technical skills, 9

Management theories

contingency approach, 36

development of, 30*f*

general administrative theorists, 31–33

historical background of management, 29

organizational behaviour (OB), 33–35, 34*f*

quantitative approach, 33

scientific management, 29–31

summary of, 37, 37*f*

systems approach, 35–36, 36*f*

Management trends, 28–37

Manager. Someone who works with and through other people by coordinating their work activities in order to accomplish organizational goals. **4**

see also management

challenges facing managers, 12–16

as decision maker, 158–161, 159*f*

described, 4–5

entrepreneurial managers, 97–98

first-line managers, 4

functions, 6–8

global perspectives, 71–72

managerial levels, 5*f*

middle managers, 4

and organizational culture, 48–53, 49*f*

organizational environment, effect of, 58–61

project manager, 252–253

roles, 8–9

skills, 9–10

top managers, 4

types of managers, 4–5

what managers do, 5–10

Managerial ethics. *See* ethics

Managerial grid. A two-dimensional grid of leadership behaviours— concern for people and concern for production—that results in five different leadership styles. 388*f*, **389**–390, 390*f*

Manuals, 336*f*

Manufacturing organizations. Organizations that produce physical goods. **510**

Market approach, 128

Market control. An approach to control that emphasizes the use of external market mechanisms, such as price competition and relative market share, to establish the standards used in the control system. **488,** 488*f*

Market economy. An economic system in which resources are primarily owned and controlled by the private sector. **81**

Market growth, 218

Market share, 218

Market structures, 102–103

Market value added (MVA). A financial tool that measures the stock market's estimate of the value of a firm's past and expected capital investment projects. **491**

Marketing boards, 57

Marketplace, 355

Maslow's hierarchy of needs theory, 419–420, 419*f*, 434

Mass customization. Providing customers with a product when, where, and how they want it. **524**–525

Mass production. The production of items in large batches. **275**

Material symbols, 47–48

Matrix structure. An organizational structure that assigns specialists from different functional departments to work on one or more projects. **279**–280, 279*f*

Maximax choice, 164

Maximin choice, 164

MBO, 337*f*

McClelland's three-needs theory, 422

McGregor's Theory X and Theory Y, 420

Means–ends chain. An integrated network of goals in which the accomplishment of goals at one level serves as the means for achieving the goals, or ends, at the next level. **189**

Mechanistic organization. An organizational design that is rigid and tightly controlled. **273**–274, 273*f*

Mentoring, 26–27, 336*f*, 412–413

Mercosur, 75

Message. A purpose to be conveyed. **292**, 296

Mexico, 324, 342, 434, 530–531

Middle managers. Managers between the first-line level and the top level of the organization who manage the work of first-line managers. **4, 7**

Middle-of-the-road management, 389, 390*f*

Minimax choice, 164, 165

Minimum-wage employees, 434–435

Mintzberg's management roles, 8, 8*f*

Mission. The purpose of an organization. **192**, 211

Money, and rewards programs, 436, 440–441

Monolingualism, 71

Moral development, 134–135, 134*f*

Motivation. The process by which a person's efforts are energized, directed, and sustained toward attaining a goal. **417**–418

and communication, 292

contemporary theories of motivation, 422–433, 432*f*

contingent workers, 435–436

early theories of motivation, 418–422

employee rewards programs, 436–439

equity theory, 428–430, 428*f*, 434

expectancy theory, 430–431, 430*f*, 431*f*

extrinsic motivation, 420

goal-setting theory, 423–424, 424*f*

hierarchy of needs theory, 419–420, 419*f*, 434

intrinsic motivation, 420

issues in, 433–439

job characteristics model (JCM), 426–427, 432

job design theory, 425–427, 427*f*

job enlargement, 425

job enrichment, 426

minimum-wage employees, 434–435

motivation-hygiene theory, 420–421, 421*f*

process, 418*f*

professional employees, 435

reinforcement theory, 425, 432

suggestions for motivating employees, 439–441

technical employees, 435

Theory X and Theory Y, 420

three-needs theory, 422

workforce diversity, 433–436

Motivation-hygiene theory. Herzberg's theory that intrinsic factors are related to job satisfaction and motivation, whereas extrinsic factors are related to job dissatisfaction. **420**–421, 421*f*

Motivators. Factors that increase job satisfaction and motivation. **421**

Multidomestic corporation. An international company that decentralizes management and other decisions to the local country. **77**

Multinational corporations (MNCs). A broad term that refers to any and all types of international companies that maintain operations in multiple countries. **77**

Multiperson comparisons, 337*f*, 349

Mystery shoppers, 311

N

National culture. The values and attitudes shared by individuals from a specific country that shape their behaviour and beliefs about what is important. **82**–85, 300, 404, 424

Natural environment. *See* sustainable management

Need. An internal state that makes certain outcomes appear attractive. **418**

hierarchy of needs theory, 419–420, 419*f*

types of needs, 419

Need for achievement (nAch). The drive to succeed and excel in relation to a set of standards. **422**

Need for affiliation (nAff). The desire for friendly and close interpersonal relationships. **422**

Need for power (nPow). The need to make others behave in a way that they would not have behaved otherwise. **422**

Need-satisfying process, 418

Negotiation skills, 462

Netherlands, 342, 434

Network organization. A small core organization that outsources major business functions. **281**

New entrants, threat of, 221

New knowledge, 103

New Zealand, 342

NGOs (nongovernmental organizations). An organization that is independent from government control and whose primary focus is on humanitarian, development, and environmental sustainability activities. **12**

No Logo: Taking Aim at the Brand Bullies (Klein), 86

Noise. Disturbances that interfere with the transmission, receipt, or feedback of a message. **293**

Nongovernmental organizations. *See* NGOs (nongovernmental organizations)

Nonprogrammed decisions. Decisions that are unique and nonrecurring and require custom made solutions. **162**–163

Nonverbal communication. Communication transmitted without words. **294**

Nonverbal cues, 302

Norming stage. The third stage of group development, which is characterized by close relationships and cohesiveness. **449**

Norms. Standards or expectations that are accepted and shared by a group's members. **453**

North American Free Trade Agreement (NAFTA). An agreement among the Canadian, American, and Mexican governments in which barriers to free trade were reduced. **74**

Norway, 434

Not-for-profit organizations, 210

Not-for-profit sector. The part of the economy that is run by organizations which operate for purposes other than making a profit (that is, providing charity or services). **12**

Nurturing, 84

O

Occupational Health and Safety Act, 325

Ohio State studies, 388*f*, 389

Omnipotent view of management. The view that managers are directly responsible for an organization's success or failure. **39**–40

On-the-job training, 336*f*

Open systems. Systems that dynamically interact with their environment. **35**

Openness, 51, 402

Operating methods, 362

Operational plans. Plans that specify the details of how the overall goals are to be achieved. **193**

Operations management. The design, operation, and control of the transformation process that converts resources into goods and services. **509**

in e-world environment, 531–532

issues in, 520–525

manufacturing organizations, 510

mass customization, 524–525

operations system, 510*f*

productivity, 510–511, 511*f*

quality goals, 523–524

quality initiatives, 521–523

role of, 509–512

service organizations, 510

strategic role of, 511–512

technology, role of, 520–521

value chain management, 512–520

Operations system, 510f

Opportunities. Positive trends in external environmental factors. **212,** 213f

Oral reports, 481f

Organic organization. An organizational design that is highly adaptive and flexible. 273f, **274**

Organization. A deliberate arrangement of people who act together to accomplish some specific purpose. **10**

adaptable organization, building, 17–18

boundaryless organizations, 280

change-capable organizations, 374f

changing organization, 11f

characteristics, 10, 10f

composition, 10

customer-responsive organization, 16

described, 10–12

effective organizations, 17f

going international, 78–80, 78f

highly reliable organizations (HROs), 173

information technology, effect of, 308

international organizations, 77–78

learning organizations, 18, 18f, 281–282

manufacturing organizations, 510

network organizations, 281

not-for-profit organizations, 210

purpose, 10

service organizations, 510

size of organizations, 11, 37f, 275

structure, 10

traditional organization, 18f

types of organizations, 12

virtual organization, 280

Organization orientation, 334

Organizational barriers, 519

Organizational behaviour (OB), 34f

Organizational behaviour (OB). The field of study concerned with the actions (behaviour) of people at work. **33–35**

Organizational change. Any alteration of people, structure, or technology in an organization. 107, **360**

see also change

Organizational communication. All the patterns, networks, and systems of communication within an organization. **291**

communication networks, 303–305, 304f

diagonal communication, 303

direction of communication flow, 302–303

downward communication, 302–303

formal vs. informal communication, 302

grapevine, 305

lateral communication, 303

upward communication, 303

Organizational culture. A system of shared meaning and beliefs held by organizational members that determines, in large degree, how employees act. **42**

changing, 369–371

continuation of, 45–46

contrasting organizational cultures, 43f

current issues, 49–53, 49f

customer-responsive culture, 51–52

described, 42

as descriptive term, 42

dimensions of, 42, 43f

diversity, support of, 52–53

dominant culture, 44

establishment, 46f

ethics and, 50, 136

innovative culture, 50–51

and internal analysis, 212

language, 48

learning about, 46–48

maintenance, 46f

managers, effect on, 48–49

material symbols, 47–48

as perception, 42

reading an organization's culture, 67–68

rituals, 47

self-assessment, 63–64

shared culture, 42

situational factors, 370

socialization, 45–46

source of culture, 44–45

stories, 46–47

strong cultures, 43–44

subcultures, 44

transmission to employees, 46–48

and value chain management, 518, 519

weak cultures, 43–44

Organizational design. The process of developing or changing an organization's structure. **266**

see also organizational structure

boundaryless organizations, 280

challenges in, 281–282

changes in, 361

common organizational designs, 277–282

contemporary organizational designs, 278–281, 278f

contingency factors, 275–277

decisions, 273–277

divisional structure, 278

entrepreneurial ventures, 106

functional structure, 278

global structural issues, 282

keeping employees connected, 281

learning organization, 281–282

matrix structure, 279–280, 279f

mechanistic organization, 273–274, 273f

network organizations, 281

organic organization, 273f, 274

project structure, 279–280, 279f

simple structure, 277–278

team structure, 279

traditional organizational designs, 277–278, 277f

virtual organization, 280

Organizational development (OD). Techniques or programs to change people and the nature and quality of interpersonal work relationships. **362**–363

Organizational effectiveness. A measure of how appropriate organizational goals are and how well an organization is achieving those goals. **478**

Organizational environment

entrepreneurial opportunities, 101–103

environmental assessment, 235–241

environmental complexity, 59

environmental uncertainty, 58–60, 59f

external environment, 54–58, 54f

general environment, 56–58

global environment. See global environment

impact of, 53–54

managers, effect on, 58–61

scanning the environment, 233

specific environment, 54–56

stakeholder relationships, 60–61

Organizational goals, 6

Organizational performance. The accumulated end results of all the organization's work activities. **478**

see also performance

concurrent control, 486

feedback control, 486–487

feedforward control, 485–486

industry and company rankings, 478–479

measures of, 478–479

organizational effectiveness, 478

productivity, 478

tools for measuring, 485–487

Organizational processes. The ways that organizational work is done. **516**

Organizational strategies. See strategies

Organizational structure. How job tasks are formally divided, grouped, and coordinated within an organization. **266**

see also organizational design

centralization, 270–272, 271f

chain of command, 268–269

changes in, 360–361

decentralization, 270–272, 271f

departmentalization, 266–268, 267f

entrepreneurial ventures, 106

and environmental uncertainty, 276

and ethics, 135–136

formalization, 272–273

global structural issues, 282

and organizational size, 275

self-assessment, 284–285

span of control, 269–270, 270f

and strategy, 275

and technology, 275–276, 276f

work specialization, 266

Organizing. A management function that involves determining what tasks are to be done, who is to do them, how the tasks are to be grouped, who reports to whom, and where decisions are to be made. **7**

communication. *See* communication

and organizational culture, 49*f*

organizational design. *See* organizational design

organizational structure. *See* organizational structure

purposes of, 266

for quality, 521–522

Orientation. Introduction of a new employee to his or her job and the organization. **334**, 342

Outsourcing, 281

Overconfidence bias, 169

P

Paralinguistics, 294

Parochialism. A narrow view of the world; an inability to recognize the differences of other people. **71**

Participative leader, 395, 396

Path–goal theory. A leadership theory that says the leader's job is to assist followers in attaining their goals and to provide direction or support needed to ensure that their goals are compatible with those of the group or organization. **394**–396, 395*f*

Pay-for-performance programs. Variable compensation plans that pay employees on the basis of some performance measure. **437**–438

Payoff matrix, 165*f*

Perception, changes in, 103

Performance. The end result of an activity. **478**

comparison of, against standard, 481–483

correction of, 483–484

economic performance, and social responsibility, 125–126

employee rewards programs, 436–439

feedback, 347–348

measurement of, 480–481, 481*f*

organizational performance. *See* organizational performance

performance appraisal, 134–135, 140–141, 337, 337*f*

and planning, 186–187

unsatisfactory performance, 337

Performance incentives, 436–439

Performance management system. A process of establishing performance standards and evaluating performance in order to arrive at objective human resource decisions, as well as to provide documentation to support those decisions. **337**

Performance orientation, 85, 86*f*

Performance-reward linkage, 430

Performance-simulation tests, 332*f*

Performance standards, 478, 481–483, 484

Performing stage. The fourth stage of group development, when the group is fully functional and works on the group task. **450**

Personal Information and Electronic Documents Act (PIPEDA), 308–309

Personal observations, 481*f*

Personality, and ethics, 135

Personality traits, 387–388, 452

PERT network. A flow chart diagram that depicts the sequence of activities needed to complete a project and the time or costs associated with each activity. **246**–248, 247*f*

Physical examinations, 332*f*, 333*f*

Physiological needs. A person's need for food, drink, shelter, sexual satisfaction, and other physical requirements. **419**

Plan B, 111

Planning. A management function that involves defining goals, establishing a strategy for achieving those goals, and developing plans to integrate and coordinate activities. **6**–7, **185**

see also planning tools and techniques

approaches, 196

contingency factors, 195–196

contingency planning, 253

criticisms of, 197–198

described, 185–186

in dynamic environments, 197, 198–199

entrepreneurial ventures, 101–105

formal planning, 186

goals, 188–193, 479

in hierarchy of organizations, 195*f*

how managers plan, 187–196

human resource planning, 327–328

informal planning, 185–186

issues in planning, 197–200

and organizational culture, 49*f*

and performance, 186–187

personal planning, 256–257

planning-controlling link, 479*f*

plans, 188, 193–196

purposes of, 186

for quality, 521

top-down approach, 196

a venture, 105

Planning tools and techniques

benchmarking, 240–241, 241*f*

breakeven analysis, 248, 249*f*

budgeting, 242, 243*f*

competitor intelligence, 236–237

contemporary planning techniques, 251–254

environmental assessment, 235–241

environmental scanning, 235–236

forecasting, 238–240, 239*f*

Gantt chart, 244, 244*f*

global scanning, 238

linear programming, 248–250, 250*f*

load chart, 245–246, 245*f*

PERT network analysis, 246–248, 247*f*

project management, 251–253

resource allocation techniques, 241–250, 242*f*

scenario planning, 253–254

scheduling, 244–248

Plans. Documents that outline how goals are going to be met and that describe resource allocations, schedules, and other necessary actions to accomplish the goals. **188**

developing plans, 193–196

directional plans, 194, 195*f*

long-term plans, 193

operational plans, 193

short-term plans, 193

single-use plan, 194–195

specific plans, 193–194, 195*f*

standing plans, 195

strategic plans, 193

types of plans, 193–195, 194*f*

Playfulness, 51

Policy. A guideline for making a decision. **162**

Political attitudes, 56

Political conditions, 56–57

"Politically correct" communication, 311–312

Polycentric attitude. The view that the managers in the host country know the best work approaches and practices for running their businesses. 71*f*, **72**

Position power. One of Fiedler's situational contingencies that described the degree of influence a leader had over activities such as hiring, firing, discipline, promotions, and salary increases. **392**

Power, 401, 414–415, 422

Power distance, 83, 85, 86*f*

Preconventional level, 135

Principled level, 135

Principles of management. Fundamental rules of management that could be taught in schools and applied in all organizational situations. **31**–32

The Principles of Scientific Management (Winslow), 29

Privacy, 497–498

Privacy Act, 308

Privacy issues, 308–309

Private sector. The part of the economy that is run by organizations which are free from direct government control; organizations in this sector operate to make a profit. **12**

Privately held organization. A company whose shares are not available on the stock exchange but are privately held. **12**

Problem. A discrepancy between an existing and a desired state of affairs. **155**

Problem-solving team. A team from the same department or functional area that's involved in efforts to improve work activities or to solve specific problems. **460**

Procedural justice. Perceived fairness of the process used to determine the distribution of rewards. **429**–430

Procedure. A series of interrelated sequential steps that a decision maker can use to respond to a structured problem. **162**

Process conflict. Conflict over how work gets done. **457**

Process departmentalization, 267*f*

Process need, 102

Process production. The production of items in continuous processes. **275**

Product departmentalization, 267*f*

Product quality dimensions, 522*f*

Production-oriented leaders, 389

Productivity. The overall output of goods or services produced divided by the inputs needed to generate that output. **478, 510**–511, 511*f*, 527–528

Professional employees, 435

Profit margin on sales ratio, 490*f*

Profit-sharing plan. An organization-wide plan in which the employer shares profits with employees based on a predetermined formula. **438**

Profitability ratios, 490*f*

Programmed decisions. Repetitive decisions that can be handled by a routine approach. **162**

Project. A one-time-only set of activities that has a definite beginning and ending point in time. **251**

Project management. The task of getting a project's activities done on time, within budget, and according to specifications. **251**–253

Project management process, 252, 252*f*

Project manager, 252–253

Project structure. An organizational structure in which employees continuously work on projects. **279**–280, 279*f*

Psychographic profiles, 103

Public pressure groups, 55–56

Public-private partnerships, 361

Public sector. The part of the economy that is controlled by government. **12**

Publicly held organization. A company whose shares are available on the stock exchange for public trading. **12**

Q

Qualitative forecasting. Forecasting that uses the judgment and opinions of knowledgeable individuals to predict outcomes. **239**, 239*f*

Quality. The ability of a product or service to reliably do what it's supposed to do and to satisfy customer expectations. **521**

as competitive advantage, 219

controlling for quality, 522–523

dimensions, of goods and services, 522*f*

goals, 523–524

leading for quality, 521–522

organizing for quality, 521–522

planning for quality, 521

quality initiatives, 521–523

Quantitative approach. The use of quantitative techniques to improve decision making. **33**

Quantitative forecasting. Forecasting that applies a set of mathematical rules to a series of past data to predict outcomes. **239**, 239*f*

Question marks, 218

R

Radical leadership, 413

Range of variation. The acceptable degree of variation between actual performance and the standard. **481**, 482*f*

Rational decision making. Making decisions that are consistent and value-maximizing within specified constraints. **158**–159, 159*f*

Readiness. The extent to which people have the ability and willingness to accomplish a specific task. **393**

Realistic job preview (RJP). A preview of a job that includes both positive and negative information about the job and the company. **333**

Reality of work, 19–20

Receiver, 297

Recognition, 440

Recruitment. The process of locating, identifying, and attracting capable applicants. 107, **328**–329, 341

Reducing resistance, 364–365, 364*f*

Reference checks, 333*f*

Referent power. Power that arises because of a person's desirable resources or personal traits. **401**

Referents. Those things individuals compare themselves against in order to assess equity. **429**

Refreezing, 357

Regional trading alliances, 73–76

Regression models, 239*f*

Regret matrix, 165*f*

Regulations, 57, 355

see also legislation

Reinforcement theory. The theory that behaviour is a function of its consequences. **425**, 432

Reinforcers. Consequences immediately following a behaviour that increase the probability that the behaviour will be repeated. **425**

Related diversification. When a company grows by combining with firms in different, but related, industries. **217**

Relationship conflict. Conflict based on interpersonal relationships. **457**

Reliability. The ability of a selection device to measure the same thing consistently. **331**

Renewal strategy. A corporate strategy designed to address organizational weaknesses that are leading to performance declines. **217**–218

Research and development (R&D). Investigative activities that an organization conducts to lead to discoveries that will help develop new products or procedures. **108**

Resistance to change, 363–365, 381–382

Resource allocation techniques, 241–250, 242*f*

breakeven analysis, 248, 249*f*

budgeting, 242, 243*f*

Gantt chart, 244, 244*f*

linear programming, 248–250, 250*f*

load chart, 245–246, 245*f*

PERT network analysis, 246–248, 247*f*

Resource evaluation, 193

Resources. An organization's assets—financial, physical, human, intangible—that are used to develop, manufacture, and deliver products or services to customers. **211**

Responsibility. The obligation or expectation to perform any assigned duties. **268**

Restraining forces, 357

Retrenchment strategy. A short-run renewal strategy. **217**–218

Return on investment (ROI), 97, 490*f*

Revenue forecast, 257–258

Reverse engineering, 237

Reverse mentoring, 412–413

Reward allocation procedures, 135

Reward power. The power a leader has to give positive rewards. **401**

Rewards programs, 436–439

RFID. An automatic identification method in which information can be stored and remotely retrieved. **517**–518

Rights view of ethics. A view of ethics that is concerned with respecting and protecting individual liberties and privileges. **133**

Risk. A condition in which a decision maker is able to estimate the likelihood of certain outcomes. **163**–164

Risk-taking, 51

Rituals, 47

Role. Behaviour patterns expected of someone occupying a given position in a social unit. **452**–453

Role clarity, 52

Roles of management. *See* management roles

Rolling forecasts, 240

Romances, workplace, 342–343

Routine technologies, 37*f*

Rule. An explicit statement that tells a decision maker what he or she can or cannot do. **162**

Russia, 76

S

Safety needs. A person's need for security and protection from physical and emotional harm, as well as assurance that physical needs will continue to be met. **419**

Sales force composition, 239*f*

Sarbanes-Oxley Act, 495

Satellite TV, 336*f*

Satisfaction, 421, 421*f*

Satisfice. To accept solutions that are "good enough." **160**

Scanability, 293

ScanLife™ Barcode, 70

Scenario. A consistent view of what the future is likely to be. **253**

Scenario planning, 253–254

Scheduling. Detailing what activities have to be done, the order in which they are to be completed, who is to do each, and when they are to be completed. **244**–248

Scientific management. The use of the scientific method to determine the "one best way" for a job to be done. **29**–31

Second Chance Program, 117

Selection devices, 332–333, 332f, 333f

Selection process. The process of screening job applicants to ensure that the most appropriate candidates are hired. **330**–334

  described, 330–331

  and ethics, 139

  reliability, 331

  selection decision outcomes, 330f

  selection devices, 332–333, 332f, 333f

  validity, 331

  and workforce diversity, 341

Selective perception, 298

Selective perception bias, 170

Self-actualization needs. A person's need to grow and become what he or she is capable of becoming. **419**

Self-assessment

  achievement, 201–202

  ambiguity, 229–230

  entrepreneurship, 114–115

  ethics, 145–146

  face-to-face communication style, 314–316

  global management, 89–90

  intuition, 176–177

  leadership styles, 409–411

  motivation to manage, 22–23

  organizational culture, 63–64

  organizational structure, 284–285

  performance feedback, 347–348

  personal planning, 256–257

  proactivity, 502–503

  productivity, 527–528

  responding to turbulent change, 377–378

  rewards, 442–443

  team building and leading, 468–469

Self-confidence, 387f

Self-efficacy. An individual's belief that he or she is capable of performing a task. **424**

Self-employment, 20

Self-managed work team. A type of work team that operates without a manager and is responsible for a complete work process or segment. **461**

Self-serving bias, 171

Sender, 296

Senior management, 7

SEO tactics, 529

Service organizations. Organizations that produce nonphysical outputs in the form of services. **510**

Service-oriented organizations, 52

Service profit chain. The service sequence from employees to customers to profit. **500,** 500f

Service quality dimensions, 522f

Sexual harassment. Any unwelcome behaviour of a sexual nature in the workplace that negatively affects the work environment or leads to adverse job-related consequences for the employee. **342**–343

Shared values, 131–132, 131f

Short-term orientation, 84

Short-term plans. Plans with a time frame of one year or less. **193**

Silent Spring (Carson), 14, 127

Simple structure. An organizational structure with low departmentalization, wide spans of control, authority centralized in a single person, and little formalization. **277**–278

Singapore, 434

Single-use plan. A one-time plan specifically designed to meet the needs of a unique situation. **194**–195

Situational approach, 36

Situational factors, 370

Situational leadership® theory (SLT). A leadership contingency theory that focuses on followers' readiness. **393**–394, 394f

Six Sigma. A quality standard that establishes a goal of no more than 3.4 defects per million units or procedures. **524**

Skill-based pay. A pay system that rewards employees for the job skills and competencies they can demonstrate. **338**–339

Skill variety. The degree to which a job requires a variety of activities so that an employee can use a number of different skills and talents. **426**

Skills. *See* management skills; specific skills

Slack time. The amount of time an individual activity can be delayed without delaying the whole project. **246**

Small business. An organization that is independently owned, operated, and financed; has fewer than 100 employees; doesn't necessarily engage in any new or innovative practices; and has relatively little impact on its industry. **98**

Social attitudes, 56

Social audits, 142

Social enterprises/ventures. Organizations that are started in response to needs within the community. **97**

Social loafing. The tendency for individuals to expend less effort when working collectively than when working individually. **455,** 464

Social need. A need of a segment of society caused by factors such as physical and mental disabilities; language barriers; and cultural, social, or geographical isolation. **122**

Social needs. A person's need for affection, belongingness, acceptance, and friendship. **419**

Social network structure. The patterns of informal connections among individuals within a group. **465**–466

Social networking websites, 307

Social obligation. A firm's engaging in social actions because of its obligation to meet certain economic and legal responsibilities. **121**

Social planning, 17

Social responsibility. A business's intention, beyond its legal and economic obligations, to do the right things and act in ways that are good for society. **14, 122**

  acceptance by employees, 379

  vs. classical view, 121

  described, 122–123

  and economic performance, 125–126

  and entrepreneurs, 99–100

  ethical imperative, 122–123

  evolution of socially responsible management, 124–125, 124f

  management and, 120–125

  vs. social obligation, 121

  vs. social responsiveness, 122, 124

  vs. socio-economic view, 121

Social responsiveness. A firm's engaging in social actions in response to some popular social need. **122,** 124

Social return on investment (SROI), 97

Social screening. Applying social criteria (screens) to investment decisions. **126**

Socialization. The process that adapts employees to the organization's culture. **45**–46

Socially responsible investing (SRI), 126

Socio-cultural conditions, 57

Socio-economic view. The view that management's social responsibility goes beyond making profits and includes protecting and improving society's welfare. **121**

South Asian Association for Regional Cooperation (SAARC), 76

Southern Cone Common Market, 75

Span of control. The number of employees a manager can efficiently and effectively manage. **269**–270, 270f

Specific environment. The part of the external environment that is directly relevant to the achievement of an organization's goals. **54**–56

Specific plans. Plans that are clearly defined and that leave no room for interpretation. **193**–194, 195f

Specific training, 335f

Stability strategy. A corporate strategy characterized by an absence of significant change in what the organization is currently doing. **217**

Stable environment, 59

Stakeholder approach, 128

Stakeholder relationships, 60–61

Stakeholders. Any constituencies in the organization's external environment that are affected by the organization's decisions and actions. **60,** 60f

Standards. *See* ISO standards; performance standards

Standing plans. Ongoing plans that provide guidance for activities performed repeatedly. **195**

Stars, 218

Start-up activities, 99

Start-up issues, 101–105

Statistical reports, 481*f*

Status. A prestige grading, position, or rank within a group. **454,** 464

Status systems, 454

Stock options. A financial incentive that gives employees the right to purchase shares of company stock, at some time in the future, at a set price. **438**–439, 439*f*

Stories, 46–47

Storming stage. The second stage of group development, which is characterized by intragroup conflict. **449**

Strategic alliances. An approach to going global that involves a partnership between a domestic and a foreign company in which both share resources and knowledge in developing new products or building production facilities. **79**

Strategic business units (SBUs). Single businesses of an organization in several different businesses that are independent and formulate their own strategies. **219**

Strategic flexibility. The ability to recognize major external environmental changes, to quickly commit resources, and to recognize when a strategic decision was a mistake. **225**

Strategic management. What managers do to develop the organization's strategies. **209**

   see also strategies
   business model, 209
   described, 208–209
   external analysis, 212–213
   importance of, 208–210
   internal analysis, 211–212
   issues in, 224–227
   not-for-profit organizations, 210
   operations management, 511–512
   strategic flexibility, 225
   strategic management process, 210–214, 211*f*

Strategic management process. A six-step process that encompasses strategic planning, implementation, and evaluation. **210**–214, 211*f*

Strategic plans. Plans that apply to the entire organization, establish the organization's overall goals, and seek to position the organization in terms of its environment. **193**

Strategies. Plans for how an organization will do what it's in business to do, how it will compete successfully, and how it will attract and satisfy its customers in order to achieve its goals, **209**

   see also strategic management
   BCG matrix, 218–219, 218*f*

business strategy, 219–224
changes in, 356
clicks-and-bricks strategy, 226
corporate portfolio analysis, 218–219
corporate strategy, 215–219
cost leadership strategy, 221
customer service strategies, 226
differentiation strategy, 222–223
e-business strategies, 225–226
focus strategy, 223
formulation of, 213
functional strategies, 224
growth strategy, 216–217
identification of, 211
implementation of, 213–214, 214*f*
innovation strategies, 226–227
levels of organizational strategy, 215*f*
new directions in organizational strategies, 225–227
and organizational structure, 275
renewal strategies, 217–218
retrenchment strategy, 217–218
stability strategy, 217
stuck in the middle, 223–224
turnaround strategy, 218
types of, 214–224

Strengths. Any activities the organization does well or any unique resources that it has. **212**

Stress. The adverse reaction people have to excessive pressure placed on them from extraordinary demands, constraints, or opportunities. **371**–373, 372*f*

Stress reduction, 372–373

Strong cultures. Organizations in which the key values are deeply held and widely shared. **43**–44

Structural variables, 366–367

Structure. *See* organizational structure

Structured problems. Problems that are straightforward, familiar, and easily defined. **162**

Stuck in the middle. A situation in which an organization is unable to develop a competitive advantage through cost or differentiation. **223**–224

Study of management, 18–20

Subcultures. Minicultures within an organization, typically defined by department designations and geographical separation. **44**

Subsidiary. *See* foreign subsidiary

Substitutes, threat of, 221

Substitution effect, 239*f*

Sunk-costs error, 170

Supervisors, 4

Suppliers, 55

Supportive leader, 395, 396

Sustainable management. The recognition by business of the close link between its decisions and activities and their impact on the natural environment. **14,** 127

   acceptance by employees, 379
   activist (dark green) approach, 128

   approaches to, 127–128, 128*f*
   evaluation of, 129
   global environment problems, 127
   legal (light green) approach, 128
   market approach, 128
   stakeholder approach, 128

Sweden, 342, 434

SWOT analysis. An analysis of the organization's strengths, weaknesses, opportunities, and threats. **212**–213

Symbolic view of management. The view that managers have only a limited effect on substantive organizational outcomes because of the large number of factors outside their control. **39,** 40–41

Symbols, and organizational culture, 47–48

System. A set of interrelated and interdependent parts arranged in a manner that produces a unified whole. **35**

Systems approach, 35–36, 36*f*

T

Task conflict. Conflicts over content and goals of work. **457**

Task groups, 449*f*

Task identity. The degree to which a job requires completion of a whole and identifiable piece of work. **426**

Task management, 389, 390*f*

Task significance. The degree to which a job affects the lives or work of other people. **426**

Task structure. One of Fiedler's situational contingencies that described the degree to which job assignments were formalized and structured. **392**

Taylor, Frederick W. 29–30

Taylor's four principles of management, 30

Team leadership, 399, 399*f*, 463

Team management, 390, 390*f*

Team structure. An organizational structure in which the entire organization is made up of work groups or teams. **279**

Teams
   creating effective teams, 461–463, 462*f*, 472–473
   cross-functional teams, 268, 449*f*, 461
   effective teams, 459–463, 462*f*, 472–473
   global teams, 464–465
   vs. groups, 460*f*
   management challenges, 463–466
   management of, 390, 390*f*
   problem-solving teams, 460
   self-assessment, 468–469
   self-managed work team, 461
   social network structure, 465–466
   supportive climate, 463
   types of teams, 460–461
   virtual team, 461
   work teams, 460–463

Technical employees, 435

Technical skills. Knowledge of and expertise in a specialized field. **9**

Technology

    anti-globalization positions, 87*f*

    automation, 362

    changes in, 361–362

    computerization, 362

    as force for change, 355

    industry and market structures, 102–103

    information technology, and communication, 305–309

    investment in, 516

    maintenance procedures, 492

    mass customization, 524–525

    and operations management, 520–521

    and organizational structure, 275–276, 276*f*

    pro-globalization positions, 87*f*

    process need, 102

    RFID, 517–518

    routine technologies, 37*f*

    training methods, 336*f*

    wireless technology, 492

    Woodward's findings on technology, 87*f*

Teleconferencing, 336*f*

Temporary employees, 435–436

Tests (employee selection), 332*f*, 333*f*

Theoretical perspectives. *See* management theories

Theory of justice view of ethics. A view of ethics in which managers impose and enforce rules fairly and impartially and do so by following all legal rules and regulations. **133**

Theory X. The assumption that employees have little ambition, dislike work, want to avoid responsibility, and must be closely controlled to perform. **420**

Theory Y. The assumption that employees can exercise self direction, accept and seek out responsibility, and consider work a natural activity. **420**

Therbligs. A classification scheme for labelling 17 basic hand motions. **30**–31

Threats. Negative trends in external environmental factors. **212**

360-degree feedback, 337*f*

Three-needs theory. McClelland's motivation theory, which says that three acquired (not innate) needs—achievement, power, and affiliation—are major motives in work. **422**

Time management program, 373

Time of consumption, 293

Time series analysis, 239*f*

Time-space constraint, 293

Times interest earned ratio, 490*f*

Timmons Model of entrepreneurial process, 100*f*

Top-down planning approach, 196

Top managers. Managers at or near the top level of the organization who are responsible for making organization-wide decisions and establishing the plans and goals that affect the entire organization. **4**

Total asset turnover ratio, 490*f*

Trade, global, 73

Trade alliances, 73–76

Traditional goal setting. An approach to setting goals in which goals are set at the top of the organization and then broken into subgoals for each organizational level. **188**–190, 189*f*

Traditional organization, 18*f*

Traditional organizational designs, 277–278, 277*f*

Traditional training methods, 336*f*

Traditional view of conflict. The view that all conflict is bad and must be avoided. **457**

Traditions, 44

Training

    employees, 335–336, 335*f*, 336*f*, 342

    leaders, 406

    methods, 336

Trait theories, 387–388, 387*f*

Transactional leaders. Leaders who lead primarily by using social exchanges (or transactions). **397**

Transformational leaders. Leaders who stimulate and inspire (transform) followers to achieve extraordinary outcomes. **397**

Transnational (borderless) organization. A type of international company in which artificial geographical barriers are eliminated. **77**–78

Trends in management, 28–37

Trust. The belief in the integrity, character, and ability of a leader. 51, 401–**402,** 462, 519

Trust-building, 149–150

Turnaround strategy. A renewal strategy for situations in which the organization's performance problems are more serious. **218**

U

Uncertainty. A condition in which a decision maker is not certain about the outcomes and cannot even make reasonable probability estimates. **164**–166, 199

    see also environmental uncertainty

Uncertainty avoidance, 84, 85, 86*f*

Unexpected situations and events, 102

Unfreezing, 357

Unified commitment, 462

Unionized organizations, 324–325

Unit production. The production of items in units or small batches. **275**

United States

    "Americanization," 85–86

    manufacturing technology, 512

    motivation, 434

    subsidiaries in Canada, 12, 80

    unionized workers, 324

Unity of command. The management principle that states every employee should receive orders from only one superior. **269**

Universality of management. The reality that management is needed in all types and sizes of organizations, at all organizational levels, in all organizational work areas, and in organizations in all countries around the globe. **19,** 19*f*

University of Iowa studies, 388*f*, 389

University of Michigan studies, 388*f*, 389

Unrelated diversification. When a company grows by combining with firms in different and unrelated industries. **217**

Unstructured problems. Problems that are new or unusual and for which information is ambiguous or incomplete. **162**–163

Upward communication. Communication that flows upward from employees to managers. **303**

Utilitarian view of ethics. A view of ethics that says that ethical decisions are made solely on the basis of their outcomes or consequences. **132**–133

V

Valence, 430

Validity. The proven relationship that exists between the selection device and some relevant job criterion. **331**

Value. The performance characteristics, features, and attributes, as well as any other aspects of goods and services for which customers are willing to give up resources. **513**

Value chain. The entire series of organizational work activities that add value at each step from raw materials to finished product. **513**

Value chain management. The process of managing the sequence of activities and information along the entire value chain. **513**–514

    benefits of, 514

    collaboration, 515–516

    coordination, 515–516

    cultural attitudes, 519

    described, 513–514

    employees and human resources, 518, 520

    goal of, 514

    implementation of, 515

    leadership, 516–517

    obstacles, 518–520, 519*f*

    and operations management, 514–520

    organizational barriers, 519

    organizational culture and attitudes, 518

    organizational processes, 516

    requirements of, 515–518, 515*f*, 519

    technology investment, 516

Value proposition. An analysis of the benefits, costs, and value that an organization can deliver to customers and other groups within and outside of the organization. **104**–105

Values. Basic convictions about what is right and wrong. **135**

Values-based management. An approach to managing in which managers establish and uphold an organization's shared values. **130**–132

Variable costs, 248

Variable pay plans, 437

Verbal intonation. An emphasis given to words or phrases that conveys meaning. **294**

Verification of application data, 333*f*

Vertical integration, 216

Videoconferencing, 336*f*

Videotape training, 336*f*

Virtual communities, 307

Virtual organization. An organization that has elements of a traditional organization, but also relies on recent developments in information technology to get work done. **280**

Virtual team. A type of work team that uses technology to link physically dispersed members in order to achieve a common goal. **461**

Virus hunters, 25–26

Visionary leadership. The ability to create and articulate a realistic, credible, and attractive vision of the future that improves on the present situation. **398**

VoIP (Voice over Internet Protocol), 308

W

Weak cultures, 43–44

Weaknesses. Activities the organization does not do well or resources it needs but does not possess. **212**

The Wealth of Nations (Smith), 29

Weber, Max, 32

Weblogs, 317

Wellness programs, 350, 373

Whistle-blowers. Individuals who raise ethical concerns or issues to others inside or outside the organization. 140, **142**

White hat tactics, 529

White-water rapids metaphor, 358, 359

Wicked problem. A problem that is impossible to solve because each attempt to create a solution changes the understanding of the problem. **17**

Wireless technology, 492

Women, and leadership, 405, 406*f*

Work, reality of, 19–20

Work-life balance, 343–345

Work sampling, 333*f*

Work specialization. The degree to which activities in an organization are subdivided into separate job tasks; also known as division of labour. **266**

Work teams. Groups whose members work intensely on a specific, common goal, using their positive synergy, individual and mutual accountability, and complementary skills. 460–463

see also teams

Work unit orientation, 334

Workbooks, 336*f*

Workforce changes, 356

Workforce diversity. The mix of people in organizations in terms of gender, race, ethnicity, disability, sexual orientation, and age, and demographic characteristics such as education and socio-economic status; the mix of people in organizations in terms of gender, race, ethnicity, age, and other characteristics that reflect differences. **14, 52**

and decision making, 183

and human resource management, 341–342

inclusive workplace culture, 53

and motivation, 433–436

and organizational culture, 52–53

orientation, 342

recruitment, 341

selection, 341

training, 342

Workplace conditions, 325

Workplace Hazardous Materials Information System (WHMIS), 325

Workplace monitoring, 497–498, 497*f*

Workplace privacy, 497–498

Workplace romances, 342–343

World-oriented view, 72

World Trade Organization (WTO). A global organization of 150 countries that deals with the rules of trade among nations. **76**

Written essays, 337*f*

Written reports, 481*f*

Written tests, 332*f*, 333*f*

NAME AND ORGANIZATION INDEX

A

Abitibi Bowater Inc., 56
Aboriginal Human Resource Development Council of Canada, 340
ABS Manufacturing and Distributing, 241
Accentra, 160
Accenture, 200
Adams, J. Stacy, 428
Adaptec, 92
Adidas, 55
Aditya, R.N., 404n
Adler, N., 465n
Agassiz, 482f
AHL, 265
Air Canada, 11, 28, 35, 181, 219, 224, 237–238, 345, 489, 492, 498
Air Canada Centre, 265
AIR MILES, 379
Airbus, 510
AJ Bus Lines, 57
Alberta Energy Company (AEC), 42
Alcoa, 122, 523
Alexander Keith's, 216, 482f
Alliance of Manufacturers & Exporters Canada, 138
Alpha Chi Omega, 387
Amazon.ca, 10, 16, 224, 228, 509
Amazon.com, 16, 54, 102, 228, 231, 397, 454, 524
America Online, 354
American Airlines, 153
American Chamber of Commerce, 205
American Express, 524
American Standard, 516, 517
Anderson, Brad, 444–445
Anderson, Ray, 120, 125
Andrus, Mark, 46
Anheuser-Busch, 79, 165–166, 483
APM Group, 123
Apparel Group, 216
Apple Computer, 17, 50, 51, 109f, 116, 198, 216, 359, 398, 521
aQuantive, 357
Arauio, Rafael, 92
ArcelorMittal, 461
Armstrong, Doug, 448
Army and Navy, 40
ASB, 307
Asch, Solomon, 453, 454f, 464
Ash, Mary Kay, 47, 398
Ask Jeeves, 355
Assembly of First Nations, 386
Atkinson, Mike, 57
Atlantic Eco Expo, 379
Atlantic Industries, 428
Atlantic Leadership Institute, 385
Au Premier Spa Urbain, 292
Audi, 426
Authors Guild, 231

Avis, 212
Aviva Canada, 268
Avolio, B.J., 397
Avon Products, 121, 397
A&W Food Services of Canada, 57
Axworthy, Lloyd, 138

B

Babcock, Mike, 448, 451, 459, 466–467
Babcock, Rob, 268
Babson College, 99
Back in Motion Rehab, 429
Baez, Danys, 259
Bagg, Jeff, 307
The Bagg Group, 307
Bakan, Joel, 85, 121
Balsillie, Jim, 96–97, 101, 106, 113
Bang & Olufsen, 223
Bank of Montreal, 123, 271, 498
Bank of Nova Scotia (Scotiabank), 74, 322, 327, 329, 334, 335, 340, 341, 345–346, 362, 388
Banks, Tim, 123
Baptiste, Michele, 340
Bard on the Beach Festival, 12
Barnard, Chester, 33
Barnes, Louis B., 390n
Barnes & Noble, 231
Barrett, Dave, 40
Barron, Millard, 391
Barrows, John, 297
Bartz, Carol, 354
Basadur, Min, 108
Basadur Applied Creativity, 17n, 108
Basur, Sheela, 254
Bayer AG, 275
BC Ferries, 505
BC Ferry and Marine Workers Union, 505
BC Hydro, 373
BCBusiness, 131
BCE, 74, 345
Beasley, M.S., 496n
The Beatles, 451
Beddoe, Clive, 238
Beer Unlimited, 481–483, 482f
Belanger, Dorys, 292
Bell, A.H., 499n
Bell, Don, 238
Bell Canada, 78, 495
Benetton Group, 362
Benimadhu, Prem, 437
Bennet, Steve, 356
Best Buy, 444–445, 513
Best Buy Canada, 311
Bethune, Gordon M., 196
Better Business Bureau, 258
beyond9to5.com, 344
Bezos, Jeff, 16, 102, 397, 454
Birk, Steve, 148

Birks, 56
BJ's Wholesale Club, 297
Black & Decker, 513
Blair, Bob, 477
Blake, Robert R., 390n
Blanchard, Ken, 393, 394f
Bloess, Rainer, 148
Bloomingdale's, 172
Blue Bird North Georgia, 530
Blue Circle Industries, 204
Blue Man Group Productions, 185, 187–188, 194, 197, 200, 458
Blue Mantle, 40
Blue Water Café, 274
BMO Field, 265
BMW, 523, 524
Bobbitt, Gordon, 491
The Body Shop, 46
Boeing Company, 39, 136, 251, 461, 510
Boeing-Rocketdyne, 461
Boman, Pär, 287
Bombardier, 77, 137, 251, 267f, 267n
Bono, 399
Bono, J.E., 387n
Bookoff, 231
Boone, J., 339n
Booz & Company (Booz Allen Hamilton), 108–109
Boralex, 272
BorderWare, 241
Boston Consulting Group, 218
Boston Pizza International, 335
BouClair, 483
BP (British Petroleum), 40, 53, 127, 296, 362, 529
Brandes, P., 439n
Branson, Richard, 46
Brasseries Unibroue, 482f
Brayer, Jean-Paul, 79
Brin, Sergey, 279
Bristol-Myers Squibb, 78
British Airways, 495, 504–505
Broadcast.com, 424
Brodbeck, F.C., 404n
Bronx Zoo, 189
Bryan, J.P., 391
Bryant, J.D., 399
Buckley, George, 39, 41, 46, 62
Buddo, Peter, 373
Buffett, Warren, 101
Bureau of Competition Policy, 57
Burger King, 203, 232
Burgin, Danny, 153
Burke, L.A., 161n
Burke, Tim, 103
Business Council on National Issues, 138
Business Development Bank of Canada, 12
BusinessWeek, 50

C

Calvin Klein, 258

Cambi General Store, 40

Cameco, 341

Campbell, Gordon, 361

Canada Line, 40, 196, 241, 246, 251

Canada Post, 11, 12, 55, 210, 362, 390–391, 407

Canada Revenue Services, 140

Canada Trust, 400

Canada's Wonderland, 55

Canadian 88 Energy, 391

Canadian Armed Forces, 362

Canadian Authors Association, 231

Canadian Business, 429

Canadian Coalition for Good Governance (CCGG), 438

Canadian Council of Chief Executives, 138

Canadian Football League (CFL), 122

Canadian Human Rights Commission, 326n

Canadian Imperial Bank of Commerce (CIBC), 122, 491, 511

Canadian Olympic Committee, 251

Canadian Paralympic Committee, 251

Canadian Policy Research Network, 418

Canadian Securities Administrators, 139, 355, 495

Canadian Tire, 10, 226

Canadian Transportation Agency, 57

Carcello, J.V., 496n

Carey, Mariah, 399

Carey, William, 105

Carlton, 523

Carmanah Technologies Corp., 100n

CarShareHFX, 102

Carson, Rachel, 14, 127

Carter, Rob, 400

Cartier, Jacques, 3

Cartoon Network, 205

Cascades, 272, 388

Caterpillar, 521

Cavanagh, Christina, 298, 306

CBC, 12, 57, 133

CEDC (Central European Distribution), 105

Celestica, 483–484

Center for Leadership Studies, 394n

Centre for Entrepreneurship Education and Development (CEED), 117

Centre for Research on Globalization, 86

Cerner, 291, 296

C.F. Martin Guitar Company (Martin Guitar), 180–181

Chandler, Alfred, 275

Chang, Steve, 280

Chapman, Clare, 422–423, 433

Chapters, 122, 208, 214

Charles Schwab, 194

The Cheesecake Factory, 510

Cheesewright, David, 396–397, 408

ChemNutra, 70

Cheol, Kim Byung, 471

Chicago Bulls, 91

Chinook Institute for Community Stewardship, 210

Chipotle Mexican Grill, 217

Cho, Fujio, 211

Choi, Barbara, 160

Christian (Chris) Frederick Martin IV, 180–181

Cirque du Soleil, 3, 4, 5, 12, 20–21, 32, 50, 51, 96

Cisco Systems, 281, 308, 362

CITES (Convention on International Trade in Endangered Species of Wild Fauna and Flora), 180

City of Ottawa, 148

City of Richmond, 241

City of Vancouver, 210, 251, 497

Clampitt, P.G., 295n

Clark, T., 75n

Clarke, Greg, 204

Club Med, 55

CN Rail, 390–391

CNN, 317, 350

Coast Guard, 505

Coca-Cola Company, 55, 203, 212, 219, 224, 232

Cochran, P.L., 123n

Cognos, 186, 235

Cohen, Jordan, 286

Coleman Trust Inc., 453

Coles, 122, 208

College of Commerce (University of Saskatchewan), 438

Comdex, 317

Communicopia, 126

Community Arts Council of Vancouver, 210

Compania Chilena de Fosforos SA, 223

Compaq, 361

COMPAS, 57

Competition Bureau Canada, 57, 208, 217

Competitive Enterprise Institute, 86

Computer Associates, 65

Confédération des syndicates nationaux, 325

Conference Board of Canada, 138, 322, 342, 437

Confucius, 151

ConocoPhillips, 391

Continental Airlines, 196

Continuity Central, 204

Coolbrands, 79

Cook, Scott, 356

Cooley, Pam, 102

Coors, 318

Cordero, Luca, 471

Corel, 33, 217, 251, 277

Corkan, Christine, 28

Corning, 461

Corporate Governance Center (Kennesaw State University), 495

Corporate Knights, 99, 123, 129

Costco, 83

Covey, Stephen, 65

Covey Center, 65

Cowell, Simon, 209

Coyne, Kevin, 369

Crosby, Sidney, 448, 463

Cuban, Mark, 424

Cullen, Alex, 148

Cushing, Richard, 151

D

Dacker, Susan, 354

Daft, R.L., 269n

Dahl Brothers Canada, 223

Daimler AG, 74

DaimlerChrysler, 225

Dalhousie University, 296

Dallas Mavericks, 92, 424

Davis, W.D., 323n

Dean, J.W.Jr., 522n

DeCenzo, D.A., 167n, 333n

Decision Lens, 461

Deere and Company, 516

Dell, Michael, 398

Dell Canada, 268

Dell Inc., 9, 15, 209, 225, 398, 513, 524

Deloitte & Touche, 204, 205

Delphi, 523

Deming, W. Edwards, 511, 511f, 511n, 512

Denghui, Ji, 80–81

DENSO, 122

Denver Nuggets, 92

Department of the Secretary of State, 210

Department of Transportation (Britain), 505

DePree, Max, 110

Detroit Red Wings, 448

Deutche Bank AG, 77, 205

DeZoot, F.T., 496n

Dharwadkar, R., 439n

Dodd, R., 128n

Dofasco, 361, 373

Dom Pérignon, 219

Domtar, 272, 345, 491

Donato's Pizza, 217

Donely, Christina, 139

Donna Karan, 219

DoubleClick, 357

Doucet, Clive, 148

Dow Chemical, 524

Dow Jones, 116

Dow Jones Industrial Average, 53

Dow Jones Sustainability Index, 149

Drucker, Peter, 6, 102

Drum, Brian, 305

Drum Associates, 305

DSA Industrial Design, 50

Dubai Ports, 20

Dun & Bradstreet (D&B), 237

DuPont, 77, 128

Duxbury, Linda, 343

E

eBay, 16, 58, 99, 103, 211, 216, 277, 309
Ebbers, Bernie, 50
Ecover, 128
Edison Electric Institute, 65
EDS, 200
Ekvall, Goran, 51
Eldis Group, 509, 512–513, 514–515, 525–526, 529
Eldridge, Matt, 290, 292
Electrolux, 208, 359
Electronic Arts Canada, 329, 435
Elizabeth II, Queen of England, 505
Ellison, Larry, 412
Emerson, David, 73
Empire Company, 11
Enbridge, 123, 129
EnCana, 42, 129
Engen, Travis, 91
Enrico, Roger, 405
Enron, 44, 181, 495
Ensign, P., 100n
Enterprise Rent-A-Car, 499, 500
Equal Employment Opportunity Commission (EEOC), 342, 349–350
Eresman, Randall, 42
Ericsson, 96, 281
Ericsson Canada, 373
Ernsrom, Bill, 318
Ernst & Young, 18, 303
Escoffier, August, 65
EthiScan Canada, 140
E*TRADE, 59
European Commission, 217
Evans, J.R., 522n
Evans, W.R., 323n
Expedia, 217
Exxon Mobil, 491

F

Facebook, 110, 210, 224, 236, 305, 307, 313, 349, 354, 357, 401
Fastow, Andrew, 495
Fayol, Henri, 31–32, 36, 269
FedEx, 55, 102, 205, 400
FedEx Kinko's, 275
Ferrari, 471
Fiat, 77
Fidelity Investments, 493
Fielder, Fred, 391–393, 392f, 395
Fields, Bill, 391
Fila, 55
Filtea, 15
Flavelle, Karen, 331
Fletcher, Stephen, 386
Follett, Mary Parker, 33
Fontaine, Phil, 386, 407
Food Town, 206

Ford Australia, 266
Ford Canada, 277
Ford Motor Company, 12, 33, 77, 524, 525
Fortune, 14, 98, 108, 232, 240, 344
Foster, Bonnie, 361
Four Points, 380
Four Seasons Hotels and Resorts, 51
Fox, Nicholas, 486
Frank, Manuela, 426
Franklin, Benjamin, 151
Freeman, R.E., 128n
Frese, M., 404n
Friedman, Andrew E., 259
Friedman, Milton, 121
Frito-Lay, 77
Fry, Art, 46
Fujian Sanming Dinghui Chemical Company, 80
Fujitsu, 437
Furlong, John, 235, 241–242, 244, 245, 246, 251, 255
Future Shop, 15, 311

G

Galanti, Richard, 83
Galbraith, Jay R., 214n
Gallup Organization, 3, 440
Ganong Bros., 215–216
Garlinghouse, Brad, 354
Garvin, D., 522n
Gasol, Pau, 92
Gates, Bill, 17, 46, 101, 235–236
Gates, Melinda, 101
Gaudrealt, Christian, 40
Gautam, Giriaj, 40
GE Aviation, 299
GE Energy, 299
GE Mobile, 96
General Cable Corporation, 4, 521
General Electric (GE), 39, 109f, 198, 225, 232, 280, 349, 356, 369, 412, 491, 524
General Motors Centre, 265
General Motors (GM), 11, 12, 80, 96, 116, 215–216, 218
General Motors (GM) Canada, 275, 345
George Weston Foods, 217
Gilbreth, Frank, 29–31, 361
Gilbreth, Lillian, 29–31, 361
Gilligan, Rich, 349–350
Giricek, Gordan, 92
Girl Guides, 55
Giving Pledge, 101
Global Entrepreneurship Monitor (GEM), 98
Global Reporting Initiative (GRI), 129
Global Witness, 127
Globalization Guide, 87n
GLOBE (Global Leadership and Organization Behaviour Effectiveness), 85, 86f, 300, 404
Globescan, 126

Glow Industries, 199
GM Canada, 80
Gnatt, Henry, 244
Godfrey, Jannike, 223
Godsoe, Peter, 388
Goldberg, Gerry, 483
Goldman, Matt, 185, 187–188, 197
Goodnight, Jim, 397
Goodyear Tire & Rubber Company, 349
Google, 55, 58, 108, 109f, 112, 116, 235–236, 279, 299, 304, 349, 354, 355, 357–358, 365, 445, 486, 493, 529, 530
Google Analytics, 531
Gore, Al, 379
Grafik Marketing Communications, 412–413
Graham, Ben, 514–515, 520, 526, 529
Gray, David, 224
Greenberg, J., 499n
Greene, Moya, 390–391, 407
Greenfield Brokerage, 180
Greenpeace, 86, 127
Greiner, Larry E., 390n
Grenny, Joseph, 370
Gretzky, Wayne, 448
Groove Networks, 317
Grupo VIPS, 79
Guerlain, 219
Gulf Canada Resources, 391

H

Hackman, J.R., 427n
Hagedom, Jim, 350
Hahn, David, 505
Haier Group, 231–232
Hale, Victoria, 187
Hansen, J.D., 499n
Hanson, Sven, 238
Harary, Ronnen, 368
Haribhai's Spice Emporium, 79
Harley-Davidson, 219
Harper, Stephen, 13
Harrah's Entertainment, 52
Harvard, 96, 286, 406
Harvard Business Review, 17, 141n, 390n, 500n
Harvard Business School, 369, 373
Harvey's, 36
Hasbro, 59
Hawken, Paul, 120
Hayne, Richard, 243
Hayward, Tony, 40
HealthSouth, 257–258
Heart and Stroke Foundation, 56
Heathrow Airport, 504–505
Hemlock, Printers, 129
Henderson, R.I., 338n
Herman Miller Inc., 110
Hermanson, D.R., 496n

Hersey, Paul, 393, 394*f*
Herzberg, Frederick, 420–422, 421*f*, 434, 437, 441
Heskett, J.L., 500*n*
Hewitt, Richard, 148
Hewitt Associates, 436–437, 479
Hewlett-Packard, 79, 82, 128, 279, 307, 361, 461, 493
Hewlett-Packard Canada, 373
Higgins, Chris, 343
Hilario, Nenê, 92
Hill, Mark, 238
Hilton, Conrad, 101
Hilton Hotels, 495
Hindustan Lever, 208
Hitachi, 79
Hitchcock, Ken, 448
Hitt, M.A., 225*n*, 522*n*
H.J. Heinz Company, 77
Hockey Canada, 448, 463
Hofstede, Geert, 83–85, 84*f*, 84*n*, 300
Holland, Ken, 448
Holmes, Diane, 148
Holt Renfrew, 224
Home Depot, 55, 56, 231, 408, 484
Home Depot Canada, 131, 400
Home Hardware, 40
Home Outfitters, 311
Home Sense, 491
Hornery, Stuart, 204
Hoskisson, R.E., 522*n*
House, R.J., 86*n*, 404*n*
House, Robert, 394–395
Houston Rockets, 91
HRMarketer.com, 339*n*
HSBC, 205
Huang, C.C., 308
Hudson's Bay Company (The Bay), 224, 311, 365, 391
Hunsaker, P.L., 301*n*
Hunt, J.G., 404*n*
Husky Energy, 477, 487, 488, 489, 493, 501
Husky Injection Molding Systems, 48, 131, 266
Husky Oil, 477
Hyde, Bill, 335
Hydro, 91
Hyundai Corporation, 46, 221

I

i2 Technologies, 412
IBM, 17, 78, 82, 109*f*, 186, 200, 235, 241, 306
IDC Canada, 336
IDEO, 50, 309
iGEN Knowledge Solutions, 280
IKEA, 56, 127, 243, 341, 515
IKI, 222
Ilies, R., 387*n*

Imasco Ltd., 400
Imperial Tobacco, 400
Inbev, 216
Indigo Books & Music, 15, 122, 208, 210–211, 212, 214–215, 224, 226, 228, 231
Indigo Books & Music & Café, 325
Indigo/Chapters, 208
Industry Week, 530
Indy 500, 241
ING Bank of Canada, 33
Innovest Strategic Value Advisers, 129
Institute of Internal Auditors, 495
Integrated Information Systems, 493
Intel, 109*f*, 198, 224, 365–366, 451, 509
Interbrand, 232
Interface Inc., 120, 125–126, 130, 143–144
Internal Revenue Services, 140
International Forum on Globalization, 86
International Institute for Sustainable Development, 86
International Monetary Fund (IMF), 74
International Organization for Standardization (ISO), 13–14, 99, 129, 523, 529
International Policy Network, 86
Intuit, 356
Intuit Canada, 46
Ipsos Reid, 281, 371, 498
IQ Partners, 307
Ireland, R.D., 522*n*
Iskat, G.J., 364
ITT Industries, 524
Iwasaki, Koyata, 350
Izod, 258

J

Jackson, Edwin, 259
Japan Booksellers Federation, 231
Japanese Ministry of Labour, 372
Java Jazz Mobile Café, 28
Javidan, M., 86*n*, 404*n*
J.D. Power and Associates, 525
Jobs, Steve, 17, 51, 116, 198, 359
Johnson, 308
Johnson, Kara, 309
Johnson, Leo, 192
Johnson & Johnson, 524
Johnson Controls Inc., 514
Johnston, David, 385, 407
Jones, T.O., 500*n*
Jong-Yong, Yun, 487
Judge, T.A., 387*n*
Jung, Andrea, 397
Jupitermedia, 317

K

Kamloops Child Development Society, 210
Kaplan, R.S., 494*n*
Ka-shing, Li, 477, 487, 501

Katz, Robert I., 9
Katz, Vivian, 148
Katzenbach, J.R., 460*n*
Kaufman, Julie, 336
Kazanijan, Robert K., 214*n*
Kempinski Hotels, 72
Kennedy, J.C., 404*n*
Kenner Toys, 59
Keung, Alice, 492
KFC (Kentucky Fried Chicken), 80, 215, 318
Khmer Internet Development Services (KIDS), 103
Kicking Horse Coffee, 192
King, Martin Luther Jr., 387, 398
Kinicki, A., 303*n*, 456*n*
Kirin, 79
Kirkpatirck, S.A., 387*n*
Kirpich, Judy, 412–413
Kirzner, Israel, 97
Klein, Naomi, 86
Knapp, Sean, 445
Kohlberg, L., 134*n*
Komex International, 138
Kotter, John, 373
Kotter, J.P., 374*n*
Kouwenhoven, Richard, 129
KPMG, 140, 142
KPMG/Ipsos Reid, 3
Kraft Canada, 351
Kraft Foods, 342, 459, 516
Kreitner, R., 303*n*, 456*n*
Krispy Kreme Doughnuts, 365
Kuhne, Eric, 204
Kumar, Sanjay, 65

L

Labatt Breweries, 79, 216, 335, 367
Lafond, Jeffrey, 237–238
Laliberté, Guy, 3, 4, 12, 20–21, 32
Lamarre, Daniel, 3, 4, 5, 12, 20, 32, 51
Lamont, Duane, 123
Lapides, P.D., 496*n*
Latham, Malcolm, 204
Lau, John Chin-Sung, 477, 487, 489, 501
Laurie, Amanda, 131–132
Lazaridis, Michael, 96–97, 101, 106, 107, 112–113
Le Bon Croissant, 221
Leafs TV, 265
Leahy, Terry, 417, 423
Lebrun, Marcel, 236
Lee, Leonard, 212
Lee, Robin, 438
Lee Valley Tools, 212, 223, 438
Legend, John, 399
Lemaire, Alain, 272
Lemaire, Bernard, 272
Lemaire, Jacques, 448
Lemaire, Laurent, 272, 388

Lemesis, G.V., 439n
Lend Lease Corporation, 204
Lepe, Belsasar, 445
Lepe, Bismarck, 445
Levi Strauss, 524
Lewin, Kurt, 357–358
Liebowitz, J., 364
Lifson, Elliot, 258–259
Lincoln, Abraham, 387
LinkedIn, 236, 305, 307, 313
Linton, Roxanne, 334
Lipschultz Levin & Gray, 24–25
L.L. Bean, 281
Loblaw Companies, 11, 123, 217, 240
Locke, E.A., 387n
Lockheed Martin, 458
Loew, Kevin, 448
London Drugs, 226
Long, Richard J., 438
Lopez, Jennifer, 199
Los Angeles Dodgers, 259
Loughridge, Ken, 465
Louis Vuitton, 219
Loveman, G.W., 500n
Lowe, Graham, 440
LoyaltyOne, 379
LVMH Moët Hennessy-Louis Vuitton SA, 219
Lymbix, 290, 294, 312

M

Macaulay, Fraser, 142
MacDougal, Deanna, 307
Mackey, John, 103
MADD (Mothers Against Drunk Driving), 56
Madison, Stacy, 46
Maeztu, Juvencio, 341
Magloire, Jamaal, 92
Magna International, 11, 44–45
Majhi, Bhagawan, 91
Major League Soccer, 265
Management, 374n
Mansbridge, Peter, 299
Manulife Financial Canada, 122
Maple Leaf Foods, 141
Maple Leaf Sports & Entertainment (MLSE),
    265, 277, 278, 283
Marketing Hall of Legends, 400
Marriott Marquis Hotel, 53
Martin, Paul, 142
Mary Kay Cosmetics, 47, 398
Maslow, Abraham, 419–420, 419f, 434, 437,
    441
MasterCard, 164–165, 165f
Masuda, Rina, 434
Matsushita, 488
Mattel, 59, 367–368, 524
Matthews, Bill, 92
Matwawana, Ed, 117
May, Ned, 359

Mayo, Elton, 34–35
McCain, Michael, 141
McCain Foods, 248, 277
McClelland, David, 422, 441
McClenahen, J., 75n
McDonald's, 217, 232, 266, 273, 365, 434,
    486–487, 511, 520
McDonald's Canada, 79, 80, 485
McElvoy, S., 497n
McGill University, 8, 9
McGrath, Judy, 399
McGregor, Douglas, 420, 441
McGuinty, Dalton, 429
McKee, Mike, 47
McKnight, William, 39
McLagan, P.A., 374n
McMaster University, 456
McNamara, Robert, 33
McNerney, James, 39, 41, 62, 369
McQuiggen, Kevin, 328
McRae, Brad, 385
McTavish's Kitchen, 92
Meckler, Alan, 317
Mega Blocks, 79
Mega Brands, 79
Memphis Grizzlies, 92
Menu Foods, 70, 72–73, 76–77, 80–81,
    87–88
Mercedes Benz, 232, 523
Merchant, Josh, 290, 292
Merrill Lynch, 77
Michael G. DeGroote School of Business at
    McMaster University, 108
Michael's, 400
Microsoft, 17, 19, 46, 48, 109f, 112, 251,
    290, 307, 354, 357, 491
Miller, 483
Miller, Jackie, 505
Miller, M.K., 161n
Milton, Robert, 181
Ming, Yao, 91
Ministry of the Environment (Ontario), 148
Mintzberg, Henry, 8–9, 8f, 8n, 452
Mississippi Power, 65
Mitsubishi Group, 238, 350
Mitsubishi Motors North America (MMNA),
    349–350
MLB (Major League Baseball), 259
Modelo, 79
Mogus, Jason, 126
Molson, 224, 491
Moscow Ballet, 387
Moses, Todd, 160
Motorola, 232, 279
Moulton, Jane S., 390n
Mountain Equipment Co-op (MEC), 123, 130
Mowat, Dave, 222
Mr. Convenience, 241
MSN, 354
MTV Networks (MTV), 185, 399

Muckler, John, 268–269
Mullally, Pam, 123
Münsterberg, Hugo, 33
Murphy, Kathy, 117
Murray, A., 338n
Murray, Bill, 291
MWH Global, 465
MySpace, 307, 349, 354, 355, 365, 401
Mystery Shopping Providers, 311

N

Naismith, James, 91
Nam Choi, Jim, 9
Nanaimo Community Gardens Society, 210
Nanaimo Conservatory of Music, 210
Napster, 16
Nardi, Tony, 258
NASA, 369, 370
NASCAR, 460
Nash, L.L., 141n
Nash, Steve, 92
National Basketball Association (NBA), 91–92,
    265, 424
National Parole Board, 57
National Speleogical Society, 493
Natura Cosmetics SA, 124
Natural Resource Canada, 130
Neal, T.L., 496n
Nelly, 299
Nelson, Rod, 505
Nestlé, 77
Nestlé USA, 516
Neto, João Vendramin, 413
New Balance Athletic Shoe, 226
Newington Olympic Village, 204
Nexen, 129
NHL, 265, 448
Nike, 49, 55, 219, 281
Nissin Foods, 47
Nitkin, David, 140
Nokia Corporation, 74, 198, 524
Nooyi, Indra, 405
Norman, Rob, 354
Norsk Hydro, 91
Nortel Networks, 57, 217, 345
Northrup Grumman Corporation, 521
Norton, D.P., 494n
Norwich Union, 309
Nova Scotia Business Hall of Fame, 400
Nowitzki, Dirk, 92
NTP, 108

O

Obama, Barack, 387
O'Brien, Larry, 148
Ocean Nutrition, 460
Oguchi, Masananga, 47
Ohio State, 389, 407

Okalik, Paul, 404
Okanagan Spring, 482f
O'Keefe, Helen, 423
O'Kelley, Johanna, 147
Olajuwon, Hakeem, 92
Omidyar, Pierre, 103
Ondrack, Dan, 403
ONE DROP Foundation, 3, 21
O'Neill, Daniel, 491
O'Neill, Jim, 76
Onex, 11
onProject, 252
Ontario Hospital Association, 495
Ontario Teachers' Pension Plan, 438
Oracle Corporation, 217, 359, 412
Oreck, Diana, 65
Orser, Barbara, 342
Ortiz, George, 222
Ortiz, Nicolas, 222
Ortiz, Oliver, 222
Ottawa Senators, 148, 268
Otto, Norbert, 111
Outward Bound School, 406
Owen, Robert, 33
Oxford, 509

P

Pacific Insight Electronics (PI), 131–132
Paddock Wood Brewing, 482f
Page, Larry, 279
Palm, 50
Palmer, Terry, 123
Panasonic Theatre, 197
PanCanadian Energy Corporation, 42
Parker, Tony, 92
Parker Brothers, 59
Participant Media, 99
Partners in Organizational Development (POD), 210
PartSelect, 509, 512, 525, 531
Patterson, Neal L., 291
Payne, Derek, 489
Pazmac Enterprises, 422
Peddie, Richard A., 265, 268, 270, 277
Peerless Clothing, 258–259
Pengrowth Energy Trust, 391
Penner, Tim, 213
PeopleSoft, 412
PepsiCo, 55, 77, 108, 215, 405, 461
Perimeter Institute of Applied Physics, 107
Perklin, Dokse, 221
Perlmutter, Dadi, 451
Perron, Don, 367
Pet Valu, 70
Peters & Co., 42
Peterson, M.F., 404n
Petrovic, Dražen, 92
PetSmart, 70

Petterson, Lynn, 149
Pfizer, 108, 286, 516
Pheonix Suns, 92
Pierce, J., 128n
Pitney Bowes Canada, 306
Pizza Hut, 215
Pooley, E., 339n
Porter, Michael, 220, 220n, 223
Portland Trailblazers, 92
Prairie General Hospital, 380–381
Pret A Manager, 217
Price, Art, 477
Proctor & Gamble Canada, 80, 213
Proctor & Gamble (P&G), 50, 108, 109f, 217, 226–227, 237, 276, 277
Progressive Conservative Party of Manitoba, 386
Project Management Institute (PMI), 251
Prokop, Brian, 42
Pronger, Chris, 451
Prudential, 53
Public Works and Services (Ottawa), 148
Purdy's Chocolates, 331
Purolator Courier, 122

Q

Qantas Airways, 16
QEII Health Sciences Centre, 458
Qinghou, Zong, 163
Quinn, Pat, 451, 466

R

Rabie, Anton, 368
Radian6, 236
Ralph Lauren, 258
Raptors NBA TV, 265
Ratcliffe, David, 65
RBC Capital Markets, 361
RCMP, 142, 342, 491
Recording Industry Association of America, 493
Reebok, 55, 281
Reisman, Heather, 208, 210, 215, 224, 228
Report on Business Magazine, 478
Research In Motion (RIM), 58, 96–97, 101, 106, 107–108, 109, 110–111, 112–113, 223, 407, 460
Revlon, 278
Richard Ivey School of Business (University of Western Ontario), 241, 298, 306
Ricoh, 127
Ricoh Coliseum, 265
RightMedia, 357
Rihanna, 513
Rio Tinto Alcan, 77, 91, 138, 491
RiskMetrics Group (RMG), 438
Ritacco, David, 509, 512, 514–515, 520, 526, 531
Ritz, Caesar, 65
Ritz-Carlton Hotels, 65–66, 310

Robbins, S.P., 167n, 333n
Robeez Footwear, 153, 158, 161, 166–167, 172, 174–175
Roberts, H.V., 522n
Robin Hood Multifoods, 491
Robinson, Andrew, 440
Robinson, Peter, 123
Rodarte, Carlos, 530–531
Roddick, Anita, 46
Rogers, Ted, 46
Rogers Communications, 46, 491
Rolex, 54
Roman Catholic Archdiocese of Regina, 40
Romanchuk, Judith, 489
Roots, 56, 244
Rosenfeld, Elana, 192
Rotman School of Management (University of Toronto), 241, 403
Roughgarden, Trish, 509
Rowe Furniture, 520
Royal Bank of Canada (RBC Financial Group), 11, 49, 122, 129, 139, 149
Royal Canadian Mint, 477
Royal Dutch Petroleum Company/Shell, 77
Royal Ontario Museum, 12, 55
Rubbermaid, 236
Ruff, Lindy, 448
Ruimin, Zhang, 231–232
Russell, R.S., 243n, 252n

S

SADD (Students Against Destructive Decisions), 56
Safeway, 12, 70
Saint-Gobain Performance Plastics, 516
Saks, 172
Salesforce.com, 236
Samsung Electronics, 109f, 471, 487
Samsung Group, 471
San Antonio Spurs, 92
San Francisco State University, 369
SAS Institute, 397
SaskPower, 335
Sasser, W.E.Jr., 500n
Saturn, 279, 470
Sauder School of Business (University of British Columbia), 237, 241
Saul, John Ralston, 85
Sawyer, J.E., 366
Scarlett, Steve, 422
[[Scaron]] koda, 511
Schering-Plough, 521
Schlesinger, L.A., 500n
Schrempp, Jürgen, 225
Schroeder, Don, 216
Schrushy, Richard, 257–258
Schulich School of Business (York University), 241
Schumpeter, Joseph, 97
Schwartz, Gerry, 208

Schwartz, Jonathan, 317
Scotia Cassels Investment Counsel, 334
Scott, Lee, 396
Scott's Miracle-Gro, 350
Sears, 12, 139, 231, 311
Sears Canada, 217
Second Life, 307, 328, 329
Segal, Alvin, 258
Segal, Moe, 258
Seidel, Marc-David, 237
Semco Group, 413
Semel, Terry, 354, 359, 369, 375
Semler, Ricardo, 413
Sens Plaza, 148
Seow, Kenny, 205
Sepomex (Servicio Postal Mexicano), 530–531
Seral, John, 299
Seres, Erika, 426
Sergesketter, B.F., 522n
Seven & i Holdings, 496
7-Eleven, 496
Shanghai Volkswagen, 232
Sharp, Isadore, 51
Sharp Corp., 434
Sharpe, R., 406n
Shaw Communications, 345
Shell Canada, 138
Shellenberger, S., 339n
Sheraton, 380
Shetty, Y.K., 241n
Shimizu, K., 225n
Shirley, Donna L., 369
Shoppers Drug Mart, 400
Siegel, Steven P., 24–25
Siemens AG, 513
Sierra Club, 147
Silverman, Matt, 259
Singapore Airlines, 226
Sitel India, 78
Sixth Line Solutions, 224
Skinner, B.F., 425
Skoll, Jeff, 99, 101, 103
Skoll Foundation, 99
Smith, Adam, 29
Smith, D.K., 460n
Smith, D.M., 499n
Smith, Fred, 102
SmithBooks, 208
Sobeys, 70
Socialinvestment.ca, 126
Society of Management Accountants of Canda, 478
Sodexho Alliance AS, 307
Sommers, David, 92
Sony Corporation, 42, 77, 198, 232, 365–366, 471, 524
Southwest Airlines, 241
Souvaliotis, Andrew, 379
SPCA (Society for the Prevention of Cruelty to Animals), 12

Spin Master, 368
Spinelli, S., 100n
Sport Otto, 111
Sports Illustrated, 259
Sprott School of Business (Carlton University), 343
Spurlock, Morgan, 232
St. Regis, 380
Stacy's Pita Chip Company, 46
Stanley Park Ecology Society, 210
Stanton, Phil, 185, 187–188, 197
Starbucks, 60, 79
Starwood, 380
Status of Women Canada, 57
Stern, David, 91–92
Sternberg, Stuart, 259
Stewart, Jon, 399
Stewart, Martha, 181
Stipe, Michael, 399
Straberg, Hans, 359
Strawberry Frog, 280
Stride Rite, 172
Stronach, Frank, 44–45
Students for a Free Tibet, 55
Suburban Hospital, 461
SUBWAY, 232, 253
Sullivan, John, 369
Sulz, Nancy, 342
Sun Life Financial, 129
Sun Microsystems, 317
Suncor Energy, 11, 129, 328, 341
Suttle, J.L., 427n
Svanberg, Carl-Henric, 40
Svenska Handelsbanken, 243, 287
Swingline, 160
Sydney Opera House, 204
Symantec, 25–26
SYSCO, 483

T

Taco Bell, 215, 232
TAG Heuer, 219
Talisman Energy, 138
Tampa Bay Devil Rays, 259
Tan, Peter, 517
Tango, 224
Tanner, Chris, 481–483
Tapscott, Don, 276
Task Force on Business Schools and Innovation, 17
Tata Group, 217
Taylor, B.W.III, 252n
Taylor, Frederick Winslow, 29–31, 36, 244, 269, 361
Taylor B.W.III, 243n
TD Canada Trust, 341
Team Canada, 448, 466
Team Canada 2010, 451
Team USA, 448

Ted's Malibu Surf Shop, 387
Telefónica, 78
Tele-Mobile, 341
TELUS Mobility, 129, 268, 341
TELUS Québec, 268
Teranet, 361
Tesco, 417, 418, 422–423, 433, 441
Tether, 103
Texas Instruments, 243, 399
Thida, Thay, 103
Thomas, Patrick, 189
3M Company, 39, 41, 44, 46, 53, 61–62, 96, 108, 109f, 365–366, 369, 524
Tiffany, Chuck, 259
Tiger Electronics, 59
Tim Hortons, 209, 216
Time Warner, 205
Timex, 54
Timken, 513
Timmons, Jeffrey, 99, 100f, 100n
TJX Companies, 491
Tomato Fresh Food Café, 40
Tom's of Maine, 131
Tonka Toys, 59
Topazi, Anthony, 65
Toronto Dominion Bank, 129
Toronto FC, 265, 277, 278
Toronto Maple Leafs, 265, 277, 278, 283
Toronto Marlies, 265, 277
Toronto Raptors, 10, 91, 92, 265, 268, 270, 277, 278, 283
Total SA, 127
Toyota Motor Corporation, 109f, 211, 224, 279, 387, 510
Training, 335n
TransCanada, 129
Transocean Drilling, 53
Transport and Communications Ministry (Mexico), 530
Transport Canada, 178, 505
TrashBusters.com, 47
Trend Micro, 280
Tulane University, 259
Tupperware, 236
Turner International Asia Pacific, 205
Twitter, 236, 294, 296, 313

U

Ugg, 513
Unilever PLC, 74, 77, 237
United Auto Workers (UAW), 80
United Breweries, 523
United Nations Global Compact, 138, 138n, 140
United Way, 10, 56
United Way of the Lower Mainland, 210
University of Alberta, 440
University of British Columbia, 85, 121, 241, 373
University of California, 518

University of Iowa, 389, 407
University of Manitoba Students Council, 386
University of Michigan, 389, 407
University of New Brunswick, 428
University of Saskatchewan, 195
University of Waterloo, 96, 385, 387, 407
University of Western Ontario, 343
University of Winnipeg, 138
Upper Canada Brewery, 482f
UPS, 55, 127, 302
Urban Outfitters, 243
Utah Jazz, 92

V

Valeo Klimasystemme GmbH, 523
Valley Springs Industrial Center, 160
Vancouver 2010, 235, 241
Vancouver City Hall, 56
Vancouver City Savings Credit Union (Vancity), 131, 222
Vancouver Foundation, 210
Vancouver Grizzlies, 91
Vancouver International Airport, 246
Vancouver Police Department (VPD), 328, 329
Vancouver Sun, 192
Varadi, Ben, 368
Verizon, 307
Verreault Navigation, 57
Verschuren, Annette, 400, 408
Viacom, 399
Vinson, Betty, 286
Virgin Group, 46
Visa, 164–165, 165f
Volkswagen AG, 511
Volvo, 243, 459
Voortman, Harry, 57
Voortman, Lynn, 57
Voortman Cookies, 57
Voyant Technologies, 318
Vroom, Victor, 430
Vrooman, Tamara, 222

W

W Hotels, 380

Wahaha, 163
Waldman, D.A., 397
Wales, Jimmy, 274
Wall Street Journal, 198, 343, 412
Wal-Mart, 55, 58, 82–83, 208–209, 215–216, 219, 221, 231, 240, 365, 425, 516, 517
Wal-Mart Canada, 70, 124, 396–397, 408
Wal-Mart International, 396–397
Warner Bros., 359
Wartick, S.L., 123n
Washbrook, Shannon, 335
Waste Management of Canada, 148
Watson Wyatt Worldwide, 305, 323
Waugh, Rick, 322, 327, 346, 388
Weafer, Vincent, 25–26
Webber, A., 406n
Weber, Max, 31–32, 32f, 36, 269
Websense, 317
Weick, Karl, 173
Welch, Jack, 280, 412
Wellmark Blue Cross & Blue Shield, 524
Wells Fargo, 524
Wendy's, 232, 434, 513, 520
Werner, M., 387n
Westcoast Energy, 74
Western Electric Company Works, 34
Western Provident Association, 309
Westin, 380
WestJet Airlines, 33, 42, 49, 209, 212, 219, 221, 223, 224, 237–238, 488, 489, 500
Westport Innovations, 99
Weyerhaeuser, 131
Whitehead, Sheila, 344
Whitman, Meg, 309
Whole Foods Market, 103, 463
Wikipedia, 274
Williamson, Terri, 199
Williams-Sonoma, 56
Willow Manufacturing, 48
Wilson, Mike, 428
Wilson, Sandra, 153, 158, 161, 166, 172, 174–175
Wilson Learning Worldwide, 92
Wink, Chris, 185, 187–188, 197
Winners, 491

Wipro, 200
Wittwer, Reto, 72
Wizards of the Coast, 59
W.L. Gore, 459
Woodward, Joan, 275, 276n
Woodward, R.W., 366
WorkSafeBC (Workers' Compensation Board of British Columbia), 211
World Bank, 33
World Economic Forum, 129
World Trade Organization (WTO), 76, 87
WorldCom, 50, 257, 286
Wormand Security, 523
WPP Group, 354

X

Xerox, 271, 279, 310, 461
Xie, Jia Lin, 403
XuZhou Anying, 80

Y

Yahoo!, 291, 354, 355, 357, 359–360, 365, 369, 370, 375–376, 424
Yahoo! Canada, 16
Yammarino, F.J., 397
Yang, Jerry, 354, 359, 369, 375–376
Yellow Pages Group, 299–300
Yogun Früz, 79
York, Pat, 329
York University, 342
YouTube, 307, 357
Yung, Chung Ju, 46
Yzerman, Steve, 448, 451, 459, 466–467

Z

Zaccardelli, Giuliano, 142
Zambonini, Ron, 186
Zapata, Gustavo Romero, 223
Zara, 90, 245
Zellers, 208–209, 224, 311, 365, 391
Zinman, David, 311
Zip, 224
Zippo Canada, 59
Zuckerberg, Mark, 110

LIST OF CANADIAN COMPANIES BY PROVINCE

British Columbia

Blue Water Café, 248
Boston Pizza International, 315
Canaccord Capital, 127, 133, 144
Canadian Petcetera, 528

Alberta

Alberta Energy Company (AEC), 42
Canadian 88 Energy, 391
ConocoPhillips, 391
Enbridge, 123, 129
EnCana, 42, 129
Gulf Canada Resources, 391
Husky Energy, 477, 487, 488, 493, 501
Komex International, 138
Shaw Communications, 345
Suncor Energy, 11, 129, 328, 341
Talisman Energy, 138
TransCanada, 129
Westcoast Energy, 74
WestJet Airlines, 33, 42, 49, 209, 212, 219, 221, 222, 224, 237–238, 488, 489, 500

British Columbia

A&W Food Services of Canada, 57
Back in Motion Rehab, 429
Bard on the Beach Festival, 12
BCBusiness, 131
BC Ferries, 505
BC Ferry and Marine Workers Union, 505
BC Hydro, 373
Best Buy Canada, 311
beyond9to5.com, 344
Blue Water Café, 274
Boston Pizza International, 335
Cambi General Store, 40
Canada Line, 40, 196, 241, 246, 251
Carmanah Technologies Corp., 100n
Chinook Institute for Community Stewardship, 210
City of Richmond, 241
City of Vancouver, 210, 251, 497
Communicopia, 126
Community Arts Council of Vancouver, 210
Electronic Arts Canada, 329, 435
HSBC, 205
iGEN Knowledge Solutions, 280
Java Jazz Mobile Café, 28
Kamloops Child Development Society, 210
Kicking Horse Coffee, 192
Sauder School of Business (University of British Columbia), 237, 241
Sixth Line Solutions, 224
Stanley Park Ecology Society, 210

Tomato Fresh Food Café, 40
TrachBusters.com, 47
Vancouver 2010, 235, 241
Vancouver City Savings Credit Union (Vancity), 131, 222
Vancouver Foundation, 210
Vancouver Grizzlies, 91
Vancouver International Airport, 246
Vancouver Police Department (VPD), 328, 329
Vancouver Sun, 192
Westport Innovations, 99
Weyerhaeuser, 131
WorkSafeBC (Workers' Compensation Board of British Columbia), 211

Manitoba

Agassiz, 482f
University of Manitoba Students Council, 386
University of Winnipeg, 138

New Brunswick

Atlantic Industries, 428
Ganong Bros., 215–216
University of New Brunswick, 428

Newfoundland and Labrador

Johnson, 308

Nova Scotia

Alexander Keith's, 216, 482f
Atlantic Eco Expo, 379
CarShareHFX, 102
Centre for Entrepreneurship Education and Development (CEED), 117
Dalhousie University, 296
Eldis Group, 509, 512–513, 514–515, 525–526, 529
Empire Company, 11
Sobeys, 70
Tether, 103

Ontario

Abitibi Bowater Inc., 56
Aboriginal Human Resource Development Council of Canada, 340
ABS Manufacturing and Distributing, 241
Air Canada Centre, 265
AIR MILES, 379
AJ Bus Lines, 57
Alliance of Manufacturers & Exporters Canada, 138
Amazon.ca, 10, 16, 224, 228, 509

Assembly of First Nations, 386
Aviva Canada, 268
The Bagg Group, 307
Bank of Nova Scotia (Scotiabank), 74, 322, 327, 329, 334, 335, 340, 341, 345–346, 362, 388
Basadur Applied Creativity, 17n, 108
Better Business Bureau, 258
BMO Field, 265
BorderWave, 241
Business Council on National Issues, 138
Business Development Bank of Canada, 12
Canada Post, 11, 12, 55, 210, 362, 390–391, 407
Canada Revenue Services, 140
Canada's Wonderland, 55
Canada Trust, 400
Canadian Armed Forces, 362
Canadian Authors Association, 231
Canadian Business, 429
Canadian Coalition for Good Governance (CCGG), 438
Canadian Council of Chief Executives, 138
Canadian Football League (CFL), 122
Canadian Human Rights Commission, 325n
Canadian Imperial Bank of Commerce (CIBC), 122, 491, 511
Canadian Olympic Committee, 251
Canadian Paralympic Committee, 251
Canadian Policy Research Network, 418
Canadian Securities Administrators, 139, 355, 495
Canadian Tire, 10, 226
Canadian Transport Agency, 57
CBC, 12, 57, 133
Centre for Research on Globalization, 86
Chapters, 122, 208, 214
City of Ottawa, 148
CN Rail, 390–391
Cognos, 186, 235
Coles, 122, 208
COMPAS, 57
Competition Bureau Canada, 57, 208, 217
Conference Board of Canada, 138, 322, 342, 437
Coolbrands, 79
Corel, 33, 217, 251, 277
Corporate Knights, 99, 123, 129
Dahl Brothers Canada, 223
Dell Canada, 268
Dofasco, 361, 373
Ericsson Canada, 140
Ethiscan Canada, 140
Food Town, 206
Ford Canada, 277
General Motors Centre, 265
General Motors (GM) Canada, 275, 345

George Weston Foods, 217
Globescan, 126
GM Canada, 80
Harvey's, 36
Heart and Stroke Foundation, 56
Hockey Canada, 448, 463
Holt Renfrew, 224
Home Depot Canada, 131, 400
Home Hardware, 40
Home Outfitters, 311
Hudson's Bay Company (The Bay), 224, 311, 365, 391
Husky Injection Molding Systems, 49, 131, 266
IDC Canada, 336
Imasco Ltd., 400
Imperial Tobacco, 400
Indigo Books & Music, 15, 122, 208, 210–211, 212, 214–215, 224, 226, 228, 231
Indigo Books & Music & Café, 325
Indigo/Chapters, 208
ING Bank of Canada, 33
Intuit Canada, 46
IQ Partners, 307
KPMG, 140, 142
KPMG/Ipsos Reid, 3
Kraft Canada, 351
Labatt Breweries, 79, 216, 335, 367
Leafs TV, 265
Le Bon Croissant, 221
Lee Valley Tools, 212, 222, 438
Loblaw Companies, 11, 123, 217, 240
LoyaltyOne, 379
Schulich School of Business (York University), 241
Scotia Cassels Investment Counsel, 334
Sears Canada, 217
Sens Plaza, 148

Shell Canada, 138
Shoppers Drug Mart, 400
SmithBooks, 208
Socialinvestment.ca, 126
Spin Master, 368
Sprott School of Business (Carlton University), 343
Status of Women Canada, 57
TD Canada Trust, 341
Team Canada, 448, 466
Team Canada 2010, 451
Teranet, 361
Tim Hortons, 209, 216
Toronto Dominion Bank, 129
Toronto FC, 265, 277, 278
Toronto Maple Leafs, 265, 277, 278, 283
Toronto Marlies, 265, 277
Toronto Raptors, 10, 91, 92, 265, 268, 270, 277, 278, 283
Transport Canada, 178, 505
University of Waterloo, 96, 385, 387, 407
University of Western Ontario, 343
Upper Canada Brewery, 482f
Voortman Cookies, 57
Wal-Mart Canada, 70, 124, 396–397, 408
Waste Management of Canada, 148
Willow Manufacturing, 48
Zellers, 208–209, 224, 311, 365, 391
Zippo Canada, 59

Prince Edward Island

APM Group, 123

Quebec

Air Canada, 11, 28, 35, 181, 219, 224, 237–238, 345, 489, 492, 498

Au Premier Spa Urbain, 292
Bank of Montreal, 123, 271, 498
BCE, 74, 345
Bell Canada, 78, 495
Birks, 56
Bombardier, 77, 137, 251, 267f, 267n
Boralex, 272
BouClair, 483
Brasseries Unibroue, 482f
Cascades, 272, 388
Cirque du Soleil, 3, 4, 5, 12, 20–21, 32, 50, 51, 96
Confédération des syndicates nationaux, 325
Coors, 318
Domtar, 272, 345, 491
Hewlett-Packard Canada, 373
Tango, 224
TELUS Mobility, 129, 268, 341
TELUS Quebec, 268
Verreault Navigation, 57
Zip, 224

Saskatchewan

Army and Navy, 40
Blue Mantle, 40
Cameco, 341
College of Commerce (University of Saskatchewan), 438
General Cable Corporation, 4, 521
SaskPower, 335
University of Saskatchewan, 195

LIST OF INTERNATIONAL COMPANIES BY COUNTRY

Australia

Alcoa, 122, 523
Apparel Group, 216
Carlton, 523
Forn Australia, 266
Lend Lease Corporation, 204
Sydney Opera House, 204
Ugg, 513
Wormand Security, 523

Belgium

Ecover, 128
European Commission, 217

Brazil

Semco Group, 413

Cambodia

Khmer Internet Development Services (KIDS), 103

Chile

Compania Chilena de Fosforos SA, 222

China

Fujian Sanming Dinghui Chemical Company, 80
Haier Group, 231–232
Shanghai Volkswagen, 232
Turner International Asia Pacific, 205
Wahaha, 163
Xuhou Anying, 80

Czech Republic

[[Scaron]] koda, 511

Denmark

Bang & Olufsen, 223

France

Airbus, 510
Dom Pérignon, 219
Guerlain, 219
Louis Vuitton, 219
LVMH Moët Hennessy-Louis Vuitton SA, 219
Saint-Gobain Performance Plastics, 516
Sodexho Alliance AS, 307
Total SA, 127

Germany

Adidas, 55
Audi, 426
Bayer AG, 275
BMW, 523, 524
Daimler AG, 74
DaimlerChrysler, 225
Deutche Bank AG, 77, 205
Sieman AG, 513
Sport Otto, 111
Valeo Klimasystemme GmbH, 523
Volkswagen AG, 511

India

Sitel India, 78
Tata Group, 217
United Breweries, 523
Wipro, 200

Italy

Benetton Group, 362
Ferrari, 471
Fiat, 77
Filtea, 15

Japan

Bookoff, 231
DENSO, 122
Fujitsu, 437
Hitachi, 79
Hyundai Corporation, 46, 221
Japan Booksellers Federation, 231
Japanese Ministry of Labour, 372
Kirin, 79
Seven & i Holdings, 496
7-Eleven, 496
Sharp Corp., 434
Sony Corporation, 42, 77, 198, 232, 365–366, 471, 524
Toyota Motor Corporation, 109f, 211, 224, 279, 387, 510
Trend Micro, 280

Lithuania

IKI, 222

Luxemburg

ArcelorMittal, 461

Mexico

Sepomex (Servicio Postal Mexicano), 530–531
Transport and Communicating Ministry (Mexico), 530

The Netherlands

Strawberry Frog, 280

New Zealand

ASB, 307

Norway

Hydro, 91

Singapore

Singapore Airlines, 226

South Africa

Haribhai's Spice Emporium, 79

South Korea

Fila, 55
Samsung Electronics, 109f, 471, 487
Samsung Group, 471

Spain

Grupo VIPS, 79
Telefónica, 78
Tele-Mobile, 341
Zara, 90, 245

Sweden

Electrolux, 208, 359
Ericsson, 96, 281
IKEA, 56, 127, 243, 341, 515
Svenska Handelbanken, 243, 287
Volvo, 243, 459

Switzerland

International Organization for Standardization (ISO), 13–14, 99, 129, 523, 529
TAG Heuer, 219
World Economic Forum, 129
World Trade Organization (WTO), 76, 87

United Arab Emirates

Dubai Ports, 20

United Kingdom

The Beatles, 451

Blue Circle Industries, 204

The Body Shop, 46

BP (British Petroleum), 40, 53, 127, 296, 362, 529

British Airways, 495, 504–505

Continuity Central, 204

Department of Transportation (Britain), 505

Global Entrepreneurship Monitor (GEM), 98

Heathrow Airport, 504–505

Inbev, 216

International Policy Network, 86

London Drugs, 226

Tesco, 417, 418, 422–423, 433, 441

Unilever PLC, 74, 77, 237

Virgin Group, 46

Western Provident Association, 309

United States

Accentra, 160

Accenture, 200

Adaptec, 92

AHL, 265

Alpha Chi Omega, 387

Amazon.com, 16, 54, 102, 228, 231, 397, 454, 524

American Airlines, 153

American Chamber of Commerce, 205

American Standard, 516, 517

America Online, 354

Anheuser-Busch, 79, 165–166, 483

Apple Computer, 17, 50, 51, 109f, 116, 198, 216, 359, 398, 521

aQuantive, 357

Ask Jeeves, 355

Atlantic Leadership Institute, 385

Authors Guild, 231

Avis, 212

Avon Products, 121, 397

Babson College, 99

Barnes & Noble, 231

Best Buy, 444–445, 513

BJ's Wholesale Club, 297

Black & Decker, 513

Bloomingdale's, 172

Blue Bird North Georgia, 530

Blue Man Group Productions, 185, 187–188, 194, 197, 200, 458

Boeing Company, 39, 136, 251, 461, 510

Boeing-Rocketdyne, 461

Booz & Company (Boo Allen Hamilton), 108–109

Boston Consulting Group, 218

Bristol-Myers Sqibb, 78

Broadcast.com, 424

Bronx Zoo, 189

Bureau of Competition Policy, 57

Burger King, 203, 232

BusinessWeek, 50

Calvin Klein, 258

Cartoon Network, 205

Caterpillar, 521

CEDC (Central European Distribution), 105

Centre for Leadership Studies, 394n

Cerner, 291, 296

C.F. Martin Guitar Company (Martin Guitar), 180–181

Charles Schwab, 194

The Cheesecake Factory, 510

ChemNutra, 70

Chicago Bulls, 91

Chipotle Mexican Grill, 217

Cisco Systems, 281, 308, 362

CITIES (Convention on International Trade in Endangered Species of Wild Fauna and Flora), 180

Club Med, 55

CNN, 317, 350

Coast Guard, 505

Coca-Cola Company, 55, 203, 212, 219, 224, 232

Coleman Trust Inc., 453

Comdex, 317

Compaq, 361

Competitive Enterprise Institute, 86

Computer Associates, 65

Continental Airlines, 196

Corning, 461

Corporate Governance Center (Kennesaw State University), 495

Costco, 83

Covey Center, 65

Dallas Mavericks, 92, 424

Decision Lens, 461

Deera and Company, 516

Dell Inc., 9, 15, 209, 225, 398, 513, 524

Deloitte & Touche, 204, 205

Delphi, 523

Denver Nuggets, 92

Department of the Secretary of State, 210

Detroit Red Wings, 448

Donato's Pizza, 217

Donna Karen, 219

DoubleClick, 357

Dow Chemical, 524

Dow Jones, 116

Dow Jones Industrial Average, 53

Dow Jones Sustainability Index, 149

Drum Associates, 305

DSA Industrial Design, 50

Dun & Bradstreet (D&B), 237

DuPont, 77, 128

eBay, 16, 58, 99, 103, 211, 216, 277, 309

Edison Electric Institute, 65

EDS, 200

Enron, 44, 181, 494

Enterprise Rent-A-Car, 499, 500

Equal Opportunity Commission (EEOC), 342, 349–350

Ernst & Young, 18, 303

E*TRADE, 59

Expedia, 217

Exxon Mobil, 491

Facebook, 110, 210, 224, 236, 305, 307, 313, 349, 354, 357, 401

FedEx, 55, 102, 205, 400

FedEx Kinko's, 275

Fidelity Investments, 493

Ford Motor Company, 12, 33, 77, 524, 525

Fortune, 14, 98, 108, 232, 240, 344

Four Points, 380

Four Seasons Hotels and Resorts, 51

Frito-Lay, 77

Future Shop, 15, 311

Gallup Organization, 3, 440

GE Aviation, 299

GE Energy, 299

GE Mobile, 96

General Electric (GE), 39, 109f, 198, 225, 232, 280, 349, 356, 369, 412, 491, 524

General Motors (GM), 11, 12, 80, 96, 116, 215–216, 218

Giving Pledge, 101

Globalization Guide, 87n

Global Reporting Initiative (GRI), 129

Global Witness, 127

GLOBE (Global Leadership and Organization Behaviour Effectiveness), 85, 86f, 300, 404

Glow Industries, 199

Goodyear Tire & Rubber Company, 349

Google, 55, 58, 108, 109f, 112, 116, 235–236, 279, 299, 304, 349, 354, 355, 357–358, 365, 445, 486, 493, 529, 530

Google Analytics, 531

Grafik Marketing Communications, 412–413

Greenfiled Brokerage, 180

Greenpeace, 86, 127

Groove Networks, 317

Harley-Davidson, 219

Harrah's Entertainment, 52

Harvard, 96, 286, 406

Harvard Business Review, 17, 141n, 390n, 500n

Harvard Business School, 369, 373

Hasbro, 59

HealthSouth, 257–258

Herman Miller Inc., 110

Hewitt Associates, 436–437, 479

Hewlett-Packard, 79, 82, 128, 279, 307, 361, 461, 493

Hilton Hotels, 495

H.J. Heinz Company, 77

Home Depot, 55, 56, 231, 408, 484

Home Sense, 491

Houston Rockets, 91

HRMarketer.com, 339n
IBM, 17, 78, 82, 109f, 186, 200, 235, 241, 306
IDEO, 50, 309
Industry Week, 530
Indy 500, 241
Intel, 109f, 198, 224, 365–366, 451, 509
Interbrand, 232
Interface Inc., 120, 125–126, 130, 143–144
Internal Revenue Services, 140
International Forum for Globalization, 86
International Institute for Sustainable Development, 86
International Monetary Fund (IMF), 74
Intuit, 356
ITT Industries, 524
Izod, 258
J.D. Power and Associates, 525
Johnson Controls Inc., 514
Johnson & Johnson, 524
Jupitermedia, 317
Kenner Toys, 59
KFC (Kentucky Fried Chicken), 80, 215, 318
Kraft Foods, 342, 459, 516
Levi Strauss, 524
LinkedIn, 236, 305, 307, 313
Lipschultz Levin & Gray, 24–25
L.L. Bean, 281
Lockheed Martin, 458
Los Angeles Dodgers, 259
Lymbix, 290, 294, 312
SADD (Students Against Destructive Decisions), 56
Safeway, 12, 70
Saks, 172
Salesforce.com, 326
San Antonio Spurs, 92
San Francisco State University, 369
SAS Institute, 397
Saturn, 279, 470
Schering-Plough, 521
Scott's Miracle-Gro, 350
Sears, 12, 139, 231, 311

Second Life, 307, 328, 329
Sheraton, 380
Skoll Foundation, 99
Southwest Airlines, 241
SPCA (Society for the Prevention of Cruelty to Animals), 12
Sports Illustrated, 259
St. Regis, 380
Stacy's Pita Chip Company, 46
Starbucks, 60, 79
Starwood, 380
Stride Rite, 172
Students for a Free Tibet, 55
Suburban Hospital, 461
SUBWAY, 232, 253
Sun Life Financial, 129
Sun Microsystems, 317
Symantec, 25–26
SYSCO, 483
Taco Bell, 215, 232
Tampa Bay Rays, 259
Task Force on Business Schools and Innovation, 17
Team USA, 448
Ted's Malibu Surf Shop, 387
Texas Instruments, 243, 399
3M Company, 39, 41, 44, 46, 53, 61–62, 96, 108, 109f, 365–366, 369, 524
Tiger Electronics, 59
Time Warner, 205
Timex, 54
Timken, 513
TJX Companies, 491
Tom's of Maine, 131
Tonka Toys, 59
Training, 335n
Transocean Drilling, 53
Tulane University, 259
Tupperware, 236
Twitter, 236, 294, 296, 313
United Auto Workers (UAW), 80
United Nations Global Compact, 138, 138n, 140

United Way, 10, 56
United Way of the Lower Mainland, 210
University of California, 518
University of Iowa, 389, 407
University of Michigan, 389, 407
UPS, 55, 127, 302
Urban Outfitters, 243
Utah Jazz, 92
Valley Springs Industrial Center, 160
Verion, 307
Viacom, 399
Visa, 164–165, 165f
Voyant Technologies, 318
Wall Street Journal, 198, 343, 412
Wal-Mart, 55, 58, 82–83, 208–209, 215–216, 219, 221, 231, 240, 365, 425, 516, 517
Wal-Mart International, 396–397
Warner Bros., 359
Watson Wyatt Worldwide, 305, 323
Websense, 317
Wellmark Blue Cross & Blue Shield, 524
Wells Fargo, 524
Wendy's, 232, 434, 513, 520
Western Electric Company Works, 34
Westin, 380
Whole Foods Market, 103, 463
W Hotels, 380
Wiards of the West Coast, 59
Wikipedia, 274
Williams-Sonoma, 56
Wilson Learning Worldwide, 92
Winners, 491
World Bank, 33
WorldCom, 50, 257, 286
WPP Group, 354
Xerox, 271, 279, 310, 461
Yahoo!, 291, 354, 355, 357, 359–360, 365, 369, 370, 375–376, 424
YouTube, 307, 357

CREDITS

Author Photos

Page xxiv, (top) Courtesy of Stephen P. Robbins, (middle) Courtesy of Mary Coulter; p. xxiv (bottom) and p. xxv, Tim Richards.

Chapter 1

Page 3, Shamil Zhumatov/Reuters /Landov; p. 13, Chris Wattie/Reuters /Landov; p. 15, © Florian Kopp/MaxXimages; p. 16, Eric Thayer/Reuters/Landov; p. 28, A.J. James/Thinkstock.

Chapter 2

Page 39, Yuriko Nakao/Reuters /Landov; p. 40, Don Healy/Leader Post; p. 46, K. Dooher Photography; p. 47, Chiaki Tsukumo/AP; p. 48 (from left to right), Ken Hurst/Shutterstock, Lisa F. Youg/Shutterstock, Brian Mueller/Shutterstock, Markos86/Shutterstock; p. 51, (top) ©Philippe Petit/Paris Match-Gamma/Ponopresse, (bottom) AP Photo/Paul Sakuma; p. 55, AP Wide World Photos; p. 56, The Canadian Press/Paul Chiasson.

Chapter 3

Page 70, Norm Betts/Bloomberg News/Landov; p. 72, Cabrera Georges/Kempinski Hotels; p. 80, Zhu Gang-FeaturesChina/Newscom; p. 82, Goodshoot/Thinkstock.

Chapter 4

Page 96, CP Photo/Kitchener-Waterloo Record- Derek Oliver; p. 101, Courtesy of Skoll Foundation; p. 102, Courtesy of Pam Cooley; p. 110, Robert Galbraith/Reuters /Landov.

Chapter 5

Page 120, © Kim Kulish/Corbis; p. 123, Photo Heather Taweel. Used with permission of APM Group; p. 129, Ric Ernst/The Province; p. 130, Mountain Equipment Co-op; p. 136, Courtesy of Boeing Aircraft Company; p. 141, The Canadian Press/Toronto Star-Aaron Harris; p. 142, Reprinted with permission of the CBC.

Chapter 6

Page 153, Wayne Leidenfrost/The Province; p. 155, Lee Jae-Won/Landov; p. 160, Gerard Burkhart/The New York Times; p. 163, Photo by Lucas Schifres/Bloomberg via Getty Images)

Chapter 7

Page 185, AP Photo/Adam Hunger; p. 187, AP Photo/Jeff Chiu; p. 189, Don Hogan Charles/The New York Times; p. 192, Peter Battistoni; p. 199, Blake Little Photography.

Chapter 8

Page 208, Wayne Cuddington/The Ottawa Citizen; p. 216, Aaron Lynett / National Post/The Canadian Press; p. 221, Colin O'Connor; p. 222, Piotr Malecki Photography; p. 223, Glenn Lowson.

Chapter 9

Page 235, Mark van Manen/Vancouver Sun; p. 236, Courtesy of Radian6; p. 243, Getty Images; p. 245, Xuroxo Lobata/Cover/International Cover; p. 253, CP Photo/Chuck Stoody.

Chapter 10

Page 265, CP Photo/J.P. Moczulski; p. 271, ©Cindy Charles/Photo Edit; p. 276, *Wikinomics: How Mass Collaboration Changes Everything*, by Don Tappscott and Antony D. Williams. © Penguin Group (USA) Inc.; p. 280, Alan Levenson.

Chapter 11

Page 290, Courtesy of Lymbix; p. 292, Frederic Jorez/Getty Images; p. 297, Areil Skelly/Getty Images; p. 299, Ann States; p. 304, Howard Cao; p. 307, Bloomberg/Getty Images.

Chapter 12

Page 322, CP/Marianne Helm; p. 329, (two photos) The Vancouver Police Department; p. 331, Dick Loek/Toronto Star; p. 335, Lucas Olenick/The Toronto Star; p. 340, Dauphin Friendship Centre; p. 344, Bill Keay/Vancouver Sun.

Chapter 13

Page 354, AP/Paul Sakuma; p. 355, Nelson Ching/The New York Times Agency; p. 362, © Robert Houser (Robert Houser.com); p. 368, Darryl James.

Chapter 14

Page 385, © Her Majesty The Queen in Right of Canada represented by the Office of the Secretary to the Governor General (2010); p. 386, (top) Mike Aporius/CP Photo Archive, (bottom) Blair Gable/Reuters/Landov; p. 391, Reuters /Landov; p. 396, The Canadian Press Images/J.P. Moczulski; p. 399, Frances M. Roberts/Newsom; p. 400, Dick Loek/GetStock.com; p. 404, CP/Jim Young; p. 405, Manish Swarup/AP Wide World Photos.

Chapter 15

Page 417, Andy Shaw/Bloomberg News/Landov; p. 424, Getty Images, Inc.; p. 426, Burkhard Schittny; p. 434, David Silverman/Getty Images; p. 435, Mark Van Manen/Vancouver Sun; p. 440, Bill Aaron/Photo Edit.

Chapter 16

Page 448, The (Canadian Press)2010(HO-COC-Dave Sandford; p. 451, Micha Bar Am/ Magnum Photos, Inc.; p. 463, Mark Matson Photography.

Chapter 17

Page 477, Adrian Wyld/CP Photo Archive; p. 483, SYSCO Corporation; p. 484, Reuters/Win McNamee/Landov LLC; p. 487, Ki Ho Park/Kistone Photography.

Chapter 18

Page 509, www.partselect.com. Used with permission of Eldis Group; p. 512, used with permission of The W. Edwards Deming Institute; p. 517, Tony Law/Redux Pictures; p. 525, AP Photo/Paul Sancya/The Canadian Press.